ON MORAL MEDICINE

Second Edition

ON MORAL

MEDICINE

Theological Perspectives in Medical Ethics

SECOND EDITION

Edited by

Stephen E. Lammers and Allen Verhey

William B. Eerdmans Publishing Company
Grand Rapids, Michigan / Cambridge, U.K.

255 Jefferson Ave. S.E., Grand Rapids, Michigan 49503 /
P.O. Box 163, Cambridge CB3 9PU U.K.

First edition 1987
Second edition 1998

Printed in the United States of America

02 01 00 99 98 7 6 5 4 3 2 1

Library of Congress Cataloging-in-Publication Data

On moral medicine: theological perspectives in medical ethics
edited by Stephen E. Lammers and Allen Verhey. — 2nd ed.
p. cm.
Includes bibliographical references.
ISBN 0-8028-4249-6 (paper : alk. paper)
1. Medical ethics. 2. Medicine — Religious aspects.
I. Lammers, Stephen E. II. Verhey, Allen.
R724.058 1998
174′.2 — dc21 97-35605
CIP

Contents

PART I: PERSPECTIVES ON RELIGION AND MEDICINE

PART III: ISSUES IN MEDICAL ETHICS

Preface to the Second Edition

The opportunity to prepare a new edition of this anthology has been both gratifying and daunting. It has been gratifying because it comes as confirmation of the success of the first edition. A decade ago it had been our hope to assemble a collection of readings that would display something of the richness of theological reflection on the issues within medical ethics when the field had been quite thoroughly secularized, that would help initiate students into this literature when most anthologies were neglecting it, and that would be a resource for those in the church, the clinic, and the academy who were curious about the relevance of the Christian tradition to questions of medical ethics. It is only fitting in the preface to this edition that we thank those who welcomed the first edition, those who used it creatively and successfully as a text or as a resource volume.

With the opportunity to do a new edition, however, came the task of revision, and it has been a daunting one. It has been daunting both because the medicine that prompts moral commentary has continued to change and because the literature that provides moral commentary has continued to grow.

The changes in medicine have required changes in many of the chapters. A decade ago there was no Human Genome Project, assisted reproductive technologies were in their infancy, physician-assisted suicide was not openly practiced or advocated, and managed care had just begun to shape medicine.

The literature in medical ethics had grown huge, and it has been enriched in the last decade by a revival of interest in religious perspectives and traditions. Among the signs of that revival have been a series of publications by The Park Ridge Center for the Study of Health, Faith, and Ethics, a new series of volumes called *Theology and Medicine*, and a new journal called *Christian Bioethics*. There has been much to choose from in revising this anthology, and the choices have been sometimes very difficult. We want to thank those who recommended changes and selections for this edition, even though we did not always follow their advice. We have retained the format of the first edition, moving from "Perspectives on Religion and Medicine" to "Concepts in Religion and Medicine" to "Issues in Medical Ethics." Some colleagues have reported that they have used the text from the back to the front, allowing the "issues" to prompt student interest in the "concepts" and "perspectives." Some colleagues have paired certain chapters in Parts I and II with consideration of the "issues" in Part III. We decided to retain both the format and our appreciation of the creativity of our colleagues who use the book in ways that fit their courses and teaching styles.

The most frequent judgment about the first edition was also the most obvious: it was big. This edition is a little bigger. Some colleagues complained about the size, and many admitted that they did not assign everything in the text, but most were glad for the size and for the opportunity to make their own selections from the readings.

We have also tried to preserve a mix of "classic" and contemporary pieces, and of course, we continue to focus on theological reflection on the issues raised by medical research and technology.

The changes include a number of new selections (67), revisions to the introductions to the chapters, and additional selections for further reading. Some of the new selections respond to new developments in health care. Some of them attend to the care of patients with AIDS. Some of them recognize the importance of nurses to health care (and the use of the first edition by nursing students and professionals).

We continue to disagree about which of us had the initial idea for this anthology, each thinking it was the other, but we agree that we would not have been able to have completed it or to have revised it without the help of many others. We are grateful to Jon Pott — and many others — at Wm. B. Eerdmans Publishing Co. for their patience with us and for their help with this project; we are grateful to authors and publishers who have permitted us to utilize their material; we are grateful to colleagues who gave advice, encouragement, and counsel; we are grateful to our secretaries, Yvonne Osmun and Karen Michmerhuizen, who supported our efforts with their own; and we are grateful to our students who continue to test our ideas of a text.

Preface to the First Edition

A little over two decades ago Kenneth Boulding first suggested that the twentieth century would witness a "biological revolution" with consequences as dramatic and profound as those of the industrial revolution of the eighteenth century.[1] The years since Boulding made his prophetic remark have seen advances in medical science and technology which have made his words seem almost reserved. Not all of the advances have been as dramatic as "cracking" the genetic code or the birth of a "test-tube baby"; not every advance has been as striking as the implantation of an artificial heart into a human patient or the electrical stimulation of the brain; but each of the advances has contributed to a rapidly expanding human control over the human and natural processes of giving birth and dying, over human genetic potential, and over behavioral performance. With the help of biological and behavioral sciences, human beings are seizing control over human nature and human destiny. That is what makes the biological revolution "revolutionary"; the nature now under human dominion is *human* nature. We are the stakes as well as the players.[1]

The new powers have raised new moral questions, and the public discussion of the complex issues raised by developments in medicine has been vigorous (and sometimes rancorous). Although the questions are raised by the developments in science and technology, they are not fundamentally scientific and technological questions. They are inevitably moral and political. Science can tell us a lot of things, but it cannot tell us what ends we ought to seek with the tools it gives us or how to use those tools without morally violating the human material on which they work. Answers to the novel questions posed by new developments in medicine always assume or contain some judgments both about the good to be sought and done and about the justice of certain ways of seeking it.

Thus among reflective people the novel questions posed by developments in medicine lead quickly to some of the oldest questions of all. The new powers have raised new moral problems, but any attempt to deal with them soon confronts fundamental questions about the meaning of life, death, health, freedom, and the person, and about the goals worth striving for and the limits to be imposed on the means to reach them. And these questions inevitably raise the most ancient question of all: What are human beings meant to be and to become? It could hardly be any different, for the nature now under human dominion is human nature.

Public discussion of the novel questions raised by these new powers has seldom candidly raised the ancient and fundamental questions about human nature and human flourishing, however. The public debate has tended to focus instead on two issues: freedom or autonomy and the weighing of risks versus benefits. This is not accidental. Many contemporary moral philosophers have identified the moral point of view with the so-called impartial perspective and have defended either a right to equal freedom or the principle of the greatest number as required by that perspective. Since the Enlightenment the project of philosophical morality has been to identify and justify some impartial and rational principle — some principle which we can and must hold on the basis of reason alone, quite apart from our loyalties and identities, quite apart from our particular histories and communities with their putatively partial visions of human flourishing.[3] The development of bioethics as a discipline, as a branch of applied philosophy, in the last two decades has led many to the task of applying that impartial perspective with its purely rational principles to the concrete and complex quandaries posed by the new developments in medical science and technology. The literature has become increasingly governed by (and limited to) utilitarian and formalist accounts of morality. There remains considerable practical discussion about which impartial principle is the *right* impartial principle, whether respect for autonomy or the greatest good for the greatest number, but the assumption still seems to be that public discourse must be limited and governed by an impartial rational principle. That assumption has affected the anthologies in medical ethics, too.

This anthology starts from different assumptions. It is our conviction that theological reflection on the issues raised by advances in medical research and technology is critically important. It is important, first, of course, for communities of faith with visions of what it means for human beings to flourish, for they want to live in faith, and to live with integrity to the identity they have been given and to which they are called. But it is also important for the broader community, for a genuinely pluralistic society requires the candid expression of different perspectives. Candid attention to the religious dimensions of morality, including medical morality, could prevent the reduction of morality to a set of minimal expectations necessary for pluralism and could remind all participants in the public discourse of broader and more profound questions about what human beings are meant to be and to become.

Classes and programs in medical ethics have sprung up all over the country in response to the new developments in medicine and the public controversy concerning them. Many of the courses are in religious studies departments; many more are in institutions which preserve and nurture a lively sense of the Christian tradition. It is primarily for such courses that we produced this anthology, but we hope it will be useful as well to a broader audience as a demonstration of the possibility and promise of candidly theological reflection about these issues.

The criteria for selection of articles for inclusion in this anthology have been these: First, the article should articulate a theological perspective; short of that, it must at least be of significant theological interest. Second, the article should be readable and interesting. Third, the articles should be representative of the diversity of theological opinion and approaches. And fourth, the articles should be either recent pieces or "classic" pieces. It was still difficult to decide what to include and what to leave out, and many of the articles listed in the suggestions for further reading in each chapter are worthy of inclusion. Nevertheless, we think we have assembled a collection which can be used in reading and in teaching to become acquainted with and appreciative of the contributions of theological reflection to medical ethics.

To produce an anthology is to be reminded of one's indebtedness to others, not only to the authors of the essays included in the anthology but also to those who have assisted us in preparing it.

We are especially grateful to Robert Burt and Richard Mouw for permission to print previously unpublished essays.

Jon Pott of William B. Eerdmans Publishing Company has been consistently patient with us and ready with his encouragement and help. Many other friends and colleagues have encouraged us in the project and advised us concerning it: Jim Childress, Rich Mouw, Stan Hauerwas, Lisa Cahill, and David Cook. A special debt of gratitude is due David H. Smith the director of the National Endowment for the Humanities seminar in medical ethics at which we met and began to collaborate on this project and a good friend and valued colleague ever since.

Our institutions have been helpful to us not only by providing leaves and sabbaticals and faculty grants, but also by supplying colleagues and support personnel and students. To mention any names means that many more whose help and support deserve acknowledgment are slighted, but we must risk at least mentioning our secretaries, Karen Michmerhuizen at Hope College and Jacqueline Wogotz at Lafayette College. And all teachers know they are indebted to their students for the simple possibility of owning the identity of teacher — and for a good deal more besides. So, thanks are due the students in IDS 454, Medicine and Morals, at Hope College, and in Religion 302, Medical Ethics, at Lafayette, on whom we have tried some of our ideas and some of these articles.

Stephen E. Lammers
Allen Verhey

Notes

1. Kenneth Boulding, *The Meaning of the Twentieth Century* (New York: Harper and Row, 1964), p. 7.

2. Pierre Teilhard de Chardin, *The Phenomenon of Man* (New York: Harper and Row, 1959), p. 229: "We must have become aware that, in the great game that is being played, we are the players as well as being the cards and the stakes."

3. Alasdair MacIntyre, *After Virtue* (Notre Dame: University of Notre Dame Press, 1981).

Part I

PERSPECTIVES ON RELIGION AND MEDICINE

Chapter One

RELIGION AND MEDICINE

The little piece from the Wisdom of Jesus ben Sirach in praise of physicians (selection 2) was written by a Jew living in a Hellenistic culture. The Hebrew tradition had explained both sickness and healing as the work of God (e.g., Exodus 15:26). In 2 Chronicles 16:23 the Chronicler chided king Asa for having "sought help from physicians" rather than from the Lord in his disease. Evidently for the Chronicler, the Lord's "healing monopoly" left little room for consulting a physician, and piety and medicine were regarded as mutually exclusive. Jesus ben Sirach saw things differently. He affirmed the tradition of divine activity in sickness and in healing, but he also affirmed the work and skill of physicians. Because God is the creator of the world — and physicians and their medicines — God can act in and through the actions of physicians and pharmacists. The sage piety of Jesus ben Sirach had no place for magic or for the invocation of Asclepius, but it did make available the empirical medicine of the Hellenistic physician to the community of faith. Religion and medicine were allies, not antagonists.

That solution, once unusual and innovative, became commonplace. People could, as Walter Rauschenbusch did much closer to our own day, give thanks to God for medicine and its practitioners, regarding doctors and nurses as "ministers of God" and their "calling" as "holy," and ask God to bless "the white light of science" (selection 1). Such prayers seem to have been answered, but the white light of science has given an aura to medicine that has prompted the question about the relation of religion and scientific medicine to be raised anew. What do religion and scientific medicine have to do with one another? That question opens up a number of other questions: Should they be kept independent of each other, our lives as Christians and as professionals or as patients divided into different compartments? Should one be subordinated to the other? What contributions does or can one make to the other? What criticisms might one make of the other? The selections here provide some perspective on these questions and ways of answering them.

Karl Barth comments on the wisdom of Jesus ben Sirach (or Ecclesiasticus), commending its "wise and prudent verdict," but he reminds his readers that neither health nor physicians are to be regarded as gods, warning against both a cult of health and idolatrous expectations of medicine. The selection is noteworthy not only for its attention to the relation of religion and medicine but also, in that context, for its definition of "health," for its rejection of body-soul dualism, and for calling attention to the effects of things like wages and housing on health.

If Barth warned against making medicine into a religion, Roy Branson points to "the religion of medicine" in selection 4. The scientific form of medicine advanced the power and the authority of the physician, providing a religious aura around the doctor. The physician is the one who holds the rational and objective knowledge that may save our lives. Given this understanding of their practice, it is not surprising that some physicians arrogated to themselves the power of life and death. Nor is it surprising that, in response, others with significant religious commitments have sought to secularize American medicine, or that more than one of the selections in this chapter criticize the pretensions of medicine as a form of idolatry. One must ask, however, how Branson's commitment to a "secular" medicine and to the "values of equality and freedom" is related to the concern of Rauschenbusch, for example, that medicine be regarded as a "holy" calling, a form of discipleship.

The critique of idolatry is not the only contribution of religion to medicine, according to most of these selections. The medical practitioner, even the duly humble medical practitioner, even the "secular" practitioner, still has the power of modern medicine at her disposal and must still confront questions of the point and purpose of our lives and medical practices as a service to them. The professional will often be unable to relieve a particular patient's suffering. Further, all that power may be used appropriately or inappropriately. And finally, even with the best of effort, the professional may err. The practice inevitably forces questions of the meaning of health and of suffering, the worth of life, the appropriate response to death, and the ambiguity of professional decisions; and these questions are inevitably religious questions.

The inevitability of such questions and the importance of religious traditions as resources for dealing with them are underscored in the article by Courtney Campbell (selection 5). Focusing on the problem of suffering, he argues that religious traditions offer resources not found in secular bioethics for the effort to give meaning to suffering by setting it in the context of a larger account of the purpose and meaning of life.

George Khushf addresses some of these questions by retrieving elements of the early Christian tradition and by setting the medical approach to sickness, suffering, and death in the context of the redemption and renewal accomplished by God. There is an analogy, Khushf claims, between illness and the human condition and between medicine and redemption. Attention to the analogical structure of healing provides a basis, he argues, not only for limiting the pretensions of medicine but also for appreciating its proper role and for discovering direction.

We should not think that these issues are only confronted by health caregivers; they are confronted by all of us. Most of us are not and will not be health caregivers. But we are all persons who will be patients. The critique of the pretensions of medicine is for us as well. We are the persons who expect miracles of medical science and who blame the physician when the miracle does not occur. The questions of meaning and purpose are ours as well. We are the persons who confront the realities of suffering and ambiguity. We all face important questions that involve the relationship of religion and medicine. Perhaps the question we might ask ourselves is, "What kind of medicine do we want?" This is not solely a question for religious people or non-religious people but a question which has implications for all of us. If we seek a medicine that will work "miracles," then it might not be surprising to find that we have created a medicine that claims for itself the power of life and death.

Suggestions for Further Reading

Bishop, Laura Jane. "Religious Perspectives on Bioethics," *Kennedy Institute of Ethics Journal* 5:4 (June 1994).

Camenisch, Paul F. *Religious Methods and Resources in Bioethics* (Dordrecht, The Netherlands: Kluwer Academic Publishers, 1994).

Fox, Renee C., and Judith W. Swazey. "Medical Morality is not Bioethics — Bioethics in China and the United States," *Perspectives in Biology and Medicine,* 27 (Spring, 1984).

Kelly, David F. *The Emergence of Roman Catholic Medical Ethics in North America: An Historical-Methodological-Bibliographical Study* (New York: Edwin Mellen, 1979).

Marty, Martin E., and Kenneth L. Vaux, eds. *Health/Medicine and the Faith Traditions: An Inquiry into Religion and Medicine* (Philadelphia: Fortress Press, 1982).

Pellegrino, Edmund D. *Helping and Healing: Religious Commitment in Health Care* (Washington, D.C.: Georgetown University Press, 1997).

Shriver, Donald W., Jr., ed. *Medicine and Religion: Strategies of Care* (Pittsburgh: University of Pittsburgh Press, 1980).

Tournier, Paul. *A Doctor's Casebook in the Light of the Bible,* trans. Edwin Hudson (London: SCM Press, 1954; New York: Harper and Row, 1960).

1 For Doctors and Nurses

Walter Rauschenbusch

We praise thee, O God, for our friends, the doctors and nurses, who seek the healing of our bodies. We bless thee for their gentleness and patience, for their knowledge and skill. We remember the hours of our suffering when they brought relief, and the days of our fear and anguish at the bedside of our dear ones when they came as ministers of God to save the life thou hadst given. May we reward their fidelity and devotion by our loving gratitude, and do thou uphold them by the satisfaction of work well done.

We rejoice in the tireless daring with which some are now tracking the great slayers of mankind by the white light of science. Grant that under their teaching we may grapple with the sins which have ever dealt death to the race, and that we may so order the life of our communities that none may be doomed to an untimely death for lack of the simple gifts which thou hast given in abundance. Make thou our doctors the prophets and soldiers of thy kingdom, which is the reign of cleanliness and self-restraint and the dominion of health and joyous life.

Strengthen in their whole profession the consciousness that their calling is holy and that they, too, are disciples of the saving Christ. May they never through the pressure of need or ambition surrender the sense of a divine mission and become hirelings who serve only for money. Make them doubly faithful in the service of the poor who need their help most sorely, and may the children of the workingman be as precious to them as the child of the rich. Though they deal with the frail body of man, may they have an abiding sense of the eternal value of the life residing in it, that by the call of faith and hope they may summon to their aid the mysterious spirit of man and the powers of thy all-pervading life.

From Walter Rauschenbusch, *Prayers of the Social Awakening* (New York: The Pilgrim Press, 1909), pp. 77-78.

2 Honor the Physician

Sirach 38:1-15

Honor the physician with the honor due him,
according to your need of him,
for the Lord created him;
for healing comes from the Most High,
and he will receive a gift from the king.
The skill of the physician lifts up his head, and
in the presence of great men he is admired.
The Lord created medicines from the earth,
and a sensible man will not despise them.
Was not water made sweet with a tree
in order that his power might be known?
And he gave skill to men that he
might be glorified in his marvelous works.
By them he heals and takes away pain;
the pharmacist makes of them a compound.
His works will never be finished; and from him
health is upon the face of the earth.
My son, when you are sick do not be negligent,
but pray to the Lord, and he will heal you.
Give up your faults and direct your hands
aright, and cleanse your heart from all sin.
Offer a sweet-smelling sacrifice, and a memorial
portion of fine flour,
and pour oil on your offering, as much as you
can afford.
And give the physician his place, for the Lord
created him;
let him not leave you, for there is need of him.
There is a time when success lies in the hands of
physicians,
for they too will pray to the Lord
that he should grant them success in diagnosis
and in healing, for the sake of preserving life.
He who sins before his Maker,
may he fall into the care of a physician.

3 The Will to Be Healthy

Karl Barth

Let us now raise the question of respect for life in the human sphere. In its form as the will to live, it will also include the will to be healthy. The satisfaction of the needs of the impulses corresponding to man's vegetative and animal nature is one thing, but health, although connected with it, is quite another. Health means capability, vigour and freedom. It is strength for human life. It is the integration of the organs for the exercise of psychophysical functions. . . .

If man may and should will to live, then obviously he may and should also will to be healthy and therefore to be in possession of this strength too. But the concept of this volition is problematical for many reasons and requires elucidation. For somehow it seems to be part of the nature of health that he who possesses it is not conscious of it nor preoccupied with it, but hardly ever thinks about it and cannot therefore be in any position to will it. . . .

If this is so, we must ask whether a special will for health is not a symptom of deficient health which can only magnify the deficiency by confirming it. And a further question which might be raised with reference to this will is whether we can reasonably affirm and seek health independently, or otherwise than in connexion with specific material aims and purposes. . . .

Yet included in the will to live there is a will to be healthy which is not affected by these legitimate questions but which, like the will to live, is demanded by God and is to be seriously achieved in obedience to this demand. By health we are not to think merely of a particular physical or psychical something of great value that can be considered and possessed by itself and therefore can and must be the object of special attention, search and effort. Health is the strength to be as man. It serves human existence in the form of the capacity, vitality and freedom to exercise the psychical and physical functions, just as these themselves are only functions of human existence. We can and should will it as this strength when we will not merely to be healthy in body and soul but to be man at all: man and not animal or plant, man and not wood or stone, man and not a thing or the exponent of an idea, man in the satisfaction of his instinctive needs, man in the use of his reason, in loyalty to his individuality, in the knowledge of its limitations, man in his determination for work and knowledge, and above all in his relation to God and his fellow-men in the proffered act of freedom. We can and should will this, and therefore we can and should will to be healthy. For how can we will, understand or desire the strength for all this unless in willing it we put it into operation in the smaller or greater measure in which we have it? And in willing to be man, how can we put it into operation unless we also will and seek and desire it? We gain it as we practise it. We should therefore will to practise it. This is what is demanded of man in this respect.

Though we cannot deny the antithesis between health and sickness when we view the problem in this way, we must understand it in its relativity. Sickness is obviously negative in relation to health. It is partial impotence to exercise those functions. It hinders man in his exercise of them by burdening, hindering, troubling and threatening him, and causing him pain. But sickness as such is not necessarily impotence to be as man. The strength to be this, so long as one is still alive, can also be the strength and therefore the health of the sick person. And if health is the strength for human existence, even those who are seriously ill can will to be healthy without any optimism or illusions regarding their condition. They, too, are commanded, and it is not too much to ask, that so long as they are alive they should will this, i.e., exercise the power which remains to them, in spite of every obstacle. Hence it seems to be a funda-

---

From Karl Barth, *Church Dogmatics,* III/4, trans. A. T. Mackay et al. (Edinburgh: T&T Clark, 1961), pp. 357-63. Used by permission.

mental demand of the ethics of the sick bed that the sick person should not cease to let himself be addressed, and to address himself, in terms of health and the will which it requires rather than sickness, and above all to see to it that he is in an environment of health. From the same standpoint we cannot count on conditions of absolute and total health, and therefore on the existence of men who are already healthy and do not need the command to will to be so. Even healthy people have great need of the will for health, though perhaps not of the doctor. Conditions of relative and subjectively total ease in relation to the psycho-physical functions of life may well exist. But whether the man who can enjoy such ease is healthy, i.e., a man who lives in the power to be as man, is quite another question which we need only ask, and we must immediately answer that in reality he may be severely handicapped in the exercise of this power, and therefore sick, long before this makes itself felt in the deterioration of his organs or their functional disturbance, so that he perhaps stands in greater need of the summons that he should be healthy than someone who already suffers from such deterioration and disturbance and is therefore regarded as sick in soul or body or perhaps both. And who of us has not constantly to win and possess this strength? A fundamental demand of ethics, even for the man who seems to be and to a large extent really is "healthy in body and soul," is thus that he should not try to evade the summons to be healthy in the true sense of the term.

On the same presupposition it will also be understood that in the question of health we must differentiate between soul and body but not on any account separate the two. The healthy man, and also the sick, is both. He is the soul of his body, the rational soul of his vegetative and animal body, the ruling soul of his serving body. But he is one and the same man in both, and not two. Health and sickness in the two do not constitute two divided realms, but are always a single whole. It is always a matter of the man himself, of his greater or lesser strength, and the more or less serious threat and even increasing impotence. It is he who has been predominantly ill and he who may be predominantly well. Or it is he who must perhaps go the opposite way from predominant health to predominant sickness. It is he who is on the way from the one or the other. Hence he does not have a specific healthy or sick life of the soul with particular dominating or subjugated, unresolved or resolved inclinations, complexes, ties, prohibitions and impulses, and then quite apart from this, in health or sickness, in the antithesis, conflict and balance of the two, an organic vegetative and animal life of the body. On the contrary, he lives the healthy or sick life of his soul in his body and with the life of his body, so that in both, and in their mutual relationship, it is a matter of his life's history, his own history. Again, he does not have a specific physical life in the sound or disordered functions of his somatic organs, his nervous system, his blood circulation, digestion, urination and so on, and then in an upper storey a separate life of the soul. But he lives the healthy or sick life of his body together with that of his soul, and again in both cases, and in their mutual relationship, it is a matter of his life's history, his own history, and therefore himself. And the will for health as the strength to be as man is obviously quite simply, and without duplication in a psychical and physical sphere, the will to continue this history in its unity and totality. A man can, of course, orientate himself seriously, but only secondarily, on this or that psychical or physical element of health in contrast to sickness. But primarily he will always orientate himself in this contrast on his own being as man, on his assertion, preservation and renewal (and all this in the form of activity) as a subject. In all his particular decisions and measures, if they are to be meaningful, he must have a primary concern to confirm his power to be as man and to deny the lack of power to be this. In all stages of that history the question to be answered is: "Wilt thou be made whole?" (Jn. 5[6]), and not: "Wilt thou have healthy limbs or be free of their sickness?" The command which we must always obey is the command to stand upright and not to fall.

From exactly the same standpoint again there can be no indifference to the concrete problems of getting and remaining well. If in the question of health we were concerned with a specific psychical or physical quantity, we might be interested at a distance in the one or the other, and seek health and satisfaction first in psychology and then in a somatic form of health, only to tire no less arbitrarily of one or the other or perhaps both, and to let things take their course. But if on both sides it is a matter of the strength to be as man, on both sides we are free from the anxious or fanatical expectation that real decisions can and must be made, but also free to give to the psychical and physical spheres the attention due to them in this respect because they are the field on which the true decisions of the will for health must be worked out. It is precisely in the continuation of his life of soul and body that the history of man must continue in the strength to be as man. What he *can* do for the continuation and therefore against every restriction of his life of soul and body, he ought to *will* to do if he is to be healthy, if he is to live in this strength, and if his history is to proceed in the strength of his being as man. In order that this strength may not degenerate into a process in which he is only driven as an object and is therefore no longer man, in order that he may remain its subject and therefore man, he must be on the watch and active for the continuation and against the constriction of his psychical and physical life. The fact that he wills to rise up and stand in this power, and not to fall into weakness, is not in the least decided by the various measures which he might adopt to maintain and protect his psychical and physical powers. He could adopt a thousand measures of this kind with full zeal and skill, and yet not possess the will to maintain this strength, thus lacking the will for health and falling in spite of all his efforts. But if he possesses the will to win and maintain this strength, it is natural that he should be incidentally concerned to take the necessary precautions to preserve and protect his psychical and physical powers, and this in a responsible and energetic way in which the smallest thing is not too small for him nor the greatest too great.

At this point, therefore, we may legitimately ask, and must do so in all seriousness, what is good, or not good, or more or less good, for the soul and body. There is a general and above all a particular hygiene of the psychical and physical life concerning the possibilities and limitations of which we must all seek individual clarity by investigation and experience and also by instruction from a third party, and to which we must all keep in questions of what we may or may not do. In such a hygiene God's gifts of sun, air and water will be applied as the most important factors, effective positively in the psychical no less than the physical sphere. Hygiene is the foundation of every prophylactic against possible illness, as it is also the main basis of therapy where illness has already commenced. We have to realise, however, that in all the negative or positive measures which may be taken it is a matter of maintaining, protecting and restoring not merely a strength which is necessary and may be enjoyed in isolation, but the strength even to be at all as man. It is because so much is at stake, because being as man is a history enacted in space and developing in, with and by the exercise of the psychical and physical functions of life, that attention is demanded at this point and definite measures must be incidentally taken by all of us. Sport may also be mentioned in this connexion. But sport has, legitimately, other dimensions, namely, those of play, of the development of physical strength and of competition, so that it may even constitute a threat to health in the true sense of the term as it now concerns us. We shall thus content ourselves with the statement that sport may form a part of hygiene, and therefore ought to do so in specific instances.

The question has often been raised, and will never find a wholly satisfactory answer, whether the measures to be adopted in this whole sphere really demand the consultation of a doctor. The doctor is a man who is distinguished from others by his general knowledge of psychical or physical health or sickness on the basis of tradition, investigation and daily renewed and corrected experience. He is thus in a position to pass an objective verdict on the psychical or physical health or sickness of others. He is capable of assisting them in their necessary efforts to maintain or regain health by his advice or orders or even, if necessary, direct intervention. What objections can there be to consulting a doctor? If we acknowledge the basic fact that we are required to will the strength to be as man, that we are thus required to will psychophysical forces, and that we are thus commanded to take all possible measures to maintain or preserve this basic power, there seems to be no reason why consultation of a doctor should not find a place among these measures. This is the wise and prudent verdict of Ecclesiasticus in a famous passage (chapter 38): "For of the Most High cometh healing . . . the Lord has created medicines out of the earth, and he that is wise will not abhor them.

. . . And he has given men skill that he might be honoured in his marvellous works. With such doth the physician heal men, and taketh away their pains. Of such doth the apothecary make a confection; and of his works there is no end, and from him is peace over all the earth" (vv. 2ff.). Therefore, "give place to the physician, for the Lord has created him; let him not go from thee, for thou hast need of him. There is a time when in their hands there is good success. For they shall also pray unto the Lord, that he would prosper that which they give for ease and remedy to prolong life" (vv. 12 ff.).

What do we have against the medical man? Apart from a general and illegitimate passivity in matters of health and sickness, the main point seems to be that there are reasons to suspect the objectivity of the knowledge, diagnosis and therapy of a stranger to whom we are required to give place and confidence at the very heart of our own history, handing over to him far-reaching powers of authority and instruction. The more a man understands the question of health and sickness correctly, i.e., the question of his own strength to be as man and therefore of the continuation of his own life history, the more he will entertain this kind of suspicion in relation to the doctor, not in spite of but just because of his science as general knowledge, and the objectiveness of his verdict, orders and interventions. Is not health or sickness, particularly when it is understood as strength or weakness to be as man, the most subjective thing that there is? What can the stranger with his general science know of this strength or weakness of mine? How can he really help me? How can I surrender into his hands?

Yet this form of argument, and the suspicion based upon it, is quite mistaken, and Ecclesiasticus is in the right against it. For it rests on a misunderstanding in which the doctor himself may share through a presumptuous conception of his position, but which may well exist only on the part of the suspicious patient. Health in the true sense of the terms as strength to be as man is not to be expected from any of the measures which can be adopted in the sphere of psychical and physical functions as a defence against sickness or for the preservation or restoration of health. There exists, more perhaps in the imagination of others than on the part of experts, or at any rate of genuine and serious experts, a medical and especially in our own day a psychological totalitarianism and imperialism which would have it that the doctor is the one who really heals. In this form, he must truly be warded off as an unpleasant stranger. There is, in fact, an ancient and in itself interesting connexion between medical and priestly craft. But both doctors and others are urgently asked not to think of the medical man as occupying the position and role of a priest. In all these or similar presumptuous forms, he will probably not be able to help even in the sphere and sense in which he might actually do so. It was probably in some such form that he confronted the woman of whom it is written in Mk. 5[26]: "She had suffered many things of many physicians, and had spent all that she had, and was nothing bettered, but rather grew worse." But in his true form, why should not the doctor be the man who is really able to assist others in his own sphere? And why should he not be looked upon in this way even when he perhaps appears in that perverted form?

In what way can he help? Can he promote the strength to be as man? No, this is something which each can only will, desire and strive for, but not procure nor attain of himself. This is something which even the best doctor can only desire for him. And he will be a better doctor the more consciously he realises his limitations in this respect. For in this way he can draw the attention of others to the fact that the main thing in getting well is something in which neither he nor any human measure can help. If he is a Christian doctor, in certain cases he will explicitly draw attention to this fact. He will then be free to help where he can and should do so, namely, in the sphere of the psychical and physical functions. In relation to these, to their organic, chemical and mechanical presuppositions, to their normal progress and its laws, to their difficulties and degeneracies, to their immediate causes, and to that which can be done in certain circumstances to promote their normal progress and prevent their disturbance, in short, to human life and its health and sickness, there exists more than individual knowledge and opinion. Within the limits of all human knowledge and ability, there are general insights the knowledge of which is based on a history, rich in errors but also in genuine discoveries, of innumerable observations, experiences and experiments, and there are also the general rules to apply this history in the diagnosis and therapy of the individual case. For in this sphere every man, irrespective of his uniqueness before God and among men, is also a specimen, a case among many cases to be classified in the categories of this science, an object to which its rules may be applied. To be sure, each is a new and individual case in which the science and its rules take on a new and specific form. It is the task and business of the doctor to find and apply the new and specific form of the science and its application to the individual case. Hence he is not for any of us an absolute stranger in this sphere. He is a relative newcomer to the extent that each case is necessarily new. But from the standpoint of his science and its practice he is a competent newcomer, and as such he deserves trust rather than suspicion, not an absolute confidence, but a solid relative confidence that in this matter he has better general information than we have, and that for the present we can hopefully submit to his judgment, advice, direction and even intervention in our own particular case. Those who cannot show this confidence ought not to trouble the doctor, nor to be troubled by him. But why should we not show this modest confidence when dealing with a modest doctor?

Ecclesiasticus is quite right to say: "The Lord has created him too." Medical art and science rest like others on a legitimate use of the possibilities given to man. If the history of medicine has been as little free from error, negligence, one-sidedness and exaggeration as any other science, in its main development it has been and still is, to lay eyes at least, as impressive, honourable and promising as, for instance, theology. There is no real reason to ignore its existence or refuse its offer. How can the doctor help? Obviously by giving free play, and removing the obstacles to the will for real health, i.e., the will to exist forcefully as man, which he cannot give to any of us but to which he may supremely exhort us. Psychical and physical illness is naturally a hindrance to this will. It restricts its development. It constitutes an external damaging of it. The doctor's task is to investigate the particular type and form of illness in any given case, to trace its causes in the heredity, constitution, life history and mode of life of the patient, and to study its secondary conditions and consequences, its course thus far, its present position and threatened progress. If humanly speaking everything depends on that will, is it not a great help to be able to learn with some degree of reliability what is really wrong, or more positively what possibilities of movement and action still remain in spite of the present injury, and within what limits one may still will to be healthy? And these limits might, of course, be extended. The doctor goes on to treat the patient with a view to arresting at least the damage, to weakening its power and effect, perhaps even to tackling its causes and thus removing it altogether, so that the patient is well again at least in the medical sphere. And even if the doctor cannot extend the limits of life available, he can at least make the restrictive ailment tolerable, or at worst, if there is no remedy and the limits become progressively narrower, he can do everything possible to make them relatively bearable. All this may be done by the doctor within the limits of his subjective mastery of his medical science and skill. He cannot do more, but at least he cannot do less. And in this way he can assist the will to live in its form as the will to be healthy. In this respect he can encourage man in the strongest sense of the word, and by removing, arresting or palliating the hampering illness he can give him both the incentive to do what he may still do, i.e., to will to be healthy, and also joy and pleasure in doing it. Having done this to the best of his ability, he should withdraw. He has no power in the crucial issue of the strength or weakness of the patient to be as man. He has no control over the will of the patient in this antithesis. Indeed, he has only a very limited power even over the health or sickness of his organs, of the psychical and physical functions in which that strength and the will for it must express themselves in conflict against the weakness. But if he does his best where he can, we must be grateful to him.

Finally, we have to remember that, when seriously posed, the whole question of measures to be adapted for the protection or recovery of the freedom of vital functions necessarily goes beyond the answers given by each of us individually. The basic question of the power to be as man, and therefore of the will for this power and therefore for real health, and the associated question of its expression and exercise, are questions which are not merely to be raised and answered individually but in concert. They are social questions. Hygiene, sport and medicine arrive too late, and cannot be more than rather feeble palliatives, if such general conditions as wages, standards of living, working hours, necessary breaks, and above all housing are so ordered, or rather disordered, that instead of counteracting they promote and perhaps even cause illness, and therefore the external impairing of the will for life and health. Respect for life in the form in which we now particularly envisage it necessarily includes responsibility for the standard of living conditions generally, and particularly so for those to whom they do not constitute a personal problem because they personally need not suffer or fear any threat from this angle, being able to enjoy at least the possibility of health, and to take measures for its protection or recovery, in view of their income, food, working hours, rest and wider interests. The principle *mens sana in corpore sano* can be a highly short-sighted and brutal one if it is only understood individually and not in the wider sense of *in societate sana*. And this extension cannot only mean that we must see to it that the benefits of hygiene, sport and medicine are made available for all, or at least as many as possible. It must mean that the general living conditions of all, or at least of as many as possible, are to be shaped in such a way that they make not just a negative but a positive preventative contribution to their health, as is the case already in varying degrees with the privileged. The will for health of the individual must therefore take also the form of the will to improve, raise and perhaps radically transform the general living conditions of all men. If there is no other way, it must assume the form of the will for a new and quite different order of society, guaranteeing better living conditions for all. Where some are necessarily ill the others cannot with good conscience will to be well. Nor can they really do it at all if they are not concerned about neighbours who are inevitably sick because of their social position. For sooner or later the fact of this illness will in some way threaten them in spite of the measures which they take to isolate themselves and which may be temporarily and partially successful. When one person is ill, the whole society is really ill in all its members. In the battle against sickness the final human word cannot be isolation but only fellowship.

4 The Secularization of American Medicine

Roy Branson

Physicians have reason to be frightened. The American Medical Association opposes national health insurance because it knows voting of such a proposal by Congress will mark the end of medicine's privileged status among professions in America. It will memorialize the transferring of power from the professional in medicine to the layman. Under the pressure of increasingly powerful outside forces, America's most cloistered profession has already begun conforming to the values, norms and practices of the society around it. Physicians know that with comprehensive health insurance Congress will be celebrating nothing less than the secularization of American medicine.

Enough has been written by sociologists and historians to demonstrate that health and disease are not purely physiological, but conditions defined by the whole matrix of human expectations, beliefs and habits. Medicine has always been practiced within the context of what a society conceived as normative in thought and action. The enormous prestige of medicine in the recent history of America derives, to a large extent, from its adherence to values and norms that have been central to American society. The problem for medicine today is that these values sometimes stand in opposition to other values, equally fundamental to American society.

Medicine continues to have faith in the inherent value of reason to discover order in empirical

---

From the *Hastings Center Studies* 1, no. 2 (1973): 17-28.

facts, continues to believe scientific and technological knowledge testify to a rational order.[1] It is an unquestioned good that man should know this order. Medicine believes man should not only discern order intellectually, but he should also act according to rationally ordered patterns. Because it adheres to the value of order in both thought and action, medicine acts according to the criterion of effectiveness. Medicine could not help but flourish in an America loyal to scientific rationality and bureaucratic efficiency.

But now values as basic to America as rationality and order are being powerfully articulated. There are increasing demands that the self-evident truths of freedom and equality of all men be extended throughout American society. It is being argued that no group has the right, because of its knowledge and effectiveness — no matter how impressive — to dictate the terms of life and death to the rest of society. Every group of experts, including medical doctors, must recognize the basic equality of all men to set the conditions of their existence. Doctors are faced with the norm they so treasure — effectiveness — losing precedence to free participation of equals as the criterion society follows in deciding problems of medical care.

This fundamental shift in emphasis from order and technical knowledge to equality and freedom, from efficiency of the expert to participation of the citizen, will affect the roles of doctor and patient. As much as loss of revenue, this is what frightens the physician. Patients will not as easily allow themselves to be treated as deviants from the doctor's marvelously rational world. They will not revere the physician as the mediator of special knowledge. Patients will quite likely regard themselves as fellow-citizens demanding technical information. Certainly any sense that medical care is a privilege that the physician mediates to those he chooses will give way to the community asserting, indeed enforcing, its right to medical care.

The Religion of Medicine

Alterations in medical care have been analyzed from the perspectives of economics and political theory. But if the controversy and deep emotion accompanying basic alterations in medical practice are to be understood, it must be realized that medicine in America has not been merely one more occupation in our economic system or an effective power bloc in American polity. Medicine's roots go deeper. If we are to understand why the conflicts over federal health care legislation have been so passionate, we must realize that medicine has acted in America as a kind of religious system, with its own symbols, values, institutions and rituals.

Robert Bellah defines religion "as a set of symbolic forms and acts which relate man to the ultimate conditions of his existence."[2] Thomas O'Dea concurs: "Religion is a response to the ultimate which becomes institutionalized in thought, practice and organization."[3] Agreement with his fellow sociologists on a functional definition of religion allows J. Milton Yinger to describe science as an attempt to deal with ultimate questions, to characterize science as a religious enterprise.

> Few men can avoid the problem of struggling with questions of salvation (how can man be saved from his most difficult problems?), of the nature of reality, of evil (why do men suffer?), and the like. Science as a way of life is an effort to deal with these questions.[4]

Science affirms that there is an ideal natural order, a set of laws or patterns, and that, as Stephen Toulmin puts it, "these ideals of natural order have something absolute about them."[5] Science has believed that ultimate questions could be answered by knowing the order it affirms. The scientist has seemed to say to his fellow men that "if we know or are aware of everything, if we understand all relevant causes and factors, we can control everything." The scientist, quintessential modern man, has genuinely believed and committed his life to what Langdon Gilkey calls "faith in the healing power of knowledge."[6]

Medicine, of course, is the healing knowledge par excellence. Medicine assumes that disorders can be treated by relying on the order science proclaims. "The science of medicine depends on the faith that it is not chance which operates, but cause."[7]

Talcott Parsons argues that while the cosmos proclaimed by traditional religion no longer dominates modern culture, society depends for its very existence on some sense of order. He suggests that the pattern of beliefs and values integrating contemporary culture is maintained by the "intellectual disciplines," among which science is pre-eminent.[8] If Parsons is right that science has replaced religion (narrowly defined) as the unifying focus of modern culture, then medicine is part of the central faith of our times.

Because medicine has identified itself so closely with science it has gained great authority as a profession. One of America's foremost sociologists of medicine, Eliot Freidson, is convinced that

> medicine is not merely one of the major professions of our time. Among the traditional professions established in the European universities of the Middle Ages, it alone has developed a systematic connection with science and technology . . . Medicine has displaced the law and the ministry from their once dominant positions.[9]

Much of the credit physicians receive for knowing the true order of things, for being experts, comes from medicine's widely proclaimed commitment to the scientific ideals of knowledge and order.

Medicine, of course, is not a purely scholarly profession. It would not be supported by the public for simply possessing knowledge. Medicine is expected to transmute science into therapy, knowledge into action. As they move from theory to practice, physicians adhere strictly to their scientific faith, trying not only to think but act in orderly fashion. Physicians who believe in a reality that is coherent regulate their actions by strict patterns of behavior. Medical doctors are committed to following procedures that have the least waste motion, that cure in the shortest amount of time. Physicians believe they should move as directly as possible from symptom to cause, from cause to treatment. The profession of medicine combines the values of scientific faith — knowledge and order — with concrete norms for regulating medical practice — effectiveness and efficiency. Medicine, then, not only conforms to what has been the fundamental perspective of modern, scientific culture, but energetically follows some of the guiding principles of pragmatic, American society. It is no wonder medicine has enjoyed enormous prestige in America.

So great has been the respect accorded medicine by American society that some commentators have come to describe it as more than an ordinary profession. Freidson believes "medicine's position today is akin to that of the state religions yesterday — it has an officially approved monopoly of the right to define health and illness and to treat illness."[10]

It is understandable that medicine would achieve such an exalted status in American society; that it would be trusted not only to control but define deviancy. What would be more appropriate than a group so obviously dedicated to order and effectiveness deciding what constitutes deviance from these values and standards?

Talcott Parsons, who has done as much as anyone to show disease to be not simply a physical condition but a social role, goes so far as to call disease the primary type of deviance in American society.[11] He does so because a person in a diseased condition cannot be effective, cannot achieve.[12] Of course, the diseased person not only violates norms regulating behavior in society. He is at fundamental odds with the natural order. Parsons follows the logic of his reasoning. He explicitly correlates illness with original sin.[13]

Freidson agrees that the stigma of having been a deviant stays with the diseased person, even after he has recovered; that someone who has received grace remains in some sense a sinner, or at least an ex-sinner. But Freidson insists that there are still important variations in society's abhorrence of disease. He suggests that two independent criteria, personal responsibility and seriousness of condition, are used to distinguish, for example, among a careless youngster sniffling from a cold, a drunk bleeding from a brawl, a bachelor suffering from venereal disease, and a gunman critically wounded in an attempted homicide.[14] Freidson's clarifications do not contradict Parsons' basic point. Indeed both men assume the same premise. "Quite unlike neutral scientific concepts like that of 'virus' or 'molecule,' the concept of illness is inherently evaluational. Medicine is a moral enterprise."[15]

Indeed, in a scientific age, where illness becomes the most ubiquitous label for deviance, medicine emerges as a crucial agent in the application of the scientific creed to a variety of problems. Consider the importance of medical testimony in courts and the influence of medical opinion in defining alcoholism and drug addiction as not strictly ecclesiastical or legal issues but as health problems. Imperceptibly, physicians, as loyal defenders of rationality, order and effectiveness, become the group that defines normality, that arbitrates orthodoxy in modern culture.[16]

Of course, physicians are not content to identify sin. They have the ability to combat it. Their knowledge of science and their extended training in applying that knowledge in a rational, disciplined manner give them confidence that evil can be purified. Men who are not in harmony with the basic order of existence can be restored. Those who have capitulated, who believe they cannot perform according to acceptable standards, can be rehabilitated. Medicine has the means.[17]

For those means to be effective the agents of order and rationality must be trusted. The sick and those responsible for them must realize that they cannot find restoration by their own efforts. They must rely on those who are competent in these matters; those who possess the proper knowledge. Furthermore, it is impossible for each practitioner to be asked to prove and re-prove his merit every time he heals. Patients must come to trust physicians as such; not the admittedly fluctuating worth of individual doctors, but the office of physician.[18] It will not do for patients to take their own medical records from one waiting room to another demanding evidence of a doctor's competence. The sick must put themselves in the hands of the professional. Patients must believe in physicians. "Their therapy depends upon faith. And we may be wise to recognize that there is a faithful quality to medical practice."[19]

The most obvious way for the diseased to show their trust in the representatives of science and their desire to return to a life of rationality and order is for patients to follow the procedures outlined for them by their physicians. It is "the patient's obligation faithfully to accept the implications of the fact that he is 'Dr. X's patient' and so long as he remains in that status he must 'do his part' in the common enterprise."[20] The patient is out of harmony with the basic order of existence. He suffers from the power of disruptive forces distorting his life. Through the course of action outlined by the physician, the patient can experience the power of rationality in his own life. By means of carefully planned actions the physician mediates the mysteries of scientific research for the benefit of ordinary, diseased patients. In the process, medicine creates a ritual system, and the doctor becomes a priest.

As is the case in all religious systems, medicine's symbols are effective because they arise from generally accepted truths. The impact of these symbols is familiar. With the separation of the priest from the layman, the mystery enshrouding the priest expands and his authority increases.

A desire to avoid contamination may be the basis for the physician's dress, but their spotless white apparel instantly conveys an aura that divides the diseased from the holy. Even when their attire cannot contribute to asepsis, physicians cling to their peculiar vestments.[21] Traditional clerics and theologians have begun to refer to their new colleagues and rivals as "the men in the white coats."[22] Technical language may be precise and convenient, but it also allows conversations among physicians which the laymen are not ready to hear. If the laymen did understand, their questions would impede the efficiency of efforts to rescue them from their grave condition.[23]

Asking a deviant for the location of records of his past actions, requiring him to give a recital of his previous deeds and present attitudes, demanding that he disrobe for a careful examination of the visible signs of his polluted state, all have good, scientific justification. They also comprise an interrogation as old as Egyptian medical rites and as intimidating as any confession taken in the Inquisition.[24] After this ritual there is no question as to where authority in the doctor-patient relationship lies.

If any doubt lingers, it is soon expelled. The fully-robed, impressively self-contained examiner pronounces a verdict on the condition of the diseased. He may grant complete absolution, saying that the problem is imaginary, or he may absolve the diseased of any guilt for his present condition; none of his past actions have led to his present deplorable state. Quite likely the inquisitor points out where there have been some past transgressions contributing to the present turmoil, and prescribes a series of penitential acts by which purity may be regained.[25] The discipline may include the purchase of objects with special powers to assist in achieving full release.[26] If the condition is serious a sentence of separation from the healthy may be pronounced. Those untouched by the corruption deserve protection, and the diseased must be encouraged to seek a new life.[27]

The authority of the physician reaches its heights when men face the ultimate threat of death. The terror is greatest because the secrecy is absolute. Nothing is more mysterious or tremendous than death, nothing more daunting. Before this final specter men become desperate for reliable knowledge of science. They gladly deliver themselves into the hands of its representative, pleading for him to effectively impose rational order on lives being drawn into chaos. As Parsons observes,

> It is striking that the medical is one of the few occupational groups which in our society have regular, expected contact with death in the course of their occupational roles. . . . It is presumed that this association with death is a very important factor in the emotional toning of the role of the physician.[28]

He goes on to say that while he believes the physician is not identical to a clergyman, he "has very important associations with the sacred."[29] Certainly the patient, desperate to achieve salvation from death, regards a physician offering him medicine with the same awe as he does a priest extending the wafer. The physician is providing a visible means by which man may receive salvation.

Parsons' own illustrations of the sacred within clinical training and practice point less in the direction of internal medicine and more towards surgery.

> Dissection is not only an instrumental means to the learning of anatomy, but is a symbolic act, highly charged with affective significance. It is in a sense the initiatory rite of the physician-to-be into his intimate association with death and the dead.[30]

If dissection of an already dead cadaver is an initiatory rite, how is cutting into a living body to be regarded? Clearly, at the present time, the medical profession itself looks on this act with the greatest awe. Medical students list surgery as a desirable specialty because it is "one which offers a wide variety of experience and in which responsibility is symbolized by the possibility of killing or disabling patients in the course of making a mistake."[31] Training to become a surgeon is the longest in medicine, and the profession has agreed that performing an operation should bring the highest financial reward of any single act in medical practice.

As for the sick, nothing in medicine frightens them more than surgery.[32] They know that the potential benefits are great. Patients feel that an operation, if survived, promises the fastest and most efficient recovery from a major illness.[33] But the sick also know that for a major operation, they must knowingly relinquish to the doctor complete control over their destiny. On previous occasions the patient has been dependent on the physician, but at no other time is the act of submission into the hands of a doctor so carefully considered, so self-conscious.

Once the decision is made, a prescribed, carefully planned sequence of actions is set in motion. The force of these lengthy preparations comes from the knowledge that they are required by the rational, orderly faith of science. Deviations will bring evil consequences, severe complications.

Days before the operation the patient enters a rigid discipline. His actions are restricted. His diet becomes even more controlled than before. The day of the operation he receives special, cleansing ministrations.

Few know exactly what transpires within the secluded area where surgery is performed. Ordinary functionaries are not allowed entrance; only those with special training. Even these enter only after purifying themselves. The surgeon himself must unvaryingly observe necessary ablutions before approaching the body. Reports indicate that drugs administered to the patient bring a deep sleep. Special ointments applied to the body complete the rituals anticipating the climactic act. Then, according to the requirements of science, the knife falls.

Of course, some are lost though their death often advances the cause of science. But sacrifice is not the culminating rite of this religion. Many recover from surgery. When they do, the religion of medicine has been able to do nothing less than ritualize the miracle of miracles. Through the surgeon's knowledge of the fundamental order of reality and his performance in the most efficient manner possible, a body has been laid to rest, and risen again.[34]

Not surprisingly, no believer testifies more zealously to his faith than the newly-recovered surgical patient. In his previous, broken condition he felt himself the least knowledgeable, least effective member of the medical community. Within the medical hierarchy it seemed appropriate that he occupy the lowest position. Grateful for his astonishing recovery, the patient regards the surgeon as high priest.

Profanation of the Religion

Except for the years from the Renaissance to the nineteenth century in the West, the physician has always been regarded as a priest. Only during the relatively brief period when faith in miraculous healing through incantation and prayer was being lost and trust in a substitute authority had not yet emerged, did the physician lose his aura of possessing sacred powers. In primitive tribes, in the high cultures of Mesopotamia, Egypt, China, India, Greece and Rome, right into the Christian Middle Ages, the physician was a religious functionary.[35]

Universally, disease was considered an evidence of sin. Not only in primitive tribes, but in Mesopotamia, Egypt, India, Mexico and Christian countries, confession necessarily preceded cure.[36] Potions with mysterious powers and rituals with guaranteed purgative effect have been prescribed by all civilizations. In Egypt, India and Greece, incubation was a central part of medical treatment.[37] The building to which the patient traveled for his healing sleep (when he was visited by the gods) were temples, presided over by physicians who were priests.[38] Especially charismatic physicians evolved from mediators of the sacred into its incarnation; for example, Akhnaten in Egypt and Aesculapius in Greece.[39]

As late as the seventeenth century the clergy were the principal healers in America.[40] Even today in America, there are hospitals with religious sponsorship, operated by ecclesiastical orders.

However, it is undeniable that from the Renaissance into the nineteenth century, medicine in the West suffered a crisis of confidence. No potion, no priesthood, no prayers, could stay the ravages of the Plague. As many people died under medical care as survived. Increasingly, the masses were unwilling to dismiss this record as the all-wise will of God. Hospitals, far from being temples, were shunned as repositories of those already enduring the final agonies of death.[41]

The recovery of medicine's influence and authority followed the rise of a new confidence in science. Though it came late, long after basic scientific discoveries, medicine finally discovered vaccines for immunizing mass populations and developed aseptic and anesthetic procedures, allowing the performance of extensive surgery.[42] Medicine had found the effective means to mediate the new, scientific world view.

The buildings where the new scientific wonders were discovered or performed ceased to be shunned as charnel houses. The population, as they had not since perhaps the days of Egypt and Greece, were awed by the new mysterious power active in these edifices. They flocked to them, seeking release from their grievous condition. Once again, in the twentieth century, the physician found amidst the marvels of scientific technology, the appropriate setting for his traditional role of wonder-worker. Never has he been more revered.

But medicine faces a crisis as challenging to its authority as the Renaissance and Enlightenment's diminished faith in the efficacy of prayer and miracle. Just as men's reliance on their own ability to think and act during that time undercut the influence of priestly physicians so today's demand for self-determination in every sector of society threatens medicine's independence of action. The process by which the laity in some parts of the West seized control of the church in the sixteenth century, the state in the eighteenth and nineteenth centuries and the economy in the twentieth, is now threatening the autonomy of science and technology. Medicine, so proudly identified as a bastion of scientific orthodoxy, must brace itself for this latest wave of reformation.[43]

Talcott Parsons identifies the present stage of reformation as an "education revolution" that insists that all institutions, groups and professions must operate in accordance with wider cultural values. Groups can find their own special areas of concern, but they must conform to the culture's general values. If they do not, if a group insists on remaining isolated, acting according to its own idiosyncratic principles, it is falling into a fundamentalism. Examples could include the American Amish, the Roman Catholic Curia, as well as such twentieth-century political movements as Fascism and Stalinism.[44] If the scientific community rejects the basic values of a culture, it too is fundamentalist.

Reformers of contemporary culture, concerned about segments of society resisting universal values, understandably concentrate their attention on the professions. From Emile Durkheim on, social philosophers have regarded the professions as pivotal elements in modern society. With the disappearance of the tribe and the weakening of the family and church, the professions have become crucial as moral orders, drawing men not only into common tasks, but common interpretations of life.[45] Parsons goes so far as to say that

> the professional complex, though obviously still incomplete in its development, has already become the most important single component in the structure of modern societies . . . the massive emergence of the professional complex, not the special status of capitalistic or socialistic modes of organization is the crucial development in twentieth-century society.[46]

As we have already noted, with the waning of faith, the clergy has differentiated into distinct professions. These newer orders of service within society have gained recognition because of their technical knowledge, their mastery of a particular set of facts and skills, but the professions have also become influential because they have been relied upon to continue the traditional function of the clergy: inculcating within individuals the overarching values of a culture.

Max Weber quite consciously called the scientific professions a "calling," with the clear religious overtones that word carries, to underline the central role of these particular professions in mediating the values of the modern, scientific age.[47] If our previous analysis is correct, medicine is the profession within the scientific callings that has most clearly assumed the function of the clergy.[48]

Protestants against this new priesthood do not dispute the technical expertise of physicians, but they do object to medical doctors thinking that mastery of scientific data qualifies them to act as moral arbiters. Influence and leadership within a society, they say, should result from adherence to universally acknowledged moral principles.

Of course physicians, and others in the scientific callings, have thought that they already lived according to the basic beliefs of the age. Certainly science has kept faith with rationality and order. It is startling to hear contemporary reformers inveighing against science as a new orthodoxy blind to more inclusive concerns. Today's reformers declare that knowledge is not sacrosanct. They demand that science recognize the priority of equality and freedom.

Appeals to equality and freedom may initially seem harmless enough. But when the reformers begin to draw out the implications of these values physicians become aware that a full-dress challenge is under way to their profession and its hallowed status. Equality means extension of power beyond the privileged few. Today's laity, like their predecessors in previous centuries, claim that equality gives them the right to participate in making decisions affecting their own lives and destiny.

Participation in medicine means invading the heart of its authority: defining the nature of disease.[49] Physicians can list a set of symptoms, but it is up to the general population to decide whether or not the condition described by the physician is normal or abnormal, acceptable or unacceptable. Definition of sin cannot be the exclusive preserve of those ordained by the community to wage war against evil.[50]

If equality means the laity involves itself to the point of defining illness, it certainly means laymen can set priorities as to which diseases are especially abhorrent, and which will receive less attention. Allocation of medical resources is the prerogative of the donors, not the functionaries receiving funds to perform designated services. Equality, for many reformers, even means that laymen retain the right to decide whether or not the method by which a physician treats a deviant conforms to generally accepted standards of behavior and practice.[51] Regional medical programs, comprehensive health planning, public review boards, and even the courts, are all ways in which laymen are already beginning to exercise authority over professionals in medicine.[52]

As this process of secularization continues, the

roles of the patient and doctor will be affected. The patient will approach the physician, not as a suppliant, but as a fellow-citizen. He will not request expiation of his condition, but affirm his right, as a member of the community, to medical care. The physician can continue to have authority, but in a much more limited sphere. The function of the physician will be much more specific. He will provide information concerning the etiology and rehabilitation of various physical disorders.

Secularization seems always to affect ritual last. As long as death, or the possibility of death, continues to strike fear in human beings, actions that are able to ward it off, or at least postpone its advent, will elicit confidence. No doubt the rite of surgery will continue to create a response of dread and awe. Certainly individual acts of healing will result in grateful patients according respect to their own physician.

But as medicine enters a new era, the rituals of cure are less impressive than the cooperative efforts of a community trying to improve its general health. The citizenry is becoming less inclined to measure the adequacy of medicine by miraculous deeds in the temple, and more interested in finding a way of life that makes spectacular cures unnecessary. Participation is moving beyond citizens asserting their control over the processes of cure to their assuming responsibility for bettering the conditions for health. The goal is not simply reforming the ministrations of physicians, but improving the health of the community to the point where their mediation is almost unnecessary.[53]

Of course, the majority of American physicians stress the dangers of this secularization of medicine. As the goal of medicine moves from cure to health, they warn that medicine's task will become much more diffuse and ill-defined. It will be less easy to integrate into a coherent pattern the knowledge needed for this expanded enterprise. It will be impossible to rely on a stable body of information to achieve specific ends. Furthermore, as the task broadens, individuals from increasingly diverse disciplines will be needed. The process of coordinating these increasingly differentiated roles will make medicine less precise. As the widened goal of health is pursued, previous standards of effectiveness in cure will be impossible to maintain. When these developments coincide with common citizens insisting on exercising their influence in medical matters, barbarism will have engulfed the orderly, scientific practice of medicine in America.[54]

The American medical community may be correct that the efficacy of their expertise is threatened by present trends. If our analysis is correct, the changes coming in American medicine are so thoroughgoing, affecting, as they do, its values, norms, roles and practices, that no one can guarantee that the future will improve on the past. However, for better or worse, one thing is certain about American medicine: it must either narrow its understanding of itself or broaden its vision.

Medicine can become one occupation among many dealing with the improvement of a community's health; that occupation responsible for the technical question of finding the physical causes and cures of disease. It can remain committed exclusively to rationality, order and effectiveness. Physicians can become ever more efficient in performing their unending round of therapeutic rituals. There is no doubt that a culture needs these tasks performed.

Or, medicine can accept the vast challenge of improving America's health. It can embrace the values of equality and freedom, and recognize the right of the whole population to involve itself in determining the nature of disease and the priorities of medical care. Medicine can redefine its task as not exclusively ceremonial, but increasingly educational. To a population with rising expectations of participation it can respond with full disclosure concerning the facts of health and cure. If physicians want to continue to enjoy the enormous respect and influence they have heretofore received in American society, they must consider assuming the crucial job of dramatizing, for the public, conditions preventing a general improvement in health.

The days when the mysteries of science could be relied upon to awe the credulous are fading quickly. Faith in the power of technical reason to save man is dead. Physicians cannot survive as mediators of the holy. With the secularization of medicine, doctors will most likely endure as civil-service technicians.

The only alternative is for physicians to launch themselves into a life where scientific knowledge gives no automatic advantage, where worth depends on sensitivity to principles known to all.

Among the most highly respected individuals in American society today are those who point out to the community those places where its disregard for basic values maims and kills; those who arouse the citizenry to correct injustices and thereby improve and save the lives of thousands.[55]

Recognition that science can no longer be a religion will lead physicians to realize that they can no longer be priests performing mysterious healing rites. Instead, physicians adopting the role of pointing out the relevance of universal values and norms to particular evils will have found a new way of life. They will be demonstrating a loyalty to the freedom, dignity and worth of man. They will have put their trust in the enduring validity of morality. They will have become prophets. The secularization of medicine may prove to be its salvation.

Notes

1. Paul Tillich, *Systematic Theology,* I (Chicago: University of Chicago Press, 1951), pp. 53-54, 72-74. Reason here refers to what Tillich called *technical reason.* "By the technical concept of reason, reason is reduced to the capacity for reasoning. Only the cognitive side of reason remains and within the cognitive realm only those cognitive acts which deal with the discovery of means for ends" (pp. 72, 73). Tillich contrasts technical reason with ontological reason. "According to the classical philosophical tradition reason is the structure of the mind which enables the mind to grasp and to transform reality. It is effective in the cognitive, aesthetic, practical and technical functions of the mind" (p. 72). Elsewhere, he identified ontological reason with ecstatic and existential reason. "Ecstatic reason is reason grasped by an ultimate concern" (p. 53). What Tillich calls ontological reason, could not be opposed to a sense of equality and freedom; but rationality, narrowly defined as technical reason, can be. Cf. Langdon Gilkey, *Religion and the Scientific Future* (New York: Harper & Row, 1970), p. 96. "Knowing for Greek philosophy, was not *techne,* knowing how to do something; it was rather *wisdom,* knowledge of the self. . . . Modern knowing is science, on the other hand; it represents objective knowledge of external structure unrelated to the self, or to the mystery of its freedom."

2. Robert Bellah, "Religious Evolution," *American Sociological Review* 29 (June 1964): 359.

3. Thomas O'Dea, *The Sociology of Religion* (Englewood Cliffs, N.J.: Prentice-Hall, Inc., 1966), p. 27; cf. Milton J. Yinger, *The Scientific Study of Religion* (New York, N.Y.: Macmillan Co., 1970), p. 7. "Religion, then, can be defined as a system of beliefs and practices by means of which a group of people struggle with these ultimate problems of human life."

4. Yinger, *The Scientific Study of Religion,* p. 12.

5. Stephen Toulmin, *Foresight and Understanding* (New York: Harper & Row, 1961), p. 57.

6. Gilkey, *Religion and the Future,* p. 52. "Use of knowledge for control over physical nature has until the present raised few moral problems, and so the model taken from engineering and medicine has seemed to validate over and over this hope for a better scientific technology" (p. 85). Cf. pp. 79, 85-89, 95, 96.

7. Lester S. King, *The Growth of Medical Thought* (Chicago: University of Chicago Press, 1963), p. 36.

8. Talcott Parsons, *The System of Modern Societies* (Englewood Cliffs, N.J.: Prentice-Hall, Inc., 1971), p. 99.

9. Eliot Freidson, *Profession of Medicine* (New York: Dodd, Mead & Co., 1970), p. xviii; cf. Talcott Parsons, "A Sociologist Looks at the Legal Profession," in *Essays in Sociological Theory* (New York: Free Press, 1949), p. 376. "Established scientific knowledge *does* constitute a highly stable point of reference. Hence the 'authority' of the relevant professional groups for interpretations can always be referred to such established knowledge."

10. Freidson, *Profession of Medicine,* p. 5.

11. Talcott Parsons, "Definitions of Health and Illness in the Light of American Values and Social Structure," in *Patients, Physicians and Illness,* ed. by E. Gartley Jaco (New York: Free Press, 1958), p. 186.

12. Ibid., p. 185; cf. Talcott Parsons, *The Social System* (New York: Free Press, 1951), pp. 437-39.

13. Parsons, "Definitions of Health and Illness," p. 175; cf. Freidson, *Profession of Medicine,* p. 231.

14. The specific examples are mine, not Freidson's.

15. Freidson, *Profession of Medicine,* pp. 208, 233, 236, 252; cf. pp. 339-40. "Furthermore, an essential component of what is said to be knowledge is the designation of illness, which, I have insisted, is in and of itself, evaluative and moral rather than technical in character."

16. Ibid., pp. 244, 248-49; cf. Parsons, *The Social System,* p. 445.

17. Parsons, "Definitions of Health and Illness," p. 178.

18. Parsons, *The Social System,* p. 439.

19. Yinger, *Study of Religion,* p. 77; cf. Eliot Freidson,

Professional Dominance: The Social Structure of Medical Care (New York: Atherton Press, 1972), pp. 119, 143.

20. Parsons, *The Social System*, p. 465.

21. Julius A. Roth, "Ritual and Magic in the Control of Contagion," *American Sociological Review* 20 (June 1957): 310-14; cf. Freidson, *Profession of Medicine*, p. 9.

22. Gilkey, *Religion and the Future*, p. 79.

23. Raymond S. Duff and August B. Hollingshead, *Sickness and Society* (New York: Harper & Row, 1968), pp. 132, 327.

24. Erwin H. Ackerknecht, *A Short History of Medicine* (New York: Ronald Press, 1968), p. 16; cf. Henry E. Sigerist, *A History of Medicine* (New York: Oxford University Press, 1951), pp. 188, 196.

25. Freidson, *Profession of Medicine*, p. 228.

26. Yinger, *Study of Religion*, p. 77.

27. Freidson, *Profession of Medicine*, pp. 228, 313-14; cf. Talcott Parsons and Renée Fox, "Illness, Therapy and the Modern Urban American Family," *Patients, Physicians and Illness*, pp. 241, 244.

28. Parsons, *The Social System*, pp. 444-45.

29. Ibid., p. 445.

30. Ibid.

31. Eliot Freidson, "Medical Personnel," *International Encyclopedia of the Social Sciences*, 2nd edition, 10, p. 107; based on data from Howard S. Becker et al., *Boys in White; Student Culture in Medical School* (Chicago: University of Chicago Press, 1961).

32. Duff and Hollingshead, *Sickness and Society*, p. 273.

33. Ibid., p. 294.

34. For a concurring analysis of surgery (though the two analyses were developed independently of each other) see Robert N. Wilson, "Teamwork in the Operating Room," *Human Organization* 12 (Winter, 1954): 9-14.

35. In addition to the works of Ackerknecht and Sigerist already cited, I am especially indebted for the historical background given by the following authors: Lester S. King, *The Growth of Medical Thought* and George Rosen, "The Hospital: Historical Sociology of a Community Institution," in *The Hospital in Modern Society*, ed. by Eliot Freidson (Glencoe, Ill.: Free Press, 1963).

36. Ackerknecht, *History of Medicine*, pp. 27-28, 31, 38; Sigerist, *History of Medicine*, pp. 188, 196.

37. Ackerknecht, *History of Medicine*, pp. 21, 41, 50.

38. Rosen, *Hospital in Society*, pp. 26, 29.

39. Ackerknecht, *History of Medicine*, pp. 21, 50.

40. Ibid., pp. 219, 220.

41. Rosen, *Hospital in Society*, pp. 26-29.

42. Ackerknecht, *History of Medicine*, p. 171; King, *Growth of Medical Thought*, p. 221; Freidson, *Profession of Medicine*, p. 16.

43. Parsons, *System of Modern Societies*, p. 99. Although Parsons does not interpret changes within medicine as a process of secularization, he does note that significant developments within the field are taking place. He analyzes the changes in medicine in terms that he elsewhere uses to describe developments in religious structures; developments which he calls secularization. See in particular, Parsons, "Some Theoretical Considerations Bearing on the Field of Medical Sociology," *Social Structure and Personality* (New York: Free Press, 1964), p. 257. "A further highly significant feature of the general process of change which has been going on is the generalization of the value complex involving health problems. This is a relatively intangible matter to which little explicit research attention has been devoted." Ibid., p. 355. Freidson does put changes within medicine in a historical continuity with secularization of institutional religion. See *Profession of Medicine*, pp. xviii, 250.

44. Parsons, *Systems of Modern Societies*, p. 100.

45. Emile Durkheim, *On the Division of Labor in Society*, trans. by George Simpson (New York: 1893); Cornelia Brookfield, *Professional Ethics and Civic Morals* (London: 1898-1900). Theodore M. Steeman, "Durkheim's Prefessional Ethics," *Journal for the Scientific Study of Religion 2* (April 1963): 163-81. C. P. Wold, "The Durkheim Thesis: Occupational Groups and Moral Integration," *Journal for the Scientific Study of Religion* 2 (Spring 1970): 17-32.

46. "Professions," the *International Encyclopedia of the Social Sciences*, 2nd edition, 12, p. 545.

47. *From Max Weber*, ed. and trans. by H. H. Gerth and C. Wright Mills (New York: Oxford University Press, 1963), pp. 129-56; Robert M. Veatch, "Medical Ethics; Professional or Universal?" Working Paper for the Institute of Society, Ethics and the Life Sciences. Hastings-on-Hudson, New York, p. 2. A comparison of professional to universal ethics in medicine.

48. Freidson, *Profession of Medicine*, pp. 335, 348.

49. Ibid., p. 206.

50. Ibid., pp. 252, 342-43, 345.

51. Ibid., pp. 345, 374; Veatch, "Medical Ethics," pp. 16-18.

52. See Barbara Ehrenreich, *American Health Empire* (New York: Random House, 1970) for criticisms of these programs and arguments for more radical proposals for community control of health care.

53. See Bellah's article "Religious Evolution" for helpful periodization of religious change. Within Bellah's stages of primitive, archaic, historic, early modern and modern, medicine might be described as in transition from historic to early modern. There is a shift from an emphasis on sacrifice to morality, from dependence on the rituals of the temple to a kind of "inner-worldly" maintenance of health. As medicine moves on from its present point of maturation there will likely be increased emphasis on each person maintaining his own health through measures that heretofore have not been considered "medical." Living a well-rounded life, with its appropriate measure of recreation, reflection and aesthetic endeavors will all be seen as part of the good, healthy life, with each person free to combine the various elements according to what is best for him. At that point, medicine will have reached Bellah's modern stage of religion, where each man echoes Jefferson's statement that "I am a sect myself." Cf. Parsons, *Social Structure and Personality*, p. 355.

54. Freidson, *Profession of Medicine*, pp. 352-53.

55. Robert F. Buckhorn, *Nader: The People's Lawyer* (Englewood Cliffs, N.J.: Prentice-Hall, Inc., 1972), p. 276. "Pollster Louis Harris ran a survey of 1,620 families in March, 1971, asking a nationwide cross-section this question: 'Do you feel that in his attacks on American industry, consumer-advocate Ralph Nader has done more good than harm, or more harm than good?' The result: a lopsided 53 percent to 9 percent agreed that Nader was doing more good than harm. . . . Louis Harris said the survey showed that, basically, the efforts of Nader 'have been extremely well received by the American public.' A poll by George Gallup taken in the same month showed that out of 1,571 persons sampled, Nader was known to 50 percent of American men and 37 percent of the women. That would be a recognition factor at the time higher than most of the announced presidential candidates."

5 Religion and Moral Meaning in Bioethics

Courtney S. Campbell

Few experiences in life seem more pointless, more suggestive that our lives are subject to powers that are arbitrary, abusive, and destructive, than the suffering and death of children. What possible account could be given to explain, let alone give meaning to such an event? Several years ago, I developed a friendship with a young couple who were anxiously awaiting the birth of their first child. What transpired, quite unexpectedly, was every prospective parent's nightmare: their child was born with serious congenital abnormalities, evidenced visibly by facial disfigurement and substantial respiratory difficulties. Following a short stay in an NICU, the neontologists indicated that though they could not be sure when death would occur, they were certain that the child's prognosis was terminal, and asked the parents for their preferences regarding continuing or stopping treatment.

How might we think about such a problem in contemporary bioethics? We might invoke a benefits versus burdens calculation or a best interests standard, or take procedural recourse to an ethics committee, perhaps recommending withdrawal of life support. Or, we might consider the cogency of arguments supporting active killing as a compassionate act to spare the child what would inevitably be a painful life, whatever its duration. But the parents did not ask those kinds of questions; they instead brought to that very difficult situation an understanding that our lives are sub-

From the *Hastings Center Report*, Special Supplement, July/August 1990, pp. 4-10.

ject to ultimate powers which are creative, nurturing, and redeeming, and a way of construing the world shaped decisively by a set of religious convictions about the purpose of life, the meaning of death, and ultimate human destiny. Within that moral vision, Angela was not seen by her parents as a tragedy to be prevented (by prenatal diagnosis and abortion) or an unwanted burden whose life could easily be shortened, but instead as a gift in need of care. With minimal medical support, my friends took Angela home to begin their family life bound together, and over the next few months gave devoted and unceasing care until she died.

I do not relate this story to say the parents' choice to care for their daughter at home rather than let her die in the hospital was ethically right or justifiable. I am still unsure about that choice, even though the subsequent care Angela received was to me an exemplary witness of how we should collectively treat the vulnerable and voiceless in our midst. Rather, my point is that a world view provided meaning in a situation that seemed pervaded by arbitrariness and cruelty, a meaning that could not be supplied or sustained by our conventional bioethics maxims about "best interests" or "substituted judgment." The tragedy seen by others, including myself, was transformed into a gift. "Suffer the little children . . . for of such is the kingdom of God."

Religion offers an interpretation or revelation of reality that responds to what Max Weber referred to as the "metaphysical needs of the human mind" to seek order, coherence, and meaning in our lives, to understand ultimate questions about our nature, purpose, and destiny. Yet, in our common endeavor to do bioethics within the limits of reason alone, the discourse necessary to sustain the traditions of moral insight and meaning embedded in the practices and values of religious communities may be characterized as "private" and so considered largely irrelevant to the overriding objectives of bioethics. Indeed, prominent scholars have given serious consideration to whether traditions of theological ethics may constructively contribute to bioethics and to the practices of health care, and the conclusion on several accounts may often be that such a moral resource is dispensable: "Bioethics, where it succeeds, shows where it does not need theology."[1]

The tensions between religious discourse and bioethics pose dual challenges of *accessibility* and *meaning*. Insofar as the incorporation of moral claims from a specific religious tradition or community is deemed to undermine the possibilities for a generally accessible bioethics discourse, the significance of religious perspectives may be very limited. Yet the criterion of accessibility may limit the moral richness of bioethics, for the costs of conformity to public discourse requirements may be the loss of meaning and content about ultimate concerns embedded in a particular tradition, whether religious (as illustrated by the story of Angela's parents) or professional (for example, medicine or nursing).

The Public Limits of Religious Discourse

If it was premature to pronounce "the death of God" in the 1960s, it seems equally mistaken to begin doing post-mortems on the demise of theological and religious perspectives in bioethics. There are nevertheless several problems posed for religious thinkers by the criterion of a generally accessible bioethics discourse, as succinctly identified by Leon Kass:

> Perhaps for the sake of getting a broader hearing, perhaps not to profane sacred teachings or to preserve a separation between the things of God and the things of Caesar, most religious ethicists entering the public practice of ethics leave their special insights at the door and talk about "deontological vs. consequentialist," "autonomy vs. paternalism," "justice vs. utility," just like everybody else.[2]

A first limit on religious discourse in bioethics, then, has to do with constructing a moral language appropriate to an interdisciplinary and public audience. Religious thinkers no longer converse only with members of a particular religious community affirming a common set of assumptions. The audience of bioethics is instead comprised of a broad range of academics and professionals, who likely do not share the same moral, let alone theological, language and concepts. In this setting, the substantive but private insights of a particular tradition may need to be translated into concepts that have public significance.

The linguistic compromises required to gain a "broader hearing," however, risk substantive compromises, since the common discourse of bioethics may not be sufficiently rich to convey the full meaning of relevant religious language. For example, the biblical concept of the "image of God" expresses a transcendent and relational understanding of the self that may be diminished by proposed equivalents of "personhood" or "autonomy," while both the motivational and substantive elements of "covenant" seem only minimally conveyed by the language of "contract." Moreover, though the principle of "beneficence" may be in the bioethics lexicon, even at its most morally demanding it is a very diluted form of "neighbor-love."

The problem of translating religious discourse into a common bioethics language, without attenuating or transforming its meaning, has for some religious thinkers illustrated the potential for cooptation involved in addressing a secular world on its terms and in its concepts. Rather than "profane sacred teachings" as Kass puts it, the alternative to this perceived compromise may be to affirm an ethic of an exemplary community that witnesses to the integrity of its religious convictions primarily in practice rather than discourse. Stanley Hauerwas, for example, has maintained that appreciating "the integrity of Christian discourse — [entails] that Christian beliefs do not need translation but should be demonstrated through Christian practices . . ."[3]

There is, to be sure, an important vocational reason for retaining the integrity of religious discourse. Unlike moral philosophers, for example, theologians do have a particular audience or constituency to whom they are accountable, namely, their various religious communities, whose historical traditions of reflection may be inadequate for the new questions of practical ethics raised by contemporary biotechnology and medicine. Part of the theological concern with addressing a public audience on generally accessible grounds, then, is that it may compromise not only a vocational responsibility to speak *out of* a particular religious tradition, but also a responsibility to speak *to* the tradition embodied in an identifiable community of believers.

Yet a third consideration to which Kass alludes is the church-state controversy, or the societal interest in preserving a wall of separation between religious and public concerns. This limit may be particularly significant in those settings where a specific kind of public bioethics is required — the articulation of public or institutional policy by advisory commissions or committees. The institutionalization of bioethics can reinforce the necessity for a generally accessible language, not only to facilitate ethical discourse among members of such commissions, but also so that they can explain and defend their recommendations to the public on grounds accessible to all.

In the process of public policymaking on bioethics issues, for example, religious themes are typically acknowledged, either through the appointment of particular commission members as representatives of a certain tradition or in public hearings in which invited representatives from a tradition present position statements. These statements may at times articulate distinctive conclusions on the issues under consideration based on the moral reasoning of a religious tradition, as exemplified by the testimony opposing the use of human fetal tissue for purposes of transplantation by Roman Catholic and Jewish scholars presented to an NIH panel in 1988. In other instances, the arguments of religious traditions may be "essentially the same" as the conclusions supported by secular moral reasoning.[4]

Whatever the contributions of religious traditions to the policy-making process, given the particular constitutional configurations of our polity the outcomes and conclusions need to be articulated and defended publicly on nonreligious, generally accessible grounds. That is, the constitutional requirements of a secular purpose for legislation and the constitutional restrictions on appeals to religious grounds as authorization for legislation impose political limits on the scope of religious argumentation.[5]

The sense that the contributions of religious discourse to contemporary bioethics are limited by these interdisciplinary, theological, and political parameters assumes of course that religious traditions have something substantively distinctive to communicate to a public, secular audience. But where might we locate these distinctive or special insights? I want to suggest that the answers to the conventional bioethics questions of "who should decide?" or "what should we do?" often —

if we felt free to allow them to do so — would push back to fundamental issues that require a substantive account of the purpose of human life and destiny. These are common questions of meaning that religious communities have devoted considerable attention to in their theologies, rituals, and practical ethics.

The Anomaly of Suffering

The nature of the accessibility-meaning dichotomy can initially be illustrated by attending to some very contested questions in contemporary bioethics. Two examples will suffice. In an influential discussion of the moral status of animals, one philosopher explains his neglect of religious argumentation for the concept of the "sanctity of life" because such views do not provide "reasoned explanation." Moreover, even sanctity of life proponents typically appeal to nonreligious reasons, since "[religious] doctrines are no longer as widely accepted as they once were."[6] Another has observed that religious arguments prohibiting active killing in medical practice have limited scope in the secular domain; even if one "eschews euthanasia on religious grounds, there will be the challenge of establishing in general terms why a secular society compassing a plurality of moral viewpoints may forbid euthanasia."[7] The constraints on religious discourse are in part its sociological inadequacy (because in our secular age purely religious appeals will not be sufficient for *public* moral reasoning), and in part its logical inadequacy (because the irrational nature of such appeals will be unsatisfactory as a foundation for *moral* reasoning). For the sake of general accessibility, then, we may be tempted to do bioethics without recourse to important sources and traditions of meaning in our culture.

Yet if we consider what is driving moral debate on both "animal rights" and euthanasia, we are likely to find what has historically been deemed a question of religious meaning right at the core, for it is difficult to discuss either of these issues without invoking the notion of "suffering." The central question in attributing moral status to animals, in Jeremy Bentham's classic formulation, is, "Can they suffer?," while arguments on euthanasia often turn on the availability of alternatives to "relieve suffering." Our moral disagreements in bioethics over whether animals should be used in research or over appropriate care of the dying may thus reflect not only (if at all) differences in moral norms, but also various understandings of the place and meaning of suffering in our lives.

Even prior to its significance for such controversial issues, the concept of suffering seems central for the most fundamental concerns of bioethics. Suffering is in part constituted by the experience of a profound assault upon or threat to our sense of self and identity that we are unable to control. It is the experience of the inexplicably arbitrary and typically destructive, of what Weber referred to as the "ethical irrationality of the world." It is perhaps such a perception of illness and disease that lies behind the Latin root (*pati*) of our "patient," meaning "the one who suffers."

Religious traditions do not have a monopoly on discourse about suffering, nor is there a univocal understanding of suffering common to all religions. It is nevertheless the case that the meaning of suffering has long been a central concern of much theological reflection and many religious communities. If such a concept is a central presupposition of both basic conceptual (what is a "patient"?) and controversial pragmatic problems in bioethics (the human treatment of animals), the traditions of religious discourse about suffering would seem to present a rich resource for substantive insights. Some conceptual comprehension of "necessary suffering" is needed, for example, to make sense of moral arguments, let alone current public referenda proposals in Oregon and Washington that would sanction active euthanasia in cases of "unnecessary" suffering.

A Journey of Meaning

Suffering is not of course an end of religious experience but a problem demanding interpretation. Religious traditions have historically tried to give meaning to suffering by placing the experience in a context of broader questions about ultimate purpose in life, and even human destiny beyond life. The "ethically irrational" is typically explained by the construction of a theodicy that reconciles the presence of evil and suffering within a concept of salvation. In Buddhism, for example, suffering may be descriptive of life within the cycle of karma. In some Western traditions, suffering has been construed as having punitive, pedagogical, or redemptive purposes in human experience, though the incompleteness of all such constructions is suggested by the paradigmatic biblical story of the suffering of Job and, in our time, by the experience of the Jews in the Holocaust. Whether suffering does have a "point" and what that point may be will vary among religious traditions. My claim, however, is that the moral intelligibility of suffering is dependent on some account, theological or philosophical, of human nature and ultimate human ends; any conception of bioethics, therefore, that purports to take suffering seriously will likewise have to consider such ultimate questions.

The substantive responses of religious traditions to questions about our origins, who we are, what the nature and purpose of life is, and what constitutes our ultimate ends, account in part of course for the practical and moral differences among traditions. While acknowledging this diversity and complexity, I want to illustrate, by drawing on one fairly common interpretation of life in religious traditions, how such ultimate perspectives can present important implications for our models of bioethics. For many traditions, a fundamental metaphor for life is that of a *journey* or *pilgrimage*. The meaning of the journey is derived in part from its *telos*, the promise of passage or deliverance, including deliverance from the ills and adversity encountered in life, and which also gives point and purpose to morality as the requirements of character and action necessary to transform the kind of people we are (human nature) into the kind of people we ought to be (human destiny).

The life given to us by powers that are ultimately creating, sustaining, and redeeming is not without its thickets and thorns, yet it is precisely through the encounter with human (evil and sin) and natural (disease) forms of opposition that progress in the journey is possible, for such experiences shape decisively the identity and character of the moral self. Thus participation in the journey is intrinsically valuable, a source of meaning through the experience of oppression, adversity, and perhaps even suffering. That meaning is constructed and explained, clarified and communicated, in stories and narratives of creation, alienation, and reconciliation told to others and retold as part of an ongoing tradition. The journey is thus as well a communal experience that involves the making of covenants and promises, the mutual binding together of former strangers for common purposes and ends, through which moral responsibilities are mediated.

This teleological account of human experience can reveal several features to us about the character of contemporary bioethics. It is part of our set of cultural assumptions that meaning is created (or not) by the autonomous individual. Consider, for example, how we understand our pervasive concern with "dying with dignity" in bioethics. A conventional explanation is that this involves returning to the patient control over his or her dying. But, as Kass has observed, it is far from clear that "dignity will reign only when we can push back officious doctors, machinery, and hospital administrators."[8] Dignity must be informed by meaning, and it is perhaps the case that we will achieve dying with meaning only as we understand the place of death within a notion of a meaningful life.

Moreover, within the vision of life as a journey, the hard cases, quandaries, and dramatic scenarios of bioethics are disclosed as but a time-slice in the narrative of a person's moral quest. A devotion to problem-solving both reflects and reinforces a cultural tendency to excise an individual from the social and temporal ties, from community and history, that present sources of meaning in moral life.

Accommodating questions of meaning in bioethics will require that we broaden its scope beyond our current fixation with problem-solving, for some problems cannot be solved but must still be faced. This broader vision involves directing attention not only to the means of medicine, such as procedures for obtaining informed consent or the regulation of research protocols, but also the purposes of medicine within the context of a life conceived as a journey. For on such an account, health will be valued not merely for its own sake, but for the end it allows us to pursue, while sickness and illness may signify not only inconvenient interruptions, but also teachers whose meaning we share with others through stories.

The journey metaphor, because it presupposes

a conception of human ends, directly confronts us with questions about the moral presuppositions of a medicine wedded to technology and conquest of the endless frontier of scientific research. Formulating what these questions are, let alone answering them, is a task made more complex by the very successes of technological medicine, which may render prior, long-standing moral or religious concepts inadequate or in need of reinterpretation. For example, the suffering for generations associated with the experience of infertility — often reinforced culturally by religious world views — may now, through various technological interventions, be transformed into an instance of unnecessary suffering.

Is suffering such an unmitigated evil, and its perduring presence such a concession to failure, that medicine ought, as many have argued, to aspire to its elimination? Or does suffering require the compassion of persons who embody the meaning of care? Such matters are particularly acute in debates over active euthanasia, where eliminating suffering involves eliminating the person who suffers. Yet a medicine that aspires to achieve such a purpose may conflict with specific religious perspectives that see suffering as less a problem to be solved than as an unavoidable part of one's journey, and which assumes meaning in the context of that journey. For example, Paul Ramsey once rhetorically inquired whether "the purpose of modern medicine is to relieve the human condition of the human condition," by which Ramsey had particularly in mind the illness, disease, and suffering all persons experience as their mortal lot. Such an objective not only commits medicine to an impossible task, but one that risks dehumanizing its practitioners and patients.

To the extent that medicine is not morally bounded, or transforms conceptual boundaries, it may summon a theological critique essentially concerned with the theme of idolatry, of making of health an absolute, the end of the human journey, rather than a value whose meaning is intelligible only within some broader account of human nature and destiny. Such a critique will thus be directed against the assertion of an unbounded dominion expressed in some definitions of health, which threaten to transform every human problem into one that is or eventually can be susceptible to medical resolution. It is directed as well against pretensions to unbridled authority and control, and unlimited knowledge in the medical context, and against the well-intentioned aspiration to alleviate the common problems of the human condition in a way that is dehumanizing. Such pretensions and aspirations frequently converge in contemporary medicine's ongoing battle with the enemy of death.

In a culture void of meaning, death must appear as the crowning surd. Its power in our culture is disclosed in the ways we seek to evade it. The vast majority of persons now die in alien environments, institutions such as hospitals and nursing homes, which shelter the living from personally confronting death and may isolate the dying from all that has comprised their journey, including, at times, their families. For the living, moreover, our culture increasingly holds out a promise of technological deliverance, through the medicine of resuscitation or organ transplantation, for example, together with empirical data on the "risk factor" — typically the probability of contracting a disease or developing a condition that has some statistically significant correlation with death — of almost every conceivable activity. We seek to evade this ultimate assault on the self and yet, as Camus's Dr. Rieux comments, it organizes our lives and medical activities. "The order of the world is shaped by death."[9]

The value of life conveyed in the journey metaphor likewise implies that religious traditions cannot (and do not) look upon death with indifference. Indeed, on some accounts, death may be perceived as the pervasive sign of the intruding presence of evil. Life is a fundamental, even if not an absolute, good; the tragedy that we ascribe particularly to premature or "untimely" death from illness or accident is in part attributable to a sense that a person's journey has been interrupted.

Yet for all the shadows cast by death, we may also respond to it not as intruder but as deliverer from a completed mortal journey. That response underlies the interpretation of death as a "blessing" found in some traditions of religious ethics, often reflected in support for practices of only caring for the dying rather than prolonging life through unceasing technological support. The issue is not so much whether we can be delivered from death, either through relying on technological sustenance or institutional isolation, but rather how we might be delivered from meaningless death. The latter requires contextualizing death in a broader vision of human life, or as passage to ultimate destiny beyond life, and through practices of ministering to the dying in a community of care. In this respect, the traditions of religious discourse witness to a conviction that death is not the overriding power that governs out lives, but is itself subject to powers that are ultimate and supreme.

The nature and purpose of life, and the place of health, medicine, suffering, and death within a vision of human nature and destiny, while integral to religious discourse, are common human questions of meaning that often seem peripheral in the quandary-centered concerns of bioethics. A central contribution of religious traditions may therefore be to broaden our moral vision by raising issues of existential interest that are not typically addressed in contemporary bioethics. Precisely because these are human questions, they require examination, lest our assumptions about pluralism and ethics consequently compartmentalize our moral lives.

Priests and Prophets

We value bioethics in a pluralistic moral culture in part because of its capacities for peaceably resolving moral conflict about difficult practical dilemmas and hard cases. The success of bioethics in problem-solving is displayed in its increasing institutionalization in health care through the establishment of hospital ethics committees, ethics consultation groups, institutional review boards, and advisory commissions at state and national levels. In these various forums, bioethics discourse is prominently shaped by an ethic of principles — autonomy, beneficence, and justice — that seems well-suited as a method of conflict resolution because such norms are deemed to command general acceptance.

In managing and regulating the moral issues that arise in the delivery of health care, bioethics provides an important service for patients, their families, and clinical practitioners. Yet, while this "priestly" role (as it might be viewed in a religious perspective) is a necessary dimension of bioethics, it is not sufficient, for bioethics should be not only a source of solutions but also a source of problems.

Part of the responsibility of bioethics is to be "prophetic," challenging to accountability the institutional and professional presuppositions of the health care system and the society of which it is a part. No ethics committee can resolve the scandal of 31.5 million medically indigent persons in this country who may not have access to any institution to begin with. The prophetic responsibility of bioethics necessarily entails probing beneath the visible manifestations of the crisis to identify the root causes of the problem *and* articulating an alternative vision of the health care system based on ideals of justice in community that may be only approximated in practice. Religious traditions can enhance recognition and implementation of this responsibility, for it is the indicting message of the biblical traditions of this culture that the poor are not to be excluded from the community of moral concern.

Moreover, religious traditions can, in several respects, be significant for reminding us of the limitations of an ethic of principles. The normative principles of bioethics are not, for example, self-applying or self-interpreting, but instead require a context of application and a content informed by moral traditions — professional, secular, and religious. In this dialogue among traditions, religious discourse can illuminate and acknowledge the validity of a moral principle, even while challenging its conceptual presuppositions.

For example, central convictions of theological anthropology in biblical traditions, such as that human beings are created in the image of God, support the notion of intrinsic human dignity and respect for personal choice conveyed in bioethics discourse by the principle of autonomy. Yet such a principle will always appear theologically limited to the extent that its conceptual assumptions reflect an isolated individual severed from community and history. The scope of autonomous choices may be limited by the relational and narrative nature of the self, whose moral identity and character are forged in process of a temporal journey rather than in discrete instances of dramatic decision making.

It would, moreover, be theologically narrow to focus on the moral self as a "decisionmaker" or "chooser." Human beings are more than the aggregate of their choices; the "person" whom one respects is an embodied self and the correlative attitude of "respect" must be holistic, acknowledging the moral significance of the bodily organism as well as concerns about liberty of action and freely willed decisions. The self is more than one's capacities for rational, cognitive activity just as the body is more than personal property. In addition, it may be misleading to understand autonomy as a moral ideal for human beings, since freedom of choice may be seriously compromised not only by illness, but also by what biblical traditions have typically designated as "sin," a condition that even Kant believed was so common and radical as to compromise the very conditions for autonomous choice.

An assessment of beneficence and justice can evoke similar kinds of overlap and critique. Beneficence conveys a sense of moral obligation and responsibility for the welfare of others, but its content and scope may seem minimalistic placed alongside norms of love and neighbor. Moral philosophers have often maintained that, beyond the fundamental requirement not to harm others, positive actions on behalf of the welfare of other persons are frequently discretionary, as suggested by the language of "imperfect duties" or "supererogation," or mediated by professional roles, such as those assumed by health care providers. The substantive requirements of love of neighbor, however, will often demand exceeding minimal or role responsibilities. The themes of self-sacrifice, assuming personal inconvenience and risk, and active seeking of the welfare of others beyond one's conventional community of concern, as displayed paradigmatically in the Christian narrative of the Good Samaritan, may entail that the discretionary takes on the character of the obligatory.

The sense that health care is a special kind of good has been an important conceptual underpinning for egalitarian schemes of allocating health care resources. This approach can be supported by the anthropology of the image of God, but it also may be qualified by a historically informed conception of preferential justice towards the poor, the oppressed, and the stranger. Justice may thus require more than a self-interested egalitarianism, namely, a commitment to give special priority to the health care needs of people and groups who have historically experienced oppression and marginalization in our culture. The preferential qualification of egalitarian justice reflects an attempt to redress inequalities stemming from natural and social "givens" with particular attention to the most vulnerable and voiceless in our society.

While religious traditions can point to the questions that need to be asked about the meaning and application of a moral principle, they can also inform judgments about what an ethic of principles neglects. For example, such an ethic assumes a sociology of strangers who share little in the way of common values and ends, and there are instances in medicine where such a situation obtains. It would be a mistake, however, to encompass all human relations, and thereby all human choices, under such a model. A richer sense of special moral relationships, embodied in families, friendships, congregations, or in professional collegiality, can attest to the moral significance religious traditions have historically placed on themes of community and covenant.

Nor do the normative principles of bioethics, to the extent that they focus our moral vision on questions of what should be done in a situation, give sufficient attention to the issue of what kind of people moral agents should be, or what kinds of virtues are necessary to sustain us in our temporal journey beyond the moment of decisionmaking. The moral teachings of religious traditions speak to matters of meekness, mercy, and purity; knowledge, temperance, and patience; gratitude, courage and kindness; faith, hope, and love; issues of moral character and identity beyond the scope of decision-oriented principles. A comprehensive bioethics may find in religious discourse about virtues and dispositions an important source of moral correction and balance, one that places our decisions about health care within the context of a fuller account of purpose and meaning in life.

Acknowledgments

I wish to thank several persons who gave me helpful criticism and needed encouragment, particularly my colleagues at The Hastings Center, Daniel Callahan, Kathleen Nolan, Susan Wolf, and Michael Zeik, all of whom read prior versions of this article; Rabbi Marc Gellman, Ronald Green, Stephen Lammers, Richard Neuhaus, Philip Turner, and Alan Weisbard, who participated in a project meeting on Religion and Bioethics where another version of this article was discussed; and James F. Childress at the University of Virginia.

Notes

1. H. Tristram Engelhardt, Jr., "Looking for God and Finding the Abyss: Bioethics and Natural Theology," in *Theology and Bioethics: Exploring the Foundations and Frontiers*, Earl E. Shelp, ed. (Boston: D. Reidel Publishing Company, 1985), p. 88.
2. Leon R. Kass, "Practicing Ethics: Where's the Action?," *Hastings Center Report* 20:1 (January/February 1990): 6-7.
3. Stanley Hauerwas, "The Testament of Friends," *The Christian Century* 107:7 (February 28, 1990): 213.
4. President's Commission for the Study of Ethical Problems in Medicine and Biomedical and Behavioral Research, *Splicing Life* (Washington, D.C.: U.S. Government Printing Office, 1982), p. 54.
5. For a more detailed account of this issue, see Kent Greenawalt, *Religious Convictions and Political Choice* (New York: Oxford University Press, 1988).
6. Peter Singer, *Animal Liberation: A New Ethics for Our Treatment of Animals* (New York: Random House, Inc., 1975), p. 21.
7. H. Tristram Englehardt, Jr., "Fashioning an Ethic for Life and Death in a Post-Modern Society," *Hastings Center Report* 19:1 (January/February 1989), Special Supplement, 8.
8. Leon R. Kass, "Averting One's Eyes, or Facing the Music? — On Dignity in Death," *Hastings Center Studies* 2:2 (May 1974): 69.
9. Albert Camus, *The Plague* (New York: Vintage Books, 1948), p. 121.

6 Illness, the Problem of Evil, and the Analogical Structure of Healing: On the Difference Christianity Makes in Bioethics

George Khushf

We must take great care to employ this medical art, if it should be necessary, not as making it wholly accountable for our state of health or illness, but as redounding to the glory of God.

Basil the Great[1]

From the start, Christians subordinated physical healing (even the miraculous sort) to the deeper spiritual healing that was given in Jesus Christ's redemptive act. The most significant human problem was not the lack of health, but rather the alienation from God, humanity, and self; i.e. not illness but sin. However, this did not mean that Christians were callous to the needs of those who were physically ill. To the contrary, as Henri Sigerist notes, the sick person "assumed a preferential position," just as did the hungry, homeless, and ostracized (Sigerist, 1943, p. 70). The task of the Christian bioethicist must be to place this concern with the sick in the broader context of the Church's understanding of the human condition

From George Khushf, *Christian Bioethics*, Volume 1, No. 1, pp. 102-20. Slightly abridged and edited from the original. Used by permission.

and God's redemptive work. In this way the legitimate role as well as limits of medicine can be properly appreciated, and concrete direction can be found for the explication of content-full bioethical norms.

For the Christian, physical problems such as sickness and poverty relate to the deeper spiritual predicament of sin in the same way that symptoms relate to a disease. This does not mean that a poor or sick person is a worse sinner than others. Rather, the physical afflictions are an expression of a brokenness in the human race (Amundsen and Ferngren, 1986, p. 45; Augustine, 1983b, book xiv, ch. 3; book xxii, ch. 22). Sin, generically understood, introduced a disorder into material creation. However, creation is not evil, and the material aspects of life cannot be ignored. Unlike gnostics, who divide the material from the spiritual and view the former as evil, Christians advance a doctrine of creation that sees body and material existence as an essential part of human identity (Amundsen and Ferngren, 1986, p. 46). Although a person's own body does indeed seem alien in the experience of illness, this does not indicate that it is evil and separable from spirit. The alienation manifests a rupture in the created identity; it reveals an assault on the unity of body and soul, not their essential difference. This assault has even been understood in terms of demonic forces; malevolent forces directly undermine the harmony of God's creation (Meeks, 1993, ch. 7; Amundsen and Ferngren, 1986, p. 54). Care for the sick amounts to assistance of the wounded, fallen in a grand cosmic battle. The problem of sickness is thus seen as an instance of a more radical problem of evil.

Although the physical problems cannot be ignored, they also cannot take center stage, just as symptomatic care cannot be given priority over treatment of disease. While it is good to relieve a patient's pain, it is better to treat an underlying infection that is causing the pain. In some cases it may even be necessary to make symptoms worse; for example, a leg may need to be broken in order to be properly reset. In the same way, healing of sickness is good, but it is subordinated to the spiritual healing that is at the heart of the Christian witness (Amundsen and Ferngren, 1986, pp. 58-59).

For the early Church, the most important role played by ministering to the sick lay not in the immediate end of physical healing, but rather in the way such healing could serve as a means through which the "good news" about God's act in Jesus Christ could be conveyed. The analogy between physical and spiritual health provided Christians with an opportunity to convey symbolically through concrete deeds of service their message of life.[2] As a physician relates to illness, so Jesus Christ relates to sin. When people see how Christians reach out to the poor and needy physically, they will be able to understand how God reaches out to sinful humanity, and they will be able to see the importance of submitting to spiritual healing as the sick submits to a physician. Through this analogical structure, people can understand that Jesus is the "Great Physician" (Augustine, 1983a, p. 90; 1980, p. 373).

Historically, the Church has thus had a twofold interest in medicine. (1) It has been concerned with assisting those who struggle in the battle of earthly life, helping them to recover so that they can continue to persevere. Medicine is here an expression of care and solidarity with the sick, and its direct concern is to confront that rupture and assault on human identity that is seen in the illness experience. Analogously, medicine is symptomatic care of the human condition, where sin is the underlying disease. (2) Medicine also can be a particular, concrete form of conveying the gospel. In this case, analogously, it is a way of treating the disease of the human condition. Through the deeds of service, medicine makes God's healing manifest in visible terms. In this case, when it is viewed as evangelism, medicine calls for reflection on the praxis of physical healing, using words to convey the manner in which the deeds are symbolically understood. The two types of medicine — symptomatic and disease oriented; i.e. the care and cure models — are thus extended analogously into two ways in which medicine can be appropriated by the Church.

Unfortunately, Christians today have lost sight of the second function of medicine, and many do not even appreciate the relativity of physical health. As noted by Numbers and Amundsen (1986, p. 3), evangelization has been displaced by a "humanitarianism" that eschews the use of medical practice as a means of conveying the gospel, arguing that such a use is "subtly coercive" and thus improper.[3] Here we clearly see a bioethic at work; one that is implicated in the broad secularization process that led to an increasing emphasis on material ends at the expense of spiritual ones. Is it coercive for a physician to move beyond symptomatic care in order to treat an underlying pathology? If not, then why is it coercive for a Christian physician in a Catholic or religiously affiliated hospital to move beyond medical care in order to address sin, which is the deeper pathology of the human condition? Although a Christian bioethic would need to carefully consider how a physician's evangelistic zeal may lead to abuses of authority, one can only dismiss the evangelistic concerns outright in a context where Christian priorities have been subverted, and where sight has been lost of the broader theological, analogical framework in which medicine and human bodily existence are rightly understood — that is, where they are understood in the framework of a Christian worldview.

The task of a Christian bioethic is to reestablish the appropriate priorities, provide the analogical framework, and work out the implications of these priorities in terms of concrete norms and virtues. This will involve placing concerns with human sickness, suffering, and death associated with medicine in the broader context of the Christian concern with redemption and renewal of humanity in the image of God. In this essay, I will sketch an outline for such a bioethic. I will begin by challenging the idolatry of health that is found in modern secular approaches to medicine. Then, I will consider how the illness experience manifests the insufficiency of fallen individuals and brings them beyond themselves to community. In the medical community one finds a knowledge base for healing that follows certain "natural" patterns that, in turn, can provide helpful analogies for the way in which spiritual sickness is healed. At the boundaries of human life, in the face of death, the insufficiency of medicine becomes apparent, and the deeper spiritual brokenness of humanity is existentially experienced. This is the root of the "problem of evil," and its "solution" is not found in theoretical theodicies, but rather in the concrete witness of the Christian community; in deeds of service coupled with proclamation about the import of such deeds. Through Christian service the true nature of healing can be understood, and the limits of medicine can be rightly appreciated. The norms that direct this particular form of service will be constitutive of a Christian bioethic, and they will guide medicine to its higher end. In this way, as Basil the Great so eloquently exhorts, the medical art will redound to the glory of God.

The Idolatry of Health

Today there is a cult of health (Skrabanek, 1994). Advertisements by national health-spa chains speak of a "baptism by sweat." Youth and strength are idealized, aging is transformed into a disease, and any form of dependence is eschewed as contrary to the dignity of the human person (Goodwin, 1991). In this context, sickness becomes the primary evil. In response to this evil, humanity mobilizes all of its resources, and "progress" is understood in terms of the development of medical knowledge and skills. "Science" becomes the savior (Herberg, 1983, ch. 4). However, in those cases where science cannot save, and where individuals fall into dependency and diminished competence, then one should "die with dignity," perhaps by euthanasia or suicide (Humphrey and Wickett, 1990). In this way the myth of the self-sufficient individual is maintained until the end.

Although the technological armamentarium of modern medicine is a recent phenomenon and it raises unique bioethical issues, the idolatry of health is not new. In a masterful discussion of the relation of ancient philosophy to medicine, Ludwig Edelstein (1967) shows how philosophers like Plato and Aristotle confronted a similar cult. Physicians of the time set forth health as the *summum bonum*, and they laid out a full regimen of diet and exercise, along with rules — can we say "norms" — about what could and could not be done (pp. 357-59). In response, philosophers argued that medicine is unable to address which ends are the appropriate ones. Medicine begins with a relative end, health, and then determines what furthers or hinders the realization of this end. But it can say nothing about how its end is to be ranked relative to other important ends (p. 360). The valuation of medicine and its ends thus depends on the supreme good of humanity, and this is determined independently of medicine (pp. 349-356).

The Christian answer to the idolatry of health and the rampant medicalization of reality will follow the same line of argumentation as that of Plato and Aristotle (McCormick, 1985, pp. 97, 106-7). However, the specificity of the Christian response will be governed by the particular end it advances; namely, by fellowship with God, and this involves renewal in the image of God, which is manifest in the person of Jesus Christ (Amundsen and Ferngren, 1986, pp. 48-49). This particular end will determine the unique content of a Christian bioethic.[4]

Edelstein also addresses another area where an interesting parallel can be drawn between the ancient and modern world. He notes that "the greatest debt of philosophy to medicine" lay in the analogy that medicine provided of the philosophical endeavor (1967, p. 360). By using medicine as a means to convey philosophical ideas, it is further relativized, the idolatry of health is undermined, and people are brought to contemplate the more important ends, which transcend the medical domain. Thus for example,

> In the beginning of the *Nichomachean Ethics,* Aristotle parallels his teaching concerning moral qualities with the teaching concerning health, because, he says, it is necessary to explain what is invisible by means of visible illustration. The soul is invisible; knowledge about it is elusive. By comparing the soul and body, that which is seemingly unreal is translated into comprehensible language. . . . In referring to medical insight the philosopher speaks of something that people can be expected to possess and that will help them to grasp the new kind of insight that they are expected to acquire through philosophy. (Edelstein, 1967, p. 361)

Christianity relates to medicine in a similar way, using it to convey a knowledge of redemption. However, in the Christian case, the capacity of medicine to provide such an analogy will be rooted in (1) a doctrine of creation, which accounts for the manner in which created things — especially human act, e.g. medical intervention — can convey a knowledge of the Creator's Act (this is the doctrine of the *analogia entis* set in the context of the *analogia fidei*), and (2) the contention that illness is at its root a manifestation of the brokenness introduced by sin and thus manifests the structure of sin. These two theological assumptions provide the conditions of the Christian use of medicine as an analogy, and they specify the unique way in which that analogy will be used to convey the "good news."

Illness as General Revelation

For the Christian, sickness is ultimately rooted in sin, individually, communally, and cosmically conceived. This does not mean sickness is the result of the personal sin of the individual who is suffering. Rather, sickness is tied to the fallenness of the human race as a whole (Amundsen and Ferngren, 1986, pp. 45-46; Augustine, 1983b, Book xxii, ch. 22).

Will Herberg summarizes the Judeo-Christian understanding of evil, when he speaks of it as "a certain spiritual perversity which tempts man to try to throw off his allegiance to the Absolute and to make himself the center of his universe" (1983, p. 54). Sin is then the "self-absolutization in rebellion against God" (p. 51). It introduces a rupture between the self and God, and this rupture then is extended into an alienation from others and self, as well. The individual becomes blind to the deeper meaning of life, trapped within an illusory, empty world of self (Niebuhr, 1953, pp. 12-18, chs. vii-viii; Niebuhr, 1984). The disordered relationships with self, others, and God are then extended into disordered communities and skewed relationships with nature. Poverty, hunger, war, and sickness, as well as destroyed environments follow. The egocentricity of sin is well exhibited in the idolatry of health, as well as the radical individualism where each person assumes self-sufficiency.

In addition to being ultimately caused by sin, illness manifests the structure of sin. The phenomenology of the illness experience reveals an experienced alienation from self, others, and God. S. Kay Toombs nicely sketches the way in which "[b]odily dysfunction necessarily causes a disturbance in the various and varying interactions between embodied consciousness and world" (1992, p. 62). Time and space shrink upon the here and now, as the lived world collapses upon the isolated self (Toombs, 1992, pp. 15, 66-70). The description Toombs gives of the way in which bodily intention is frustrated could be taken as an account of the bondage of the will, associated since Augustine with human sinfulness (Toombs, 1992, pp. 62-63, 70-76; Augustine, 1980b; see also Paul's Epistle to Romans 7:14-24). As possibility constricts, individuals lose the power to deliver themselves. Drew Leder elaborates on this in his account of the phenomenology of pain, which is associated with illness, showing how "when beset by pain, the body surfaces as Other, something disharmonious with mind" (Leder, p. 98). Further, "[p]ain forces itself between self and other, introducing an existential rift" (p. 99). As pain increases, one's ability to interact in community decreases, even as pain makes painfully clear one's dependency on others and community. "Pain recalls us to our finitude and dependency, dragging us back into the mundane world" (p. 98). The illusion of self-sufficiency is shattered, and one is brought to self-transcendence; motivated to move beyond self to the others who can help.

Illness thus is revelatory of the human condition in general, although the specific content of that revelation is ambiguous, and thus is in need of interpretation by those who understand its deeper import. Because illness is related in its ultimate cause to sin and manifests, albeit ambiguously, its structure and thus the human predicament, illness comes within the purview of the activity of the Church and provides unique opportunities for Christian witness.

Medicine as Analogy

Through illness individuals become aware of their insufficiency and they turn to others for help. However, most people do not appreciate the full revelatory function of illness — that it discloses a deep brokenness that is there already, and not brought about for the first time by the sickness. Instead, people think of the dis-integration of self and the alienation from community and God as a consequence of sickness, rather than as something unveiled in and by sickness. For them, the loss of self-sufficiency is an aberrant state; a fall from the "normal" independence of the individual. The need to turn to community for assistance is thus viewed as a temporary lapse, necessitated by the individual's inability to maintain somatic integrity.

Many people look to medicine as the primary way of combating the dis-integration that attends illness. Through the physician one finds the mediation of the communal knowledge by which wholeness can be restored. However, paradoxically, the physician heals by way of a process that initially exacerbates the alienation of the patient from self and others (Khushf, 1992). In modern medicine, "health" is understood in terms of "normal" anatomy and physiology (Foucault, 1973), as well as the negation of those natural forces that negate normal function (Mainetti, 1992). By identifying the pathoanatomical or pathophysiological truth value of a given clinical manifestation of illness, the physician can map the patient's condition on to the body of knowledge possessed in the medical domain, and thereby determine the appropriate intervention needed to restore somatic function, minimize the debilitating effects if such function cannot be restored, or at least provide prognosis (Englehardt, 1986, ch. 5). Through the diagnostic process the patient's illness experience is translated into a disease description, which accounts for all factors in terms of a closed world of material, interrelated causes (Englehardt, 1992; Khushf, 1992). The living subject is thereby transformed into an object — what Toombs refers to as body-as-scientific-object — and placed in the totalizing world of science (Toombs, 1992, pp. 76-81). The biological substratum of personal life is then manipulated in a way that brings it into accord with statistical norms of acceptable function (Boorse, 1975).

This process of objectivization and manipulation is distancing and dehumanizing, further intensifying the experience of alienation that attends illness (Leder, 1992, p. 96). In a sense, the patient is killed, divested of soul (Khushf, 1992, p. 294). This point regarding the metaphorical death of the patient has been well made by Michel Foucault and Richard Zaner, when they note how the "anatomical body" into which physicians transform their patients has the status of a corpse; namely, that corpse in gross anatomy laboratory on which all physicians receive their initial training (Toombs, 1992, p. 78). "[A]s a scientific object, a particular body is simply an exemplar of *the* human body (or of a particular class of human bodies) and, as such, it may be viewed independently from the person whose body it is" (Toombs, 1992, p. 79). Once the dysfunction of "body" is appropriately addressed, then it is often assumed that the physician's responsibility qua physician is finished, and the integration of personal life is expected to follow naturally thereafter. Following the metaphorical death comes a renewed integration, a resurrection (Khushf, 1992, p. 294).

In this account of medicine we find a rich analogy for understanding the Christian message. Instead of the anatomical and physiological archetype, one has the image of God that is manifest in Jesus Christ. The knowledge of this standard is found in the Christian community, and it is mediated by those who have been themselves transformed from the old ways of sin into the new way that is according to the Image of God. Likewise, the way of this transformation involves death; a giving up of self, and a submission to others, ultimately to an Other, God, who works for individuals a work that they are not able to accomplish by themselves.

In a more extensive discussion it would be fruitful to develop the analogy in some detail, showing what I think are very significant parallels between the process of modern medicine and the way of salvation that is at the heart of the Christian message. The analogy between medicine and spiritual healing make the medical discipline an important profession for the Christian, especially when services are offered freely to those who cannot otherwise afford them (as God's grace is offered freely). When the charitable act of physical healing is coupled with confession that makes clear how the deeds symbolically convey God's salvific work, medicine can obtain a sacramental character.[5] For the purpose of this essay, however, it will be enough to identify the analogy, and to note again that, for the Christian, priority of importance will be given to the deeper spiritual concerns. Suffering, sickness, and medicine will be understood within the broader theological framework. Instead, our question will be: what implications does this parallel have for the practice of medicine and the norms of a Christian bioethic? Before we can answer this question we will first need to consider an approach to medicine that is different from the disease-oriented one outlined above.

Today many people in the field of medicine are criticizing the disease-oriented approach to medicine, and they are advocating a "care ethic" that puts greater emphasis on addressing the disruption of the lived body associated with the illness experience. There is a call for "holistic medicine" that goes beyond the "disease" and ministers to the "illness," including the altered relation of the patient to self and community. Medicine will then focus on "the process of reconstructing the shattered domain" (Leder, 1992, p. 102; see also Toombs, 1992, p. 82).

The emphasis on "care" resonates well with an attempt to alleviate symptoms, which has always been a part of medical practice. However, "the care ethic" also arises as a response to perceived deficiencies in the dehumanizing objectivization of the patient that is, as discussed above, at the heart of modern scientific medicine.[6] The disease-oriented approach seems especially inappropriate in cases of chronic illness or where it is unlikely that such treatment will be successful and the patient is near death. In these cases, the metaphorical killing of the patient becomes the final word; it is not followed by the re-integration that arises naturally from restored physiological function. Rather, it is followed by literal death. For this reason, the indignity of the disease-oriented approach — the dehumanization that is a part of its method — does not seem warranted, and one looks for another response to the illness experience; one that addresses the needs of the whole person and does not simply focus on the biological substratum.

While the disease-oriented approach is closely tied to the scientific worldview and it will be relatively constant across cultures (at least in principle, because the anatomy and physiology is relatively constant across cultures), the care-oriented approach will be much more dependent on the particular cultural understandings of self, community, and God (Khushf, 1992, pp. 283-88; Hauerwas, 1978, p. 148). For this reason, Christians can accept much of what is found in the disease-oriented approach to medicine. They can openly acknowledge a degree to which all are implicated within a closed world of interrelated causes. As long as the scientific account of the world recognizes its limits, it is fully in accord with Christianity (Jockey, 1978; Herberg, 1983, p. 21). However, when one focuses on the lived body disruption and not just the body-as-scientific-object, then uniquely Christian values, especially the understanding of sickness, suffering, and death, will play a constitutive role in defining an ethic of care.

There will be a conflict between Christianity and the more naturalistic oriented approaches to the alienating experiences that attend illness. Many of the care-oriented approaches to medicine do not appreciate the revelatory function of illness — that it discloses a disruption at the heart of the human condition. Instead, they view the alienation from self, other, and God as caused by the biological dysfunction. Although there will be an attempt to minister to the person as a whole, the personal problems are still given a material, physiological etiology. In this way they are medicalized. The response will often involve coping strategies that seek to eliminate the awareness of the alienation or dull its perception; e.g. pain relief becomes a central focus (Skelly, 1994). The intent is to restore as much as possible of the illusion of self-sufficiency; an illusion that often goes under the name of "autonomy." In contrast, Christianity reverses the relation between the spiritual and material. Instead of taking the disintegration of self and community as an epiphenomenon of physiological dysfunction, the latter is understood as a symptom of sin, which is the deeper personal dis-integration. Christianity will thus resist the medicalizing of human reality associated with the attempts to develop a "holistic" medicine.[7] Instead, it will seek to appropriately place the limits of medicine, and it will develop the revelatory function of the illness experience so that it discloses the deeper import of sickness and suffering. A Christian "ethic of care" will not be primarily a form of medicine, but rather a broader ministry, which accounts for and appropriates medicine within its concern with spiritual well-being.

Just as individuals must recognize their insufficiency in certain illness experiences and go beyond self to others (the medical community), so too the insufficiency of medicine must be recognized. This is something many are unwilling to do. However, when one moves from the center of everyday medicine to its boundaries, where the reality of death cannot be escaped and the inability of medicine to alleviate suffering becomes apparent, then the plight of the human condition can be glimpsed. At these boundaries, illness and death are again revelatory, and they point to an answer that lies beyond self and the medical community.

The "Problem of Evil" as the Human Predicament

The brokenness manifest in the illness experience and made especially apparent at the boundary conditions of human life is not just that of the one who is ill. It is a brokenness that is also experienced by those who are intimately related to the ill person, and even by those who observe the plight and seek to understand it. Parents and close friends, for example, also experience an alienation from self and from others as they are implicated in the sufferings of their child or friend. This alienation manifests a need to go beyond self and secular community, although the character of the answer does not become apparent in a natural way. A Christian ethic of care must appreciate the way in which the disruptions associated with the illness experience open outward to the broader disruptions associated with the problem of evil. Without the proclamation that properly diagnoses the human predicament and conveys the "good news" about what God has done to heal, there is an ambiguity and absurdity in certain experiences of "natural evil" (such as a child's suffering) that cannot be overcome medically or philosophically. This is because there is an alienation from God that can only be bridged from beyond self, in the community of faith, which extends God's mediation of true life.

To appreciate the full character of the human predicament, consider the following situation: there is a young girl, burnt from head to foot, racked with pain and looking with unwillingly dry eyes to her father, who is sitting as near as he can, but afraid to touch her bandaged body; afraid that his embrace will cause more pain than comfort. This is a God-fearing family, simple in belief but faithful. Now, however, as the father looks helplessly upon his child, perceiving the "why?" in her stare, he is confused, unable to place his present experience in the broader context of understanding that attends his faith, and he is groping for the spiritual source and help that can minister to the hurt of his suffering daughter. In this father's particular, very concrete experience, where the surdity of unwarranted pain confronts the simple understanding of belief, the "problem of evil" finds its existential source (Hauerwas, 1990).

In this account of father and daughter we have a dis-integration of self and community that extends beyond the immediate consequences of the physiological etiology. There is a sense of meaning and human purpose that is shattered by the very existence of a child's suffering, and it cannot be healed simply by treating the burn. This sense of absurdity is intensified in the case of terminal illness — for example, when a child is dying of leukemia, as recounted so powerfully in Peter DeVries' *The Blood of the Lamb* (1969). A true ethic of care will minister to this deep crisis in meaning, and not simply attempt to dull or view the physical, emotional, and spiritual pain associated with the experience.

Philosophers have attempted to conceptually articulate the existential crisis through the classical formulation of the problem of evil. "How can an omnipotent, omnibenevolent God permit such evil?" "Is this experience not the refutation of theism?" In the "classical theodicies" one begins with the three propositions regarding God's omnipotence, omnibenevolence, and the presence of evil, and then one qualifies their meaning and seeks to establish a conceptual framework in which contradiction is overcome (Hick, 1978). Or, in the same general vein, one can soften the paradox by denying one of the conceptually articulated propositions in the collision — for example, one can deny God's omnipotence, as does Harold Kushner in his popular *When Bad Things Happen to Good People* (1981), or, with the Christian Science practitioner, one can deny the reality of evil. In each case, one assumes that we are in a position where we can in principle understand; where we can conceptually resolve the paradox and determine the context that rightly "places" pain and suffering. Why make this assumption? Further, it is assumed that the "existential crisis" is sufficiently captured in the philosophical articulation, so that one can answer the crisis by answering the philosophically formulated "problem of evil." This implies that the deep healing humanity needs is conceptual. The healer is then the person who provides the right ideas and conceptual framework for overcoming the absurdity.

This approach fails to do justice to our full humanity. Just as certain medicalizing, naturalist approaches err by focusing on the body at the expense of the broader spiritual and intellectual dimensions, this approach ignores the concrete needs of human material existence; it ignores body, emotions, and much more. How many really would be satisfied with a nice conceptual framework when confronted with the suffering of their little child? In such moments all ideological solutions are empty and shallow. Offering such solutions involves a fundamental misapprehension about the character of the problem. The pain and suffering that confronts belief is not just that physiological pain that is, for example, in the child. That pain particularizes a deep brokenness that is not just here or there, but lies behind and confronts every and all human endeavors, including the endeavor to conceptually grasp and address the problem of evil. The deep suffering is not just the pain and suffering that one seeks to reconcile with omnipotence and omniscience, conceptually understood. It is the very absurdity, experienced in the contradiction that is the problem of evil. It is this contradiction that challenges the broader framework of meaning and existentially confronts individuals with the absence of an omnipotent, omnibenevolent God. The conceptual aporia called "the problem of evil" and the disrupted life-world associated with the illness experience each particularize in their own way that "problem of evil" called "sin" that is at the heart of the human predicament. An ethic of care that ministers to this primordial disruption should not focus only on the conceptual dimension, just as it should not focus only on the somatic dimension. By appreciating the congruence of the somatic and conceptual forms of disruption, one can move beyond those attempts that address the human predicament in a fragmented way and one can turn to the root problem.

From the Christian perspective it must be affirmed that one will only be able to fully understand when God's Kingdom has come. Only then will we be in a position where we no longer see through a glass dimly, and where the deep contradictions of the present life are overcome. To use a Hegelian idiom, it is important to remember that the Owl of Minerva takes flight at dusk, after a given form of life has fully blossomed (Hegel, 1967, p. 13). Only then can philosophy paint its conceptual grey on grey, and only then will the question and answer to the problem of evil obtain its philosophical form. Until then we live in the absurdity of a human condition that is both redeemed and yet to be redeemed. In this context, the role of the healer is not to convey a purely conceptual reconciliation, nor is it to simply restore somatic function. It is rather to convey an existential reconciliation, which anticipates and proleptically makes present the coming perfection of the Kingdom of God. Theodicy, as an appropriate response to the need seen in and as the problem of evil, must thus be Christian healing.[8]

Christian Healing

Healing involves the mediation of life. In Christianity the paradigm of such healing is found in Jesus Christ, "the one mediator between God and men" (1 Timothy 2:5). He provides the Image of God, the archetype of spiritual health. Through the cross, Christ took on the brokenness that humanity could not bear, redeeming those who could not redeem themselves. He entered into the condition and suffering, even the sinfulness, of those who had become alienated from spiritual life, and thereby mediated that life. Through the resurrection it became manifest that such self-giving was not futile, but bore within it the hope of a new, deeper existence, one that goes beyond that which is presently experienced (Khushf, 1993b, pp. 29-33).

In faith — the simple confidence in the prospect of that new life — the followers of Jesus emulate "the way" of death and resurrection (John 14:6). They too enter into the sufferings of others and thereby convey the life of Christ, just as Christ conveyed the life of God (Khushf, 1993a, ch. 4). When one enters into another's suffering, one takes that suffering upon oneself. For example, one comes and cries with the father whose child is dying of leukemia. Rather than stay at a distance and provide conceptual answers, one comes down into the confusion and uncertainty of the situation, never knowing exactly how to respond or what one can do (this is part of the uncertainty, and makes many people unwilling to visit those in grief or suffering). But one comes with a paradigm of life; namely, the gospel of Jesus Christ. Through this message, hope is brought into a situation where there is no hope. One comes with a confidence that the seemingly unredeemed and unredeemable suffering (in human terms) is overcome in a form of life that cannot yet be grasped, or, to the degree it is now seen, it is only seen "through a glass dimly" (1 Corinthians 13:12). By following this way of humility, the witness becomes conformed to the Image of God, and as a reflection of that Image makes the way of healing known to the one who is suffering. This is the form of Christian care. By entering into the suffering of the sufferer, by suffering-with (mit-leiden) the alienated other, the healer establishes a community that transcends the form of community from which the sufferer became alienated in the illness experience (Hauerwas, 1985, p. 223).

Since the problem of evil that characterizes the human condition has material, intellectual, and spiritual dimensions, the Christian response will not just involve the spiritual dimension by itself. Christianity is concerned with the whole person, and there is a "preferential love" for those who experience misery. Thus the proclamation in words and deeds of the message about healing (salvation) will also involve the use of natural means to respond to physical needs (Catechism of the Catholic Church, 1994, p. 588). Food will be gathered for the hungry, money for the poor, and medicine will be used to heal the sick. By "caring" for the needy physically, the Church will witness to the way God cares for humanity. The invisible will be made visible in the works of mercy. This essay has elaborated on the way this can take place in medicine.

It is important, however, for the Christian to appropriately direct the concern with physical misery such as sickness so that it does not veil its central concern with the healing of sin. Unfortunately, in many of the "Christian" hospitals and for many physicians a sense of their deeper calling has been lost. They have forgotten that the rupture in human identity does not first take place when one is ill or when a loved one is suffering. Rather, the fallen condition becomes manifest in these experiences. By disclosing the fallen character of humanity and thus the need for grace, "natural evils" provide a special opportunity for the Church to bear witness (John 9:3; 11:4). They make people more receptive to accepting the message of life. The task of a Christian bioethic should be to order the practice of medicine so that it responds to this opportunity; so that it unveils rather than veils the deeper healing offered by the Church.

In this essay I have considered the basic framework for the development of this bioethic. The task is now to work out its implications in the many particulars that constitute the content of a bioethic. Thus one will need to consider the dynamics between physician and patient, noting as well the way in which this relation is extended into one between Christian witness and hearer of the Word, and the way the physician can coordinate with other healers such as the minister or priest. One will need to consider the withholding and withdrawing of treatment, framing the debate with a recognition of the higher end of humanity and thus the limits of medicine. At an institutional level, one will need to ask what it means to develop a Christian hospital, or perhaps a Christian managed care plan. In each case one will not just look at supererogatory acts or motivation that is separate from norms (McCormick, 1995). Neither will one just consider the type of community needed to sustain medical practice (Hauerwas, 1985). One will be concerned with a fundamental, radical transformation of all acts so they are reordered toward their higher ends. The result will be an ethic of care that takes seriously the call of Christ on all those in the health care arena who would live their lives in his service.

Acknowledgment

I would like to thank Mark J. Cherry and Gerald McKenny for their critical comments and suggestions on an earlier draft of this essay.

Notes

1. This is from Basil the Great's Long Rule 55, quoted in Amundsen (1982, p. 338).

2. For an early use of this analogy, see John 9. The healing of the blind man is used analogous[illegible] how God gives sight to those who are in the[illegible] of sin. For Augustine this blind man symbo[illegible] human race, and the blindness is rooted in sin [illegible] tractate xliv). This passage in John is especially instructive since it explicitly raises the question about an individual's personal responsibility for sickness, and it points to sickness as an opportunity to manifest the works of God (9:2-3).

3. This shift from evangelization to humanitarianism can be found among most Christian denominations, especially the more liberal, main-line ones. For a discussion of the shift among Baptists, see Weber (1986, esp. p. 305).

4. In this essay I will not consider why a person would want to accept this end. Here it is simply assumed that one is working within the framework of Christian commitment, and one is considering what implications such commitment has for the norms of a Christian bioethic.

5. Hauerwas points to this sacramental function when he outlines the way in which the healer makes God present (1985). However, he does not sufficiently address the nature or "what" of presence, focusing purely on the fact or "that" of presence.

6. On the ambiguities of care and the different needs to which an ethic of care responds, see Hauerwas (1978).

7. Holistic medicine is often a substitute for a content-full tradition in a contemporary, pluralistic culture where one does not want the commitment associated with a tradition like Christianity. It then involves a rival account of human flourishing — an account that is often rooted in the myths of self-sufficiency outlined earlier in this essay. It should also be noted that there are many different types of holistic medicine, each with a different understanding of the human good.

8. Hauerwas (1990) is moving toward such an approach to the problem of evil when he recognizes that modern medicine has been viewed as a theodicy (ch. iii), and when he suggests that we need to move beyond medical solutions and come to a practice that is rooted in Christian community. Unfortunately, he does not say much about what such practice would involve other than being present to the sick person. How does this "Christian" presence distinguish itself from all the ways in which nonchristians are present to the sick?

References

Amundsen, D. W. (1982). "Medicine and faith in early Christianity," *Bulletin of the History of Medicine* 56, 326-50.

Amundsen, D. W., and Ferngren, G. (1986). "The Early Christian Tradition," in R. L. Numbers and D. W. Amundsen (eds.), *Caring and Curing: Health and Medicine in the Western Religious Traditions,* Macmillan Publishing Company, New York, pp. 40-64.

Augustine (1980a). "On the Creed: A Sermon to Catechumens," in P. Schaff (ed.), *Nicene and Post-Nicene Fathers of the Christian Church,* First Series, Vol. III, Wm. B. Eerdmans Publishing Company, Grand Rapids, Michigan, pp. 369-75.

Augustine (1980b). "On the Spirit and the Letter," in P. Schaff (ed.), *Nicene and Post-Nicene Fathers of the Christian Church,* First Series, Vol. V, Wm. B. Eerdmans Publishing Company, Grand Rapids, Michigan, pp. 80-114.

Augustine (1983a). "Expositions on the book of Psalms," in P. Schaff (ed.), *Nicene and Post-Nicene Fathers of the Christian Church,* First Series, Vol. VIII, Wm. B. Eerdmans Publishing Company, Grand Rapids, Michigan.

Augustine (1983b). "The City of God," in P. Schaff (ed.), *Nicene and Post-Nicene Fathers of the Christian Church,* First Series, Vol. II, Wm. B. Eerdmans Publishing Company, Grand Rapids, Michigan, pp. 1-511.

Boorse, C. (1975). "On the distinction between disease and illness." *Philosophy and Public Affairs,* 5, 49-68.

Catechism of the Catholic Church (1994). Liguori Publications, Liguori, Montana.

Curzer, H. J. (1993). "Is Care a Virtue for Health Care Professionals?," *Journal of Medicine and Philosophy,* 18, 51-69.

De Vries, P. (1969). *The Blood of the Lamb,* Little, Brown and Co., Boston.

Edelstein, L. (1967). "The Relation of Ancient Philosophy to Medicine," in O. Temkin and C. L. Temkin (eds.), *Ancient Medicine: Selected Papers of Ludwig Edelstein,* The Johns Hopkins Press, Baltimore, pp. 349-66.

Engelhardt, H. T. (1986). *The Foundations of Bioethics,* Oxford University Press, Oxford.

Engelhardt, H. T. (1992). "Observer Bias: The Emergence of the Ethics of Diagnosis," in J. L. Peset and D. Gracia, *The Ethics of Diagnosis,* Kluwer Academic Publishers, Dordrecht, pp. 63-71.

Foucault, M. (1975). *The Birth of the Clinic,* A. M. S. Smith (trans.), Vintage Books, New York.

Goodwin, J. S. (1991). "Geriatric Ideology: The Myth of the Myth of Senility," *Journal of the American Geriatrics Society* 39 6, 627-31.

Hauerwas, S. (1978). "Care," in W. T. Reich, *The Encyclopedia of Bioethics,* Vol. I, Free Press, New York, pp. 145-50.

Hauerwas, S. (1985). "Salvation and Health: Why Medicine Needs the Church," in E. Shelp (ed.), *Theology and Bioethics,* D. Reidel Publishing Company, Dordrecht, pp. 205-24.

Hauerwas, S. (1990). *Naming the Silences: God, Medicine, and the Problem of Suffering,* Wm. B. Eerdmans Publishing Company, Grand Rapids, Michigan.

Hegel, G. W. F. (1967). *Hegel's Philosophy of Right,* T. M. Knox (trans.), Oxford University Press, London.

Herberg, W. (1983). *Judaism and Modern Man,* Atheneum, New York.

Hick, J. (1978). *Evil and the God of Love,* Harper & Row, New York.

Humphrey, D., and Wickett, A. (1990). *The Right to Die,* The Hemlock Society, Eugene, Oregon.

Jockey, S. (1978). *The Road of Science and the Ways of God,* University of Chicago Press, Chicago.

Khushf, G. (1992). "Post-modern Reflections on the Ethics of Naming," in J. L. Peset and D. Gracia (eds.), *The Ethics of Diagnosis,* Kluwer Academic Publishers, Dordrecht.

Khushf, G. (1993a). *Deconstructing General Hermeneutics/(Re)Constructing a Biblical Hermeneutic,* University Microfilms International, Ann Arbor, Michigan.

Khushf, G. (1993b). 'Die Rolle des "Buchstabens" in der Geschichte des Abendlands und im Christentum," in H. U. Gumbrecht and K. L. Pfeiffer, *Schrift,* Wilhelm Fink Verlag, München.

Kushner, H. S. (1981). *When Bad Things Happen to Good People,* Schocken Books, New York.

Leder, D. (1992). "The Experience of Pain and Its Clinical Implications," in J. L. Peset and D. Gracia (eds.), *The Ethics of Diagnosis,* Kluwer Academic Publishers, Dordrecht, pp. 95-105.

Mainetti, J. A. (1992). "Embodiment, Pathology, and Diagnosis," in J. L. Peset and D. Gracia (eds.), *The Ethics of Diagnosis,* Kluwer Academic Publishers, Dordrecht, pp. 79-93.

McCormick, R. (1985). "Theology and Bioethics: Christian Foundations," in E. Shelp (ed.), *Theology and Bioethics,* D. Reidel Publishing Company, Dordrecht, pp. 95-113.

Niebuhr, R. (1953). *The Nature and Destiny of Man,* Vols. I and II, Charles Scribner's Sons, New York.

Niebuhr, R. (1984) "Sin," in A. Cohen and M. Halverson (eds.), *A Handbook of Christian Theology,* Abingdon Press, Nashville.

Sigerist, H. (1943). *Civilization and Disease,* Ithaca, New York.

Skelly, F. J. (1994). "Price of Pain Control," *American Medical News* (May 16), 13-15.

Skrabanek, P. (1994). *The Death of Humane Medicine,* St. Edmundsbury Press Ltd., Bury St. Edmunds, Suffolk.

Toombs, S. K. (1992). *The Meaning of Illness: A Phenomenological Account of the Different Perspectives of the Physician and Patient,* Kluwer Academic Publishers, Dordrecht.

Weber, T. P. (1986). "The Baptist Tradition," in R. Numbers and D. Amundsen (eds.), *Caring and Curing,* Macmillan Publishing Company, New York, pp. 288-316.

Chapter Two

THEOLOGY AND MEDICAL ETHICS

Long before medical ethics became a distinct field of inquiry, Christians and others with religious convictions had considered moral questions raised by health care and had tried to answer them in ways appropriate to the ways they talked of God and of the causes of God. It is not surprising, therefore, that these theological traditions were retrieved when developments in medicine prompted public concern and conversation in the decade of the sixties. As Daniel Callahan reported autobiographically, "When I first became interested in bioethics in the mid-1960s, the only resources were theological or those drawn from within the traditions of medicine, themselves heavily shaped by religion."[1] Nor is it surprising that theologians played an important role in what LeRoy Walters called the "renaissance of medical ethics."[2]

After the "renaissance," however, came the "enlightenment" of medical ethics. When the new questions and quandaries of medical ethics captured the attention of the media and the courts and legislatures, many thought it necessary to frame the arguments in what could be regarded as a common (and secular) moral language, a moral Esperanto. The *Belmont Report,* issued in 1978 by the National Commission for the Protection of Human Subjects, epitomized this approach by privileging an ethic of universal principles (autonomy, beneficence, and justice). Such principles were taken to transcend particular communities and specific identities; they were regarded as unbiased by any particular religious convictions. Medical ethics was, in a word, secularized.

In that same year James Gustafson published the article which stands at the head of this chapter (selection 7). In it he observed that a good deal of the literature on medical ethics, even when written by people trained as theologians, made no explicit reference to theological traditions or to religious convictions. He acknowledged that there are sometimes good reasons for bracketing one's religious convictions but lamented nevertheless the neglect of the relevance of religious traditions and theological reflection to issues in the ethics of health care. The first question set before the readers of this chapter, then, is whether it makes sense to share in Gustafson's lament. Does theology have a contribution to make to medical ethics? Should people with religious convictions set them aside in order to engage in public discussion about issues in bioethics? Can medical ethics be theological? Should it be?

If one shares Gustafson's lament, then the hard work begins. A second set of questions becomes inescapable: What is the contribution of theology to medical ethics? And how should theological reflection about these issues be conducted? The essays in this chapter set forth proposals concerning how best to construe that contribution and to engage in theological reflection about the issues in medical ethics.

Paul Ramsey, in the preface to *The Patient as Person* (selection 8), writing at the beginnings of the "renaissance" of medical ethics, proposed that we attend to certain "canons of loyalty" or "relationally objective norms," as he called them in another place, and he was not "embarrassed" to invoke the biblical notion of covenant to help defend and define our duties. He simply spoke his mind and gave his reasons, and the indebtedness of a mind or of reasons to a theological tradition was not assumed (not by Ramsey, at least) to limit the relevance of one's normative conclusions.

When the other essays are compared with Ramsey's preface, a number of methodologically significant questions emerge. One such question concerns the appropriate mode of moral reflection. If Ramsey concentrates on the constraints imposed by certain "canons of loyalty," Richard McCormick would direct attention and actions toward certain goods which should be achieved (and never repudiated). And if both Ramsey and McCormick focus in their different ways on choices about what should be done, others like Karen Lebacqz criticize such "decision-oriented" modes of moral reflection and focus instead on identity and community, proposing that questions of character and vision be given first and central consideration (see selection 12).

To some extent, these proposals simply rehearse the old debate in philosophical ethics about whether the appropriate mode of moral reflection is deontological, teleological, or aretological — whether, that is, conduct should be examined in terms of its conforming to some rule which ought to be obeyed, or in terms of its realizing some end which should be achieved, or in terms of its coherence with a virtuous character. In a theological account of morality, however, the mode of moral reflection will have to be appropriate to the way God is judged to be related to human moral agents and their conduct — and that judgment will have to be coherent with the sources acknowledged as authoritative in and for the community. One might note, for example, Ramsey's emphasis on covenant, McCormick's attention to the creative design and redemptive intention of God, and among those who focus on character some account of the story Christians tell and long to live.

A second methodologically significant question has to do with the relation of theological reflection on medical ethics to a "natural" morality. Ramsey's confidence that he could speak publicly as a Christian assumed that medicine was a "natural" covenant with canons of loyalty that had been formed (or "decisively influenced"[3]) by the Judeo-Christian tradition. McCormick is representative of the natural law tradition of Roman Catholicism with its confidence that certain values and goods are rooted in "natural inclinations" and, because they can be known by any rational person, the basis for conversation and consensus. Stanley Hauerwas, on the other hand, urged theologians not "to downplay the distinctiveness of their theological convictions in the interest of societal harmony" (selection 11), and he has been a persistent critic of the "enlightenment" effort to discover an ethic that transcends particular communities and their traditions. Lisa Sowle Cahill (selection 9) provides a thoughtful account of the contrast between the "natural law" approach and the more "confessional" approach of people like Hauerwas. She provides, moreover, an argument that these approaches are "not mutually exclusive but complementary."

Even if she is right, however, there remains the question of style. Both Gustafson and Cahill (and Campbell in the previous chapter, selection 5) distinguish a "priestly" and a "prophetic" style. Gustafson's essay honored the "radically prophetic stance" of some theologians but challenged them to exercise the priestly task of helping people with the real choices open to them in their social and historical contexts. People suffer, after all, not only from their historical contexts but also within them. On the other hand, one might honor the "priestly concern" of those who care for people within the context of existing institutions and current practices, whose legitimacy (or at least inevitability) they assume, but warn them that we are all at risk of being coopted by the establishment without the "countercultural" edge of more prophetic voices.

Finally, there is the question of sources for theological reflection about medical ethics. To be sure, there are many sources, and the relations between them are frequently complex. There are the sciences, for example, and one might argue that whatever one says theologically should not contradict what we know scientifically. Medical traditions, political and legal traditions, traditions in moral philosophy, as well as the Christian tradition play a role in theological reflection; and the Christian tradition includes not only ecclesiastical statements and liturgical practices but also, of course, the canonical part of that tradition, Scripture. There is, moreover, the experience of human beings, and especially the experience of the poor and oppressed. All of these are sources, but how are they related to each other, and is any one of them authoritative compared to the others? That Scripture has authority is accepted by almost all Christians, and all of the essays in this chapter make at least passing reference to it, but there are clearly different views about how Scripture functions authoritatively. Ramsey invoked "the biblical norm of *fidelity to covenant*" as backing for his approach. Hauerwas objected to such a use of Scripture; instead, he used Scripture to remember the story of Job's friends — and the story of God's presence — and so to train Christians for presence to the sick and suffering. The essay by Margaret Farley (selection 13) is quite clear both about the "primacy of women's experience as a source for theology and ethics" and about the importance of a "feminist hermeneutical principle" when reading and using Scripture as a source.

These are hard and complex questions. But they are worth pondering and discussing if one is at all sympathetic with Gustafson's lament, if one is at all discontent with the secular and minimal approaches to medical ethics which exclude or neglect the profound questions which care for the suffering inevitably raises.

Notes

1. Daniel Callahan, "Religion and the Secularization of Bioethics," *Hastings Center Report,* Special Supplement: "Theology, Religious Traditions, and Bioethics," 20, no. 4 (July/August 1990): 2.

2. LeRoy Walters, "Religion and the Renaissance of Medical Ethics," in *Theology and Bioethics: Exploring the Foundations and Frontiers,* ed. Earl E. Shelp (Dordrecht: D. Reidel Publishing Company, 1985), pp. 3-16.

3. Paul Ramsey, *Ethics at the Edges of Life* (New Haven: Yale University Press, 1978), p. xiv.

Suggestions for Further Reading

Bouma, Hessel III, Douglas Diekema, Edward Langerak, Theodore Rottman, Allen Verhey. *Christian Faith, Health, and Medical Practice* (Grand Rapids: William B. Eerdmans Publishing Company, 1989).

Callahan, Daniel, and Courtney S. Campbell, eds. "Theology, Religious Traditions, and Bioethics," A Special Supplement, *The Hastings Center Report* 20, no. 4 (July/August 1990), pp. 1-24.

Camenisch, Paul F., ed. *Religious Methods and Resources in Bioethics* (Dordrecht: Kluwer Academic Publishers, 1994).

Gustafson, James M. *The Contributions of Theology to Medical Ethics* (Milwaukee: Marquette University Press, 1975).

Gustafson, James M., and Stanley M. Hauerwas, eds. *Theology and Medical Ethics.* Issue of *The Journal of Medicine and Philosophy* 4 (December 1979).

Kilner, John F. *Life on the Line* (Grand Rapids: William B. Eerdmans Publishing Company, 1992).

MacIntyre, Alasdair. "Can Medicine Dispense with a Theological Perspective on Human Nature?" In *The Roots of Ethics,* edited by Daniel Callahan and H. Tristram Englehardt (New York: Plenum Press, 1981).

Shelp, Earl E., ed. *Secular Bioethics in Theological Perspective* (Dordrecht: Kluwer Academic Publishers, 1996).

Shelp, Earl E., ed. *Theology and Bioethics: Exploring the Foundations and Frontiers.* (Dordrecht: D. Reidel, 1985).

Tubbs, James B. Jr. *Christian Theology and Medical Ethics: Four Contemporary Approaches* (Dordrecht: Kluwer Academic Publishers, 1996).

Verhey, Allen, and Stephen E. Lammers, eds. *Theological Voices in Medical Ethics* (Grand Rapids: William B. Eerdmans Publishing Company, 1993).

Verhey, Allen, ed. *Religion and Medical Ethics: Looking Back, Looking Forward* (Grand Rapids: William B. Eerdmans Publishing Company, 1996).

Wheeler, Sondra Ely. *Stewards of Life: Bioethics and Pastoral Care* (Nashville: Abingdon, 1996).

7 Theology Confronts Technology and the Life Sciences

James M. Gustafson

That persons with theological training are writing a great deal about technology and the life sciences is clear to those who read *The Hastings Center Report, Theological Studies* and many other journals. Whether *theology* is thereby in interaction with these areas, however, is less clear. For some writers the theological authorization for the ethical principles and procedures they use is explicit; this is clearly the case for the most prolific and polemical of the Protestants, Paul Ramsey. For others, writing as "ethicists," the relation of their moral discourse to any specific theological principles, or even to a definable religious outlook is opaque. Indeed, in response to a query from a friend (who is a distinguished philosopher) about how the term "ethicist" has come about, I responded in a pejorative way, "An ethicist is a former theologian who does not have the professional credentials of a moral philosopher."

Much of the writing in the field is by persons who desire to be known as "religious ethicists" if only to distinguish themselves for practical reasons from those holding cards in the philosophers' union. Exactly what the adjective "religious" refers to, however, is far from obvious. If it refers to something as specific as "Christian" or "Jewish," or even "Protestant" or "Catholic," presumably writers would be willing to use the proper term. Again Ramsey is to be commended; one can ask for nothing more forthright than his 1974 declaration, "I always write as the ethicist I am, namely a Christian ethicist, and not as some hypothetical common denominator." If "religious ethicists" would even say what the "religious dimensions" of the problems were, we could place the adjective in some frame of reference: Tillichian, Deweyan, Luckmannian, Geertzian or what have you.

The difficulties in formulating a theological (and not merely moral) confrontation with technology and the life sciences are real, and not just apparent, as any of us who have written in this area knows. Unless the intended readership is one internal to the theological community, communication problems are exacerbated beyond the ordinary. Much of the writing is done for persons who are making policy or choices in the areas of technology, biological experimentation and clinical medicine. While there is a self-consciously Catholic constituency among these professional persons (for example, the member of the National Federation of Catholic Physicians' Guilds who sponsor *The Linacre Quarterly*), and while there may well be constituencies from the evangelical wing of Protestantism, most of the professional persons the writers seek to influence are judged not to be interested in the theological grounds from which the moral analysis and prescription grows. (I recall attending a party after a day of meetings with biologists and physicians at which a biologist, made friendlier by the ample libations provided, said to me, "Say something theological, Gustafson." I had the presence of mind to utter a guttural and elongated "Gawd.")

Not only is the audience frequently uninterested in the theological principles that might inform moral critique, but also the problems that are addressed are defined by the non-theologians, and usually are problems that emerge within a very confined set of circumstances. Should one cut the power source to a respirator for patient *y* whose circumstances are *a, b,* and *c?* Although the stakes are much higher, this is not utterly dissimilar to asking whether $8.20 an hour or $8.55 an hour ought to be paid to carpenters' helpers in Kansas City. Even a clear and well developed principle of distributive justice would not easily answer the latter question. To ask what "theology" might say to that question is patently more difficult. Obviously it is not easy to give a clearly theological answer to a question that is formulated so

From *Commonweal* 105 (June 16, 1978): 386-92. Used by permission.

that there are no theological aspects to it. To make the practical moral question susceptible to any recognizably theological answer requires nursing, massaging, altering, and maybe even transforming processes. When these processes are completed one might discover that a different set of issues are under discussion from those that originated the interaction.

To respond to specific questions requires more acumen in moral reasoning than it requires theological learning and acumen. I am sure that the writers of the manuals in medical moral theology were well schooled in the tractates on the Trinity; the bearing of those texts on their medical moral discussions, however, is at best remote. It is quite understandable, then, that theology (either as doctrine from an historic tradition, or ideas about the "religious dimensions" of life) tends to be displaced in the attention of the writer by ethical theory and by procedures of practical moral reasoning.

In the Catholic tradition with its continued development of natural law as a basis for ethics an intellectual legitimation for the autonomy of moral theology developed; the natural moral order was itself created by God so the natural order was God's order. Ethical analysis and prescription were theological in principle; moralists were theologians by being moralists. Enough said about theology. Unfortunately, in this tradition the resources and dimensions of theological reflection became confined to a basic theological authorization for ethics, and almost nothing more. And the ethical questions were stirred by particular acts about which judgments of moral rightness or wrongness could be made. It did not occur to these moralists, for example, to wonder if the prophets' critiques of the worship of Baal might not provide, by an act of imagination if not by well developed analogy, some basis for a theological criticism of the excessive scrupulosity that the moral enterprise itself might promote.

A brute fact, and a source of some embarrassment in discourse with the professionals in technology and the life sciences, is the lack of consensus among theologians on some rather simple matters. What is it that theologians think about and write about? What is the subject matter of theology? The high degree of *anomie* among practicing theologians, and the uncertainty among some as to what defines their work as theological, is hardly an asset to any interaction between "theology" and technology and the life sciences. A tired old story from the years of the banquet circuit of the National Conference of Christian and Jews comes to mind. A priest, a Protestant minister and a rabbi were asked to respond to the same question. The priest began, "The Church teaches that. . ." The rabbi began, "The tradition teaches that. . ." The minister began, "Now I think that. . ." There are very good historical and intellectual explanations for the extension of a kind of Protestant *anomie* to the theological enterprise as a whole, but explanations of why it is hard to answer the simple question "what is the subject matter of theology?" do little to identify a melody in a collective cacophonous response. I can readily cite coherent passages from Tillich on technology, Barth on clinical medical moral problems, Rahner on the uses of genetic knowledge, and Ramsey on why Richard McCormick's Jesuit probabilism requires a rigorist response, but I see no way in which I can find among them a basis for a generalization about how theology confronts technology and the life sciences.

We know what many of the *moral* issues are in technology and the life sciences; we are not sure what the "religious" or *theological* issues are. While debate continues about what moral principles ought to be decisive in determining courses of action in the life sciences and technology, at least the principles under debate can be formulated with some conceptual precision. Much of the literature deals with such matters as the rights of individuals, the preservation of individual self-determination, the conditions under which others might exercise their own self-determination, and the consideration of what benefits and whose good might justify overriding the rights of individuals. Certain principles are invoked constantly: informed consent, risk-benefit ratios, distributive justice, and so forth. There are procedures for justifying particular judgments; there are complex prescriptions like double-effect.

Nothing of comparable detail and precision exists in the more strictly theological realm of discourse; and for various theological reasons the sorts of questions a previous generation asked — such as "What is God doing in these circumstances?" or "What is God saying to us through these crises?" — appear to be very odd and unanswerable. Ethics provides a basis for a new casuistry that is indispensable as long as the issues are framed by the professional persons who have to make particular choices, and as long as the terms of discussion are those on which there can be some consensus, namely ethical terms. No doubt there can be a theological justification for the casuistry, but then there can also be a lot of other, non-theological justification for it. The ethical questions have become fairly clear, and to an ethical question one gives an ethical answer, whether one is a physician, engineer, philosopher or theologian. The theological questions are not clear, and as a result frequently even those writers trained in theology neither attempt to make them clear, nor attempt to answer those that can be asked.

Matters of Belief

I have long believed and often said, that many of the debates that are passionately conducted within the framework of ethics are misplaced, and that the issues that divide persons are matters of beliefs (whether theological in function or in fact, or whether moral or something else we need not decide here) and loyalties which determine our value choices. Paul Ramsey's Beecher Lectures at Yale, from which came the widely read *The Patient as Person*, provoked a discussion between an internist and surgeon both of whom worked in the renal program. The internist was much taken by Ramsey's argument and vehemently supported the Uniform Anatomical Gifts Act, an act stipulating in precise detail the consent procedures for using an organ from a corpse. The surgeon strongly expressed the opinion that hospitals and their staff ought legally to be authorized to "salvage" from corpses any usable organs that might benefit the health and prolong the life of patients. There certainly are ways to deal with the controversy between these two that might lead to some agreement — that might determine whether to pay the carpenters' helpers $8.20 or $8.55 an hour. The precision of the debates at the level of casuistry is not to be demeaned. But the difference between these two physicians really stemmed from more general beliefs and valuations, and these divergences will not be settled, or even addressed, by the latest refinement of the principle of double-effect and its application to cases in the operating room.

Who ought to address these differences? What is the agenda for exploring them? What are the grounds for convictions about the "limit questions," to use Stephen Toulmin's phrase? In a most technical sense, perhaps, these are not yet "theological" questions; but surely they demand a response that is more "theological" than casuistic. And surely there are resources in the religious traditions, in speculative natural theologies, and in the discussions of "religious dimensions" that can be used at least to frame the questions and explore answers to them.

A different example reveals the need for another kind of discourse which at least approaches "theology" if it is not theology. How one understands the relation of self and society, how this relationship is interpreted and conceptualized has profound effects upon the outcome of very specific answers to specific questions. I shall illustrate this too simply by suggesting that the competing metaphors used to depict this relationship are the mechanistic and the organic. The first understands society basically in contractual terms; society is a structure that individuals voluntarily agree to institute and develop. The second understands society, obviously, in organic terms; society is a network of interrelatedness and interdependence in which the relations of the parts are "internal" (I do not intend to invoke a whole Hegelian view by using this term), and in which the development of the well-being of the whole must be considered, if not supreme, at least on par with the well-being of its individual members. The population geneticist tends to take the latter view; when he or she speaks of "benefits," the reference is to the human species. When the ecologist speaks of benefits, the reference is to the well-being of life on the planet. Physicians and most persons writing about ethical issues in medicine and the life sciences have consciously or implicitly adopted the more mechanistic metaphor, and not without some good reasons. Those who use the organic metaphor are more ready to justify overriding an individual "right." If there is any plausibility to my observations, it is fair to ask who is responsible to think about such matters of basic perception, in this case of the relations of individuals to society.

What data and warrants support alternative views, and which view in the end appears more adequate?

Another example refers more specifically to Christians and their doctrinal differences. I have argued elsewhere that Karl Rahner's apparent openness to certain kinds of experimentation on humans is a reasonable conclusion from his philosophical and theological anthropology, and from his understanding of the relations of grace and nature. This openness so alarmed Paul Ramsey that he described it as "remarkably like a priestly blessing over everything, doing duty for ethics" and yet Rahner's attitude rests firmly on theological and philosophical grounds.

If one does not like Rahner's openness (which is really very guarded and has several severely restraining principles) one has to argue with his theological and philosophical anthropology and with his views of the relations of grace and nature. If one is persuaded that Rahner's theology is the best available for the Catholic Church today (and the number of dissertations sympathetically exploring his thought suggest that quite a few people are so persuaded), then one ought to come out in moral theology somewhere within the range of his conclusions. If one is concerned that Rahner's openness is morally dangerous in its potential consequences, perhaps one ought to examine one's own theological anthropology, and one's own views of grace and nature. The proper argument is not to be confined to the consequences of relatively closed or open positions but must pursue the question further, to the adequacy of doctrines of God and different anthropologies. A *real* theological discussion then becomes unavoidable.

In the course of such an argument an apparently astounding matter might be seen, namely that one's theological convictions and their articulation in principles about the character of ultimate reality and about human life have a fundamental bearing on one's attitude toward the life sciences and technology. This bearing, in fact, might be more significant in determining one's particular moral preferences than the specific principles chosen to justify a particular decision. It might turn out that passionate ethical debates about technology and the life sciences are missing the crucial point where the real differences lie, and (my goodness!) "ethicists" might have to become theologians! They might find an agenda that would give them something distinctive to do!

To be trained in theology should alert one to aspects of discussion that are otherwise hidden. Several years ago a number of us participated in an intensive conference with research and clinical geneticists. One of the papers was rather more utopian in outlook than the others; its author limned out a vision of the vast benefits to the human race that would accrue from vigorous pursuit of genetic research. I call such scientists "hawks." The paper generated a very passionate discussion, mostly by other scientists and clinicians. Among them were the "doves." Indeed, the rhetoric in the discussion was what those of us alert to religious language could only call apocalyptic. One could interpret the whole discussion as a contest between competing eschatologies: prospects for a universal salvation pitted against prospects for eternal annihilation. The arguments were finally not about matters of hard science; there were some discussions about whose extrapolations from the known to the unknown were most reliable, and about the time frame in which certain possibilities (such as cloning of humans) might occur. But what really divided the disputants were questions that traditionally have been judged to be religious in character.

Most apparent was the question "For what can we hope?" And that could not be answered without asking, in effect, "In whom can we trust?" and "In what can we trust?" Also in dispute were answers to the question "What is desirable?" — which to my mind, incorrigibly saturated with biblical and theological language, becomes "What are proper objects of our love?" I feel I do not unduly alter what went on there if I say we were in the midst of a discussion of hope, faith and love. We were also in a discussion of the proper objects of hope, faith and love. No one proposed the Pauline answer, "Your hope is in God." Or the more general Christian answer, "Trust in God." Or the Augustinian answer, "God is the proper object of desire." But the discussion was about whether one should trust chance, or the evolutionary process with minimal intervention, or scientists and statesmen who have power to intervene. The house could readily have been divided between the Augustinians and Pelagians on other questions: the extent of "free will" and the depths of human corruption. It cannot be said that my intervention, in which I pointed out these themes, turned the conversation to one about theology, and certainly about Christian theology, as a subject in itself. I do believe, however, that something dawned in the consciousness of some participants: theology might not provide answers you like to accept, but it can force questions you ought to be aware of. To paraphrase the title of an article by H. Richard Niebuhr, in these circumstances theology is not queen, but servant.

This article ought to have made clear my criticisms of the interchange between theology and technology and the life sciences as long as that interchange is confined merely to the "ethical." With equal severity I would criticize those who confine the theological discussion to *Zeitgeist,* ethos and other comparably general terms. To be honored in such theologians is their radically prophetic stance. They know golden calves when they see them, and they see them sooner than persons preoccupied with how to get from one oasis to the next in the Sinai of contemporary culture and society. I have been accused, in my preoccupation with some matters of a casuistic sort, of "rearranging the deck chairs on the *Titanic.*" Valid charge. My equally nasty retort to those critics is that they think the only proper response is to jump in the North Atlantic and push the icebergs away.

Whether or not one uses the religious language of idolatry, the attack on ethos and *Zeitgeist* implies a call to radical repentance, to a turning away from the Baals of technology whose reliability is bound to fail, and to whom cultural devotion can only lead to desolation for the coming generations. What the culture is to turn from is clear; that it is to return to Yahweh is not necessarily proclaimed. That persons and society are in bondage to the powers of technology, that they are looking for a "salvation" in medical therapy that therapy cannot give them, these are poignantly indicated by the contemporary prophets. That the need is for liberation from bondage, and that some fundamental conversion of individuals and of ethos is required, these points are well made. The sickness is "global" and the antidote must be sufficient for the poison. The creative and exasperating French Protestant Jacques Ellul is one such prophet; he works out of a highly biblical and confessional theology. Not only technology and science, but programs of social revolution and churches feel the sting of his prophetic rhetoric. For him and others like him, technology tends to become reified as a demonic power which only the power of the crucifixion can overcome.

Myopic casuists need strong enough lenses to see the point of the radical theological critics. On the other hand, the perspectives of the radical prophets make conversation with persons who specialize in technology and the life sciences very difficult. If they cannot address the specific and concrete manifestation of the ethos (if it can be said to exist independently) in the particularities of cases and policy choices, if they cannot show how their theologies address the issues as they arise out of specific activities, conversation never gets down to the ground. Many theologians who are critics of culture write for other theologians and for a half-converted religious readership even when they are writing as theologians of culture — technological culture, "modern" culture, or what have you. Indeed, often when they write about the *need* for theology to be engaged in criticism of technological and scientific culture, they are addressing a like-minded group. Why not *test* the need and the practice on an endocrinologist who researches testosterone levels?

Sometimes it turns out that those who are famous as prophetic critics of culture have nothing very specific to say about any particular event in technology and the use of the life sciences. We are told, for example, that a theology of hope addresses social and cultural issues. It turns out that the principal point of the address is that present institutions and cultural values are ephemeral and relative, and we ought not to absolutize them. Thanks a lot! Any student of the history of science and technology knows that. That does not assist the committees on experimentation on human subjects on which I sit to decide whether protocol #6172 is acceptable from a moral perspective. That particular *Titanic* has not yet sunk, and there is merit in arranging things so that it can stay afloat for some time in the future, or at least in organizing things so the lifeboats can be used effectively. Theology cannot push the icebergs away. It might at least help to develop the radar technology that aids in avoiding them.

The moralists find a vocabulary enabling them to interact with the professionals from technology and the life sciences; this tends to limit the theological questions. The prophetic theologians find a vocabulary that is somewhat "theological" in some sense which enables them to interact with other theologians and with other prophetic critics of the ethos; this tends to limit their capacities to relate to the specific occasions in which critical choices have to be made.

Since this is my occasion for broadsides, yet another group of writers can be noted. They are those concerned about the relations between "religion" and "science." Frequently both terms are abstractions: these writers are not concerned about the relations of Judaism to human genetics. They frequently publish in that very interesting journal called *Zygon*. Their intention is to humanize technology and science with some sense of the sacred, and to scientize theology with arguments that presumably support "religion." While it is the case that all modern theology continues to reel from the impact of the Enlightenment, and that theologians continue to find philosophical bases on which to justify the existence of religion (or "the religious" as some like to call it), on the whole this synthetic enterprise is not in the best of repute philosophically, scientifically, or theologically and for some substantial reasons.

"Sciences are a fundamental resource for theology," writes Ralph Wendell Burhoe, a person seldom cited by professional theologians but more widely known than Van Harvey or Gordon Kaufman or David Tracy by groups of scientists interested in the relations of science and religion. Burhoe is confident. He writes, "I suggest that before this century is out we shall see all over the world an increasing integration of information from the sciences into the heart of the belief systems of traditional religions. I prophesy human salvation through a reformation and rehabilitation of religion at a level superior to any reformation in earlier histories, a level high above that of Jasper's axial age as that was above the primitive religions of 10,000 B.C. . . . The new religious and theological language will be as high above that of five centuries ago as contemporary cosmology is above the Ptolemaic, as contemporary medicine, agriculture, communications and transportation concepts are above those of the fifteenth century." Burhoe's program is in sharpest contrast with those theologians that Kai Nielsen has called "Wittgensteinian fideists" who separate religious consciousness and language from scientific consciousness and language in such a way that the former is virtually rendered immune from any criticism by the latter.

In effect the writers of whom Burhoe is fairly typical aspire to develop both theology and ethics on the basis of science, and the life sciences seem to have a privileged place in these proposals. The enterprise is not novel, and different proposals come forward from it about the biological bases for ethics, for knowledge of ultimate reality, and for other matters. Now, no less than in previous decades, it is fraught with difficulties that have frequently been indicated by philosophers of science, philosophers of religion, and moral philosophers. Inferences from scientific data and theories to theological and ethical conclusions are often weakly warranted. The enterprise has the merit of a challenge, however. Can we think theologically and ethically on the basis of what we know about biology? If we find an affirmative answer to the question unacceptable, at least we have to give our reasons for that, and we are left with the chore of figuring out just how knowledge of biology relates to ethics and theology. That is a philosophical and theological problem as important for one aspect of culture as the relation of Marxist theory to ethics and theology for another.

What can be anticipated about theology's "confrontation" with technology and the life sciences? I have amply distributed my criticisms so that few, if any, theologically trained writers in this field are exempt, including myself. I have not described the social, historical and institutional contexts in which the discussions increasingly occur. As far as the ethical responses are concerned, what was a lively, interdisciplinary enterprise even a decade ago has increasingly become a separate profession, if only because the volume of literature has exponentially increased so that it takes a fulltime effort to be in control of it. Theologically trained writers had a prominence a decade ago that is receding and will continue to do so. Their prominence was in part the effect of the concern that religious communities had for practical moral questions, a concern that moral philosophers, until very recently, looked upon with haughty disdain. Now philosophers, physicians and many other professions are contributing a larger portion of the literature than was the case. Separate institutes, national commissions, advisory committees and other organizations have come into being. Theologically trained persons have not been excluded from participation in these, and indeed continue to be significant contributors, but insofar as the contribution of the "theologians" has been and continues to be "practical moral philosophy," the basis of their being attended to is shared by practitioners who are at least as skillful as they are. Competence in argumentation is the criterion by which their contributions will be judged, and a number of them will continue to be highly respected.

Usage and Interpretation

But what if "theologians" choose to be clearer about what the theological issues, or the "religious dimensions," are in the life sciences and technology? I grant that some anxieties will arise. There is not a wide world waiting to hear about these ideas, since they do not immediately assist in determining what constitutes a just distribution of health care resources. There may, however, be more people out there who are interested than we presently recognize. Traditional theological language, and perhaps also the efforts to decontaminate its historical particularities with the language of natural theology or of religious dimensions, will require some skillful usage and significant interpretation. Timidity might be as much a restraining factor as are the objectively real problems in undertaking such discourse. Theologians and other religious thinkers seem highly self-conscious of their own cultural relativity; they often forget that other areas of thought share the same plight. It will have to be accepted that not everyone in that highly esteemed secular technological culture will be interested in the contributions of theologians, but that some persons (even some with social power) might.

In the meantime there are still a large number of people who attend churches, and who seem not fully alienated from traditional religious language and practice. They fall sick, have unexpected pregnancies, vote for legislators who in turn vote on health insurance plans and funding of research. Catholic moral theologians are more conscious of that constituency than are Protestants. Perhaps there is quite a bit to be done to help these persons understand technology in the light of their religious faith and convictions!

In the matters I have been discussing as in so many others, my impression is that much theological or "religious" writing is directed to the justification of an enterprise in the eyes of persons who are not really interested enough to care whether the justification is adequate or not. (I worked for years on a book *Can Ethics Be Christian?* with the nagging sense that most persons who answer in an unambiguous affirmative would not be interested in my supporting argument, that a few fellow professional persons might be interested enough to look at it, and that for those who believe the answer is negative the question itself is not sufficiently important to bother about.) While theologians ought to continue to participate competently in the public debates about matters of technology and the life sciences, they would also do well to attend to the home folks who *might* care more about what they have to say. I am not suggesting that theologians are the best retail communicators, but that the historically identifiable religious communities are fairly obvious loci to be taken into account in writing theology and theological ethics in relation to technology and the life sciences.

It is the "religious ethicists" who have most to be anxious about, in my judgment. They will have either to become moral philosophers with a special interest in "religious" texts and arguments, or become theologians: Christian theologians, or natural theologians, or "religious dimensions" theologians. Only indifference to what they are writing, or exceeding patience with inexcusable ambiguity, can account for the tolerance they have enjoyed.

8 Preface to *The Patient as Person*

Paul Ramsey

The problem of medical ethics that are especially urgent in the present day are by no means technical problems on which only the expert (in this case, the physician) can have an opinion. They are rather the problems of human beings in situations in which medical care is needed. Birth and death, illness and injury are not simply events the doctor attends. They are moments in every human life. The doctor makes decisions as an expert but also as a man among men; and his patient is a human being coming to his birth or to his death, or being rescued from illness or injury in between.

Therefore, the doctor who attends *the case* has reason to be attentive to the patient as person. Resonating throughout his professional actions, and crucial in some of them, will be a view of man, an understanding of the meaning of the life at whose first or second exodus he is present, a care for the life he attends in its afflictions. In this respect the doctor is quite like the rest of us, who must yet depend wholly on him to diagnose the options, perhaps the narrow range of options, and to conduct us through the one that is taken.

To take up for scrutiny some of the problems of medical ethics is, therefore, to bring under examination at once a number of crucial human moral problems. These are not narrowly defined issues of medical ethics alone. Thus this volume has — if I may say so — the widest possible audience. It is addressed to patients as persons, to physicians of patients who are persons — in short, to everyone who has had or will have to do with disease or death. The question, What ought the doctor to do? is only a particular form of the question, What should be done?

This, then, is a book *about ethics,* written by a Christian ethicist. I hold that medical ethics is consonant with the ethics of a wider human community. The former is (however special) only a particular case of the latter. The moral requirements governing the relations of physician to patients and researcher to subjects are only a special case of the moral requirements governing any relations between man and man. Canons of loyalty to patients or to joint adventurers in medical research are simply particular manifestations of canons of loyalty of person to person generally. Therefore, in the following chapters I undertake to explore a number of medical covenants among men. These are the covenant between physician and patient, the covenant between research and "subject" in experiments with human beings, the covenant between men and a child in need of care, the covenant between the living and the dying, the covenant between the well and the ill or with those in need of some extraordinary therapy.

We are born within covenants of life with life. By nature, choice, or need we live with our fellowmen in roles or relations. Therefore we must ask, What is the meaning of the *faithfulness* of one human being to another in every one of these relations? This is the ethical question.

At crucial points in the analysis of medical ethics, I shall not be embarrassed to use as an interpretative principle the Bible norm of *fidelity to covenant,* with the meaning it gives to *righteousness* between man and man. This is not a very prominent feature in the pages that follow, since it is also necessary for an ethicist to go as far as possible into the technical and other particular aspects of the problems he ventures to take up. Also, in the midst of any of these urgent human problems, an ethicist finds that he has been joined — whether in agreement or with some disagreement — by men of various persuasions, often quite different ones. There is in actuality a community of moral discourse concerning the claims of persons. This is the main appeal in the pages that follow.

Still we should be clear about the moral and

From Paul Ramsey, *The Patient as Person* (New Haven: Yale University Press, 1970), pp. xi-xviii.

religious premises here at the outset. I hold with Karl Barth that covenant-fidelity is the inner meaning and purpose of our creation as human beings, while the whole of creation is the external basis and condition of the possibility of covenant. This means that the conscious acceptance of covenant responsibilities is the inner meaning of even the "natural" or systemic relations into which we are born and of the institutional relations or roles we enter by choice, while this fabric provides the external framework for human fulfillment in explicit covenants among men. The practice of medicine is one such covenant. *Justice, fairness, righteousness, faithfulness, canons of loyalty,* the *sanctity* of life, *hesed, agapé* or *charity* are some of the names given to the moral quality of attitude and of action owed to all men by any man who steps into a covenant with another man — by any man who, so far as he is a religious man, explicitly acknowledges that we are a covenant people on a common pilgrimage.

The chief aim of the chapters to follow is, then, simply to explore the meaning of *care,* to find the actions and abstentions that come from adherence to *covenant,* to ask the meaning of the *sanctity* of life, to articulate the requirements of steadfast *faithfulness* to fellow man. We shall ask, What are the moral claims upon us in crucial medical situations and human relations in which some decision must be made about how to show respect for, protect, preserve, and honor the life of fellow man?

Just as man is a *sacredness in the social, political order,* so he is a *sacredness in the natural, biological order.* He is a sacredness in bodily life. He is a person who within the ambience of the flesh claims our care. He is an embodied soul or ensouled body. He is therefore a sacredness in illness and in his dying. He is a sacredness in the fruits of the generative process. (From some point he is this if he has any sanctity, since it is undeniably the case that men are never more than, from generation to generation, the products of human generation.) The sanctity of human life prevents ultimate trespass upon him even for the sake of treating his bodily life, or for the sake of others who are also only a sacredness in their bodily lives. Only a being who is a sacredness in the social order can withstand complete dominion by "society" for the sake of engineering civilizational goals — withstand, in the sense that the engineering of civilizational goals cannot be accomplished without denying the sacredness of the human being. So also in the use of medical or scientific technics.

It is of first importance that this be understood, since we live in an age in which *hesed* (steadfast love) has become *maybe* and the "sanctity" of human life has been reduced to the ever more reducible notion of the "dignity" of human life. The latter is a sliver of a shield in comparison with the awesome respect required of men in all their dealings with men if man has a touch of sanctity in this his fetal, mortal, bodily, living and dying life.

Today someone is likely to say: "Another 'semanticism' which is somewhat of an argument-stopper has to do with the sacredness or inviolability of the individual."[1] If such a principle is asserted in gatherings of physicians, it is likely to be met with another argument-stopper: It is immoral not to do research (or this experiment must be done despite its necessary deception of human beings). This is then a standoff of contrary moral judgments or intuitions or commitments.

The next step may be for someone to say that medical advancement is hampered because our "society" makes an absolute of the inviolability of the individual. This raises the spectre of a medical and scientific community freed from the shackles of that cultural norm, and proceeding upon the basis of an ethos all its own. Alternatively, the next move may be for someone to say: Our major task is to reconcile the welfare of the individual with the welfare of mankind; both must be served. This, indeed, is the principal task of medical ethics. However, there is no "unseen hand" guaranteeing that, for example, *good* experimental designs will always be morally *justifiable.* It is better not to begin with the laissez-faire assumption that the rights of men and the needs of future progress are always reconcilable. Indeed, the contrary assumption may be more salutary.

Several statements of this viewpoint may well stand as mottos over all that follows in this volume. "In the end we may have to accept the fact that some limits do exist to the search for knowledge."[2] "The end does not always justify the means, and the good things a man does can be made complete only by the things he refuses to do."[3] "There may be valuable scientific knowledge which it is morally impossible to obtain. There may be truths which would be of great and lasting benefit to mankind if they could be discovered, but which cannot be discovered without systematic and sustained violation of legitimate moral imperatives. It may be necessary to choose between knowledge and morality, in opposition to our long-standing prejudice that the two must go together."[4] "To justify whatever practice we think is technically demanded by showing that we are doing it for a good end . . . is both the best defense and the last refuge of a scoundrel."[5] "A[n experimental] study is ethical or not in its inception; it does not become ethical or not because it turned up valuable data."[6] These are salutary warnings precisely because by them we are driven to make the most searching inquiry concerning more basic ethical principles governing medical practice.

Because physicians deal with life and death, health and maiming, they cannot avoid being conscious or deliberate in their ethics to some degree. However, it is important to call attention to the fact that medical ethics cannot remain at the level of surface intuitions or in an impasse of conversation-stoppers. At this point there can be no other resort than to ethical theory — as that elder statesman of medical ethics, Dr. Chauncey D. Leake, Professor of Pharmacology at the University of California Medical Center, San Francisco, so often reminds us. At this point physicians must in greater measure become moral philosophers, asking themselves some quite profound questions about the nature of proper moral reasoning, and how moral dilemmas are rightly to be resolved. If they do not, the existing medical ethics will be eroded more and more by what it is alleged *must* be done and technically *can* be done.

In the medical literature there are many articles on ethics which are greatly to be admired. Yet I know that these are not part of the daily fare of medical students, or of members of the profession when they gather together as professionals or even for purposes of conviviality. I do not believe that either the codes of medical ethics or the physicians who have undertaken to comment on them and to give fresh analysis of the physician's moral decisions will suffice to withstand the omnivorous appetite of scientific research or of a therapeutic technology that has a momentum and a life of its own.

The Nuremberg Code, The Declaration of Helsinki, various "guidelines" of the American Medical Association, and other "codes" governing medical practice constitute a sort of "catechism" in the ethics of the medical profession. These codes exhibit a professional ethics which ministers and theologians and members of other professions can only profoundly respect and admire. Still, a catechism never sufficed. Unless these principles are constantly pondered and enlivened in their application they become dead letters. There is also need that these principles be deepened and sensitized and opened to further humane revision in face of all the ordinary and the newly emerging situations which a doctor confronts — as do we all — in the present day. In this task none of the sources of moral insight, no understanding of humanity of man or for answering questions of life and death, can rightfully be neglected.

There is, in any case, no way to avoid the moral pluralism of our society. There is no avoiding the fact that today no one can do medical ethics until someone first does so. Due to the uncertainties in Roman Catholic moral theology since Vatican Council II, even the traditional medical ethics courses in schools under Catholic auspices are undergoing vast changes, abandonment, or severe crisis. The medical profession now finds itself without one of the ancient landmarks — or without one opponent. Research and therapies and actionable schemes for the self-creation of our species mount exponentially, while Nuremberg recedes.

The last state of the patient (medical ethics) may be worse than the first. Still there is evidence that this can be a moment of great opportunity. An increasing number of moralists — Catholic, Protestant, Jewish and unlabeled men — are manifesting interest, devoting their trained powers of ethical reasoning to questions of medical practice and technology. This same galloping technology gives all mankind reason to ask how much longer we can go on assuming that what can be done has to be done or should be, without uncovering the ethical principles we mean to abide by. These questions are now completely in the public forum, no longer the province of scientific experts alone.

The day is past when one could write a manual on medical ethics. Such books by Roman Catholic moralists are not to be criticized for being deductive. They were not; rather they were commendable attempts to deal with concrete cases. These manuals were written with the conviction that moral reasoning can encompass hard cases, that ethical deliberation need not remain highfalutin but can "subsume" concrete situations under the illuminating power of human moral reason. However, the manuals can be criticized for seeking finally to "resolve" innumerable cases and to give the once and for all "solution" to them. This attempt left the impression that a rule book could be written for medical practice. In a sense, this impression was the consequence of a chief virtue of the authors, i.e., that they were resolved to think through a problem, if possible, *to the end* and precisely with relevance and applicability in concrete cases. Past medical moralists can still be profitably read by anyone who wishes to face the challenge of how he would go about prolonging ethical reflection into action.

Medical ethics today must, indeed, be "casuistry"; it must deal as competently and exhaustively as possible with the concrete features of actual moral decisions of life and death and medical care. But we can no longer be so confident that "resolution" or "solution" will be forthcoming.

While no one can do ethics in the medical and technological context until someone first does so, anyone can engage in the undertaking. Anyone can do this who is trained in one field of medicine and willing to specialize for a few years in ethical reasoning about these questions. Anyone can who is trained in ethics and willing to learn enough about the technical problems to locate the decisional issues. This is not a personal plea. It is rather a plea that in order to become an ethicist or a moral theologian doctors have only to quit resisting being one. An ethicist is only an ordinary man and a moral theologian is only a religious man endeavoring to push out as far as he can the frontier meaning of the practice of a rational or a charitable justice, endeavoring to draw forth all the actions and abstentions that this justice requires of him in his vocation. I am sure that by now there are a number of physicians who have felt rather frustrated as they patiently tried to explain to me some technical medical circumstance I asked about. At the same time, I can also testify to some degree of frustration as I have at times patiently tried to explain some of the things that need to be asked of the science and methods of ethics. Physicians and moralists must go beyond these positions if we are to find the proper moral warrants and learn how to think through moral dilemmas and resolve disagreements in moral judgment concerning medical care.

To this level of inquiry we are driven today. The ordinary citizen in his daily rounds is bound to have an opinion on medical ethical questions, and physicians are bound to look after the good moral reasons for the decisions they make and lead society to agree to. This, then, is a plea for fundamental dialogue about the urgent moral issues arising in medical practice.

No one can alter the fact that not since Socrates posed the question have we learned how to teach virtue. The quandaries of medical ethics are not unlike that question. Still, we can no longer rely upon the ethical assumptions in our culture to be powerful enough or clear enough to instruct the profession in virtue; therefore the medical profession should no longer believe that the personal integrity of physicians alone is enough; neither can anyone count on values being transmitted without thought.

To take up the questions of medical ethics for probing, to try to enter into the heart of these problems with reasonable and compassionate moral reflection, is to engage in the greatest of joint ventures: the moral becoming of man. This is to see in the prism of medical cases the claims of any man to be honored and respected. So might we enter thoughtfully and actively into the moral history of mankind's fidelity to covenants. In this everyone is engaged.

Notes

1. Wolf Wolfenberger, "Ethical Issues in Research with Human Subjects," *Science* 155 (January 6, 1967): 48.

2. Paul A. Freund, "Is the Law Ready for Human Experimentation?" *Trial* 2 (October-November, 1966): 49; "Ethical Problems in Human Experimentation," *New England Journal of Medicine* 273, No. 10 (September 10, 1965): 692.

3. Dunlop (1965), quoted in Douglass Hubble, "Medical Science, Society and Human Values," *British Medical Journal* 5485 (February 19, 1966): 476.

4. James P. Scanlan, "The Morality of Deception in Experiments," *Bucknell Review* 13, No. 1 (March, 1965): 26.

5. John E. Smith, "Panel Discussion: Moral Issues in Clinical Research," *Yale Journal of Biology and Medicine* 36 (June, 1964): 463.

6. Henry K. Beecher, *Research and the Individual: Human Studies* (Boston: Little Brown, 1970), p. 25.

9 Can Theology Have a Role in "Public" Bioethical Discourse?

Lisa Sowle Cahill

Religious groups indubitably have been active in pressing their bioethical concerns in the public arena of the United States. One thinks preeminently of the efforts of the Roman Catholic Church and its representatives, or of religiously motivated "pro-life" activists, who quite visibly aim to influence public perceptions and policies on reproductive issues such as abortion and infertility therapies, and on dilemmas of life-prolongation, such as withdrawal of artificial nutrition and direct euthanasia. Have these church-based efforts any legitimacy in public policy formulation and if so, on what grounds? Or are they attempts to foist particularistic religious convictions on a pluralistic and otherwise free society, in violation of our prized tradition of separation of church and state?

At the same time that religious involvement in policy formation may seem unduly aggressive to some, from the perspectives of bioethics literature and medical practice or research, it often appears that theology brings little to bioethics which is even identifiably religious. When one inspects the work of individual theologians rather than ecclesial bodies — and especially when one advances beyond the well-tread ground staked out around abortion to tangle with issues such as genetic research or national health insurance — it may seem that religious faith and theological reflection fail to offer any guidance that could not have been arrived at by other means. Although "theologians" and "Christian ethicists" frequently address bioethics issues both in clinical settings and in print, even major figures such as Paul Ramsey and Richard McCormick often limit or avoid directly religious appeals in the interest of expanding their audience and hence influence. One might thus ask whether the result has any specifically theological stamp to it.

If by "theological" is meant a specific and unique line of religious argument entailing conclusions that also manifest a religious imprint, then theology is scarce in bioethics. Even clearly theological foundations, premises, and commitments do not necessarily lead to substantive moral principles, to arguments, or much less to concrete conclusions of a directly religious character, even though they may be endorsed strongly by religious groups. At the same time, the presence in bioethics of persons with theological training or with religious affiliations continues to give theology influence, even though this may not manifest itself in the explicit justification of moral conclusions. But it is more appropriate to construe theological contributions as overlapping and coinciding with philosophical ones, than to see secular, philosophical bioethics and religious, theological bioethics as two distinct or even competing entities.

As I see it, public bioethical discourse (or public policy discourse) is actually a meeting ground of the diverse moral traditions that make up our society. Some of these moral traditions have religious inspiration, but that does not necessarily disqualify them as contributors to the broader discussion. Their contributions will be appropriate and effective to the extent that they can be articulated in terms with a broad if not universal appeal. In other words, faith language that offers a particular tradition's beliefs about God as a sole warrant for moral conclusions will convince only members of that tradition. But faith commitments can legitimately motivate participants in public discussion to see a moral consensus consistent with their faith while at the same time be congenial to members of other moral traditions, the persuasion of whom may be the object of religious groups and theologians who argue and act for social change.

A Commitment to Dialogue and Openness

As James Gustafson has indicated, theology rarely yields precise and concrete directives for bioethical decisionmaking, or commends insights and actions inaccessible to nonreligious persons. But theology does have a critical function in "public" discourse, if the edge of religious commitment can be sharpened so as to cut through cultural assumptions.[1] Theologians and religious groups can introduce the civil community to insights borne by their own traditions, *on the assumption that and provided that* these traditions are not sheerly insular nor the civil community a wholly foreign country in which values with originally religious sponsorship are entirely unintelligible.

One should not, moreover, approach the issue of the contribution of theology to bioethics on the assumption that there exists some independent realm of secular or philosophical discourse, privileged as more reasonable, neutral, or objective, and less tradition-bound, than religious discourse. If such a realm is posited, then theology is seen potentially as entering it to be talkative, or remaining outside it in silence. To speak of distinctly secular language and arguments also implies that to be intelligible, religious or theological language must undergo some sort of "translation" into the lingua franca — into some different vocabulary universally understood. But this is a distorted understanding both of religious traditions and their theologies, and of what happens in "public" discourse about bioethics.

Bioethical discussions (and other "public" or intertraditional discussions of ethics) begin in situations of common *practical* interest; a dilemma about the nature of a *practical* moral obligation gives a common starting-point. A real or envisioned situation of moral agency presents questions and stimulates participants to think theoretically. Discussion partners come to be so on the basis of such situations, and they enter them as persons from quite different, yet sometimes shared, or overlapping, moral and religious communities. Attempts to fashion a life together, a life that necessarily involves moral obligations and decisions, force us to arrive at some mutual understanding of what that would mean — especially in its practical results. Yet we do not participate in this process via an objective, traditionless, secular version of philosophical reasoning. The preeminent and supposedly neutral vocabulary of public policy debates in the U.S. today (liberty, autonomy, rights, privacy, due process) itself comes out of a rather complex but distinct set of political, legal, philosophical, moral, and even religious *traditions*. Though these are far from universal to humankind, they have over a three-hundred-year period come to be constitutive of a certain shared North American perspective. As Jeffrey Stout puts it, there is no privileged vantage point "above the fray."[2]

To follow Stout's evocative terminology,[3] there is also no universal and neutral language, no "Esperanto," into which theological language can be translated. Moreover, it is mistaken to expect theologians to adopt some sort of "pidgin," implying that, even if not philosophically fluent, theologians ought to try to master some dominant language, a language rising above all special commitments and points of view, the language in which those no longer hampered by an immigrant, ghetto mentality are already conversing. What ethicists do manage, as they speak beyond but always out of their native traditions, is what Stout (reinterpreting the term from Claude Levi-Strauss) calls "bricolage," a borrowing of what is not only handy but appropriate and communicative in jostling, negotiating, and persuading toward a common moral sense.

It is also useful to keep in mind that ethical discourse occurs on different levels and in different contexts, and that differentiated methods and goals may be appropriate to each. In a reminder to this effect, James Gustafson distinguishes four complementary modes of ethics: analytical ethics, public policy ethics, narrative ethics, and prophetic ethics.[4] The first, which Gustafson calls "ethical discourse," is aimed at finding moral justifications for specific actions and decisions, while the interrelated modes of narrative and prophetic discourse present larger questions about worldview, community identity, and basic values. Public policy discourse can be "ethical discourse" when it is more disciplined and distanced from the actual political process. But policy discourse can also be carried out by persons with institutional roles, who ask practical questions. In such a case, bioethics is not "purely" ethical because it deals with the "enabling and limiting conditions" of practical social options, rather than with a more philosophical delineation of the ideally good society, institution, or policy.[5]

Using Gustafson's categories, one will note that policy discussions occur precisely in the arena in which some common courses of action must be agreed upon, despite less agreement at the "metaethical" level. To construct a language of "principles" that will serve this purpose is a necessary achievement, however limited. We will also discover that even analyses at the highest theoretical levels take place within some "narrative" traditions, that is, within communities shaped by, to use Gustafson's language, "formative narratives."[6] Both ethical and institutional varieties of policy discussion also occur within narratives, or at least on the basis of narratives that may be partially transcended as common ground is sought. Consensus-shaping policy efforts search for and build on the existing ground shared by traditions; they seek to illumine the aspects of a narrative that can encompass more particular stories.

Like narrative ethics, prophetic ethics advances special agendas over against common views or practices, and does so both by "indictment," and by "utopian" visions that can raise human aspirations.[7] Prophetic ethics has as its agenda the introduction of particular values into the mainstream, to shift the geography of the ground occupied in common, that is to say, to reconfigure the governing narrative.

It follows that it is best to construe "public discourse" not as a separate *realm* into which we can and ought to enter tradition-free, but as embodying a *commitment* to civil exchanges among traditions, many of which have an overlapping membership, and which meet on the basis of common concerns. The language of "secular" and "publicly accessible" serves exactly to exhort persons from traditions to adopt a stance of dialogue and openness, of mutual critique, of commitment to consensus and to hammering out institutions and policies that will affect the common life for "the better," as defined on the broadest consensus we can achieve. It is a commitment to the dialogic and consensual mode of discourse, or perspective, or attitude, or stance, that is indicated by the expectation that religious and other traditions will make public rather than particularistic appeals. in addressing civil society or the body politic.

Community with Others

In struggling toward a conclusion within the "public" realm of discourse, Christians, Jews, or other religious persons will of course be influenced by their religiously based values. They will look for ways to live in community with others — that is, in the many communities in which they participate — that are consistent with their religious way of being (say, as a covenant people, or as disciples), as well as with their theoretical or theological reflection on the way of life. Biblical, especially New Testament, models exist for this sort of approach. St. Paul, for instance, borrows freely from the surrounding culture (as in the "vice lists" of *1 Corinthians* 5:11, and 6:9-10) in his writings about morality. Paul seems to feel no necessity to carve out something that is uniquely Christian in morality, for its own sake. His primary concern is to discern that sort of activity is appropriate for persons with a special religious identity. Then, on concrete moral issues he accepts or rejects cultural practices in view of their relation to the communal vocation of discipleship. Although Christianity poses profound questions about "worldly" power, authority, and values, it does not necessarily demand that all moral expectations which are not specifically Christian be set aside or judged irrelevant to the Christian portrayal of the moral life. As Wayne Meeks has observed, the New Testament literature expresses a process of "resocialization" in the early church, in which new social relationships and identities were forged, even though Christians might simultaneously continue to live as members of other communities with their own values, sometimes overlapping with Christian values, and sometimes challenged by them.[8]

Meeks has also suggested that the importance of religious commitment for ethics lies in its function to form communities that then interact with the broader culture in provocative ways. Just as the biblical narratives were generated by a social environment in which the new religious identity of Christianity served a critical function, so Christian communities today mediate their religious commitment into society through a "hermeneutics of social embodiment" of the biblical witness.[9] The relevance of religion to bioethics does not lie primarily in any distinct or specific contribution to the process of moral argumentation, nor in lifting up "religious" behaviors, defensible only on faith, revelation, or church authority. Rather it depends on the formation of socially radical communities that challenge dominant values and patterns of social relationship, not by withdrawing from the larger society, or by speaking to it from outside, but by participating in it in challenging and even subversive ways.

A Countercultural Edge

It is important that, in thinking bioethically, theologians hone the critical edge of religious or theological interest. To be more specific, a person from a Jewish or Christian religious tradition might have sensibilities and interests that would make her or him more attuned to certain biblically based themes, such as the well-being of creation, God's providence, human responsibility, and human finitude and sinfulness.[10] Other themes include love of neighbor and a "preferential option for the poor" and vulnerable, mercy to others as God is merciful to us, forgiveness of others as we expect to be forgiven by God, and repentance for our sins. In nonreligious terms these themes cash out as service, not only autonomy; solidarity and integration within the community; the dignity of all human beings, and special advocacy for the most vulnerable; sensitivity to our own finitude and limits that we confront in all the projects we undertake. Recognizing and retaining the countercultural edge of such commitments is the first task of the theologian, even as he or she acknowledges that it will have few direct payoffs in particular bioethical decisions and analyses.

For instance, invoking the narrative, prophetic mode, Protestant theologians Stanley Hauerwas and Allen Verhey criticize decisions to let severely abnormal newborns die. They draw on Christian themes without claiming either that these themes *require* particular decisions, or that *only* these themes would enjoin decisions to sustain life. Hauerwas claims, "The cross provides a pattern of interpretation which allows one to locate the pointlessness of suffering within a cosmic framework,"[11] while Verhey maintains that "the eschatological vision of Christianity — and the entire Jesus story — enlists us on the side of life and health in a world where death and evil still apparently reign." This vision also "calls us to identify with and to serve especially the sick and the poor, the powerless and the despised, and all those who do not measure up to conventional standards."[12] Although many Christians would no doubt see acceptance of death as an appropriate choice for some infants, they would agree nonetheless that the tradition would make such choices a rare exception within an ethos of nurturance and sacrifice.

Hauerwas and Verhey represent a somewhat more biblical and confessional strand within Christian theology; their audience is characteristically the Christian community itself. Hence they emphasize the specifically Christian "narrative" and themes, while "prophetically" exhorting the community to create patterns of moral action that correspond to its religious commitments. A contrasting approach is represented by Roman Catholicism. Catholic moral theology historically has manifested a greater interest in explicitly "public" discourse and has in its service developed a "natural law" moral language claiming to analyze with some precision shared human (not religious) values. While doctrines such as creation, humanity's status as "image of God," and the supernatural destiny of human beings lie in the background of the natural law approach, it still assumes that there are basic human characteristics and values which obtain cross-culturally, and which ought to provide a basis for moral thinking and social order. The nature and extent of these "basics," as well as their practical implications, provide the often controversial subject matter of ethics. As articulated by Joseph Fuchs, S.J., Catholic ethics is based in faith in the sense of a deep personal "giving and entrusting" to God, but "no concrete ethics" can be developed out of faith so understood. Thus, Catholic ethics "has generally presented itself as a philosophical ethics: its reflections, its principles, and its reasonings differ hardly at all, in a formal sense, from those of a philosopher."[13]

Yet even contemporary natural law thinkers are increasingly ready to recognize the "postmodern" emphasis on contextualism, particularity, and tradition, and hence also to recognize that Catholic natural law thinking, while aiming at the "universal," is worked out within a historically particular religious tradition: Christianity as Catholicism. Nonetheless, the tradition continues to represent a commitment to cross-traditional communication, aiming at the broadest community possible. In the modern papal encyclicals from John XXIII forward, the community addressed has even been global, for example, in regard to the "universal common good," on issues such as arms control and international development. In narrower political communities, such as the nation, local prelates may work to raise moral consciousness about issues whose practical importance they consider not to be limited to their own church. Their effectiveness in achieving this goal — and even their legitimacy in attempting to achieve it — depends on their success in framing the moral issues in terms that can in fact strike a responsive chord in a constituency formed from a plurality of communities within the larger political order.

If religiously motivated speakers from particular traditions are to contribute to the sort of public consensus that can support policy initiatives, they will need to do so on the basis of moral quandaries, moral sensibilities, moral images, and moral vocabulary shared among other religious and moral traditions (as an ethics without tradition does not exist.) Such morally formative factors are not sheerly "universal" nor need they be. Consensus in and about the public order is contingent not on genuine universality, but on intelligibility and persuasiveness within a community of communities broad enough to encompass the society to be ordered. (This is not to deny that at least at a very fundamental level, the whole human race might be considered a "community," sharing certain minimal moral insights in common. But even if so, such insights would *practically* demand to be worked into consistent moral expectations and social institutions within derivative communities shaped historically in more differentiated ways.)

In the United States, a Roman Catholic example of the explicitly intertraditional appeal is the writings and addresses of Joseph Cardinal Bernardin. During the 1984 presidential election, Bernardin shaped a moral vision ("the consistent ethic of life") based on the interconnection of "life issues," including but not limited to abortion, capital punishment, and nuclear war. Although obviously a religious leader wielding both religious and moral authority, Bernardin does not advance his position on specifically religious grounds. In a recent address focused on abortion (Georgetown University, March 20, 1990), Bernardin tried to persuade his audience that the moral issue of who decides should not overwhelm the issue of what it is that is decided. Specifically, how does a community grant or refuse the recognition of "humanity" in debatable cases? Appealing for a consensus that "at the very heart of public order is the protection of human life and basic human rights," Bernardin asks, "What happens to our moral imagination and social vision if the right to life is not protected for those who do not look fully human at the beginning or end of life?" Recognizing that a large percentage of Americans do not identify themselves either with pro-choice or pro-life positions, the Cardinal "invites" this constituency to agreement that the human fetus is a value to be protected, and thus to "join us in setting significant limits to abortion."[14] His intended audience may or may not come to concur that although early fetuses do not "look" human, they deserve the full protection due children and adults; nor may it be persuaded that the limits on abortion ought to be "significant." This point here is rather that Bernardin's identity as a religious leader does not disqualify his participation in the public debate, and his success in this forum will depend precisely on his ability to join issues in a way that can elicit or instigate broad agreement. No politician, philosopher, or "humanist" marches into the contest armed only with the sharp sword of reason, stripped naked of the costume of any moral culture — however invisible he or she might wish that clothing to be. Each will succeed on demonstrated ability to find and enlarge the common ground on which originally disparate forces can be joined around a mutual cause.

Jeffrey Stout's notion of a "creole" language is illuminating here: a language that begins as a simplified "bridge dialect" to enable communication among unconnected communities, but "eventually gets rich enough for use as a language of moral reflection (e.g., the language of human rights)."[15] Bernardin puts his case in the vocabulary of public order, human life, and basic human rights, hoping to be persuasive on grounds that are not narrowly "Catholic" or "religious." Where Bernardin and other Roman Catholic representatives might differ with historically more biblical communities and theologians such as Stanley Hauerwas and Allen Verhey is in the former's confidence that essential and recognizable human values (e.g., human life) ground any cultural specifications; in their stronger belief that religion supports these human values; and in their optimism about the ability of discussion partners in good faith to come to agreement not only on what the basic values are, but on how they should be implemented practically. Hauerwas and Verhey would emphasize the critical or "witnessing" function of religion (its narrative and prophecy), while Fuchs and Bernardin would stress the motivation it gives to join in moral analysis and public efforts towards consensus on better social institutionalization of "human" values (the contributions it makes to ethical discourse and to policy). As Gustafson has argued, these contributions are not mutually exclusive but complementary.

Roles of Theology in Bioethics

The role of theology in bioethics is, first of all, to clarify for the religious community itself what the shape of its life should be in the relevant areas. Even within the community, however, theology will yield fewer specific norms than it will more fundamental affirmations of the values and commitments that should undergird the identity and challenge the decision-making of religious persons. Indeed, articulating moral norms will usually require the interaction of religious values and theological reflection with other sources, such as philosophy, the natural and social sciences, and careful analysis of implications and consequences. The second role of theology is to move the religious community toward active participation in the broader or overlapping communities with which its members are in some way affiliated, and in which specific norms and policies for those communities are hammered out. Beginning especially from questions of common practice, theology can influence policy through a prophetic function that challenges the civil community to consider more seriously values and alternatives which other traditions and established forms of life may have neglected. Theology also contributes at a more precise analytic level, in which a common language of moral analysis is forged by traditions that are on speaking terms, and which, more importantly, share a commitment to mutual criticism and to progress toward consensus.

Notes

1. James M. Gustafson, *The Contributions of Theology to Medical Ethics* (Milwaukee: Marquette University Theology Department, 1975).

2. Jeffrey Stout, *Ethics After Babel: The Languages of Morals and Their Discontents* (Boston: Beacon Press, 1988), p. 282.

3. Stout, *Ethics After Babel*, p. 294.

4. James M. Gustafson, "Moral Discourse About Medicine: A Variety of Forms," *The Journal of Medicine and Philosophy* 15:2 (1990): 125-42.

5. Gustafson, "Moral Discourse," 140-41.

6. Gustafson, "Moral Discourse," 137.

7. Gustafson, "Moral Discourse," 130-31.

8. Wayne Meeks, *The Moral World of the First Christians* (Philadelphia: Westminster Press, 1955), p. 126.

9. Wayne Meeks, "A Hermeneutics of Social Embodiment," *Harvard Theological Review* 79:1-3 (1986): 176-86.

10. Gustafson, *Contributions of Theology*, pp. 18-25.

11. Stanley Hauerwas, "Reflections on Suffering, Death, and Medicine," in *Suffering Presence: Theological Reflections on Medicine, the Mentally Handicapped, and the Church* (Notre Dame: University of Notre Dame Press, 1986), 31.

12. Allen Verhey, "The Death of Infant Doe: Jesus and the Neonates," in *On Moral Medicine: Theological Perspectives in Medical Ethics*, Stephen E. Lammers and Allen Verhey, eds. (Grand Rapids: Eerdmans, 1987), 492.

13. Joseph Fuchs, " 'Catholic' Medical Moral Theology?," in *Catholic Perspectives on Medical Morals*, Edmund D. Pellegrino et al., eds. (Dordrecht: Kluwer, 1989), pp. 85, 83.

14. As quoted by Thomas H. Stahel, "Cardinal Bernardin on the 'Forgotten Factor' and Other Gaps in the Abortion Debate," *America* 162:13 (1990): 354-56.

15. Stout, *Ethics After Babel*, 294.

10 Theology and Bioethics

Richard A. McCormick

As we enter neighborhood homes, many of us have been quickened with the peculiar hospitality of a sign that reads: "Beware of dog." There are doubtless many people around who believe that an analogous sign is in place when a theologian is present to discuss the ethical dimensions of biomedicine. Theologians just may bite. Or perhaps worse, they may not. At their worst they are seen as extremely dangerous. At their best, they are harmless, that is, useless. For these reasons they should preferably be out of sight, or at least on a short leash. Perhaps Alasdair MacIntyre had something like this in mind when he observed:

> Theologians still owe it to the rest of us to explain why we should not treat their discipline as we do astrology or phrenology. The distinctiveness and importance of what they have to say, if it is true, make this an urgent responsibility.[1]

Clearly implied in MacIntyre's ultimatum is the conviction that theologians have not successfully articulated the "distinctiveness and importance of what they have to say." Faintly implied — unless I misread him — is the assertion that they really cannot because they do not have that much to say. An urgent task is thus transformed into an impossible one — and under threat of relabeling as *disciplina astrologica.* I like neither the odds nor the possible outcome. But to avoid the latter I must risk the former.

From Richard McCormick, *Hastings Center Report,* Volume 19, No. 3, May/June 1989, pp. 5-10. © The Hastings Center. Used by permission.

Theology and Faith

Both terms in my title need explication and narrowing if I hope to avoid unthreatening generalizations and verbal incontinence. First, then, *theology.* Theology starts when faith begins reflecting on itself. This pirates the definition of Anselm of Canterbury: *fides quaerens intellectum* (faith seeking understanding). Two things should be stated at the outset. First, there are different faiths (for example, the Catholic faith, the Jewish faith, the Muslim faith). Second, the communities in which these faiths originate exist in history and therefore must continually reappropriate their inheritance in changing times and diverse circumstances — often with different purposes in view. On the first count it is clear that there can be radically different theologies, and on the second that there can be many theologies within an individual faith community. This means, of course, that how theology is said to relate to bioethics can vary from community to community, and within the same community at varying times.

Let me narrow the proportions of my "urgent responsibility" by saying, first, that I will speak as an adherent of the Catholic faith (it is the only one I know from experience) and therefore will understand theology as reflection on *that* faith only and second, that I make no claims that my reflections are the *only* theology of that faith. Rather my reflections should be seen as one possible way of approaching the subject, and are not meant to detract from the validity or beauty of any other faith or theology.

But such narrowing is not enough. I must make explicit the implications of the statement that theology is reflection on *faith.* There is the danger in our time that the term "faith" will be collapsed into a bloodless, intellectualistic acceptance of credal statements. When "I believe" is sterilized into mere affirmation of propositions, faith has lost its heart and soul. In this sense Johannes B. Metz states: "Christ must always be thought of in such a way that he is never merely thought of."[2] Merely to "think of" Christ is to trivialize Him, to reduce Him to one more (among many) observable historical event, to an example of humane benevolence. For the person of Christian faith, Jesus Christ is God's immanent presence, His love in the flesh.

Let me borrow from the late Joseph Sittler at this point.[3] Sittler has noted that the theme of the biblical narratives is God's "going out from Himself in creative and redemptive action towards men." He refers to "God's relentless gift of Himself," "the undeviating self-giving God," "the total self-giving God." Jesus Christ is no less than God's self-giving deed. The response of the believer to this person-revelation is the total commitment of the person known as faith.

For the believer, God's self-disclosure in Jesus is at once the self-disclosure of ourselves and our world. The response to this personal divine outpouring is not a dead and outside-observer "amen." It is a faith-response empowered by the very God who did the redemptive and restorative deed in Jesus Christ and is utterly and totally transforming — so much so that St. Paul must craft a new metaphor to articulate it. We are "new creatures" plain and simple. Faith is the empowered reception of God's stunning and aggressive love in Jesus.

Faith, then, is the proper term "to point to the total commitment of the whole person which is required by the character of the revelation."[4] When I speak of theology (as relating to bioethics), it is theology as reflection on *that sense of faith* that I speak. I emphasize this because there are many influences tempting us to treat theology primarily as reflection on credal statements hammered out as communicative and protective vehicles of a more profound and original happening (God's self-communication and our response to it). For one thing, it is much easier to deal with credal statements, since faith itself, being a *response to God,* exceeds the reach of human language. For another, the historical religious communities that provide the context of the faith-response have myths and symbols that differentiate them and there is the temptation to confuse these with faith itself. Finally, the temptation becomes almost irresistible when these myths and symbols lead to distinct ethical codes.

Theology and Ethics

My second introductory qualifier concerns *bioethics.* Bioethics is a subspecies of ethics. There has been a tendency to equate ethics with "quandary ethics."[5] Symbols of this abound. We are fascinated and fixed by the tangled casuistry of plug-pulling, palliation decisions, proxy determinations. Cases are newsworthy eye-catchers and amenable to legal resolution. Thus courses in bioethics are loaded with *Quinlan, Jobes, Fox, Storar, Conroy, Baby M,* pregnancy reduction, testing for seropositivity, triage decisions, dilemmas about confidentiality. Test me by picking up any issues of the *Hastings Center Report.* It is no diminishment of casuistry to say that it does not all of ethics make, especially an ethics that calls itself Christian, most especially one that claims to be *theological.*

An ethic that claims to be theological will root itself in God — God's actions and purposes. Its primary referents will be God's relation to us, and ours to God. The prime analogate of the term "morality" will be this relationship. The most basic language — not the only — of theological ethics builds around goodness and badness, not rightness and wrongness of actions, since goodness-badness is basically vertical and has its aortal lifeline to the God-relationship.

In slightly different words, a Christian theological ethic is founded on the fact that something *has been done* to and for us, and that something is Jesus. There is a prior action of God at once revelatory and response-engendering that provides the entire grounding and meaning of the Christian ethic.

When I mention Christian theological ethics, I think primarily of those foundations that deserve the name theological. These foundations can be summarized in a systematic way with six assertions.[6]

> God's self-disclosure in Jesus Christ as self-giving love allows of no further justification. It is the absolutely ultimate fact. The acceptance of this fact into one's life is an absolutely originating and grounding experience.
>
> This belief in the God of Jesus Christ means that "Christ, perfect image of the Father, is already law and not only lawgiver. He is already the categorical imperative and not just the font of ulterior and detailed imperatives."[7]
>
> This ultimate fact reveals a new basis or context for understanding the world. It gives it a new (Christocentric) meaning. As a result of God's concrete act in the incarnation, "human life has available a new relation to God, a new light for seeing, a new fact and center for thinking, a new ground for giving and loving, a new context for acting in this world."[8]
>
> This "new fact and center for thinking" that is Jesus Christ finds its deepest meaning in the absoluteness and ultimacy of the God-relationship. Outside the God-relationship efforts to know ourselves and be ourselves fully are doomed to falter.
>
> This God-relationship is already shaped by God's prior act in Jesus (self-giving). The Christian moral life therefore is a recapitulation in the life of the believer of the "shape of the engendering deed' to use Sittler's language.
>
> The empowered acceptance of this engendering deed (faith) totally transforms the human person. It creates new operative vitalities that constitute the very possibility and the heart of the Christian moral life.

I stress these points because there has been, and still is, a tendency to conceive of Christian ethics as norms derived from Jesus' pronouncements. There are such sayings recorded in the New Testament. But to reduce Christian ethics to such sayings is to trivialize it. When the Christian thinks of Christian ethics (or moral theology — I treat them as identical here), he or she thinks primarily of what Jesus has done to and for us, and therefore of *who we are.*

In and through Jesus we know what the God-relationship is: total self-gift. For that is what God is and we are created in His image. To miss this is, I believe, to leave the realm of Christian ethics.

Levels of Ethics

There is another aspect to the notion of "ethics" (and therefore bioethics) that needs mentioning. There are four levels at which the term can be understood where rightness or wrongness of conduct is concerned.[9] These distinctions are not often made but I think them critical if we are to gain precision in speaking of the relation of theology in bioethics.

First, there is what we might call an *essential* ethic. By this term we mean those norms that are regarded as applicable to all persons, where one's behavior is but an instance of a general, essential moral norm. Here we could use as examples the rightness or wrongness of actions of killing, contracts, or promises, and all actions whose demands are rooted in the dignity of the person.

Second, there is an *existential* ethic. This refers to the choice of a good that the individual as individual should realize, the experience of an absolute ethical demand addressed to the individual. For instance, an individual might conclude that his or her own moral-spiritual life cannot grow and thrive in the health care environment, hence that this work ought to be abandoned. Or, because of background, inclination, talent, etc., an individual might choose to concentrate time and energy on a particular aspect of health care.

Third, there is *essential Christian* ethics. By this we refer to those ethical decisions a Christian must make precisely because he or she belongs to a community to which the non-Christian does not belong. These are moral demands made upon the Christian *as Christian.* For instance, to regard fellow workers as brothers and sisters in Christ (not just as autonomous, to-be-respected persons), to provide a Christian education for one's children, to belong to a particular worshipping community.

Fourth, there is an *existential Christian* ethics — these ethical decisions that the Christian *as individual* must make, for example, to undertake the ministry of the priesthood.

The Task of Theological Ethics

With these introductory notes on faith and ethics as background, I want now to consider whether theology really makes any difference — beyond moral philosophy — in bioethical discussions. Let me begin by citing James Gustafson:

> For theological ethics . . . the first task in order of importance is to establish convictions about God and God's relations to the world. To make a case for how some things really and ultimately are. . . .[10]

I agree with Gustafson's description of the first task of theological ethics, though it is clear we would disagree significantly about "how some things really and ultimately are." How, then, are they, "really and ultimately?" In its *Declaration on Euthanasia* the Congregation for the Doctrine of the Faith made reference to "Christ, who through his life, death and resurrection, has given *a new meaning to existence.*"[11] If that is true (and Christians believe it is), then to neglect that meaning is to neglect the most important thing about ourselves, to cut ourselves off from the fullness of our own reality.

If Christ has given "a new meaning to existence," then presumably that new meaning will have some relevance for key notions and decisions in the field of bioethics. At this point it is a fair question to ask: what is this new meaning?

Theological work in the past decade has rejected the notion that the sources of faith are a thesaurus of answers. Rather they should be viewed above all as narratives, as a story. From a story come perspectives, themes, insights, not always or chiefly direct action guides. The story is the source from which the Christian construes the world theologically. In other words, it is the vehicle for discovering and communicating this new meaning.

Let me attempt to disengage some key elements of the Christian story, and from a Catholic reading and living of it. One might not be too far off with the following summary.

> God is the author and preserver of life. We are "made in His image." Thus life is a gift, a trust. It has great worth because of the value He is placing in it.
>
> God places great value in it because He is also (besides being author) the end and purpose of life.
>
> We are on a pilgrimage, having here no lasting home.
>
> God has dealt with us in many ways. But his supreme epiphany of Himself (and our potential selves) is His Son Jesus Christ.
>
> In Jesus' life, death and resurrection we have been totally transformed into "new creatures," into a

community of the transformed. The ultimate significance of our lives consists in developing this new life.

The ultimate destiny of our combined journeys is the "coming of the Kingdom," the return of the glorified Christ to claim the redeemed world.

Thus we are offered in and through Jesus Christ eternal life. Just as Jesus has overcome death (and now lives), so will we who cling to Him, place our faith and hope in Him, and take Him as our law and model.

This good news, this covenant with us has been entrusted to a people, a people to be nourished and instructed by shepherds.

This people should continuously remember and thereby make present Christ in His death and resurrection at the Eucharistic meal.

The chief and central manifestation of this new life in Christ is love for each other (not a flaccid "niceness," but a love that shapes itself in the concrete forms of justice, gratitude, forbearance, chastity, etc.), especially for the poor, marginal sinners. These were Jesus' constant companions.

For the Catholic Christian, this is "how some things really and ultimately are." In Jesus we have been totally transformed. This new life or empowerment is a hidden but nonetheless real dimension of our persons, indeed the most profoundly real thing about us.[12] I have already suggested the integrating shape of our lives from this faith-perspective: the self-gift of *agape.* But what does all of this have to do with bioethics? I want to reject two possible extremes from the outset. The first extreme is that faith gives us concrete answers to the problems of *essential* ethics.

The second extreme is that faith has no influence whatsoever on bioethics. It would seem strange indeed if what Sittler calls "the invasion of the total personality by the Christ-life" had no repercussions on one's dispositions, imagination, and values.

How, then, does faith exercise its influence? I will take my lead from Vatican II. In an interesting sentence, "The Constitution on the Church in the Modern World" states:

> Faith throws a new light on everything, manifests God's design for man's total vocation, and thus directs the mind to solutions which are fully human.[13]

The nature of this "new light" is that it reveals human existence in its fullest and most profound dimensions. The effect of this new light is to "direct the mind." To what? "Solutions which are fully human." The usage "fully human" I take to mean a rejection of any understanding of "a new meaning to existence" that sees it as foreign to the human, and radically discontinuous with it.

Reason Informed by Faith

The Catholic tradition has encapsulated the way faith "directs the mind to solutions" in the phrase "reason informed by faith." Reason informed by faith is neither reason *replaced* by faith, nor reason *without* faith. It is reason shaped by faith.[14]

"Reason informed by faith" is shorthand for saying that the reasoner (the human person) has been transformed and that this transformation will have a cognitive dimension through its invasion of consciousness. I think it true to say that the more profound the faith, the greater and more explicit will be the Christian consciousness — which is a way of saying that how faith (and theology) affects ethics can be seen best of all in the saints. But even we nonsaints ought to be able to give an intelligible account of theology's influence. That account is destined to be more or less incomplete because the transformation worked by faith is at a very profound level not totally recoverable in formulating consciousness.

With that in mind, I suggest that theology can relate to bioethics in three distinct but overlapping ways. I shall call these ways *protective, dispositive,* and *directive.*

Protective

Moral philosophers, following St. Thomas, have identified basic inclinations toward goods that define our well-being or flourishing. Even though these inclinations can be identified as prior to acculturation, still they exist as culturally conditioned. We tend toward values as perceived. And the culture in which we live shades our perceptions of values, a point made by Philip Rieff, who refers to "reasons that have sunk so deeply into the self that they are implicitly understood."[15] He argues that decisions are made, policies set not chiefly by articulated norms, codes, regulations, and philosophies, but by these "reasons" that lie below the surface. Our way of perceiving the basic human values and relating to them is shaped by our whole way of looking at the world.

An example from bioethics will help here. As Daniel Callahan has pointed out, several images of human beings and their relation to the basic human values are possible.[16] First, there is the power-plasticity model. In this model, nature is alien, independent of humans, possessing no inherent value. It is capable of being used, shaped, and dominated by humans. We see ourselves as possessing an unrestricted right to manipulate it in the service of our goals. Death is something to be overcome, outwitted. Second, there is the sacro-symbiotic model. In its religious forms, nature is seen as God's creation, to be respected and heeded. Nature is a trust; we are not masters, but stewards. In secular forms, humans are seen as part of nature. Nature is a teacher and we must live in harmony and balance with it. Death is but a rhythm of nature, to be gracefully accepted.

The model that seems to have sunk deep and shaped our moral imaginations and feelings — and our perception of basic values — is the power-plasticity model. We are corporately *homo technologicus.* The best solution of the dilemmas created by technology is more technology. We tend to eliminate the maladapted condition (defective newborns, retarded persons) rather than adjust the environment to it; this is our cultural bias.

It can be persuasively argued that the peculiar temptation of a technologically advanced culture such as ours is to view and treat persons functionally. Our treatment — at least all too often — of the aged is a sorry symptom of this. The elderly are probably the most alienated members of our society. More and more of them spend their declining years in homes for senior citizens, in chronic care hospitals, in nursing homes. We have shunted them aside. Their protest is eloquent because it is helplessly muted and silent. But it is a protest against a basically functional assessment of their persons. "Maladaptation" is the term used to describe *them* rather than the environment. This represents a terribly distorted judgment of the human person.

I want to argue that faith can be protective against such a collapse. It should and, I believe, does sensitize us to the meaning of persons, to their inherent dignity regardless of functionability. In this sense it aids us in staying human by underlining the truly human against cultural pressures to distort it. Faith exercises this protective function by steadying our gaze on the basic human values that are the parents of more concrete norms and rules.

Let me put this another way. I have noted that the single, dominating, all-pervasive vitality in Jesus was the God-relationship. The human goods that define our flourishing (life and health, mating and raising children, knowledge, friendship, enjoyment of the arts) while desirable and attractive in themselves, are *subordinate* to this structural God-relationship.[17] Yet it is the characteristic of the redeemed but still messy human condition to make idols, to pursue these basic goods *as ends in themselves.* This is the radical theological meaning of secularization: the loss of the context that relativizes and subordinates these basic goods and prevents our divinizing them. The goods are so attractive that our constant temptation is to center our being on them as ultimate ends, to cling to them with our whole being.

Jesus' love for us is, of course, primarily empowerment. But it is also, in its purity and righteousness, the standard against the type of collapse known as idolatry. Whatever He willed for us and did for us, He did within the primacy and ultimacy of the God-relationship. His love, as standard, suggests the shape of our Christian love for each other. It is conduct that reminds others of their true dignity, of their being and destiny, and therefore that pursues, supports, and protects the basic human goods *as subordinate.*

Dispositive

The Christian of profound faith will reflect in his or her dispositions the very shape of that faith. That shape, as I have noted, is the self-gift we call charity, love of God in others, charitable action. In an illuminating study, Edmund Pellegrino shows how the central dynamism of charity can shape moral choice within medicine.[18] He argues that charity will influence (1) the way the three dominant principles of medical ethics (beneficence, autonomy, justice) are interpreted; (2) the way the physician-patient relationship is construed; (3) the way certain concrete choices are made. For instance, where beneficence is concerned, Pellegrino claims that some form of benevolent self-effacement (arguable on mere philosophical grounds) is a *minimum* obligation in an agapeistic ethic. The Christian physician sees him- or herself called to perfection, to imitate Jesus' healing. In this perspective appeals to exigency, fiscal survival, self-protection, or the canons of a competitive environment are morally feeble, even totally unacceptable. Similarly, where justice is concerned, faith-full Christians will go beyond the strict calculus of duties and claims and exercise a "preferential option" for the very ones whose moral claims on society are difficult to establish: the poor, the outcasts, the sociopaths, the alcoholic, the noncompliant in the care of their own health.

When he turns to the physician-patient relationship, Pellegrino argues that a charity-based ethic would reject notions of health care as a commodity transaction, of the physician as a businessman. It would reject likewise the relationship as one of contract for services, or as one primarily for profit. The covenantal model is most consistent with the perspectives and dispositions generated by charity.

Let me take another aspect of an ethic rooted in Christian faith, an aspect that may also be considered dispositive. It is the pascal mystery, the death-resurrection of Christ. Christians are accustomed to viewing aging, suffering, and dying within these perspectives.

Take aging as an example. Perhaps the most prominent quality of the lives of the elderly is dependence. Yet, as Theodore Minnema points out, we are notoriously resistant to the idea of dependence.[19] Our national consciousness is shaped by the Declaration of Independence. And similar perspectives frame our individual attitudes. Dependence is vulnerability. Independent autonomy is exalted as a key maker of dignity. On this view there is a certain negativity that attaches to the passive virtues (meekness, humility, patience). Yet Christ's supreme dignity was manifest in dependence: "Not my will, but thine be done."

For this reason Drew Christiansen has developed a "theology of dependence."[20] For most of our adult lives we ignore the dependence that ties us to other men and women. Christiansen sees this avoidance of dependence as mistaken. Dependence is an opportunity, a call to let ourselves go, to open up to God, to cling in trust to a power beyond our control, to see more clearly than ever the source and end of life.

Dependence on others should be a sign of our more radical dependence on God. Since our freedom is intended to lead us to a deeper union with God, it is an interesting paradox that our deep dependence on God establishes our own radical independence: independence in dependence.

Thus from a theological perspective, dependent old age should represent a flowering not a wilting.

Very similar things can be said about suffering and dying. From the perspective of faith, just as aging is not mere dependence and weakening, so suffering is not mere pain and confusion, dying is not merely an end. These must be viewed, even if mysteriously, in terms of a larger redemptive process: as occasions for a growing self-opening after Christ's example, as various participations in the paschal mystery. Such perspectival nuances may not solve clinical dilemmas nor are they in any way intended to glorify suffering and dying. But they powerfully suggest that in approaching such realities healing can never be seen as mere fixing; autonomy is not a mere "being left alone," but a condition for life-shaping, care is never merely material provision, but a "being with" that reinforces a sense of worth and dignity; dying can never be seen as "cosmetized passing" whose dignity is measured by the accumulation of minutes.

Directive

The biblical materials or stories that pass along the events that are the occasion of faith yield certain perspectives or themes that shape consciousness, and therefore constitute faith's informing of reason. I have attempted elsewhere to identify some of the themes that structure our ethical deliberation in biomedicine as the following: Life as a basic, but not absolute value; the extension of this evaluation to nascent life; the potential for human relationships as that aspect of physical life to be valued; the radical sociality of the human person; the inseparability of the unitive and procreative goods in human sexuality; and permanent heterosexual union as normative.[21]

Let me take just the first to illustrate the "directive" influence of theology on bioethics — life as a basic but not absolute good.

The fact that we are pilgrims, that Christ has overcome death and lives, that we will also live with Him, yields a general value judgment on the meaning and value of life as we now live it. It can be formulated as follows: life is a basic good but not an absolute one. It is *basic* because, as the Congregation for the Doctrine of the Faith worded it, it is the "necessary source and condition of every human activity and of all society."[22] It is not *absolute* because there are higher goods for which life can be sacrificed (glory of God, salvation of souls, service of one's brethren, etc.). Thus in John: "There is no greater love than this: to lay down one's life for one's friends."[23] Laying down one's life for another cannot be contrary to the faith or story or meaning of humankind. It is, after Jesus' example, life's greatest fulfillment, even though it is the end of life as we now know it. Negatively, we could word this value judgment as follows: death is an evil but not an absolute or unconditioned one.

This value judgment has immediate relevance for care for the ill and dying. It issues in a basic attitude or policy: not all means must be used to preserve life. Why? Pius XII in a Congress of Anesthesiologists stated: "A more strict obligation would be too burdensome for most people and would render the attainment of the higher, more important good too difficult. Life, health, all temporal activities are in fact subordinated to spiritual ends."[24] In other words there are higher values than life in the living of it. There are also higher values in the dying of it.

What Pius XII was saying, then, is that forcing (morally) one to take *all* means is tantamount to forcing attention and energies on a subordinate good in a way that prejudices a higher good, even eventually making it unrecognizable as a good. Excessive concern for the temporal is at some point neglect of the eternal. An obligation to use all means to preserve life would be a devaluation of human life, since it would remove life from the context or story that is the source of its ultimate value.

Thus the Catholic tradition has moved between two extremes: medicomoral optimism or vitalism (which preserves life with all means, at any cost no matter what its condition) and medicomoral pessimism (which actively kills when life becomes onerous, dysfunctional, boring). Merely technological judgments could easily fall into either of these two traps. The medically effective could begin to define the humanly beneficial.

Thus far theology. It yields a value judgment and a general policy or attitude. It provides the framework for subsequent moral reasoning. It tells us that life is a gift with a purpose and destiny. Dying is the last or waning moments of this "new creature." At this point moral reasoning (reason informed by faith) must assume its proper responsibilities to answer questions like: What means ought to be used, what need not be? What shall we call such means? Who enjoys the prerogative and/or duty of decisionmaking? What is to be done with now incompetent, or always incompetent patients in critical illness? The sources of faith do not provide concrete answers to these questions.

The directive importance of such general themes can be indicated by an example. Several years ago, in Louisville, I participated on a panel on the artificial heart. The panel included the mandatory Protestant (Robert Nelson), Catholic, and Jew (the late Isaac Franck) along with Dr. Allan Lansing, medical director of Humana Heart Institute. The question arose as to whether the artificial heart works. Dr. Lansing stated: "When Bill DeVries and I decide that it doesn't work, the program will stop." I jumped on that and asked: "If the artificial heart gives you only an extra ten hours of life, or ten days, does it work?" Somewhat to my surprise — but not really as I look back on the incident — my colleague and friend Dr. Franck mumbled audibly, "it works." Theology was only thinly disguised in such a reaction. I do not believe the Christian story would support such a response, however, for it views life and death in light of the paschal mystery and this has a relativizing influence on both.

What I am proposing, therefore, is that theology can influence bioethics in very important ways. Its function is not a *direct* originating influence on concrete moral judgments at the essential level — but on "morally relevant insights" in the words of Franz Böckle.[25] On this view faith and reason compenetrate to produce a distinct consciousness, a consciousness with identifiable cognitive dimensions or facets. I have tried to identify three such dimensions, overlapping as they are, as *protective* (or corrective), *dispositive*, and *directive*.

Cumulatively, such influences attempt to show how faith informs reason. I believe the outcome of such "informing" is a distinct — though not utterly mysterious — way of viewing the world and ourselves and of hierarchizing values. To claim that such distinct outlooks and onlooks (theology) have nothing to do with bioethics is either to separate faith from one's view of the world (which is to trivialize faith by reducing it dualistically to an utterly other-worldly thing), or to separate one's view of the world from bioethics (which is to trivialize bioethics by isolating it from the very persons it purports to serve).

Notes

1. Alasdair MacIntyre, "Theology, Ethics and the Ethics of Medicine and Health Care," *Journal of Medicine and Philosophy* 4 (1979): 435-43.

2. Johannes B. Metz, *Followers of Christ* (Ramsey, N.J.: Paulist, 1978), pp. 39-40.

3. Joseph Sittler, *The Structure of Christian Ethics* (New Orleans: Louisiana State University Press, 1958).

4. Sittler, *Structure of Christian Ethics*, p. 46.

5. Cf. Edmund Pincoffs, "Quandary Ethics," *Mind* 80 (1971): 552-71.

6. I have taken these from my earlier essay "Theology and Bioethics: Christian Foundations" in Earl E. Shelp, ed., *Theology and Bioethics* (Dordrecht: D. Reidel, 1985), pp. 95-113.

7. Encino Chiavacci, "The Grounding for the Moral Norm in Contemporary Theological Reflection," in *Readings in Moral Theology, No. 2,* Charles E. Curran and Richard A. McCormick, S.J., eds. (Ramsey, N.J.: Paulist, 1980), pp. 291-92.

8. Sittler, *Structure of Christian Ethics,* p. 18.

9. I take these distinctions from Norbert Rigali, S.J., "On Christian Ethics," *Chicago Studies* 10 (1971): 227-47.

10. James M. Gustafson, *Ethics From a Theocentric Perspective. V. II Ethics and Theology* (Chicago: University of Chicago Press, 1984), p. 98.

11. Sacred Congregation for the Doctrine of the Faith, *Declaration on Euthanasia* (Vatican City: Vatican Polyglot Press, 1980); *Origins* 10 (1980): 154-57.

12. Karl Barth, *The Knowledge of God and the Service of God According to the Teaching of the Reformation* (London: Hodder and Stoughton, 1938), p. 95.

13. *The Documents of Vatican II* (New York: America Press, 1966), p. 209.

14. Vincent MacNamara, *Faith and Ethics* (Washington, DC: Georgetown University Press, 1985), pp. 117-21.

15. Philip Rieff, *The Triumph of the Therapeutic Uses of Faith After Freud* (New York: Harper and Row, 1966).

16. Daniel Callahan, "Living with the New Biology," *Center Magazine* (July-August 1972): 4-12.

17. Cf. Richard A. McCormick, S.J., *Health and Medicine in the Catholic Tradition* (New York: Crossroad, 1984), pp. 37-38.

18. Edmund Pellegrino, "Agape and Ethics: Some Reflections on Medical Morals from a Catholic Christian," forthcoming in *Catholic Perspectives on Medical Morals: Foundational Issues,* v. 34 (Kluwer Academic Publishers).

19. Theodore Minnema, "Human Dignity and Human Dependence," *Calvin Theological Journal* 16 (1981): 5-14.

20. Drew Christiansen, S.J., "The Elderly and Their Families: The Problems of Dependence," *New Catholic World* 223 (1980): 100-104.

21. Cf. Richard A. McCormick, S.J., "Theology and Biomedical Ethics," *Logos* 3 (1982): 25-43.

22. *Declaration on Euthanasia.*

23. John 15:13.

24. Pius XII, *AAS* 49 (1957), pp. 1031-32.

25. Franz Böckle, "Glaube und Handeln," *Concilium* 120 (1976): 641-47.

11 Salvation and Health: Why Medicine Needs the Church

Stanley Hauerwas

A Text and a Story

While it is not unheard of for a theologian to begin an essay with a text from the Scripture, it is relatively rare for those who are addressing issues of medicine to do so. However I begin with a text, as almost everything I have to say is but a commentary on this passage from Job 2:11-13:

> Now when Job's friends heard of all this evil that had come upon him, then came each from his own place, Eliphaz the Temanite, Bildad the Shuhite, and Zophar the Na'amathite. They made an appointment together to come console with him and comfort him. And when they saw him from afar, they did not recognize him; and they raised their voices and wept; and they rent their robes and sprinkled dust upon their heads toward heaven. And they sat with him on the ground seven days and seven nights, and no one spoke a word to him, for they saw that his suffering was very great.

I do not want to comment immediately on the text. Instead, I think it best to begin by telling you a story. The story is about one of my earliest friendships. When I was in my early teens I had a friend, let's call him Bob, who meant everything to me. We made our first hesitant steps toward growing up through sharing the things young boys do — i.e., double dating, athletic activities, and endless discussions on every topic. For two years we were inseparable. I was extremely appreciative of Bob's friendship, as he was not only brighter and more talented than I, but also came from a family that was economically considerably better off than my own. Through Bob I was introduced to a world that otherwise I would hardly know existed. For example, we spent hours in his home playing pool in a room that was built for no other purpose; and we swam in the lake that his house was specifically built to overlook.

Then very early one Sunday morning I received a phone call from Bob requesting that I come to see him immediately. He was sobbing intensely but through his crying he was able to tell me that they had just found his mother dead. She had committed suicide by placing a shotgun in her mouth. I knew immediately I did not want to go to see him and/or confront a reality like that. I had not yet learned the desperation hidden under our everyday routines and I did not want to learn of it. Moreover I did not want to go because I knew there was nothing I could do or say to make things even appear better than they were. Finally I did not want to go because I did not want to be close to anyone who had been touched by such a tragedy.

But I went. I felt awkward, but I went. And as I came into Bob's room we embraced, a gesture that was almost unheard of between young men raised in the Southwest, and we cried together. After that first period of shared sorrow we somehow calmed down and took a walk. For the rest of the day and that night we stayed together. I do not remember what we said, but I do remember that it was inconsequential. We never talked about his mother or what had happened. We never speculated about why she might do such a thing, even though I could not believe someone who seemed to have such a good life would want to die. We did what we always did. We talked girls, football, cars, movies, and anything else that was inconsequential enough to distract our attention from this horrible event.

As I look on that time I now realize that it was obviously one of the most important events in my life. That it was so is at least partly indicated by

---

how often I have thought about it and tried to understand its significance in the years from then to now. As often as I have reflected on what happened in that short space of time I have also remembered how inept I was in helping Bob. I did not know what should or could be said. I did not know how to help him start sorting out such a horrible event so that he could go on. All I could do was be present.

But time has helped me realize that this is all he wanted — namely, my presence. For as inept as I was, my willingness to be present was a sign that this was not an event so horrible that it drew us away from all other human contact. Life could go on, and in the days to follow we would again swim together, double date, and generally waste time. I now think that at the time God granted me the marvelous privilege of being a presence in the face of profound pain and suffering even when I did not appreciate the significance of being present.

Yet the story cannot end here. For while it is true that Bob and I did go on being friends, nothing was the same. For a few months we continued to see one another often, but somehow the innocent joy of loving one another was gone. We slowly found that our lives were going in different directions and we developed new friends. No doubt the difference between our social and cultural opportunities helps explain to some extent our drifting apart. Bob finally went to Princeton and I went to Southwestern University in Georgetown, Texas.

But that kind of explanation for our growing apart is not sufficient. What was standing between us was that day and night we spent together under the burden of a profound sadness that neither of us had known could exist until that time. We had shared a pain so intense that for a short period we had become closer than we knew, but now the very pain that created that sharing stood in the way of the development of our friendship. Neither of us wished to recapture that time, nor did we know how to make that night and day part of our ongoing story together. So we went our separate ways. I have no idea what became of Bob, though every once in a while I remember to ask my mother if she has heard about him.

Does medicine need the church? How could this text and this story possible help us understand that question, much less suggest how it might be answered? Yet I am going to claim in this essay that it does. Put briefly, what I will try to show is that if medicine can be rightly understood as an activity that trains some to know how to be present to those in pain, then something very much like a church is needed to sustain that presence day in and day out. Before I try to develop that thesis, however, I need to do some conceptual groundbreaking to make clear exactly what kind of claim I am trying to make about the relationship of salvation and health, medicine and the church.

Religion and Medicine: Is There or Should There Be a Relation?

It is a well-known fact that for most of human history there has been a close affinity between religion and medicine. Indeed that very way of putting it is misleading, since to claim a relation suggests that they were distinguished, and often that has not been the case. From earliest times, disease and illness were not seen as matters having no religious import but rather as resulting from the disfavor of God. As Darrel Amundsen and Gary Ferngren have recently reminded us, the Hebrew scriptures often depict God promising

> health and prosperity for the covenant people if they are faithful to him, and disease and other suffering if they spurn his love. This promise runs through the Old Testament. "If you will diligently hearken to the voice of the Lord your God, and do that which is right in his eyes, and give heed to his commandments and keep all his statutes, I will put none of the diseases upon you which I put upon the Egyptians; for I am the Lord, your healer" (Exod. 15:26). ([2], p. 92)

This view of illness was not associated only with the community as a whole, but with individuals. Thus in Psalm 38 the lament is

> There is no soundness in my flesh because of thy indignation; there is no health in my bones because of my sin. . . . My wounds grow foul and fester because of foolishness. . . . I am utterly spent and crushed; I groan because of the tumult of my heart. . . . Do not forsake me, O Lord! O my God, be not far from me! Make haste to help me, O Lord, my salvation! (vv. 3, 5, 8, 21-22)

Amundsen and Ferngren point out this view of illness as accompanied by the assumption that acknowledgment of and repentence for our sin was essential for our healing. Thus in Psalm 32:

> When I declared not my sin, my body wasted away through my groaning all day long. For day and night thy hand was heavy upon me; my strength was dried up. . . . I acknowledged my sin to thee, and I did not hide my iniquity; I said, "I will confess my transgressions to the Lord"; then thou didst forgive the guilt of my sin. (vv. 3-5) ([2], p. 93)

Since illness and sin were closely connected it is not surprising that healing was also closely associated with religious practices — or, put more accurately, healing was a religious discipline. Indeed Amundsen and Ferngren make the interesting point that since the most important issue was a person's relationship with God the chief means of healing was naturally prayer. That clearly precluded magic and thus the Mosaic code excluded soothsayers, augurs, sorcerers, charmers, wizards, and other such figures who offered a means to control or avoid the primary issue of their relation to Yahweh ([2], p. 94). They also suggest that this may have been why no sacerdotal medical practice developed in Israel particularly associated with the priesthood. Rather, the pattern of the Exodus tended to prevail, with illness and healing more closely associated with prophetic activity.

The early Christian community seems to have done little to change these basic presuppositions. If anything it simply intensified them by adding what Amundsen and Ferngren call the "central paradox" in the New Testament:

> Strength comes only through weakness. This strength is Christ's strength that comes only through dependence upon him. In the Gospel of John, Christ says: "I have said to you, that in me you may have peace. In the world you have tribulation; but be of good cheer, I have overcome the world" (16:33). "In the world you have tribulation." It is simply to be expected and accepted. But for the New Testament Christian no suffering is meaningless. The ultimate purpose and meaning behind Christian suffering in the New Testament is spiritual maturity. And the ultimate goal in spiritual maturity is a close dependence upon Christ based upon a childlike trust. ([2], p. 96)

Thus illness is seen as an opportunity for growth in faith and trust in God.

Because of this way of viewing both the positive and negative effect of illness, Amundsen and Ferngren note that there has always been a degree of tension in the way Christians understand the relation between theology and secular medicine, between the medicine of the soul and the medicine of the body.

> According to one view, if God sends disease either to punish or to test a person, it is to God that one must turn for care and healing. If God is both the source and healer of a person's ills, the use of human medicine would circumvent the spiritual framework by resorting to worldly wisdom. On another view, if God is the source of disease, or if God permits disease and is the ultimate healer, God's will can be fulfilled through human agents, who with divine help have acquired the ability to aid in the curative process. Most Christians have asserted that the human agent of care, the physician, is an instrument of God, used by God in bringing succor to humankind. But in every age some have maintained that any use of human medicine is a manifestation of a lack of faith. This ambivalence in the Christian attitude, among both theologians and laity, has always been present to some degree. ([2], p. 96)

Nor is it possible to separate or distinguish religion and medicine on the basis of a distinction between soul and body. For as Paul Ramsey has reminded us, Christians affirm that God has created and holds us sacred as embodied souls ([14], p. xiii). Religion does not deal with the soul and medicine with the body. Practitioners of both are too well aware of the inseparability of soul and body — or perhaps better, they know the abstractness of both categories. Moreover when religion too easily legitimates the independence of medical care by limiting medicine to mechanical understanding and care of the body, it has the result of making religious convictions ethereal in character. It may be that just to the extent Christianity is always tempted in Gnostic and Manichean directions it accepts too willingly a technological understanding of medicine. Christians, if they are to be faithful to their convictions, may not ever be able to avoid at least potential conflict between their own assumptions about illness and health and how the ill should be cared for and the assumptions of medicine. One hopes for cooperation, of course, but structurally the possibility of conflict between church and medicine cannot be excluded, since both entail convictions and practices concerned with that same subject.

Put differently, given Judaism and Christianity's understanding of humankind's relation with God — that is: how we understand salvation — health can never be thought of as an autonomous sphere. Moreover, insofar as medicine is a specialized activity distinguished from religious convictions, you cannot exclude the possibility that there may well be conflict between religion and medicine. For in many ways the latter is constantly tempted to offer a form of salvation that religiously may come close to idolatry. The ability of modern medicine to cure is at once a benefit and potential pitfall. Too often it is tempted to increase its power by offering more than care, by offering in fact alleviation from the human condition — e.g., the development of artificial hearts. That is not the fault of medical practitioners, though often they encourage such idolatry; rather the fault lies with those of us who pretentiously place undue expectations on medicine in the hope of finding an earthly remedy to our death. But we can never forget that the relation between medicine and health, and especially the health of a population, is as ambiguous as the relation between the church and salvation.

In the hope of securing peace between medicine and religion, two quite different and equally unsatisfactory proposals have been suggested. The first advocates a strong division of labor between medicine and religion by limiting the scope of medicine to the mechanism of our body. While it is certainly true that medicine in a unique way entails the passing on of the wisdom of the body from one generation to another, there is no way that medical care can be limited to the body and be good medicine [10]. As Ramsey has reminded us again and again, the moral commitment of the physician is not to treat diseases, or populations, or the human race, but the immediate patient before him or her ([14], pp. 36, 59). Religiously, therefore, the care offered by physicians cannot be abstracted from the moral commitment to care based on our view that every aspect of our existence is dependent upon God.

By the same token the clergy, no less than physicians, are concerned about the patient's physical well-being. No assumptions about technical skills and knowledge can legitimate the clergy retreating into the realm of the spiritual in order to claim some continued usefulness and status. Such a retreat is as unfaithful as abandoning the natural world to the physicist on the grounds that God is a God of history and not of nature. For the church and its officeholders to abandon claims over the body in the name of a lack of expertise is equivalent to reducing God to the gaps in scientific theory. Such a strategy is not only bad faith but it results in making religious convictions appear at best irrelevant and at worse foolish.

The second alternative to accepting the autonomy of medicine from our religious convictions seeks to maintain a close relationship by resacralizing medical care. Medicine requires a "holistic vision of man" ([7], p. 9), because the care it brings is but one aspect of salvation. Thus the church and its theology serve medical care by promoting a holistic view of man, one that can provide a

> comprehensive understanding of human health [that] includes the greatest possible harmony of all man's forces and energies, the greatest possible spiritualization of man's bodily aspects and the finest embodiment of the spiritual. True health is revealed in the self-actualization of the person who has attained that freedom which marshals all available energies for the fulfillment of his total human vocation. ([7], p. 154)

Such a view of health, however, cannot help but pervert the kind of care that physicians can provide. Physicians rightly maintain that their skill primarily has to do with the body, as medicine promises us health, not happiness. When such a general understanding of health is made the goal of medicine, it only results in making medical care promise more than it can deliver. As a result, we are tyrannized by the agents of medicine because we have voluntarily vested them with too much power. It is already a difficult task in our society to control the expectations people have about modern medicine; we only compound that problem by providing religious legitimacy to this overblown understanding of health. Certainly we believe that any account of salvation includes questions of our health, but that does not mean that medicine can or ever should become the agency of salvation. It may be a fundamental judgment on the church's failure to help us locate wherein our salvation lies that so many today seek a salvation through medicine.

Can Medical Ethics Be Christian?

The already complex question of the relation between religion and medicine only becomes more confusing when we turn our attention to more recent developments in medical ethics. For even though religious thinkers have been at the forefront of much of the work done in the expanding field of "medical ethics," it is not clear that they have been there as religious thinkers. Joseph Fletcher [5], Paul Ramsey [15], James Gustafson [6], Charles Curran [4], Jim Childress [3], to name just a few, have done extensive work in medical ethics, but often it is hard to tell how their religious convictions have made a difference for the methodology they employ or for their response to specific quandaries. Indeed it is interesting to note how seldom they raise issues of the meaning or relation of salvation and health, as they seem to prefer dealing with questions of death and dying, truth-telling, etc.

By calling attention to this fact by no means do I wish to disparage the kind of reflection that has been done concerning these issues. We have all benefited from their careful analysis and distinctions concerning such problems. Yet one must wonder if, by letting the agenda be set in such a manner, we have already lost the theological ball game. For the very concentration on "issues" and "quandaries" as central for medical ethics tends to underwrite the practice of medicine as we know it, rather than challenging some of the basic presuppositions of medical practice and care. Because of this failure to raise more fundamental questions, concerns that might provide more access for our theological claims are simply never considered.

There are at least two reasons for this that I think are worth mentioning. The first has to do with the character of theological ethics itself. We tend to forget that the development of "Christian ethics" is a relatively new development [8]. It has only been in the last hundred years that some have styled themselves as "ethicists" rather than simply theologians. It is by no means clear that we know how to indicate what difference it makes conceptually and methodologically to claim our ethics as Christian in distinction from other kinds of ethical reflection. In the hopes of securing great clarity about their own work many who have identified their work as Christian have nonetheless assumed that the meaning and method of "ethics" was determined fundamentally by non-Christian sources. In a sense the very concentration on "medical ethics" was a godsend for many "religious ethicists," as it seemed to provide a coherent activity without having to deal with the fundamental issue of what makes Christian ethics Christian.

This can be illustrated by attending to the debate among Christian ethicists concerning whether Christian moral reasoning is primarily deontological or consequential. This debate has been particularly important for medical ethics, as obviously how you think about non-therapeutic experimentation, truth-telling, transplants, and a host of other issues seems to turn on this issue. For instance, Joseph Fletcher, who wrote one of the first books by a Protestant in medical ethics, has always argued in favor of a consequential stance, thus qualifying the physician's commitment to an individual patient in the name of a greater good [5]. In contrast, Paul Ramsey has emphasized that the "covenant" of the physician with the patient is such that no amount of good to be done should override that commitment [14].

It is interesting to note how each makes theological appeals to support his own position. Fletcher appeals to love as his basic norm, interpreting it in terms of the greatest good for the greatest number, but it remains unclear how his sense of love is theologically warranted or controlled. Ramsey provides a stronger theological case for his emphasis on "covenant" as a central theological motif, but it is not clear how the many "covenants of life with life into which we are born" require the covenant of God with a particular people we find in Scripture. Ramsey's use of covenant language thus underwrites a natural law ethic whose status is unclear both from a theological and/or philosophical perspective.[1]

What is interesting about the debate between Fletcher and Ramsey is that it could have been carried on completely separate from the theological premises that each side claimed were involved. For the terms of the debate — *consequential* and *deontological* — are basically borrowed from philosophical contexts and are dependent on the presuppositions of certain philosophical traditions. Of course that in itself does not mean that such issues and concepts are irrelevant to our work as theologians, but what is missing is any sense of how the issue as presented grows, is dependent on, or informed by our distinctive commitments as theologians.

The question of the nature of theological ethics and its relation to the development of ethical reflection in and about medicine is further complicated by our current cultural situation. As Ramsey has pointed out, we are currently trying to do the impossible — namely, "build a civilization without an agreed civil tradition and [in] the absence of a moral consensus" ([13], p. 15). This makes the practice of medicine even more morally challenging, since it is by no means clear how one can sustain a non-arbitrary medicine in a genuinely morally pluralistic society. For example, much of the debate about when someone is "really" dead is not simply the result of our increased technological power to keep blood flowing through our bodies, but witnesses to our culture's lack of consensus as to what constitutes a well-lived life and the correlative sense of a good death. In the absence of such a consensus our only recourse is to resort to claims and counterclaims about "right to life" and "right to die," with the result of the further impoverishment of our moral language and vision. Moreover, the only way to create a "safe" medicine under such conditions is to expect physicians to treat us as if death is the ultimate enemy to be put off by every means. Then we blame physicians for keeping us alive beyond all reason, but fail to note that if they did not we would not know how to distinguish them from murderers.

Alasdair MacIntyre has raised this sort of issue directly in his "Can Medicine Dispense with a Theological Perspective on Human Nature?" Rather than calling attention to what has become problematic for physicians and surgeons — issues such as when it is appropriate to let someone die — he says he wants to direct our attention to what is still taken for granted, "namely, the unconditional and absolute character of certain of the doctor's obligations to his patients" ([12], p. 120). The difficulty is that modern philosophy, according to MacIntyre, has been unable to offer a persuasive account of such an obligation.

> *Either* they distort and misrepresent it *or* they render it unintelligible. Teleological moralists characteristically end up by distorting and misrepresenting. For they begin with a notion of moral rules as specifying how we are to behave if we are to achieve certain ends, perhaps *the* end for man, the *summum bonum*. If I break such rules I shall fail to achieve some human good and will thereby be frustrated and impoverished. ([12], p. 122)

But MacIntyre notes that this treats moral failure as if it is an educational failure and lacks the profound guilt that should accompany moral failure. More importantly, such an account fails entirely to account for the positive evil we know certain people clearly pursue.

Moral philosophers who tend to preserve the unconditional and absolute character of the central requirements of morality, however, inevitably make those "oughts" appear as if they are arbitrary. What they cannot do is show how those oughts are rationally entailed by an account of man's true end. Kant was only able to do so because he continued the presupposition (which he failed to justify within his own philosophical position) that "the life of the individual and also of that of the human race is a journey toward a goal" ([12], p. 127). Once that presupposition is lost, however, and MacIntyre believes that it has been lost in our culture, then we lack the resources to maintain exactly those moral presuppositions that seem essential to securing the moral integrity of medicine.

Such a situation seems ripe for a theological response, since it might at least be suggested that it thus becomes our task as theologians to serve our culture in general and medicine in particular by supplying the needed rationale. Yet, MacIntyre argues, such a strategy is doomed, since the very intelligibility of theological claims has been rendered problematic by the ethos of modernity. Therefore, just to the extent theologians try to make their claims in terms offered by modernity, they only underwrite the assumption that theological language cannot be meaningful.

This kind of dilemma is particularly acute when it comes to medicine. For if the theologian attempts to underwrite the medical ethos drawing on the particular convictions of Christians, just to the extent those convictions are particular they will serve only to emphasize society's lack of a common morality. Thus theologians, in the interest of cultural consensus, often try to downplay the distinctiveness of their theological convictions in the interest of societal harmony. But in the process we only reinforce the assumption on the part of many that theological claims make little difference for how medicine itself is understood or how various issues are approached. At best theology or religion is left with justifying a concern with the "whole patient," but it is not even clear how that concern depends on or derives from any substantive theological conviction that is distinguishable from humanism.

Almost as if we have sense that there is no way to resolve this dilemma, theologians and religious professionals involved in medicine have tended to associate with the patients' rights movement. At least one of the ways of resolving our cultural dilemma is to protect the patient from medicine by restoring the patient's autonomy over against the physician. While I certainly do not want to underestimate the importance of patients recovering a sense of medicine as an activity in which we play as important a role as the physician, the emphasis on the patient's rights over against the physician cannot resolve our difficulty. It is but an attempt to substitute procedural safeguards for what only substantive convictions can supply. As a result our attention is distracted from the genuine challenge we confront for the forming of an ethos sufficient to sustain a practice of medicine that is morally worthy.

Pain, Loneliness, and Being Present: The Church and the Care of the Ill

I can offer no "solution" to the issues raised in the previous section, as I think they admit of no solution, given our social and political situation. Moreover, I think we will make little headway on such matters as long as we try to address the questions in terms of the dichotomies of religion and medicine or the relation between medical ethics and theology. Rather, what is needed is a restatement of the issue. In this section I will try to do that by returning to my original text and story to suggest how they may help remind us that more fundamental than questions of religion and morality is the question of the kind of community necessary to sustain the long-term care of the ill.

Indeed, part of the problem with discussing the question of "relation" in such general terms as "medicine" and "religion" is that each of those terms in its own way distorts the character of what it is meant to describe. For example, when we talk in general about "religion" rather than a specific set of beliefs, behaviors, and habits embodied by a distinct group of people, our account always tends to be reductionistic. It makes it appear that underlying what people actually believe and do is a deeper reality called "religion." It is as if we can talk about God abstracted from how a people have learned to pray to that God. In like manner we often tend to oversimplify the nature of medicine by trying to capture the many activities covered by that term in a definition or ideological system. What doctors do is often quite different from what they say they do.

Moreover, the question of the relation of theology to medical ethics is far too abstract. For when the issue is posed in that manner it makes it appear that religion is primarily a set of beliefs, a world view, that may or may not have implications for how we understand and respond to certain kinds of ethical dilemmas. While it is certainly true that Christianity involves beliefs, the character of those beliefs cannot be understood apart from its place in the formation of a community with cultic practices. By focusing on this fact I hope to throw a different perspective on how those who are called to care for the sick can draw upon and count on the particular kind of community we call the church.

I do not intend, for example, to argue that medicine must be reclaimed as in some decisive way dependent on theology. Nor do I want to argue that the development of "medical ethics" will ultimately require the acknowledgment of, or recourse to, theological presuppositions. Rather all I want to try to show is why, given the particular demands put on those who care for the ill, something very much like a church is necessary to sustain that care.

To develop this point I want to call attention to an obvious but often overlooked aspect of illness — namely, that when we are sick we hurt and are in pain. I realize that often we are sick and yet not in pain — e.g., hardening of the arteries — but that does not ultimately defeat my general point, since we know that such an illness will lead to physical and mental pain. Nor am I particularly bothered by the observation that many pains are "psychological," having no real physiological basis. Physicians are right to insist that people who say they have pain, even if no organic basis can be found for such pain, are in fact, in pain, though they may be mistaken about what kind of pain it is.

Moreover I am well aware that there are many different kinds of pain, as well as intensity of pains. What is only a minor hurt for me may be a major trauma for someone else. Pain comes in many shapes and sizes and it is never possible to separate the psychological aspects of pain from the organic. For example, suffering, which is not the same as pain since we can suffer without being in pain, is nonetheless akin to pain inasmuch as it is a felt deficiency that can make us as miserable as pain itself.[2]

Yet given these qualifications it remains true that there is a strong connection between pain and illness, an area of our lives in which it is appropriate to call upon the skills of a physician. When we are in pain we want to be helped. But it is exactly at this point that one of the strangest aspects of our being in pain occurs — namely, it is impossible for us to experience one another's pain. That does not mean we cannot communicate to one another our pain. That we can do, but what cannot be done is for you to understand and/or experience my pain as mine.

This puts us under a double burden because we have enough of a problem learning to know one another in the normal aspects of our lives, but when we are in pain our alienation from one another only increases. For no matter how sympathetic we may be to the other in pain, that very pain creates a history and experience that makes the other just that much more foreign to me. Our pains isolate us from one another as they create worlds that cut us off from one another. Consider, for example, the immense gulf between the world of the sick and the healthy. No matter how much we may experience the former, when we are healthy or not in pain we have trouble imagining and understanding the world of the ill.

Indeed the terms we are using are still far too crude. For we do not suffer illness in and of itself, but we suffer this particular kind of illness and have this particular kind of pain. Thus even within the world of illness there are subworlds that are not easily crossed. Think, for example, of how important it is for those suffering from the same illness to share their stories with one another. They do not believe others can understand their particular kind of pain. People with heart disease may find little basis of communion with those suffering from cancer. Pain itself does not create a shared experience; only pain from a particular kind and sort. Moreover the very commonality thus created separates the ill from the healthy in a decisive way.

Pain not only isolates us from one another, but even from ourselves. Think how quickly people with a terribly diseased limb or organ are anxious for surgery in the hope that if it is just cut off or cut out they will not be burdened by the pain that makes them not know themselves. This gangrenous leg is not mine. I would prefer to lose the leg rather than face the reality of its connection to me.

The difficulties pain creates in terms of our relation with ourselves is compounded by the peculiar difficulties it creates for those close to us who do not share our pain. For no matter how sympathetic they may be, no matter how much they may try to be with and comfort us, we know they do not want to experience our pain. I not only cannot, but I do not want to, know the pain you are feeling. No matter how good willed we may be, we cannot take anther's pain as our pain. Our pains divide us and there is little we can do to restore our unity.

I suspect this is one of the reasons that chronic illness is such a burden. For often we are willing to be present and sympathetic with someone with an intense but temporary pain — that is, we are

and their presence, even though we have been unwilling to face that reality while we were healthy.

But what do these somewhat random and controversial observations have to do with helping us better understand the relation between medicine and the church and/or the story of my boyhood friendship with Bob? To begin with the latter, I think in some ways the mechanism that was working during that trying time with Bob is quite similar to the mechanism that works on a day-to-day basis in medicine. For the physician, and others concerned with our illness, are called to be present during times of great pain and tragedy. Indeed physicians, because of their moral commitments, have the privilege and the burden to be with us when we are most vulnerable. The physician learns our deepest fears and our profoundest hopes. As patients, that is also why so often we fear the physician, because she/he may know us better than we know ourselves. Surely that is one of the reasons that confidentiality is so crucial to the patient-physician relation, since it is a situation of such intimacy.

But just to the extent that the physician has been granted the privilege of being with us while we are in pain, that very experience creates the seeds of distrust and fear. We are afraid of one another's use of the knowledge gained, but even more deeply we fear remembering the pain as part of our history. Thus every crisis that joins us in a common fight for health also has the potential for separating us more profoundly after the crisis. Yet the physician is pledged to come to our aid again and again, no matter how we may try to protect ourselves from his/her presence.

The physician, on the other hand, has yet another problem, for how can anyone be present to the ill day in and day out without learning to dislike, if not positively detest, our smallness in the face of pain. People in pain are omnivorous in their appetite for help, and they will use us up if we let them. Fortunately the physician has other patients who can give him distance from any patient who requires too much. But the problem still remains how morally those who are pledged to be with the ill never lose their ability to see the humanity that our very suffering often comes close to obliterating. For the physician cannot, as Bob and I did, drift apart and away from those whom he or she is pledged to serve. At least they cannot if I am right that medicine is first of all pledged to be nothing more than a human presence in the face of suffering.

But how can we account for such a commitment — the commitment to be present to those in pain? No doubt basic human sympathy is not to be discounted, but it does not seem to be sufficient to account for a group of people dedicated to being present to the ill as their vocation in life. Nor does it seem sufficient to account for the acquiring of the skills necessary to sustain that presence in a manner that is not alienating and the source of distrust in a community.

To learn how to be present in that way we need examples — that is, a people who have so learned to embody such a presence in their lives that it has become the marrow of their habits. The church at least claims to be such a community, as it is a group of people called out by a God who, we believe, is always present to us, both in our sin and our faithfulness. Because of God's faithfulness we are supposed to be a people who have learned how to be faithful to one another by our willingness to be present, with all our vulnerabilities, to one another. For what does our God require of us other than our unfailing presence in the midst of the world's sin and pain? Thus our willingness to be ill and to ask for help, as well as our willingness to be present with the ill is no special or extraordinary activity, but a form of the Christian obligation to be present to one another in and out of pain.

Moreover, it is such a people who should have learned how to be present with those in pain without that pain driving them further apart. For the very bond that pain forms between us becomes the basis for alienation, as we have no means to know how to make it part of our common history. Just as it is painful to remember our sins, so we seek not to remember our pain, since we desire to live as if our world and existence were a pain-free one. Only a people trained in remembering, and remembering as a communal act, their sins and pains can offer a paradigm for sustaining across time a painful memory so that it acts to heal rather than to divide.

Thus medicine needs the church not to supply a foundation for its moral commitments, but rather as a resource of the habits and practices necessary to sustain the care of those in pain over the long haul. For it is no easy matter to be with the ill, especially when we cannot do much for them other than simply be present. Our very helplessness too often turns to hate, both toward the one in pain and ourselves, as we despise them for reminding us of our helplessness. Only when we remember that our presence is our doing, when sitting on the ground seven days saying nothing is what we can do, can we be saved from our fevered and hopeless attempt to control others' and our own existence. Of course to believe that such presence is what we can and should do entails a belief in a presence in and beyond this world. And it is certainly true many today no longer believe in or experience such a presence. If that is the case, then I do wonder if medicine as an activity of presence is possible in a world without God.

Another way of raising this issue is to ask the relation between prayer and medical care. Nothing I have said about the basic pledge of physicians to be present to the ill entails that they should not try to develop the skills necessary to help those in pain and illness. Certainly they should, as theirs is an art that is one of our most valuable resources for the care of one another. But no matter how powerful that craft becomes, it cannot in principle rule out the necessity of prayer. For prayer is not a supplement to the insufficiency of our medical knowledge and practice; nor is it some divine insurance policy that our medical skill will work; rather, our prayer is the means that we have to make God present whether our medical skill is successful or not. So understood, the issue is not whether medical care and prayer are antithetical, but how medical care can ever be sustained without the necessity of continued prayer.

Finally, those involved in medicine need the church as otherwise they cannot help but be alienated from the rest of us. For unless there is a body of people who have learned the skills of presence, the world of the ill cannot help but become a separate world both for the ill and/or those who care for them. Only a community that is pledged not to fear the stranger — and illness always makes us a stranger to ourselves and others — can welcome the continued presence of the ill in our midst. The hospital is, after all, first and foremost a house of hospitality along the way of our journey with finitude. It is our sign that we will not abandon those who have become ill simply because they currently are suffering the sign of that finitude. If the hospital, as too often is the case today, becomes but a means of isolating the ill from the rest of us, then we have betrayed its central purpose and distorted our community and ourselves.

If the church can be the kind of people who show clearly that they have learned to be with the sick and the dying, it may just be that through that process we will better understand the relation of salvation to health, religion to medicine. Or perhaps even more, we will better understand what kind of medicine we ought to practice, since too often we try to substitute doing for presence. It is surely the case, as Paul Ramsey reminds us, "that not since Socrates posed the question have we learned how to teach virtue. The quandaries of medical ethics are not unlike that question. Still, we can no longer rely upon the ethical assumptions in our culture to be powerful enough or clear enough to instruct the profession in virtue; therefore the medical profession should no longer believe that the personal integrity of physicians alone is enough; neither can anyone count on values being transmitted without thought" ([14], p. xviii). All I have tried to do is remind us that neither can we count on such values being transmitted without a group of people who believe in and live trusting in God's unfailing presence.

Notes

1. Ramsey's position is complex and I certainly cannot do it justice here. His emphasis on "love transforming natural law" would tend to qualify the point made above. Yet it is also true that Ramsey's increasing use of covenant language has gone hand in hand with his readiness to identify certain "covenants" that need no "transformation." Of course he could object that the covenant between doctor and patient is the result of Christian love operating in history.

2. For a fuller account of the complex relation between pain and suffering see [11].

3. I am indebted to a conversation with Dr. Earl Shelp for helping me understand better the significance of this point.

References

[1] Amundsen, D., and Ferngren, G. 1982. "Medicine and Religion: Pre-Christian Antiquity." In M. Marty and K. Vaux, eds., *Health/Medicine and the Faith Traditions,* pp. 53-92. Philadelphia: Fortress Press.

[2] Amundsen, D., and Ferngren, G. 1982. "Medicine and Religion: Early Christianity Through the Middle Ages." In M. Marty and K. Vaux, eds., *Health/Medicine and the Faith Traditions,* pp. 93-132.

[3] Childress, J. 1981. *Priorities in Biomedical Ethics.* Philadelphia: Westminster Press.

[4] Curran, C. 1978. *Issues in Sexual and Medical Ethics.* Notre Dame, Ind.: University of Notre Dame Press.

[5] Fletcher, J. 1954. *Morals and Medicine.* Boston: Beacon Press.

[6] Gustafson, J. 1975. *The Contributions of Theology to Medical Ethics.* Milwaukee: Marquette University Press.

[7] Haring, B. 1973. *Medical Ethics.* South Bend, Ind.: Fides Publishers.

[8] Hauerwas, S. 1983. "On Keeping Theological Ethics Theological." In A. MacIntyre and S. Hauerwas, eds., *Revisions: Changing Perspectives in Moral Philosophy,* pp. 16-42. Notre Dame, Ind.: University of Notre Dame Press.

[9] Hauerwas, S. 1982. "The Retarded, Society and the Family: The Dilemma of Care." In S. Hauerwas, ed., *Responsibility for Devalued Persons.* Springfield, Ill.: Charles C. Thomas.

[10] Hauerwas, S. 1982. "Authority and the Profession of Medicine," In G. Agich, *Responsibility in Health Care,* pp. 83-104. Dordrecht, Holland: Reidel.

[11] Hauerwas, S. 1979. "Reflections on Suffering, Death, and Medicine," *Ethics in Science and Medicine* 6:229-37.

[12] MacIntyre, A. 1981. "Can Medicine Dispense with a Theological Perspective on Human Nature?" In D. Callahan and H. Englehardt, eds., *The Roots of Ethics,* pp. 119-38. New York: Plenum Press.

[13] Ramsey, P. 1973. "The Nature of Medical Ethics." In R. Neatch, M. Gaylin, and C. Morgan, eds., *The Teaching of Medical Ethics,* pp. 14-28. Hastings-on-Hudson, N.Y.: Hastings Center.

[14] Ramsey, P. 1970. *The Patient as Person.* New Haven: Yale University Press.

12 Bio-ethics: Some Challenges from a Liberation Perspective

Karen Lebacqz

The Task

In Lewis Carroll's delightful story *Alice in Wonderland,* Alice has a tendency to change size, not always at will. On once such occasion, the following dialogue ensues:

"Don't squeeze so," said the Dormouse to Alice.

"I can't help it. I'm growing," she replied.

"You've no right to grow *here.*"

"Don't talk nonsense; you know you're growing, too."

"Yes, but *I* grow at a reasonable pace, and not in that ridiculous fashion."

These words describe all too accurately what many of us feel today in the face of the so-called "biological revolution": sitting next to something that appears to be growing at a ridiculous rate, we feel "squeezed" and are tempted to cry out: "You've no right to grow *here.*" Wonderland, or bad dream? Current arguments posit one or the other: proponents hold out visions of miraculous cures for human ailments and new freedoms in human living, while opponents raise the spectre of Huxley's *Brave New World.* Perhaps the only thing on which both would agree is that developments in biomedical technology threaten to change the nature of our existence.

From *Faith and Science in an Unjust World.* Report of the *World Council of Churches' Conference on Faith, Science and the Future,* vol. 1: Plenary Presentations, ed. Roger L. Shinn (Geneva: World Council of Churches, 1980), pp. 272-81. Used by permission.

Rather than undertake a direct discussion of ethical dilemmas raised by biomedical research and technological capacity, I wish to raise a more profound question related to our sense of being "squeezed." The great church historian Ernest Troeltsch once said: "If the present social situation is to be controlled by Christian principles, thoughts will be necessary which have not yet been thought, and which will correspond to this new situation as the older forms met the need of the social situation in earlier ages."[1]

In the conviction that advances in biomedical technology require the development of "thoughts which have not yet been thought," I shall focus on the *way* we analyse ethical issues in biomedical arenas. That is, my concern will be methodological rather than substantive. In particular, I shall argue that the predominant western approach to bio-ethical issues suffers serious limitations and should be challenged in the light of some emerging ethical reflection, particularly that of feminist and liberation theology.

Bio-Ethics: The Prevailing Approach

Most contemporary writings in bio-ethics share certain characteristics. While the following list would not apply uniformly, it does suggest the predominant characteristics of the field.

1. Decision-Orientation

Like much current social ethics, both philosophical and theological, contemporary bio-ethics is largely decision-oriented. It focuses on such questions as: "Should we operate on this newborn infant with a congenital defect?", "Should we permit recombinant DNA research?" and so on. Indeed, most has been "crisis-oriented," dealing not simply with action decisions in medical research and care, but with catastrophic events rather than routine questions about delivery of care.[2]

In short, we have focused on *doing the right things.* This discussion of the right thing to do has resulted in increased clarity about the nature and meaning of some ethical dilemmas, some movement towards resolution of important ethical dilemmas in particular cases, and agreement about basic ethical principles applicable to certain bio-ethical dilemmas.

Nonetheless, the decision-orientation of contemporary bio-ethics has serious flaws. First, it tends to give the impression that there is *one* correct decision in every dilemma and that our only task is to find the "right" answer. It ignores the possibility that every possible action may embody some important values and that what may be at stake is not finding the "right" answer but choosing among competing values.

Second, traditional normative ethics considers at least three questions: (1) which actions are right; (2) what makes a person "good" or virtuous; and (3) what constitutes the "ideal state" or structure of human society. The decision-orientation of contemporary bio-ethics focuses on the first of these. With some exceptions, two important aspects of normative ethics have been largely ignored.

2. Individualistic Orientation

Most contemporary bio-ethics is also individualistic. It begins with the concerns of individual patients or physicians as they encounter dilemmas. Indeed, much contemporary bio-ethics takes as its starting place the "physician-patient relationship."[3]

This focus reflects the western, white culture from which such discussions originate, and is not adequate to explain the needs and experiences of most of the world. In many localities and countries, the major health questions have nothing to do with physicians and how they treat patients, but have instead to do with poor housing, inadequate sewage systems, and so on. In other localities, health care is provided through massive bureaucracies in which the primary problem may be that of getting *access* to a physician, not how one is treated once one finally sees her or him.[4] In a social structure where there is no access to physicians for major portions of the population, or in which one's "physician-patient relationship" comprises no more than 2 percent of one's medical and health care, a bio-ethics that takes the "physician-patient relationship" as normative is simply inapplicable. What is needed is an approach that focuses on systems and institutions and that takes seriously the entire web of relationships in the delivery of care, of which the presumed "physician-patient relationship" is only one.

3. Ahistorical Approach

Partly because of the search for norms and principles that are generally applicable, bio-ethics as currently practised tends to be ahistorical. It is assumed that once the "right" answer is found, it will be correct for all similar cases; little discussion is given to the changing historical setting within which bio-ethical decisions are made and whether this setting might affect the correctness of the decision. Resulting norms tend to be rigid.[5] While not all theorists agree with the "absolutist" position that, for example, rejects all abortion as unethical, most assume that once the proper "exceptions" are found, they hold irrespective of historical circumstance.

The "contextual" or "situational" approach to ethics, which gained popularity in the United States during the 1960s, attempted to correct this ahistorical rigidity by refusing to accept any "absolutes." However, in its own way it remains ahistorical: by failing to specify clearly *which* aspects of a situation or *which* historical changes make a difference, it also tends to focus on the immediate situation and loses any historical "bite." It leaves one with the impression that historical settings either do not matter at all, or that there is no way to sort out which do and which do not; thus, it fails to specify criteria for deciding which historical contexts are "morally relevant."

4. Scientific Evidence as Normative

Most bio-ethics today operate out of the dominant western scientific worldview, in which science sets criteria for the acceptability of evidence. The results are, first, a minimizing of the value of individual or group experience, and second, a blurring of the value-laden nature of "facts" or data.

It is not uncommon, for example, to hear an ethicist say that medical personnel or scientists must provide the "facts" or evidence in the case. While personal experiences are not totally ignored, they tend to be discredited: "feelings" are not an adequate basis for ethical decision-making; only logical analysis of "facts" will do. This tends to take the decision away from those most intimately involved, for they are often not in possession of all the data and are also inclined to be emotional in their responses.

Moreover, it tends to obfuscate the value-laden nature of data. Data are not value-free. We make choices about what to look for, how to measure what we find, and how to present it. Professional training determines to a large extent how we structure inquiry and how we interpret the results of the inquiry. In addition, prior value assumptions shape our interpretation and presentation of data. (E.g. is there a 50 percent chance of having a normal child, or a 50 percent chance of having a defective child? Note that the term "defective" is itself a value judgment, not a statement of fact.)

5. Grounding of Norms

Most discussions of bio-ethical issues, particularly those by Christian ethicists, either accept a wide variety of grounding sources for norms or fail to specify the grounding of particular norms; there is also little discussion of the movement from theological presuppositions to particular norms.[6] For example, in his influential book *The Patient as Person*, Ramsey introduces a number of Judeo-Christian affirmations such as *hesed* (steadfast love), covenant (faithfulness), and the like. In his discussion of concrete issues, however, he turns to norms derived from medical sources such as the Nuremberg Code with its requirement for informed consent. The link between the two sources — if, indeed, there is any — is not clear, and it is often not clear how Ramsey incorporates his Christian principles into an otherwise Kantian perspective.

It is understandable, of course, that Christian ethicists working in the field of bio-ethics would incorporate a broad base for normative statements. Many operate out of a "natural law" tradition or approach in which they affirm as a part of their Christian belief a general set of norms available to all persons and not necessarily distinctive for Christians.[7] Moreover bio-ethics must speak to lawyers, scientists, politicians, and others who do not operate out of a specifically Christian approach. It therefore behooves the Christian ethicist not to be overly narrow.

Nonetheless, the failure to specify the grounding for norms results in confusion and disagreement as to (1) what norms there are, if any; (2) which are applicable to the situation; (3) how they are to be interpreted, e.g. does "justice" require protection of the vulnerable or simply equal treatment?; and (4) how to weigh and balance conflicting norms, e.g. does the potential social good outweigh the requirement to seek informed consent in certain types of research or genetic screening programs? In particular, we need to know whether it makes a difference to do bio-ethics as a "Christian" and, if so, what that difference is.

Challenges and Alternatives

I shall here suggest some major alternatives to the prevailing mode of doing bio-ethics, drawing primarily on contemporary work in feminist and liberation theology.[8] I shall also indicate the sorts of questions that these alternative approaches would suggest, though it will not be possible here to answer these questions or to put them into full context.

1. Patterns of Meaning and Structural Concerns

Liberation theologians and feminists are primarily concerned not with choosing the right action, but with structures and patterns of meaning.

I believe that this is partly why there has been little attention in these writings to bio-ethical issues, important though technological advances in biomedicine may be for the lives of women and other members of oppressed and disadvantaged groups. At a recent conference on Ethical Issues in Reproductive Technology: Analysis by Women, questions about whether *in vitro* fertilization is right or wrong were transmuted into questions about who holds the power to make such decisions, what the impact of all biomedical technologies combined is on the lives of women in this society, and so on.[9] In short, questions about what is right and wrong to *do* were ignored in favor of questions about the nature of the social structures and mythologies that support these technologies.

Other liberation theologians argue that it is not merely the shape of *particular* social institutions and structures that must be analysed, but the shape of the entire *age* or epoch. For example, Roy Sano argues that Asian American liberation theologians and people turn to apocalyptic rather than prophetic literature because apocalyptic literature gives a better base from which to observe the interweavings of the various powerful institutions.[10] Dussel argues that what is at stake is recognizing the shape of evil in any and all institutions.[11] Feminist theologians analyze the myths that undergird particular institutions by defining the "masculine" and "feminine" in society.[12] Thus, it is not simply particular institutions that are to be analyzed ethically, but the thought structures, myths, and loyalties that permit those institutions to exist. The very shape of the scientific worldview may be at stake.

Applied to the biomedical arena, these insights would suggest some new questions to be asked: What images of health, disease, normalcy, womanhood, sexuality, etc. undergird the present delivery of health care and development of new biomedical technologies? Who or what are our current idols? Where are our loyalties? What is the relationship between the development of new biomedical technologies and nuclear power, communications technology, and so on? The primary ethical questions have to do with the shape and interrelationship of the dominant social structures and their impact on the lives of those who are oppressed. It is in part a theological question, having to do with our loyalties and whether we give our allegiance to anything other than God — even to the scientific worldview.

2. Story and Community

As soon as one asks about patterns of meaning, one moves beyond looking at the specific decision to asking how that decision fits into the context of a life. The particular decision may either make sense or be muted in its total context within the person's life. Thus, questions of character, integrity, and virtue come to have central significance, and the telling and shaping of one's life story is crucial to the ethical task.[13]

The women's movement and feminist theology in particular have stressed the importance of life stories as the groundwork for theology. As women share their experiences, they locate patterns of meaning that emerge and give theological dimension. Theology and ethics, thus, are born of experience and its coherence in a life story.[14]

But this is partly because the interpretative framework brought to one's own life story has political significance. As women commonly put it, "the personal is political." This means that the entire context in which one interprets one's own story also matters. And so a concern for story and its patterns of meaning results in a concern for community. Indeed, it is often only when women are together in community that they make the transition from saying, "I'm depressed" — an interpretative framework provided by the dominant western scientific worldview — to saying "I'm oppressed" — an interpretation possible within the context of a liberating community.

Applied to the field of bio-ethics, this concern for story and community would suggest that we ask not: "Should this woman have an abortion?" but: "What is this woman's story? What are the interpretative frameworks that give meaning to her life? Does she have a supportive community? Is she oppressed? Will the abortion be liberating for her? Will it be community-building or community destroying?"

The concern for story and community that arises from feminist and liberation perspectives is akin to Ramsey's concern for covenant, Lehmann's focus on koinonia, and H. R. Niebuhr's concern for accountability structures, in that it focuses on one's relationship within a group. However, I believe that feminist and liberation theologians are more true to the biblical perspective when they go beyond Ramsey, Lehmann, and Niebuhr to the point of seeing one's *identity* as in some way intimately related to that group. Ramsey talks about covenants between physician and patient as though no others need be involved, whereas women and members of oppressed groups argue that those in existence today have sufficient continuity with those of the past to be able to stand in their stead and receive what was their due. This is a radically different notion of identity and I believe that it is one of the contributions that a feminist or liberation theology might make to the field of bio-ethics.

3. History (or "Herstory," as Feminists Say)

What has just been said makes clear that feminists and liberation theologians also require a *historical* ethic — an ethic that takes seriously the oppression of people through time and asks: "Is something that was appropriate yesterday still appropriate today? Will it be appropriate tomorrow?" Yesterday's oppressions are not simply forgotten, but must be rectified today. Thus, for example, no interpretation of justice may be proffered that fails to account for retribution and compensation for past injury. Perhaps most important, this focus on history requires the rewriting of history, with a view to lifting up the role of women and other oppressed peoples — to locating the "fore-mothers" as well as the "fore-fathers" of current medical practice and technological innovation.

Applied to the area of bio-ethics, this historical view would certainly preclude an absolute and unyielding "yes" or "no" to technological innovations. More important, however, it would require a second look at the history of development of biomedical technologies to ask how that history is perceived from the perspective of oppressed peoples, how it impacts on their lives and possibilities, and so on. One is tempted to suggest that from this perspective serious questions need to be raised about whether these technologies should be developed in the absence of basic nutritional, health, and medical care in "third world" countries.

4. Experiential Approach

To argue for the importance of history, and for the reclaiming of one's story, is also to argue for new interpretative frameworks. Thus, new criteria for evidence are emerging. Scientific data are *not* the only source of meaningful interpretation; the life histories and shared experiences of oppressed groups are the primary "facts" to be considered. Most feel that only those who have had such experiences can communicate them accurately. Thus, there is a tendency to shift from a dependence on experts to a focus on the layperson.

This new approach also suggests that there may be numerous valid value systems, not one "right" approach. At the same time, as the above analysis has shown, the primary loyalty is always to those who are oppressed, and it is their interpretations and perspectives that are given most validity.

Applied to the ethical issues posed by technological advances in medicine and science, the questions become obvious: What is the experience of women who want desperately to become pregnant and are unable to conceive? Why do they want this so desperately — i.e. what in the system creates this need? How does the development of these technologies affect the chances for life and health of the "Third World"? And, perhaps most important, are these developments really "advances" at all? Finally, a participatory decision-making model, perhaps involving community as well as individual participation, might be called for with respect to each technology and to the scientific enterprise as a whole.

Sources for Ethics

Since the question of norms is no longer the only question asked, the issue of grounding of norms is broadened to ask about sources of ethical insight. From the above, it is clear that a primary source for both feminists and liberation theologians is the experience of the oppressed group. Indeed, Cone goes so far as to assert that only those who are "black" can talk about God in the United States.[15]

Taking the experiences of the oppressed as central to the theological task has led some feminists to move beyond Christianity altogether, and to assert that the grounding for theological insight lies in women's bodies (e.g. menstruation and bodily cycles), dreams, and rituals.[16] Others retain a closer adherence to biblical insight, but with the proviso that the biblical message be measured and interpreted by the experiences of the oppressed.[17]

Serious questions remain for feminists and liberation theologians at this point. Is there a different norm or ethic for each group? Or is there only one ethical system, but that one discernible only by the oppressed? Is there a "natural law" or insight into ethical stances and norms provided by the natural (e.g. women's bodies)? Until such methodological questions are addressed systematically, the impact of these new approaches cannot be fully assessed. It is difficult to know thus far what the impact on bio-ethics might be of new approaches to the source of ethical insight.

Conclusions

It is not the rate of growth of biomedical technologies *per se* that make us feel "squeezed." Rather, it is the threat they present to the meaning structures of our world. This essay is submitted in the hopes of initiating the task of creating "thoughts which have not yet been thought" and which will meet the social situation of our day. Wonderland, or nightmare? Much depends on our perspective. Will we open that perspective to the challenge of the oppressed and incorporate into the doing of bio-ethics the message of liberation theology?

Notes

1. Ernst Troeltsch: *The Social Teachings of the Christian Churches* (New York: Harper Torchback Edition, 1960), p. 1012.

2. I have criticized this "crisis" approach in an earlier essay. See Karen Lebacqz: "Peter and His Doctor." *Journal of Current Social Issues,* Fall 1975. At the same time, I wish to emphasize that I have also tended to adopt the decision-orientation in my own writings in the field of bio-ethics. Thus, the purpose of this essay is not to assign blame to those who take such an approach, but to try to be cognizant of its limits.

3. While examples are legion, one of the best known is Paul Ramsey's important volume, *The Patient as Person* (New Haven: Yale University Press, 1970).

4. I personally have not had a sustained "physician-patient relationship" with any single physician for more than 16 years; I find that my single most important problem is getting *to* the doctor — it routinely takes two hours of telephoning, two hours of waiting, and at least four contacts with clerks, receptionists, nurses, and others before I see the physician for what is generally a maximum of ten minutes. Since I am a relatively well-situated and well-educated health care consumer, I can only imagine how such problems might be multiplied for those who are less fortunate.

5. This is particularly a problem when norms are turned into governmental regulations. The norm "seek informed consent" still permits some flexibility; however, a law mandating informed consent does not permit the same flexibility.

6. Several recent volumes attempt to address this problem. See Philip Wogaman: *A Christian Method of*

Moral Judgment (Philadelphia: Westminster Press, 1976).

7. For example, in his discussion of proxy consent for children, Richard McCormick argues that there are certain values that all human beings ought to uphold, and that therefore one may give consent on behalf of a child in order to foster those values. See "Proxy Consent in the Experimentation Situation." *Perspectives in Biology and Medicine,* Vol. 18, No. 1, 1974.

8. Two words of explanation are in order here. First, much "feminist" theology *is* liberation theology and can be classified under that general heading. However, some feminist theologizing does not fit neatly under the liberation approach, and I have therefore chosen to specify that I am drawing from both types of theological thought as they are emerging.

Second, feminist and liberation theologies are not the only sources of some of the alternative insights and approaches specified here. A number of male theologians and ethicists from the dominant tradition have fostered one or another of these concerns, e.g. the Niebuhr stress on community, the work of Gustafson, Stanley Hauerwas, and others on character and virtue, James McClendon's stress on biography. Nonetheless, I shall take the theology from feminists and liberation thinkers as my baseline for this analysis.

9. Held at Amherst, Massachusetts, 24-29 June 1979.

10. Roy Sano: "Ethnic Liberation Theology: Neo-Orthodoxy Reshaped or Replaced?" *Christianity and Crisis,* 10 November 1975. Others who are using apocalyptic literature and suggesting that it is the entire shape of the age that must be analysed and criticized include William Stringfellow: *An Ethic for Christians and Other Aliens in a Strange Land* (Waco, Texas: Word Books, 1973), and William Coats: *God in Public: Political Theology Beyond Niebuhr* (Grand Rapids, Michigan: William B. Eerdmans, 1974).

11. Enrique Dussel: *Ethics and the Theology of Liberation* (New York: Orbis Books, 1978).

12. See, for example, Jo Freeman (ed.): *Women: a Feminist Perspective* (Palo Alto: Mayfield, 1979); Anne Koedt et al.: *Radical Feminism* (New York: Quadrangle/The New York Times Book Co., 1973); Mary Daly: *Gyn/Ecology: the Metaethics of Radical Feminism* (Boston: Beacon Press, 1978); Sheila Collins: *A Different Heaven and Earth* (Valley Forge, Pa.: Judson, Press, 1974); Mary Vetterling-Braggin et al.: *Feminism and Philosophy* (Totawa, N.J.: Littlefield, Adams and Co., 1977); Rosemary Reuther: *Religion and Sexism* (New York: Simon and Schuster, 1974).

13. For example, in *Beyond Mere Obedience,* Dorothee Sölle describes the life story of a woman who broke many of the conventions of her day and whose life would probably be judged by most to include some unethical acts. Nonetheless, within the context of her total life, she has gone "beyond mere obedience" into a life of freedom, and she expresses some virtues and character that override her particular misdoings.

14. Sheila Collins is particularly emphatic on this point. See *A Different Heaven and Earth,* op. cit., and "Reflections on the Meaning of Herstory" and "Theology in the Politics of Appalachian Women," in Carol Christ and Judith Plaskow: *Womenspirit Rising* (New York: Harper and Row, 1979).

15. James Cone: *A Black Theology of Liberation* (New York: J. B. Lippincott, 1970). It is not clear whether "black" refers to skin color necessarily or whether those of like spirit but different skin color might be "black."

16. See essays by Plaskow, Goldenberg, Washburn, and Christ in *Womanspirit Rising,* op. cit.

17. See essays by Trible, Fiorenza, McLaughlin in *Womanspirit Rising,* op. cit.

13 Feminist Theology and Bioethics

Margaret A. Farley

The aim of this essay is to explore the connections between feminist theology and issues in the field of bioethics. I have construed the task largely as a descriptive one; that is, I shall try to indicate some basic contours of feminist theology and some ways in which the values it emphasizes bear on the vast network of ethical issues related to the biological sciences, technology, and medicine. In addition, and in order to press the question of possible contributions by feminist theology to bioethics, I shall focus on the particular implications of feminist theology for the development and use of reproductive technology.

To some extent, the connection between the concerns of feminist theology and bioethics is obvious. Whatever else feminist theology does, it proceeds from a methodological focus on the experience of women, and whatever feminist ethics does, it begins with a central concern for the well-being of women. Medical ethics (as a part of bioethics) can be expected to share in some important way this focus and this concern, if for no other reason than that women constitute the majority of those who receive and provide health care ([46], pp. 119, 125; [33]). Beyond this, however, traditional religious views of women associate them symbolically and literally with nature, with the body, with human relationships, with reproduction — all themes for feminist theological critique and reconstruction, all foci for major concerns of bioethics in its broadest dimensions. The obviousness of the connection between these two disciplines, however, does not in itself give us the present and potential lines of mutual influence.

Before beginning a closer look at the relation between feminist theology and bioethics, three caveats are perhaps in order. That is, it is helpful to identify some forms of relation which we should *not* expect to find.

First, we should not expect to find feminist theology articulating for bioethics fundamental values or moral principles which are in every way unique to a feminist theological perspective. Few contemporary theological ethicists who take seriously the task of making explicit the connection between religious beliefs and ethical action claim for their theologies exclusive access to moral insight in the formulation of commonly held norms ([19], p. 9; [18], p. 119; [14], pp. 84-90; [13], p. 26).[1] It is not only religious belief, or theology, or a particular theology that can ground, for example, a requirement to respect persons, or a principle of equality, or a rational system of distributive justice. Likewise, it is not only feminist theology that can ground a view of human persons as fundamentally interpersonal and social, or that can formulate a view of nature that requires human stewardship rather than exploitation. Still, theologies do yield ethical perspectives that are unique in some respects, moral points of view that claim hermeneutically privileged insights, even particular moral action-guides that chart frontiers for human decision. Feminist theology is no exception in this regard. Indeed, it may have a more explicit ethical entailment than many other theologies. Moreover, its critical function may provide an essentially new perspective on some issues in bioethics.

Second, there is no one definitive form of feminist theology which can be looked to as representing all of its possible implications for bioethics. Theology in general is pluralistic on many levels. Feminist theology is not just one among many options in theology; it is itself pluralistic on many of the same levels as is theology generally. Thus, there are feminist theologies that are centered in ancient forms of goddess worship, and

From Margaret A. Farley, "Feminist Theology and Bioethics," in Earl E. Shelp, ed., *Theology and Bioethics: Exploring the Foundations and Frontiers* (Dordrecht: D. Reidel Publishing Co., 1985), pp. 163-86. Used with kind permission of Kluwer Academic Publishers.

others that locate themselves, with important distinctions, in the Jewish or Christian biblical traditions, and still others that move beyond any historical traditions at all. There are diverse perspectives within particular traditions, too — perspectives that vary as much as process theology varies from medieval scholasticism. So clear have the differences in feminist theologies become that typologies abound in a growing effort to compare and contrast them ([36], pp. 214-234; [10], pp. 7-36; [31]). This wide divergence must be kept carefully in mind while we, nonetheless, explore a rather remarkable convergence of basic ethical concerns, values, and to some extent, norms for action.

Third, while it is not difficult to identify some parameters of an ethic which derives from and/or is reinforced by feminist theology, the kind of systematic development necessary to bring basic values to bear on very specific bioethical issues remains in important respects still to be undertaken. Indeed, feminist theology as such is at beginning points in its systematic formulation. While monumental strides have been taken by feminist biblical scholars, theologians, and historians ([4], [36], [39], [10], [42]), sustained theological synthesis is new on the horizon, at least for the Christian tradition [36]. Even newer is a systematic comprehensiveness and depth on the ethical side of feminist theology [14]. The import of the still limited development of feminist theology and ethics lies in the general conviction of most theologians that there is no easy route from the sources of religious faith to the specific insights needed for many of the radically new questions generated by scientific and medical capabilities. This conviction is mirrored in the reservations, though not final condemnation or approval, which many feminist theologians and ethicists express regarding, for example, some technologies of reproduction ([14], p. 37; [36], p. 226). It is also mirrored in the recognition of the necessity of collaboration with disciplines other than theology and ethics for the gradual forging of moral perspectives on the multitude of issues which a comprehensive bioethics may address.

There are limits, then, to the connections presently discernible between feminist theology and bioethics. Within those limits, however, lie meeting points, challenges, resources, of potential critical importance to both disciplines. We turn first to the methods, sources, and relevant themes of feminist theology.

Feminist Theology

Of all the themes in feminist theology which have direct bearing on issues in bioethics, three can be raised up for central consideration. These are the themes of (1) relational patterns among human persons, (2) human embodiment, and (3) human assessment of the meaning and value of the world of 'nature'. Feminist theology's development of these themes includes an articulation of basic ethical perceptions and leads to the formulation of some ethical action-guides. Moreover, attention to the emergence and treatment of these themes illuminates important methodological decisions which, as we shall see, constitute not only central commitments for feminist theology but possible warrants for ethical arguments in bioethics.

Patterns of Relation

Feminism, in its most fundamental sense, is opposed to discrimination on the basis of sex. It opposes, therefore, any ideology, belief, attitude, or behavior which establishes or represents such discrimination. In terms of social structure, feminism is opposed, then, to patriarchy. This opposition has the ultimate aim of equality among persons regardless of gender. To achieve this aim, however, feminism is necessarily pro-woman. Since discrimination on the basis of sex — or sexism — has been and remains pervasively discrimination against women, feminism aims to correct this bias by a bias for women, however temporary or prolonged that bias must be. A bias for women includes a focal concern for the well-being of women and a taking account of women's experience in coming to understand what well-being demands for women and men.

Feminist theology perceives profound discrimination against women in traditions of religious patriarchy. The major work of feminist theologians to date has been the unmasking of beliefs, symbols, and religious practices which establish and foster this discrimination. What they have found are massive tendencies in religious traditions to justify patterns of relationship in which men dominate women. Within the history of Christianity, for example, the major pattern of relationship between women and men has been one of dominance and subjugation. This has been sustained through a variety of beliefs about the essential inferiority of women to men and the need for a hierarchical order in social arrangements. Theological assessments of woman's nature, like many philosophical assessments, were based on views of a fundamental dualism within humanity. In these views, women and men are distinguished as polar opposites, representing body or mind, emotion or reason, passivity or activity, dependence or autonomy. The female-identified pole is always inferior to the male. Even when men and women are considered complementary in their duality, complementarity never means equality when it comes to role-differentiation. Thus, for example, men are to be primary agents, leaders, initiators; women are helpers, followers, supporters. More than this, women are often symbolically associated with evil. They are perceived as temptresses, to be feared as the threat of chaos to order, carnality to spirituality, weakness to strength. Even when women are exalted as symbols of virtue rather than vice, they bear the liabilities of impossible expectations and the burden of mediating 'femininity' to men [35].

Feminist theology's critique of religious traditions goes further, however, to the central symbols of faith. Feminists argue, for example, that Christianity's traditional formulation of a doctrine of God is itself a sexist warrant for discrimination against women. Though the Christian God transcends gender identification, personal metaphors for God are strongly masculine. This is true in the biblical tradition as well as in theological formulation of the doctrine of the Trinity. Moreover, Christian faith is centered in a savior who is male. Hence, there is a strong tendency in this tradition to consider men more appropriate as representatives of God in the human family, society, and the church. Indeed, traditional Christian theology has often granted the fullness of the *imago Dei* to men, yielding it only derivatively and partially to women. Thus is sealed the primary role of men in the human community. But more than this, feminist theologians point to the character of the Christian God as it is frequently drawn ([2]; [4]). That is, God is portrayed as sovereign, transcendent, requiring submission from human persons. It is on this model of relationship (dominance and submission) that human relationships are then patterned. Hence, as God is to God's people, so man is to woman, husband to wife, pastor to congregation, and on and on through the many forms of human life.

Some feminists have argued that the Christian view of the human self and its ideal development is also determined by the submissive role of persons in relation to God. That is, the height of Christian virtue is thought to be often portrayed as patient suffering and self-sacrificial love, and the mode of Christian action as humble servanthood. Women are socialized into these ideals in a way that men are not, for men can imitate the autonomy and agency of God in their role as God's representatives. Doctrines of sin which stress the evil of prideful self-assertion serve as a caution to men, but they only reinforce the submissiveness which already characterizes women [24]. Nietzsche's critique of Christianity as a religion for weaklings and victims can then be applied to the effect of Christian faith on women if not on men [5].

What emerges in feminist theology (in relation to Christianity, but here a harbinger of systematic developments in relation to other historical religions as well) is an analysis of what are judged to be oppressive patterns of relationship and ideologies which foster them. These patterns of oppression are identified not only in relations between men and women but in every human relation where the pattern is one of domination and subjugation on the basis of sex or race or class or any other aspect of persons which is used to deny full humanity to all. Given the radical nature of the feminist critique of Christianity (a critique which ultimately reaches to every major doctrine — of God, creation, redemption, the human person, sin and grace, the church, eschatology), feminist theologians either move away from Christianity altogether, or they take up the task of critical reconstruction of Christian theology. In either case, they have by and large moved to develop a view of human relations characterized by equality and mutuality, in which both autonomy and relationality are respected.

Feminist theologians who take up the task of

restoring and reconstructing Christian theology 'beyond the feminist critique' argue that there are fundamental resources within the tradition which are not ultimately sexist and which can be brought to bear precisely as a challenge to sexism. With feminist hermeneutical methods, for example, biblical resources are available which reveal a God who does not need to compete with human beings for sovereignty, who comes forth from freedom in order to call forth freedom from human persons; a God who is able to be imagined in feminine as well as masculine terms [42], for whom 'friend' or 'partner' are more apt metaphors then 'king' or 'logos' ([20]; [39]). Reformulations of gender-assignment within the doctrine of the Trinity free a male-identified God from some of the limits of the human imagination and, indeed, from some of the problems which parent/child metaphors retain both for the life of God in itself and the relation of God to human persons. The prophetic traditions in the Old and New Testaments provide biblical grounds for challenging religious as well as secular institutions, or in other words, "every elevation of one social group against others as image or agent of God, every use of God to justify social domination and subjugation" ([36], p.23). Biblical and historical studies using a feminist hermeneutic yield evidence of Christian community organized not on the model of sexist hierarchy but on the bases of equality and reciprocity [10].

It might be argued that what feminist theology is doing offers no new insights regarding patterns of human relationships. When it argues for equality between women and men, it simply extends to women the insights of liberalism. When it concerns itself with economic structures as well as political, it only blends a form of Marxism with liberalism. When it raises up the importance of mutuality, it follows the theoretists of sociality — George Herbert Mead, Martin Buber, John MacMurray. When it criticizes notions of Christian love as self-sacrifice, it just gets clear on what has been taught all along. When it analyzes claims for self-determination and active participation in all the spheres of human life, it only repeats the agenda of liberation theology.

Feminist theologians are drawing on all these sources of insight. Like feminists in general, however, they conclude that none of these other traditions or movements adequately address the oppression of women. This is not just a failure of extension. Rather, it represents a fundamental need for deeper analysis of the contexts of human life, concepts of the human self, and categories of human relation. From the hermeneutical vantage point of the experience of women — of their oppression and their achievements, their needs and contributions, their freedom and their responsibilities — feminist theology assumes groundbreaking work on questions of human relationships.

It has not been open to feminist theology, for example, simply to appropriate a view of the human person which makes autonomy paramount as the ground of respect or the primary principle to be protected in social relations. The issue of relationality as equiprimordial with autonomy as a feature of human personhood has pressed itself on feminist theologians from the experience of women. It is this that has demanded continued analysis of the nature of human relations and has led to historical and biblical studies of, for example, Christian communities, and to theological studies of the very nature of God (as relational). But if feminist theology cannot ignore relationality, neither has it been able to let go of autonomy as an essential feature of personhood [40]. Romantic returns to organic notions of society where relation is all, each in her place, without regard for free agency or for personal identity and worth which transcends roles — these are options that feminists judge can only repeat forms of oppression for women. It is this conviction that prompts continued biblical and theological studies of the compatibility of autonomy with dependence on God, the coincidence of activity and receptivity in peak experiences of relation, and social models which both protect individuality and promote the common good.

In another example, feminist theology has not been able to critique and then ignore interpretations of the differences between women and men. The whole enterprise of feminist theology still has something to do with demythologizing and deontologizing these differences, yet taking persons seriously as woman-persons and man-persons. Faced with these issues, feminist theology has had to take account of insights from the biological and behavioral sciences, and from philosophy. It has also had to maintain a focus on the concrete experience of women in systems where roles and spheres of human life are gender-specific. Refusal to defer these issues prompts unique probing of the fundamental possibilities and requirements of human relations, whether intimate or public. There is potential universal relevance for all human relationships in a move, for example, from traditional ideas of gender 'opposites', or even gender opposite 'complements', to ideas of gender 'analogies', where the primary focus is on similarity rather than difference [45].

Pluralism in feminist theology, of course, leads to some profoundly different choices regarding historical forms of human relationships. As in feminism generally, disagreements can be on the level of strategy (is there any possibility of radically transforming existing religious traditions?); or on the analysis of the cause of oppression (whether it is most fundamentally religion, or culture in a more general sense, or the conspiracy of men, or economics, etc.); or even on important characteristics of the model of relation to be advocated (do exclusivity and separatism contradict the values of equality and mutuality?). Such disagreements are extremely serious, and it would be a mistake to underestimate them. Still, there is basic unanimity among feminist theologians on the values that are essential for nonoppressive human relationships — the values of equality, mutuality, and freedom.[2] The depth of significance given to these values is testified to, not denied, in the disagreements they entail. For feminist theologians who finally reject traditional religious traditions as irretrievably sexist, the alternative is a 'women's culture' which can incorporate these values despite the impossibility of transforming existing religions or society at large. For feminist theologians who continue to stand within their traditions, the alternative is a radical restructuring of institutions and a radical revision of religious doctrine and practice.

Embodiment

The second theme in feminist theology which has particular bearing on issues of bioethics is the theme of human embodiment. Less needs to be said about this theme, since an understanding of it follows directly upon many of the concerns we have already explored regarding patterns of human relationships. There is, however, a clear history of association of ideas that we must trace if we are to see the import of this theme both for feminist theology and bioethics.

Body/spirit is in many ways the basic dualism with which historical religions have struggled since late antiquity. Women, as we have already noted, have been associated with body, men with mind. Those who have speculated on the reasons for this have generally noted the tendency to locate the essence of woman in her childbearing capabilities. Women's physiology has been interpreted as 'closer to nature' than men's in that many areas and functions of a woman's body seem to serve the human species as much as or more than they serve the individual woman [24]. Moreover, women's bodies, in this interpretation, are subject to a kind of fate — more so than men's. Women are immersed in 'matter', in an inertness which has not its own agency. This is manifest not only in the determined rhythms of their bodily functions, but in a tendency to act from emotion rather than from reason, and in women's 'natural' work which is the caring for the bodies of children and men.

Whatever the reasons women have been associated with the body, they have thereby also been associated with the going evaluations of human bodiliness and matter in general. Historical religions which have made this connection have frequently devalued the body in relation to the spirit. Despite resistance from basically world-affirming attitudes in Judaism, and despite an ongoing conflict with positive Christian doctrines of creation and incarnation, both of these traditions incorporated negative views of the human body (and especially women's bodies). In late antiquity, Judaism was influenced by world-denying attitudes of Near Eastern gnosticism and mysticism. Christianity absorbed these same influences in its very foundations, along with Greek philosophical distrust of the transitoriness of bodily being.

Integral to views of the human body have been views of human sexuality. Once again, despite traditional influences toward positive valuation (of sexuality as a part of creation, as implicated in the very covenant with God, etc.), strongly negative judgments have been brought in. From ancient blood taboos, to Stoic prescriptions for the control of sexual desire by reason, to Christian doctrines of the consequences of original sin, fear and suspicion regarding the evil potentialities of sex have reigned strong in the Western conscience. So great, in fact, has been the symbolic power of sex in relation to evil that there seems to have been "from time immemorial", as Paul Ricoeur puts it, "an indissoluble complicity between sexuality and defilement" ([30], p. 28).

Central to the association of women with bodiliness has been the interpretation of their sexuality as more 'carnal' than men's, again 'closer to nature', more animal-like, less subject to rational control. Disclosure of this historical view of women's sexuality came as a surprise to many feminists whose direct learning from religious traditions had tended to be the opposite — that is, that women are less passionate than men, and hence more responsible for setting limits to sexual activity. The reversal in this regard has its roots, too, in religious traditions, and reflects the tendency we have seen before to identify women with evil, on one hand, and place them on a pedestal, on the other [3]. In either case, women's identity remains closely tied to the way they relate to their bodies, and in either case, women have learned to devalue their bodies. For women themselves, Freud's comment on beliefs about menstruation, pregnancy, and childbirth held true: ". . . it might almost be said that women are altogether taboo"([12], p. 75).

With the rise of feminist consciousness, all past interpretations of the meaning of women's bodies were called into question. Women's turn to their own experience for new interpretations of embodiment was not a simple process, however. Feminist theology, like feminism in general, has continually modified original insights, not settling once and for all a meaning for every woman's experience. Thus, a beginning feminist response to past religious and cultural associations of women with their bodies was a rejection of their association. Anatomy was *not* destiny; women were not to be identified with their bodies any more than were men; women could transcend their bodies through rational choices. Such a response paradoxically freed women, however, to take their bodies more seriously. Rather than abstract from bodiliness, reinforcing a dichotomy between body and mind, women soon moved to 'reclaim' their bodies — to claim them as their own, as integral to their selfhood and their womanhood. This entailed new practical and theoretical approaches. Reflecting on their experiences, woman shared insights and interpretation, formulated new symbols, expanded and revised understandings of human embodiment as such [43].

Struggling to move beyond the dualism of body and self that had limited them for so long, feminist philosophers and theologians used a phenomenological method to describe what it means to *be* a body as well as *have* a body, to understand their own bodies as ways of being inserted into the world, as structured centers of personal activity, as body-subjects not just body-objects [28]. From an understanding of themselves as embodied subjects, women 'reclaim' their bodies not just by taking them seriously and 'living' them integrally, but by refusing to yield control of them to men. New intimate self-understandings and new philosophical and theological anthropologies yield new personal and political decisions.

The World of Nature

The third theme in feminist theology which is potentially relevant to issues in bioethics is the meaning and value of the world of nature. Feminist theologians' concern for this theme is directly influenced by their concern for patterns of human relations and for the world as the place of human embodiment.

Just as women have been thought of in religious and cultural traditions as 'close to nature', so the world of nature has been symbolized as female. This is a clue to the difficulties which feminist theologians have with past beliefs and attitudes regarding nature. They find, in fact, a correlation between patterns of domination over women and efforts at domination over nature ([36], pp. 72-85; [37], pp. 57-70).

Perceptions of nature change through history, of course, and its symbolism is always to some extent ambivalent. Nature has been exalted in importance beyond the being and culture of humans, or reduced to a tool for humans; it has been viewed as the cosmic source of life and goodness, or a mysterious force to be feared and fled or controlled. All of these interpretations of nature mirror similar identifications of the essence of woman. However, especially in the history of Christian thought, a pattern emerges which raises serious questions for feminist theology.

Despite the fact that a Christian worldview and specific Christian teaching have supported 'sacramental' views of the whole of creation, sometimes especially of nature (as revelatory of the fidelity, the presence, the grandeur and the graciousness of the living God), Christianity has nonetheless also tended to trivialize the value of nature. Ascetic theologies sometimes reduced nature to a transitory illusion, a distraction from 'higher things', in the manner of some Hellenistic philosophies. Christian leaders sometimes forbade the study of nature as dangerous or a waste of time. When nature and culture were paired among traditional dualisms, nature was assigned the value of the negative pole.

Similarly, while there is a strong tradition in Christian thought requiring reverence for and stewardship of nature, there is also strong support for a way of relating to nature which sees it only as something to be used, dominated, controlled by human persons ([19], p. 7). In this latter view, because nature has no value of its own, it can be treated as the private property of humanity (or of individuals), with no limits on its exploitation or manipulation short of the limits of human persons' own self-interest. Where total possession is permitted, the concept of 'rape' does not apply.

Rosemary Ruether traces a history of Western attitudes toward nature which moves from an early ascetical 'flight' from nature to a modern 'return' to nature ([36], p. 82). The rise of scientific research in the seventeenth century helped secularize a view of nature, fostered a perception of it as intrinsically rational, penetrable, manageable. Unintended negative consequences of scientific and technological development, visible from the nineteenth century on, produced romantic reactions calling for a different sort of return to nature — a restoration of 'pure' nature, uncontaminated and unalienated by human intervention. All of these attitudes toward nature, however, represented pieces of the pattern of hierarchical domination and subjugation — domination through possession and control, whether through denigration, or exploitation, or the expectation of mediated happiness and identity through 'keeping' nature as a haven for some (despite the suffering this in turn might cause for others) ([36], p. 85; [37]).

Feminist theology argues, alternatively, for a view of nature consonant with a view of a God who takes the whole of creation seriously, and a view of creation which does not see predatory hierarchy as the basis of order. Nature, in this view, is valuable according to its own concrete reality, which includes an interdependence with embodied humanity. It is limited in its possibilities, which precludes its moral use as the battleground for the ultimate challenge to human freedom. Human intelligence and freedom are not barred from addressing nature, but measures for understanding and just use are lodged both in nature itself and in ethical requirements for relations among persons.

Feminist Theological Ethics

Given this overview of themes in feminist theology, it may be possible to identify some characteristics of a feminist theological ethic, moving still closer to connections with issues in bioethics. We have, for example, seen enough of feminist theology to draw some conclusions regarding the *methods* likely to characterize any ethics that derives from it. First in this regard is a sense in which feminist theology and ethics can be said to be concerned with objective reality, and hence to presuppose methodologically some access to an intelligible reality. The work of these disciplines began, after all, as a result of what was at base a new understanding of the reality of women. Like feminism in general, feminist theology had its origins in women's growing awareness of the disparity between received traditional interpretations of their identity and function within the human community and their own experience of themselves and their lives. The corresponding claim that gender role-differentiation and gender-specific limitations on opportunities for education, political participation, economic parity, etc., are discriminatory was based on the argument that past interpretations of women's reality were simply wrong. That is, past theories failed to discover the concrete reality of women and represented, in fact, distorted perceptions of that reality. Moreover, the attitudes and policies they fostered often did violence to that reality.

It would be a mistake to label feminist theology and ethics in any simple sense 'naturalistic', though the term is not wholly inappropriate. Feminist theology does not, obviously, reduce to a natural or behavioral science. Nor does it rely for its access to reality on human reason alone. And while feminist theological ethics searches for and proposes universally valid norms, it does so in a way that acknowledges the historical nature of human knowledge and the social nature of the interpretation of human experience. The fact that present insights may be superseded by future ones, and that present formulations of specific principles may change, does not contradict either the methodological requirement of attending to concrete reality or the methodological presupposition that the accuracy and adequacy of theories can be tested against that reality.

Closely aligned with all of this is the methodological commitment to begin with and continue a primary focus on the experience of women ([25]; [36], pp. 12-13). This is often coupled with the qualification that no claims are made for the universality of women's experience in relation to human experience. There is a claim made, however, that until a theology based on women's experience is developed, traditionally assumed universal claims for a theology based on men's experience will continue to render inadequate if not inaccurate the major formulations of religious belief.

A methodological commitment to the primacy of women's experience as a source for theology and ethics goes significantly beyond a simple focusing of attention, however. It yields, in addition, a feminist hermeneutical principle which functions in the selection and interpretation of all other sources. While not every feminist theologian articulates this principle in exactly the same way, it can be expressed as strongly as "Whatever diminishes or denies the full humanity of women must be presumed not to reflect the divine or an authentic relation to the divine, or to reflect the authentic nature of things, or to be the message or work of an authentic redeemer or a community of redemption" ([36], p. 19). As is to be expected, this principle functions in importantly different ways in different feminist theologies. In some, for example, it leads to the rejection of the authority of the Bible altogether [41]; in others it allows the relativization of the authority of some texts [10]; in still others it leaves all texts standing as a part of an authoritative revelation, but renders their meaning transformed under a new feminist paradigm [42]. The same is true for theological doctrines, historical events, and for sources of theology and ethics which can range from the comparative study of religions to philosophical and scientific writings and schools of thought.

A focus on women's experience, the use of a feminist hermeneutical principle, and a concern for the lived experience of women precisely as disadvantaged, can constitute for feminist theological ethics the bias for women which is the earmark of feminism in general. If this is chosen as a strategic priority, feminist theological ethics can be methodologically oriented ultimately as an ethic whose concerns include the well-being of both women and men, both humanity and the world of nature. Its theological center will depend on its ultimate warrants for these concerns.

Finally, in regard to method, feminist theological ethics has been open to both deontological and teleological patterns of reasoning ([14], pp. 12-13). On the one hand, for example, the very notion of 'strategic priority', as well as a strongly 'ecological' view of reality, implies a concern for consequences, an ethical evaluation of means in relation to ends and parts in relation to wholes, a relativization of values in situations of conflict. On the other hand, demands of the concrete reality of persons are such that some attitudes and actions can be judged unethical precisely because they contradict values intrinsic to that reality. The sorting out of what ultimately determines a specific obligation is the task of ethics, but neither of these modes of reasoning is ruled out for feminist theological ethics.

When we turn from method to *substance* in feminist theological ethics, we perhaps need only summarize the ethical import of what we have seen in regard to feminist theological themes. Thus, an ethic derived from feminist theology understands the well-being of persons in a way that takes account of their reality as embodied subjects (and hence includes considerations of persons as historical beings, living in social and cultural contexts, identified with yet transcending systems and institutions; as beings whose actuality includes potentiality for development as well as vulnerability to diminishment; beings constituted by complex structures of freedom, physiology, intelligence, affectivity, etc.; beings which are essentially interpersonal and social; beings which are unique as well as common sharers in humanity). It is an ethic which gives important status to principles of equality and mutuality. It holds together principles of autonomy and relationality. It gives ethical priority to models of relationship characterized by collaboration rather than competition or hierarchical gradation. Finally, it does not isolate an ethic of human relations from ethical obligations to the whole of nature. These sound like a list of ideals, high rhetoric which any ethic may incorporate somehow. Some test of it can be made by turning now to issues in bioethics.

Feminist Theology and Bioethics

Feminist theology offers something of a distinctive perspective on many issues that we today include under the general rubric of bioethics. This is because women's lives are deeply implicated in areas of personal medical care, public health, and the development and use of biomedical technologies. Feminist theology also gains from analyses of issues arising in these areas, for here the lived experience of women reveals some of the central opportunities and limitations of the human condition. Here it is that "reflection upon the goals, practices, and theories of medicine validates philosophical reflection upon many issues that have traditionally been of concern to women," but ignored by the traditional disciplines of philosophy and theology ([46], p. 120).

We can explore the interrelation between feminist theology and bioethics in a number of ways. Thus, we can examine the perspective offered by feminist theology on the principles usually considered central to bioethics — principles of, for example, nonmaleficence and beneficence, veracity and fidelity, as well as autonomy, mutuality, and justice. We can also look to numerous specific issues for which feminist theology and ethics can be expected to have special relevance — issues such as abortion and sterilization, medical care of the elderly, psychiatric treatment of women, medical settings for childbirthing, conflict between nursing roles and moral rules, the use of amniocentesis for gender selection, models of doctor/patient relationships in a culture and in relation to a profession marked by sexism. Among these and other possibilities, however, let me select for consideration the issue of the development and use of reproductive technologies.[3] A feminist theological approach to this issue may, in even a brief attempt, show some of the implications of feminist theology for understanding both context and principles in the area of bioethics.

The potentialities of reproductive technology have for some time caught the attention of feminists. It raises issues, however, on which unanimity of view does not exist. Some feminists have argued that the ultimate source of women's oppression is their physiological capability of bearing children. While physical motherhood can constitute individual and social power, it also renders women powerless — before nature, before men, before their children, before society (which judges them, and which determines the conditions under which their children must grow). In the face of this powerlessness, and the suffering it entails, technology offers a solution. Indeed, in an extreme view, women's liberation can only be achieved with a revolution not only against forms of society, but against nature itself. Thus, Shulamith Firestone argued for the "freeing of women from the tyranny of their reproductive biology by every means available", including technology which could separate women once and for all from a gender-identified responsibility for reproduction ([11], p. 238).

This was a relatively early position, however, and strong disagreement has come from other feminists on a variety of grounds. Many consider the analysis of the causes of oppression to be wrong ([21], pp. 87-91). Others see in the development of reproductive technologies a new means of devaluing women, rendering them "expendable in the procreative process" ([14], p. 37). Still others argue that some uses of technology, such as amniocentesis for the purpose of gender selection, will pit women against themselves [26].

Feminists agree on at least two things with regard to these questions. First, the history of women's experience in relation to the power and process of reproduction is, indeed, a history of great pain. While fertility, pregnancy, and childbirth have been a source of women's happiness and fulfillment, and on occasion for powerful expressions of great human love and enduring fidelity to duty, they have also been the locus of a cumulative burden of immense oppression and suffering. The twentieth-century incursion of technology into reproduction (the 'medicalization' of pregnancy and childbirth) has often added to this suffering, extended this oppression.

Second, and closely following, feminists are in agreement that the development and use of reproductive technology cannot be evaluated apart from its concrete, sociocultural context. This context has been, and remains, an "historically specific social order in which positions of power and privilege are disproportionately occupied by men" ([7], p. 41). As long as sexism continues to characterize the lived world which women know, technology will have different consequences for women and for men. Far from freeing women from unnecessary burdens in reproduction, further technological development may result in greater bondage.

Given these agreements, however, neither feminism in general or feminist theology renders wholly negative judgments on reproductive technology. One obvious reason for this is that such technology can take many forms. Evaluations of developments of contraceptives, childbirth procedures, methods of abortion, artificial insemination, *in vitro* fertilization, fetal diagnosis, cloning, and many other technologies can hardly be lumped together in a single comprehensive judgment. Only a total antitechnology approach could yield that. Generally, despite deep ambivalence toward reproductive technologies, feminists can affirm that

> natural-scientific breakthroughs represent genuine gains in human self-understanding. The widespread social irresponsibility of medical practice, exacerbated by male monopoly of the medical profession that is only now changing, must not be confused with the value of scientific discoveries ([14], pp. 169-170).

Science and technology have, in fact, been instruments of reform at times, even in regard to almost intractable problems of sexism ([32], pp. 22, 83, 136).

But if a single ethical judgment cannot be made for all forms of reproductive technology, then it will be helpful here to narrow our focus still more to one form. Once again, this will have implications beyond itself for reproductive technology more generally, but we cannot expect thereby to have resolved all questions. The form of technology that I will consider is *in vitro* fertilization for the purpose of producing a child (that is, not just as a procedure for the purpose of scientific research with no intention of bringing a child 'to term'). As a technology, it raises the issue of profound change in human modes of reproduction, not just the issue of improving present modes.

One place to begin a feminist analysis of *in vitro* fertilization (with embryo transfer or some other form of providing for gestation) is with women's experience to date of technology in the area of pregnancy and birth. As we have already noted, this is in many respects not a happy experience. Recent studies have helped to make visible the difficulties women have had in this regard ([44]; [22]; [29]; [17]; [5]). Recalling these difficulties can help us to formulate the questions that need to be asked of *in vitro* fertilization. If, for example, the use of medical technology in relation to childbirth has been oppressive to women, or to their children, in what way has it been so? One response to this question is that it has contributed to the alienation of women from their bodies, their partners, and their children (by, for example, moving childbirth into settings appropriate primarily for the treatment of disease, isolating mothers both from 'women's culture' and their spouses, regimenting the presence of mothers with their babies, etc.);[4] and that it has placed women in a network of professional relations which unjustifiably limit their autonomy (in the matter of a 'patient'). Does the development and use of *in vitro* fertilization hold this same potential for alienation, albeit in different ways? From a feminist theological perspective, the question can be: Does *in vitro* fertilization violate (or is it in accord with) feminist understanding of embodiment, norms for relationships, and concerns for the common good? The following considerations hold this question as their backdrop.

For many feminists the sundering of the power and process of reproduction from the bodies of women would constitute a loss of major proportions. Hence, the notion of moving the whole process to the laboratory (using not only *in vitro* fertilization but artificial placentas, et al.) is not one that receives much enthusiasm. On the other hand, *in vitro* fertilization is not perceived as a procedure which necessarily violates the essential embodying of reproduction. If its purpose is primarily to enable women who would otherwise be infertile to conceive a child, it becomes a means precisely to mediate embodiment. Feminists generally oppose the kind of sacralization of women's reproductive organs and functions that would prohibit all technological intervention. In fact, desacralization in this regard is seen as a necessary step in the breaking of feminine stereotypes and the falsification of anatomy as destiny. Moreover, feminist interpretations of sexuality are very clear on the validity of separating sexuality from reproduction. Without contradiction, however, they also affirm *in vitro* fertilization as a significant potential factor in separating sexuality from reproduction, oviating the series of 'natural' physical connections between sexual intercourse and the fertilization of an ovum by male sperm. Indeed, it is a failure of imagination which sees this as the only way in which integrated sexuality can be related to reproduction. All in all, then, while human embodiment remains a central concern in a feminist analysis of *in vitro* fertilization, it does not thereby rule out the ethical use of this technology.

Feminists are generally clear on the need to understand and experience childbearing in an active way. Pregnancy and childbirth are not events in relation to which women should be wholly passive ([14], pp. 169, 246-247). Part of taking active control and responsibility regarding their reproductive power can include a willingness to use technology insofar as it makes childbearing more responsible, less painful, and more safe. Sometimes discernment of just these consequences for technology is difficult, but the fact that it is called for indicates, again, that *in vitro* fertilization is not ruled out in principle.

Perhaps the most troubling aspect of *in vitro* fertilization, and of other technologies which actually empower reproduction, is the question of primary agency and responsibility. This question in itself has many sides. For example, women's previous experience with reproductive technology suggests that (at least in the concrete context of present societies) women's own agency is likely to be submerged in the network of multiple experts needed to achieve *in vitro* fertilization. Far from this accomplishing a liberation of women from childbearing responsibilities, it can entail "further alienation of our life processes" ([36], p. 227). Moreover, efforts to restrict and share the agency of professionals often move only in the direction of what some feminists fear as collectivism or state control, the "total alienation of one's life to institutions external to one's own control and governed by a managerial elite" ([36], p. 226). In any case, without a drastic change in the composition of society and the professions, widespread use of *in vitro* fertilization could, it seems, make it difficult for women to achieve or sustain control of human reproduction.

But does it matter whether women or men, parents or scientists, control reproduction? Feminists argue that those who will bear the responsibility for childrearing should have primary agency in decisions about childbearing — not just because it is their right if they are to bear the burden of such responsibility, but because this is required for the well-being of offspring. "Only those who are deeply realistic about what it takes to nourish human life *from birth onward* have the wisdom to evaluate procreative choice" ([14], p. 173).[5] Reproductive technologies that divorce decisions for childbearing from childrearing fail to take seriously the basic needs of children for not only material resources but personal relation and support, in contexts that allow the awakening of basic trust and the development of fundamental autonomy ([34], p. 258; [27], p. 65).[6] It is not only women who, in principle, can make these choices ([34], p. 262),[7] but it is 'parents', not just 'scientific facilitators' or society at large or any persons who are unprepared to take responsibility at an intimate as well as comprehensive level for our children. Such problems of agency are complex and sobering in the face of technological capabilities such as *in vitro* fertilization. They are not, in principle, intractable, perhaps not even in practice. They need not rule out the ethical use of *in vitro* fertilization, but they occasion grave moral caution.

Yet another consideration prompted by *in vitro* fertilization (and other reproductive technologies) regards the developing capability for 'selection' of offspring — from among many candidates (differentiated by gender, bodily health, intellectual capacity, etc.). The problem of 'discards' in *in vitro* fertilization is larger than the discernment of grave embryonic anomalies. For some feminists this capability can erode moral and religious obligation to accept all sorts of persons into the human community. In so doing, it undermines basic feminist principles of equality, inclusiveness, mutuality, and toleration of difference and of 'imperfection' ([7], p. 42). *In vitro* fertilization need not, of course, be used in this way. But once again, a voice of caution is raised.

Underlying all of these considerations is what might be called the need to measure *in vitro* fertilization according to norms of justice. If justice in its deepest sense can be understood as treating persons in truthful accordance with their concrete reality (a concrete reality which must be interpreted as best we can), then all the issues of embodiment, nondiscrimination, agency, responsibility, inclusive care, are issues of justice. They are not focused only on individuals, but on the human community. They converge in the fundamental question, 'How are we to reproduce ourselves as human persons?' They press us to new theories of justice which extend a requirement for 'just parenting' in relation to all human children. They include, then, too, questions of the meaning and value of *in vitro* fertilization in a world threatened by overpopulation, in countries where not every existing child is cared for, in communities where grave needs of children require the resources of science and technology. Questions of macroallocation of scarce goods and services may finally be unresolvable, but they cannot be ignored. At the very least, in this instance, they preclude justifications of *in vitro* fertilization on the basis of any absolute right to procreate.

A feminist analysis of *in vitro* fertilization remains provisional. It yields, however, the following position: Negatively there are not grounds for an absolute prohibition of the development and use of technology such as *in vitro* fertilization; positively, such technology may aid just and responsible human reproduction. The presence of certain circumstances, or certain conditions, sets limits to its ethical development and use — circumstances such as (a) high risk of injury to the well-being of either parent or child; (b) a context unconducive to the growth and development of any child produced (unconducive because, for example, no one is prepared to offer the child basic human personal relationship); (c) an intention to produce a child to be used as means only in relation to the producers' ends (as, for example, if the child is produced merely for the sake of the advance of scientific research, or for the duplication of one's own self without regard for the child's development into an autonomous self); (d) failure to meet criteria of distributive justice (when it is determined that other basic human needs place legitimate prior claims on the resources involved). Such conditions rule out spectres of human laboratory 'farms'. They also tell us something about the conditions for *any* ethical decisions regarding human reproduction, not just decisions made in the context of reproductive technology.

With this, then, we have one example of the relation between feminist theology and an issue in bioethics. My development of the issue must remain more suggestive than exhaustive of the particular ethical values and ultimate theological warrants that feminist theologians may offer. My suspicion is that future work in this area of bioethics will bring careful reflection on questions that I have not, within the limits of this essay, addressed at all; questions, for example, of women's interpretation not only of birth but of death, and women's evaluation of the strength of 'quality of life' claims in relation to sanctity-of-life principles. Whatever lines along which a feminist bioethics may develop, however, it will never be far from central concerns for human embodiment, for the well-being of women-persons on a par with the well-being of men-persons, for newly just patterns of relationship among all persons, and for the balanced care of the whole world of both nonpersonal and personal beings.

The Divinity School
Yale University
New Haven, Connecticut, U.S.A.

Notes

1. For a contrary emphasis, see ([15], p. 48).

2. To the argument that separatist feminist movements do indeed contradict these values (by affirming a new form of elitism, by simply 'reversing' the order in the hierarchy of men and women, etc.), the response is

sometimes given that separation does not entail domination, and that elitism is no more a necessarily substantial charge against separatist feminism than it is against any religious sectarianism. It is more difficult for some separatists to answer the criticism that they are duplicating oppressive patterns of 'identifying an enemy'.

3. Reproductive technologies include all those technologies which relate to human reproduction. They are sometimes differentiated from technologies of genetic engineering, though I do not in this essay maintain a sharp separation. For some helpful distinctions, see ([27], pp. 8-10).

4. 'Tales of horror' are told more and more in recent sociological studies in this regard. However, it should be noted that very recently there have come significant changes — changes, for example, such as an increase in home birthing, the provision of birthing rooms in hospitals, the rise once again of the profession of midwifery, etc. Some feminists express concern that some new movements, such as natural childbirth, incorporate an alienating technology just as previous methods did ([44], pp. 183-198; [22], pp. 628-630).

5. I am not, here, focusing on the grounds for women's right to procreative choice which are often central to feminist arguments — that is, a right to bodily integrity or a right to privacy. One reason I am not focusing on those grounds is that *in vitro* fertilization *can* be understood to prescind from women's bodies in a way that, for example, abortion cannot.

6. This can be maintained without conflicting with contemporary concerns for 'too much mothering', etc.

7. Nor should it be the exclusive prerogative of women. When it is this, it justifies a male dismissal of obligation regarding childbearing — something feminists have long been concerned to oppose.

Bibliography

[1] Carr. A.: 1982, 'Is A Christian Feminist Theology Possible?' *Theological Studies* 43, 279-97.

[2] Christ, C. P.,: 1977, 'The New Feminist Theology: A Review of the Literature', *Religious Studies Review* 3, 203-12.

[3] Cott, N. F.: 1978, 'Passionlessness', *Signs* 4, 227-28.

[4] Daly, M.: 1973, *Beyond God the Father,* Beacon, Boston.

[5] Daly, M.: 1978, *Gyn/Ecology: The Metaethics of Radical Feminism,* Beacon, Boston.

[6] Donegan, J. B.: *Women and Men Midwives: Medicine, Morality, and Misogyny in Early America,* Greenwood Press, Westport, Connecticut.

[7] Elshtain, J. B.: 1982, 'A Feminist Agenda on Reproductive Technology', *Hastings Center Report* 12, 40-43.

[8] Farley, M. A.: 1975, 'New Patterns of Relationship: The Beginnings of a Moral Revolution', *Theological Studies* 36, 627-46.

[9] Farley, M. A.: 1976, 'Sources of Sexual Inequality in the History of Christian Thought', *The Journal of Religion* 56, 162-76.

[10] Fiorenza, E. S.: 1983, *In Memory of Her: A Feminist Reconstruction of Christian Origins,* Crossroad, New York.

[11] Firestone, S.: 1971, *The Dialectic of Sex: The Case for Feminist Revolution,* Bantam, New York.

[12] Freud, S.: 1918, 'The Taboo of Virginity', *Collected Papers,* Vol. 8, pp. 70-86.

[13] Gustafson, J. M.: 1975, *The Contributions of Theology to Medical Ethics,* Marquette University Press, Milwaukee.

[14] Harrison, B. W.: 1983, *Our Right to Choose: Toward A New Ethic of Abortion,* Beacon, Boston.

[15] Hauerwas, S.: 1978, 'Can Ethics Be Theological?' *The Hastings Center Report* 8, 47-49.

[16] Heyward, C.: 1979, 'Ruether and Daly: Theologians Speaking and Sparking, Building and Burning', *Christianity and Crisis* 39, 66-72.

[17] Lebacqz, K.: 1975, 'Reproductive Research and the Image of Woman', in Fischer, C. B. et al., *Women in a Strange Land,* Fortress, Philadelphia.

[18] McCormick, R. A.: 1983, 'Bioethics in the Public Forum', *Milbank Memorial Fund Quarterly* 61, 113-26.

[19] McCormick, R. A.: 1981, *How Brave A New World? Dilemmas in Bioethics,* Doubleday, Garden City, New York.

[20] McFague, S.: 1982, *Metaphorical Theology,* Fortress, Philadelphia.

[21] Mitchell, J.: 1971, *Woman's Estate,* Vintage, New York.

[22] Oakley, A.: 1979, 'A Case of Maternity', *Signs* 4, 606-631.

[23] O'Brien, M.: 1981, *The Politics of Reproduction,* Routledge and Kegan Paul, London.

[24] Ortner, S.B.: 1974, 'Is Female to Male as Nature is to Culture?' in M. Z. Rosaldo and L. Lamphere (eds.), *Woman, Culture and Society,* Stanford University Press, Stanford, pp. 67-87.

[25] Plaskow, J.: 1980, *Sex, Sin, and Grace,* University Press of America, Washington, D.C.

[26] Powledge, T. M.: 1981, 'Unnatural Selection: On Choosing Children's Sex', in H. B. Holmes et al. (eds.), *The Custom-Made Child? Women-Centered Perspectives,* Humana Press, Clifton, New Jersey, pp. 193-99.

[27] President's Commission for the Study of Ethical Problems in Medicine and Biomedical and Behavioral Research: 1982, *Splicing Life,* U.S. Government Printing Office, Washington, D.C.

[28] Rawlinson, M. C.: 1982, 'Psychiatric Discourse and the Feminine Voice', *The Journal of Medicine and Philosophy* 7, 153-77.

[29] Rich, A.: 1976, *Of Woman Born: Motherhood as Experience and Institution,* Prometheus, Buffalo.

[30] Ricoeur, P.: 1967, *The Symbolism of Evil,* Harper, New York.

[31] Robb, C. S.: 1981, 'A Framework for Feminist Ethics', *The Journal of Religious Ethics* 9, 48-68.

[32] Rosenberg, R.: 1982, *Beyond Separate Spheres: Intellectual Roots of Modern Feminism,* Yale University Press, New Haven.

[33] Rothman, B. K.: 1979, 'Women, Health, and Medicine', in J. Freeman (ed.), *Women: A Feminist Perspective,* Mayfield, Palo Alto, pp. 27-40.

[34] Ruddick, S.: 1980, 'Maternal Thinking', *Signs* 6, 342-67.

[35] Ruether, R. R. (ed.): 1974, *Religion and Sexism: Images of Women in the Jewish and Christian Traditions,* Simon and Schuster, New York.

[36] Ruether, R. R.: 1983, *Sexism and God-Talk: Toward A Feminist Theology,* Beacon, Boston.

[37] Ruether, R. R.: 1981, *To Change the World,* Crossroad, New York.

[38] Russell, L.: 1982, *Becoming Human,* Westminster, Philadelphia.

[39] Russell, L.: 1979, *The Future of Partnership,* Westminster, Philadelphia.

[40] Saiving, V.: 1981, 'Androgynous Life: A Feminist Appropriation of Process Thought', in S. G. Davaney (ed.), *Feminism and Process Thought,* Edwin Mellen Press, New York, pp. 11-31.

[41] Stanton, E. C. (ed.): *The Original Feminist Attack on the Bible: The Woman's Bible,* Arno, New York.

[42] Trible, P.: 1978, *God and the Rhetoric of Sexuality,* Fortress, Philadelphia.

[43] Washbourn, P.: 1979, *Becoming Woman: The Quest for Spiritual Wholeness in Female Experience,* Harper, New York.

[44] Wertz, R. W., and Wertz, D. C.: 1977, *Lying-In: A History of Childbirth in America,* Free Press, New York.

[45] Whitbeck, C.: 1984, 'A Different Reality: Feminist Ontology', in C. Gould (ed.), *Beyond Domination: New Perspectives on Women and Philosophy,* Rowman and Allenheld, Totawa, N.J., pp. 64-85.

[46] Whitbeck, C.: 1983, 'Women and Medicine: An Introduction', *The Journal of Medicine and Philosophy* 7, 119-33.

Chapter Three

THE PROFESSION AND ITS INTEGRITY

When Christians "profess" their faith they commit themselves to God and to God's cause. From *profateri* (to confess, own, acknowledge), *profession* first meant "the declaration, promise, or vow made by one entering a religious order" (*Oxford English Dictionary,* s.v. profession). In a religious context the requirement of integrity upon the "professor" is clear and compelling, even if sometimes complex. The term has been secularized, however, and applied to other occupations which require special knowledge or skill. This chapter confronts the reader with two basic questions: first, whether the professions of medicine and nursing still declare, promise, or vow anything which would make a requirement of integrity clear and compelling, if sometimes complex; and second, whether and, if so, how the professions of medicine and nursing are related to a profession of the Christian faith.

The first question may be framed in a number of different ways: Should the professions of medicine and nursing be understood as value-free collections of skills learned by training and accessible to consumers or as a value-laden form of human activity constituted as much by the ends they seek as the skills they use? Can medical and nursing ethics be done by articulating and applying the goods and standards implicit in the profession or only by specifically applying norms learned outside the profession, whether by reason or revelation? Is the expertise and authority of the professional only technical or also, in some sense, moral? Is professional excellence a technical matter or a moral matter as well? Does it make sense for a physician or nurse to introduce a moral claim by saying, "As a physician (or nurse) I think . . ."?

The excerpt from Veatch below rejects the claim to a special professional ethic (selection 17) as fallacious and dangerous. The other essays agree in defending a professional ethic which is not simply the application of universal and rational norms to special techniques. But the agreement that there is a professional ethic does not entail agreement about what it is or about how to describe and defend it. The disagreements extend to different assessments of the famous Hippocratic Oath and are related in turn to different understandings of the healing traditions and their communities.

These different understandings of the medical community do not stand by themselves. They are related to our understanding of the relationship between the medical community and the larger society. Stephen E. Lammers points out (in selection 19) how different expectations of the medical professional about the treating of AIDS patients are related to our understanding of the relationship of the medical professional to the larger society as well as to the medical profession's understanding of itself as having something to profess.

If there is a professional ethic, then the question of the relation of a medical profession to a Christian profession will be as important to those who would reflect theologically about medical ethics as the question of the relation of an impartial and rational perspective to a Christian perspective (an issue raised in the previous chapter). Thomas Sydenham's eloquent and powerful description of "the doctor" (selection 20) is suggestive of some of the ways a Christian profession nurtured and sustained a medical professional. In Sydenham's remarks there seems to be a powerful identification of the Christian profession and the medical profession, or at least a neat harmony between the declaration a physician makes as a Christian and the declaration a Christian makes as a physician. Other Christian voices have been raised in prophetic protest against medicine and what was taken to be the ethos of physicians; the Christian profession has been set over against the medical profession. The readings from Florence Nightingale (selection 21) raise the question of the relation of the Christian profession to the nursing profession in terms of what is "added," but perhaps the possibility (or necessity) of a creative tension or even transformation should not be overlooked, both for medicine and nursing.

Another question here, of course, is the theological resources to be brought to bear on the medical and nursing professions. Florence Nightingale attends especially to the model of Christ's healing ministry. William F. May (selection 18) highlights the features of covenant in the biblical tradition. Allen Verhey (selection 16) attends to native senses of gratitude and dependence, of a tragic fault, of responsibility to the transcendent and suggests that these be informed by the biblical narrative. None of the authors claim to be exhaustive, but their suggestions nevertheless can — and should — be subjected to critical review in terms of their appropriateness to medicine and nursing and their adequacy to the Christian profession.

Perhaps Sydenham's "profession" and Nightingale's advice sound quaint, even naive, today. The medical and nursing professions have become considerably more complex, and the Christian profession has perhaps become less confident. But those who would search for and live with integrity, while they not only stand in plural communities and traditions but also own, acknowledge, profess their causes, will celebrate Sydenham's declaration and Nightingale's maxims. Perhaps a pleasant harmony of medical and nursing professions and Christian profession no longer exists, but it may honor Sydenham and Nightingale to strike the discordant note if integrity with what has been promised or vowed requires it.

Suggestions for Further Reading

Barnard, David. "The Physician as Priest," *Journal of Religion and Health* 24 (Winter 1985): 272-86.

Beauchamp, Tom L., and Laurence B. McCullough. *Medical Ethics: The Moral Responsibilities of Physicians* (Englewood Cliffs, N.J.: Prentice-Hall, 1984).

Brody, Howard. *The Healer's Power* (New Haven: Yale University Press, 1992).

Cameron, Nigel de S. *Life and Death After Hippocrates: The New Medicine* (Wheaton, Ill.: Crossway Books, 1991).

Cassell, Eric. *The Healer's Art* (New York: Lippincott, 1976).

Campbell, Alastair V. *Professional Care: Its Meaning and Practice* (Philadelphia: Fortress, 1984).

DuBose, Edwin R. *The Illusion of Trust: Toward a Medical Theological Ethics in the Postmodern Age* (Dordrecht, The Netherlands: Kluwer Academic Publishers, 1995).

Etziony, M. B. *The Physician's Creed: An Anthology of Medical Prayers, Oaths and Codes of Ethics Written and Recited by Medical Practitioners Through the Ages* (Springfield, Ill.: Charles C. Thomas, 1973).

Gustafson, James M. "Professions as Callings," *Social Science Review* 5 (December 1982): 501-15.

Hauerwas, Stanley. "Authority and the Profession of Medicine," in *Responsibility and Health Care*, edited by G. Agich (Dordrecht, the Netherlands: D. Reidel, 1982), pp. 83-104.

Hilfiker, David. *Not All of Us Are Saints: A Doctor's Journey with the Poor* (New York: Hill and Wang, 1994).

Kass, Leon. "Professing Ethically: On the Place of Ethics in Defining Medicine," *JAMA* 249 (March 11, 1983): 1305-10.

Lebacqz, Karen. *Professional Ethics: Power and Paradox* (Nashville, Tenn.: Abingdon, 1985).

Lifton, Robert Jay. *The Nazi Doctors: Medical Killing and the Psychology of Genocide* (New York: Basic Books, 1989).

May, William F. *The Physician's Covenant* (Philadelphia: Westminster, 1983).

McKenny, Gerald M., and J. R. Sande (eds.). *Theological Analysis of the Clinical Encounter* (Dordrecht, The Netherlands: Kluwer Academic Publishers, 1994).

Pellegrino, Edmund D. *The Christian Virtues in Medical Practice* (Washington, D.C.: Georgetown University Press, 1996).

Smith, Harmon M., and Larry R. Churchill. *Professional Ethics and Primary Care Medicine* (Durham: Duke University Press, 1986).

14 The Hippocratic Oath

The Hippocratic Oath

I swear by Apollo Physician and Asclepius and Hygieia and Panaceia and all the gods and goddesses, making them my witnesses, that I will fulfil according to my ability and judgment this oath and this covenant:

To hold him who has taught me this art as equal to my parents and to live my life in partnership with him, and if he is in need of money to give him a share of mine, and to regard his offspring as equal to my brothers in male lineage and to teach them this art — if they desire to learn it — without fee and covenant; to give a share of precepts and oral instruction and all the other learning to my sons and to the sons of him who has instructed me and to pupils who have signed the covenant and have taken an oath according to the medical law, but to no one else.

I will apply dietetic measures for the benefit of the sick according to my ability and judgment; I will keep them from harm and injustice.

I will neither give a deadly drug to anybody if asked for it, nor will I make a suggestion to this effect. Similarly I will not give to a woman an abortive remedy. In purity and holiness I will guard my life and my art.

I will not use the knife, not even on sufferers from stone, but will withdraw in favor of such men as are engaged in this work.

Whatever houses I may visit, I will come for the benefit of the sick, remaining free of all intentional injustice, of all mischief and in particular of sexual relations with both female and male persons, be they free or slaves.

What I may see or hear in the course of the treatment or even outside of the treatment in regard to the life of men, which on no account one must spread abroad, I will keep to myself holding such things shameful to be spoken about.

If I fulfil this oath and do not violate it, may it be granted to me to enjoy life and art, being honored with fame among all men for all time to come; if I transgress it and swear falsely, may the opposite of all this be my lot.

From Ludwig Edelstein, "The Hippocratic Oath: Text, Translation and Interpretation," in Oswei Temkin and C. Lillian Temkin, eds., *Ancient Medicine* (Baltimore: Johns Hopkins University Press, 1967), pp. 3-63. Used by permission.

15 The Hippocratic Oath Insofar as a Christian May Swear It

Blessed be God the Father of our Lord Jesus Christ. Who is blessed for ever and ever; I lie not.

I will bring no stain upon the learning of the medical art. Neither will I give poison to anybody though asked to do so, nor will I suggest such a plan. Similarly I will not give treatment to women to cause abortion, treatment neither from above nor from below. But I will teach this art, to those who require to learn it, without grudging and without an indenture. I will use treatment to help the sick according to my ability and judgment. And in purity and holiness I will guard my art. Into whatsoever houses I enter, I will do so to help the sick, keeping free from all wrongdoing, intentional or unintentional, tending to death or to injury, and from fornication with bond or free, man or woman. Whatsoever in the course of practice I see or hear (or outside my practice in social intercourse) that ought not to be published abroad, I will not divulge, but consider such things to be holy secrets. Now if I keep this oath and break it not, may God be my helper in my life and art, and may I be honoured among all men for all time. If I keep the faith, well; but if I forswear myself may the opposite befall me.

From W. H. S. Jones, *The Doctor's Oath: An Essay in the History of Medicine* (New York: Cambridge University Press, 1924), pp. 23-25. Used by permission.

16 The Doctor's Oath — and a Christian Swearing It

Allen Verhey

The Hippocratic Oath is the most familiar of that long line of oaths, prayers, and codes by which doctors have transmitted an ethos to members of their profession. Indeed, it is sometimes simply called "the doctor's oath." In our age, however, enamored of novelty and confident of its technological powers, familiarity seems to have bred, if not contempt,[1] at least the sort of quaint regard which relegates ancient documents to the historian's museum of curiosities. It is my intention, nevertheless, to suggest that there are lessons to be learned — or relearned — from this oath and its history, lessons which can be instructive concerning a professional ethic for physicians and the possible contributions of theology to that ethic.

The intention ought not be misunderstood. I will not suggest that the Hippocratic Oath is an adequate and comprehensive foundation for a professional ethic today. I will not call upon doctors and moralists concerned with medical ethics to swear it again. I will not deny that the invocation of Apollo, Asclepius, Hygeia, Panacea, and all of the gods and goddesses sounds quaint to modern ears or claim that such an invocation can be made with Christian integrity. I will not deny that the ancient institutions presupposed in the oath for the learning and practice of medicine differ

Reprinted with permission from *Linacre Quarterly*, vol. 51, no. 2, pp. 139-58. 850 Elm Grove Road, Elm Grove, WI 53122. Subscription rate: $20 per year; $5 per single issue. Slightly abridged and edited from the original. Used by permission.

from their contemporary counterparts. And I will not recommend the stipulations of the oath as a code to simplify the address to the dilemmas and quandaries posed by medical practice.

That list of disclaimers, it may easily be observed, involves every part of the oath. It may prompt the question of what is to be salvaged. But the lessons to be gleaned from this ancient document are not to be found in its content so much as in certain features of its history and its method. I want to suggest that there are lessons to be learned (1) from its reformist intention; (2) from its treatment of medicine as a practice with intrinsic goods and standards; and (3) from setting these standards in a context which expressed and evoked an identity and recognized one's dependence upon and indebtedness to a community and to the transcendent. Finally, I want to suggest (4) that there is a lesson for Christians who would contribute to the discussions of bioethics in the early Church's adoption and revision of the doctor's oath. In an age when medicine's powers flourish, but its ethos flounders, the ancient oath may help us to attend to ways of doing medical ethics which are not currently popular. I undertake, therefore, both to describe certain features of the ancient oath and to defend them as having some promise for the contemporary consideration of medical ethics in comparison to certain features of the current literature.

The Reformist Intention

According to Ludwig Edelstein, interpreter of the oath, the Hippocratic Oath was not formulated by the great Hippocrates himself, but by a small group of Pythagorean physicians late in the fourth century B.C. Edelstein observes that the oath was a minority opinion, "a Pythagorean manifesto," written against the stream and intending the reform of medicine.[2]

For centuries before the oath, ancient physicians had provided poison for those whom they could not heal, had counted abortifacients among the tools of their trade, and had been disposed to the use of the knife instead of the less invasive use of dietetics and pharmacology. Moreover, they had sometimes been guilty of injustice and mischief toward their patients, and sometimes quite shamelessly broken confidences.

When the little sect of Pythagoreans set out to reform the condition of medicine, they found no help in the law, which forbade neither suicide nor abortion. They could plainly find no help in the conventional behavior of physicians in antiquity. Nor did they find help in any "philosophical consensus," for, insofar as there was any agreement about these issues, it worked against the Pythagorean position. Platonists, Cynics, and Stoics could honor suicide as a courageous triumph over fate. Aristotelians and Epicureans were much more circumspect, but they did not forbid suicide. And abortion was typically considered essential for a well-ordered state. The arguments between Pythagoreans and other Greek philosophers must have seemed as interminable and as conceptually incommensurable as any contemporary moral argument. The minority status of their opinions, however, did not dissuade the Pythagoreans.

The point is not to defend the oath's absolute prohibitions of abortion and euthanasia and surely not to defend Pythagorean philosophy or the premises it might supply to defend such prohibitions.[3] The point is rather to call attention to this feature of the oath's method and history, that in spite of their minority position, the convictions of this community led them and moved them to reform. They refused to be satisfied with the medicine they saw around them. They refused to reduce medical morality to what the law allowed or what some philosophical consensus determined. They intended the reform of medicine.

The lesson, I suggest, for the contemporary discussion of medical ethics is that some, at least, should take courage to investigate and articulate a medical ethic which may stand at some remove from conventional behavior and attitudes within the profession and which may be based on convictions and standards more particular and profound than legal and contractual obligations or some minimal philosophical consensus. Communities with convictions about what human persons are meant to be and to become, with visions of what it means for embodied persons to flourish and thrive, have an opportunity and vocation to think through the art of medicine from their own perspectives.

The recent literature on medical ethics has not owned such an agenda. Indeed, the moral convictions and visions of particular communities typically have been tolerated and trivialized in the literature. On the one hand, there is an insistence that everyone's moral point of view should be respected. On the other hand, there has been an insistence that the only arguments which may count publicly are those which can be made independent of a distinctive moral point of view. This simultaneous tolerance and trivialization is accomplished by making the autonomy of the agent the highest human good, by making contracts between such autonomous agents the model of human relationships, and by focusing almost exclusively on the procedural question of who should decide.[4] The ancient enterprise of attempting to understand and communicate the intrinsic good of human persons and of some human relationships and activities has been largely abandoned. Attempts to articulate communities' or traditions' address to those ancient questions may be tolerated if the "good" is kept to themselves, relegated resolutely to a "private" arena and, thus, trivialized. It may not even be tolerated if the "good" is announced as "public" good, for then it threatens to restrict and subvert autonomy. Such recent literature on medical ethics has provided — and can provide — only a "thin theory of the good,"[5] only a shriveled and dangerously minimal construal of the moral life in its medical dimensions. We find, in much contemporary medical ethics, for example, a readiness to insist on procedures to protect autonomy but a reticence to provide any advice about the morally proper uses of that autonomy and a dismissal of the idea that physicians should be the ones to give such advice.

The Hippocratic Oath, however, can remind us that the current focus on autonomy and contracts and procedural questions provides only a minimal account of medical morality. It can encourage us to own a fuller vision of medical morality and to seek the reform of medicine in the light of that vision.

The Pythagoreans' reform movement finally triumphed. The oath gradually moved from the status of a countercultural manifesto to a historic document which formed and informed the ethos of physicians for centuries. The explanation for this triumph was not any philosophical triumph by the Pythagoreans; their influence, never great, waned. Their reform, however, articulated not just Pythagorean moral premises and conclusions, but standards inherent in medicine when it is seen as a practice with certain intrinsic goods. They situated these standards in a context which provided and formed identity and which recognized dependence and indebtedness to a community and to the transcendent. These standards finally won the support of another minority community, a community which did move to dominance in Western culture — the Christian Church. These features of the oath explain its triumph. They are still instructive and, after more than two millennia, again innovative. They can help form the "fuller vision" of medical morality which may once again call for and sustain the reform of medicine.

Medicine as a Practice

The Pythagoreans began with their own convictions about human flourishing. But one of these convictions concerned the moral significance of the crafts, the arts, the *teknē*.[6] The Pythagoreans honored the arts, especially music and medicine, as having moral and, indeed, ontological significance. Therefore, they did not simply apply Pythagorean premises to morally neutral medical skills; instead, they tried to educe and elucidate the moral significance of the craft, the art, the *teknē* of medicine itself. Because this Pythogorean attitude to the crafts came to be dominant in late philosophical schools, notably the Stoics,[7] the Pythagorean reform of medicine flourished while Pythagorean philosophy waned.

In striking an intriguing contrast to most contemporary literature on medical ethics, which so often picks an ethical theory (whether Mill's or Rawls's or Nozick's or . . .) and applies it to dilemmas faced by medical practitioners, the Pythagorean conviction about the crafts allowed and required one to identify the good implicit in the craft and to articulate the standards coherent with the good of the craft. According to the oath, then, the doctor is obligated not because he is a Pythagorean, but because he is a doctor, and his obligations consist not only of standards based on Pythagorean doctrine but also of standards implicit in medicine.

The oath treats medicine as a craft, an art, a *teknē*, or to use Alasdair MacIntyre's terms,[8] as a practice, not simply a set of technical skills. That is to say, it treats medicine as a form of human activity with goods internal to it and standards of excellence implicit in it, not simply as an assortment of skills which can be made to serve extrinsic goods with merely technological excellence.

The goal of medicine, the good which is intrinsic to the practice, is identified by the oath as "the benefit of the sick." To benefit the sick is not simply the motive for taking up certain ethically neutral skills nor merely an extrinsic end to be accomplished by ethically neutral technical means.[9] It is, rather, the goal of medicine as a practice, and so it governed the physician's use of his skills in diet, drugs, and surgery, and the use of his privileged access to the patient's home and privacy. This intrinsic good entailed standards of professional excellence which could not be reduced to technological excellence.

The pattern is repeated again and again in the oath. Its prohibitions of active euthanasia, of assisting in suicide, and of abortion, for example, were not argued on the basis of Pythagorean premises; they were given as standards of a practice whose goal is to benefit the sick. Because the ends intrinsic to medicine are to heal the sick, to protect and nurture health, to maintain and restore physical well-being, limits could be imposed on the use of skills within the practice. The skills were not to be used to serve alien ends, and the destruction of human life — either the last of it or the first of it — was seen as an alien and conflicting end. The point was not that one would fail to be a good Pythagorean if one violated these standards, although that is true enough, but rather that one would fail to be a good medical practitioner. The good physician is not a mere technician; he is committed by the practice of medicine to certain goods and to certain standards.

The notoriously difficult foreswearing of surgery, even on those who stand to benefit from it, is also founded on the notion of medicine as a practice. Edelstein is probably right in tracing this stipulation to the Pythagorean preference for dietetics and pharmacology as modes of treatment,[10] but the foreswearing in the oath did not appeal to any uncompromising Pythagorean position about either the appetitive and dietetic causes of illness or the defilement of shedding blood. It rather articulated a standard for medical practice whose goal is to benefit the sick: namely, don't attempt what lies beyond your competence. To benefit the sick was not merely a motive, but the good intrinsic to medicine, and to put the patient at risk needlessly — even with the best of intentions — can be seen to violate medicine understood as such a practice. There was, therefore, no universal prohibition of surgery, only the particular prohibition of surgery by those ill-equipped to attempt it. That standard may well have been of particular relevance to Pythagorean physicians, but one need not have been a Pythagorean to accept its wisdom as a standard of practice.

The stipulations concerning decorum are yet another example. They can be readily understood against the background of Pythagorean asceticism and the proverbial "Pythagorean silence,"[11] but again, the oath presented them not as Pythagorean stipulations, but as standards of medicine understood as a practice. The goal of the practice, "the benefit of the sick," was repeated in this context even as the (necessary) intrusion into the privacy, the homes, of the sick was acknowledged. The physician's access to the intimacies of the patient's body and household and his exposure to the vulnerability of the patient and his household were granted and accepted for the sake of the goal intrinsic to medicine. To use such access for any other end or to make public the vulnerability to which the physician was made privy was seen to subvert the relation of such access and such exposure to the end of medicine. It debased the patient who should be benefited. It vitiated medicine as a practice and, therefore, the standards prohibiting sexual relations with patients and prohibiting breaches of confidentiality were implicit in medicine as a practice.

These standards could be further explicated,[12] and, if the point of this essay were to treat the oath as a code, then the further explication would be necessary. But that is not the point. It is not my claim that the oath provides an unexceptionable code of conduct. The standards of a practice at any particular time are not immune from criticism. The point is to call attention to this feature of the oath's method, that it construes medicine as a practice. It does not provide a timeless code for medicine, but there are standards of excellence appropriate to and partly definitive of the practice, whose authority must be acknowledged, and there is a good intrinsic to the practice which must be appreciated and allowed to govern the skills and to form and reform the standards. The lesson, I suggest, for the contemporary discussions of medical ethics, is that those who seek the constant reform of medicine should also construe medicine as a practice with implicit goods and standards.

That is a hard but important lesson in a culture as bullish on technology and as pluralistic in values as our own. There is a constant tendency to reduce medicine to a mere — but awesome — collection of techniques that may be made to serve extrinsic goods, themselves often reduced to matters of taste.

The technology of abortion is a telling example. In *Roe v. Wade*, the Court declared that a woman's decision with respect to abortion was a private matter between herself and her physician. It recognized that the moral status of the fetus was controverted, but it held that the fetus is not a *legal* person and so is not entitled to the protection the law extends to persons. It wanted to leave the moral controversy about the status of the fetus within that private arena of the decision a woman and her doctor would make. The court presumed (and suggested by calling the decision to abort a "medical decision") that the professional ethos of physicians would limit abortions, even if abortion were legalized and it might have been, if there had been a vivid sense of medicine as a practice.[13] The legal license was interpreted by many (both women and physicians) as a moral license and the outcome has been a callous and frightening disregard for fetal life and welfare. The protests — usually applying some extrinsic good or extrinsic standard — have been long and loud and have sometimes exhibited callous disregard for the rights of women with respect to their own bodies and ignored the legitimate controversy about the status of the fetus. The opportunity for medicine to reassert itself as a practice, different from the practice of politics or the marketplace, has almost been lost. But the lesson of the oath is that the attempt is both possible and worthwhile.

The notion of medicine as a practice stands in marked contrast to a good deal of the current literature concerning the professions in general and medicine in particular. Michael Bayles, for example, would reject the normative characteristics of the professions, including medicine.[14] He reduces the professions to skills learned by training and made accessible to consumers. The professions, on this view, are not justified or guided by any intrinsic good but by "the values of a liberal society."[15] Thus, there are no standards implicit in the practice but only "ordinary norms" to be applied in professional contexts.

The problems with such a view are manifold. One is linguistic. "Professional" and "unprofessional" continue to be used evaluatively and, moreover, with respect to excellences not merely technical.

The notion of applying ordinary norms to medical dilemmas is also problematic. It is naive and presumptuous to suppose that a moral philosopher or theologian can boldly put to flight a moral dilemma by expertly wielding a sharp principle or some heavy theory.[16] And how shall we select the "ordinary norms" to apply? Justice is surely relevant, but there is more than one theory of justice. Good ends surely ought to be sought in medicine, too, but shall we use St. Thomas Aquinas or John Stuart Mill to define a good end? The values of society may be important, but none of us, I trust, has forgotten the atrocities committed when Hitler's vision of a "third reich" was applied to medicine.

I am much more comfortable with Bayles's "values of a liberal society" than with Hitler's "third reich," but I am not so much more confident about the practice of politics than the practice of medicine that I would make the professional ethic dependent upon our political ethic. Indeed, I wonder whether a society is truly "liberal" if it tailors the professions to a liberal society's (minimal) vision of the good. A liberal society can be guilty of trivializing ancient wisdom about human flourishing when it renders the professions, including medicine, merely instrumental skills to satisfy consumer wants.

Bayles's application of his "ordinary norms" to medicine leads to minimal moral claims and, because the minimal character of the claims is not acknowledged, to a truncated and distorted medical ethic. There is, for example, no limit to "professional services" when a profession is basically skills accessible to consumers: laetrile, genetic testing for sex determination, plastic surgery to win the Dolly Parton look-alike contest, all become the sphere of the professional-entrepreneur. Immoral clients cannot be refused on the basis of "professional integrity," for there is no such thing. Bayles is aware of the problem posed by clients who would use professional skills for ends which are morally questionable but which do not clearly violate the "ordinary norms," and he presents two options for dealing with such clients. The "no difference" option quite candidly leaves no room for integrity of any kind and renders the professional the "animated tool" of the consumer.[17] The second option permits the physician to refuse services to such clients on the basis of "moral integrity," but this "moral integrity" is represented as strictly personal and private rather than professional.[18]

Bayles's attempt to reduce professional norms to "ordinary norms" applied in a medical context, to give one more example, leads to a minimal and truncated version of the prohibition of sexual intercourse with patients.[19] The ordinary norm he provides, that sexual intercourse requires the free consent of both parties, is itself a dangerously minimal account of sexual ethics. It does provide a justification for the prohibition, but it does not discount either the possibility or the importance of a "professional" justification, that the (necessary) access to the patient's privacy and vulnerability must be guided by and limited to the "good" of medicine and not be used for extrinsic ends (even when they are freely chosen or consented to).

The debate about the crafts, about the professions, is an ancient and an enduring one. The lesson of the oath is that we should not too readily accept the notion of medicine as a collection of skills accessible to consumers. We should not identify our task as simply applying universal and rational norms of conduct to medicine and to the quandaries faced within it.[20]

If the *ṭeknē* of medicine is construed simply in terms of its techniques or skills, learned by training and accessible to consumers, then, of course, it is morally neutral. Skill in pharmacology enables one to be a good healer or a crafty murderer. But if a *teknē* is more than technique, if it has its own goal and its own virtues, then it is hardly morally neutral. Then some moral wisdom about living as a finite body may exist within the practice of medicine and within those communities and traditions which learn and teach medicine as a practice. Then medicine's fragile capacity to resist being co-opted by an alien ideology, even a liberal ideology (not to mention the "third reich"), can be strengthened and nurtured. The lesson of the oath, I suggest, is that for some, at least, the task should be to defend the vision of medicine as a practice while educing and elucidating the goods and standards implicit in that practice.

The Hippocratic Oath had its origins among the Pythagoreans who had the courage to attempt the reform of medicine and the wisdom not merely to apply Pythagorean premises to medicine but to construe it as a practice. It was handed down not as legislation but as voluntary rule imposing voluntary obedience. Its power to reform was not coercive or simply rationally persuasive; its power to reform was its power to form character and a community which nurtured it. It did not set its standards in a context of legal sanctions or in a context of impartial rationality. It set these standards in a context which expressed and evoked an identity and recognized one's dependence upon and indebtedness to both a community and the transcendent. To those features of the oath we turn next.

Identity, Community, and the Transcendent

The oath, like all oaths and promises, was a performative declaration rather than a descriptive one. It did not just describe reality; it altered it. The one who swore this oath was never the same "one" again. The one swearing this oath adopted more than a set of rules and skills; he or she adopted an identity. The goods and standards of medicine as a practice were owned as one's own and gave shape to integrity with one's identity. Therefore, "physician" was a description not only of what one knew or of what one did or of what one knew how to do, but of who one was. Henceforth, one examined questions of conduct in this role not as an impartial and rational agent, calculating utility sums, say, but as a physician. Integrity with this identity called for the physician to exert himself on behalf of the patient at hand, even the patient-scoundrel at hand, without calculating the greatest good for the greatest number. Indeed, to allow that question, to bear toward the patient the kind of impartial relation which makes it plausible, was to lose one's identity, to forfeit one's integrity.

This feature of the oath calls our attention to the moral significance of "identity." Once again the lesson of the doctor's oath sets a different agenda than the one contemporary medical ethics has generally undertaken. Contemporary medical ethics usually adopts the perspective of impartial rationality, either in the form of utilitarianism or in the form of contract theory.[21] To adopt any such impartial perspective, however, requires the doctor's alienation from his own moral interests and loyalties *qua* physician, from himself and from his special relationship to his patient. Doctors are asked, indeed, obliged, by this perspective to view the project and passion of their practice as though they were outside objective observers.

They are asked by this approach to disown — and for the sake of morality — the goods and standards they possess as their own and which give them their moral character as physicians.[22]

The perspective of impartial rationality is not to be disowned. It can enable conversation between people with different loyalties and the adjudication of conflicting interests, and it can challenge the arbitrary dominance of one perspective over another. To be made to pause occasionally and, for the sake of analysis and judgment, to view things as impartially as we can is not only legitimate, but also salutary. But such an ethic remains minimal at best, and if its minimalism is not acknowledged, it can distort the moral life. Physicians — and patients — cannot consistently live their moral lives like that with any integrity. The Hippocratic Oath calls our attention to the importance of a physician's identity, character, and integrity. Such an approach might recover the importance of performative rituals like swearing an initiatory oath, and it would surely attend not only to the ways in which acts effectively realize ends, but also to the ways in which acts express values and form character.[23]

The oath expressed and evoked an identity, but it was an identity which recognized its dependence upon and indebtedness to a community and the transcendent.

The oath bound one to a community where not only the requisite skills were taught, but where the requisite character and identity were nurtured. The doctor swore to live in fellowship (Gk.: *koinosasthai*) with his teacher, to share a common life with him. He pledged, moreover, to teach the art to his teacher's sons, to his own sons, and to all who wanted to learn not simply the skills, but also the practice. Here was not an autonomous individual practitioner, utilizing his skills for his private good and according to his private vision of the good or as contracted by another to accomplish the other's "good." The doctor who swore the oath stood self-consciously in a community and in a tradition. He acknowledged gratefully his dependence upon this community and tradition, his indebtedness to his teacher, and his responsibility to protect and nurture the practice of medicine.[24]

This section of the oath is often criticized.[25] It is accused of fostering a medical guild where obligations to colleagues take priority over obligations to patients, so that medical incompetence and malpractice are usually covered up and the incompetent and unscrupulous (protected by the guild) do further harm to patients. The charge is a serious one, and the profession's reluctance to discipline its members makes it cogent. The fault is not with the oath, however, but with the corruption of the oath in the absence of a commitment to medicine as a practice. When there is such a commitment, it governs relations with colleagues as well as patients, and protecting and nurturing the practice — both the requisite skills and the requisite character — enable and require communal discipline. The failure of the profession to discipline itself adequately may be traced not to the perspective of the oath but to the dismissal of the perspective of the oath.

Today the training for medicine has shifted to university-based medical schools, which pride themselves on their scientific detachment from questions of value in their dispassionate pursuit of the truth. Such a context can virtually sponsor the construal of medicine as a collection of skills and techniques to be used for extrinsic goods which are not matters of truth but matters of taste.[26] Then there is no community of people committed to a practice and under its standards; there is only the camaraderie of those who have undergone the same arduous routine. Then the profession lacks both a commitment to a practice which makes discipline possible and a genuine enough community to make discipline a nurturing as well as a punishing activity.

The stress on community in the oath can help call our attention to the moral necessity of attending to the institutions, communities, and traditions within which the physician's identity is nurtured. Adding courses in medical ethics taught by philosophers or theologians to the curricula of medical schools may be important, but it is neither essential nor sufficient. Indeed, if such courses are co-opted as token evidence of the moral concern of the institution, or if clinical instructors abdicate the responsibility for difficult decisions to "the moral expert," the results could be counter-productive. It is more important to have teachers chosen and rewarded not only for their excellent skills but also for their excellence in medical practice — chosen and rewarded not only for their ability to teach the skills, but also for the ability to model the practice. The philosopher or theologian may then have an important role as participant in — and mid-wife for — a continuing dialogue between such teachers and their students about the goods and standards implicit in medicine as a practice. In such a continuing dialogue there will surely be continuing conflicts, but so any living tradition is passed down.

No less important than institutions where doctors are trained are institutions within which they practice and the communities within which they live, including the religious communities. That religious communities might nurture and sustain the identity of physicians is, of course, suggested by the doctor's oath itself. The physician acknowledged his dependence upon and indebtedness to not only the community of doctors, but also the transcendent.

The opening line called all the gods and goddesses as witnesses to this oath, and the last line puts the doctor at the mercy of divine justice. The invocation of the gods and their divine retribution served, of course, to signify the solemnity of the oath and the stringency of the obligations. More than that, however, was accomplished by the oath's piety, by its recognition of our dependence upon and indebtedness to transcendent power which bears down on us and sustains us. A narrative is provided, a narrative which helps inform identity and helps sustain community, a narrative which supports and tests the practice of medicine. The deities named are a lineage. Apollo, the god of truth and light, here invoked as "Apollo Physician," is the father of Asclepius. Asclepius, the father of medicine and the patron of physicians and patients, had two daughters, Hygeia and Panacea, or "Health" and "All-heal," the goddesses of health maintenance and therapy.[27] It is a story of the divine origins and transmission of the work physicians are given and gifted to do. To undertake the work of a physician was to make this story one's own story, to continue it and embody it among human beings. They were not tempted to "play God" or to deny their subordinate role, but they were supported and encouraged in their ministrations by this story. In serving patients in their practice, they continued a narrative that had its beginnings among the gods. They were not tempted to magic by this story,[28] but they were enabled to acknowledge the mystery of healing, the subtle and profound connections of the spirit and the body.[29]

This feature of the oath can remind us of the religious dimensions of medicine and medical morality. It is a hard but important lesson for an age as noisily secular as ours. The oath, I think, is an example of the moral significance of a natural piety, the importance of what Calvin would call a *sensus divinitatis,* the sense of the divine. This natural piety includes the sense of gratitude for the gifts of life and of the world, a sense of dependence upon some reliable, but dimly known order, a sense of some tragic fault in the midst of our world, and a sense of responsibility to the inscrutable power Who stands behind the gifts and the order and Who judges the fault.[30] One can do worse, I think, than name this other wrongly; one could understand (misunderstand) this other as the "enemy" of his own work, as a deluding power, or one could deny or (like so much of the contemporary literature) ignore this other and these senses. The oath adopted neither of those forms of distrust;[31] rather, it set the practice of medicine in the context of a natural piety, in the context of a sense of gratitude, of dependence, of tragedy, and of responsibility to the transcendent. Such a natural piety can still nourish and sustain the physician's calling. Its responsiveness to the transcendent can protect the physician both from the presumption of "playing God" and from the reductionism of plying the trade for hire. It remains part of the fuller vision of medicine.

The Christian's Swearing It

The triumph of the doctor's oath may finally be attributed to the triumph of a new religion in the ancient world. Christianity adopted it as its own, finally presenting it in a Christian form, "The Oath According to Hippocrates Insofar as a Christian May Swear It." There were certain revisions, to be sure, but the continuity of the Christian version with the ancient oath is undeniable. Both the continuity and the revisions are instructive for Christian theologians and communities who take part in the current discussions of bioethics.

First, note the adoption and reiteration of the standards of the Hippocratic Oath. There are some minor variations in the stipulations governing the practice — the operation clause is omitted, even "unintentional" harm (negligence) is forbidden, the prohibition of abortion is amplified — but the similarity is the striking thing. The claim is not that here finally we have a Christian code to be used and applied to current dilemmas. The claim is rather that there is a lesson here for those Christians who would contribute to the conversations about medical ethics. The lesson is that Christian ethics does not disown "natural" morality. It does not construct an ethic *ex nihilo,* out of nothing. It selects and assimilates the "natural" moral wisdom around it in terms of its own truthfulness and in terms of its integrity with the Christian vision. The theologians who would contribute to the conversation about bioethics must first listen attentively and respectfully to "natural" moral wisdom concerning medicine. Then they can speak responsively and responsibly about the adoption and selection of certain standards as coherent with reason, with medicine construed as a practice, and with the Christian vision.

"The Oath Insofar as a Christian May Swear It" offers a second lesson for theologians interested in medical ethics. Note the two obvious changes. The first is that the practice and its standards were set in the context of a Christian identity and of the Christian story. God, the Father of our Lord Jesus Christ, was invoked rather than Apollo et al.; the physician cast himself on the mercy of His justice. Once again, the invocation of God and His retribution served not only to signal the solemnity of the oath and the stringency of the obligations, but also to set the physician's identity and practice in the context of a story which has its beginnings with God. This feature was expressed visibly as well. "The Oath Insofar as a Christian May Swear It" — or at least some copies of it — was written in the shape of a cross.[32] The one who swore such an oath adopted the physician's identity as a follower of Christ, "Who took our infirmities and bore our diseases" (Matt. 8:17; cf. Is. 53:4). A Christian identity nurtured, sustained, and shaped the physician's identity for those who took such an oath seriously.

The second obvious change is the reduction of duties to one's teacher. Historically, this change is understandable. Medical instruction had shifted from artisan families and guilds to universities and eventually to faculties of medicine. The Church itself was, for centuries, the nurturing and sustaining institution and community for medicine. It chartered and administered the universities; it dominated the curriculum; its pervasive ethos ruled the professions.[33] Morally, the change was required by setting the oath in the context of the Christian story, for that story makes service the mark of greatness as well as of gratitude. So, it was inevitable that service to the patient was emphasized rather than obligations to teachers. The Christian story of breaking down the barriers that separate people, moreover, made it inevitable that the emphasis shifted from professional elitism to open access to the community of service.

What Is the Lesson Here?

The lesson here is not that we should attempt to reintroduce "Christendom" or even the patterns of medical instruction of that time. Notwithstanding the impossibility of such an attempt, the dominion of the Church was marked by parochialism as well as majesty, by pettiness as well as grandeur, by obscurantism as well as learning. The reformist intention does not lead back to Christendom for either medicine or the Church. There is little hope for a Christian medical ethic that proceeds by way of a theological triumphalism, that claims to have truth, if not captive, at least cornered. The lesson is rather that Christian medical ethics cannot proceed with integrity if it always restricts itself to articulating and defending standards of the practice or certain applications of impartial principles of philosophy or law to medical dilemmas. It is lamentable that so little of the work in medical ethics by Christian theologians candidly and explicitly attends to the Christian story and its bearing on medicine.[34] It is lamentable for the communities of faith out of which these ethicists work, for they want to live in faith, to live in integrity with the identity they have been given and to which they are called. But it is also lamentable for the broader community, for a pluralistic society profits from the candid expression of different perspectives. Candid attention to the theological dimensions of morality could prevent the reduction and distortion of morality to a set of minimal expectations necessary for pluralism and remind all participants in such a culture of broader and more profound questions about what human persons are meant to be and to become. The integrity to think about and talk about the relevance of the Christian story is the second lesson of "The Oath Insofar as a Christian May Swear It."

The first lesson of "The Oath Insofar as a Christian May Swear It" was that Christian ethics does not disown "natural" morality. The Christian story does not force those who own it to disown either medicine as a practice or human rationality. The second lesson of "The Oath Insofar as a Christian May Swear It" is that Christians concerned with medical ethics should have the integrity to set medicine in the context of the Christian story, to form, inform, and reform medicine. The first lesson stands against any premature sectarian stance, against opting prematurely for either a sectarian community or a sectarian medicine.[35] The second lesson stands against any simple identification of a Christian ethic either with universal and rational principles or with a professional ethic, against, for example, sanctifying contract theory by identifying it with "covenant."[36] The task is to transform or, to put it less presumptuously, to qualify[37] a rational ethic and a professional ethic by candid attention to the Christian story.

There will be tensions, of course. With respect to decisions about the refusal of treatment, for example, a universal and rational ethic may emphasize the patient's autonomy, but a professional ethic may emphasize the physician's commitment to the life and health of his or her patient, and a theological ethic may emphasize dispositions formed and informed by a story where the victory over death is a divine victory, not a technological victory, where people need not stand in dread of death, but may not practice hospitality toward it.[38] These tensions and their resolution will require the careful attention of those who make it their task to think about medicine and who care about the Christian story as the story of our life, our whole life.

Finally, it may be observed that theological reflection, even when it is presumptuous enough to talk about "transformation," does not represent an alien imposition upon the practice of medicine. As we have seen, the tradition of medicine as a practice is at home in piety. Loyalty to God, the Father of our Lord Jesus Christ, fulfills and redeems natural piety. The native senses of gratitude and dependence, of a tragic fault in the midst of our world, and of responsibility, are not disowned by a theological approach, but informed and reformed by the Christian story. The current literature on bioethics stands at risk of ignoring that story, of neglecting those resources. Christians have a vocation to identify and articulate the significance of the Christian story for medicine not only because that agenda stands comfortable in an ancient tradition, but also because it will serve both integrity within the Christian community and humanity with medical practice. To renege on this opportunity and vocation will diminish not only the communities of faith, but the art of medicine as well.

Notes

1. The attitude of Robert Veatch toward the oath can only be characterized as contempt. He argues that the oath is morally "dangerous." See Robert Veatch, *A Theory of Medical Ethics* (New York: Basic Books, 1981), pp. 18-26, 79-107, and especially 141-69. See also his "The Hippocratic Ethic: Consequentialism, Individualism, and Paternalism," *No Rush to Judgment,* ed. by David Smith and Linda M. Bernstein (Bloomington, Ind.: Poynter Center, 1978), pp. 238-64; "Medical Ethics: Professional or Universal?" *Harvard Theological Review,* 65:4 (Oct., 1972): 531-39; and *Death, Dying, and the Biological Revolution* (New Haven: Yale University Press, 1976), pp. 171, 172. Veatch criticizes both the basis and

the content of the oath. The basis is criticized because the oath is based on a special professional ethic rather than on universal rational moral norms. The content is criticized because the oath is construed as consequentialist, individualist, and paternalistic.

2. Edelstein, Ludwig, "The Hippocratic Oath: Text, Translation and Interpretation," *Ancient Medicine* ed. by Oswei Temkin and C. Lillian Temkin (Baltimore: Johns Hopkins University Press, 1967), pp. 3-63. I am convinced by Edelstein concerning the Pythagorean origins of the oath. Even if it originated in some other community, however, it would still have had the intention to reform ancient medicine, and that is the feature of the oath to which I would call attention.

3. For example, the Pythagorean premise concerning the status of the fetus was supplied by a physiology which took the seed to be clot of brain containing the warm vapors whence came soul and sensation. The Pythagorean asceticism, which justified intercourse only as the necessary condition for procreation, surely affected their perspective on abortion. See Edelstein, op. cit. It is important to observe, however, that the oath, while coherent with Pythagorean doctrines and beliefs (as Edelstein shows), does not simply apply Pythagorean doctrine *to* medicine (as Edelstein presumes to have shown). The oath draws *from* medicine the morality to guide and limit the behavior of physicians. See section 2, "Medicine as a Practice" and reference 6 below.

4. So, for example, Robert Veatch, *A Theory of Medical Ethics.* See the review by Allen Verhey, "Contract — or Covenant?" *Reformed Journal* 33:9 (Sept. 1983): 23, 24.

5. The phrase, of course, is John Rawls's. See, e.g., *A Theory of Justice* (Cambridge, Mass.: Harvard University Press, 1971), pp. 396ff. The complaint about "the thin theory of the good" in the contemporary literature echoes Daniel Callahan, "Minimalist Ethics," *Hastings Center Report* 11:6 (Oct. 1981): 19-25.

6. Edelstein recognizes the importance of the Pythagorean attitude toward the crafts (e.g., "the Professional Ethics of the Greek Physician" in his *Ancient Medicine,* pp. 319-48, p. 327), but he fails to recognize that it warrants construing medicine as a practice of intrinsic goods and implicit standards (e.g., ibid., n. 21). The same failure marks Veatch's use of Edelstein (e.g., *A Theory of Medical Ethics,* p. 21).

7. *Precepts* and *On Decorum,* later writings in the Hippocratic corpus, are probably Stoic in origin; see Edelstein, op. cit.

8. On the notion of a practice, see Alasdair MacIntyre, *After Virtue* (Notre Dame: University of Notre Dame Press, 1981), pp. 175-78.

9. Veatch's criticism of the oath's "consequentialism" relies heavily on the oath's commitment to "the benefit of the sick." Veatch's understanding of the oath at this point makes "benefit" an extrinsic good and, moreover, renders benefit definable in terms of the physician's (or the patient's) private preferences. I am convinced that this is a misunderstanding. The *teknē* of medicine is not construed in the oath as morally neutral skills accessible to consumers; it is not just a "means" even to health; it is a human activity of inheriting and learning and teaching and applying a wisdom about living with a finite body. See further E. Pellegrino and D. Thomasma, *A Philosophical Basis of Medical Practice* (New York: Oxford University Press, 1981); and Stanley M. Hauerwas, "Authority and the Profession of Medicine" (Manuscript). That Veatch misunderstands the oath at this point is obvious when he suggests — quite against the oath's own straightforward prohibition — that the oath's concern for benefit of the patient could permit participation in bringing about the death of an infant (*A Theory of Medical Ethics,* pp. 15-26).

10. Edelstein, "The Hippocratic Oath," op. cit., pp. 21-33.

11. Ibid., pp. 33-39.

12. See especially Leon Kass, "The Hippocratic Oath: Thoughts on Medicine and Ethics," a lecture given on Nov. 12, 1980, in the seminar series sponsored by the program in the Arts and Sciences Basic to Human Biology and Medicine and the American Medical Students' Association, at the University of Chicago.

13. The court's use of Edelstein's study of the Pythagorean origins of the Hippocratic Oath, unfortunately, tended to reinforce the position that extrinsic goods and standards may be applied to medicine but that goods and standards intrinsic to medicine do not exist. At the very time the court laid a heavy burden on physicians by calling abortion a "medical decision," it weakened physicians' resolve and ability to resist this culture's tendency to construe medicine as a set of skills to satisfy consumer wants.

14. Bayles, Michael, *Professional Ethics* (Belmont, Calif.: Wadsworth Publishing Co., 1981). See also Alan Goldman, *The Moral Foundations of Professional Ethics* (Tutowa, N.J.: Rowman and Littlefield, 1980).

15. In Goldman's view, op. cit., the justification and guidance are provided by a modified utilitarianism.

16. See further Arthur L. Caplan, "Ethical Engineers Need Not Apply: The State of Applied Ethics Today,"

Science, Technology and Human Values, 6:33 (Fall, 1980): 24-32.

17. This is, of course, Aristotle's definition of a slave. See Paul Ramsey, *Ethics at the Edges of Life* (New Haven: Yale University Press, 1978), pp. 45-158.

18. Bayles, op. cit., pp. 52ff.

19. Ibid., p. 21.

20. Veatch, *A Theory of Medical Ethics,* op. cit., is a case in point.

21. Again, Veatch, ibid., is a case in point.

22. See further Stanley Hauerwas, *Truthfulness and Tragedy: Further Investigations in Christian Ethics,* (Notre Dame: University of Notre Dame Press, 1977), pp. 23-25; and Bernard Williams, "A Critique of Utilitarianism," in J. J. C. Smart and Bernard Williams, *Utilitarianism: For and Against* (New York: Cambridge University Press, 1973), pp. 100-18.

23. Childress, James, *Priorities in Biomedical Ethics* (Philadelphia: Westminster Press, 1981), p. 82, citing Max Weber, *Max Weber in Economy and Society,* nicely distinguishes "goal-rational" and "value-rational" conduct.

24. Veatch's charge that the oath is "individualistic" (*A Theory of Medical Ethics,* pp. 154-59, and "The Hippocratic Ethic," pp. 255-59) fails to recognize this communal character of the practice of medicine in the oath. The oath, indeed, seems much more cognizant of the social and historical character of medicine than Veatch himself for whom independent and autonomous individuals contract for medical services. Veatch's accusation cannot stand; it can, in fact, be turned against Veatch's own position, for it is Veatch's contract model which protects and perpetuates the individualism of modern liberalism and sets medicine in the ethos of the marketplace. Veatch's contract theory may provide a minimal amount of medical morality, but unless its minimalism is acknowledged, it can distort medical morality into the most arid form of individualism, quite incapable of nurturing or supporting other than contractual relationships. See further James Childress, "A Masterful Tour: A Response to Robert Veatch," *Journal of Current Social Issues* 4:12 (Fall 1975): 20-25.

25. See, e.g., William F. May, "Code and Covenant or Philanthropy and Contract?" in *Ethics in Medicine: Historical Perspectives and Contemporary Concerns,* ed. by Stanley J. Reiser, Arthur J. Dyck, and William J. Curran (Cambridge, Mass.: MIT Press, 1977), pp. 65-76 (an expanded and revised form of an essay first published in *Hastings Center Report* [Dec. 1975]: 29-38).

26. See further William F. May, *Notes on the Ethics of Doctors and Lawyers,* a Poynter Pamphlet (Bloomington, Ind.: Poynter Center, 1977), pp. 16-21; and his "Normative Inquiry and Medical Ethics in Our Colleges and Universities," in *No Rush to Judgment,* pp. 332-61.

27. Kass, op. cit.

28. See Edelstein, "Greek Medicine in Its Relation to Religion and Magic," op. cit., pp. 205-46.

29. Kass, op. cit.

30. See further James M. Gustafson, "Theocentric Interpretation of Life," *The Christian Century,* July 30-Aug. 6, 1980, p. 758; and *Ethics from a Theocentric Perspective* (Chicago: Chicago University Press, 1981), pp. 129-36.

31. See H. R. Niebuhr, *The Responsible Self* (New York: Harper & Row, 1963), pp. 115-18.

32. Jones, W. H. S., *The Doctor's Oath: An Essay in the History of Medicine* (New York: Cambridge University Press, 1924), pp. 23-25. See facsimilies in W. H. S. Jones, *The Doctor's Oath,* frontispiece and p. 26.

33. May, *Notes on the Ethics,* op. cit., pp. 16, 17; and "Normative Inquiry," op. cit.

34. See James M. Gustafson, "Theology Confronts Technology and the Life Sciences," *Commonweal* 2:5 (June 1978): 386-92. See also Stanley Hauerwas, "Can Ethics Be Theological?" *Hastings Center Report* 5:8 (Oct. 1978): 47, 48. To his credit, Robert Veatch introduces the notion of "covenant" into his *A Theory of Medical Ethics.* Unfortunately, it is unclear how, if at all, the religious significance of covenant affects his understanding of the contract between physician and patient. Indeed, the meaning of "covenant" seems to be reduced to the notion of "contract." For some of the differences between contract and covenant (and for an outstanding example of theological reflection on medical ethics focusing on the notion of covenant), see William May, "Code and Covenant," op. cit.

35. Stanley Hauerwas calls for the formation of "a sectarian community" ("Authority and the Profession of Medicine," p. 22).

36. As Robert Veatch, *A Theory of Medical Ethics,* op. cit.

37. See James M. Gustafson, *Can Ethics Be Christian?* p. 173 *et passim.*

38. See further, Allen Verhey, "Christian Community and Identity: What Difference Should They Make to Patients and Physicians Finally?" *Linacre Quarterly* 52:2 (May 1985).

17 From "Medical Ethics: Professional or Universal?"

Robert M. Veatch

There is an obvious tone of idealism in the claim that the individual laymen's inputs into decision-making should be maximized. The professional would rightly claim that this, if carried to extremes, would complicate his task to the point of absurdity. He would have to spend hours explaining the technical details and policy options to each patient. For choices which are ethically trivial and technically complex this is just impossible. The more trivial the value alternatives involved, the less technically complex the choices have to be to make informed decision-making by the layman needlessly wasteful. Laymen are willing to spend more time and money paying professionals to clarify the options for them when the decision involves experimental heart surgery than when it involves which brand of antacid to use. This does not mean, however, that the layman should not be routinely consulted for decisions such as whether to use a generic name drug which should be cheaper but (under present FDA controls) perhaps more variable than the brand name drug.

Nevertheless, the professionals are right. It is logically and logistically impossible to defer every decision to the layman. This does not mean, however, that the decision reverts to the professional in his professional role because of his superior technical skills, his unique set of norms, or his superior ability in reaching ethical judgments. It may revert to him — it must in many cases — but it will revert to him as another human being with no necessarily superior decision-making skills. He may be using the layman's system of values. If he is dedicated, he will try to do so when it does not conflict with his own and will consciously withdraw from the case when it does; but he may be using a system which is quite at odds with the patient's. If the secondary factors of group identification and cultural system of meaning are significant in the decision-making process, the odds may be quite good that it is different from the patient's. When we are dealing in trivialities in medically serious situations such as the brand of compress to use to close a serious arterial wound, the value system conflict may be nearly irrelevant, but we should not overlook the fact that it is still there. A system of decision-making which is rooted in a universal, human ethic may still call on the professional to make many decisions; it certainly will insist that he practice his trade ethically; but the decisions he makes will be made within a universal frame of reference, one which is not unique to the profession he is practicing.

The conclusion to which one is led is that medical ethics must not be thought of as a special "professional ethic" at all, but as a specific application of the universal norms of ethical action. Those traditional and more modern codes of ethics and professional responsibility which are rooted in relativistic norms which cannot be universalized must be distinguished from those which have more universal foundations. The universally rooted principles of medical ethics are extremely important for curbing certain kinds of excesses and hastily conceived actions. The professional codes of medical ethics, on the other hand, are not only irrelevant — if that were the case we could just ignore them. They are actually dangerous diversions which lead professionals to believe that there is a special type of ethics appropriate for their own professional discipline. Rather, we must first reject the fallacy of generalization of expertise — that expertise about the technical facts of a given area also gives one expertise in the evaluative factor required for deci-

Excerpt from "Medical Ethics: Professional or Universal?" by Robert M. Veatch, in the *Harvard Theological Review* 65 (1972): 531-59.

sion-making in that area. . . . Special norms or a special process of balancing norms cannot exist for a professional group without collapsing into ethical relativism and particularism. Expertise in ethical decision-making in questions relevant to a profession may reside in certain members of that profession, but other members of that profession may be particularly deficient in that skill, and on balance there is no evidence of a quantum difference in this regard between professionals and laymen. Finally, although professional review committees may be appropriate for certain limited functions, such as protecting the interests of the profession from the gross offenses of certain of its members, without the premises which have just been rejected, there is no theoretical reason for relying on these committees for adjudication of disputes within a professional area. There is some empirical evidence suggesting that they are not particularly effective and may actually be harmful by diverting the attention of other groups which may take up the cases. Let us hope that, if medical ethics is to emerge as an independent discipline, it is a special case of the universal norms of ethical behavior and not as a special professional ethic.

18 Code and Covenant or Philanthropy and Contract?

William F. May

When it first broke in the news the Summer of 1975, the case of the Marcus twins (gynecologists at a teaching hospital in New York City) posed in vivid circumstances several difficult and illuminating problems in professional ethics; problems which worry both laymen and doctors. The usual analysis of such problems, which appeals to the language of Philanthropy and Contract, boggles at the Marcus case. The categories of Code and Covenant (which are related to Philanthropy and Contract as *genera* to *species*) offer at least the beginnings of solutions to the professional ethical problems embodied in the case.

The Marcus brothers were physicians who, although technically expert (they wrote one of the best current textbooks on gynecology) and professionally and sympathetically involved, allowed themselves to become addicted to barbiturates, to miss appointments, and to offer consultation, diagnosis, and treatment while under the observable influence of drugs. They retained skill and expertise enough, however, to refrain from killing any of their patients. Their colleagues and the institutions in which they worked were slow to blow the whistle on them.

The Marcus case poses ethical problems for the professional. At what point is a doctor who pre-

---

From *Ethics in Medicine: Historical Perspectives and Contemporary Concerns*, ed. Stanley J. Reiser et al. (Cambridge: MIT Press, 1977), pp. 65-76.

willing to be present as long as they work at being "good" sick people who try to get well quickly and do not make too much of their discomfort. We may initially be quite sympathetic with someone with a chronic disease, but it seems to be asking too much of us to be compassionate year in and year out. Thus the universal testimony of people with chronic illness is that their illness often results in the alienation of their former friends. This is a problem not only for the person who is ill but also for those closely connected with that person. The family of a person who is chronically ill often discover that the very skills and habits they must learn to be present to the one in pain creates a gulf between themselves and their friends. Perhaps no case illustrates this more poignantly than a family that has a retarded child. Often they discover it is not long before they have a whole new set of friends who also happen to have retarded children [9].

Exactly because pain is so alienating, we are hesitant to admit that we are in pain. To be in pain means we need help, that we are vulnerable to the interests of others, that we are not in control of our destiny. Thus we seek to deny our pain in the hope that we will be able to handle it within ourselves. But the attempt to deal with our pain by ourselves or to deny its existence has the odd effect of only increasing our loneliness. For exactly to the extent I am successful, I create a story about myself that I cannot easily share.

No doubt more can be and needs to be said that would nuance this account of pain and the way it tends to isolate us from one another. Yet I think I have said enough that our attention has been called to this quite common but all the more extraordinary aspect of our existence. Moreover, in the light of this analysis I hope we can now appreciate the remarkable behavior of Job's friends. For in spite of the bad press Job's comforters usually receive (and in many ways it is deserved!), they at least sat on the ground with him for seven days. Moreover they did not speak to him, "for they saw that his suffering was very great." That they did so is truly an act of magnanimity, for most of us are willing to be with sufferers, especially those in such pain that we can hardly recognize them, only if we can "do something" to relieve their suffering or at least distract their attention. Not so with Job's comforters. They sat on the ground with Job doing nothing more than being willing to be present in the face of his suffering.

Now if any of this is close to being right, it puts the task of physicians and others who are pledged to be with the ill in an interesting perspective. For I take it that their activity as physicians is characterized by the fundamental commitment to be, like Job's comforters, in the presence of those in pain.[3] At this moment I am not concerned to explore the moral reason for that commitment, but only to note that in fact physicians, nurses, chaplains, and many others are present to the ill as none of the rest of us are. They are the bridge between the world of the ill and the healthy.

Certainly physicians are there because they have been trained with skills that enable them to alleviate the pain of the ill. They have learned from sick people how to help other sick people. Yet every physician soon learns of the terrible limit of his/her craft, for the sheer particularity of the patient's illness often defies the best knowledge and skill. Even more dramatically, physicians learn that using the best knowledge and skill they have on some patients sometimes has terrible results.

Yet the fact that medicine through the agency of physicians does not and cannot always "cure" in no way qualifies the commitment of the physician. At least it does not do so if we remember that the physician's basic pledge is not to cure, but to care through being present to the one in pain. Yet it is not easy to carry out that commitment on a day-to-day, year-to-year basis. For none of us have the resources to see too much pain without the pain hardening us. Without such a hardening, something we sometimes call by the name of professional distance, we fear we will lose the ability to feel at all.

Yet the physician cannot help but be touched and, thus, tainted by the world of the sick. Through their willingness to be present to us in our most vulnerable moments they are forever scarred with our pain — a pain that we the healthy want to deny or at least keep at arm's length. They have seen a world we do not want to see until it is forced on us, and we will accept them into polite community only to the extent they keep that world hidden from us. But when we are driven into that world we want to be able to count on their skill scribes drugs for himself misusing his technical expertise? At what point does a professional's duty to laymen override his duties to his fellow professionals? At what point does professional courtesy become professional whitewash? Is there a duty to a profession, as distinct from a duty to those individuals who practice the profession and those who benefit from its practice? These problems tend to concern the layman more than the experts in moral philosophy. Professional moralists tend to apply their analytical skills to issues they find intellectually interesting. They tend to solve moral puzzles rather than outline the foundations for professional character. They have produced in recent years elegant work on abortion, euthanasia, organ transplants, scarce medical resources and other subjects tantalizing at a theoretical level. The layman meanwhile is concerned with more prosaic questions. He wonders whether the doctor's real loyalty is to the patient or to the guild. Are medical societies, hospitals, and other health agencies ready and willing to weed out incompetent or unscrupulous practitioners? Will the profession find ways of challenging those doctors who order unwarranted surgery, charge fees that always press against the ceiling, play Ping Pong with referrals, process patients through their office with the speed of sales, or commit the sick to the hospital with indecorous haste?

Such blatantly unethical behavior (perhaps its self-evident wrongness explains why the professional moralist seldom attends to it) stirs the layman's anger. The profession seems to belong to an elite, utterly beyond the reach of his criticism. Certainly the physician is beyond serious challenge from the nurse and the social worker. His professional hegemony is well-nigh total over other health professionals. As long as doctors are in scarce supply and badly distributed, they are also beyond the reach of consumer criticism — except through the melodramatic, spotty, random, and sometimes, in its own right, unjust resort to the malpractice suit. For the same reason to date, they have not been seriously limited — except for the demands of paperwork — by outside agencies — the government, Blue Shield, and insurance companies. Under current conditions, the maintenance of professional standards of conduct depends largely on the doctor's own internal sense of professional obligation and on the willingness of the profession to enforce standards of conduct on its members.

This essay on the basis of professional ethics will therefore divide into two questions: why, despite the existence of medical codes and enforcement procedures, is the medical profession reluctant to engage in serious self-criticism? How are the concepts of code and covenant useful in interpreting professional duties and in establishing their obligatory power?

When the *New York Times* first carried its story on the Marcus brothers, it seemed a potentially scandalous reminder that the profession is loath to accept responsibility for professional discipline. The death of the gynecologists exposed both the ineffectualness of the well-intentioned New York Medical Society and the possible lack of zeal of the teaching hospital in protecting patients from two derelict professionals.

As it turned out, the case was not quite so pure an instance of *noblesse néglige* as it first appeared. The New York Hospital did write a letter terminating the services of the gynecologists. (Unfortunately for the reputation of the hospital and the profession, the termination date set in the letter preceded their death only by seventeen days, and, at a stage so far along the road of addiction that the body weight of these six footers at death was 115 and 100 pounds each.) Officials also made the point that the work of professionals is always monitored by colleagues in the hospital but they conceded that such controls would not apply to the Marcus brothers' private practice. In this as in other cases of solo practice, the patient — certainly the unsophisticated patient — is unprotected by the profession from its incompetent or unscrupulous members.

Whatever the final disposition of the Marcus brothers' case, a fundamental problem remains — and grows — that deserves the attention of moralists; that is, the tension in medical ethics between obligations to patients and obligations to one's fellow professionals. The tendency in the profession is to take the latter duties more seriously than the former. Professional ethics has traditionally had two social vectors: one concerned with behavior toward patients or clients; the other, with conduct toward one's colleagues. When concern for colleagues prevails, professional ethics reduces itself to courtesy within a guild. Certain arguable responsibilities to patients (such as informing them about incompetent treatment) are not simply eclipsed, they are professionally denied, that is, they are viewed as a breach of the discretionary bonds that pertain within the guild. Thus an inversion occurs. A report on incompetent or unethical behavior to patients becomes a breach in "professional ethics," that is, a breach in courtesy.

There are many reasons both material and ideological for the reluctance of doctors to engage in professional self-criticism and regulation. First, like any professional group, doctors find themselves in a complex, interlocking network of relations with fellow professionals: they extend favors, incur debts; exchange referrals; intertwine personal histories. The bond with fellow professionals grows, while ties with patients seem transient. Further, any society organized around certain ends tends to generate a sense of community among professional staff members serving those ends. This experience of collegiality becomes an end in its own right and subtly takes precedence over the needs of the population served. Hence criticism gets muted.

Second, professional self-regulation may be even more difficult to achieve in medicine because self-criticism seems somewhat more natural to lawyers and academicians whose work goes on in an adversarial or, at least, a disputatious setting. The doctor, however, has a special role in relation to his patients, quasi-priestly-parental, which seems more severely subverted by criticism. Trust is a very important ingredient in the relationship; criticism seems outside the boundaries of professional behavior.

Third, the doctor's authority, while great, is precarious. The analogy often drawn between the authority of the modern doctor and the traditional power of the parent and priest obscures an important difference between them in the security of their status. The modern doctor's position, while exalted, is inherently less stable. Apotheosized by many of his patients, he is resented bitterly if his hand slips publicly but once. The reason for this instability lies in differing sources of authority. Parents and priests in traditional society derived their authority from sacred powers perceived to be creative, nurturant, and beneficent. Given this positive derivation of power, human defect in the authority figure could be tolerated. The power of good would prevail despite human lapse. The modern doctor's authority, however, is reflexively derived from a grim negativity; that is, from the fear of death. This self-same power of death that exalts him and makes him the most highly paid, the most authoritative, professional in the modern world threatens to bring him low if through his own negligence, unscrupulousness or incompetence, he endangers the life of his patient. Thus while the modern physician enjoys much more prestige and authority than the contemporary teacher or lawyer, his position as a professional is, in one sense, more precarious than theirs. Resentment against him is potentially much greater. Professional self-criticism in academic life or in the law seems like child's play compared with medicine. The slothful teacher deprives me merely of the truth; the negligent lawyer forfeits my money, or, at worst, my freedom; but the incompetent doctor endangers my life. The stakes seem much higher in the case of medicine. The profession is tempted to draw its wagons around in a circle when any of its members are challenged.

Fourth, Americans of all walks of life have a morally healthy suspicion of officiousness. They are loath to press charges against their neighbors or colleagues. They are peculiarly sensitive to the injustice and hypocrisy of those who are zealous about the sliver in their neighbor's eye while unmindful of the beam in their own. Better, then, to comply with moral standards in one's own professional conduct, but, beyond that, to live and let live. It is difficult, after all, to tell the difference between an honest mistake and culpable negligence. Who can know enough about a particular medical case to second-guess the physician in charge? Is it not better to keep one's mouth shut? Must a person be his colleague's keeper?

This revulsion against officiousness deserves sympathy, but it fails to respect fully the special moral situation of the professional. Professionals are those who, on the basis of their special knowledge and competence, claim final right to pass judgment (in professional matters) on colleagues or would-be colleagues. The state board honors and supports this right when it establishes licensing procedures under the control of professionals and backs up these procedures by prosecuting imposters and pretenders. In effect, the state sanctions a monopoly (a limitation on the supply of professionals) from which, to be sure, patients profit, but also from which the professional profits — handsomely, financially. If the professional were in fact a free-lance entrepreneur (as the myth would have it) without the protection of the monopoly, he would not fare nearly so well.

Professional accountability therefore cannot be restricted to the question of one's own personal competence; it includes also the question of the competence of the guild. The right to pass judgment on colleagues carries with it the duty so to judge; otherwise doctors profit from a monopoly established by the state without enforcing those standards the need for which alone justified the monopoly. The license to practice is based on the prior license to license. If the license to practice carries with it the duty to practice well, the license to license carries with it the duty to judge and monitor well.

Ethical standards sag and falter when they are no longer accepted as universally binding. The usual test of whether an individual holds an ethical principle to be universally valid is whether he concedes its application not only to others but to himself. No one can make of himself an exception. The famous confrontation between King David and Nathan the prophet was devoted to that point. The king who makes judgments and enforces laws shall live by the law himself.

Today, however, in professional ethics, the test of moral seriousness may depend not simply upon personal compliance with ethical principles, but upon the courage to hold others accountable. Otherwise, the doctor's oath to his patients has yielded to the somewhat tarnished majesty of the guild.

A fifth and final cause for reserve in pressing for disciplinary action is neither exclusively modern nor American. It is prepared for in principle as far back as the Hippocratic Oath. The ancient oath made an important distinction between two sets of obligations: those that pertain to the doctor's treatment of his patients and those he accepts toward his teacher and his teacher's progeny. Obligations to one's fellow professionals flow from an original indebtedness of the student to his teacher; consequently, they acquire a gravity that makes them take procedure over obligations to patients.

To explore this distinction in obligations, we will need to press back into alternative ways of conceptualizing professional ethics and corresponding perceptions of its binding power. For this reason, in the second section of this essay, we will examine certain root terms for interpreting professional obligation, specifically the concepts of code, covenant, philanthropy, and contract. This investigation will take us beyond the somewhat narrower issue of professional discipline with which we began, but it remains a topic of which, in closing, we will need to return.

The Hippocratic Oath is a useful place to begin not only because of its prominence in medicine, but because it forces reflection on the distinction between code and covenant. The oath itself includes three elements: first, codal duties to patients; second, covenantal obligations to colleagues; and, third, the setting of both within the context of an oath to the gods, specifically, the gods of healing.

The duties of a physician toward his patients, as elaborated in the oath, include a series of absolute prohibitions (against performing surgery, assisting patients in attempts at suicide or abortion, breaches in confidentiality, and acts of injustice or mischief toward the patient and his household, including sexual misconduct); more positively, the physician must act always for the benefit of the sick (the chief illustration of which is to apply dietetic measures according to the physician's best judgment and ability), and, more generally, to keep them from harm and injustice.

The second set of obligations, directed to the physician's teacher, his teacher's children and his own, require him to accept full filial responsibilities for his adopted father's personal and financial welfare, and to transmit without fee his art and knowledge to the teacher's progeny, his own, and to other pupils, but only those others who take the oath according to medical law.

In his monograph on the Hippocratic Oath, Ludwig Edelstein characterizes those obligations that a physician undertakes toward his patients as an ethical code and those assumed toward the professional guide and its perpetuation as a covenant. Just why this difference in terminology is appropriate, Edelstein does not say. In my judgment, the chief reason for resorting to the word covenant in describing the second set of obligations is the fact of indebtedness. The doctor may have duties to his patients, but he owes something to his teacher. He is the beneficiary of goods and services received to which his filial services are responsive. This is one of the hallmarks of covenant. Both the Hammurabi Code and the Mosaic Law detail those statutes that will give shape to a civilization; in this respect, they are alike. But the biblical covenant differs in that it places the moral duties of the people within the all-important context of a divine act of deliverance: "I am the Lord thy God who brought thee out of the land of Egypt, the house of bondage." Thus the promises which the people of Israel make at Mt. Sinai to obey the statutes of God are responsive to goods already received. Analogously, in the Hippocratic Oath, the physician undertakes obligations to his teacher and his progeny out of gratitude for services already rendered. It will be one of the contentions of this essay that the development of the practice of modern medicine, for understandable reasons, has tended to reinforce this particular and ancient distinction between code and covenant and opted for code as the ruling ideal in relations to patients, but not with altogether favorable consequences for the moral health of the profession.

The Hippocratic Oath, of course, includes a third element: the vow or religious oath proper, directed to the gods. "I swear by Apollo, the physician, and Aesculapius and health and all-heal and all the Gods and Goddesses that, according to my ability and judgment, I will keep this oath and stipulation." A religious reference appears again in the statement of duties to patients: "In purity and holiness I will guard my life and art"; and the promise-maker finally petitions: "If I fulfill this oath and do not violate it, may it be granted to me to enjoy life and art . . . ; if I transgress it and swear falsely, may the opposite of all this be my lot."

This religious oath, in the literal sense, makes a "professional" out of the man who takes it. He professes or testifies thereby to the power of healing of which his duties to patients and his obligations to his teacher are a specification. Swearing by Apollo and Aesculapius is at the ontological root of his own state of his life. He professes those powers by which his own state of being is altered. Henceforth he is a professional, a professor of healing.

It is an intriguing, but not quite resolvable, question as to whether this oath is an ingredient of a covenant or simply a part of the full meaning of a code. In some respects, it is like a covenant. The physician makes a promise which has a reference to the gods from whom the profession of healing is ultimately derived. This religious promise becomes then the basis for that secondary promise or covenant which the physician makes to care for his teacher and for those duties which he undertakes toward his patients. His promise by the gods gives gravity and shape to the whole. Yet in two important respects the oath itself differs from a biblical covenant: it offers no prefatory statement about the actions of the divine to which the human promise is responsive; and, second, its form is such as to deemphasize the responsive nature of the physician's action, for he swears *by* the gods instead of promises *to* the gods to undertake his professional duties.

Similarly, the question can be raised as to whether this religious vow should be interpreted as part of the full meaning of a code, but, to argue this case, the concept of code needs to be expanded to include more than it means currently in the medical profession.

The word "code" in current professional ethics usually has two meanings — depending on the way in which professional duties are mediated. It can refer alternatively to those *unwritten* and habitual modes of behavior that are transmitted chiefly in a clinical setting from generation to generation of physicians or those *written* codes, beginning with the Hippocratic Oath and concluding with the various AMA codes that have had wide currency in this country. Technical proficiency is the prized ideal in the informal codes of behavior passed on from doctor to doctor; the ideal of philanthropy (that is, the notion of gratuitous service to humankind) looms larger in the more official, engraved tablets of the profession.

Code, however, covers a third form of activity — above and beyond habitual modes of behavior and collections of written statutes — it refers also to special languages, coded messages, and solemn oaths within special groups. It is this third aspect of code which may be most illuminating; for it implies a special initiation, a profession of allegiance, the possession of a key, and a mutual understanding available only to those who have undergone an alteration in their being which privileges them to use the codebook, the vocabulary, and the technical proficiency.

This third dimension of code prompted us to suggest that the religious vow in the Hippocratic Oath might be interpreted in codal as well as covenantal terms. The professional not only enters into a relationship with a patient, a colleague, or a guild, but also makes a *profession* in and through which his being is altered. He recognizes that his subsequent life for good or ill is derived from this profession. Whenever the medical guild fails to recognize this third aspect of code, it reduces itself to the ideal of technical proficiency alone or it tries to elevate itself to the compensatory and ultimately pretentious concept of philanthropy.

The Current Codal Ideal of Technical Proficiency

Both the ideal of technical proficiency and the skills that go with it are transmitted largely in a clinical setting. A code operating in this milieu shapes human behavior in a fashion somewhat similar to habits and rules. A habit, as Peter Winch has pointed out,[1] is a matter of doing the same thing on the same kind of occasion in the same way. A moral rule is distinct from a habit in that the agent in this instance *understands what is meant* by doing the same thing on the same kind of occasion in the same way. Both habits and rules are categorical, universal, and to this degree historical, in that they do not receive their authority from particular events by which they are authorized or legitimated. They remain operative categorically on all similar occasions. *Never* assist patients in attempts at suicide or abortion, or *never* break a confidence except under certain specified circumstances.

A code is usually categorical and universal in the aforementioned senses but not in the sense that it is binding on any and all groups. Hammurabi's code is obligatory only for particular peoples. Moreover, inner circles within certain societies — whether professional or social groups — develop their special codes of behavior. We think of code words or special codes of behavior among friends, workers in the same company, or professionals within a guild. These codes offer directives not only for the content of action, but also for its form. In its concern with appropriate form, a code, partly understood, moves in the direction of the aesthetic. It becomes less concerned with what is done or why it is done than with how it is done; so reduced, a code becomes preoccupied with matters of style and decorum. Thus medical codes include directives not only on the content of therapeutic action, but also on the fitting style for professional behavior including such matters as dress, discretion in the household, fitting behavior in the hospital, and prohibitions on self-advertisement.

Insofar as a code becomes more exclusively concerned with style, image, and decorum, it runs the danger of detaching itself from its ontological root. Style functions to protect the stylist from the assaults of life (and death) and to preserve him also from any alterations in his own being. This tendency to move ethics in the direction of aesthetics, rather than ontology, is conveniently illustrated in the work of the modern novelist who is most associated with the aesthetic ideal of a code — Ernest Hemingway. The ritual killing of a bull in the short stories and novels of Hemingway offers a paradigm for the professional; the bullfighter symbolizes an ethic in which stylist performance becomes everything: ". . . the bull charged and Villalta charged and just for a moment they became one. Villalta became one with the bull and then it was over" (*In Our Time,* Hemingway). For the Hemingway hero, there is no question of permanent commitments to particular persons, causes, or places. Robert Jordan of *For Whom the Bell Tolls* does not even remember the "cause," "power," or "profession" for which he came to Spain to fight. Once he is absorbed in the ordeal of war, the test of a man is not a cause to which he is committed but his conduct from moment to moment. Life is a matter of eating, drinking, loving, hunting, and dying well; Jordan can no longer "profess" a cause or sustain a long-term commitment; just like Catherine in *A Farewell to Arms,* he must die. Hemingway writes about lovers, briefly joined, but rarely about marriage or the family. Just for a moment, lovers become one and then it is over.

The bullfighter, the wartime lover, the doctor — all alike — must live by a code that eschews involvement; for each there comes a time when the thing is over; matters are terminated by death. At best, one can hope to escape from the pain of time; thus the aesthetic aspires to the timeless. Men must learn to live beautifully, stylishly, fittingly. Discipline is all, according to the aesthetic code. There is a right and a wrong way to do things. And the wrong way usually results from a deficiency in technique or from an excessive preoccupation with one's ego. The bad bullfighter either lacks technique or he lets his ego — through fear or vanity — get in the way of his performance. The conditions of beauty are technical proficiency and a style wholly purified of disruptive preoccupation with oneself. Literally, however, when the critical moment is consummated, it is over, it cannot shape the future. Partners must fall away; only the code remains.

For several reasons, the medical profession has been attracted to the aesthetic ideal of code for its interpretation of its ethics. First, such a code requires one to subordinate the ego to the more technical question of how a thing is done and done well. At its best, the discipline of a code cultivates the aesthetic. It encourages a proficiency that is quietly eloquent. It conjoins the good with the beautiful. Since the technical demands of medicine have become so great, the standards of the guild are largely transmitted by apprenticeship to those whose preeminent skills define the real meaning of the profession. All the rest is a question of disciplining the ego to the point that nervousness, fatigue, faintheartedness, and temptations to self-display (including gross efforts at self-advertisement) have been smoothed away.

A code is additionally attractive in that it does not in and of itself, encourage personal involvement with the patient; and it helps free the physician of the destructive consequences of that personal involvement. Compassion, in the strictest sense of the term, "suffering with," has its disadvantages in the professional relationship. It will not do to pretend that one is the second person of the Trinity, prepared with every patient to make the sympathetic descent into his suffering, pain, particular form of crucifixion, and hell. It is enough to offer whatever help one can through finely honed services. It is important to remain emotionally free so as to be able to withdraw the self when those services are no longer pertinent, when, as Hemingway says, "it is over." Such is the attraction of the codal ideal of technical proficiency.

The Ideal of a Covenant

A covenant, as opposed to a code, has its roots in specific historical events. Like a code, it may give inclusive shape to behavior, but it always has reference to a specific historical exchange between partners leading to a promissory event. Edelstein was quite right in distinguishing code from covenant in the Hippocratic Oath. Rules governing behavior toward patients have a different ring to them from the fealty which a physician owes to his teacher. Loyalty to one's instructor is founded in a specific historical event — that original transaction in which the student received his knowledge and art. He receives, in effect, a specific gift from his teacher which deserves his life-long loyalty, a gift that he perpetuates in his own right and turn, as he offers his art without fee to his teacher's children and his own progeny. Covenant ethics is responsive in character.

In its ancient and most influential form, a covenant usually included the following elements: first, an original experience of gift between the soon-to-be covenanted partners; and, second, a covenant promise based on this original or anticipated exchange of gifts, labors, or services. However, these temporal and contractual elements of a covenant were but two aspects of a tripartite concept: a covenant included not only an involvement with a partner in time, and a responsive contract, but the notion of a change of being; a covenanted people is a people changed utterly by the covenant. This third aspect of covenant is, like the third aspect of the concept code, ontological in nature. The aesthetic code attempts to remove style from time; a contract has a limited duration in time, but a covenant imposes a change on all moments. A mechanic can act under a contract, and then, when not fixing the piston, act without regard to the contract, but a covenanted people is covenanted while eating, sleeping, working, praying, stealing, cheating, healing, or blundering. Paul remarks, in effect, "When you eat, eat to the glory of God, and when you fast, fast to the glory of God, and when you marry, marry to the glory of God, and when you abstain, abstain to the glory of God."[2] When the professional is initiated, he is covenanted, and the physician is a healer when he is healing, and when he is sleeping, when he is practicing, and when he is malpracticing. A covenant changes the shape of the whole life of the covenanted. It changes the totality of the subsequent life of the covenanted in two ways: first, it contains very specific contractual obligations; the law of Moses, and the Talmudic code based on this law, changed the life of the covenanted by specifying not only the way in which God was to be worshipped, but in their methods of stewing kids; a physician contracts not only to do no harm, but specifically to educate free of charge other professionals' kids. However, the covenant changes are not restricted to the codified and specified changes. It alters the covenanted pervasively in his being; at the beginning of the oath, the physician seals himself, and his whole life, to the gods through his profession. This second change is ontological.

The scriptures of ancient Israel are littered with such covenants between men and controlled throughout by that singular covenant which embraces all others. The covenant between God and Israel included the aforementioned elements: (1) a gift (the deliverance of the people from Egypt); (2) an exchange of promises (at Mt. Sinai); and (3) the shaping of all subsequent life by the promissory event. God "marks the forehead" of the Jews forever, as they respond by accepting an inclusive set of ritual and moral commandments by which they will live. These commands are both specific enough to make the future duties of Israel concrete (e.g., love the Lord thy God with all thy heart . . .) so as to require a fidelity that exceeds any specification.[3]

For some of the reasons already mentioned, the bond of covenant, in the classical period, tended to define and bind together medical colleagues to one another, but it did not figure large in interpreting the relations between the doctor and his patients. The doctor receives his professional life from his teacher; this gift establishes a bond between them and prompts him to assume certain life-long duties not only toward the teacher (and his financial welfare), but toward his children. This symbolic bond with one's teacher acknowledged in the Hippocratic Oath is strengthened in modern professional life by all those exchanges between colleagues to which reference was made in the opening section of this essay — referrals, favors, personal confidences, and collaborative work on cases. Thus loyalty to colleagues is a responsive act for gifts already, and to be, received.

Duties to patients are not similarly interpreted in the medical codes as a responsive act for gifts or services rendered. This is the essential feature of covenant conspicuously missing in the interpretation of professional duties to patients from the Hippocratic Oath to the modern codes of the AMA. Compensatorily, the profession has tended to elaborate the codal ideal of philanthropy.

Philanthropy versus Covenantal Indebtedness

The medical profession includes in its written codes an ideal that Hemingway never shared and that seldom looms large in the ethic of any self-selected inner group — the ideal of philanthropy. The medical profession proclaims its dedication to the service of mankind. This ideal is implicitly at work in the Hippocratic Oath and the culture out of which it emerged;[4] it continues in the Code of Medical Ethics originally adopted by the American Medical Association at its national convention in 1847 and it is elaborated in contemporary statements of that code.

This ideal of service, in my judgment, succumbs to what might be called the conceit of philanthropy when it is assumed that the professional's commitment to his fellow man is a gratuitous, rather than a responsive or reciprocal, act flowing from his altered state of being. Statements of medical ethics that obscure the doctor's prior indebtedness to the community are tainted with the odor of condescension. The point is obvious if one contrasts the way in which the code of 1847 interprets the obligations of patients and the public to the physician, as opposed to the obligations of the physician to the patient and the public. On this particular question, I see no fundamental change from 1847 to 1957.

Clearly the duties of the patient are founded on what he has received from the doctor:

> The members of the medical profession, upon whom is enjoined the performance of so many

> important and arduous duties, toward the community, and who are required to make so many sacrifices of comfort, ease, and health for the welfare of those who avail themselves of their services, certainly have a right to expect and require that their patients should entertain a just sense of the duties which they owe to their medical attendants. (Art. II, Sect. 1, "Obligations of Patients to Their Physicians," Code of Medical Ethics, American Medical Association, May 1847; Chicago: A.M.A. Press, 1897.)

In like manner, the section on the Obligations of the Public to Physicians (Art. II, Sect. 1) emphasizes those many gifts and services which the public has received from the medical profession and which are the basis for its indebtedness to the profession.

> The benefits accruing to the public, directly and indirectly, from the active and unwearied beneficiaries of the profession, are so numerous and important that physicians are justly entitled to the utmost consideration and respect from the community.

But turning to the preamble for the physician's duties to the patient and the public, we find no corresponding section in the code of 1847 (or 1957) which founds the doctor's obligations on those gifts and services which he has received from the community. Thus we are presented with the picture of a relatively self-sufficient monad, who, out of the nobility and generosity of his disposition and the gratuitously accepted conscience of his profession, has taken upon himself the noble life of service. The false posture in all this blurts out in one of the opening sections of the 1847 code. Physicians "should study, also, in their deportment so as to unite tenderness with firmness, and condescension with authority, so as to inspire the minds of their patients with gratitude, respect and confidence."

I do not intend to demean the specific content of those duties which the codes set forth in their statement of the duties of physicians to their patients, but I am critical of the setting of context in which they are placed. Significantly the code refers to the *Duties* of Physicians to their Patients but to the *Obligations* of Patients to their Physicians. The shift from "Duties" to "Obligations" may seem slight, but, in fact, I believe it is a revealing adjustment in language. The AMA thought of the patient and the public as *indebted* to the profession for its services but the profession has accepted its *duties* to the patient and public out of noble conscience rather than a reciprocal sense of indebtedness.

Put another way, the medical profession imitates God not so much because it exercises power of life and death over others, but because it does not really think itself beholden, even partially, to anyone for those duties to patients which it lays upon itself. Like God, the profession draws its life from itself alone. Its action is wholly gratuitous.

Now, in fact, the physician is in very considerable debt to the community. The first of these debts is already adumbrated in the original Hippocratic Oath. He is obliged to someone or some group for his education. In ancient times, this led to a special sense of covenant obligation to one's teacher. Under the conditions of modern medical education, this indebtedness is both substantial (far exceeding the social investment in the training of any other professional) and widely distributed (including not only one's teachers but those public monies on the basis of which the medical school, the teaching hospital, and research into disease, are funded).

In view of the fact that many more qualified candidates apply for medical school than can be admitted and many more doctors are needed than the schools can train, the doctor-to-be has a second order of indebtedness for privileges that have almost arbitrarily fallen his way. While the 1847 code refers to the "privileges" of being a doctor it does not specify the social origins of those privileges. Third, and not surprisingly, the codes do not make reference to that extraordinary social largesse that befalls the physician, in payment for services, in a society where need abounds and available personnel is limited. Further, the codes to not concede the indebtedness of the physician to those patients who have offered themselves as subjects for experimentation or as teaching material (either in teaching hospitals or in the early years of practice). Early practice includes, after all, the element of increased risk for patients who lay their bodies on the line as the doctor "practices" on them. The pun in the word but reflects the inevitable social price of training. This indebtedness to the patient was most recently and eloquently acknowledged by Judah Folkman, M.D., of Harvard Medical School in a Class Day Address.

> In the long run, it is better if we come to terms with the uncertainty of medical practice. Once we recognize that all our efforts to relieve suffering might on occasion cause suffering, we are in a position to learn from our mistakes and appreciate the debt we owe our patients for our education. It is a debt which we must repay — it is like tithing.
>
> I doubt that the debt we accumulate can be repaid our patients by trying to reduce the practice of medicine to a forty-hour week or by dissolving the quality of our residency program just because certain groups of residents in the country have refused, through legal tactics, to be on duty more than every fourth or fifth night or any nights at all.
>
> And, it can't be paid by refusing to see Medicaid patients when the state can't afford to pay for them temporarily.
>
> But we can repay the debt in many ways. We can attend postgraduate courses and seminars, be available to patients at all hours, teach, take recertification examinations; maybe in the future even volunteer for national service; or, most difficult of all, carry out investigation or research.[5]

The physician finally is indebted to his patients not only for a start in his career. He remains unceasingly in their debt in its full course. This continuing reciprocity of need is somewhat obscured for we think of the mature professional as powerful and authoritative rather than needy. He seems to be a self-sufficient virtuoso whose life is derived from his competence while others appear before him in their neediness, exposing their illness, their crimes, or their ignorance, for which the professional, as doctor, lawyer, or teacher, offers remedy.

In fact, however, a reciprocity of giving and receiving is at work in the professional relationship that needs to be acknowledged. In the profession of teaching, for example, the student needs the teacher to assist him in learning, but so also the professor needs his students. They provide him with regular occasion and forum in which to work out what he has to say and to rediscover his subject afresh through the discipline of sharing it with others. Likewise, the doctor needs his patients. No one can watch a physician nervously approach retirement without realizing how much he has needed his patients to be himself.

A covenantal ethics helps acknowledge this full context of need and indebtedness in which professional duties are undertaken and discharged. It also relieves the professional of the temptation and pressure to pretend that he is a demigod exempt from human exigency.

Contract or Covenant

While criticizing the ideal of philanthropy, I have emphasized the elements of exchange, agreement, and reciprocity that mark the professional relationship. This leaves us with the question as to whether the element of the gratuitous should be suppressed altogether in professional ethics. Does the physician merely respond to the social investment in his training, the fees paid for his services, and the terms of an agreement drawn up between himself and his patients, or does some element of the gratuitous remain?

To put this question another way: is covenant simply another name for a contract in which two parties calculate their own best interests and agree upon some joint project in which both derive roughly equivalent benefits for goods contributed by each? If so, this essay would appear to move in the direction of those who would interpret the doctor-patient relationship as a legal agreement and who want, on the whole, to see medical ethics draw closer to medical law.

The notion of the physician as contractor has certain obvious attractions. First, it represents a deliberate break with more authoritarian models (such as priest or parent) for interpreting the role. At the heart of a contract is informed consent rather than blind trust; a contractual understanding of the therapeutic relationship encourages full respect for the dignity of the patient, who has not, because of illness, forfeited his sovereignty as a human being. The notion of a contract includes an exchange of information on the basis of which an agreement is reached and a subsequent exchange of goods (money for services); it also allows for a specification of rights, duties, conditions, and qualifications limiting the agreement. The net effect is to establish some symmetry and mutuality in the relationship between the doctor and patient.

Second, a contract provides for the legal enforcement of its terms — on both parties — and thus offers both parties some protection and recourse under the law for making the other accountable for the agreement.

Finally, a contract does not rely on the pose of philanthropy, the condescension of charity. It presupposes that people are primarily governed by self-interest. When two people enter into a contract, they do so because each sees it to his own advantage. This is true not only of private contracts but also of that primordial social contract in and through which the state came into being. So argued the theorists of the eighteenth century. The state was not established by some heroic act of sacrifice on the part of the gods or men. Rather men entered into the social contract because each found it to his individual advantage. It is better to surrender some liberty and property to the state than to suffer the evils that would beset men apart from its protection. Subsequent enthusiasts about the social instrumentality of contracts[6] have tended to measure human progress by the degree to which a society is based on contracts rather than status. In the ancient world, the Romans made the most striking advances in extending the areas in which contract rather than custom determined commerce between people. In the modern world, the bourgeoisie extended the instrumentality of contracts farthest into the sphere of economics; the free churches, into the arena of religion. Some educationists today have extended the device into the classroom (as students are encouraged to contract units of work for levels of grade); more recently some women's liberationists would extend it into marriage; and still others would prefer to see it define the professional relationship. The movement, on the whole, has the intention of laicizing authority, legalizing relationships, activating self-interest, and encouraging collaboration.

In my judgment, some of these aims of the contractualists are desirable, but it would be unfortunate if professional ethics were reduced to a commercial contract. First, the notion of contract suppresses the element of gift in human relationships. Earlier I verged on denying the importance of this ingredient in professional relations, when I criticized the medical profession for its conceit of philanthropy, for its self-interpretation of the great giver. In fact, this earlier criticism was not an objection to the notion of gift but to the moral pretension of a profession whenever it pretends to be the exclusive giver. Factually, the professional is also the beneficiary of gifts received. It is unbecoming to adopt the pose of spontaneous generosity when the profession has received so much from the community and from patients, past and present.

But the contractualist approach to professional behavior falls into the opposite error of minimalism. It reduces everything to tit for tat. Do no more for your patients than what the contract calls for. Perform specified services for certain fees and no more. The commercial contract is a fitting instrument in the purchase of an appliance, a house, or certain services that can be specified fully in advance of delivery. The existence of a legally enforceable agreement in professional transactions may also be useful to protect the patient or client against the physician or lawyer whose services fall below a minimal standard. But it would be wrong to reduce professional obligation to the specifics of a contract alone.

Professional services in the so-called helping professions are directed to subjects whose needs are in the nature of the case rather unpredictable. The professional deals with the sickness, ills, crimes, needs, and tragedies of humankind. These needs cannot be exhaustively specified in advance for each patient or client. The professions therefore must be ready to cope with the contingent, the unexpected. Calls upon services may be required that exceed those anticipated in a contract or for which compensation may be available in a given case. These services moreover are more likely to be effective in achieving the desired therapeutic result if they are delivered in the context of a fiduciary relationship that the patient or client can really trust.

Contract and covenant, materially considered, seem like first cousins; they both include an exchange and an agreement between parties. But, in spirit, contract and covenant are quite different. Contracts are external; covenants are internal to the parties involved. Contracts are signed to be expediently discharged. Covenants have a gratuitous, growing edge to them that spring from ontological change and are directed to the upbuilding of relationships.

There is a donative element in the upbuilding of covenant — whether it is the covenant of marriage, friendship, or professional relationship. Tit for tat characterizes a commercial transaction, but it does not exhaustively define the vitality of that relationship in which one must serve and draw upon the deeper reserves of another.

This donative element is important not only in the doctor's care of the patient but in other aspects of health care. In a fascinating study of *The Gift Relationship*, the late economist Richard M. Titmuss compares the British system of obtaining blood by donations with the American partial reliance on the commercial purchase and sale of blood. The British system obtains more and better blood, without the exploitation of the indigent, which the American system has condoned and which our courts have encouraged when they refused to exempt non-profit blood banks from the antitrust laws. By court definition, blood exchange becomes a commercial transaction in the United States. Titmuss expanded his theme from human blood to social policy by offering a sober criticism of the increased commercialism of American medicine and society at large. Recent court decisions have tended to shift more and more of what had previously been considered as services into the category of commodity transactions with negative consequences, he believes, for the health of health delivery systems.[7] Hans Jonas has had to reckon with the importance of voluntary sacrifice to the social order in a somewhat comparable essay on "Human Experimentation."[8] Others have done so on the subject of organ transplants.

The kind of minimalism that a contractualist understanding of the professional relationship encourages produces a professional too grudging, too calculating, too lacking in spontaneity, too quickly exhausted to go the second mile with his patients along the road of their distress.

Contract medicine encourages not only minimalism, it also provokes a peculiar kind of maximalism, the name for which is "defensive medicine." Especially under the pressure of malpractice suits, doctors are tempted to order too many examinations and procedures for self-protection. Paradoxically, contractualism simultaneously tempts the doctor to do too little and too much for the patient — too little in that one extends oneself only to the limits of what is specified in the contract, yet, at the same time, too much in that one orders procedures useful in protecting oneself as the contractor even though not fully indicated by the condition of the patient. The link between these apparently contradictory strategies of too little and too much is the emphasis in contractual decisions on self-interest.

Three concluding objections to contractualism can be stated summarily. Parties to a contract are better able to protect their self-interest to the degree that they are informed about the goods bought and sold. Insofar as contract medicine encourages increased knowledge on the part of the patient, well and good. Nevertheless the physician's knowledge so exceeds that of his patient that the patient's knowledgeability alone is not a satisfactory constraint on the physician's behavior. One must at least, in part, depend upon some internal fiduciary checks which the professional (and his guild) accept.

Another self-regulating mechanism in the traditional contractual relationship is the consumer's freedom to shop and choose among various vendors of services. Certainly this freedom of choice needs to be expanded for the patient by an increase in the number of physicians and paramedical personnel. However, the crisis circumstances under which medical services are often needed and delivered does not always provide the consumer with the kind of leisure or calm required for discretionary judgment. Thus normal marketplace controls cannot be relied upon fully to protect the consumer in dealings with the physician.

For a final reason, medical ethics should not be reduced to the contractual relationship alone. Normally conceived, ethics establishes certain rights and duties that transcend the particulars of a given agreement. The justice of any specific contract may then be measured by these standards. If, however, such rights and duties adhere only to the contract, then a patient might legitimately be persuaded to waive his rights. The contract would solely determine what is required and permissible. An ethical principle should not be waivable (except to give way to a higher ethical principle). Professional ethics should not be so defined as to permit a physician to persuade a patient to waive rights that transcend the particulars of their agreement.

The donative mode seems to provide for a more satisfactory analysis than the philanthropic or the contractual, but it shares their flaws. Analysis based on donative elements suggests that the professional fulfills his contract, lives up to his specified technical code, and then, gratuitously, throws in something extra to sweeten the pot. All of these modes allow the professional to evade the uncomfortable and demanding ontological implications of Initiatory Code, Covenant as Chosen, and Profession as Transformation. The ontological changes implied in Secret Code, Covenanted People, and Profession of a mystery are complete changes in substance which affect the total life of the professional. A carpenter who contracts to build a chair, when he eats an ice cream cone, does not eat it as a carpenter, nor, when he gets his union card, does he imply that his initiation has changed him utterly, relating him, before everything else, to the mystery of chair making or shellac. A profession of a mystery, in theological terms changes one from damned to saved; in professional terms, from a man who studies medicine, to a man who at all times embodies healing. Malpractice, then, is rather like the sin against the Holy Ghost, uncomfortable for those sinned against, but utterly negating the identity of the sinner. A professional eats to heal, drives to heal, reads to heal, comforts to heal, rebukes to heal, and rests to heal. The transformation is radical, and total. The Hippocratic Oath, under this ontological aspect, can be summarized: *aut medicus aut nihil;* from this moment, I am a healer or I am (literally) nothing. He takes his identity from that which he professes, and that which he professes, to which he is covenanted, whose code he will embody, transcends him and transcends his colleagues.

Transcendence and Covenant

Two characteristics of covenantal ethics have been developed in the course of contrasting it with the ideal of philanthropy and the legal instrument of contracts. As opposed to the ideal of philanthropy that pretends to wholly gratuitous altruism, covenantal ethics places the service of the professional within the full context of goods, gifts, and services received; thus covenantal ethics is responsive. As opposed to the instrument of contract that presupposes agreement reached on the basis of self-interest, covenantal ethics may require one to be available to the covenant partner above and beyond the measure of self-interest; thus covenantal ethics has an element of the gratuitous in it.

We have to reckon now with the potential conflict between these characteristics. Have we developed our notion of covenant too reactively to alternatives without paying attention to the inner consistency of the concept itself? On the one hand, we had cause for suspecting those idealists who founded professional duties on a philanthropic impulse, without so much as acknowledging the sacrifice of others by which their own lives have been nourished. Then we have reasons for drawing back from those legal realists and positivists who would circumscribe professional life entirely within the calculus of commodities bought and sold. But now, brought face to face, these characteristics conflict. Response to debt and gratuitous service seem opposed principles of action.

Perhaps our difficulty results from the fact that we have abstracted the concept of covenant from its original context within the transcendent. The indebtedness of a human being that makes his life — however sacrificial — inescapably responsive cannot be fully appreciated by totaling up the varying sacrifices and investments made by others in his favor. Such sacrifices are there; and it is lacking in honesty not to acknowledge them. But the sense that one is inexhaustively the object of gift presupposes a more transcendent source of donative activity than the sum of gifts received from others. For the biblical tradition this transcendent was the secret root of every gift between human beings, of which the human order of giving and receiving could only be a sign. Thus the Jewish scriptures enjoin the covenanted people: when you harvest your crops, do not pick your fields too clean. Leave something for the sojourner, for you were once sojourners in Egypt. Farmers obedient to this injunction were responsive, but not simply mathematically responsive to gifts received from the Egyptians or from strangers now drifting through their own land. At the same time, their actions could not be construed as wholly gratuitous. Their ethic of service to the needy flowed from Israel's original and continuing state of neediness and indebtedness before God. Thus action which, at a human level, appears gratuitous, in that it is not provoked by a specific gratuity from another human being, at its deepest level is but gift answering to gift. This responsivity is theologically expressed in the New Testament as follows: "In this is love, not that we loved God, but that He loved us . . . if God so loves us, we also ought to love one another" (1 John 4:10-11). In some such way, covenant ethics shies back from the idealist assumption that professional action is and ought to be wholly gratuitous and from the contractualist assumption that it be carefully governed by quotidian self-interest in every exchange.

A transcendent reference may also be important in laying out not only the proper context in which human service takes place but also the specific standards by which it is measured. Earlier we noted some dangers in reducing rights and duties to the terms of a particular contract. We observed the need for a transcendent norm by which contracts are measured (and limited). By the same token, rights and duties cannot be wholly derived form the particulars of a given covenant. What limits ought to be placed on the demands of an excessively dependent patient? At what point does the keeping of one covenant do an injustice to obligations entailed in others? These are questions that warn against a covenantal ethics that sentimentalizes any and all involvements, without reference to a transcendent by which they are both justified and measured.

Further Reflections on Covenant

So far we have discussed those features of a covenant that affect the doctor's conduct toward his patient. The concept of covenant has further consequences for the patient's understanding of his role as patient, for the accountability of health institutions, for the placement of institutional priorities within other national commitments, and, finally, for such collateral problems as truth-telling.

Every model for the doctor-patient relationship establishes not only a certain image of the doctor, but also a specific concept of the patient. The image of the doctor as priest or parent encourages dependency in the patient. The image of the doctor as skillful technician encourages the patient to think of himself as passive host to a disease. The doctor and his technical procedures are the only serious agent in the relationship. The image of the doctor as covenanter or contractor bids the patient to become a more active participant both in the prevention and the healing of disease. He must bring a will-to-live and a will-to-health to the partnership.

Differing views of disease are involved in these differing patterns of relationship to the doctor. Disease today is usually interpreted by the layman as an extraordinary state, discrete and episodic, disjunctive from the ordinary condition of health. Illness is a special time when the doctor is in charge and the layman renounces authority over his life. This view, while psychologically understandable, ignores the build-up, during apparent periods of health, of those pathological conditions that invite the dramatic breakdown when the doctor "takes over."

The cardiovascular accident is a case in point. Horacio Fabrega[9] has urged an interpretation of disease and health that respects more fully the processive rather than the episodic character of both disease and health. This interpretation, I assume, would encourage the doctor to monitor more continuously health and disease than ordinarily occurs today, to share with the patient more fully the information so obtained, and to engage the layperson in a more active collaboration with the doctor in health maintenance.

The concept of covenant has two further advantages for defining the professional relationship, not enjoyed by models such as parent, friend, or technician. First, covenant is not so restrictively personal a term as parent or friend. It reminds the professional community that it is not good enough for the individual doctor to be a good friend or parent to the patient, it is important also that whole institutions — the hospital, the clinic, the professional group — keep covenant with those who seek their assistance and sanctuary. Thus the concept permits a certain broadening of accountability beyond personal agency.

At the same time, however, the notion of covenant also permits one to set professional responsibility for this one human good (health) within social limits. The professional covenant concerning health should be situated within a larger set of covenant obligations that both the doctor and the patient have to other institutions and priorities within the society at large. The traditional models for the doctor-patient relationship (parent, friend) tend to establish an exclusivity of relationship that obscures these larger responsibilities. At a time when health needs command $120 billion out of the national budget, one must think about the place that the obligation to the limited human good of health has amongst a whole range of social and personal goods for which men are compacted together as a society.

Although a covenantal ethic has implications for other collateral problems in biomedical ethics, I will restrict myself simply to one final issue that has not been viewed from the perspective of covenant: the question of truth-telling.

Key ingredients in the notion of covenant are promise and fidelity to promise. The philosopher J. L. Austin drew the distinction, now famous, between two kinds of speech: descriptive and performative utterances. In ordinary declarative or descriptive sentences, one describes a given item within the world. (It is raining. The tumor is malignant. The crisis is past.) In performative utterances, one does not merely describe a world; in effect, one alters the world by introducing an ingredient that would not be there apart from the utterance. Promises are such performative utterances. (I, John, take Thee, Mary. We will defend your country in case of attack. I will not abandon you.) To make or to go back on a promise is a very solemn matter precisely because a promise is world-altering.

In the field of medical ethics, the question of truth-telling has tended to be disposed of entirely as a question of descriptive speech. Should the doctor, as technician, tell the patient he has a malignancy or not? If not, may he lie or must he merely withhold the truth?

The distinction between descriptive and performative speech expands the question of the truth-telling in professional life. The doctor, after all, not only tells descriptive truths, he also makes or implies promises. (I will not see you next Tuesday. Despite the fact that I cannot cure you, I will not abandon you.) In brief, the moral question for the doctor is not simply a question of telling truths, but of being true of his promises. Conversely, the total situation for the patient includes not only the disease he's got, but also whether others desert him or stand by him in his extremity. The fidelity of others will not eliminate the disease, but it affects mightily the human context in which the disease runs its course. What the doctor has to offer his patient is not simply proficiency but fidelity.

Perhaps more patients could accept the descriptive truth if they experience the performative truth. Perhaps also they would be more inclined to believe in the doctor's performative utterances if they were not handed false diagnoses or false promises. That is why a cautiously wise medieval physician once advised his colleagues: "Promise only fidelity!"

The Problem of Discipline Revisited

The conclusion of this essay is not that covenantal ethics should be preferred to the exclusion of some of those values best symbolized by code and contract. If we return to the problem of discipline with which we began, we can see that both alternatives have resources for professional self-criticism.

Those who live by a code of technical proficiency have a standard on the basis of which to discipline their peers. The Hemingway novel, especially *The Sun Also Rises* is quite clear about this. Those who live by a code know how to ostracize deficient peers. Indeed, any "in-group," professional or otherwise, can be quite ruthless about sorting out those who are "quality" and those who do not have the "goods." Medicine is no exception. Ostracism, in the form of discretely refusing to refer patients to a doctor whose competence is suspected, is probably the commonest and most effective form of discipline in the profession today.

Defendents of an ethic based on code might argue further that deficiencies in enforcement today result largely from too strongly developed a sense of covenantal obligations to colleagues and too weakly developed a sense of code. From this perspective, then, covenant is the source of the problem in the profession rather than the basis for its amendment. Covenantal obligations to colleagues inhibit the enforcement of code.

A code alone, however, will not in and of itself solve the problem of professional discipline. It provides only a basis for excluding from one's own inner circles an incompetent physician. But, as Eliot Freidson has pointed out in *Professional Dominance,* under the present system, the incompetent professional, when he is excluded from a given hospital, group practice, or informal circle of referrals, simply moves his practice and finds another circle of people of equal incompetence in which he can function. It will take a much stronger, more active, and internal sense of covenant obligation to patients on the part of the profession to enforce standards within the guild beyond local informal patterns of ostracism. In a mobile society with a scarcity of doctors, local ostracism simply hands on problem physicians to other patients elsewhere. It does not address them.

Code patterns of discipline not only fall short of adequate protection for the patient, they also fail to be collegially responsible to the troubled physician. To ostracize may be the lazy way of handling a colleague when the professional society fails altogether to make a first attempt at remedy and to address the physician himself in his difficulty.

At the same time, it would be unfortunate if the indispensable interest and pride of the medical profession in technical proficiency were allowed to lapse out of an expressed preference for a professional ethic based on covenant. Covenant fidelity to the patient remains unrealized if it does not include proficiency. A rather sentimental existentialism unfortunately assumes that it suffices morally for human beings to be "present" to one another. But in crisis the ill person needs not simply presence but skill, not just personal concern but highly disciplined services targeted on specific needs. Code behavior, handed down from doctor to doctor, is largely concerned with the transmission of technical skills. Covenant ethics, then, must include rather than exclude the interests of the codes.

Neither does this essay conclude with a preference for covenant to the total exclusion of the interests of enforceable contract. While the reduction of medical ethics to contract alone incurs the danger of minimalism, patients ought to have recourse against those physicians who fail to meet minimal standards. They ought not to be dependent entirely upon disciplinary measures undertaken within the profession. There ought to be appeal to the law in cases of malpractice and for breach of contract explicit or implied.

On the other hand, a legal appeal cannot be sustained in the case of an injustice without assistance and testimony from physicians who take their obligations to patients and their profession seriously. If, in such cases, fellow physicians simply gather around and protect their colleague like a wounded elephant, the patient with just cause is not likely to get far. Thus the instrument of contract and other avenues of legal redress can be sustained only by physicians who have a sense of obligation to the patient and the profession. Needless to say, it would be better for all concerned if professional discipline and continuing education were so vigorously pursued within the profession as to cut down drastically on the number of cases that needed to reach the courts.

The author inclines to accept covenant as the most inclusive and satisfying model for framing questions of professional obligation. Covenant fidelity includes the code duty to become technically proficient; it includes the obligation to meet the minimal terms of contract, but it also requires much more. Moreover, this surplus of obligation may be to the final advantage not only of patients but also of medical colleagues. The Marcus case, or, if not that one, others like it, suggest a failure in covenant responsibilities not only to patients but to troubled colleagues.[10]

Notes

1. *The Idea of Social Science and Its Relation to Philosophy* (New York: Humanities Press, 1985).

2. A paraphrase of Rom. 4:5-8 and 1 Cor. 10:31.

3. The most striking contemporary restatement of an ethic based on covenant is offered by Hemingway's great competitor and contemporary as a novelist — William Faulkner. See especially "Delta Autumn" and "The Bear" and *Intruder in the Dust.*

4. See P. Lain-Entralgo, *Doctor and Patient* (New York: McGraw-Hill, 1969), for his analysis of the classical fusion of *techne* with *philanthropia,* and how skill in

the art of healing combined with a love of mankind defines the good physician.

5. *New York Times,* Op. Ed. Page, June 6, 1975.

6. Sir Henry Sumner Maine, *Ancient Law* (London: Oxford University Press, 1931).

7. Titmuss does not acknowledge that physicians in the United States have helped prepare for this commercialization of medicine by their substantial fees for services (as opposed to salaried professors in the teaching field or salaried health professionals in other countries).

8. See "Philosophical Reflections on Experimenting with Human Subjects," pp. 903-16 below.

9. Horacio Fabrega, Jr., "Concepts of Disease: Logical Features and Social Implications," *Perspectives in Biology and Medicine,* Vol. 15, No. 4, Summer 1972.

10. This is a revised version of an article that first appeared in *The Hastings Center Report* 5 (December 1975): 29-38.

19 AIDS and the Professions of Healing: A Brief Inquiry

Stephen E. Lammers

Introduction

It is not controversial to claim that AIDS has presented the healing professions with a number of challenges, both technical and moral. In this essay I will speak about the particular challenges AIDS has presented to the healing professions, challenges which had as much to do with our societal circumstances as they had to do with the particulars of the disease itself in the late 1980s. What has not been widely celebrated is that there is a consensus within the medical and nursing professions that AIDS patients should be treated even though the patients can be a threat to the caretaker. What I hope to show is how fragile is that consensus, especially fragile because our current moral philosophy is not particularly helpful to us at this point.

This second point is not particularly controversial. Stephen Toulmin pointed up the difficulties of a certain type of philosophy in his essay, "How Medicine Saved the Life of Ethics."[1] In that article Toulmin argues that when philosophers began attending to modern medicine, they moved away from some debates that they had been having

---

This paper was originally prepared for a symposium at Hope College in 1988. I would like to thank the students and faculty at Hope. Their questions led me to correct some of my errors. The rest of them are my own.

and moved towards a more fruitful, in Toulmin's eyes, understanding of human beings, especially human beings in community. Toulmin argues that philosophers had to start attending to the real needs of human beings, instead of worrying about their feelings. In addition, they had to go beyond the discussion of principles to the analysis of cases; thirdly, they had to start thinking about the professional settings within which the particular tasks and duties of so many of us arise, and finally, there was some attention once again to concepts such as equity and reasonableness. Principles alone did not enable persons to talk about professional matters. What Toulmin does not report is that there was a cost of doing medical ethics that way and that much of the cost was borne by the medical professionals, who were being told by the philosophers, and sometimes the theologians, that they had to learn more ethics. Needless to say, this was a message that was not often received with a welcome by the healing professions.[2]

At the same time that they were being asked to learn the language of modern ethics, health professionals confronted AIDS. We ought to notice that those persons in the medical profession who are treating AIDS patients are "teaching," and this by example, lessons in ethics which most of us will be unwilling to learn, and in many cases, to honor. I will return to this later.

I. The Situation of Medicine Today

The healing professions have been under increasing pressure from the larger society. I am going to use the term "the healing professions," although it shall be clear shortly that I am going to focus upon medicine and not upon all of the healing professions. From time to time, I will notice how nursing, for example, might be similar or different from medicine, but nursing is not my main focus of attention. This has more to do with the limitations of time and space and not a lack of inherent interest in the topic.

One pressure comes from members of public interest groups and regulatory agencies who find the costs of health care to be exorbitant and who suggest that members of certain healing professions are greedy and that they are not careful with the public and private monies which they have been given for their work. In addition, there is a concern that medicine has become enamored of expensive technologies. One fairly recent consequence has been the introduction of DRG's, Diagnostic Related Groups, a way of categorizing hospital admissions and trying to give hospitals incentives to hold their costs down. Briefly, what this system does is to limit the amount of reimbursement a hospital can receive for a particular admission, depending upon the diagnosis. Hospitals are given a certain amount, for, say, a gall bladder case. If they can have the patient go home before they spend that money, the hospital can keep the difference. In such a payment plan, hospitals are no longer paid for each and every little thing that they do for and with the patient; they are paid by the case. There are proposals that physicians should receive reimbursement the same way. Obviously, this puts pressures upon hospitals and healers to perform more efficiently. It also should be clear that in their search for efficiency, healers might be tempted to display some biases, preferring younger patients to older ones, for example. These and other problems with DRG's could form the basis of another inquiry; for our purposes it is sufficient to note that the AIDS crisis came upon American medicine at a time when that medicine was under increasing scrutiny about the way in which medicine was practiced, especially the expense of modern medicine.[3]

This has not been the only pressure upon American medicine. At the same time that medicine was being criticized for being wasteful with the public's resources, other persons suggested that healers have been acting immorally, in that they have not permitted patients to exercise their wishes. The term used to describe this phenomenon is medical paternalism. What is argued is that healers assume that they know what is best for persons and they often ignore what patients want. In some forms, this argument asserts that modern medicine, which is often a medicine between strangers, assumed attitudes from the past, when medicine was practiced between friends. We do not have to determine whether such a golden age ever existed. All we know is that what is claimed is that physicians assumed that they knew what was best for their patients and often proceeded to act on what they thought they knew, instead of being guided by their patients. It is argued that this was immoral and should be stopped. Thus the effort to teach ethics to healers so that they will act appropriately.

There are good reasons why people might hold this latter point of view. After all, if the practice of medicine is understood primarily as the application of scientific knowledge, then the knowledge of science is not going to be of much help in resolving ethical questions. Indeed, according to some commentators, it is precisely the assumption that "doctor knows best" that causes many of our current problems in medical ethics. For what has been assumed, so say the critics, is a "generalization of expertise" which is unwarranted.[4]

Thus, healers were undergoing at least two different but not necessarily unrelated crises when AIDS came upon the scene. The first crisis had to do with health care costs and the second with the understanding of the profession. AIDS presented a number of problems, some of which are obvious and others which were not so obvious:

1. AIDS is a wasting disease. The body's immune system, compromised by the disease, cannot fight off ordinary infections. Thus persons with AIDS undergo often a long period where they decline through a number of hospitalizations. Thus far, medical science has been able to do little to reverse this course of events. Among the most devastating effects of AIDS is the diminishing of cognitive capacities in many AIDS patients. It is the case that many AIDS patients are "not themselves" from time to time while they are diseased and this presents difficult problems for physicians who are trying to determine what their wishes are. Further, AIDS is an expensive disease to treat. Often there are many hospitalizations.
2. Persons with AIDS die, and the persons dying are often in the prime of life. Dying is difficult enough to deal with for healers; we know that beginning medical students are more fearful of death than the general population. When the dying is happening to people who are not old, it is harder on those who care for them.
3. AIDS often occurs in persons who are already stigmatized, if not by one or another member of the healing professions, by some members of the society at large. Thus persons who are homosexual or IV drug users, the two groups thus far most ravaged by this disease in our society, are persons often at the margins of our culture. Here the healing professions sometimes reflect the attitudes of the larger society, in that they join in the stigmatization,[5] and sometimes reflect an older perspective which promised care to anyone, no matter how they contracted their disease. Note that in this case, there are two reasons for the stigmatizing to occur. First, the persons who have AIDS often are engaged in behaviors that many Americans find reprehensible, and second, the disease itself often marks the victim.
4. AIDS threatens the healer. There have been a small number of persons in healthcare who appear to have converted to seropositive status as a result of their occupational exposure to the virus and not as a result of other activities. That is, they show signs of having been exposed to the AIDS virus. The expectation is that they will go on to develop AIDS.

   While the statistical possibility of becoming seropositive is small, the danger to the healthcare worker is perceived by many to be large, precisely because most persons who are seropositive go on to develop AIDS. As a result of this perceived danger, some healers have refused to care for patients either who are seropositive or who in fact have AIDS.
5. But that is only the most dramatic threat. AIDS threatens the healer because of the age of the victim; the young residents who take care of most of the AIDS patients in many public hospitals are closer to AIDS patients in age than their elderly dying patients or the dying infants they may see on the neonatal intensive care wards. This has led to what one author referred to as "AIDS burnout," when the young house officer simply becomes overwhelmed by the psychological toll of the disease.[6] What seems to be especially difficult is to go on in the face of one's own fears and the sense of inevitability that so far is part of the reality of AIDS.
6. Healers are put in a very odd situation, in that they are asked by their own profession to treat persons when such treatment may harm not only the healer but the healer's family. AIDS is passed by contact with body fluids, primarily semen and blood, and if the healer becomes

seropositive, so might the spouse. Let me give an example here.

In one scenario, a pregnant nurse (obviously, it could have been a pregnant physician) was worrying about a recent admission to the ICU because of the nurse's fear that the AIDS patient would suffer a cardiac arrest and she could not find a mouthpiece to create an airway to begin resuscitation while awaiting the crash cart and the team of physicians. In fact the patient suffered the arrest and she gave mouth to mouth resuscitation while awaiting assistance. In this case, not only was the nurse threatened, but also her fetus.

7. When there was a refusal to treat, this refusal to treat has been met with public criticism by the professions of nursing and medicine, although they are not the only ones involved. It is argued that healers have an affirmative obligation to treat persons. There is some tension between this claim and the AMA's statement that physicians have a right to choose their own patients, but the more recent AMA statements have been leaning in the direction of claiming that physicians have a duty to treat that is primary and their freedom of choice is secondary.[7]

While we recognize that some healers continue to give care to AIDS victims, others refuse and they are criticized. This leads me to my central question. On what basis do we ask these men and women to provide this care?

II. Societal Context for the Discussion of Professional Obligations

If we were asked to justify requiring healers to assist the victims of AIDS, what might we say? Most of us, I suspect, would want to make arguments that would lead to the conclusion that physicians have an obligation to treat AIDS patients. We would want to do this because although we may not be at risk for AIDS, or at least we are under the illusion that we are not at risk, we still may become the victim of some disease which is threatening to the healer and would like medical treatment.

It would seem, at first glance, that there are reasons to be fearful that we might not be treated. I want to use the recent work of Robert Bellah and others to make this point.

In their work, *Habits of the Heart*, Bellah and his colleagues attempt first to describe and then to critique some of the assumptions of what they take to be the dominant culture of American society, especially the American middle class.[8] Since it is from that class that the vast majority of physicians come, it would seem fair to look to this work for some indication of what one might think is being thought by the typical physician.

Bellah wants to argue that we have four languages which we might use in America to explain ourselves to one another. The first is the language of biblical religion, the second of the republican tradition, which focused on the good of the state. The third is the language of utilitarian individualism and the fourth is that of expressive individualism. According to Bellah, the last two languages are the languages that we use to explain ourselves to one another. The languages of republicanism and biblical religion have lost their power in our culture. According to Bellah, most middle class Americans do not use these languages to explain themselves, either to themselves or to one another. That was not always the case but is the case today. Before we turn to the present, let us take a quick look at the languages of the past.

What is the language of republicanism? This tradition grows out of the classical traditions of Greece and Rome. It assumes that both civic virtue and self-interest are the motivations of citizens. One participates in public life as a way of moral education and one attempts to achieve both justice and public good.

The biblical tradition is carried by Christianity and Judaism. In America, Protestant Christianity is its most influential carrier. One attempts to create a community in which a genuine human life can be lived. One did this under the judgment of a God who cherished you but also held you accountable if your actions led to the destruction of that genuine human life.

But it is the other two traditions which are the focus of much of Bellah's observations and criticism. In the perspective of the topic at hand, we can use the work of Bellah to ask how a health care worker who came at the world using the languages of individualism would understand their situation in terms of the AIDS epidemic.

Bellah starts by describing individualism, since he thinks that all four traditions do agree about one thing with respect to individualism. His claim is that all four traditions believe that the individual has inherent value. The biblical tradition might put this more strongly, claiming that the person was sacred, but there is agreement among all the traditions about the inherent dignity of the individual. There is disagreement, however, about the question, which has priority, the individual or the social order? The republican and biblical traditions claim that the social order is primary, the traditions of utilitarian and expressive individualism claim that the individual is primary.

Utilitarian individualism assumes that there are certain basic appetites, including the desire for power and the fear of sudden death at the hands of others. All of us are assumed to act to maximize our interests relative to those ends. Society arises out of a contract between self-interested individuals. There is a connection between an economic understanding of existence and this tradition.

Expressive individualism arises in reaction to utilitarian individualism. It argues that there is a core of uniqueness at the center of each person, and this core ought to find ways of developing and expressing itself. This core is not necessarily opposed to the center of every other person. Thus, it is possible for persons who hold this view to merge with other persons in their personal journey to express their own uniqueness.

What are the consequences of these views as they appear in our culture? First, argues Bellah, persons holding these views tend to see their lives as encompassed only by their job and their family, if they have one. There is little conception of a public life apart from a social life with like-minded individuals. Nor is one's work related to public goods. Second, one looks at situations in terms of what benefits and risks they represent for the self. In this context, associating with AIDS patients, especially early in the epidemic, was clearly a risky business and should be avoided. The method of transmission was not known for certain and it appeared even then that the disease was going to be fatal. Our hypothetical utilitarian individualist, for example, would have no reason for associating with AIDS patients, especially when one took into account that the conception of the social world was encompassed by the family. What the rational utilitarian would do in these circumstances would be to avoid AIDS people.

Many physicians wanted to take this route. Yet inevitably, they were subjected to criticism by their peers. We might want to try to explain this criticism by some theory of a social contract, that there is some kind of agreement between a person who will be a physician and the rest of society. In return for the privileges of medicine, there will be some risks.

The social contract is explicitly mentioned in an interesting paper on this topic, and it is rejected as an adequate basis for the discussion of the issue. In a remarkable article in *The Journal of the American Medical Association*, Drs. Abigail Zuger and Steven H. Miles discuss what they call a rights model, a contract model, and a virtue model. Let me give their descriptions of these models and then make some observations about them.[9]

In the rights model, the patient's right to care creates a duty on the part of healers. The duty is imposed upon the professions but not directly upon the individual healer. It is society which must make arrangements for the provision of medical treatment. This has the consequence that only two classes of physicians have obligations to care for patients who are infectious or who otherwise present a risk to the healer. These would be persons who work in emergency medicine or persons who work in public hospitals. A private practitioner could refuse to treat, under the rights model, on the grounds that he or she is simply exercising a civil liberty which is properly theirs. Thus the rights model gives the person who is ill a right to treatment, but it is a right which must be met by the society only and not the individual physician or nurse. If one is not treated, one has a claim against the larger society for not providing the treatment, but no reason to criticize a particular physician.

There is a second alternative, and here Zuger and Miles examine a version of the contract model. In that model, the assumption is that the contract is between the patient and the physician. The contract imposes a fiduciary obligation on the physician to act in the patient's best interest and to provide competent treatment. Voluntariness is preserved on both sides; the physician can leave after having made alternative provision for medical treatment. Alternatively, the patient may leave the physician at any time. The contract model does protect the infectious patient in that the physician is obligated to provide competent treatment and less than competent care cannot be provided in order to minimize the risk of infection. Note that the physician and patient allow both sides freedom about entering the treatment situation. If the physician does not wish to treat infectious patients, he or she is free to refuse to treat. Zuger and Miles are not content with either of these alternatives. They leave patients vulnerable and as far as Zuger and Miles are concerned, they do not capture what is at stake in speaking about a physician's responsibility to patients in the face of danger to the physician.

Thus Zuger and Miles proceed to discuss a third alternative, a virtue model. Let me quote directly from the article, in order to give a sense of the flavor of the argument that is being made.

> A virtue-based medical ethic has powerful implications for the care of contagious patients in general, and HIV-infected patients in particular. It recognizes that all HIV-infected persons are in need of the healing art — for counseling and reassurance, if nothing else. It mandates, as well, that because of their prior voluntary commitment to the *professio* of healing, physicians are obliged to undertake the *officia* of caring for these patients. Individual physicians who fail to perform these *officia* are falling short of an excellence in practice implicit in their professional commitment.[10]

Thus Zuger and Miles come to what they call the moral art of medicine. Yet I fear that the moral art of medicine is one which is going to be difficult to sustain in our society.

First, notice the arcane language the authors use in order to explain the obligations of the physician, or in my language, the healers. For example, they speak of the end of medicine as a *professio.* It simply is not part of our vocabulary to speak of these matters in this way. Medicine, in modern parlance, has not one end but many, depending upon what the patient wishes.

Second, notice not simply the language but the implications of the language. The language is a language which involves certain moral commitments, commitments which have costs associated with them, costs in terms of time and materials. The patient's good is to be sought, not some other good or goods. AIDS is not cheap to treat and to ask healers to commit themselves to the treatment of persons with AIDS means that other diseases will go untreated. In an age which wishes to cut the costs of medical treatment, there is something ironic about criticizing healers for refusing to treat AIDS victims and at the same time asking them to cut the costs of medical care in general. If we wish to have AIDS victims treated, then we will have to pay for it. This is what we do not want to have to do. Thus right at the beginning of the process, we can identify difficulties. Indeed, the professional may wish to treat the AIDS victim but in so doing the professional is making difficulties for another of society's wishes, that the cost of medical care should come down.

But there are further problems. How is a society which uses the language of utilitarian and expressive individualism identified by Robert Bellah going to sustain the vision which has been articulated by Zuger and Miles? The languages of utilitarian and expressive individualism are opposed to the language of virtue. Indeed, one might want to argue that these later languages are set up on the assumption that it would be better if we had a society that did not depend upon virtuous persons in order to be a good society and that we certainly do not go out of our way to produce them.

III. Some Uncomfortable Conclusions

This, of course, leaves us in a paradoxical situation. The behavior of the professional is clearly countercultural. That is to say, what is being maintained is a way of life apart from that of a larger society. We need a vision of what it means to be a healer that is not sustained nor, possibly, sustainable by the moral languages used in the larger society. We are in the odd circumstance of being dependent upon a profession but being unable to articulate the basis of our dependence, and absent that, our sense of what we might have as our responsibilities towards that profession. Further, without any expectation on the part of society, the profession has no conception of when it is or when it is not meeting its responsibilities to the society in which it finds itself. Finally, it should be clear by now that the treatment of AIDS, insofar as it is understood as a duty by the medical profession, has implications for the cost of medicine.

There are two alternatives which one might wish to consider at this point. One alternative would be to declare that if medicine wishes to develop in its practitioners the sense of virtue which is noted above, medicine will have to develop a community of its own to sustain that vision, since that vision is not sustained by the larger society. In this alternative, medicine would have to create its own community to sustain the kind of vision needed to create the kind of persons necessary to care for people with AIDS.

There is another alternative which has been explored by Stanley Hauerwas. Hauerwas would not have medicine create its own community but rely upon a community called church in order to sustain the persons who would practice an appropriate medicine. Hauerwas argues that only in such a community would it be possible to sustain the vision necessary to have these virtues, and to pass that story on to those who would be practitioners of the arts of medicine.[11] Such a vision of the community is an appealing one, in that it involves a willingness to have a medicine which is fallible, which is finite, which is humble in the face of mortality. What Hauerwas suggests, if only by implication, is that the larger society as presently constituted could not sustain such a vision.

Thus far I have been focusing on the responsibilities of the caretakers of the AIDS patient, responsibilities which, if I read the literature aright, we wish to say that the healers have but which we are not easily able to justify. Further, when we find a language which makes that obligation clear, it rings strangely in our ears; we are not quite sure what to do with it. Indeed, it intrigues me that most of the work done in modern ethical theory is not of much help here, since the emphasis upon freedom allows the healer to ignore the cries of the victim on the grounds that the healer is simply exercising his or her freedom. It seems that we are in the curious circumstance of having to learn from behavior that we cannot explain to ourselves, at least not with the languages of the majority culture.[12] We will have to learn, not simply a new set of problems as Toulmin suggested but a new moral philosophy, one learned this time by watching persons who appear to act rightly but who explain to us in languages most of us have difficulty understanding why it is that they do what they do.

But that takes me away from the point that I have been trying to come to for some time. What is at stake is not simply the responsibility of the healer to the victim, but the responsibilities of the larger society both to the victims and to the healers. That issue remains unaddressed in most of the literature. It remains unaddressed because the larger society has been unwilling to look upon the AIDS crisis as one in which it has been implicated. If there is one thing that one could learn by working one's way through Randy Shilts's book *And the Band Played On,* it is precisely this.[13] We are implicated, however, not only insofar as we are at risk for becoming an AIDS victim ourselves but also in the sense that we are being offered a chance to learn something about ourselves and our society and how we respond to difficult human situations. In this sense, we are comfortable in our righteousness criticizing the physician or nurse who refuses to treat AIDS people and at the same time unwilling to either support what they do with our own presence or in some other way that commits us to care for those persons stigmatized by the larger society. Someone else will do it for us and then we will not have to ask ourselves how we shall deal with it. What is appalling in reading Shilts is to see how the many deaths in the gay community were not thought of as important as deaths in other communities; Shilts's favorite comparison is between the way in which the federal government mobilized for Legionnaire's disease and the way in which it did not mobilize for AIDS victims. While I do not think that Shilts has shown his implicit claim to be true, it is probable that a cure for AIDS could have been found if the United States had been willing to throw enough research dollars at the problem, I am sympathetic to his claim that not enough was done to help AIDS victims. I am also convinced that he is correct when he claims that this was not done because of who the victims were, or at least, who the vast majority of the victims were.

I am not suggesting that we need to become experts in the care of AIDS patients; that is not the point. The issue is how we support those persons who care for AIDS patients and those patients themselves and what we are willing to commit to treating this particular disease. Most importantly, how we understand who we are as we do this and the reasons that we offer to one another are going to be important.

It is also going to be important that we begin working on what we owe to one another in terms of medical treatment. Whether or not AIDS had come along, the current difficulties in health financing would have developed and we as a society are having difficulties facing up to them. With AIDS, we have to face up to them, to our responsibilities to victims of a disfiguring disease, and also to our responsibilities, if any, to the professionals that we expect to care for these persons. It may seem odd to include our responsibilities to the healer, but I do this because I fear that we are in a situation in which the patient runs the risk of being excluded from the moral community and then the healer who treats that patient will be excluded as well. Once you are no longer held to be responsible for your actions, you are excluded from the moral community. William May writes powerfully of how this happens to the elderly in our society, when we no longer hold them responsible for what they do and who they are.[14] I worry that in holding professionals responsible to care for us, even in praising them when they do that at risk to themselves, we might reinforce the notion that we (and by the "we" here I include all of us who will be patients) do not have any moral responsibilities in this area. We are not obligated to challenge one another to aspire to something greater. We do not challenge ourselves to try to find ways of assisting them in their illness, nor do we find ways to express our concern for them. In effect, we have excluded them from our world.

Here, it seems to me, we might appropriate Zuger and Miles's language for our own purposes, to argue for an understanding of the relationship of the self to the larger world which understands the self as having a vocation. To do that would be to ask us to abandon what Bellah calls our dominant languages. That choice is ours. If we do not do it, we will remain in the anomalous situation described above, where we can admire those persons who care for AIDS victims, but find it difficult to honor them. Further, we will set ourselves apart from both them and their patients, forgetting, of course, that one day we will be the patients. The alternative is to join with them and support them as they do their tasks, not in the blind adulation which so often marked the American love affair with medicine in the past, not in awe of medicine's technological skill which marks so much of the discussion of medicine today, but with an attitude of appreciation for what has occurred. Let me be clear, that it is not just the fact that AIDS victims were treated that we should appreciate, but that we learned that it is still possible in this society to envision our world in such a way that victims can be attended to. William May rightly reminds physicians that they must constantly remind themselves of what they owe their patients; without them the physician would not have a practice.[15] It seems to me that it would not be inappropriate for those of us who will be patients to remind ourselves of what we owe our physicians when they treat others, like ourselves, who are possessed by dangerous diseases.

Notes

1. *Perspectives in Biology and Medicine* 25: 4 (Summer 1982): 736-50.

2. There is no denying that those persons who were philosophers and theologians and who were invited into the medical setting had to learn the language of medicine.

3. Obviously, American medicine has gone much further in its attempts to control costs since this essay was originally written. Those further developments do not change the claim being made here, that AIDS came upon a medicine newly conscious of its responsibility to control costs.

4. Robert Veatch, "Generalization of Expertise," *Hastings Center Studies* 1:2 (1973): 29-40.

5. For an account of how stigmatization can occur, cf. Douglas Shenson, "When Fear Conquers," *The New York Times Magazine,* February 28, 1988, pp. 34ff. Shenson points out the similarities between AIDS and leprosy.

6. Robert Wachter, "Sounding Board: The Impact of the Acquired Immunodeficiency Syndrome on Medical Residency Training," *New England Journal of Medicine* 314 (1986): 177-80.

7. Cf. "American College of Physicians Ethics Manual," *Annals of Internal Medicine* 103 (1984): 129-

37, at 131-32. Cf. also, American Medical Association Council on Ethical and Judicial Affairs, *Report on Ethical Issues Involved in the Growing Aids Crisis* (November 1987).

It must be said that the AMA does not demand that each and every practitioner treat AIDS patients but it does insist that the practitioner should not exclude a class of patients from practice because they are HIV positive or have AIDS. In short, it is not something about which the practitioner is totally free; there are obligations which must be fulfilled, even if they do not have to be fulfilled in person. By this standard, those physicians who refuse to treat AIDS patients and who do not make provision for care fail to meet their affirmative duty. I am not claiming that this is an entirely satisfactory resolution of the question. All that should be noted is that the practitioners have lost some of their freedom; they cannot simply walk away from patients.

8. Robert Bellah et al., *Habits of the Heart: Individualism and Commitment in American Life* (Berkeley: University of California Press, 1985).

9. Abigail Zuger, MD, Steven H. Miles, MD, "Physicians, AIDS, and Occupational Risk," *JAMA* 258:14 (October 9, 1987): 1924-28.

10. Ibid., 1927.

11. Stanley Hauerwas, "Salvation and Health: Why Medicine Needs the Church," *Suffering Presence* (Notre Dame: University of Notre Dame Press, 1986), pp. 63-83.

12. I cite only one article. John Arras has written a fine article on the responsibility of physicians to treat AIDS patients. At the end of the day, the most powerful part of the argument is his reference to the history of practice of physicians in the past. All his reference to ethical theory does not do the necessary work of convincing us that, indeed, physicians have duties towards people with AIDS. Cf. John Arras, "The Fragile Web of Responsibility: AIDS and the Duty to Treat," *Hastings Center Report* 18:2 (April/May 1988): 10-20.

13. Randy Shilts, *And the Band Played On: Politics, People, and the AIDS Epidemic* (New York: St. Martin's, 1987).

14. William May, "The Aged: Their Virtues and Vices," in *The Patient's Ordeal* (Bloomington: Indiana University Press, 1991), pp. 120-41.

15. William May, *The Physician's Covenant* (Philadelphia: The Westminster Press, 1983).

20 The Doctor

Thomas Sydenham

It becomes every man who purposes to give himself to the care of others, seriously to consider the four following things: — First, that he must one day give an account to the Supreme Judge of all the lives entrusted to his care. Secondly, that all his skill and knowledge and energy have been given him by God, so they should be exercised for His glory and the good of mankind, and not for mere gain or ambition. Thirdly, and not more beautifully than truly, let him reflect that he has undertaken the care of no mean creature, for, in order that we may estimate the value, the greatness of the human race, the only begotten son of God became himself a man, and thus ennobled it with His divine dignity, and, far more than this, died to redeem it. And, fourthly, that the doctor, being himself a mortal man, should be diligent and tender in relieving his suffering patients, inasmuch as he himself must one day be a like sufferer.

From Edward F. Griffith, ed., *Doctors by Themselves*, 1951. Courtesy of Charles C. Thomas, Publisher, Springfield, Illinois.

21 The Nurse's Profession

Florence Nightingale

. . . Does not the Apostle say: "I count not myself to have apprehended: but this one thing I do, forgetting those things which are behind, *and reaching forth unto those things which are before, I press toward* the mark for the prize of the *high calling* of God in Christ Jesus"; and what higher "calling" can we have than Nursing? But then we must "press forward." . . .

When the head and the hands are very full, as in Nursing, it is so easy, so very easy, if the heart has not an earnest purpose for God and our neighbour, to end in doing one's work only for oneself, and not at all — even when we seem to be serving our neighbours — not at all for them or for God. . . .

But "can we not see ourselves as God sees us?" is a still more important question. For while we value the judgments of our superiors, and of our fellows, which may correct our own judgments, we must also have a higher standard which may correct theirs. We cannot altogether trust them, and still less can we trust ourselves. And we know, of course, that the worth of a life is not altogether measured by failure or success. We want to see our purposes, and the ways we take to fulfil such charge as may be given us, as they are in the sight of God. "Thou God seest me."

And thus do we return to the question we asked before — how near can we come to Him whose name we bear, when we call ourselves Christians? How near to His gentleness and goodness — to His "authority" over others?

And the highest "authority" which a woman especially can attain among her fellow women must come from her doing God's work here in the same spirit, and with the same thoroughness, that Christ did, though we follow him but "afar off."

Lastly, it is charity to nurse sick bodies well; it is greater charity to nurse well and patiently sick minds, tiresome sufferers. But there is a greater charity even than these: to do good to those who are not good to us, to behave well to those who behave ill to us, to serve with love those who do not even receive our service with good temper, to forgive on the instant any slight which we may have received, or may have fancied we have received, or any worse injury.

If we cannot "do good" to those who "persecute" us — for we are not "persecuted": if we cannot pray "Father, forgive them, for they know not what they do" — for none are nailing us to a cross: how much more must we try to serve with patience and love any who use us spitefully, to nurse with all our hearts any thankless peevish patients! . . .

Let us be on our guard against the danger, not exactly of thinking too well of ourselves (for no one consciously does this), but of isolating ourselves, of falling into party spirit — always remembering that, if we can do any good to others, we must draw others to us by the influence of our characters, and not by any profession of what we are — least of all, by a profession of Religion. . . .

We have been, almost all of us, taught to pray in the days of our childhood. Is there not something sad and strange in our throwing this aside when most required by us, on the threshold of our active lives? Life is a shallow thing, and more especially *Hospital* life, without any depth of religion. For it is a matter of simple experience that the best things, the things which seem as if they most would make us feel, become the most hardening if not rightly used.

And may I say a thing from my own experience? No training is of any use, unless one can learn (1) to feel, and (2) to think out things for oneself. And if we have not true religious feeling and purpose, Hospital life — the highest of all things *with* these — *without* them becomes a mere

From Rosalind Nash, ed., *Florence Nightingale to Her Nurses: A Selection from Miss Nightingale's Addresses to Probationers and Nurses of the Nightingale School at St. Thomas's Hospital* (London: MacMillan and Co., Limited, 1914).

routine and bustle, and a very hardening routine and bustle.

. . . Without deep religious purpose how shallow a thing is Hospital life, which is, or ought to be, the most inspiring! For, as years go on, we shall have others to train; and find that the springs of religion are dried up within ourselves. The patients we shall always have with us while we are Nurses. And we shall find that we have no religious gift or influence with them, no word in season, whether for those who are to live, or for those who are to die, no, not even when they are in their last hours, and perhaps no one by but *us* to speak a word to point them to the Eternal Father and Saviour; not even for a poor little dying child who cries: "Nursey, tell me, oh, why is it so dark?" Then we may feel painfully about them what we do not at present feel about ourselves. We may wish, both for our patients and Probationers, that they had the restraints of the "fear" of the most Holy God, to enable them to resist the temptation. We may regret that our own Probationers seem so worldly and external. And we may perceive too late that the deficiency in their characters began in our own.

For, to all good women, *life* is a prayer; and though we pray in our own rooms, in the Wards and at Church, the end must not be confounded with the means. We are the more bound to watch strictly over ourselves; we have not less but more need of a high standard of duty and of life in our Nursing; we must teach ourselves humility and modesty by becoming more aware of our own weakness and narrowness, and liability to mistake as Nurses and as Christians. Mere worldly success to any nobler, higher mind is not worth having. Do you think Agnes Jones, or some who are now living amongst us, cared much about worldly success? They cared about efficiency, thoroughness. But that is a different thing.

We must condemn many of our own tempers when we calmly review them. We must lament over training opportunities which we have lost, must desire to become better women, better Nurses. That we all of us must feel. And then, and not till then, will *life* and *work* among the sick become a prayer.

For prayer is communion or cooperation with God: the expression of a *life* among his poor and sick and erring ones. But when we speak with God, our power of addressing Him, of holding communion with Him, and listening to His still small voice, depends upon our will being one and the same with His. *Is* He our God, as He was Christ's? To Christ He was all, to us He seems sometimes nothing. Can we retire to rest after our busy, anxious day in the Wards, with feeling: "Lord, into Thy hands I commend my spirit," and those of such and such anxious cases; remembering, too, that in the darkness, "Thou God seest me," and seest them too? Can we rise in the morning, almost with a feeling of joy that we are spared another day to do Him service with His sick? —

Awake, my soul, and with the sun,
Thy daily stage of duty run.

Does the thought ever occur to us in the course of the day, that we will correct that particular fault of mind, or heart, or temper, whether slowness, or bustle, or want of accuracy or method, or harsh judgments, or want of loyalty to those under whom or among whom we are placed, or sharp talking, or tale-bearing or gossiping — oh, how common, and how old a fault, as old as Solomon! "He that repeateth a matter, separateth friends"; and how can people trust us unless they know that we are not tale-bearers, who will misrepresent or improperly repeat what is said to us? Shall we correct this, or any other fault, not with a view to our success in life, or to our own credit, but in order that we may be able to serve our Master better in the service of the sick? . . .

This is the spirit of prayer, the spirit of conversation or communion with God, which leads us in all our Nursing silently to think of Him, and refer it to Him. When we hear in the voice of conscience *His* voice speaking to us; when we are aware that He is the witness of everything we do, and say, and think, and also the source of every good thing in us; and when we feel in our hearts the struggle against some evil temper, then God is fighting *with* us against envy and jealousy, against selfishness and self-indulgence, against lightness, and frivolity, and vanity, for "our better self against our worse self." . .

And let me say a word about self-denial: because, as we all know, there can be no real Nursing without self-denial. We know the story of the Roman soldier, above fourteen hundred years ago, who, entering a town in France with his regiment, saw a sick man perishing with cold by the wayside — there were no Hospitals then — and, having nothing else to give, drew his sword, cut his own cloak in half, and wrapped the sick man in half his cloak.

It is said that a dream visited him, in which he found himself admitted into heaven, and Christ saying, "Martin hath clothed me with his garment": the dream, of course, being a remembrance of the verse, "When saw we thee sick or in prison, and came unto thee?" and of the answer, "Inasmuch as ye have done it unto one of the least of these my brethren, ye have done it unto me." But whether the story of the dream be true or not, this Roman soldier, converted to Christianity, became afterwards one of the greatest bishops of the early ages, Martin of Tours. . . .

Suppose we dedicated this "School" to Him, the Divine Charity and Love which said, "Inasmuch as ye do it unto one of the least of these my brethren" (and He calls all our patients — all of us, His brothers and sisters) "ye do it unto me" — oh, what a "Kingdom of Heaven" this might be! Then, indeed, the dream of Martin of Tours, the soldier and Missionary-Bishop, would have come true! . . .

When a Patient, especially a child, sees you acting in all things as if in the presence of God — and none are so quick to observe it — then the names he or she heard at the Chaplain's or the Sister's or the Night Nurse's lips become names of real things and real Persons. There *is* a God, a Father; there *is* a Christ, a Comforter; there *is* a Spirit of Goodness, of Holiness; there *is* another world, to such an one.

When a Patient, especially a Child, sees us acting as if there were *no* God, then there but too often becomes no God to him. Then words become to such a child mere words. . . .

Above all, let us pray that God will send real workers into this immense "field" of Nursing, made more immense this year by the opening out of London *District* Nursing at the bedside of the sick poor at home. A woman who takes a sentimental view of Nursing (which she calls "ministering," as if she were an angel), is of course worse than useless. A woman possessed with the idea that she is making a sacrifice will never do; and a woman who thinks any kind of Nursing work "beneath a Nurse" will simply be in the way. But if the right woman is moved by God to come to us, what a welcome we will give her, and how happy she will soon be in a work, the many blessings of which none can know as we know them, though we know the worries too! . . .

Nurses' work means downright work, in a cheery, happy, hopeful, friendly spirit. An earnest, bright, cheerful woman, without that notion of "making sacrifices," etc., perpetually occurring to her mind, is the real Nurse. Soldiers are sent anywhere, and leave home and country for years; *they* think nothing of it, because they go "on duty." Shall *we* have less self-denial than they, and think less of "duty" than these men? A woman with a healthy, active tone of mind, plenty of work in her, and some enthusiasm, who makes the best of everything, and, above all, does not think herself better than other people because she is a "Nightingale Nurse," that is the woman we want. . . .

I must have moral influence over my Patients. And I *can* only have this by *being* what I appear, especially now that everybody is educated, so that Patients become my keen critics and judges. My Patients are watching me. They know what my profession, my calling is: to devote myself to the good of the sick. They are asking themselves: does that Nurse act up to her profession? This is no supposition. It is a fact. It is a call to us, to each individual Nurse, to act up to her profession.

We hear a good deal nowadays about Nursing being made a "profession." Rather, it is not the question for *me: am I* living up to my "profession"?

Part II

CONCEPTS IN RELIGION AND MEDICINE

Chapter Four:

LIFE AND ITS SANCTITY

Advances in medical science and technology have served the good of life. Evidence for that claim is not hard to marshal. Infant mortality rates have dropped; life expectancy has increased; certain death-dealing childhood diseases have been defeated.

The same advances have confronted us with new choices, alternatives, between life and death. Illustrations of those choices fill this volume: Shall we abort a fetus diagnosed as suffering from a fatal genetic defect? Shall we strive to keep a terminally ill patient alive? Shall we continue the research and development of expensive technological devices in the service of the good of the lives of a few when other goods or other lives might be served by allocating that money and energy elsewhere? Human beings have today a quite remarkable control over life and dying, a control undreamt of not long ago. Accompanying such control is, however, an equally remarkable responsibility.

When people try to take that responsibility seriously, they think about life and the appropriate disposition toward it. People confronted with choices of life or death significance are likely to ask themselves about "life and its sanctity."

The phrase "life and its sanctity," of course, is not unambiguous. It does not make clear whether all life or only human life is included. It does not make clear whether it is *bios* or *zoē*, biological life or spiritual life, which is due respect. "Sanctity" carries a religious connotation not always welcome to the non-religious and sometimes adjudged idolatrous by the religious. The deepest ambiguity of all, however, may be that the phrase does not settle the relation of the good of life to other goods.

The phrase is open to more than one justification, to more than one interpretation, and so, to more than one sort of application. Its ambiguity conspires with its importance to require reflection about this concept in the context of the advances in medicine.

Reflection about life and its sanctity is at home in the great religions of the world and surely in Christianity. The Christian scriptures reveal a God who intends life and forbids trespass upon it. The traces of this intention are found in creation (e.g., Genesis 2:4b-7), in a rainbow (e.g., Genesis 9:1-17), in a commandment (e.g., Exodus 20:13), in an empty tomb (e.g., John 11:23-26, I Corinthians 15), and in a vision (Revelation 21:1-8). Christian theologians, however, can give different accounts of "life and its sanctity," accounts which bear in different ways on the choices that confront us. The attempt to think both clearly and Christianly about this issue will be served by careful attention to the selections gathered here and by raising certain questions about them.

Some of these questions have been introduced in earlier chapters. For example, the questions of the relation of Christian moral reflection to a "natural" morality may be raised again by comparing Barth, Gustafson, and Stith. For Barth, the reverence due life is seen in Christian perspective, for human dignity is an "alien dignity," a dignity which does not derive from life itself, or from human beings themselves, but from God's dealings with human beings.[1] A similar argument was made by Helmut Thielicke[2] whose notion of "alien dignity" is retrieved and interpreted by Karen Lebacqz in selection 26.

Roman Catholic thought is as capable as Protestant of articulating this notion of "alien dignity,"[3] but it has typically attended much more self-consciously and confidently to an impartial perspective, a natural law perspective. So, too, Richard Stith (selection 25) appeals to universal moral "intuitions" and defends and explicates the "sanctity of life" as a universal and rational principle.[4]

James Gustafson's essay (selection 24) attends neither to the deliverances of theology alone nor to the wisdom of a natural morality alone but to their relationship. He asks a quite different question: "In what ways might the religious belief qualify the human experience?" He begins with an appreciative understanding of the human experiences of the value of life, of the plurality of values, and of valuing things for their utility or for themselves; and he seeks to qualify and to reorient those experiences by belief in the transcendence of God and in the God who is transcendent. One might ask what is gained and lost by these different judgments about the relations of theological reflection to "natural" morality.

The question of the mode of moral analysis also resurfaces. For example, Barth focuses on the command of God and calls for the obedience of the faithful to the command of God in the moment. Gustafson explicitly rejects this language in favor of the language of values, dispositions, and intentions. For his part, Stith explicitly rejects the language of value to explicate the meaning of sanctity and articulates rules of practice on the basis of this principle. Karen Lebacqz, in her feminist retrieval of the notion of "alien dignity," is concerned fundamentally with our moral vision and with the correction in it that can come with the lens of this notion. If we see people in this way, we will also see reasons to protect people and to regard them as equals; such an image of persons can shape both personal relationships and social structures. It is worth asking which of these models is an appropriate strategy for thinking about "life and its sanctity."

The question to which such self-conscious methodological decisions must finally be addressed, of course, is the meaning of "life and its sanctity." How can and should we think clearly and Christianly about this phrase? How shall we articulate and describe this sanctity? According to one eminent bioethicist, "The belief in the sanctity of human life is the belief that each moment of biological life of every member of our species is of infinite value."[5] It is worth observing that none of the essays in this chapter take such a view or propose such a belief. Such a definition confuses "the sanctity of life" with a crude vitalism. But if "sanctity" does not name an "infinite value," does it still name a value? Or does it name an attitude of awe and reticence?

If we have decided what we mean by "sanctity," how shall we defend it? Should we reject, as Barth does, any effort to defend the notion on the basis of "a law of nature and reason" — or should we search for precisely such a justification for the sake of public discourse? If we start with human experience, should we, like Stith, be content with naming our common intuitions — or should we, like Gustafson, both appreciate human experience and insist on qualifying it by the experience of God's transcendence? Should we defend it by appealing to the commandment, "Thou shalt not kill," or does the sanctity of life name a reason the commandment itself was given? Is it the splendid dignity of the human creature that evokes (and justifies) reverence, and if so, is that dignity something "alien" to that creature or something "naturalized"?

And if we have decided what we mean by "sanctity" and how we should defend it, then we will have made considerable progress toward knowing how we should apply it. These are hard but important questions, the answers to which will determine the way one addresses other hard and important questions, the concrete questions posed by advances in medicine and humanity's unprecedented control over human life and dying.

Notes

1. See also Paul Ramsey, "The Morality of Abortion," in *Life and Death: Ethics and Options,* ed. Daniel H. Labby (Seattle: University of Washington Press, 1968), pp. 60-93.

2. Helmut Thielicke, "The Doctor as Judge of Who Shall Live and Who Shall Die," in *Who Shall Live?* ed. Kenneth Vaux (Philadelphia: Fortress Press, 1970).

3. Josef Fuchs, *Natural Law* (New York: Sheed and Ward, 1965); Norman St. John-Stevas, *The Right to Life* (New York: Holt, Rinehard and Winston, 1963).

4. One might fruitfully compare, for example, the position of Stith with the position Edward Shils develops on the basis, not of Christianity, but of a "deeper, proto religious 'natural metaphysic'" ("The Sanctity of Life" in Labby, *Life or Death, Ethics and Options,* p. 9).

5. Baruch A. Brody, "A Historical Introduction to Jewish Casuistry on Suicide and Euthanasia," in *Suicide and Euthanasia* ed. Baruch A. Brody (Dordrecht, the Netherlands: Kluwer Academic Publishers, 1989), pp. 39-75, p. 39. Following that definition Brody argues that traditional Judaism is *not* committed to "the sanctity of life" so understood.

Suggestions for Further Reading

Amundsen, Darrel W. *Medicine, Society, and Faith in the Ancient and Medieval Worlds* (Baltimore: The Johns Hopkins University Press, 1996).

Callahan, Daniel. "The Sanctity of Life," in *Updating Life and Death,* edited by Donald R. Cutler, with commentaries by Julian Pleasants, James M. Gustafson, and Henry K. Beecher (Boston: Beacon Press, 1969), pp. 181-250.

Callahan, Daniel, Gilbert Meilaender, Christine Whitbeck, William M. Smith, M. Therese Lysaught, William E. May, Eric Cassell. "The Sanctity of Life Seduced: A Symposium on Medical Ethics," *First Things* no. 32 (April 1994): 13-28.

Clouser, Danner K. "The Sanctity of Life: An Analysis of a Concept," *Annals of Internal Medicine* 78 (1973): 119-25.

Crane, Diana. *The Sanctity of Social Life: Physician's Treatment of Critically Ill Patients* (New York: Russell Sage Foundation, 1975).

Hartt, Julian. "Creation, Creativity, and the Sanctity of Life," *The Journal of Medicine and Philosophy* 4 (December 1979): 418-34.

Kilner, John F. *Life on the Line: Ethics, Aging, Ending Patients' Lives, and Allocating Vital Resources* (Grand Rapids: William B. Eerdmans Publishing Company, 1992).

Nelson, Robert J. *Human Life: A Biblical Perspective for Bioethics* (Philadelphia: Fortress Press, 1984).

Ramsey, Paul. "The Sanctity of Life," *Dublin Review* 241 (Spring 1967): 3-21.

Shils, Edward, et al. *Life or Death: Ethics and Options* (Seattle: University of Washington Press, 1968).

Thomasma, David C. *An Apology for the Value of Human Life* (St. Louis: Catholic Health Association of the United States, 1983).

Weber, Leonard J. *Who Shall Live?* (New York: Paulist Press, 1976).

22 Genesis 2:4b-7

In the day that the LORD God made the earth and the heavens, when no plant of the field was yet in the earth and no herb of the field had yet sprung up — for the LORD God had not caused it to rain upon the earth, and there was no man to till the ground; but a mist went up from the earth and watered the whole face of the ground—then the LORD God formed man of dust from the ground, and breathed into his nostrils the breath of life; and man became a living being.

---

23 Respect for Life

Karl Barth

Those who handle life as a divine loan will above all treat it with respect. Respect is man's astonishment, humility and awe at a fact in which he meets something superior — majesty, dignity, holiness, a mystery which compels him to withdraw and keep his distance, to handle it modestly, circumspectly and carefully. It is the *respicere* of an object in face of which his attitude cannot be left to chance or preference or even clever assessment, but which requires an attitude that is particularly appropriate and authoritatively demanded. This compulsion does not derive from life itself and as such. Life does not itself create this respect. The command of God creates respect for it. When man in faith in God's Word and promise realises how God from eternity has maintained and loved him in his little life, and what He has done for him in time, in this knowledge of human life he is faced by a majestic, dignified and holy fact. In human life itself he meets something superior. He is thus summoned to respect because the living God has distinguished it in this way and taken it to Himself. We may confidently say that the birth of Jesus Christ as such is the revelation of the command as that of respect for life. This reveals the eternal election and love of God. This unmistakably differentiates human life from everything that is and is done in heaven and earth. This gives it even in the most doubtful form the character of something singular, unique, unrepeatable and irreplaceable. This decides that it is an advantage and something good and worthwhile to be as man. This characterises life as the incomparable and non-recurrent opportunity to praise God. And therefore this makes it an object of respect.

It is really surprising that the Christian Church and Christian theology have not long ago urged more energetically the importance for ethics of so constituent a part of the New Testament message as the fact of the incarnation, instead of resorting, in the vital question why man and human life are to be respected, to all kinds of general religious expressions and to the assertions of non-Christian humanism. The assurances of the latter that the value of human life rests on a law of nature and reason sound quite well. But on this basis they are extremely insubstantial, and it is clear that nature and reason can always be used to prove something very different from respect for man. They also have the disadvantage that by "human life" they understand either his very one-sided intellectual existence, "the infinite value of the human soul," on the one side, or his equally one-sided material existence and prosperity on the other. They have the further drawback of always being bound up with illusory overestimations of his goods, abilities and achievements which can only prove detrimental to the respect which ought really to be paid. And somewhere there obviously lurks the ambiguity that, although reference is made to man, humanity, the dignity of man, etc., it is not really man himself who is intended but all sorts of things, ideas, advances and aims which in effect man has only to serve, for which he has only to let himself be used, and for the sake of which he can at any moment be dropped and sacrificed.

In contrast to every other, the respect of life which becomes a command in the recognition of the union of God with humanity in Jesus Christ has an incomparable power and width. For in this recognition it is really commanded with the authority of God Himself and therefore in such a way that there can be no question whatever of disregard as an alternative. Intellectualistic and materialistic one-sidedness in answer to the question of what human existence is all about is thus excluded by the grounding of the command in this recognition because the human life in question, the life of the man Jesus, cannot be divided into psychical or physical but compels us to offer the respect demanded by God to the whole man in his ordered unity of soul and body. The usual

From Karl Barth, *Church Dogmatics*, III/4, trans. A. T. Mackay et al. (Edinburgh: T&T Clark, 1961), pp. 336-43. Used by permission.

overestimations of man and human nature are also excluded, because the distinction of human existence brought about in Jesus Christ is to be seen wholly as grace and therefore only in humility. And finally on the basis of this recognition there can be no question of man's life being secretly honoured again as only the vehicle and exponent of an idea or cause superimposed upon him. For human life itself and as such is seen in the person of the man Jesus to be the matter about which God is concerned and therefore man must also be concerned in His service. In respect of the recognition of the command in the sense which now occupies us the Christian Church and Christian theology have an incomparable weight to throw into the scales. They and they alone know exactly why and in what sense respect for life is demanded from us, and demanded in such a way that there can be no evasions or misunderstandings.

But what does respect for life mean? We have spoken of astonishment, humility, awe, modesty, circumspection and carefulness. Application must now be made to our particular theme. What matters is not something but someone, the real man before God and among his fellows, his individual psycho-physical existence, his movement in time, his freedom, his orientation to God and solidarity with others. What matters is that everyone should treat his existence and that of every other human being with respect. For it belongs to God. It is His loan and blessing. And it may be seen to be this in the fact that God himself has so unequivocally and completely acknowledged it in Jesus Christ. What, then, can be the meaning of respect in relation to this object?

First, it obviously means an adoption of the distance proper in face of a mystery. It is a mystery that I am, and others too, in this human structure and individuality in which we recognise one another as of the same kind, each in his time and freedom, each in his vertical and horizontal orientation. This is indeed an incomprehensible and in relation to ourselves intangible fact, inexhaustible in its factuality and depth and constantly adapted to give us pause. Those who do not know *respicere* in face of it, those who are not startled and do not feel insignificant and incompetent in its presence, those who think they can understand and master and control it, do not know what obedience is. All human life as such is surrounded by a particular solemnity. This is not the solemnity of the divine, nor of the ultimate end of man. Life is only human and therefore created, and eternity as the divinely decreed destiny of man is only an allotted future. But within these limits it is a mystery emphasised and absolutely distinguished by God Himself. As such it must always be honoured with new wonder. Every single point to be observed and pondered is in its own way equally marvelous — and everything is equally marvelous in every human existence. First, then, we have simply to perceive this, and once we have done so we have not at any price to relinquish or even to lose sight of this perception. We must be awake to this need to keep our distance, and always be wakeful as we do so.

But a mere theoretical and aesthetic wonder is not enough. On the contrary, the theoretical and aesthetic wonder which rightly understood forms the presupposition for everything else, must itself have a practical character if it is to be the required respect. And this means that human life must be affirmed and willed by man. We hasten to add that it must be affirmed and willed as his own with that of others and that of others with his own. Egoism and altruism are false antitheses when the question is that of the required will to live. My own life can no more claim my respect than that of others, but neither can that of others. Although they are not the same, but each distinct, the homogeneity and solidarity of all human life is indissoluble. But what is the will to live understood in this sense? Obviously, because to life there also belongs the freedom of this will, it is determination and readiness for action in the direction of its confirmation. That we should spontaneously perceive and affirm the reception of life as a divine loan in its character as a favour shown, a possession entrusted and an opportunity offered to us, is obviously what is expected of us as those who possess it, who are alive. But if this perception and confirmation is our act, it must consist in our making of our life the use prescribed by its nature as seen in these points. What is important is that according to the measure and within the limits of his individuality, and in the time granted to him, each should exist — always in orientation to God and solidarity with others — as this rational creature, attentively, unreservedly and loyally confessing his human existence in willing responsibility to the One to whom he owes it. We cannot live in obedience accidentally, irresolutely, without plan or responsibility. We cannot in obedience let ourselves go or be driven. We cannot and must not seriously tire of life. For it is always an offer waiting for man's will, determination and readiness for action. And it is to be noted that this is real respect for life. In this form as the will to live it is more than passive speculation in face of its mystery. It is the respect which its mystery demands. We really see it as the mystery it is in the fact that we will to live it and accept it responsibly. A life which is not affirmed and willed, which is irresolute, irresponsible and inactive, is necessarily a life without mystery. And against the constant threat of egoism, there is always the safeguard and corrective of recollection that the real human life is the one which is lived in orientation to God and co-ordination with others. The last is particularly important from the practical standpoint. The will to live which is the form of respect for life will always be distinguishable from an inhuman and irreverent will to live contrary to the command, by the fact that it considers the existence and life of others together with its own, and its own together with that of others.

But having considered and said this, we must also show that the commanded respect for life includes an awareness of its limitations. We have already mentioned these. We refer to the creaturely and the eschatological limitations. These cannot diminish respect for life, much less abrogate it. But it is necessarily modified and characterised by the fact that the life to which it is paid has these limitations. As the reverence commanded of man it is not limitless. As such it has within itself its own limitation. Its limitation is the will of God the Creator Himself who commands it, and the horizon which is set for man by the same God with his determination for eternal life. Life is no second God, and therefore the respect due to it cannot rival the reverence owed to God. On the contrary, it is limited by that which God will have from the man who is elected and called by Him. For the life of man belongs to Him. He has granted it to him as a loan. And He decides in what its right use should consist. He also decrees and decides in His command in what man's will to live should at any moment consist or not, and how far it should go or not go as such. And what God will have of man is not simply that he should will to live for himself and in co-existence with others. God can also will to restrict man's will to live for himself and in co-existence with others. He can weaken, break and finally destroy it. He actually does this. And when He does, obedience may not be withheld from Him. As Creator and Lord of life, He has also the right to will and do this, and if He does, then He knows well why it must be so, and in this too He is man's gracious Father. In relation to man, He has much more in mind than what man can see here and now in the fulfilment of his life-act. He has determined him for eternal life, for the life which one day will finally be given him. He is leading him through this life to the other. The respect for life commanded by Him cannot then be made by man a rigid principle, an absolute rule to be fulfilled according to rote. It can only try to assert and maintain itself as the will to live in the one sense understood by man, whether in relation to his own life or that of others. Respect for life, if it is obedience to God's command, will have regard for the free will of the One who has given life as a loan. It will not consist in an absolute will to live, but in a will to live which by God's decree and command, and by *meditatio futurae vitae*, may perhaps in many ways be weakened, broken, relativised and finally destroyed. Being prepared for this, it will move within its appointed limits. It can always be modest. And it will not on this account be any the less respect for life. It will be so in this modesty and in readiness for it. When we come to questions of detail, we shall see how important it is to remember this reservation, or rather this closer definition. Respect for life without this closer identification could be the principle of an idolatry which has nothing whatever to do with Christian obedience.

But this reservation must now be strictly and sharply qualified. This inwardly necessary relativisation of what is required of us as respect for life, this recollection of the freedom of the controlling and commanding God and of eternal life as the limitation of this present life, must not be forgotten for a single moment. But the application of this reservation, the reference to it and the corresponding modesty, cannot have more than the character of an *ultima ratio*, an exceptional case.

They arise only on the frontiers of life and therefore of the respect due it. Hence it is not true that respect for life is alternately commanded and then not commanded us. Neither is it true that alongside the sphere of this respect there is a sphere in which it is not normative, or only partially so. However much we understand by this respect and therefore by the commanded will to live is limited and relativised by God's free will and man's determination for a future life, this relativisation never means that man is released from this respect. The one God, who is of course the Lord of life and death, the Giver of this life and that which is to come, will in all circumstances and in every conceivable modification demand respect for life. He will never give man liberty to take another view of life, whether his own or that of others. Indifference, wantonness, arbitrariness or anything else opposed to respect cannot even be considered as a commanded or even a permitted attitude. Even the way to these frontiers — the frontiers where respect for life and the will to live can assume in practice very strange and paradoxical forms, where in relation to one's own life and that of others it can only be a matter of that relativised, weakened, broken and even destroyed will to live — will always be a long one which we must take thoughtfully and conscientiously, continually asking and testing whether that *ultima ratio* really applies. The frontiers must not be arbitrarily advanced in any spirit of frivolity or pedantry; they can be only reached in obedience and then respected as such. Recollection of the freedom and superior wisdom, goodness and controlling power of God, and recollection of the future life, cannot then form a pretext or excuse for attitudes and modes of action in which many may actually evade what is commanded within these limits. They are frontiers which are necessarily set by God, and cannot be claimed as emancipations of man. This will be best understood by those who do not treat respect for life as a principle set up by man. Even on these frontiers they will not see a relaxation of the command or exception to the rule, but only a relaxation of that which they think they should understand and offer as obedience when they accept it as a summons to the will to live. Even here there will be required of them a new and deeper understanding of the will to live, which *ultima ratione* can now take the form of a broken and even destroyed will to live, and, if it be the will of God, must necessarily do so. Yet if it is an obedient and not frivolous will, if it is not wantonness and self will, it must always be the will to live, and therefore the practical form of respect for life.

?

questions of right to die must be examined case by case

suicide is never right

24 The Transcendence of God and the Value of Human Life

James M. Gustafson

Throughout this paper I shall keep in view two general areas of reference, two sources of understanding. One is human experience: of the values of human life, and of valuing. The other is Christian theology, or at least certain affirmations made in the intellectual life of faith which pertain to the valuing of human life. Any discourse which attempts to move theology and ethics by necessity must keep these two areas and sources in view. If theological principles and affirmations pertain to human moral values, they do so in two ways. Either they are principles and affirmations which include within the divine purposes those purposes which are moral, that is, which stipulate human moral values, ends, rules, etc., or the religious community infers certain moral values, ends, rules, etc., to be consistent, coherent, harmonious, consonant with affirmations about God. If claims are made for transformation, emendation, penetration, alteration, re-orientation of human experience through religious faith, those claims are in principle subject to virtually empirical investigation. These are two pitfalls in the efforts to relate theology and ethics in general which I wish to avoid. On the one hand are the temptations to deduce too much from theological principles for ethics, a pitfall more characteristic of the religious rhetoric of some continental Protestants than of either Roman Catholic or American Protestant theologians, e.g., the claim that what is morally right is determined by the command of God in the moment. On the other hand are the temptations to separate the ethical discourse from the theological, confining the significance of the theological to soteriology, and finding the resources for the ethical only in what (hopefully) all men can accept in common as the human and the moral.

My procedure will be to discuss three general affirmations in an exploratory way, seeking to make clear the relations between Christian belief in the transcendence of God (and the God who is transcendent) and human experience in each. The first is: Human physical life is not of absolute value, but since it is the indispensable condition for human values and valuing, the burden of proof is always on those who would take it. The second is more complex: Human life has *many values.* Some of these adhere to individuals, others adhere to the relations between persons in interpersonal situations, others adhere to human collectivities, and some adhere to all three. These values are not always in harmony with each other in particular human circumstances. The third is this: Human valuing of others involves several kinds of relations, and several aspects of individual experience; it is no simple single thing either descriptively or normatively.

I. Human Physical Life is not of Absolute Value

Human physical life is not of absolute value. But it is the indispensable condition for human values and valuing, and for its own sake is to be valued. Thus the burden of proof is always on those who would take it. The delicacy of discerning what value is to be given to human physical life under particular circumstances when it is not valued absolutely presents one of the principal practical moral problems men have to face.

H. Richard Niebuhr, in *Radical Monotheism and Western Culture,* stated the broad outlines of the affirmation of the nonabsolute value of all created things from a theological perspective. He closes his chapter, "The Idea of Radical Monotheism," with the following words. "Radical monotheism dethrones all absolutes short of the principle of being itself. At the same time it reverences

From the *Catholic Theological Society of America Proceedings* 23 (1968). Used by permission.

every relative existent. Its two great mottoes are: 'I am the Lord thy God; thou shalt have no other gods before me' and 'Whatever is, is good.' "[1] The theme is a very familiar one in a great deal of Protestant theology. Kierkegaard wrote about the difficulties of being absolutely related to the absolute, and relatively related to the relative; Paul Tillich's idea of the "protestant principle" functioned to provide men with a point of transcendence from which all finite gods could be assessed with presumed freedom and objectivity.[2] Nothing has been exempted from the edges of this theological sword, including religion (as it is distinguished in Barth, Bonhoeffer, and many followers, from faith). The intention of many Protestant writers in this vein has been primarily religious and theological; they intend to preserve the majesty of God from confusion with lesser majesties, they intended to make the claim that God alone is worthy of absolute trust and reliance, that is, of absolute faith; they intended to drive men to faith in God by preaching the unworthiness of lesser gods. A few writers have moved on to develop some of the ethical inferences that can be drawn from the theological point; the Niebuhr brothers, for example, show in part what it means for the political community to confess that God alone is the Lord. It is not unfair, however, to charge almost all of the Protestant giants who perceived the dangers of idolatry with failing to deal with many of the hard cases in which men must judge what the proper reverence is for various relative existents.

Here we see the serious ethical limitations of affirmations of the transcendence of God if the moral inference drawn from it is vaguely the relativity of all things that are not God. A veritable host of conclusions could be drawn from this vagueness. Some of these can be easily listed. 1) Since only God is absolute, all other things are *equally* relative to him and to each other. No one, however, wishes to take this line. 2) Quite different would be this; since the importance of the doctrine of transcendence is to show the majesty and virtual mystery of God, once we see the relativity of all things in relation to him, we have exhausted the theological resources for determining the values of the relativities of life. We are on our own to explore pragmatically the great varieties of human schemes for the ordering of existents in relation to each other: reason, power, utility and other values, and many other things can be brought together in whatever combination to keep life surviving. 3) God, in his absoluteness, had the good sense to foresee the problem of the relativity of all things, and had the good judgment to designate certain persons and institutions with the authority to order the relativities in relation to each other. So men ought to obey these divinely authorized minds and powers, whether ecclesiastical or political. 4) Since man, according to Scripture and his own estimate of himself, is the "highest" being in the created order, all relative things are to be ordered according to his valuations. These empirically might be wrong; but if we can know what man is essentially we can know how normatively all relative things are to be ordered for man's well-being. Which conclusion one accepts will set something of the course he takes in dealing with the question of when human physical life can be taken.

When we turn from theology to human experience, we see that it is not necessary for a person to believe in the transcendence of God in order to affirm the relativity of institutions, religious, morals, physical life, and what have you.[3] Historical and cultural relativism, whatever their intellectual origins might be, are part of the conventional wisdom. And even long before there were tags to put on these notions, men had learned that circumstances of human experience often required them to alter things they professed to be of absolute value, whether these were physical life processes or institutions. "Kill or be killed," the slogan drummed into some of us during the Second World War, has a natural history predating myths of creation. One's own life is to be valued more than the life of the one who attacks, at least under most conditions — if he attacks first, if he has malicious intent, if he seeks to destroy not only one's own life but those of others, if you are under orders to kill him before he kills you in the game of war, etc. But many other things have been valued above human life; the honored legends and narratives of the things men have been willing to die for, all point to the development of human convictions about things to be valued more than physical life itself — justice, liberty of conscience, exemplary witness to a belief, as well as things valued less highly by most people. It is not hard for most men to believe that physical life is not of absolute value, though in the time of assassinations, it is hard to accept the fact that others do not believe it.

How might belief in the transcendence of God qualify, alter, modify, man's understanding of, and response to, the non-absolute human values, and particularly the value of human physical life? If there are theological grounds for accepting the finite values as non-absolute, and if there are experiential grounds for this, in what ways might the religious belief qualify the human experience? I shall not give all the possible answers to these questions, but only some which I deem to be very important.

First, created life is accepted as a gift; it has an author and a source beyond itself, and we and all the other forms of life are dependent on that author and source. Life is given to us; even if man succeeds in creating new physical life, he remains the recipient of a multitude of gifts which make this possible. Thus one could spell out a number of the characteristics of the relationship between man and God which in turn would qualify man's disposition toward the created values around him: man is a *dependent* creature, dependent upon God and upon his fellows — this he remembers in his relationships and responses; man is the recipient of good things which are not of his creation, including his own physical life — this brings a response of *gratitude* both to God and the persons and institutions which sustain the goodness of his life, etc.

Second, since only God is absolute, man must remember his finitude, not to mention his deformed existence. This, as the Protestant theological interpreters of culture remind us, requires that man always be brought under question by himself and by others, that he never absolutize his powers, his acts, his judgments. The requirement, in traditional religious terms, of humility constantly qualifies his tendencies to absolutize the relative.

Third, man is *accountable* to the author and source of life for his use and cultivation of life, including human physical life. He is responsible (in terms of accountable) to God for the ways in which he cares for, preserves, sustains, cultivates, and, in his limited capacity, creates life around him. His disposition is that of the free servant; not servile but acknowledging that his human vocation is under God.

Fourth, in his participation in the created order, man is *responsive* to the *developments and purposes which are being made possible* for him under the power and gifts of life from God. He responds not only to the immediacies of possibilities, but to the course of developments which the transcendent God is making possible and ultimately governing. This fourth brings us to a critical point, in my judgment, in Protestant theologies which most substantiate the first affirmation of this paper. That is, insofar as the transcendent God is the One beyond the Many (H. R. Niebuhr), or the unspeakable ground of being (Tillich), he is peculiarly devoid of meaningful content, and thus man is left almost no substantial theological resources in the determination of the values and purposes which ought to govern his participation in the created order, including his use of human physical life. The human ingenuity left for man to depend on in the absence of theological resources is not to be denigrated; out of reflections on human life man does develop views of the "values" which are human, and which are to be developed and sustained. But the God who is transcendent is not the totally unknown God, and thus there are more resources than man's reflection on his own existence alone.

Since the *sine qua non* of other relative values and of valuing is the existence of human physical life, it is valued and is to be valued with a high priority. To take it is to render it impossible for the other person to experience any values, and for him to contribute to the life of the community in such valued ways as it might be possible to do. Thus, while human physical life is not an absolute value, it is to be preserved unless there are substantial grounds for regarding other values to be of greater significance in the particular circumstances in which judgments are made. Human physical life is the primary gift of God on which all other gifts to man are dependent; this vacuous platitude suddenly becomes cogent when assassins' bullets remove from the human community the values of a great man's life, not only values to himself but to the human community.

Human Life Has Many Values

Human life has many values. These values are not always in harmony with each other in particular circumstances. Indeed, there is no fixed timeless order of priority of the values of human life which *a priori* determines what ought to occur in all particular circumstances. Put theologically, while God's purposes for man might be summed up in some generalized unitary conception, such as "He wills man's good," man's good is a complex and not simple notion. Indeed, the religious consciousness of Christianity and Judaism has always recognized that God's purposes are multiple and not single in human life. Put in the language of human experience, men have always been aware that human life cannot exist without both freedom and order, without both love and justice, without both peace and freedom or peace and justice, and that these sometimes conflict with each other and with the value of particular human physical lives in particular circumstances.

The God who is transcendent is not a totally unknown God. People who have acknowledged him to be the Lord have historically discerned his activity in the course and purposes of events, in the lives and deeds of particular men, in the responses men have made to each other and to him. They have written accounts of human life in which they have interpreted experience in the light of the purposes of God, the values God confers upon life. They have written in propositional form some of the predicates which they have deduced from the activities of God; God is love, God is just, God is merciful, God is wrathful, God is the creator, God is the redeemer, God is the judge, God is righteous, etc. Many of these accounts and purposes are directly moral in their content; they pertain to what God wills that human life should be if it is in accord with his activities and his purposes, his will in the double sense of what he does and what he requires. To be sure, certain purposes of God are more dominant than others: his redemptive purpose triumphs over his wrath, for example, as Jonah was disappointed to find out. But in particular circumstances the significance of his redemptive purposes might well include his wrath, as religious sentimentalists often fail to see. He is loving, but the forms of his loving are at least as complex as the forms of human loving — sometimes he loves through the provision of an order, a pattern of rules for life, sometimes through spontaneity and boundless mercy, sometimes through the preservation of peace, and sometimes through the break-up of oppressive and unjust peace. Religious men, like others, long to leap to a simple unitive understanding of God's will and purpose, for if they can be true believers in such, they can provide simpler statements of what life in the human world is to be. But the impulse violates both Christian beliefs about the God who is transcendent and the complexity of the life created by him in which his purposes are to be fulfilled. God values many things in human life.

In my judgment, the most current simplification is that God wills the human, a simplification which has ecumenical auspices. The human, it turns out, is either something men are presumed to know intuitively, or it is something which must be spelled out in more rationally defensible terms, which is to open the door to complexity. It may well be that God wills the human, but the human, like the good, is not a simple notion.[4]

The things which human beings value, quite properly, are at least as many, and at least as inconsistent with each other in particular circumstances as are the purposes of God. What common human experience knows about this was depicted philosophically several decades ago by Nicolai Hartmann.[5] Not only is there a plurality of values which are abrasive to each other, but there is a plurality of virtues; indeed, Hartmann wrote about the antinomy of values and of virtues. In his rigorous atheism and his rigorous assertion of the moral autonomy of men, Hartmann painted one of the most awesome pictures of human responsibility I have encountered. One might, however, learn from his phenomenological accounts of moral life without necessarily agreeing with his metaphysics and his anthropology. Human values are many, and many things which men value can be ethically and theologically justified. They do not fall into a neat pattern of priorities which smooths the abrasiveness of particular situations.[6]

Do the Christian beliefs about the God who is transcendent bear any importance upon the choices men make in the ordering of human values in the conduct of life? Or, is one left with a plurality in the transcendent matched by a plurality in the human sphere? In this brief paper I cannot explicate my answers fully. They would, however, take the following line. Since the transcendent God is not a capricious being, man can discern the fundamental directionality of his purposes for human life. There is an orientation, an intention, which sheds its light upon which intentions and values are proper for man. And, as I indicated in the first part of this paper, man is accountable to God, whose purposes can be in part explicated, in the conduct of his affairs. One also receives his knowledge of God's purposes as a gift of light and direction in the conduct of his actions. But this directionality, which can be translated into a generally applicable ordering of human values, does not resolve the conflicts that are bound to be present in the hard cases of moral judgment. Although God is loving, and wills that men shall be loving, love is not *prima facie* consistent with the preservation of human life under all circumstances. If one chooses to say that love is consistent with man's well-being, one has only moved the problem over from one term to the other, without specifying it more carefully.

Further, the transcendence of God has personal meaning only if one has trust in the God who is transcendent, only if there is a gratitude to him, loyalty to him, a sense of obligation to him. Given this faith, then, the religious believer is obligated to seek to discern (not alone, but in the company of the people of God) what the transcendent God's purposes are for the conduct of life with its plurality of human values. But given a measure of plurality of God's purposes, there is no guarantee of man making a risk-proof moral judgment, either in God's or in men's sights. There is no prior guarantee of hitting the mark morally. Given the finitude of men, and the plurality of values discerned in human experience, there is no guarantee *a priori* of moral rectitude in all circumstances. Given man's sin (not explicated here), there is need both for guidance from the communities' beliefs about God, and for the mercy which he grants to all people. The Christian beliefs about the God who is transcendent give guidance in the ordering of life with its plurality of values.

III. Human Valuing

Human valuing is complex and not simple. It involves several kinds of relations, and several aspects of individual experience. A rehearsal of the theories of human valuation is no more possible than a rehearsal of theories of value in this brief paper. To keep the topic manageable I shall confine my discussion to two principal aspects of the experience of valuing. One is valuing things and other persons for their utility, not only for one's own purposes, but for purposes of the human community. The other is valuing things and persons for themselves. My interest in this distinction here is to suggest some of the different characteristics of human responses, and of personhood, which are properly involved in each of these two aspects. The first suggests a mode of life which is largely one of problem-solving, of achievement of specific purposes or ends, and tends to slip into a flat, mechanistic view of experience. It reduces the sense of awe and wonder. The second suggests a mode of life which is spiritually profound, but tends to slip into the denigration of rationality, of the necessity for specification of ends and means. Both modes of life are advanced under religious auspices; the first is strong in the proposals of those who affirm the advances of technology and urbanization, and share the optimistic spirit that sometimes pervades successful problem solvers. (My personal conviction is that the thinness of such theologically sponsored views is becoming clear with the compounding of human failures and tragedies.) The second is strong in the proposals of radically personalistic Christians, who, in some of their rhetoric, appear to suggest that the organization of persons to be useful to achieve certain ends (particularly in the church) compromises what men are meant to be for each other. The double tendency is not new, of course; one can gain insight into it from reading the theology of St. Augustine, among others from the past.

It would be folly to try to argue that only a belief in the transcendence of God can justify the more personalistic vision of life, with its responses to other persons of awe, wonder, joy, reverence, and profound respect. Certain aspects of contemporary youth culture manifest this kind of valuing while at the same time rebelling against traditional religious beliefs; the relations between young people are "beautiful" in a meaningful way to them. (My son, for example, wrote recently to a friend, "The real world is beautiful, and you are part of it.") The grounds for the fresh appropriation of the Kantian principle that persons are to be treated as ends in themselves and not as means, are more a revulsion against the institutionalization of values of utility which appear to be "dehumanizing" than they are religious beliefs.

I believe it would be equally a folly to argue that no theological support can be given for the instrumental value, the utility value, of persons. If God is intent upon the preservation and cultivation of life, including as it must, men's lives in relation to each other and in relation to the rest of nature, a view of men as functionaries for the achievement of purposes consistent with those larger purposes is proper, and in order. There is an ordering activity in life, with its impositions of duties and obligations, its assignment of tasks and the requirement of their fulfillment, which is part of God's purpose for man.

The general phenomenon of valuing, then, has many aspects, and cannot be reduced to a simple notion, nor be grounded in a simple set of ultimate requirements. In "using" another person one is valuing him for his function in the social economy of life; one values his wife, even, in part for her utility — in providing for the mundane needs of the family (doing laundry, cooking meals, shopping, cleaning the house, etc.) and in fulfilling needs for affection and even sexual gratification. But relations other than utility between persons also include valuing; not all valuing of persons is reducible to utility. To respect another is to acknowledge his value, as is to reverence another, appreciate another, care for another, preserve the life of another, sustain another, love another, honor another. The valuing carried by these notions suggests in each instance an aspect of the value of the other for his own sake, an intrinsic value to the other. These notions suggest aspects of the experience of valuing, and the relationship with the other, which acknowledge the mystery, the autonomy, the value of the existence, of the other. They also suggest that the self, in such valuing, is not simply calculating in a rational way how the other fulfills one's own desires, interests, and needs, or even the interests and needs of the society. Rather they involve the affections, the emotive life of the person.

Belief in the transcendence of God is not a necessary personal condition for proper maintenance of either the utility or the intrinsic values of persons. To claim that it is a necessary condition would be to take on the obligation to prove that those who believe in the transcendence of God are better "valuers" than are those who do not believe. Christian belief in the God who is transcendent, however, does, can, should, and ought to inform and direct the valuing experiences of Christians, and the relations they have with each other and with nature.

To spell this out, I would develop two themes. One is the effect of this belief on the dispositions of the persons who believe it. To accept life as a gift, to acknowledge dependence on God for life, to acknowledge one's finitude and disobedience in humility, would all (if there is some wholeness to the person) predispose one to have respect, reverence, honor, appreciation, and love for others, and for the world. In the life of praise and adoration, of confession and repentance, which are part of the expression of this belief, of the response to the transcendence of God, the affections are nourished, and the dispositions directed toward the response of respect, honor, appreciation, etc. The calculative rationality of valuations for utility is tempered and impregnated by the sensibilities, dispositions, and affections nourished in religious faith.

The second theme is the effect that the beliefs about the God who is transcendent would have in conditioning the ends and purposes for which the experience of utilization of others would be directed. Since these ends and purposes can be specified in consistency with the purposes of God who is known in Christian faith, and since ends and purposes which are inconsistent with such knowledge of God would be illicit, the utilization of other persons and of nature would be informed by the affirmations made about the God who is transcendent.

The legitimate claims of Christian thought with reference to God's transcendence and the values of human life could be summarized in the following terms. All created things, including human physical life, are of non-absolute value. Yet as gifts of God they are to be nourished, cared for, protected, developed, etc. The transcendent God is a known God, and the knowledge of his purposes gives direction to the ordering of life's values, but not with such clarity that man is exempted from the responsibility to judge and act in his finite condition. The relation of the believers to God in trust, gratitude, obedience, etc., places upon them the willingness and the obligation to make their orderings of values cohere with God's purposes. It also effects their personal existences; impregnating their affections and intentions, their dispositions and their purposes.

That these explorations require further precision, elaboration, and correction, goes without saying. Their fundamental warrant is this: they maintain the interaction between the positive theological affirmations of the Christian faith on the one hand, and human experience of values and of valuing on the other.

Notes

1. H. Richard Niebuhr, *Radical Monotheism and Western Culture* (New York: Harper, 1960), p. 37.

2. S. Kierkegaard, *Concluding Unscientific Postscript* (Princeton: Princeton Univ. Press, 1944), pp. 358-68. Paul Tillich, *The Protestant Era* (Chicago: Univ. of Chicago Press, 1948), pp. 161-81.

3. Theologians of various religious persuasions seem to take some pride in the possible historical connection between the belief in God's transcendence and the "secularization" of life, which might be restated "the relativization of all of life" in actual practice. It may make them personally happier to be with the world, but their positive attitude does not in itself resolve the problems of how to differentiate the better and the worse in the secular.

4. I have given some attention to this in two recent articles. See J. M. Gustafson, "Two Approaches to Theological Ethics," *Union Seminary Quarterly Review* 23 (June 1968): 337-48, and "New Directions in Moral Theology," *Commonwealth* 87 (Feb. 23, 1968): 617-23.

5. N. Hartmann, *Ethics*, Vol. II, *Moral Values* (London: G. Allen and Unwin, 1932), esp. pp. 407-43.

6. See J. M. Gustafson, "A Christian Approach to the Ethics of Abortion," *Dublin Review*, No. 514, pp. 346-64, for the way in which this affirmation of plurality affects a particular moral decision and how it is made.

25 Toward Freedom from Value

Richard Stith

Introduction

Few would wish for a world where life would always be preserved indefinitely and at all costs, for we feel that life ought sometimes to give way to other human aspirations. At the same time, most of us hold inviolable the life of every individual, regardless of its usefulness for the achievement of our heart's desires.

We have, then, two intuitions: that life must not be destroyed, but that it need not be always preserved; that every person's life is infinitely valuable, but that other things may sometimes be more valuable; that human life has sanctity, but that death may occasionally be welcomed. As we seek to map out even a crooked frontier separating these two sovereign intuitions, we soon learn that each lays claim to perhaps the entire territory of the other, and that neither will remain satisfied for long with those apparently "convenient" compromises represented by distinctions between "active and passive" or "ordinary and extraordinary." If life has infinite value, how can we passively abandon it when its preservation becomes burdensome? Or, if we can indeed abandon it, perhaps it has little value after all, and therefore may be violated. So we discover not only that we cannot easily draw a clear line of separation between our two intuitions, but also that each seeks to annihilate the other.

If we wish to intervene to prevent either side from suffering a total rout, we must begin by find-

From *The Jurist* 38 (Winter 1978). Used by permission.

ing high ground from which we can describe the proper limits of each. That is, we must develop an appealing and understandable theory of the nature and limits of the prohibition on taking human life.[1]

Here again is our dilemma: if we set the value of life low enough to account for the moral[2] intuition that we need not preserve life at all costs, we have set it too low to account for our other intuition that we ought not to kill no matter what benefits we might gain. On the other hand, if we raise the value of life to the point where no benefits are weighty enough to justify killing, we soon discover that we have committed ourselves to a surely excessive effort to eliminate death. It is my belief that our error here does not lie in valuing "mere" life or "quality" life too highly or too lowly, but rather springs from the ordinary use of the word "value." Is there no other word available? Is there no attitude, besides that of "valuing," which we take to life? I suggest that we already know and name the attitude for which we are searching: "reverence." And we also speak often about the aspect of life which accounts for our attitude of reverence: "sanctity." Unfortunately, life's *sanctity* is ordinarily confounded, or even identified, with its *value* — so that to say that life has sanctity is popularly taken to mean that it has great (or even absolute or infinite) value. Yet it is my contention that sanctity and value are radically different, and that it is precisely thinking in terms of value which obscures and may destroy our sense of the demands of human life. Only by first overthrowing the rulership of value-thought can contemporary man hope to *think* clearly about what he still already knows.

Why not kill? This essay seeks to say what there is about human life[3] as we perceive it which could account for our moral intuition that killing is wrong. In the first part of the essay, it will be argued that the value of life cannot account for the prohibition on killing for two reasons: (1) we often give life such a low "value" that this value alone would be insufficient to preclude permission to kill, and (2) we would not feel killing to be forbidden even if we were to value life infinitely. The value of life, even when made absolute, cannot preclude the taking of life. This is so not because of any defect in life, but because of the impotence of the concept and attitude called valuing. Because all valuing is for a type (or essence), I will argue, it can demand only that a quantity or quality of life exist, but never that a particular person live or be allowed to live. (To debate quantity vs. quality of life is thus *already* depersonalizing, no matter which side one takes.)

Having attacked the notion of valuing and having demonstrated the inadequacy of the attitude we take to life when we value it, in the second part of this essay, I shall describe and distinguish the attitude of reverence, the object of which has sanctity rather than value. Here it will be argued that the sanctity of life primarily demands nonviolation — rather than preservation — of life, and therefore can both forbid the taking of life and coexist with the nonpreservation of life. Thus, both our original intuitions can be affirmed: sanctity makes the individual *matter*, in a way which value does not, and yet does not demand his preservation at all costs.

Dependency, however, raises difficult problems for the meaning of sanctity. If someone's life is dependent upon our actions, is there a difference between causing death and not preserving life? This dilemma is most often currently discussed in the medical context, but it is surely as ancient as the helplessness of every newborn. Its solution, I shall argue, lies not in behavioral but in intentional criteria for actions violative of the sanctity of life.

Finally, some practical consequences of the theory of sanctity will be developed. The demands of sanctity will be described first vis-à-vis medical patients and then as a guide to social and economic planning.

I. The Insufficiency of Value

Not all of us regard killing as always wrong. Most make an exception for self-defense; many do so in cases ranging from war and capital punishment to selective euthanasia. But all of us are *reluctant* to kill. Why?

Perhaps the most frequent answer to this question is "because of the value of life." Indeed, advocates of an absolute prohibition on, say, capital punishment or euthanasia are wont to cite "the *infinite* value of life." And for people used to translating all ethical and policy issues into "value" terminology, these answers are quite understandable. After all, why *would* we protect life unless it had value? And how could the value of life *never* be outweighted unless it were infinite?

Nevertheless, it is my contention here that the value of life cannot adequately explain our reluctance to kill, that some other factor is at work. I shall try to demonstrate this thesis by first showing that even where life's value is clearly insufficient to outweigh other relevant values, we do not kill. Therefore, more than the *value* of life must matter to us. Further, I shall show that even if life had infinite value, this alone could not make killing wrong in many situations where we refrain from killing. And so, again, I conclude that we regard life as having more than value and in subsequent sections will move beyond value in search of the missing element that explains our intuitions.

Sometimes life is not valued highly. For example, many doctors would be willing not to use "extraordinary" measures in order to preserve the lives of persons able to live only a very short time in any event.[4] Such minimal amounts of life are seemingly considered not valuable enough in themselves to require the costs of heroic treatment. Yet at the same time, these physicians are apparently reluctant to kill actively and deliberately in order to avoid equivalent future costs. Why? Do these doctors see something else in life besides its value?

Even a healthy normal life may have insufficient "value" to outweigh other considerations. I am not referring here to the oft-cited case of martyrdom where someone sacrifices his own life for the sake of some noble ideal,[5] but rather, I am speaking of those instances where we value our own *and others'* lives less than comfort and convenience — as is the case with all limitations on "safety." Without a doubt we could individually and collectively live far more safely and so protect life better if we were willing to put up with the accompanying decline in life's "quality."

Nowhere is this fact more obvious than in the question of speed limits. By not drastically lowering the speed limit, our various governments and their constituencies are with statistical *certainty* allowing tens of thousands of violent deaths to occur. Nor do these deaths occur only to those who have chosen to "assume the risk" of driving. Pedestrians and dependents (e.g., children) are also killed; and given our society and economy, even those who "choose" to drive can hardly be said to have much choice in the matter. The simple fact is that thousands upon thousands of innocent and unwilling victims of traffic accidents die each year because our society and government do not want the decline in mobility and in GNP which would be caused by a speed-limit reduction.

And yet my torts teacher, Guido Calabresi, found no takers when he presented to our law school class the hypothetical case of a god who offered us an equivalent increase in societal well-being if we would agree to kill one thousand persons on an altar each year. Why this difference? Why was the class simultaneously willing (albeit with qualms) to let many die in traffic deaths and unwilling to produce the same benefits by the "sacrifice" of a lesser number?[6]

No adequate answer to these questions is possible, I submit, as long as we persist in treating human lives merely as valued objects. The way we regard people, which includes a reluctance to destroy them, has very little analogy to the way we treat that which we value, as we can see again by turning to the "potentiality-actuality" continuum — first in regard to things we value (money and justice, for example) and second in regard to human life.

Now, an object which is valued when we have it (in "actuality"), is also valued when we *could* have it (in "potentiality"). True, we discount the value of the latter by the time, trouble, and uncertainty involved. But we would surely think someone at least confused who were stingy with money that he did not wish to have it in the first place. Or again, we would doubt the sincerity of someone who strongly resisted increased injustice and yet also opposed increased justice.

But in an age of individualism and of possible overpopulation, this strange stance seems to be exactly what many people take toward other human beings. As individuals and as a society, many of us do not wish more children, do not consider them a net value when considering their possible existence. Yet once a child is born (or once it is conceived), killing is for most of us out of the question — even if the child is still "unwanted." This reluctance to destroy that which we never wanted to begin with would border on insanity if we were speaking of something we merely valued.

We cannot explain our disinclination to kill by saying simply that we value human life, because sometimes we do not value it and yet are still reluctant to kill.

I have so far argued that life's value is sometimes relatively too low to be sufficient to prevent killing and that we should look elsewhere for reasons not to kill. However, I suspect that at least some of us will not be ready to give up on value this easily. Not knowing what else we may find, some may be appropriately cautious about casting loose from what may seem the only firm mooring for the protection of life. "Should we not," some of us might ask, "find ways instead to increase the value we give to life, even at the cost of a larger population, more respirators, and even more bicycles?"

I want to cut off this last hope in the value of life by arguing that even if we somehow could agree that human life had *infinite* value, we would not necessarily prohibit killing. Only when this has been shown will the inadequacy of value be sufficiently clear to send us in search of a new base on which to anchor the protection of life.

Let us assume, then, for the sake of argument, that human life has infinite value, meaning that a human being is so valuable, of such great worth, that no other kind of entity (thing, relationship, or whatever) or combination of entities can ever be preferable to such a being. In other words, insofar as we choose rationally that which is most valuable, we would *never* choose something else instead of a living human being. Consequently, we would never destroy such a being, no matter what other kinds of benefits we might realize.

But, I submit, we might well destroy such a being for the sake of the *same* kinds of benefits (i.e., human life). Indeed, if we felt that human life were of infinite value, we might well feel morally compelled to kill, whenever such killing would save more lives than those lost.[7] We would promote capital punishment, for example, if it were the only effective means of deterring a greater number of killings. We also would kill a healthy person if his vital organs were needed to save his two ailing siblings.

We might also kill for reasons other than saving life. If life were really of infinite value but our resources were limited, would we not favor those who were more fertile and/or lived longest at least cost? Would we not like some kind of "breeder," to put to sleep the fat and the sick to make room for more people to replace them? If every single life had tremendous value, we would want as many as we could afford, for as long as possible, even if this meant destroying those requiring greater care, resources, or space.

Nor would we avoid comparing the lives we valued, and perhaps killing would result. Even if all lives had infinite value, we would have no rational objection to killing whenever an equal *substitute* were available. Even if I valued Austro-Hungarian gold coins infinitely, I would not have any objection to exchanging equivalent coins. So, too, I would not object, say, to killing the newborn if they could be quickly replaced and extra inconvenience compensated for. Moreover, I would actually *prefer* to destroy and replace if the quality of what I have could be in any way improved. Even if I valued those coins infinitely (in that I would give *anything* else to have even one), I no doubt would rather have one without a scratch. Similarly, even though I value every baby infinitely, I would prefer to have one of maximum quality, as long as it is easy to have "defective" ones sent back to their maker and new ones substituted. No value of human life can preclude killing simply to improve life's quality.

These last examples begin to reveal the reason why no amount of *valuing* of human life, not even infinite valuing, can be in harmony with our intuitive regard for life: we think that the *individual* matters, whereas anything which we merely value can be *substituted* for something relevantly identical. In other words, all valuing (in common with many other attitudes) is and must be for *types* (or essences), and not for mere particular examples of such types. No matter how highly I value gold coins, there is no possible reason I would prefer one to another if both partook equally of value-conferring characteristics. If we only *valued* human life, we would otherwise treat people as substitutable; since we do not so treat them, we must do more than value them.

Nor can we make do with value by saying that we value the individual examples of the type, rather than the type itself. Such a clarification is no doubt true, in that we do not value some kind of disincarnate type called "human life" any more than I value the abstract type of gold coins. But my point is that as long as the individuals are described as valuable only because they are human beings (i.e., examples of this type), they become substitutable. That is, if I value the set called "individual human beings," I cannot object to the substitution or maximization of the members of this set, even where this involves killing.

Someone might object here that I have misunderstood the way we value human beings; we do not value them merely as examples of the human species, but for their qualities as "unique" persons. Now, although it is certainly commonplace to hear that everyone is unique and therefore valuable, I regard such talk as a meaningful intuition seeking to express itself in meaningless value terminology. For even if people are all unique (which is quite uncertain except in the sense that they are not identical), it seems impossible that we could value them infinitely for their unique characteristics, primarily because the differences are just not so important. I do not care about a stranger in his uniqueness (his never-to-be repeated fingerprints, or his special facial appearance), but in his humanity. It is only his humanity, in fact, which I know with any degree of certainty, but this knowledge suffices to make me reluctant to kill him. Again, even if all people are unique, we can hypothetically imagine the existence of absolutely identical siblings. Would our reluctance to kill one to save the others be in any degree lessened by their lack of uniqueness? I think not, but obviously something other than valuing their individual or collective uniqueness must be at the root of our reticence. We must somehow explain how the *individual* thus matters to us, in the sense that we are reluctant to kill him even when he is exactly identical to his fellows.

II. The Alternative of Sanctity

What is the moral status of human life? What is there about human life, as we perceive it, which makes us reluctant to destroy it even where we are not interested in producing or preserving it? We have seen that "the value of life" cannot adequately explain our deference to life: Even if human life had an infinite value, *individual* human beings would not necessarily be morally protected. But in fact the value of life is often treated as far less than infinite. *A fortiori* valuing of life cannot give it the protection we think it deserves.

We need, therefore, an alternative way to conceptualize our moral recognition of life, a way different from saying "we value life" or "life has value." Before we can even begin to argue about whether or not we *ought* to have the attitudes we have to human life, we must adequately describe the attitudes we *do* have, and "valuing" is not an adequate description.

In particular, we need to explain how we can at once not wish to maximize the quantity (in numbers of years) of life, and yet seek to prevent the killing of every individual simply because he belongs to the type we call "people." We need to find an attitude which is both universally applicable to all human beings and particularly applicable to every individual, making us reluctant to kill even those we do not highly value. We already experience this attitude: I submit that when we contemplate killing someone, our mind does in fact recoil in a way unrelated to any worry about the destruction of something valuable. We feel that we simply ought not to kill, that life is not to be *violated* by us, that life is not entirely subject to our value-judgment and disposal. What name can we give to our regard for life?

Perhaps the first hurdle we must overcome is the modern tendency to identify all affirmative attitudes with some sort of valuing. The world and thought are today assumed to consist entirely of "facts" and "values." Is our reticence about killing due to some empirical fact of life? If not, conventional thought takes it to be a "value-judgment" about life. For such a mind-set, our proof that life cannot be consistently valued sufficiently to prevent killing could be evidence only that our reluctance is irrational and arbitrary.

Against such narrowness, we must show that value-language is a trap and prison of the mind, and that the moral world has a multitude of curious creatures in it — many of whom are at least as fascinating as those two beasts of burden called "fact" and "value."[8]

Our method, then, in the following few pages will be to look at three further attitudes which it is often claimed we take or should take to life: love, respect, and reverence. In each case, we shall first seek phenomenologically to distinguish the given attitude from valuing, in order both to prove that there do exist moral stances other than valuing and to get a better hold on the particular proposed alternative. Then, second, we shall ask whether the suggested attitude is one which would describe adequately our feelings and behavior toward human life.

Love

There is, of course, a loose sense of the word "love" which would seem to apply to many valued objects. I might say that I love steak or horses or diamonds — and mean little more than that I value them.

But love in the full sense in which we say we love God, or a spouse, or a friend, is not normally used for *things,* no matter how highly we value them. We cannot translate all value into love. More surprisingly, the converse is also true: we cannot translate our feelings for those we love into value terminology. "I love my wife" has a very different feel to it than "I value my wife." The latter, of course, seems at first objectionable because of its instrumentalist connotation; one suspects that I care about my wife only because I have some *use* for her. But the antagonism between love and value is even deeper. If anything, it sounds more inappropriate to eschew instrumentalism and to say "I consider my wife to have intrinsic value."

No doubt I can speak of valuing our marriage, but to speak of my wife herself having value seems to demean her — not because of a connotation of instrumental value, but because the very idea of valuing her seems to reduce her to a good or commodity to be prized and even priced. Such an attitude is at least different from, if not incompatible with, love. I appear in some way to have set myself above her and to be evaluating and preferring her, rather than unselfconsciously delighting in her in the way of *eros* and giving myself to her in the way of *agape.* Indeed, to speak solely in value terms of a beloved seems so misguided as to be nearly absurd.

Love is radically different from valuing. Moreover, at least some loves care about the beloved as an *individual,* while valuing regards only types. As we saw earlier, valuing is willing to *exchange,* to accept substitutes of at least equal value. Such willingness is quite appropriate for value since, as we have noted, valuing proceeds from a value-judgment, an evaluation, and it would be silly not to value two entities equally if both were judged to have the same valued characteristics — i.e., to be the same value type. Love, by contrast, is often not willing to accept substitutes, even identical ones. Even if God were to promise me that He would immediately substitute an identical person (or more than one) for my wife if I would let Him take her away, I would refuse. I do not want someone *like* her; I want *her.*

The fact that one cannot give sufficient reasons for one's love is directly related to the fact that one cares about the beloved as an individual and not as a type. If one were to claim that any characteristics of the beloved could fully account for one's love, then one would be saying that anyone else of the same type would be equally loved. But many lovers would not say this. Love can be for particular individuals instead of for types.[9]

Could this love be the alternative to valuing for which we are searching? Could it be that we are reluctant to kill because we love other people, even strangers? Without even beginning to discuss the complex question of whether love precludes killing but allows not preserving life, which the attitude for which we are looking must do, we must reject love. For although love may indeed care for individuals, in a way which valuing does not, this love cannot be extended to all human beings. This is so, not only because such love is too intimate and too scarce a commodity, but also because to universalize it is to destroy its particularly. That is, if we were to love all people simply as people rather than as "John" and "Mary," we would be treating the object of love as a type — i.e., "people." But it is the very non-type caring of love which makes the individual matter. Therefore, we can never fully love individuals simply because they are people. Someone who says he loves people cannot mean love in our sense here and may mean rather in the sense of liking a type.[10] Such "people-liking" may well be no more incompatible with killing individuals than is the people-valuing which we have discussed at length above.

The love alternative, then, will not work, but it has shown at least this much: We are looking for an attitude which finds significance in individuals, but not *only* in individuals — because it must be an attitude which can be for all human beings simply because they are such. We must somehow find a way to respond to this *type* called "people" in a way which nevertheless cares about individual examples of this type.

Respect

Let us look at the *feeling,* similar to admiration and esteem, which we call "respect."[11] In many circumstances, this feeling cannot easily be translated into value-talk.[12] I might tell a judge of my respect for his court, but I would be unlikely to tell him how I valued it. Valuing again seems connected to using, or at least implies congruence with one's desires; the judge is normally not interested in how desirable I find his court's judgments. Just as valuing seemed unloving in regard to a spouse, so here it seems disrespectful in regard to a court. Its evaluative boldness seems necessarily to obscure a court's particular kind of dignity, no matter how highly I finally rank the court in my scale of values.

Nor can we respect just anything we value. I can value diamonds, but do I make sense if I say "I respect diamonds"? The answer is obvious. The important point is not that I am silly or overly materialistic, but that the sentence does not make sense. It would perhaps be wrong of me, but certainly not senseless, to say, "I value diamonds more than anything else in the world." Nor is the problem that diamonds cannot be valued as ends in themselves, or that they are merely desired but not obligatory ends. I can say, "I think diamonds ought to exist for their own sake," or "Everyone has an obligation to produce a maximum number of diamonds." Yet it sounds like gibberish to say, "I respect diamonds." We would be dumbfounded by such a statement during a conversation.

Similarly, we cannot sensibly say, "I respect honor," though certainly many value it. Honor and diamonds just do not seem to be the proper *kind* of object for respect. The same holds for happiness, which has been proposed again and again as the final end of all action. We cannot say, "I respect happiness." Whether or not eudaemonism or hedonism has been refuted is irrelevant here. It certainly is possible to think of happiness as having great value, yet it is not possible even to imagine it as an object of respect.

If someone were to ask why we could not feel respect for goods of such obviously high value, we might well respond "But they don't *do* anything! How can I say I respect them?" Agency, the ability to act or to participate in action, seems necessary (though not sufficient) for respect. So we can respect intelligence but not good looks, and courage but not honor. We respect not goods or goals, but virtues — not only moral virtues but also what might be called "directed powers."

Moreover, even where the object of valuing appears to be the same as the object of respecting, our stance toward it is quite different. "I value intelligence" has a different feel from "I respect intelligence." The former puts intelligence into my sphere of action and speaks of the preference it has; the latter steps back and accords the virtue of intelligence its own proper sphere of action. The first is a holding and the second a releasing.

Undoubtedly, to respect people means something important other than to value them. In a sense, respect discerns the personhood of human beings as creatures able to persevere powerfully and creatively in their aims. And although this agency is usually discovered in people one-at-a-time, it might be that all human beings are at least potentially capable of some kinds of "virtue" (e.g., moral virtue).[13] If potential virtue is sufficient for respect-worthiness, then perhaps respect is the individual and universal attitude to human life which we are seeking. Or, again, if the human *species* generates respect in us, perhaps this feeling can be appropriate even for individuals in themselves unworthy of respect. In this way, too, respect might be the feeling we seek toward human life.

Without denying the tremendous human importance of respect felt for others (and the even greater importance to human dignity of respect *shown* — i.e., treating people as though they had various virtues even when they may not), we cannot accept respect as an adequate description of our attitude to human life primarily because respect not only does not prevent killing, but it also may even cause it. Someone we respect, after all, may be a friend or an enemy. If he is the latter, then our feeling of respect for his prowess can only increase our determination to act well against him. True, we would do so with appropriate acknowledgment and consideration for his ability, and thus our opposition would not demean him, but it might lead to his destruction. Surely among the greatest epic stories are those in which two heroes seek with all due respect to kill each other.

Reverence

Valuing feels demeaning in contrast to revering, just as it did in contrast to loving and to respecting. The sentence "I value God" seems rather presumptuous and can hardly mean that I revere Him. To talk of valuing art or law, again, is to give them less importance than to speak of reverence for them. Reverence acknowledges a nobility in its object which valuing does not, a quality we may call "sanctity."[14]

The inequality of value and sanctity can be shown in still another way: As with respect, reverence for many objects of value would be nonsensical. Happiness and honor can no more be revered than they can be respected. They are just not the proper *kind* of object for reverence. We do not and cannot revere goods or goals *as such.*[15] Therefore, we cannot revere those entities which can never present themselves to us except as desired goods or goals, and we can revere other entities which we value, such as people, only by seeing them differently than we do when valuing them.

Value is not necessary for sanctity, any more than it is sufficient. One may well not like going to church, yet behave reverentially each Sunday. One might even resent an ugly church while feeling reverence once inside. Reverence, after all, harkens back a bit to its linguistic root of *vereri*— "to fear." There is no necessary correlation between that which we revere and that which we like or value. Consequently, we may well not seek to produce or preserve many objects which partake of sanctity for us — e.g., ugly churches.[16]

Nor does the revered have to have the "virtues" of the respected. I can feel reverence for churches, even if at the same time I do not have a feeling of respect for them (because I regard them as inert objects). Only if I attribute some dynamic qualities to churches in addition to their sanctity can I also feel respect for them. That which we revere does not have to have actional virtues, as did that which we respect.

And unlike love, reverence does not need to fasten *only* upon the individual in order to make him matter. Reverence can be for types, e.g. "churches" or "people." But instead of making and having its types, as does valuing, reverence lets them be. Reverence is reticent and hesitant before that which has sanctity. It seeks to leave room for its object. Above all, it seeks not to violate the object of its concern. But not to violate that which we revere means necessarily not to violate any individual examples of the revered. Because valuing seeks actively to promote its type, it cannot be bothered with individuals, but seeks to use them in furtherance of its goal. Because reverence is a largely passive withdrawing, a "letting be" of its type, it must move back from every individual instance of that type. The only way not to destroy human life is not to destroy *any* human lives.

All valuing seeks to dominate the world. Individual entities as they exist have no significance; what matters is the production and preservation of various valued types. People, facts, matter, the stuff of being become mere resources to be used in the maximization of values. All that exists is expendable, because only the abstractions we have here called "types" count. Even if these types are considered to have intrinsic or infinite value, rather than only an instrumental value, the individual examples of these types (including human beings) are reduced to the status of desired goods and can be destroyed and exchanged at will. No wonder, then, that valuing feels bold and arrogant in contrast to the other attitudes we have examined; a world we only value is a world entirely subject to our evaluation and control.

Reverence, by contrast, eschews domination. It steps back before the "sanctity" of that which is revered, and thus necessarily before every particular which has sanctity. A limit is given to us and to our schemes of domination. We can no longer destroy and rebuild as we wish, but must accept and accommodate being, even the being of individuals. If I revere human life, if I say it has sanctity, then rather than making and controlling it, I acknowledge and defer to it; I let it be. That which has sanctity is beyond the scope of our rightful judgment; even to evaluate it seems presumptuous and wrong. True, I may sometimes (but not necessarily or always) have a kind of attraction to what I revere. But even here my feeling is not the achieving and holding stance which accompanies valuing, but is rather an appreciative awe or delight.

Both universal and individual, both not violative and not necessarily preservative, reverence remedies the deficiencies of valuing, loving, and respecting and provides an adequate concept descriptive of our feelings and behavior toward human life and, in particular, of our reluctance to kill.

Are there no exceptions to the demand that human life not be violated? At first sight it may seem that there is no kind of human killing with which we feel totally at ease, that reverence always shrinks before violence toward human life.

Still, the existence of many traditional permissions to kill must give us pause. The sanctity of life in itself would seem to prohibit capital punishment, for example: Although one can argue that such punishment does not reduce the "value" of life (because by treating the destruction of life as the greatest deterrence and retribution, capital punishment obviously treats life as the greatest good), it clearly does not treat life as something inviolable. So there must be in the minds of ardent supporters of capital punishment some exceptions to the sanctity of human life — perhaps the notion that one voluntarily forfeits one's sanctity by committing a capital crime. Proponents of voluntary euthanasia or assisted suicide would likewise seem to be arguing that one can by choice give up the sanctity of one's own life. Perhaps they are right, although sanctity seems to me something one cannot easily turn off.

But it is at least clear that a low value alone cannot destroy sanctity, cannot create exceptions to reverence for life. Valuing and revering are two separate stances toward the world. One cannot argue from the judgment that a handicapped newborn has a low value life to the conclusion that his life has no sanctity and may be taken. (Nor, of course, can one make the opposite argument that because his life has sanctity it has a high or infinite value, and so an indefinite amount of resources must be expended in keeping him alive.) Moreover, there seems no obvious way to "balance" a life's low value against its sanctity; being entirely different creatures, value and sanctity have no common scale (such as "usefulness" or "satisfaction") by which they could be weighted against each other. We return to a much more specific discussion of practical policy toward life below. Here our only point is to say that the sanctity of life creates at least a prima facie demand not to kill anyone, and that the mere fact that life sometimes lacks highly valued qualities cannot create an exception to this demand.

The same point should be noted with regard to respect and virtue: Because we can revere that which we do not respect, the fact alone that a coward does not call forth respect in everyone cannot prove that everyone does not or should not feel reverence for his life. Human life may have sanctity even when it is neither valued nor respected.

Is the moral significance of the sanctity of life exhausted by a rule forbidding killing? Does reverence for life demand only that we not kill? It would seem not. Rather, the sanctity of life is a foundation, perhaps the only foundation, for all ethical principles which make individual people a matter of moral significance.

All moral attitudes which, like valuing, *demand* something must be indifferent as between individual examples of that which they seek. Only an attitude, such as reverence, which seeks to *respond* to something necessarily has regard for every individual example of the object of its concern. Only a responding can make individuals even have "reality," in the full sense of that which must necessarily be accepted and taken into account in planning how to use the things of the world. Now the word given to individuals who have this reality, who have a final and fundamental moral significance, is "persons." Reverence, by requiring the nonviolation of human life, raises in the soft clay of value the hard rocks of persons. We can *recognize* persons, we can distinguish and make each one matter, not only in spite of the fact that they are all identical *qua* human but because of this fact. Because we revere people's lives, we cannot care only about their quantity or quality; we are suddenly aware of them as individuals who cannot be sacrificed to the whole.

What does the sanctity of human life then entail, besides not killing? The answer to this question may be: everything. All interpersonal morality and all human rights may be derivable from the sanctity of life. For that which has sanctity must be seen as always also an end in itself. Our deference to it prevents us from using it in any destructive way. Metaphorically, we are forced to leave a "space" around persons, not unlike the empty and unused space in churches, within which they can manifest themselves. "Rights" demarcate this space: The necessary supports for personal integrity, such as health, acquire a derivative sanctity which demands their nonviolation. And reverence is not indifferent to personal flourishing in this space, but in service and in delight waits for human fulfillment.

Unfortunately, the attempt to construct an entire moral system founded solely on sanctity is beyond the hope of this article. And it may well be that there are other appropriate objects of reverence (such as nature, truth, or beauty) whose sanctity is not derived from that of human life. Yet even if the sanctity of life could not stand alone, it could provide an invaluable basis for other moral principles. Justice, in particular, requires as its necessary starting point the identification of those *to whom* one must be just. It needs both to know the type on which it is to operate, i.e., human life, and to separate this type into persons. It needs to operate on individuals, but in a world of pure value, individuals cannot easily matter. Reverence for human life lets justice know where to start, lets it know for whom to ready its tools of equal regard.

Perhaps such explanation of the significance of life's sanctity seems overly abstract. Let us then speak frankly of some of the direct effects which a rule against killing may have on our moral life.

Without the sanctity of life, justice is a sham. If we must be fair to the interests of everyone existing, but need not let them remain existing, we effectively undercut all demands of justice. If we must relieve the oppressed unless we kill them, then we will probably choose the latter and easier way. The idea of justice to the weak might never even occur to us if we could get rid of others, instead of having to deal with them, when they get in our way. That justice must be founded on the inviolability of the individual is so obvious it would not be worth stating were it not sometimes overlooked in the way we treat the handicapped. On the one hand, we have today a great awareness of our responsibility for just treatment of those dependent on us as evidenced, for example, by frequent declarations of child and handicapped rights. But on the other hand, we have the "common practice" of infanticide of handicapped newborns.[17] We seem to take a schizophrenic attitude toward these dependent people: we insist that we must treat them justly if they are around, but that we may make sure they die when they first arrive. I submit that the latter allowance must in the long run either destroy the rights even of the older handicapped or else convert these very rights to a pressure to kill them while they are young.

Similarly, the demand for a universal high "quality of life" masks a monstrous choice unless it is accompanied by the recognition of life's sanctity. For there are two ways to ensure that everyone living has a high quality of life: raise the quality of all lives, or eliminate those of low quality. Without the sanctity of life to exclude the less arduous second alternative, any increase in the urgency or degree of the quality of life demanded may lead to mass killing. Achieving top quality life may be felt too expensive, drawn-out, and problematic a process, and death may be found preferable. Already this seems the plight of the "defective" newborn, but unless at some point the quality-of-life ethic is supplemented by the sanctity of life, no one with any quality deficiency can be secure. Without sanctity, we are all likely to be aided only when and to the extent that aid is cheaper than poison. Whether our "defects" are physical or mental, economic or educational, only sanctity can ensure that others see these lacks as reasons to help us rather than to destroy us.

Lastly, the sanctity of life grants us an appreciation of the dignity and meaning of the human condition which we could not otherwise have. This fact was brought home to me last year when I spoke to a meeting of an association of parents of retarded children. During my speech, I had gingerly expressed sympathy for the "burdens" of such children. Afterwards a number of parents came up to me to say that they did not think of their children as "burdens"; they were just "their children," although they did have needs others did not.

Yet surely, I thought, any parent deciding whether or not to let such a newborn child die would perceive these burdens. And then I realized that these people were *not* making such choices. For them, their children were a *given*, something they simply accepted and, indeed (as I later saw), came to delight in.

Now this prochild attitude is possible, I submit, because the sanctity of life not only does not correspond to life's value but also tends to exclude a consideration of its value. Valuing is preferring; preferring is choosing. All valuation implies the possibility of an alternative to the thing valued. But here there is no occasion to compare the child's existence with its nonexistence, and to come up with the feeling that it is a burden, because the sanctity of life excludes the possibility of killing the child.

Would we be likely to call these children "vegetables," or otherwise to denigrate them, if we accepted them and sought to help them? I think not. Yet if we saw killing as an option, could we avoid comparison and evaluation?[18] To allow killing leads us to evaluate and so to "devaluate" those whom we might kill, even if we do not do so. To eliminate the option of killing does not so much cause handicapped life to be given an erroneously high "value" as place it beyond all valuation and valuing. Handicapped lives become not merely valued, highly or lowly, but appear as the given objects of appreciation and delight.

Sanctity, in sum, by asserting the reality and importance of the individual makes possible or at least facilitates all attitudes which focus on particular persons.[19] It overthrows the depersonalizing tyranny of value, and presents others insistently to us. We must then take them into account and perhaps respond with delight, compassion, justice, or respect. Without the sanctity of human life, could even love long survive? Would it make any sense at all, say, to love a handicapped newborn if he were thought of only as a defective human-type specimen? But if we revere him first, perhaps we will come also to love him.

III. "Do Not Act or Fail to Act in Order to Have Someone Die"

Taking as data our usual feelings and behavior toward human life, we have sought to give them a name. We have focused on the curious fact that we often do not desire human life as a good or goal, and yet are deferentially reluctant to violate it in general or in its individual examples. "Valuing" was rejected as a name for this stance, primarily because such a bifurcated regard for valued objects would be irrational. Exploring more deeply, we also discovered that valuing seems improperly demeaning to human life and this fact likewise demanded an alternative to value. At the same time, love, respect, and reverence were examined; of these, reverence matched up best with the way we treat human life. Reverence does not treat life as a desired good to be achieved (as valuing would), but rather bows before the sanctity of human life, refusing to destroy any individual people (as valuing would not).

What behavior results from reverence for life? What pattern of actions is compatible both with the demand to accept life and with the permission not to achieve or maintain it? How can we both not act destructively against life and also not prolong it indefinitely?

The simplest answer to these questions is no doubt that we must not ourselves cause death, but also need not preserve life. The inviolability of life gets interpreted in a kind of spatial metaphor, so that as long as we do not "trespass" upon life we have not violated it, even though at the same time we do not come to its rescue when we see it threatened. In other words, we may not "kill," but may "allow to die"; we may not "actively" terminate life, but may "passively" stand back and let it end. Life, in this view, sets limits to our action, but not to our inaction.

Now we shall see shortly that this concept of the demands of life is quite inadequate, but we should first recognize that it is clearly founded upon more than life's value. It seeks reverently to step back before life, not to violate it. No moral theory based solely upon the *value* of life could explain such behavior; to distinguish a causing and an allowing which have the same valued (or disvalued) consequences for life would be highly irrational.

Therefore, we can already conclude that all valid criticism even of these crude distinctions must take into account the attitude of reverence out of which they may arise. That is, no one can validly be driven to support active killing simply because he believes that passive letting die is permissible. To make such a distinction, he may be operating out of a sense of life's sanctity. He is against active killing because it clearly violates life; he approves of passive letting die because he *thinks* it does not. If one argues that he is inconsistent in the way he *values* life, one has missed his point. If one argues that the active-passive distinctions themselves are meaningless, then one forces him to reevaluate his approval of letting die, rather than his disapproval of killing.

Put generally, the common moral allowance of lethal inaction, omission, passivity and the like cannot be used as a persuasive moral precedent for active killing. No refutation of the distinction between these two types of behavior can justify the latter, because the very reason the former is allowed is that it is thought to be distinguishable from the latter.

With all this said, we must nevertheless insist upon the inadequacy of all interpretations of reverence for life solely as "not causing death." Such an approach would work only if the meaning of "cause" were clear and if the intention of the moral agent were irrelevant to reverence. However, neither of these propositions is true: Causal terminology is highly elastic, and reverence involves an *attitude* of deference as well as nonviolative *behavior* toward life.

All conditions "but for" which a given death would not have occurred are necessary causes of death. Yet few are sufficient causes of death. My driving a car today may well be the *sine qua non* precondition of someone else's death. At the same time, my firing a bullet at someone would not cause his death if he were wearing a bullet-proof vest. If the sanctity of life precluded all necessary causes of death, it would prohibit the automobile; if it demanded only that no person act in a way sufficient to cause death, shooting people in the chest would not violate that sanctity.

Of course, death is far more *likely* in the latter than in the former case. Could we simply say that we must not act in such a way that we make death highly probable for others? Unfortunately, no. If I carefully hide a vial of poison in a tree, hoping that some child will find it and drink it, I have surely violated the sanctity of life even if it is extraordinarily unlikely that my wish will be fulfilled. But at the same time, few would condemn me equally for voting no to lower the speed limit to 20 m.p.h., or for giving my dying aunt requested pain-killing medication, even where these actions probably or even certainly will cause death.

The difficulty in causal terminology is even clearer if we move to the situation of *dependency*, whether another person needs my help to survive. If I fail to feed my child, I can be simultaneously and correctly said to have "caused her death" and to have "let her die." The "no trespassing" metaphor for the sanctity of life does not work here. We live in constant interaction with others; human life is not like some holy altar which we could refrain from touching at all. Indeed, "not touching" may itself violate life. That is, as long as anyone in any way depends upon my actions (a most frequent occurrence), then any omission by me may be as much a necessary or sufficient cause of death as an action could be. To say that dependent persons need not be helped is to say that we may cause their death by omission just as surely as we cause the death of independent persons by action. Yet requiring of us that we never omit any treatment where this omission tends to result in death is equivalent to requiring that we never cease any treatment which preserves life — something which our reverent intuition tells us is not demanded by life's sanctity. Causal terminology either permits killing or demands preserving life. But both are intuitively wrong. Therefore, such terminology is inadequate.[20]

Moreover, regardless of whether or not a particular action is labeled a "cause," I seem a trickster if I aim effectively to bring about someone's death, but claim not to have violated the sanctity of life. If I let my child run in the street hoping that she will be run over, I have killed her even if I could be said not to have "caused" her death. If I fail to give my wife the medicine she needs to survive, in order to collect her insurance, again I cannot honestly claim to abide by the sanctity of life, even if her disease is officially listed as "cause" of death. Both our idea of morality, which focuses on the intention of the moral agent, and reverence for life itself, which is an inner deference to the sanctity of life before it is an outer step back, seem to preclude my intent to bring about another's death by the clever use of inaction to produce a lethal situation under my control.

Should we then throw out the use of the word "cause" in explaining the demands of sanctity, and substitute the word "intent"? I do not think so. "Not causing death" is too fundamental a human response to ignore. But the word "intent" itself has a causal content: I cannot be said to place my pen in my pocket with the intent that it reach the moon unless I have posited some causal connection between my pocket and the moon. And at the same time, our analysis has been frustrated by our inability to label the morally significant causes of death. Could we not use *intent* to identify *cause*? Could we not say that an action or omission causes death if it is intended to result in death or does so? The vial of poison may be far less dangerous than my car, but I *intend* it, *wish* to kill children. Therefore, placing it in the tree is contrary to the sanctity of life even if driving is not.

In other words: if I see myself wishing for someone's death and choosing means which I hope will bring about his death, then I have acted against the sanctity of life even if the means chosen consist only in a passive withholding of life supports. More concisely, the practical rule resulting from life's sanctity is the following: "*Do not act or fail to act in order to have someone die.*"

Again, let me emphasize that we have not claimed that the sanctity of life is absolute; if it is not, then clearly no rules derived from it can be absolute. This rule would then be only a *prima facie* one, with some exceptions. However, we have not here discovered any exceptions. No one I know of has explained convincingly how life can lose sanctity or how sanctity can be weighed, say, against value. And in any event, description of the operation and limits of this rule is simpler if we state it without exceptions, and we shall adopt this simpler treatment in the rest of this essay.

Perhaps the most troublesome aspect of this rule is not what it prohibits, but what it permits. Purposely bringing about someone's death surely seems to violate the sanctity of life however it is accomplished. But we may well feel that knowingly causing someone's death, even if his death is not desired, also shows a lack of reverence for life. If I fail to give my wife her medicine simply out of laziness rather than out of malice, knowing, however, that she will die as a result, have I not killed her? If I shoot a burglar in the head, is my action in accord with reverence for his life, even if I only wish to stop him from stealing my watch and hope by some miracle that he survives? In other words, is intent here only a matter of purpose (the "in order to" is the rule formulated above), or is it also a matter of "forseeable consequences"?

It seems to me that there may be at least some sets of foreseeable consequences which are so bound up with our desired goals that they cannot be morally separated. Can I blow up a fat man stuck in the entrance to a cave, wishing only that the cave be opened and not that he be killed? I think not. But still our rule may stand, because if I do intend consequences bound up tightly with my immediate desires, I am held back by the rule. Perhaps the scope of protection afforded by the sanctity of life varies from person to person; some people may sincerely feel themselves wishing for certain foreseeable consequences of their actions while others sincerely do not. Reverence for life could still be said to require that we not act or fail to act with lethal intent. Besides, we are not here claiming that reverence for life means *only* not acting in order to bring about death, but rather that it means *at least* not so intending death. It may mean more, or it may not.

Moreover, I think that the force of this objection to the permissiveness of our rule is greatly diminished by pointing out that a given consequence of an action or omission does not automatically become moral merely because it is not prohibited by this particular rule. We are clearly responsible for all the foreseen and foreseeable results of our moral decisions. But our responsibility may be formulated in terms other than those involving reverence for life alone. Do love and familial obligation allow me to put my laziness ahead of my wife's life? I should think not, even if I in no way can be said to wish her to die. May I shoot a burglar in a fashion obviously likely to result in his death? Justice and prudence might condemn me, even if reverence did not. May we leave a worker trapped in a coal mine as long as we do not *wish* for his death? Surely human sympathy, as well as economic justice, demand that we save him, even if neglecting him is not intentional murder. In other words, our rule is intended to be supplemented by other moral norms, based perhaps on justice, sympathy, and charity. It says only, for example, that I may not fail to give alms to a beggar hoping that he will die.[21] It does not say that I may withhold alms hoping to buy a chocolate sundae. Surely I ought to help him, or at least do my fair share to meet a societal obligation to help him, if his death is otherwise imminent. But unless I ignore him out of a death wish, out of malice against his life, I have not clearly shown a lack of reverence for life.

Perhaps the prime contrast between valuing and revering is that the first seeks to preserve its object while the second does not. The first controls, the second does not. Our maxim prohibiting an antilife intention, but permitting unintended effects harmful to life, is an application of reverence to the complexity of causation and of human dependency which is quite in keeping with the noncontrolling ethos of the principle applied.

"Do not act or fail to act in order to have someone die" both liberates and disciplines us. It frees us from the idea that life is so precious that it must receive priority in all our hopes and plans. It tells us that as long as we never wish for someone's death or act on this wish, we may strive for things other than life. Life is revered while the good life is pursued. Yet the maxim also keeps us away from the countermistake of thinking that because death is sometimes acceptable, human lives may be taken for the sake of noble aims. By making sense of our intuition that life must not be destroyed but need not be preserved, it keeps us off the slippery slope to the dangerous moral abyss where human life is as expendable as the individual things we value.

IV. Applications of the Maxim

Much more investigation needs to be done into the implications of the sanctity of human life. We have in this article described at length only a "nonviolation" requirement of reverence for life, and have specified only the minimal maxim "Do not act or fail to act in order to have someone die." The sanctity of human life surely grounds behavior other than this alone, just as the sanctity of churches demands more than not intentionally vandalizing them. Nevertheless, in an effort to provide as much help as possible in matters of life and death, we shall now seek to understand some ethical consequences of the sanctity of life, as we have so far discerned it, in two areas: medical care and public policy.

The Ethics of Medical Care

A tripartite decision procedure (in all cases where death of the patient is a possibility) would seem adequately to adhere to the maxim developed above.

First of all, medical choices must be for the sake of something other than death. According to our maxim, we may never choose to act or not to act in order to bring about death. Therefore, if we assume that all choices are motivated, there must be some end other than death motivating our choice of treatment. Now, this requirement is not particularly onerous. Other ends are almost always present as possible motivating factors. But it does mean that the hypothetical "costless" patient, whose continued existence was no burden at all to himself or to anyone else, could not be gratuitously dispatched because of, say, the low value or quality of his life. We must always be acting *for* something else, not simply *against* life. And this means also, for example, that a parent or doctor caring for a handicapped newborn could not act or fail to act in any degree out of an elitist desire to put an end to such a life because it is undignified or embarrassing. Wherever a death wish is operative in a decision not to care for a newborn, the decision violates the sanctity of life.

Second, that for the sake of which the decision is made may never be something which can be obtained only by means of the patient's death. I cannot say, for example, "I didn't pull the plug to kill him, but only to collect his insurance" (or ". . . to collect his heart"). Since there is no way I can collect the insurance unless he dies, and since I know death is a necessary means to my end, I do intend death in pulling the plug. The point seems obvious in this case, but it can be more subtle. For example, it might well be in keeping with our maxim for the parents of a handicapped child to refuse a life-saving operation which is so expensive that it would economically ruin the family; there it is quite possible that the parents are still hoping and praying that their child will live. But it would not be permissible to refuse a life-saving operations because the expenses of bringing up the surviving child would be too great; here the parents are in fact wishing the death of the child. Note that in both cases, the motivation for refusal of the operation is to save money, and the almost certain consequence is death. Nevertheless, there is an important moral difference between them. Only in the second case are the costs the parents seek to avoid the "costs of continued life" (rather than only "costs of the operation"); only in the second case are the money benefits the "benefits of death" (rather than only the "benefits of not operating"). Only in the second case do the parents omit the operation *in order* to have death occur.

Third, our maxim must never be applied alone, must always be used together with other moral norms. We must never assume that a particular action or omission is permissible simply because it is not done in order to have someone die. Social justice, contract, sympathy, charity, and all the relevant norms of a complex moral universe must be at least tacitly considered before fatal damage is done. So, for example, besides not seeking to get rid of burdensome newborns, one should also not unjustly neglect them, especially where such neglect is likely lethal.

Pope Pius XII, in his oft-quoted medical address of November 24, 1957, seems to address himself to this third point. He there declares that only failure to provide the "ordinary" means of support would constitute what we have here called "neglect." "Extraordinary" supports would go beyond what justice and charity demand, and so they need not be provided:

> "Natural reason and Christian morals say that man (and whoever is entrusted with the task of taking care of his fellowman) has the right and the duty in case of serious illness to take the necessary treatment for the preservation of life and health. This duty that one has toward himself, toward God, toward the human community, and in most cases toward certain determined persons, derives from well ordered charity, from submission to the Creator, from social justice and even from strict justice, as well as from devotion toward one's family.
>
> "But normally one is held to use only ordinary means — according to circumstances of persons, places, times, and culture — that is to say, means that do not involve any grave burden for oneself or another."[22]

The Pope's permission here to withhold extraordinary life supports is, I suggest, misinterpreted if it is taken to mean that supports may be withheld *in order* to have someone die. Note that he does not even directly mention the sanctity of life in his above enumeration of the norms governing withholding of care. Apparently, he is taking for granted that no actual attack on life is involved, and therefore he considers only the moral principles governing the extent of affirmative duties of care. Indeed, he later adds that even the withholding of extraordinary means (specifically, resuscitation attempts) is subject to two additional norms, both directly relevant to our concept of the sanctity of life:

> Even when it causes the arrest of circulation, the interruption of attempts at resuscitation is never more than an indirect cause of the cessation of life, and one must apply in this case the principle of double effect and of '*voluntarium in causa.*'[23]

Double effect and *voluntarium in causa* are roughly equivalent to the maxim of intention developed in this essay.[24] What the Pope seems to be saying is that if life supports involve extraordinary hardship, then justice *et al.* do not require that they be given — provided, of course, that the intention of the omission is to avoid the hardship rather than to achieve death.

The simple "ordinary-extraordinary" distinction is no doubt a useful rule of thumb, which normally would sufficiently protect life. It is quite unlikely that one would omit the ordinary means of life (e.g., food) unless one's purpose were to kill; and it is quite likely that extraordinary means would be omitted to avoid hardship to the patient or to others. Nevertheless, ordinary means *might* be withheld from a patient without an operative death wish by the physician (e.g., out of deference to the patient's wishes). Similarly, extraordinary means *might* be withheld in order to have a dependent patient die. So, if one treats the papal distinction as authority, one should always point out that even extraordinary care must not be withheld in order to have death occur.

Are these guidelines unduly restrictive? On the contrary, they are at once a protection for the patient and a freedom for those caring for him. The patient knows that he will not be purposely violated in his weakness, though he must also modestly acknowledge that his welfare is not the center of the moral universe. The physician knows that he is free to seek the good of the patient, of his family, and of all others affected, without the fear of death as the ultimate evil — as long as he never wishes for death and acts on this wish. He might, in my opinion, accede to the family's wish to care for a handicapped child at home rather than at the hospital, even if he thought this meant certain death for the child. His goal here might well be to provide a more loving environment for the child, and a wish for death might be far from his mind. Or, as already suggested, he could discontinue a necessary life-saving treatment at the request of a competent patient, having in mind only respect for the patient's autonomy and not a desire for the patient's death. He could, perhaps, inject a dose of morphine into a dying patient, where no other pain-killer were available, even though he knew that the dose were sufficiently high eventually to cause death. He would be acting to relieve suffering, not to achieve death, and would not be disappointed if the patient survived. Or he could disconnect "unnatural" or "undignified" life supports from a comatose patient, out of deference to aesthetic sensibilities, as long as no intent to achieve death were present and no injustice or other wrong were being done.

"Quality of life" criteria might be relevant to such decisions. The fact that a dying patient has at best only a short and/or comatose existence left could be taken into account in deciding whether further burdens on patient, family, medical personnel, and society are worthwhile. Additional resuscitations might seem to do little good where the patient could at best gain only a few hours more of possible unconscious life; and avoiding pointless draining of the hospital staff and perhaps physical abuse of the patient (e.g., broken ribs) might seem a sufficient reason not to resuscitate. In other words, the low benefits to be gained by treatment could be considered as well as the costs to be avoided. Where the sum were negative, the treatment might be discontinued in order to save these costs rather than in order to achieve death.

However, we must again emphasize that this calculus is subject to two very important strictures. First of all, in this cost-benefit weighing neither the "costs of life" nor the "benefits of death" can have any place whatsoever. It is one thing to discontinue a procedure which is a burden and is doing little good; it is quite another to terminate a life which is itself thought burdensome. Second, justice and other moral norms must be brought into play. If parents refuse an expensive operation on their handicapped newborn because they do not want to waste their resources on what their doctor calls a "defective," they are not clearly failing to revere life. They are not trying to kill him, just to save money. Nevertheless, although such a parental decision is not the moral equivalent of murder, it does seem to me quite probably a violation of familial obligation, and a gross injustice if not by the parents then by the society which does not fairly share this financial burden. In not falsely calling such calculated neglect murder, we do not and must not forget the callous selfishness which may motivate our abandonment of those who depend on us for their lives. Here again the sanctity of life must be considered not alone, but as the undergirding of justice. Without the sanctity of life, talk of justice is a sham because we can eliminate those with a claim on us. But without justice, lethal discrimination is easy. Both are necessary. Sanctity must guarantee that individual persons are recognized and not destroyed, and then justice must ensure all persons are treated fairly.[25]

The Ethics of Public Policy

A similar procedure would be applicable to political decision-making.

First, the sanctity of life would preclude any policy choices, whether by action or omission, done in order to bring about death. Most obviously, capital punishment would not be permissible, unless some relevant exception to life's sanctity exists. Its immediate purpose is without a doubt the taking of human life. But more subtle uses of death would likewise be disallowed. We could not individually or collectively withhold food from drought-stricken foreigners, even if they are our enemies, if our purpose is to have them decimated. We also could not allow famine in order to "teach a lesson" to other countries about the benefits of birth control. One cannot judge the morality of private or governmental actions only by their efforts; it is not that we must never allow anyone to die around the world, but rather that we cannot make death a goal of our programs or nonprograms.

And even where death is not obviously a goal,

we must be very careful not to include in our cost-benefit calculations any of the "costs of life" or the "benefits of death," because if we do we are unavoidably intending the deaths necessary to eliminate such costs or to achieve such benefits. So, for example, as far as our maxim is concerned, it would seem permissible to leave the speed limit at 55 m.p.h. in order to maintain economic efficiency, even knowing that thousands of persons will thus be killed. We do not here desire their deaths, and may even impose safety requirements to minimize the number of fatal accidents. Death is acquiesced in rather than hoped for. However, it would be impermissible to include in a cost-benefit analysis of various suggested speed limits items such as savings on Social Security benefits as the old are killed or the net economic gain by the elimination of other "marginal" members of society, i.e., members whose consumption is expected to be greater than their production (such as the chronically unemployed). This point cannot be overemphasized, because an advancing medical technology and an increasing marginal population may soon force difficult decisions upon us. Even though these "benefits of death" are real, they must be ignored in policy-making. We must simply shut our eyes to such benefits, and of regard for the sanctity of life, in policy-making for highways, hospitals, and the care of the dependent — at home and abroad. Analysts must, when necessary, submit "inaccurate" figures on the total costs and benefits of various proposed policy options, in order not to allow the benefits of death to have any weight in public planning.[26]

Lastly, and as always, we must never think only of life's sanctity. A high speed limit may be imprudent or unjust even if not irreverent to life. Do pleasure and profit outweigh the enormous violence of traffic deaths? We cannot honestly avoid this question simply by pointing out that we are sorry about these deaths, are looking for means to prevent them, and are compensating those who survive.

We can speak clearly about the ways we act toward other people only if we do not force all morality into value-talk, but allow words such as "sanctity" to develop an independent resonance. The ethical norms developed in this essay are the echoes of sanctity, and, as such, are meant to be taken seriously. Yet words are prior to echoes, and first of all is freedom of value-free speech.

—The generous assistance of
the St. Louis University School
of Medicine made possible this article.

Notes

1. By "life" or "human life" I mean "living humans." This meaning, I take it, is that most commonly understood in speaking of the value or sanctity of human life. To "value human life" thus means to "value people" — except that the first phrase focuses upon those valued as simply alive, while the second pulls us away from the question of life or death and toward the complexities of social existence. Put another way, human life is the foundation which all people have in common; to value life is thus to value people simply because of this foundation rather than because of their maturity, personality, or whatever. A newborn baby is perhaps the clearest example of naked human life.

By contrast, I do not in this essay take seriously the frequent way of speaking which treats life as a thing which may be "given to" or "taken from" someone. For an organism, to live is to *exist.* The idea that existence (life) is a separate entity which can be added to or subtracted from a person seems to me a worthy subject for reflection, but only indirectly and confusedly applicable to the question of whether or not we may destroy people. When I say "taking human life," I mean eliminating it, not removing it.

2. Except where otherwise stated, this essay deals entirely with morality, and with the moral underpinning of law, rather than with law itself.

3. Implicit here is that there is phenomenologically something *about life* which makes us reluctant to kill. We do not refrain from killing *only* out of obedience to a disincarnate moral rule not to kill, whether that rule derived from God or from ourselves. We genuinely care about not harming people, and therefore are already reluctant to destroy them prior to explicit reflection upon God's commands or upon the moral rules which we personally would like everyone to follow.

Furthermore, we do not feel such rules themselves to be arbitrary or to have a status no higher than our desires. Rightly or wrongly, we feel that they are an expression of human dignity rather than *only* of formalized self-interest or will. In this essay, I argue that this dignity cannot be called "value."

4. See the 1973 A.M.A. statement condemning intentional mercy killing but allowing cessation of extraordinary life support, reprinted and criticized for inconsistency in the important article by J. Rachels, "Active and Passive Euthanasia," *New England Journal of Medicine* 292:2 (January 9, 1975): 78-80. Rachels in turn has been criticized (rightly, in my opinion) by T. Sullivan for misunderstanding the A.M.A. position. See "Active and Passive Euthanasia: An Impertinent Distinction?" in *The Human Life Review* 3:3 (Summer, 1977): 40-46. Sullivan's distinctions are similar, but not identical, to those developed below.

5. Nor am I here or elsewhere in this essay thinking of intentional suicide. The primary method of this essay (placing human life before us, and asking our attitude toward it) is simply not easily adaptable to an examination of self-killing. Perhaps our conclusions are nevertheless applicable to suicide: See the powerful attempt by Germain Grisez to grapple with suicide within a project in many ways similar to that of this essay in "Suicide and Euthanasia," *Death, Dying and Euthanasia*, edited by D. Horan and D. Mall (Washington: University Publications of America, 1977), pp. 742-817.

6. For Calabresi's own explanation of this kind of discrepancy, which differs from my own, see "Reflections on Medical Experimentation in Humans," *Daedalus* 98:2 (Spring, 1969): 387-405.

7. Note that I am here assuming only that life has an infinite *exchange* value, i.e., that we would exchange an infinite amount of anything else for one life. If one life were taken to provide infinite *satisfaction*, then we might be indifferent between preserving one life or many. Such infinite satisfaction-value would be even less able to prevent killing than would infinite exchange value, for although it would refute the claim that we ought to kill one person to save 2 or 50 (by affirming that one person has as much value as 50), it would also be indifferent to killing 50 to save one — i.e., it would affirm that no value would thus be lost.

8. Further political and historical studies would be of immense help in a struggle for liberation from value, perhaps along the lines suggested by Karl Mannheim in *Ideology and Utopia* (New York: Harcourt, Brace and World, 1936), p. 82:

> . . . [T]he fact that we speak about social and cultural life in terms of values is itself an attitude peculiar to our time. The notion arose and was diffused from economics, where the conscious choice between values was the starting point of theory. This idea of value was later transferred to the ethical, aesthetic, and religious spheres, which brought about a distortion in the description of the real behavior of the human being in these spheres. Nothing could be more wrong than to describe the real attitude of the individual when enjoying a work of art quite unreflectively, or when acting according to ethical patterns inculcated in him since childhood, in terms of conscious choice between values.

9. A particular entity is distinguished not by *what* it is but by *where* it is in space-time. I can think abstractly of a table, but I cannot think of, say, the third identical table I am about to build unless I mentally insert it into space-time and imagine it existing sequentially with the first two. Only if they have differing space-time coordinates can two entities of the same type be distinguished. Only if they so exist, consequently, can they be *thought* of as particular individuals; the mind otherwise knows only quantity and quality, not particulars.

Put another way, one might say that "location" is part of the essence of an individual. In searching for a way of thinking which can respect the individuality of people, we are thus looking for a mode of thought which can take such location seriously.

10. The religious person, however, may mean that he loves God, that God loves all persons individually, and that he thus indirectly loves all those loved by his Beloved as individuals. This alternative to valuing is not insignificant, but its exploration here would take us too far from the common realm of philosophy and phenomenology.

11. The word "respect" is also used for actions which may be quite unconnected to *feeling* respect. So, for example, one might "act respectfully" in church, even though one felt reverence rather than respect. Or one might treat an authority with respect, even though one felt only fear. Or one might respect someone's rights, in the sense simply of not violating them, while feeling nothing at all or even contempt for them. Our concern here is to describe only the feeling we call respect, not the many actions we call by the same name.

12. Certainly value requires more to be treated as a component of respect and a measure of human dignity, as happens in Marvin Kohl's "Voluntary Beneficent Euthanasia," in *Beneficient Euthanasia* (Buffalo: Prometheus Books, 1975), p. 133.

13. So Michael Polanyi, in *The Tacit Dimension* (Garden City: Doubleday, 1966), pp. 51-52 writes:

"... [H]owever greatly we may love an animal, there is an emotion which no animal can evoke and which is commonly directed toward our fellow men. I have said that at the highest level of personhood we meet man's moral sense, guided by the firmament of his standards. Even when this appears absent, its mere possibility is sufficient to demand our respect.

"[B]oth this moral sense and our respect for it presuppose an obedience to commands accepted in defiance of the immemorial scheme of self-preservation which had dominated the evolutionary process up to this point."

Kant, too, makes the capacity for moral action a basis for respect for humanity, although he sometimes appears to be thinking of a feeling more akin to what is below called "reverence," rather than to what is here called respect. See, e.g., *Critique of Practical Reason* (Indianapolis: Liberal Arts Press, 1956), pp. 99ff.

14. D. Callahan, in *Abortion: Law, Choice, and Morality* (New York: Macmillan, 1970), may be correct about some of the behavioral consequences of the sanctity of life, but he and others he cites (e.g., Gustafson at p. 325) too quickly assume that sanctity can be only a kind of value. He simply asserts that "when we speak of 'the sanctity of life,' we are . . . speaking of . . . the value we attach to human life" (p. 326). Daniel Maguire, too, despite his seeming awareness of the nature of sanctity, seems to equate it with value. *Death by Choice* (New York: Schocken Books, 1974), pp. 92-93, 156-57.

15. The sanctity of life may, however, be to some degree analogous to the "sanctity" of goods which are owned by another. We leave such goods alone, or feel numinously uneasy with them if we steal them, not because we value them *or* disvalue them, but simply because they are not properly within our control. Note that such "sanctity" necessarily has a transcendent origin : a book is more than a mere book if it is someone else's book. God's ownership of life could be the explanation of *this* kind of sanctity, or there might be a better explanation. In any event, our experience of human life seems not identical to our rather more cool and uncaring deference to the property of others. The sanctity of life may be thus not reducible to the sanctity of property, even of divine property.

16. Churches are used here as a familiar example of that which appears to have sanctity. However, sanctity need not be found only in religious contexts. A history of art teacher has told me of a recent sale of a large piece of land in which buyer and seller quarreled over who should pay the enormous costs of removing certain unsaleable monumental sculptures which neither party wanted or valued. Clearly the simplest and cheapest solution would have been to destroy the sculptures and cart away the pieces. But "the sanctity of art" made this impossible. At the same time, the low value of the works of art justified doing little or nothing to preserve them from gradual destruction by the weather.

17. Robertson, "Involuntary Euthanasia for Defective Newborns: A Legal Analysis," *Stanford L. Rev.* 27 (1975): 213, 214. Robertson is speaking primarily of passive (or "negative") euthanasia; but see *Pediatric News,* February, 1977, for a report of the 1974 Sonoma Conference on neonatal ethics where seventeen out of twenty panelists approved the possible use of active (or "positive") intervention to end the life of a presumably handicapped infant. Most graphic is the documentary film "Who Should Survive?" produced by the Kennedy Foundation in 1971, in which a mongoloid newborn is intentionally let die by his parents and the hospital staff.

18. See David Mall's analysis of human objectification in his essay "Death and the Rhetoric of Unknowing," in *Death, Dying, and Euthanasia, op. cit.,* pp. 659-61.

19. Such tremendous functional significance cannot, of course, justify a personal or societal belief in the sanctity of life. If one "believes" in life's sanctity only because such a belief is useful, then one in fact is only *pretending* to believe — and this pretense will be dropped in private at any time, and in public whenever it becomes too costly. Only if we believe that life *really* has sanctity can we reap the full benefits of this belief.

20. That is, it is inadequate unless one adopts and uses highly conventional definitions of "cause." So, for example, one could say that only the omission of a pre-existing duty can "cause" death. But then one must develop a full description of all prior duties to others before one can make sense of a requirement not to cause death. Such a prerequisite does not seem in keeping with the immediacy of the demand for reverence for life and seems difficult or impossible to fulfill in the area of morality. But cf. the excellent application of this data to the conventions of legal causation in G. Fletcher, "Prolonging Life," *Wash. L. Rev.* 42 (1967): 999-1016.

21. Note that such a hope would be joined here with an attempt to effectuate it. A *mere* hope for someone's death, which is not the motive for an action or an omission, might not be precluded by reverence for life.

22. "The Prolongation of Life," reprinted in *Death, Dying and Euthanasia, op. cit.,* pp. 283-84.

23. Ibid., p. 286.

24. For a summary of the meaning of these terms in traditional Catholic moral theology, see T. O'Donnell, *Morals in Medicine* (Westminster: Newman Press, 1960), pp. 39-44.

25. Adequately to develop the proper medical-legal applications of this moral rule would require an additional article. Nevertheless, a few remarks can be made on its legal usefulness and limits.

Because of the extremely subjective nature of the "in order to," it may well be that our legal institutions are unsuited to the full enforcement of the maxim. Even so, the maxim could be a legislative guide in that lawmakers could ask themselves whether or not a proposed legal rule would make it *easy* for those with lethal intent to be successful. "Death with dignity" legislation could be carefully limited to ensure that it is at least *likely* that treatment withdrawals occur to achieve dignity rather than to achieve death. "Proxy" or "substitute" decisions (especially by interested parties) for an incompetent patient could, for example, be strictly limited, in keeping with fiduciary principles. The "trustee" for the patient's life should have far less freedom to refuse life-saving treatment than the patient himself would have, in order to avoid the possibility of the patient being taken advantage of.

But the idea of "specific intent" is not entirely unheard of in our law. It has had a place in the criminal law (see e.g., Rollin M. Perkins, *Criminal Law*, Second Edition [Mineola, New York: Foundation Press, 1969], pp. 762-64) and in recent constitutional law dealing with the intent to segregate (see *Village of Arlington Heights v. Metropolitan Housing Development Corporation*, 97 S.Ct. 555, 563-66 [1977]). Enacting into law a prohibition on the withdrawal of even "extraordinary" or "undignified" life-supports with the specific intent to end life, could serve the salutary function of clarifying and guiding medical decisions, even if because of evidentiary obstacles the laws were seldom if ever enforced. To omit such a prohibition could promote the misunderstanding that the more dependent a person becomes, the less sanctity his life has.

Yet there can never be full legal-moral congruence. The law can never forbid all omissions designed to cause death, but only lethal omissions of a prior legal duty. Law would over-extend itself if it were to prohibit, say, failure to give money to beggars with the secret intent that they die. And, too, it might be appropriate legally, by way of excuse rather than of justification, to allow intentional killing *in extremis* (e.g., lifeboat cannibalism) and/or to show mercy for merciful motives. For all these reasons, our maxim seems most appropriately considered only a guide for law making, rather than an absolute legal rule.

26. Cost-benefit analysts, in other words, must go beyond a pluralistic willingness to have their findings considered only one factor, along with morality and other influences, in policy decisions. If the "benefits of death" are to have zero weight in such decisions, but if other costs and benefits are to be taken into account, then the proposed "inaccurate" figures must at some point be made available. See M. W. Jones-Lee, *The Value of Life: An Economic Analysis* (Chicago: University of Chicago Press, 1976), pp. 3ff for a discussion of the pluralistic or "restricted" theory of policy decision. Mr. Jones also provides an excellent review of the literature on value of life vs. value of safety which is sensitive at various points to the possibility that some people's lives might be found to have a net negative economic value under those modes of analysis which do not rely entirely on gross output measurement, e.g. pp. 33, 43-46.

26 Alien Dignity: The Legacy of Helmut Thielicke for Bioethics

Karen Lebacqz

This experience of rejection made me think that there was no God, because in moments of rejection like that one I feel I am no good. And if I am no good, how can there be any God? Am I not made in the image and likeness of God?[1]

With these haunting words, Ada Maria Isasi-Diaz points not only to the painful realities of racism and sexism in our midst but also to the centrality of the image of God for theological ethics and to the intimate link between that image and the valuation of human beings. "If I am no good, how can there by any God? Am I not made in the image and likeness of God?" What does it mean to be made in the image and likeness of God and how does it relate to our valuation as persons?

No modern ethicist has elaborated the link between the image of God and the valuing of persons with more care than the great German theologian Helmut Thielicke. Twenty-five years ago Thielicke provided the reflections on theological foundations for Houston's first international conference on ethics in medicine and technology. In "The Doctor as Judge of Who Shall Live and Who Shall Die,"[2] Thielicke suggested that there are two ways to view people: in terms of their utility, or in terms of their "infinite worth." Thielicke opted for their infinite worth, and based that option on his understanding of the "alien dignity" of persons.

In this essay, I will explore briefly the theological roots and meaning of "alien dignity" in Thielicke's thought, and then develop the legacy of this term for the task of health care ethics today by illustrating its implications in several arenas of medicine and health care. Although there are problems with the concept of alien dignity, I will argue that it provides a rich legacy for protecting and equalizing human beings, for requiring personal responsibility, for attending to structural problems in health care, and for seeing humans as fundamentally relational.

Alien Dignity and the Image of God

The "incommensurable, incalculable worth of human life,"[3] argued Thielicke, does not reside in any immanent quality of human beings, but in fact that we are created and redeemed by God. Our worth is imparted by the love bestowed on us by God. Human worth is thus an "alien dignity," given in the relationship between humans and God. It is the image of God in us that gives us our alien dignity.

The image of God in humans was not, for Thielicke, a given attribute or property, such as rationality or even freedom.[4] Rather, "the divine likeness rests on the fact that God remembers [us]. . . ."[5] The image of God is not our own immanent or ontic dignity, not some quality such as rationality that "imitates" the character of the divine, but rather a statement of our relationship to God. To speak of the *imago Dei* is to speak of God's love for us. God creates us in love, calls us in love, and redeems us in love; and it is this love that creates the image of God in us and gives us our worth. The image of God is not substantive, but relational.

Human worth is therefore "alien" in the sense that it comes to us from God. It is "that alien dignity which is grounded in and by [the one] who does the giving."[6] As a *proprium*, a true ontic possession or attribute in the strict sense, it belongs only to Christ.[7] The divine likeness of human beings is fulfilled only in Christ. Only in Christ is there the immediacy of relation to God that con-

From Allen Verhey, ed., *Religion and Medical Ethics: Looking Back, Looking Forward* (Grand Rapids: Eerdmans,1996), pp. 44-60.

stitutes the *imago Dei,* and that was destroyed in the "Fall." The immediacy thus lost is restored in Christ, and so we participate in this divine likeness through Christ. God "remembers" us and draws us back into proper relationship, and herein lies the image of God.

The image of God is therefore ineffable and difficult to describe concretely, since it does not consist in specific characteristics or attributes that can easily be named.[8] For Thielicke, the divine image in humans was like a mirror reflecting the glory of God. Like a mirror, the image goes dark when the source of light is withdrawn: "it possesses only borrowed light."[9]

The *imago Dei* is thus, substantively, a representation of agape — of God's love for humans. It is therefore also agape that recognizes and realizes the *imago Dei,* seeing the other person in her standing before God rather than in her "utility" value for me. It is agape that allows us to love our enemies, not identifying them with their opposition to us, but seeing in them the children of God.[10]

For Thielicke, then, to speak of the alien dignity of human beings is to speak of their infinite worth. It is to speak of their relationship to God, and of the love with which they are held by God. It is to speak of what God has "spent" on human beings, the love poured out that creates an unimpeachable worth possessed by "even the most pitiful life."[11] To speak of alien dignity is to speak of the individual destiny received from God, of the indivisible totality of the person, of the person's standing in the eyes of God.

Problems with Alien Dignity

"Alien dignity" may not be a comfortable term today, especially for feminists and others from oppressed groups. Two problems are immediately evident. First, to speak of dignity as "alien" is to imply that it is not truly "ours." If the source is outside humans, then it seems something that is "not us." If it is only reflective of a light that originates elsewhere, then it seems that it could too easily be removed. To see dignity as "alien" thus seems to remove it too much from the *humanum* and to make it precarious.

In our post-Enlightenment world, and particularly since the human potential movement, the Western world has tended to stress the dignity and potential that are inherent to humans. We want a dignity that is *precisely* ours, that is so much a part of us that there can never be any recognition of us without an acknowledgment of that dignity. To suggest that one's dignity is "alien" and comes from outside may perhaps make us think that it is therefore more vulnerable to attack or erosion. We are probably more comfortable today with a notion of *intrinsic* dignity, as this notion would imply something so inbuilt that it can never be taken away.

Second, Thielicke's notion that alien dignity is like the reflection of a mirror in which all light comes from outside may appear to posit human beings as empty vessels. All value, all light, all dignity appear to come from God and from God alone. Thielicke's God seems distant and omnipotent. The gulf between the divine and the human seems virtually unbridgeable. Thielicke's alien dignity, the mirror reflecting God's light, seems to pose an all-powerful God and an all-empty human being: "the *imago Dei* depends on the reflecting of alien light, a process which is always under the control of the glory of God which casts the reflection."[12] Any sense of divine-human partnership seems fragile at best. We appear to have a process in which humans are at most pawns in a game controlled by God.

Such a transcendent, omnipotent God has been abandoned in many contemporary theologies. Liberation and feminist theologians tend instead to speak of a vulnerable God who suffers with us or of a partnership between humans and God. How else are we to explain the suffering of children who are abused by their parents or of oppressed peoples everywhere? An omnipotent God who fails to intervene in human suffering seems a cruel hoax.[13]

We might wonder, then, whether Thielicke's notion of alien dignity is theologically and ethically adequate. Does it create too fragile a dignity, not sufficiently rooted in human nature itself? Does it pose a God too remote and removed for an age of liberation that needs a God who suffers with us?

Within the scope of this essay, I cannot fully address these questions. Nonetheless, I believe that such doubts may arise from a misreading of the implications of Thielicke's work, and that Thielicke's core notion of alien dignity offers protections and insights badly needed today. I will illustrate this claim by pointing to five implications of alien dignity and their application in bioethics.

Implications of Alien Dignity for Ethics

1. *Alien Dignity* Protects *People*

That human dignity is "alien" does mean that it comes from outside me; it does not arise from within me. But for Thielicke, it is also integral to me. Since it is given to me in my very creation by God, since it is bestowed from the beginning with God's love, it is always present with me. It is therefore intimately mine, as truly mine as any of my characteristics and far more enduring. My youth will surely pass, my beauty will fade, but my alien dignity does *not* dim, in Thielicke's view.

Precisely because human dignity is "alien," it does not have to be *earned,* and it cannot be *lost.* It does not depend on my skin color, my sex, my sexual orientation, my intelligence, or any other particular characteristic or achievement. It does not depend on "works."[14] Precisely because it is "alien" to me, it cannot be given away by me or taken away by others. It is both alien and inalienable. It is indelible, a mark put on us by God's love that permeates our being to the core. Since the alien dignity of humans depends only on God's love, and since God's love is constant and enduring, so is the dignity of each person.

To speak of alien dignity is therefore precisely a way of securing the basic inalienable worth of every person. Alien dignity *protects* people. They are inviolable. "Even the most pitiful life" retains its dignity, and its incommensurable, incalculable worth. Because of this worth, humans may not be subjected to the dictatorial rule of technical capacities.[15]

The concept of alien dignity thus provides a strong base for responding to difficult bioethical questions such as when to cease treatment. In "House Calls to Cardinal Jackson," David Schiedermayer struggles to explain why he continues to treat a 79-year-old woman who has been "mindless, lights-on-but-nobody's-home" for over ten years.[16] In trying to explain why he does not withdraw her feeding tube, Schiedermayer speaks of the daughter's love for the old woman and also of the fire that still burns in her green eyes. Then he asks:

> What is it that gives a person dignity? What is that inner grace that projects out toward the doctor, so that he, despite his intellect and education and training and skills, is taken aback? . . . The dignified are above reproach. You can't take dignity away from the dignified.[17]

Schiedermayer speaks here of the dignity of a woman who no longer functions as she once did. There is something about Cardinal Jackson that makes her inviolable to him, in spite of her advanced age and her mental incompetence. This something, which Schiedermayer calls her dignity, is what Thielicke would have called her alien dignity. For Thielicke, it is the worth that does not fade with age nor dim with incompetence because it comes from God.[18] Schiedermayer finds it harder to name the source of the dignity. He mentions not the love of God but the love of Cardinal Jackson's daughter, the hardship of Cardinal Jackson's life, the sense that we cannot abandon her after her history of discrimination and mistreatment.

While Schiedermayer does not name the same source of dignity that Thielicke would name, his understanding of the inviolability conferred by that dignity comes very close to Thielicke's. For Thielicke, alien dignity of humans means that others can never be treated simply for their instrumental value. They cannot be a means to an end for me. Their technical or utilitarian capacities do not define their worth. Hence, they do not lose their worth when they cease to function or when their capacities diminish.

In *The Ethics of Sex,*[19] for example, Thielicke argues against prostitution because it entails the instrumentalization of a human being. Such instrumentalization — turning the other into an instrument for my pleasure or satisfaction — is contrary to the alien dignity that prevents another from being simply a means to my ends.

Elsewhere, Thielicke argues that one can never fully possess another human being. To try to do so would be to destroy him at the center of his being.[20] One cannot split off parts of a person or objectify that person, but must deal with the whole person, with the "indivisible totality of a human being."[21] Only this is recognition of the alien dignity of the other.

Nor are others subject to the fickle nature of our emotions. To see another as the bearer of an alien dignity means that our regard for that other will remain even when her or his importance for us diminishes.[22]

Thus, in none of these ways can we take away the dignity of the other. Alien dignity protects the other from our vagaries, from objectification or instrumentalization, from our lust for possession or for power, from our imposition of our goals and purposes. If Cardinal Jackson's daughter tired of caring for her mother and ceased to love her, the old woman would not lose her dignity, in Thielicke's view.

In the medical arena, the inviolable worth of the other means that no one could simply be used, for example, as an organ bank. It means that research on human beings must respect those persons as whole beings, even if they are convicted criminals or the "most pitiful" of mental patients.[23] The notion of alien dignity provides fundamental protections against using persons as means to the ends of others, against objectifying people, against the intrusions of power to oppress the powerless.

2. *Alien Dignity* Equalizes *People*

If the first implication of alien dignity is the protection of persons, the second is the equalization of persons. Since human worth is not earned or achieved, but given by God, no one is "worth" more than others. All were bought for a price, and therefore all carry an incalculable value. The worth of human life for Thielicke was "incommensurable" — it is not possible to measure one person's worth against another. Genuine agape, which recognizes the alien dignity in the other, "does not degrade the other person." Rather, it honors the other, and puts the other "on the same level" as the one doing the loving.[24] Alien dignity has an equalizing effect.

This is reinforced by understanding that alien dignity would never allow the other to be dealt with simply in utilitarian terms. The "use value" or "social contribution value" of the person is not the person's true value. Only the alien dignity, the love poured out by God, represents the true value of the person. This value is unique, individual, incommensurable.

Operating out of this understanding of alien dignity would therefore prevent some approaches to the allocation of health care resources. In his study of medical directors of kidney dialysis and transplant facilities, John Kilner found that "more than half of the directors would assess the different social value of various candidates" for dialysis or transplant, and "less than a third would institute a more egalitarian random selection."[25] Thielicke's understanding of alien dignity would suggest that such attempts to measure the social worth of candidates for dialysis violates the incommensurable dignity of each.

In "The Doctor as Judge of Who Shall Live and Who Shall Die," Thielicke tackled directly the problem of insufficient resources to help those who might live with medical intervention. He recognized explicitly that at times, difficult choices must be made and some must be chosen to live while others die. Under these circumstances, humans will make the best choices they can. Considerations of social worth may in fact enter those choices. But there can never be, for Thielicke, an easy conscience about this choice. "One must simply run the risk of making the decision — and be prepared in so doing to err, and thereby to incur guilt."[26] When we must choose some to live at the price of death for others, we should experience that choice as wounding. These are the wounds that "must not be allowed to heal."[27] They touch on a deep "metaphysical" guilt that is built into the very structure of human existence[28] and that, ironically, makes us sound and healthy. Not to experience such guilt would be a sign that we forget the alien dignity and hence equality of all; to experience it is a sign that we recognize the alien dignity and equal worth of each. To do so is to be in partnership; thus, experiencing metaphysical guilt means that we remain fundamentally in relationship and hence healthy.

To say that alien dignity equalizes people is not to say that it makes everyone the same. The great diversity of human life is never denied by Thielicke. Indeed, he held to some traditional notions, for example of the differences between men and women and of the roles appropriate to them. But even in the midst of recognizing these differences, Thielicke held that women were right to demand respect because their alien dignity makes them "equal before God."[29] Women's different *roles* did not affect women's basic *worth* or *equality* with men, which is secured by their alien dignity. Similarly, people's different roles or status in life do not affect their basic value, which is secured by their alien dignity. Precisely because we are made in the image and likeness of God, we cannot be rejected as being "no good." Whatever our race, color, sex, class, or social status, we are all equal in the eyes of God.

From the notion of alien dignity, then, might come an appreciation not only of the protectability of humans, but of their equality without diversity. As the Human Genome Project continues to locate and define the many genes that make up human beings, it will be increasingly important to find a grounding for understanding equality in the midst of diversity. Our history of genetic discrimination indicates all too graphically how easy it is for human communities to establish genetic norms and discriminate against those who do not fit the norm.[30] As the Human Genome Project progresses, there is the danger that we will make judgments of social worth based on individual genomes. Troy Duster charges that we are opening a "backdoor" to eugenics, legitimizing social discrimination under the name of genetic science as we seek to correct "defective" genes.[31] Some will be judged not to have "normal" genes, others to have "superior" genes. Such judgments are exactly what the concept of "alien dignity" prevents. To accept diversity and yet affirm equality may be the most important challenge that lies before us in the realm of genetics. Thielicke's notion of alien dignity captures the underlying premise of equal worth amidst differing manifestations of human life.

3. Alien Dignity Requires Personal *Response*

For Thielicke, the alien dignity of the other required an "I-Thou" relationship. Agape must be immediate, improvisational, non-routinized.[32] For Thielicke, there is no escaping personal responsibility by assuming that institutions or others will take over. The institutionalization of agape was therefore problematic: "Does not the Samaritan's ministry of mercy become inconceivable, is it not altered in its very substance, the moment it is institutionalized? . . ."[33] Thielicke cautioned against the "welfare state," because "no one is ever summoned personally" or need take personal responsibility in it.[34] In the welfare state, care would be "rationalized," and this very rationalization would kill the agape element in it.[35] Thus, the agape that responds to the alien dignity of the other, and in so responding realizes that dignity, must always be a personal response.

In the arena of health care, such a view may be an important corrective to the assumption that "others" or "the system" will provide. In the United States, for example, 95 percent of elderly people live not in nursing homes but in the community, dependent on care by family, friends, or hired workers. More than 80 percent are cared for by families, and in 75 percent of these cases, the caregiver is a woman. Most of these women are over the age of fifty and not always in the best of health themselves.[36]

On the one hand, Thielicke would probably applaud these women. They have chosen positively, lovingly, and willingly to care for elderly spouses or parents. They exhibit agape. They assume personal responsibility.

On the other hand, the fact that 75 percent of the care is being done by women should make us ask, Where are the men? In Thielicke's view, no one should escape from personal response to and responsibility for the needs of others. A society that allows some to escape responsibility while others carry the burden would not meet with Thielicke's approval. Since Thielicke did not believe that a ministry of mercy could be institutionalized without losing something of its basic character, the institutionalization of caring as "women's work" or a "female function" might also violate his understanding of the need for personal responsibility. Thus, alien dignity could provide correctives to some societal arrangements.

4. Alien Dignity Requires Structural *Response*

Thielicke's resistance to the institutionalization of care might be particularly problematic today for liberation theologians who stress the structural nature of injustice. It might seem at first glance that Thielicke's understanding of alien dignity would militate against nationalized health care or against a universal program such as that currently proposed by the Clinton administration. True, Clinton stressed personal responsibility in presenting his proposal to the nation. Responsibility is one of the principles presumably embedded in the design of the program.[37] Nonetheless, Clinton's program would require massive intervention on state and national levels to ensure access to health care for all American citizens and legal residents. Since Thielicke argued against routinization of care, one might wonder whether this I-Thou approach to alien dignity would undercut the Clinton plan.

Yet before we draw this conclusion, some nuancing is in order. It is true that Thielicke argued against the welfare state. The rationalization or routinizing of care, he asserted, ran counter to what is characteristic of Christian love of the neighbor.[38] He was particularly troubled by the argument that the welfare recipient could "claim" welfare as a right, and that claiming such a right would be seen to honor the dignity of the person in ways that offering charity or agape does not.[39] But one must understand why Thielicke was troubled in order to understand the structural implications of his reflections on the welfare state. In spite of his reservations, his understanding of the implications of alien dignity pushes in the direction of a structural response to social and personal ills.

Thielicke's resistance to "rights" and preference for agape or charity was based on the understanding that love never degrades the other, but must treat the other as a true partner. "Rights" or claims separate people and force them into antagonistic relationships. Not antagonism, but a partnership "in the ultimate dimension" was, for Thielicke, the goal of all Christian action.[40] Precisely because of the alien dignity of the other, that other is meant to be seen as a person in the sight of God, never merely as an object. But if the other is a subject, contended Thielicke, then the other can never be left as the mere passive recipient of our actions. To do so is to degrade the other.

By the same token, poverty can never be accepted as the other person's fate.[41] The other must not simply be helped or sustained in poverty, but must "be restored to economic independence."[42] I have argued elsewhere that such restoration is implied by the Jubilee image of justice.[43] Such restoration requires structural undergirding. Rehabilitation was, for Thielicke, a proper undertaking of the state.[44]

In fact, for Thielicke the other must not simply be restored and helped to move out of poverty, but must be prevented from moving into poverty in the first place. "What is more urgently needed is preventive action."[45] Prevention, however, requires structural response: "a social order in which the right to gainful employment is assured and in which possibilities are created for the attainment of economic independence by way of education, financial credits, and the like."[46] Only such a structural, preventive response would constitute in Thielicke's view a genuine partnership or expression of agape.

Thus it is true that Thielicke argued for a limited role for the state and would not have condoned either the Marxist analysis or the more extensive welfare state supported in some liberation treatises today. At root, he understood agape to be a deeply personal response, and he shied away from any institutional response that would relieve personal responsibility. He feared the "impersonal machine" that would take away direct person-to-person care.[47] Nonetheless, his understanding of alien dignity also required preventive and structured response, in order to support the dignity of the other and the true partnership between people and between people and the state. Most significantly, it required not simply "charity" but moving people to a place of restored autonomy and self-support. Thielicke recognized the structural components of poverty and other human ills, and his understanding of alien dignity required attention to these components. To argue that the social order must guarantee a "right to gainful employment" is to take a large step toward structural justice.

By extension from this reasoning, I believe that we could also see in Thielicke's work the structural demands for a system of universal health care. If, as President Clinton said in his address to the nation, health care is crucial to the security necessary in order for people to make free choices and take risks for the future, then health care would be one of the structural demands of agape. Universal access to basic health care would recognize the alien dignity of all.

5. *Alien Dignity Is* Relational

It is clear by now that Thielicke's concept of alien dignity is relational through and through. To have dignity is to be in relation.

First, it is to be in relation to God, who gives the dignity by investing love in people. Thus, one cannot speak of alien dignity without speaking of God's relationship to humankind. The very concept depends on relationality. Indeed, it connotes relationality, since for Thielicke alien dignity is not an "ontic" possession but precisely a statement of our relationship to God.

Second, to have alien dignity is to be in relation to people. It is others who realize our dignity by acting out of agape, out of a perspective of who we are before God. The term thus implies not only our "vertical" relation to God but also our "horizontal" relation to others.

Alien dignity is therefore very *personal,* but it is not *private* or atomistic. Dignity derives *between* beings — between humans and God, between humans and other humans. Thielicke called alien dignity "teleological, not ontological."[48] By this he meant that it does not refer to human characteristics or status, but to the purposes for which we are created by God. The term implies connections between beings and a fundamental covenant of life with life. To speak of alien dignity is therefore always to point us to relationship, interdependence, and covenant.

In this relationality, love is central. It is God's love that establishes the alien dignity of humans. It is human love that recognizes and realizes it. Once we know that God, like every mother, loves precisely the vulnerable and weak ones, then we know how irrevocable is the dignity of the poor and outcast. "If I am no good, how can there be any God? Am I not made in the image and likeness of God?" Our fate is not sealed by our actions or by the judgments of others about us, but by the love of God for us. Alien dignity is a Christological concept for Thielicke.

This notion of relationality also has important implications for contemporary bioethics. Criticisms of the current stress on "autonomy" are now legion.[49] Increasingly, bioethicists are searching for an approach to ethics that neither isolates the individual nor manufactures a false autonomy, but places the individual in social context, recognizing the role of family, of fiduciary relationships, of diminished autonomy. Feminists have been particularly keen on stressing caring and relationship as central to the tasks of ethics.

Thielicke's notion of alien dignity fits well with these concerns. Cardinal Jackson's dignity was not dependent on her mental capacity, but rather on her relationships. Significantly, as Schiedermayer struggled with what gave Jackson her dignity, he pointed both to past relationships and to present ones, both to relationships of harm and to relationships of love. Cardinal Jackson's unassailable dignity came for him in part because of the love that her daughter still held for her. But it also came because a history of discrimination and mistreatment required a form of reparations — of refusing to abandon now one who had been abandoned in the past. In his own way, Schiedermayer attempts to establish a covenant that would assure Cardinal Jackson and her family that her dignity remained evident and appreciated. Cardinal Jackson does not have to have autonomy in order to be in relationship, to be the recipient of duties such as reparations on the part of others, to be loved and recognized. Her dignity — what Thielicke would call her alien dignity — is relational and implies covenant.

In response to Isasi-Diaz, Schiedermayer might say that the fact that she has experienced racist rejection in the past is precisely what gives her an inviolable dignity, just as it has contributed to that dignity for Cardinal Jackson. A relationship need not be one of love in order to remind us of the inviolable dignity of the other. Alien dignity requires a relational understanding of human life.

Conclusions

When Helmet Thielicke spoke to the first international conference on ethics in medicine and technology twenty-five years ago, health care ethics was in its infancy. The Human Genome Project, Kevorkian's "suicide machine" — these were unknowns. Abortion was not legal in the United States, in vitro fertilization clinics were not dotting the landscape as they now do. Much has changed in the intervening years.

Yet much has also remained the same. The genome project, assisted suicide, legalized abortion, in vitro fertilization — these modern developments raise ancient questions: should there be limits to human intervention in nature; when if at all is it permissible to take human life; should human bodies be bought and sold? At the root of these questions lies the ever present dilemma of the valuing of human life. What does it mean to be human, and what gives human life its worth?

It is to these foundational questions that Thielicke addressed his understanding of alien dignity. "If I am no good, how can there be any God? Am I not made in the image and likeness of God?" queries Isasi-Diaz. For Thielicke, being made in the image and likeness of God meant that each person gained an alien dignity that stamped a fundamental worth on that person — a worth so central and ineradicable that nothing done by oneself or by others could ever remove it. If there is a God, and if God is good, then so are we, for we are made in the image of God.

To be sure, Thielicke's precise formulation of alien dignity raises some problems. Although he speaks of partnership "in the ultimate dimension," it is not clear whether his understanding of alien dignity implies a true partnership between humans and God. His God seems distant and wholly "other," his human beings perhaps a bit too empty. Human dignity seems removed, perhaps a bit too alien.

Yet in spite of these problems, there is an enduring legacy here to which we would do well to attend. The notion of alien dignity provides considerable protection to human beings. It keeps us from being used as objects of others' desires or schemes and from being swept up in the instrumentalization of human life. This may be important for our consideration as we move toward increasing technological imperatives. Alien dignity also has a powerful equalizing vector, which may be important as we struggle to understand how to do ethics in the midst of diversity. Alien dignity requires both the immediacy of love and personal responsibility on the one hand, and on the other hand structures that undergird true partnership. It neither lets us off the hook nor reduces ethical action to mere sentimentality.[50] Finally, alien dignity requires a relational view of human beings. Such a focus on relationality is consonant with many feminist approaches to ethics, and provides an important corrective to the contemporary stress in bioethics on autonomy.

Notes

1. Ada Maria Isasi-Diaz, "Las Palmas Reales de Ada," in Katie G. Cannon et al. (The Mudflower Collective), *God's Fierce Whimsy* (New York: Pilgrim Press, 1985), 106.

2. Helmut Thielicke, "The Doctor as Judge of Who Shall Live and Who Shall Die," in Kenneth Vaux, ed., *Who Shall Live? Medicine, Technology, Ethics,* (Philadelphia: Fortress Press, 1970).

3. Thielicke, "Doctor as Judge," 170.

4. Helmut Thielicke, *Theological Ethics, Volume 1: Foundations,* ed. William H. Lazareth (Philadelphia: Fortress Press, 1966), 151.

5. Helmut Thielicke, *Theological Ethics,* vol. 1, 165.

6. Helmut Thielicke, *Theological Ethics,* vol. 1, 170.

7. Helmut Thielicke, *Theological Ethics,* vol. 1, 171.

8. Helmut Thielicke, *Theological Ethics,* vol. 1, 159.

9. Helmut Thielicke, *Theological Ethics,* vol. 1, 177.

10. Thielicke, *The Ethics of Sex,* trans. John W. Doberstein (New York: Harper & Row, 1964), 32.

11. Thielicke, "*Doctor as* Judge," 172.

12. Helmut Thielicke, *Theological Ethics,* vol. 1, 180.

13. See, e.g., Wendy Farley, *Tragic Vision and Divine Compassion: A Contemporary Theodicy* (Louisville, Ky.: Westminster/John Knox Press, 1990); Joanne Carlson Brown and Carole R. Bohn, eds., *Christianity, Patriarchy, and Abuse: A Feminist Critique* (New York: Pilgrim Press, 1989).

14. It also does not depend on faith, but only on the image of God. Thus, even the nonbeliever would have dignity.

15. Thielicke, "Doctor as Judge," 186.

16. David Schiedermayer, "The Case: House Calls To Cardinal Jackson," *Second Opinion* 17, no. 4 (April, 1992): 35-40.

17. Schiedermayer, "The Case," 39.

18. Indeed, for Thielicke, her dignity would remain even if there was no fire in her eyes and no love proffered by her daughter.

19. Thielicke, *Ethics of Sex,* 33.

20. Thielicke, *Ethics of Sex,* 61.

21. Thielicke, *Ethics of Sex,* 63.

22. Thielicke, *Ethics of Sex,* 27.

23. See The National Commission for the Protection of Human Subjects, *Research Involving Those Institutionalized as Mentally Infirm,* DHEW #OS-78-0006, and *Research Involving Prisoners,* DHEW #OS-76-131.

24. Thielicke, *Theological Ethics, Volume 2: Politics,* ed. William H. Lazareth (Philadelphia: Fortress Press, 1969), 305.

25. John K. Kilner, "Selecting Patients When Resources Are Limited: A Study of U.S. Medical Directors of Kidney Dialysis and Transplantation Facilities," *American Journal of Public Health* 78, no. 2 (1988): 146.

26. Thielicke, "Doctor as Judge," 166.

27. Thielicke, "Doctor as Judge," 173.

28. Thielicke, "Doctor as Judge," 164.

29. Thielicke, *Ethics of Sex,* 12.

30. Troy Duster, *Backdoor to Eugenics* (New York: Routledge, 1990). See also John Horgan, "Eugenics Revisited," *Scientific American* 268, no. 6 (June 1993): 122-31.

31. Duster, *Backdoor to Eugenics,* 122-31.

32. Helmut Thielicke, *Theological Ethics,* vol. 2, 291.

33. Helmut Thielicke, *Theological Ethics,* vol. 2, 291.

34. Helmut Thielicke, *Theological Ethics,* vol. 2, 292.

35. Helmut Thielicke, *Theological Ethics,* vol. 2, 294.

36. See Tish Sommers and Laurie Shields, *Women Take Care: The Consequences of Caregiving in Today's Society* (Gainesville, Fla.: Triad Publishing, 1987), 21.

37. *American Health Security Act of 1993,* Sept. 7, 1993, section 10 (Washington, D.C.: Bureau of National Affairs, 1993).

38. Helmut Thielicke, *Theological Ethics,* vol. 2, 300.

39. Helmut Thielicke, *Theological Ethics,* vol. 2, 304.

40. Helmut Thielicke, *Theological Ethics,* vol. 2, 305.

41. Helmut Thielicke, *Theological Ethics,* vol. 2, 306.

42. Helmut Thielicke, *Theological Ethics,* vol. 2, 306.

43. See Karen Lebacqz, *Justice in an Unjust World* (Minneapolis: Augsburg Publishing House, 1987), ch. 7.

44. Helmut Thielicke, *Theological Ethics,* vol. 2, 307.

45. Helmut Thielicke, *Theological Ethics,* vol. 2, 306.

46. Helmut Thielicke, *Theological Ethics,* vol. 2, 306.

47. Helmut Thielicke, *Theological Ethics,* vol. 2, 313.

48. Helmut Thielicke, *Theological Ethics,* vol. 1, 154.

49. See, e.g., Marshall B. Kapp, "Medical Empowerment of the Elderly," *Hastings Center Report* (July-August, 1989): 5-7, George J. Agich, "Reassessing Autonomy in Long Term Care," *Hastings Center Report* (November-December 1990): 12-17.

50. Some feminist texts that take "caring" or love as central to ethics do run the risk of dealing only with immediate relationships and failing to provide structural supports. See, for example, Nel Noddings, *Caring: A Feminist Approach to Ethics and Moral Education* (Berkeley: University of California Press, 1984).

Chapter Five:

DEATH AND ITS (IN)DIGNITY

If life has "sanctity," what of death? How is death to be understood, or imagined? What posture should we take towards it? What attitudes or dispositions are appropriate? Those are the questions which this chapter invites you to consider. They are by no means simple questions, but answers to them will shape conduct in dying and in caring for the dying.

Do we understand death well, for example, if we understand it as an illusion? Mary Baker Eddy, founder of Christian Science, took this view; "Death," she said, "is but another phase of the dream that existence can be material. . . . Life is real, and death is the illusion."[1] This way of understanding and dealing with death, however, has been blocked for most Christians by the celebration of a (material) creation that stands at the beginning of its story and by the harsh reality of the death of Jesus that stands at the center of it. Death is real; it is efforts to deny its reality — whether in metaphysical idealism, in religious repudiations of material reality, in funeral customs that give corpses rosy cheeks, or in medical behaviors that deny mortality — that seem illusory.

If it is folly to deny death, might we domesticate it? Do we understand death well if we understand it simply as the end of the life of biological organism? as a "natural" event? as a "fact of life," so to speak? Death is, of course, the end of the life of a biological organism, and if all persons are mortal, death is surely "natural" enough, but it may be argued that such an account of death reduces the human person to biological organism. Human persons are distinguished from other biological organisms in part by the fact that they know that they will die. The terror of death is not just that it is something that happens in this world but that it seems to have the last word. Pascal said it well, "The last act is tragic, however happy all the rest of the play is; at the last a little earth is thrown upon our head, and that is the end forever."[2]

The saddest of the laments found in scripture, Psalm 88 (selection 27), may have said it even better. The man is sick; he has evidently been sick since he was a boy, and now he suffers his way towards his death. The last word of the Psalm, the last word for this psalmist, is "darkness." That's what makes it the saddest of the laments. Other laments end with a vow to give praise to God or with the expression of the certainty that God will hear their prayer and rescue them — but not Psalm 88. Death and darkness have the last word. The terror of death is not simply the termination of existence but the threatened unraveling of meaning, the destruction of relationships, the lordship of chaos.[3]

The selection from Nicholas Wolterstorff's *Lament for a Son* (selection 28) neither denies nor domesticates death. His confidence that the last word belongs to God, however, and not to death allows him to face both the reality and the horror of the death of his son, and he makes the claim that such confidence is exhibited in the mourning of "aching visionaries."

William F. May (selection 29) points out the poverty of efforts to deny or to domesticate death, attending to "the sacral power of death." Death, he says, is a religious reality, and the confrontation with death is inevitably a confrontation with a power that confounds the efforts of human beings to master it. Only thus can we explain the simultaneous evasion and obsession with death in our culture. May admits that religious communities, including the Christian Church, have sometimes conspired with the culture to deny or to domesticate — or to master — death. By attending, however, to the death and resurrection of Jesus, May finds resources for the Church to deal honestly with the threatening and real power of death and to form conduct toward the dying.

The connections between our understandings of death, our attitudes toward it, and our behavior toward the dying are also the central concern of the essay by Paul Ramsey (selection 30). The slogan "Death with Dignity" may be unobjectionable, but behind it Ramsey finds ideologies suspiciously hospitable to death. Death is, Ramsey insisted, to be regarded as an enemy; it is for Christian theology a "conquered enemy," but it is and remains an enemy. It is, Ramsey insisted, an evil; it may be "a good evil" if the prospect of it and the dread of it teach us "to number our days" and to spend them with some point and purpose, but it remains an evil. Death is, according to Ramsey, "an indignity"; he would permit "a calculus of comparative indignities," but he would not permit us to regard death as having a dignity of its own or in itself. To forget that death is "an indignity," an insult to the embodied and irreplaceable character of human persons and their lives, to forget that death is an evil, to forget that it is an enemy, forms us to indifference and carelessness toward human persons and their lives.

There are many questions one might ask of Ramsey. Does he do justice to nature? Does he do justice to the word of God, "You are dust, and to dust you shall return" (Gen. 3:19)? And even friendly critics have wondered whether such an understanding of death implies human (and medical) defiance of natural mortality, efforts to preserve life as long as technically possible. The essay by Oliver O'Donovan (selection 31) raises this question and attempts to answer it by situating Ramsey's principle of the coinherence of body and soul more clearly within the context of the Christian gospel and its affirmation of resurrection. An important methodological question lies just below the surface here: Was it Ramsey's effort to speak to anyone who would listen (and not just Christians) which led to silence about the resurrection? Conversely, is the gain in both confessional integrity and internal intelligibility in O'Donovan's commentary on Ramsey made by sacrificing the possibility of persuading those who belong to other communities and who do not enter the conversation already affirming the resurrection of Christ as "the first fruits of those who have died" (1 Corinthians 15:20)?

The essay by O'Donovan provides a commentary not only on Ramsey but also on the different traditions behind and within affirmations of "the immortality of the soul," on the one hand, and "the resurrection of the body," on the other. The contrast was important to both Ramsey and May, and as O'Donovan remarks, to most of Western theology since the First World War. O'Donovan admits that this focus on resurrection was a "revolutionary" development, but he claims that it represents a "rediscovery" of the original Christian understanding of death and of ourselves.

The questions of this chapter are not just methodological and metaphysical; they are finally practical questions about how to live while we are dying, about how to treat a dying patient. There is the question, for example, already mentioned, about whether Ramsey's view entails a technological defiance of death. If O'Donovan is right, it does not; but the question of the appropriate use of technology remains. If May is right, there are ways in which technology can be made to serve life — not just biological survival, but the embodied and communal life of those threatened by death. Death and its threats of alienation from our flesh, from community, and from God can make their power felt in a hospital and in the sort of medicine that would resist death by its technological orientation toward biological survival. In May's account of the various ministries of the Church to the dying there are important clues about how to limit and guide technology so that it may serve patients in their flesh, and in their communities, and in their relationship with God. Not the least important of these clues is the observation that the attempt to master death by technological intervention grows sometimes presumptuous, sometimes desperate, and sometimes ironically alienating.

These are practical matters, but the force of this chapter is that our practices are inevitably connected with our imagination, that our choices are formed by our convictions, that our behaviors are shaped by our vision and understanding. How do you see death? And how might that shape your conduct in the face of it?

Notes

1. Mary Baker Eddy, *Science and Health with Key to the Scriptures* (Boston: First Church of Christ, Scientist, 1934), pp. 427-28.

2. Blaise Pascal, *Pascal's Pensées* (New York: E. P. Dutton & Co., 1958), no. 210, p. 61.

3. See further Allen Verhey, "Meditation: Is the Last Word 'Darkness'?," in Allen Verhey (ed.), *Religion and Medical Ethics: Looking Back, Looking Forward* (Grand Rapids: Eerdmans, 1996), pp. 146-50.

Suggestions for Further Reading:

Aries, Philippe. *Western Attitudes Toward Death: From the Middle Ages to the Present,* translated by Patricia M. Ranum (Baltimore: Johns Hopkins University Press, 1974).

Bailey, Lloyd R., Sr. *Biblical Perspectives on Death* (Philadelphia: Fortress, 1979).

Bottum, J. "All That Lives Must Die," *First Things,* no. 63 (May 1996): 28-32.

Bresnahan, Jim. "Catholic Spirituality and Medical Interventions in Dying," *America* 164 (June 22-29, 1991): 670-75.

Cullmann, Oscar. "Immortality of the Soul or Resurrection of the Dead," in *Immortality and Resurrection,* edited by Krister Stendahl (New York: Macmillan, 1965).

Gunderman, Richard B. "What Can Medical Science Contribute to Theological Ethics? Musings on Mortality," in Lisa Sowle Cahill and James F. Childress, (eds.), *Christian Ethics: Problems and Prospects* (Cleveland: The Pilgrim Press, 1996), pp. 152-65.

Jüngel, Eberhard. *Death: The Riddle and the Mystery* (Philadelphia: Westminster, 1974).

Kilner, John F., Arlene B. Miller, Edmund D. Pellegrino, (eds.). *Dignity and Dying: A Christian Appraisal* (Grand Rapids: William B. Eerdmans Publishing Company, 1996).

Steinfels, Peter, and Robert M. Veatch (eds.). *Death Inside Out* (New York: Harper and Row, 1975).

Tolstoy, Leo. *The Death of Ivan Ilyich,* translated by Lynn Solotaroff (New York: Bantam, 1981).

Westphal, Merold. *God, Guilt, and Death* (Bloomington, Ind.: Indiana University Press, 1984).

27 Psalm 88

O Lord, my God, I call for help by day;
I cry out in the night before thee.
Let my prayer come before thee,
incline thy ear to my cry!

For my soul is full of troubles,
and my life draws near to Sheol.
I am reckoned among those who go down to the Pit;
I am a man who has no strength,
like one forsaken among the dead,
like the slain that lie in the grave,
like those whom thou dost remember no more,
for they are cut off from thy hand.
Thou hast put me in the depths of the Pit,
in the regions dark and deep.
Thy wrath lies heavy upon me,
and thou dost overwhelm me with all thy waves. *Selah*
Thou has caused my companions to shun me;
thou hast made me a thing of horror to them.
I am shut in so that I cannot escape;
my eye grows dim through sorrow.
Every day I call upon thee, O Lord;
I spread out my hands to thee.
Dost thou work wonders for the dead?
Do the shades rise up to praise thee? *Selah*
Is thy steadfast love declared in the grave,
or thy faithfulness in Abaddon?
Are thy wonders known in the darkness,
or thy saving help in the land of forgetfulness?

But I, O Lord, cry to thee;
in the morning my prayer comes before thee.
O Lord, why dost thou cast me off?
Why dost thou hide thy face from me?
Afflicted and close to death from my youth up,
I suffer thy terrors; I am helpless.
Thy wrath has swept over me;
thy dread assaults destroy me.
They surround me like a flood all day long;
they close in upon me together.
Thou hast caused lover and friend to shun me;
my companions are in darkness.

28 *Lament for a Son*

Nicholas Wolterstorff

Standing on a hill in Galilee Jesus said to his disciples:

> Blessed are those who mourn,
> for they shall be comforted.

Blessings to those who mourn, cheers to those who weep, hail to those whose eyes are filled with tears, hats off to those who suffer, bottoms up to the grieving! How strange, how incredibly strange!

When you and I are left to our own devices, it's the smiling, successful ones of the world that we cheer. "Hail to the victors." The histories we write of the odyssey of humanity on earth are the stories of the exulting ones — the nations that won in battle, the businesses that defeated their competition, the explorers who found a pass to the Pacific, the scientists whose theories proved correct, the athletes who came in first, the politicians who won their campaigns. We turn away from the crying ones of the world. Our photographers tell us to smile.

"Blessed are those who mourn." What can it mean? One can understand why Jesus hails those who hunger and thirst for righteousness, why he hails the merciful, why he hails the pure in heart, why he hails the peacemakers, why he hails those who endure under persecution. These are qualities of character which belong to the life of the kingdom. But why does he hail the mourners of the world? Why cheer tears? It must be that mourning is also a quality of character that belongs to the life of his realm.

From Nicholas Wolterstorff, *Lament for a Son* (Grand Rapids: Eerdmans, 1987), pp. 84-86.

Who then are the mourners? The mourners are those who have caught a glimpse of God's new day, who ache with all their being for that day's coming, and who break out into tears when confronted with its absence. They are the ones who realize that in God's realm of peace there is no one blind and who ache whenever they see someone unseeing. They are the ones who realize that in God's realm there is no one hungry and who ache whenever they see someone starving. They are the ones who realize that in God's realm there is no one falsely accused and who ache whenever they see someone imprisoned unjustly. They are the ones who realize that in God's realm there is no one who fails to see God and who ache whenever they see someone unbelieving. They are the ones who realize that in God's realm there is no one who suffers oppression and who ache whenever they see someone beat down. They are the ones who realize that in God's realm there is no one without dignity and who ache whenever they see someone treated with indignity. They are the ones who realize that in God's realm of peace there is neither death nor tears and who ache whenever they see someone crying tears over death. The mourners are aching visionaries.

Such people Jesus blesses; he hails them, he praises them, he salutes them. And he gives them the promise that the new day for whose absence they ache will come. They will be comforted.

The Stoics of antiquity said: Be calm. Disengage yourself. Neither laugh nor weep. Jesus says: Be open to the wounds of the world. Mourn humanity's mourning, weep over humanity's weeping, be wounded by humanity's wounds, be in agony over humanity's agony. But do so in the good cheer that a day of peace is coming.

29 The Sacral Power of Death in Contemporary Experience

William F. May

Theological reflection on the subject of death usually has an air of unreality because it has no contact with death as it is actually experienced by men in its sacral power. This is especially true of theology in an age that likes to think of itself as secular without remainder. Presumably there are no religious realities left to contend with. Men are relatively self-sufficient and autonomous, blessedly free of the incubus of religion in all its forms. The gospel has only to address itself to a world-come-of-age, commanded and populated by secular men.

Theologians of the secular persuasion may be right when they attempt to free the gospel from its earlier, uncritical ties with religion, but they are wrong when they assume that religion is dead. While religions, in the sense of official historical traditions, may indeed have entered a period of decline, the experience of the sacred is still very much with us. Nowhere is this more apparent than in the contemporary experience of death. . . .

Death in Its Religious Reality

Pastors rarely approach the gravely ill without noticing immediately the evasions and the brave lies that encircle the dying. Doctors often refuse

From *Social Research* 39 (Autumn 1972). Used by permission of the publisher and the author.

to inform the patient of his true condition in the case of a terminal illness. Needless to say, most families cooperate readily with the doctor and his instructions.

A heavy silence surrounds death. I believe that this painful reticence has a source more profound than our childlike submission to the advice of a doctor. For the instructions of a doctor would not hold for a minute if men felt they had recourse in their words and actions against death. In fact, where else except from the dying has the doctor himself learned his reticence? He has seen too many men avoid asking the big question about their illness. Or he has heard them ask the question without being certain that they really wanted an answer.

Despite some charges to the contrary (which I will discuss later), I do not think of the doctor as the villain of the piece in this conspiracy of silence. Silence has its origin in the awesomeness of death itself. Just as the Jew, out of respect for the awesomeness of God, would not pronounce the name of Yahweh, so we find it difficult to bring the word *death* to our lips in the presence of its power. This is so because we are at a loss as to how to proceed on the far side of this word. Our philosophies and our moralities desert us. They retreat and leave us wordless. Their rhetoric, which seemed so suitable on other occasions, suddenly loses its power, and we may well wonder whether our words themselves are not caught up in a massive, verbose, uneasy flight from death, while we are left with nothing to say, except to "say it with flowers."

Without provision against death, our rituals and ceremonies are characterized by a powerful flight from its presence. This is a phenomenon that has already received savage treatment at the hands of satirists in the Anglo-Saxon world: Aldous Huxley, *After Many a Summer;* Muriel Spark, *Memento Mori;* Evelyn Waugh, *The Loved One;* and most recently, Jessica Mitford, *The American Way of Death.* Interestingly enough, all are English writers, and three of the four focus on the American attitude toward death. They are wrong, however, when they suggest that Americans believe in a triumph of technology over death by virtue of which they reduce death to the incidental or the unreal. Rites are evasive not because Americans react to death as trivial or incidental but because they feel an inner sense of bankruptcy before it. The attempts at evasion and concealment are pathetic rather than casual. The doctor's substitute diagnoses and vague replies and the undertaker's allusions to the "loved one" or to the "beautiful memory picture" reflect a culture in which men sense their own poverty before this event.

Men evade death because they recognize in the event an immensity that towers above their resources for handling it. In effect, death (or the reality that brings it) is recognized as some sort of sacred power that confounds the efforts of man to master it. James Joyce uses a particularly gloomy expression to convey this sense of death as sacred power in *Ulysses* — "*Dio Boia*" — the "Hangman God." Joyce happens to import the phrase into English literature from the Italian, but the reality of which he speaks crosses national boundaries — death recognized as the power before which all human efforts are ineffectual longings to no avail; death admitted as the reality that may have inspired philosophers to meditate but brings these meditations to their conclusion, that may have crowned the hero or martyr with renown but eventually drags into oblivion even those whom it has lifted up; death honored as the power that unravels every human community, taking those fervent little intersections of human want — husband and wife, lovers, father and son — and eventually forcing all these intersecting lines to honor its presence with the rigid parallels of the graveyard.

So understood, death is not merely a biological incident that ends human life. It reaches into the course of life, gripping the human heart with love, fear, hope, worry, and flight, long before the end itself is reached. Whenever the concert is over, the meal is digested, or the career turns barren in one's hands, a man experiences the quiet, disturbing fall from life to death. Because death is more than the incident of biological demise, it is difficult to do justice to its scope without falling into parody of the psalmist's sense of the omnipresence of God. For the power that brings death besets men on every side. It drives men from behind as they flee into frenetic activities — the pursuit of career, virtuosity, or the display of some glory — hoping to escape their metaphysical solitude by outlining themselves against a dark background. It confronts men frontally as they mount their battles against their threatening enemies, whether that enemy happens to be soldier, competition, or sibling. It lies in wait and ambushes from the side — the young, the high-minded, and the frivolous — with the unexpectedness of a clipping at a football game. It stirs beneath human life in the profoundest of pleasures, as it touches with melancholy the marriage bed or as it ladens with guilt the relations between the generations. And at night, it settles down from above and breathes gently within men who are weary with all other forms of fleeting, fighting, and sidestepping death and who long now for sleep and the surcease of care.

If, in some such fashion, men experience death as a religious reality, then one might expect the language of religion to describe most appropriately man's primordial attitude toward the onslaught of the event. This is in fact the language that Joyce chooses in the opening passage of the *Dubliners*. A young boy — friend to a dying priest — muses on the word "paralysis," and offers therein a fine description of religious awe. "Paralysis . . . It sounded to me like the name of some maleficent and sinful being. It filled me with fear and yet I longed to be near it and to look upon its deadly work."[1] Joyce's description captures beautifully that ambivalence of spirit that the phenomenologists of religion have recognized in all religious feeling and which they have variously termed: "awe," "dread," "astonishment," "wonder," or "amazement." A peculiar ambivalence, a strange vibration, a sort of motionless motion obtains in the religious man, an attentiveness somewhat akin to the attention that a hummingbird gives to a flower, when its wings beat furiously and yet it hovers at the spot. This is the way men relate to death in its dreadful reality.

The analysis has uncovered so far two basic responses to the event of death in contemporary culture: concealment and obsession. Only the category of the sacred explains their connection. Men are tempted to conceal death or to hold themselves enthralled before it only because they recognize death as an overmastering power before which all other responses are unavailing.

Geoffrey Gorer, the English sociologist, in his essay "The Pornography of Death,"[2] brings together the phenomena of obsession and concealment by appeal to the religious category of *taboo*. On the one hand, death is a taboo subject, the unmentionable event; on the other hand, death (and violence) is an obsession at every level of our culture. Gorer finds the solution to this oddity in a comparison with the Victorian attitude toward sex. A prudish culture in which personal sexual life is a taboo subject is also likely to develop simultaneously a pornographic obsession with sex. In contemporary culture, argues Gorer, the personal event of death has replaced sex as a taboo subject: Death has replaced copulation and birth as the unmentionable. At the same time, an obsession with violence has dominated our age. Concealment and obsession go together in the same culture.

The chief feature of pornography, of course, is an obsession with the sex-act abstracted from its normal human emotion which is love; the pornography of death therefore is an obsession with death abstracted from its natural human emotion which is grief. For the sake of his thesis Gorer might be altogether satisfied with the development of the James Bond movie. When the sexual act is abstracted from love it becomes somewhat repetitive and dull; therefore, pornographic literature rescues its readers from boredom by filling the fantasy with the sex-act performed in an endless variety of ways, each more elaborate or intense than the last. Interest is removed altogether from love to the technology of the act itself. Correspondingly, when death is abstracted from grief the same restless elaboration of technology occurs. It is difficult to maintain interest in the subject of death unless violence is done in a variety of ways. Thus technicians in violence have to equip James Bond with the ultimate in a death-dealing car that surpasses with exquisite ingenuity the death-dealing instruments that General Motors has already put on the road. And the makers of the movie *Thunderball* bring both lines of pornography to their absurd conclusion, inasmuch as lovemaking and murdering are somehow managed underwater.

The fascination with death in pornography and the concealment of death in the liturgies of polite society are both rooted in religious feeling. It is a religious enthrallment with death that eventuates in the strategies of helpless evasion in the homelike atmosphere of the funeral parlor and in the pornographic experimentations of the entertainment industry.

The traditional belief in the immortality of the soul does not seem to provide men with a sense of resource against the threat of death. In this respect the consciousness of the twentieth century has undergone a radical break with the recent Western past. Christian theologians from the Church Fathers through the Reformers of the sixteenth century held to a doctrine of the immorality of the soul. This doctrine was continued in an altered form by many theologians and philosophers (particularly those of idealist persuasion) in the eighteenth through the late nineteenth century. But today the situation has changed. Naturalists among the philosophers dismiss the doctrine of the immortality of the soul as just so much idealistic vaporing. Psychoanalysts interpret the longing for immortality as a perpetuation of infantile desires. Social critics have condemned the doctrine for its encouragement of an attitude of otherworldly indifference to social ills. Existentialists have opposed the doctrine because it distracts a man from his most essential task as an authentic human being: the appropriation of his own finitude and morality. Even modern biblical scholars have rejected the doctrine as they usually distinguish today between the primitive Christian hope of the resurrection of the body and the Hellenic-idealist doctrine of the immortality of the soul.

This is not to say that a belief in the immortality of the soul has had its defenders in Germany, England, America, and France. Dualists of the stripe of Unamuno have tried to reckon with the heart's longing for eternal life, along with the mind's crushing sense of death. Even existentialists, such as Marcel, have made appeal to the existence of a beloved community that transcends the empirical order of death. Finally, and somewhat less grandly, the ordinary man likes to think of himself as immortal, or at least, invulnerable. Tolstoy has observed[3] that the passion for finding out the "cause" of someone else's death is a way of satisfying oneself that the other fellow died accidentally or fortuitously by virtue of special circumstances affecting him (but not me). This shabby impulse, however, is hardly a serious expression of the traditional confidence in the immortality of the soul. Rather it is the hedonist's inveterate bargaining for a little more time in which to dawdle over just one more last cigarette.

Despite traces of contemporary belief in the immortality of the soul, the minister is ill advised to rely on it in the presence of death. Nowhere is the bankruptcy of the doctrine so evident as in a certain type of Protestant funeral service in which the minister strains to give the impression that the person "lives on" in the trappings of the service itself. The minister disastrously seeks to "personalize" the service, not by simple reference to the name and biography of the deceased, but by including his alleged favorite hymns, poems, prayers, and songs. We are supposed to have the impression that we are in the presence of a kind of *aurora borealis* of the dead man's personality, shimmering miraculously in the darkest hour of grief. Instead, however, the minister gives the sad impression that he has a repertory of three or four such "personalized" services, designed like Sears Roebuck seat covers to fit any and all makes and models of cars. Its ill-fitting imposition upon the dead man only reminds us ever so forcibly and comfortlessly that he is, indeed, dead.

Theological Reflection on Death

The attempt to cover up death in the funeral service is an unmitigated disaster for the church, preceded and prepared for by the church's failure to reckon with death in its own preaching and pastoral life. Many persons have said that they have never heard their minister take up frontally in a sermon the question of their own dying. This state of affairs, once again, is not entirely the fault of the professional. People tend to expect from the church service an hour's relief from the demons that plague them in the course of the week. In this atmosphere sermons on death would seem intrusive and unsettling. Better to avoid them and protect this hour from everything that jangles the nerves — even though the service comes to an end and the demons must be faced once again on Monday, fully intact, unexorcized, and screeching. The melancholic effect of this arrangement is that the church offers a temporary sanctuary, a momentary respite, from one's secret apprehensions about death, but inevitably they take over once again, without so much as a candid word of comfort intervening.

To preach about death is absolutely essential if Christians are to preach with joy. Otherwise they speak with profound melancholy of men who have separated the church from the graveyard. They make the practical assumption that there are two Lords. First, there is the Lord of the Sabbath, the God who presides over the affairs of cheerful Philistines while they are still thriving and in good health. Then there is a second Lord, a Dark Power about whom one never speaks, the Lord of highways, wrecks, hospitals, and graveyards who handles everything in the end. Under the circumstances, there can be no doubt as to which of the two Lords is the more commanding power. The death-bringer God already encroaches upon the sanctuary itself, inasmuch as people gathered there are so unsettled as to refuse to hear of his name.

The Christian faith, however, does not speak of two parallel Lords. The Lord of the church is not ruler of a surface kingdom. His dominion is nothing if it does not go at least six feet deep. The church affirms the one Lord who went down into the grave, fought a battle with the power of death, and by his own death brought death to an end. For this reason the church must be unafraid to speak of death. It is compelled to speak of death as the servant of Jesus Christ, the Crucified and Risen Savior, who has freed men from the power of the Unmentionable One.

But even when the church speaks about the subject, does the church evade it? Is theological reflection on the subject of death itself a method of circumlocution? Existentialism, after all, from Kierkegaard to Heidegger, has made men sensitive to the way in which objective discourse on the subject of death may be a way of escaping from one's own personal destiny as a creature who dies. Camus has condemned Christian thought on the subject of death for placing, in effect, theological screens before the eyes of the condemned.[4] Apparently the Christian hope of eternal life only serves to divert attention from the stark condition of life in the flesh. "The order of the world is shaped by death," says one of the heroes of *The Plague*.[5]

At the outset, then, by way of reply, it must be argued that Christian reflection, far from screening death from view actually tears away the screens and forces men to look at death and to look toward their own dying. This is an unavoidable focus of a faith that has to reckon with the factual dying of its Savior. Even if men wanted to avoid death, they cannot if they look toward such a savior. In fact, he exposes the flimsiness of the partitions that men raise in order not to have to consider death. The purpose of this comment is not to outdo the existentialist in pessimism but to lay the only sure basis for Christian hope, a hope that is not based on screens, mirrors, or sentiment. It is based on the good news that men do not have to go beyond Jesus for a knowledge of death in its fullest scope; death is not an additional realm alongside of Jesus terrorizing men from the side.

Death in Jesus

In the light of Jesus Christ it is possible to explore the scope of death as it threatens a man in his three most fundamental identities as a human being. Death threatens a man's identity with his flesh, with his community, and with his God. (Insofar as the doctrine of the immortality of the soul abstracted the question of future life from these three fundamental identities, it tended to offer an impoverished if not ghostly sense of future existence.)

A man is clearly identified with his flesh. He is not a ghost. The body is more important to his identity than words to a poet. He both controls his world and savors his world, and reveals himself to others, in and through the living flesh. Part of the terror of death is that it threatens a man with a loss of identity with his flesh, an identity which is essential to him in at least these three ways.

First, man's flesh is the means to his control of his world. Except as he uses his flesh instrumentally (feet for walking, hands for working, tongue for talking) he could not relate to the world by way of mastery and control. When death therefore threatens to separate him from his flesh, it threatens him first with a comprehensive loss of possession and control of his universe. Death meets him as the dispossessor (Luke 12:15-21), even though he retaliates as best he can against his loss of control with an assortment of insurance policies. Quite shrewdly the medieval moralists saw a special connection between the capital sin of avarice and old age. Avarice is the special sin in which a man focuses his life on his possessions. The closer a man gets to the time of his dispossession, the more fiercely he clings to what he has and the more suspicion he feels toward all those who would dispossess him with indecorous haste.

Second, a man's flesh is more than instrumental, it is also the site for the disclosure of the world to him, the world which he will never be able to reduce to property but which is there for the savoring. Except that flesh is sensitive, susceptible, and vulnerable, a man could not be open to the world as it pours in upon him in a wild profusion of colors, sounds, and feelings. He could not fall under the spell of powers that both enchant and terrify him. When death therefore threatens to separate him from flesh it threatens also to separate him from the propertyless creation, the world which he may not control but which is his for the beholding in ritual, art, and daily routine.[6]

Third, flesh is more instrumental than and more sensitive to the world; it is also revelatory. A man reveals himself to his neighbor in and through the living flesh. He is inseparable from his countenance, gestures, and the physical details of his speech. Part of the terror of death, then, is that it threatens him with a loss of his revelatory power. The dreadfulness of the corpse lies in its claim to be the body of the person, while it is wholly unrevealing of the person. What was once so expressive of the human soul has suddenly become a mask.

We have referred to the *threat* of separation from the flesh in each case not only because a man can anticipate it before it occurs, but also because this separation does not occur all at once. It is shocking to encounter a young man who is dying and recognize a spirit that is still alive with its original power and promise while the flesh abandons it. Or again it is possible to look upon the aged whose spirits have long since absented themselves while their bodies persist so mindlessly alive.

Part of the melancholy of this loss of identity is no frontal assault can be launched against it. The fear of death only intensifies insofar as a man plunges deeper into his possessions as a way of securing himself against the day of his dispossession, or gives himself over to the frenetic carnivals of a death-ridden age as a way of savoring his world, or takes daily inventory of his physical appearance in the quest ceremonies before the morning mirror.

Death not only threatens a man with separation from the flesh; it also tears him away from his community. This threat has already been anticipated in the discussion of the revelatory power of the flesh. Death means the unraveling of human community. It divides husband and wife, father and son, and lovers from one another. Not even the child is exempt from this threat. In demanding the reassurance of a voice, the touch of a hand at bedtime, he shows that he knows all the essential issues involved in a sleep that is early practice in dying. Death threatens all men with final separation, exclusion, and oblivion. And again, this threat is operative beforehand, as the fear of oblivion can prompt men to force their way into the society of others in ways which are ultimately self-isolating.

But death also threatens men with separation from God. This is the terror of death that men have never fully faced because they have never wholly honored the presence of God. But it is the terror of which all others are but prologue and sign. Men fear separation from their flesh because they know life in and through their flesh. They fear separation from community because they know life in and through their community. But what are these compared with separation from God, who is the source of life in the flesh and life in the community? This question remains partly rhetorical for all men inasmuch as they do not know fully what they ask. But it was the last question on the lips of the One whom Christians worship and adore in his cry of abandonment from the cross.

Jesus knew death in all its dimensions. The creed puts it: He "suffered under Pontius Pilate, was crucified, dead and buried; he descended into Hell." His death, like others, meant separation from the flesh. The narratives are utterly factual in detail about his ordeal in the flesh. He suffered dispossession: the king with no subjects, the teacher with no pupils, the healer who bleeds. He suffered severance from the world, reduced as it was to a sop of vinegar, the darkness of the sixth hour, and a spear in his side; and he, like all other men before and after him, suffered the final conclusion of his life in the unrevealing corpse.

His death meant also separation from community. One can see this separation at work beforehand in the persecution of the high priest, the ambiguities of the Roman governor, the fickleness of the crowds, the betrayal of Judas, the cowardice of Peter, and the sleepiness of followers in Gethsemane. It was consummated in his burial when he, like all other men, was removed from sight.

Finally Jesus experienced what men know only

through him: separation from God. The Son of God cries out, "My God, my God, why hast thou forsaken me?" The Son of God descends into the region that stands under the naked terror of the absence of God and stands fast there for every man.

Because the Son of God has done this, the Christian cannot be content simply to tell horror stories about the ravaging power of death. If in looking toward Jesus, he looks toward death in its full terror and power, so also he looks toward the Savior who exposes death in its ultimate powerlessness. No final power remains to death, if death itself has become the event in which Jesus exposes the powerfulness of God's love. Death can still menace, but it can no longer make good on its threats. In Jesus' death, God, flesh, and community are indissolubly met in self-expending love. For this reason, it is no longer necessary to stare in the mirror, worrying about the defeat of one's flesh, or to plunge into communities, worried about exclusion at their hands, or to lift up one's eyes to heaven, attempting in a blind fury of good works to force the presence of God. For the Savior who is identified, soul and body, with men in his descent is the one who remains their Lord in his ascent, to bring men new life — bodily, together, in the presence of God.

Life in Jesus

Usually when a man asks the question of eternal life, he wonders simply whether he will continue to live beyond the grave. Putting the question this way, he assumes that a human being can be separated from his ties with his flesh, community, and God. This is the assumption by virtue of which the doctrine of the immortality of the soul, in some of its versions, actually led to an impoverishment of the notion of eternal life. Eternal life, in effect, became an eternalization of death, as the soul projected itself endlessly into the future — deprived of everything that formerly made it jubilant with life. Cut off from its ties with its flesh, community, and God, the soul so imagined is spectral and wraith-like. Its daydreams about the future have turned into ghoul-ridden nightmares.

The Risen Christ, however, cuts through the nonsense of these daydreams about eternity with the sharp actuality of his life. He is not ghoulishly divested of a body; on the contrary, he shows himself to his disciples, his flesh still bearing the marks of his crucifixion. He is not banished from community like a spook (whose appearance always causes men to scatter and run); on the contrary, his appearance among men is such as to establish and nourish human community. Neither is he greviously separated from God; the account of his resurrection is followed by the acknowledgment of his ascension. This testimony to the ascension of Christ excludes the fantasy of a ghostly Savior drifting in the nether world between God and men. His proximity to God, in turn ("at the right hand of the Father"), is at the basis of his power to create a full-bodied life for his community among men.

Correspondingly, the eternal life that Jesus imparts to men is neither spectral or rootless. Jesus extends to men the specific hope of future life in the body. "We wait for adoption as sons, the redemption of our bodies" (Rom. 8:23). Wholly consistent with this promise of a glorified body is the apostolic assurance of a new heaven and a new earth to which the body gives access. Man is not destined to live on perpetually in the tedium of a worldless "I." Neither however will he live on in isolation from his fellow. Jesus imparts eternal life to him through a community. As Ephesians puts it, "God . . . made us alive together in Christ" (2:4, 5). The word "together" in the passage does not convey the incidental bit of intelligence that others beside oneself are involved in the resurrection, as though men were like strangers, temporarily herded together to receive a fortune from a benefactor whom each knew in his private way. Rather God creates in the community of disciples a freedom for each other that would not be there except through participation in his life.

Finally eternal life means bodily life, together, in the *presence* of God. Resurrection means intimacy with God. Jesus says to the thief on the cross, "Today you will be with me in paradise" (Luke 23:43). The Christian hope is not simply for a deathless, endless life in which relations between a man, his body, and his neighbor have been set in order. To center hope on a perfected world alone is eschatological atheism. If God exists, eternal life cannot be defined apart from his presence. Without him the perfection of this world would be like the sterile order of a house that a woman kept immaculate for no other end than its own tidiness, as though she did not desire the presence of her husband. In the humblest of marriages the vital presence of the husband belongs to the joy of the house, so the presence of God fills out the joy of heaven.

Eternal life is the future destiny of man, but participation in this life is not reserved to the future alone. Just as death is not simply an event at the end of life but overtakes men by way of fear, worry, and disease in the present moment, so also the resurrection is not an event wholly reserved for the other side of the grave. Men can live now in the power of the resurrection. Surely the martyr faced death with hope in his heart for the future glory, yet he did so in the present enabling power of the resurrection. Otherwise the fullness of God fills only the future, fills only the far side, powerless finally to redeem the present and powerless to sustain men in the agony of dying itself. Men can look forward to the coming ages of his kindness toward them because he stands with them already on this side of the grave.

The fact of the resurrection of Christ, however, does not mean that the Christian is altogether removed from the experience of natural grief and sorrow. Were it otherwise, the Christian should be able to face his own death without a tremor, and he should be able to walk confidently into the sickroom, contending with its silence by "talking up" a victory that has not yet, apparently, reached the ears of those who await an imminent defeat. This is a professional Christian cheerfulness, a grisly boy-scoutism, for which there is no justification in Scripture. The apostle Paul expressed himself carefully: Only "when this corruptible *shall* have put on incorruption . . . *shall* there come to pass the saying that is written, Death is swallowed up in victory" (I Cor. 15:54, italics added). The Christian knows grief in this life. He is not granted on this side of the grave a pure, steadfast, confident, and transparent sense of his limits — or the limits of his neighbor — before God. He tastes of eternal life in Christ, but not a life that removes him from death and the sting of death. The work of death is still very much evident in the inner and the outer man. Death remains the last enemy. Not until the gift of life beyond the limit has been granted to man is it possible for him to say wholeheartedly:

O Death, where is thy victory?
O Death, where is thy sting?

This death does not mean, however, that nothing of importance has occurred. Although the Christian does not yet know an eternal life without death, he has reckoned in Christ with an eternal life under the conditions of death, that permits him to live hopefully in the crisis of his neighbor's death and his own. This is the basis for the witness of the church to the dying.

The Church's Behavior Toward the Dying

Let it be said at the outset that the church cannot act as though it possesses something that the dying lack. A demoralizing feature of illness for any patient is the condescending cheerfulness of nurses and friends, whose very display of good health reminds the mortally ill that they are about to be dispossessed of their world. The church cannot behave in such a way as to add yet another possession, i.e., Christian hope, that distinguishes the Christian from the unbeliever or the sorely tried believer who is mortally ill.

This consideration, however, produces an oddity. Does the Christian somehow have to assume the *unreality* of the resurrection in order to avoid removing himself from his fellowman? Must he ignore the resurrection so as not to appear like a self-assured Christ-dispenser in the sickroom? Does he find himself saying, in effect, that the resurrection has taken place but that its fruits are a long way off for all of us and therefore nothing has occurred that need disturb the humanity of my response to your illness and imminent death?

Actually, the reverse is the case. It is precisely in the absence of a sense of the resurrection that the Christian is tempted to think solely in terms of those possessions he has to offer the sick. He makes the painful assumption that he must be a God-producer, a Christ-dispenser, or a religious magician in the sickroom. Failing miserably, of course, at all these roles, he feels keenly his poverty. He makes a lame effort to produce the decisive and healing word, only to stutter and to fall silent. In the absence of a sense of resurrection he feels the terrifying lack of a gift between himself and the dying, a frightening guilt of silence between them. He is inclined therefore with every healthy fiber of his being to shy away from the dying to avoid his own poverty.

The resurrection of Christ frees a man for approach to the dying not because it arms him with a possession to give, but because it frees him from all this worry and confusion about possessions. Christ is already the decisive gift between the living and the dying, the mediator between them. There is no need to produce Christ in the sickroom when he is already there in advance of a man's approach. The Christian is mercifully free, therefore, to offer whatever secondary gifts he can — of anxiety, suffering, money, words, friendship, and hope — letting them be, whenever possible, signs of a divine love which they do not produce.

The Church's Witness and Separation from the Flesh

It is angelism to assume that the sole witness of the church to the dying and the bereaved is the testimony of theology alone. A ministry to the flesh is a true and valid ministry. It need not be supposed that Christian witness is invariably something more than this. Admittedly the apparatus of medicine — doctors, nurses, and sanitary hospitals — can function as a shield behind which the larger community of health protects itself from contact with the dying. But this need not be the case. There is no reason why the machinery of modern medicine — awesome and impersonal though it is — may not yet serve human purposes and therefore function as a sign of a life that exceeds its own powers to heal. To do this, however, some sensitivity must be shown toward the several crises that a man experiences in his flesh.

It was noted earlier that sickness and death involve a traumatic loss of control over one's world. A man who has brutally exploited his body as an instrument of aggression against his world suddenly suffers a heart attack. The very flesh through which he exercised mastery suddenly explodes from within. He is helpless in the hands of others, unable even to control disturbing noises down the hall. Under these circumstances the apparatus of medicine can be frightening; it demonstrates to him his helplessness and therefore reminds him of the poverty of all his attempts to solve the problem of his existence through mastery alone. The machinery of medicine thus assumes the terrifying shape of a parable of judgment. It brings his past life to nought. At the same time, however, the apparatus of medicine can be a testimony to grace. It does after all serve the body; and in this it can be a mute sign of the Lord whose mastery took the form of life-giving and life-comforting service. Seen in this light, it is the special task of the church not to ignore the work of medicine as a sub-Christian activity but to accompany and to criticize it in such a way as to help it to serve this end of service.

The second crisis for the flesh is the loss of the world in its uncontrolled splendor and diversity. A toothache has a way of reducing the world to itself. Unfortunately, the apparatus of medicine, dedicated as it is to the medical recovery of the patient, presents the hospitalized patient with a functional but blank and abstract environment, devoid of the irrelevant details that make up a truly human existence. (Yeats once registered his complaint against the scientific formula H_2O by observing, "I like a little seaweed in my definition of water.") Many European hospitals admirably manage to maintain gardens as part of their grounds. A functionally irrelevant expense, perhaps, in an institution dedicated to treating and discharging people as fast as it can, but some patients, after all, are discharged for burial, and it is well to maintain a sign for them of a world that has not shrunk to the final abstraction of their irremediable pain.

The third crisis for the flesh is the imminent loss of its revelatory power. The falterings of the body in old age increasingly prevent it from being expressive of the soul in its full dignity. There is warrant here for a sensitive ministry to the body in its infirmities which extends to the humblest of details in the daily routines of eating and cleansing. Upon death, moreover, there is warrant for a funeral service in which the body is not treated as a disposable cartridge to be thrown away like garbage. This argument for a fitting disposal of the remains, however, is hardly an apology for present-day funeral practice. Quite the contrary, it opens the way for an even more savage criticism of these practices. Precisely because the body has been (and will be) what it is only by the power of God to glorify it, it cannot become in Christian practice a lewd object of the mortician's craft. It is one thing for the mortician to minimize the violence done to the body by death, but it is quite another thing for him to impose upon the deceased the suggestion of a character other than its own. Only too often today Uncle John is not allowed to die. He must be prettied up with rouge on his cheeks and his casket opened so that his friends can see his face forced into a smile. Poor Uncle John never smiled in his life, but now he does — beatifically. It is not only the beautification of Uncle John, but his beatification that one attempts to achieve. The church won't canonize him but the mortician will. One is supposed to go to the funeral parlor, look on the face of the corpse, and say about Uncle John, "Doesn't he look natural?" which, of course, is the one thing he does not look. Let death be death. There is no reason to add to its hideousness by mocking the inability of the dead to reveal themselves.

The Witness of the Church and Separation from Community

One of the most devastating features of terminal illness is the fear of abandonment.[7] Sickness has already isolated the patient from his normal identity in the community. Strong and authoritative, he is now relatively helpless; gregarious by nature, he suddenly finds friends exhausting. Ironically the very apparatus by which the community ministers to his physical need isolates him further. The modern hospital segregates the sick and the dying from their normal human resources. One doctor has observed that in an Arabian village a grandmother dies in the midst of her children and grandchildren, cows and donkeys. But our high level of technological developments leads simply to dying a death appropriate to one's disease — in the heart ward or the cancer ward.[8]

Most desolating of all is the breakdown of communication between the dying patient, the doctor, and the nearest of kin. Substitute diagnoses are sometimes justified on the grounds that they establish an emotional equilibrium (homeostasis) essential to the health and comfort of the patient, but this justification ignores the fact that evasiveness can itself be emotionally disturbing. It is demoralizing for everybody concerned to get stuck with a lie, because, once told, life tends to organize itself around it. Even when the lie isn't working, even when it produces the anguish of suspicion, isolation, and uncertainty, the doctor may rely on it to keep his own relation to the patient in a state of equilibrium. Homeostasis, in other words, is a problem not only for the patient but also for the doctor and for the family. The family also grows accustomed to the explanation and enmeshes itself more deeply in the demands of make-believe. It seems too late for everybody concerned to recover an authentic relationship to the event. Isolated by evasion and lies, the patient is driven out of community before his time. He has forced upon him a premature burial. While trying to avoid the fact of death, the community actually reeks of death, for it has already excluded him.

It would be wrong, however, to make the doctor the scapegoat here and therefore to underestimate woefully the problems of sharing the truth. This was the mistake of a group of psychiatrists in the previously referred to study of *Death and Dying: Attitudes of Patient and Doctor.*[9] The psychiatrists reported that 69 to 90 percent of physicians (depending on the specific study) were not in favor of informing the patient in cases of mortal illness. Meanwhile on the basis of their own interviews with patients, the psychiatrists reported that approximately 82 percent of patients in terminal cases actually wanted to be informed of their true condition. Several psychiatrists explained this discrepancy between the apparent desire of patients and the actual performance of doctors by appeal to the psychological defects of doctors or to faults in their training: (1) they are more afraid of death than other professional groups; (2) they shy away from dealing with chronic and terminal cases because such cases are a blow to the doctor's professional self-esteem; (3) they receive inadequate preparation in medical school for coping with the problem of handling terminal cases.

Doubtless, all these observations are valid in given instances, but I found the psychiatrists breathtakingly naïve in the evidence they accepted as proof that patients really want to know the truth. First, it is not clear that patients are so willing to talk about the possibility — or the inevitability — of their own death *with their own doctor,* as the percentages reported by the psychiatrists in their interviews with patients would indicate. Dr. Samuel Feder indirectly admitted this fact when he observed that "all . . . patients, when they were asked to see me as a 'new doctor,' reacted with great anxiety."[10] All but two of the patients, however, were delighted to discover that he was "only" a psychiatrist. He admits that this was a unique experience for him as a psychiatrist. Obviously patients were glad that "he was not one of those other doctors — those other doctors being the bearers of bad tidings."

Dr. Feder interpreted these anxiety reactions as proof that people knew that they were going to die. Therefore the doctors had no excuse for avoiding the subject. I interpret them, however, as proof that these people were frightened of hearing just this verdict from their own doctors. The doctor in charge is less approachable on this subject precisely because he is the keeper of desolate truths. By the same token, the psychiatrist is more accessible since he brings no final verdict. If this analysis is correct, then the doctor's reticence to discuss the subject cannot be written off solely as a question of his own fear of death or his oversensitive, professional self-esteem. The sacral dimensions of death are too awesome to admit of easy professional solution. The problem of isolation cannot be solved by handing out truth like pills since the truth itself can have a disturbing and an isolating effect.

Yet there are ways in which people can reach out to one another in word and actions and maintain some measure of solidarity before the overwhelming event of death. It would be pretentious to outline these ways since they are not fully given to men except in the concrete case. Nevertheless it is possible to clarify (and perhaps even to clear the way of) certain obstacles that men face in their behavior toward the dying. They divide very simply into those of word and deed.

The Problem of Words

Perhaps we are especially inhibited in our talk with the dying because the alternatives in language seem so poor. There are several types of discourse available to us: (1) direct, immediate, blunt talk; (2) circumlocution or double-talk; (3) silence (which can be, of course, a mode of sharing, but oftentimes, is a way of evading); and (4) discourse that proceeds by way of indirection.

Too often we assume (especially as Americans) that the only form of truth-telling is direct, immediate, blunt talk. Such talk seems to be the only alternative to evasive silence or circumlocution On the subject of sex, for example, we assume that the only alternative to the repressions of a Victorian age is the tiresome, gabby explicit discussion of sex we impose upon the adolescent from junior high forward. So also on the subject of death we assume that truth-telling requires something approaching the seminar in loquacity. But obviously gabby bluntness in the presence of one dying is wholly inappropriate. It reckons in no way with the solemnity of the event. To plead for the explicit discussion of diagnosis or prognosis with every patient in clinical detail would be foolhardy. But the alternative to blunt talk need not be double-talk, a condescending cheerfulness, or a frightening silence. There is such a thing as *indirect* discourse in both love and death.

Perhaps examples of what I mean by indirection will suffice. One doctor reports that many patients instinctively brought up the question of their own death in an indirect form. Some asked him, for example, whether he thought they should buy a house, marry, or have plastic surgery done to their face. The doctor realized that the answer, "Yes, surely, go ahead — " in a big, cheerful voice was an evasion. Meanwhile the answer, "No," was a summary reply which would have made further discussion impossible. He found it important however to convey to them somehow that he recognized the importance of the question. From that point on, it was possible to discuss their uncertainties, anxieties, and fears. Some kind of sharing could take place. It was not necessary to dwell on the subject for long; after its acknowledgment it was possible to proceed to the details of daily life without the change of subject seeming an evasion.

Indirection may be achieved in another way. Although it may be too overbearing to approach the subject of death frontally under the immediate pressure of its presence, a kind of indirection can be achieved if death is discussed in advance of a crisis. The minister who suddenly feels like a tongue-tied irrelevancy in the sickroom gets what he deserves if he has not worked through the problem with his people in a series of sermons or in work sessions with lay groups. Words too blunt and inappropriate in the crisis itself may, if spoken earlier, provide an indirect basis for sharing burdens.

The language of indirection is appropriate behavior because, as it has been argued throughout, death is a sacred event. For the most part, toward the sacred the most fitting relation is indirect. The Jew did not attempt to look straight on Yahweh's face. A direct, immediate, casual confrontation was impossible. But avoidance of God's presence was not the only alternative. It was given to the Jew to hold his ground before his Lord in a relation that was genuine but indirect. So also, it is not necessary to dwell directly on the subject of death interminably or to avoid it by a condescending cheerfulness wholly inappropriate to the event. It is possible for two human beings to acknowledge death, be it ever so indirectly, and to hold their ground before it until they are parted.

The Problem of Action

Deeds are no easier to come by than words in extremity. Everyone grows uneasy. When nothing is left to be done toward the dying, a man is inclined to pay his respects, look at his watch, and fish out an excuse that fetches him home. Perhaps, however, our discomfort stems partly from a view of action somewhat inappropriate to overwhelming events. T. S. Eliot once said that there are two types of problems we face in life. In one case, the appropriate question is: what are we going to do about it? In the other case: how do we behave toward it? The deeper problems in life are of the latter kind.

But unfortunately as Americans, and especially as Americans in those professions that get tinged with a slight messianic pretension — medicine and the minister — we are used to tackling problems in terms of the first question, and are left somewhat bereft, therefore, when that question is inappropriate to the crisis. If all we can say is, What are we going to do about it?, then the dying indeed (and our own death) is a fatal blow to professional self-esteem. But this is not the only question we can ask ourselves in crisis. In extremity it may not be possible to do something about a tragedy, but this inability need not altogether disable our behavior toward it.

The Witness of the Church and the Threat of Separation from God

Since this is the threat in which the name of God appears, it is assumed that the special witness of the church in this case is theology. It may indeed be theology — but neither invariably nor exclusively so and certainly not theology conceived as a series of truths that provide men with access to God while putting them at a comforting distance from the sting of death. Such a theology, while trying to screen death from view, would only succeed in shielding men from the presence of God. For who is God as the Christian knows him? He is the God and Father of Jesus Christ, crucified and risen from the dead. Possessed by Jesus Christ, the church is not removed from the sting of existence come to an end. Rather it lives by a concrete existence that cuts into death with all the power of God's love to make death itself the very instance of that love. Because this is the case, the church cannot shield death from view without seeking — foolishly — to place theological screens before the eyes of the redeemed.

The witness of the church to the presence of God is not always direct and verbal. This fact has already been anticipated in our discussion of death. Just as an authentic acknowledgment of death can take place within the limits of indirect discourse, so also an authentic witness to Jesus Christ can occur without the inevitable footnote giving reference to his name. The Christian sense of the presence of God can express itself indirectly in the way in which the Christian responds to other levels of crisis. The calm with which he offers friendship in crisis may count for more than theological virtuosity in testifying to God's presence. The worry with which he offers advice will reveal more than the advice itself when he is really stricken with a sense of God's absence. But even in the case of failure he cannot, with Christian consistency, take his failure too seriously. God is the ultimate presence in death, whether men succeed in testifying to him or not. Neither life, nor death, nor the failure of Christians, will be able to separate men from the love of God. This is the message of Rom. 8 and the substance of Christian witness. When the church fails by its words and deeds to make this witness to the dying, let the dying among her members be brave enough to make this witness to the church.

Notes

1. James Joyce, *The Dubliners* (New York: The Modern Library), p. 7.

2. Reprinted as an appendix in his book, *Death, Grief, and Mourning* (Garden City, N.Y.: Doubleday & Co., 1965).

3. Leo Tolstoy, *The Death of Ivan Ilyich* (New York: Boni and Liveright), p. 8. See also Sigmund Freud, "Thoughts for the Times on War and Death," *Collected Papers*, Vol. IV, 1915, trans. Joan Riviere (London: The Hogarth Press, 1925), p. 305.

4. "In Italian museums are sometimes found little painted screens that the priest used to hold in front of the face of condemned men to hide the scaffold from them." Albert Camus, *The Myth of Sisyphus and Other Essays*.

5. Albert Camus, *The Plague*, trans. Stewart Gilbert (London: Hamish Hamilton, 1948), p. 123.

6. Karl Rahner has argued that the severance of a man from his flesh may mean not the loss of a world but rather a release of the soul from the more restricted world it knows in the flesh to an all-cosmic relationship that transcends the limitations of life within the province of a body. Even so Rahner must admit that this eventuality, if it be our destiny, is precisely the future which death, in its darkness, obscures. As we know it now, death threatens to separate us from the flesh and so banish us from that sight through which the world is disclosed. See Karl Rahner, *On the Theology of Death*, pp. 29ff.

7. "The dying patient faces emotional problems of great magnitude, including fear of death itself, fear of the ordeal of dying and the devastating fear of abandonment." See Ruth D. Abrams, M.S., "The Patient with Cancer — His Changing Pattern of Communication," *New England Journal of Medicine*, Vol. 274, No. 6, p. 320.

8. Bryant M. Wedge, in discussion at the conclusion of a symposium on *Death and Dying: Attitudes of Patient and Doctor*, sponsored by the Group for the Advancement of Psychiatry, Symposium No. 11, Vol. V.

9. See especially the essay by Herman Feifel, "The Function of Attitudes Toward Death," Ch. V in *Death and Dying: Attitudes of Patient and Doctor*, pp. 633-37.

10. Samuel L. Feder, "Attitudes of Patients with Advanced Malignancy," Chap. III in *Death and Dying: Attitudes of Patient and Doctor*, pp. 614-20.

30 The Indignity of "Death with Dignity"

Paul Ramsey

Never one am I to use an ordinary title when an extraordinary one will do as well! Besides, I mean to suggest that there is an additional insult besides death itself heaped upon the dying by our ordinary talk about "death with dignity." Sometimes that is said even to be a human "right"; and what should a decent citizen do but insist on enjoying his rights? That might be his duty (if there is any such right), to the commonwealth, to the human race or some other collective entity; or at least, embracing that "right" and dying rationally would exhibit a proper respect for the going concept of a rational man. So "The Indignity of Death" would not suffice for my purposes, even though all I shall say depends on understanding the contradiction death poses to the unique worth of an individual human life.

The genesis of the following reflections may be worth noting. A few years ago,[1] I embraced what I characterized as the oldest morality there is (no "new morality") concerning responsibility toward the dying: the acceptance of death, stopping our medical interventions for all sorts of good, human reasons, *only* companying with the dying in their final passage. Then suddenly it appeared that altogether too many people were agreeing with me. That caused qualms. As a Southerner born addicted to lost causes, it seemed I now was caught up in a triumphal social trend. As a controversialist in ethics, I found agreement from too many sides. As a generally happy prophet of the doom

From the *Hastings Center Studies* 2 (May 1974): 47-62.

facing the modern age, unless there is a sea-change in norms of action, it was clear from these premises that anything divers people agree to must necessarily be superficial if not wrong.

Today, when divers people draw the same warm blanket of "allowing to die" or "death with dignity" close up around their shoulders against the dread of that cold night, their various feet are showing. Exposed beneath our growing agreement to that "philosophy of death and dying" may be significantly different "philosophies of life"; and in the present age that agreement may reveal that these interpretations of human life are increasingly mundane, naturalistic, and antihumanistic when measured by *any* genuinely "humanistic" esteem for the individual human being.

These "philosophical" ingredients of any view of death and dying I want to make prominent by speaking of "The Indignity of 'Death with Dignity.'" Whatever practical agreement there may be, or "guidelines" proposed to govern contemporary choice or practice, these are bound to be dehumanizing unless at the same time we bring to bear great summit points and sources of insight in mankind's understanding of mankind (be it Christian or other religious humanism, or religiously-dependent but not explicitly religious humanism, or, if it is possible, a true humanism that is neither systematically nor historically dependent on any religious outlook).

Death with Dignity Ideologies

There is nobility and dignity in caring for the dying, but not in dying itself. "To be a therapist to a dying patient makes us aware of the uniqueness of each individual in this vast sea of humanity."[2] It is more correct to say that a therapist brings to the event, from some other source, an awareness of the uniqueness, the one-for-allness of an individual life-span as part of an "outlook" and "onlook" upon the vast sea of humanity. In any case, that is the reflected glory and dignity of caring for the dying, that we are or become aware of the unique life here ending. The humanity of such human caring is apt to be more sensitive and mature if we do not lightly suppose that it is an easy thing to convey dignity to the dying. That certainly cannot be done simply by withdrawing tubes and stopping respirators or not thumping hearts. At most, those omissions can only be prelude to companying with the dying in their final passage, if we are fortunate enough to share with them — they in moderate comfort — those interchanges that are in accord with the dignity and nobility of mankind. Still, however noble the manifestations of caring called for, however unique the individual life, we finally must come to the reality of death, and must ask, what can possibly be the meaning of "death with dignity"?

At most we convey only the liberty to die with human dignity; we can provide some of the necessary but not sufficient conditions. If the dying die with a degree of nobility it will be mostly their doing in doing their own dying. I fancy their task was easier when death as a human event meant that special note was taken of the last words of the dying — even humorous ones, as in the case of the Roman Emperor who said as he expired, "I Deify." A human countenance may be discerned in death accepted with serenity. So also there is a human countenance behind death with defiance. "Do not go gently into that good night," wrote Dylan Thomas. "Old age should rage and burn against the close of day; Rage Rage against the dying of the light." But the human countenance has been removed from most modern understandings of death.

We do not begin to keep human community with the dying if we interpose between them and us most of the current notions of "death with dignity." Rather do we draw closer to them if and only if our conception of "dying with dignity" encompasses — nakedly and without dilution — the final indignity of death itself, whether accepted or raged against. So I think it may be more profitable to explore "the indignity of 'death with dignity.'" "Good death" (euthanasia) like "Good grief?" is ultimately a contradiction in terms, even if superficially, and before we reach the heart of the matter, there are distinctions to be made; even if, that is to say, the predicate "good" still is applicable in both cases in contrast to worse ways to die and worse ways to grieve or not to grieve.

"Death is simply a part of life," we are told, as a first move to persuade us to accept the ideology of the entire dignity of dying with dignity. A singularly unpersuasive proposition, since we are not told what sort of part of life death is. Disease, injury, congenital defects are also a part of life, and as well murder, rapine, and pillage.[3] Yet there is no campaign for accepting or doing those things with dignity. Nor, for that matter, for the contemporary mentality which would enshrine "death with dignity" is there an equal emphasis on "suffering with dignity," suffering as a "natural" part of life, etc. All those things, it seems, are enemies and violations of human nobility while death is not, or (with a few changes) need not be. Doctors did not invent the fact that death is an enemy, although they may sometimes use disproportionate means to avoid final surrender. Neither did they invent the fact that pain and suffering are enemies and often indignities, although suffering accepted may also be ennobling or may manifest the nobility of the human spirit of any ordinary person.

But, then, it is said, death is an evolutionary necessity and in that further sense a part of life not to be denied. Socially and biologically, one generation follows another. So there must be death, else social history would have no room for creative novelty and planet earth would be glutted with humankind. True enough, no doubt, from the point of view of evolution (which — so far — never dies). But the man who is dying happens not to be evolution. He is part of evolution, no doubt; but not to the whole extent of his being or his dying. A crucial testimony to the individual's transcendence over the species is man's problem and his dis-ease in dying. Death is a natural fact of life, yet no man dies "naturally" nor do we have occasions in which to practice doing so in order to learn how. Not unless the pursuit of philosophy is a practice of dying (as Plato's *Phaedo* teaches) and that I take to be an understanding of the human being we moderns do not mean to embrace when we embrace "death with dignity."

It is small consolation to tell mortal men that as long as you are, the death you contribute to evolution is not yet; and when death is, you are not — so why fear death? That is the modern equivalent to the recipe offered by the ancient Epicureans (and some Stoics) to undercut fear of death and devotion to the gods: as long as you are, death is not; when death is, you are not; there's never a direct encounter between you and death; so why dread death? Indeed, contrary to modern parlance, those ancient philosophers declared that death is *not a part of life;* so, why worry?

So "death is not a part of life" is another declaration designed to quiet fear of death. This can be better understood in terms of a terse comment by Wittgenstein: "Our life has no limit in just the way in which our visual field has no limit."[4] We cannot see beyond the boundary of our visual field; it is more correct to say that beyond the boundary of our visual field *we do not see.* Not only so. Also, we do not see the boundary, the limit itself. There is no seeable bound to the visual field. *Death is not a part of life* in the same way that the boundary is not a part of our visual field. Commenting on this remark by Wittgenstein, James Van Evra writes: "Pressing the analogy, then, if my life has no end in *just the way* that my visual field has no limit, then it must be in the sense that I can have no experience of death, conceived as the complete cessation of experience and thought. That is, if life is considered to be a series of experiences and thoughts, then it is impossible for me to experience death, for to experience something is to be alive, and hence is to be inside the bound formed by death."[5] This is why death itself steadfastly resists conceptualization.

Still, I think the disanalogy ought also to be pressed, against both ancient and contemporary analytical philosophers. That notion of death as a limit makes use of a visual or spatial metaphor. Good basketball players are often men naturally endowed with an unusually wide visual field; this is true, for example, of Bill Bradley. Perhaps basketball players, among other things, strive to enlarge their visual fields, or their habitual use of what powers of sight they have, if that is possible. But ordinarily, everyone of us is perfectly happy within the unseeable limits of sight's reach.

Transfer this notion of death as a limit from space to time as the form of human perception, from sight to an individual's inward desire, effort and hope, and I suggest that one gets a different result. Then death as the temporal limit of a life-span is something we live toward. That limit still can never be experienced or conceptualized; indeed death is *never* a part of life. Moreover, neither is the boundary. Still it is a limit we conative human beings know we live *up against* during our life-spans. We do not live toward or up against the side-limits of our visual-span. Instead, within that acceptable visual limit (and other limits as well) as channels we live toward yet another limit which is death.

Nor is the following analogy for death as a limit of much help in deepening understanding. ". . . The importance of the limit and virtually *all* of its significance," writes Van Evra, "derives from the fact that the limit serves as an ordering device" — just as absolute zero serves for ordering a series; it is not *just* a limit, although nothing can exist at such a temperature. The analogy is valid so far as it suggests that we conceive of death not in itself but as it bears on us while still alive. As I shall suggest below, death teaches us to "number our days."

But that may not be its only ordering function for conative creatures. Having placed death "out of our league" by showing that it is not a "something," or never a part of life, and while understanding awareness of death as awareness of a limit bearing upon us only while still alive, one ought not forthwith to conclude that this understanding of it "exonerates death as the purported snake in our garden." Death as a limit can disorder no less than order the series. Only a disembodied reason can say, as Van Evra does, that "the bound, not being a member of the series, cannot defile it. The series is what it is, happy or unhappy, good or bad, quite independently of any bound as such." An Erik Erikson knows better than that when writing of the "despair and often unconscious fear of death" which results when "the one and only life cycle is not accepted as the ultimate life." Despair, he observes, "expresses the feeling that the time is short, too short for the attempt to start another life and to try out alternate roads to integrity."[6]

It is the temporal flight of the series that is grievous (not death as an evil "something" within life's span to be balanced, optimistically or pessimistically, against other things that are good). The reminder that death is *not a part of life,* that it is only a boundary never encountered, is an ancient recipe that can only increase the threat of death on any profound understanding of human life. The dread of death is the dread of oblivion, of there being only empty room in one's stead. Kübler-Ross writes that for the dying, death means the loss of every loved one, total loss of everything that constituted the self in its world, separation from every experience, even from future possible, replacing experiences — nothingness beyond. Therefore, life is a time-intensive activity and not only a goods-intensive or quality-intensive activity. No matter how many "goods" we store up in barns, like the man in Jesus' parable we know that this night our soul may be required of us (Luke 12:13-21). No matter what "quality of life" our lives have, we must take into account the opportunity-costs of used time. Death means the conquest of the time of our lives — even though we never experience the experience of the nothingness which is natural death.

"Awareness of dying" means awareness of *that;* and awareness of that constitutes an experience of ultimate indignity in and to the awareness of the self who is dying.

We are often reminded of Koheleth's litany: "For everything there is a season, and a time for every matter under heaven: a time to be born and a time to die; a time to plant, and a time to pluck up what is planted," etc. (Eccles. 3:1, 2). Across those words of the narrator of Ecclesiastes the view gains entrance that only an "untimely" death should be regretted or mourned. Yet we know better how to specify an untimely death than to define or describe a "timely" one. The author of Genesis tells us that, at 180 years of age, the patriarch Isaac "breathed his last; and he died and was gathered to his people, old and full of years . . ." (Gen. 35:29). Even in face of sacred Scripture, we are permitted to wonder what Isaac thought about it; whether he too knew how to apply the category "fullness of years" *to himself* and agreed his death was nothing but timely.

We do Koheleth one better and say that death cannot only be timely; it may also be "beautiful." Whether such an opinion is to be ascribed to David Hendin or not (a "fact of life" man he surely is, who also unambiguously subtitled his chapter on euthanasia "Let There Be Death"),[7] that opinion seems to be the outlook of the legislator and physician, Walter Sackett, Jr., who proposed the Florida "Death with Dignity" Statute. All his mature life his philosophy has been, "Death, like birth, is glorious — let it come easy."[8] Such was by no means Koheleth's opinion when he wrote (and *wrote* beautifully) about a time to be born and a time to die. Dr. Sackett also suggests that up to 90 percent of the 1,800 patients in state hospitals for the mentally retarded should be allowed to die. Five billion dollars could be saved in the next half century if the state's mongoloids were permitted to succumb to pneumonia, a disease to which they are highly susceptible.[9] I suggest that the physician in Dr. Sackett has atrophied. He has become a public functionary, treating taxpayers' pocketbooks under the general anesthesia of a continuous daytime soap opera entitled "Death Can Be Beautiful!"

"Death for an older person should be a beautiful event. There is beauty in birth, growth, fullness of life and then, equally so, in the tapering off and final end. There are analogies all about us. What is more beautiful than the spring budding of small leaves; then the fully-leaved tree in summer; and then in the beautiful brightly colored autumn leaves gliding gracefully to the ground? So it is with humans." These are words from a study document on Euthanasia drafted by the Council for Christian Social Action of the United Church of Christ in 1972. An astonishing footnote at this point states that "the naturalness of dying" is suggested in funeral services when the minister says "God has called" the deceased, or says he has "gone to his reward," recites the "dust to dust" passage, or notes that the deceased led a full life or ran a full course!

Before this statement was adopted by that Council on Feb. 17, 1973, more orthodox wording was inserted: "Transformation from life on earth to life in the hereafter of the Lord is a fulfillment. The acceptance of death is our witness to faith in the resurrection of Jesus Christ (Rom. 8). We can rejoice." The subdued words "we can rejoice" indicate a conviction that *something* has been subdued. The words "acceptance of death" takes the whole matter out of the context of romantic naturalism and sets it in a proper religious context — based on the particular Christian tenet that death is a conquered enemy, to be accepted in the name of its Conqueror. More than a relic of the nature mysticism that was so luxuriant in the original paragraph, however, remain in the words, "Death for an older person should be a beautiful event. There is beauty in birth, growth, fullness of life and then, *equally so,* in the tapering off and final end." (Italics added.) I know no Christian teaching that assures us that our "final end" is "equally" beautiful as birth, growth, and fullness of life. Moreover, if revelation disclosed any such thing it would be contrary to reason and to the human reality and experience of death. The views of our "pre-death morticians" are simply discordant with the experienced reality they attempt to beautify. So, in her recent book, Marya Mannes writes "the name of the oratorio is euthanasia." And her statement "dying is merely suspension within a mystery," seems calculated to induce vertigo in face of a fascinating abyss in prospect.[10]

No exception can be taken to one line in the letter people are being encouraged to write and sign by the Euthanasia Societies of Great Britain and America. That line states: "I do not fear death as much as I fear the indignity of deterioration, dependence and hopeless pain." Such an exercise in analyzing *comparative indignities* should be given approval. But in the preceding sentence the letter states: "Death is as much a reality as birth, growth, maturity, and old age — it is the one certainty." That logically leaves open the question what sort of "reality," what sort of "certainty," death is. But by placing death on a parity with birth, growth, maturity — and old age in many of its aspects — the letter beautifies death by association. To be written long before death when one is thinking "generally" (i.e. "rationally"?) about the topic, the letter tempts us to suppose that men can think generally about their own deaths. Hendin observes in another connection that "there is barely any relation between what people think that they think about death and the way they actually feel about it when it must be faced."[11] Then it may be that "the heart has its reasons that reason cannot know" (Pascal) — beforehand — and among those "reasons," I suggest, will be an apprehension of the ultimate (noncomparative) indignity of death. Talk about death as a fact or a reality seasonally recurring in line with birth or planting, maturity and growth, may after all not be very rational. It smacks more of whistling before the darkness descends, and an attempt to brainwash one's contemporaries to accept a very feeble philosophy of life and death.

Birth and death (our *termus a quo* and our *terminus ad quem*) are not to be equated with any of the qualities or experiences, the grandeur and the misery, in between, which constitute "parts" of our lives. While we live toward death and can encompass our own dying in awareness, no one in the same way is aware of his own birth. We know that we were born in the same way that we know *that* we die. Explanations of whence we came do not establish conscious contact with our individual origin; and among explanations, that God called us from the womb out of nothing is as good as any other; and better than most. But awareness of dying is quite another matter. That we may have, but not awareness of our births. And while awareness of birth might conceivably be the great original individuating experience (if we had it), among the race of men it is awareness of dying that is uniquely individuating. To encompass one's own death in the living and dying of one's life is more of a task than it is a part of life. And there is something of indignity to be faced when engaging in the final act of life. Members of the caring human community (doctors, nurses, family) are apt to keep closer company with the dying if we acknowledge the loss of all worth by the loss of him in whom inhered all worth in his world. Yet ordinary men may sometimes nobly suffer the ignobility of death.

By way of contrast with the "A Living Will" framed by the Euthanasia Society, the Judicial Council of the AMA in its recent action on the physician and the dying patient had before it two similar letters. One was composed by the Connecticut Delegation:

> *To my Family, my Physician,*
> *my Clergyman, my Lawyer —*
>
> If the time comes when I can no longer actively take part in decisions for my own future, I wish this statement to stand as the testament of my wishes. If there is no reasonable expectation of my recovery from physical or mental and spiritual disability, I, ... , request that I be allowed to die and not be kept alive by artificial means or heroic measures. I ask also that drugs be mercifully administered to me for terminal suffering even if in relieving pain they may hasten the moment of death. I value life and the dignity of life, so that I am not asking that my life be directly taken, but that my dying not be unreasonably prolonged nor the dignity of life be destroyed. This request is made, after careful reflection, while I am in good health and spirits. Although this document is not legally binding, you who care for me will, I hope, feel morally bound to take it into account. I recognize that it places a heavy burden of responsibility upon you, and it is with the intention of sharing this responsibility that this statement is made.

A second letter had been composed by a physician to express his own wishes, in quite simple language:

> *To my Family, To my Physician —*
>
> Should the occasion arise in my lifetime when death is imminent and a decision is to be made about the nature and the extent of the care to be given to me and I am not able at the time to express my desires, let this statement serve to express my deep, sincere, and considered wish and hope that my physician will administer to me simple, ordinary medical treatment. I ask that he not administer heroic, extraordinary, expensive, or useless medical care or treatment which in the final analysis will merely delay, not change, the ultimate outcome of my terminal condition.

A comparison of these declarations with "A Living Will" circulated by the Euthanasia Society reveals the following signal differences: neither of the AMA submissions engages in any superfluous calculus of "comparative indignities";[12] neither associates the reality of death with such things as birth or maturation; both allow death to be simply what it is in human experience; both are in a general sense "pro-life" statements, in that death is neither reified as one fact among others nor beautified even comparatively.[13]

Everyone concerned takes the wrong turn in trying to "thing-ify" death or to beautify it. The dying have at least this advantage, that in these projects for dehumanizing death by naturalizing it the dying finally cannot succeed, and death makes its threatening visage known to them before ever there are any societal or evolutionary replacement values or the everlasting arms or Abraham's bosom to rest on. Death means *finis,* not in itself *telos.* Certainly not a telos to be engineered, or to be accomplished by reducing both human life and death to the level of natural events.

"Thing-ifying" death reaches its highest pitch in the stated preference of many people in the present age for *sudden* death,[14] for death from unanticipated internal collapse, from the abrupt intrusion of violent outside forces, from some chance occurrence due to the natural law governing the operation of automobiles. While for a comparative calculus of indignities sudden *unknowing* death may be preferred to suffering knowingly or unknowingly the indignity of deterioration, abject dependence, and hopeless pain, how ought we to assess in human terms the present-day absolute (noncomparative) preference for sudden death? Nothing reveals more the meaning we assign to human "dignity" than the view that sudden death, death as an eruptive natural event, could be a prismatic case of death with dignity or at least one without indignity. Human society seems about to rise to the moral level of the "humane" societies in their treatment of animals. What is the principled difference between their view and ours about the meaning of dying "humanely"? By way of contrast, consider the prayer in the Anglican prayer book: "From perils by night and perils by day, perils by land and perils by sea, and *from sudden death,* Lord, deliver us." Such a petition bespeaks an age in which dying with dignity was a gift and a task (*Gabe und Aufgabe*), a liberty to encompass dying as a final act among the actions of life, to enfold awareness of dying as an ingredient into awareness of one's self dying as the finale of the self's relationships in this life to God or to fellowman — in any case to everything that was worthy.

Man Knows that He Dies

Before letting Koheleth's "a time to be born and a time to die" creep as a gloss into *our* texts, perhaps we ought to pay more attention to the outlook on life and death as expressed in the enchantment and frail beauty of those words,[15] and ask whether that philosophy can possibly be a proper foundation for the practice of medicine or for the exercise of the most sensitive care for the dying.

That litany on the times for every matter under heaven concludes with the words, "What gain has the worker from his toil?" (Eccles. 3:9). In general, the author of Ecclesiastes voices an unrelieved pessimism. He has "seen everything that is done under the sun," in season and out of season. It is altogether "an unhappy business that God has given to the sons of men to be busy with" — this birthing and dying, planting and uprooting; "all is vanity and seeking after wind" (Eccles. 1:3b, 14). So, he writes with words of strongest revulsion, "I hated life, because what is done under the sun was grievous to me"; "I hated all my toil and gave myself up to despair . . ." (Eccles. 2:17, 18a, 20).

After that comes the litany "for everything there is a season" — proving, as Kierkegaard said, that a poet is a man whose heart is full of pain but whose lips are so formed that when he gives utterance to that pain he makes beautiful sounds. Koheleth knew, as later did Nietzsche, that the eternal recurrence of birth and death and all things else was simply "the spirit of melancholy" unrelieved, even though there is nothing else to believe since God died.[16] (The Pope knows; he was at the bedside.)

"Death with dignity" because death is a "part" of life, one only of its seasonal realities? If so, then the acceptable death of all flesh means death with the same signal indignity that brackets the whole of life and its striving. Dying is worth as much as the rest; it is not more fruitless.

"For the fate of the sons of men and the fate of the beasts is the same; as one dies so dies the other. They all have the same breath, and man has no advantage over the beasts; for all is vanity" (Eccles. 3:19). "Death with dignity" or death a part of life based on an equilibration of the death of a man with the death of a dog? I think that is not a concept to be chosen as the foundation of modern medicine, even though both dogs and men are enabled to die "humanely."

Or to go deeper still: "death with dignity" because the dead are better off than the living? "I thought the dead who are already dead," Koheleth writes in unrelieved sorrow over existence, "more fortunate than the living who are still alive; and better than both is he who has not yet been, and has not seen the evil deeds that are done under the sun" (Eccles. 4:2, 3). Thus the book of Ecclesiastes is the source of the famous interchange between two pessimistic philosophers, each trying to exceed the other in gloom: First philosopher: More blessed are the dead than the living. Second philosopher: Yes, what you say is true; but more blessed still are those who have never been born. First philosopher: Yes, wretched life; but few there be who attain to that condition!

But Koheleth thinks he knows some who have attained to the blessed goal of disentrapment from the cycles in which there is a time for every matter under heaven. ". . . An untimely birth [a miscarriage] is better off [than a living man], for it [a miscarriage] comes into vanity and goes into darkness, and in darkness its name is covered; moreover it has not seen the sun or known anything; yet it finds rest rather than he [the living]" (Eccles. 6:3b, 4, 5). So we might say that death can have its cosmic dignity if untormented by officious physicians, because the dying go to the darkness, to Limbo where nameless miscarriages dwell, having never seen the sun or known anything. Thus, if dying with dignity as a part of life's natural, undulating seasons seems not to be a thought with much consolation in it (being roughly equivalent to the indignity besetting everything men do and every other natural time), still the dying may find rest as part of cosmic order, from which, once upon a time, the race of men arose to do the unhappy business God has given them to be busy with, and to which peaceful darkness the dying return.

Hardly a conception that explains the rise of Western medicine, the energy of its care of the dying or its war against the indignity of suffering and death — or a conception on which to base its reformation! Dylan Thomas's words were directed against such notions: "The wise men at their end know dark is right, / Because their words had forked no lightning."

There is finally in Ecclesiastes, however, a deeper strand than those which locate men living and dying as simply parts of some malignly or benignly neglectful natural or cosmic order. From these more surface outlooks, the unambiguous injunction follows: Be a part; let there be death — in its time and place, of course (whatever that means). Expressing a deeper strand, however, Koheleth seems to say: Let the natural or cosmic order be whatever it is; men are different. His practical advice is: Be what you are, in human awareness apart and not a part. Within this deeper understanding of the transcendent, threatened nobility of a human life, the uniqueness of the individual human subject, there is ground for awareness of death as an indignity yet freedom to encompass it with dignity.

Now it is that Koheleth reverses the previous judgments he decreed over all he had seen under the sun. Before, the vale of the sunless not-knowing of a miscarriage having its name covered by darkness seemed preferable to living; and all man's works a seeking after wind. So, of course, there was "a time for dying." But now Koheleth writes, ". . . There is no work or thought or knowledge or wisdom in Sheol, to which you are going" (Eccles. 9:10b). While the fate of the sons of men and the fate of the beasts are the same, still "a living dog is better than a dead lion"; and to be a living man is better than either, because of what Koheleth means by "living." "He who is joined with all the living has hope" (Eccles. 9:4), and that is hardly a way to describe dogs or lions. Koheleth, however, identifies the grandeur of man not so much with hope as with awareness, even awareness of dying, and the misery of man with the indignity of dying of which he, in his nobility, is aware. "For the living know that they will die," he writes, "but the dead know nothing. . ." (Eccles. 9:5). Before, the dead or those who never lived had superiority; now, it is the living who are superior precisely by virtue of their awareness of dying and its indignity to the knowing human spirit.

Therefore, I suggest that Koheleth probed the human condition to a depth to which more than twenty centuries later Blaise Pascal came. "Man is but a reed, the feeblest in nature, but he is a thinking reed . . . . A vapor, a drop of water, is sufficient to slay him. But were the universe to crush him, man would still be nobler than that which kills him, for *he knows that he dies,* while the universe knows nothing of the advantage it has over him. Thus our whole dignity consists in thought."[17] (Italics added.)

So the grandeur and misery of man are fused together in the human reality and experience of death. To deny the indignity of death requires that the dignity of man be refused also. The more acceptable in itself death is, the less the worth or uniqueness ascribed to the dying life.

True Humanism and the Dread of Death

I always write as the ethicist I am, namely, a Christian ethicist, and not as some hypothetical common denominator. On common concrete problems I, of course, try to elaborate analysis at the point or on a terrain where there may be convergence of vectors that began in our ethical outlooks and onlooks. Still one should not pant for agreement as the hart pants for the waterbrooks, lest the substance of one's ethics dissolve into vapidity. So in this section I want, among other things, to exhibit some of the meaning of "Christian humanism" in regard to death and dying, in the confidence that this will prove tolerable to my colleagues for a time, if not finally instructive to them.

In this connection, there are two counterpoised verses in the First Epistle of St. John that are worth pondering. The first reads: "Perfect love casts out fear" (which being interpreted means: Perfect care of the dying casts out fear of one's own death or rejection of their dying because of fear of ours). The second verse reads: "Where fear is, love is not perfected" (which being interpreted means: Where fear of death and dying remains, medical and human care of the dying is not perfected). That states nothing so much as the enduring dubiety and ambiguity of any mortal man's care of another through his dying. At the same time there is here applied without modification a standard for unflinching care of a dying fellowman, or short of that of any fellow mortal any time. That standard is cut to the measure of the perfection in benevolence believed to be that of our Father in Heaven in his dealings with mankind. So there is "faith-ing" in an ultimate righteousness beyond the perceptible human condition presupposed by those verses that immediately have to do simply with loving and caring.

Whatever non-Christians may think about the *theology* here entailed, or about similar foundations in any religious ethics, I ask that the notation upon or penetration of the human condition be attended to. Where and insofar as fear is, love and care for the dying cannot be perfected in moral agents or the helping professions. The religious traditions have one way of addressing that problematic. In the modern age the problematic itself is avoided by various forms and degrees of denial of the tragedy of death which proceeds first to reduce the unique worth and once-for-all-ness of the individual life-span that dies.

Perhaps one can apprehend the threat posed to the dignity of man (i.e. in an easy and ready dignifying of death) by many modern viewpoints, especially those dominating the scientific community, and their superficial equivalents in our culture generally, by bringing into view three states of consciousness in the Western past.

The burden of the Hebrew Scriptures was man's obedience or disobedience to covenant, to Torah. Thus sin was the problem, and death came in only as a subordinate theme; and, as one focus for the problematic of the human condition, this was a late development. In contrast, righteousness and disobedience (sin) was a subordinate theme in Greek religion. The central theme of Greek religious thought and practice was the problem of death — a problem whose solution was found either by initiation into religious cults that promised to extricate the soul from its corruptible shroud or by belief in the native power of the soul to outlast any number of bodies. Alongside these, death was at the heart of the pathos of life depicted in Greek tragical drama, against which, and against the flaws of finitude in general, the major character manifested his heroic transcendence. So sin was determinative for the Hebrew consciousness; death for the Greek consciousness.

Consciousness III was Christianity, and by this, sin and death were tied together in Western man's awareness of personal existence. These two foci of man's misery and of his need for redemption — sin and death — were inseparably fused. This new dimension of man's awareness of himself was originally probed most profoundly by St. Paul's Letter to the Romans (5-7). Those opaque reflections, I opine, were once understood not so much by the intellect as along the pulses of ordinary people in great numbers, in taverns and market places; and it represents a cultural breakdown without parallel that these reflections are scarcely understandable to the greatest intelligences today. A simple night school lesson in them may be gained by simply pondering a while the two verses quoted above from St. John's Epistle.

The point is that according to the Christian saga the Messiah did not come to bring boors into culture. Nor did he bear epilepsy or psychosomatic disorders to gain victory over them in the flesh before the interventions of psychoneurosurgery. Rather is he said to have been born *mortal* flesh to gain for us a foretaste of victory over sin and death where those twin enemies had taken up apparently secure citadel.

Again, the point for our purposes is not to be drawn into agreement or disagreement with those theological affirmations, and it is certainly not to be tempted into endless speculation about an after-life. Crucial instead is to attend to the notation on the human condition implied in all that. Death is an enemy even if it is the last enemy to be fully conquered in the Fulfillment, the eschaton; meanwhile, the sting of death is sin. Such was the new consciousness-raising that Christianity brought into the Western world. And the question is whether in doing so it has not grasped some important experiential human realities better than most philosophies, whether it was not attuned to essential ingredients of the human condition vis-à-vis death — whatever the truth or falsity of its theological address to the condition.

The foregoing, I grant, may be an oversimplification; and I am aware of needed corrections more in the case of Hebrew humanism than in the case of Greek humanism. The New Testament word, "He will wipe away every tear from their eyes, and death shall be no more, neither shall there be mourning nor crying nor pain any more, for the former things have passed away" (Rev. 21:3, 4), has its parallel in the Hebrew Bible: "He will swallow up death forever, and the Lord God will wipe away tears from all faces . . ." (Isa. 25:8). Again, since contemplating the Lord God may be too much for us, I ask only that we attend to the doctrine of death implied in these passages: it is an enemy, surely, and not simply an acceptable part of the natural order of things. And the connection between dread of death and sin, made most prominent in Christian consciousness, was nowhere better stated than in Ecclesiastes: "This is the root of the evil in all that happens under the sun, that one fate comes to all. Therefore, men's minds are filled with evil and there is madness in their hearts while they live, for they know that afterward — they are off to the dead!"

One can, indeed, ponder that verse about the source of all evil in the apprehended evil of death together with another verse in Ecclesiastes which reads: "Teach us so to number our days that we may apply our hearts unto wisdom." The first says that death is an evil evil: it is experienced as a threatening limit that begets evil. The second says that death is a good evil: that experience also begets good. Without death, and death perceived as a threat, we would also have no reason to "number our days" so as to ransom the time allotted us, to receive life as a precious gift, to drink the wine of gladness in toast to every successive present moment. Instead, life would be an endless boredom and boring because endless; there would be no reason to probe its depths while there is still time. Some there are who number their days so as to apply their hearts unto eating, drinking and being merry — for tomorrow we die. Some there are who number their days so as to apply their hearts unto wisdom — for tomorrow we die. Both are life-spans enhanced in importance and in individuation under the stimulus of the perceived evil of death. Knowledge of human good or of human evil that is in the slightest degree above the level of the wild beasts of the field is enhanced because of death, the horizon of human existence. So, debarment from access to the tree of life was on the horizon and a sequence of the events in the Garden of Paradise; the temptation in eating the fruit of the tree of knowledge of good and evil was because that seemed a way for mortal creatures to become like gods. The punishment of that is said to have been death; and no governor uses as a penalty something that anyone can simply choose to believe to be a good or simply receive as a neutral or dignified, even ennobling, part of life. So I say death may be a good evil or an evil evil, but it is perceived as an evil or experienced indignity in either case. Existential anxiety or general anxiety (distinguishable from particular fears or removable anxieties) means anxiety over death toward which we live. That paradoxically, as Reinhold Niebuhr said, is the source of all human creativity and of all human sinfulness.

Of course, the sages of old could and did engage in a calculus of comparative indiginities. "O death, your sentence is welcome," wrote Ben Sira, "to a man worn out with age, worried about everything, disaffected and beyond endurance" (Ecclus. 41:2,3). Still death was a "sentence," not a natural event acceptable in itself. Moreover, not every man grows old gracefully in the Psalms; instead, one complains:

> Take pity on me, Yahweh,
> I am in trouble now.
> Grief wastes away my eye,
> My throat, my inmost parts.

For my life is worn out with sorrow,
My years with sighs;
My strength yields under misery,
My bones are wasting away.
To every one of my oppressors
I am contemptible,
Loathsome to my neighbors,
To my friends a thing of fear.
Those who see me in the street
Hurry past me.
I am forgotten, as good as dead, in their hearts,
Something discarded. (Ps. 31:9-12)

What else is to be expected if it be true that the madness in men's hearts while they live, and the root of all evil in all that happens under the sun, lies in the simple fact that every man consciously lives toward his own death, knowing that afterward he too is off to the dead? Where fear is — fear of the properly dreadful — love and care for the dying cannot be perfected.

Unless one has some grounds for respecting the shadow of death upon every human countenance — grounds more ultimate than perceptible realities — then it makes good sense as a policy of life simply to try to outlast one's neighbors. One can, for example, *generalize,* and so attenuate our neighbors' irreplaceability. "If I must grieve whenever the bell tolls," writes Carey McWilliams, "I am never bereft: some of my kinsmen will remain. Indeed, I need not grieve much — even, lest I suggest some preference among my brethren, should not grieve much — for each loss is small compared to what remains."[18] But the solace, we know, is denied the dead who have lost everything making for worth in their world. Realistic love for another irreplaceable, noninterchangeable individual human being means, as Unamuno wrote, care for another "doomed soul."

In this setting, let us now bring into consideration some empirical findings that in this day are commonly supposed to be more confirmatory than wisdom mediated from the heart.

In the second year anatomy course, medical students clothe with "gallows humor" their encounter with the cadaver which once was a human being alive. That defense is not to be despised; nor does it necessarily indicate socialization in shallowness on the students' part. Even when dealing with the remains of the long since dead, there is special tension involved — if I mistook not a recent address by Renée Fox — when performing investigatory medical actions involving the face, the hands, and the genitalia. This thing-in-the-world that was once a man alive we still encounter as once a communicating being, not quite as an object of research or instruction. Face and hands, yes; but why the genitalia? Those reactions must seem incongruous to a resolutely biologizing age. For a beginning of an explanation, one might take up the expression "carnal knowledge" — which was the best thing about the movie bearing that title — and behind that go to the expression "carnal *conversation,*" an old, legal term for adultery, and back of both to the Biblical word "knew" in "And Adam *knew* his wife and begat. . . ." Here we have an entire anthropology impacted in a word, not a squeamish euphemism. In short, in those reactions of medical students can be discerned a sensed relic of the human being bodily experiencing and communicating, and the body itself uniquely speaking.

Notably, however, there's no "gallows humor" used when doing or observing one's first autopsy, or in the emergency room when a D.O.A. (Dead on Arrival) is brought in with his skull cleaved open. With regard to the "newly dead" we come as close as we possibly can to experiencing the incommensurable contrast between life and death. Yet those sequential realities — life and death— here juxtaposed never *meet* in direct encounter. So we never have an impression or experience of the measure and meaning of the two different worlds before which we stand in the autopsy and the emergency room. A cadaver has over time become almost a thing-in-the-world from which to gain knowledge of the human body. While *there* a little humor helps, to go about acquiring medical knowledge from autopsies requires a different sort of inward effort to face down or live with our near-experience of the boundary of life and death. The cleavage in the brain may be quite enough and more than enough to *explain* rationally why this man was D.O.A. But, I suggest, there can be no gash deep enough, no physical event destructive enough to account for the felt difference between life and death that we face here. The physician or medical student may be a confirmed materialist. For him the material explanation of this death may be quite sufficient rationally. Still the heart has its reasons that the reason knows not of; and, I suggest, the awakening of these feelings of awe and dread should not be repressed in anyone whose calling is to the human dignity of caring for the dying.

In any case, from these empirical observations, if they be true, let us return to a great example of theological anthropology in order to try to comprehend why death was thought to be the assault of an enemy. According to some readings, Christians in all ages should be going about bestowing the gift of immortality on one another posthaste. A distinguished Catholic physician, beset by what he regarded as the incorrigible problems of medical ethics today, once shook his head in my presence and wondered out loud why the people who most believe in an afterlife should have established so many hospitals! That seems to require explanation, at least as against silly interpretations of "otherworldliness." The answer is that none of the facts or outlooks cited ever denied the reality of death, or affirmed that death ever presents a friendly face (except comparatively). The explanation lies in the vicinity of Christian anthropology and the Biblical view that death is an enemy. That foundation of Western medicine ought not lightly to be discarded, even if we need to enliven again the sense that there are limits to man's struggle against that alien power.

Far from the otherworldliness or body-soul dualism with which he is often charged, St. Augustine went so far as to say that "the body is not an extraneous ornament or aid, but a part of man's very nature."[19] Upon that understanding of the human being, Augustine could then express a quite realistic account of "the dying process":

> Wherefore, as regards bodily death, that is, the separation of the soul from the body, it is good to none while it is being endured by those whom we say are in the article of death [dying]. For the very violence with which the body and soul are wrenched asunder, which in the living are conjoined and closely intertwined, brings with it a harsh experience, jarring horribly on nature as long as it continues, till there comes a total loss of sensation, which arose from the very interpenetration of flesh and spirit.[20]

From this Augustine correctly concludes: "Wherefore death is indeed . . . good to none while it is actually suffered, and while it is subduing the dying to its power. . . ." His ultimate justifications attenuate not at all the harshness of that alien power's triumph. Death, he only says, is "meritoriously endured for the sake of winning what *is* good. And regarding what happens after death, it is no absurdity to say that death is good to the good, and evil to the evil."[21] But that is not to say that death as endured in this life, or as life's terminus, is itself in any way good. He even goes so far as to say:

> For though there can be no manner of doubt that the souls of the just and holy lead lives in peaceful rest, yet so much better would it be for them to be alive in healthy, well-conditioned bodies, that even those who hold the tenet that it is most blessed to be quit of every kind of body, condemn this opinion in spite of themselves.[22]

Thus, for Biblical or later Christian anthropology, the only possible form which human life in any true and proper sense can take here or hereafter is "somatic." That is the Pauline word; we today say "psychosomatic." Therefore, for Christian theology death may be a "conquered enemy"; still it was in the natural order — and as long as the generations of mankind endure will remain — an enemy still. To pretend otherwise adds insult to injury — or, at least, carelessness.

There are two ways, so far as I can see, to reduce the dreadful visage of death to a level of inherently acceptable indifference. One way is to subscribe to an interpretation of "bodily life" that reduces it to an acceptable level of indifference to the person long before his dying. That — if anyone can believe it today, or if it is not a false account of human nature — was the way taken by Plato in his idealized account of the death of Socrates. (It should be remembered that we know not whether Socrates' hands trembled as he yet bravely drunk the hemlock, no more than we know how Isaac experienced dying when "fullness of years" came upon him. Secondary accounts of these matters are fairly untrustworthy.)

Plato's dialogue *The Phaedo* may not "work" as a proof of the immortality of the soul. Still it decisively raises the question of immortality by its thorough representation of the incommensurability between mental processes and bodily processes.

Few philosophers today accept the demonstration of the mind's power to outlast bodies because the mind itself is not material, or because the mind "plays" the body like a musician the lyre. But most of them are still wrestling with the mind-body problem, and many speak of two separate languages, a language for mental events isomorphic with our language for brain events. That's rather like saying the same thing as Socrates (Plato) while claiming to have gone beyond him (Søren Kierkegaard).

I cite *The Phaedo* for another purpose: to manifest one way to render death incomparably welcomed. Those who most have mature manhood in exercise — the lovers of wisdom — have desired death and dying all their life long, in the sense that they seek "in every sort of way to dissever the soul from the communion of the body"; "thought is best when the mind is gathered into herself and none of these things trouble her — neither sounds nor sights nor pain nor any pleasure — when she takes leave of the body. . . ." That life is best and has nothing to fear that has "the habit of the soul gathering and collecting herself into herself from all sides out of the body." (Feminists, note the pronouns.)

Granted, Socrates' insight is valid concerning the self's transcendence, when he says: "I am inclined to think that these muscles and bones of mine would have gone off long ago to Megara and Boeotia — by the dog, they would, if they had been moved only by their own idea of what was best. . . ." Still Crito had a point, when he feared that the impending dread event had to do with "the same Socrates who has been talking and conducting the argument" than Socrates is represented to have believed. To fear the loss of Socrates, Crito had not to fancy, as Socrates charged, "that I am the other Socrates whom he will soon see, a dead body." Crito had only to apprehend, however faintly, that there is not an entire otherness between those two Socrates *now*, in this living being; that there was unity between, let us say, Socrates the conductor of arguments and Socrates the gesticulator or the man who stretched *himself* because his muscles and bones grew weary from confinement.

The other way to reduce the dreadful visage of death is to subscribe to a philosophy of "human life" that reduces the stature, the worth, and the irreplaceable uniqueness of the individual person (long before his dying) to a level of acceptable transiency or interchangeability. True, modern culture is going this way. But there have been other and better ways of stipulating that the image of death across the human countenance is no shadow. One was that of Aristotelian philosophy. According to its form-matter distinction, reason, the formal principle, is definitive of essential humanity. That is universal, eternal as logic. Matter, however, is the individuating factor. So when a man who bears a particular name dies, only the individuation disintegrates — to provide matter for other forms. Humanity goes on in other instances. Anything unique or precious about mankind is not individual. There are parallels to this outlook in Eastern religions and philosophies, in which the individual has only transiency, and should seek only that, disappearing in the Fulfillment into the Divine pool.

These then are two ways of denying the dread of death. Whenever these two escapes are *simultaneously* rejected — i.e., if the "bodily life" is neither an ornament nor a drag but a part of man's very nature; and if the "personal life" of an individual in his unique life-span is accorded unrepeatable, noninterchangeable value — then it is that Death the Enemy again comes into view. Conquered or Unconquerable. A true humanism and the dread of death seem to be dependent variables. I suggest that it is better to have the indignity of death on our hands and in our outlooks than to "dignify" it in either of these two possible ways. Then we ought to be much more circumspect in speaking of death with dignity, and hesitant to — I almost said — thrust that upon the dying! Surely, a proper care for them needs not only to know the pain of dying which human agency may hold at bay, but also care needs to acknowledge that there is grief over death which no human agency can alleviate.

Notes

1. Paul Ramsey, "On (Only) Caring for the Dying," *The Patient as Person* (New Haven: Yale University Press, 1971).

2. Elisabeth Kübler-Ross, *On Death and Dying* (New York: Macmillan, 1969), p. 247.

3. Schopenhauer's characterization of human history: if you've read one page, you've read it all.

4. Wittgenstein, *Tractatus,* 6.4311.

5. James Van Evra, "On Death as a Limit," *Analysis* 31 [5] (April, 1971): 170-76.

6. Erik Erikson, "Identity and the Life Cycle," *Psychological Issues,* I, [1] (New York: International University Press, 1959).

7. David Hendin, *Death as a Fact of Life* (New York: W. W. Norton, 1973).

8. Reported in *ibid.,* p. 89.

9. The *Florida Times-Union,* Jacksonville, Fla., Jan. 11, 1973.

10. Marya Mannes, *Last Rights* (New York: William Morrow, 1973), p. 6 (cf. 80, 133).

11. Hendin, *Death as a Fact of Life,* p. 103.

12. What, after all, is the point of promoting, as if it were a line of reasoning, observations such as that said to be inscribed on W. C. Field's tombstone: "On the whole I'd rather be here than in Philadelphia"?

13. I may add that while the House of Delegates did not endorse any particular form to express an individual's wishes relating prospectively to his final illness, it recognized that individuals have a right to express them. While it encouraged physicians to discuss such matters with patients and attend to their wishes, the House nevertheless maintained a place for the conscience and judgment of a physician in determining indicated treatment. It did not subsume every consideration under the rubric of the patient's right to refuse treatment (or to have refused treatment). That sole action-guide can find no medical or logical reason for distinguishing, in physicians' actions, between the dying and those who simply have a terminal illness (or have this "dying life," Augustine's description of all of us). It would also entail a belief that wishing or autonomous choice makes the moral difference between life and death decisions which then are to be imposed on the physician-technician; and that, to say the least, is an ethics that can find no place for either reason or sensibility.

14. Cf. The report of a Swedish survey by Gunnar Biörck, M.D., in *Archives of Internal Medicine,* October, 1973; news report in the *New York Times,* Oct. 31, 1973.

15. In the whole literature on death and dying, there is no more misquoted sentence, or statement taken out of context, than Koheleth's "time to be born and a time to die" — unless it be "Nor strive officiously to keep alive." The latter line is from an ironic poem by the nineteenth century poet Arthur Hugh Clough, entitled, "The Latest Decalogue":

Thou shalt not kill; but need'st not strive
Officiously to keep alive,
Do not adultery commit;
Advantage rarely comes of it:
Thou shalt not steal; an empty feat,
When it's so lucrative to cheat:
Bear not false witness; let the lie
Have time on its own wings to fly:
Thou shalt not covet; but tradition
Approves all forms of competition.
The sum of all is, thou shalt love
If anybody, God above:
At any rate, shalt never labor
More than thyself to love thy neighbor.

16. Nietzsche, *Thus Spake Zarathustra,* especially XLVI and LXVI.

17. Pascal, *Pensées,* p. 347.

18. Wilson Carey McWilliams, *The Idea of Fraternity in America* (Berkeley: University of California Press, 1973), p. 48.

19. Augustine, *City of God,* Book I, Chapter XIII.

20. Ibid., Book XIII, Chapter VI.

21. Ibid., Book XIII, Chapter VIII.

22. Ibid., Book XIII, Chapter XIX.

31 Keeping Body and Soul Together

Oliver O'Donovan

An admirer of Paul Ramsey's work has recently complained that in his later writing, and specifically in his writing on medical ethics since "The Patient as Person" in 1970, there is "much less direct appeal to theological warrants."[1] Whether or not this will stand as a generalization, there appears to be one striking counter-example, Ramsey's contribution to the *Hastings Center Studies* feature on "Facing Death" in 1974, an article entitled "The Indignity of 'Death with Dignity.'"[2] The occasion for that article, the author tells us, was his alarm at the sudden popularity of the view (his own, as well as that of many others) that the use of officious medical technique in the care of the dying should be discouraged (p. 47). In it he set out, in the first place, to chart the "'philosophical' ingredients of any view of death and dying," and, in the second "to exhibit some of the meaning of 'Christian humanism' in regard to death and dying" (p. 56). The result was a discussion so steeped in theological warrants that the two respondents, Robert S. Morison and Leon Kass, while acknowledging extensive practical agreement with Ramsey, hardly knew what to make of parts of it. Their three-cornered discussion has always seemed to me to be of especial interest, and that for three reasons. First, it succeeds in demonstrating what Ramsey set out to demonstrate: that the agreement about the unofficious care of the dying was a contingent coalition of divergent spiritual and intellectual viewpoints. Secondly, Ramsey's own article provides a striking example of his appeal to theological warrants in medical ethics, as well as of the ambiguities which make that appeal less decisive than it might be. And yet, thirdly, I would judge that it is something more than a personal declaration of sombre grandeur, but has integrity as an articulation of the Christian view of death.

My purpose in this essay is to concentrate on one particular theological theme of which Ramsey makes use in that article, as frequently in his other writings: the appeal to a unitary view of human nature, that is, to the mutual coinherence of body and soul. It is a familiar enough contention to anyone who has read Ramsey at all widely, that the chief errors of contemporary moral thought, whether about sexual freedom, nuclear deterrence, or euthanasia, are attributable to an over-spiritualisation of human action.[3] The only surprising thing about the appearance of this contention in ". . . Death with Dignity" might seem to be the lateness of its arrival there (p. 59, at the foot of the thirteenth of sixteen pages)! I shall however be drawing attention to some other surprising features. For Ramsey's use of this and other theological warrants in this article is strangely difficult to pin down. Not only did the argument prove difficult for sympathetic respondents from outside the Christian tradition to understand, let alone sympathise with; but it also involved Ramsey in some surprisingly evasive moves from the point of view of Christian theology itself. I take this fine piece of writing, then, as my starting-point for what will be at once a defense, an interpretation and, I hope, a refinement of a central thesis in theological anthropology, from which Ramsey launches his medical ethics as well as much else.[4]

Given the complexity of the article it may not be officious to offer an analytic summary of it, illuminating its structure, which, while thoroughly and soundly built, has been obscured both by the author's own use of art to conceal art and by an editorial disposition of sub-headings which savours of despair.[5] As I have indicated, the article falls into two parts: the first concerned with the "'philosophical' ingredients of any view of death and dying," the second with the "Christian humanism" which Ramsey himself, unwilling to

---

Published as "Ne pas séparer l'âme du corps," trans. M.-B. Mesnet, *Ethique* xi (1994): 64-89. The English version is published here for the first time with permission of the author.

speak as "some hypothetical common denominator," intends to profess. The word "philosophical" is placed by Ramsey himself in quotation marks. And that is because this first part of the article constitutes, in effect, a sustained *criticism* of traditional philosophical wisdom about death, a criticism summed up in a mocking misquotation from Dylan Thomas: "The wise men at their end know dark is right, because their words had forked no lightning."[6] Philosophy, in attempting to reconcile human beings to their death, has sold life short. The criticism embraces Aristotle and Plato (though the *Phaedo* is discussed in a tone of deep appreciation) and a horde of popular modern philosophers for which Ramsey does not attempt to disguise his scorn. It must also, by implication, embrace the Jewish wise men, Rabbi Meir and Maimonides, whom Kass holds out as examples. For Kass and Ramsey see the task of the philosopher differently. Kass, though he admits the dangers in judging doctrines by their moral "usefulness," understands the philosopher's duty as exhortation: "how *should* Socrates or Isaac or Ramsey or Kass or any human being regard . . .the fact that we must each and all die?"[7] For Ramsey it is interpretation: what is the truth about human dignity in the face of death? And Ramsey, at the very beginning of his article, does not conceal from us what he thinks the truth is, which philosophers, simply by attending to their own business, ought to have been able to see: it is that human dignity is not found *in* dying, but is brought *to* dying. Ramsey's standard of philosophical truth is found in the famous Pascal *Pensée*, which designates man as "a thinking reed" who "knows that he dies . . . All our dignity, then, consists in thought."[8]

Kass, too, of course, assents to a version of this thesis. He, too, does not look to death itself as the source of man's dignity in dying. He contends that death is "neutral with respect to dignity"; for dignity is "something that belongs to a human being and is displayed in the way he lives, and hence something not easily taken away from him."[9] But Ramsey means, and understands Pascal to mean, something more negative about death than Kass could stomach. The very occasion for dignity is afforded by the fact that death is itself an *indignity*, in response to which the "human countenance" must be made to appear. On the one hand the therapist, and on the other the dying patient must bring to the event from outside it that sense of human worth which will enable it to appear. And this means encompassing "nakedly and without dilution" the fact that death is an indignity. What the philosophers should have grasped, as the fundamental ingredient of any view of death and dying, is that human mortality and human dignity are in dialectical contradiction. If the one evokes the other, it is not by sympathy but by antithesis.

The objection to received philosophical wisdom is then pursued in two stages. In the first Ramsey knocks together two characteristic consolations which attempt to accommodate human mortality to the life-projects of human agents. On the one hand, there is the claim that death is part of life; on the other, the claim that death is not part of life; either of which, if it were the whole truth, would be consoling. For we could be reconciled to the naturalness of death in the one case; or in the other we could dismiss it as something which, by definition, lies outside our ken. But neither is true. Or, perhaps we should say, neither is true except in such a way that the other is equally true. Death is not a part of life in such a way that it can be encompassed within our life-projects and so made comfortable; neither is it beyond our ken in such a way that it does not in fact impinge upon our life-projects and trouble them. It is a boundary; and a boundary is neither simply within the field nor simply beyond it. We live "up against" this limit during our life-spans. And whatever good may come to us from the fact that the limit is there, whatever creativity or virtue it may evoke, it does so because it is dreaded. Refusing to be accommodated within, and refusing to absent itself beyond our scope as human agents, it confronts us as the ultimate No to all that we aspire to be and do.

The second stage of the argument takes its cue from the saying of Koheleth (Ecclesiastes) that there is "a time to die" (3:2), and examines the grounds that philosophers have found for denying the character of death as the negation of the human. Koheleth himself, as Ramsey argues at the end of this section, knew better than those who had torn this thread out of the fabric of his thought. "Koheleth seems to say: Let the natural or cosmic order be whatever it is; men are different" (p. 55). And what Koheleth seems to say is, in Ramsey's view, what all philosophers ought to say instead of attempting to accommodate death within the sequence of life-experiences, and praising it for its fittingness. Philosophical "morticians" falsely ascribe to death the capacity to carry its own immanent meaningfulness, to be a *telos* when it is in fact no more than a *finis.* There is to be sure, a legitimate way in which we can reach the conclusion that death is, on this or that occasions, *to be chosen:* that is, when it appears as the least of a number of possible indignities which the sufferer is compelled to choose among. But such an analysis of "comparative indignities" cannot justify talk of death's "beauty." Philosophy has struck an abstract posture which overlooks our human horror of death in order to think "generally." Against it Ramsey quotes another Pascal saying: "The heart has its reasons which reason does not know."[10] But he quotes it without entirely accepting the opposition of reason and heart which Pascal suggests. For the heart's reasons are genuine reasons; and philosophy which refuses to listen to the heart's reasons in its dread of death simply makes itself less than fully rational. Koheleth, when properly read, affords an example of what philosophy can say truly in the face of man's mortality; and so does Pascal.

All of which, as is evident enough, is Ramsey's way of making philosophy rebuke philosophy. He has allied himself (and not for the first time) with the existentialist philosophers in their contest with idealist metaphysics.[11] One of the questions he must face is how far "Christian humanism" can walk in this company without being consumed by it. For the moment it is enough to observe that in one feature of his exposition he is self-consciously dependent upon them. Kass complains of "Ramsey's frequent weaving back and forth between a subjective perspective on a particular death in its individuality . . . and an objective perspective on human mortality itself."[12] Such weaving, Ramsey would reply, is precisely what philosophy must do if it is to attend to its business. The dialectic between subjective dread, on the one hand, and objective recognition of the harmony of death and nature on the other, provides philosophers with the agenda for their thinking. If philosophy (as Plato, or Maimonides) refuses to attend to the dialectic, what has it left to think about? But if (as Koheleth, or Pascal) it does attend to it, then a further question arises: where, if anywhere, is it to turn for a resolution? Ramsey, for his part, turns to "Christian humanism."

Where, we may ask, is this turn meant to bring us? For there is more than one kind of resolution to the antinomy which we might envisage as the proper goal of our thought. Does Ramsey have in mind an evangelical reconciliation, in which biological homogeneity and humane distinctiveness will embrace and kiss each other? Or does he envisage a resolution in thought alone, which will ground their opposition in metaphysics and show why it must always arise? This question is connected with another. When Ramsey turns to "Christian humanism" is that phrase meant to introduce a *theological* interpretation of human nature, a moment in the proclamation of the Christian Gospel? Or is he pointing us to something that is less decisively of faith, to a Christian wisdom that can prescind from evangelical proclamation and proceed on its own? On two occasions in what follows he invites non-Christians "whatever [they] may think about the *theology* here entailed . . ." to attend to the "penetration of human condition" (56, 57). Yet those who know Ramsey's theoretical explorations of how Christ "transforms" the law of nature, will not expect to find him advancing an unambiguously "natural" account of human existence as that which properly belongs to Christendom.[13] If it is true that the argument of this second major section of Ramsey's article is not theological, it is also true that it is shaped by theology, and that evangelical proclamation lurks in its shadows. In order to illustrate this, I propose to read the first part of it (IIA) twice: once in order to trace its most obvious course, which seems to allow no place for evangelical reconciliation, and then a second time in order to notice the indications which point us towards one. Both readings are facilitated by a comparison with a published sermon of thirteen years before, entitled (after Donne) *Deaths Duell,* on which Ramsey drew heavily for this part of his article.[14]

The section begins with a twofold quotation from 1 John 4:18: "Perfect love casts out fear," and "Where fear is, love is not perfected." The same pair of sayings had served as a text for *Deaths Duell.* In what follows most of Ramsey's attention is directed to the second member of this pair, which he applies to the question of dying in the following paraphrase: "Where fear of death and dying remains, medical and human care of the dying is not perfected" (56). Fear, in other words, is the source of that medical officiousness which troubles the dying unnecessarily, as well as of other attempts to remove the human countenance from death, some of them masquerading under the slogan "death with dignity." One or another species of the denial of death operates to prevent that humane keeping-of-company which ought to be the truest form of care. It is in support of this thesis that Ramsey then turns to the assertion of Saint Paul that sin and death are connected — an assertion which differentiates Christianity, in his view, both from the Hebrew concern with sin and the Hellenistic concern with death. Death brings sin after it. And with this claim Christianity "has grasped some important experiential human realities" better than most philosophies (57). Not that it was not anticipated in the Old Testament: again, Koheleth can be quoted. Nor can we say that this "existential anxiety" is without possibilities for good; for the Psalmist was able to pray "Teach us to number our days that we may apply our hearts to wisdom."[15] The point is simply that such wisdom as springs from the knowledge of our mortality arises from *dread.* And in recognising the fact, and the equally striking fact that dread lies behind our refusal of love because it generates self-protection, Christianity has unmasked the pretensions of philosophy to accommodate death within the scheme of things. It has also made sense, as philosophy cannot otherwise do, of such instinctual responses to death as the "gallows humour" by which medical students negotiate their earliest engagements with the dissection of a corpse.

On this first reading of section IIA, then, which is the more straightforward reading, it contains no evangelical reconciliation, but merely points to elements of a theological anthropology which will ground the antinomy of mortality and human aspiration. The link between sin and death, in which death brings sin after it, highlights the fact that we cannot ignore the dread of death nor regard it as merely circumstantial weakness of mind; for it lies at the root of that universal failure of love which is the core of the human tragedy. There is no doubt from which source Ramsey derived this train of thought: it is from Reinhold Niebuhr, quoted at a significant moment as saying that anxiety over death is the source of all human creativity and of all human sinfulness.[16] The same train of thought featured prominently in *Deaths Duell.* But comparison of the two writings turns up a startling contrast. In the earlier essay Ramsey treated the thesis *death brings sin after it* merely as the preparation for a more important antithesis, and criticised any one-sided affirmation of it as "a return to the Greek religious consciousness and a breakdown of the Biblical tradition that is without parallel."[17] And he named "present-day existentialism" as one of the factors in that breakdown. The more profoundly Christian connexion between sin and death, Ramsey then argued, is found in the contrary assertion that *sin brings death after it.* The importance of this assertion lay in the fact that it constituted a "redefinition" of life and death, determining the locus of each in relation to the object of our human love and belief: "We *live* by faith; or else in lack of faith living according to the flesh we die."[18] The Christian Gospel, therefore, proclaims a reconciliation of humanity with mortality, for it proclaims that eternal life is present here and now, even under the conditions of mortality. Thus, Ramsey concluded, "perfect love casts out any fear over the loss of life," and this, the first member of the pair of sayings, proves (despite an early impression to the contrary) to be the more Christian because it is the more evangelical statement.[19]

We are struck, first of all, by the simple absence of this material from ". . . Death with Dignity." At first reading, Ramsey has turned his back on the evangelical emphasis which he was previously at pains to give — the connexion between sin and death in Christian thought. But a second reading does something to qualify this impression. He paraphrases the first part of his text as follows: "Perfect care of the dying casts out fear of one's own death or rejection of their dying because of fear of ours." The standard for care of the dying, he adds, is "cut to the measure of the perfection in benevolence believed to be that of our Father in Heaven"; and then, seizing on the word "believed" (which gives the impression of having been dragged in) he adds: "So there is 'faith-ing' in an ultimate righteousness beyond the perceptible human condition." Behind the perception that death brings lovelessness after it, there lies the proclamation that by faith in divine love we may overcome the lovelessness that death brings. All that is said in a moment, before the unbeliever is invited to prescind from theology and attend to the "notation upon" the human condition. In no more than a moment, too, Ramsey reminds us (in a passage which did not come ready-made from *Deaths Duell*!) that the Messiah was born as mortal flesh "to gain for us a foretaste of victory over sin and death." It becomes clear, then, that we are not meant to forget that Christianity has an evangelical proclamation to make, arising from the connexion of death and sin; but still there is no hint of the conclusion in the earlier piece, that a one-sided emphasis on existential anxiety is in danger of reverting to paganism, and that the Christian connexion between death and sin is better expressed as "sin draws death after." The implied criticism of Niebuhr has now been withdrawn. In 1974 Ramsey, writing with more explicitly apologetic motives perhaps, does not want to distance himself from Niebuhr, but simply to recall what he once taught us.

Thus we turn to the final section (IIB), which is the climax of the argument. It begins with the assertion of body-soul unity, the theological goal, as we may now see, to which the article has been tending. Ramsey has expounded this principle from many sources on many different occasions. Here he takes his lead from Augustine's *City of God*, with no more than a passing allusion to Saint Paul, which, however, I quote in order to comment later on what it omits: "Thus for Biblical or later Christian anthropology, the only possible form which human life in any true and proper sense can take here or hereafter is 'somatic.' That is the Pauline word; today we say psychosomatic" (60). The natural conclusion from this anthropology is that death (though theologically it may be a *conquered* enemy) is, in the natural order, an enemy still. Ramsey then outlines two alternative strategies of thought for reducing "the dreadful visage of death." If we are not prepared to follow either of these "escapes," he will conclude, then "Death the Enemy again comes into view" (62). One of these strategies is Plato's, the other Aristotle's. Plato reduces *bodily life to indifference*, by arguing for the self-sufficient immortality of the dissevered soul, "gathering and collecting herself into herself . . . out of the body." Aristotle reduces the *uniqueness of individual life to interchangeability*, vesting all the value and worth of human kind in the species rather than the individual.

Ramsey's pincer-movement appears to be a fairly simple one. Either the soul is immortal and self-sufficient (and so the individual is unarmed by death); or the value of humanity resides in the species (and so the death of individuals is of little moment); or, the value of humanity residing in individuals and the soul being bound up in the death of the body, death is dreadful. The dreadfulness of death is thus argued as an implication of some fundamental Christian postures over against classical paganism; and that is why Christians should find themselves at one with existentialists in calling the bluff of idealist or naturalist evasions. But on inspection the argument appears to face at least two difficulties. Does the Christian affirmation of "somatic" existence imply the affirmation of *both* the arms of Ramsey's pincer, the one rejecting Plato the other Aristotle? If we are to say so, then we need to lay a better foundation than is afforded by the simple assertion of body-soul unity. For psychosomatic unity, as it stands, also describes Aristotle's position; and if Ramsey wishes to differentiate Christian anthropology from the Aristotelian alternative, he will have to say more than he has done to characterise it as a view which conceives human value as not only bodily but individual.[20] The second difficulty we may allow Kass to express: "He should . . . be willing *in principle* to embrace current biochemical research which aims to retard the process of aging and greatly extend our life expectancy. . . . I suspect he would, on principle, refuse. His heart may know the reasons why . . . but his reason's reasons — at least those given in this paper — would not tell him or us why not."[21]

The programme of Ramsey's discussion has been to move from a disagreement internal to philosophy, in which existential anxiety in the face of death demands to be taken more seriously than palliating naturalist and idealist philosophies have taken it, to a Christian anthropology which grounds existential anxiety in two metaphysical assertions, the connexion of sin and death and the unity of body and soul. It appears, however, that the second of these two assertions, the principle of body-soul unity, is not strong enough to bear the weight which Ramsey puts on it. It will not rule out, on the one hand, an Aristotelian settlement which accepts individual perishability for the sake of species-survival; and it will not rule out, on the other, a defiance of natural mortality (by technique, if it can be done) which might seem to be the inevitable implication of the existential struggle which Ramsey admires. My argument will be that this undeniable weakness in Ramsey's anthropological foundations is not systemic, but that it arises from the apologetic strategy of the article, by which he encouraged his readers too readily to prescind from the theological context and so deprived his contentions of the full range of their interpretative force. We have already shown how, in his handling of the first assertion, he suppressed what had seemed to him elsewhere to be the more important aspect of the Christian association of sin and death, and how with it he surrendered the ground from which he could criticise the existentialist philosophies with which he was strategically allied. We must proceed by showing how he has done the same with the second assertion, the most persistently Ramseyan of the two and the one with which our own chief interest on this occasion lies. By positing the principle of body-soul unity in isolation from its context in the Christian gospel, Ramsey has left it weaker in explanatory force than it should be, and has accordingly failed to display the full intelligibility of his own position.

Leon Kass might have found an answer, had he come across *Deaths Duell*, to the challenge he threw down about research to avert aging. The reasons Ramsey would adduce for refusing such research emerge clearly enough there, from an elegant quotation of Donne: "When thou thinkest thyself swallowed, and buried in affliction . . . Christ Jesus shall remove thy grave stone, and give thee a resurrection; but if thou thinkest to remove it by thine own wit, thine own power, or favour of potent friends, *Digitus Dei non est hic*, the hand of God is not in all this, and the stone will lie upon thee, till thou putrefy into desperation, and thou shalt have no part in this . . . resurrection."[22] Expressed in a plainer style, the same answer can be found in some words of Niebuhr: "The hope of the resurrection . . . implies that the condition of finiteness and freedom, which lies at the basis of human existence, is a problem for which there is no solution by any human power. Only God can solve this problem."[23]

The road which leads from psychosomatic unity to an endeavour of technique to keep body and soul together, is blocked by an act of God. The decisive intervention of divine power is the warning that we must not (even if we could) secure the unity of body and soul by the strivings of practical ingenuity. But in ". . . *Death with Dignity* the resurrection is scarcely mentioned."[24] Denying himself an appeal to this central affirmation of the Christian creed, Ramsey has denied himself the means of delimiting his position effectively and of refusing the unwelcome inference which Kass would make him draw from it.

The resurrection, however, plays more than a merely limiting role in relation to psychosomatic unity. It is, in fact, the intellectual foundation of it in Christian thought. It is the resurrection, rather than the principle of body-soul unity *in abstracto*, which performs the crucial task of criticising the idealist "over-spiritualisation" of human action in modern thought. And at this point we may have to acknowledge another coalition of otherwise divergent viewpoints; for there are, of course, other critiques of idealism, other assertions of the materialist affirmation of the human body, than that which a Christian will feel bound to make.[25] But in *Deaths Duell* Ramsey made clear enough the theological roots of his own materialism. The first page of that sermon proceeds tightly by the following steps: (i) Christianity (speaking through the mouth of Saint Paul) improved upon both Hebrew and Hellenistic thought by tying sin and death together. (ii) It is implied in this conjunction that death is an act of divine judgment, in which "God withdrew his perduring power." (iii) And it is implied in that view of death that there is no inherent immortality of the soul, which would be, in effect a "robbery of God." Conversely, the denial of the authentic Christian belief in the resurrection of the body is grounded in an "ultra-spiritual estimate of man." Conclusion: Christian belief in resurrection and Hellenistic belief in the immortal soul are, therefore, opposed to each other.

This argument places Ramsey in the mainstream of an almost twentieth-century theological consensus, and in order to demonstrate the character of this consensus, I beg indulgence for a brief and sketchy historical excursus. It could almost be said that an opposition between idealist "spiritualisation" and Christian "materialism," based on belief in the resurrection, is the hallmark of all Western theology which postdates the great theological upheaval of the 1920s. It is common to all the diverse schools of Protestant theology, however differently they relate to the resurrection to history.[26] It is proclaimed as a datum of Biblical research by the "Biblical theology" school.[27] Historical New Testament criticism plunges into the task of separating the "pre-Easter" from the "post-Easter" elements of the Gospel tradition. Thomists claim for St. Thomas the decisive articulation of a materialist Christian anthropology.[28] Reform-minded Roman Catholics challenge the Western Catholic tradition over the "shrinkage" of Easter.[29] Eastern Orthodox theologians recall that resurrection was central to the theology of the Greek fathers.[30] "Christian materialism" then survives the collapse and demise of all the leading mid-century schools of theology, and emerges, fresh and as though new-minted, in the historical dialectics of the neo-Hegelians.[31]

I take as an early manifesto for this twentieth-century consensus a small book by Karl Barth dating from 1926, *The Resurrection of the Dead*.[32] In it Barth addresses the fifteenth chapter of 1 Corinthians, the chapter about the resurrection, and argues that it is the key to the whole epistle and, more sweepingly, to the whole of Saint Paul's proclamation of the Gospel. In light of the resurrection all the issues of life and death are seen clearly and judged (p. 107). In this context Barth advances his criticism of romantic idealism, in which the main outline of what Ramsey will later want to say is already apparent. The Last Things of Christian proclamation are not the ultimate possibilities of human life; they are the end of all things — not in the sense of being their goal but as their termination (p. 109f.). Death relativises all the abundant possibilities of life by putting a close to them (p. 113). Human aspirations cannot include death within their purposes, however spiritual. Life after death is not a possibility *within* a uniform cosmos which we can comprehend. The Gospel proclaims a *bodily* resurrection in order to reprove our "wanton play of imagination with respect to the invisible," and this challenges at its root all ideas of an immanent human fitness for immortality. The overcoming of death is a new world, unbelievable, inaccessible apart from the fact that God has simply confronted us with it (p. 157). Paul's opponents at Corinth, says Barth (and makes no secret of thinking that nineteenth-century idealism was their natural intellectual milieu) played down the general resurrection because it confronted them with the alien "other" of divine activity. But without the general resurrection, the resurrection of Christ could be only a meaningless isolated miracle (p. 122), not a true appearance of the divine horizon (p. 162). The "parousia" of Christ at the end of history is the surfacing of the subterranean stream which has run from the resurrection of Christ (p. 176). The resurrection is, therefore, already the decisive conquest of death and the inauguration of the new world.

Sixty years ago this was revolutionary. It is hard to find any eighteenth or nineteenth-century voices which would assert the centrality of the resurrection of Christ as almost all twentieth-century voices have agreed in asserting it. The mood of the nineteenth century is set by Schleiermacher's cool estimate that "the disciples recognised in Jesus the Son of God without having the faintest premonition of his resurrection and ascension, and we too may say the same of ourselves; moreover neither the spiritual presence which he promised, nor all that he said about his enduring influence upon those who remained behind, is mediated through either of these two facts."[33] But, of course, it was not original to the nineteenth century romantics to suggest that the salvific meaning of Christ's death could be explained on its own, without reference to the resurrection. In Western theology this assumption can be traced back at least as far as Anselm's *Cur Deus Homo*. And the corollary of it was a view of death which vested the hope of the believer in the immortality of the soul, and, at its worst, repudiated the body. We may observe this tradition at its most marked in the popular Lutheran piety of the early eighteenth century, as represented to us in the texts used by J. S. Bach for his church cantatas, with their constantly recurring prayers of longing for death.[34] Nobody ever told Bach or his contemporaries that "the only possible form which human life in any true and proper sense can take here or hereafter is 'somatic.'"[35]

The Christian anthropology, then, to which Ramsey appeals to insistently is hardly the anthropology of the whole Christian tradition. If we are to affirm (as I, with him, would do) that this is authentic Christian anthropology, then we have to support our claim with another: that the revolution which swept the body to the centre of Christian thought earlier this century was a genuine rediscovery of elements of an original Christian understanding.

Where did the twentieth-century revolution spring from? Its sources are complex. On the philosophical side it is part of the general repudiation of idealism in the inter-war period, and so has negative affinities with the philosophical turn to materialism which occurred at the same time. More profoundly, however, it is the fruit of an accumulating weight of biblical and historical scholarship in at least three areas. It reflects the development in patristic scholarship, which made theologians aware of the central place played by the resurrection of the body in early Christian anti-Platonist polemic. This is the more impressive as it occurs in a theological milieu which, as some modern objectors are inclined to feel, had already made dangerously extensive concessions to Platonic dualism; yet however great the concessions may have been, the Fathers characteristically viewed the resurrection of the body as a battle-line which could not be abandoned. It reflects also the discovery of late Jewish apocalyptic and its role in shaping the categories of the New Testament. It reflects, in the third place, a new appreciation of the materialist character of psychological terms in Biblical Hebrew, and the disembarrassment of such words as *nephesh* and *leb* of the irrelevant overtones which "soul" and "heart" had acquired from other sources. The assertion that body-soul unity is the "Biblical" anthropology is based on a study of *Hebrew* words; though the Greek New Testament, it is true, often reflects Hebrew word-usage, as in the famous text about "losing one's soul" and "saving it," where *psyche* is properly the equivalent of the Hebrew *nephesh.*

But the claim for a "Biblical" concept of man as a unitary psychosomatic being cannot be sustained on the basis of Hebrew lexicography alone. It is quite clear that Jewish writers of the New Testament era allowed themselves a much greater eclecticism, of terminology and conceptualisation, than would ever be encountered in the Psalms. Compare the entirely "materialist" cry of Psalm 30:9, "Will the dust praise thee? Will it tell of thy faithfulness?," with the famous passage from the Book of Wisdom (3:1ff.) which declares that "the souls of the righteous are in the hand of God," and adds that "in the eyes of the foolish they *seem* to have died, and their departure was *thought* to be an affliction . . . but they are at peace" (emphasis added). And before we dismiss this as an aberration in a work deeply influenced by Hellenism, we have to account for a saying of Jesus himself, as we find it in St. Matthew's Gospel (10:28), hardly the most Hellenistic of Jewish writings: "And do not fear those who kill the body but cannot kill the soul."[36] Even Saint Paul compares the body to a tent in which we conduct our pilgrimage, to be replaced after death by a more permanent dwelling (2 Cor. 5:1ff.) However true it may be that *psyche* in the New Testament does not mean what it means in Plato's *Phaedo,* it is clear that the New Testament writers are quite at home with the concept of an "inner man" — the phrase itself comes from Ephesians (3:16) — and are prepared to evoke this hidden level of human existence to give support to the believer's hope in the face of death. There is, of course, a great difference between the way they handle it and the way that it is handled in the Platonic tradition. But the point is that it is not the conceptual structure *itself* which differentiates New Treatment anthropology from Platonic. The conceptual structure is plastic and adaptable, responding to the ideas that the writers had to express, which are not exactly those which the Psalmists had to express.

The difference lies in the fact that the apostles of the earliest church made the resurrection of Jesus the centre of their proclamation, and it was this that forbade them to *develop* a dual conception of man as body and soul (which they could perfectly well *admit*) in the direction of an objectifying alienation of the body. Thus we find in their writings, too, something that can be called, not inappropriately, "body-soul unity" — though we might be wiser to find ourselves another term, since the effect of the words "unity" and "dualism" is to reduce all the options inflexibly to two. I prefer to speak of a Christian *identification* with the body, as opposed to an *objectification* of the body which marks the idealist tradition. Even where the discussion has not to do with death — notably at Corinthians 6:12ff., where the theme is sexual morality — the ground of identification with the body is the claim that God has made upon the bodily life of a man by the resurrection of Christ. "The body is not meant for immorality but for the Lord, and the Lord for the body. And God raised the Lord, and will also raise us up by his power. Do you know that your bodies are members of Christ?"

The principle of psychosomatic unity, then, has no *free-standing* authority for Christian thought, but rides on the principle that the resurrection of Christ is central to Christian faith and the resurrection of all mankind to Christian hope. It is in this context that the Christian will wish to give his assent to the saying, "Embodiment is the end of all God's works."[37]

It remains for me to plead that the positions which Ramsey maintained in ". . . Death with Dignity" cohere around this central theological affirmation. This part of my argument can only be effected by a doctrinal sketch, which will be as unsatisfactory as such sketches always are — for it is the cartoonist's fate that his pencil-lines must seem too sweeping and dogmatic.

At the root of idealism, and therefore of the idealist view of human nature which Ramsey, with the majority of twentieth-century theologians, wishes to contest, is the contrast between appearance and reality. Idealism takes its bearings from the sharp difference between what it is to *be* a human being and what it is to *observe* one; and in its attempt to discern what is real, it follows those clues which are given by the hidden subjectivity of human existence, that which we know only in ourselves and not in other people. To speak, with Plato, of "the soul" is to use only one of the terms by which idealist philosophies have identified the hidden reality of what it is to be a human being. One may speak equally of "spirit" or of "mind" — the latter term drawing attention to the common conviction that the hidden reality is connected with the phenomenon of mental awareness, of world and of self.

To think of reality as hidden, is not, of course, to think of it as beyond knowledge — with such a contention philosophy would merely rule itself out. We know the hidden world because it is the source of the intelligible form with which appearances are presented to us; it is the intelligible principle behind their intelligibility. But knowledge can only be acquired by a philosophical askesis, by stripping away appearances and unmasking their pretensions to be the reality which they present. Idealism embodies the suspicion of appearances, the conviction that they create delusions which must be overcome. And so it is with its treatment of death. When Ramsey criticises idealist philosophers for not taking existential anxiety about death seriously enough, the truth probably is (as Kass hints) that they *have* taken it seriously — as a delusion! They have treated it as a form of the vulgar acceptance of what merely seems to be. Thus the *Phaedo* takes the form of a dialogue, in which the distress of Socrates' friends is overcome by his own philosophic calm. A dialogue, too, the most striking of the romantic expressions of calm before death, Matthias Claudius's "Der Tod und das Mädchen," famous from Schubert's unforgettable setting:

'Vorüber! ach, vorüber
Geh, wilder Knochenmann!
Ich bin noch jung, geh, Lieber!
Und rühre mich nicht an.'

'Gib deine Hand, du schon und zart Gebild,
Bin Freund und komme nicht zu strafen.
Sei gutes Muts! Ich bin nicht wild,
Sollst sanft in meinen Armen schlafen.'[48]

Christian opposition to idealism is based on a different view of the relation of appearance to reality. The distinction between them is, of course, recognised in the biblical depiction of human nature: "Man looks on the outward appearance, but the Lord looks on the heart" (1 Samuel 16:7). Yet the distinction is developed differently. If in Platonism the essence of the inner man is self-conscious awareness (or "Mind"), with the biblical "heart" we encounter a conception of inwardness as a source of practical agency. The hidden man deliberates and originates action; it is not the philosopher who demonstrates our need to reckon with him, but the schemer, whose impassive face conceals elaborate plans for the downfall of the righteous. And that means that the hidden reality will not remain hidden, but will burst into appearance and manifest itself, as the intentions of the heart finally bear fruit in action. In the teaching of Jesus in the synoptic Gospels it is constantly repeated that the hidden must eventually publish itself: "Either make the tree good and its fruit good, or make the tree bad and its fruit bad; for the tree is known by its fruit. You brood of vipers! how can you speak good, when you are evil? For out of the abundance of the heart the mouth speaks. The good man out of his good treasure brings forth good, and the evil man out of his evil treasure brings forth evil" (St. Matthew 12:33-5). Appearances are not insulated against the hidden reality; there is no stable distance between them which will allow illusion to be indefinitely sustained. The appearance of ultimate annihilation which death presents is to be overcome, then, not by being seen through by the wise, but by being abolished and replaced with a truer appearance. The difference between the immortality of the soul and the resurrection of the dead is the difference between an esoteric reconciliation and a public one.

The resurrection was not named among the traditional Four Last Things of Christian thought — an arbitrary list, deservedly toppled long since from its place in the doctrinal textbooks. One might say that resurrection unmasks the pretensions of death to be a Last Thing, by superseding it as a Later-than-last Thing, and so demonstrating that it was never more than a penultimate thing. But from this it follows that death can no longer be regarded (though ever so philosophically, and in despite of appearances) as the goal towards which life in the body is ordered, the *telos* which sets the coping stone on its achievement. In the sonorous Coverdale version of the ninetieth Psalm we are accustomed to say that "we bring our years to an end as a tale that is told," a claim that seems to be false on at least two points. For, by whatever means our years come to their end, it is not we who bring them to it, unless we are in that small and unhappy group of those who end their own lives by violence. And when, however, our years come to their end, their end gives them no perceptible narrative coherence; rather, death comes bounding into them to disrupt whatever narrative coherence they might have been in course of achieving. Think of the difficulty which confronts every biographer in attempting to include the subject's death in the story of his life! Only fiction-writers can integrate death pleasingly into a narrative wholeness; and that is because characters who die in fiction exist only to die, whereas characters who die in life have existed to live. We would do better to choose a less sonorous but more truthful modern translation of the Psalmist's words: "Our years peter out in a whimper."

Behind the pretension of death to provide a *telos* for life there lies a way of looking at life itself. Or perhaps we should say, there lie several ways of looking at it; for not every philosophy that can be grouped under the umbrella-title of "idealism" will look at life in precisely the same way. Yet every way of looking at life that tries to find in it a thread of meaning which will make death its climax will seem to the Christian perspective to have sold life short. Of the tendency of Platonism to engender a suspicion of the body, and to ally itself with a Manichaean dread of sexuality and sense, more than enough has been said in this century by the voices of robust materialism, Jewish, Christian and unbelieving. We need not pursue that side of things further here. Less has been said (though some of it has been very memorable) of the life-renouncing character of modern romanticism.[39] In the Claudius poem we find an epitome not merely of the romantic view of death but of the romantic spirit as such, which trades heavily on death in order to project its vision of life. The secret meaningfulness of death which it uncovers is that the true goal of life is exhaustion. To live as though to become a pile of embers, burnt out in a momentary blaze of brilliant and unearthly luminosity, such is the aspiration which romanticism, in many forms, commends to us. And against that aspiration authentic Christianity will find itself forced to contend for all that is represented by the empty tomb of Easter. Bodily life is not given us in order for it to collapse spectacularly under the weight of the spirit; it is given to sustain spiritual life, and in turn to be renewed by it. Life is for life, not for the abnegation of life.

In this context we may take up a crucial charge that Kass has made against Ramsey: that he has not given nature its due (p. 76). Let us try to meet it, on Ramsey's behalf, by turning it round against Kass himself. He writes that "decline and death are a part of life, an integral part which cannot be extruded without destroying the whole" (p. 76). At the level of a purely biological teleology, that is obviously undeniable. But does it raise no difficulties for the wider concept of "nature" to which Kass would recall us, that is, the concept of an ordered teleological system which embraces the whole? When he describes life as a "bitter-sweet bargain" (p. 79), ought he not to sense an element of tension between this and the confident "very good" of Rabbi Meir and Maimonides? Whether he ought or no, it is a matter of simple intellectual history that the majority of moderns have claimed to find here such a sharp conflict between the biological and the humane, between *bios* and *zōē*, that they have declared the idea of an overarching natural order simply untenable. The would-be vindicator of nature has something more to do than simply read natural purposes off biology.[40] I would think that Ramsey has grasped more subtly what kind of teleological vindication the concept of "nature's due" requires. Yet he has failed to point us to the fulcrum on which Christian thought has believed it could comprehend a harmonious balance of *bios* and *zōē*: the new act of God which transforms the one to be the adequate vehicle of the other.

I think it was an error of exposition on Ramsey's part to embark on his account of "Christian humanism" from the connexion between sin and death. In the internal logic of Christian thinking such a connexion is reached only in the second place, from the way death is understood in the light of the vindication of life. To see death as the emblem of divine judgment requires that we have first seen life as an emblem of divine acquittal. Because God has said his final "Yes" to the world, we may understand the mysterious and world-denying absurdity of death as God's penultimate "No", the No which supports the Yes by refusing all forms of uncreation and destruction in the human will. The assertion that Christ's *death* is redemptive comes second (*pace* Anselm and Schleiermacher) to the assertion that his *resurrection* is redemptive.[41] Deutero-Isaiah's suffering servant, who bore the sin of many (Isa. 52:13–53:12) depends for intelligibility upon the prophet's message of divine liberation through the conquests of Cyrus. Even the Yahwist's picture of the encroachment of mortality in the wake of human disobedience is not self-standing; for the primaeval history of Genesis 1-11 could be no part of faith otherwise than as a preface to the story of God's blessing of the nations through Abraham's seed. The purposiveness of condemnation is never perspicuous in itself. It gains its perspicuity only in the light of the purposiveness of vindication.

I do not wish to underestimate the difficulty which thought encounters in handling the connexion of physical death with moral condemnation. No thinker of any sophistication (and least of all one who had learned from Jesus' words in John 9:3) could allow a simple concept of equivalence or desert between the two. Yet in ruling out the crudely superstitious ways in which the connexion might be made, we should not fail to recognise it as an inescapable task for any theism — even, perhaps, for any metaphysic. If we cannot discern moral purposiveness in what merely "happens," then events and meaning will simply fall apart. It is open to Morison to think of meaning as *imposed* upon the raw material of fate by human form-giving — though even he may one day have to explain how *such* a material is susceptible of *such* a form![42] But if anything more is to be said about nature than that it is "inevitable," then the task of discerning moral purpose is already upon us. The Christian view of death as the emblem of divine judgment is one way in which that task may be approached. Maimonides approaches it no less resolutely in another way. The argument is not whether, but only how our connexions between the physical and the moral are to be drawn.

The resurrection can thus be seen to undergird Paul Ramsey's assertions about the natural teleology of life and death: that death is not the fitting *telos* of human life taken as a whole, but only of one aspect of human life, its aspect as wilful rebellion against the created order. There remains to be considered another assertion, standing somewhat apart from these, which plays an important part in the argument of ". . . Death with Dignity," and is contested by Leon Kass: the importance of the individual as an irreplaceable bearer of human value. This, too, has to be seen as an implication of the resurrection; and in order to show how this is so, I shall analyse it as a contention about the *historical teleology* of human life.

The question has engaged the participants in contemporary Christian-Marxist dialogue as to whether the historical teleology on which the Marxist hope for the future is founded is inevitably totalitarian in structure, in that it sacrifices the interests of every prior generation that the later generations may enjoy true communism.[43] Where, it has been asked, is the justice of a final order which cannot reconcile the well-being of present members with the sacrifices of those who made it possible? The bald assertion that the sacrifices of preceding generations are compensated for by the achievement of the common goal seems to be formally totalitarian — which is to say that it does not permit the question of justice between generations to be raised, but makes the rights of the future stipulatively determinative of the duties of each present generation. One could, of course, soften the formal rigour of this position. Without denying that the question of justice could in principle be raised, one might appeal to the natural generosity of any generation to its successors (who are, after all, dependent upon it for the world they are to inherit) and urge that the question of justice should not dominate our thinking about the humanity of the future. That is excellent counsel, just so long as the question is posed that way round, in terms of the duties of present generations to the future. But what of the recipients of such generosity? Do they find themselves in a position in which their preferred status as inheritors of the goal of history makes them guilty, self-accusing, and therefore ill at ease with the welfare which their predecessors laboured to give them? That this is not entirely an idle worry may be judged from the characteristic demoralisation of every "post-war" generation, which confronts the task of living up to an infinite sacrifice made on its behalf and finds that the terms of daily existence do not permit it to discharge its debt.

Present generations have no monopoly on generosity, and they can hardly so determine to be generous to their successors that their successors will be deprived of any possibility of being generous in return. Yet the generation which inherits the goal of history has no comparable opportunity for sacrificing itself for its successors. In the earliest Christian church there was a group of believers who were sufficiently troubled by the prospect of a preferred status as to think that if the Lord were to return in their day, they could hardly welcome him if the Christian dead (who at this stage cannot have been numerous) were to be excluded. It was not that the Lord was insufficient to make his people happy; it was that the people lacked the conditions for being made happy if they were not to meet the Lord together. One answer to this anxiety would have been to say that the Lord would never come, but that each succeeding generation would live its life on the same terms as each preceding one. The answer which Saint Paul actually gave that anxious group was different: — "We who are left alive until the Lord comes shall not forestall those who have died . . . the Christian dead will rise, then we who are left alive shall join them" (1 Thessalonians 4:15-17).

The resurrection promises a reconciliation of the diastasis of history, and so makes historical teleology possible. This, in my view, is the heart of the difference between Ramsey and Aristotle. Aristotle makes no claims for history; it is that conclusion, rather than the form-matter distinction, which allows him to seek consolation for individual death in the succession of generations and the perpetuation of the human race. He has no problem of justice in the diastasis of history; for if no generation inherits the goal of humanity's striving, the balance of justice between generations has never been upset. Each generation participates equally in the ongoing life of the race; each, as its moment comes, relinquishes its place to another. But Messianic faith of any description, Jewish, Christian or Marxist, is debarred from Aristotle's settlement; for its hope for history has upset the balance and has made the later generations more completely human than the earlier — which lies uneasily with another aspect of Messianic faith, that the goal of history can effect the just reconciliation of all claims. The question is whether historical teleology can be made consistent with itself; and to that question the hope of resurrection offers a positive answer.

Kass has accused Ramsey, very effectively, of being too closely identified with "the stress on 'the unique worth of the individual,'" which "connects together the mainstream of today's secular thought and its severed theological source, from which Paul Ramsey still takes his watering."[44] In reply to that accusation we first of all draw attention to what Kass concedes, that Ramsey's affirmation of the non-exchangeability of individual human beings is not free-standing. He has not posited the individual *in abstracto*, as the seat of consciousness or self-awareness or reason, and declared that he has discovered where the good of human existence lies. That is precisely the Cartesian move which his principle of psychosomatic unity is intended to reject. His affirmation of the individual springs from the eschatological affirmation that each person is to be recalled to an irreplaceable presence before the judgment seat of God. But from there we may take a further step: this eschatological affirmation is not "individualist" in the sense in which that term is used as a reproof. For the irreplaceable presence of the individual at the end of time is itself an aspect of the presence of the whole human community. It is true that the resurrection grounds the eternal value of the individual. But it does so, not by backing the claim of the individual against the community, but by doing away with the notion of *replacement* as applied to any part of the human community — which is why we could approach the question as well by way of the replacement of earlier by later generations. In the context of a historical *telos,* replacement is injustice; and the fundamental point behind Ramsey's contention for the individual is justice as a feature of perfected humanity.

We may never forget, indeed, that in Paul Ramsey we have to do with a thinker who has attempted more thoroughly than most to articulate the meaning of justice as a feature of the good of society. He can hardly be mistaken for an atomistic contractarian, reducing the whole social good to a list of individual rights, nor for an anti–social subjectivist, elevating inward integrity in defiance of community claims. If, in ". . . Death with Dignity" as occasionally elsewhere, he has found it possible to shed a few sympathetic tears for the late blooms on the Cartesian rose-bush (all the while hacking vigorously at the roots), we may treat it as a characteristically dialectical moment of self-concealment in self-disclosure.

Notes

1. Stanley Hauerwas, *Against the Nations* (Minneapolis: Winston Press, 1985), p. 49.

2. *Hastings Center Studies* 2:2 (May 1974): 47-62. Despite the author's insistence on every word of his title, I shall abbreviate as ". . . Death with Dignity."

3. See for example *Christian Ethics and the Sit-In* (New York: Association Press, 1961), pp. 37f.; *Nine Modern Moralists* (Englewood Cliffs, N.J.: Prentice-Hall, 1962), pp. 105-9; "A Christian Approach to the Question of Sexual Relations Outside Marriage," *Journal of Religion* (1965): 102; *The Just War* (New York: Scribners, 1968), pp. 49f., 221-25; *Fabricated Man* (New Haven: Yale University Press, 1970), pp. 36-38, 86-90, 130-38; *The Patient as Person* (New Haven: Yale University Press, 1970), pp. xiii, 187-88, 193; *Ethics at the Edges of Life* (New Haven: Yale University Press, 1978), pp. 139, 180. I am grateful for the assistance of David Attwood in locating these references.

4. I shall confine my use of the two responses, interesting as each is, to illuminating Ramsey's position. This means, in effect, making use only of Kass ("Averting one's eyes, or facing the music? — On dignity in death," *loc. cit.* pp. 67-80), who has succeeded in putting into sharp focus the issues between Ramsey and his own position, shaped by the Jewish tradition. The interest of Morison's briefer response ("The last poem: the dignity of the inevitable and necessary," ibid., pp. 63-66) lies chiefly in the unsuspected convergences which appear between its professed neo-paganism and some of the existentialist positions viewed with sympathy by the Christian writer. As a criticism of Ramsey it is weakened by a failure to grasp his meaning at crucial points. But does Morison's use of a quotation from Alfred Kazin (p. 66) that "art is the fusion of suffering with form" leave him very far removed from Niebuhr's opinion that the fear of death is the source of all human creativity? And does not the point of unconscious sympathy sharpen the suspicion, which Ramsey himself articulated on an earlier occasion, that existential anxiety leads us back to the pagan consciousness?

5. The bare bones of the analysis on which my exposition is based are as follows:

Introduction: a defence of the title (p. 47-48 col. 1).

I. Philosophical ingredients of a view of death:
   A. Statement of position (p. 48 col. 1: "There is nobility . . ." — col. 2: ". . . to grieve or not to grieve")
   B. The meaning of death as a limit (p. 48 col. 2 "'Death is simply a part . . .'" — p. 50 col. 2 ". . . awareness of the self who is dying.")
   C. The alleged fittingness of death (p. 50 col. 2 "We are often reminded . . ." — p. 56 col. 1 ". . . the worth or uniqueness ascribed to the dying life.")

II. Christian humanism:
   A. Love and fear (p. 56 col. 1 "I always write . . ." — p. 59 col. 2 ". . .the human dignity of caring for the dying.")
   B. The anthropological alternatives (p. 59 col. 2 "In any case, from these empirical . . ." — p. 62)

6. Thus Ramsey, p. 55, attributing philosophical resignation to the failure of philosophical vitality. What Thomas wrote, however, was:

> Though wise men at their end know dark is right,
> Because their words had forked no lightning they
> Do not go gentle into that good night.

That is, the philosophers do not match their acceptance of death in theory with an acceptance in practice. Their words have forked no lightning for *them* to see their way by! (*Collected Poems 1934-52* [London: Dart, 1966], p. 159). Ramsey picks up this hint on p. 60, somewhat mischievously suggesting that Plato's account of Socrates' fortitude in death may not be trustworthy.

7. Kass, p. 71.

8. B. Pascal, *Pensées,* no. 347.

9. Kass, pp. 68f.

10. Pascal, *Pensées,* no. 277.

11. See especially the use he makes of existentialist inspiration in his writing on sexual morality, "Jean-Paul Sartre: Sex in Being" in *Nine Modern Moralists* (Englewood Cliffs, N.J.: Prentice-Hall, 1962), and "A Christian Approach to the Question of Sexual Relations Outside of Marriage," *Journal of Religion* 1965 (published in Britain as: *On Flesh* [Nottingham: Grove Books, 1975]).

12. Kass, p. 70.

13. See *Nine Modern Moralists,* chs. 5-9 inclusive.

14. University Park: Pennsylvania State University, 1961. The sermon contains a number of passages on which Ramsey has drawn for his 1974 article: — on p. 1, the relation of Christianity to Greek and Hebrew views of death (cf. ". . . Death with Dignity," p. 57 col. 1); on p. 3 the two parts of the text 1 John 4:18 (cf. p. 56 col. 1), the reference to Ecclesiastes 9:3 (cf. p. 57 col. 2, but with the reference not given), and the use of Pascal's *Pensée* 347 (cf. p. 55 col. 2); on p. 5 love as respect for the shadow of death upon the face of another (cf. p. 58 col. 2). These are the obvious debts. In addition there are places where the thought of ". . . Death with Dignity" becomes clearer when it is seen to carry an allusion to an argument which was developed in *Deaths Duell*: such is the reference to " 'faith-ing' in an ultimate righteousness" (p. 56 col. 2), which demands to be read in the light of p. 6 of the sermon.

15. Psalm 90:12, curiously misattributed by Ramsey to Ecclesiastes.

16. I have not traced the source of the quotation, though the sentiment is common enough in Niebuhr's writings. A more comprehensive treatment of Ramsey's theological debt to Niebuhr would illuminate a good deal. We find in *The Nature and Destiny of Man* sources for several observations in ". . . Death with Dignity": the criticism of Epicurus (I p. 98, II p. 9); the preoccupation of Hellenistic thought with finitude (II p. 58) *finis* and *telos* (II p. 293); the "testimony of the heart" (II p. 294); and in *Faith and History* (p. 170) the alternative strategies of the "worldly" and "other-worldly religions." All of which may conceal from us how Ramsey has, without naming him, turned against Niebuhr at a critical point. Take the crucial passage, *The Nature and Destiny of Man* (I pp. 173-76) (New York: Scribner Library edition, 1964). Niebuhr first distinguishes two ways of connecting sin and death, using Augustine's saying "It is by sin that we die and not by death that we sin." The latter connexion is purely pagan; the former is rabbinic, Pauline and preferable. However, even the rabbinic-Pauline view has the odour of dualism lingering over it, and obscures the organic relation of death and nature. There is another Pauline view, expressed in 1 Cor. 15:56, "The sting of death is sin," which is much better. It attributes no evil to death, but only to the fear of death (which is pride concealing its own mortality). This is the "general biblical view." This "general biblical view" which Niebuhr favours is the view which Ramsey thinks in danger of reverting to paganism if it is not balanced out, that "death brings sin after." The "rabbinic-Pauline view," which Niebuhr damns with faint praise is Ramsey's own preferred view, that "sin brings death after." Niebuhr and Ramsey (in *Deaths Duell*) would each incline to accuse the other of temporising with paganism. In ". . . Death with Dignity" the qualified criticism of Niebuhr's preferred emphasis is suppressed; but only by an implicit denial of the distinction between that and the rabbinic-Pauline view. Paul's teaching that sin brings death after is made the theological chapter-heading for the exposition of Niebuhr's view! Ramsey will never, in fact, assert with Niebuhr that "death is no evil though it is an occasion for evil, namely the fear of death" (I p. 167). And that is because Ramsey has not accepted the starting-point of Niebuhr's anthropology, which is the dialectic of nature and freedom. Kass accuses Ramsey of failing "to give nature her due" (p. 76), and would, no doubt, be much happier with the generous concessions that Niebuhr will make to the mutual implication of nature and death. But it is at least arguable that Ramsey has understood better what a theology of the natural order requires when he refuses to follow Niebuhr's example of giving everything to nature with one hand, only to take it away with the other.

17. *Deaths Duell*, p. 5.

18. *Deaths Duell*, p. 6.

19. "This is the more basic direction of things . . . than that expressed by those other statements (which are also true), that death draws sin after, and where fear is, love is not perfected," p. 7. Contrast the impression given on p. 3: "The truth of this (i.e. where fear is love is not perfected) we have to discover by more profound insight. . . ."

20. He has, of course, said that according to Aristotelian philosophy, "reason, the formal principle, is definitive of essential humanity. That is universal, eternal as logic. Matter, however, is the individuating factor" (61). But this is not sufficient. For Aristotle believes (in contradistinction to Plato) that the universal is not "separable" from the particular, but exists only as it is instantiated particularly. He therefore fulfils the formal requirement of believing that the particular body and the universal reason are inseparably united. Ramsey needs a criterion that goes beyond that formal requirement.

21. Kass, p. 79.

22. Once again Ramsey's commonplace book defeats the commentator. The quotation does not appear to be from Donne's "Death's Duell."

23. *The Nature and Destiny of Man* II, p. 295.

24. It appears, as though by reflection in a mirror, when Ramsey praises the "more orthodox wording" of a church statement on p. 51.

25. It would appear that both Morison and Kass would give assent to some form of the body-soul unity principle. A striking example of its use outside a Christian context is given by Hans Jonas, in his article about the 1968 Harvard report advocating criteria for "brain-death": "I see lurking behind the proposed definition of death . . . a curious revenant of the old soul-body dualism. Its new apparition is the dualism of brain and body. In a certain analogy to the former it holds that the true human person rests in (or is represented by) the brain, of which the rest of the body is a mere subservient tool" (*Philosophical Essays* [University of Chicago Press, 1974], p. 139).

26. Thus it is held by Barth (reference below), Niebuhr (*Nature and Destiny of Man* II, pp. 294-98), Bultmann (*Theology of the New Testament*, London: SCM, 1955, I, pp. 192-203) and Tillich (*Systematic Theology* III [Chicago: University of Chicago Press, 1963], pp. 409-14).

27. See, for example, Oscar Cullmann, *Immortality of the Soul or Resurrection of the Dead?* (London: Epworth Press, 1958).

28. See Etienne Gilson, *The Spirit of Mediaeval Philosophy* (New York: Scribners, 1936), pp. 168-88.

29. See Karl Rahner, "Dogmatic Questions on Easter," *Theological Investigations* IV (London: Darton Longman & Todd, 1966), pp. 121-33.

30. See Georges Florovsky, "The 'Immortality' of the Soul," *Creation and Redemption* (Belmont, Mass.: Nordland, 1976), pp. 213-40.

31. See J. Moltmann, *God in Creation* (London: SCM, 1985), pp. 244-75.

32. Karl Barth, *The Resurrection of the Dead*, tr. H. J. Stenning (London: Hodder & Stoughton, 1933).

33. F. Schleiermacher, "The Christian Faith," ed. H. J. Mackintosh and J. S. Stewart (Edinburgh: T&T Clark, 1928), p. 418.

34. This feature was highlighted by Albert Schweitzer (*J. S. Bach*, vol. I, tr. E. Newman [New York: Dover, 1966; 1st ed. 1911], pp. 169f.) who, however, misunderstood it as a personally distinctive feature of Bach's own outlook rather than as a cultural commonplace. Though universally exemplified in the Bach corpus, it is most striking in the Easter cantatas, where we might have expected the theme of resurrection to prevail. Thus in BWV 31 the librettist (S. Franck) prays: "Letzte Stunde, brich herein, mir die Augen zuzudrücken!," and in BWV 158 we take up the words of a hymn by J. G. Albinus, "Welt, ade, ich bin dein müde." In BWV 6 the theme is set by a metaphorical treatment of the words of Luke 24:29, "the day is far spent." The most notable exception is BWV 4, which has a text drawn throughout from Luther's hymn, "Christ lag in Todesbanden." The Reformation had, indeed, given a sharper definition to the resurrection than either the late-mediaeval inwardness which preceded it or the age of science and sensibility which succeeded it. It was never, therefore, banished from the edges of Christian consciousness, and in some traditions maintained a stronger presence throughout the seventeenth and into the eighteenth century. Handel's "Messiah," which does altogether more justice to the resurrection than we will usually find in Bach, has as its text an Anglican catena of Scripture quotations supplied by C. Jennens. And it was in the preaching of an Anglican seventeenth-century divine, John Donne, that Ramsey found a congenial model for his own proclamation of the resurrection in *Deaths Duell.*

35. Ramsey, ". . . Death with Dignity," p. 60.

36. The parallel in St. Luke's Gospel (12:4) conforms much more closely to our expectations of a "Hebraic" anthropology: "Do not fear those who kill the body, and after that have no more that they can do."

37. A saying of the eighteenth-century theologian F. C. Oetinger, taken up by Moltmann (op. cit., p. 244).

38. "'Pass me by, pass me by, Go away, wild skeleton! I am still young — go, dear Death, and do not touch me.' 'Give me your hand, you lovely and tender creature; I am your friend and do not come to punish. Be comforted! I am not wild. You will sleep gently in my arms.'" Text and translation from *The Penguin Book of Lieder*, ed. and tr. S. S. Prawer (Harmondsworth, Middlesex: Penguin, 1964), pp. 38f.

39. See, for example, the classic analysis of romanticism in D. de Rougemont, *Passion and Society*, tr. M. Belgion (London: Faber, 1956 rev.)

40. As Kass himself will elsewhere acknowledge. See his *Toward a More Natural Science* (New York: Free Press, 1985) p. 346ff.

41. Following Karl Barth (*Church Dogmatics* IV/1 [Edinburgh: T&T Clark, 1956], p. 313) and Jürgen Moltmann (*The Crucified God* [London: SCM, 1974], pp. 178-87).

42. Morison, p. 66: ". . . the whole business of life (is) the study of how to give form and dignity to suffering."

43. See C. Davis, *Theology and Political Science* (Cambridge: Cambridge University Press, 1980).

44. Kass, p. 69.

Chapter Six

HEALTH AND HEALING

What do we do when we distinguish health from illness? More than one thing, it seems. First we indicate an attitude toward a condition; we approve of health and show our disapproval of disease. Second, we assign responsibility. Ill persons are relieved of certain responsibilities but they are expected to seek a physician, who will be assigned responsibility for their care. A third thing we do is sanction certain patterns for dealing with a condition: hospitalization, confinement, avoidance, quarantine, etc. Therefore, the way we define health is important; our definition will guide certain evaluations, determine certain responsibilities, and even suggest the appropriateness of certain responses. When we would define health, we must explore the relationship of health to other human goods, the relationship of health to the responsibilities of both individuals and the medical profession, and the relationship of health and conventional modes of treating and coping with illness.

Let us examine the relationship of health to other values. More than one of the selections in this chapter calls attention to a cult of health in our culture (see also Khushf, selection 6). Its icons may be omnipresent images of young muscled bodies; its disciplines, performed "religiously," of course, diet and exercise; its temples, health-spas. In the cult of health, health is the greatest good, the *summum bonum;* all of life must be oriented toward this good. In the Christian tradition health is a good, surely, but not the greatest good, and it will be suspicious of definitions of health — and of patterns of life — which make health the *summum bonum*.

If, for example, we follow the World Health Organization's (in)famous definition of health as a state of "complete physical, mental, and social well-being," then human flourishing is identified with (or reduced to) health. But if health and human flourishing are rendered equivalent, then we will have lost the capacity to weigh the good of health against other goods. And if we lose that capacity, we become unable to understand Paul's words in 2 Corinthians cited below (selection 32). Paul evidently thought of health as a good but not the only good and certainly not the greatest good. Note that he does not belittle his suffering by negating it either as a mere external affliction that does not affect the inner person or as an illusion that has no reality. His contentment is not mere resignation but participation in Christ and his suffering, his weakness for the sake of God's cause in the world. The selection from Karl Barth (selection 33) may be regarded as an extended commentary on these words of Paul.

Dennis Sansom (selection 37) raises the issue of the relation of health to other human values quite explicitly. He reminds us that the good of health is itself properly oriented toward other goods, other goals. That by itself is a challenge to the cult of health. Sansom also asks us to consider, however, what the goals of health ought to be, to consider what health is good for, what specific goods ought to order and govern our pursuit of health. He asks us, for example, to judge whether the goal of health is to be an autonomous individual or to live faithfully in community. And he argues that a health care system ordered and governed by the first of these options has led to some of the difficulties of health care in America. Is he right? If we agree with him, how should we speak of the goals of health?

The next question is the relationship of health and responsibility. We often think of illness, not only as the opposite of health, but as a result of some accident or fate, a matter over which we have no control. The sudden fever of children, the appendicitis attack, the injury inflicted by a tornado — these all seem like paradigm cases of the loss of health. When we become ill, we adopt the sick role. Part of that role is an exemption from our usual responsibilities while we assume the responsibility of trying to become well.

LeRoy Walters, however, argues (in selection 35) that this model of relating health and individual responsibility may need to be modified. He points out that we are far more responsible for the condition of our health than we usually recognize. If we abuse our bodies with alcohol or tobacco, we have no one to blame but ourselves when we suffer from cirrhosis of the liver or lung disease. While it may be true that we are not responsible for all illness from which we suffer, we are responsible for much of it. If persons are responsible for their health or their sickness, if "health is a duty," may we blame the sick for their condition? And if we blame them, does that mean that we have less responsibility to care for them in their illness and to attempt to restore to them their health?

Any analysis of health and responsibility which focuses solely upon individuals will turn out to be faulty, however, for there are social conditions which cause individual illness. Factories which emit poisonous fumes, plants which dump their waste products into rivers which supply drinking water, poverty which makes proper prenatal care inaccessible — these are all causes of illness over which the individual may have little or no control. This is not to say that other persons do not have responsibility for the creation of such conditions, but it is to point out that the responsible agent and the affected person may not be one and the same. How should we relate individual health and collective or societal responsibility to each other, in terms of both becoming ill and becoming well again?

The question of the relation between health and responsibility has a particular importance for health caregivers. Daniel Callahan's objections to the WHO definition (in selection 36) include his claim that the result of such broad definitions is that physicians are given too much responsibility, in that they become the caretakers of complete human well-being. A more modest sense of responsibility might be nurtured by Walters's observation that the contribution of medicine to human health has frequently been overrated. And it might be protected by a narrower definition of health, perhaps, as the absence of disease or infirmity.

Jan van Eys and Kenneth Vaux, however (in selection 34), propose that physicians should be concerned with the whole person and not simply a particular disease process. Though they worry about health becoming an idol and offer a scathing critique of American culture, does their position open up the possibility for the kind of expansion of the physician's role Callahan fears? Can we define health in such a way as to restrict and restrain the responsibilities of physicians while at the same time calling on them to care for the whole person? How should we relate health, the responsibility of physicians, and Van Eys's and Vaux's claim that our current standard of health discriminates against the aged, the unborn, and anyone physically different?

Finally, the issue of the relationship of health and the conventional models of coping with and treating illness needs to be considered. If we define health too broadly, we tend to want to treat social problems and spiritual problems and deviancy and crime and numerous other problems on the medical model; but should we? And if we define health too narrowly, as the absence of disease or infirmity, we tend to allow physicians to redescribe the patient's experience of illness solely in terms of an objective description of pathology. Such a redescription risks transforming the living subject into a manipulable object, first in our imagination but finally in our actions toward that subject who has become object. If that occurs, to admit to being sick is to invite objectification, manipulation, and the conventional models for treating disease.

How can we understand health in a way that will grant to medicine its appropriate (and modest) place in its service to health while restricting the medical model and attending to other ways of ministering to the sick? How can we acknowledge the applicability of the anatomical and physiological assessment and treatment of the patient without objectifying and manipulating the patient (and without simply compartmentalizing the care of a patient)? Can we define health to allow analytic precision, scientific medicine, and an appreciation of the interrelatedness of life? And can we understand health in a way that will nurture physicians and nurses who will care for the whole person through their care of the body?

Suggestions for Further Reading

Caplan, Arthur L., H. Tristram Engelhardt, Jr., and James J. McCartney, eds. *Concepts of Health and Disease: Interdisciplinary Perspectives* (Reading, Mass.: Addison-Wesley, 1981).

Dubos, Rene. *Mirage of Health* (Garden City, N.Y.:Doubleday, 1959).

Harakas, Stanley. *Health and Medicine in the Eastern Orthodox Tradition: Faith, Liturgy, and Wholeness* (New York: Crossroad, 1990).

Holifield, E. Brooks. *Health and Medicine in the Methodist Tradition* (New York: Crossroad 1986).

Illich, Ivan. *Medical Nemesis: The Expropriation of Health* (New York: Pantheon, 1975).

Marty, Martin. *Health and Medicine in the Lutheran Tradition: Being Well* (New York: Crossroad, 1983).

McCormick, Richard A. *Health and Medicine in the Catholic Tradition: Tradition in Transition* (New York: Crossroad, 1984).

Peel, Robert. *Health and Medicine in the Christian Science Tradition: Principle, Practice, and Challenge* (New York: Crossroad, 1988).

Seybold, Klaus, and Ulrich B. Mueller. *Sickness and Healing,* trans. by Douglas Stott (Nashville: Abingdon, 1978).

Smith, David Horton. *Health and Medicine in the Anglican Tradition: Conscience, Community, and Compromise* (New York: Crossroad, 1986).

Snyder, Graydon F. *Health and Medicine in the Anabaptist Tradition: Care in Community* (Valley Forge, Pa.: Trinity Press International, 1995).

Sweet, Leonard I. *Health and Medicine in the Evangelical Tradition: "Not by Might nor Power"* (Valley Forge, Pa.: Trinity Press International, 1994).

Vaux, Kenneth L. *Health and Medicine in the Reformed Tradition: Promise, Providence, and Care* (New York: Crossroad, 1984).

32 2 Corinthians 12:7-10

To keep me from being too elated by the abundance of revelations, a thorn was given me in the flesh, a messenger of Satan, to harass me, to keep me from being too elated. Three times I besought the Lord about this, that it should leave me; but he said to me, "My grace is sufficient for you, for my power is made perfect in weakness." I will all the more gladly boast of my weaknesses, that the power of Christ may rest upon me. For the sake of Christ, then, I am content with weaknesses, insults, hardships, persecutions, and calamities; for when I am weak, then I am strong.

33 Sickness and Illusion

Karl Barth

We have so far accepted the fact that man has the strength to be as man, that he can will and affirm it as such, and that he can therefore will and adopt the corresponding measures of this will in the sphere of his vital functions of soul and body. We have understood disease as merely the weakness opposed to this strength, as that which is not to be willed but contested in the will to live, as the shadow which recedes as it were before health and the will for health. This is one aspect of the matter. But there are two very different aspects, and we must now try to explain that the will to be healthy is in relation to them. We may begin by saying generally that sickness is not an illusion, even though there is such a thing as illusory sickness and therefore those who are ill only in their imagination. . . .

If we see the problem of psychical and physical health and sickness properly in its unity, and this unity itself from a higher standpoint, i.e., in the light of the question of the strength or weakness to be as man, we can only regard and treat the victim of imaginary ailments as one who is really very ill, although not in the way that he thinks. We certainly cannot ridicule him, or find in him support for the general proposition that all sickness is an illusion. Sickness is no illusion, whether in relation to the opposing will to live in the true and secondary sense, or objectively as a different condition from the real strength to be as man and the freedom of secondary vital forces, or in relation to God as the Creator of human life and the will to live.

The tenet that sickness is an illusion is the basic negative proposition which in the seventies of the last century the American Mary Baker Eddy said that she did not lay down but "discovered" through the authoritative inspiration of a book now regarded as canonical, namely, *Christian Science.* What was at first a small group of adherents has since spread to all parts of the world in the form of religious societies which are particularly popular among the upper and middle classes and more especially among women. Karl Holl has depicted and done it almost too much justice in a careful study entitled "Scientismus" (*Ges. Aufs. Z. Kgsch.,* III, 1928, p. 460 f.). The positive basis of this teaching is that God is the only reality, that he is Spirit and that the whole creation is only a reflection of his spiritual essence. Apart from God there are only powers, which in reality are only thoughts. All matter as such represents a mere appearance, and the same is true of all such associated features as sin, sickness, evil and death. Man as the image of God always was and is and shall be perfect. Everything that contradicts this perfection is in reality only an illusion and misunderstanding rooted in the forgetfulness of God, which in turn evokes fear. And fear is the true basis of all illness; indeed, it is actually illness itself. For fear creates a picture of illness which then falls externally upon the body. "You maintain that an ulcer is painful; but that is impossible, for matter without mind is not painful. The ulcer merely reveals by inflammation and swelling an appearance of pain, and this appearance is called an ulcer." The true and physical man is not touched by it. He is only as it were enveloped in a mist and has disappeared from consciousness. Evil is unreal. "Take away fear, and at the same time you have also removed the soil on which sickness thrives." Jesus was and is the embodiment of truth which scatters and breaks through the mist of these false appearances. The power bestowed and the task presented by Him consist in recognising that God is Spirit and that man belongs to Him and is eternally at one with the God who is Spirit. It thus consists in freeing oneself from the false appearances of sin (which even Mrs. Eddy puts first), sickness and death. For death, too, is only man's "disappearance from our level of conscious-

From Karl Barth, *Church Dogmatics,* III/4, trans. A. T. Mackay et al. (Edinburgh: T&T Clark, 1961), pp. 363-73. Used by permission.

ness." Supremely, this power and task are identical with prayer, in which everything evil really subsides into nothingness. Any other measures, and especially the well-meant action of the doctor, are a sin against the first commandment. Medical diagnosis, which Mrs. Eddy regards as particularly evil, is replaced by "mind-reading," which is possible at a great distance and in which the thought images which dominate the sufferer are noted. Medical treatment is supplanted by prayer, in which it can only be a matter of acknowledging the cure already effected by God, of understanding His completed work and of initiating it in the patient. The "healer" — the name given to the active members of the Christian Science Association — is not then to rouse and fortify the will of others through his own, but simply to make a free path in the sufferer for the divine operation. "Call to mind the presence of health and the fact of harmonious existence, until the body corresponds to the normal condition of health and harmony."

This doctrine has several features which remind us of the message of the New Testament, and which are of course derived from it: the recognition of fear as the basic evil in man's relation to God; an unconditional trust in the efficacy of prayer; and bold reference to a work already completed by God. But these are all devalued by the fact that they are related to a view which has nothing to do with that of the New Testament but in the light of it can only be described as utterly false. The fact that Christian Science can undoubtedly point to successes in healing — as well as to disastrous failures — cannot of itself commend it to Christians. As is well-known, the magicians of Pharaoh could do quite a number of things. And the concession that Karl Holl (*loc. cit.*, p. 477) is willing to make, namely, that its positive presupposition at least is correct, is one which cannot really be made to it. God is indeed the basis of all reality. But He is not the only reality. As Creator and Redeemer He loves a reality which is different from Himself, which depends upon Him, yet which is not merely a reflection nor the sum of His powers and thoughts, but which has in face of Him an independent and distinctive nature and is the subject of its own history, participating in its own perfection and subjected to its own weakness. As the coming of the kingdom, the incarnation of the Word and the death and resurrection of Jesus Christ in His true humanity are not just an appearance, so it is with man in general, whether in his nature or perversion, in his psychical being or his physical, in his divine likeness or his sin and transgression. It is because Mrs. Eddy did not understand this that sin, evil and death — in conquest of which Jesus Christ did not "disappear from our level of consciousness" but actually died on the cross — are for her mere "appearances" of human thinking, and redemption is only the act of man in which he submerges himself in God and leads a life submerged in God in order that God may work in him, putting an end to those "appearances" or thought images and bringing to light the perfection of psychical essence which was never lost, the presence of health and the fact of harmonious being. On this point we can only say that both the Old and New Testaments regard not only God and man, not only sin and death and their conquest, but also sickness in a different light. They certainly do not see it as an illusion, and its conquest as the dispelling of this illusion. Whether Christian Science is really "science" need not occupy us here. But there can be no doubt that it is not "Christian" science.

Sickness is real. Certainly, as an encroachment on the life which God has created, it is not real in the same way as God is. In what sense, then, is it real? We shall take up this point in a moment, but we may begin by simply observing that if man, even the sick man, is really healthy in the strength which he still has and can still exert to be as man, then the weakness which opposes this strength is not as such an appearance but is effective and real, so that his will for health already meets a hard "object" in this primary and essential sense. But the same is also true of the impairing of his psychical and physical powers which takes place in illness. His transition from health to sickness, the resistance which illness offers to his health, the effort and trouble which it costs if he or the doctor adopts the appropriate measures against it, the obstinacy with which it maintains itself in spite of all these measures, the triumphs which it can enjoy in spite of them — these are not all plays of the imagination, but real events in the real history of the real man. And the will to live as the will for health is a serious act of obedience to a serious command of God because man is not dealing with a fake or imaginary opponent but with an enemy which is in some sense real. Yet the question arises what kind of reality this is. And we must try to explain this if we are to understand more deeply and seriously what the will to be healthy really means and does not mean. Again, however, two different aspects open up before us.

The one aspect which dominates the field in the Old and New Testament Scriptures, and which has always to be remembered first materially, is the one in which sickness is a forerunner and messenger of death, and indeed of death as the judgment of God and the merited subjection of man to the power of nothingness in virtue of his sin. From this standpoint, sickness like death itself is unnatural and disorderly. It is an element in the rebellion of chaos against God's creation. It is an act and declaration of the devil and demons. To be sure, it is no less bound to God and dependent on Him than the creature which He created. Indeed, it is impotent in relation to him in a double way. For like sin and death it is neither good nor is it willed and created by God at all, but is real, effective, powerful and menacing only as part of that which He has negated, of His kingdom on the left hand, and therefore with its nullity. But in accordance with the will of God and under His reign it is necessarily dangerous — as the forerunner and messenger of death, the executor of God's final sentence — to the man who has fallen from God and become His enemy.

What does health mean as the power to be as man, and what do the vital functions of soul and body mean as the sphere for the exercise of this strength, if sickness is this reality, if it is an element and sign of the power of the chaos threatening creation on the one hand, and on the other an element and sign of God's righteous wrath and judgment, in short, an element and sign of the objective corruption which is related and corresponds to human sin and from which there is no deliverance apart from the mercy of God in Jesus Christ? . . .

What does health mean from this standpoint, and what is the meaning of the will to be healthy in the primary and secondary senses in which we have hitherto understood it?

The following consideration suggests itself. When seen in this way, sickness is a superior power in relation to which there can be no question at all of health or the will to be healthy. What is man with his health and will for health in face of the invasion of the realm of death to which he himself has deliberately opened the defences? What is he in face of the divine judgment by which he is overtaken in this assault? What can he do in this situation? What can the whole field of ethics tell him in these circumstances? What is there left to will? Strength to be as man? Psycho-physical powers? Is it not almost grotesque from this standpoint to try even to think of a human determination, let alone of human measures, along the lines considered? Are not faith and prayer the only real possibilities in face of this reality of sickness?

But this whole consideration is only defeatist thinking, and not at all Christian. It overlooks the fact that the command of God is not withdrawn but still in force, namely, that man must will to live and not die, to be healthy and not to be sick, and to exercise and not neglect his strength to be as man and the remaining psycho-physical forces which he has for this purpose, and thus to maintain himself. This command has not been revoked even for sinful man forfeited to the judgment of God, and it is not for him to counter God with speculations whether obedience to it is possible or offers any prospects. Unquestioning obedience is his only option if he is not to bring himself into greater condemnation. Again, this consideration overlooks the fact that the realm of death which afflicts man in the form of sickness, although God has given it power and it serves as an instrument of His righteous judgment, is opposed to His good will a Creator and has existence and power only under His mighty No. To capitulate before it, to allow it to take its course, can never be obedience but only disobedience towards God. In harmony with the will of God, what man ought to will in face of this whole realm on the left hand, and therefore in face of sickness, can only be final resistance. Again and supremely, this consideration overlooks the fact that God Himself is not only Judge but faithful, gracious and patient in His righteous judgment, that He Himself has already marched against that realm on the left, and that He has overcome and bound its forces and therefore those of sickness in Jesus Christ and His sacrifice, by which the destroyer was himself brought to destruction. Those who know this, and therefore that they are already helped in this matter, can only reply to the faithfulness of God with a new unfaithfulness if they try to fold their hands and sigh and ask what help there is or what more they can will. Within the modest limits in which this is still possible they must will what God has already willed and indeed definitely fulfilled in Jesus Christ concerning sickness and that whole kingdom on the left hand. With God they must say No to it without asking what the result will be or how much or little it will help themselves or others, without enquiring whether it is not rather feeble and even ridiculous to march into action in accordance with this No. A little resolution, will and action in face of that realm and therefore against sickness is better than a whole ocean of pretended Christian humility which is really perhaps the mistaken and perverted humility of the devil and demons.

There is, of course, a right deduction to be drawn from the fact that sickness is real in this sense, i.e., as an element and sign of the power of chaos and nothingness, and therefore as an element and sign of the judgment of God falling on man. The right deduction is that all resistance to sickness, all human willing of the strength to be as man, all human affirmation, cultivation and promotion of the vital forces of body and soul, is necessarily in vain if God is not God; if He does not live, speak, act and make Himself responsible for man; if this whole cause is not first and supremely His own cause; if His is not the judgment on man from which we cannot escape; if His is not the grace which is the meaning of this judgment; and above all if His is not the judgment on the destroyer and destruction itself which by reason of man's sin can have a little space, but which can have only the space allowed and allotted by God, and in relation to which God is absolute Lord and conclusive Victor. Without or even against God there is, of course, nothing that man can will in this matter. And if faith in Him and prayer to Him cannot be a refuge for weak-willed and defeatist Christians who are lazy, cowardly and resigned in face of His and their enemy, we must also say with the same certainty that if the conflict enjoined upon man in this matter is to be meaningful, faith in Him and prayer to Him must never be lost sight of as its *conditio sine qua non,* but continually realised as the true power of the will required of man in this affair. They cannot replace what is to be modestly, soberly and circumspectly, but energetically, willed and done by man. They cannot replace his determination to exercise his little strength to be as man, and thereby to maintain himself. They cannot replace hygiene, sport and medicine, or the social struggle for better living conditions for all. But in all these things they must be the orientation on the command of God which summons man inexorably, and with no possible conditions, to will and action. They must be the orientation on the righteous judgment of God in recognition of which man constantly discovers, and again without murmuring or surrender, the limitation of his willing and doing and its consequences. Above all, they must be the orientation on the inexhaustible consolation of the promise, on true and effective encouragement by the One who as the Creator of life primarily espouses this as His own cause, and fights and has already conquered for us in the whole glory of His mercy and omnipotence. It is true that without Him, without the orientation on Him, all ethics, all human willing and doing, can only be futile and impotent in relation to the superiority of evil which opposes us also in the form of sickness; and worse still, that it can only be rebellion against the judgment of God and therefore increase its severity. But it is also true, and even more so, that human willing and acting with God, and in orientation on Him, and with faith and prayer to Him, whatever the outcome, has the promise which man cannot lack, and the fulfilment of which he will soon see, if he will simply obey without speculation. Those who take up this struggle obediently are already healthy in the fact that they do so, and theirs is no empty desire when they will to maintain or regain their health. . . .

But the fact is undeniable that sickness has also another aspect. For health, like life in general, is not an eternal but a temporal and therefore a limited possession. It is entrusted to man, but it does not belong to him. It is to be affirmed and willed by man as a gift from God, yet not in itself and absolutely, but in the manner and compass in which He gives it.

We have defined health as the power to be as man exercised in the powers of the vital functions of soul and body. And we have defined sickness as the impairing of this power, as crippling and hampering weakness. We have seen that in the antithesis, contrast and conflict of these two determinations of human life we have to do with a real event in the existence of the real man. And we have first attempted to evaluate this event from the angle from which it presents itself as the collision of normal being, as willed, created and ordered by God, with its negation, so that it is brought under the threat of abnormality and even destruction. On this view it can be understood only as man's encounter with the realm of death and therefore the experience of God's judgment. We have been able to describe the required human attitude, the will to live and to be healthy, only in terms of the resistance and conflict of faith and prayer appealing to the grace and gracious power of God. And if we have now to draw attention to another aspect of the same matter, there can be no question — we are irresistibly prevented by the biblical witness concerning health and sickness — of looking away again from this first aspect or even trying to relativise or weaken it. Sickness is one of the elements in the situation of man as he has fallen victim to nothingness through his transgression, as he is thus referred wholly to the mercy of God, but as he is summoned by this reference to hope and courage and conflict. Not a single word of what we have said in this connexion can be retracted or even limited. It must not be lost sight of or forgotten in whatever we may have to add.

What is there to be added? Simply that, quite apart from his transgression, quite apart from his abandonment to the power of nothingness, and quite apart from the consequent visitation of God's judgment upon him, the life of man, and therefore his health as the strength to be as man in the exercise of the powers of all his vital functions of life, is a life which even according to God's good will as Creator, and therefore normally and naturally, begins and ends and is therefore limited. Man does not possess the power to be as man in the same way as God has His power to be as God, nor does he have power over his vital functions as God has His power as Creator, Ruler and merciful Deliverer of His creature. It does not belong to him to be and to live as God. Rather, he may see the goodness of God the Creator in the fact that to his life and strength and powers a specific space is allotted, i.e., a limited span. He may and should exercise them in it and not in the field of the unlimited. They are adapted for it, for development and application within it. Within its confines he may and should be as man in their possession and exercise. Within its confines he stands before God, and at the limit of this span God is mightily for him and is his hope. Just because it is limited, it is a kind of natural and normal confirmation of the fact that by God's free grace man may live through Him and for Him, with the commission to be as man in accordance with the measure of his strength and powers, but not under the intolerable destiny of having to give sense, duration and completeness to his existence by his own exertions and achievements, and therefore in obvious exclusion of the view that he must and may and can by his own strength and powers eternally maintain, assert and confirm himself, attaining for himself his own dignity and honour. The eternal God Himself guarantees all this, and tells him that He does so by giving him a life that is temporal and therefore limited. In this way it always remains in His hand both in its majesty and in its littleness. In itself and as such this fact cannot be an object of complaint, protest or rebellion, nor can the fact that man must make the concrete discovery that his life and therefore his health and strength and powers are not an unlimited reality, but that he is impeded in their possession and exercise, that weakness is real as well as strength, that there is destruction as well as construction, obstruction as well as development. This is all the more terrible because it is just from this direction that we find ourselves threatened by death and judgment. But is it really surprising and shocking in itself? The life of man, his commission, and his strength to fulfil it, are not limited accidentally but by God, and therefore not to his destruction but to his salvation. Inevitably, then, he always in some way comes up concretely against this boundary of his life. Inevitably he must grow old and decline. Inevitably he must concretely encounter his Creator and Lord and therefore God's omnipotence and mercy. But is it merely a question of necessity? In the correct sense, is it not true to say that, no less than in his unimpeded movement within these confines, this is also a possibility. May it not be that genuine freedom to live can and must be concretely realised in the fact that in the impeding and impairing of his life he is shown that neither his life nor he himself is in his own hand, but that he is in God's hand, that he is surrounded by him on all sides, that he is referred wholly to Him, but also that he is reliably upheld by Him? Does not this freedom begin at the very point where we are confronted by the hard actuality of the insight that "Christ will be our consolation"? But what if sickness as the concrete form of weakness, of destruction, of the impairing of his strength and powers, of growing old and declining, is the hard actuality which ushers in this genuinely liberating insight? What if it is not only the forerunner and messenger of death and judgment, but also, concealed under this form, the witness to God's creative goodness, the forerunner and messenger of the eternal life which God has allotted and promised to the man who is graciously preserved and guided by Him within the confines of his time?

34 A Declaration of Faith and Health

Jan Van Eys and Kenneth Vaux

American medicine is in a state of crisis that touches the heart of our lives and our faith. This crisis is expressed in numerous and obvious ways: the excesses in the care of the terminally ill, where death is fought even when life is no longer possible; the belief that scientific insights will give us objective solutions to the problem of the disposition of the unwanted or defective conceptus or newborn; the unwarranted assurance that investigational approaches to diseases are therapeutic; the obsession with preventive medicine as a way to achieve control over disease and life. It is customary to hold these problems to be the consequence of an autocratic and paternalistic medical establishment enamored of its own power and knowledge. However, attempts at dealing with medicine's ethical shortcomings on the basis of that hypothesis have not only failed, but the problem is accelerating.

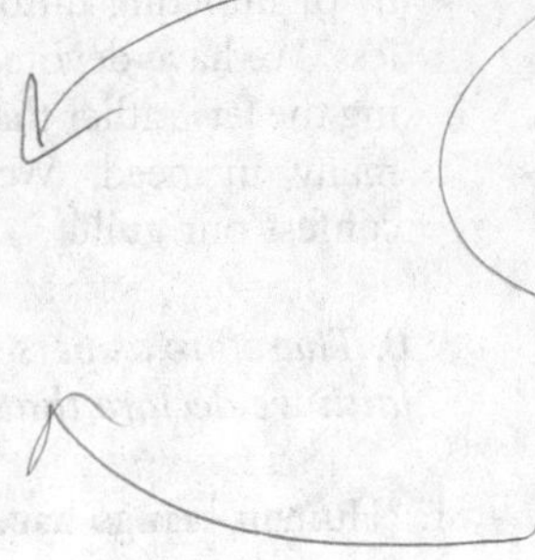

This health crisis is fundamentally a crisis of faith and theology. It results from an idolatry that threatens the very fabric of our society and the rightness of our relationship with God. We seem to have made idols of the body, health, and life. We feel that we can rely on our own power to procure unlimited life for ourselves through pursuing health. We think of threats to health as a calamity; we consider physical disease an evil to be exorcised at all costs.

Karl Barth's theology offers a wise corrective to this attitude. This theology was steeped in the faith expressed in and derived from the Heidelberg Catechism, which defines idolatry clearly and concisely: "It is to imagine or possess something in which to put one's trust in place of or beside the one true God who has revealed himself in his Word" (400th Anniversary Edition, Pilgrim, 1963, p. 158). The very heart of that faith is expressed in the Catechism's first question, "What is your only comfort, in life and in death?," and in its answer:

> That I belong — body and soul, in life and in death — not to myself but to my faithful Savior, Jesus Christ, who at the cost of his own blood has fully paid for all my sins and has completely freed me from the dominion of the devil; that he protects me so well that without the will of my Father in heaven not a hair can fall from my head: indeed, that everything must fit his purpose for my salvation. Therefore, by his Holy Spirit, he also assures me of eternal life, and makes me wholeheartedly willing and ready from now on to live for him [p. 17].

Amid the political realities of early Nazi Germany, Barth felt idolatry threatening the very fabric of faith. The Barmen Declaration followed, long before the church recognized the dangers inherent in the worship of an absolute state. When health becomes an idol, it is the human person, subject to morbidity and mortality, that is adored and served. In modern America, health is seen as personal freedom from abnormality. This view rejects even wholesome aging as a lack of health. Since the norm of health is self-derived, those who are functionally imperfect or different from the self-centered standards are arbitrarily rejected. In the guise of health, we practice an insidious form of discrimination.

It is not the relief from pain, the healing of disease, the prevention of suffering that is our idolatry. It is the need for perfection according to our own measure that creates the crisis in religion. But in matters of health, not humanity in itself but humanity's relationship to God should be the measure of all things. It is not necessary to have a sound body in order to be accepted by God. The doctrine of creation and incarnation repudiates that heresy once and for all. Neither is it possible to be in harmony with God when we neglect those acts of healing of which we are capable.

This poverty of faith, this rampant idolatry, generates a crisis of a proportion almost unparalleled in human history. The way we view ourselves will determine how we attempt to shape our destiny. Making an idol of medicine is alienating us from the sovereignty of God. It is both a problem of the individual believer and the collective responsibility of church and synagogue. The church must guide its flock to remain in harmony with God, reminding people that God's mercy is unfailing despite humanity's misdoings.

So great do we perceive this crisis to be that we feel the urgent need to formulate a declaration on faith and health. We hereby submit that declaration for consideration by all persons of faith.

A Declaration of Faith and Health

A. Preamble:

1. "For no one of us lives, and equally no one of us dies, for himself alone. If we live, we live for the Lord; and if we die, we die for the Lord. Whether therefore we live or die, we belong to the Lord" (Rom. 14:7-8).
2. A grave deficit in our religious faith has led us to make an idol of medicine. This is a threat to humankind's relationship to God. We seek unlimited life for ourselves, striving to achieve it through our own power. We are guilty thereby of inflicting untold suffering on the helpless. We have devoted ourselves to aggrandizing the few rather than to seeking relief for the many in need. We humbly and sincerely confess our guilt.

B. Therefore as persons of faith we declare that:

1. "Human beings have been given great power to conquer disease and alleviate suffering. It is God's gift that we may extract succor from his creation. We must reject the false doctrine that such relief of suffering and cleansing of disease is our own doing, rather than God's mercy to us. We must reject the idolatrous belief that

the prolongation of life at all costs constitutes a good that glorifies God. Just as it is a sin to appear before God without being summoned, so it is a sin to refuse to appear when God's summons is unmistakable.

2. We must acknowledge God's call to relieve the suffering of others just as we seek relief from suffering for ourselves. We must confess our lack of wholeness and our need for healing. It is our physical suffering that so often confronts us with that need. God's mercy, in providing relief for our own pain, should make us mindful of our responsibility to alleviate the suffering of others.
3. We are able to ease and, often, to prevent suffering. Not to use our knowledge in order to prevent unnecessary pain is to reject God's mercy. We must confess our manifold unwillingness to be used by God to help others.
4. We must reject the false doctrine that health is the absence of disease and that, therefore, it is within our power to maintain health. The prevention of disease is a good insofar as it allows us to stop unnecessary suffering. However, our obsession with personal health alienates us from the world and denies God's sovereignty over us. "For the mind that is set on the flesh is hostile to God; it does not submit to God's law, indeed it cannot; and those who are in the flesh cannot please God" (Rom. 8:7-8).
5. There are many victims of our idolatry. We often sacrifice the helpless, the children, and the elderly to our search for physical cures and our endless attempts to prolong life. The weakest among us is precious to God; his mercy and grace extend to all. When entrusted with the care of the helpless, we must become channels for God's mercy through our medical knowledge, while accepting his grace when he deems it more merciful to deliver them from all suffering. As we treat the helpless, so do we treat God (Matt. 25:45-46).

C. Those persons who are entrusted with the care of the ill will declare that:

1. Learning about diseases, understanding their causes, exploring their prevention and attempting their cure are moral obligations for humanity in general and the medical community in specific.
2. Patients represent suffering humanity, whatever their afflictions. Some diseases are inherent in our finite bodies, but many are either inflicted on defenseless persons or, by human inaction, are allowed to strike. However noble may be our quest to conquer disease, we must never forget how much our sins contribute to human suffering.
3. The goal of medicine is the prevention of disease and the restoration of the sick to full health. Physicians must remember that withholding the application of effective treatment *and* making promises based on unproven theories equally are abuses of their privileged status. We must not lead physicians into the temptation to do either.
4. We must be concerned with whole persons, not just with physical problems. Disease that others have inflicted on them confronts patients with evil in their fellow human beings. Disease that was inherent in their own bodies confronts them with dread of latent evil in themselves. The task of physicians is healing as well as cleansing. At times this means demonstrating the power of good to the patients; at other times it means helping people become at ease with themselves. When Jesus saw the paralyzed man descend through the roof and forgave his sins, he challenged us by asking, "Is it easier to say, 'Your sins are forgiven you,' or to say 'Stand up and walk'?" (Luke 5:23).
5. We must reject the false doctrine that our medical knowledge gives us power over the unborn and the voiceless. Our idolatry too often turns our nurturing of children into abuse, and our caring for the elderly into procedures tantamount to terminal torture.

D. Therefore the church will affirm that:

1. In Paul's words: "My brothers [and sisters], I implore you by God's mercy to offer your very selves to him: a living sacrifice, dedicated and fit for his acceptance, the worship offered by mind and heart. Adapt yourselves no longer to the pattern of this present world, but let your minds be remade and your whole nature thus transformed. Then you will be able to

discern the will of God, and to know what is good, acceptable and perfect" (Rom. 12:1-2).

2. We must approach both our own pain and others' needs with Paul's words in mind, lest we continue to idolize physical perfection, maintained at all costs.
3. We acknowledge the absolute sovereignty of God and recognize that health is God-given; enjoyed by being right with God; and made possible through God's infinite mercy to all who earnestly seek him.

Science, technology, and medicine are gifts of God, given for the protection and enhancement of life on earth. Our public theology and ethics must become again a fitting vehicle for the continued inspiration and conveyance of the biomedical project, a project that promises great blessing for the human family. Medicine must forsake its propensity to allow materialistic or value-free norms to direct its momentum. Rather, the scientific enterprise must celebrate and honor our moral and spiritual heritage.

3- questions about health

35 In Search of Health

LeRoy Walters

In the past, "health" seemed to be a relatively simple and straightforward concept. However, in recent years increasing controversy has surrounded that concept. To illustrate, here are two quotations. The first is taken from a 1973 article by Peter Sedgwick, a British social scientist:

> All departments of nature below the level of mankind are exempt both from disease and from treatment. The blight that strikes at corn or at potatoes is a human invention, for if man wished to cultivate parasites rather than potatoes (or corn) there would be no "blight" but simply the necessary foddering of the parasite-crop. Animals do not have diseases either, prior to the presence of man in a meaningful relation with them. . . . Outside the significance that man voluntarily attached to certain conditions, there are no illnesses or diseases in nature.

The second quotation appears in the preamble to the constitution of the World Health Organization (WHO): "Health is a state of complete physical, mental and social well-being and not merely the absence of disease or infirmity."

Three questions are raised by these quotations. First, how broadly should the concept of health be construed or applied? Second, is health a natural norm or an arbitrary label? And third, is health to be considered a minimum, a maximum, or something in between, some sort of golden mean?

It is easy for the concept of health to become

so broad that it ends up as virtually the equivalent of happiness — or even salvation. This breadth is one of the problems of the WHO definition. If one enjoys "a state of complete physical, mental, and social well-being," what else remains to be enjoyed? For the sake of clarity and simplicity I will consider only the health of bodies, not that of minds or of whole societies. Thus, I will accept only the first aspect of the WHO definition: health is a state of "physical well-being."

With this narrowed definition it is then possible to assert that (physical) health is a natural norm and not merely an artificial construct. In the mental health field mere social deviancy is often labeled as mental illness. In the realm of physical health, however, I think there will be a broad consensus on what is or is not healthy. A deer or a person riddled with cancer is unhealthy, as is the shattered victim of a serious auto accident. On the positive side, we have relatively clear concepts of healthy athletes and even healthy squirrels.

The WHO definition would require that health be a maximum: *complete* physical well-being and not merely the absence of disease or infirmity. In my view, this definition requires too much. Complete physical well-being sounds like an ideal which few of us are likely ever to attain. On the other hand, a bare minimum of well-being seems inadequate to satisfy our concept of health. Therefore, I suggest that we regard physical health as a kind of mean. In other words, health is functional normality or, in the words of Leon R. Kass, "the well-working of the [physical] organism as a whole."

physical health

I

Although it is generally assumed that medical care has contributed significantly to the health of human beings, that contribution is frequently overrated. According to Victor Fuchs, a health economist at Stanford University, it was not until well into the 20th century that the average patient had a better than 50-50 chance of being helped by the average physician.

During the past 200 years most of the change in longevity has been due to a reduction in death rates at early ages. "Normal" life expectancy has lengthened very little: for example, between 1900 and 1970 the average life expectancy of persons who reached the age of 65 increased by only one and one-half years.

Much of the improvement in health during the 19th and 20th centuries — especially prior to the mid-1930s — is attributable to better nutrition, falling birth rates, rising living standards, and public health measures: primarily the chlorination of water, the pasteurization of milk, and indoor plumbing. Consider, for example, the case of the "pneumonia-diarrhea" complex. During the 19th century infants and children frequently caught infections which led to chronic diarrhea; the diarrhea in turn often weakened the children's resistance so severely that they became ill with pneumonia and died. In New York City, deaths from this syndrome fell about 80 percent between 1900 and 1930 — this before the advent of antibiotics (statistics from *Who Shall Live?*, by Victor R. Fuchs [Basic Books, 1974]).

It must in fairness be conceded that since 1935 medicine *has* contributed significantly to health, particularly the health of infants and children. Antibiotics and vaccines have been developed for the control of diphtheria, typhoid fever, polio, measles, influenza, and certain types of pneumonia. This record of success in the conquest of infectious diseases has sometimes been called the "Golden Age of Medicine."

In dealing with the chronic diseases of adults, however, medicine has not been able to achieve similar increases in life expectancy. Intractable chronic diseases are some of the major killers of our time: heart disease, cancer, stroke. Many of the medical measures used in "treating" them are only palliative; some are also highly expensive. Kidney dialysis, for example, costs approximately $30,000 per year and does nothing to improve the patient's underlying disease. And there is always the possibility that medical care will do harm as well as good: through the side-effects of radiation, drug reactions, infections contracted in hospitals, or the aftereffects of surgery.

In sum, with the exception of antibiotics and vaccines — especially in the case of infants and children — medical care has not made as significant a contribution to health as is sometimes supposed. Indeed, modern medicine has made only slight progress toward the conquest of chronic diseases.

This may be very different in 1999

II

In several recent publications on the quest for health there has been a rather decisive shift away from the search for medical cures and toward the issues of personal responsibility for one's own health status. One way into this issue has been to consider the major causes of death in persons 15-24 years of age. Among white males, the five leading causes of death are, in order, motor accidents, other accidents, suicide, cancer, and homicide. Only one of these five is a disease, strictly defined.

Dean Lester Breslow and his colleagues at the UCLA School of Public Health have recently completed a series of studies investigating correlations between health practices and physical health status. Inductively, these researchers have discovered seven "rules" which seem to correlate very well with both general healthiness and longevity:

1. Don't smoke cigarettes.
2. Get seven or eight hours of sleep each night.
3. Eat breakfast.
4. Keep your weight down.
5. Drink moderately.
6. Exercise daily.
7. Don't eat between meals.

The Breslow group reports some startling findings in connection with these rules. The physical health status of individuals over 75 who followed all the rules is about the same as that of people aged 35-44 who observe fewer than three. A person who adheres to at least six of the seven rules has at age 45 a life expectancy 11 years longer than someone who has followed fewer than four. And we may note in passing that "visit your doctor regularly" does not appear on the list!

A further illustration: Victor Fuchs, in *Who Shall Live?*, recounts "The Tale of Two States," Utah and Nevada. Of course, not all Nevadans live in Las Vegas, and not all residents of Utah are abstemious Mormons. But these two adjacent states, with similar income levels and similar numbers of physicians and hospital beds per capita, are at opposite ends of the spectrum in average health status. Adult death rates for Nevada are generally 40-50 percent higher than for Utah. Deaths resulting from cirrhosis of the liver and lung cancer among males in their 30s are almost *seven* times as high in Nevada as in Utah.

The upshot of all these statistics would seem to be our life style may have more of an impact on our dying from certain diseases than all the most modern techniques of medical care. Thus, rather than asserting that health is a right, we may need to concede that, at least in certain respects, health is a duty.

Several caveats are in order, lest we overstate the case. Debilitating and even lethal genetic diseases do exist, and a change of life style usually cannot improve the health status of persons suffering from such diseases. There are also environmental determinants of health; e.g., toxic substances in the air, which cannot be controlled by those who are victims of their effects. However, for most of us there remains a significant realm in which our own voluntary behavior and life style have a direct and substantial impact on our personal health status.

III

At the level of public policy, we are faced with a number of difficult questions. How much of the nation's "health" dollar should go into the medical-care sector, and how much should be invested in building tennis courts and jogging tracks or in ensuring adequate nutrition for children? Then, within the medical-care sector, what type of health programs should receive highest priority: ones for crisis medicine, like kidney dialysis, or health-maintenance and preventive-medicine programs?

Another dilemma involves who should pay health-care costs which arise from the patient's own negligence or overexuberant style of life. This problem will become even more serious if a comprehensive program of national health insurance is ever enacted. In the words of one wry commentator: "Utah may be unwilling to pay for the sins of Nevada."

There are also dilemmas to be faced at a more personal level. Physical health is important, and a certain minimum level of health is essential to achieving any other goals in life. Yet there may be times when the benefit of health comes squarely into conflict with other important values — such as responding to friends or working to attain excellence or being faithful to one's Christian commitment.

To illustrate how this conflict may arise, let me cite a few autobiographical lines from a letter of an early Christian missionary, the Apostle Paul:

> Five times the Jews have given me the thirty-nine strokes; three times I have been beaten with rods; once I was stoned; three times I have been shipwrecked, and for twenty-four hours I was adrift on the open sea. I have been constantly on the road; I have met dangers from rivers, dangers from robbers, dangers from my fellow-countrymen, dangers from foreigners, dangers in towns, dangers in the country, dangers at sea, dangers from false friends. I have toiled and drudged, I have often gone without sleep; hungry and thirsty, I have often gone fasting; and I have suffered from cold and exposure. [II Cor. 11:24-47, NEB]

By his own admission, Paul was guilty of violating at least two of the seven rules for good health: he did not always get seven or eight hours' sleep per night, and on occasion he probably skipped breakfast.

So we are left with a paradox. Bodily health is an important value, and we have a duty to promote our own health. Yet there may be times when other important values — like friendship, or excellence, or fidelity to one's Christian commitment — should take precedence over the quest for health.

36 The WHO Definition of "Health"

Daniel Callahan

There is not much that can be called fun and games in medicine, perhaps because unlike other sports it is the only one in which everyone, participant and spectator, eventually gets killed playing. In the meantime, one of the grandest games is that version of king-of-the-hill where the aim of all players is to upset the World Health Organization (WHO) definition of "health." That definition, in case anyone could possibly forget it, is "Health is a state of complete physical, mental, and social well-being and not merely the absence of disease or infirmity." Fair game, indeed. Yet somehow, defying all comers, the WHO definition endures, though literally every other aspirant to the crown has managed to knock it off the hill at least once. One possible reason for its presence is that it provides such an irresistible straw man; few there are who can resist attacking it in the opening paragraphs of papers designed to move on to more profound reflections.

But there is another possible reason which deserves some exploration, however unsettling the implications. It may just be that the WHO definition has more than a grain of truth in it, of a kind which is as profoundly frustrating as it is enticingly attractive. At the very least it is a definition which implies that there is some intrinsic relationship between the good of the body and the good of the self. The attractiveness of this relationship is obvious: it thwarts any movement toward a dualism of self and body, a dualism

From the *Hastings Center Studies* 1, no. 3 (1973): 77-87.

which in any event immediately breaks down when one drops a brick on one's toe; and it impels the analyst to work toward a conception of health which in the end is resistant to clear and distinct categories, closer to the felt experience. All that, naturally, is very frustrating. It seems simply impossible to devise a concept of health which is rich enough to be nutritious and yet not so rich as to be indigestible.

One common objection to the WHO definition is, in effect, an assault upon any and all attempts to specify the meaning of very general concepts. Who can possibly define words as vague as "health," a venture as foolish as trying to define "peace," "justice," "happiness," and other systematically ambiguous notions? To this objection the "pragmatic" clinicians (as they often call themselves) add that, anyway, it is utterly unnecessary to know what "health" means in order to treat a patient running a high temperature. Not only that, it is also a harmful distraction to clutter medical judgment with philosophical puzzles.

Unfortunately for this line of argument, it is impossible to talk or think at all without employing general concepts; without them, cognition and language are impossible. More damagingly, it is rarely difficult to discover, with a bit of probing, that even the most "pragmatic" judgment (whatever *that* is) presupposes some general values and orientations, all of which can be translated into definitions of terms as general as "health" and "happiness." A failure to discern the operative underlying values, the conceptions of reality upon which they are based, and the definitions they entail, sets the stage for unexamined conduct and, beyond that, positive harm both to patients and to medicine in general.

But if these objections to any and all attempts to specify the meaning of "health" are common enough, the most specific complaint about the WHO definition is that its very generality, and particularly its association of health and general well-being as a positive ideal, has given rise to a variety of evils. Among them are the cultural tendency to define all social problems, from war to crime in the streets, as "health" problems; the blurring of lines of responsibility between and among the professions, and between the medical profession and the political order; the implicit denial of human freedom which results when failures to achieve social well-being are defined as forms of "sickness," somehow to be treated by medical means; and the general debasement of language which ensues upon the casual habit of labeling everyone from Adolf Hitler to student radicals to the brat next door as "sick." In short, the problem with the WHO definition is not that it represents an attempt to propose a general definition, but that it is simply a bad one.

That is a valid line of objection, provided one can spell out in some detail just how the definition can or does entail some harmful consequences. Two lines of attack are possible against putatively hazardous social definitions of significant general concepts. One is by pointing out that the definition does not encompass all that a concept has commonly been taken to mean, either historically or at present, that it is a partial definition only. The task then is to come up with a fuller definition, one less subject to misuse. But there is still another way of objecting to socially significant definitions, and that is by pointing out some baneful effects of definitions generally accepted as adequate. Many of the objections to the WHO definition fall in the latter category, building upon the important insight that definitions of crucially important terms with a wide public use have ethical, social, and political implications; defining general terms is not an abstract exercise but a way of shaping the world metaphysically and structuring the world politically.

Wittgenstein's aphorism, "don't look for the meaning, look for the use," is pertinent here. The ethical problem in defining the concept of "health" is to determine what the implications are of the various uses to which a concept of "health" can be put. We might well agree that there are some uses of "health" which will produce socially harmful results. To carry Wittgenstein a step further, "don't look for the uses, look for the abuses." We might, then, examine some of the real or possible abuses to which the WHO definition leads, recognizing all the while that what we may term an "abuse" will itself rest upon some perceived *positive* good or value.

Historical Origin & Context

Before the task is undertaken, however, it is helpful to understand the historical origin and social context of the WHO definition. If abuses of that definition have developed, their seeds may be looked for in its earliest manifestations.

The World Health Organization came into existence between 1946 and 1948 as one of the first major activities of the United Nations. As an outcome of earlier work, an Interim Commission to establish the WHO sponsored an International Health Conference in New York in June and July of 1946. At that Conference, representatives of 61 nations signed the Constitution of the WHO, the very first clause of which presented the now famous definition of "health." The animating spirit behind the formation of the WHO was the belief that the improvement of world health would make an important contribution to world peace; health and peace were seen as inseparable. Just why this belief gained ground is not clear from the historical record of the WHO. While there have been many historical explanations of the origin of World War II, a lack of world health has not been prominent among them; nor, for that matter, did the early supporters of the WHO claim that the Second World War or any other war might have been averted had there been better health. More to the point, perhaps, was the conviction that health was intimately related to economic and cultural welfare; in turn, that welfare, so it was assumed, had a direct bearing on future peace. No less important was a fervent faith in the possibilities of medical science to achieve world health, enhanced by the development of powerful antibiotics and pesticides during the war.

A number of memorandums submitted to a spring 1946 Technical Preparatory Committee meeting of the WHO capture the flavor of the period. The Yugoslavian memorandum noted that "health is a prerequisite to freedom from want, to social security and happiness." France stated that "there cannot be any material security, social security, or well-being for individuals or nations without health . . . the full responsibility of a free man can only be assumed by healthy individuals . . . the spread of proper notions of hygiene among populations tends to improve the level of health and hence to increase their working power and raise their standard of living. . . ." The United States contended that "international cooperation and joint action in the furtherance of all matters pertaining to health will raise the standards of living, will promote the freedom, the dignity, and the happiness of all peoples in the world."

In addition to those themes, perhaps the most significant initiative taken by the organizers of the WHO was to include mental health as part of its working definition. In its memorandum, Great Britain stated that "it should be clear that health includes mental health," but it was Dr. Brock Chisholm, soon to become the first director of the WHO, who personified what Dr. Chisholm himself called the "visionary" view of health. During the meeting of the Technical Preparatory Committee he argued that: "The world is sick and the ills are due to the perversion of man; his inability to live with himself. The microbe is not the enemy; science is sufficiently advanced to cope with it were it not for the barriers of superstition, ignorance, religious intolerance, misery and poverty. . . . These psychological evils must be understood in order that a remedy might be prescribed, and the scope of the task before the Committee therefore knows no bounds."

In Dr. Chisholm's statement, put very succinctly, are all of those elements of the WHO definition which led eventually to its criticism: defining all the problems of the world as "sickness," affirming that science would be sufficient to cope with the causes of physical disease, asserting that only anachronistic attitudes stood in the way of a cure of both physical and psychological ills, and declaring that the cause of health can tolerate no limitations. To say that Dr. Chisholm's "vision" was grandiose is to understate the matter. Even allowing for hyperbole, it is clear that the stage was being set for a conception of "health" which would encompass literally every element and item of human happiness. One can hardly be surprised, given such a vision, that our ways of talking about "health" have become all but meaningless. Even though I believe the definition is not without its important insights, it is well to observe why, in part, we are so muddled at present about "health."

Health & Happiness

Let us examine some of the principal objections to the WHO definition in more detail. One of them is that, by including the notion of "social well-being" under its rubric, it turns the enduring problem of human happiness into one more medical problem, to be dealt with by scientific means. That is surely an objectionable feature, if only because there exists no evidence whatever that medicine has anything more than a partial grasp of the sources of human misery. Despite Dr. Chisholm's optimism, medicine has not even found ways of dealing with more than a fraction of the whole range of physical diseases; campaigns, after all, are still being mounted against cancer and heart disease. Nor is there any special reason to think that future forays against those and other common diseases will bear rapid fruits. People will continue to die of disease for a long time to come, probably forever.

But perhaps, then, in the psychological and psychiatric sciences some progress has been made against what Dr. Chisholm called the "psychological ills," which lead to wars, hostility, and aggression? To be sure, there are many interesting psychological theories to be found about these "ills," and few techniques which can, with some individuals, reduce or eliminate antisocial behavior. But so far as I can see, despite the mental health movement and the rise of the psychological sciences, war and human hostility are as much with us as ever. Quite apart from philosophical objections to the WHO definition, there was no empirical basis for the unbounded optimism which lay behind it at the time of its inception, and little has happened since to lend its limitless aspiration any firm support.

Common sense alone makes evident the fact that the absence of "disease or infirmity" by no means guarantees "social well-being." In one sense, those who drafted the WHO definition seem well aware of that. Isn't the whole point of their definition to show the inadequacy of negative definitions? But in another sense, it may be doubted that they really did grasp that point. For the third principle enunciated in the WHO Constitution says that, "the health of all peoples is fundamental to the attainment of peace and security. . . ." Why is it fundamental, at least to peace? The worst wars of the 20th century have been waged by countries with very high standards of health, by nations with superior life-expectancies for individuals and with comparatively low infant morality rates. The greatest present threats to world peace come in great part (though not entirely) from developed countries, those which have combatted disease and illness most effectively. There seems to be no historical correlation whatever between health and peace, and that is true even if one includes "mental health."

How are human beings to achieve happiness? That is the final and fundamental question. Obviously illness, whether mental or physical, makes happiness less possible in most cases. But that is only because they are only one symptom of a more basic restriction, that of human finitude, which sees infinite human desires constantly thwarted by the limitations of reality. "Complete" well-being might, conceivably, be attainable, but under one condition only: that people ceased expecting much from life. That does not seem about to happen. On the contrary, medical and psychological progress have been more than outstripped by rising demands and expectations. What is so odd about that, if it is indeed true that human desires are infinite? Whatever the answer to the question of human happiness, there is no particular reason to believe that medicine can do anything more than make a modest finite contribution.

Another objection to the WHO definition is that, by implication, it makes the medical profession the gate-keeper for happiness and social well-being. Or if not exactly the gate-keeper (since political and economic support will be needed from sources other than medical), then the final magic-healer of human misery. Pushed far enough, the whole idea is absurd, and it is not necessary to believe that the organizers of the WHO would, if pressed, have been willing to go quite that far. But even if one pushes the pretension a little way, considerable fantasy results. The mental health movement is the best example, casting the psychological professional in the role of high priest.

At its humble best, that movement can do considerable good; people do suffer from psychological disabilities and there are some effective ways of helping them. But it would be sheer folly to believe that all, or even the most important, social evils stem from bad mental health: political injustice, economic scarcity, food shortages, unfavorable physical environments, have a far greater historical claim as sources of a failure to achieve "social well-being." To retort that all or most of these troubles can, nonetheless, be seen finally as symptoms of bad mental health is, at best, self-serving and, at worst, just plain foolish.

A significant part of the objection that the WHO definition places, at least by implication, too much power and authority in the hands of the medical profession, need not be based on a fear of that power as such. There is no reason to think that the world would be any worse off if health professionals made all decisions than if any other group did; and no reason to think it would be any better off. That is not a very important point. More significant is that cultural development which, in its skepticism about "traditional" ways of solving social problems, would seek a technological and specifically a medical solution for human ills of all kinds. There is at least a hint in early WHO discussions that, since politicians and diplomats have failed in maintaining world peace, a more expert group should take over, armed with the scientific skills necessary to set things right; it is science which is best able to vanquish that old Enlightenment bogeyman, "superstition." More concretely, such an ideology has the practical effect of blurring the lines of appropriate authority and responsibility. If all problems — political, economic, and social — reduce to matters of "health," then there ceases to be any way to determine who should be responsible for what.

The Tyranny of Health

The problem of responsibility has at least two faces. One is that of a tendency to turn all problems of "social well-being" over to the medical professional, most pronounced in the instance of the incarceration of a large group of criminals in mental institutions rather than prisons. The abuses, both medical and legal, of that practice are, fortunately, now beginning to receive the attention they deserve, even if little corrective action has yet been taken. (Counterbalancing that development, however, are others, where some are seeking more "effective" ways of bringing science to bear on criminal behavior.)

The other face of the problem of responsibility is that of the way in which those who are sick, or purportedly sick, are to be evaluated in terms of their freedom and responsibility. Siegler and Osmond elsewhere in this issue discuss the "sick role," a leading feature of which is the ascription of blamelessness, of non-responsibility, to those who contract illness. There is no reason to object to this kind of ascription in many instances — one can hardly blame someone for contracting kidney disease — but, obviously enough, matters get out of hand when all physical, mental, and communal disorders are put under the heading of "sickness," and all sufferers (all of us, in the end) placed in the blameless "sick role." Not only are the concepts of "sickness" and "illness" drained of all content, it also becomes impossible to ascribe any freedom or responsibility to those caught up in the throes of sickness. The whole world is sick, and no one is responsible any longer for anything. That is determinism gone mad, a rather odd outcome of a development which began with attempts to bring unbenighted "reason" and free self-determination to bear for the release of the helpless captives of superstition and ignorance.

The final and most telling objection to the WHO definition has less to do with the definition itself than with one of its natural historical consequences. Thomas Szasz has been the most eloquent (and most singleminded) critic of that sleight-of-hand which has seen the concept of health moved from the medical to the moral arena. What can no longer be done in the name of "morality" can now be done in the name of "health": human beings labeled, incarcerated, and dismissed for their failure to toe the line of "normalcy" and "sanity."

At first glance, this analysis of the present situation might seem to be totally at odds with the tendency to put everyone in the blame-free "sick role." Actually, there is a fine, probably indistinguishable, line separating these two positions. For as soon as one treats all human disorders — war, crime, social unrest — as forms of illness, then one turns health into a normative concept, that which human beings must and ought to have if they are to live in peace with themselves and others. Health is no longer an optional matter, but the golden key to the relief of human misery. We *must* be well or we will all perish. "Health" can and must be imposed; there can be no room for the luxury of freedom when so much is at stake. Of course the matter is rarely put so bluntly, but it is to Szasz's great credit that he has discerned what actually happens when "health" is allowed to gain the cultural clout which morality once had. (That he carries the whole business too far in his embracing of the most extreme moral individualism is another story, which cannot be dealt with here.) Something is seriously amiss when the "right" to have healthy children is turned into a further right for children not to be born defective, and from there into an obligation not to bring unhealthy children into the world as a way of respecting the right of those children to health! Nor is everything altogether lucid when abortion decisions are made a matter of "medical judgment" (see *Roe vs. Wade*); when decisions to provide psychoactive drugs for the relief of the ordinary stress of living are defined as no less "medical judgment"; when patients are not allowed to die with dignity because of medical indications that they can, come what may, be kept alive; when prisoners, without their consent, are subjected to aversive conditioning to improve their mental health.

Abuses of Language

In running through the litany of criticisms which have been directed at the WHO definition of "health," and what seem to have been some of its long-term implications and consequences, I might well be accused of beating a dead horse. My only defense is to assert, first, that the spirit of the WHO definition is by no means dead either in medicine or society. In fact, because of the usual cultural lag which requires many years for new ideas to gain wide social currency, it is only now coming into its own on a broad scale. (Everyone now talks about everybody and everything, from Watergate to Billy Graham to trash in the streets, as "sick.") Second, I believe that we are now in the midst of a nascent (if not actual) crisis about how "health" ought properly to be understood, with much dependent upon what conception of health emerges in the near future.

If the ideology which underlies the WHO definition has proved to contain many muddled and hazardous ingredients, it is not at all evident what should take its place. The virtue of the WHO definition is that it tried to place health in the broadest human context. Yet the assumption behind the main criticisms of the WHO definition seem perfectly valid. Those assumptions can be characterized as follows: 1) health is only a part of life, and the achievement of health only a part of the achievement of happiness; 2) medicine's role, however important, is limited; it can neither solve nor even cope with the great majority of social, political, and cultural problems; 3) human freedom and responsibility must be recognized, and any tendency to place all deviant, devilish, or displeasing human beings into the blameless sick-role must be resisted; 4) while it is good for human beings to be healthy, medicine is not morality; except in very limited contexts (plagues and epidemics) "medical judgment" should not be allowed to become moral judgment; to be healthy is not to be righteous; 5) it is important to keep clear and distinct the different roles of different professions, with a clearly circumscribed role for medicine, limited to those domains of life where the contribution of medicine is appropriate. Medicine can save some lives; it cannot save the life of society.

These assumptions, and the criticisms of the WHO definition which spring from them, have some important implications for the use of the words "health," "illness," "sick," and the like. It will be counted an abuse of language if the word "sick" is applied to all individual and communal problems, if all unacceptable conduct is spoken of in the language of medical pathologies, if moral issues and moral judgments are translated into the language of "health," if the lines of authority, responsibility, and expertise are so blurred that the health profession is allowed to preempt the rights and responsibilities of others by redefining them in its own professional language.

Abuses of that kind have no possibility of being curbed in the absence of a definition of health which does not contain some intrinsic elements of limitation — that is, unless there is a definition which, when abused, is self-evidently *seen* as abused by those who know what health means. Unfortunately, it is in the nature of general definitions that they do not circumscribe their own meaning (or even explain it) and contain no built-in safeguards against misuse, e.g., our "peace with honor" in Southeast Asia — "peace," "honor"? Moreover, for a certain class of concepts — peace, honor, happiness, for example — it is difficult to keep them free in ordinary usage from a normative content. In our own usage, it would make no sense to talk of them in a way which implied they are not desirable or are merely neutral: by well-ingrained social custom (resting no doubt on some basic features of human nature) health, peace, and happiness are both desired and desirable — good. For those and other reasons, it is perfectly plausible to say the cultural task of defining terms, and settling on appropriate and inappropriate usages, is far more than a matter of getting our dictionary entries right. It is nothing less than a way of deciding what should be valued, how life should be understood, and what principles should guide individual and social conduct.

Health is not just a term to be defined. Intuitively, if we have lived at all, it is something we seek and value. We may not set the highest value on health — other goods may be valued as well — but it would strike me as incomprehensible should someone say that health was a matter of utter indifference to him; we would well doubt either his sanity or his maturity. The cultural problem, then, may be put this way. The acceptable range of uses of the term "health" should, at the minimum, capture the normative element in the concept as traditionally understood while, at the maximum, incorporating the insight (stemming from criticisms of the WHO definition) that the term "health" is abused if it becomes synonymous with virtue, social tranquility, and ultimate happiness. Since there are no instruction manuals available on how one would go about reaching a goal of that sort, I will offer no advice on the subject. I have the horrible suspicion, as a matter of fact, that people either have a decent intuitive sense on such matters (reflected in the way they use language) or they do not; and if they do not, little can be done to instruct them. One is left with the pious hope that, somehow, over a long period of time, things will change.

In Defense of WHO

Now that simply might be the end of the story, assuming some argument can be reached that the WHO definition of "health" is plainly bad, full of snares, delusions, and false norms. But I am left uncomfortable with such a flat, simple conclusion. The nagging point about the definition is that, in badly put ways, it was probably on to something. It certainly recognized, however inchoately, that it is difficult to talk meaningfully of health solely in terms of "the absence of disease or infirmity." As a purely logical point, one must ask about what positive state of affairs disease and infirmity are an absence of — absent from what? One is left with the tautological proposition that health is the absence of non-health, a less than illuminating revelation. Could it not be said, though, that at least intuitively everyone knows what health is by means of the experiential contrast posed by states of illness and disease; that is, even if I cannot define health in any positive sense, I can surely know when I am sick (pain, high fever, etc.) And compare that condition with my previous states which contained no such conditions? Thus one could, in some recognizable sense, speak of illness as a deviation from a norm, even if it is not possible to specify that norm with any clarity.

But there are some problems with this approach, for all of its commonsense appeal. Sociologically, it is well known that what may be accounted sickness in one culture may not be so interpreted in another; one culture's (person's) deviation from the norm may not necessarily be another culture's (person's) deviation. In this as in other matters, commonsense intuition may be nothing but a reflection of different cultural and personal evaluations. In addition, there can be and usually are serious disputes about how great a deviation from the (unspecified) norm is necessary before the terms "sickness" and "illness" become appropriate. Am I to be put in the sick role because of my nagging case of itching athlete's foot, or must my toes start dropping off before I can so qualify? All general concepts have their borderline cases, and normally they need pose no real problems for the applicability of the concepts for the run of instances. But where "health" and "illness" are concerned, the number of borderline cases can be enormous, affected by age, attitudinal, and cultural factors. Worse still, the fact that people can be afflicted by disease (even fatally afflicted) well before the manifestation of any overt symptoms is enough to discredit the adequacy of intuitions based on how one happens to feel at any given moment.

A number of these problems might be resolved by distinguishing between health as a norm and as an ideal. As a norm, it could be possible to speak in terms of deviation from some statistical standards, particularly if these standards were couched not only in terms of organic function but also in terms of behavioral functioning. Thus someone would be called "healthy" if his heart, lungs, kidneys (etc.) functioned at a certain level of efficiency and efficacy, if he was not suffering physical pain, and if his body was free of those pathological conditions which even if undetected or undetectable could impair organic function and eventually cause pain. There could still be dispute about what should count as a "pathological" condition, but at least it would be possible to draw up a large checklist of items subject to "scientific measurement"; then, having gone through that checklist in a physical exam, and passing all the tests, one could be pronounced "healthy." Neat, clean, simple.

All of this might be possible in a static culture, which ours is not. The problem is that any notion of a statistical norm will be superintended by some kind of ideal. Why, in the first place, should anyone care at all how his organs are functioning, much less how well they do so? There must be some reason for that, a reason which goes beyond theoretical interest in statistical distributions. Could it possibly be because certain departures from the norm carry with them unpleasant states, which few are likely to call "good": pain, discrimination, unhappiness? I would guess so. In the second place, why should society have any interest whatever in the way the organs of its citizens function? There must also be some reason for that, very possibly the insight that the organ functioning of individuals has some aggregate social implications. In our culture at least (and in every other culture I have ever heard of) it is simply impossible, finally, to draw any sharp distinction between conceptions of the human good and what are accounted significant and negatively evaluated deviations from statistical norms.

That is the whole point of saying, in defense of the WHO definition of health, that it discerned the intimate connection between the good of the body and the good of the self, not only the individual self but the social community of selves. No individual and no society would (save for speculative, scientific reasons only) have any interest whatever in the condition of human organs and bodies were it not for the obvious fact that those conditions can have an enormous impact on the whole of human life. People do, it has been noticed, die; and they die because something has gone wrong with their bodies. This can be annoying, especially if one would, at the moment of death, prefer to be busy doing other things. Consider two commonplace occurrences. The first I have alluded to already; dropping a heavy brick on one's foot. So far as I know, there is no culture where the pain which that event occasions is considered a good in itself. Why is that? Because (I presume) the pain which results can not only make it difficult or impossible to walk for a time but also because the pain, if intense enough, makes it impossible to think about anything else (or think at all) or to relate to anything or anyone other than the pain. For a time, I am "not myself" and that simply because my body is making such excessive demands on my attention that nothing is possible to me except to howl. I cannot, in sum, dissociate my "body" from my "self" in that situation; my self is my body and my body is my pain.

The other occurrence is no less commonplace. It is the assertion the old often make to the young, however great the psychological, economic, or other miseries of the latter: "at least you've got your health." They are saying in so many words that, if one is healthy, then there is some room for hope, some possibility of human recovery; and even more they are saying that, without good health, nothing is possible, however favorable the other conditions of life may be. Again, it is impossible to dissociate good of body and good of self. Put more formally, if health is not a sufficient condition for happiness, it is a necessary condition. At that very fundamental level, then, any sharp distinction between the good of bodies and the good of persons dissolves.

Are we not forced, therefore, to say that, if the complete absence of health (i.e., death) means the complete absence of self, then any diminishment of health must represent, correspondingly, a diminishment of self? That does not follow, for unless a disease or infirmity is severe, it may represent only a minor annoyance, diminishing our selfhood not a whit. And while it will not do to be overly sentimental about such things, it is probably the case that disease or infirmity can, in some cases, increase one's sense of selfhood (which is no reason to urge disease upon people for its possible psychological benefits). The frequent reports of those who have recovered from a serious illness that it made them appreciate life in a far more intense way than they previously had are not to be dismissed (though one wishes an easier way could be found).

Modest Conclusions

Two conclusions may be drawn. The first is that some minimal level of health is necessary if there is to be any possibility of human happiness. Only in exceptional circumstances can the good of self be long maintained in the absence of the good of the body. The second conclusion, however, is that one can be healthy without being in a state of "complete physical, mental, and social well-being." That conclusion can be justified in two ways: (a) because some degree of disease and infirmity is perfectly compatible with mental and social well-being; and (b) because it is doubtful that there ever was, or ever could be, more than a transient state of "complete physical, mental, and social well-being," for individuals or societies; that's just not the way life is or could be. Its attractiveness as an ideal is vitiated by its practical impossibility of realization. Worse than that, it positively misleads, for health becomes a goal of such all-consuming importance that it simply begs to be thwarted in its realization. The demands which the word "complete" entails set the stage for the worst false consciousness of all: the demand that life deliver perfection. Practically speaking, this demand has led, in the field of health, to a constant escalation of expectation and requirement, never ending, never satisfied.

What, then, would be a good definition of "health"? I was afraid someone was going to ask me that question. I suggest we settle on the following: "health is a state of physical well-being." That state need not be "complete," but it must be at least adequate, i.e., without significant impairment of function. It also need not encompass "mental" well-being; one can be healthy yet anxious, well yet depressed. And it surely ought not to encompass "social well-being," except insofar as that well-being will be impaired by the presence of large-scale, serious physical infirmities. Of course my definition is vague, but it would take some very fancy semantic footwork for it to be socially misused; that brat next door could not be called "sick" except when he is running a fever. This definition would not, though, preclude all social use of the language of "pathology" for other than physical disease. The image of a physically well body is a powerful one and, used carefully, it can be suggestive of the kind of wholeness and adequacy of function one might hope to see in other areas of life.

37 Why Do We Want to Be Healthy? Medicine, Autonomous Individualism, and the Community of Faith

Dennis Sansom

Eric J. Cassell, in *The Nature of Suffering and the Goals of Medicine,* observes that the medical profession is now realizing that an exclusive interest in the patient's "physical biology" does the patient an injustice. "[I]llness is a biopsychosocial phenomenon and cannot be completely described in any lesser terms. It is not that patients with diseases also have psychological or social problems, the sick are sick in all dimensions simultaneously."[1] Suffering due to pain attacks the whole person, not just a particular body part, because it debilitates the person's relationships to family, others, work, recreation, future goals, and assumed obligations. This is why, when we lose our health because of suffering from pain, we feel attacked. We value health because it is a condition by which we have enough strength (whether physical, psychological, interpersonal, and/or spiritual) to live as humans, having a personal center from which we hope to organize our lives into a meaningful whole.

The loss of health challenges our personal integrity. It disrupts our ability to be centered in the world, because it makes us too feeble to continue with the ways we have been ourselves up to that point. On a simple level we expect health care and medicine to restore our health, but actually the expectations are greater than merely removing pain from our bodies. We expect health care and medicine to help secure our integrity as humans when suffering due to pain overwhelms us.

In a sense we look to health care and medicine to empower us when we become weak due to suffering from pain. We want empowerment because we value our integrity, and we know we need health to fulfill our goals in life. Health requires power. Karl Barth notes, in *Ethics,* that the concept of health implies power as well. "[Our life] wills to be lived also in the maintaining and achieving of its possibilities, in *power.* To be healthy is to be in possession of one's physical and intellectual powers. It is to will what is necessary to achieve and assert these powers."[2] Since power must be included in an understanding of health, then it is easy to see why we expect empowerment from health care agencies and medicine. With the loss of health, we need power to regain it.

Yet it's not enough just to link health and power, and ill-health and the need for empowerment. If power is understood as the ability to accomplish certain ends, goals, or purposes (i.e., *telos*), then the *telos* determines what kind and amount of power is necessary for us. The *telos* which guides a person informs her of the means by which she lives meaningfully within society. It also defines the nature and use of power. Therefore, if we are to understand why we want to be healthy, we not only need to understand personhood, power, and the value of the health care industry, but we also need to understand our society's *telos.* Hospitals, medicine, and health care in general manifest our societal moral commitments, and it is in observing these manifestations that we see the large differences between the effects of what I shall call the "autonomous individualism of the Enlightenment" and "the community of faith of Christianity" upon our expectations for health care.

Since our society is complex, it is always risky to generalize about it, but I will venture to say that to a great extent our society's *telos* is shaped by one aspect of the Enlightenment's moral agenda — autonomous individualism. Of course that pe-

From Dennis Sansom, *Christian Scholar's Review* 23 (March 3, 1994): 300-306. Used by permission.

riod of intellectual growth and religious tolerance had many good effects (e.g., ending the sectarian wars, promoting personal responsibility in moral matters, and encouraging intellectual rigor and creativity), but we have funneled the Enlightenment's legacy into the single value of personal autonomy, which has become the moral *telos* of our liberal democracy.

The autonomous adult who freely chooses her own moral principles and who produces effectively in our free market economy is the pinnacle of our society. We are committed to removing as many obstacles as possible to achieving this autonomous, self-made personhood. We accept only those restrictions of our own choosing. Ill-health is obviously a restriction, and if in our society we are primarily committed to establishing conditions in which we can live, move, and work according to our own choosing, then we pressure the health industry to restore our autonomy. We expect the industry to take away health obstacles, and the greatest of these obstacles is death. Certainly, no one thinks that medical science can make us immortal, but nonetheless we act in a practical sense as though medical science can keep extending our lives indefinitely. We insist that medical science keep finding cures for all fatal diseases and genetic maladies, and we keep utilizing as many life-prolonging technologies as possible until the only time we choose to die is when we artificially are kept alive beyond our own sense of dignity.

In August, 1987, Daniel Callahan wrote the controversial article "Limiting Health Care for the Old?" and in it he maintained that our inability to know when to die has put undue pressures upon health care in our society. Callahan is bothered primarily by three urgent issues.[3] First, "an increasing large share of health care is going to the elderly." Second, "the elderly, in dying, consume a disproportionate share of health care costs." And third, the elderly use most of the medical technology primarily to prolong their lives. According to Callahan, we have these pressing concerns in health care because we assume that we can extend middle age with medicine's accomplishments. Because we assume that health care can keep us middle-aged, and we do not want to grow old and suffer the restrictions of aging, we conclude we do not have to grow old.

However, this attitude is the problem, according to Callahan. "By pretending that old age can be turned into a kind of endless middle age, we rob it of meaning and significance for the elderly."[4] In trying to push back the experience of death and dying, we forget our mortality and become ignorant and incapable of learning how to grow old.

We are mortal, no doubt about it, and we need to consider our mortality as part of our destiny and not deny it. However, we keep demanding that medical science invent new life-prolonging technology so that we can be resuscitated one more time to prevent death. What is missing in our modern moral vocabulary is what Callahan is urging us to revive — "a fresh vision of what it means to live a decently long and adequate life, what might be called a 'natural life span.'"[5] We need to recognize that we have physical and temporal limitations, and that knowing when to die is one of the most important attitudes to cultivate in our personal pilgrimages. The desire to stay autonomous without restrictions eventually compels us either to forget a practical sense of our mortality or to deny it.

To remedy this attitude, Callahan proposes three principles for public policy.[6] First, due to our sense of a collective social obligation, the government should help people to live out their natural life span. Second, what life-extending technology is used should be restricted to the application of the first principle. And third, beyond a patient's natural life span, the government should provide only for the relief of suffering.

Not everyone agrees with Callahan's article. Amitai Etzioni is typical of negative criticism against it.[7] Etzioni believes that Callahan's argument starts down a slippery slope with no place to stop. The argument is built on too many ambiguous ideas whose meanings would have to be changed only slightly for Callahan not to want to live with the consequences. For instance, the term "elderly" fluctuates according to death rates, general health trends, and size of population. It is conceivable that population pressures and environmental deterioration could make fifty-five-year-old people "elderly" and subject to the denial of some health care under Callahan's limitations.

Etzioni is also afraid that Callahan's policy would cause intergenerational strife between the

young and old, making the old inferior. According to Etzioni, discrimination against the elderly is contrary to democracy and undermines our society. Furthermore, Etzioni thinks Callahan would probably not want to impose draconian restrictions on cigarette smokers who disproportionately tax society's medical budget, even though he wants to impose draconian restrictions on the elderly because they do disproportionately burden society.

In Etzioni's eyes, Callahan oversteps the bounds of democracy. Yet Callahan does find a sympathic reader in Stanley Hauerwas, of Duke University. Like Callahan, Hauerwas sees one of the major issues in health care to be society's moral assumptions. In the book *Naming the Silences: God, Medicine, and the Problem of Suffering,* Hauerwas criticizes in his typical fashion the Enlightment's legacy of autonomous individualism.

> In a way, modern medicine exemplifies the predicament of the Enlightenment project, which hopes to make society a collection of individuals free from the bonds of necessity other than those we choose. In many ways that project has been accomplished, only now we have discovered that they very freedom we sought has, ironically, become a kind of bondage.[8]

Autonomous individualism is crippling society, and one way we suffer by it is in health care. As a liberal society, we want fewer and fewer inhibitions, and obviously illness and death are major restraints which prevent us from realizing the goals we choose for ourselves. We thus demand that medical science cure our illnesses and prolong our lives. We create technologies to help keep death farther from us and to give us more control of our lives.

Of course, to admit our finitude we do not need to eliminate health care or life-prolonging technology. Yet medicine should help us fulfill our creaturely limitations, not be a symptom of our practical denial of them.

Hauerwas does criticize Callahan for not being more precise about the meaning of "natural life span" and "tolerable death."

> The problem with Callahan's recommendation for a recovery of these notions is that such concepts remain far too formal. He talks, for example, about having "one's life possibilities accomplished," but what precisely does that mean? I should like to live long enough to have read all of Trollope's novels twice — but even if I accomplished that, I suspect I would want to try it three times. . . . But in the end the crucial issue is not whether one's death seems offensive to others, rather the kind of expectations we ought to have so that death, perhaps even an untimely death, is an event to be accepted — accepted with sorrow, but accepted nevertheless.

According to Hauerwas, Callahan does not go far enough in rejecting autonomous individualism, because he still assumes that our lives are our own making, but in fact, according to Hauerwas, it is truer to admit that "we more nearly discover rather than create our lives."[10]

Callahan's ideas of "natural life span" and "tolerable death" lack coherence outside of a moral tradition which enables a person to integrate her life from birth to death under what Hauerwas calls a narrative unity. The concept of narrative unity is a key notion for Hauerwas. It refers to the way a community defines the meaning of life from birth to death according to that community's moral and spiritual traditions. Such a tradition enables us to realize that illness and death need not be alien to us but can be events, as painful and as sad as they are, which do not necessarily destroy our lives' integrity and meaning.

> Interestingly, a life experienced as a narrative unit is one in which events are not experienced or remembered as foreign. A kind of fatalism in which one's life is seen as fundamentally out of control, in which one is a victim of time, is rendered impotent by a narrative construal, which allows one to integrate one's misfortunes into an ongoing framework.[11]

The Christian affirmations that our lives with all their blemishes and illnesses are not alien to God and that God promises to live with us and empower us even in our death provide a narrative unity in which sickness and dying do not rob one of a *telos.*

Theology becomes a way of telling ourselves that in the midst of our tragedies and sufferings we have a unity which cannot be taken away because the unity is given by God, and because of this theological narration about our lives in God we do not need to exhaust our lives and natural resources by trying to prevent the inevitability of illness and death. We expect medicine to give us enough power when needed to fulfill our places within the community which has given us our destinies through its moral and spiritual traditions.

Yet from the Enlightenment's legacy we expect medicine to empower us to overcome our restrictions, and this is a different justification for health care. According to Hauerwas, medicine in the Enlightenment tradition becomes a secular theodicy in which we try to justify our lives by trying to deny our creaturely finitude and the natural consequences of being mortal. With our fixation upon life-prolonging technologies we even think medicine can control our greatest foe — death. Instead of religious faith providing a hope by which we believe evil and death will not destroy our *telos*, medicine usurps the role of faith by saying that we do not need to appeal to God or a transcendent hope to integrate our lives but through science and technology we can obtain our *telos*.

If it is true, as Hauerwas implies, that underneath our appreciation and expectations for modern medicine lies a theodicy, then we ask a lot of it. We ask it to change reality. There are different kinds of theodicies. The one undergirding the Enlightenment's rationale for medicine is an "ontological theodicy," by which we desire to alter our creaturely limitations and thereby show that we can change reality to conform to our desires.

One of the consequences of the Enlightenment's *telos* of autonomous individualism is that we are exhausting our resources to pay for a health care system in which we hope that our mortality can be checked. But we can look at medicine in another way. Instead of seeing medicine as an "ontological theodicy," we can see it as a "soul-making theodicy" (to borrow a phrase from John Hick's interpretation of Irenaeus' theodicy). That is, medicine can help us mature our souls, our identity as moral and spiritual beings, by providing us with enough power when we are ill so that we can continue to live virtuously towards others and God. In this sense our *telos* in life is not autonomous individualism but living virtuously within a community of people in whom we find our purpose. If living virtuously before God within a community is our goal in life, then what we expect out of medicine is to help us have enough physical power to exhibit those virtues which build up the community in which we find our narrative unity. There comes the time in which we need to exhibit how a virtuous person dies, affirming in our dying the moral and spiritual commitments by which we discovered our own unity within the community's stories of faith. Medicine does its greatest service when it assists us in this *telos*.

We learn what is a "natural life span" and a "tolerable death" by living in a community in which we see and learn from others who have discovered their own narrative unity through their faith in God. By living in a community of faithful people who are shaped by the life, teachings, death, and resurrection of Jesus Christ, we see how people integrate their lives, how they deal with sickness and dying. The model of these relationships equips us to integrate our lives and to accept our limitations, even illness and dying. In knowing that our meaning as humans is found in what we derive and contribute to the legacy of the community of faithful people, we expect of medicine to help us bear witness to the Gospel of Jesus Christ.

Of course, in the community of faith we want just as much as in the Enlightenment's tradition to alleviate excruciating pain, to save the lives of our children, to cure diseases, and to keep ourselves healthy, but the primary difference is the goal for medicine. As long as we think our *telos* is autonomous individualism, then we will pressure medicine to empower us to overcome more and more of our physical limitations, to change our finite nature. In a sense what happens in a society shaped by the ethos of autonomous individualism is that the very plausible and common sense desire to stay healthy is distorted into the desire to live without illness and dying, a form of practical immortality.

But if our *telos* is to live faithfully within a community of people who treasure its particular spiritual and moral tradition, then we ask medicine to restore our health to us so that we may fulfill our role within the community of faith. We don't ask of medicine to do the impossible, i.e., help us to pretend we are immortal, but we ask of it to help us be healthy enough to act in ways indicative of a person who knows that the *telos* of life is not dominating over the restrictions of our natural finitude but living faithfully towards God within the community of faith.

Certainly, this justification for medical care does not prohibit further research or life-prolonging treatments. When illness or injury obviates our natural life span, then we need medical science to help us to live. But the question is — what is our natural life span? We find an answer within a community of people who understand that life's purpose is in being faithful to our spiritual and moral legacy, our families, our community of faith, and to the continuation of this tradition of believers in God. The best that we can determine within our own finitude and *telos* is that our natural life span is the amount and level of health it takes to fulfill this level of faithfulness. It may come early or it may come late. It may come with grief or it may come with peace. But all along the ultimate focus of our life becomes not how much of life we can enjoy or how much we get out of it, but how we can live and die as a faithful person. We value medical care because it can help us fulfill that *telos*.

Notes

1. Eric J. Cassell, *The Nature of Suffering and the Goals of Medicine* (Oxford: Oxford University Press, 1991), p. 206.

2. Karl Barth, *Ethics*, edited by Dietrich Braun, translated by Geoffrey W. Bromiley (Edinburgh: T. and T. Clark, 1981), pp. 129-30.

3. Daniel Callahan, "Limiting Health Care for the Old," in *Taking Sides: Clashing Views on Controversial Bioethical Issues*, third edition, edited by Carol Levine (Guilford, Connecticut: Dushkin Publishing Group, 1989), pp. 328-29.

4. Callahan, p. 331.

5. Callahan, p. 330.

6. Callahan, pp. 331-32.

7. Amitai Etzioni, "Spare the Old, Save the Young," Levine, ed., in *Taking Sides*, pp. 333-37.

8. Stanley Hauerwas, *Naming the Silences: God, Medicine, and the Problem of Suffering* (Grand Rapids: William B. Eerdmans, 1990), p. 108.

9. Hauerwas, pp. 108-9.

10. Hauerwas, p. 111.

11. Hauerwas, p. 119.

Chapter Seven:

NATURE AND ITS MASTERY

The report of some new scientific or medical breakthrough is likely to be greeted by both shouts of celebration and cries of alarm. The reasons for this may be many, but surely one of the reasons is that people have different dispositions toward nature and its mastery. Some will see in the new powers to intervene purposefully in natural processes the possibility and the promise of doing genuine good; they, of course, celebrate human mastery over nature. Others will see in the new powers the pride that sets humanity over nature rather than in it, and they complain and warn that nature will yet master presumptuous humanity.

There are reasons, too, for different dispositions toward nature, and some of them at least are religious reasons, reasons formed by a response to God and informed by reflection about God's relations to human beings and to the nature on which they depend and try to master.

Such reflection is sometimes founded on Scripture, and it can in fact be found already in Scripture. There is, for example, the blessing of God upon humanity at creation:

> Be fruitful and multiply, and fill the earth and subdue it; and have dominion over the fish of the sea and over the birds of the air and over every living creature that moves upon the earth (Genesis 1:28).

This verse has frequently provided a kind of "proof-text" for those who would celebrate human dominion or mastery over nature.[1] The historical and canonical context for these words, however, may affect the way these words shape our disposition toward nature and its mastery. If they were originally written (as many biblical scholars claim) to a people exiled to Babylon, powerless and hopeless, according to the ordinary canons of judgment, subdued and dominated themselves, then they were words of encouragement and hope. But what was blessing in one historical context may become curse in another — in the twentieth century with its technological power and pride, for example — or at least so say some who are more suspicious of technology.

The canonical context may also shape our understanding of this text and our attitudes toward nature. Scripture speaks not only of human dominion but of an intimate bonding of human beings with nature, in creation (signaled by the common root of *'adam,* "man," and *admah,* "earth"), in the curse (Genesis. 3), and decisively in the visions of renewal and shalom (e.g. Isaiah 11:6-9, Romans 8:18-25). The larger story is enough, perhaps, to remind us that we are part of nature and not simply transcendent over it, that the creation is "good," and that human beings are responsible to God for caring for it. Then our reading of "dominion" in Genesis 1 may well be that we are stewards of nature and not simply sovereigns over it. Such, at least, is the position of James Childress in selection 43.

The creation is "good," but it is not god. There was in the ancient near east a number of nature deities. Ba'al, for example, was a Canaanite fertility god who, it was believed, controlled the fertility of both womb and field; this nature deity's name meant "master." The people of God were liberated from this "master" and constantly warned against the worship of such gods. Those warnings against nature deities surely contributed to a desacralization of nature among the people of God. And that religious "disenchantment" of nature surely contributed in turn to the modern readiness to "master" nature. Today, however, some ask whether there is not a new god, a new idol, a new thing on which human beings found their hopes: technology. Daniel Callahan raises the question of extravagant and idolatrous expectations of technology in a profound way in selection 41.

It is important, of course, to say that God is God — but may human beings "play God"? The essay by Allen Verhey (selection 42) sorts through some of the meanings of the phrase and concludes not only that it means different things to different people, but also that it can be used appropriately both to warn against a certain perspective on technology and to invite people to use technology in service to the cause of God.

The issues, however, are too important to rely on slogans about "playing God," and the essays collected here raise a number of important questions about nature and its mastery. One such question is how to understand technology. Is it, as Francis Bacon — and Joseph Fletcher (in selection 40) — said, simply knowledge as power over nature in the service of human well-being? Or is it, as C. S. Lewis said (in selection 39), not simply ever "Man's power over Nature" but also always "a power of some men over other men with Nature as its instrument"? Gerald McKenny (selection 44) examines and challenges the understanding of technology in what he calls the Baconian project. He accuses conventional approaches to bioethics of complicity in this Baconian project, and he attends to the work of a number of critics of this understanding of technology, displaying their alternative accounts not only of technology but of nature and tradition and embodiment.

A related question concerns the relation of human beings to both nature and to technology. C. S. Lewis warns of "the abolition of man" if we reduce humanity to "Nature" and fail to limit and guide technology by the absolute values of what he calls the Tao. Joseph Fletcher, on the other hand, celebrates rationality and control as distinctive characteristics of both humanity and technology.

Finally, the question of the relation of technology and values must be considered. Is technology morally neutral, a set of tools with which to build the sort of world we already want? Are technological innovations, that is, simply a function of our values? Or do they shape values as well? Worth pausing over is Callahan's observation that some technologies have become socially enforced after being introduced as a way of increasing our options. If one agrees with Callahan about the need for a "cultural super-ego," where will it find the power to limit and to guide technology? From a corrective vision of ourselves in relation to nature? Or should we attempt to apply the objective moral norms which Lewis refers to as the "Tao" in order to limit and guide technology? Or should we calculate the consequences as best we can and direct innovation to the greatest good for the greatest number? What should we make of Fletcher's proposal to test technology "by a new morality of love"? Does "love" mean in the setting of society to achieve the greatest good for the greatest number? Should we, and can we, understand love in terms of the same narrative by which Christians try to understand themselves in relation to God? James Childress suggests that theology can both shape the way we see the situation and back certain principles used to assess technological innovation. He recommends attention to the consequences, to the weighing of risks and benefits, but he rejects utilitarianism, insisting on a just distribution of the risks and benefits, and urging attention to what he, following Max Weber, calls "value-rational" as well as "goal-rational" human action. He acknowledges the ambiguity of many concrete decisions about technological innovation; among his most interesting suggestions is that society should shift the burden of proof from those who are suspicious of technology to those who urge us to go forward with it.

Reports of scientific breakthroughs are likely to continue to be greeted by both shouts of celebration and cries of alarm. The assessment of particular technologies will remain sometimes difficult and ambiguous. Our dispositions and assessments, however, should be formed and informed by an appropriate vision of nature and its mastery. This chapter invites you to consider the way you envision humanity in relation to nature and both in relation to the God who has ordered and redeemed both it and us.

Notes

1. Lynn White, Jr., "The Historical Roots of Our Ecological Crisis," *Science* 155 (March 10, 1967): 1203-07.

Suggestions for Further Reading

Anderson, Bernhard W. "Human Dominion over Nature." In *Biblical Studies in Contemporary Thought,* edited by Miriam Wood (Somerville, Mass.: Green Hadden, 1975).

Cahill, Lisa Sowle, and Margaret A. Farley. *Embodiment, Morality, and Medicine* (Dordrecht, The Netherlands: Kluwer Academic Publishers, 1995).

Childress, James. "The Place of Autonomy in Bioethics," *Hastings Center Report,* 20:1 (1990): 12-17.

Campbell, Courtney. "Body, Self, and the Property Paradigm," *Hastings Center Report,* 22:5, 34-42.

Ellul, Jacques. *The Technological Society,* translated by John Wilkinson (New York: Knopf, 1965).

Geyer, Alan. "The EST Complex at MIT: The Ecumenical-Scientific-Technological Complex." *Ecumenical Review* (October 1979): 372-80.

Gustafson, James M., *Intersections: Science, Theology, and Ethics* (Cleveland, Ohio: The Pilgrim Press, 1996).

Illich, Ivan D. "Technology and Conviviality," in *To Create a Different Future,* edited by Kenneth Vaux (New York: Friendship Press, 1972).

Jonas, Hans. "Technology and Responsibilities: Reflections of the New Tasks of Ethics," in *Philosophical Essays* (Englewood Cliffs, N.J.: Prentice-Hall, 1974).

Kass, Leon R. *Toward a More Natural Science: Biology and Human Affairs* (New York: The Free Press, 1985).

Midgley, Mary. *Science as Salvation: A Modern Myth and Its Meaning* (London and New York: Routledge, 1992).

Reiser, Stanley Joel. *Medicine and the Reign of Technology* (New York: Cambridge University Press, 1978).

Shinn, Roger, ed. *Faith and Science in an Unjust World: Report of the World Council of Churches' Conference on Faith, Science and the Future,* Vol. I (Philadelphia: Fortress, 1980).

38 Ode on a Plastic Stapes

Chad Walsh

for Dr. Rufus C. Morrow, surgeon

What God hath joined together man has put
Asunder. The stapes of my middle ear
Rests in some surgical kitchen midden.
Good riddance to an otosclerotic pest.
And welcome to the vibrant plastic guest
That shivers at each noise to let me hear.

What would the theologians make of this?
The bone God gave me petered out and failed.
But God made people, too. One of them sawed
A dead bone off and put a new one in.
I hear now through a storebought plastic pin.
Where God's hand shook, his creature's skill
availed.

Dig where they bury me and you will find
A skeleton of bone perfected in plastic.
Gleam down the buried years, synthetic bone,
Await the judgment of the Resurrection,
The shining glory or the sharp correction
When calendars and clocks read chiliastic.

Will my old stapes rise, expel my plastic?
Do I own or do I merely borrow?
God is no divorce court judge. What man
Hath joined together, he will not put asunder.
Praise God who made the man who wrought
this wonder,
Praise God, give thanks tomorrow, and
tomorrow.

---

39 The Abolition of Man

C. S. Lewis

It came burning hot into my mind, whatever he said and however he flattered, when he got me home to his house, he would sell me for a slave.

Bunyan

'Man's conquest of Nature' is an expression often used to describe the progress of applied science. 'Man has Nature whacked' said someone to a friend of mine not long ago. In their context the words had a certain tragic beauty, for the speaker was dying of tuberculosis. 'No matter,' he said, 'I know I'm one of the casualties. Of course there are casualties on the winning as well as on the losing side. But that doesn't alter the fact that it is winning.' I have chosen this story as my point of departure in order to make it clear that I do not wish to disparage all that is really beneficial in the process described as 'Man's conquest,' much less all the real devotion and self-sacrifice that has gone to make it possible. But having done so I must proceed to analyse this conception a little more closely. In what sense is Man the possessor of increasing power over Nature?

Let us consider three typical examples: the aeroplane, the wireless, and the contraceptive. In a civilized community, in peace-time, anyone who can pay for them may use these things. But it cannot strictly be said that when he does so he is exercising his own proper or individual power over Nature. If I pay you to carry me, I am not therefore myself a strong man. Any or all of the three things I have mentioned can be withheld from some men by other men — by those who sell, or those who allow the sale, or those who own the sources of production, or those who make the goods. What we call Man's power is, in reality, a power possessed by some men which they may, or may not, allow other men to profit by. Again, as regards the powers manifested in the aeroplane or the wireless, Man is as much the patient or subject as the possessor, since he is the target both for bombs and for propaganda. And as regards contraceptives, there is a paradoxical, negative sense in which all possible future generations are the patients or subjects of a power wielded by those already alive. By contraception simply, they are denied existence; by contraception used as a means of selective breeding, they are, without their concurring voice, made to be what one generation, for its own reasons, may choose to prefer. From this point of view, what we call Man's power over Nature turns out to be a power exercised by some men over other men with Nature as its instrument.

It is, of course, a commonplace to complain that men have hitherto used badly, and against their fellows, the powers that science has given them. But that is not the point I am trying to make. I am not speaking of particular corruptions and abuses which an increase of moral virtue would cure: I am considering what the thing called 'Man's power over Nature' must always and essentially be. No doubt, the picture could be modified by public ownership of raw materials and factories and public control of scientific research. But unless we have a world state this will still mean the power of one nation over others. And even within the world state or the nation it will mean (in principle) the power of majorities over minorities, and (in the concrete) of a government over the people. And all long-term exercises of power, especially in breeding, must mean the power of earlier generations over later ones.

The latter point is not always sufficiently emphasized, because those who write on social matters have not yet learned to imitate the physicists by always including Time among the dimensions. In order to understand fully what Man's power over Nature, and therefore the power of some men over other men, really means, we must picture the race extended in time from the date of its emergence to that of its extinction. Each generation

From C. S. Lewis, *The Abolition of Man* (London: William Collins Sons & Co. Ltd., 1946). Used by permission.

exercises power over its successors: and each, in so far as it modifies the environment bequeathed to it and rebels against tradition, resists and limits the power of its predecessors. This modifies the picture which is sometimes painted of a progressive emancipation from tradition and a progressive control of natural processes resulting in a continual increase of human power. In reality, of course, if any one age really attains, by eugenics and scientific education, the power to make its descendants what it pleases, all men who live after it are the patients of that power. They are weaker, not stronger: for though we may have put wonderful machines in their hands we have preordained how they are to use them. And if, as is almost certain, the age which had thus attained maximum power over posterity were also the age most emancipated from tradition, it would be engaged in reducing the power of its predecessors almost as drastically as that of its successors. And we must also remember that, quite apart from this, the later a generation comes — the nearer it lives to that date at which the species becomes extinct — the less power it will have in the forward direction, because its subjects will be so few. There is therefore no question of a power vested in the race as a whole steadily growing as long as the race survives. The last men, far from being the heirs of power, will be of all men most subject to the dead hand of the great planners and conditioners and will themselves exercise least power upon the future. The real picture is that of one dominant age — let us suppose the hundredth century A.D. — which resists all previous ages most successfully and dominates all subsequent ages most irresistibly, and thus is the real master of the human species. But even within this master generation (itself an infinitesimal minority of the species) the power will be exercised by a minority smaller still. Man's conquest of Nature, if the dreams of some scientific planners are realized, means the rule of a few hundreds of men over billions upon billions of men. There neither is nor can be any simple increase of power on Man's side. Each new power won *by* man is a power *over* man as well. Each advance leaves him weaker as well as stronger. In every victory, besides being the general who triumphs, he is also the prisoner who follows the triumphal car.

I am not yet considering whether the total result of such ambivalent victories is a good thing or a bad. I am only making clear what Man's conquest of Nature really means and especially that final stage in the conquest, which, perhaps, is not far off. The final stage is come when Man by eugenics, by pre-natal conditioning, and by an education and propaganda based on a perfect applied psychology, has obtained full control over himself. *Human* nature will be the last part of Nature to surrender to Man. The battle will then be won. We shall have 'taken the thread of life out of the hand of Clotho' and be henceforth free to make our species whatever we wish to be. The battle will indeed be won. But who, precisely, will have won it?

For the power of Man to make himself what he pleases means, as we have seen, the power of some men to make other men what *they* please. In all ages, no doubt, nurture and instruction have, in some sense, attempted to exercise this power. But the situation to which we must look forward will be novel in two respects. In the first place, the power will be enormously increased. Hitherto the plans of educationalists have achieved very little of what they attempted and indeed, when we read them — how Plato would have every infant 'a bastard nursed in a bureau,' and Elyot would have the boy see no men before the age of seven and, after that, no women,[1] and how Locke wants children to have leaky shoes and no turn for poetry[2] — we may well thank the beneficent obstinacy of real mothers, real nurses, and (above all) real children for preserving the human race in such sanity as it still possesses. But the man-moulders of the new age will be armed with the powers of an omnicompetent state and an irresistible scientific technique: we shall get at last a race of conditioners who really can cut out all posterity in what shape they please. The second difference is even more important. In the older systems both the kind of man the teachers wished to produce and their motives for producing him were prescribed by the *Tao**— a norm to which the teachers themselves were subject and from which they claimed

*What Lewis calls the *Tao* is "the doctrine of objective value, the belief that certain attitudes are really true, and others really false, to the kind of thing the universe is and the kinds of things we are." *The Abolition of Man* (New York: Macmillan, 1962), p. 29. — Ed.

no liberty to depart. They did not cut men to some pattern they had chosen. They handed on what they had received: they initiated the young neophyte into the mystery of humanity which over-arched him and them alike. It was but old birds teaching young birds to fly. This will be changed. Values are now mere natural phenomena. Judgements of value are to be produced in the pupil as part of the conditioning. Whatever *Tao* there is will be the product, not the motive, of education. The conditioners have been emancipated from all that. It is one more part of Nature which they have conquered. The ultimate springs of human action are no longer, for them, something given. They have surrendered — like electricity: it is the function of the Conditioners to control, not to obey them. They know how to *produce* conscience and decide what kind of conscience they will produce. They themselves are outside, above. For we are assuming the last stage of Man's struggle with Nature. The final victory has been won. Human nature has been conquered — and, of course, has conquered, in whatever sense those words may now bear.

The Conditioners, then, are to choose what kind of artificial *Tao* they will, for their own good reasons, produce in the Human race. They are the motivators, the creators of motives. But how are they going to be motivated themselves? For a time, perhaps, by survivals, within their own minds, of the old 'natural' *Tao*. Thus at first they may look upon themselves as servants and guardians of humanity and conceive that they had a 'duty' to do it 'good.' But it is only by confusion that they can remain in this state. They recognize the concept of duty as the result of certain processes which they can now control. Their victory has consisted precisely in emerging from the state in which they were acted upon by those processes to the state in which they use them as tools. One of the things they now have to decide is whether they will or will not, so condition the rest of us that we can go on having the old idea of duty and the old reactions to it. How can duty help them to decide that? Duty itself is up for trial: it cannot also be the judge. And 'good' fares no better. They know quite well how to produce a dozen different conceptions of good in us. The question is which, if any, they should produce. No conception of good can help them to decide. It is absurd to fix on one of the things they are comparing and make it the standard of comparison.

To some it will appear that I am inventing a factitious difficulty for my Conditioners. Other, more simple-minded, critics may ask 'Why should you suppose they will be such bad men?' But I am not supposing them to be bad men. They are, rather, not men (in the old sense) at all. They are, if you like, men who have sacrificed their own share in traditional humanity in order to devote themselves to the task of deciding what 'Humanity' shall henceforth mean. 'Good' and 'bad,' applied to them, are words without content: for it is from them that the content of these words is henceforward to be derived. Nor is their difficulty factitious. We might suppose that it was possible to say 'After all, most of us want more or less the same things — food and drink and sexual intercourse, amusement, art, science, and the longest possible life for individuals and for the species. Let them simply say, This is what we happen to like, and go on to condition men in the way most likely to produce it. Where's the trouble?' But this will not answer. In the first place, it is false that we all really like the same things. But even if we did, what motive is to impel the Conditioners to scorn delights and live laborious days in order that we, and posterity, may have what we like? Their duty? But that is only the *Tao*, which they may decide to impose on us, but which cannot be valid for them. If they accept it, then they are no longer the makers of conscience but still its subjects, and their final conquest over Nature has not really happened. The preservation of the species? But why should the species be preserved? One of the questions before them is whether this feeling for posterity (they know well how it is produced) shall be continued or not. However far they go back, or down, they can find no ground to stand on. Every motive they try to act on becomes at once a *petitio*. It is not that they are bad men. They are not men at all. Stepping outside the *Tao*, they have stepped into the void. Nor are their subjects necessarily unhappy men. They are not men at all: they are artefacts. Man's final conquest has proved to be the abolition of Man.

Yet the Conditioners will act. When I said just now that all motives fail them, I should have said all motives except one. All motives that claim any validity other than that of their felt emotional weight at a given moment have failed them. Everything except the *sic volo, sic jubeo* has been explained away. But what never claimed objectivity cannot be destroyed by subjectivism. The impulse to scratch when I itch or to pull to pieces when I am inquisitive is immune from the solvent which is fatal to my justice, or honour, or care for posterity. When all that says 'it is good' has been debunked, what says 'I want' remains. It cannot be exploded or 'seen through' because it never had any pretensions. The Conditioners, therefore, must come to be motivated simply by their own pleasure. I am not here speaking of the corrupting influence of power nor expressing the fear that under it our Conditioners will degenerate. The very words *corrupt* and *degenerate* imply a doctrine of value and are therefore meaningless in this context. My point is that those who stand outside all judgements of value cannot have any ground for preferring one of their own impulses to another except the emotional strength of that impulse. We may legitimately hope that among the impulses which arise in minds thus emptied of all 'rational' or 'spiritual' motives, some will be benevolent. I am very doubtful myself whether the benevolent impulses, stripped of that preference and encouragement which the *Tao* teaches us to give them and left to their merely natural strength and frequency as psychological events, will have much influence. I am very doubtful whether history shows us one example of a man who, having stepped outside traditional morality and attained power, has used that power benevolently. I am inclined to think that the Conditioners will hate the conditioned. Though regarding as an illusion the artificial conscience which they produce in us their subjects, they will yet perceive that it creates in us an illusion of meaning for our lives which compares favourably with the futility of their own: and they will envy us as eunuchs envy men. But I do not insist on this, for it is mere conjecture. What is not conjecture is that our hope even of a 'conditioned' happiness rests on what is ordinarily called 'chance' — the chance that benevolent impulses may on the whole predominate in our Conditioners. For without the judgement 'Benevolence is good' — that is, without re-entering the *Tao* — they can have no ground for promoting or stabilizing their benevolent impulses rather than any others. By the logic of their position they must just take their impulses as they come, from chance. And Chance here means nature. It is from heredity, digestion, the weather, and the association of ideas, that the motives of the Conditioners will spring. Their extreme rationalism, by 'seeing through' all 'rational' motives, leaves them creatures of wholly irrational behaviour. If you will not obey the *Tao*, or else commit suicide, obedience to impulse (and therefore, in the long run, to mere 'nature') is the only course left open.

At the moment, then, of Man's victory over Nature, we find the whole human race subjected to some individual men, and those individuals subjected to that in themselves which is purely 'natural' — to their irrational impulses. Nature, untrammelled by values, rules the Conditioners and, through them, all humanity. Man's conquest of Nature turns out, in the moment of its consummation, to be Nature's conquest of Man. Every victory we seemed to win has led us, step by step, to this conclusion. All Nature's apparent reverses have been but tactical withdrawals. We thought we were beating her back when she was luring us on. What looked to us like hands held up in surrender was really the opening of arms to enfold us for ever. If the fully planned and conditioned world (with its *Tao* a mere product of the planning) comes into existence, Nature will be troubled no more by the restive species that rose in revolt against her so many millions of years ago, will be vexed no longer by its chatter of truth and mercy and beauty and happiness. *Ferum victorem cepit:* and if the eugenics are efficient enough there will be no second revolt, but all snug beneath the conditioners, and the Conditioners beneath her, till the moon falls or the sun grows cold.

My point may be clearer to some if it is put in a different form. Nature is a word of varying meanings, which can best be understood if we consider its various opposites. The Natural is the opposite of the Artificial, the Civil, the Human, the Spiritual, and the Supernatural. The Artificial does not now concern us. If we take the rest of the list of opposites, however, I think we can get a rough idea of what men have meant by Nature and what it is they oppose to her. Nature seems to be the spatial and temporal, as distinct from what is less fully so or not so at all. She seems to be the world of quantity, as against the world of quality: of objects as against consciousness: of the bound, as against the wholly or partially autonomous: of that which knows no values as against that which both has and perceives value: of efficient causes (or, in some modern systems, of no causality at all) as against final causes. Now I take it that when we understand a thing analytically and then dominate and use it for our own convenience we reduce it to the level of 'Nature' in the sense that we suspend our judgements of value about it, ignore its final cause (if any), and treat it in terms of quantity. This repression of elements in what would otherwise be our total reaction to it is sometimes very noticeable and even painful: something has to be overcome before we can cut up a dead man or a live animal in a dissecting room. These objects *resist* the movement of the mind whereby we thrust them into the world of mere Nature. But in other instances too, a similar price is exacted for our analytical knowledge and manipulative power, even if we have ceased to count it. We do not look at trees either as Dryads or as beautiful objects while we cut them into beams: the first man who did so may have felt the price keenly, and the bleeding trees in Virgil and Spenser may be far-off echoes of that primeval sense of impiety. The stars lost their divinity as astronomy developed, and the Dying God has no place in chemical agriculture. To many, no doubt, this process is simply the gradual discovery that the real world is different from what we expected, and the old opposition to Galileo or to 'body-snatchers' is simply obscurantism. But that is not the whole story. It is not the greatest of modern scientists who feel most sure that the object, stripped of its qualitative properties and reduced to mere quantity, is wholly real. Little scientists, and little unscientific followers of science, may think so. The great minds know very well that the object, so treated, is an artificial abstraction, that something of its reality has been lost.

From this point of view the conquest of Nature appears in a new light. We reduce things to mere Nature *in order that* we may 'conquer' them. We are always conquering Nature, because 'Nature' is the name for what we have, to some extent, conquered. The price of conquest is to treat a thing as mere Nature. Every conquest over Nature increases her domain. The stars do not become Nature till we can weigh and measure them: the soul does not become Nature till we can psychoanalyse her. The wresting of powers *from* Nature is also the surrendering of things *to* Nature. As long as this process stops short of the final stage we may well hold that the gain outweighs the loss. But as soon as we take the final step of reducing our own species to the level of mere Nature, the whole process is stultified, for this time the being who stood to gain and the being who has been sacrificed are one and the same. This is one of the many instances where to carry a principle to what seems its logical conclusion produces absurdity. It is like the famous Irishman who found that a certain kind of stove reduced his fuel bill by half and thence concluded that two stoves of the same kind would enable him to warm his house with no fuel at all. It is the magician's bargain: give up our soul, get power in return. But once our souls, that is, our selves, have been given up, the power thus conferred will not belong to us. We shall in fact be the slaves and puppets of that to which we have given our souls. It is in Man's power to treat himself as a mere 'natural object' and his own judgements of value as raw material for scientific manipulation to alter at will. The objection to his doing so does not lie in the fact that this point of view (like one's first day in a dissecting room) is painful and shocking till we grow used to it. The pain and the shock are at most a warning and a symptom. The real objection is that if man chooses to treat himself as raw material, raw material he will be: not raw material to be manipulated, as he fondly imagined, by himself, but by mere appetite, that is, mere Nature, in the person of his dehumanized Conditioners.

We have been trying, like Lear, to have it both ways: to lay down our human prerogative and yet at the same time to retain it. It is impossible. Either we are rational spirit obliged for ever to obey the absolute values of the *Tao*, or else we are mere nature to be kneaded and cut into new shapes for the pleasures of masters who must, by hypothesis, have no motive but their own 'natural' impulses. Only the *Tao* provides a common human law of action which can over-arch rulers and ruled alike. A dogmatic belief in objective value is necessary to the very idea of a rule which is not tyranny or an obedience which is not slavery.

I am not here thinking solely, perhaps not even chiefly, of those who are our public enemies at the moment. The process which, if not checked, will abolish Man, goes on apace among Communists and Democrats no less than among Fascists. The methods may (at first) differ in brutality. But many a mild-eyed scientist in pince-nez, many a popular dramatist, many an amateur philosopher in our midst, means in the long run just the same as the Nazi rulers of Germany. Traditional values are to be 'debunked' and mankind to be cut out into some fresh shape at the will (which must, by hypothesis, be an arbitrary will) of some few lucky people in one lucky generation which has learned how to do it. The belief that we can invent 'ideologies' at pleasure, and the consequent treatment of mankind as mere ὕλη, specimens, preparations, begins to affect our very language. Once we killed bad men: now we liquidate unsocial elements. Virtue has become *integration* and diligence *dynamism,* and boys likely to be worthy of a commission are 'potential officer material.' Most wonderful of all, the virtues of thrift and temperance, and even of ordinary intelligence, are *sales-resistance.*

The true significance of what is going on has been concealed by the use of the abstraction Man. Not that the word Man is necessarily a pure abstraction. In the *Tao* itself, as long as we remain within it, we find the concrete reality in which to participate is to be truly human: the real common will and common reason of humanity, alive, and growing like a tree, and branching out, as the situation varies, into ever new beauties and dignities of application. While we speak from within the *Tao* we can speak of Man having power over himself in a sense truly analogous to an individual's self-control. But the moment we step outside and regard the *Tao* as a mere subjective product, this possibility has disappeared. What is now common to all men is a mere abstract universal, an H. C. F., and Man's conquest of himself means simply the rule of the Conditioners over the conditioned human material, the world of post-humanity which, some knowingly and some unknowingly, nearly all men in all nations are at present labouring to produce.

Nothing I can say will prevent some people from describing this lecture as an attack on science. I deny the charge, of course: and real Natural Philosophers (there are some now alive) will perceive that in defending value I defend *inter alia* the value of knowledge, which must die like every other when its roots in the *Tao* are cut. But I can go further than that. I even suggest that from Science herself the cure might come. I have described as a 'magician's bargain' that process whereby man surrenders object after object, and finally himself, to Nature in return for power. And I meant what I said. The fact that the scientist has succeeded where the magician failed has put such a wide contrast between them in popular thought that the real story of the birth of Science is misunderstood. You will even find people who write about the sixteenth century as if Magic were a medieval survival and Science the new thing that came in to sweep it away. Those who have studied the period know better. There was very little magic in the Middle Ages: the sixteenth and seventeenth centuries are the high noon of magic. The serious magical endeavor and the serious scientific endeavour are twins: one was sickly and died, the other strong and throve. But they were twins. They were born of the same impulse. I allow that some (certainly not all) of the early scientists were actuated by a pure love of knowledge. But if we consider the temper of that age as a whole we can discern the impulse of which I speak. There is something which unites magic and applied science while separating both from the 'wisdom' of earlier ages. For the wise men of old the cardinal problem had been how to conform the soul to reality, and the solution had been knowledge, self-discipline, and virtue. For magic and applied science alike the problem is how to subdue reality to the wishes of men: the solution is a technique; and both, in the practice of this technique, are ready to do things hitherto regarded as disgusting and impious — such as digging up and mutilating the dead. If we compare the chief trumpeter of the new era (Bacon) with Marlowe's Faustus, the similarity is striking. You will read in some critics that Faustus has a thirst for knowledge. In reality, he hardly mentions it. It is not truth he wants from his devils, but gold and guns and girls. 'All things that move between the quiet poles shall be at his command' and 'a sound magician is a mighty god.'[3] In the same spirit Bacon condemns those who value knowledge as an end in itself: this, for him, is to use as a mistress for pleasure what ought to be a spouse for fruit.[4] The true object is to extend Man's power to the performance of all things possible. He rejects magic because it does not work,[5] but his goal is that of the magician. In

Paracelsus the characters of magician and scientist are combined. No doubt those who really founded modern science were usually those whose love of truth exceeded their love of power; in every mixed movement the efficacy comes from the good elements not from the bad. But the presence of the bad elements is not irrelevant to the direction the efficacy takes. It might be going too far to say that the modern scientific movement was tainted from its birth: but I think it would be true to say that it was born in an unhealthy neighbourhood and at an inauspicious hour. Its triumphs may have been too rapid and purchased at too high a price: reconsideration, and something like repentance, may be required.

Is it, then, possible to imagine a new Natural Philosophy, continually conscious that the 'natural object' produced by analysis and abstraction is not reality but only a view, and always correcting the abstraction? I hardly know what I am asking for. I hear rumours that Goethe's approach to nature deserves fuller consideration — that even Dr. Steiner may have seen something that orthodox researchers have missed. The regenerate science which I have in mind would not do even to minerals and vegetables what modern science threatens to do to man himself. When it explained it would not explain away. When it spoke of the parts it would remember the whole. While studying the *It* it would not lose what Martin Buber calls the *Thou*-situation. The analogy between the *Tao* of Man and the instincts of an animal species would mean for it new light cast on the unknown thing, Instinct, by the only known reality of conscience and not a reduction of conscience to the category of Instinct. Its followers would not be free with the words *only* and *merely*. In a word, it would conquer Nature without being at the same time conquered by her and buy knowledge at a lower cost than that of life.

Perhaps I am asking impossibilities. Perhaps, in the nature of things, analytical understanding must always be a basilisk which kills what it sees and only sees by killing. But if the scientists themselves cannot arrest this process before it reaches the common Reason and kills that too, then someone else must arrest it. What I most fear is the reply that I am 'only one more' obscurantist, that this barrier, like all previous barriers set up against the advance of science, can be safely passed. Such a reply springs from the fatal serialism of the modern imagination — the image of infinite unilinear progression which so haunts our minds. Because we have to use numbers so much we tend to think of every process as if it must be like the numeral series, where every step, to all eternity, is the same kind of step as the one before. I implore you to remember the Irishman and his two stoves. There are progressions in which the last step is *sui generis* — incommensurable with the others — and in which to go the whole way is to undo all the labour of your previous journey. To reduce the *Tao* to a mere natural product is a step of that kind. Up to that point, the kind of explanation which explains things away may give us something, though at a heavy cost. But you cannot go on 'explaining away' for ever: you will find that you have explained explanation itself away. You cannot go on 'seeing through' things for ever. The whole point of seeing through something is to see something through it. It is good that the window should be transparent, because the street or garden beyond it is opaque. How if you saw through the garden too? It is no use trying to 'see through' first principles. If you see through everything, then everything is transparent. But a wholly transparent world is an invisible world. To 'see through' all things is the same as not to see.

Notes

1. *The Boke Named the Governour,* I. iv: 'Al men except physitions only shulde be excluded and kepte out of the norisery.' I. VI: 'After that a childe is come to seuen yeres of age . . . The most sure counsaile is to withdrawe him from all company of women.'

2. *Some Thoughts Concerning Education,* § 7: 'I will also advise his *Feet to be wash'd* every Day in cold Water, and to have his Shoes so thin that they might leak and *let in Water,* whenever he comes near it.' § 174: 'If he have a poetick vein, 'tis to me the strangest thing in the World that the Father should desire or suffer it to be cherished or improved. Methinks the Parents should labour to have it stifled and suppressed as much as may be.' Yet Locke is one of our most sensible writers on education.

3. *Dr. Faustus,* 77-90.

4. *Advancement of Learning,* Bk. I (p. 60 in Ellis and Spedding, 1905; p. 35 in Everyman Edn.).

5. *Filum Labyrinthi,* i.

40 Technological Devices in Medical Care

Joseph Fletcher

A mass circulation magazine recently ran a two-page advertisement by General Electric which showed an eight-year-old boy at play in the fields. The ad explained how an implanted pacemaker maintains a 92 per minute beat in Brian Coe's heart. The caption read, "This boy's heart runs on batteries." Such devices are at work in patients from six-month-old girls to ninety-four-year-old men. "Helping people live longer," said the advertisement, "is progress of the most important kind."

The Terms and Ideas We Use

When we submit technological devices to ethical analysis, we need first to be clear about what we mean by "technological" and what we mean by a "device." Too often, I think, we use the concept of technology in a narrow way, doing less than justice to its practitioners and their triumphs. In the popular image, for example, the term "technology usually connotes a gadget, a mechanical tool or arrangement of some kind. Indeed, the common error is precisely to conceive of technology as a matter of mechanics. And the same is true of devices — they are thought of as more or less ingeniously "devised" mechanical tools or arrangements. But this mechanical model is far from adequate for the ethical evaluation of technology as it plays its part (an increasingly essential part) in medical care.

Arnold Toynbee has spoken of "technology's relentless progress," and it is my own belief that technology, with its often revolutionary innovations in how we do things, is the source or cause of the most pressing problems of ethics. Either it poses perennial problems of good and evil in significantly new forms, or it confronts us with new problems of conscience, new in the sense that they are unanticipated and often even seemingly bizarre. This happens in medicine fully as much as in industry or war or communications or any other field. In a moment we shall have occasions to look at some typical examples.

But first, there are various ways to think technology. Another word for it could be "techniquery." It is indeed a matter of devices or of "devising" ways and means. It is at bottom a matter of process, innovation, method. Nevertheless, technology is far more than merely ingenious. It is a knowledgeable combination of information and skill, of know-what (science) and know-how (technology). In its bluntest definition, it is applied science. It is the scientifically disciplined and sophisticated invention of devices to serve the ends or goals or "goods" we cherish. In medicine these ends are health and life and psychophysical well-being. As a matter of means and ends, therefore, technology is of the greatest direct ethical concern. Perhaps the best definition is Webster's: "the totality of the means employed to provide objects necessary for human sustenance and comfort."[1]

But let me repeat: technology — perhaps especially in medicine — is far from being a matter of mechanics only. The "hardware" is less important than the "software." In medicine, the systems engineering of technology is not only mechanical but also chemical, biological, physical, psychological, and surgical. . . .

The Influence of Technology

Technology . . . is changing more than just man's environment and his tools: it is changing man himself. Hence our recent more mature and scientific interest in ecology. "Once men start down the technological road," says Roger Revelle, "they can-

---

Reprinted from *Who Shall Live* by Kenneth Vaux,

not turn back. Once they have bitten into the fruit of the tree of knowledge, there can be no return to Eden."[2] As I put it sometime ago at the Mayo medical center, we have reached the end of the age of innocence, that is, of ignorance, and the end of ignorance means the end of alibis and excuses.[3]

Every widening or deepening of our knowledge of reality and our control of its forces adds to our ethical problems; knowledge and control are the ingredients of both freedom and responsibility. Less and less are we the helpless and therefore nonmoral victims of whatever life happens to bring us — and by "life" here I mean not only circumstances but the vital principle of biological life itself. Knowledge and virtue have always been coupled, as by Confucius and Socrates — an association recently reexamined by the English biologist C. H. Waddington in his essay *The Ethical Animal*,[4] and by Rene Dubos in *Adapting Man*.[5]

As Pascal thought, the problem of ethics is "*travailler à bien penser*," "to work hard at good thinking." Not feeling or guessing, but thinking and knowing. "Let us," he said, "strive to think well — therein is the principle of morality."[6] And Kant called ethics "practical reason." In this spirit we can say that the heart of the problems of medical ethics is the science and technology at stake in them, along with a willingness to see our values and goals in the fresh light of fresh developments, and even to add to or abstract from them as the data suggest. I would be the first to echo the opinion of J. Robert Oppenheimer, who said, "I believe the strength and soundness of Christian sensibility, the meaning of love and charity, have changed the world at least as much as technological developments." But as Oppenheimer suggests, I want to insist that it is in love working with technology, not in love alone, that we find the key to human hopes. . . .

The Ethical Problems Posed

The picture of what has happened in the technology of medicine and paramedical care fills us, ambivalently, with fear and confidence, assurance and doubt — both as to the facts themselves and as to the value-meaning of the facts, their ethical significances. For example, how are we to regard the prospect of human hibernation for short periods (hours or days) and later for longer periods (months or years), as cryonics develops from its present uses as "deep freeze" for surgical purposes? What will the surgical use of laser beams ultimately entail (besides the dangers of the so-called death ray)? Genetic control of the basic human constitution by microbiological manipulation of "code" material, DNA and RNA, is at hand. Is there any cause to be squeamish or chary about using techniques for cosmetic changes of human features, figure, complexion, skin color, and even physique? Or the more radical technology of chemotherapy in controlling fatigue, relaxation, alertness, mood, sleep, personality, perception, and fantasies? Lurking behind all such questioning is the factor of control: We wonder whether we may establish and exercise management of the very essentials of personal identity and existence. The question really is not whether we can but whether we should. We can do it, but the ethical question is: Ought we to?

Chemotherapy is far less challenging morally than the immediate or prospective manipulations of psycho-pharmacology, for example, in changing the chemical composition of the nervous system, its neurons and chemical transmitters of impulses, or than the chemical control and improvement of memory and learning (even, theoretically, programmed dreams). The very concepts of choice, chance, self, and rationality, so central to classical or traditional reasoning, may have to be altered or even "reconceptualized."

Take the notion of "identity," a notion so prominent in the current rhetoric of psychology, especially under the influence of Erikson's thesis about the identity crisis. Given the present and future trends in cyborg medicine, one may well ask: Who is it that functions physiologically with borrowed or artificial veins and arteries (whether synthetic or plastic), bone structures, prosthetic devices, cardiac implants — including even donated aortas or whole hearts — audio and visual aids, manipulators and pedipulators, donated kidneys, or artificial dialysis for kidney function, artificial kidneys and hearts powered by isotopic energy, and many other technological devices, logically ending in a sort of *ultima ratio* with transplanted brains?

Who is the child born as a result of predetermined sex, germinal selection, genetic control, and artificial mutations — and after birth modified not only by cyborg technology but by chemical and electronic means, for example, by effective appetite controls and weight controls, electric brain stimulation by electrodes and surgical subcuts, endocrine alterations, and the like?

For just as we once reached the point at which diabetics could regulate the sugar in their blood systems, so we will have autocontrol of mood and intelligence. Who, then, is who? How will we think of it when theoretical brain transplants become operational? As they say, today's "science fiction" is tomorrow's science.

Who *is* the recipient patient — is he the pre-operative person or the donor? This kind of basic conceptual question, like the one about when and what is death, will inevitably change not only the language but also the mental constructs with which we think about moral values, ethical responsibility, and even the very notion of the moral agent himself.

What are our licit or morally justifiable choices, initiatives, and purposes as we employ the technology of medicine? What are the values we should seek or preserve — such as freedom from pain, health, euphoria, even life itself — and in what order of relative desirability are we to rank them? What comes first as the *summum bonum,* in the sense that, if necessary, all else is to be subordinated or sacrificed? Life? Self-image? Personal survival? Social welfare? In the conventional wisdom nearly all such questions have been almost ignored, or their answers complacently assumed. But technology has a way of undermining conventions, of changing the world, and with it our values and priorities.

The Problem of Control

As I remarked earlier, my own opinion is that, morally, the heart of the matter is control. The question is whether human beings may choose or make the conditions of life, health, and death. (I am sure that death control, as in direct or indirect euthanasia, is as much a part of modern medicine as birth control and health control are.) The key to control, however, is initiative. True control of life puts the initiative in man's hands; that is, it is a matter of choice. Nothing not chosen has ethical importance. Babies born by chance rather than choice may be precious, but their birth is amoral if not actually immoral. A patient who dies in personality-blotting suffering, or after personality is gone and irretrievable, may be an object of compassion, but his actual dying is nonmoral and his own relationship to it is either amoral or immoral, as is that of his medical servants as well.

What we do when we can do it, by our own choice, initiative, and purposiveness, is moral action — either right or wrong, as the case may be. If we refuse to do what we can when we can, on the ground that we may not or ought not to take the initiative, this is nonmoral and antiethical — I would even add "subhuman," because truly human acts are moral, that is, free and responsible. For example, not to take the initiative by using a Bennett valve and mask in a case of respiratory failure on the operating table might in a concrete situation be a responsible decision to let the patient go. Such a decision might, for example, be made for a nonagenarian patient with grievously metastasized cancer. But *never* to revive artificially a patient whose respiration fails would be immoral, that is, it would be a refusal to exercise initiative and choice. It would be irresponsible and therefore immoral.

A great deal of ethical reasoning in the past has been of this immoral kind — arguing against initiative and human control on grounds that it is allegedly "unnatural" or "against nature." That kind of ethics simply cannot survive in a technological civilization. "Nature" and "human nature" are no more fixed and finished than any of the other concepts moralists like to posit. In Catholic moral theology it used to be held that we are only tenants of our bodies, that we may not alter them because we have only their usufruct, not their dominion. As stewards, not proprietors, of our bodies we have charge only of the *bene esse,* not of the *esse.* Hence, no mutilation was morally justified, except to preserve life. This ruled out donations of organs such as kidneys and ovaries, as well as free decision for or against the new transformations possible as a result of scientific and technical development. But that old morality of nature is being superseded, happily, by a new morality of love. What this means, for example, is that those who have courage will gladly risk the sacrifice of one of their kidneys for a friend, thus deliberately reducing their own survival quotient by half; or that a nun who has embraced the vocation of childlessness will eagerly donate an ovary to a sterile patient.

The new morality of situation ethics has little patience with those who object in principle to heart transplants from cadaveric donors. Such a position has been taken by Dr. Werner Forssmann, chief surgeon at the Düsseldorf Evangelical Hospital and Nobel prize winner in medicine for 1956. In commenting on Christian Barnard's successful transplants in South Africa, he said such transplants are morally dangerous because they involve a third person, the donor, as well as the doctor and the recipient patient, and because they offend against the medical rule *nil nacere,* "hurt nothing." There is a danger, of course, that surgeons will sacrifice the chances of one patient for the sake of the other, that this will lead, for example, to executing criminals in order to get vital organs, and to an inequitable tendency to select recipients on the basis of wealth, personal friendship, or politics. On the other hand, most Catholic moralists already say that "it is morally permissible to transfer parts from a corpse to a living person,"[7] and in Dr. Barnard's interview with the pope no objections were voiced. I am myself convinced that we must stick to the maxim of most moralists, *abusus non tollit usum,"* the abuse of the thing does not bar its use." As Raymond Queneau once said, "The people who whine about naughty robots and inhuman machinery have never proved anything except their own lack of imagination and fear of liberty."[8] As the old saw put it, "conscience" gets a lot of credit that belongs to cold feet.

Dr. Forssmann also believes that it was wrong to put a pig's liver in a dying woman in Buenos Aires — presumably on the ground that heterografts or xenogenic (i.e., interspecific) transplants are "unnatural." By this logic we would, for example, have to give up the transplantation of monkeys' thymus glands into cancerous patients' thighs in an effort to let the antibodies help in the struggle against the neoplasm. This will be a hard kind of classicism to maintain as immunosuppressive techniques overcome the rejection reaction, and as better antigen typing and tissue preservation are developed.[9] It is a matter of time, that is all, until herds of animals are raised directly for human spare parts — cows, swine, chimpanzees, and the like. Already, barely on the threshold of transplant technique, we have only a sad short-supply of paired organs (livers, lungs, hearts) for postmortem donation, and of nonpaired organs (kidneys, ovaries, testes) for pre- or postmortem donation. Even if we could discourage the present subethical practice of burying or burning (cremating) precious vital organs — here is immorality ritualized — there still would be a need for interspecific supplies.

One of the ethical issues at stake, then, is whether any procedure or process is, as such, to be proscribed as always wrong for some intrinsic reason. A hundred years ago dissection of human bodies was forbidden, so that grave robber and medical student meant the same thing; yet all that is gone by now — a mythology demythologized. For some people abortion is still held to be immoral in all cases except when necessary to preserve the life and/or health of a patient. But unlike this absolutism (really a mystique) of the old morality, the new morality decides the right or the wrong of medical treatments relatively, according to the factors in each situation. If, for example, there is at least a 25 percent chance that a PKU child (phenylketonuric) will be born of a union of PKU heterozygotes, producing a retarded child, why not abort? Especially if normal children can be adopted or conceived by artificial insemination from a donor? Why submit to the cruel working of subhuman physical nature? Technology by its very principle and method substitutes human control for nature's control — and holds, indeed, that control is a word appropriate only to the moral decisions of people and inappropriate to the determinism of mindless processes. As a writer in the *British Medical Journal* once put it very simply, "Each case must be judged on its merits." . . .

"Playing God"

At this point somebody always cries, "You are playing God!" I think the only honest and constructive reply is, "Yes, we are." This is part of the meaning of the Bible's creation and "fall" myths. By gaining know-what and know-how we become responsible, by eating the fruit of the tree of knowledge we make ourselves "like God" — whose superiority is threatened by man's inquiry and invention. But that old, primitive God is dead, that God of the gaps, the God whose majesty and power derived from man's ignorance. That God was God because of human ignorance and fear, and he has been dying by inches with the advance of human knowledge and control over life and death which knowledge brings to man. In the matter of human knowledge we are indeed "playing the God of the gaps." If such achievements as ectogenetic reproduction, genetic control, and the production (not creation) of life in a test tube shakes anybody's faith, then his God is only one that plugs up the gaps in his knowledge, a hypothesis of ignorance. If we have to say goodbye to God because science solves the mysteries of life and technology gives us control of life, then our God is only a doomed idol.

What we need then is a new God. It is better to believe in God as creator, the creative principle behind all the workings of nature and of human achievement. He is as much the will and the love behind a test tube as behind "natural phenomena." This God can be worshiped as the other no longer can. After all, as Eric Ambler once said, "If there is such a thing as a super-human law, it is administered with subhuman inefficiency."[10]

We must get rid of that obsolete theodicy which imagines that God is not only the cause but the builder of nature and its works, and not only the builder but the manager — so that it is God himself who is the efficient as well as the final cause of earthquake and fire, of life and death, with the logical inference that "interference with nature" (which is precisely what medicine and technology are) is "playing God." That God is dead.

As I have expressed it in the *Atlantic Monthly,* in an article about neonatal defects such as the Down's syndrome, "The belief that God is at work directly or indirectly in all natural phenomena is a form of animism or simple pantheism. If we took it really seriously, all science, including medicine, would die away because we would be afraid to 'dissect God' or tamper with His activity. Such beliefs are a hopelessly primitive kind of God-thought and God-talk, but they hang on long after theologians generally have bid them good-bye."[11]

Some decisions are less radically problematic, although equally statistical. For example, we debate whether it is wise to give mass smallpox vaccinations, since postvaccinal encephalitis is fairly common whereas the risk of getting smallpox, at least in industrially mature societies, is not great. How shall we figure the probabilities? Here, it seems to me, the differential consideration is that the risk of getting smallpox is low precisely because of the preventive practice of mass vaccination. But it is not a simple moral question, comparable to "doing all we can for the patient" in clinical medicine.

We are pursued by ambivalences as much as by ambiguities. For example, diabetics were in mortal danger until we found the insulin treatment, yet they still could not risk pregnancy and childbirth. Now we can deliver them safely, but with what result? The result is an increase in diabetes, the spread of a genetic defect. There is always a risk of cancer to kidney recipients from cancerous donors. Synthetics have unexpected side effects, as was found with Chloromycetin (chlorophenicol) which has been connected with leukemia and aplastic anemia. Artificial hearts fueled with isotopic energy may spread radiation. But will that be any worse, or more lethal, than smog, water pollution, air pollution, and highway traffic? After a few years the danger to the cyborg himself can be serious; for example, leukemia may result. If only two or three more years of life are possible, is it worth the trouble and expense of a cardiac substitute? If a patient says, "No I don't want it," is that suicide? As hemodialysis improves it will foreseeably increase the incidence of suicide, because patients will weary of it all. If a man has been deterioratively paralyzed by a massive stroke and wants to give his heart to a much younger wife because hers is failing, is that suicide? Or is it an act of sacrificial love, realized by technology?

A Serious Conclusion

The Faustian question plagues some people when they discuss technology and morality; it takes possession of them and inhibits them — for example, Jacques Ellul.[12] Will man's growing power over his life and world be his undoing? Like Faust, is he selling his soul for knowledge, power, and riches; and are these things nothing more than what Sorokin called "sensate" values?[13] Or, to vary the figure, are we too Promethean, stealing the fire from heaven and the gods — to our own mortal danger?

Jean Rostand is right to warn us, "Let us not give ourselves the airs of demigods, or even of demiurges, when we have only been petty magicians."[14] We do not want to be trapped by a Promethean intoxication, or in a bad bargain of Faustian proportions. And we must not suppose that know-how, as in technology, is of itself enough to show us what is good or worth seeking. On the contrary, we must guard against what Veblen called "the trained incapacity of the specialist," his inability to consider what lies outside his expertise. Perhaps the correct model for modern medicine, in its partnership with the engineers and biologists, is the space probe program of the National Aeronautics and Space Administration in which the design and fabrication of hardware and the operations system are all subjected to a careful testing of their impact on the astronauts themselves, the human needs at stake. Good science (which is itself an ethical phrase) unites facts and values. As Lawrence Granberg has put it, "The very language of our most basic science, quantum mechanics, is the language of expectation and of probability amplitudes."[15]

Kant said two things filled him with awe: the starry heavens above and the moral law within.[16] If, by the first, he meant a sincere humility before the order and power of nature, we can agree; but not if he meant simply acceptance of nature without human interference or manipulation. As to the moral imperative, the "oughtness" of human beings, if he meant the sense of obligation and aspiration, especially to and for human welfare, we can go along with Kant, but not if by "law" he meant ethical rules, or final or universal or "natural" prescriptions of right and wrong regardless of changing needs and situations. There are no hard and fast rules, no fixed norms, no moral recipes.

Dr. Delford Stickel at Duke's medical center has declared that situation ethics, as I have formulated it, "provides a useful and helpful frame of reference within which to deal with the moral aspects" of medical problems, and that it "can foster a quality of responsibility which is in keeping with the best traditions of Western medicine."[17] Let me add, then, that we can only have a choice between three methods of moral decision-making: (1) moral absolutism, (2) anomic indifference, and (3) pragmatic situation ethics.

The first, absolutist ethics, has been the traditional method. Life and death are regarded as a divine monopoly, dependent on the will of God — either directly by special providence or indirectly through delegated processes of nature, presumably including such devices as sexual passion, menstrual cycles, senescence, gangrene, melanoma, and heart failure. On this view it has been wrong to try to be "equal with God" by exerting birth and death control, to say nothing of our many forms of health control.

The second method, the anomic and indifferent (acedic) one, is unconcerned about whether medical control is good or evil. It looks upon such questions as "adiaphora," morally neutral. On this basis we could be eager either to push technology or to restrain it without regard to right-wrong questions, merely accepting human controls as self-validating and *sui justificatis.*

The third alternative, situation-ethics, finds technology neither good nor evil in and of itself. Its standard of the good is human well-being; and technology at any place, in any time, of any form, is therefore right or wrong according to whether it detracts or contributes to the good, that is, human need.

This morality finds life good sometimes, and death good sometimes — depending on the situation, on the case or the context. Life is not good in itself, nor is death evil as such. Drugs and prosthetics and transplants, all forms of medical techniquery, are subject to the same ethical contingency. The question to ask about any technological device is not what is right or which one is good, but *when* are they right and *when* are they good. The answer is never prefabricated, in heaven or on earth. The decision lies with us. The age of innocence is gone. We have eaten the apple, the fruit of the tree of knowledge.

Katherine Mansfield once said, "At the end, truth is the only thing worth having; it's more thrilling than love, more joyful and more passionate." She was mistaken. Truth is sought for love's sake, not for its own sake. And love is for people — patients, neighbors, family and friends, fellow human beings.

Notes

1. *Webster's Seventh New Collegiate Dictionary* (Springfield, Mass.: G. & C. Merriam Company, 1967).

2. *Boston Globe,* 1 January 1967.

3. See Joseph Fletcher, "Medicine's Scientific Developments and Ethical Problems," in *Dialogue in Medicine and Theology,* ed. Dale White (Nashville: Abingdon Press, 1968), pp. 103-33.

4. C. H. Waddington, *The Ethical Animal* (Chicago: University of Chicago Press, 1960).

5. Rene Dubos, *Adapting Man* (New Haven: Yale University Press, 1965).

6. H. F. Steward, ed., *Blaise Pascal's Pensées* (New York: Pantheon, 1950), p. 83.

7. See, e.g., Robert White, M.D., and Charles Curran, Th.D., "The Morality of Human Transplants," *The Sign* (March 1968): 19-30.

8. Jean Rostand, *Can Man Be Modified?* trans. Jonathan Griffin (New York: Basic Books, 1959), p. 62.

9. Rejection may be solved by studying how mothers for nine months avoid rejecting the fetus which consists of foreign or alien tissue! The secret might well be in the placenta. (In all animal life, even the lowly earthworm, the rejection mechanism occurs.)

10. Eric Ambler, *A Coffin for Dimitrios* (New York: Dell, 1939), p. 9.

11. Bernard Bard and Joseph Fletcher, "The Right to Die," *Atlantic Monthly* 221, no. 4 (April 1968): 64.

12. See Jacques Ellul, *The Technological Society* (New York: Knopf, 1967), esp. pp. 428-36.

13. See Pitirim A. Sorokin, *Social and Cultural Dynamics* (New York: American Book Co., 1937).

14. Rostand, *op. cit.,* p. 25.

15. Lawrence Granberg, unpublished paper in the physics department at the University of Virginia, Charlottesville, Virginia.

16. Emmanuel Kant, *Critique of Practical Reason,* trans. T. K. Abbott (London: Longman Green & Co., 1923), p. 260.

17. Delford L. Stickel, M.D., "Ethical and Moral Aspects of Transplantation," *Monographs in the Surgical Sciences* (Baltimore: Williams and Wilkins, 1966), 3, no. 4, p. 292.

41 Science: Limits and Prohibitions

Daniel Callahan

The special power of Sigmund Freud's contribution to the analysis of "civilization and its discontents" lay in his unwillingness to engage in easy talk of liberation, to raise the question of altruism and its widening drive for community in the most tentative way only, and to reserve his most probing dissection for those deepest of human pathologies which stand in the way of happiness. If there is ever to be, to use Philip Rieff's term, a "science of limits" for technology, Freud's sober, anti-visionary spirit provides a healthy starting point. The question is not so much what should be done with technology, and what goods should be sought, but what boundaries should not be transgressed in the process. Yet to speak of "boundaries" in the full sense of the term is to recognize the importance of Freud's stress on the "cultural super-ego," which establishes psychological limits deep within the unconscious of entire societies. The route to a rational and humane technology is through the culture's unconscious, where its ultimate premises and values lie hidden from sight.

There are at least two reasons why a science of technological limits is needed. First, limits need to be set to the boundless hopes and expectations, constantly escalating, which technology has engendered. Advanced technology has promised transcendence of the human condition. That is a false promise, incapable of fulfillment. Human desires are infinite and cannot be achieved by the finite means of technology.

From the *Hastings Center Report* 3 (November 1973): 5-7.

Second, a science of technological limits is necessary in order that the social pathologies resulting from technology can be controlled. These pathologies can be introduced either by attempts to impose new technologies, or by attempts to correct the harms wrought by technology through the introduction of sanctions against those who, not having introduced the technology in the first place, are supposed to compensate personally for its extant hazards. While technology can and does cure, save and free, it can also become the vehicle for the introduction of new repressions in society, both because it provides ever more precise methods of controlling human behavior and also because fear in the face of its excesses can engender social terrorism as a defensive, corrective response.

Yet the temptation to a casual, irrational, anti-technological spirit must be resisted. The most important perception is to understand and accept the fact that man is a technological animal. It makes no sense to talk of *Homo sapiens* without technology or to distinguish man from technology. A science of technological limits cannot be built upon hostility to technology, which has always turned out historically to be self-defeating, setting the stage for a new spiral of unrestricted expectations. Together with the cultural, political, philosophical and religious systems which the human race has developed, science and technology can take their place among the greatest of human achievements.

To speak of "limits" at all is to introduce a dour note in the face of those achievements, yet one which should be embraced in all its rigor. I mean by a "science of limits" a system of prohibitions, denials and interdictions which establishes the limits of technological aggressiveness, hopes and mandates. The word "No" perfectly sums up what I mean by a limit — a boundary point beyond which one should not go. Technological development has been subject both to a tyranny of individualism and a tyranny of survival; neither knows how to say No. Individualism does not know how to deny anything to the private self. The cult of survival does not know how to say No to the needs of the community and the species.

A science of limits must, as a minimal demand, be able to establish the legitimacy of prohibitions, repressions and interdictions in the use of technology. The first required interdiction is a sharp dampening of the unchecked and uncorrected technological imagination. This dampening should take its point of departure from the biological reality principle that, however much human beings need technology, it cannot provide the full measure of human happiness, and will in fact lead to misery if, in a lust for infinite possibility, the reality principle is set aside even for a moment. This is essentially a task for the cultural super-ego, which could curb the desire for technological infinity and transcendence by scaling down the emotional and visionary demands made upon technology in the first place — by putting in their place a sense of radical finiteness, even a sense of guilt for demanding too much.

I do not want to be misunderstood. I am not proposing that we cease the careful rational analysis of the possibilities, good and bad, of new technologies; far more of that kind of analysis is needed. I am only proposing that we not continue to be caught in a cultural situation in which, our technological imagination out of hand, we are then forced to make judgments on technological givens which in a more prudent society might not have been present at all. Only a cultural super-ego imbued with an innate skepticism toward technological infinity, a spontaneous sobriety in the face of futuristic scenarios which would lure us into unrealistic hopes, and a healthy repugnance toward those who would, by the siren song of happiness and plenty, lure us away from our doubts and inhibitions, will suffice.

The second interdiction must take its rise from a social reality principle. By that principle I mean the inherent resistance that groups and populations initially and ordinarily feel toward efforts to force new technologies upon them, or toward bearing socially imposed penalties in order to control technology. The history of technology shows that specific developments are almost always justified on the ground that they will increase freedom of choice and maximize voluntary options. That same history, however, also shows how short-lived the new freedoms are. Specified choices — usually in the name of a "responsible" use of freedom — quickly make the new options mandatory, either by law, economic force or social custom. When horses were still available, the automobile was introduced as an optional, alternative mode of transportation; that choice is now gone. Genetic counseling was originally hailed as a means of giving people the freedom to choose the avoidance of a defective child, if they wanted to avail themselves of that option. But signs are already present that they will in the future be considered socially irresponsible if they do not make use of their "free" choice to choose against bearing defective children.

The repetition of the historical pattern which sees free choices quickly become mandatory suggests a modest wisdom: assume, in trying to judge the benefits and harms of any new technology, that its use will eventually become a socially enforced requirement. And assume, as well, that if there are some hazardous by-products from the technology, everyone will be forced to pay for them, however innocent they may have been in introducing them.

The second interdiction, then, must be a prohibition of careless meddling in social orders and structures by technologists and, beyond that, a refusal to believe that the answer to the derangements of society is technological. There is no reason whatever to assume that all problems can be solved by technological solutions, and no reason to assume either that it is even good to seek a technological answer. It is precisely these assumptions which need to be denied. As matters now stand, nothing is allowed to compete with technology, so deeply ingrained is the tendency to give it the first crack at any serious issue.

Moreover, there is no reason to presume that technological advances must be taken advantage of once they are available. The most noxious combination is the joining of technological possibility with demands for survival. Survival obsessions wipe out choices and options — that is their power and why they are invoked. When survival and technology join hands, a technological imperative is introduced: the technology must be used.

The third interdiction springs from a psychological reality principle. By that principle I mean the fact that human beings are not at all likely to give up their attempts to find happiness through technology. The new burst of technological fervor, already foreshadowed in the marriage of psychological technology to counter-culture mysticism and communitarianism, shows that people are not disillusioned with technology, despite superficial indications of an anti-technological mood. But if people will not cease to hope for happiness through technology, how can they be expected to impose upon themselves the restrictions necessary to ground their hopes in reality and thus limit them? In one way only. There must be deeply imbedded in the cultural super-ego the profound perception that violent reactions against technology carry within them the seeds of a subsequent collapse once again in the face of the seductions of technology. That has been the historical rhythm of the matter, where the juxtaposition of the fundamental human need for technology and the harms wrought by technology present a dilemma which cannot and will not be resolved.

The third interdiction, necessary in light of the psychological reality principle of technology, is that there must be an intuitive censorship of visions of a non-technological society. The only possibility of a check to an over-investment of hope in technology is, paradoxically, the existence of checks against an overinvestment of hopes in non-technology. Needed is a scaling down of technology and a rational control of it — neither its deification nor its denial. Interdictions against an infinitizing of technological promise, impossible of fulfillment, will become feasible only when the extremes of hope and despair have been once and for all excluded.

No substitute for technology has yet been found for the primary human business of facilitating adaptation and preservation; and no one urged to give up technology can fail to miss that fact. Nor has any substitute been found for the economic strength which technological societies provide. The irreversibility of technology — whatever the theory of the matter, that is the historical realty — poses the most important obstacle to its management. Since people cannot go back on technology, they find themselves impelled to go forward, to avoid returning to that which lies behind them, and to seek that which technology has yet to deliver — and will not deliver. A limit to *always* going forward is needed; when to go forward and when not to is the question.

The only possible hope for the development of an interdictory cultural super-ego lies in a shift from viewing technology as a vehicle for saving and satisfying individuals, to one which roots its values in the needs of the community: basic health and economic needs, the sustaining of viable educational institutions, the preservation of natural resources, clean air and water, and a cultural life which provides physical and aesthetic enrichment.

Naturally, even to suggest a list of this kind — noncontroversial enough on its face — does not take us far toward determining what a sufficient *level* of these goods would be. The fact that technological societies work from a very high baseline of desires and expectations, perceived as "necessities," poses the most stubborn difficulty. The main work of an interdictory cultural super-ego would be to lower the base-line of expectation and demand, neutralizing the sense of restlessness, unrequited desire, and obsessive attempts to achieve still more happiness through technology that are the marks of advanced industrial societies. A downward shift in demand can emerge only from a social rather than an individual ethic.

The most difficult task in creating a rational social ethic which can win support and dig itself into the cultural super-ego is that of finding the proper balance between the rights of individuals and those of the community. Societies and historical circumstances differ, and for just that reason there is no possibility of abstractly establishing the proper balance for every community at every given moment in time. In technological societies, the individualistic demands made upon technology can have the effect of creating a false sense of scarcity. If every individual wants everything, and believes he or she has a right to it as a necessary condition of personal self-realization, then scarcity becomes psychologically endemic, with every person so affected living under a constantly perceived threat of degradation or annihilation.

It is much easier to proclaim the need for community-centered rather than individual-centered thinking than to work through the ethical difficulties this stance engenders. Once the community (or the species) has been given moral preeminence, there can be a very rapid descent to persecution and tyranny in the name of the common good. Is there any middle ground between an unlimited individualism, which can generate terror, and an unlimited regard for the community, which can generate no less terror? Only in two ways: by establishing upper limits to what individuals can demand and expect, and internal restraints on the harm a community may do to individuals in the name of its own welfare.

Lacking an instinct for limitations and prohibitions, society has at present no real way to judge and control technology. When intrinsic limits are denied, and every proposal for a limit subjected to tests which no prohibition could pass, then all possibility for rational communal behavior ceases. The stage is then set for force to be applied.

The greatest need Freud saw was that of reconciling human beings to civilization. The individualism underlying technology has made that task more difficult than ever. Technology has given the private person illusory arms with which to better fight off civilization and its repressive demands. The possibility of altruism, which Freud defined as an impulse to merge with others in the community, is ever hard pressed; egoism drives us in another direction.

The individual will always have to bargain with society and with nature. Technology has made a better bargain possible. But that possibility is constantly threatened by the demand for a perfect bargain. That will never be possible. That insight is the foundation of a science of limits.

42 "Playing God" and Invoking a Perspective

Allen Verhey

Should human beings play God? It is a question frequently raised in discussions of bioethics and of genetics. The question is sometimes asked rhetorically, as though the answer is obvious: "Human beings should not play God!"[1] Sometimes the question is set aside as if it were not a serious question, as though human beings have no choice but to play God, as though it is what human beings do. "The question is not whether we will play God or not, but whether [we will play God responsibly or not]" (Augenstein, 1969, p. 145).

We are sometimes invited to play God, and we are sometimes warned against it, but before we decide whether to accept the invitation or to heed the warning, it would be good to know what it means to "play God."

When my daughter, Kate, was very young, she once invited the rest of the family to play "52-semi." She was holding a deck of cards, obviously eager to play. But when we asked for an explanation of this game, she would give none, only repeating her invitation to play "52-semi." Finally we said, "OK, Katie, let's play '52-semi'." She threw the cards up into the air and, when they had fallen back to the floor, commanded triumphantly, "Now pick 'em up." She had gotten her trucks mixed up, confusing "52-semi" with "52 pickup" but suddenly — too late — we knew what she meant. Should human beings "play God"? It depends, you see, on what it means to "play God."

Unfortunately, the phrase does not mean just one thing; it means different things to different people in different contexts. That is hardly surprising, I suppose, given the fact that neither "play" nor "God" are simple terms. Moreover, sometimes the phrase is used in ways that have nothing to do with either "play" or "God."

In one recent survey of the uses of the phrase, Edmund Erde decided that the phrase is meaningless. Using the phrase as though it meant something, he said, "... is muddle-headed" (Erde, 1989, p. 594); moreover, he regarded the phrase not only as "non-sensical," but also as "unconstitutional or blasphemous" (Erde, 1989, p. 599), even "immoral" (Erde, 1989, p. 594). Erde demanded that, for the phrase to be meaningful, it must mean a single moral principle, and a universal moral principle at that. That seems a bit much to ask.

This article undertakes to sort through at least some of the uses of this phrase. I hope to indicate that the phrase does not so much state a principle as invoke a perspective on the world; a perspective from which other things, including scientific and technological innovations in genetics — and the phrase itself — are meaningful. I hope to indicate that we must be attentive not only to particular moral problems raised by genetic engineering but also to the perspective from which we examine and evaluate these new powers and problems. And I hope to suggest, finally, the relevance of a perspective in which "God" is taken seriously and "play" playfully.

The President's Commission report on *Splicing Life* (1982) would seem a good place to begin. The commission noted the concerns voiced about "playing God" in genetics and, to their credit, undertook to make some sense of the phrase. It even invited theologians to comment on the phrase and its relevance to genetic engineering. The "view of the theologians" is summarized in a single paragraph.

> [C]ontemporary developments in molecular biology raise issues of responsibility rather than being matters to be prohibited because they usurp powers that human beings should not possess.... Endorsement of genetic engineering, which is praised for its potential to improve the human

From Allen Verhey, "'Playing God' and Invoking a Perspective," *The Journal of Medicine and Philosophy* 20 (1995): 347-64. Used with kind permission from Kluwer Academic Publishers.

> estate, is linked with the recognition that the misuse of human freedom creates evil and that human knowledge and power can result in harm (President's Commission, 1982, pp. 53-54).

There is much here that could reward a closer analysis. It is clear that the theologians rejected the warnings against "playing God" when those warnings were understood as warnings against usurping powers that are properly God's — but how else might they be understood? The theologians evidently thought that the notion of "responsibility" might be suggestive. It is indeed suggestive, and I will return to it. The President's Commission, however, decided to leave the notion of responsibility to God aside. It decided that the phrase "playing God" does not have "a specific religious meaning" (President's Commission, 1982, p. 54).

If, in stating this, the Commission had meant simply that the phrase does not mean one thing, and that the meaning of the phrase varies with the particular religious tradition and perspective within which it might be used, then one could hardly object. However, the Commission proceeded to assert that "at its heart" the phrase was "an expression of a sense of awe [in response to extraordinary *human* powers] — and concern [about the possible consequences of these vast new powers]" (President's Commission, 1982, p. 54). The Commission simply translated the warnings against "playing God" into a concern about the consequences of exercising great human powers (Lebacqz, 1984, p. 33).

The Commission reduced the meaning of the phrase to secular terms and made "God" superfluous. "At its heart," according to the Commission, the phrase "playing God" has nothing to do with "God." Moreover, there is nothing very playful about "playing God" either. The human powers in genetics and their possible consequences are too serious for playfulness.

"Playing God" might mean what the Commission interpreted it to mean, something like, "Wow! Human powers are awesome. Let's not play around!" It evidently does mean something like that to many who use the phrase. Such an interpretation of the phrase is hardly trivial, but it is also not very useful to guide or limit human powers. Moreover, it is worth pointing out that the President's Commission invoked a particular perspective in interpreting the phrase, and it then used the phrase as shorthand to invoke that perspective when interpreting developments in genetics.

The President's Commission highlighted one very important feature of contemporary culture, the hegemony of scientific knowledge. "Since the Enlightenment," it said, "Western societies have exalted the search for greater knowledge" (President's Commission, 1982, p. 54). Scientific knowledge, beginning with Copernicus, has both "dethrone[d] human beings as the unique center of the world" and delivered "vast powers for action" into their hands (President's Commission, 1982, pp. 54-55).

Leroy Augenstein had made the same point in *Come, Let Us Play God.* Science has taught us the hard lesson that human beings and their earth are not "the center of the universe" (Augenstein, 1969, p. 11), but it is now putting into human hands powers and responsibilities "to make decisions which we formerly left to God" (Augenstein, 1969, p. 142). Borrowing the phrase of Dietrich Bonhoeffer, Augenstein described this situation as humanity's "coming of age" (Augenstein, 1969, p. 143).

Where this is the context for talk of "playing God," it is not surprising that "God" is superfluous, that "God" is not taken seriously when we try to make sense of the phrase. Bonhoeffer, after all, described humanity's "coming of age" as an effort to think the world "*etsi deus non daretur*" ("as though God were not a given") (Bonhoeffer, 1953, p. 218). Science has no need of God "as a working hypothesis" (Bonhoeffer, 1953, p. 218); in fact, it is not even permitted for science *qua* science to make use of "God." There are assumptions operative in this perspective, however, not only about "God" but about humanity, knowledge, and nature as well. With respect to humanity, science has taught us that we are not "the center of the universe." However, science has not taught us where we do belong. As Nietzsche aptly put it, "since Copernicus man has been rolling from the center into x" (cited in Jüngel, 1983, p. 15). Once human beings and their earth were at the center. They did not put themselves there; God put them there, and it was simply accepted as a matter of course that they *were* there. After Copernicus had shown that they were not at the center, humanity was left to fend for itself (or simply to continue "rolling"). This positionlessness was the new assumption, and it entailed that humanity had to attempt to secure (if somewhat anxiously) a place for itself — and what better place than at the center. After Copernicus, humanity was not simply at the center, it had to *put* itself at the center, make itself *into* the center. Fortunately, the very science that destroyed the illusion that humanity was at the center gave to humanity power in the world and over the world. Such mastery, however, has not eliminated human insecurity and anxiety; in fact, the new powers and their unintended consequences evoke new anxieties.

In this context "playing God" *etsi deus non daretur* might well be interpreted as "an expression of a sense of awe [before human powers] — and concern [about unanticipated consequences]" (President's Commission, 1982, p. 54).

There are assumptions concerning knowledge, too. The comment of the President's Commission that "[s]ince the Enlightenment, Western societies have exalted the search for greater knowledge" (President's Commission, 1982, p. 54) requires a gloss. They have exalted a particular kind of knowledge, the knowledge for which they reserve the honorific term "science."

It is simply not the case that the search for knowledge only began to be exalted with the Enlightenment. Thomas Aquinas, for example, had exalted the search for knowledge long before the Enlightenment, affirming "all knowledge" as "good." He distinguished, however, "practical" from "speculative" (or theoretical) sciences, the difference being that the practical sciences are for the sake of some work to be done, while the speculative sciences are for their own sake (Aquinas, Commentary on Aristotle's *On the Soul*, I, 3; cited in Jonas, 1966, p. 188).

That classical account (and celebration) of knowledge must be contrasted with the modern account epitomized in Francis Bacon's *The Great Instauration* and "exalted" in Western societies. In Bacon all knowledge is sought for its utility, "for the benefit and use of life" (Bacon, [1620] 1960, p. 15). The knowledge to be sought is "no mere felicity of speculation" (Bacon, [1620] 1960, p. 29), which is but the "boyhood of knowledge" and "barren of works" (Bacon, [1620] 1960, p. 8). The knowledge to be sought is the practical knowledge that will make humanity "capable of overcoming the difficulties and obscurities of nature" (Bacon, [1620] 1960, p. 19), able to subdue and overcome its vexations and miseries. "And so those twin objects, human knowledge and human power, do really meet in one" (Bacon, [1620] 1960, p. 29). The knowledge "exalted" in Western societies is this power over nature which presumably brings human well-being in its train.

In the classical account, theory (or the speculative sciences) provided the wisdom to use the practical sciences appropriately. The modern account may admit, as Bacon did, that for knowledge to be beneficial humanity must "perfect and govern it in charity" (Bacon, [1620] 1960, p. 15), but science is "not self-sufficiently the source of that human quality that makes it beneficial" (Jonas, 1966, p. 195). Moreover, the compassion (or "charity") that responds viscerally to the vexations and miseries of humanity will urge us to *do something* to relieve those miseries, but it will not tell us *what thing* to do. Bacon's account of knowledge simply arms compassion with artifice, not with wisdom (O'Donovan, 1984, pp. 10-12). For the charity to "perfect and govern" human powers and for the wisdom to guide charity, science must call upon something else. But upon what? And how can humanity have "knowledge" of it? Knowledge of that which transcends "use" — and transcends the "nature" known scientifically, even the "human nature" known scientifically — has no place in Bacon's theory.[2]

Knowledge of that which might guide and limit the human use of human powers was the subject of classical theory, but not of the Enlightenment "search for greater knowledge." In this context there is no place for either "play" (because play is not "useful"[3]) or "God" (because God is transcendent and will not be used).

With the different assumptions concerning knowledge come different assumptions concerning nature, too. The Baconian project sets humanity not only over nature but against it. The natural order and natural processes have no dignity of their own; their value is reduced to their utility to humanity — and nature does not serve humanity "naturally." Nature threatens to rule and to ruin humanity. Against the powers of nature, knowledge promises the power to relieve humanity's miseries and "to endow the human family with new mercies" (Bacon, [1620] 1960, p. 29). The fault that runs through our world and through our lives must finally be located in nature. Nature may be — and must be — mastered (Jonas, 1966, p. 192).

This is the perspective invoked by the President's Commission. From this perspective "playing God" has nothing to do with either "play" or "God." Rather it is concerned with human scientific knowledge and power over nature and it raises doubts about the taken-for-granted assumption that human well-being will come in the train of such knowledge and power.

Religious people have sometimes celebrated this Baconian perspective and its quest for scientific knowledge and technical power — and have sometimes lamented it. Some who have lamented it have raised their voices in protest against almost every new scientific hypothesis (witness Galileo and Darwin) and against almost all technological developments (for example, anesthesia during childbirth). These evidently regard scientific inquiry as a threat to faith in God and technical innovation as an offense to God. These lament a "humanity come of age" and long to go back to a former time, a time of our childhood (if only we knew the way!). They regret a world *etsi deus non daretur* and wish to preserve the necessity of "God" in human ignorance and powerlessness. But such a "God" can only ever be a "God of the Gaps" and can only ever be in retreat to the margins.

It is an old and unhappy story in Christian apologetics that locates God's presence and power where human knowledge and strength have reached their (temporary) limit. Newton, for example, saw certain irregularities in the motion of the planets, movements which he could not explain by his theory of gravity, and in those irregularities he saw, he said, the direct intervention of God. When later astronomers and physicists provided a natural explanation for what had puzzled Newton, "God" was no longer necessary. And there is the old joke of the patient who, when told that the only thing left to do was to pray, said, "Oh, my! And I didn't even think it was serious." The God of the Gaps is only invoked, after all, where doctors are powerless.

In the context of such a piety, when there is a defensive faith in the God of the Gaps, "playing God" means to encroach on those areas of human life where human beings have been ignorant or powerless, for there God rules, there only God has the authority to act. In this context "playing God" means to seize God's place at the boundaries of human knowledge and power, to usurp God's authority and dominion. In this context it is understandable that humanity should be warned, "Thou shalt not play God."

Once again the phrase is used not so much to state a principle as to invoke a perspective. To be sure, such warnings serve to remind humanity of its fallibility and finitude, and such warnings are salutary. There are, however, at least two problems with this perspective and with such warnings against "playing God."[4]

The first and fundamental problem with this perspective is that the God of the Gaps is not the God who is made known in creation and in scripture. The God of creation and scripture made and sustains the order we observe and rely upon. To describe that order in terms of scientific understanding does not explain God away; it is to give an account of the way God orders God's world. The order of the world comes to us no less from the gracious hand of God than the extraordinary events humans call "miracles." "Nature" is no less the work of God than "grace." The world and its order are not God, but they are God's. They are the work of God. And, to understand the world and its order as God's is not to understand it in a way that prohibits "natural scientific" explanations. It is to be called to serve God's cause, to be responsible to God in the midst of it.

The second problem with this perspective and with such warnings against "playing God" is that they are indiscriminate; they do not permit discriminating judgments. There are some things which we already know how to do (and so can hardly be said to trespass the boundaries of human ignorance and powerlessness), but which we surely ought never to do. And there are some things (including some things in genetics) which we cannot yet do, but which we must make an effort to learn to do if God is God and we are called to "follow" one who heals the sick and feeds the hungry. The warning against "playing God" in this perspective reduces to the slogan "It's not nice to fool with Mother Nature (at least not any more than we are currently comfortable with)." Ironically, then, the warning enthrones "nature" as god rather than the One who transcends it and our knowledge of it.

Some other religious people celebrate the advances of science and the innovations of technology, urging humanity bravely to go forward, uttering a priestly benediction over the Baconian project. These sometimes use the phrase "playing God," too, usually in inviting humanity to "play God". Joseph Fletcher, for example, responded provocatively to the charge that his enthusiasm for genetic technology amounted to a license to "play God" by admitting the charge (Fletcher, 1970, p. 131) and by making the invitation explicit; "Let's play God," he said (Fletcher, 1974, p. 126).

The "God" Fletcher invited us to "play" was still the God of the Gaps (Fletcher, 1970, p. 132), the God at the edges of human knowledge and power. For Fletcher, however, "that old, primitive God is dead" (Fletcher, 1970, p. 132; 1974, p. 200). Dead also are the "taboos" which prohibited trespass on the territory of that God's rule (Fletcher, 1974, p. 127), the "fatalism" that passively accepted the will of that God (Fletcher, 1974, p. 128), and the "obsolete theodicy" (Fletcher, 1970, p. 132) that attempted to defend that God. "What we need," he said, "is a new God" (Fletcher, 1970, p. 132), but Fletcher's "new God" bore a striking resemblance to the God of the eighteenth century deist, and indifference to a God so conceived is inevitable; life may proceed — and "playing God" may proceed — *etsi deus non daretur.*

Although Fletcher said little more about this "new God," he did say that "any God worth believing in wills the best possible well-being for human beings" (Fletcher, 1974, p. xix). Fletcher's "new God" turns out to be a heavenly utilitarian, and this God, too, humanity must "play."

So, the invitation to "play God" comes to this: humanity should use its new powers to achieve the greatest good of the greatest number of people (not intimidated by "taboos"), to take control over "nature" (not enervated by "fatalism"), to take responsibility, to design and make a new and better world, to substitute for an absent God. "It was *easier* in the old days," Fletcher said (1974, p. 200),

> to attribute at least some of what happened to God's will — we could say with a moral shrug that we weren't responsible. Now we have to shoulder it all. The moral tab is ours and we have to pick it up. The excuses of ignorance and helplessness are growing thin.

Notice what has happened to responsibility. Fletcher underscores human responsibility, but we are responsible not so much *to* God as *instead of* God.[5] That shift puts an enormous (and messianic) burden on genetics, a burden which leaves little time for "play."

The phrase "playing God" here does state a principle, namely, utility, but it also does more than that — it invokes a perspective, a perspective in which the God of the Gaps is superfluous, in which humanity is maker and designer, in which knowledge is power, and in which nature must be mastered to maximize human well-being. Such a perspective makes the invitation to "play God" — and much else in Fletcher's discussion of genetics — meaningful.

Christians may welcome Fletcher's burial of the God of the Gaps, but they still wait and watch and pray not for the invention of some "new God" but for the appearance of the one God who continues to create, preserve, and redeem humanity and its world. Moreover, Fletcher's invitation to "play God" need not seem blasphemous to those trained to "imitate God," to "follow" God, to be disciples of the one who made God present among us. But, to map the path of discipleship and imitation as "the utilitarian way" must seem strange to those who know the law and the prophets, and the gospels.

It seemed strange, at least, to Paul Ramsey. In Ramsey's usage, although we are usually warned against "playing God," we are sometimes encouraged to "'play God' in the correct way" (Ramsey, 1978, p. 203) — and God is no utilitarian. "God," Ramsey said (1978, p. 205),

> is not a rationalist whose care is a function of indicators of our personhood, or of our achievement within those capacities. He makes his rain fall upon the just and the unjust alike, and his sun to rise on the abnormal as well as the normal. Indeed, he has special care for the weak and the vulnerable among us earth people. He cares according to need, not capacity or merit.

These divine patterns and images are, according to Ramsey, at "the foundation of Western medical care" (Ramsey, 1978, p. 205).

One might expect Ramsey, then, simply to echo Fletcher's invitation to "play God" while engaging him and others in conversation concerning who this God is whom we are invited to "play." However, he also (and more frequently) warned against "playing God." The phrase itself, he admitted, is "not [a] very helpful characterization" (Ramsey, 1970b, p. 90), but he used it to name — and to warn against — an "attitude," an "outlook," certain "operating, unspoken premises" at work in western scientific culture (Ramsey, 1970b, p. 91), and to invite a different perspective on the world.

The fundamental premise of the perspective Ramsey warns against is that "God" is superfluous. "Where there is no God . . . ," he said (Ramsey, 1970b, p. 93), there humanity is creator, maker, the engineer of the future (Ramsey, 1970b, pp. 91-92), and there nature, even human nature, may be and must be controlled and managed with messianic ambition (Ramsey, 1970b, pp. 92-96). Where "God" is superfluous and human beings are cast in this role of "the maker," there morality is reduced to the consideration of consequences, knowledge is construed simply as power, and nature — including the human nature given to humanity as embodied and communal — is left with no dignity of its own.

Ramsey's warnings against "playing God" are not immediately identified with a particular moral rule or principle; rather, they challenge the wisdom and the sufficiency of the assumptions too much at work in Western culture. It is not that some "God of the Gaps" is threatened. It is not simply that human powers are awesome or that the consequences of "interfering with nature" are worrisome, as the President's Commission suggested. It is rather that the fundamental perspective from which we interpret our responsibilities is critically important to seeing what those responsibilities are (Ramsey, 1970b, pp. 28, 143).

The fundamental perspective which Ramsey recommends and to which he contrasts "playing God" is "to intend the world as a Christian or as a Jew" (Ramsey, 1970b, p. 22), i.e., *etsi deus daretur* — and not just any old *deus* (nor Fletcher's "new God") but the God who creates and keeps a world and a covenant. That means, among other things, that the end of all things may be left to God. Where God is God and not us, there can be a certain eschatological nonchalance. From this perspective, our responsibilities, while great, will not be regarded as being of messianic proportion. There will be some room, then, for an ethic of means as well as the consideration of consequences (Ramsey, 1970b, pp. 23-32), for reflection about the kind of behavior which is worthy of human nature as created by God, as embodied and interdependent, for example.

When joined with such reflection, Ramsey's warnings that we should not play God do provide some prohibitions. When joined with an interpretation of human procreation, for example, the warning against "playing God" bears the prohibition against putting "entirely asunder what God joined together," against separating "*in principle*" the unitive and procreative goods of human sexuality, against reducing procreation either to biology or to contract (Ramsey, 1970b, pp. 32-33), and that prohibition supports in turn a series of more particular prohibitions, for example, a prohibition against artificial insemination using the sperm of a donor (Ramsey, 1970b, pp. 47-52).

When joined with an interpretation of the patient as "*a sacredness in the natural, biological order*" (Ramsey, 1970a, xiii), the "edification" drawn from the warning against "playing God" includes prohibitions against deliberately killing patients, including very little patients, for the sake of relieving their (or another's) suffering, against using one without consent, even a very little one, even one created in a petri dish, to learn to help others.

Ramsey warns against "playing God," against trying to substitute for an absent God, against trying to "be" God, but there remains room for "playing God" *etsi deus daretur*. Indeed, as we have seen, Ramsey can invite people to "'play God' in the correct way" (Ramsey, 1970a, p. 256). Such "playing" is not to substitute for an absent God, not to "be" God, but to "imitate" God (Ramsey, 1970a, p. 259), to follow in God's way like a child "playing" a parent.

In both the warning and the invitation a perspective is invoked, an outlook which assumes that God is God and not us, that humanity is called to honor and to nurture the nature God gave, that knowledge of that which transcends use is possible, and that the fault that runs through our lives and our world is not simply located in nature but in human pride or sloth.

One who — like me — shares this perspective will make sense of the phrase "playing God" in the light of this perspective. Sometimes it will be appropriate to sound a warning against "playing God", and sometimes it will be appropriate to issue an invitation to "play God" in imitation of God's care and grace. Permit me to focus on the invitation to "play God" — and first to underscore the invitation to "play."[6] Many have complained that "playing God" is serious stuff and regretted the implication of "playfulness" in the phrase (e.g., Lebacqz, 1984, p. 40, n.19). Some "play," however, can be very serious indeed — as anyone who plays noon-hour basketball knows quite well. "Playfulness" is quite capable of being serious, but it is not capable of being purely instrumental.

When Teilhard de Chardin said that "in the great game that is being played, we are the players as well as . . . the stakes" (1961, p. 230), he created a powerful image to call attention both to the extraordinary powers of human beings and to the awesome consequences of exercising those powers. No wonder playfulness seems inappropriate. Precisely because the stakes are high, however, it may be apt to set alongside Teilhard's image a Dutch proverb: "It is not the marbles that matter but the game" (quoted in Huizinga, 1950, p. 49). When the stakes are high, or even when the stakes alone are taken seriously, then one is tempted to cheat in order to win. And when one cheats, then one only pretends to play; the cheat plays neither fair nor seriously.

Play, even marbles, can be serious, but it cannot be purely instrumental; it cannot allow attention to be monopolized by the stakes, by the consequences of winning or losing. When our attention is riveted by Teilhard's image that we are "the stakes," it may well be important to allow our imagination to be captured by his image that we are "the players," too. Then we may be able to avoid reducing the moral life to a concern about consequences, even where the stakes are high. We may be able to avoid reducing ourselves to makers and designers and our existence to joyless and incessant work. We may see that we are at stake, not just in the sense of some plastic destiny our powers may make but already in the imagination, in the image of ourselves with which human creativity begins (Hartt, 1975, pp. 117-134).

The invitation is an invitation to "play," but it is more specifically an invitation to "play God," and that invitation requires attention to the God whom we are invited to play. In the foreword to *Should Doctors Play God?* Mrs. Billy Graham wrote (1971, p. vii),

> [i]f I were an actress who was going to play, let's say, Joan of Arc, I would learn all there is to learn about Joan of Arc. And, if I were a doctor or anyone else trying to play God, I would learn all I could about God.

That seems a prudent strategy for an actress — and good advice for people called to imitate God. The invitation to "play God," to cast ourselves playfully in the role of God, invites theological reflection; it invites reflection about "God."

The invitation goes out to all, not just to Christians. When ancient Greek physicians swore the Hippocratic Oath by Apollos, Aesclepius, Hygiea, Panacea and all the gods and goddesses, they invoked a story. Healing had its beginnings among the gods, and the Hippocratic physician swore to make that story their own. And when the temple to Aesclepius in the Areopagus was inscribed with the message that, like a god, Aesclepius healed both rich and poor without discrimination, a path was laid out for physicians to follow.

The invitation goes out to all, but reflection about God is always formed and informed by the particular stories and communities within which it is undertaken, and Christians will heed this invitation in the light of their own tradition and its talk of God. We play God in response to God, imitating God's ways and providing human service to God's cause. Our responsibility to God limits and shapes an account of what we are responsible for in God's good world — and its genetics.

Permit me, then, simply to select a few images of God in the Jewish and Christian tradition and to suggest something of their relevance to "playing God" in genetics. Two of these images are regularly invoked in these discussions: creator and healer — and the third is often overlooked: God is the one who takes the side of the poor.

First, then, what might it mean playfully to cast ourselves in the role of the creator? This, of course, has been the topic of much discussion. If I read the story right, however, to cast ourselves in the role of the creator might mean something too much overlooked. It might mean that we look at the creation and at its genetics and say to ourselves, "God, that's good." It might mean, that is, first of all, to wonder, to stand in awe, to delight in the elegant structure of the creation and its DNA. It would mean a celebration of knowledge which was not simply mastery. It would mean an appreciation of nature — and of human nature — as given, rather than a suspicion of it as threatening and requiring human mastery.

And if I read the story right, it might mean a second thing too much overlooked. It might mean to take a day off, to rest, to play. But we have already talked of that.

It also means, of course, a third thing, a thing seldom overlooked in these discussions — that human creativity is given with the creation. Human beings are created and called to exercise dominion in the world — and I see no reason to suppose that such creativity and control does not extend to genetics. It is not "Mother Nature" who is God, after all, in the Christian story. Human creativity and control, however, are to be exercised in response to God, in imitation of God's ways, and in service to God's cause. That's a part of the Christian story, too, a part of the store usually captured in describing ourselves as stewards and our responsibility as stewardship.

We can discover something of God's cause, the cause stewards serve, in a second feature of the story. God is the healer. Jesus, the one in whom God and the cause of God were made known, was a healer. We discover there that the cause of God is life, not death; the cause of God is human flourishing, including the human flourishing we call health, not disease. What does it mean to cast ourselves playfully in the role of God the healer? It means to intend life and its flourishing, not death or human suffering. Therefore, genetic therapy, like other therapeutic interventions which aim at health, may be celebrated. Healing is "playing God" the way God plays God. Genetic therapies, however, are still mostly (but not completely) a distant hope. The more immediate contributions of genetics to medicine are in genetic diagnosis. And where there are therapeutic options, these too may be celebrated. However, genetic diagnoses without therapeutic options are sometimes deeply ambiguous.

Prenatal diagnoses, for example, are frequently ambiguous. Already we can diagnose a number of genetic conditions in a fetus, and the number is constantly growing. For most of these there is no therapy. The tests allow parents to make a decision about whether to give birth or to abort. How shall we "play God" here in ways responsible to God? If God's cause is life rather than death, then those who would "play God" in imitation of God will not be disposed to abort; they will not celebrate abortion as a "therapeutic option."

There are, I think, genetic conditions which justify abortion. There are conditions like Tay-Sachs which consign a child not only to an abbreviated life but to a life subjectively indistinguishable from torture. And there are conditions like Trisomy 18 which are inconsistent not only with life but with the minimal conditions for human communication. Pre-natal diagnosis — and abortion — can be used responsibly. However, when some children with Down's Syndrome are aborted because they have Down's, there seems to exist a reasonable possibility that prenatal diagnoses have been — and will be — used irresponsibly. When the slogan about "preventing birth defects" is taken to justify preventing the birth of "defectives," those who do not measure up to the standards or match the preferences of parents, then there are reasons to worry a little, to worry that the disposition of a good "parent" will change from the sort of uncalculating nurturance that can evoke and sustain trust from children to the sort of calculating nurturance that is prepared to abandon or abort the offspring who do not match specifications. "Playing God" the way God plays God — or, if you will, the way God plays "parent" — would sustain care for the weak and the helpless, and for the little ones who do not measure up.

Genetic therapy, I said, may be celebrated as service to God's cause of health. It is to "play God" as God plays God. However, to use this knowledge and technology responsibly it must be aimed at "health," not genetic enhancement. The distinction between intervening for health and intervening for genetic enhancement may be a slippery one, but casting ourselves playfully in the role of God the healer will encourage us to make such a distinction and to abide by it. Eugenics is not the way to "play God" the way God plays God.

Consider, finally, this third image: God is one

who takes the side of the poor. What would it mean to cast ourselves in the role of one who takes the side of the poor? It would mean, at the very least, I think, a concern for social justice. It would mean, for example, to ask about the allocation of resources to the human genome project. When cities are crumbling, when schools are deteriorating, when we complain about not having sufficient resources to help the poor or the homeless, when we do not have the resources to provide care for all the sick, is this a just and fair use of our society's resources? Is it an allocation of social resources that can claim to imitate God's care and concern for the poor?

Having raised that question, let me focus instead on the sharing of the burdens and benefits of the human genome project itself. Who bears the burdens? Who will benefit? And is the distribution fair? Does it fit the story of one who takes the side of the poor and powerless?

If we cast ourselves in this role, if we attempt to mirror God's justice and care of the poor and powerless, we will not be eager to create human life in order to learn from it with the intention of destroying it after we have learned what we can from it. We will not be eager to use the unborn for experiments to learn some things that would benefit others, even if it were a great benefit, even if it would benefit a great number of others. And we would be cautious about stigmatizing some as diseased and others as carriers.

But consider also the sharing of benefits. Who stands to benefit from the human genome initiative? Will genetic powers be marketed? Presumably they will, given the patenting of microorganisms. And so the rich may get richer while the poor still watch and pray. Will the poor have access to health-care benefits that their taxes helped develop? Since health care reform has died in Congress again, can we have any confidence that genetic technology will be available to the uninsured or to those with public insurance? Or will insurance companies use genetic information to screen candidates for insurance? Will the category of "preexisting condition" be redefined to make it easier for insurance companies to make a still larger profit? Will genetic information be included in actuarial tables? Will corporations use genetic information to screen applicants in order to hire those with greatest promise of long-term productivity? The point of these questions is not simply to lament our failure to accomplish health care reform. It is to suggest that "playing God" as God plays God will be attentive not only to intriguing questions about the frontiers of technology and science but also to mundane questions about fairness, about the effect of such innovations on the poor. If we are to "play God" as God plays God, then we have a pattern for imitation in God's hospitality to the poor and to the stranger, to the powerless and to the voiceless, to those who are different from both us and the norm, including some genetic norm. If we are to "play God" as God plays God, then we will work for a society where human beings — each of them, even the least of them — are treated as worthy of God's care and affection.

This has been just a selection of images of God, and I admit that the moves to claims about genetic interventions were made far too quickly. But enough has been said, I hope, to suggest the importance of the invitation to play God as God plays God. Enough has been said, I hope, to suggest the importance of the perspective in terms of which we think about genetics and in terms of which we make sense not only of our powers but of the phrase "playing God."

Notes

1. Ted Howard and Jeremy Rifkin, for example, ask their readers *Who Should Play God?* in the title of their book (1977), but a reader who expects an extended discussion of the question or a reasoned defence of an answer will be disappointed. The question is evidently rhetorical and the answer is "no one."

2. To be sure, Bacon recommended his "great instauration" as a form of obedience to God, as a restoration to humanity of the power over nature which was given at creation but lost through the fall. Indeed, he prays "that things human may not interfere with things divine, and that . . . there may arise in our minds no incredulity or darkness with regard to the divine mysteries" (Bacon, [1620] 1960, pp. 14-15). Even so, such mysteries have no theoretical place in Bacon's account of knowledge.

3. Jonas (1966, p. 194) contrasts the relations of leisure to theory in the classical and modern traditions. In the classical account leisure was an antecedent condition

for speculative knowledge, for contemplation; in modern theory leisure is an effect of knowledge (as power), one of the benefits of that knowledge that provides relief from the miseries of humanity, including toil. "Wherefore," Bacon says ([1620] 1960, p. 29), "if we labor in thy works with the sweat of our brows, thou wilt make us partakers of . . . thy sabbath."

4. This account of "playing God" was the one rejected by the theologians consulted by the President's Commission (1982, p. 53).

5. On the shift from theodicy to "anthropodicy" see Becker (1968, p. 18) and Hauerwas (1990, pp. 59-64).

6. A delightful essay by Jan van Eys (1982) also underscores the invitation to "play" in the phrase "play God," unfortunately, van Eys treats "play" as a kind of psychological therapy and so renders it instrumental finally.

References

Augenstein, L.: 1969, *Come, Let Us Play God,* Harper & Row, New York.

Bacon, F.: 1960 [1620], *The New Organon and Related Writings,* F. H. Anderson (ed.), The Liberal Arts Press, Bobbs-Merrill Co., Indianapolis.

Becker, E.: 1968, *The Structure of Evil,* George Braziller, New York.

Bonhoeffer, D.: 1953, *Letters and Papers from Prison,* E. Bethge (ed.), R. H. Fuller (trans.), Macmillan Company, New York.

Erde, E.: 1989, "Studies in the Explanation of Issues in Biomedical Ethics: (II) On 'On Play[ing] God,' Etc.," *The Journal of Medicine and Philosophy,* 14: 593-615.

Fletcher, J.: 1970, "Technological devices in medical care," in K. Vaux (ed.), *Who Shall Live? Medicine, Technology, Ethics,* Fortress Press, Philadelphia, pp. 115-42.

Fletcher.: 1974, *The Ethics of Genetic Control: Ending Reproductive Roulette,* Anchor Books, Garden City, New York.

Graham, R.: 1971, "Foreword," in C. A. Frazier (ed.), *Should Doctors Play God?,* Broadman, Nashville.

Hartt, J.: 1975, *The Restless Quest,* United Church Press, Philadelphia.

Hauerwas, S.: 1990, *Naming the Silences: God, Medicine, and the Problem of Suffering,* William B. Eerdmans, Grand Rapids.

Howard, T., and Rifkin, J.: 1977, *Who Should Play God?,* Dell Publishing Co., New York.

Huizinga, J.: 1950, *Homo Ludens: A Study of the Play-Element in Culture,* Beacon Press, Boston.

Jonas, H.: 1966, *The Phenomenon of Life: Toward a Philosophical Biology,* Dell Publishing Co., New York.

Jüngel, E.: 1983, *God as the Mystery of the World,* Guder (trans.), William B. Eerdmans Publishing Company, Grand Rapids.

Lebacqz K.: 1984, "The ghosts are on the wall: a parable for manipulating life," in R. Esbjornson (ed.), *The Manipulation of Life,* Harper & Row, San Francisco, pp. 22-41.

O'Donovan, O.: 1984, *Begotten or Made?,* Oxford University Press, Oxford.

President's Commission for the Study of Ethical Problems in Medicine and Biomedical and Behavioral Research: 1982, *Splicing Life: A Report on the Social and Ethical Issues of Genetic Engineering with Human Beings,* U.S. Government Printing Office, Washington, D.C.

Ramsey, P.: 1970a, *The Patient as Person: Explorations in Medical Ethics,* Yale University Press, New Haven.

Ramsey, P.: 1970b, *Fabricated Man: The Ethics of Genetic Control,* Yale University Press, New Haven.

Ramsey, P.: *Ethics at the Edges of Life: Medical and Legal Intersections,* Yale University Press, New Haven.

Teilhard de Chardin: 1961, *The Phenomenon of Man,* B. Wall (trans.), Harper and Row, New York.

van Eys, J.: "Should doctors play God?," *Perspectives in Biology and Medicine,* 25: 481-85.

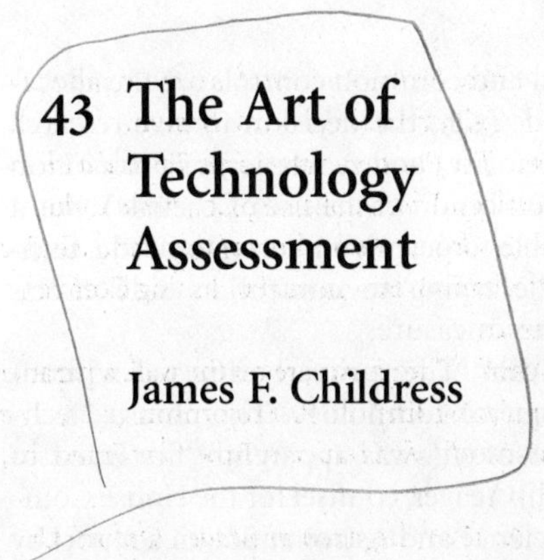

43 The Art of Technology Assessment

James F. Childress

Technology, Assessment, and Control

"It was the best of times, it was the worst of times, it was the age of wisdom, it was the age of foolishness." These words, which Charles Dickens uses for the French Revolution in *A Tale of Two Cities*, could easily apply to our discourse about technology. Positive and negative superlatives abound. We are quick to applaud or to disapprove. Rarely do we grasp the ambiguity of technology and the necessity of subtle and nuanced evaluations. Our public policies will not be responsible until we grasp this ambiguity and deal with it in relation to moral principles and values.

In the late 1950s and early 1960s, many commentators declared that the modern world had lost interest in, or the capacity to answer, big questions such as the meaning of life and the goals of our institutions. Social scientists such as Daniel Bell announced the "end of ideology," philosophers such as Peter Laslett observed that "political philosophy is dead," and theologians such as Harvey Cox noted the decline of religion. According to Cox, the secular city was emerging, and its inhabitants would be pragmatic and profane, interested only in what will work in this world. All these interpretations converged: individuals and communities are no longer interested in, or able to deal with, ideology, metaphysics, and mystery.[1] Some interpreters even went so far as to say that the important issues are merely technical and can be handled by the technicians or experts. President Kennedy expressed this viewpoint in the early '60s, when he held that the real issue today is the management of industrial society — a problem of ways and means, not of ideology. As he put it, "the fact of the matter is that most of the problems, or at least many of them, that we now face are technical problems, are administrative problems [requiring] . . . Very sophisticated judgments which do not lend themselves to the great sort of 'passionate movements' which have stirred this country so often in the past."[2]

The obituaries for ideology, social and political philosophy, and religion were premature — as the events of the last twenty years have demonstrated. In the rapid growth of various religious communities and in the conflicts over civil rights, the war in Vietnam, abortion, and technology, it became clear that interest in the big questions was only dormant or overlooked in the rush to embrace new trends.

For the most part, those who wrote the obituaries for meaning and value in the modern world were quite sanguine about technological society and the technocrats who would run it without worrying about larger perspectives. But while they praised technological man, others such as Jacques Ellul viewed him with distrust and disdain.[3] However, their debates lacked subtlety and discrimination largely because the protechnologists and the antitechnologists tended to agree that the issue was technology as such (or at least modern technology as such). As a result, they obscured the importance of assessing and controlling particular technologies.

Unfortunately, these global perspectives endure. Two examples can be found in recent books. In *The Republic of Technology: Reflections on Our Future Community*, Daniel Boorstin, the Librarian of Congress, connects the growth of technology with the (alleged) decline of ideology: "Technology dilutes and dissolves ideology. . . . More than any other modern people we have been free of the curse of ideology."[4] Holding that we are most human when we are making and using tools, Boorstin is enthusiastic about technology as such.

An example of a global perspective that is negative toward technology (at least within one area of medicine) is Stanley Reiser's *Medicine and the*

Reign of Technology. Reiser, a historian of medicine, traces the development of various diagnostic technologies such as the stethoscope and concludes that they have increasingly alienated physicians from patients. Because they provide external, objective signs, the physician no longer relies on his own personal contact with the patient for diagnosis. Thus, the physician concentrates on the measurable aspects of illness rather than on human factors. "Accuracy, efficiency, and security are purchased at a high price," Reiser contends, "when that price is impersonal medical care and undermining the physician's belief in his own medical powers." The physician, he says, must rebel against this "reign of technology."[5]

It is interesting that both Boorstin and Reiser choose "political" metaphors and images when they discuss technology: "republic," "reign," and "rebellion." And despite their different responses to technology, both appear to hold a form of technological determinism, either hard or soft. Technology determines social relationships, for example, between patient and physician. Not only are there problems with this determinism which makes technology an independent variable, but it is not accurate or helpful to approach technology as such, to offer global praise or blame. More precise and discriminate judgments are required if we are to reap the benefits and avoid the evils of particular technologies. One attempt in the last fifteen years to provide a way to control technologies through public policy is *technology assessment.* I want to examine the art of technology assessment, its possibilities and its limitations.

For our purposes, "technology" can be defined as the "systematic application of scientific knowledge and technical skills for the control of matter, energy, etc., for practical purposes."[6] I shall concentrate on biomedical technologies: the technologies (techniques, drugs, equipment, and procedures) used by professionals in delivering medical care. Examples include insulin, the totally implantable artificial heart, kidney dialysis, CAT scanners, and in vitro fertilization.

We assess technologies in order to be able to "control" them responsibly through our public policies.[7] Public policy is a purposive course or pattern of action or inaction by government officials. Public policies designed to "control" technologies may operate in many different ways. The most typical and common controls are the allocation of funds (e.g., the decision to give research on cancer priority) and regulation or prohibition (e.g., the prohibition of the use of Laetrile). But it is also possible to permit and even to fund a technology while trying to control its side effects through other measures.

Control cannot be properly directed without an assessment of technology. The phrase "technology assessment" was apparently first used in 1966 by Philip Yeager, counsel for the House Committee on Science and Astronautics, in a report by the House Subcommittee on Science, Research and Development chaired by Congressman Emilio Q. Daddario (D-Conn.), later the first head of the Office of Technology Assessment. Basically, technology assessment is a comprehensive approach, considering all the possible or probable consequences, intended and unintended effects, of a technology on society. It is thus multidisciplinary and interdisciplinary.

Against some interpreters and practitioners of technology assessment, I would argue that it is "an art form," not a science.[8] As an art form, it is basically the work of imagination which is indispensable for judgment-making. All sorts of methods can be used, and technology assessment should not be identified with any particular methods. Before policy makers had access to systems analysts, and the like, they consulted astrologers, and, on the whole, Hannah Arendt once suggested, it would be better if they still consulted astrologers! I want to show that technology assessment can be more than a narrow technique and that, as a broad approach, drawing on several different methods, it is an indispensable art.

Theological Convictions

Technology assessments will draw on theological (or quasi-theological) convictions as well as on moral principles and values. Before turning to the latter, I want to indicate how general theological convictions provide perspectives on and engender attitudes toward technology, often through perspectives on and attitudes toward nature.[9] It should be noted that Christian (and Jewish) convictions reflect certain tensions which may be creative or destructive.

On the one hand, the Christian tradition affirms the goodness of creation, holding that nature is not an enemy to be assaulted. On the other hand, it also leads to what Max Weber called "the disenchantment of the world" or "the rationalization of the world."[10] Its stress on God's transcendence tends to exclude spirits in nature who need to be approached with awe, and it thus frees nature for man's dominion.

Another tension can be seen in the distinction between sovereignty over nature and stewardship of nature. Although the Christian tradition has sometimes engendered (or at least supported) attitudes of human sovereignty over nature,[11] its dominant theme is human stewardship, deputyship, or trusteeship. While the sovereign is not accountable, the trustee is accountable to God and for what happens to nature. Human action takes place within a context in which humans are ultimately responsible to God as the sovereign Lord of life, Creator, Preserver, and Redeemer. Within this perspective of trusteeship, we cannot be satisfied with a short-term view of responsibility. For example, there is penultimate responsibility to and for future generations; it is not legitimate to slight this responsibility by asking, What has posterity ever done for us? And there is penultimate responsibility to and for nonhuman nature, not only because "nature bats last"!

Some theological critics reject the image of stewardship or trusteeship because it involves *dominium terrae.* But it is irresponsible to neglect or to repudiate human control over nature. The issue is not control (technology) but, rather, the ends, effects, and means of control (technology). This control is not total or unlimited; it is not absolute dominion. It is limited and constrained by nature itself, by moral principles and rules, and by ultimate loyalty and responsibility to God. It is not necessary or desirable to conceive these limits and constraints in terms of "rights" (e.g., rights of trees) as though we can imagine moral requirements only when we can invoke rights. However important rights are — and they are very important — we can conceive moral limits on our control of nature without appealing to them.

The ends of *dominium terrae* are also subject to criticism. If there is a hierarchy of interests, and if human interests are dominant, they should not be construed narrowly — for example, in terms of material goods. Nor should they exclude the goods of nature which are not reducible to human interests. Theologically, the propensity of human beings to construe their interests narrowly and to exclude nonhuman interests or goods is explained in terms of sin. Because humanity is fallen, its control over nature will frequently be misdirected and even destructive. In addition, as we will see when we discuss process later, procedures and mechanisms for reducing the effects of sin are indispensable; even though they cannot eradicate sin, they can lessen its destructiveness.

According to some theological critics, the image of stewardship or trusteeship is also suspect because it appears to separate human beings and nonhuman nature. To be sure, this image depends on a distinction between humanity and nature, but it does not imply an invidious separation. Humanity is part of nature. But, created in the image of God, it is a distinctive, even unique, part of nature. In addition, there may be a hierarchy of value with humanity at the apex. However much we need to emphasize the continuity between humanity and nature, discontinuity, at least as distinction, is still evident and important. Even as part of nature, humanity can still be a steward and trustee for nature.

Furthermore, to distinguish humanity and nature is not to deny their interdependence. Humanity should recognize its solidarity, its community of interests, with nature, because what affects nonhuman nature also affects humanity. It is not necessary or desirable, however, to focus on oneness or organic harmony or to develop a process theology in order to support an adequate ethic. It is possible, for example, to develop adequate limits on human control over nature from a perspective of conflict between humanity and nature in a fallen world. As Gerhard Liedke argues, such a perspective would hold that nonhuman nature is more than material, for, at the very least, it is a rival partner in a conflict. And it needs protection to ensure its participation as an equal in this conflict.[12] Furthermore, recognizing nature in this way is compatible with an attitude of awe and wonder that supports limits on human control over nature.

Although general theological (or quasi-theological) convictions provide perspectives and engender attitudes, they are not by themselves sufficient for the assessment of technologies. For such a task, we need an ethical bridgework or framework to connect these convictions, perspectives, and attitudes with judgments about technologies. Such a bridgework or framework will consist, in part, of general principles and values. But theological convictions, along with the perspectives they provide and the attitudes they engender, do not merely serve as warrants for moral principles and values. They also shape interpretations of situations to which we apply principles and values. Consider, for example, beliefs about death in debates about technologies to prolong and extend life. If a society views death as an enemy, always to be opposed, it will be inclined to provide funds to develop life-prolonging and life-extending technologies and to use them even when the expected quality of life is poor. An adequate critique would thus include convictions, perspectives, and attitudes that shape interpretations of situations, as well as moral principles and values.

Because it is not possible here to establish all the important connections between theological convictions, moral principles and values, and interpretations of situations, I shall assume several principles and values in order to trace their implications for the assessment of technologies.[13] Unless a single principle or value is accepted as overriding, conflicts and dilemmas are inevitable. As Guido Calabresi and Philip Bobbitt emphasize in *Tragic Choices*, tragedy is largely a cultural phenomenon: it depends on the principles and values of the individual or the society.[14] This point was underlined during a 1979 visit to the People's Republic of China with an interdisciplinary and interprofessional delegation interested in ethics, public policy, and health care. Frequently members of our delegation asked Chinese policy makers, health care professionals, and others how they handle some of our "problems" such as refusal of treatment. The most common response was: "That's not a problem here. It doesn't exist here." Sometimes this response reflected the stage of technological development; often, however, it reflected the unimportance of some Western principles and values such as autonomy, privacy (for which there is no Chinese word), and other ingredients of individualism.[15]

Principles and Values in Technology Assessment

I now want to indicate how technology assessment might proceed and, in particular, what principles and values it ought to consider. Nothing in its logic requires that it be as narrow as it sometimes is. Its practitioners need not be what John Stuart Mill called "one-eyed men" attending only to the "business" side of life.[16]

1. Any technology assessment depends to a great extent on the principle of proportionality — proportion between the probable good and bad effects of technologies. This principle is expressed in various methods used to assess technologies, for example, cost-benefit analysis and risk-benefit analysis, which are only "new names for very old ways of thinking" (as William James said of pragmatism). They represent attempts to systematize, formalize, and frequently to quantify what we ordinarily do. For example, outside Canton, patients in a commune hospital formed their own risk-benefit analysis of traditional Chinese herbal medicine and Western medicine, both of which were available. They said, "Chinese medicine might not help you, but it won't hurt you. Western medicine might help you, but it also might hurt you."

I shall concentrate on *risk* and *benefit*, viewing risk as one sort of cost, i.e., cost as threat to safety, health and life. The terms "risk" and "benefit" are perhaps not the best. Risk includes both amount or magnitude of harm and probability of harm. When we juxtapose benefit and risk, we are likewise interested in the magnitude and probability of benefit. It would be more accurate then to say that we need to balance the probability and magnitude of harm and the probability and magnitude of benefit. But since that expression is too cumbersome, I will use the common formulation of *risk-benefit analysis*.

Risk-benefit analysis involves what has been called "statistical morality."[17] Risks are everywhere, and one major question is how far we are willing to go in order to reduce the risks of premature mortality, morbidity, and trauma. Let us concentrate on mortality and ask the troubling question: How much is it worth to save a life (really to postpone death since lives are never really saved)? Or what is the value of a life? Consider the controversy over the Pinto. Apparently in 1973 Ford officials decided not to install a safety device that would prevent damage to the Pinto's gasoline tank in rear-end collisions. According to some reports, this device would have cost eleven dollars per vehicle or 137 million dollars for the whole production run. It is not accurate to say that Ford valued human life at eleven dollars. Rather, using a figure of approximately $200,000 per life, it concluded that the safety device should not be used because its costs outweighed its benefits.[18]

Economists propose two different ways to determine the value of life.[19] First, discounted future earnings. This approach tends to give priority to young adult white males. Thus a program to encourage motorcyclists to wear helmets would be selected over a cervical cancer program. Second, a willingness to pay. The question is not how much we would be willing to pay in order to avoid certain death, but how much we would be willing to pay to reduce the risk of death. How is willingness to pay determined? By finding out how much all those who are affected would be willing to pay, summing up the individual amounts, and then dividing by the anticipated number of deaths prevented. While it might be possible to study actual behavior (e.g., in the workplace), one promising approach uses opinion polls to determine, for example, how much a community would be willing to pay in taxes for a technology that would reduce the chances of death after a heart attack.

Although it may be impossible to avoid valuing lives (at least implicitly) in technology assessment, criticisms abound. Religious critics contend that life has infinite or absolute value. But their criticism is not serious insofar as it is directed against policies that do not do everything possible to reduce the risk of death. Judaism and Christianity, to take two examples, do not hold that life is an absolute value, superior to all other values. Both traditions honor martyrs who refuse to value life more highly than other goods such as obedience to the divine will. Furthermore, there is a difference between negative and positive duties, and the duty not to kill is more stringent than the duty to save lives.

Other critics hold that it is immoral to put a value on life. But we all have life plans and risk budgets.[20] Our life plans consist of aims, ends, and values, and our risk budgets indicate the risks to our health and survival we are willing to accept in order to realize some other goods. Health and survival are conditional, not final, values. A society might justly choose to put more of its budget into goods other than health and survival, as I argued in *Priorities in Biomedical Ethics*. Such a choice may be more political, i.e., to be resolved through the political process in terms of the community's values, or even aesthetic. One way to make this choice is to determine a community's willingness to pay for different goods.

An extension of these religious and moral objections opposes the calculation of consequences. Utilitarianism has sometimes been depicted as "ethics in cold blood." But, as I will argue later, consequences are always morally relevant even if they are not always morally decisive. This objection to calculation of consequences may simply be an objection to doing self-consciously and openly what we have to do. For example, Steven Rhoads argues that we should do a little dissembling since to put a public value on life would shock the community and perhaps lead to callousness.[21] In effect, he offers consequentialist grounds for not openly pursuing consequentialism.

These various objections to valuing lives do not hold. For the most part, they are not even aimed at the right targets. And it would be useful for us as individuals and members of a community to ask how much we are willing to spend to reduce the risk of death (in brief, to put a value on life).

It is obvious that value considerations determine what counts as benefit and what counts as harm. They also determine how much particular benefits and harms count, how much weight they should have in the calculation. An adequate risk-benefit analysis needs to keep in play a wide range of values to identify, weight, and balance benefits and harms. Analysts tend to prefer the hard, quantifiable variables, rather than the soft variables that are less susceptible to quantification. But a "narrow" cost- or risk-benefit analysis fails to convey the richness of our moral values and principles.

2. Value considerations not only shape our perceptions of benefits and harms, they also "dictate the manner in which uncertainty as to the potential diverse consequences will be resolved."[22] To some analysts, the absence of evidence that harm will result is taken as evidence that the harm will not result, and so forth. The resolution of uncer-

tainty, then, will reflect the value judgments of the analyst, whether he uses his own values or reflects the society's values. Description and evaluation cannot be separated even in the determination of the probability of harm because of "opposing dispositions or outlooks toward the future" such as confidence and hope or fear and anxiety.[23]

In the face of uncertainty, a procedural suggestion seems justified.[24] In the past, technology has been presumed innocent until proven guilty. ("Guilt" and "innocence" are used metaphorically to refer to risk-benefit analysis.) But in the light of our experiences in the last twenty years, we cannot be satisfied with this approach: we should, perhaps, presume that technology is guilty until proven innocent. The burden of proof and of going forward should be placed on the advocates of a technology who hold that its benefits will outweigh its harms. Such a shift in the *onus probandi* would not signal opposition to technological development. It would only indicate that we have not been sufficiently attentive to the harmful side effects and second-order consequences in technological development and that we intend to correct this deficiency.

A version of this procedure is mandated for the Food and Drug Administration, which cannot approve drugs for use outside research until they have been shown to be safe and efficacious. In effect, research may go forward (within the limits sketched in Chapter 3 of my *Priorities in Biomedical Ethics* [Philadelphia: Westminster, 1981], "Human Subjects in Research"), research may even be funded (in accord with priorities sketched in Chapter 4 of the same book, "Allocating Health Care Resources"), but let's not introduce a technology until we have determined with a reasonable degree of assurance that its probable benefits will outweigh its probable harms. This procedure will not harass or arrest technology.

3. It is not sufficient for a technology to have a favorable risk-benefit ratio; its proponents should also show that its risk-benefit ratio is more favorable than alternative technologies or even no technology at all. For example, if both X and Y have favorable risk-benefit ratios, they may not be equally acceptable if Y's ratio is more favorable. Many critics of technology call on society to consider alternative technologies, particularly technologies that emphasize the values of smallness and the integrity of person, community, and nature.[25] To a great extent, the issue is again the range of values that should be invoked for risk-benefit analysis.

4. We should seek to minimize risks by *some* reduction in the probability and amount of the benefit we seek, if that is the only way to minimize the risks. Because we have duties to do no harm and to benefit others, we are responsible for balancing harms and benefits in an imperfect world. But, *ceteris paribus,* the principle of not harming others (including imposing risks) takes priority over the principle of benefiting others; thus, we should minimize risks even at some reduction in the magnitude and/or probability of the benefit. Although this principle is sound, it is difficult to specify how far we should go to minimize risks, short of making it impossible to realize the benefit we seek.

5. In the long run, "the reversibility of an action should . . . be counted as a major benefit; its irreversibility a major cost."[26] Thus, reversibility of a technology and its effects should be preferred over irreversibility. Why should reversibility have this privileged position? Surely, if we could realize the ideal social order on earth, we would prefer that it be irreversible and imperishable. But precisely because of the *uncertainties* about probabilities and magnitudes of benefits and harms, we should be particularly cautious about technologies with apparently irreversible effects. The "preservation of future options" is an important goal, and it requires, for example, special concern about the destruction of an animal species and about nuclear waste.

Let me summarize these points about the principles of proportionality, the first consideration in technology assessment. We should balance the probabilities and amounts of benefits and harms. Value considerations will influence all aspects of the balance, including what counts as benefits and harms, how much they count, and how uncertainty is to be resolved. If lives are valued in public policy by determining how much people are willing to pay, the process of valuing lives is not inherently objectionable and may even be illuminating. Procedurally, the advocates of a technology should demonstrate its innocence before it is implemented and should show that its risk-benefit ratio is more favorable than any alternative technologies. We should minimize risks even when we reduce (within limits) the probability and amount of benefit. Finally, reversibility is a benefit, irreversibility a cost.

Limiting Principles

Most flaws in contemporary technology assessments can be traced to the perspective of utilitarianism — the moral, social, and political doctrine that acts and policies are to be judged by their consequences and effects. It is an end-result view of life. After my praise for the principle of proportionality, the reader may wonder whether I am not at least a "closet utilitarian." After all, isn't the principle of proportionality roughly what the utilitarians mean by the principle of utility — maximizing net benefit relative to harm? Any adequate moral, social, or political theory must include the principle of proportionality or the principle of utility. In a world that is not ideal, it is impossible always to do good and to avoid harm. Often doing good produces at least the risk of harm. The principle of proportionality or utility requires that we weight and balance these benefits and harms when they come into conflict and that we try to produce a net benefit (or, when considering only bad states of affairs, the best of the alternatives). Whatever we call this principle, it is required by any adequate morality.

But we can accept the principle of proportionality or utility without accepting utilitarianism, which may be stated more sharply as the doctrine that right and wrong are determined *only* by the consequences of acts or policies. It makes the utility the *only* principle (act-utilitarianism) or the *primary* principle (rule-utilitarianism). And it distorts many technology assessments by restricting the range of relevant moral considerations. In particular, it concentrates on aggregative rather than distributive matters and it ignores other moral limits such as "rights" (which it frequently translates into "interests").

Utilitarian assessors sum up the interests of various individuals and groups to be affected by the technology, and they use this summation to determine our policy toward that technology. Although they may take account of wider and wider ranges of impacts and interests, they frequently overlook how burdens and harms are distributed. "Acceptable level of risk" of a technology, for example, should not be considered only in terms of the summed-up interests of the society. Principles of justice require that we consider the distribution of risks and benefits.

This issue can be sharpened by an examination of four possible patterns of distribution of risks and benefits. (1) The risks and benefits may fall on the same party. For example, in most therapy, the patient bears the major risks and stands to gain the major benefits. (2) One party may bear the risks, while another party gains the benefits. For example, in nontherapeutic research, the subject bears risks, while others in the future will gain the benefits. Or we may gain the benefits of some technologies that will adversely affect future generations. (3) Both parties may bear the risks, while only one party gains the benefits. For example, a nuclear-powered artificial heart would benefit the user but would impose risks on other parties as well as on the user. (4) Both parties may gain the benefits, while only one party bears the risks. For example, persons in the vicinity of a nuclear power plant may bear significantly greater risks than other persons who also benefit from the plant. These patterns suggest the importance of considerations of distributive justice. As an Advisory Committee on the Biological Effects of Ionizing Radiations reports:

> For medical radiation, as well as for certain uses of radiation in energy production, the problem of balancing benefits and costs is complicated by issues of ethics and discrimination. As an example, increased years of life expectation or increased economic productivity can be a useful measure of health benefit in some contexts. If, however, these parameters are used to balance the benefit-cost equation against the elderly with limited life expectancy or those with limited productivity, important values of society will have been overlooked.[27]

Utilitarianism in technology assessment often fails to take account of other limits because of its particular view of rationality. Max Weber drew classic distinctions between types of social action: "goal-rational" (*zweckrational*), "value-rational" (*wertrational*), affective, and traditional types of action. For our purposes, the first two, which I introduced in Chapter 4 of *Priorities in Biomedical Ethics,* are the most important. Value-rational conduct involves "a conscious belief in the absolute value of some ethical, aesthetic, religious, or other form of behavior, entirely for its own sake and independently of any prospects of external success."[28] Goal-rational conduct involves reasoning about means to ends. It is a form of "instrumental rationality," involving the choice of effective (and efficient) means to given ends. It has been dominant not only in technology but also in technology assessment. By stressing limits, I have tried to include another type of rationality that may modify instrumental rationality by setting boundaries and constraints on the pursuit of goals.

Instrumental rationality tends to exclude value-rational considerations because they do not fit easily into the schema of means and ends. Just as I suggested about policies of the allocation of resources, we might choose policies toward technologies not because they *achieve* certain goals, but because they *express* certain values. They are expressive, symbolic, or representative. This range of considerations frequently involves *gestures,* not only *tasks.* For example, we might approach nature to make it serve our needs, or to express a certain attitude toward or relationship with it. As Laurence Tribe indicates, technology assessors typically ask what are society's current values regarding nature and they treat nonhuman life merely in relation to those values. But suppose society asked seriously, How should we value nature, including wildlife? And suppose the society came to the conclusion that it should treat nature with respect. Although this conclusion would not necessarily imply that the society would never give human interests priority over nature, "the very process of according nature a fraternal rather than an exploited role would shape the community's identity and at least arguably alter its moral character." As Tribe suggests, the decision maker's own identity might be at stake, for in choosing policies toward technologies, "the decision-maker chooses not merely how to achieve his ends but what they are to be and who he is to become."[29] Who are we and who shall we be? These are considerations of agent-morality that do and should influence our technology assessments.

Process

One critical issue in technology assessment is often overlooked; process. Process is largely a matter of who should decide — that is, who should make the assessment, and how. It is possible to argue that technology assessors do not overlook process. Rather, they judge processes by their results. They ask whether particular processes "pay off" in producing the best possible outcomes — that is, the best possible predictions, evaluations, and controls of technology. When this judgment of processes by their results is combined with the view that we should judge technologies by their predicted consequences for human interests, as measured by preferences, there is one obvious conclusion: the *experts* should make the assessment. This viewpoint simply perpetuates the myth of the end of ideology even while trying to control technology.

Its critics are numerous and vocal. Many of them are concerned with processes of evaluation and decision-making in some independence of their results. In technology assessment, the demand for public participation has become widespread and has encouraged the language of "participatory technology."[30] The World Council of Churches Church and Society Conference on "Faith, Science and the Future" at the Massachusetts Institute of Technology in July 1979 emphasized "a just, participatory and sustainable society." As the general secretary of the WCC, Philip Potter, put it in his address at the MIT conference, "a just and sustainable society is impossible without a society which is participatory." He continued:

> In the present situation of science and technology, they are not really participatory, or rather they are forced to be biased on the side of those who wield economic and political power. There is little sign that they are on the side of the oppressed, the deprived and the marginalized, or simply the people.[31]

It is no exaggeration to claim that "the central issue in technology assessment concerns democratic theory."[32] Involving the public, and especially the individuals and groups affected by the technology, expresses the value of equal concern and respect. It should be built not so much on anticipated results as on the right to treatment as an equal.[33] Processes of public participation in technology assessment are essential to embody this right to treatment as an equal, as one whose wishes, choices, and actions count. In addition, fairness, a principle derived from the principle of equal concern and respect, applies to specific procedures that may be used for public participation (e.g., adversary hearings and public forums). These values and principles are independent of the results of the procedures and processes.

Emphasizing that technology requires a "new ethics of long-range responsibility," Hans Jonas notes the "insufficiency of representative government to meet the new demands on its normal principles and by its normal mechanics."[34] In a lighter vein, H. L. Mencken once said, "I do not believe in democracy, but I admit that it provides the only really amusing form of government ever endured by mankind." He went on to describe democracy as "government by orgy," an orgy of public opinion. Obviously, it is necessary to devise procedures and mechanisms that can both satisfy independent principles and values and sustain effective and disciplined public participation in technology assessment. The creation of such procedures and mechanisms may presuppose that we transcend interest-group liberalism.

Temporal Perspective

As currently practiced, technology assessment tends to "find opportunities for making judgments and taking action only at those points in which a new development in technology occurs."[35] Why? Perhaps because the utilitarianism back of much technology assessment is forward-looking, or because many assessors believe that what we now have is good, or because they believe that we cannot undo what has already been done. Whatever the reason, technology assessment for the most part predicts and evaluates for the future and is less interested in the evaluation of technologies already developed. Langdon Winner argues that we need not only "technology assessment" but also "technology criticism," which can look at the past and the present as well as the future, which can look at long-term trends of technological development as well as at particular technologies, and which can look at the society as well as the technologies it produces.[36]

Winner's concerns are legitimate, but technology assessment, properly understood, can encompass them. It should be an ongoing process, dealing not only with the introduction of a technology but also with its impact as it is implemented. For example, there was no systematic assessment of the technology of renal dialysis in the 1950s and 1960s, but it has received careful scrutiny since its introduction, widespread use, and funding by the Government. While it is difficult to make adjustments once societal momentum has reached a certain point, we have learned and are continuing to learn from the experience with dialysis, and our experience may improve our policies in other areas. Among the numerous questions that remain about dialysis are whether it is worth the cost (already over one billion dollars a year), whether the money could have been spent better elsewhere, and whether we are able to cope with the successes of technologies (e.g., prolongation of life vs. quality of life of dialysis patients). Nevertheless, our struggle with these questions, and others, may illuminate present and future technology assessments.

Another point needs to be made about temporal orientation. Historical perspective may bring a cautionary tone to discussions of technology assessment. In a fine essay, entitled "Technology Assessment from the Stance of a Medieval Historian," Lynn White, Jr., directs our attention away from the easily measured factors to what he calls the "imponderables" and insists that technology assessment requires "cultural analysis" since the impact of a technology is filtered through the culture and the society.[37] Among his several case studies is alcohol, which was distilled from wine as a pharmaceutical at Salerno, the site of Europe's most famous medical school. How, he asks, could anyone have offered an assessment of alcohol in the twelfth century? Alcohol was praised in medieval literature as a pharmaceutical with beneficial effects for chronic headaches, stomach trouble, cancer, arthritis, sterility, falling or graying hair, and bad breath. It was supposed to be good for people who had a "cold temperament." But then widespread drunkenness and disorder became problems. To shorten the history, we have problems of traffic deaths and cirrhosis of the liver. White observes, "A study group eight centuries ago, equipped with entire foresight, would have failed at an assessment of alcohol as we today fail."

Although White's point is not always clear, it appears to be that technologies touch on many aspects of life (e.g., psychological and sociological factors) that cannot be determined with great precision. What will happen in the interactions between technologies and society, culture, and psyches is an "imponderable." His lesson is salutary. History is ironic, and we can only be modest about *(a)* our ability to *predict* effects, *(b)* our ability to *assess* effects, and *(c)* our ability to *control* effects. It is true, as a character in *Death Trap* puts it, that "nothing recedes like success." While modesty is in order because our abilities are indeed limited, we have no choice but to try to predict, to assess, and to control in the light of moral principles and values.[38]

Notes

1. See Harvey Cox, *The Secular City* (Macmillan Co., 1965); Daniel Bell, *The End of Ideology* (Free Press of Glencoe, 1960), especially "An Epilogue: The End of Ideology in the West"; and Peter Laslett (ed.), *Philosophy, Politics and Society,* First Series (Oxford: Basil Blackwell, Publisher, 1957), "Introduction."

2. Arthur Schlesinger, Jr., *A Thousand Days* (Houghton Mifflin Co., 1965), p. 644. See also William Lee Miller, *Of Thee, Nevertheless, I Sing* (Harcourt Brace Jovanovich, 1975), pp. 78-95. These themes were prominent in President Kennedy's commencement speech at Yale University in 1962.

3. Jacques Ellul, *The Technological Society,* tr. from the French by John Wilkinson (Vintage Books, 1964).

4. Daniel J. Boorstin, *The Republic of Technology: Reflections on Our Future Community* (Harper & Row, 1978).

5. Stanley Joel Reiser, *Medicine and the Reign of Technology* (Cambridge University Press, 1978).

6. This definition is a modification of the definition offered in *Assessing Biomedical Technologies: An Inquiry Into the Nature of the Process,* by the Committee on the Life Sciences and Social Policy, National Research Council (Washington, D.C.: National Academy of Sciences, 1975), p. 1.

7. The term "control" is anathema to many critics of contemporary society and technology, perhaps especially in religious contexts; some critics have retreated into the private sphere because technology appears to be out of control or because the issues are thought to be cultural rather than political. For a valuable discussion of "autonomous technology," see Langdon Winner, *Autonomous Technology: Technics-out-of-Control as a Theme in Political Thought* (MIT Press, 1977).

8. Joseph F. Coates, "The Identification and Selection of Candidates and Priorities for Technology Assessment," *Technology Assessment,* Vol. 2, No. 2 (1974), p. 78. For an overview of technology assessment, see LeRoy Walters, "Technology Assessment," in Reich (ed.), *Encyclopedia of Bioethics,*. Vol. 4, pp. 1650-54.

9. See James M. Gustafson, *The Contributions of Theology to Medical Ethics,* The 1975 Pere Marquette Theology Lecture (Marquette University Press, 1975). In a critique of most, if not all, theological approaches to technology and life sciences, Gustafson castigates casuists and moralists for their myopia and prophetic theologians for their inability to deal with specifics. See James M. Gustafson, "Theology Confronts Technology and the Life Sciences," *Commonweal,* June 16, 1978, pp. 386-92.

10. Weber drew the phrase "disenchantment of the world" (*Eutzauerung der Welt*) from Friedrich Schiller. See Max Weber, *The Protestant Ethic and the Spirit of Capitalism,* tr. by Talcott Parsons (Charles Scribner's Sons, 1958), esp. pp. 105 and 221-22, n. 19, and H. H. Gerth and C. Wright Mills (eds.), *From Max Weber: Essays in Sociology* (Oxford University Press, 1958), p. 51.

11. Lynn White, Jr., "The Historical Roots of Our Ecologic Crisis," *Science,* March 10, 1967.

12. Gerhard Liedke, "Solidarity in Conflict," in *Faith and Science in an Unjust World: Report of the World Council of Churches' Conference on Faith, Science and the Future,* Vol. 1, Plenary Presentations, ed. by Roger Shinn (Fortress Press, 1980), pp. 73-80. In contrast, Charles Birch's presentation in the same volume stresses oneness and harmony and calls for a process theology ("Nature, Humanity and God in Ecological Perspective," pp. 62-73).

13. For some of these principles, see Beauchamp and Childress, *Principles of Biomedical Ethics.*

14. Calabresi and Bobbitt, *Tragic Choices* (New York: W. W. Norton, 1978).

15. See James F. Childress, "Reflections on Socialist Ethics," and H. Tristram Englehardt, Jr., "Bioethical Issues in Contemporary China," *The Kennedy Institute Quarterly Report,* Fall 1979, pp. 11-14 and 4-6.

16. Mill, "Bentham," in Warnock (ed.), *Utilitarianism, On Liberty, Essay on Bentham,* pp. 92 and 105.

17. Warren Weaver, "Statistical Morality," *Christianity and Crisis,* Jan. 23, 1961, pp. 210-15. In Chapter 4 of *Priorities in Biomedical Ethics* (Westminster Press, 1981), I introduced Thomas Schelling's idea of "statistical lives." For a fuller analysis of risk, see James F. Childress, "Risk," in Reich (ed.), *Encyclopedia of Bioethics,* Vol. 4, pp. 1516-22.

18. For a discussion, see George I. Mavrodes, "The Morality of Chances: Weighing the Cost of Auto Safety," *The Reformed Journal,* March 1980, pp. 12-15.

19. See Steven E. Rhoads (ed.), *Valuing Life: Public Policy Dilemmas* (Westview Press, 1980), especially his chapter "How Much Should We Spend to Save a Life?" pp. 285-311. His formulations have shaped this paragraph.

20. These are Charles Fried's terms as introduced in the chapter 4 of James Childress, *Priorities in Biomedical Ethics.*

21. Rhodes, "How Much Should We Spend to Save a Life?" pp. 305-6.

22. Harold P. Green, "The Risk-Benefit Calculus in Safety Determinations," *George Washington Law Review,* Vol. 43 (1975), p. 799.

23. James M. Gustafson, "Basic Ethical Issues in the Biomedical Fields," *Soundings,.* Summer 1970, p. 153.

24. National Academy of Sciences, Panel on Technology Assessment, *Technology: Processes of Assessment and Choice.* Report to the Committee on Science and Astronautics, U.S. House of Representatives, July 1969 (Washington, D.C.: Government Printing Office, 1969), pp. 33-39.

25. For a defense of "intermediate technologies," see E. F. Schumacher, *Small Is Beautiful* (Harper & Row, 1973); for a defense of "alternative technology," see David Dickson, *The Politics of Alternative Technology* (Universe Books, 1975). For a critique of these movements, see Witold Rybczynski, *Paper Heroes: A Review of Appropriate Technology* (Doubleday & Co., 1980).

26. National Academy of Sciences, *Technology: Processes of Assessment and Choice,* p. 32.

27. Advisory Committee on the Biological Effects of Ionizing Radiations, National Research Council, *Considerations of Health Benefit-Cost Analysis for Activities Involving Ionizing Radiation Exposure and Alternatives* (Washington, D.C.: National Academy of Sciences, 1977), p. 150.

28. Weber, *Max Weber on Law in Economy and Society,* p. 1. It should also be obvious from my argument that I believe that it is both possible and desirable to have rational deliberation about the ends that are chosen. They are not merely arbitrary. Yet, as I suggested in Chapter 4 of *Priorities in Biomedical Ethics,* the selection of some ends is mainly political and even aesthetic.

29. Laurence Tribe, "Technology Assessment and the Fourth Discontinuity: The Limits of Instrumental Rationality," *Southern California Law Review,* June 1973, pp. 657, 634-35. See also Laurence Tribe, "Policy Science: Analysis or Ideology," *Philosophy and Public Affairs,* Fall 1972, pp. 66-110. Tribe's discussion has been important for this chapter, especially for this paragraph and the previous one. For another critique of the assumptions of much technology assessment, see Carroll Pursell, "Belling the Cat, Critique of Technology Assessment," *Lex et Scientia,* Oct.-Dec. 1974, pp. 130-45.

30. See James D. Carroll, "Participatory Technology," *Science,* Vol. 171 (1971), pp. 647-53.

31. Philip Potter, "Science and Technology: Why Are the Churches Concerned?" in *Faith and Science in an Unjust World,* Vol. 1, Plenary Presentations, pp. 26-27. For the reports and recommendations, see *Faith and Science in an Unjust World,* Vol. 2, ed. by Paul Abrecht (Fortress Press, 1980). For a critical analysis of the conference, see Alan Geyer, "The EST Complex at MIT: The Ecumenical-Scientific-Technological Complex," *Ecumenical Review,.* October 1979, pp. 372-80, and other essays in that issue (e.g., those by Ian Barbour and Ole Jensen).

32. Harold P. Green, "Cost-Risk-Benefit Assessment and the Law: Introduction and Perspective," *George Washington Law Review,* August 1977, p. 908.

33. For the principle of equal concern and respect, see Ronald Dworkin, *Taking Rights Seriously.*

34. Hans Jonas, "Technology and Responsibility: Reflections on the New Tasks of Ethics," *Philosophical Essays: From Ancient Creed to Technological Man* (Prentice-Hall, 1974), pp. 18-19.

35. Langdon Winner, "On Criticizing Technology," in Albert H. Teich (ed.), *Technology and Man's Future,* 2d ed. (St. Martin's Press, 1977).

36. Ibid.

37. Lynn White, Jr., "Technology Assessment from the Stance of a Medieval Historian," *Medieval Religion and Technology: Collected Essays* (University of California Press, 1978), pp. 261-76.

38. This chapter originated in a lecture for a Conference on the Technological Society and the Individual sponsored by the Program on Social and Political Thought at the University of Virginia in 1978. It was

subsequently delivered in modified form at Whitworth College (1979), at a symposium on Religious Belief in the Age of Science and Technology sponsored by the Religion Club of the University of Virginia (1980), at Earlham School of Religion as one of the 1980 Wilson Lectures, and at Miami University (Ohio) as one of the 1980 Wickenden Lectures. It has been strengthened by various comments and suggestions I received in these settings. I am particularly grateful to Dante Germino who, alas, will not be satisfied that I have answered his criticisms.

44 Bioethics, the Body, and the Legacy of Bacon

Gerald P. McKenny

In Book III of the *Republic*, while discussing the training for the guardians of his ideal city, Plato addresses the role of medicine in their formation. His underlying question is how the pursuit of health can be so managed that medicine serves rather than hinders or dominates our moral projects. This question in turn breaks down into several more specific questions: How much attention or vigilance should we devote to our bodies in the effort to optimize their capacities? How much control should we allow physicians to exercise over our bodies? What ends, individual and collective, should determine what counts as a sufficiently healthy body? What limits should we observe in our efforts to improve our bodily performance and remove causes of suffering? (Plato, 403c-407a)

Ludwig Edelstein, the historian of ancient Greek medicine, reminds us of the context for these questions. Ancient physicians advocated the notion that without a high level of health no other goods are possible and that even the healthy should follow the dictates of physicians, which were comprehensive enough to require an almost continuous monitoring of one's bodily life. Fearing that to follow these dictates would make one a slave of the body and of one's physician, a major task of philosophers such as Plato was to oppose

Excerpted and adapted from the forthcoming book *To Relieve the Human Condition: Bioethics, Technology, and the Body*, by Gerald P. McKenny, by permission of the State University of New York Press.

the glorification of health, the excessive vigilance it involved, and the underlying claim that health is the highest human good (Edelstein, 1967, pp. 357-59).

Had the term bioethics existed in Plato's time, there is little doubt that the questions he raised would have constituted its agenda. Yet these questions are virtually absent from the mainstream agenda of the enterprise we call bioethics. This would perhaps be less of a problem if the analogies between the ancient Greek estimation of the pursuit of bodily perfection and our own were not so strong. But if the analogies are so strong, why has contemporary bioethics not taken up Plato's agenda? I shall argue that one reason is that our obsession with bodily perfection occurs under a moral imperative that originated with the rise of modern technology and that, in the writings of Francis Bacon and René Descartes, looks to medicine for its actualization. Modern medicine, with its immense capacities to intervene into and reorder the body, continually holds out the promise of fulfilling this imperative. The imperative is to eliminate suffering and to expand the realm of human choice — in short, to relieve the human condition of subjection to the whims of fortune or the bonds of natural necessity. The complicity of standard forms of bioethics in this Baconian project, as I call it, impoverishes bioethics in two ways. First, while relief of suffering and expansion of choice are laudable goals, standard bioethics provides no moral framework within which to determine what kinds of suffering should be eliminated and which choices are best. Medicine is therefore called upon to eliminate whatever anyone might consider a burden of finitude. Second, standard bioethics is incapable of addressing moral implications of the way technological medicine constructs and controls the body. The result of this twofold impoverishment is that standard bioethics is silent on many of the most urgent moral questions raised by the technological transformation of medicine. These are the questions Plato raised: the attention or vigilance we should devote to the state of our bodily health relative to other matters, the degree of control over our bodies we should surrender to medicine, the individual and collective ends that determine what counts as adequate health, and the limits to improving our bodies and eliminating suffering.

The failure to address these and related questions cannot be overcome by a better bioethical theory of the standard variety. For such questions pose the problem of the place of the body — its health, its capacities, its susceptibility to illness and suffering, and its mortality — in a morally worthy life, and for reasons that will become clear below, standard forms of bioethics cannot address these issues. Accordingly, I argue that the task of bioethics is to explore the moral significance of the body as it is expressed in particular moral and religious traditions — a moral significance that is denied in the efforts of the Baconian project to rescue the body from fortune or necessity.

The argument proceeds in three sections. The first section shows why standard bioethics is incapable of answering Plato's questions by tracing the former to a moral discourse which replaced traditional ways of understanding the moral significance of the body, the pursuit of health, and the suffering connected with illness. I argue that this modern discourse underwrites the Baconian project and prevents challenges to its technological utopianism from being heard. Section two briefly examines the work of critics of the Baconian project and their alternatives to it. These criticisms and alternatives fall roughly under three headings: nature, tradition, and the body. In the final section I illustrate the kind of inquiry I believe bioethics should pursue in response to the Baconian project by showing how the view of the moral significance of the body in Christianity answers Plato's questions.

I. Standard Bioethics and the Baconian Project

Standard bioethics, I have claimed, is unable to answer Plato's questions because it forms part of a moral discourse that excludes or marginalizes those questions. To demonstrate this requires a combined hermeneutical and critical investigation of standard bioethics, which can 1) account for the kinds of questions standard bioethics raises about the contemporary practice of medicine, the range of concerns it addresses, and the moral issues it believes are at stake, and 2) identify the range of concepts, objects, norms of reasoning, etc. that comprise the discourse of standard bioethics and show how they prevent the latter from articulating the moral insights and concerns of the kind of moral discourse represented by Plato's questions. Obviously, I cannot provide more than a sketch of such a hermeneutical-critical investigation here, but I hope to show how the triumph of standard bioethics coincides with the loss, or at least the suppression, of another kind of moral discourse — one that places the pursuit of health in the context of the pursuit of a good life within the limits set by fate or necessity — and its replacement by a new moral discourse — one that is dedicated to overcoming the human subjection to natural necessity.

In order to describe this process I will begin by sketching some rather formal features of medical and religious moral traditions. The accounts are formal — I do not claim that they describe any single historically identifiable practice or community. Nor do I claim that premodern societies were marked by practices that conformed to a unified moral vision that is now lost. Instead I offer these accounts as instances of a range of moral concerns that characterized premodern practices and communities but that modern moral discourse disavows and disallows.

An adequate description of medicine as a traditional practice would clarify the relation between knowledge and technical skill on the one hand and health as an end for the particular patient being treated on the other hand. As such, medicine is a practical art. It assumes an understanding of health as a standard of bodily excellence or "an activity of the living body in accordance with its excellences" (Kass, 1985, p. 174). But it also recognizes that this standard must be specified with reference to each person, so that the task is to determine the nature and degree of health appropriate for a particular patient. Hence medicine requires general knowledge about excellent bodily functioning, insight into the relation of this functioning to the capacities and roles of a particular patient, and awareness of the possibilities and limitations of facilitating or restoring functioning for this particular patient. It is impossible to achieve competence without this threefold knowledge because one can identify a skilled practitioner only by her ability to fulfill the possibilities and observe the limitations of bodily health for a particular patient.

Three important points follow. First, the standards and ends of medicine exist in a complex relation to the practice itself: medicine is not a set of technical skills in the service of ends that can be described apart from standards of excellence of bodily functioning, but what this excellence is for any given patient involves more than the body. Second, these standards need not and will not be static. Hence there is room in principle for technological change and for growth of insight. As with any practice, "conceptions of goods and ends which are the technical skills serve . . . are transformed and enriched by . . . extensions of human powers and by . . . regard for its own internal goods" (MacIntyre, 1984, p. 193). But, third, this transformation and enrichment will occur within the recognition of health as a mortal good and of human beings as destined to suffer disease and die (Kass, 1985, p. 163).

I now turn to the characteristics of the moral authority of a religious tradition. These characteristics may or may not be explicit; for some persons they may be almost entirely customary. An adequate description of such a tradition would include its account of the nature and proper ends of human beings and of the virtues that either constitute those ends or enable one to attain them. It would also include an account of how one attains the proper ends of life, the obstacles (both internal and external) one encounters, the authorities (official or unofficial) that lead and instruct one, and the powers (for example, divine grace) that assist one. Such a tradition will also include norms, rules, and prohibitions. These specify actions or modes of conduct that are either required or ruled out in order to engage in this way of life. For example, both the major precepts of the natural law in Thomas Aquinas and the five moral precepts in Theravada Buddhism specify the necessary conditions for embarking on a way of life devoted to reaching the higher ends in each tradition. One justifies these precepts by showing how that way of life depends upon observing them. Without some such norms and prohibitions it would be impossible for that way of life to be the distinctive form of belief and practice that it is. Moreover, from within such a way of life, these norms, rules and prohibitions will have a casuistical framework in which they are refined, contested, and sometimes abandoned; conflicts between them are resolved; and rules and authorities for interpreting them are identified and contested.

Such a tradition will possess two characteristics relevant to health and illness. First, it will provide an account of how bodily health is related to the ends of life, what degree of health is necessary to attain those ends, and how suffering thwarts or helps one to realize those ends. Second, when technology brings new areas of bodily life into the realm of medical intervention, both those ends themselves and certain norms and prohibitions will place limits on the pursuit of health and the means by which it is pursued.

These characteristics of medical and religious traditions are absent in the modern moral discourse that challenged these traditions. This modern discourse, or so I argue, accounts for the cultural content on which bioethics draws. Charles Taylor's reconstruction of the sources of the modern moral self offers one fruitful way of understanding this discourse (Taylor, 1989). What follows relies heavily on key elements of Taylor's interpretation, though I alter it, add to it, and apply the resulting product to medicine. One of the chief characteristics of the modern moral discourse according to Taylor is the moral valuation of ordinary life. For Protestant Christianity human effort is fruitless in attaining salvation, which comes through divine grace alone. Hence rather than directing one's life toward the attainment of moral and religious perfection, human effort is to be directed toward serving the needs of one's neighbors. This is done by engaging in the pursuits of ordinary life such as family and work. But if the needs of one's neighbors are to be met, one's work must be disciplined and effective. It became clear beginning with Francis Bacon that effectiveness would require an instrumental approach to nature, ultimately including human nature, in order to fulfil its moral project. In this spirit Bacon praised the mechanical arts and disparaged speculative science for doing nothing "to relieve and benefit the condition of man" (Bacon, 1960, pp. 71-72; cf. Taylor, 1989, p. 213).

The instrumental approach to nature was supported by a theological conviction that God has ordered it for the preservation and enhancement of human life. Nature is therefore governed by divine providence as in the Stoic and medieval cosmos, but the conception of a providential order has changed. The ancient and medieval conception of nature as a teleological order from which a hierarchy of ends could be derived was replaced by the burgeoning conception of nature as a law-governed mechanism, susceptible to human control and neutral regard to ends — an order, therefore, which permits human control for the purposes of human preservation and well-being. As Taylor argues, from this perspective Baconian science could be viewed as an avenue to the fulfillment of Protestant moral and religious aspirations. Its turn from contemplation of nature to control of nature allowed nature to be used for its proper twofold purpose; to glorify God (rather than serve as an end in itself) and to benefit human beings (1989, pp. 231-33).

Up to this point, the roots of modern morality are in Protestant Christianity. But as Taylor emphasizes, radical Enlightenment thinkers such as Jeremy Bentham were able to understand their secular agenda as a superior way of affirming ordinary life and expressing benevolence. According to them, the affirmation of ordinary life meant being true to the demands of ordinary human nature and so identifying good with pleasure and evil with pain. The Protestant commitment to meeting the needs of the neighbor now became a set of obligations to prevent and remove the causes of pain and to maximize the quantity of pleasure. As Taylor argues, this made it possible for the first time to put the relief of suffering (and the avoidance of cruelty) at the center of the social agenda. This emphasis on the relief of suffering in turn resulted in a new standard for all remaining conceptions of religious, moral, and legal order: do they lessen the amount of suffering in the world or contribute to it? (1989, p. 331). From now on all these conceptions of order would have to present their credentials for relieving suffering to gain admission to the moral realm, credentials few such conceptions could produce.

Not surprisingly, this new moral agenda was closely connected with the loss of the belief in divine providence that had sustained the Protestant moral enterprise. Ever since the nominalists it had been difficult to support belief in divine providence on philosophical grounds, and as the mechanistic explanation of nature reached its climax with Newton, providential and the remaining teleological approaches to nature were both discredited. Confidence in a providential order therefore gave way to a growing emphasis on the need to extract the preservation and enhancement of human life from an indifferent nature by means of technological labor. This has implications for the approach to suffering. While the loss of ideas of providence or a meaningful cosmic order removes the incentive to find any religious or cosmic meaning for suffering, the mechanization of nature means that suffering from natural causes is no longer an inevitable feature of the world but is, to the extent that human beings are capable of controlling nature, an object of human responsibility. Hence the new worldview both requires the elimination of suffering and makes it possible.

The contrasts with traditional ways of life are clear. First, the meaning of bodily life, which was once determined by an account of its excellent functioning and limited by its subjection to fortune, will now be determined by its susceptibility to technological control. The medical wisdom of learning the limits of healing and accepting the morality of the body will yield to Bacon's admonition to call no disease incurable and, even more presciently, to orient medical knowledge to the prolongation of life (Bacon, 1894, pp. 163, 166-68). Second, the concern with the preservation and enhancement of ordinary human nature combined with the concern to relieve suffering means that health will become an end in itself rather than a condition or a component of a virtuous life. Medical care will be devoted to relieving and eliminating suffering wherever it is found rather than to the management of health for the pursuit of virtue. Third, rules and prohibitions limiting what can be done to the body to relieve suffering will appear to be at best insufficiently concerned about suffering and at worst arbitrary and even cruelly insensitive.

This combination of technological control over nature (including the human body) and a moral commitment to relieve suffering by preventing the harms and eliminating all the conditions and limitations that threaten bodily life accounts for a large part of the nature and task of medicine in the modern era. The unquestioned commitments to technological control of the body for the sake of eliminating "misery and necessity" constitute much of what I call the Baconian project. But there is one more chapter to the story. A second aspect of the modern moral framework is what Taylor calls inwardness (1989, pp. 370-76). Inwardness has deep Augustinian and Cartesian roots, but during the Romantic period it surfaced in the inner conviction of the importance of one's own natural fulfillment. The idea is not only that each individual is unique and original but that this uniqueness and originality determines how he or she ought to live. There is an obligation (more aesthetic than moral) for each person to live up to his or her originality. What follows from this is the importance contemporary moderns place on free self-determination. Together with the ideal of universal benevolence, self-determination also leads to the idea of the subject as bearer of rights of immunity and entitlement. From this follows expectations that the expansion of the reign of technology over the body should be accompanied by, and in fact should make possible, the expansion of the reign of human choice over the body, and that medicine should enable and enhance whatever pattern of life one chooses.

Taylor argues that the Victorian era brought together these Enlightenment and Romanticist trends and bequeathed them to us — along with a view of history as a story of moral progress over our forebears, a progress marked by our greater sensitivity to and eradication of suffering and our greater latitude for human choice (1989, pp. 393-96). This view enabled the Victorians to be convinced of their moral progress over the age of religion even as it enables their successors in this century to be convinced of their moral superiority over the Victorians. As a result, medicine is based on practices and techniques of control over the body rather than on traditions of wisdom about the body. The task of public policy is to negotiate rights of immunity and entitlement rather than to determine the place of health, illness, and medical care in a well-lived and responsible life and in a good community. Traditional moral injunctions that limit or inhibit what medicine can do appear arbitrary, but there is no broader framework to evaluate and criticize the commitments of modern medicine. In the absence of such a framework the commitment to eliminate all suffering combined with an imperative to realize one's uniqueness leads to cultural expectations that medicine should eliminate whatever anyone might consider to be a burden of finitude or to provide whatever anyone might require for one's natural fulfillment. This does not mean that individual conceptions of this burden or this fulfillment are necessarily arbitrary. But it does mean that modern moral discourse provides no vocabulary with which to deliberate about what makes some such conceptions better or worse than others.

This brief sketch of modern moral discourse allows us to identify the major cultural values that standard bioethics draws upon and expresses in its agenda and content. The connection of these values to the Baconian project helps explain the silence of standard bioethics on questions that challenge that project. Moreover, it shows us how this discourse, with its new ways of conceptualizing and objectifying the body and nature, and its new moral valuations, makes it impossible for the moral questions and insights of the discourse of traditional ways of life to gain a hearing. In the modern discourse, moral convictions about the place of illness and health in a morally worthy life are replaced by moral convictions about the relief of suffering and the expansion of choice, concepts of nature as ordered by a telos or governed by providence are replaced by concepts of nature as a neutral instrument that is brought into the realm of human ends by technology, and the body as object of spiritual and moral practices is replaced by the body as object of practices of technological control. From this new perspective the moral and practical concerns of traditional discourses are obfuscated, marginalized, or rejected.

However, four points must be made clear. First, I do not believe that there once was a golden age when medical care was grounded in a robust view of the good or that individual choices now are necessarily arbitrary. Nor do I believe that it is possible or desirable to reverse the technological revolution in medicine and simply return to traditional ways of life. Still less do I believe that publicly enforced consensus about these matters is possible or desirable. On the contrary, efforts to retrieve tradition must take account of the advantages of technology. My argument is the more modest one that modern moral discourse provides no vocabulary with which to deliberate about the meaning of corporeality, what moral purposes the body serves, what goods health should serve, or what limits the control of our bodies by technology should observe. Hence it allows for no discussion of what kinds of suffering should be eliminated, what kinds of choices human beings should make, and what role technology should play in all of this. Second, I do not argue that a commitment to the methods, theories, or principles of standard bioethics entails an explicit endorsement of the Baconian project. But neither is standard bioethics neutral with regard to that project. Negatively, the rejection of all substantive judgments about the moral meaning of bodily life and the ends technological control over the body should serve eliminates any in-principle objection to the Baconian project. Positively, standard bioethics fosters commitments to the elimination of suffering and the expansion of human choice within the moral constraints set by modern moral theories. Third, my account simply identifies some features of the modern moral framework and does not do justice to the rigor with which some bioethicists have articulated and balanced these features. Finally, I do not wish to imply that none of the concerns of standard bioethics are valid or that the alternative I suggest can do without some of these concerns.

Nevertheless my account allows for two conclusions that highlight the obstacles any challenge to standard bioethics must face. First, in regard to technology, it shows how the reign of technology expresses, and is perhaps in part produced by, the deepest moral commitments of modernity: the commitments to eliminate suffering and expand the range of human choices. If I am right about this, modern technology does not render traditional moralities obsolete or call for a new morality so much as it expresses and carries out an existing (modern) morality. Nor does it merely signal a will to dominate nature that levels all moral values and leads to nihilism, as many humanist and existentialist critics of technology charge. Rather, modern technology is surrounded and infused by a certain kind of moral purpose. That this was the case for early prophets of technology is clear to Albert Borgmann in his summary of the projects of Francis Bacon and René Descartes.

> The main goal of these programs seems to be the domination of nature. But we must be more precise. The desire to dominate does not just spring from a lust of power, from sheer human imperi-

> alism. It is from the start connected with the aim of liberating humanity from disease, hunger, and toil, and of enriching life with learning, art, and athletics (Borgmann, 1984, p. 36).

Indeed, one of the most characteristic features of technological medicine is the confidence among its practitioners that the elimination of suffering and the expansion of human choice, in short, the relief of human subjection to fate or necessity, are (so long as abuses in implementation are avoided) unambiguous goods whose fulfillment is made possible by technology — a confidence standard bioethics supports and defends. The moral purpose that surrounds technology and the moral confidence it inspires is precisely what makes it so difficult to criticize the reign of technology in medicine — a task that would be relatively easy were modern technology simply nihilistic or were the moral purpose it represents unambiguously flawed.

Second, the foregoing account shows why moderns allow medicine to extend its authority over new areas of life. But it offers an additional reason why standard bioethics was able to usurp much of this authority. This reason refers not to the claim of standard bioethics to articulate a common morality in place of a parochial ethic internal to medicine but to its greater success in giving individual persons a sense of control over the powers of medicine. Once again, the challenge to standard bioethics faces a significant obstacle from this perspective. For it is not immediately clear and is difficult to show how standard bioethics has actually failed to give authority and control over technology to individuals rather than to medicine or to society through medicine (as I argue below from a perspective informed by Michel Foucault), or that gaining such control for its own sake is not the ultimate purpose of bioethics.

It is one thing, therefore, to challenge the self-understanding of standard bioethics by pointing out the moral discourse that lends it its agenda, content, and plausibility; it is quite another (and much more difficult) thing to argue that its moral purpose and its understanding of human freedom are inadequate and to argue for an alternative agenda and content for bioethics. Fortunately, as the following section indicates, arguments for such an alternative are as old as the bioethics movement itself.

II. Critics and Alternatives

One set of alternatives to the Baconian project comes from James Gustafson and Hans Jonas, who argue that 1) the Baconian project entails a flawed view of nature and of the relation of humanity to nature, and that 2) modern technology renders the utopian quest for control over nature perilous to humanity and to nature in general. The emphasis on the perils of modern technology in the second point lends a consequentialist flavor to their projects, but their responses to the first point lead them to develop normative conceptions of the human, based on a more adequate understanding of humanity and nature, that extend and qualify the consequentialism and limit technology. Gustafson emphasizes broader and longer-range goods by arguing that both the findings of the sciences and the capacities of modern technology require us to construe human beings as participants in larger human and nonhuman wholes whose well-being is threatened by devotion to human goods pursued in disregard to those larger wholes. Jonas emphasizes an intrinsic good, namely responsibility itself, which arises within and is endorsed by nature itself, and whose possible future existence must be preserved against actions (often supported by ordinary consequentialist calculations) that threaten to turn humanity into a mere product.

Gustafson stands within the ethic of ordinary life which, we have seen, gave rise to the Baconian project. His starting points echo Bacon: humanity is that species which "naturally and properly" extends control over necessity to secure its survival and well-being (Gustafson, 1981, pp. 3-4). Biomedicine, in Baconian fashion, confronts nature as a threat to human survival and well-being that must be overcome (1984, p. 274). However, for Gustafson modern technology requires us to reject the utopian confidence that nature can be reduced to the service of human needs and desires. First, modern technology opens up a huge gap between our technological capacities and our knowledge and control over their far-reaching effects. Second, both science and technology make it clear that the natural world is not ordered only — ultimately nor even primarily — to human survival and well-being. While a Bacon or a John Locke could be confident that God's purposes could be fulfilled by reducing nature to human control and using it, in Locke's terms, "for the Support and Comfort of their being," Gustafson knows that nature does not guarantee such support and comfort, and that if human benefit continues to be the only criterion for intervention the results will likely be catastrophic for human beings and for the rest of nature.

The solution is neither conformity to nature as a fixed order nor control over it for human benefit, but rather participation in the dynamic divine ordering of interdependent wholes (1984, pp. 279-92). Premodern conformity and modern control both yield to a complex determination of the proper ends, scope, and limits of intervention (1984, pp. 298-315). Hence while Gustafson attaches primary moral significance to those points at which interventions into and reorderings of natural, social, and interpersonal processes become possible, this is not because these are the points at which suffering is eliminated and choices are expanded, but because they raise the question of where to draw the fine lines between proper human flourishing and threats to human and other natural wholes. In the case of medicine, this means recognizing the limits to the legitimate needs that can be met by the available resources, taking account in the development and implementation of new kinds of intervention of consequences which affect broader wholes and occur over longer time spans, and accepting the ultimate limits to what medicine can do in the face of death and disease (1984, pp. 272-76).

For Jonas, modern utopianism reverses the ancient priority of *theoria* over *techne:* human perfectability is no longer found in emulation of a timeless object of contemplation but in human power over the realm of necessity. But modern technology makes this utopianism dangerous. First, the roots of modern technology are in mechanistic science, which by rendering the natural world (ultimately including humanity) both manipulable by human action and neutral with respect to value, made possible control of a nature (including humanity) devoid of any intrinsic norm that would set limits to such control (Jonas, 1974, pp. 45-80). Second, the "dymanics of endless progress" intrinsic to modern technology — its cumulative nature in which each state of progress creates cognitive and material conditions that bring about further progress — ensure that technology will overtake any effort to realize — indeed even to formulate — any ideal that would direct it (1979; 1984, pp. 126-28). The result is that modern technology is both utopian and nihilistic: it clings to the notion that human perfection is to be realized through progressive control over the realm of necessity while nullifying or surpassing any substantive ideal designed to direct it. In the case of biomedicine it is no longer necessary to spell out, as Bacon and Descartes began to do, the utopia medicine will usher in; it is enough simply to keep pushing the frontiers of life extension, genetic control, forestalling of aging, etc.

This utopianism could radically alter human nature and even turn humanity into a product of our own making. Does human nature demand to be protected against this fate? If so, on what grounds? The task is to identify a certain conception of the human that we have a duty, on the grounds that it is an objective good, to maintain against threats posed to it by our technological power. In a long and complex argument Jonas reconstructs a post-Darwinian, anti-materialist teleology of nature to arrive at the notion of responsibility itself as this good, with the correlative duty (largely but not entirely negative) not to foreclose by technological remaking or by destruction of the natural world the possibility of there being future responsible beings (1984, pp. 25-135).

Gustafson's recognition of intervention into nature as fundamental to human beings and his emphasis on the divine ordering of nature as dynamic entails a more positive stance toward the Baconian project, including a qualified openness to biomedical alterations of human nature, than Jonas, with his concern to preserve humanity as it is and his conviction that nature ratifies this concern, allows. Yet in another sense Gustafson is less Baconian than Jonas, whose chief concern is ultimately anthropocentric. In any case, however powerful their critiques, Gustafson and Jonas share a thin conception of the human which exposes the problem with any effort to oppose the Baconian project by appealing primarily to nature. The problem is that nature itself is too indeterminate a criterion to rule on particular biomedical interventions and, as the alternative paradigms of responsibility and participation indicate, endorses too many versions of the proper stance toward our technological capacities. Gustafson does recognize that it is unreasonable to ask nature alone to provide a conception of the human sufficient to resolve most bioethical issues. But while he rightly points to the need for communities of moral formation and discourse to fill this gap, neither he nor Jonas articulates the convictions and practices that would define such a community and render its moral judgments determinate, nor do they consider that different communities may well have radically different interpretations of nature and its moral significance.

The second set of alternatives to the Baconian Project, those of Stanley Hauerwas and Leon Kass, finds limitations to technological utopianism in the very nature of medicine itself as an inherently moral practice. However, medicine as such a practice is not self-sufficient; it depends either upon a biology and a customary yet reflective morality to determine the kind of human flourishing, with its limitations, at which medicine aims (Kass), or upon a church to sustain by its story-formed virtues the practices of caring that would otherwise, in the face of the inevitable tragedy of human finitude, yield to efforts to eliminate suffering at any cost (Hauerwas).

For both Hauerwas and Kass, medicine is morally committed 1) to the well-functioning of individual patients and 2) to caring for those whom medicine cannot cure or restore. This twofold commitment, moreover, is for both of them derived from the role of medicine in attaining or expressing goods and moral values connected with our embodied life rather than from general moral principles. Hauerwas and Kass differ, however, on which of these two commitments is fundamental, and this difference, I would argue, is grounded in their alternative views of the moral significance of embodiment. For Kass the moral significance of embodiment is found in a life that displays the excellences of embodied life through cultivation of virtues and capacities, and elevates its necessities through custom (as, for example, table etiquette and clothing, respectively, elevate the fundamental dependencies involved in metabolism and the need for protection from the elements) (Kass, 1985, pp. 276-98, 318-45; 1994). Health is either a condition for or is partly constitutive of human flourishing as defined in these terms. Kass therefore begins with health or wholeness as the end of medicine. Given this end, he then recognizes that for individual persons it is realized approximately, under conditions of finitude and vulnerability (1985, pp. 157-246). Hauerwas begins with the opposite point, namely with finitude and vulnerability. Medicine is a tragic profession whose very moral identity, which is found in its commitment to caring for patients when curing is not possible, derives from its limitations. Accordingly, the moral tasks of our embodied life are to determine how our finitude and our subjection to suffering may become part of our moral projects and to care for those whose suffering is pointless and cannot be cured (Hauerwas, 1986, pp. 23-38, 159-81).

From this fundamental difference the key features of their respective accounts follow. For Kass the Baconian project arises from the loss of teleology. Echoing Jonas, Kass argues that the fundamental problem with the Baconian project is its denial of the ethical significance of the natural. The Baconian project is grounded in a modern form of science that seeks to control nature rather than to determine which human aspirations are natural, and in a modern form of ethics that manages our desires and wishes rather than determining which of them represent genuine human aspirations. Modern science and ethics therefore complement each other, and together they remove us from the ordinary understandings of the meaning of embodiment imbedded in our customs and taboos. The results for medicine follow accordingly: the disconnection of our desires and wishes from nature means that medicine is called upon to exert ever greater control over the body in order to fulfill yet more arbitrary wishes and desires. Despite its moral core, medicine is vulnerable to Baconian aims precisely because its knowledge of the meaning of embodiment is only implicit and is thus in need of science and ethics. The antidote to Bacon, then, lies in a biology that articulates the meanings of embodiment and customs that actualize these meanings in institutions and practices.

For Hauerwas the Baconian project follows not so much from the loss of teleology as from the loss of the tragic. The Baconian project denies the tragedy medicine inevitably faces because it deals with beings who are particular, and whose bodies thus do not conform to the relative certainties of a general science, and finite, thus ensuring the ultimate failure of medicine (1977, pp. 184-202). In its denial of the tragic, the Baconian project is for Hauerwas the product of modernity more generally: since moderns have no tradition that enables them to accept tragedy they are unable to find any moral significance in any kind of suffering and therefore call upon medicine to eliminate it all. Bacon and his followers confirm the view that all suffering is pointless and, with their promise to eliminate it by technology, foster illusions about our finitude and subjection to suffering. These illusions about the power of medicine lead to its control over our lives, to the dangerous (because it involves killing those who cannot be cured) and impossible quest for the elimination of disease, and to the abandonment of those whom medicine cannot cure — those who remind us of our own, and medicine's, limitations. In order to resist these forces, medicine is quite radically in need of a particular community (for Hauerwas, the church). First, medicine can restrict itself to the bodily functioning and the care of individual patients only if there are other practices in the community that address the inevitable suffering that accompanies such a restriction. Second, both the demands of care and the pressures to reject and abandon those who remind us of our limitations require a community whose habits embody reconciliation with the suffering other. Third, the role of medicine itself is ultimately determined by a community's understanding of what kinds of suffering fit into its moral projects and how.

There are problems with these projects taken together and separately. First, both overestimate the caring and the contribution to human flourishing that can legitimately be ascribed to medicine. It is both more realistic and ethically more sound, I would argue, to abandon ideals of doctors as gifted with special abilities (or time) to care and special insight into the good, and instead to view medicine as a *techne* which takes its place within a particular community's own forms of caring and is directed to its understanding of the good. (This does not mean, however, that physicians should not be caring people or that they have no role in attainment of the good. Surely physicians should help patients to achieve their goods, determine their capacities for pursuing these goods, and educate them about the likely effects pursuing these goods will have upon their health. In addition, some physicians will, as individuals, also occupy caring roles or be experts in their community's understanding of the good.) Second, Kass seems to think that an adequate account of the proper meaning of embodiment can be found in some entity called "the" western tradition. Hauerwas is right to oppose to this the necessity of a particular community with particular convictions and practices. But, third, Hauerwas tells us very little about the moral projects that at least some kinds of suffering are supposed to serve. A Kassian critique of Hauerwas would rightly insist that a description of these projects requires an articulation of the moral significance of the body that Hauerwas has not yet supplied. In the following section I take a first step toward such an articulation.

The third kind of approach links the Baconian project to a set of discourses and practices regarding the body that, by bringing the body under the seeing eye of clinical-laboratory medical science and the intervening hand of technology, renders it analyzable and manipulable. For these critics, who include Michel Foucault, Drew Leder, and Richard Zaner, the formation of these discourses and practices completed the process initiated by Bacon and Descartes in which medicine allocates to itself both the problem of human finitude (the subjection of the body to disease, decay, and death) and the task of resolving it. Foucault goes on to show how this same analyzability and manipulability subjects the body to efforts to optimize its capacities and increase its usefulness in accordance with certain interests of modern societies.

Leder and Zaner both begin with the hermeneutical displacement that occurs when the patient's illness narrative is replaced by a disease description. In Zaner's terms, this displacement is grounded in alternative kinds of relation to the body and the substitution of one, the body "in itself" as a material object — a strange body apprehended by and for the Other in a narrative of biological processes — for the other, my lived body which is "for-itself" — my embodied subjectivity narrated in accounts that link illness to various factors in the life-world (Zaner, 1988, pp. 95-97; 1981, pp. 48-50). For Leder and Zaner this hegemony of the body of the Other has dehumanized medicine and rendered it incapable of responding adequately to all but acute conditions, whose causes and cures, unlike those of most conditions, can usually be accounted for in abstraction from the patient's being-in-the-world. Leder and Zaner trace the origin of the body of the Other to Descartes. Zaner argues that Descartes's dualism — not between body and soul but between the ordinary experience of the body (in which the union of body and soul is not problematic) and the body as machine — made possible a scientific basis for anatomy and physiology, which for Descartes require treating the body as an inanimate corpse. He then went on to regard the inanimate corpse as the truth of the body (1988, pp. 115-25). But why privilege the truth of the body as corpse, especially when, according to Zaner, Descartes conceded the superiority for clinical purposes of the body of ordinary experience? The reason, Leder argues, is Descartes's quest for a solution to the existential threats of disease, decay, and death, which he hoped could be met by relegating them to a sphere of objectification and quantification where medical science and technology would eventually eliminate them from humanity (Leder, 1990, pp. 138-41). Hence the result I referred to above, in which medicine gains the authority to formulate and resolve the problem of finitude. In Foucault's terms "health replaces salvation": in place of the spiritual techniques and practices one engaged in when suffering or death was unavoidable, the techniques and practices of medicine aim at eliminating or postponing disease and death (cf. Rose, 1994).

Foucault argues that the body as machine also makes it possible to optimize the capacities of bodies and increase their usefulness, both of individuals and of the society as a whole. Through a wide range of interacting forces — the sciences of medicine and public health, dissemination of health information and advertising, forms of screening and monitoring, etc. — bodies of individuals and populations are now measured against norms related to utility, amenability to profitable investment, capacity for being usefully trained, and prospects of survival, death, and illness (Foucault, 1980, pp. 121-23, 172). By internalizing and acting according to these norms, we come to desire, for ourselves and others, bodies that approximate the norms (1983, p. 208; 1987, pp. 10-11). As a result, modern societies can accomplish through our own choices and desires what they could never have accomplished by force. Eugenics is a case in point. Where eugenic goals once required suppression of the desire of some to procreate, they now operate through stimulation (by health information, advertising, prenatal and neonatal monitoring and screening, and the fear of having an imperfect child in a society that values and constantly measures persons with reference to their usefulness) of the desire for a perfect child.

Leder and Zaner are quite right to draw attention to the role of the body of the Other in the constitution of the subject through the experience of illness and our responses to it. They also help break the hold of the Baconian project by emphasizing that the body of the Other, as that which escapes and thwarts my intentionality, is not merely a product of objectifying science and technology but one way in which the body reveals (often by concealing) itself in experience, thus overcoming the effort to isolate the body of the Other from the subject. But Leder and Zaner are mistaken in believing that the Baconian project can be overcome by reincorporating the body of the Other into the lived body. This belief assumes that the lived body is a genuine expression of embodied selfhood, so that by reorienting medicine to the lived body we recover an essential, nonalienated self as the basis of medical practice in contrast to the alienation of self and the dehumanization of medicine that, they argue, results from the primacy of the body of the Other in Baconian medicine. The problem, as many observers have pointed out, is that the lived body is also marked by the attitudes and practices of one's society or particular way of life. The lived body too is in part a social body, and not a pure expression of self. Medicine oriented to the lived body will still involve techniques of monitoring the body, disciplines, and even the formation of desires and choices — all of which not only express but also form our subjectivity.

This, of course, brings us to Foucault, who seeks to show how technological control of the body is connected with the production of certain kinds of bodies and the formation of certain kinds of subjects. And if this is always the case with any way of interpreting and acting upon the body (as ascetics have always realized) then it also forces us to realize that the task is not to recover an essential humanity behind these attitudes and practices but to determine what kinds of bodies and subjects we should cultivate. From this perspective, the most significant point about the Baconian project is not the alienation it involves or the "dehumanized" medicine it causes. Rather, the significant points are, first that the body of the Other — the body in its susceptibility to disease, suffering, and death — is construed through attitudes and practices that reduce it to an object of technological control rather than attitudes and practices that find moral and spiritual significance precisely in the otherness of the body, and second, that this reduction of the body of the Other to technological control is connected with a vast range of norms, institutions, forms of knowledge, techniques of monitoring, etc. which increasingly form our bodies, in large part by already having formed (and been formed by) our desires to eliminate suffering and our choices for what we have now come to regard as a good body. In short, as I argued in the first section, a set of attitudes and practices grounded in one discourse of the body has been substituted for another, and the task of bioethics is to determine what set of attitudes and practices should form our bodies and ourselves as subjects, whether those of the Baconian project or some other. But this requires a move from the genealogical (in Foucault's sense) task of pointing out how various attitudes and practices form us to the ethical task of determining which ones *should* form us.

III. The Moral Significance of the Body in Christianity

The problem is that if the genealogist of Baconian medicine is right, we have already been formed by the Baconian project in a way that determines our answer to the ethical question in its favor. The challenge to the Baconian project must come from a set of interpretations and practices regarding the body that constitutes an alternative to Baconian medicine. I will now try to show how certain Christian convictions would, if fully developed, make it possible to understand how Baconian medicine has formed us as subjects and to answer Plato's questions regarding the attention or vigilance we should exercise over our bodies, the control we should give medicine over our bodies, the ends that should determine what counts as a sufficiently healthy body, and the limits we should observe in improving our bodies and eliminating suffering. Underlying this alternative is a fundamental conviction that the attempt to render our bodies free from suffering and wholly subject to our choices is morally impoverishing — that the kind of vigilance over the body it entails produces subjects who are incapable of understanding the nature and meaning of embodiment, of recognizing and accepting the limits of medicine, of caring adequately for those who embody those limits and who fall victim to our efforts to deny them, and of rightly ordering the goods of the body (including those made possible by technology). The remainder of this section spells out this conviction.

The Christian discourse that subjugates medicine to the moral uses of suffering is connected with a subject formed by certain attitudes and practices regarding the body. What distinguishes these attitudes and practices from their modern counterparts is their refusal to separate the body of the Other from the subject. Rather, they recognize that the body of the Other is inextricable from the subject, so that the subject is separated from and within itself. This understanding of the body can be traced to Paul, for whom, as Rudolf Bultmann and a succession of later scholars have concluded, "the *soma* [body] is not a something that outwardly clings to a man's real *self* (to his soul, for instance), but belongs to its very essence, so that we can say man does not *have* a *soma;* he *is soma* . . ." (Bultmann, 1951, p. 194). In phenomenological terms, the body for Paul is a lived body; it is oneself as related to the external world. But according to Bultmann, the body for Paul is also that in which one experiences oneself as "subjected to an occurrence that springs from a will other than [one's] own" (1951, p. 196). The body, then, is oneself as separated from oneself. Phenomenologically speaking, this is the body of the Other: oneself as subject to powers external to one's own willing or intentionality. And it brings with it the temptation to allow the separation within the subject to become a separation in which, as in Gnosticism, the body becomes alien and foreign to the subject (1951, p. 199). The refusal of Paul — in contrast to Plato as well as the

Gnostics — to resolve the problem of alterity by separating the body from the true subject as alien to the latter is highly significant. For it means that for him the alterity recognized by all of these ancient writers does not occur between the subject and something external to it, but within the subject itself. Hence a Christian view of the body will understand the body of the Other as integral to the subject and will therefore interpret alterity — the body as it escapes the dominion of will and intentionality — as the separation of the subject from and within itself.

But for Paul, in contrast to some phenomenological accounts, the body of the Other is not altogether negative. While it poses the threat of wresting one from oneself (i.e. sin), it also harbors the promise, fulfilled in the resurrection of the body, of redemption, which is itself the work of a power that escapes one's will and intentionality (Bultmann, pp. 198, 201). In short, the body of the Other is for the Christian inseparable from the determination of the subject by sin and grace, so that the body of the Other is the key to the Christian meaning of embodiment and to the attitudes and practices that carry that meaning. Since illness and bodily imperfection are primary occasions in which the body of the Other breaks through the body as expression of will and intentionality — the state of being at one with oneself — it is appropriate for Christians to view illness and healing in analogy (though not in a causal relationship) to sin and redemption (cf. Khushf, 1995). Hence one way in which illness or bodily imperfection has served the moral projects of Christians is as an occasion for meditation on sin and the need for grace, and the disciplines and ways of monitoring the body Christians have developed have sought to form subjects accordingly.

From this perspective Descartes's effort to separate himself as a subject from his body prone to disease, decay, and death, or more generally, the quest to make the body perfect and perfectly subject to our choices, can only be understood as a denial of the moral and spiritual significance of the body. And the disciplines and ways of monitoring of the body and its processes that carry out this quest produce subjects constituted by their denial of the body of the Other. This denial prompts the use of medicine to eliminate all traces of the body of the Other in their own bodies. Medicine is accordingly called upon to postpone death, stall or reverse biochemical aging processes, restore youthful anatomical features, and in general eliminate or alter anything that is unwanted. Just as significantly, this denial of the Other equates the meaning of embodiment with control over the body. When the body of the Other is denied, the end of life may become a desperate quest for control through physician-assisted death.

From a Christian perspective, therefore, when one monitors and acts upon one's body in a way that denies the body of the Other, one becomes incapable of the use of illness and bodily imperfection to form oneself in an awareness of sin and grace. One wrongly supposes that medicine can resolve the crisis of alterity and overcome the separation of the subject by rendering the body the full expression of one's will and intentionality. But this denies the limits of medicine, which does not expel the Other but only delays his inevitable appearance, and which cannot dispel the deeper question of sin and redemption. Moreover, those who deny the body of the Other end up affirming it in a most ironic way, since efforts to perfect the body and bring it under the realm of choice do not restore the body to the willing and choosing subject but instead place it under the hegemony of a society that produces the subjects whose desires and choices enable it to accomplish its normalizing ambitions.

Acceptance of the body of the Other that separates the subject from and within itself is the condition for receptivity to the body of the Other in a second sense, as the suffering of the Other. The Baconian project fails from this perspective because it does not address and in fact contributes to this kind of suffering. Just as the Baconian-Cartesian subject is formed by monitoring and acting upon himself in accordance with societal standards for the body, so he internalizes his society's concern with producing other bodies that approximate these standards. His compassion for the suffering of others is thus formed by and expressed in these normalizing processes. The suffering of the other is elicited and responded to in terms of utility, efficiency, prospects of healthy survival, etc. Medicine exercises compassion by measuring individuals against these norms and helping them to approximate them to the highest degree possible. But as Edith Wyschogrod has argued (with respect to postmodern, not Christian, ethics), such a subject is incapable of responding to the pain of the Other because it never allows the Other to break through the codes (such as those of normalization) that inscribe the body in the text of society (Wyschogrod, 1990, pp. 98-99, 103-4; 1995, pp. 26-27). It is not surprising, therefore, that as Hauerwas argues, compassion for the suffering results in elimination of the sufferer who will never approximate the standards. It is also not surprising that as Baconian medicine keeps increasing the standards for a "normal" body in a society that measures and calculates bodies according to these standards, the marginalization of those whose bodies cannot meet the standards is increased and their worth in the eyes of society is diminished. On the other hand, acceptance of the vulnerability of the body that separates the subject from itself opens up a receptivity to the Other that resists reducing the Other to social codes (Wyschogrod, 1990, p. 99). In Hauerwasian terms, a subject for whom the susceptibility of the body to suffering and death is integral to interpretations of and actions upon the body may welcome the other who reminds us of the limits of medicine or whose body refuses to conform to the normalizing demands of society.

This understanding of the body has direct and thoroughgoing implications for the practice of medicine and the care for the ill more generally in a community formed according to this understanding. First, such a community is prepared to recognize and accept the limits of medicine and to reorganize health care around this recognition. It is becoming clear to many observers that the quest of medicine to find a "magic bullet" cure for every disease or unwanted condition has been founded on an exaggeration of certain accomplishments of medicine in this century (Golub, 1994). The prevalence and persistence of chronic diseases, the yawning gap between genetic diagnosis and effective therapy, the growing resistance of bacterial strains to antibiotics — these and many other similar factors assure us that the Baconian quest to eliminate suffering is not only being delayed but is an illusion. This is not to deny the many accomplishments of technological medicine — to the contrary, my point is that once we accept the limits of medicine in elimination suffering, we will be in a better position to use technology, as part of a more general commitment to caring, in ways that help more and more people to live better with conditions that can not be eliminated. But if chronic conditions, the gap between diagnosis and therapy, and the like will characterize medicine for the foreseeable future, then from a Christian perspective Baconian medicine has done those who suffer from these factors a double disservice. By defining all suffering as pointless and holding out the false promise of eventually being able to eliminate it all, it has discouraged them from coming to understand what for Christians is the truth of the body (namely, one's place in the drama of sin and redemption) while also failing to provide adequate resources and other support for those who, due to the limitations of medicine in general or for a particular patient, cannot be cured. Because the Christian approach to the body and to bodily suffering as I have described it is committed to the transformation of suffering into the moral and spiritual projects I have identified, it is in a position not only to recognize and accept the limits of medicine in eliminating suffering but to form a practice of health care that assigns a much higher place to the forms of care and support that enable people to live with their conditions in such a way that they can accomplish the transformation.

Second, because a community formed according to this understanding of the body denies that all incurable suffering is pointless or that the worth of one's life is determined by how closely one conforms to societal standards of bodily perfection, it will see no "need" to eliminate those who suffer in order to spare them a life of suffering. It is necessary at this point to understand Baconian medicine in relation to the larger society that it makes possible but that also supports it. The Baconian project is bound up with an entire social and economic system that virtually demands that we be independent of the need to care for others or be cared for by them. Those who cannot or can no longer maintain their independence or control over their bodies are therefore abandoned to specialized forms of care which, due to the devaluation of this kind of care and support in view of the priorities of Baconian medicine criticized in the previous paragraph, are unable to meet their needs. In these circumstances we are taught to value independence and control over our bodies and to fear their loss far more, I surmise, than our predecessors were. To the same extent we are inclined to deny the moral worth of those who cannot or can no longer exercise independence or control their bodies, including ourselves. In this context it is clear why many would kill others to spare them a life of suffering or call for assistance in dying as a way to regain control and independence. But for a subject constituted by the body of the Other, loss of control over the body may signal an occasion for oneself and others to grasp the truth of the body: the need for grace and the experience of it through the care of families and communities who recognize their duty to care in such circumstances. This is not to idealize or romanticize the loss of control; it can be a deeply troubling experience for everyone involved. Nor does it by itself resolve the status of those who are irreversibly incapable of responding to the care of others or whose incurable pain or tragic sense of abandonment at the end of life precludes accomplishment of any moral or spiritual transformation of suffering. My point is only that from a Christian perspective one does not lose one's moral worth or one's moral task in life simply because one has lost independence or control of one's body. A community committed to this perspective would form its institutions and order its health care priorities accordingly. In the case of the dying, this would involve a rather thoroughgoing redirection of resources from efforts to extend life to efforts to develop more effective comfort care, including pain relief, high quality nursing care, and support of family caregivers.

Third, members of a community formed by this approach to the body would no longer measure themselves or others by the norms of a society bent on producing bodies designed for optimal levels of productivity, beauty, and success. Because the body is no longer measured, calculated, and valued according to such norms, the need to reorder it in accordance with these norms disappears. In such a community, the uses of medicine to eliminate all traces of the body of the Other, some of which I referred to above, would simply disappear. This does not mean that all uses of medicine to enhance bodily functioning would disappear, but it does involve two implications. The first is that members of such a community will find the place of the pursuit of health and bodily excellence within the space opened up by the body of the Other and the moral and spiritual tasks and duties it entails for oneself and for others. The second is that it is clear how little is contributed to this task by efforts to draw lines between, say, treatment of a disease and enhancement of a trait. Rather, the process of discernment requires determination of how one's own body, with its capacities and limitations, best carries out the tasks and duties just mentioned and orders the rest of life in accordance with them.

In his study of sexual renunciation in early Christianity Peter Brown shows how "Christian attitudes to sexuality delivered the death-blow to the ancient notion of the city as the arbiter of the body" (Brown, 1988, p. 437). A subject formed by the body of the Other in the twofold sense I have described possesses both the self-regarding and other-regarding moral commitments to frame a way of practicing health care that is capable of rejecting as arbiters of the body Baconian medicine and the society that underwrites it. But this interpretation of the body is, of course, only the beginning. It indicate the attitudes and practices Christians should bring to occasions of suffering but does not tell us specifically what kinds of suffering should be eliminated or what choices should be made with regard to the capacities of technology. It tells us in general what priorities a health care system organized around these moral convictions should have but does not tell us in detail how to order the goods of the body. It shows how the twofold imperative of Baconian medicine fails on its own terms insofar as it delivers the body over to society rather than to human freedom and increases certain kinds of suffering in its effort to eliminate other kinds. But it does not offer a detailed alternative to the Baconian project. And if contemporary Christians are to reject Baconian medicine as arbiter of the body in the same way that their ancient predecessors rejected the Roman city, there is a final and much more important deficiency. That is the need for a concrete community (including health care institutions) to form subjects according to these attitudes and practices regarding the body as fully as the broader society forms subjects by the attitudes and practices of the Baconian project.

Sources

Bacon, Francis, 1894, *Works of Lord Bacon*, edited by Joseph Devey, London: George Bell and Sons

Bacon, Francis, 1960, *The New Organon and Related Writings*, edited by Fulton H. Anderson, New York: Liberal Arts Press

Borgmann, Albert, 1984, *Technology and the Character of Everyday Life: A Philosophical Inquiry*, Chicago: University of Chicago Press

Brown, Peter, 1988, *The Body and Society: Men, Women, and Sexual Renunciation in Early Christianity*, New York: Columbia University Press

Bultmann, Rudolf, 1951, *Theology of the New Testament*, vol. 1, New York: Scribners

Edelstein, Ludwig, 1967, *Ancient Medicine: Selected Papers of Ludwig Edelstein*, edited by Owesei Temkin and C. Lilian Temkin, Baltimore: Johns Hopkins Press

Foucault, Michel, 1980, *Power/Knowledge: Selected Interviews and Other Writings*, 1972-1977, edited by Colin Gordon, New York: Pantheon Books

Foucault, Michel, 1983b, "The Subject and Power," Afterword to Hubert L. Dreyfus and Paul Rabinow, *Michel Foucault: Beyond Structuralism and Hermeneutics*, Chicago: University of Chicago Press, pp. 208-26

Foucault, Michel, 1987, "The Ethic of Care for the Self as a Practice of Freedom," in James Bernauer and David Rasmussen, eds., *The Final Foucault*, Cambridge, Mass.: Massachusetts Institute of Technology Press, pp. 1-120

Golub, Edward S., 1994, *The Limits of Medicine*, New York: Times Books

Gustafson, James M., 1981, *Ethics from a Theocentric Perspective*, vol. l: *Theology and Ethics*, Chicago: University of Chicago Press

Gustafson, James M., 1984, *Ethics from a Theocentric Perspective*, vol. 2: *Ethics and Theology*, Chicago: University of Chicago Press

Hauerwas, Stanley, 1977, *Truthfulness and Tragedy: Further Investigations into Christian Ethics*, Notre Dame, Ind.: University of Notre Dame Press

Hauerwas, Stanley, 1986, *Suffering Presence: Theological Reflections on Medicine, the Mentally Handicapped, and the Church*, Notre Dame, Ind.: University of Notre Dame Press

Jonas, Hans, 1974, *Philosophical Essays: From Ancient Creed to Technological Man*, Chicago: University of Chicago Press

Jonas, Hans, 1979, "Toward a Philosophy of Technology," *Hastings Center Report 9*, no. 1 (February), pp. 34-43

Jonas, Hans, 1984, *The Imperative of Responsibility: In Search of an Ethics for the Technological Age*, Chicago: University of Chicago Press

Kass, Leon R., 1985, *Toward a More Natural Science: Biology and Human Affairs*, New York: The Free Press

Kass, Leon R., 1994, *The Hungry Soul: Eating and the Perfection of Our Nature*, New York: The Free Press

Khushf, George, 1995, "Illness, the Problem of Evil and the Analogical Structure of Healing: the Difference Christianity Makes in Bioethics," *Christian Bioethics* 1, pp. 102-20

Leder, Drew, 1990, *The Absent Body*, Chicago: University of Chicago Press

MacIntyre, Alasdair, 1984, *After Virtue*, 2nd edition, Notre Dame, Ind.: University of Notre Dame Press

Plato, *The Republic*

Taylor, Charles, 1989, *Sources of the Self: The Making of the Modern Identity*, Harvard University Press

Wyschogrod, Edith, 1990, *Saints and Postmodernism: Revisioning Moral Philosophy*, Chicago: University of Chicago Press

Zaner, Richard M., 1981, *The Context of Self: A Phenomenological Inquiry Using Medicine as a Clue*, Athens, Ohio: Ohio University Press

Zaner, Richard M., 1988b, *Ethics and the Clinical Encounter*, Englewood Cliffs, N.J.: Prentice-Hall

Chapter Eight

CARE OF PATIENTS AND THEIR SUFFERING

Medical personnel confront suffering on a daily basis. How does a medicine shaped by Christian convictions understand suffering? What stance does it take towards it? One of the perennial temptations is to deny the seriousness of suffering, and Christians are, perhaps, especially tempted to negate suffering as a mere external and "earthly" reality in the enthusiastic flight to a better and other world. If we can deny the reality of suffering, we feel more comfortable ourselves. But this sort of "Gnostic" dualism was called a heresy early in the church's history.

If the first temptation is avoided, a second awaits us. It is easy and comfortable to think of suffering as constituted solely by physical pain. If Bradley Hanson is to be believed (selection 46), that is not the experience of the sufferer; and if the Christian tradition is to be believed, the external person, the body, is never quite so neatly separated from the inner person. But while the Christian tradition of an embodied soul or ensouled body may keep us from either denying suffering or reducing it to physical pain, what does it contribute positively to our understanding of suffering and to our response to it? "Well," you say. "It teaches us to be compassionate towards the sufferer." But what is it to be compassionate? Compassion is a visceral response to the suffering of another. So far, so good. It moves us to want to do something in response to another's suffering. A little further, and still unobjectionable. We see suffering, and we want to do something — anything — to put a stop to it. With this small step a divide has suddenly opened up between what may be called a "modern" compassion and an ancient virtue. The ancient virtue fit the story of one who, God with us, made the human cry of lament his own cry; "modern" compassion wants to stop the crying. The ancient virtue was the strength to suffer with others; "modern" compassion wants to put an end to the suffering, and by whatever means necessary. When we celebrate the "modern" compassion, the ancient virtue sounds suspiciously like an invitation to masochism and a license for sadism; suffering should be eliminated, after all, not shared.

But perhaps there are reasons to be suspicious of the "modern" compassion, too. Perhaps the "modern" compassion is a failure — or at least a temptation — of the Baconian project described by Gerald McKenny in the previous chapter. One should be grateful, of course, for the successes of medical technology in response to human suffering, thankful for any little token of God's good future. The ancient virtue itself, after all, does not delight in suffering but in God's cause and in the neighbor's good. It was surely compassion that prompted the gradual development of a medical science and technology that no longer leave us quite so helpless and hopeless in the face of the sad stories of human suffering and premature dying. But the suspicion of more than one of the essays in this chapter is that modern medicine is tempted to neglect an ancient virtue and to distort compassion into its "modern" counterfeit.

Compassion tells us, in view of suffering, to do something, but it does not tell us what thing to do. Given our confidence in the Baconian project, it is not surprising that the thing to do is to use the tool at hand. "Modern" compassion simply (and blindly) arms itself with superior technique, relying not on wisdom but on artifice against suffering.

This modern counterfeit moves those unskilled in medical technology to assign the sufferer to the care of those armed with artifice, to abandon the sufferer to medicine, and so to remove the suffering. And then it moves those skilled with such tools, those armed with artifice, to attempt to give the story a happy ending by their technology; and if and when they fail, it licenses their withdrawal since they cannot do the patient any "good" any more — as if the only good were the elimination of mortality or suffering. Meanwhile, such patients, abandoned by both friends and experts, and surrounded by technology rather than by a community that knows and shares their suffering, suffer alone and pointlessly.

This chapter asks you to consider the meaning of care. It invites you to consider the shape of a compassion armed not only with artifice but with wisdom, and not only with wisdom but with faith. To equip compassion with wisdom, it is necessary first to attend to the suffering, and it is there that the chapter begins.

W. H. Auden gives us a tour of a surgical ward and an initiation into the world of the suffering in selection 45. His observations, confirmed by the testimony of sufferers, call attention to at least three marks of the suffering of the sick. There is a marginalization, or "isolation," of the sufferer; "we stand elsewhere." There is a simultaneous identification with and alienation from the body; "who when healthy can become a foot?" And there is a loss of voice; the "groans they smother."

Bradley Hanson's description of his suffering (selection 46) corroborates Auden's analysis, especially the marginalization of the sufferer, but he writes as one who has recovered his voice and as one who interprets his suffering as a divine pedagogy. He has learned, he says, to share the suffering of others and to share the suffering of Christ. He has learned the ancient virtues of compassion and patience.

The essay by M. Therese Lysaught (selection 49) identifies those same three marks of the suffering of patients, but she shows that medicine can sometimes ironically reinforce a patient's suffering rather than relieving it. A patient can suffer not only from a disease but from the treatment for it. Margaret Mohrmann, too (selection 48), is attentive to the ways in which medicine can further isolate the patient, can silence (or neglect) the patient's voice, and can identify the patient with the patient's body (or disorder) while reinforcing the experience of the body as the enemy. The challenge of medicine as a "ministry" to the suffering is not just to "feel compassion," nor simply to master a technique. The first challenge is to get to know the patient so that one can recognize their suffering. One context for this would presumably be the practice of taking a patient's history; Mohrmann's complaint that this practice is "significantly flawed" and her proposal to nurture a practice of listening to the patient's story are worth pausing over. It may be hard to "listen," of course, to one struck dumb by suffering; a compassion armed with wisdom will be prepared to practice a silent and empathetic presence that can break the desolating isolation of suffering and nurture the readiness of a patient both to tell their story and to begin to write "the next chapter."

The other selections in this chapter focus on the resources of the Christian tradition for both sufferers and those who would care for them. Together with some of the other essays they attempt to arm compassion not only with artifice but with faith. Lysaught sets suffering and care in the context of the liturgical tradition of the Anointing of the Sick. She argues that the ritual offers "an alternative vision of the world" and of our suffering; it offers community to the otherwise marginalized, an appreciation of the embodied life of a mortal self when we feel both reduced to body and alienated from it, and a voice, a witness, not only to the suffering but of the suffering.

Earl Shelp and Ronald Sunderland (selection 47) retrieve New Testament materials on suffering, especially the stories of the healing ministry of Jesus, in order to provide a model for a Christian response to people with AIDS. The stories present Jesus as compassionate and "as a combatant"; Jesus' compassion moves him not to judge but to heal, to oppose with his power the power of death and sickness. They contrast the New Testament materials with later theological efforts which train us to respond to suffering, they suggest, by trying to figure out what wrong had been done or what lesson was to be learned.

One might usefully compare the suspicion of suffering as pedagogical in the essay by Shelp and Sunderland with the account by Hanson of his suffering as a school. And one might contrast the importance of appeals to "sharing in Christ's suffering" or "sharing in the cross" in some of other essays with the effort of Shelp and Sunderland to make "a clear distinction" between suffering "for Christ's sake" and suffering due to disease or disability. That same "clear distinction" allows them to focus on Jesus as "combatant" in his healing ministry as the model for Christian compassion and discipleship in response to the suffering caused by disease and disability. One might ask whether they are at risk of underwriting the "modern" compassion with their distinction and emphasis. Conversely, one must ask whether a Christian account of compassion may neglect the stories of Jesus' healing ministry. Without such stories to guide our response to suffering what we called the ancient virtue may be at risk of complacent acceptance of suffering.

Stanley Hauerwas and Charles Pinchas (selection 50) revisit the descriptions of patience in Cyprian, Tertullian, Augustine, and Aquinas. They find in that ancient Christian virtue and in those commentaries on it a strength to recognize the sadness of our lives and of our world and to endure it without giving up hope. Without the strength to acknowledge truthfully the brokenness of our world and the limits of our power, caretakers are tempted to remove all traces of pain and suffering, even if that finally requires the removal of the sufferers. Without the readiness to bear evils without inflicting them, we will not learn to care for those we cannot cure. Patience is not Stoic fatalism, not complacent indifference to suffering; but they also contrast patience not only to Stoicism but also to the restless impatience and limitless desires of modern patients, who demand the medical miracle that will eliminate their mortality and vulnerability to suffering. They contrast it, if you will, to a "modern" compassion. And they retrieve it as a resource for equipping compassion both with wisdom and with faith in the patient care of God, as a resource for restoring another ancient virtue.

Suggestions for Furthur Reading

Cassell, Eric J. *The Nature of Suffering and the Goals of Medicine* (New York: Oxford University Press, 1991).

Dougherty, Flavian, C.P. *The Meaning of Human Suffering* (New York: The Human Sciences Press, 1982).

Dyck, Arthur J. *On Human Care* (New York: Abingdon, 1977).

Farrar, Austin *Love Almighty and Ills Unlimited* (New York: Doubleday, 1961).

Fichter, Joseph Henry. *Religion and Pain: The Spiritual Dimensions of Health Care* (New York: Crossroad, 1981).

Hauerwas, Stanley. *God, Medicine, and Suffering* (Grand Rapids: Wm. B. Eerdmans Publishing Co., 1994).

Kliever, Lonnie D., ed. *Dax's Case: Essays in Medical Ethics and Human Meaning* (Dallas, Texas: Southern Methodist University Press, 1989).

May, William F. *The Patient's Ordeal* (Bloomington, Indiana: Indiana University Press, 1991).

McGill, Arthur C. *Suffering: A Test of Theological Method* (Philadelphia: Westminster, 1982).

Nouwen, Henri. *The Wounded Healer* (Garden City, N.Y.: Doubleday, 1972).

McKenny Gerald P., and Jonathan R. Sande. *Theological Analysis of the Clinical Encounter* (Dordrecht, The Netherlands: Kluwer Academic Publishers, 1994).

Ricoeur, Paul. *The Symbolism of Evil* (Boston: Beacon Press, 1967).

Sabatino, Frank G. "AIDS as a Spiritual Journey," *Second Opinion* 18, no. 1 (July 1992): 94-99.

Sölle, Dorothee. *Suffering,* trans. by Everett Kalin (Philadelphia: Fortress, 1975).

Taylor, Rodney L., and Jean Watson, eds. *They Shall Not Hurt: Human Suffering and Human Caring* (Boulder, Colorado: Colorado Associated University Press, 1989).

45 Surgical Ward

W. H. Auden

They are and suffer; that is all they do;
A bandage hides the place where each is living,
His knowledge of the world restricted to
The treatment that the instruments are giving

And lie apart like epochs from each other
— Truth in their sense is how much they can
bear;
It is not like ours, but groans they smother —
And are remote as planets; we stand elsewhere.

For who when healthy can become a foot?
Even a scratch we can't recall when cured,
But are boist'rous in a moment and believe

In the common world of the uninjured, and
cannot
Imagine isolation. Only happiness is shared,
And anger, and the idea of love.

46 School of Suffering

Bradley Hanson

The School of Suffering has a demanding curriculum that includes practical experience as well as thinking and reading. The practical requirements makes this school different from any humanly designed institution of higher learning, for most of its students have not requested entrance. Admission usually happens to one rather than is sought. Yet once one becomes a student in the School of Suffering, one finds that it has a distinguished faculty.

My own recent illness thrust me into the school and although I am not a biblical scholar, I was impelled to seek out one of its greatest teachers, the apostle Paul, and to especially ponder his Second Epistle to the Corinthians. I found that Paul has four major lessons on suffering. His first two lessons cast light on my experience of suffering and in turn were confirmed and illuminated by that experience. His third lesson is rather advanced for me, and I have only begun to comprehend it. The fourth is well beyond me, and I can do little more than identify it.

I

Paul's first lesson is that the sufferer is not forgotten, because God cares and often expresses his caring through the comfort given by other people. I learned this the hard way over a period of about four months when I endured increasing pain. I learned to distinguish between levels of pain. At the lowest level is an ache. While it is a bother, if one becomes engaged in something the ache is forgotten. The next level is a mild pain, sharper and more noticeable than an ache. Yet again if one becomes fully involved in some activity or conversation, the mild pain is forgotten. As the level of pain increases, the pain occupies more and more of one's consciousness. At the upper limit pain crowds out awareness of anything else; this is excruciating pain. A notch below is what I came to call intense pain, in which pain occupies nearly all of one's awareness; other things are noticed only as peripheral and subordinate to the pain. One cannot forget about intense pain. As the weeks passed the visits of intense pain came more often and lasted longer.

One result of the pain was that I was pushed to the margins of life. Many things that I enjoyed had to be given up — playing football with my sons, attending a concert or a play, spending an evening in conversation with friends, and the enjoyable activities that remained became clouded by pain. Life became dull and uninteresting as it took all available energy just to get through the day's minimum duties.

Not only is existence on the margins of life flat, it tends to be lonely. My friends and associates were at the center, and I felt increasingly like a crippled child left on the sidelines while other children play a game. Adding to the sense of loneliness was a certain privacy about my experience of physical pain. Much suffering has a communal character. When a family member dies, the survivors share their common grief. When a minority endures discrimination, they have many common elements in their experience. But few of the people around me know first hand what it was to endure chronic intense pain. There are many who suffer like this, with no one near who fully understands their plight. Whatever the particular circumstances, being pushed to the margins of life in some form or other is nevertheless a universal feature of human suffering.

It is precisely because all genuine suffering includes psychological and social dimensions as well as the physical, that comfort from others is so terribly important. The sufferer longs to be assured that others care, and that others are striving to relieve the suffering. To feel abandoned, alone in one's suffering, would crush the sufferer with an unbearable burden.

The powerful need for this assurance was brought home to me late one night in September. I awoke as usual about 2 a.m. with intense pain. Usually it had lasted 30-45 minutes, but this night it kept on and on. After about two hours I began to cry, not a gentle weeping but great gasps. I felt unable to stand up to the pain any longer, and I cried out in anguish at being overwhelmed. My cries were also a call to my wife that I needed her. She awoke and held and stroked me. The pain did not cease for some time, but her presence made it more tolerable.

A few days later Paul's words caught my eye, "But God, who comforts the downcast, comforted us by the coming of Titus . . ." (II Cor. 7:6 RSV). When Paul speaks of comfort, he uses it against the Old Testament background in which comfort includes deliverance as well as tender stroking (e.g. Isaiah 40:1, 2). The news that the Corinthian church had taken Paul's severe letter well delivered him from his anxiety; but first he mentions that the mere arrival of his friend and associate Titus was a comfort.

Paul sees this ordinary series of events in theological perspective. The arrival of his friend with good news encourages Paul who has been afflicted with anxieties and conflicts in his work; but it is ultimately God who has comforted him through Titus. "But God, who comforts the downcast, comforted us by the coming of Titus." Thus for Paul the aid that one human being gives to another is a human transaction grounded in and manifesting the character of God, "The Father of mercies and God of all comforts" (II Cor. 1:3).

When strong and privileged socially concerned Christians hear that God comforts sufferers through other people, they are likely to hear only a call to be active in relieving the suffering of others, but that is not what *sufferers* need to hear. To issue such an ethical challenge to those who suffer is to increase their trouble by laying another burden on them. The strong and privileged are able to give; the sufferer needs first of all to receive. So Paul's first word to those Corinthian Christians who endure sufferings with him is to bless "The God and Father of our Lord Jesus Christ, the Father of mercies and God of all comfort, who comforts us in all our afflictions . . . " (II Cor. 1:3, 4). If those who suffer are to interpret the meaning of their suffering within the Christian perspective, they need to know they are not abandoned in their suffering. Others care, and God cares. This word of comfort rather than a word of moral challenge is the first lesson in learning the Pauline meaning of suffering.

II

Paul's second lesson is that those who have received comfort from God in their suffering are called to give comfort to other sufferers, for God "comforts us in all our affliction, so that we may be able to comfort those who are in any affliction . . ." (II Cor. 1:3,4). Paul's "so that" expresses purpose.

Of course, Paul's audience and his own situation shape what he says. Paul speaks as a man who has endured much affliction yet has lived through it all; and his audience are Christians in Corinth and the province of Achaia who also were no strangers to suffering. Paul does not consider those whose suffering is such that they do not live through it or fail to receive comfort in their suffering. He considers only those cases in which people are able to learn something from their suffering. He also is not speaking to non-sufferers, even though they might be eager to help those less fortunate. The admission fee to this particular lesson on suffering is high — it requires suffering, for comfort is received only in suffering. It is sufferers who are given comfort "so that" they may comfort others.

It is true that Paul's "we" in II Cor. 1:3-11 refers primarily to himself, but the plural "we" likely indicates that the pattern of affliction and comfort so dramatically exemplified in the apostle's existence has wider application. He certainly does not set himself totally apart from the Corinthians whom he also recognizes as sharing in comfort and suffering.

So Christians who have been comforted in their suffering may affirm as part of its meaning that their experience of suffering and comfort includes God's call to comfort others and that the experience itself equips them to do it. There is a psychological aspect to this, because someone who has experienced a certain kind of affliction is peculiarly equipped to help others with that affliction. Having known poverty first hand can enable one to more fully understand the plight of the poor and to bring genuine comfort. To be sure, deliverance from suffering often requires also the technical knowledge of a physician or economic changes on a broad front. Still, direct experience of suffering and comfort gives a depth and sensitivity to compassion which is irreplaceable in the total effort to comfort the afflicted.

The truth of this lesson began to dawn on me one night shortly before entering the hospital. My wife was helping me use a heat lamp, and we began to talk about the meaning of my suffering. I had to admit that the most prominent feature of the suffering up to this point had been its emptiness of purpose. There had been no goal which I could affirm and strive for, except to fight against the pain and seek healing. The suffering itself was an experience of passivity, of being acted upon by negative forces beyond my control. The pain was a harsh reminder of the blind physical roots of life, an irrational reminder without purpose. I felt kinship with the insect accustomed to living in the supportive environment of black soil suddenly turned on its back in the sun, legs moving helplessly. The brute physical reality of pain was devoid of meaning. The only glimmer of meaning I could own at this time was that I now felt much greater sympathy for others who had to suffer, especially those who had to endure chronic pain without hope of relief.

Upon further reflection after my suffering was over, I came to see that the scope of "suffering with others" should not be unduly extended by overdramatized portrayals of the Christian life, which picture the concerned Christian as suffering with the afflicted. There are tendencies toward this sort of rhetoric in Dorothee Sölle's book *Suffering.*

There are at least three distinct ways for Christians to bring comfort through sharing in the suffering of others. One way is to have concern and sympathy for those who suffer and to express it in some concrete way. Such active compassion is an expression of love for neighbor. Paul's collection for the needy in Jerusalem appealed to this sort of compassion.

Another way to bring comfort by sharing in the sufferings of others is by enduring the same suffering they do (e.g. to starve with the starving). Very infrequently would one choose to suffer with others in this way and only when it would serve some constructive end.

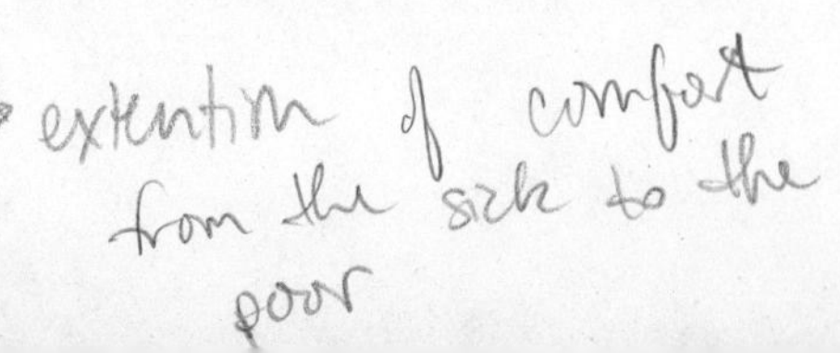

A third way to share in the suffering of others is through profound identification with them. Paul does not define suffering for us; but a good definition is that a person is suffering when being acted upon in such a way that the person wishes strongly that his or her state were different.[1] If the sun is shining on one during a hot summer's day walk, one is uncomfortable but not suffering. If one were forced to walk 20 miles in scorching heat, one would suffer. The wish that one's state were otherwise would be very powerful indeed. Using this definition to suffer with another would mean that the other's suffering would have such a deep impact on a person that one would fervently wish that the other's state (and one's own) would be changed. Parents who agonize over the serious illness of their child genuinely suffer; their anxiety causes them to lose sleep, to weep, etc. To suffer with another in this way requires a profound identification with that other person; the other's welfare is intimately linked with one's own.

While Christians frequently exhibit active concern for others in affliction, they seldom actually suffer with them. This should be honestly recognized. When there was mass starvation recently in Cambodia, I prayed for them and sent contributions through Oxfam and church. This and other manifestations of compassion are good, but it is not suffering.

A final comment about receiving comfort in order to comfort others. It would be reading too much into Paul to infer from this lesson that God *sends* suffering in order to build character. That pedagogical view of suffering may or may not be true, but Paul does not consider such a question of justification for suffering. He begins with the fact of suffering and comfort, and says that God sends *comfort* at least in part so that those who are comforted may be able to comfort others.

Paul also sees this principle of "comforting as one has been comforted" in theological depth, for Christians are to comfort others "with the comfort with which we ourselves are comforted by God" (II Cor. 1:4). This brings us back to the foundation of Paul's first lesson — the ultimate source of comfort is not our own skill or personality but God's compassion for His creatures.

III

The third Pauline lesson is that suffering Christians share in the suffering of Christ. I found this to be the most difficult lesson to understand and appropriate. Two obstacles stood in the way.

I encountered the first obstacle when I read Second Corinthians while in the hospital. When I first read Paul's list of his own sufferings in II Cor. 11:23-29, I felt that my own affliction from pain did not qualify as suffering that shares in the suffering of Christ. Paul mentions sufferings from persecution as a Christian missionary — he was imprisoned, beaten, lashed, and stoned. He also speaks of hardships that came with being a traveling missionary — the dangers of first-century travel, hunger, and cold. On top of all that was the anxiety he felt as an apostle for all the churches.

My suffering found no place among those listed by Paul. I was not persecuted for the faith. About the only hazard I faced in carrying out my vocation as a professor of religion was a loss of muscle tone from sedentary work. And while some Christians can confess anxiety over the church, I could not recall losing any sleep for that reason. If only persecution, hardship, and anxiety for the faith could count as sharing in the sufferings of Christ, then I, and by far most American Christians, were left out.

Later, after serious study of Paul's thought, two things led me to include myself as having shared in Christ's suffering. One is that Paul refers to two personal afflictions which were very likely physical. In II Cor. 1:8 he mentions "the affliction we experienced in Asia" which brought him very near death. And in II Cor. 12:7 he alludes to his "thorn." Although Paul never tells us exactly what either of these were, the bulk of commentators think that the indications make physical afflictions the best guess.

The second reason is that Paul does not set himself totally apart from other Christians, for he says that they are comforted when they "patiently endure the same sufferings that we suffer" (II Cor. 1:6). It could hardly be literally true that they experienced the same sufferings as the well-traveled apostle. It is likely that other Christians at Corinth underwent some persecution, especially the Jewish Christians, but such opposition most likely focused on Paul as the instigator of changes (Acts

18:12-17). While the disciplic pattern of suffering/death and resurrection is most vividly evident in the apostle's life, still he recognizes its presence in the more ordinary lives of other Christians as well.

It is very doubtful that Paul meant to set strict boundaries to what sort of sufferings share in the sufferings of Christ. The specific afflictions he cites from his own experience are merely examples, and even these examples are varied, including anxiety, illness, and physical disability. It seems likely that Paul would agree with I Peter 4:12-19 that suffering as a murderer or wrongdoer would not count, but he opens the circle beyond the persecution cited by Peter to include any innocent suffering. Thus those Christians whose more settled circumstances do not expose them to persecution and hardship for the faith will still at times have sufferings which bring them to share in the sufferings of Christ.

Having surmounted the first obstacle, another still loomed ahead: What does it *mean* to share in Christ's sufferings? A number of commentators think that at least part of what Paul means is connected with his beliefs about the end times. C. K. Barrett points out that there was a Jewish notion of the "sufferings of the Messiah" which did not mean that the Messiah himself would suffer but that the age of the Messiah would be a time of tribulation prior to eternal bliss. Paul probably believed that Jesus had taken most of this end-time tribulation upon himself, yet in the brief time remaining before the end some of this messianic suffering had "overflowed to" Jesus' followers. "For as we share abundantly in Christ's sufferings" (II Cor. 1:5) is perhaps better rendered ". . . as the sufferings of Christ overflow to us."[2]

If these commentators are correct, there is the question what this can mean for us today. When Paul believed that the Christians of his time were living in the last days, the idea of sharing in the end-time woes with Christ lent drama and rich meaning to their suffering. It might have given a sense of high privilege to be among this chosen band. But what happens after 1900 years have elapsed and belief in the imminent end has waned? Most of the power in this interpretation of suffering is lost.

Of course, it is not impossible to view the course of human history in Paul's framework if one lengthens the end time considerably, but it is difficult not to lose the vibrancy of that belief unless one believes this nearly 2000-year end-time era is about to close. Jehovah's Witnesses, Seventh Day Adventists, and dispensationalist minded Christians can resonate to this interpretation of sharing in Christ's suffering, but it leaves me unmoved. For me, and I suspect for most mainline church-goers, its power has been dissipated by the passage of time and numerous failed prophecies of when the end would come. We simply do not approach each day thinking this might be the day when Christ returns.

The more important and durable meaning of sharing in Christ's suffering depends on Paul's conception of the relationship between Christ and believers as expressed in the terms "Body of Christ" and "in Christ." Considerable historical study is required to grasp what Paul might have meant with these expressions, for they are many-leveled metaphors. Eduard Schweizer's discussions of these terms are a happy contrast to numerous murky treatments of Paul's mysticism. Much of what Schweizer says can be grouped under three heads.

First, Schweizer says that when Paul speaks of the body of Christ and being in Christ, he is following the Jewish way of thinking in terms of spheres, in which there are certain places or spheres where God's lordship is experienced more directly than in other places, e.g. the temple. Such a sphere of life could bear the stamp of a man such as Abraham, Jacob, or Moses. When Paul speaks of the church as the body of Christ, he is speaking of the place or sphere bearing the stamp of Christ.[3]

Secondly, "body of Christ" has several rich overtones which make it especially suitable as a metaphor for the community/sphere in which Christ's stamp is manifest. One level of its meaning is always the historical body of Christ sacrificed on the cross. In Paul's day this reminder that God expressed His love for people supremely in that physical realm counteracted common Hellenistic tendencies to escape from the physical world into some pure spiritual realm. For Christians the body is the appropriate place and means for meeting and serving others. By extension the Christian community is also appropriately called the body of Christ, because in this down-to-earth sphere people are accepted by God on the basis of Christ's bodily sacrifice and are called to obedient service. Life in this community bears the stamp of Christ. "Life in the body of Christ is identical with life 'in Christ'."[4]

Thirdly, Schweizer says that the expressions "body of Christ" and "in Christ" are also part of Paul's translation of Jesus' call to discipleship for a Hellenistic audience. When Jesus called Matthew and others to be his disciples, it meant to come with him as he traveled from place to place, but after the resurrection that sort of accompaniment was no longer possible. Discipleship to Christ needed reinterpretation. Paul translated Jesus' call to discipleship into spatial images readily understandable to the Hellenistic mind already accustomed to calling a social group a "body" and to thinking in Platonic and Stoic fashion of the world as the body in which God dwells as its soul. It was not a great step for them to think of the Christian community as the body in which Christ dwells.[5]

What had special appeal to the Hellenistic audience was to say that following Christ would mean being glorified with him and elevated above the trials of this physical world; but to say only this would have falsified the account of Christian discipleship. Paul had to say that following Christ also means obedience to Him in daily life with its defeats as well as its victories. Indeed, following the crucified Christ means that his disciples cannot expect to be delivered from the ills of life; their way will also include suffering and death.

I think the idea of discipleship is the key to a contemporary interpretation of how Christians share in Christ's suffering. My own experience of suffering suggests how the relationship of lord and disciple can be understood to involve participation in the Lord's suffering. There were a few people who shared by suffering to the extent that they suffered with me; above all it was my wife, to a lesser extent my children and parents. There were friends and other relatives who were concerned and sympathetic to my situation, yet could hardly be said to suffer with me. What seems to account for the difference between the sympathizers and the fellow sufferers is that those who suffered with me were so closely identified with me that I was included in their sense of self; their own identity as persons was closely intertwined with me as husband, father, or son.

There is a useful analogy here to the believer's participation in the sufferings of Christ, although the basis of the participation is the relationship of disciple to lord rather than husband and wife, father and children, son and parents. The identity of the disciple is inseparably linked with the lord, and the identity of the lord with his disciples ("Saul, Saul, why do you persecute me?" Acts 9:4). Christ's relationship with his disciples belongs to his very being as Christ; he cannot be Christ all by himself. The relationship of disciples with Christ is also constitutive of their being; they cannot be Christians apart from identifying with Christ as their lord.

The relationship of Christ with his disciples is asymmetrical, for the relationship rests on his choosing them while it is their secondary place to respond to the lord's call. Therefore the sufferings of Christians are also Christ's sufferings fundamentally because Christ identifies himself so closely with his church. If a concerned parent hurts when the child hurts, how much more does Christ share in the suffering of his people. So our sufferings are his primarily because he makes them his. He wills to include us in his own being as Christ the lord.

Secondarily, disciples of Christ are called to recognize that suffering is an integral part of Christian discipleship. If they hope to be glorified with Christ, they should also expect to share in his suffering by following the way that includes suffering. To identify with the crucified one as lord is to include in one's own self-definition the expectation of suffering. When the son of a Nigerian territorial ruler came to medical school in the United States, he refused to do some dirty work expected of beginning medical students in the hospital. That lay outside his self-definition, and he was prepared to drop out of the university rather than do that menial work. Suffering does not lie outside the self-definition of Christians.

Because the disciple's identity is dependent upon that of the lord, the disciple's sufferings are not just his or her own but are a sharing in the lord's suffering. That is to say, the disciple's identity is patterned after the lord's identity. So when the disciple of Christ suffers, it is not simply sharing in a common human experience as it is when one laughs or plays; it is more importantly a sharing in the specific way of Jesus Christ.

Not every path of discipleship follows that way. Suffering cannot be ignored, but one after another religious leaders point a way out of it, and suffering is usually regarded as a sign that disciples are failing to follow their leader. Jesus Christ leads his disciples more deeply into suffering, for he himself went into the depths of suffering before the resurrection. Thus while suffering comes to every human being, Christians can believe that their suffering is not alien to their relationship to Christ, but an integral part of it. Even as Christ shares in their suffering by virtue of his identification with his church, so also Christians share in his suffering by following his way.

I have found that this Pauline lesson is not as easily appropriated as the first two. To be sure, I take comfort in the thought that Christ has so closely identified himself with the community of believers that he makes their suffering his own. That is a reassuring expression of God's love for me. But the idea that suffering is an integral part of Christian discipleship is contradictory to human inclinations. I am very much like that African medical student who refused to do menial work. I shy away from including suffering in my self-definition.

My tendency is to assume that it is my *right* to be healthy, to be able to run, to have good eyesight and hearing, to have the normal functioning of all my limbs and organs. I believe it is my right to be happy, and I become enraged at any violation of these rights. Thus I deny my creatureliness, for I assume that God (or "life") owes me happiness as though the cosmic order were established by some grand social compact like a club or nation. I do not want to admit that as a creature, whatever I have has been given to me. Certainly health and happiness are goods which I should seek, but there is no cosmic bill of rights which guarantees that I should have them.

Just as Paul's lesson goes against our denial of creaturely limits, so it also goes against our tendency to deny being disciples of Christ. I definitely think of myself as a "Christian" or a "believer in Jesus Christ." I realize that when those terms are properly understood, they include discipleship, but my inclination is not to understand myself as one who is called to obediently follow the way of Christ, a characteristic basic to discipleship. I am more interested in what comfort Christ can give to me than in the summons to follow him. So I tend to ignore the call to take up my cross and follow him even when the cross has knocked me flat on my back. The resistance to being a disciple is strong.

Christ did not claim any right to a happy normal life (not even equality with God was a thing to be grasped). He accepted God's call to service and followed it through suffering and death. "A disciple is not above his teacher." So Christians need to include suffering in their self-definition. Not that they should welcome affliction or go looking for it, but there should be a recognition that suffering is both an inevitable risk for human creatures and an integral element in Christian discipleship.

Because my resistance to discipleship is so strong, I have barely opened the book on this lesson. Yet in an elementary way I have found that suffering brings lord and disciple into closer fellowship. I am drawn closer to Christ as I more fully appreciate the nature of the sufferings that he endured. The sheer physical pain must have been excruciating and prolonged. Scholars often downplay this because it is not unique to Jesus, but having known extended intense pain myself, I marvel at anyone voluntarily undergoing great pain. Adding to Jesus' suffering was the sense of abandonment by most disciples. And depending on the interpretation of Jesus' words, "My God, my God, why hast thou forsaken me?" most terrifying of all may have been abandonment by God and apparently meaningless suffering. Since my illness, I have felt a bond with anyone who suffers pain or illness. I am even drawn closer to Christ, for in some sense he suffered for me.

Being drawn closer to the suffering Christ has revealed that discipleship is a fulfilling relationship of deeper fellowship between lord and disciple. In this relationship the disciple finds fulfillment in surprising ways. There has been a glimpse of the truth that through following the lord's way of suffering, my own true identity is being fashioned, for it is mysteriously intertwined with Christ.

IV

Yet another lesson that Paul teaches about suffering is that it has the potential for being a means through which God's power can be revealed to others. Paul accepted his thorn in the flesh when told, "My grace is sufficient for you, for my power is made perfect in weakness" (II Cor. 12:9). Besides whatever else it means that God's power is made perfect in weakness, it means that the divine power is especially evident when the human vessel is weak (II Cor. 4:7). God's power is more apparent when his will is accomplished in and through one who lacks the human power of strength, beauty, wealth, etc. So Paul gladly boasts of the weaknesses evident in his own sufferings, because through them God's power is plainly revealed to others.

This too is a teaching difficult to appropriate, and it may be that it does not have as wide an application as the previous lessons. It seems presumptuous to regard one's own affliction as a vehicle for God's revelation except when circumstances clearly warrant it. I know of nothing in my own suffering that made it a means for divine revelation to others. One cannot assume that one's suffering is automatically being used in this way, but one can certainly pray that God will so use it and one can seek to be open to the grace that will make that possible. If it turns out that one's suffering becomes a medium of revelation to others, that is grounds for seeing yet another profound meaning in one's suffering.

V

Very likely Paul has other lessons on suffering, but these are enough for one term. Learning Paul's lessons is not easy, because the required involvement in suffering is a very high tuition to pay for the School of Suffering. Yet more than enough suffering will come to every Christian over a lifetime even without choosing it, so it is good that Christians can draw upon Paul's insights. When we can affirm for ourselves some of his rich meaning in suffering, then we too can paradoxically rejoice in our suffering at the same time that we long for deliverance.

Notes

1. Cf. David R. Mason, "Some Abstract, Yet Crucial, Thoughts About Suffering," *Dialog* 16 (Spring 1977): 94-96.

2. C. K. Barrett, *A Commentary on the Second Epistle to the Corinthians* (New York: Harper & Row, 1973), pp. 61-62.

3. Eduard Schweizer, *Jesus* (Richmond: John Knox, 1971), p. 110.

4. Ibid., p. 113.

5. Eduard Schweizer, *Lordship and Discipleship* (London: SCM, 1960), pp. 104-13.

47 AIDS and the Church

Earl E. Shelp and
Ronald H. Sunderland

Illness in Christian Perspective

The question of how to account for the existence of illness, suffering, and tragedy as integral parts of daily life has preoccupied the human psyche throughout history. In particular, the Christian church has struggled with the relationship of illness to faith. The Gospels provide little insight regarding the role of illness and suffering in creation. Issues of how to justify the ways of God seem to have been unimportant to Jesus, who clearly gave priority to the urgency of proclaiming the gospel. We seemingly cannot forgo our human preoccupation with attempts to explain illness and suffering, but apparently Jesus did not join these discussions. He was too busy going about healing the sick, casting out demons, and, in so doing, manifesting God's compassion and love toward the afflicted. The church attempts to keep a balance between these two functions, engaging in acts of compassion and support to people in need and reflecting theologically on the relationship of this ministry to the church's confession and mission. If the New Testament is a guide, ministry must remain in the forefront of the church's activity. But theology as critical reflection on the work of ministry is not a secondary function. Rather, each function informs and corrects the other; each fulfills a servant role, so that the church's work may be done.[1]

It is important to pursue this interrelationship with respect to the AIDS epidemic. The dimensions of this crisis, the needs of people with AIDS, and societal reactions to people with AIDS demand a response from the church. We must discover the appropriate form such a response must take, as to both the nature of compassionate ministry and the theological imperatives by which care and concern are shaped and corrected. In the course of exploring these issues, we will discover that the scriptures do not offer simple answers to questions related to the existence of illness and suffering. Rather, they call the people of God to serve their neighbors. At this moment, that includes people with AIDS.

New Testament Perceptions of Suffering

The New Testament recognizes suffering as a part of daily living that must be accepted and endured with fortitude. The troubles to be borne in this earthly existence are of little consequence compared to the life that is "hidden with Christ in God" (Col. 3:3). The New Testament, however, addresses sufferings at three levels. First, some afflictions clearly were the consequences of imprisonment and persecution because of the believer's witness to faith in Jesus Christ as Lord. Thus was Stephen stoned to death. Second, suffering may be the result of oppression by one person or group of another person or group. The most frequently cited biblical example is the oppression of the weak and helpless by the wealthy and powerful. Third, pain and suffering may be due to disease or physical or mental disability.

Suffering "For Christ's Sake"

Peter refers to suffering "for Christ's sake," for example, when he warns his readers that they may suffer "trials of many kinds." These trials come so that their faith "may prove itself worthy of all praise, glory, and honour when Jesus Christ is revealed" (1 Peter 1:6-7). Paul expresses the same thought frequently. Writing to the Corinthians, he offers the example of his faithful witness:

> As God's servants, we try to recommend ourselves in all circumstances by our steadfast endurance: in distress, hardships, and dire straits; flogged, imprisoned, mobbed; overworked, sleepless,

> starving. . . . Dying we still live on; disciplined by suffering, we are not done to death; in our sorrows we have always cause for joy; poor ourselves, we bring wealth to many; penniless, we own the world."
>
> (2 Corinthians 6:4-5, 9-10)

One of the richest sources of this image is in the eleventh chapter of the same letter:

> Five times the Jews have given me the thirty-nine strokes; three times I have been beaten with rods; once I was stoned; three times I have been shipwrecked, and for twenty-four hours I was adrift on the open sea. I have been constantly on the road; I have met dangers from my fellow-countrymen, dangers from foreigners, dangers in towns, dangers in the country, dangers at sea, dangers from false friends.
>
> (2 Corinthians 11:23-26; see also, for example, Romans 8:19; 13-19; 1 Corinthians 4:9-13; 2 Corinthians 1:8-11; 4:8-12, 16-18)

These "trials of many kinds" were anticipated in phrases attributed to Jesus in the Beatitudes: "How blest you are, when you suffer insults and persecution and every kind of calumny for my sake. Accept it with gladness and exultation, for you have a rich reward in heaven; in the same way they persecuted the prophets before you" (Matt. 5:11-12). Suffering "for Christ's sake" on the part of his followers is thus incorporated into the suffering for the sake of righteousness that characterizes both Old and New Testaments. In the Old Testament, it is linked to the concept of the Suffering Servant. In the New Testament, Peter recognizes that such human suffering participates in the suffering of Christ:

> My dear friends, do not be bewildered by the fiery ordeal that is upon you, as though it were something extraordinary. It gives you a share in Christ's sufferings, and that is cause for joy; and when his glory is revealed, your joy will be triumphant. . . . If anyone suffers as a Christian, he should feel it no disgrace, but confess that name to the honour of God.
>
> (1 Peter 4:12-13, 16)

Such passages often seem to be advanced in support of the claim that when suffering in the form of physical illness is experienced, it ought to be accepted and endured as an ordeal in the sense intended by Peter: that is, a trial sent to test the believer's faith. A clear distinction, however, should be made as to the source of the suffering before physical hardship and illness are so linked, as will be noted.

Suffering as a Result of Oppression

The Gospels note a second source of suffering against which Jesus cried out in protest, and which is to be opposed at every point: suffering that results from human injustice and oppression of the poor. Luke begins his record of Jesus' ministry with the account of the visit to Nazareth. The words from Isaiah 61 are applied to the ministry of Jesus: "[The Lord] has sent me to announce good news to the poor" (Luke 4:18). The announcement is clearly intended to address the concerns that so roused the prophets: the need to proclaim liberation to broken victims and release to the captives. It is usual to link with these phrases the complementary passages from Isaiah. Thus, the Gospel calls for the loosing of the fetters of injustice, untying the knots of the yoke, snapping every yoke, and setting free those who have been crushed. To the cry for compassion toward the crushed is added the call to proclaim recovery of sight to the blind and to clothe the naked, provide hospitality to the homeless poor, feed the hungry, and satisfy the needs of the wretched (Isa. 58:6-10). In denouncing the religious authorities, Jesus pointed to their greed: "Beware of the doctors of the law. . . . These are the men who eat up the property of widows, while they say long prayers for appearance' sake; and they will receive the severest sentence" (Luke 20:45-47).

Luke is not alone among the Evangelists in identifying Jesus as championing the cause of the poor and oppressed, but his gospel is noteworthy for this emphasis. With Matthew, Luke cites Jesus' reply to John's disciples, who sought confirmation that Jesus was really "the coming one." Jesus' ministries of healing and liberation were explicit signs of the reign of God — for those who had eyes of faith to see. The fact that, in the liberating actions of Jesus, John possessed all the evidence he needed to satisfy his uncertainty leads to only one conclusion: the power of God is present in Jesus. In its presence, evil — in the form of oppression of the innocent, injustice levied against those too weak to speak for themselves, or exclusion of the humble from the community's concern and care — is being overturned. The message is clear. Evil cannot continue to exist in the presence of God's love.

The hospitality of the Kingdom is extended without hesitation to those whom society has oppressed or ignored: the poor, the crippled, the lame, and the blind (Luke 14:21), those whose homes are the city's streets and alleys (v. 21) or the roads and hedges of the countryside (vs. 23-24). Such gracious acts are extended to people who, because of their very weakness, even their failure to thrive, are unable to return the gift of hospitality. That they cannot is the best reason for inviting them. The inability of the poor to return the kindness is the measure of their need of it. The words and actions of Jesus are those of confrontation: the causes and consequences of poverty, injustice, and exclusion from the community are to be opposed. Not only will those who oppress the poor not inherit the kingdom; even those who fail to minister to the least of the Lord's brothers and sisters will go away to eternal punishment, "to the eternal fire that is ready for the devil and his angels" (Matt. 25:41). Jesus accused the Pharisees of having no care for justice and love of God, and the lawyers of loading men with intolerable burdens (Luke 11:42, 46). The scene in the temple in which the money-changers' tables were overthrown and the pigeons freed from their cages expresses the same sense of outrage at the afflictions imposed on the poor. For the robbery being practiced involved not only the fraudulent activities of the money-changers against worshipers, but the stealing of this house from God. "Moreover, the thefts from me were not limited to the Temple precincts, as Jeremiah knew, but included the dog-eat-dog practices outside the Temple by men who then took part in the worship (Jer. 7:8-15)."[2]

Jesus' work in the temple was a prophetic sign of God's wrath, in accordance with God's desire to make God's house a place of worship for all nations. God had promised to bring foreigners and gather the outcasts to rejoice in the benefits of the temple (Isa. 56:6-8). "It was this promise which Jesus fulfilled and which the priests repudiated, so that this episode becomes an epitome of the Messiah's whole career."[3] As a result, Christians are not urged to accept or tolerate such affliction with passive resignation; they are bidden to lift the yoke of oppression and to fill the role of champions of the downtrodden. The followers of Jesus walk in his footsteps only if they are filled with a like concern for the poor (we discuss this theme more comprehensively in chapter 4).

Suffering Due to Disease or Disability

Just as injustice cannot exist in the presence of the Lord's anointed, neither can sickness endure against God's power. The citing of the Isaianic passages (Luke 4:18-19) signals Luke's emphasis on Jesus' ministry to the poor and oppressed, included among whom, true to the Old Testament passages, are the sick and disabled in body and mind. This aspect of the discussion should be set in the context of the attribution of causality for sickness and affliction, and the perceived relationship between illness or disability and ritual defilement, that has characterized Judeo-Christian thought. Judaism struggled with the notion that sickness was a consequence of sin and therefore a punishment. Acts of healing were acknowledged by proving to a priest that the symptoms of disease or disability had vanished, whereupon the priest declared that the defilement was lifted and the formerly disabled person was restored to the community and to the full benefits of the law. Ritual defilement resulted from any affliction, since it was axiomatic that the disease would not have occurred if the victim's relationship with God was not disordered.[4]

It is in this context that the ministry of Jesus to the sick should be set. Jesus was at pains to discard the ancient attribution of illness or disability as punishment for some act of disobedience of God's law: that is, as God's retribution for human sin. The tradition was long and deep. Sirach, or ben Sira, the author of Ecclesiasticus, declared in the second century B.C. that

> From the beginning good things were created
> for the good,
> and evils for sinners.

The chief necessities of human life
are water, fire, iron, and salt,
flour, honey, and milk,
the juice of the grape, oil, and clothing.
All these are good for the godfearing,
but turn to evil for sinners.

There are winds created to be agents of
retribution,
with great whips to give play to their fury;
on the day of reckoning, they exert their force
and give full vent to the anger of their Maker.
Fire and hail, famine and *deadly disease*,
all these were created for retribution;
beasts of prey, scorpions and vipers,
and the avenging sword that destroys the
wicked.
They delight in carrying out his orders,
always standing ready for his service on the
earth;
and when their time comes, they never disobey.
(Ecclesiasticus 39:25-31;
emphasis added)

Sirach clearly reflected a popularly held perception against which Jesus protested. John records the disciples' questioning of Jesus regarding a blind man: "Rabbi, who sinned, this man or his parents? Why was he born blind?" Jesus responded: "It is not that this man or his parents sinned; he was born blind so that God's power might be displayed in curing him" (John 9:2-3). Jesus rejected the notion that God had deliberately disabled this man — and, conceivably, others — on account of sin, or merely to provide an opportunity to demonstrate God's power. Indeed, Mark presents Jesus as requiring the disciples to keep silent concerning such acts lest they be regarded by the populace as merely displays of power designed to coerce a positive response to the gospel — and thus be misunderstood. Luke records that Jesus was challenged to explain the sufferings of the innocent: for example, the Galileans slaughtered by Pilate and the eighteen upon whom the tower of Siloam fell (Luke 13:1-9). An easy solution would be to say, echoing Job's friends, that the fate of the Galileans overtook them in the providence of God, a just punishment for some iniquity of which they were doubtless guilty. While it is precisely this theory that Jesus rejects, he does not advance any alternative explanation at this point.[5] The question of the problem of suffering is unanswered, for Jesus treats the story, and another that he raises, as parables. And the whole issue of the parables is the urgency of the gospel. It is this urgency which is offered as the basis for the Johannine statement: "While daylight lasts we must carry on the work of him who sent me; night comes, when no one can work. While I am in the world I am the light of the world" (John 9:4-5).

The issue for Jesus is the primacy of the gospel. He had come into Galilee "proclaiming the Gospel of God" (Mark 1:14). What followed, whether teaching, confronting, ministering compassionately, or healing, was the manifestation of the power of God at work: "If it is by the finger of God that I drive out the devils, then be sure the kingdom of God has already come upon you" (Luke 11:20). The healing acts were entailed by the message he proclaimed. Nothing, including disease and devils, could impede the progress of the kingdom's unveiling or withstand its power. Hence, the Markan "secret": the healing acts would only be correctly perceived when people recognized them as outbreaks of the kingdom's presence. In any other context, they would appear as mere "signs and wonders," which Jesus refused the Pharisees.

When one turns to examine how Jesus acted when confronted by human distress arising from disease and disability, the evidence is overwhelming: Jesus responded at every opportunity to relieve such affliction. Healing was often performed in a manner indicative of confrontation with illness. The Gospels identify Jesus as engaged in two types of healing activity: the driving out of demons and the healing of the sick and physically disabled. The twelve disciples were sent out with instructions to heal the sick, raise the dead, cleanse lepers, and cast out devils (Matt. 10:8). In Capernaum, the crowds brought to him all who were ill or possessed by devils (Mark 1:3). To Pharisees who urged him to escape from Herod, he replied, "Go and tell that fox, 'Listen: today and tomorrow I shall be casting out devils and working cures'" Luke 13:32). The separate identification of the two activities suggests two functions. In the case of demon possession, the confrontation with evil is emphasized, but such actions are viewed in the context of the struggle between the power of the evil one and the power of God. Edward Schillebeeckx notes, "As Jesus pursues his ministry and manifests himself, this in itself is regarded by the evil powers as an act of aggression (Mk. 1:23-24 and parallels; 5:7ff. and parallels, 9:20-25). Against the evil and hurtful results produced by these powers Jesus sets only good actions, deeds of beneficence."[6]

The exorcisms are presented to show that God's eschatological kingdom is now present. Illness in general, however, was a sign of disorder in God's creation that ends with physical death. While sickness and death are customarily assumed to be evidence of the activity of evil, the healing of the sick is set in the context of the announcement of the kingdom and of Jesus' compassion for those who, because of their illness, are unable to live life to its fullest. Again and again, he is represented as reaching out to people at their points of need. Acts 10:38 states that witnesses can bear testimony to all that he did in the Jewish countryside and in Jerusalem: he went about doing good and healing all who were oppressed by the devil, "actively showing pity for the sick and those who by the standards of that time were held to be possessed by 'the demon' or by 'demons,' 'the prisoners' whom the eschatological prophet was to set free (Isa. 61:1-2)."[7] The commitment of Jesus on behalf of people in distress became the basis for the early church's emphasis on the preaching of the "glad tidings of Jesus Christ" (Mark 1:1). The Gospels report that the response of Jesus to those whose lives were disordered was one of tenderness and compassion. Nothing aroused his anger more spontaneously than unfeeling and uncaring legalists who saw not the distress of a person crippled in mind or body but an opportunity to moralize on the basis of some fine point of the Torah (Mark 3:1-6; see also Matt. 23:23: "You pay tithes of mint and dill and cummin; but you have overlooked the weightier demands of the Law, justice, mercy, and good faith. . . . Blind guides! You strain off a midge, yet gulp down a camel!").

The intensity of Jesus' response to human suffering is illustrated in the story of the healing of a man with a crippled hand (Mark 3:1-6). The healing is necessary on the Sabbath, since in Hebrew thought not to heal the man would leave him nearer to death — for sickness is proximity to death.[8] That is, the struggle against sickness is a struggle to save the sufferer from the power of death and the threat it poses. Since sickness opposes the Creator God's saving power, it must be righted and the creation restored. Jesus is the Redeemer in whom the mercy of God is present. What is new in his ministry is that the beneficiaries of God's mercy are not the religious authorities and legal scholars but those considered outsiders: the poor, the disabled, the sick, and the bereaved. Jesus made himself accessible to those who needed him, ignoring conventional limitations and thus according proper recognition to those who were cast out of society for whatever reason. Consistently, he met people at their particular points of need and addressed those needs. Jesus is presented as a combatant, constantly opposing with his power those forces that kept people in subjugation. Whatever held people back from experiencing the fullness of the gospel must be confronted and its power to do so destroyed. Thus, the sick were healed, the disabled returned to full activity, and the oppressed freed.

When Jesus welcomed the sick and disabled with open arms, he presented a potent model to his followers. The manner in which churches and their members respond to people with AIDS is an indication of the degree of seriousness with which they follow the example of Jesus. A response of love and compassion — an open-arms response — is demanded of God's people. It is a mandate expressly given by Jesus, as, for example, in the parable of the Judgment (Matt. 25:31-46). Further, such a response is a sign of God's gracious love, not only to people with AIDS and to their loved ones but to the wider community. It announces for all to see and hear that the kingdom is being realized, that it is taking shape in the world. If AIDS, in fact, means that the sick person has fallen into death's realm of power, loving acceptance of people with AIDS announces that God's saving power takes the field against death's destructive power.

During a recent hospitalization, a young man who knew that his struggle with numerous infections occasioned by AIDS was reaching its inevitable end drew comfort from the knowledge that his membership in a local church had led to the development of a support group for AIDS patients in the congregation. During the final days of his struggle he was visited by members of the group.

His family gathered to support him. He was distressed that his family, in particular, would remember him racked with pain and broken by disease. With a supreme effort, he spent some time with each family member, leaving each with a message of how important was their support and love and how strong his love was for them. The ministry of the religious community was one of the undergirding forces in the hospital room, both for the patient and for his family. It symbolized God's gracious and reconciling love. Such compassion is a first call upon God's people in the crisis created by the AIDS epidemic.

The "Problem of Suffering"

In marked contrast to the fact that Jesus was concerned to show compassion to the afflicted rather than to establish the causes of disease and disability, Western scholars have tended to be preoccupied with the latter concern, connecting their response to issues of morality. The church's response to sickness and disability has been influenced by both emphases, which have existed side by side in Western culture. The ministry of compassion, so integral to the ministry of Jesus, is manifested, for example, in the establishment of an infirmary in Rome as early as the late fourth century, a logical development of Christian charity. The commandment to love the neighbor (Matt. 19:19; 22:39; Mark 12:31-33) was not simply a piece of advice, it was a categorical imperative. Love for the neighbor can be manifested in a variety of ways, but spiritual concern must never take precedence over immediate material or physical help for those in need, as the Letter of James bluntly states: "Religion that is pure and undefiled before God and the Father is this: to visit orphans and widows in their affliction" (1:27, RSV).

The visitation, care, and comfort of the afflicted became an obligation incumbent upon all Christians and was repeatedly stressed in early Christian literature. This duty to attend the sick and the poor conferred on them a preferential position that has lasted until now. The example of Christ was followed in the mid-third century when, during an outbreak of plague, Christians ministered to plague victims. In a letter by Dionysius written in A.D. 263, he describes how "our brethren were unsparing in their exceeding love and brotherly kindness. They held fast to each other and visited the sick fearlessly and ministered to them continually, serving them in Christ. . . . And many who cared for the sick and gave strength to others died themselves . . . so that this form of death, through the great piety and strong faith it exhibited, seemed to lack nothing of martyrdom."[9] The commitment to the outcast sick is evident in the nineteenth century exemplified by Fr. Damien on the island of Molokai, and into the twentieth century, with Mother Teresa and countless nameless people for whom the needs of the sick and dying become a call to ministry.

Yet this often sacrificial gesture of compassionate response has been accompanied by efforts to explain the existence of pain and suffering in terms of retribution. For example, Calvin identified two purposes served by suffering caused by such events as pestilence, disease, poverty, or any other suffering in body or mind. First, suffering is punishment for high crimes and misdemeanors against God, a punishment justly deserved. Calvin prayed that God's chastisements — the affliction of disease or poverty, for example — would be effective for the reformation of the sufferer's life. In this sense, suffering has an expiatory force which imparts the assurance to the believer that guilt is thereby atoned, reflecting the Talmudic statement that the one who has suffered in this life is thereby assured of rewards in the life to come. Second, suffering is perceived to have an educational purpose. Calvin directed ordained pastors who visit those afflicted by disease or "other evils" to

> console them by the word of the Lord, showing them that all which they suffer and endure comes from the hand of God, and from his good providence, who sends nothing to believers except for their good and salvation. . . . Moreover, if he sees the sickness to be dangerous, he will give them consolation, which reaches farther, according as he sees them touched by their affliction; that is to say, if he sees them overwhelmed by the fear of death, he will show them that it is no cause for dismay to believers, who having Jesus Christ for their guide and protector, will, by their affliction, be conducted to the life on which he has entered.

> By similar considerations he will remove the fear and terror which they may have of the judgment of God.[10]

This manner of presenting poverty and disease — and, in fact, misfortune generally — has endured into modern Western usage and remains a powerful influence on contemporary attitudes to disease and disability. During a morning TV news presentation late in 1986, the parents of a promising college athlete who had died during 1986 were interviewed. Asked what meaning they attached to their son's death, his mother responded that God had made their son an example to other youth "so that millions might live." The same attribution of suffering is evident in the tracts left in hospital waiting areas or placed on bedside tables that carry such messages as: *Sickness is an opportunity to mature inwardly; The Lord does not place burdens upon us that are more than we can bear; Affliction is God's test of our faith; we must pray for strength.*

It seems that either the experience of personal affliction or the awareness of suffering in another person inevitably drives humanity back to the question asked poignantly by the psalmists: Why do righteous people suffer? Attempts to answer that question seem endless. The Hebraic perception of God, which attributed all phenomena to a divine purpose, was carried over into early Christendom and remains a pervasive influence in much "folk religion." As the Renaissance paved the way ultimately for the enhancement of the sciences, however, larger and larger areas of human life were explained on the basis of a growing body of scientific data. Included in this explosion of knowledge was the matter of illness. A small group of British scientists was convened in the late 1950s to review the relationship between religion and science. The group recalled that in the Middle Ages people crowded into churches to seek deliverance from plagues, whereas twentieth-century societies dig drains and educate the public concerning matters of hygiene. Whereas primitive societies prayed for rain and abundant harvests, we invest resources in water conservation and teach third world countries the benefits of fertilizers and crop rotation. When humans were forced to account for phenomena they could not understand, the tendency was to fall back upon the age-old measure of attributing causality to some unfathomed divine purpose.

The problem arose, however, that as rational explanations emerged to account for more and more areas of human experience, the extent of experience ascribed to a purposive God began to shrink. Now that science can explain in intricate detail the manner in which viruses enter and affect the human body, and how the body's immune system defends itself against such attacks, it is tempting to divide human experience into two (or more) parts, granting science control over one while retaining the control of religion over the other. This is a mistake. To assert that some sort of hedge can be planted in the country of the mind to mark the boundary where a transfer of authority takes place is a twofold error. First, it presupposes an intolerable dichotomy of existence. Second, it invites "science" to discover new things and thence gradually take possession of that which "religion" once held.[11] Soon, God becomes no longer necessary because the gap between the explained and the unexplained is closed. If this image is applied to the science of medicine, any attempt to remove disease from the arena of medicine to that of religion assumes the same dichotomization, an untenable position. God does not reserve certain areas of life in which to dabble. In particular, AIDS was not "sent" on some divine intention to communicate a message; for example, to remind humans that God retains some areas in which to manifest initiative.

There is a second and more disturbing objection to the notion that the answer to suffering is to be found in some divine purpose. Dorothee Sölle put the issue forcefully when she objected to what she termed "theological sadism." For her, "Christian masochism" had "so many features that merit criticism: the low value it places on human strength; its veneration of one who is neither good nor logical but only extremely powerful; its viewing of suffering exclusively from the perspective of endurance; and its consequent lack of sensitivity for the suffering of others." But what bothered Sölle was not the well-meaning attempts of onlookers to comfort a disabled person; such attempts may be genuine efforts to speak in comfort and compassion. Her greatest discomfort and anger arose because "the picture changes as soon as theologians, in a kind of overly rigorous application of the masochistic approach, sketch in as a companion piece a sadistic God." Her concern was that such a God who causes affliction and suffering is presented as one who demands the impossible and then tortures people.[12]

As this chapter was being written, a father sat for three weeks at the bedside of his dying twenty-eight-year-old son. He dealt with his grief out of images derived from the Middle Ages. He stated simply that what was happening was God's will, which he had no alternative but to accept. When the chaplain asked how he would feel if he were to discover that his son's imminent death was not "willed" by God but that instead God "grieved" over the death of one of God's children, he dismissed the image without consideration. The chaplain did not return to the theological issue; at that moment such a discussion was not appropriate. The father's conviction that his son's death was at God's behest was his only source of comfort. It might have been easier to accept his perception if his consolation had been deep and genuine. But it was as if he were engaged in a never-ending struggle to hold back the waters of bitterness behind a narrow dike, with his finger plunged into a fissure through which the waters seeped, constantly threatening to become a surge that would overwhelm him. Similarly, a hospital chaplain recounted a ten-year-old patient's struggle to come to terms with his diagnosis of AIDS. Who knows the source of the child's images? Had some well-meaning relative, friend, or pastor sought to comfort him by suggesting gently that God had "chosen" him? He sat up in bed and cried out, "Why did God choose me? I did not want to be chosen!"

These images of God are derived from perceptions of God's transcendence that leave little room for immanence such as manifested in the life of Jesus of Nazareth, who sat beside a woman alienated from her community, or who crouched in a dusty village street alongside another threatened woman. These biblical pictures contrast sharply with the image of a transcendent God, far removed from human concerns except to use them as teaching opportunities. It is right to criticize radically all attempts to reconcile God with misery or, worse, to represent God as sanctioning misery. Such a God, who uses affliction merely or primarily to reprove, correct, or educate, cannot be separated from the accusation of injustice. If God "comes to a sufferer only with pedagogical intent,"[13] then God seems deaf to the anguished protest of a ten-year-old child or any other person with AIDS, on whose behalf all must cry out for justice and compassion.

To attribute suffering to an all-powerful God who uses such power to inflict pain and misery upon humanity flies in the face of the incarnation of God's love in Jesus Christ. Such love is expressed in an active goodwill toward people, moved by a genuine sensitivity to their deepest needs. This type of love includes, but is not limited to, compassionate sympathy. Sympathy indeed has received a bad press, with the contemporary emphasis by social scientists on terms such as "empathy." Sympathy involves being present with a person — weeping with the sad, rejoicing when there is cause for celebration. It is comforting for one who is sick to know that he or she is not alone and that others care. "Empathy," on the other hand, is a construct that more fully expresses a human attempt to speak of God's love. The term involves a relationship between the helper and the afflicted person in which the helper knows, or can imagine, the depth of the pain and struggle the other is experiencing. It is a relationship that opens the possibility of change or, if that is not possible, assures the struggler that the helping person has the ability to enter into the feeling of helplessness or even despair and know what it means. If these images may be applied validly to God's love, they suggest that God is in touch with our pain, that God "feels" our anguish and is affected by it. This conception is in stark contrast to the Greek notion of divine impassibility that has permeated traditional theism, a notion that sharply restricts the biblical perception of divine love that is responsive to human suffering.

The idea that God's knowledge of the world is complete and unchanging implies that God has determined every aspect of the world, down to the last detail. Nothing can happen that is not immutably known. There is little provision for creaturely freedom in such a fixed system. Process theology, on the other hand, sees God's creative activity as based upon responsiveness to the world. Since the very meaning of actuality involves internal relatedness, God as an actuality is essentially related to the world. Since actuality as such is partially self-creative, future events are not determined. Even perfect knowledge, process theologians argue, cannot know the future. Thus, God does not wholly control the world. God's power, even creative power, is persuasive, not coercive.[14]

Process thought has three immediate consequences for this inquiry. First, it provides a theological basis for the assertion that God does not select specific diseases to punish certain human behaviors. If God's power is persuasive, not controlling, finite actualities can fail to conform to the divine aims for them. Deviations from divine aims may give rise to evil. Since deviation is possible, though not necessary, evil is not necessary. It is the *possibility* of deviation that is necessary, and that makes the *possibility* of evil necessary. The risk in all this for humanity is that a new actuality may develop which introduces a novel element into creation. It may add to the variety of existence, and so to the value that can be enjoyed. But the new reality may be a strain of virus which leads not to enjoyment but to discord.[15] Human immunodeficiency virus (HIV) surely falls into this category. If the intention had been to exclude the possibility of all discord, God would simply have abstained from creating a world altogether, and so have guaranteed the absence of all suffering. Risk is part of the created order, a price paid for freedom, God's trump card. Thus, God does not "send" AIDS for some retributive purpose (such a thought flies in the face of the New Testament witness to a loving God). Rather, God "risked" creating a world in which HIV could develop.

The second consequence of process thought centers around the question of persuasiveness vs. control. It is on just this issue that conservative Christians oppose radically any stance to the left of their own positions. "Fundamentalist" and "liberal" Christians may fight over matters of ecclesiology and biblical and historical theology, but what is at stake is the political issue of management styles and measures of control and freedom. This battle has certainly invaded areas of ethics and theology in accounting for human suffering, but it also plays a key role in the form that pastoral care takes — for example, in shaping attitudes toward people with AIDS. Care and compassion can be offered to people in need without attempting to coerce them into adopting the caregiver's religious commitments. It is appropriate for ministries to reflect religious and moral values; it is not appropriate, however, to expect the other person to adopt those values as the *conditions* for the relationship and the care.[16]

Both the Hebrew scriptures and the New Testament characterize God as choosing to deal freely with humanity. God offers humanity choices. The question then is whether the choices made are trivially or morally evil or are genuine attempts at responsible living. This matter of choice is always unambiguous. It is the choice expressed by Joshua to the Israelites: "Hold the Lord in awe then, and worship him in loyalty and truth. Banish the gods whom your fathers worshipped beside the Euphrates and in Egypt, and worship the Lord. But if it does not please you to worship the Lord, choose here and now whom you will worship. . . . I and my family, we will serve the Lord" (Josh. 24:14-15). The choice is presented as sharply by Jesus to the rich young ruler: "Jesus said to him, 'If you wish to go the whole way, go, sell your possessions, and give to the poor . . . and come, follow me'" (Matt. 19:21).

The fact of freedom places the responsibility for decision and choice on the only one who can assume such responsibility, the person who must decide. The attempt to control the choices of others is a constant temptation for caregivers. One of the temptations is to reject a person who has made a decision with which one disagrees or, more pointedly, which is offensive to one's own moral judgment. It is also tempting to use the power implicit in the role of the caregiver to overwhelm the person who needs help and to make help contingent upon the adoption of an "acceptable" lifestyle.[17]

This raises the third consequence of process thought for this inquiry. It is logical to argue that if God's relationship with humanity is persuasive, that characteristic should be the model for our own interpersonal relationships. It should apply particularly to the role of caregiver. If persuasion, rather than control, is the divine mode of relation, this manner of doing things is expected of believers. These images of relationship — offer, freedom, and persuasion — are true to the gospel. The object of preaching the gospel is "full life" (John 10:10). That invitation is offered, but in large measure it is up to each of us how that full life will be appropriated. God's creative purpose for humanity is loving because God is always a completely *gracious* God. God's aim for people is existence that they experience as intrinsically good. But God is not in complete control. We are in part responsible for who we are and what we shall become. We are certainly responsible for the choices we make and for their consequences. The freedom God offers humanity is therefore risky, but it is a necessary risk if there is to be the chance for greatness. Thus the question as to whether God is indictable for evil reduces to the question of whether the positive values enjoyed by the higher forms of life and experience are worth the risk of the negative values; namely, the sufferings. Should humans, therefore, risk possible suffering in order to have at least the possibility of intense enjoyment? Process theologians Cobb and Griffin respond affirmatively, explaining that the divine reality is an Adventurer who not only enjoys humanity's experience of the pitch of enjoyment but who also experiences sufferings.[18] God knows what it is like to taste the bitter waters of our valleys of Marah (Ex. 15:23).

The desert plains across which lie our paths, as we press forward looking for Canaan, that land flowing with milk and honey, are broken by more than one valley of Marah. The ancient pilgrimage of the children of Israel remains a prototype for all. AIDS is but the latest tragedy to evoke from humanity the age-old question, "Why, Lord? Why me?"

It has been suggested that from the most primitive of ancient cultures to the more highly developed religious forms, humanity has always struggled with the tragedy of affliction, resolving the paradox of life pockmarked by suffering by attributing disease and disability to the gods' anger at human failure and sin. Primitive Hebrew thought incorporated this concept, and much of contemporary Christian "folk religion" reflects it. Yet the biblical response is one of affirmation. It does not answer the question, "Why me?" other than to remind us, through metaphor, that we are called to be children of our Father in heaven, who makes the sun rise on good and bad alike and sends the rain on the honest and dishonest (Matt. 5:45). We are assured that God makes those whom society denigrates God's people. It is salutary to remember that the first epistle of Peter was addressed to just such people: domestics, street sweepers, laborers, and Gentiles. The writer's joy is in seeing people who once were "no people" becoming "God's people." Those who had not previously received mercy were now recipients of God's mercy. Nobodies were receiving the dignity and the joy of being God's children. Is there any comfort for a patient in the theological notion that his or her God, who has rejoiced in human achievements and enjoyments, now shares in the pain and physical discomfort of his or her dying?

There is no formula for erasing the pain and anguish of people with AIDS and of their loved ones. Moreover, as sick and disabled people constantly remind those who just stand around, one who has not experienced catastrophic crisis cannot know the feelings it evokes in the sufferer. But in the face of such pain, the witness of scripture is plainly and simply stated: God is a God of unfathomable love who tends people like a shepherd tends the flock. The human analogy is of a loving parent who loves to the uttermost. This affirmation moves Paul to reassure his readers that nothing can separate people from the love of God revealed in the Christ. Not persecution, hunger, nakedness, peril, or sword; not illness, disability, or AIDS. But our thoughts are not God's thoughts; neither are our ways God's ways. We do not rise to Paul's level of maturity but continue to judge from our human point of view. We cannot say, with the apostle, that "worldly standards have ceased to count in our estimate of any man" (2 Cor. 5:16). So we continue to place people in categories, creating new groups of "the poor" from whom, because they do not fit our stereotypes, we distance ourselves.

Notes

1. For an elaboration of this theme, see *The Pastor as Theologian*, Earl E. Shelp and Ronald H. Sunderland, eds. (New York: Pilgrim Press, in press).

2. Paul S. Minear, *The Gospel According to Mark*, vol. 17 of the Layman's Bible Commentary, Balmer H. Kelly, ed. (Atlanta: John Knox Press, 1960), p. 109.

3. Ibid.

4. This was the case, for example, with respect to leprosy. In this respect, it is important to recognize that the term to which reference is made in the Jewish scriptures and in the New Testament carried a different connotation from that of the disease known commonly as leprosy in the twentieth century. The leprosy of the

ancient Near East actually encompassed a range of dermatological disorders that seldom approached the seriousness or evoked the level of fear with which today's leprosy (Hansen's disease) is associated. Such common skin diseases as psoriasis, eczema, and other common rashes and lesions were probably included under the general heading of "leprosy."

The real suffering of lepers was not so much due to physical discomfort as to the isolation and ostracism that sufferers met in the general community. It is a similar isolation and ostracism experienced by people with AIDS that links the two. More important, given this association, the response of Jesus to people with leprosy suggests the model for the response of God's people to people AIDS.

5. T. W. Manson, *The Sayings of Jesus* (London: SCM Press, 1954), p. 273.

6. Edward Schillebeeckx, *Jesus: An Experiment in Christology* (New York: Crossroad Publishing Co., 1985), p. 184.

7. Ibid., p. 180.

8. For a development of the concept that illness and affliction place the sick person "nearer to death," see Klaus Seybold and Ulrich B. Mueller, *Sickness and Healing* (Nashville: Abingdon Press, 1981). They state, "The sick person as such has fallen into death's realm of power, not only because sickness possibly brings death . . . but because sickness *eo ipso* belongs to death's domain" (p. 123).

9. *Nicene and Post-Nicene Fathers,* Series 2, Philip Schaff and Henry Wace, eds., vol. 1, *Eusebius* (Grand Rapids: Wm. B. Eerdmans Publishing Co., 1979), p. 307.

10. John Calvin, *Tracts and Treatises on the Doctrine and Worship of the Church,* vol. 2 (Grand Rapids: Wm. B. Eerdmans Publishing Co., 1958), p. 127.

11. Charles A. Coulson, *Science and Christian Belief* (Chapel Hill, N.C.: University of North Carolina Press, 1955), p. 19.

12. Dorothee Sölle, *Suffering* (Philadelphia: Fortress Press, 1975), p. 22.

13. Ibid., p. 26.

14. John B. Cobb, Jr., and David Ray Griffin, *Process Theology: An Introductory Exposition* (Philadelphia: Westminster Press, 1976), pp. 51-52.

15. The philosopher Alfred North Whitehead suggests that, to the extent that conformity to the divine aims is incomplete, there is evil in the world. New actualities or realities (such as AIDS) may lead not to enjoyment but to discord, a term Whitehead uses to refer to physical or mental suffering which is simply evil in itself, whenever it occurs. See Alfred North Whitehead, *Religion in the Making* (New York: Macmillan Co., 1926), p. 60, and *Adventures of Ideas* (New York: Macmillan Co., 1933), pp. 329-30, 342.

16. See James A. Wharton, "Theology and Ministry in the Hebrew Scriptures," in Earl E. Shelp and Ronald Sunderland, eds., *A Biblical Basis for Ministry* (Philadelphia: Westminster Press, 1981), pp. 62-69.

17. See Alan Keith-Lucas, *Giving and Taking Help* (Chapel Hill, N.C.: University of North Carolina Press, 1972), p. 9.

18. Cobb and Griffin, p. 74.

48 Stories and Suffering

Margaret E. Mohrmann, M.D.

Paying Attention

We should not read the Bible for lists or rules or for direct answers to most of our specific moral questions. Nevertheless, scripture is a unique and inescapable authority for Christian ethics, although not an absolute judge (only God is absolute).[1] Therefore, let us consider what can be found in our reading of scripture.

There is a long tradition in Christian thought, dating back to at least Augustine (in *De doctrina Christiana,* for example), that teaches us that understanding scripture requires that we come to it prepared to be changed by it.[2] From the standpoint of theological ethics, it is for that change, rather than for any rules or answers, that we go to scripture. Christian ethics, as Richard McCormick has written, is not norms and principles but transformation.[3]

> Do not be conformed to this world, but be transformed by the renewing of your mind, so that you may discern what is the will of God — what is good and acceptable and perfect. (Rom. 12:2)

The crux of biblically informed ethics is that the story of God's love for us is transformative. It has the power to shape us into the sorts of persons who want and are able to discern what is good, and who then can and will act morally. That story also has the power to shape the church into the sort of community that enables and encourages both the transformation and the empowered action of its members.

To what end is this transformation? There is only one encompassing purpose: to love God with all our being and to love our neighbors as ourselves. The scripture that transforms us comes to us as story, and thereby teaches us to see that our lives and the lives of those we love and serve are also stories and not random collections of disconnected episodes. The transforming story is one that both reveals and compels love. The narrative form of scripture and the agape command that is at the heart of the ethics of the Bible are inseparably intertwined. The story makes no sense without its meaning of love; the love it compels has no content without the narrative that shows us what love is and how love acts.

The metaphor of ever-expanding, ever-clearer vision has long been used in Christian thought to describe this process of transformation, the process of moral and spiritual growth toward the mind of Christ. The more our minds are renewed by the transforming power of God, the more clearly we can see: see what loving God and our neighbor means; see the injured person by the side of the road; see the Samaritan who comes with healing for us; see all the pain, all the suffering that perhaps we would rather not see; see both the infinitely precious object and the incalculably high cost of love. To be transformed is to live and love with open eyes.

In her powerful and painful book on suffering, Dorothee Sölle tells us that, just as freedom from pain is nothing but death, so freedom from suffering is only a blindness that fails to perceive suffering.[4] The truth we must hear, as ministers of medicine, is that we must first see the suffering if we are to help relieve it, and that we cannot see it without in some sense experiencing it. To be transformed, to love with open eyes, is to join in the suffering of the world, as Jesus did.

The story of Jesus' suffering is the basis for the belief that it was his very participation in our pain that makes our salvation possible. Likewise, it is our willingness to see, and thereby to partake of, the suffering of those we wish to serve that makes our service effective.

In love's service there is no substitute for seeing, recognizing, hearing (to use another metaphor)

From Margaret E. Mohrmann, M.D., *Medicine as Ministry* (Cleveland, Ohio: The Pilgrim Press, 1995), pp. 62-88. Edited slightly from the original. Used by permission.

those who are suffering. To acknowledge a sufferer in all her anguish is to begin the process of restoring her to full personhood.[5] In Arthur Miller's play *Death of a Salesman,* Willy Loman's wife seems to understand the crucial role of recognition, for she pleads the case of her desperate husband this way: "He's a human being, and a terrible thing is happening to him. So attention must be paid. He's not to be allowed to fall into his grave like an old dog. Attention, attention must be finally paid to such a person."[6]

Paying attention to those who suffer — hearing their pain, seeing their damaged selves as damaged selves and not just as vehicles for interesting diagnoses — means, more than anything, listening to the stories they have to tell us. In 1985, Richard Baron wrote a thought-provoking essay in the *Annals of Internal Medicine* titled "I Can't Hear You While I'm Listening." He makes the essential point that we need to take human experience as seriously as we do anatomy and pathology.[7] To do this, we must hear what our patients have to tell us about their experiences.

The more than twenty years I have spent being a doctor have taught me two things that constitute, I believe, the heart of medical practice. One is the importance of the physician's silent presence with those whose lives she or he has changed forever by information and intervention, a presence that allows a true sharing of the burdens of knowledge and fear that pass between healer and sufferer. I shall say more about this silent presence in the final chapter when I speak of the importance of being with the patient through the suffering.

The other thing I have learned is how to take a history — or, rather, how to hear a story. I believe that much of what we teach medical students about taking medical histories from their patients is significantly flawed. We teach them, in effect, how not to listen, how not to hear the human experiences that have brought the patients to seek their help. We accomplish this by teaching the student to force the patient's experience into a prefabricated structure that sorts and separates information in ways foreign to the patient's story as it has been lived.

Anyone who teaches clinical medicine will have observed that hospitalized patients in medical centers often love the green third-year medical students assigned to them, and look upon them as their primary doctors during their hospital stay. I am sure there are many reasons for this phenomenon, but one in particular, I am convinced, is that the students have not yet "mastered" history taking as it is taught to them.

Students are given an enormous list of questions to ask and, usually, some method of selecting the appropriate questions for particular complaints. However, they cannot remember all the questions, and they get nervous, playing doctor for the first time. When they go in to take a history, they often end up just listening to the patient's flow of words, hoping that somehow the answers will appear by chance or that something in the monologue will jog from their memory some question to ask. They do not yet know enough to direct the story into the structured lines that they are taught to use. Consequently, their patients feel that they have finally been heard by someone.

If I were now teaching medical students about taking histories from patients, the first thing I would tell them is that all the lists of questions are to be used, but only to flesh out the story. The questions may clarify details, or stimulate further revelations, or recall a rambling storyteller to the main plot, but they are never a substitute for the story itself. There is much to be learned from the way patients tell their own tales of suffering: what they emphasize, the chronology as they have experienced it, the side events that sound unrelated to us but clearly are not to them, what they fear it all means. Only when we hear all of this can we dare to insert our own questions — about whether a certain symptom is also present, or whether the pain has this or that character — so that the answers fit into the patient's story. Otherwise, the answers create simply our own story: a description of a patient whom we have not heard, a human experience we have not touched.

Understanding illness is mostly a matter of getting the description right, and the description involves far more than just a diagnosis. Diagnosis is one of the extraordinary powers given to physicians, the power of naming. I know, however, that more often than not we get the name wrong, or at least dramatically incomplete. We often get the diagnosis right, but diagnostic labels primarily serve as shorthand tags that physicians find useful for encompassing a theory of pathophysiology and related treatment. A diagnosis is not always a helpful or meaningful label for the illness as experienced by the patient. The following examples illustrate this point.

In Flannery O'Connor's letters, she occasionally spoke of the lupus that was her constant companion and that eventually killed her at the age of thirty-nine. However, when she was very anemic, she did not speak of anemia — much less of bone marrow suppression — as her problem; she spoke of fatigue. When, only a month before her death, she referred to her illness, she did not mention circulating immune complexes, or even nephritis and renal failure. She said simply, "The wolf, I'm afraid, is inside tearing up the place."[8] Her experience was not systemic lupus erythematosus. It was, rather, her awareness of the chaotic, destructive, wolflike gnawing inside that she knew was gradually but inexorably disassembling, "tearing up" her self.

John Updike's story "From the Journal of a Leper" is told by a man who suffers from psoriasis. Although we have learned to laugh at the phrase "the heartbreak of psoriasis," how he describes the disease makes it clear that heartbreak may be a truer name for the illness than the term psoriasis, which he calls "a twisty Greek name it pains me to write." Here is his description.

> I am silvery, scaly. Puddles of flakes form wherever I rest my flesh. Each morning, I vacuum my bed. My torture is skin deep: there is no pain, not even itching; we lepers live a long time, and are ironically healthy in other respects. Lusty, though we are loathsome to love. Keensighted, though we hate to look upon ourselves. The name of the disease, spiritually speaking, is Humiliation.[9]

It is important to get diagnoses right: to recognize psoriasis and lupus, cancer and schizophrenia, AIDS and alcoholism. However, it is no less important to get the name of the illness right. It is no less important to recognize that for the sufferer the name of the disease, spiritually speaking, is humiliation or fear or malaise or endless pain or loneliness or despair or the end of a career or the end of a life. It is no less important to recognize that this is a human being to whom a terrible thing is happening and, whatever other name this terrible thing bears, its name is tragedy. There is nothing harder or less sentimental than Christian realism. Christian realism knows how to call a tragedy a tragedy, and not some other "twisty Greek name."

Tragedies come in all shapes and sizes, minor and major, but they all have three things in common: they are sad stories; they have flawed heroes; and they represent conflicts of good intentions or, more often, gatherings of evil possibilities.[10]

I have said enough about the importance of stories, and of recognizing our patients' lives and histories as stories; I shall not belabor the definition of tragedy as a story. However, I want to emphasize the adjective "sad." Being Christian does not spare us from the sorrow evoked by all that our open eyes see. On the contrary, the concentrated gaze of Christian realism allows us to experience true Christian sorrow[11] with and for those who suffer. This sorrow is not the sentimental, effortless tears we shed for distant starving children on the evening news. It is rather a deep, aching, compelling sorrow that breaks our hearts even while it motivates and empowers our resolve to understand and to love. It is a sorrow that binds us to those we serve as surely as Jesus' tears bound him to Lazarus, Martha, and Mary.

Our sorrow is for the flawed heroes of the sad story, the ones who suffer the action of the tale. "Flawed," in this context, has at least two meanings. Medically, it implies the defect of disease: the disintegration or unwholeness caused by the attack on self-identity that illness inflicts. In a Christian sense, it also implies the imperfection of sinfulness we all bear: sick and well alike, we are all flawed heroes in our own stories.

The word "hero" is at least as interesting. It seems somewhat out of place in the midst of discussion of sad stories and tragic suffering. However, I suggest that identifying sufferers as the heroes within their own stories is a healing move,[12] similar to the healing power evoked by recognition of the complex stories of our patients' lives.

A sometimes difficult corollary of seeing the patient as hero is that the physician is *not* the hero; this adjustment of perspective is probably salutary. We often hear and speak of the heroism of modern medicine, with the term invariably referring to "heroic" actions by members of the medical professions — the desperate fight to save a life with resuscitation techniques, the gallant flight of a transplant team to retrieve a life-saving organ, the dedicated twenty-four-hour efforts of intensive care nurses and doctors. All these people seem heroic; they certainly may be of critical importance to their patients. But they are not the true heroes in these stories.

To do one's job well and thoroughly is an excellent accomplishment, but it is not heroic. To bear the suffering that disease and its remedies bring can be heroic. As William May puts it, "the heavy burden of heroism in medicine falls not on the physician but on the patient and the patient's family."[13] The label of hero belongs only to those who bear the burden of the heroism.

Recognizing the patient as hero should make us think twice about imposing the burden of our own heroics on one who might not choose that particular form of courage. More important, it should add considerably to the reempowering of a person otherwise trapped in the impotence of illness. Such reempowering requires the patient's reintegration, the restoration of his wholeness. It begins with our enabling the patient to regain her voice by our paying attention to her and her story. The process continues with our unwavering recognition of who the hero truly is in this tragedy.

The perception of the true owner and protagonist of the story evokes a much richer sense of patient autonomy than most discussions of medical ethics allow. With our transformed, open eyes we can see the one who suffers as a person in all his wholeness — a person with self-creating relationships and with an intact and meaningful life story into which the present suffering can be incorporated and, therefore, comprehended.

Beyond any minimalist notion of respecting a patient's right to determine his or her own fate, we can now see this burdened hero as the only one who knows all the threads of the story well enough to weave them into the next panel of the tapestry. That panel's colors and textures and design can be congruent with all that has gone before only if the hero who lives within the tapestry, and those who have been allowed to share it, can direct the weaving. Somewhat less metaphorically, it has been said of the patient's autonomy that "the freedom we must honor is not the arbitrary freedom to will one thing one moment and another the next, but the freedom to establish an identity and to maintain integrity."[14]

I speak of "empowering" the patient, but this may have become too glib a catchword. It requires clarification if it is to fit into a specifically Christian ethical proposition. The power I speak of is the gleaming, grueling power that streams through these words of Paul to the Christians at Rome:

> We also boast in our sufferings, knowing that suffering produces endurance, and endurance, and endurance produces character, and character produces hope, and hope does not disappoint us, because God's love has been poured into our hearts through the Holy Spirit that has been given to us. (Rom. 5:3-5).

"We also boast in our sufferings." This is not a frivolous notion of enjoyment, no masochistic reveling in pain. There is too much in scripture and theology to warn us against choosing suffering for its own sake. The solemn "joy" of suffering is only in knowing where it can lead: to endurance, to character, to hope, to the love of God.

"Suffering produces endurance." In the rolling Latin of the Vulgate, this statement is *tribulation patientiam operatur,* which can also be translated "tribulation produces patience." To be a patient is to be one who is patient, one who endures. To be a patient is to be one who suffers not only in the sense of feeling pain but also in the sense of allowing the pain, of acknowledging and incorporating it as a true thing that is actually happening and that must be dealt with as such. The power of acknowledgment and incorporation — the power to exercise the freedom to establish an identity and to maintain integrity — is the power available to and essential for the suffering ones we wish to serve. It is the power that our recognition of their suffering can evoke and enhance.

It should be clear, then, that in speaking of patience, of endurance, I am not talking about a "stiff upper lip." I am not talking about a foolish, isolating, and fundamentally impotent refusal to admit the presence of pain and to seek its elimination. The stolid, stoical "patience on a monument" that denies its need for healing is not the Christian virtue of patience.

The first known moral essay in Christian history, written around the year 200 C.E. by Tertullian, was entitled *De patientia,* "On Patience."

Tertullian makes the pivotal point that the Stoic ideal of patience is designed to result in resignation. In contrast, Christian endurance produces hope. The difference is crucial.

The Christian virtue of patience is the power that looks suffering square in the face, sees it for what it is, and then decides what is to be done about it. It is in this process of clear vision, open acknowledgment, and careful decision that endurance produces character, the sort of character that is full of the hope that neither suffering nor anything else in all creation will ever be able to separate us from the love of God (Rom. 9:35, 39).

Writing the Next Chapter

We who minister to the ill in the name of the faithful community are transformed by the Word of God to be persons who can see. We can now perceive the tragedy that befalls "the patient one" as a sad story centered around a flawed hero. Our perception helps empower in the sufferer a hopeful and virtuous endurance so that she or he also may look upon the tragedy with open eyes and work with us to discern what is to be done, what is, in Paul's words, "good and acceptable and perfect."

It sounds as though we may finally have arrived at the point where we shall have to talk about more traditional medical ethics — about problem solving, about what is to be done. Maybe.

William May, in *The Patient's Ordeal,* makes a distinction, which he attributes to T. S. Eliot, between two sorts of problems. One type of problem raises the question "What are we going to do about it?"; the other asks, "How are we going to behave toward it?" May proposes that many, if not most, of the problems we seek to solve in responding to the suffering of our neighbors are those of the latter sort.[15] For example, if I am coping with the news of a disease likely to be fatal to me, there are things I must do: I must make decisions about therapy, get my affairs in order, and the like. However, these sorts of decisions surely take a back seat to, and in fact depend on, my response to the second question about how I shall behave toward this news. I must first ponder how I choose to conduct the rest of my life in the light of the new, self-shattering information. I must consider how to complete my life in a way that is congruent with who I am and congruent with the way I have lived my life thus far.

The metaphor that leads us to seek "solutions" to our problems may reveal more than we have realized about the intricate process of problem solving. In their book about the largely unnoticed prevalence of metaphorical language in our everyday speech, Lakoff and Johnson tell the story of a young man who was learning to speak English. When he encountered the phrase "the solution of a problem," he adopted with enthusiasm the chemical metaphor that no longer stands out for native speakers familiar with it.[16] His explanation of the image is worth considering as an alternative to the usual notion that to solve a problem is to eliminate it.

When the young man heard "the solution of a problem," he pictured a huge vat of solvent in which problems of various types are suspended. In order to get any particular problem into solution, it is necessary to alter the chemical nature of the solvent. The problem will then become dissolved and seem to disappear. However, if the solvent is altered again, perhaps to handle another problem, the first problem may precipitate; it may come out of solution and, once again, cloud its fluid environment.

Reclaiming the chemical basis of the metaphor of problem solving reminds us that the solution of a problem may at times depend not on its removal but on a change in its environment. "Solutions" may require alterations in the other aspects of one's life that now have to adjust to this new problem in order to fit it in, and thus solve it by assimilating it. It is also worth remembering that later adaptations to newer dilemmas may make old problems reappear, an experience likely to be familiar to most of us.

Some problems, like strep throat or a broken arm, can be eliminated sooner or later. In contrast, many others, like chronic arthritis, alcoholism, cancer, grief — indeed, virtually all the afflictions that entail the kinds of suffering that call for virtuous and hopeful endurance — can find their "solutions" only by being acknowledged and incorporated into the embracing whole of a lifetime's narrative. "Incorporate" is the Latin-based equivalent of the Anglo-Saxon word "embody." What some problems need is embodiment: they need to be given bodies that allow them to fit into the story, forms that are compatible with the story. The rich nuances of the forgotten metaphor embedded in the notion of problem solving can, therefore, lead us toward the adoption of a different metaphor to explain our task. I suggest that we can offer more to those we serve by consciously adopting the metaphor of *story*, so that we can see the process of healing as a process not of solving problems, but of giving narrative form to the events. It is the process of "writing the next chapter."

The stories of all our lives have always been under joint authorship. I may rightly consider myself to be the chief author of my own tale (although, at times, "editor" seems to be the better word, because my life typically happens to me while I am making other plans, and much of my task seems to be to correct the spelling and the punctuation). However, I am well aware that there has been no time when I have been the sole contributor to this work. Parents and siblings, school friends and teachers, children and colleagues, all the people we love and those to whom we commit ourselves — all these people participate in varying degrees in writing the chapters of our life stories. In addition, when a time of medical crisis arrives, the members of the healing community — the pastor and the physician, the comforter and the therapist — will also be part of the composition that solves the problem by continuing the narrative. Together with the family and friends who are old hands at this particular manuscript, they will help the flawed hero embody this newest sad episode within the story of his or her life.

There are several criteria for the writing of that next chapter. First, it has to be part of the hero's story and no one else's. It is undeniably true that our contributions to the stories of those we serve are themselves important parts of our own narratives. However, it is essential that we remember whose crises we are involved in and that we ensure that the paragraphs we add are crafted to fit those persons' tales and not our own.

Second, the next chapter has to make sense. It has to fit the story as it has unfolded to that point. There is no sense in trying to tack the last chapter of *Anna Karenina* onto the first half of *Gone with the Wind.* Scarlett would never have thrown herself in front of a train, even if there had been any railroad tracks left in Georgia, and there is no point in considering such an incongruous outcome.

The meaning of the next chapter must include and somehow continue the themes that have defined the hero's life. This requirement may entail a strenuous examination of previous parts of the story in order for the significance of past activities to be understood, so that the content can be continued even if the activities themselves cannot, because of changes wrought by illness or injury. The process of ensuring continuity may call for an expansion or an altered comprehension of the meanings that animate the story, but such rethinking characterizes healing and growth in their most basic forms.

The work of finding new interpretations and new expressions for the essential meanings of one's life satisfies the third criterion of a good chapter: the new chapter should be able to lead the story on to the other chapters that are to follow. It must be not only continuous with what has gone before but also generative of what is to come: the re-formed, reintegrated life of a whole person.

Sometimes, when the next chapter is actually the final chapter in the story, it leads to the continuation of important threads of the hero's tale in the lives of those who have shared the story. Sometimes the succeeding chapters can be read only in the lives of those left behind to remember and to sustain the meaning of that memory.

The next chapter in the hero's story may be the last chapter, or it may be a chapter so shattering that finding strands of continuous meaning and creative hope seems scarcely possible. To acknowledge this is to recognize once again the part of the story we are concerned with is indeed a tragedy. Beyond all poetic talk of the tragedy as a sad story about a flawed hero, the fact remains that tragedy is dark confusion and chaos swirling around a conflict of good intentions and, most painfully, a gathering of evil possibilities.

The conflict that characterizes tragedy is perhaps most evident in situations that ask for impossible decisions, situations that seem to need ethics consultants. A good example is the case of Debbie, . . . in which the good of preserving life comes into uncompromising conflict with the good of relieving suffering, and the evil of failing to respond to pain confronts head-on the evil of ending a life. However, the multiple evils and conflicting goods that create and intensify suffering appear long before that final decision point is reached. It is characteristic of the tragedy of human suffering that it is always a compound insult; the attack is always on more than one front.

Many authors have correctly described illness as an assault on the identity of the patient, or have explained it in terms of damage to the person's wholeness. Others have spoken of a fundamental internal division, a violent separation of the parts of the self that were created to live an integrated life. William May's way of putting it — which I find particularly applicable to an understanding of the communal nature of healing — is that our human identity is best understood in three dimensions: that of the body, our physical presence in the world; that of the community, our relations with each other; and that of the ultimate, our perception of transcendent reality, our connection to God.[17]

With this compound notion of identity, illness can be understood as a simultaneous assault at all three levels, physical, communal, and religious. One conclusion to be drawn from such a perspective is that, to be fully restorative, healing must attend to all three levels. Such an approach affirms the point made in the Introduction that healing involves all segments of the healing community — medical, lay, and clerical. Medicine is a ministry in which doctors are not the only ordinands.

I shall analyze briefly each of these dimensions of healing, and the response to each by the part of the community most closely related to it. However, I wish to make it clear from the start that such a pairing off of the three levels of suffering and the three categories of healers, while it may create neat rhetorical parallels, belies the actual interplay of real patients and real ministers. There is and there should be considerable overlap among these three areas; I do not want my assignment of apparently separate tasks to obscure the complexity of our interactions with those we serve..

Having made this disclaimer, I can say that the physical dimension of illness, which involves a disruption of the patient's unique embodied state in some fashion, is preeminently the domain of the medical professional. It is the obligation of the physician, nurse, or therapist to witness materially to the will of the community to relieve suffering and to reestablish the patient's physical participation in the world of sense, activity, and communication.

Specifically, much can be said about the primacy of the physician's obligation to relieve suffering: to do everything possible to alleviate the illness, to remove the impediment to health, to attend to the patient's physical well-being. One can find innumerable warrants for the doctor's task in scripture, especially in the healing work of Jesus. Although Jesus asked some interesting questions of his patients, he never suggested to them that they would be better off just bearing their pain. Jesus' consistent willingness to relieve physical suffering adds a necessary qualifier and counterbalance to any discussion of the glorious endurance that suffering can produce.

The sort of suffering of which Paul speaks in Romans, the "tribulation that produces patience," must satisfy at least two criteria in order to be productive of the endurance that strengthens character and engenders hope. First, the suffering must be unavoidable. This ineluctability can mean either that the suffering cannot be eliminated — the pain is intractable, the loss irretrievable, the prognosis undeniable — or that what is required for its elimination is unacceptable — a loss of consciousness, say, or a renunciation of deeply held principles.

Second, it must be possible for the suffering in question to produce those goods of endurance and character and hope. There is no point in talking about character building when the torture is so intense and shattering that there may be virtually no self left to be strengthened or to comprehend the idea of hope. Moreover, there is no point in talking about the productivity of suffering when the one who suffers has no discernible capacity to learn from the experience — a person in irreversible coma, for example, or perhaps a newborn infant. As William May writes, "suffering does not always ennoble."[18] It can crush rather than strengthen its bearer.

Therefore, while we recognize and understand the creative potential in suffering, we also know that we are not asked to bear unnecessary suffering. We know that there is some pain that cannot lead to more abundant life. Our Christian hope is built partly upon the assurance that God does not test us beyond our power to endure, but always provides means of escape (1 Cor. 10:13). Such avenues of escape are often under our control. We may not test God's children more rigorously than God would by blocking access to the escape routes God provides.

The suffering that a serious illness inflicts results not only from the assault on the person's physical well-being and sense of embodiment, [19] but also from the threat to that person's relations with those who comprise his or her community. For example, the physician may fully be able to relieve the devastating physical pain of a severe burn, but the psychic pain of permanent disfigurement and its inevitable alteration of relationships does not respond to analgesics. The damage done to a person's self-identification as part of a community can be healed only by the ministrations of that community.

Just as it is the doctor's task to witness to the will to relieve physical suffering and restore the patient's damaged embodiment, so it is the task of the community to witness to the will to sustain relationship with the injured one. In so doing, the community confirms the patient's continued identity as a whole and treasured member. By our refusal to allow suffering to separate the patient from us, we repeat the truth that nothing can separate us from the love of God. We also proclaim an essential fact about human existence, theologically understood: none of the negative aspects of life — sickness and crime and grief and meanness and pain — is absolute in this world. Their elimination is not required for us to be able to live a fully human existence.[20] What is required for a truly human life is not the absence of pain but the presence of others, the maintenance of living bonds with other human beings. It is these relations that are threatened during any self-assaulting illness. As part of their healing, those who suffer require from us assurance that our relationships with them endure.

Sickness is isolating; one of the pains that any serious illness inflicts is the pain of loneliness. The loneliness cannot be completely overcome, because illness is, ultimately, an intensely personal experience. However, the loneliness that accompanies suffering, though it may still be present, can be stripped of much of its ability to destroy if it is transformed into a sign of the patient's unique and central position within a community that focuses its healing love on him or her.

Flannery O'Connor wrote, "I have never been anywhere but sick. In a sense sickness is a place, more instructive than a long trip to Europe, and it's always a place where there's no company, where nobody can follow."[21] She would probably be quick to acknowledge that she wrote this in a letter to a close friend whose weekly correspondence and frequent visits were part of a network of relationships that kept O'Connor unshakable in her identity and capable of stunningly creative work through all her years of living in that lonely place called sickness. She would also be quick to remind us — and it is important that we not forget — that, despite that supportive network, she could still write this kind of statement and know it to be true.

The third dimension of illness is its assault on one's relation to God. This is the level of suffering to which ordained clergy especially are called to respond. Serious illness shatters our understanding of the way the world works by bringing into question God's power to protect us and even God's love for us.

I considered briefly the possibility of devoting part of this book to questions of theodicy, to the problem we have in reconciling a belief in both God's goodness and God's omnipotence with the obvious presence of evil and suffering in the world. I have chosen, however, not to linger on theodicy, not only because there has already been much written on the subject, most of which focuses appropriately on our misunderstanding of power as an attribute of God, but also because I do not think that it is a particularly helpful emphasis for those who wish to minister to the suffering. None of us wants to be in the role of Job's comforters; we want to be real comforters, real healers. That task requires attention not to the fine points of theological doctrine but to the reality of the patient's experience of pain and to our certainty of God's love.

The theological witness needed to reestablish and reaffirm the patient's relationship to God is the witness of the cross and its double message that evil is real and God is good. It is a message that both validates the reality of the suffering and denies that the pain is absolute. Suffering is real (we cannot accept the stance of Christian Science); suffering may not always be explainable (we are not God, but creatures bound in time); but suffering is not the ultimate reality (we are not lost out here in the stars). And nothing can separate us from the love of God.

Suffering produces hope, "because God's love has been poured into our hearts through the Holy Spirit that has been given to us" (Rom. 5:5). It is, finally, that truth — the truth of God's love in our hearts — that we bring to those who suffer when we treat their bodies, when we sustain our relationships with them, when we assure them that the pain working at them is being vanquished by the love working for them. From these overlapping responses to the several dimensions of illness we can enable in those we serve and in ourselves the transformation of vision that we need, not only to see the suffering itself, but also to see the meaning of the pain.

Notes

1. James M. Gustafson, introduction to *The Responsible Self,* by H. Richard Niebuhr (New York: Harper and Row, 1963), p. 22.

2. Charles M. Wood's *Formation of Christian Understanding* (Valley Forge, Pa.: Trinity Press, 1981) teaches much the same lesson as Augustine.

3. Richard A. McCormick, "Theology and Bioethics: Christian Foundations," in *Theology and Bioethics,* ed. E. Shelp (Dordrecht, Netherlands: D. Reidel Publishing Company, 1985).

4. Dorothee Sölle, *Suffering* (Philadelphia: Fortress Press, 1975), pp. 37-39.

5. Howard Brody, *Stories of Sickness* (New Haven, Conn.: Yale University Press, 1987), p. 125.

6. Arthur Miller, *Death of a Salesman,* in *The Portable Arthur Miller,* ed. Harold Clurman (New York: Viking Press, 1971), p. 50.

7. Richard J. Baron, "An Introduction to Medical Phenomenology: I Can't Hear You While I'm Listening," *Annals of Internal Medicine* 103 (1985): 606-11.

8. Flannery O'Connor, *The Habit of Being,* ed. Sally Fitzgerald (New York: Random House, 1980), p. 591.

9. John Updike, "From the Journal of a Leper," in *Problems and Other Stories* (New York: Alfred A. Knopf, 1979), p. 181.

10. Hessel Bouma et al., *Christian Faith, Health, and Medical Practice* (Grand Rapids, Mich.: Eerdmans, 1989), pp. 124-32.

11. Arthur C. McGill, *Suffering: A Test of Theological Method* (Philadelphia: Westminster Press, 1968).

12. Rita Charon, "Doctor-Patient/Reader-Writer: Learning to Find the Text," *Soundings* 72 (1989): 147.

13. William F. May, *The Patient's Ordeal* (Bloomington: Indiana University Press, 1991), p. 3.

14. Bouma et al., *Christian Faith,* p. 15.

15. May, *Patient's Ordeal,* pp. 3-4.

16. George Lakoff and Mark Johnson, *Metaphors We Live By* (Chicago: University of Chicago Press, 1980), pp. 143-44.

17. May, *Patient's Ordeal,* pp. 9-12.

18. Ibid., p. 50.

19. "Embodiment" here is not intended to signal the varied philosophical and experiential nuances that the term carries in, for example, feminist thought. In the context of this book, embodiment refers simply to the fact of human physicality, especially as it seizes our attention in situations of pain and disease.

20. Ibid., p. 153.

21. O'Connor, *Habit of Beings,* p. 163.

49 Patient Suffering and the Anointing of the Sick

M. Therese Lysaught

A physician, reflecting on the early days of his medical training, recounts a relationship with a patient suffering from a rare form of bone cancer. He recalls the following:

> In the hospital, it was the habit [of this patient] to roam the halls late at night after his wife and small children had gone to their lodging. I never asked him whether it was pain that kept him moving or perhaps loneliness and a simple desire for conversation. One night, having completed my work for the day, feeling too tired to read on my own, and facing no other prospect but to give in to sleep, I felt like talking.
>
> On that night, and on other nights following, we discussed nothing in particular. Our conversation might turn to his aspirations at work . . . or to my thoughts about medicine. For a time he would talk about his plans for the future as though they were still foremost in his mind, but before long he would lapse into the past tense and grow sullen. I think that a part of him was looking for encouragement, but what little I knew of his condition made medical reassurance nearly impossible. I hid from his pain by focusing on the bright side of things. It was a kind of dishonesty, though at that early point in my medical training I did not recognize it as such. What we had was better than silence, but we never really talked.
>
> One night, after I had been away for several days, I met him again in the semidark hallway near the nurses' station. He was asking a nurse to bring something to his room . . . For some reason, she proceeded to introduce the two of us — a rare event by hospital standards. Equally strange, neither he nor I spoke up to say that we already knew one another. I put out my hand to shake his, and he started to do the same; then it hit me: his arm was missing. It had been amputated as part of his treatment. I should have anticipated the amputation . . . but it came as a surprise to me. In the instant before my hand withdrew and I looked down, at a loss for what to say or do, I caught in his eyes a look of sorrow, perhaps even shame. I begged his pardon, but we did not speak further . . . We never met again. (Gunderman 15-16)

A week or so later, the patient dies, and the rapidity of the deterioration and the injustice of the illness creates a crisis for the physician. He feels that he has failed this patient, though not medically as this was not his patient. He senses that he has failed morally, although according to the principles and canons of biomedical ethics, he has done nothing 'wrong.' The physician is disturbed that nothing in his medical training or in his medical ethics prepared him, guided him, instructed him in how to attend to this man's pain and suffering.

As it did with this physician, suffering confronts us, compels us, and condemns us. It confronts us with shock that can upheave our unified, positive, progressive vision of our world, our lives, and our selves. It compels us to act — to alleviate it or to flee from it — in order to restore our sense of unity shattered by its eruption into our present. It condemns us — our fictions of unity, peace, and invulnerability, our factual self-centeredness and complicity in its creation and sustenance, our paralysis in its face and our evasion of responsibility.

Suffering similarly confronts theological theory, accusing it of being ephemeral and inadequate, assuming the role of a problematic, a contradiction, a paradox. It compels us to speak words that comfort and justify. It condemns all theorizing that posits a metastructure more important than the real and everyday or that posits a God who could cause or allow suffering, convicting it of

---

From M. Therese Lysaught, "Patient Suffering and the Anointing of the Sick," *The Cresset,* February 1992, pp. 15-21. Used by permission.

complicity and generativity of conditions, of privileging an airtight image of God that we have created over the chaos of those who suffer.

Suffering similarly convicts biomedical ethical theory. In confronting biomedical ethics, the physical and social suffering of patients rarely finds itself addressed adequately. The reality of this suffering condemns a biomedical ethics that privileges the construction of clean and clear formulaic principles aimed primarily at facilitating the decision-making of medical practitioners and that allies itself with a theoretical structure which cannot account for the suffering of patients — a suffering which is the *raison d'être* for medicine and the locus for much of the moral significance of medicine. As for this physician, the sufferings of patients compel us to look beyond biomedical ethics.

This essay, then, undertakes three tasks. Part one offers a construction of some of the philosophical commitments of biomedical ethics, arguing that these prevent it from adequately conceptualizing two crucial characteristics of patients: (1) the fact that they are suffering and (2) religious/moral interpretations patients give to their own suffering. In order to highlight this problem, part two describes some of the dynamics of suffering as drawn from narratives of patients and phenomenological analyses of suffering. Finally, part three reflects on one way in which the Christian tradition has incorporated these dimensions of sickness and suffering into its corporate life, namely the Rite of the Anointing of the Sick.

Biomedical Ethics and its Theoretical Alliances

Biomedical ethics failed this physician, failed to give him the conceptual or moral tools with which to act or to understand his lack of actions. It failed to convict his actions as wrong, although he profoundly knew that he had behaved badly. What do we mean by 'biomedical ethics' in this context, and why do they often fail to provide the necessary guidance or illumination?

Biomedical ethics might profitably be understood as a 'discourse' in the Foucauldian sense. Arthur Frank defines discourses as "cognitive mappings of the body's possibilities and limitations, which bodies experience as already there for their self understanding . . . These mappings form the normative parameters of how the body can understand itself" (Frank 48). By situating themselves at the intersection of a number of discourses offered by societies, individuals formulate what Frank calls a 'code' by which we understand, and hence navigate, both the world and our identities. Biomedical ethics, then, insofar as it offers societal expectations of normative ideals of individual performance, might be understood to function in part as an agent of social regulation.

This might seem a strange categorization for those of us familiar with a biomedical ethic that speaks the language of principles, rights, autonomy, and decision-making. But the power of this description is evident in H. Tristram Englehardt's *Foundations of Bioethics.* Englehardt is the most articulate and forthright spokesperson for the majority position in biomedical ethics, namely 'pluralist biomedical ethics.'[1] Pluralist biomedical ethics see themselves as a "general attempt at secular ethics," derived form the "logic of pluralism," a logic which seeks to describe a neutral framework for the peaceable resolution of controversies. (Englehardt 6, 11, 39)

To create this framework, pluralist biomedical ethics utilize normative anthropological and sociological dualisms that structure the liberal philosophy of pluralist society. The taken-for-granted dichotomies of mind/body, reason/desire, public/private, lead Englehardt to make some bold claims. First of all, he posits the moral landscape as bifurcated into "two tiers" mirroring traditional distinctions between public and private. These "two tiers" of the moral life he names the "peaceable secular community" and "particular moral communities" (54). The "peaceable secular community" functions as a conceptual space in which public disputes are resolved by 'rational' (i.e., impartial, unprejudiced, anonymous, universal) arguments made by rational beings "anywhere in the cosmos" who have transcended the boundaries of their particular communities (10, 81, 105); ethical reasoning and moral judgments derive authority through correlations with procedures of this general standpoint and not from any particular content.

While the second tier, particular moral communities, is the locus of moral content and meaning, these communities rely on premises that, because of their particularity, "cannot be secured by [rational] argument," so that judgments of these communities cannot be validated as "rationally" authoritative (54). Particularities and affectivities, commitments nurtured within particular moral communities, which for our purposes means especially *religious* commitments and convictions, therefore, cannot be admitted as premises in rational moral arguments. While moral agents live their lives within particular, substantial, concrete communities, for moral purposes they must disembed themselves from these attachments if they wish to function in the public, moral domain.

Englehardt also provides criteria for membership in the "peaceable secular community,' criteria that are necessary insofar as "not all humans are equal . . . [as he says] persons, not humans, are special" (104). The criteria, namely, rationality, self-consciousness, and a sense of worthiness of blame and praise, define a being as an autonomous moral agent. A body — a human body — does not qualify one to be a moral agent; correlatively, bodies are not theoretically required for moral agency. Bodies tend to be practical correlatives of moral agents, but they have no moral or rational value or content.

This distinction between 'persons' and 'humans' greatly simplifies the task of biomedical ethics. Engelhardt argues that there are only two methods by which to resolve an ethical controversy; agreed-to-procedures or force. The autonomy of the members of the 'peaceable secular community' constrains society and other persons from using 'unconsented-to' force against them. But 'non-persons,' who can make no claim to autonomy, are not protected from such force.

Thus, a contradiction becomes apparent. On the one hand, a primary object of pluralist biomedical ethics is 'bodies,' and the task is to authorize legitimate use of force against bodies — for example, who decides what is to be done with a particular (now incompetent) body; when do we stop sustaining a body; when do we let new-born but malformed bodies expire; should we kill bodies; whose body will have access to health care? But this same human body does not count as a legitimate epistemological or even anthropological moral resource. Moral subjectivity is equated with rational mind, and 'knowledge' is available only of those things predicated as accessible to all minds; human embodiment, the locus of human illness and suffering and the site of the practice of medicine, are overlooked.[2]

The Sufferings of Patients

The patient's suffering and pain convict the physician of moral failing.[3] If biomedical ethics were to attend to the embodied sufferings of patients, what might they discover?

If nothing else, they would discover that the sufferings of the sick differ widely. This fact alone renders suffering inaccessible to biomedical ethics (see Smith 261). Not only are different kinds of sufferings associated with different kinds of illnesses — emergency traumatic injury vs. chronic illness vs. terminal illness that moves rapidly vs. a life-threatening condition that persists for twenty years vs. illness that has intense social stigmas — but each individual body will be inscribed differently by the intersection of the cultural discourses of class, race, gender, age, religion, science, and politics with the individual's personal history. The matrix comprised of these intersections of discourses, relationships, and histories, provides our ongoing identity, the code by which each individual deciphers and negotiates the world. In instances of suffering, this 'code' is broken.

In spite of this irreducible particularity, phenomenological and autobiographical accounts of suffering note three consistent dynamics. In the first dynamic, experiences of illness or pain often re-situate patients *vis-à-vis* their bodies, re-ordering taken-for-granted relationships between "self" and "body." Experiences of illness serve as a reminder that "selves" depend on the integrity of bodies, that health and lives are radically contingent. In illness the body often moves from the background to the forefront of perception, and patients increasingly identify their selves with their bodies, a move which also unfortunately often encourages medical professionals to do the same. Some describe this aspect of patients' experiences as "essentially on ontological assault" in which the body becomes the enemy, interposing itself between "us and reality," standing "opposite the self" (Pellegrino/Thomasma 207-8), challenging a culturally instilled sense of the transcendence of self over body.

While this reorientation can be illuminating, more likely it can be alienating. Pain and illness can first effect alienation by counteracting "the human being's capacity to move out beyond the boundaries of his or her own body into the external, sharable world" (Scarry 13). Restrictive and dissociative, pain "chains down our thoughts," breaks connections between "body" and "world." In addition to impeding motion beyond personal boundaries, pain also alters the nature of these boundaries: "It is the intense pain that destroys a person's self and world, a destruction experienced spatially as either the contraction of the universe down to the immediate vicinity of the body or as the body swelling to fill the entire universe" (Scarry 35). The body can become one's "world" as pain occupies more and more of one's consciousness and crowds out awareness of anything else. Alienation can also be effected by experiencing the body as the "enemy," the "agent of the agony."

Secondly, patients often experience a loss or usurpation of their "voice." Voice may literally be "lost" as a function of pain, or legitimate "voice" may be denied or repressed because it does not fit with normative medical or moral language. As Elaine Scarry notes, one characteristic of physical pain is that, for the most part, it is "inexpressible." While I can *tell you* of my pain, for example, there is no way for you to truly grasp its reality — either *that* it is real, or how real, how intense it is; your doubt of my pain cannot be decisively dispelled (4). This inexpressibility, this unsharability, can isolate patients from those close to them and prevent them from effectively communicating their distress to medical practitioners. Moreover, Scarry continues, "pain does not simply resist language, but [can] actively destroy it, bringing about an immediate reversion to a state anterior to language, to the sounds and cries a human being makes before language is learned" (Scarry 4). (An alternative suggestion is that these sounds actually *are* the language of pain.) It can achieve this effect because physical pain resists objectification. Undoubtedly, this characteristic of pain underlies medicine's tendency to identify patients with their bodies: this identification is a first step in trying to "objectify" the pain, to give it the referent, the object, that it lacks. As Arthur Frank notes, illness can also result in "the loss of capacity to express through the body" (Frank 85).

But in many ways, the medical establishment furthers the patient's experience of loss of voice. As many have noted, when it comes to medicine, the patient is a "stranger in a strange land" (Engelhardt 256); medicine is foreign country filled with unfamiliar languages and customs. Kleinman, for example, perceptively comments on how medical facilities seem designed to be navigated only by those who are familiar with them. Often, patients' lack of knowledge of the language of medicine can intimidate them, leaving them speechless. When patients do "find" their voice, they often speak of the "lived experience" of their illness in non-scientific and often subjective "common-sense ways accessible to all lay persons in their social group" (Kleinman 4). But, all too often, in order to participate in the medical cure, patients must conform themselves to the world of medicine rather than vice versa, learning its language; their accounts of their own illness are translated into the language of the profession.

Kleinman notes that practitioners "have been taught to regard with *suspicion* patients' illness narratives and causal beliefs" (17). Physicians often feel they have to sift out meaning from confused and messy narratives of patients, listening selectively "so that some aspects are carefully listened for and heard (sometimes when they are not spoken), while other things that are said — and even repeated — are literally not heard" (Kleinman 52, 16; Scarry 6-7). 'Subjective' experiences of patients' illnesses become 'objective' categorized diseases. Moreover, not only are patients' narratives at times suspect, but at times, as a result of the "inexpressibility" of their pain, patients' claims of illness or pain are doubted, if not explicitly denied, especially in the cases of the chronically ill patients or in cases where the "explanatory framework" of medicine has not yet shifted to allow an illness into "reality." (Contemporary examples of this might include early sufferers of AIDS and chronic fatigue syndrome.) Alternatively, patients who reject a diagnosis of disease, or who do not conform to acceptable modes of dealing with a diagnosis, may be labelled as "in denial"; the physiological "interpretation" is given higher epistemic status than the patient's lived experiential interpretations. Patients, along with their voices, can be rendered inadequate, unhelpful, wrong, inactive, silenced.

But, just as a crucial characteristic of suffering is its ability to dissolve and destroy language, a first step toward dissolving and destroying suffering, then, is linguistic. As pain and suffering "resist objectification in language" and de-objectify the world, they can be overcome only by "forcing [them] into avenues of objectification," an objectification correlated with the body in which they reside (Scarry 5, 6, 17; see also Sölle 70-72). We find this same notion of "objectification" in descriptions of "work." Work, an inextricably social process, is the vehicle through which we "objectify" ourselves, a multi-directional process through which the "self" is constituted and through which the self constitutes the "world." Dorothee Soelle employs this concept to suggest that "working on" suffering is best understood as "transforming the act of suffering into purposeful activity . . . nothing [she maintains] can be learned from suffering unless it is worked through" (126).

A fundamental shape that this work takes in the lives of the ill and suffering is that of creation of 'narratives.' As Kleinman notes, "the illness narrative is a story the patient tells, and significant others retell, to give coherence to the distinctive events and long-term course of the suffering" (49). Kleinman further affirms that not only does the story reflect the experience of illness, "but rather it contributes to the experience of symptoms and suffering" (49). Arthur Frank confirms this process, noting that "in illness, the body finds itself progressively unable to express itself in conventional codes. Sometimes, with the right kind of support, it creates a new code" (85).

It is noteworthy that Frank remarks, "with the right kind of support." The dynamics of suffering in illness all contribute to a sense of isolation and marginalization voiced by many who have been ill. Consequently, this process of narrative creation depends on the resources, options, and opportunities offered to the individual by the social situation. Often these prove insufficient. But importantly, those who initiate this narrative process need not be the victims of suffering themselves; in fact, often they cannot be. Thus Kleinman includes as a "core clinical task" what he calls "empathetic witnessing. That is the existential commitment to be with the sick person and to facilitate his or her building of an illness narrative that will make sense of and give value to the experience" (54; see also Scarry 6). This corporate dimension is indispensable in the dissolution of suffering, for the sufferer to move from the state of isolation caused by the destruction of her world, through expression and communication to solidarity through which change is possible. Thus, potential for deriving meaning from suffering lies not in some inherent quality suffering possesses, nor in the abilities of its victims. It lies rather in the resources offered by society and in the willingness of individuals to participate in this process, to enter into solidarity, to pay "attention" to those who suffer.

Suffering and Illness in a Liturgical Framework

Given the secular commitments of pluralist biomedical ethics described in section one, the Christian community might seem an unlikely place to turn to find resources to aid and inform our physician. But Christian tradition has, from its earliest beginnings, been significantly committed to attending those who suffer. This commitment has led to the development of practices which in their contemporary forms attend to many of the dynamics of suffering outlined above and thereby shape contemporary Christian relationships to suffering, both individual and communal. In this third section, I would like to focus on one practice in particular — liturgical rites of anointing and healing. For our purposes, I will draw on the Roman Catholic tradition's Sacrament of the Anointing of the Sick.

Before turning to the Rite, it is important to highlight the centrality of suffering and healing in Christian practice. Healing of the sick was one of three primary activities associated by the Evangelists with Jesus' ministry, inextricably linked with his preaching and teaching. John Dominic Crossan, in a recent article, attends to this fact and suggests that Jesus' particular bodily practices (i.e., eating and healing) embodied his message and had radical religiopolitical ramifications. Crossan locates his argument within the matrix of anthropological claims that correlate regulation of bodily boundaries with regulation of social boundaries. Drawing on Mary Douglas, Peter Farb, and George Armelagos, as well as Pierre Bourdieu and Caroline Walker Bynum, Crossan begins with the position that in Jesus' Jewish culture, who one ate with defined and identified one's location in the social matrix: "those decisions about what we eat, where we eat, when we eat, and above all, with whom we eat . . . form a miniature map of our social distinctions and hierarchies" (1195). It probably would have been rare, we can imagine, to find a Jew eating with a Samaritan or a Pharisee with a tax collector. Furthermore, bodies who were sick, menstruating or dead were denoted as ritually "unclean" and would have been categorized as those one ought not touch, let alone eat with. Thus, food customs and illness customs provided clear social divisions, with some designations excluding people entirely.

Within this matrix, Crossan argues, Jesus' proclamation of the advent of the Kingdom of God contained a radical social challenge. Crossan maintains that Jesus' practices and message championed a radically egalitarian "reciprocity of open eating and open healing" (Crossan 1195). Thus we find Jesus scandalizing onlookers by those he chooses to eat with (tax collectors and sinners, taking water from a Samaritan woman). Parables tell of the kinds of people he healed — lepers, the blind, the lame, a woman "with a flow of blood" — those understood within the culture to be blemished or unclean. And importantly, in these parables it is clear that Jesus often healed by touch, as Crossan notes:

> [Jesus] healed the illness by refusing to accept the official quarantine, by refusing to stay separate from the sick person, by touching him [or her], and thereby confronting others with a challenge and a choice. By so doing, of course, he was making extremely subversive claims about who defined the community, who patrolled its boundaries, who controlled its entries and exits, who, in other words, was in charge." (1197)

Crossan implies that these two practices — open eating and open healing — were identifiable marks of what he calls the "Jesus movement." Those who had been healed were enjoined only to carry the message, and those who carried the message were charged to carry with them no other provisions but to trust that message and miracle would open the homes and hearths of those they healed. These two practices are embodied in the contemporary Church in the Eucharist and in the practice of ministry to the sick. While this is not the place to argue for a stronger liturgical and ecclesial understanding of the constitutive nature of the latter practice, I would like to suggest that Christian liturgies of healing, at least as represented in the Roman Catholic Rite, are both responsive to the existential situation of those who suffer and continue to embody the meaning that Jesus' healing practices suggest.

As can be seen from the text of its Introduction, the *Rite of Anointing and Pastoral Care of the Sick* responds to a number of the dynamics of the sufferings of patients noted in part two above. First of all, the Rite is fundamentally liturgical, reconfigured from its earlier privatized forms in light of the Second Vatican Council call to liturgical renewal. Properly liturgical actions embody and intend the Church as a whole, and the Introduction to the Rite stresses this corporate dimension:

> Like the other sacraments, these too have a communal aspect, which should be brought out as much as possible when they are celebrated. . . . The faithful should clearly understand the meaning of the anointing of the sick so that these sacraments may nourish, strengthen, and express faith. It is most important for the faithful in general, and above all for the sick, to be aided by participating in it, especially if it is to be carried out communally. ("Rite of Anointing" 191)

The communal context of the action emphasizes that, overagainst the social and cultural realities of isolation and marginalization that attend illness, the sick are not alone. The ecclesial community continues to understand them as included, and in fact, to be an integral part of the community: "If one member suffers in the body of Christ, which is the Church, all the members suffer with him" (I Corinthians 12:26) ("Rite of Anointing" 190). This bond is reinforced in the ritual actions of touch — the laying on of hands and the anointing.

In addition to communal support being integral to ameliorating the burdens of suffering, in part two Scarry, Kleinman, Sölle and others further suggested the importance of "working on" or "transforming the suffering into purposeful activity." The Rite of Anointing of the Sick as a liturgical act can be understood as 'work' in precisely this sense. On the one hand this dimension can be seen etymologically, as the Greek term 'leitourgia' is derived from the two terms 'leos' (people) and 'ergou' (work). 'Liturgy' is precisely 'work' done by all the people in the Body of Christ. Equally importantly, in the Rite, it is 'work' done by the sick person. The sick person is not understood as passive and, in fact, is enjoined special duties and activities which give meaning to their suffering.

> The sick in return offer a sign to the community: In the celebration of the sacrament they give witness to their promises at baptism to die and be buried with Christ. They tell the community that in their present suffering they are prepared to fill up in their flesh what is lacking in Christ's sufferings for the salvation of the world. . . . And the sick are *believed* to be and seen as productive members of the community, contributing to the welfare of all by associating themselves freely with Christ's passion and death. . . . In the sacrament, the faith of the sick person gives us, the healthy, a sign — an embodiment — of the words of Paul to Timothy: 'You can depend on this: If we have died with him, we shall also live with him. If we hold out to the end, we shall also reign with him' (2 Tim. 2:12). (*Study Text,* 20-21.)

The sick are challenged not to isolate themselves from the community, not to withdraw in embarrassment or fear. They are called to continue acting as a part of the body of Christ, called to forge ahead in the face of their difficulties, modelling discipleship and so serving as "ministers to the whole church in their illness" (*Study Text,* 41). In this way, "meaningless" suffering — of which suffering associated with illness is especially a case — is given a use, purpose, meaning.

Finally, we noted in part two that illness inflicts suffering partly by breaking apart a person's "code" — that set of discourses, relationships, and histories by which one understands and interprets one's world and identity. The Rite addresses this in two ways. On the one hand, most of those to whom this Rite reaches inhabit a 'code' derived partly from Christian formation and partly from secular culture. In instances of illness, especially in contemporary Western culture, part of the crisis of illness is created by presuppositions supplied by secular culture. For example, illness can pose a grave threat not only to psychological identity but also to physical security in a culture that values to the point of ideology the idea of individual autonomy. By preaching and living the gospel of a God who is essentially dependent and self-giving, the sacramental rite informs those who practice it with an alternative vision of the world.

On the other hand, as we noted above, Kleinman and others advocate that those involved with the sick encourage the creation of 'narratives.' While this is important, the Church, especially through the practice of the Rite of Anointing of the Sick, invites those who suffer to locate their narratives in an ongoing story, to learn anew the stories of others who have suffered and the interpretations they give their experiences, to truly hear — possibly for the first time — what it means to worship a God whose relationship to humanity was revealed on a cross.

Sacraments and Medical Ethics?

It might be objected that all this is well and good, but it doesn't really aid us in the difficult task of making day-to-day decisions about which technologies to use, and when, and for how long. But the power of the simple dynamic involved in these liturgical rites is easy to underestimate when compared to the power exercised by biomedical technologies and interventions. Like Jesus' practices of open eating and open healing, Christian understandings of suffering, illness, and healing embodied in the rites and liturgies of common worship challenge contemporary cultural understandings. The Church's 'discourses' challenge those of secular society. They refuse to locate a creature's value solely in its rationality, refusing to accept the designation 'enemy' for the realities of suffering and death, refusing to validate a posture that is closed to the world and fearful and ostracizing of those who are 'other.'

Those physicians and patients formed by ecclesial practices of Christian communities will find themselves navigating the world of medicine and biomedical ethics along a different path, for what they see as 'persons,' 'threats,' 'dilemmas,' and even 'the world' may differ significantly from their colleagues. For the physician whose story opened these reflections, the Sacrament of the Anointing of the Sick might have supplied him with alternative understandings of sufferings and a disposition toward openness and vulnerability that would have enabled him to reach out to the patient with a touch that healed. As importantly, it might have opened him to the touch of the patient that would have left him with the hopeful memory of shared community in addition to the empty sorrow of aloneness.

Notes

1. I would assert the case for three approaches to biomedical ethics: (1) pluralist — represented by Engelhardt, and the work of Beauchamp and Childress in *Principles;* (2) an ethics of medicine — represented by Leon Kass, as well as Pellegrino and Thomasma in *A Philosophical Basis;* and (3) Roman Catholic biomedical ethics — represented by Richard A. McCormick, S. J., Lisa Sowle Cahill, and Charles E. Curran.

2. It is important to emphasize here that I am distinguishing between medical ethics and medicine. Clearly medicine attends to bodies and the bodily in a significant manner, both conceptually and practically. My remarks are directed solely at medical ethics at this point.

3. On the other hand, I do not distinguish too clearly between the notions of 'suffering' and 'pain.' The distinction, which is commonly employed, relates suffering to one's self and identity, while pain is understood primarily in bodily terms. Although it is now rather standard to make this distinction, and the distinction can be helpful within certain arguments, I would resist making it too clear-cut, as I am concerned that it might buy into a mind/body dualism that will only exacerbate the problems I am trying to address.

Works Cited

Beauchamp, Tom and James Childress. *Principles of Biomedical Ethics,* 2nd edition. New York: Oxford University Press, 1983.

Bourdieu, Pierre. *An Outline of a Theory of Practice.* New York: Cambridge University Press, 1977.

Bynum, Caroline Walker. *Holy Feast and Holy Fast: The Religious Significance of Food to Medieval Women.* Berkeley: The University of California Press, 1987.

Cahill, Lisa Sowle. "Can Theology Have a Role in 'Public' Bioethical Discourse?" *Hastings Center Report 20.4* A Special Supplement, July/August: 1-14, 1990.

Campbell, Courtney. "Religion and Moral Meaning in Bioethics." *Hastings Center Report 20.4.* A Special Supplement, July/August: 4-10, 1990.

Cassell, Eric. "Recognizing Suffering," *Hastings Center Report 21* May-June 1991: 24-31.

Crossan, John Dominic. "The Life of a Mediterranean Jewish Peasant." *The Christian Century 108* December 18-25, 1991: 1194-1200.

Elshtain, Jean-Bethke. *Public Man, Private Woman.* Princeton, N.J.: Princeton University Press, 1981.

Engelhardt, H. Tristram, Jr. *The Foundation of Bioethics.* New York: Oxford, 1986.

Frank, Arthur. "For a Sociology of the Body: An Analytical Review," in *The Body,* Mike Featherstone, Mike Hepworth, and Bryan Turner, eds. London: Sage Publications, Ltd., 1991.

Finkelstein, Joanne L. "Biomedicine and Technocratic Power." *Hastings Center Report 20.4* July/August: 13-16, 1990.

Gunderman, Richard B. "Medicine and the Question of Suffering." *Second Opinion* 14: 15-25, 1990.

1979. "Rite of Anointing and Pastoral Care of the Sick." *Instruction on the Revised Roman Rites.* London: Collins.

Heller, Agnes. *Everyday Life.* Tr. G. L. Campbell. New York: Routledge and Kegan Paul, 1984.

Kleinman, Arthur, M.D. *The Illness Narratives: Suffering, Healing and the Human Condition.* New York: Basic Books, Inc., 1988.

McGill, Arthur C. *Suffering: A Test of Theological Method.* Philadelphia, Pa.: Westminster Press, 1982.

Musser, Donald M., 1987. "On the Edge of Uncertainty: Twenty Years with Cancer." *Second Opinion* 5: 121-27, 1982.

National Council of Catholic Bishops. *Study Text 2: Pastoral Care of the Sick and Dying.* Washington, D.C.: Office of Publishing Services, United States Catholic Conference, 1984.

Pellegrino, Edmund and David Thomasma. *A Philosophical Basis of Medical Practice: Toward a Philosophy and Ethic of the Healing Profession.* New York: Oxford University Press, 1981.

Scarry, Elaine. *The Body in Pain: The Making and Unmaking of the World.* New York: Oxford University Press, 1984.

Smith, David H. "Suffering, Medicine and Christian Theology," in *On Moral Medicine: Theological Perspectives in Medical Ethics.* Stephen E. Lammers and Allen Verhey, eds. Grand Rapids: William B. Eerdmans Publishing Company, 1987.

Sölle, Dorothee. *Suffering.* Trans. Everett R. Kalin. Philadelphia: Fortress Press, 1975.

Springstead, Eric. *Simone Weil and the Suffering of Love.* Cambridge, Mass: Cowley Publications, 1986.

Turner, Bryan. *The Body and Society: Explorations in Social Theory.* Oxford: Basil Blackwell, 1984.

Weil, Simone. *Waiting on God.*

Wendell, Susan. "Toward a Feminist Theory of Disability." *Hypatia* 4.2 (Summer): 104-24, 1989.

Wind, James P. "What Can Religion Offer Bioethics?" *Hastings Center Report* 20.4 A Special Supplement, July/August: 18-20, 1990.

50 Practicing Patience: How Christians Should Be Sick

Stanley Hauerwas and Charles Pinchas

The subject of the physician's art is called "a patient." We are, of course, the most impatient of patients. Yet the very fact that we are still called patients provides an opportunity for reflection on what difference it might make for how we, as Christians, come to know ourselves as patients who are truly patient. By exploring what it means for the Christian to embody the virtue of patience, I hope at least to suggest . . . what difference it makes to be a Christian [and] what that difference might mean for specific problems arising from the modern practice of medicine.

There are at least two unusual aspects to this way of proceeding that should be highlighted at the beginning. The first has to do with the retrieval of the virtues for modern ethics and, secondly, the centrality of one particular virtue for the practice of modern medicine. Emphasizing the importance of the virtues for how one thinks about ethics, and in particular medical ethics, has only recently begun.[1] There are many reasons why the virtues have been neglected in modern Western ethics, but perhaps the most significant factor in their recovery is their unavoidability if one wishes to provide any coherent account of the tradition in which one is standing.[2] What is particularly important for my purposes is to show how the absence of a thick account

From a forthcoming book by Stanley Hauerwas and Charles Pinchas. Slightly abridged and edited from the original. Used by permission of the University of Notre Dame Press.

of the virtues makes any consideration of the virtues or a virtue in medicine far too abstract. In other words, the great problem with becoming a patient is that too often the first time we are forced to exercise patience is when we become sick, and that is probably the worst time to begin to be patient. It's hard enough knowing how to be patient when you are well, let alone when you become ill. So, if we are to understand the inescapable importance of patience as a virtue, we cannot begin by considering the patient in the context of medicine — which may well mean that I will test your patience even as I must ask you to bear with me as I explore how Christians have understood patience as integral to the Christian life.

The second unusual aspect of my approach is the identification of patience as a significant virtue. If the virtues in general have been ignored in recent moral reflection, the virtue of patience has even been less prominent, which creates the problem of knowing how to begin to think about patience since we have such a dearth of examples.[3] Happily, however, patience has played a prominent role in Christian accounts of the moral life, and I propose to begin where those accounts begin — namely, with God.

For example, Cyprian begins his *On the Good of Patience* by observing that philosophers also claim to pursue the virtue of patience, but "their patience is as false as is their wisdom." For how can anyone be either wise or patient unless he knows the wisdom and patience of God? In contrast, Christians

> are philosophers not in words but in deeds; we exhibit our wisdom not by our dress, but by truth; we know virtues by their practice rather than through boasting of them; we do not speak great things but we live them. Therefore, as servants and worshipers of God, let us show by spiritual homage the patience that we learn from heavenly teachings. For that virtue we have in common with God. In Him patience has its beginning, and from Him as its source it takes its splendor and dignity. The origin and greatness of patience proceeds from God its Author. The quality that is dear to God ought to be loved by man.[4]

According to Cyprian, God's patience is clearly shown by the way he endures profane temples, replete with earthly images and idolatrous rites meant to insult God's majesty and honor. Yet no where is God's patience more clearly exemplified than in the life of Christ. Tertullian likewise observes that the patience of God made it possible for him to be conceived in a mother's womb, await a time for birth, delay growing up, and even when grown up to be less than eager to receive recognition, having himself baptized by his own servant. Throughout his ministry, he cared for the ungrateful and even refrained from pointing out the betrayer who was part of his own company.

> Moreover, while He is being betrayed, while He is being led up "as sheep for a victim" (for "so He no more opens His mouth than a lamb under the power of the shearer'), He to whom, had He willed it, legions of angels would at one word have presented themselves from the heavens, approved not the avenging sword of even one disciple.[5]

Tertullian and Cyprian alike make much of Matthew 5:43-48, since the refusal to return evil for evil is the very character of God, and, accordingly, through imitation, the way the sons and daughters of God are made perfect. As Tertullian says, "In this principal precept the universal discipline of patience is succinctly comprised, since evil-doing is not conceded even when it is deserved."[6] Such patience is not only in the mind, according to Tertullian, but in the body, for "just as Christ exhibited it in his body so do we. By the affliction of the flesh, a victim is able to appease the Lord by means of the sacrifice of humiliation. By making a libation to the Lord of sordid raiment, together with scantiness of food, content with simple diet and the pure drink of water in conjoining fasts *to all this*; this *bodily* practice adds a grace to our prayers for good, a strength of our prayers against evil; this opens the ears of Christ *our* God, dissipates severity, elicits clemency."[7] Thus, that which springs from a virtue of the mind is perfected in the flesh, and, finally, by the patience of the flesh, does battle under persecution.[8]

Suicide is, accordingly, out of the question. Job is the great exemplar in this regard, resisting his wife's suggestion that he should curse God and die. Augustine calls upon those who would kill themselves under persecution to look to "this man," meaning both Job and Christ. Like true martyrs who neither seek our death nor invite it prematurely, they ought to bear all patiently rather than "to dare death impatiently." According to Augustine, all that can be said to those who have killed themselves under persecution is "Woe unto them which have lost patience!"[9]

Augustine, following Tertullian and Cyprian, maintains that only that patience which is shaped by Christ is true patience. As he says, "properly speaking those are patient who would rather bear evils without inflicting them, than inflict them without bearing them. As for those who bear evils that they may inflict evil, their patience is neither marvelous nor praiseworthy, for it is not patience at all; we may marvel at their hardness of heart, but we must refuse to call them patient."[10] Such patience cannot come from "the strength of the human will,"[11] but rather must come as a gift of the Holy Spirit. The name of that gift is, of course, charity:

> without which in us there cannot be true patience, because in good men it is the love of God which endureth all things, in bad men the lust of the world. But this love is in us by the Holy Spirit which was given us. Whence, of Whom cometh in us love, of Him cometh patience. But the lust of the world, when it patiently bears the burdens of any manner of calamity, boasts of the strength of its own will, like as of the stupor of disease, not robustness of health. This boasting is insane: it is not the language of patience, but of dotage. A will like this in that degree seems more patient of bitter ills, in which it is more greedy of temporal good things, because more empty of eternal.[12]

Aquinas, like Tertullian, Cyprian, and Augustine, maintains that true patience is that which comes from God. Like them, he is aware that many people seem to display patience without the gift of the Spirit, but the problem with construing patience as a "natural virtue" is that it is not shaped by the appropriate sadness and joy constitutive of Christian patience. For Aquinas, a true understanding of our place as creatures must include an insuperable sadness and dejection about our condition. Christ's suffering on the cross exemplifies the sorrow that must be present in every Christian's life.[13] Christians must "be saddened by their own frailty, by the suffering present in the world, and by their inability to change either fundamentally."[14]

From Aquinas's perspective, the problem is how to prevent sadness, which we appropriately feel, from becoming depression, despair, or apathy. "Patience is to ensure that we do not abandon virtue's good through dejection of this kind."[15] Patience makes us capable of being rightly saddened without succumbing to the temptation to give up hope. A patience-formed sadness produces joy because each is the effect of charity. Such a joy

> makes us delight in the divine good as shared by us . . . can be impeded by something contrary to it, (so that) our joy can be mingled with sadness, in the sense that we grieve over what opposes this participation in the divine good in ourselves, or in our neighbors, whom we love as ourselves.[16]

Lee Yearly rightly suggests that Aquinas's account of patience combines two different, even apparently paradoxical, attitudes. Christians must judge our earthly life according to the standard evident in God's goodness, yet they must also adhere to the future good of possible union with God and the present good evident in God's manifestations in the world and in people's lives. Neither side of such an attitude can be lost. We must persist in such sadness, yet that very sadness must not be allowed to overwhelm the pursuit of the good, the accurate recognition of its forms, and a correct belief about the world's ultimate character. "This attitude is distinctive enough that it can arise, Aquinas thinks, only from the theological virtues. Charity's friendship with God is most crucial, but the attitude manifest in patience also rests on faith and displays the mean between presumption and despair that appears in hope."[17]

Christian patience, like all the virtues that come from charity, is a gift. There are, of course, semblances of the virtues, and patience in particular, is frequently confused with the virtues not formed by charity. For example, there is a kind of tempered optimism in which people

> either rest too confidently on their past experiences of overcoming dejection or manifest a phlegmatic or unreflective disposition at inappropriate times. Their optimism, then, reflects a

> flawed hope that is close to dullness or presumption. It displays an untempered attitude that expresses itself in the naive belief that all will turn out for the best.[18]

Christians have no such wan hope, sustained as they are by a patience that looks to our misfortunes, even the misfortune of our illness and death, as part of our service to one another as God's people.

Such patience, as I suggested above, is exactly that for which those committed to the creation of a world without God have no time. Our lives are constituted by what Albert Borgmann characterizes as a kind of addiction to hyperactivity. Believing, as we do, that we live in a world of infinite possibilities, we find ourselves constantly striving, restless for what we are not sure.[19] We call our restlessness freedom, but too often such freedom seems more like fate, especially when we get exactly what we strive after only to discover that it does not satisfy — thus the peculiar combination in modern life that seems to conjoin an attitude of metaphysical indeterminism with Stoic fatalism.

As Christians, of course, we should not be surprised to discover that our world is constituted by impatience. Tertullian ascribed to the devil the creation of impatience, since the devil could not endure the patience God exemplified in creation. According to Tertullian, the devil passed to Eve that same impatience when, through his speech, he "breathed on her a spirit infected with impatience: so certain is it that she would have never sinned at all, if she had honoured the divine edict by maintaining her patience to the end."[20] She passed her impatience on to Adam which in turn produced sons. The very impatience that "had immersed Adam and Eve in death, aught their son, too, to begin with murder." That murder was the fruit of impatience, as Cain impatiently refused his God given obligation to his brother.[21]

Yet surely medical care has been one of God's gifts which is our prerogative to use as a hedge against the impatience of the world. To care for one another when we cannot cure is surely one of the many ways we serve one another patiently. To be committed to alleviating the other's pain in a manner that makes all other considerations irrelevant makes no sense if we have not been made to be patient people. Yet it is surely the case that the powers of impatience have breathed on the practice of modern medicine and, accordingly, have led it to promise more than it can or should deliver. In the frustration of being unable to meet impatient expectations, we are threatened with a medicine that in the name of relieving suffering, kills.

Christians are, of course, as implicated in this strange reversal as our non-Christian neighbors. But these issues are far too serious to play, "Who is to blame?" The challenge is rather whether Christians have any contribution to make that would help us discover the proper limits of our care of one another through the office of medicine. It is not the Christian's task to suggest new and better theories about medical care, though some Christians engaged in that care may have some contributions to make. Rather, if Christians have anything to offer, it is to be patients who embody the virtue of Christian patience.

To be patient when we are sick requires first that we learn how to practice patience when we are not sick. God has given us ample resources for recovering the practice of patience. First and foremost, we have been given our bodies which will not let us do whatever we think we should be able to do.[22] We are our bodies and, as such, we are creatures destined to die. The trick is to learn to love the great good things my body makes possible without hating my body, if for no other reason than the death of my body is also my death. To practice the patience of the body is to put on the way to holiness as we learn that we are not our own creations.

Secondly, we have been given one another. To learn to live with the unavoidability of the other is to learn to be patient. Such patience comes not just from our inability to have the other do our will, but more profoundly is constituted by the love that the presence of the other can and does create in us. For our loves, like our bodies, contain our deaths. Such love, if it is not to be fearful of its loss, must be patient. Patience names the time required for the constitution of the story that we must be able to tell together, the story that in fact constitutes our love.[23]

Thirdly, we have been given time and space for the acquisition of habits that come from worthy activities such as growing food, building shelters, spinning cloth, writing poems, playing baseball. Such activities not only take time but create time by forcing us to take first one step and then another. Moreover, these activities must be passed on to future generations through tradition-constituted practices and stories. Patience constitutes our ability to tell such stories well so that we and our children may be rightly entertained.

These resources, these practices of patience — and there are others — are not simply "there," but are shaped by the narrative of God's patient care of the world. This is but another way of insisting, with Aquinas, that it is impossible to have patience without charity — that is, without friendship with God. Put simply, our very ability to take the time to enjoy God's world, when we are well as when we are sick, depends on our recognition that this is God's world.

Yet when we are sick, talk of joy seems too much a gesture of false courage. Still, Aquinas maintained that the sadness occasioned by our own and other's illness is not to be denied. The acknowledgment of such sadness is part of the Christian gift for sustaining the ill and those who care for the ill. To be a patient who has been formed by the virtue of patience, however, is to be a patient who does not believe that life is an end in itself. Indeed, a patient formed by patience knows that the enemy is neither illness nor the death that it intimates, but the enemy is all that would tempt us to be impatient or fatalistic in the face of our "bad luck."

If we as Christians could be such patient patients — and there is every reason to think that we can — I suspect that we might well have a witness to make to our non-Christian neighbor. We might even have something to say, not only about the kind of people who should be called to be physicians and nurses, but the kind of training they should receive as well. To do that we would have to take the risk of being different, but then that is no great risk for a people, who because they have learned to be patient, have all the time in the world for such worthy work.[24]

Notes

1. A welcome exception is *Virtue and Medicine: Explorations in the Character of Medicine,* edited by Earl E. Shelp (Dordrecht: D. Reidel Publishing Company, 1985). Karen Lebacqz's essay, "The Virtuous Patient" (pp. 275-88), is particularly relevant for what I am trying to do in this essay. Lebacqz argues that three virtues — fortitude, prudence, and hope — are central to the task of being a patient. My only difficulty with her account is knowing from whence such virtues come. William May has also developed the importance of the virtues in his "The Virtues in a Professional Setting" in *Medicine and Moral Reasoning,* edited by K. W. M. Tulford, Grant Gillet, and Janet Martin Soskice (Cambridge: Cambridge University Press, 1994), pp. 75-90. For an overview of recent work in medical ethics on the importance of virtue see my article "Virtue and Character" in the new edition of the *Encyclopedia of Bioethics.*

2. Alasdair MacIntyre's *After Virtue* (Notre Dame: University of Notre Dame, 1984) is, of course, the best account not only of why the virtues have been ignored in modernity but of why the virtues must be unavoidably located within traditional-shaped practices if they are to make any sense.

3. I was first made aware of the significance of patience as a virtue by struggling with John Howard Yoder's account of non-violence as embodied in Christ's cross. Yoder observes that apparent complicity with evil, which the nonresistant stance allegedly involves, has always been a stumbling block to nonpacifists. In response, Yoder points out

> that this attitude, leaving evil to be evil, leaving the sinner free to separate himself from God and sin against man, is part of the nature of *agape* itself, as revealed already in creation. If the cutting phrase of Peguy, "*complice, c'est pire que coupable,*" were true, then God Himself must needs be the guilty one for making man free and again for letting His innocent Son be killed. The modern tendency to equate involvement with guilt should have to apply *par excellence,* if it were valid at all, to the implication of the all-powerful God in the sin of His creatures. God's love for men begins right at the point where He permits sin against Himself and against man, without crushing the rebel under his own rebellion. The word for this is divine *patience* not complicity." (*The Original Revolution* [Scottdale, Penn.: Herald Press, 1971], pp. 64-65).

Drawing on Yoder, I argued in *The Peaceable Kingdom: A Primer in Christian Ethics* (Notre Dame: University of Notre Dame Press, 1983) that hope and patience are central Christian virtues (pp. 102-6).

4. Cyprian, *De Bono Patientia: A Translation with an Introduction and Commentary,* by Sister M. George Edward Conway, S.S.J. (Washington, D.C.: The Catholic University Press of America, 1957), p. 65. Cyprian's account of patience closely parallels Tertullian's earlier treatise, "On Patience." The latter can be found in Volume III of *The Ante-Nicene Fathers* (Grand Rapids: Eerdmans, 1989), pp. 707-17. Augustine drew on both Tertullian and Cyprian for his "On Patience," which can be found in *A Library of Fathers of the Holy Catholic Church, Anterior to the Division of the East and West,* translated by Members of the English Church (Oxford: John Henry Parker Press, 1937), pp. 542-62. Sister Conway provides a very helpful comparison of these three treatments of patience.

5. Tertullian, p. 708.

6. Ibid., p. 711. Cyprian's reflections on Matthew are found on pages 68-69.

7. Tertullian, p. 715.

8. Cyprian observes that the Christian should not hasten to revenge the pain of persecution, since vengeance is the Lord's. "Therefore, even the martyrs as they cry out and as they hasten to their punishment in the intensity of their suffering are still ordered to wait and to show patience until the appointed time is fulfilled and the number of martyrs is complete" (p. 89).

9. Augustine, pp. 550-51.

10. Augustine, p. 554. Aquinas uses this quote to counter the claim that patience is not a virtue, since it can sometimes be found in wicked men. See *Summa Theologica,* translated by Fathers of the English Dominican Province (Chicago: Encyclopedia Britannica, 1952), II-II, 136, 1, 2.

11. Augustine, p. 551.

12. Augustine, pp. 557-58. Augustine, like all Christian theologians, makes constant appeals to scripture in support of this argument — I Corinthians 13:4 being, of course, the central text. Charity must form patience, but it is equally the case that charity needs patience. In a remarkable passage Cyprian says,

> Charity is the bond of brotherhood, the foundation of peace, the steadfastness and firmness of unity: it is greater than both hope and faith; it excels both good works and suffering for the faith; and, as an eternal virtue, it will abide with us forever in the kingdom of heaven. Take patience away from it, and thus forsake, it will not last; take away the substance of enduring and tolerating, and it attempts to last with no roots or strength. Accordingly, the apostle when he was speaking about charity joined forbearance and patience to it, saying: Charity is magnanimous, charity is kind, charity does not envy, is not puffed up, is not provoked, thinks no evil, loves all things, believes all things, hopes all things, endures all things. By this he showed that charity can persevere steadfastly because it has learned how to endure all things. And in another place he says: bearing with one another in love, taking every care to preserve the unity of the Spirit in the union of peace. He proved that neither unity nor peace can be preserved unless brothers cherish one another with mutual forbearance and preserve the bond of unity with patience as intermediary. (p. 81)

13. I am indebted to Lee Yearley's wonderful account of Aquinas's view of patience in his *Mencius and Aquinas: Theories of Virtue and Conceptions of Courage* (Albany: State University of New York Press, 1990), pp. 136-43. Crucial for understanding Aquinas's views is the significance of his account of the passions, and in particular, sadness as a passion. See *Summa Theologia,* I-II, 35-39. Yearley, quite rightly, observes that Aquinas thinks his understanding of the place of sadness in the Christian life is the crucial difference between Stoicism and Christianity. The Christian cannot seek to be free of sadness for without the appropriate sadness we lack the ability to be joyful.

The Stoics' understanding of the passions was much more complex than they are usually given credit for. See, for example, Martha Nussbaum's treatment of Stoicism in her *The Therapy of Desire: Theory and Practice in Hellenistic Ethics* (Princeton: Princeton University Press, 1994), pp. 356-438. Nussbaum, quoting Seneca, observes,

> "Where you take greatest joy you will also have the greatest fear." Just as there is unity among the virtues, all being forms of correct apprehension of the self-sufficient good, just as there is a unity to the passions — and also to their underlying dispositional states. But this means, too, that there is a unity to the cure of the passions. "You will cease to fear, if you cease to hope . . . Both belong to a soul that is hanging in suspense, to a soul that is made anxious by concern with the future." The world's vulnerable gifts, cherished, give rise to the passionate life; despised, to a life of calm. "What fortune does not give, she cannot take away." (pp. 388-89)

Against such a background the importance of Aquinas's insistence that Christians are the most passionate of people can be understood not only as a claim about what we must be as Christians, but also as a claim about the way the world is. If God, at least the God that Christians worship, does not exist, then our joy and our sadness, schooled by our hope, is a lie.

14. Yearley, p. 137. Josef Pieper, however, rightly notes that Thomas's account of patience does not entail passivity. Patience is a necessary component of fortitude, which as Pieper observes seems incongruous for many people because for them patience has come

> to mean an indiscriminate, self-immolating, crabbed, joyless, and spineless submission to whatever evil is met with or worse, deliberately sought out. Patience, however, is something quite other than indiscriminate acceptance of any and every evil: "The patient man is not the one who does not flee from evil, but the one who does not allow himself to be made inordinately sorrowful thereof." To be patient means to preserve cheerfulness and serenity of mind in spite of injuries that result from the realization of the good. Patience does not imply the exclusion of energetic, forceful activity, but simply explicitly and solely the exclusion of sadness and confusion of heart. Patience keeps man from the danger that his spirit may be broken by grief and lose its greatness. Patience, therefore, is not the tear-veiled mirror of a "broken" life (as one might easily assume in the face of what is frequently presented and praised under this name), but the radiant embodiment of ultimate integrity. In the words of Hildegard of Bingen, patience is 'the pillar which nothing can soften.' And Thomas, following Holy Scripture (Luke 21:19), summarizes with superb precision: 'Through patience man possesses his soul.' (*The Four Cardinal Virtues* [Notre Dame: University of Notre Dame Press, 1966], p. 129).

15. Aquinas, *Summa Theologica,* II-II, 136, 4, 2. Yearley highlights this wonderful passage.

16. Aquinas, *Summa Theologica,* II-II, 28, 2. I am using Yearley's translation of this passage. Crucial for sustaining such joy in the midst of sadness is the kind of materialism required in the Christian belief in the Incarnation and Resurrection. Our belief in the bodily Resurrection — that is, that the Resurrection is not so much a throwing off of our human flesh but rather an exchanging of our present body for a new body so that we may dwell in a new heaven and a new earth — means that the Christian's hope that "all manner of things shall be well" can never by a facile optimism that evades the reality of pain. As Dr. Jim Fodor observed to me

> simply to encourage people to see things differently, while leaving things as they are, is to reinforce their slavery, the reinforcement of which is all the more insidious precisely because it is disguised as a proclamation of the truth to set us free. Christianity, in other words, is not merely a way of "regarding," "looking at," or "interpreting" reality. Christianity is not a "theory" but a way of life, a way of discipleship. And discipleship is concrete, specific; it occurs — or fails to occur — in particular practices and patterns of engagements, relationships, suffering and worship. Thus the importance of the practice of "bodily patience" for guarding against the tendency, all too common among many modern Christians, to affirm "the primacy of the spiritual" to the neglect of the material conditions of redemption. The practical, material display of Christian virtue necessary for patience is finding a gift from God and not something we cultivate willfully or from our own strength, apart from God's help. In fact, patience is often something we reluctantly accept, if at all, and then only after a long and painful struggle to acknowledge our creaturely limits and sense in which most things in our life remain out of control.

17. Yearley, p. 139.

18. Yearley, p. 139. Yearley notes that Aquinas did not examine the semblances of practice in the systematic manner in which he explored the semblances of courage. Yet given patience's close relation to endurance, the crucial aspect of courage, Yearley rightly uses the semblances of courage to suggest analogies for how Aquinas might have understood the semblances of patience.

Though the comparison of the semblances of patience (and courage and other virtues) with true patience are usually negative, it is a mistake to assume that positive comparisons are not also a possibility. Since we are God's good creatures we should expect to find in those who are not Christians indications of God's patience. The problem, then, is not that non-Christians fail to exhibit any of the virtues, but that they do and because they do they are just as likely to display them in ways that may be either destructive and/or constructive. The Christian advantage is to be part of God's people, which makes us vulnerable to the judgments of others who have acquired the wisdom necessary to understand the interrelation of the virtues.

19. Albert Borgmann, *Crossing the Postmodern Divide* (Chicago: University of Chicago Press, 1992), pp. 97-102.

20. Tertullian, p. 710. Gerald J. Schiffhorst in a similar fashion argues that in *Paradise Lost* Milton

> relies on patience to express the Christian's proper response to the divine will while ironically revealing the anti-heroism of Satan, whose blind impatience reverses what Milton called the "better fortitude" of patience. Satan's struggle to fight God is undercut by the "pleasing sorcery" of a false heroism whereas Adam learns to arm himself with patience "to overcome by suffering" what God will unfold. The centrality of "patience as the truest fortitude" (*Samson Agonistes,* 654) in revealing this fundamental contrast demonstrates the importance of the virtue in the poem. ("Satan's False Heroism in *Paradise Lost* as a Perversion of Patience," *Christianity and Literature* 38, 2 [Winter, 1984]: 13)

Schiffhorst provides a very helpful contrast of Christian patience with Stoic indifference by noting the difference between the Christian understanding of providence and the Stoic idea of fortune. He notes that

> the basic Christian-pagan distinction helps us recall that Christ's victory over death was a victory over Fortune, and so the virtuous Christian can have everlasting life by imitating Christ's perfect patience. As Miles Coverdale says in his important Elizabethan treatise on patience, "the impatient man complains against God and ascribes prosperity to his own wisdom, blaming blind Fortune for adversity. Without ascribing dispassionate Stoic virtues to Satan, we can nevertheless say that his false heroism is rooted in a stubborn pride and that he exhibits all the passions of the impatient man: wrath, despair, grief, and envy." (pp. 14-15)

For a wonderful collection of essays on patience, see Gerald J. Schiffhorst, ed., *The Triumph of Patience: Medieval and Renaissance Studies* (Orlando: University Presses of Florida, 1978). Particularly interesting is Elizabeth Kirk's entitled, " 'Who Suffreth More Than God?': Narrative Redefinition of Patience in *Patience* and *Piers Plowman,*" pp. 88-105. She not only provides a wonderful commentary on the medieval poet of the *Pearl,* but ends with a delightful quote from Chaucer's Parson that she thinks contains everything written large in *Patience* and *Piers Plowman.*

> Patience, that is another remedie agayns Ire, is a vewru that suffreth swetely every mannes goodness, and is nat wroth for noon harm that is doon to hyn. . . . This vertu maketh a man lyk to God, and maketh hym Goddes owene deere child, as seith Crist. This vertu disconfiteth thyn enemy. And therfore seith the wise man, If thow wolt vengukysse thyn enemy, lerne to suffre. . . . And understond wel that obedience is parfit, whan that a man dooth gladly and hastily, with good herte entirely, al that he should do. (p. 102)

21. Tertullian, p. 710. As a pacifist I find Tertullian's suggestion that our violence lies in our impatience as intriguing as it is persuasive.

22. I am acutely aware, as anyone must be after the work of Foucault, that appeals to the "body" are anything if they are not problematic. Recent historical work that helps us better understand why Paul could think that nothing was more "spiritual" than the body or the body as the peculiarly "spiritual" I think has great potential for helping us rethink the relation of Christian practices and the practice of medicine. I have in mind such works as Peter Brown's *The Body and Society: Men, Women and Sexual Renunciation in Early Christianity* (Boston: Faber, 1988) and my colleague Dale Martin's wonderful book, *The Corinthian Body* (New Haven: Yale University Press, forthcoming). Particularly important is a better understanding of the "therapy of desire" characteristic of Christian practice in contrast to the assumptions of Galen and the other hellenistic philosophical schools. For example, we need a Christian account parallel to Nussbaum's *The Therapy of Desire.* Brown's book is obviously a good beginning to understand better what Augustine and Aquinas understood far better than we about the nature of the passions. I am indebted to Mr. Thomas Harvey, a graduate student at Duke, for a paper in which he explored how Augustine provided an alternative to Galen's understanding of the body.

23. I am aware that the emphasis on patience as the virtue essential to the doctor-patient relationship may appear particularly perverse, since it seems to make the patient even more powerless. There is rightly an asymmetry between the doctor and patient inasmuch as the physician has authority that the patient does not or

should not have. Once, however, it is understood that medicine names an activity in which doctor and patient are jointly involved, I think it can also be understood how patience works in such a relationship not so much as to increase the possibilities of abuse of power but to decrease the possibility of such misuse. Crucial in this respect, is how Christian patience requires the Church for its display. Without the kind of friendship, dependency, trust, and mutual nurturing imbedded in the worship of God, patience always risks the possibility of becoming malformed. . . .

24. I am indebted to Dr. Jim Fodor and Mr. Scott Saye for their critique of this essay, as well as for their suggestions for how it might be improved.

Chapter Nine:

RESPECT FOR PERSONS AND THEIR AGENCY

There is in medical ethics a lot of talk about "persons." And there are in medical ethics important disagreements about what it means to be a person — and about whether the fact that human persons have (or are) bodies is relevant to the meaning of their being "persons." Reflecting those disagreements there have been other discussions about who counts as a person and about the meaning of the moral requirement of "respect for persons."

The talk about "persons" achieved currency as a language of protest. It may be useful to recall some of the protests at the beginning of modern bioethics. There was a protest against what was frequently called the "depersonalization" of modern medicine. Hospital chaplains and others complained that technological medicine threatened to reduce the patient to a part of nature. To register that protest and to insist that healing not be regarded simply a matter of curing the body by scientific medicine, hospital chaplains and others called attention to "the whole person."[1]

There was a protest against experiments which made human beings into "guinea pigs." The revelations at Nuremberg of the Nazi experiments — and subsequent revelations of human experimentation in this country, too — provoked outrage and complaint. The resulting protest frequently accused the experimenters of violating the respect due persons, and frequently invoked Kant's second formulation of the categorical imperative, that persons must always be treated as ends and never merely as means.

There was a suspicion of the physicians who performed putatively therapeutic procedures upon patients "for their own good" but without their consent. The suspicion grew into a protest against the power of some people, even benevolent and well-meaning people, over other people. As earlier protests against the unchecked power of kings and priests had insisted on respect for persons, so the protest against the benevolent but despotic physician called for attention to the rights of patients as persons.

Another protest was prompted by the allocation of what was a scarce medical resource. In 1962 the Admissions and Policies Committee of the Seattle Artificial Kidney Center at Swedish Hospital made decisions about who would have access to the recently developed, but clearly effective, dialysis machine — made decisions, that is, about who would live and who would die — on the basis of *ad hoc* comparisons of the social worth of those who needed it. Shana Alexander, correspondent for *Life* magazine, gave it the name "the Seattle God Committee,"[2] and many protested against reducing the worth of persons to their value on some utilitarian calculus.

In all of these cases, protests and cries for reform invoked the language of "person." It is little wonder, perhaps, that the ground-breaking works of Joseph Fletcher and Paul Ramsey, *Morals and Medicine* and *The Patient as Person,* each emphasized the importance of the notion of "person" to moral reflection about medicine. Beneath this superficial agreement, however, there were profound disagreements about who counted as a person, about the relation of "person" and body, and about what moral requirements were included in the principle of respect for persons.

This chapter invites you to enter the fray. Who counts as a person? What does it mean to be a person? And what does it mean to be counted and respected as a person? These questions are of obvious importance to debates about abortion and the removal of life support for a human being in persistent vegetative state, but one's vision of person has much broader implications, as many of the essays in this chapter make clear.

The chapter begins with the question about "who counts as a person?" and with Joseph Fletcher's claim that neo-cortical function is "the key" to personhood (selection 51). Although he sometimes used "human" and "person" interchangeably, it is clear that he meant to distinguish between them; a human being, a member of the species, counts as a person if and only if he or she has the capacity for thought.

Oliver O'Donovan approaches the question quite differently (selection 52). He takes his cue from the parable about the Good Samaritan, and his essay may be regarded as an extended commentary on the question of the lawyer, "Who is my neighbour?", and on Jesus' reply. He rejects the effort to identify "criteria of personhood," arguing that we discover someone as a person only in personal engagement. Parents can discover the "personhood" of their fetus in the commitment to care for their child; researchers are unlikely to discover the personhood of the fetus in their decision to treat it as a "thing" from which they can learn. Although he rejects the effort to identify "criteria of personhood," he does propose a criterion for judging when personal engagement with another being is *appropriate*, namely, the "appearance" of a human being. One "may protest," he says, that this "simply begs the whole question," but he defends his argument against the charge of circularity. Do you agree?

Stanley Hauerwas (selection 53) argues that the notion of "person" no longer serves to protect the powerless and to protest injustices done to them; it serves now, he claims, as "a permissive notion," permitting doctors, researchers, and the rest of us to do as we wish with those who do not count as persons. He questions the question, arguing that it imperils not only fetuses, dying patients, and "defective" infants, but also the very practices and institutions which have been charged to care for them.

The question "Who counts as a person?" forces any who would answer it back to some vision of what it means to be a person. The second question this chapter asks you to consider, therefore, is "What does it mean to be a person?" The essays by Gilbert Meilaender and Lisa Sowle Cahill in this chapter (selections 54 and 55) insist that any answer to that question attend to the "embodiment" of persons. Both reject "dualism" and its effort to think of the "person" and the body as separate things, and both reject the reduction of "person" to "merely" body.

Meilaender describes the great contenders about the meaning of "person" at the beginning of bioethics — and still — as the dualism of Fletcher, which located the morally valuable in the capacities for thought and choice and which reduced the body to manipulable nature, and a vision, Paul Ramsey's vision, of the coinherence of body and soul.

Cahill compares an "old" dualism of Western culture (and of the Church) and the "new" dualism of modern science. She finds in both the requirement of mastering the body, although the means are different. She argues for a view of the self as embodied and for affirmation of our embodiment; in that context she also argues that an integrated and positive view of body and mind does not exclude "an ordering of the body in relation to a social vision." She retrieves early Christian sources to show that the body — and its discipline — can serve "as a countersign to hierarchy and domination," as a sign of a society of mutuality, equality, and compassion.

These two essays are alike in their emphasis on "embodiment" and in their suspicion of a medical ethics founded on a view of the person as autonomous choice-maker, but it is worth noting the different emphases. Meilaender, like Paul Ramsey, underscores the inviolability of the individual, of each human person, each "someone who, as a living body, has a history." Cahill, on the other hand, emphasizes that human beings are, by their very embodiment, social creatures.

Robert Jenson (in selection 56) acknowledges that physicians encounter "two sides" of the patient. This duality gives rise to the tensions between a scientific or technological attitude toward patients and an attitude toward patients appropriate to respect for them as fellow persons. He rejects any dualism which would "compartmentalize" these two sides and any reductionism which would ignore one side in order to deal with the other. As long as patients are embodied selves, physicians will have to struggle with this two-sidedness of the embodied selves who are their patients.

The dispute about the meaning of personhood is displayed sometimes in controversy about the status of the fetus, or in arguments about the definition of death, or in different assessments of technological interventions into procreation, or in different proposals for the care for the sick and dying, and again and again in discussions within medical ethics. Even when not on display, however, visions of personhood shape and form how a situation is described and how principles are applied in medical ethics. Such is surely the case with the principle of "respect for persons." And the third question this chapter asks you to consider is "What does it mean to be counted and respected as a person?" The remaining essays in this chapter suggest answers to that question.

It is axiomatic in much of the literature on medical ethics that respect for persons entails respect for their autonomy. Jim Gustafson acknowledges that respect for persons requires respect for their freedom, but he reminds us that the scope of our freedom is not as vast as is sometimes claimed, that our freedom is both limited and made possible by the determinate, embodied, and communal features of a human life. Respect for persons entails, Gustafson claims, also that we "respect their bodily natures" and that we respect them not only as individuals but as members of their communities, some of which are not of their own choosing.

In the final selection within this chapter David Thomasma describes and defends "respect for persons" as central to Judeo-Christian morality, to the Hippocratic tradition of medicine, and to Western political and philosophical thought. He describes the meaning, the implications, of "respect for persons" by invoking the norms identified by the *Belmont Report* of the National Commission for the Protection of Human Subjects: autonomy, beneficence, non-maleficence, and justice. "Respect for persons" may not have precisely the same foundations or identical implications in the traditions of religion, medicine, and philosophy, but both the foundations and the implications are close enough to enable a wide conversation and a consensus about medical ethics. Thomasma's effort to articulate and defend a moral consensus stands in sharp contrast to the suspicion of attempts to find a consensus voiced by Hauerwas earlier in this chapter.

The questions posed, then, include not only "Who counts as a person?," "What does it mean to be a person?," and "What does it mean to be respected as a person?," but also whether, in answering such questions, we should search for consensus or for the difference Christian convictions can make or, somehow, for both. Religious commitments, Thomasma argues, reinforce these norms, but it is also clear that religious commitments can shape those norms, nudging justice, for example, toward a special concern for the poor and disenfranchised who are often, in our society, not respected as persons.

Notes

1. For example, Richard C. Cabot and Russell L. Dicks, *The Art of Ministering to the Sick* (New York: Macmillan, 1936). Another source for the emphasis on "the whole person" was Paul Tournier, *A Doctor's Casebook in the Light of the Bible* (trans. Edwin Hudson; London: SCM, 1954).

2. Shana Alexander, "They Decide Who Lives, Who Dies," *Life* 53 (November 9, 1962): 102-4.

Suggestions for Further Reading

Callahan, Daniel. "Can the Moral Commons Survive Autonomy?" *Hastings Center Report* 26, no. 6 (November-December 1984): 41-42; with responses by Robert Veatch, "Which Grounds for Overriding Autonomy are Legitimate?," pp. 42-43; Willard Gaylin, "Worshiping Autonomy," pp. 43-45; and Bonnie Steinbock, "Liberty, Responsibility and the Common Good," pp. 44-47.

Campbell, Courtney. "On James F. Childress: Answering That of God in Every Person," in Allen Verhey and Stephen E. Lammers (eds.), *Theological Voices in Medical Ethics* (Grand Rapids: William B. Eerdmans Publishing Company, 1993), pp. 127-56.

Childress, James F. *Who Should Decide? Paternalism in Health Care* (New York: Oxford University Press, 1982).

Dyck, Arthur J. *On Human Care* (Nashville: Abingdon, 1977).

Faden, Ruth R., Tom L. Beauchamp, and Nancy P. King. *A History and Theory of Informed Consent* (New York: Oxford University Press, 1986).

Lammers, Stephen E. "Autonomy and Informed Consent," in David H. Smith (ed.), *Respect and Care in Medical Ethics* (Lanham, Maryland: University Press of America, 1984).

Lebacqz, Karen. *Professional Ethics: Power and Paradox* (Nashville: Abingdon, 1985).

Reich, Warren. "Toward a Theory of Autonomy and Informed Consent," in *The Annual of the Society of Christian Ethics,* 1982, edited by Larry Rasmussen, pp. 191-215.

Thomasma, David C. "Freedom, Dependency, and the Care of the Very Old," *Journal of the American Geriatrics Society* 32, no. 12 (December 1984): 906-14.

Veatch, Robert M. *A Theory of Medical Ethics* (New York: Basic Books, 1983).

Veatch, Robert M. "Abandoning Informed Consent," *Hastings Center Report* 25, no. 2 (March/April, 1995): 5-12.

Verhey, Allen "Luther's 'Freedom of a Christian' and Patient Autonomy," in John F. Kilner, Nigel M. de S. Cameron, and David Schiedermayer (eds.), *Bioethics and the Future of Medicine: A Christian Appraisal* (Grand Rapids: William B. Eerdmans Publishing Company, 1995), pp. 81-92.

51 Four Indicators of Humanhood — The Enquiry Matures

Joseph F. Fletcher

Jean Rostand describes a meeting of French Catholic intellectuals; they spoke of a prosecution for infanticide following the thalidomide disaster of the Sixties.[1] Morvan Lebesque: "After centuries of morality, we still cannot answer questions like those raised by the trial in Liège. Should malformed babies be killed? Where does man begin?" Father Jolif: "No one knows what man is any longer."

That is the situation, exactly. Whether or not we ever knew in the past what man is, in the sense of having a consensus about it, we do not know now. To realize this, make only a quick scan of the wild confusion and variety on the subject gathered together by Eric Fromm and Ramon Xirau in their historical compendium.[2]

First There Was One

Yet it is this question, how we are to define the *humanum,* which lies at the base of all serious talk about the quality of life. We cannot appraise quality or enumerate human values if we cannot first say what a human being is. The *Hastings Center Report* (November 1972) published a shortened version of an essay of mine in which I made a stab at this problem, under the title "Indicators of Humanhood: A Tentative Profile on Man."[3]

From the *Hastings Center Report* 4 (December 1975): 4-7.

In substance I contended that the acute question is what is a *person;* that rights (such as survival) attach only to persons; that out of some twenty criteria one (neocortical function) is the cardinal or hominizing trait upon which all the other human traits hinge; and then I invited those concerned to add or subtract, agree or disagree as they may. This was intended to keep the investigation going forward, and it worked; the issue has been vigorously discussed pro and con.

What crystals have precipitated? Without trying to explore them in any detail, as each of them deserves to be, four different traits have been nominated to date as the singular *esse* of humanness; neocortical function, self-consciousness, relational ability, and happiness — the last being included more in a light than a heavy vein. Various additional criteria of the optimal or *bene esse* kind are mentioned in a growing correspondence, but no argument *against* any one of them has been offered: e.g., one correspondent (Robert Morison) wants concern for the meek and dependent stipulated under my eighth trait, "concern for others."

But on the question which one of the optimal traits and capabilities is the *sine qua non,* the essential one without which no combination of the others can add up to humanhood, there are now four contenders in the running. It should be noted at the outset that of the four discrete cardinal criteria thus far entered, none of them is mutually exclusive of any of the others, any more than the optimal indicators are (sense of time, curiosity, ideomorphous identity, obligation, reason-feeling balance, self-control, changeability, etc.). The decisive question therefore appears to be about precondition. Which one of these traits, if any, is required for the presence of the others? To answer this is to find *the* criterion among the criteria.

Now There Are Four

I. Michael Tooley of Stanford contends that the real precondition to "having a serious right to life" or to being the kind of moral entity we call a person, as in the Sixteenth Amendment sense, is subjectivity or self-awareness (no. 2 in my original list). He called it "the self-consciousness requirement."[4] As he points out, fetuses and infants lack that requirement. Machines have no consciousness at all, and therefore may be sacrificed in a competing values situation. Animals are probably not self-conscious, although a few pet lovers claim they are. Once a growing baby's neurological "switchboard" gets hooked up, allowing consciousness of self to emerge, he or she is a person. (Mind is, as Dubos points out, a verb — not a noun; it is not something given but acquired, a process rather than an event.[5] It is what the mind does, not what it is.) So runs Tooley's thesis.

II. Richard McCormick of the Kennedy Center for Bioethics at Georgetown University, on another tack, says "the meaning, substance, and consummation of life is found in human relationships," so that when we try to make quality of life judgments ("and we must"), as in cases of diseased or defective newborns, "life is a value to be preserved only insofar as it contains some potentiality for human relationships."[6] On this basis anencephalics certainly, and idiots probably, lack personal status, with a consequent lack of claim rights. If you lack what he calls "the relational potential" (what I call "the capability to relate to others," no. 7) you cannot be human. "If that potential is simply nonexistent or would be utterly submerged and undeveloped in the mere struggle to survive, that life has achieved its potential" and we need not save it from death's approach.

III. When a pediatrician at the Texas Medical Center (Houston), whose work takes her daily into a service for retarded children, heard me at a grand rounds expound my suggestion that minimal intelligence or cerebral function is the essential factor in being human, she rejected it: "I know a little four-year-old-boy, certainly 20 minus or an idiot on any measurement scale and untrainable, but just the same he is a human being and nobody is going to tell me different. He is happy and that makes him human, as human as you or I." By "human" she meant morally, not only biologically. She described the child's affectionate response to caresses and his constant euphoria. I thought of my neighbor's kitten and recalled the euphoria symptom as happiness without any reason for it, and I remembered Huxley's *Brave New World* where everybody was happy on drugs — except the rebellious intellectuals. I asked her if she really meant to say that euphoria qualifies us for humanhood. I took her silence to be an affirmative answer.

The Original Indicators of Humanhood: A Tentative Profile of Man

Positive Human Criteria

1. Minimal intelligence
2. Self-awareness
3. Self-control
4. A sense of time
5. A sense of futurity
6. A sense of the past
7. The capability to relate to others
8. Concern for others
9. Communication
10. Control of existence
11. Curiosity
12. Change and changeability
13. Balance of rationality and feeling
14. Idiosyncrasy
15. Neo-cortical function

Negative Human Criteria

1. Man is not non- or anti-artificial
2. Man is not essentially parental
3. Man is not essentially sexual
4. Man is not a bundle of rights
5. Man is not a worshiper

IV. As far as I can yet see, I will stand by my own thesis or hypothesis that neocortical function is the key to humanness, the essential trait, the human *sine qua non.* The point is that without the synthesizing function of the cerebral cortex (without thought or mind), whether before it is present or with its end, the person is nonexistent no matter how much the individual's brain stem and mid-brain may continue to provide feelings and regulate autonomic physical functions. To be truly homo sapiens we must be sapient, however minimally. Only this trait or capability is necessary to *all* of the other traits which go into the fullness of humanness. Therefore this indicator, neocortical function, is the first-order requirement and the key to the definition of a human being. As Robert Williams of the University Medical Center (Seattle) puts it, "Without mentation the body is of no significant use."[7]

Discussion Goes On

This search for a *shared* view of humanness, a consensus, may not find a happy ending. James Gustafson's (University of Chicago Divinity School) skepticism about reaching agreement has now been graduated into skepticism also about applying whatever criterion we might agree to.[8] He thinks now that "intuitive elements, grounded on beliefs and profound feelings," would color our judgments seriously. More sharply, Rostand warns us (p. 66) that looking for a single trait is "a temptation for the fanatics — and there are always fanatics everywhere — to think that his adversary is less human than himself because he lacks some mental or spiritual quality." In scientific and medical circles I find that a *biological* definition is thought to be feasible, but not a list of moral or psychological traits — to say nothing of picking out only one cardinal trait subsumed in all the rest.

One slant on the problem is to deny the problem itself, not as insoluble but as specious (no pun intended). For example, William May of Catholic University, trying to justify the prohibition of abortion, objects to "the thought of Fletcher, Tooley, and those who would agree with them" that membership in a *species* is of no moral significance.[9] He argues that we are human by virtue of what we are (our species), not what we achieve or do. A member of the biological species is, as such, a human being. Thus, we would be human if we have opposable thumbs, are capable of face-to-face coitus and have a brain weighing 1400 grams, whether a particular brain functions cerebrally or not. (I put in the thumbs and coitus to exclude elephants, whales and dolphins, the only other species having brains as big or bigger than man's.) In this reasoning the term "human" slides back and forth between meaning sometimes the biological, sometimes the moral or personal, thus combining the fallacy of ambiguity with the fallacy of ostensive definition. ("He has opposable thumbs, therefore he is a person.")

Tristram Englehardt of the Texas Medical Branch (Galveston) takes a different path: he renounces not the need to define humanhood but the attempt to single out any one crucial or essential indicator.[10] Instead, he is synoptic in the same manner that René Dubos has so superbly shown us in *Man Adapting* and *So Human an Animal.* Englehardt distinguishes the biological from personal life but follows a multifactorial, non-univocal line. Indeed, he points precisely to the traits elected in all three of the major univocal definitions discussed here; together they compose his own — cerebral function, self-consciousness, and relationship or the societal dimension. Yet it is difficult, studying his language, not to believe that he gives cerebral function the determinative place, as when he says that "for a person to be embodied and present in the world he must be conscious in it," but follows that up by adding, "The brain is the singular focus of the embodiment of the mind, and in its absence man as a person is absent" (p. 21).

Being careful in all this is supremely important. Leonard Weber of Detroit urges "caution in adopting a neocortical definition of death" because this is tantamount to a definition of personhood, although he doesn't throw it out of court. He further asks us to make sure "the biological is not being under-valued as a component of human life."[11] On both scores I agree. I take "caution" to mean carefulness, which is always in order, and I certainly want to affirm our physical side, since why even talk of cerebral function apart from a cerebrum? "Mind is meat" may be too crass, but I agree that it contains a vital truth.

Rapprochement?

To Tooley and McCormick I would want to say, "You are on sound ground, so far. Of all the optimal traits of a full and authentic human life, I am inclined with you to give top importance to awareness of self (Tooley's cardinal and my optimal trait no. 2) and to the capacity for interpersonal and social relations (McCormick's cardinal and my optimal traits no. 7 and no. 8)." But I still want to reason that *their* key indicators are only factors at all because of *my* key criterion — cerebral function. Is this not an issue to be carefully weighted?

Rizzo and Yonder of Canisius College, Buffalo, have argued the case for the neocortical definition.[12] Their conclusion is that "when there is incontrovertible evidence of neocortical death, the human life has ceased." To Professor Tooley and Father McCormick I would say, "Neocortical death means that both self-consciousness and other-orientedness are gone, whereas neither non-self-consciousness nor inability to relate to others means the end of neocortical activity." Just remember amnesia victims when self-consciousness is proposed as the key; just remember radically autistic and schizophrenic patients when the relational key is proposed. The amnesiac has lost his identity, his selfhood, and the psychotic is still *thinking,* no matter how falsely and in what disorder. On these grounds we cannot declare that such individuals are no longer persons, just as we cannot do so at some levels of mental retardation. Only irreversible coma or a decerebrate state is ground for such a serious determination. It seems that possibly the neocortical key is more conservative than some observers of the ethical debate suppose.

The importance of self-awareness is obvious. Abraham Maslow has taught this generation that much. Being able to recognize and respond to others is of the greatest importance to being truly human, as Gordon Allport's interpersonalism made plain. But as Julius Korein, the New York University neurologist, tells us, "Basic to the definition of the death of an individual is identification of the irreversible destruction of that critical component of the system which represents the essence of the person," and that essence, he says, is "cerebral death."[13] The "vegetable" patient, no matter how many spontaneous vital functions may be continuing, is dead, a nonperson, but not at the point he appears to be incapable of self-perception or of relational affect — only when neurologic diagnosis determines that cerebral function has ended permanently.

The non-neocortical theories (or paraneocortical) fail because they do not account for all cases. "Neocortical death," on the other hand, *necessarily* covers all other criteria, because they are by definition impossible criteria when neocortical function is gone. The key trait must be one that covers all cases, no matter how infrequently they are seen clinically. Incidentally but not unimportantly, the neocortical indicator is *medically* determinable, whereas Tooley's and McCormick's are not.

If it proves that very many ethicists feel these issues about a sound hypothesis for the *humanum* are crucial, those whose training has been in the humanities will need the help and advice of psychiatrists, psychologists, and neurologists and brain specialists, to teach us the limiting principles involved and expedite our discussion.

Notes

1. J. Rostand, *Humanly Possible: A Biologist's Notes on the Future of Mankind,* trans. by L. Blair (New York: Saturday Review Press, 1973), p. 8.

2. E. Fromm and R. Xirau, *The Nature of Man* (New York: Macmillan, 1968).

3. The full text is "Medicine and the Nature of Man," in *The Teaching of Medical Ethics,* ed. by R. M. Veatch, W. Gaylin and C. Morgan (Hastings-on-Hudson, N.Y.: Institute of Society, Ethics and the Life Sciences, 1973), pp. 47-58. It appeared also in *Science, Medicine and Man* I (1973): 93-102.

4. M. Tooley, "Abortion and Infanticide," *Philosophy and Public Affairs* 2 (Fall, 1972): 37-65.

5. R. Dubos, *Man Adapting* (New Haven: Yale University Press, 1965), p. 7n.

6. R. A. McCormick, "To Save or Let Die: The Dilemma of Modern Medicine," *Journal of the American Medical Association* 229 (July 8, 1974): 172-76.

7. R. H. Williams, *To Live and To Die* (New York: Springer-Verlag, 1974), p. 18.

8. J. M. Gustafson, "Basic Ethical Issues in the Biomedical Fields," *Soundings* 53 (1970): 177; and "Mongolism, Parental Desires, and the Right to Live," *Perspectives in Biology and Medicine* 16 (Summer, 1973): 529-57.

9. W. May, "The Morality of Abortion," *Catholic Medical Quarterly* 26 (1974): 116-28.

10. H. T. Englehardt, Jr. "The Beginnings of Personhood: Philosophical Considerations," *Perkins* (School of Theology) *Journal* 27 (1973): 20-27.

11. L. J. Weber, "Human Death or Neocortical Death: The Ethical Context," *Linacre Quarterly* 41 (May 1974): 106-13.

12. R. F. Rizzo and J. M. Yonder, "Definition and Criteria of Clinical Death," *Linacre Quarterly* 40 (November 1973): 223-33.

13. J. Korein, "On Cerebral, Brain, and Systemic Death," *Current Concepts of Cerebrovascular Disease* 8 (May-June 1973): 9.

52 Again: Who Is a Person?

Oliver O'Donovan

'And he, desiring to justify himself, said to Jesus, "And who is my neighbour?"' Moral theologians have never tired of pointing out that Jesus did not answer the question in the terms in which it was put. The student of the law knew that he had an obligation to care for a certain class of person, called 'neighbours'; accordingly, he asked for criteria by which he would recognize members of this class. Jesus offered him no criteria, but told a story illustrating how someone discharged the obligation of neighbour-love — someone who might quite plausibly have been held to be outside the category, 'neighbour', because he was not a Jew. 'Which of the three, do you think, proved neighbour to the man who fell among the robbers?' 'The one who showed mercy on him.'

There are at least three ways in which the answer of Jesus defeats the hidden presuppositions of the lawyer's question. In the first place, Jesus' answer clearly implied a 'universalist' doctrine of neighbourhood, whereas the lawyer, we must suppose, had in mind some kind of racial restriction. That is the most obvious, and perhaps least dramatic challenge that Jesus makes to his questioner. In the second place, Jesus' story shows *how* we identify our neighbour; from our active engagement with him in caring for him, sympathizing with him, protecting him. There is, in other words, an epistemology implied in the story; at the *end* of this engagement we can say that the neighbour-

From Oliver O'Donovan, "Again, Who Is a Person?," in J. H. Channer, ed., *Abortion and the Sanctity of Human Life* (Exeter: The Paternoster Press), pp. 125-37. Used by permission.

hood of the two men had become apparent. It would never have become clear *whether* a Samaritan and a Jew could be neighbours, if the Samaritan, like the lawyer, had waited for the question to be answered speculatively before he attended to the Jew at the roadside. The truth of neighbourhood is known in engagement; we act in commitment to someone *as* a neighbour, and thus *prove* the neighbourhood. In the third place, this is a story about how a Jew learned who his neighbour was. He learned it, not by serving him, but by being served by him. And this, perhaps, is the most scandalous element in Jesus' story: that a Jew could *need* a Samaritan as his neighbour, that the natural relation (as he saw it) of patron and client could be reversed, and that he would solve the speculative problem about Samaritans as neighbours not even by caring for a Samaritan in need, but by being cared for, in his need, by a Samaritan.

And who, then, is a person?

The term 'person' is clearly intended to be a universal term, in the way that 'neighbour' is. The question has already taken cognizance of the first challenge that Jesus offered to the lawyer. My case is a very simple one: that the question about 'personhood' has to take notice also of the second and third challenges which Jesus made. That is to say: *(a)* that we can recognize someone as a person only from a stance of *prior moral commitment* to treat him or her as a person, since the question of what constitutes a person can never be answered speculatively; and *(b)* that we know someone as a person as that person is disclosed in his or her personal relations to us, that is, as we know ourselves to be not simply the subject of our own attention to the other, but to be the object of the other's attention to us. On the basis of point *(a)* my account of personhood will be called (and deserves to be called) 'existentialist' — and it is no worse for that, but simply recognizes a fundamental truth about human knowledge which could be found in the New Testament long before anyone declared that it was 'existentialist', namely, that certain kinds of knowledge are given to us only within an active commitment of faith and obedience: 'If any man's will is to do his will, he shall know whether the teaching is from God' (John 7:17). On the basis of point *(b)*, however, we can claim to be safe from the solipsistic tendency into which popular existentialism has too often degenerated. We are not saying that personhood is *conferred* upon the object simply by our willingness to treat him or her as a person. Rather the opposite: we *discover* the personhood of the other by his personal dealings with us. We hold, therefore, to an existentialist *anthropology.* What is required of us is a commitment to be open to the other *as another human agent,* to be open to interaction with him in every form. The term 'person', too, must carry with it this implication of the old term 'neighbour', that we find ourselves with somebody 'next to' us, like us, equal to us, acting upon us as we upon him, as much a subject to whom we become object as he is object to our subject. And this presupposes a doctrine of human nature, and an understanding that we who encounter the equal and opposite other are, with him, mankind.

I

In the first place, then, there are no 'criteria of personhood' by which a person could be recognized independently of, or prior to, *personal engagement.* To say this is to say something about humanity: that members of our species are knownn (at least to one another) *in a way* that members of other animal species are not known. We may recognize a duck abstractly, by simple observation, and distinguish it from a goose. In the same way, of course, we may distinguish a human being from an elephant; but such observational recognition falls short of the kind of knowledge that it is appropriate for one human being to have of another. And, notoriously, it does nothing to answer the moral questions about our fellow human beings which are posed for us by medical technology. When we ask whether someone in an irreversible coma is a 'person' or not, it does no good to answer that he is not an elephant. We want to know whether he still is that same human agent, with whom we have engaged as fellow agents in the business of life, and to whom we therefore owe a brotherly loyalty, or whether he is no longer 'he'. And the point I wish to make is that no conceivable set of purely observational criteria can answer that question positively or negatively for us. It might seem that we could answer it negatively, by adducing certain information about his brain activity (which is not what it was when we used to meet him for lunch and discuss politics). It might seem that we could answer it positively, by showing that the vital functions of respiration and heartbeat are as spontaneously active as they used to be when he tasted wine and drew on his pipe. But both answers would miss the point: it was not his brain that we conversed with about the by-elections. It was he, the agent, the person; and although there would be no possibility of such engagement *without* the functioning brain, respiration and heartbeat, what we met and talked with was not simply the sum of those functions, but another category of subject altogether.

We met *him* — I say 'the person', but it is very important not to think that 'the person' is another *kind* of constituent, like 'the brain' or 'the heart', only different. It would be quite wrong, for example, to say that we met 'the mind'. What we met, simply, was 'Michael', the human being as irreducibly individual, irreplaceable, a member of a species, certainly, but not accounted for simply as 'an instance of kind X', but only as *himself*. To all this the word 'person' points. It is, therefore, from a logical point of view, a category mistake to try to demonstrate the presence or absence of a person by proving that this or that biological or neurological function is present or absent. It is a category mistake to say that a new conceptus cannot be a person until there is brain activity; it is a category mistake to say that it must be a person because there is an individual genetic structure. (I shall be defending a different use of this genetic evidence in a minute; for the moment I merely remark on the impropriety of this use.) For, whatever criteria we take, we end up by reducing the notion of personhood to that one constituent of human functioning.

It has seemed to some that they could evade the implications of this categorical difference by treating personhood as an epiphenomenon supervening upon the presence of biological and neurological functions, and so depending upon them without, nevertheless, being reducible to them. But our thought cannot grasp 'the person', in his unique particularity, by thinking along this route. The most that it can reach is a group of second-order capacities, different in kind from the biological or neurological functions, but no less genetic than they are. It can reach what we call 'personality', which is the cluster of behavioural and relational attributes which characteristically belong to human beings as a kind. It is a common misunderstanding of talk about persons to think that it is interchangeable with talk about personality — as though the difference between the concrete and the abstract meant nothing — or with talk about some aspect of personality, such as the capacity for relationship. But in speaking of the human person we are not speaking of any kind of capacity nor of any kind of attribute. Our argument has not been that we can know persons by *observing* their capacity for relationship. We have said that we know them *in* relationship, which is to say, when we abandon the observer's stance altogether and commit ourselves to treating them *as* persons. Of course, persons are intended for relationship, and will therefore (barring accidents) develop the personal attributes and capacities. But that is a very different thing from taking these attributes as a supposedly objective criterion for determining their status as persons. Personality *discloses* personhood; it does not constitute it. Personal attributes develop, as self-consciousness develops; but persons do not develop, for they are not in the category of quality but of substance.

There is a sermon by Austin Farrer which opens with an account of how he visited a friend who was in an irrecoverable coma; he spoke his name and took his hand, and was profoundly moved to feel the dying man's hand close firmly upon his own in a responsive grasp. But sadly, he reflected, the appearance of relationship was deceptive. The grasp was to be explained as the spontaneous response of the local nerves in the palm of the hand, habituated by years of handshaking; the friend himself was too far gone to know his name or respond to a touch. Now, I put this observation to a neurosurgeon friend of mine, and he was quite uncomprehending. To him it was far from obvious that a deeply comatose person could not hear and respond in some way, and he himself would never discount any such sign, however remote, of awareness. Like many of us when we become fascinated by medical explorations of consciousness, Austin Farrer tried to 'know too much'. Of course, this comatose person's response was not unambiguous; we may well wonder what to make of it, since from an observer's point of view it is quite inconclusive. Farrer's sermon goes on to talk of babies' smiles and wind. Again, what we see is inconclusive; we don't know that a baby is smiling, but we don't know that it is not. Personal presence emerges out of hiddenness, through ambiguous signs, to the point of clear disclosure, and then retreats into ambiguity and hiddenness at the end. There is no sign of behaviour of which we can say, 'There he is present! There he has gone!' — short of death itself, of course, and even there there are ambiguities too obvious to be mentioned. All we can do is *act personally,* as person or as friend.

The importance of this, when applied to the question of human life in its beginnings, the unborn child from conception to birth, is that it allows us to acknowledge the *mysteriousness* of what it is that lives in the womb. No one, I suppose, can have been the parent of a child without experiencing bafflement and amazement at the incomprehensibility of what thought encounters there. It is certainly not what we normally encounter when we engage with some object as a 'person'. Parents have to go *beyond the phenomenon,* and, at first almost playfully, attribute personhood to the living being in the womb — and this playful projection continues in some measure even after birth, as we see in the case of smiles and wind. But it would be quite wrong to imagine that this was simply a sentimental and arbitrary embroidery on some otherwise-specifiable cold sober 'facts' about the fetus. Nobody knows any cold sober facts; they merely observe the ambiguous phenomenon. This commitment of the parents to going beyond the phenomenon, treating the fetus as a baby, and then the newborn baby as a person, is actually *necessary,* if they are to care properly for it and if the baby is ever to develop those 'personal' characteristics which are not themselves personhood but communicate it. Furthermore, it is not arbitrary to think that the fruit of the human womb will, given the right care, develop to the point of evincing personhood through personal characteristics. Parents who do this know what the natural goal of a pregnancy is, and act in expectation of that goal's being reached. In their commitment to that goal, their engagement with the unborn child as their baby, the possibility arises of their knowing their child as a person.

But what is true of the parents in particular has to be true of the whole community. All those who assist in the pregnancy (medically or otherwise) are equally committed to welcoming the new life. And those who have no involvement with *this* pregnancy are nevertheless encouraged to see it sympathetically from the same point of view, and by so doing learn the attitudes which will be important to them when and if they are parents. The commitment of parenting, in other words, is not a private and particular commitment only of *these* parents to *this* fetus, but a generic commitment of a community and its culture to personal care for fetuses in general. This commitment is important for the community's ability to recognize and welcome new members, and will be reflected subsequently in its care for children. Only a very confused culture, such as ours is presently, can arbitrarily treat one fetus in one way and another in another. The confusion must be resolved into a general cultural attitude to the unborn human. And if that attitude does not arise from the practice of parenting, where will it arise from?

I take the practice of *experimenting on embryos* as the clearest indication of what the alternative attitude to the unborn child is. Abortion as such does not express a decisive concept of the fetus; it is the mere *refusal* of parenthood, and can be defended sometimes as the disposal of an impersonal piece of tissue and sometimes as the overruling of one person's rights in favour of another's. Once we confront experiment, however, the philosophy is quite explicit: an embryo is manipulable tissue, which has the double advantage to the researcher of being at one and the same time human tissue, with a high degree of individual organization, and non-personal.

Once again, this philosophy goes beyond the phenomenon, and commits itself in action to a view of the embryo which cannot be demonstrated objectively. Non-personhood is every bit as unsusceptible of proof as personhood. The philosophy is demanded not by the phenomena of human beginnings but by the internal requirements of the commitment to scientific experiment itself. Experiment objectifies, assigns its subject to the status of 'thing' — that is the logic of the undertaking. This does not in itself invalidate all experiment on human beings, but it does require a careful structure of symbolic safeguards — requirements of informed consent etc. — which exist to remind us all that the experimenter's perspective on the human subject is an abstraction, and potentially a dangerous one. No comparable safeguards exist in experiment on human embryos, nor could they be introduced without abolishing all useful research. We may therefore regard as purely speculative any suggestions about kinds of research which might be compatible with treating the embryo as a person, and simply say that for practical purposes experiment embodies and requires the decision not to treat it so. And that decision arises from the practice, and not vice versa.

We have to choose, then, between the alternative practices of scientific experiment and parenting as providing rival matrices for the commitment we have to unborn children as a class. This choice cannot be arbitrated existentially, but only on the basis of what is true about the world. In demanding that our common attitude should be formed by the commitment to parenthood, not by the commitment to scientific knowledge (for all the goods of mastery of disease which it promises us), we base ourselves on the truth that those whom we treat as persons when they are yet unborn, become *known* to us as persons when they are children; and that this truth is utterly hidden from us by the alternative practice. The fundamental incompatibility of these two perspectives is ultimately expressed as the decision either to know human beings personally, or not to know them so. The decision to 'play God' — to reidentify the human object — is also, and inescapably, a decision *not* to 'play many', to close ourselves off from the modes of mutual knowledge which essentially belong to the community of mankind.

II

Having said that discerning persons is a matter of commitment to moral engagement, we must add a second point: there are criteria of *appropriateness* for our engaging with other beings as persons in fidelity. It might be thought that the doctrine that we *know* persons only as we *treat* them as persons opened the door to all kinds of fantasy. What do we make, for example, of people who treat their pets or their plants as persons? Certainly the response they get is ambiguous, but that we allowed to be no obstacle; so is the response from the comatose man or the newborn baby ambiguous, but it is appropriate, nevertheless, to commit ourselves to them. Is it equally appropriate to commit ourselves to our plants? No; for, as we made it clear in the beginning, our existential commitment is founded on an anthropology. The commitment to the other is rationally justified because he and we are alike mankind. It is appropriate to commit oneself in engagement with mankind, as it is not with plants; which is not to say that some kind of commitment may not be appropriate also in dealing with plants, but not the kind of commitment that treats them as persons.

'But this,' someone may protest, 'simply begs the whole question. We started off asking whether certain doubtful beings — comatose patients and unborn babies — were really human beings in the full sense of being persons, and you told us that we would discover whether they were only if we assumed that they were and committed ourselves accordingly. Now you tell us that we must, after all, make up our minds *in advance* whether someone is a human being before we know whether to commit ourselves.' The appearance of circularity here is, however, only momentary. For we said also that there was a purely observational level at which we could 'know' human beings and distinguish them from elephants in the same way that we know ducks and distinguish them from geese. This is not knowing 'humanely' — that is as a human being *ought* to know another human being — but it is a form of knowledge, a knowledge of the human *phenomenon* which can render intelligible and appropriate the commitment to treating someone 'as a person'. The question then becomes: what are the criteria for discerning the human *phenomenon?* What is the human 'appearance', or human 'face,' which invites us to commit ourselves to it in expectation and hope of meeting the human 'person'? But this question in turn cannot be answered simply as it stands, for phenomena themselves develop and unfold in time; the more one investigates an object, the more the phenomenon of that object unfolds. Take, for example, a famous shock-scene in Bergman's film *The Seventh Seal.* The hero approaches from behind a figure seated, slightly crouched, upon a rock, and taps him on the shoulder. As he does so, the figure slumps over and his head lurches round at an unnatural angle, to reveal that his eyes have been picked out and that it is nothing but a rotted corpse. The initial phenomenon of a living human being has quickly developed into something quite different. So we might frame the question in this way: how far into the phenomenon do we have to go before we have a sufficient basis for recognizing a human being to whom we may show humane fidelity?

But even in this form the question is misleading. The hero was not *wrong* to think he saw a living human being. That is what makes the shock shocking. It was perfectly appropriate for him to tap this figure on the shoulder, as one might arrest the attention of someone taking a nap. It would not have been appropriate for him to *go on* treating that figure as a living human being; but he had sufficient warrant to *approach* him in that way. It would have been inappropriate, indeed morally wicked, for him to transfix him with an arrow like a beast of prey, for such phenomenal evidence as he had suggested that he had to deal with a living man. So we need to get away from any form of the question which implies that there is a level of proof to be reached before we have warrant to interact with someone as a human being. Rather, the initial appearance of the human form is immediate, and immediately commands a committed humane response. If that appearance then breaks down and turns into something else, then we recognize we have made a mistake and abandon our 'committed' response. But we respond to the 'human face', the immediate self-presentation of humanity, and not to any measure of proof.

Consider the following scenario. The obstetrician cuts the umbilical cord, and the nurse washes the baby, weighs it, takes measures to protect it against infection, wraps it in a blanket to keep it warm; and then, of course, the parents talk to it, call it by its name, try to attract its attention, console its cries. But then the baby shows signs of being in trouble, and in a few minutes dies. It was pointless talking to it, calling it by its name, attracting its attention, for its eyes are sightless, its ears without hearing. But in the first moments it appeared normal. And when we say that the parents were right to *treat* it as a normal child until they knew it was *not* a normal child, we are not merely recommending that one should be on the safe side when in doubt. We are saying that the *only* proper response to the human appearance is the humane response. There could not be any question of *doubt* until the first deviant phenomena occurred; to profess doubt earlier than that would be the purest bad faith. The immediate appearance of a child was a quite sufficient warrant for commitment in those initial moments. (Does this example, perhaps, give us a paradigm for how we may think about natural fetal wastage by spontaneous abortion?)

To say that we respond to the 'immediate appearance' of a human being does not mean that we cannot learn to discern the human appearance more accurately. The first explorers who encountered pigmy peoples may have been in some justifiable doubt as to whether this was the human race or not. Today nobody could be justified in professing doubt on the matter. Many of us might make the mistake of supposing that someone was dead, when the skilled eye of a physician would suspect a coma. We can, in other words, learn to trace the genetic patterns of the human phenomenon and identify some appearances — which lie outside our common experience — as belonging properly to the phenomenon of humanity and others as not doing so. This point is of great importance in assessing the claim on our attention made by the human embryo.

Earlier generations had perfectly legitimate difficulties in recognizing an unborn child (in embryo state) as a human being. The discontinuities of appearance were striking, and, of course, the embryo was never observed alive. Consequently they hypothesized a moment of 'animation' in which this strange body was transformed and brought to life by the coming of the soul. We may compare this kind of thinking to early anthropological speculations about the Bantu races, which tried to show essential discontinuities with the Caucasian races. Subsequent scientific exploration of the phenomena has discredited the impression of such discontinuities. Similarly, scientific study of embryology has laid to rest the notion of a major physiological discontinuity in human development between embryo and fetal stage. Genetic studies have, on the other hand, indicated a major discontinuity at conception, when the parental genotypes re-form into a new genome, the distinct endowment of the new conceptus. (This has meant, not only that the history of the embryo/fetus can no longer be conceived as including a moment of 'animation', but that it can no longer be extended back to include the history of the sperm before conception.)

Our generation cannot avoid the implications of this knowledge. Our recognition of the human face is improved, and we can now see it in the embryo, even in the invisible blastocyst and zygote, where our ancestors could not. This means that pre-modern speculations about the animation of the fetus are now empty of all probative force. (I say this, because there remains among some Anglican Christians a curious belief that this question can be settled simply on the basis of Christian tradition.) This is not to subordinate theology *in principle* to science. Rather, it is to point out that such theological speculations were always *empirical in intent*, lacking only the investigative resources to reach accurate conclusions. And to say that these pre-modern discussions have no probative force is not to say that they have no value for our thinking on the question. They have great *critical* value, in that they expose and refute the philosophical pressures which, then as now, exercise an improper *a priori* influence on what ought to be empirical judgments.

To sum up. The scientific evidence about the development of the unborn child does not prove that the unborn child is a person, because that cannot in principle be proved. We cannot accept any equation of personhood with brain-activity, genotype, implantation, or whatever — for that is to reduce personhood, which is known only in personal engagement, to a function of some observable criteria. However, what the scientific evidence does is to clarify for us the lines of objective continuity and discontinuity, so that we can identify with greater accuracy the 'beginning' of any individual human existence. It is, of course, a purely 'biological' beginning that biology discloses to us; how could it be otherwise? In adopting it as the sufficient ground of respect for the human being, we are not declaring that personhood is merely biological. We are, rather, exploring the presuppositions of personal commitment. The only ground we have for risking commitment in the first encounters with the new human being is biological 'appearance'.

One of the most potent philosophical ingredients from which the giddy modern cocktail of technological materialism is mixed is the idealist distrust of appearances. It has, of course, become almost customary in these days to proclaim emancipation from a 'Cartesian' body-soul dualism, and there can be few intellectual evils which have not been attributed to this source by someone or other. For the most part, however, the emancipation has proved to be an empty boast. The very least that would be implied by it would be a willingness to get a hold on human appearances once again. It would imply that we stopped treating the bodily manifestations of humanity, its genetic and physiological structures, as though we had entirely seen through them and knew that there was nothing there. It would imply that we stopped talking and acting as though we shared some secret knowledge about a real humanity that was disclosed apart from physical appearances. It would imply that we stopped throwing up specious oppositions between 'personalist' and 'biologistic' conceptions of the human being. It is true, as we have emphasized, that the human person resists exhaustive analysis, that it has its root in the mystery of divine vocation whereby God confers our individual existence upon us as he calls us by our names. But to that secret calling there is no public audio-link. We know another person by his unfolding manifestation through appearances, and we know him to be something more than the sum of the appearances only as we attend with seriousness to what the appearances manifest. The Samaritan, who proved to be the Jew's neighbour, was the one traveller upon that road who reckoned that he could trust the evidence of his eyes: 'When he saw him, he had compassion.'

53 Must a Patient Be a Person to Be a Patient? Or, My Uncle Charlie Is Not Much of a Person but He Is Still My Uncle Charlie

Stanley Hauerwas

As a Protestant teaching at a Catholic university, I continue to learn about problems I had no idea even existed. For example, recently I was called down for referring to Catholics as "Roman Catholics." I had been working on the assumption that a Catholic was a Roman Catholic; however, it was pointed out to me that this phrase appeared only with the beginning of the English reformation in order to distinguish a Roman from an Anglo-Catholic. A Catholic is not Roman, as my Irish Catholic friend emphatically reminded me, but is more properly thought of simply as Catholic.

I recount this tale because I think it has something to do with the issue I want to raise for our consideration. For we tend to think that most of our descriptions, the way we individuate action, have a long and honored history that can be tampered with only with great hesitation. Often, however, the supposed tradition is a recent innovation that may be as misleading as it is helpful.

That is what I think may be happening with the emphasis on whether someone is or is not a "person" when this is used to determine whether or what kind of medical care a patient should receive. In the literature of past medical ethics the notion of "person" does not seem to have played a prominent role in deciding how medicine should or should not be used vis-à-vis a particular patient. Why is it then that we suddenly seem so concerned with the question of whether someone is a person? It is my hunch we have much to learn from this phenomenon as it is an indication, not that our philosophy of medicine or medical ethics is in good shape, but rather that it is in deep trouble. For it is my thesis that we are trying to put forward "person" as a regulative notion to direct our health care as substitute for what only a substantive community and story can do.

However, before trying to defend this thesis, let me first illustrate how the notion of "person" is being used in relation to some of the recent issues of medical ethics. Paul Ramsey in his book, *The Patient as Person,*[1] uses the notion of person to protect the individual patient against the temptation, especially in experimental medicine, to use one patient for the good of another or society. According to Ramsey, the major issue of medical ethics is how to reconcile the welfare of the individual with the welfare of mankind when both must be served. Ramsey argues that it is necessary to emphasize the personhood of the patient in order to remind the doctor or the experimenter that his first responsibility is to his immediate patient, not mankind or even the patient's family. Thus Ramsey's emphasis on "person" is an attempt to provide the basis for what he takes to be the central ethical commitment of medicine, namely, that no man will be used as a means for the good of another. Medicine can serve mankind only as it does so through serving the individual patient.

Without the presumption of the inviolability of the "person," Ramsey thinks that we would have no basis for "informed consent" as the controlling criterion for medical therapy and experimentation. Moreover, it is only on this basis that doctors rightly see that their task is not to cure disease, but rather to cure the person who happens to be subject to a disease. Thus, the notion of "person" functions for Ramsey as a Kantian or deontological check on what he suspects is the utilitarian basis of modern medicine.

However, the notion of "person" plays quite a

From *Connecticut Medicine* 39 (December 1975).

different function in other literature dealing with medical ethics. In these contexts, "person" is not used primarily as a protective notion, but rather as a permissive notion that takes the moral heat off certain quandaries raised by modern medicine. It is felt if we can say with some assuredness that X, Y, or Z is not a person, then our responsibility is not the same as it is to those who bear this august title.

Of course, the issue where this is most prominent is abortion. Is the fetus a human person? Supposedly on that question hang all the law and the prophets of the morality of abortion. For if it can be shown that the fetus is not a person, as indeed I think it can be shown, then the right to the care and protection that modern medicine can provide is not due to the fetus. Indeed, the technological skill of medicine can be used to destroy such life, for its status is of no special human concern since it lacks the attribute of "personhood."

Or, for example, the issue of *when* one is a person is raised to help settle when it is morally appropriate to withdraw care from the dying. If it can be shown, for example, that a patient has moved from the status of being a person to a non-person, then it seems that many of the difficult decisions surrounding what kind and the extent of care that should be given to the dying becomes moot. For the aid that medicine can bring is directed at persons, not at the mere continuation of our bodily life. (Since I will not develop it further, however, it is worth mentioning that this view assumes a rather extreme dualism between being a person and the bodily life necessary to provide the conditions for being a person.)[2]

Or, finally, there are the issues of what kind of care should be given to defective or deformed infants in order to keep them alive. For example, Joseph Fletcher has argued that any individual who falls below the 40 I.Q. mark in a Stanford-Binet test is "questionably a person," and if you score 20 or below you are not a person.[3] Or Michael Tooley has argued that young infants, indeed, are not "persons" and, therefore, do not bear the rights necessary to make infanticide a morally questionable practice.[4] Whether, or what kind, of medical care should be given to children is determined by whether children are able to meet the demands of being a person. You may give them life-sustaining care, but in doing so you are acting strictly from the motive of charity since nothing obligates you to do so.

As I suggested at the first, I find all this rather odd, not because some of the conclusions reached by such reasoning may be against my own moral opinions, or because they entail practices that seem counter-intuitive (e.g., infanticide), but rather because I think this use of "person" tends to do violence to our language. For example, it is only seldom that we have occasion to think of ourselves as "persons" — when asked to identify myself, I do not think that I am a person, but I am Stanley Hauerwas, teacher, husband, father or, ultimately, a Texan. Nor do I often have the occasion to think of others as persons. I do sometimes say, "Now that Joe is one hell of a fine person," but so used, "person" carries no special status beyond the naming of a role. If I still lived in Texas, I would, as a matter of fact, never use such an expression, but rather say, "Now there is a good old boy."

Moreover, it is interesting to notice how abstract the language of person is in relation to our first-order moral language through which we live our lives and see the kind of issues I have mentioned above. For example, the reason that we do not use one man for another or society's good is not that we violate his "person," but rather because we have learned that it is destructive of the trust between us to do so. (Which is, in fact, Ramsey's real concern, as his case actually rests much more on his emphasis on the "covenant" between doctor and patient than on the status of the patient as a "person.") For example, it would surely make us hesitant to go to a doctor if we thought he might actually care for us only as a means of caring for another. It should be noted, however, that in a different kind of society it might well be intelligible and trustworthy for the doctor rightly to expect that his patient be willing to undergo certain risks for the good of the society itself. I suspect that Ramsey's excessive concern to protect the patient from the demands of society through the agency of the doctor is due to living in an extraordinarily individualistic society where citizens share no good in common.

Even more artificial is the use of "person" to try to determine the moral decision in relation to abortion, death, and the care of the defective newborn. For the issues surrounding whether an abortion should or should not be done seldom turn on the question of the status of the fetus. Rather, they involve why the mother does not want the pregnancy to continue, the conditions under which the pregnancy occurred, the social conditions into which the child would be born. The question of whether the fetus is or is not a person is almost a theoretical nicety in relation to the kind of questions that most abortion decisions actually involve.

Or, for example, when people are dying, we seldom decide to treat or not to treat them because they have or have not yet passed some line that makes them a person or non-person. Rather, we care or do not care for them because they are Uncle Charlie, or my father, or a good friend. In the same manner, we do not care or cease to care for a child born defective because it is or is not a person. Rather, whether or how we decide to care for such a child depends on our attitude toward the having and caring for children, our perception of our role as parents, and how medicine is seen as one form of how care is to be given to children.[5] (For it may well be that we will care for such children, but this does not mean that medicine has some kind of overriding claim on being the form that such care should take.)

It might be felt that these examples assume far too easily that our common notions and stories are the primary ones for giving moral guidance in such cases. The introduction of the notion of "person" as regulatory in such matters might be an attempt to find a firmer basis than these more historically and socially contingent notions can provide. But I am suggesting that is just what the notion of "person" cannot do without seriously distorting the practices, institutions, and notions that underlay how we have learned morally to display our lives. More technically, what advocates of "personhood" have failed to show is how the notion of person works in a way of life with which we wish to identify.

Yet, we feel inextricably drawn to come up with some account that will give direction to our medical practice exactly, because we sense that our more immediate moral notions never were, or are no longer, sufficient to provide such a guide. Put concretely, we are beginning to understand how much medicine depended on the moral ethos of its society to guide how it should care for children, because we are now in a period when some people no longer think simply because a child is born to them they need regard it as their child. We will not solve this kind of dilemma by trying to say what the doctor can and cannot do in such circumstances in terms of whether the child can be understood to be a "person" or not.

As Paul Ramsey suggests, we may have arrived at a time when we have achieved an unspeakable thing: a medical profession without a moral philosophy in a society without one either. Medicine, of course, still seems to carry the marks of a profession inasmuch as it seems to be a guardian of certain values — that is, the unconditional commitment to preserve life and health; the responsibility for justifying the patient's trust in the physician; and the autonomy of the physician in making judgments on others in the profession. But, as Alasdair MacIntyre has argued, these assumed virtues can quickly be turned to vices when they lack a scheme, or, in my language, a story that depends on further beliefs about the true nature of man and our true end.[6] But such a scheme is exactly what we lack, and it will not be supplied by trying to determine who is and is not a "person."

The language of "person" seems convenient to us, however, because we wish to assume that our medicine still rests on a consensus of moral beliefs. But I am suggesting that is exactly what is not the case and, in the absence of such a consensus, we will be much better off to simply admit that morally there are many different ways to practice medicine. We should, in other words, be willing to have our medicine as fragmented as our moral lives. I take this to be particularly important for Christians and Jews, as we have been under the illusion that we could morally expect medicine to embody our own standards, or, at least, standards that we could sympathize with. I suspect, however, that this may not be the case, for the story that determines how the virtues of medicine are to be displayed for us is quite different from the one claimed by the language of "person."[7] It may be then, if we are to be honest, that we should again think of the possibility of what it might mean to practice medicine befitting our convictions as Christians or Jews. Yet, there is a heavy price to be paid for the development of such a medical practice, as it may well involve training and going to doctors whose technology is less able to cure and sustain us than current medicine provides. But, then, we must decide what is more valuable, our survival or how we choose to survive.

Notes

1. Paul Ramsey, *The Patient as Person* (New Haven: Yale University Press, 1970).

2. For a more extended analysis of this point, see my *Vision and Virtue: Essays in Christian Ethical Reflection* (Notre Dame, Ind.: Fides Press, 1974).

3. Joseph Fletcher, "Indicators of Humanhood," *Hastings Center Report,* November, 1972, pp. 1-3; also see my response in "The Retarded and the Criteria of Human," *Linacre Quarterly,* November 1973, pp. 217-22.

4. Michael Tooley, "A Defense of Abortion and Infanticide," in Joel Feinberg (ed.), *The Problem of Abortion* (Belmont: Wadsworth Publishing Co., 1973), pp. 51-91.

5. For an extended analysis of these issues, see my "The Demands and Limits of Care: Ethical Reflections on the Moral Dilemma of Neonatal Intensive Care," *American Journal of Medical Science,* March-April 1975, pp. 269-91.

6. Alasdair MacIntyre, "How Virtues Become Vices: Values, Medicine and Social Context," *Evaluation and Explanation in the Biomedical Services* (Dordrecht: Reidel, 1975), pp. 97-111.

7. For I would not deny that advocates of "person" as the regulatory notion of medical care are right to assume that the notion of person involves the basic libertarian values of our society. It is my claim that such values are not adequate to direct medicine in a humane and/or Christian manner.

54 *Terra es animata:* On Having a Life

Gilbert Meilaender

To live the risen life with God is, presumably, to be what we are meant to be. What can we conclude about our duties to the dying from the medieval belief that we join the hosts of heaven as "animated earth"?

For the past quarter century bioethics has been a booming business in this country. In part that may be because humanists found here a field in which they could compete with scientists for grant money. In larger part, it is surely because medical advance has forced certain problems upon our attention. But, at least in part, it must also be because some of the concerns of bioethics impinge upon everyday life — upon the lives of most people, and at some of the crucial moments of life, in particular birth and death. Bioethics could not have boomed as it has were it not a reflection of some of our central concerns.

I will examine some of the issues that have emerged in bioethical discussions of death, dying, and care for the dying as a way of thinking about what it means to have a life. In particular, I will focus on a concept that has risen to great prominence in our thinking: the concept of a person. Two competing visions of the person — and the relation of person to body — have unfolded as bioethics has developed, and in my view, the wrong one has begun to triumph. We have tried to handle our substantive disagreements on this

From the *Hastings Center Report* 23, no. 4 (1993): 23-32. © The Hastings Center. Used by permission of the publisher and the author.

question by turning to procedural solutions — in particular, advance directives — trusting that they presume no answer to the disputed question. We are, however, beginning to see how problematic such a procedural solution is, how flawed and even contradictory much thinking about advance directives has been. What we need, I will suggest, is to recapture the connection between our person and the natural trajectory of bodily life.

That will be the course of my argument. But, as a way of framing the issues, I begin in what is likely to seem a strange place: with the thought of some of the early Christian Fathers about heaven and the resurrection of the dead. They were attempting to relate the body's history to their concept of the person's optimal development. In so doing, they provide a different and illuminating angle from which to see our present concerns.

Patristic Images of the Resurrection of the Body

In his *City of God* Saint Augustine describes the human being as *terra animata,* "animated earth."[1] Such a description, contrary in many ways to trends in bioethics over the last several decades, ought to give pause to anyone inclined to characterize Augustine's thought simply in terms of a Neoplatonic dualism that ignores the personal significance of the body. It may, in fact, be our own constant talk of "personhood" that betrays a more powerful tendency toward dualism of body and self.

This same Augustine, however, found himself puzzled at the thought of the resurrection body. What sort of body will one who dies in childhood have in the resurrection? "As for little children," Augustine wrote, "I can only say that they will not rise again with the tiny bodies they had when they died. By a marvelous and instantaneous act of God they will gain that maturity they would have attained by the slow lapse of time" (22.14). This is, in fact, a question to which a number of the Church Fathers devoted thought.[2]

Origen, for example, understood that throughout life our material bodies are constantly changing. How, then, can the body be raised? He appealed (in good Platonic fashion) to the *eidos,* the unchanging form of the body. Despite the body's material transformations, its *eidos* remains the same as we grow from infancy, through childhood and adulthood, to old age. (For Origen this *eidos* is not the soul; it is the bodily form united with the soul in this life and again in the resurrection. J. N. D. Kelly comments that Origen was charged with having held that resurrected bodies would be spherical; he may have held such a view, in keeping with the Platonic theory that a sphere is the perfect shape.)

From there it is not a long step to suppose that since the *eidos* of each resurrected body will be perfect, it will in every instance be identical in qualities and characteristics. Thus, Gregory of Nyssa, though differing from Origen in some respects, held that in the resurrection our bodies will be freed from all the consequences of sin — including not only death and infirmity, but also deformity and difference of age. This is a view not unlike Augustine's. Bodies may have a (natural) history, but the bodily form is unchanging. That form is the human being at his or her optimal stage of development, the person as he or she is truly meant to be (I write "he or she" not simply to conform to current canons but because Augustine, for example, took trouble to note that the sexual distinction — but not the lust which, in our experience, accompanies it — would remain in the resurrection. All defects would be removed from the resurrected body, but "a woman's sex is not a defect" [*CD* 22.17]. And although intercourse and childbirth will be no more in the resurrection, "the female organs . . . will be part of a new beauty." This is perhaps what C. S. Lewis had in mind when he wrote of the resurrection: "What is no longer needed for biological purposes may be expected to survive for splendour."[3]

Against Origen's notion that the resurrected body would be a purely spiritual *eidos,* Methodius of Olympus held that the body itself — not just its form — would be restored in the resurrection. He based his claim less on a developed philosophical argument than on the resurrection of Jesus, who was raised in the same body that had been crucified (complete, we may recall, with the nail prints in his hands).

Such issues continued to occupy the attention of theologians for centuries to come. For Saint Thomas, the form of the body is the rational soul, and the body reunited with that soul in the resurrection need not reassume all the matter that had ever been its own during temporal life. Rather, as Thomas suggests in the *Summa contra gentiles,* the resurrected man "need assume from that matter only what suffices to complete the quantity due."[4] The "quantity due" is whatever is "consistent with the form and species of humanity." This means that if one had died at an early age "before nature could bring him to the quantity due," or if one had suffered mutilation, "the divine power will supply this from another source" (4.81.12). Saint Thomas is emphatic — against what may have been Origen's view — that our risen bodies will not be purely spiritual. Like Christ's they will have flesh and bones, but in these bodies there will not be "any corruption, any deformity, any deficiency" (4.86.4). Nor, it appears, will there be differences of age; for all will rise "in the age of Christ, which is that of youth [young adulthood], by reason of the perfection of nature which is found in that age alone. For the age of boyhood has not yet achieved the perfection of nature through increase; and by decrease old age has already withdrawn from that perfection" (4.88.5).

Modern Images of the Resurrection

At least to my knowledge, this sort of speculation becomes much rarer after the Reformation — perhaps because Protestants were less inclined to go beyond biblical warrants, even when an intriguing and potentially significant question beckoned. In the fifteenth and last of his charity sermons, Jonathan Edwards does say of heaven: "There shall be none appearing with any defects either natural or moral."[5] And more recently Austin Farrer has approached these questions by asking how it is possible for us to "relate to the mercy of God beings who never enjoy a glimmer of reason."[6] If there never was a speaking and loving person, Farrer asks, where is the creature for God to immortalize? He is less troubled by those who have lost the speaking and loving personhood that once was theirs: God can immortalize them, though Farrer does not tell us whether they are immortalized free of defects or even age differences. But what of those in whom reason never developed? "The baby smiled before it died. Will God bestow immortality on a smile?" Farrer contemplates, without being satisfied by, the possibility that "every human birth, however imperfect, is the germ of a personality, and that God will give it an eternal future" — a speculation not entirely unlike that of some of the early Fathers. And he realizes that there may be some who, though retarded, are not completely without reason — though he never asks, then, what sort of eternal future might be theirs.

If we can overcome both our enlightened bemusement at such speculation and our Protestant refusal to learn from questions that admit of no answer, if instead we enter into the spirit of such questioning, we may find ourselves rather puzzled. Could such a monochromatic heaven really be heavenly? All of us thirty-five-years old, well endowed with (identical?) reasoning capacities? If each of the saints is to see God and to praise the vision of God that is uniquely his or hers, and if the joy of heaven is not only to see God but to be enriched by each other's vision, then why should we not look through the eyes of persons who are very different indeed? Is not the praise of a five-year-old different from that of a thirty-five-year-old, and, again, from that of a seventy-five-year-old? Why should not these distinct and different visions be part of the vast friendship that is heaven? Perhaps it is easier to understand the tendency to eliminate any defects from heaven, but even there, when they closely touch personal identity, we may find ourselves rather puzzled. Edwards was, for example, confident that there would be neither moral nor *natural* defect in heaven. Yet he was willing to grant that friends will know each other there. But if the stump that should have been my leg has shaped the person who I am, the person who has been your friend for forty years, it is hard to know exactly what our heavenly reunion is to be like when the stump is replaced by a perfectly formed leg. "Will God bestow immortality on a smile?" As likely, I should think as that the mother of that child will meet one upon whom God has, in Augustine's words, bestowed in "a marvelous and instantaneous act . . . that maturity they would have attained by the slow lapse of time." We might set against Farrer's view the comment of his fellow Anglican David Smith, who writes that "at the very least it would be hard for Anglicans to hold that a being who might be baptized was lacking in human dignity."[7]

Perhaps I begin to wax too enthusiastic in my own speculations, but the point is worth pondering. To live the risen life with God is, presumably, to be what we are meant to be. It is the fulfillment and completion of one's personal history. To try to think from that vantage point, therefore, is to imagine human life in its full dignity. And to try, however clumsy the speculation, to adopt this vantage point for a moment is to think about what it means to have a life. The questions I have been considering invite us to think about our person, our individual self. Does it have a kind of timeless form? A moment in life to which all prior development leads and from which all future development is decline? A moment, then, in which we are uniquely ourselves? Or is our person simply our personal history, whether long or short, a history inseparable from the growth, development, and decline of our body?

There is some reason to think — or so I shall suggest in what follows — that much contemporary thought in ethics has a great deal in common with Origen. In an age supposedly dominated by modes of thought more natural and historical than metaphysical, we have allowed ourselves to think of personhood in terms quite divorced from our biological nature or the history of our embodied self. In the words of Holmes Rolston, our "humanistic disdain for the organic sector" is "less rational, more anthropocentric, not really *bio*-ethical at all," when compared to a view that takes nature and history into our understanding of the person.[8] Or, put in a more literary vein, the view I will try to explicate is that expressed by Ozy Froats in Robertson Davies's novel, *The Rebel Angels.* Froats, a scientist, is discussing his theories about body types with Simon Darcourt, priest and scholar. Froats believes there is little one can do to alter one's body type, a dismaying verdict for Darcourt, who had hoped by diet and exercise to alter his tendency toward a round, fat body. Froats says of such hopes:

> To some extent. Not without more trouble than it would probably be worth. That's what's wrong with all these diets and body-building courses and so forth. You can go against your type, and probably achieve a good deal as long as you keep at it. . . . You can keep in good shape for what you are, but radical change is impossible. Health isn't making everybody into a Greek ideal; it's living out the destiny of the body.[9]

Terra es animata.

Ozy Froats's notion of having a life is not, however, the vision that seems to be triumphing in bioethics. And, to the degree that developments in bioethics both reflect and shape larger currents of thought in our society, those developments merit our attention.

Contra Ozy Froats

The language of personhood has been central to much of the last quarter century's developments in bioethics. It was there at the outset when, in 1972, in the second volume of the *Hastings Center Report,* Joseph Fletcher published his "Indicators of Humanhood: A Tentative Profile of Man." The language had not yet solidified, since Fletcher could still use "human" and "person" interchangeably. But the heart of his view was precisely that which would, in years to come, distinguish clearly between the class of human beings and the (narrower) class of persons.

Among the important indicators (by 1974 Fletcher would declare it fundamental[10]) was "neo-cortical function." Apart from cortical functioning, "the *person* is non-existent." Having a life requires such function, for "to be dead 'humanly' speaking is to be ex-cerebral, no matter how long the body remains alive." And, in fact, being a person has more to do with being in control than with being embodied. Among the indicators Fletcher discusses are self-awareness, self-control (lacking which, one has a life "about on a par with a paramecium"), and control of existence ("to the degree that a man lacks control he is not responsible, and to be irresponsible is to be subpersonal"). Human beings are neither essentially sexual nor parental, but the technological impulse *is* central to their being. ("A baby made artificially, by deliberate and careful contrivance, would be more *human* than one resulting from sexual roulette.")

Even if, in the briskness with which he can set forth his claims, Fletcher makes an easy target, he was not without considerable influence — and it may be that he discerned and articulated where bioethics was heading well before the more fainthearted were prepared to develop the full consequences of their views. Certainly the understanding of personhood that he represents is very different from Augustine's "animated earth" or Ozy Froats's sense that one must live out the destiny of the body. Views of that sort have generally been labeled "vitalism," and their inadequacy assumed.

This is especially evident in our attitude toward death and toward those who are dying. To confront our own mortality or that of those we love is to be compelled to think about our embodiment and about what it means to have a life.[11] How we face death, and how we care for the dying, are not just isolated problems about which decisions must be made. These are also occasions in which we come to terms with who we are, recognizing that we may soon be no more. The approach of death may seem to mock our pretensions to autonomy; at the least, we are invited to wonder whether wisdom really consists in one last effort to assert our autonomy by taking control of the timing of our death. Contemplation of mortality reminds us that our identity has been secured through bodily ties — in nature, with those from whom we are descended; in history, with those whose lives have intertwined with ours. We are forced to ask whether the loss of these ties must necessarily mean the end of the person we are. Such issues, fundamental in most people's lives, have been involved in arguments about how properly to care for the dying, as we can see if we attempt to bring to the surface two contrasting views within bioethics about what it means to have a life.

Having a Life: View 1

For some time the distinction between "ordinary" and "extraordinary" care dominated bioethical discussions of care for the dying. It provided categories by which to think about end-of-life decisions. When this language began to be widely used — and, indeed, it did filter quite often into ordinary, everyday conversation — its chief purpose was a simple one. The perception, in many ways accurate, was that patients needed moral language capable of asserting their independence over against the medical establishment. They needed to be able to have ways of justifying treatment refusals, ways of resisting overly zealous — even if genuinely concerned — medical caregivers. A widespread sense that patients found themselves confronting a runaway medical establishment lay behind arguments that "extraordinary" or "heroic" care could rightly be refused and that no one had a moral obligation to accept such care. Over against a runaway and powerful medical establishment, this language sought to restore a sense of limits and an acceptance of life's natural trajectory. The language proved inadequate, however, meaning too many different things to different people. But it was not simply inadequate; it was also a language that did not, taken by itself, lend stature to the increasingly prominent concept of personhood. And that concept has been used to broaden significantly the meaning of "useless" or "futile" treatment, by divorcing the person from the life of the body.

In recent years we have seen a spate of articles seeking to define futility in medical care. Care that is futile or useless has in the past been considered "extraordinary" and could be refused or withheld. But what do we mean by futility? Years ago, when I was younger and more carefree, I used to enjoy going out at night in the midst of a hard snowstorm to shovel my driveway. In a sense, this was far from futile, since its psychological benefits were, I thought, considerable. But if the aim was a driveway clear of snow, it was close to futile. Well before I had finished, if the snow was coming hard, the driveway would again be covered. Sometimes I'd do it again before coming in, though aware that those inside were laughing at me. But if the goal was a driveway clear of snow, it just could not be accomplished, no matter how hard I worked while the snow was falling. "In Greek mythology, the daughters of Danaus were condemned in Hades to draw water in leaky sieves. . . . A futile action is one that cannot achieve the goals of the action no matter how often repeated."[12]

This sense of futility we all understand, even if we realize that it may be difficult to apply with precision in some circumstances. Thus, for example, the comatose person (unlike the person in a persistent vegetative state) is reasonably described as "terminally ill." Because the cough, gag, and swallowing reflexes of the comatose patient are impaired, he or she is highly susceptible to respiratory infections and has a life span usually "limited to weeks or months."[13] Because these reflexes are not similarly impaired in the PVS patient, he or she may live years if nourished and cared for. It makes sense, therefore, to describe most medical care for the comatose person as futile, and we understand readily, I think, the language of futility in that context. It is not as obvious, however, that the same language is appropriate in referring to the PVS patient.

Recent discussions make clear that, in light of such problems, "futility" has gradually come to mean something else — and something quite different. If the sense of futility described above is termed "quantitative" (referring to the improbability that treatment could preserve life for long), a rather different sense of futility is now termed "qualitative." Thus, some have argued, treatment that preserves "continued biologic life without conscious autonomy" is qualitatively futile.[14] It is effective in keeping the earth that is the body animated — effective, but, so the argument goes, not beneficial because what is central to being a person cannot be restored.

How ambivalent we remain on these questions becomes evident, however, when we contrast that view with a recent article, "New Directions in Nursing Home Ethics."[15] The authors argue that the standard view of autonomy that has governed so much of our thinking about acute care in the hospital context is not applicable to the nursing home patient. There we need a new notion of "autonomy within community." This may not be the best language to make their point, however, since the authors want to do more than just envision the person within his community of care. They are also concerned to see his medical condition, his chronic needs, his dependence, as internal to the person. Thus, they seek a

> notion of moral personhood that is not abstracted from the individual's social context or state or physical and mental capacity. . . . For now the caring constitutes the fabric of the person's life . . . and the reality of the moral situation is that the person must embrace dependency rather than resisting it as a temporary, external threat.

The aim here is no longer to fend off the threat external to this person and return the patient to an autonomous condition; instead, the aim is to rethink autonomy, to take into it a loss of self-mastery, to accept dependence in order "to give richer meaning to the lives of individuals who can no longer be self-reliant." Perhaps we might even say that the aim is to help the chronically ill person live out the destiny of the body.

How can it be, in essentially the same time and place where this argument is put forward, that we should be moving rapidly away from such an understanding of the person in so many discussions of "futile" medical care? When Dr. Timothy Quill assisted his patient Diane to commit suicide, he did it, he said, to help her "maintain . . . control on her own terms until death." The hands are the hands of Dr. Quill, but the voice is that of Joseph Fletcher, an increasingly powerful voice in our society.

Having a Life: View 2

Around the time that Fletcher was publishing his indicators of humanhood, one of the other great figures in the early years of the bioethics movement, also a theologian, was writing that the human being is "a sacredness in the natural biological order. He is a person who within the ambience of the flesh claims our care. He is an embodied soul or an ensouled body."[16] In those words of Paul Ramsey the vision of the human being as *terra animata* was forcefully articulated. As "embodied souls" we long for a fulfillment never fully given in human history, for the union with God that is qualitatively different from this life — which longing can never, therefore, be satisfied by a great quantity of this life. But as "ensouled bodies" our lives also have a shape, a trajectory, that is the body's. Our identity is marked, first, by the bodily union of our parents, a relationship that then gradually takes on a history. We are a "someone who" — a someone who has a history — and though we may long for that qualitatively different fulfillment, we never fully transcend the body's history in this life. To come to know who we are, therefore, one must enter that history.

It is a history that may be cut short at any time by accident or illness, but in its natural pattern it moves through youth and adulthood toward old age and, finally, decline and death. That is the body's destiny. As Hans Jonas has suggested, we exist as living bodies, as organisms, not simply by perduring but by a constant encounter with the possibility of death.[17] We constantly give up the component parts of our self to renew them, and our continued life always carries within itself the possibility that these exchanges may fail us. Eventually we are worn down, unable any longer to manage the necessary exchanges. The fire goes out, and we are no longer "animated" earth.

To point to some moment in this history as the moment in which we are most truly ourselves, the vantage point from which the rest of our life is to be judged — not just another of the many moments in which we are persons, but a moment at which, presumably, we have personhood — is to suppose that we can somehow extricate ourselves from the body's natural history, can see ourselves whole. It is even, perhaps, to suppose that in such a moment we are rather like God, no longer having our personal presence in the body.

It is not too much to say that two quite different visions of the person — Fletcher's and Ramsey's — have been at war with each other during the three decades or so that bioethics has been a burgeoning movement. But it is equally clear that one view has begun to predominate within the bioethics world and perhaps within our culture more generally. Among the peculiarities of our historicist and purportedly antiessentialist age is the rise to prominence of an ahistorical and essentialist concept of the person. On this view, it is not the natural history of the embodied self but the presence or absence of certain capacities that makes the person. Indeed, we tend to think and speak not of being a person but of having personhood, which becomes a quality added to being. The view gaining ascendancy does not think of dependence or illness as something to be taken into the fabric of the person and lived out as part of one's personal history. It pictures the real person — like Origen's spherical *eidos* — as separate from that history, free to accept or reject it as part of one's person and life. Moreover, to be without the capacity to make such a decision is to fall short of personhood.

This view is not required by any of the standard approaches to bioethical reasoning or any of the basic principles (such as autonomy, beneficence, and justice) so commonly in use. What we do with such principles depends on the background beliefs we bring to them. Those benefits determine how wide will be the circle of our beneficence and whether our notion of autonomy will be able to embrace dependence. The problems we face lie less with the principles than with ourselves. We have lost touch with the natural history of bodily life — a strange upshot for *bio*ethics, as Holmes Rolston noted. How wrong we would be to suppose that ours is a materialistic age, when everything we hold central to our person is separated from the animated earth that is the body.

Embodied Souls sans Competence

It might be, however, that I have overlooked something important. If in some cases we judge care futile when the capacity for independence is gone, and if in other cases of chronic illness we take the need for continual care into the very meaning of personal life, perhaps — one might suggest — the difference lies in what different people want, how they choose to live. One patient chooses to live on; another sees no point in doing so. Hence, the key is autonomous choice, which remains at the heart of personhood. All we need do is get people to state their wishes — enact advance directives — while they are able. Then, if the day comes when others must make decisions for them, we will not have to delve into disputed background beliefs about the meaning of personhood. We will have a procedure in place to deal with such circumstances.

In the wider sweep of history, living wills are a very recent innovation, but the debate about their usefulness or wisdom coincides with the quarter century in which bioethics has grown as a movement.[18] And when we are told that, within a month after the Supreme Court's *Cruzan* decision, 100,000 people sought information about living wills from the Society for the Right to Die, we can understand that this is not an issue for specialized academic disciplines alone. The term "living will" was coined in 1969, and the nation's first living will law (in California) was passed in 1976 — prompted, it seems, by the Karen Quinlan case. By now most states have enacted laws giving legal standing to living wills, and in 1991 the federal

Patient Self-Determination Act went into effect, requiring hospitals to advise patients upon admission of their right to enact an advance directive. In a relatively short period of time, therefore, the idea of living wills (and other forms of advance directives, such as the health care power of attorney) seems to have scored an impressive triumph. If we have no substantive agreement on what it means to be a person or have a life, the living will offers a process whereby we can deal with substantive disagreement. Each of us autonomously decides when our life would be so lacking in personal dignity as to be no longer worth preserving, and we pretend that such a process masks no substantive vision of what personhood means.

But it does, of course. Such a procedural approach brings with it a certain vision of the person: to be a person is to be, or have the capacity to be, an autonomous chooser, to take control over one's personal history, determining its bounds and limits. This substantive view turns out to have a life of its own and — we are beginning to see — can lead in several quite different directions. For a time, perhaps, all choices of once autonomous patients are honored. You choose to die when your ability to live independently and with "dignity" wanes; I choose to live on even when my rational capacities are gone. Each of us is treated as we have stipulated in advance. But then a day comes — and, indeed, is upon us — when the vision of the person hidden in this process comes to the fore.

The Paradox of Autonomy

If the person is essentially an autonomous chooser, then we will not forever be allowed to choose to live on when our personhood (so defined) has been lost. Living wills had, for the most part, been understood as a means by which we could ensure that we were not given care we would no longer have wanted, care that preserved a life regarded as subpersonal and no longer worth having. But in principle, after all, the process could be used to other ends. One could execute a living will directing that everything possible be done to keep oneself alive, even when one's "personal" capacities had been irretrievably lost. What then?

In a case somewhat like this, Helga Wanglie's caregivers answered that question by seeking a court order to stop the respirator and feeding tube that were sustaining her life. Mrs. Wanglie was an eighty-seven-year-old woman who, because of a respiratory attack, lost oxygen to her brain. She did not recover and remained in a persistent vegetative state. Although the costs of her care were covered by the family's insurance policy, the hospital still sought permission to remove life support. In some relatively minor ways, her case does not fit perfectly the hypothetical situation I considered above, for she had no living will. What she had, though, was a husband who was her guardian and who refused to consent to the withdrawal of treatment, believing she would not have wanted him to do so. Also, the medical caregivers went to court challenging her husband's suitability as guardian, rather than directly seeking court approval to terminate treatment.[19] But as Alexander Morgan Capron notes, when the caregivers first announced their intention to go to court, they stated that "they did not 'want to give medical care they described as futile.'"

Thus, in the Wanglie case, at least in the minds of the caregivers, personhood defined in terms of the right autonomously to determine one's future gave way to personhood defined in terms of the present possession of certain capacities.[20] For those who lack such rational capacities, further care is understood as futile — whatever they might previously have stipulated while competent. Similarly, when Schneiderman and his colleagues develop their "qualitative" understanding of futility, they make clear its impact on cases like this one. "The patient has no right to be sustained in a state in which he or she has no purpose other than mere vegetative survival; the physician has no obligation to offer this option or services to achieve it."[21] Ironies abound here. At the heart of the bioethics movement has been an assertion of personal autonomy for patients, which was, of course, ordinarily understood as ensuring their ability to be rid of unwanted treatment. But having built autonomy into the center of our understanding of personhood, having indeed (after *Roe v. Wade)* claimed that such autonomy flows from our right of privacy and may be asserted on our behalf even by others when we are unable to assert our wishes, having used patient autonomy as a hammer to bludgeon into submission paternalistic physicians, we suddenly rediscover the responsibility of physicians to consider what is really best for the patient, to make judgments about when care is futile. We suddenly do an about face. Against past autonomous patient choice for continued treatment even after "personhood" has been lost, we now assert medical responsibility not to provide present care that is "futile."

Helga Wanglie's caregivers and those who would assert a "qualitative" notion of personhood are both right and wrong — though not in the ways they suppose. They are right in that there is no reason to think that my physicians should forever be bound by what I stipulate (when I am forty-five and in good health) about my future care. That is, they are right in thinking that autonomy alone is far too thin an account of the person and that physicians must concern themselves with patients' best interests, not just their requests or directives. But they are wrong in supposing that care for me becomes futile simply because I have irretrievably lost the higher human capacities for reasoning and self-awareness. They are also confused; for the vision of the person guiding them where they are right is incompatible with the vision of the person at work where they are wrong. In supposing that care for me becomes futile when I have lost my powers of reason (even though I may not be terminally ill), they express a vision of the person that divorces personhood from organic bodily life. They decline to take into their understanding of the person defect, dependence, or disability. But in judging that caregivers need not be bound forever by directions I have stipulated in advance, when my condition was quite different from what it has now become, they accept the need to live out the body's history, and they decline to give privileged status to the person's existence at one earlier moment in time.

Rethinking the *Eidos*

If we could develop an increased sense of irony about the course the bioethics movement has taken, we might be well positioned to think about the important questions for everyday life with which it here deals. The ironies are a clue to our confusions. Is it not striking that just at the moment when the idea of living wills seems to have triumphed, when federal law has required hospitals to make certain we know of our right to execute an advance directive, bioethicists should begin to wonder whether living wills are not themselves problematic? Having gotten what we thought we wanted — a law undergirded by a certain vision of the person — we begin to discern problems.

Thus, for example, John A. Robertson has had "Second Thoughts on Living Wills."[22] There are, he notes, spheres of life in which we do not hold a person to an understanding he or she had previously stated. We do not, for example, hold surrogate mothers to contracts. Yet, we are reluctant to recognize that when Meilaender becomes incompetent — severely demented, let us say — his interests may well shift. We prefer to suppose that his person was complete and perfect at some earlier point in his development — when say, at age forty-five he executed a living will. We hesitate to consider that what the forty-five-year-old Meilaender thought should be done to and for a demented Meilaender may not be in the latter's best interest. His life circumstances have changed drastically; he has become more simply and completely organism and less neocortex. If we would care for him, we must take that into account. And if we do not take it into our reckoning, if we blindly follow whatever directions the forty-five-year-old Meilaender gave, it is not clear that we can really claim to have the best interests of *this* patient — the Meilaender now before us — at the center of our concern.

Something like that is Robertson's argument, and it makes good sense. For it essentially denies that we should think of the person as a perfect *eidos* captured at a moment in time, and, less directly, it invites us to think of the person as a someone who has a history, as animated earth. But that is not really Robertson's intent. He sees that the living will has become essentially "a device that functions to avoid assessing incompetent patient interests," but his real aim is to encourage us to take up "the difficult task of determining which incompetent states of existence are worth protecting." This can only land him back in the muddle from which he is trying to escape. He is back to thinking of personhood as something added to existence — and well on his way, therefore, to the conception of personhood that gave rise to an emphasis on autonomy, which in turn suggested the living will as a useful way to exercise our autonomy, which — or so he thinks — is a path strewn with "conceptual frailties." He wants us not to live out the destiny of the body but to escape it.

Life as "Someone Who"

To have a life is to be *terra animata,* a living body whose natural history has a trajectory. It is to be someone who has a history, not a someone with certain capacities or characteristics. In our history this understanding of the person was most fully developed when Christians had to make sense of the claim that in Jesus of Nazareth both divine and human natures were joined in one person.[23] Christians did not wish to say that there were really two persons (two sets of personal characteristics) in Christ; hence, they could not formulate his personal identity in terms of capacities or characteristics. They could speak of his person only as an individual with a history, a "someone who." The personal is not just an example of the universal form; rather, the general characteristics exist in and through the individual person. And we can come to know such persons only by entering into their history, by personal engagement and commitment to them, not by measuring them against an ideal of health or personhood.

Perhaps such an understanding of the person is also available to us through reflection upon our life as embodied beings. "Embodiment is a curse only for those who believe they deserve to be gods."[24] If Origen's account of the resurrected body seems to have lost much of what we mean by embodiment, he had at least this excuse: he genuinely believed that God intended to make humankind divine. That bioethics — and our culture more generally — is in danger of losing the body in search of the person is harder to understand, unless in our own way we believe that we deserve to be gods.

James Rachels, arguing that ethics must and can get along quite well without God, has recently distinguished between biological and biographical life, arguing that only the second of these is of any value to us.[25] Biological life has instrumental value, since apart from it there is no possibility of realizing biographical life, but biological life without the possibility of self-consciousness and self-control can be of no value to us. In such a state we no longer have any interest in living, and we cannot be harmed if our life is not preserved.

Perhaps, though, such arguments do not take seriously enough the *terra* of which we are made. What Rachels never explains, for example, is why one's period of decline is not part of one's personal history, one's biography. As John Kleinig suggests, "Karen Ann Quinlan's biography did not end in 1975, when she became permanently comatose. It continued for another ten years. That was part of the tragedy of her life."[26] From zygote to irreversible coma, each life is a single personal history. We may, Kleinig notes, distinguish different points in this story, from potentiality to zenith to residuality. But the zenith is not the person. "Human beings are continuants, organisms with a history that extends beyond their immediate present, usually forward and backward. What has come to be seen as 'personhood,' a selected segment of that organismic trajectory, is connected to its earlier and later phases by a complex of factors — physical, social, psychological — that constitutes part of a single history."

Indeed, it is not at all strange to suggest that even the unaware living body has "interests." For the living body takes in nourishment and uses it; the living body struggles against infection and injury. And if we remember "the somatic dimensions of personality, as expressed for instance in face and hands,"[27] we may recognize in the living body the place — the only place — through which the person is present with us. This does not mean that the person is "merely" body; indeed, in such contexts the word "merely" is always a dangerous word. As bodies we are located in time, space, and history; yet, we also transcend that location to some degree. Indeed, from the Christian perspective with which I began, it is right to say that, precisely because we are made for God, we indefinitely transcend our historical location. But it is as embodied creatures that we do so, and our person cannot be divorced from the body and its natural trajectory. This is not vitalism; it is "the wisdom of the body" (p. 358). It is the wisdom to see that every human life is a story and has a narrative quality — a plot to be lived out. That story begins before we are conscious of it, and, for many of us, continues after we have lost consciousness of it. Yet, each narrative is the story of "someone who" — someone who, as a living body, has a history.

Caught as we are within the midst of our own life stories, and unable as we are to grasp anyone else's story as a single whole, we have to admit that only God can see us as the persons we are — can catch the self and hold it still. What exactly we will be like when we are with God is, therefore, always beyond our capacity to say. But it will be the completion of the someone who we were and are, and we should not, therefore, settle for any more truncated vision of the person even here and now.

Notes

1. St. Augustine, *De civitate Dei,* trans. Henry Bettenson (New York: Penguin Books, 1972), 20.20. Future citations will be given by book and chapter number within parentheses in the body of the text.

2. For much of what follows about the early Fathers I draw upon J. N. D. Kelly, *Early Christian Doctrines* (New York: Harper & Row, 1960), pp. 464-79. I am indebted to Robert Wilken for drawing my attention to Kelly's discussion.

3. C. S. Lewis, *Miracles* (New York: Macmillan, 1947), p. 166.

4. Saint Thomas Aquinas, *Summa contra gentiles,* trans. Charles J. O'Neil (Notre Dame: University of Notre Dame Press, 1975), 4.81.12. Future citations will be given by book, chapter, and paragraph number within parentheses in the body of the text.

5. Jonathan Edwards, *Works,* vol. 8, *Ethical Writings,* ed. Paul Ramsey (New Haven: Yale University Press, 1989), p. 371.

6. Austin Farrer, *Love Almighty and Ills Unlimited* (Garden City, N.Y.: Doubleday & Company, 1961), p. 166. For his discussion more generally, see the Appendix, "Imperfect Lives," pp. 166-68.

7. David H. Smith, *Health and Medicine in the Anglican Tradition* (New York: Crossroad, 1986), p. 10.

8. Holmes Rolston III, "The Irreversibly Comatose: Respect for the Subhuman in Human Life," *Journal of Medicine and Philosophy* 7 (1986): 337-54.

9. Robertson Davies, *The Rebel Angels* (New York: Penguin Books, 1983), pp. 249ff.

10. Joseph Fletcher, "Four Indicators of Humanhood: The Enquiry Matures," *Hastings Center Report* 4, no. 6 (1974): 4-7.

11. I have discussed this from another angle in chapter 8 of *Faith and Faithfulness* (Notre Dame: University of Notre Dame Press, 1991).

12. Lawrence J. Schneiderman, Nancy S. Jecker, and Robert R. Jonsen, "Medical Futility: Its Meaning and Ethical Implications," *Annals of Internal Medicine* 112 (June 1990): 949-54.

13. E. Cranford, "The Persistent Vegetative State: The Medical Reality (Getting the Facts Straight)," *Hastings Center Report* 18, no. 1 (1988): 27-32.

14. Schneiderman et al., "Medical Futility," p. 952.

15. Bart Collopy, Philip Boyle, and Bruce Jennings, "New Directions in Nursing Home Ethics," special supplement, *Hastings Center Report* 21, no. 2 (1991): 1-16.

16. Paul Ramsey, *The Patient as Person* (New Haven: Yale University Press, 1970), p. xiii.

17. Hans Jonas, "The Burden and Blessing of Mortality," *Hastings Center Report* 22, no. 1 (1992): 34-40.

18. For the historical information that follows I rely upon George J. Annas, "The Health Care Proxy and the Living Will," *NEJM* 324 (25 April 1991): 1210-13.

19. Alexander Morgan Capron, "In Re Helga Wanglie," *Hastings Center Report* 21, no. 5 (1991): 26-28.

20. My distinction here bears some similarities to James Childress's distinction between autonomy as an end state and autonomy as a side constraint. Cf. his *Who Should Decide? Paternalism in Health Care* (New York: Oxford University Press, 1982), p. 64.

21. Schneiderman et al., "Medical Futility," p. 952.

22. John A. Robertson, "Second Thoughts on Living Wills," *Hastings Center Report* 21, no. 6 (1991): 6-9.

23. I have discussed this point more fully (and acknowledged my indebtedness for it to Oliver O'Donovan) in *Faith and Faithfulness,* pp. 45-47.

25. James Rachels, *Created from Animals: The Moral Implications of Darwinism* (New York: Oxford University Press, 1990), pp. 198ff.

26. John Kleinig, *Valuing Life* (Princeton: Princeton University Press, 1991), p. 201.

27. Rolston, "Irreversibly Comatose," p. 352.

55 "Embodiment" and Moral Critique: A Christian Social Perspective

Lisa Sowle Cahill

"Embodiment" is frequently lifted up as central in critiques of the Western moral tradition on both sex and medicine. Yet the prominence of this theme is in some respects puzzling. After all, talk and practice in these two areas could hardly be more explicit about having the "body" as a key concern. Indeed, ethics as discourse about human relations and practices is always at some level about the body. . . .

What, then, could be intended by current appeals to recover the significance of the body for moral discourse? Most ethicists use the theme of embodiment to counteract a dualism about body and mind in which the body tends to come off as the inferior partner in an uneasy relationship. Contemporary ethicists, both religious and philosophical, see the integration of body and mind or spirit as a value and goal. Yet, somewhat paradoxically, choice, consent, and autonomy can be so central in (Western) moral and policy discussions that protection of freedom serves to justify almost any medical or technological manipulation of his or her body that an informed moral agent elects. Moreover, liberal moral theory about choice rarely succeeds in integrating the body and the embodied agent or self with their social context. Integration needs to occur not only between body and mind, but also among body, mind, and society. The body is always central in defining the self, while in all cultures, the meaning of the body reflects and augments social relationships. To understand the significance of embodiment for bioethics, it will be useful to set references to the body in sexual and medical ethics against broader discussions of body and society in philosophical, anthropological, and religious discourse. In so doing, it must be noted that society influences and shapes the bodily experience of the self not only in negative, repressive ways, but also in positive, expressive ways.

A thesis I want to develop is that a positive, integral view of the self as embodied and as intrinsically social does not require the rejection of control of the body in relation to the values of an encompassing social order. To advance this thesis, I will review dualism in the Western tradition, including modern versions of it which focus on autonomy; will examine recent critiques of mind-body dualism; and will examine the proposal, differently elaborated by Michel Foucault and Mary Douglas, that the self-understanding and social agency of the embodied self reflects and reinforces social organization. Drawing on their work as well as that of Peter Brown, I will use Christian sources to show that the disciplined body can and has functioned as a countersign to hierarchy and domination, and as an inaugural sign of a new social order characterized by solidarity and equality. Consequences for the practice of medicine follow from changed relationships in general, and in particular from Christian symbolization of the new order through the experiences of bodily illness, pain, healing, and death.[1]

Dualism and Western Tradition

A matter of concern for many ethicists is a body-spirit dualism which pervades Western (North Atlantic) culture, and which was expressed in Christian tradition by a negative view of the body as unruly and in need of control. In contemporary medical practice, we find a different but not unrelated objectification of the body as the site of technical intervention, and as the material or even

---

From L. Sowle Cahill and M. A. Farley, *Embodiment, Morality, and Medicine* (Dordrecht: Kluwer Academic Publishers, 1995): 199-214. Slightly abridged and edited from the original. Used with kind permission from Kluwer Academic Publishers.

property regarding which autonomous persons exercise free consent.

This dualism about the body's relation to the mind or spirit has not been a problem to the same degree in many other cultures and religions. Islam and Judaism assume a strong integration of body and spirit, even though those traditions, like others, are occasionally beset by dualistic strands and the denigration of women's bodies. ([5], pp. 23-55). African religious traditions see the body as so essential to the person that the physical integrity of the body is crucial to the individual's successful passage into the afterlife ([5], pp. 141-53). Similarly, in many Asian philosophical traditions (for instance, those of India, China, Japan), the mind-body relation might be better described as a symbiotic "polarity" within an integrated whole, than as a "duality" ([1], p. 159). Moreover, the relation of mind to body becomes in these traditions not a philosophical or epistemological problem of the reconciliation of two diverse elements, but a practical matter of improved integration of the self through ritual and self-cultivation or training.

> The process may proceed by the mind's training the body or the body's training the mind. In the former case, the mind sets a pattern for the body to follow; in the latter the body leads the mind (through controlled breathing, for example) to a state of tranquility or creativity. . . . The unity of mind and body is not to be discovered, but achieved ([10], p. xviii).

June O'Connor's account of abortion in Japan shows precisely that it is through a *ritual practice* of recognizing the aborted fetus that issues of women's choice to abort, the social circumstances of the abortion, women's and men's emotions about the event and their physical parenthood, and the physical-spiritual existence of the unborn child are brought into conjunction and addressed, if not resolved ([5], pp. 93-111).

In much of the Western tradition, however, mind and body have often been seen as discrete entities whose conjunction is uncertain, posing a philosophical problem. Modern science builds a strictly material body, and locates the causes of its illness and health in material causes, tending thereby to erode both the interdependence of spiritual and physiological states, and the connectedness of the embodied self with other elements and presences in the cosmos ([18], p. 133). Many place the blame on Descartes and his metaphor of the body as "machine" (e.g., [5], pp. 169-83). By philosophically privileging thought over physical existence as constitutive of the person, Descartes laid the way for later disembodiments and dehistoricizations of subjectivity, and for the body's deprivation of its role in knowledge and in moral valuation.

But Western dualism did not originate in the seventeenth century. While Aristotle cultivated virtue through practical wisdom in daily, bodily, social life, other ancient Greek philosophers deliberated on the distance between the world of lived experience and the world of unmediated truth and goodness. The heights of spiritual and intellectual accomplishment seemed to require escape from the exigencies and tensions of physical function and survival. The Platonists, and to a lesser extent the Stoics, armed their approach to the body with asceticism and rational direction, an approach attractive to many later Christian authors. On the one hand, the problematic body is subject to an impressive number of "contingencies," such as the need for food and shelter, and the liability to torture and imprisonment. On the other, when the drive to fulfill its own needs becomes stronger than the rational purposes by which one tries to channel or restrain them, the body seems to have a "mind of its own" ([13], pp. 130-31). In dualistic views of the body and mind or spirit, body still defines self insofar as the virtues of rationality and asceticism move to center stage precisely in reaction to bodily realities.

Body and Self in Christianity

One finds, if anything, an anti-dualism about the body in the gospels. God's reign is realized in the life and ministry of a man formed bodily in the womb of a woman, a man who in his very walking, sleeping, eating, drinking, talking, touching, fasting, night-watching, pain, and death makes present the compassion of God for human suffering. Human persons are drawn into God's own love and life through the resurrection of their bodies. In earthly existence, the healing of illness is linked to faith, and human beings are called to alleviate the physical hunger, nakedness, and pain of neighbors and enemies alike.

St. Paul may reflect some of the anxieties of the philosophers when he laments that "I delight in the law of God, in my inmost self, but I see in my members another law at war with the law of my mind and making me captive to the law of sin which dwells in my members" (Rom 7:22-23). But despite his appreciation of the recalcitrance of the body in conforming to spiritual aims, Paul more generally understands "flesh" in terms of any sinful turning from God or captivity to the world and its powers. "Spirit" as flesh's opposite transforms not only the mind but the whole person to a life of righteousness through the indwelling Spirit of God. Certainly, notwithstanding its potentially hierarchical uses, Paul's master metaphor of the Christian community as "Body of Christ" depends on the literal incorporation of disciples in all their physical reality. In his reaction against prostitution, he insists, "The body is not meant for immorality, but for the Lord, and the Lord for the body. . . . Do you not know that your bodies are members of Christ? . . . Do you not know that your body is a temple of the Holy Spirit within you . . . ? . . . So glorify God in your body" (1 Cor 6:13-20).

Ambivalence toward the body assumed a higher profile in the tradition, however, as Christians battled and were in the process influenced by, gnostic and other dualistic worldviews. An early example is Origin, who, like Plato, saw the differences among creatures as marks of their deviation from an original unity of being, and who was reputed at least to have had himself castrated by a doctor in order to avoid either sexual incontinence or the appearance of immorality in his spiritual relationships with women ([2], p. 168). Augustine is another great thinker whose dualistic inclinations were eventually reconciled to but never eliminated from his defense of the body against Manichean assaults on marriage and childbearing. Though Augustine defined procreation of offspring as a "good" of marriage (*On the Good of Marriage*, 6-7, trans. Deferrari), he was nevertheless able to speculate that in the Garden of Eden conception might have been accomplished by a passionless act of the will (*City of God*, XIV, trans. Dods).

Despite the ultimate victory of the orthodox Christian view that the body is not only essential to the person, but is good as created and redeemed, the uncertainty of much of the tradition's investment in that view led not only to now-incredible theological proposals, but also to much agony of human spirit and body alike. "The very matter-of-fact manner in which monastic sources report bloody, botched attempts at self-castration by desperate monks shocks us by its lack of surprise" ([2], p. xviii).

Dualism in Contemporary Views

The "old" dualism of Western culture, reinforced historically by Christianity, saw the body (especially the sexual body) as the enemy of rational control and requiring subjugation. A "new" dualism, which sees the body as raw material for choice and intervention, is exercised via the technical and instrumental rationality guiding much of modern science. . . . Defining instrumental reason as the calculation of maximum efficiency in pursuing means to a given end, Charles Taylor notes its evidence "in the prestige and aura that surround technology," making us believe that "we should seek technological solutions even when something very different is called for" ([19], pp. 5-6).

The reign of informed consent in bioethics today is a symptom of technical rationality operating within a lingering body-mind dualism. The self is defined as an autonomous, private, and self-constituting will. After Nuremburg, we may hardly forget that the principle of consent is important to maintain the dignity and inviolability of persons. However, the near absoluteness and self-sufficiency of this criterion in moral decisions about medical care and research reveals a modern version of the idea that the body is inferior and essentially alien to personal freedom. The rhetoric of choice promoting a legal right to physician-assisted suicide or euthanasia is a glaring example, as is the array of "new reproductive technologies" designed to take advantage of all available means to force the realization of the self's chosen aims. The body relates to the self's freedom primarily as matter to be manipulated, matter which when resistant to the self's elected projects, may and must be overcome or circumvented.

It would be foolish to repudiate all forms of medical resistance to bodily limitations or failures, or to conform the identity of the self to physiological capacities (as do patriarchal definitions of women's roles). The issue is not a choice between bodiliness and freedom, but the appropriate integration of the self *as* body, mind, will, and spirit. The moral exclusions and permissions a wise and practicable integration would entail are no simple matter to define, and no doubt cannot be defined finally or abstractly. Suffice it to say that a naturalist morality of the body, a libertarian morality of the will, a rationalist morality of the intellect, and a fundamentalist morality of divine command all fail to meet the standard of a nuanced and experientially true approach to moral agency. All the constitutive dimensions of the self should be mutually engaged and allowed to carry some normative moral force.

One dangerous consequence of holding informed consent not only as necessary but as the sufficient principle of bioethics is that to do so keeps out of our range of vision broader social relations which impinge on the identity of the self and its "free" choices, including relations and practices focused on the body. Obvious examples are gender, race, and class expectations that make choices less than free, or that create blindnesses and injustices which cannot be redressed by focusing narrowly on providing information and eliciting a decision. . . . The informed consent criterion also tends to neglect positive moral experiences and values which may be important to moral identity but which are not captured by the simple ideal of well-informed choice. . . .

Embodiment as a Critical Theme in Sexual and Medical Ethics

It is in sexual ethics that the appeal to embodiment has been most visible. This appeal typically supports a claim that traditional moral norms have been defined in the abstract (with authority attributed to God or to nature), and with inadequate attention to the normative value of the actual, embodied experience of sex. For example, to define procreation as the principal purpose of sexual intercourse is to neglect if not ignore other aspects of sexual experience, such as pleasure, intimacy, and homoeroticism. These aspects might also define goods and values whose claim should be recognized in moral choices. No doubt it *is* actual experience in precisely such dimensions that the experientially incommensurate norms are intended to control. In this sense, they do address sexual reality, even if only to assert a norm over against it. But this fact only verifies the critique: received sexual norms themselves do not build constructively on the embodied experience of the persons they are aimed to address. As far as sex is concerned, then, the corrective advanced via "embodiment" is the counteraction of repressive attitudes toward the body with a more positive attitude toward the fullness of its capacities, an important feature of which is the potential of the sexual body for intimacy and pleasure as well as for procreation.

Because it is derived from biological sex as its social interpretation, gender also enters into the positive reconstrual of the body. Specifically, women's bodies are affirmed as constituting selves who are equal to men in moral agency and moral value. Women's reproductive capacities in no way signal lesser rational or volitional abilities, nor should women's roles be constrained or accorded lesser value on account of women's distinctive reproductive contributions. Women's bodies are a source of moral knowledge equal to, if somewhat different from, that yielded by the male embodied experience.

In medicine, the point commonly advanced by means of the theme of embodiment is that the "patient" whose body is manipulated is also a "person" who is embodied. The self is constituted by the person's materiality as much as by his or her intellectual, spiritual, and psychological dimensions. The body enters into the subjectivity of the person, mediates that subjectivity to the world, and is a medium through which the world and other persons interact with the subject as embodied self. In the words of Merleau-Ponty, "the body expresses total existence, not because it is an external accomplishment to that existence, but because existence comes into its own in the body" ([14], p. 166). Bodies are not just living organisms which as such become the objects of scientific, technical interventions. Bodies are the spatiality and temporality of selves, and it is to person — not only to bodies — that medical professionals must respond. In medicine, the corrective which "embodiment" brings is a holistic view of the person. In addition to the unity of self and body, this holism extends to a unity of all the physical parts and processes of the body in their personal and social meanings.

It is just this emphasis on holism that often brings sexual discourse into conjunction with biomedical talk of the significance of body, especially in the case of the medical relevance of biological sex socially mediated as gender. The self as embodied is quite strongly constituted by the social significance of gender as an elaboration of maleness or femaleness. Medical practice can become oppressive to women to the extent that it incorporates patriarchal gender models in its approach to women's health. A revealing treatment of the practical interpenetration of sexual and medical discourses is Emily Martin's *The Woman in the Body* ([12]). In the medicalization of women's reproductive processes, the female body is often objectified in a way reflecting cultural views of women's passivity and inferiority. The obstetrician, for instance, often assumes the role of "supervisor or foreman" of a labor process in which two images complete: "the uterus as a machine that produces the baby and the woman as laborer who produces the baby" ([12], p. 63). If Gerda Lerner is right that patriarchy is the first and paradigm case of oppression ([11]) then we will not be surprised to see further objectification of the bodies of those in "lower" racial, ethnic, and class groups, all of which are compounded when the medical subject/object is a woman.

In overview, Western authors writing today . . . are almost unanimously inclined to see dualism as bad and integration as a value, and to affirm that the body's contribution to selfhood is not only essential but is a component of the highest levels of human value and accomplishment, such as love, friendship, moral insight, and art. Contemporary Western affirmations of embodiment as a value may be seen to address three axes along which the body is understood, each structured by an internal polarity. Affirmations of embodiment are generally intended to move perception and practice away from the first pole in each set, and toward the second. These axes are *dualism — integration* (of body and mind, reason, or spirit); *denigration — affirmation* (of the body as part of the person); and *control — freedom* (presence or absence of a definite social ordering of the parts and processes of one's own body, as well as of one's own person in relation to the bodies of others). The third move in combination with the first two has a somewhat paradoxical effect at the level of moral practice and public policy. There we find a cultural and philosophical insistence on the freedom to control, reshape, or even kill the body as a prerequisite of genuine moral agency and as a form of resistance to the heteronomous control of social institutions which serve the vested interests of some groups of individuals in control over the bodies of others.

We find examples in the phrasing of the morality of avoiding or undertaking parenthood as a matter of reproductive choice, and when sexual morality is phrased as a matter of creating or constructing one's own sexual identity. The merits of both agendas lie in their unmasking definitions of the body's moral significance which employ a rhetoric of the biologically natural to disguise social power relationships. However, such critiques would be strengthened by the development of positive alternative ways to bring freedom back into interdependence with the body, and with the other material and social conditions of freedom. Charles Taylor instructs us that any nontrivial "choice" reflects a set of value priorities which at the very least highlight the realms of moral conduct which are of highest importance, and which reflect a dialogical community of other moral agents ([19], p. 39).[2] Freedom as a moral value makes no sense without a material and social context.

The Body as Symbol of Social Organization

A lesson that we learn in different ways from Mary Douglas and Michel Foucault is that the individual body is always interpreted and ordered to reflect social relationships. It is both a symbol of those relations and a medium through which they are realized, realigned, or replaced. Conceptions of the individual body and of the social body are interdependent. Interestingly, writers who explore the social history behind the early Christian religious world often draw on Mary Douglas and, less centrally, on Foucault. (Peter Brown [2] cites both in his bibliography; see John Dominic Crossan [6], p. 77) for a discussion of Mary Douglas.)[3] A counterpoint to the social interpretation of the body is the fact that the body is to some extent a biological given. Presumed "universals" of human embodiment include need for food and shelter, sexuality and reproduction, pain and pleasure, health and disease, aging and death. At the same time many commentators on embodiment focus on the variety of ways in which such embodied experiences as these have been understood and on how religious understandings of embodiment have changed or remain in need of change.

Foucault writes precisely to resist the "universals" of reason and nature by showing that experience and knowledge are thoroughly historical. He argues that our self-consciousness, our freedom, our values, and our very construal of what is central in our own experience are created by social practices which represent and perpetuate power relationships. Part of the originality of his contribution lies in his demonstration that in order to shape the self at its deepest levels, power does not need to coerce consciousness or behavior directly. Power determines consciousness through a comprehensive set of strategies which focus on the body (whether through hospitals, prisons, insane asylums, education, theories of sex, and — across all of these — modern medicine), and which determine the parameters within which we imagine our identity and our options. Foucault convincingly displays the ways in which power "controls" bodies as a positive and constructive force, not just by repression and constraint. He writes of "deployment" of discourses or "regimes" of knowledge and power which induce people to construct reality on their terms. He regards the whole notion of "sexuality" as such a discourse ([9]). He illustrates how Christian confessional practice and medical-psychiatric discourses about sex, supposedly responsible for repression, have actually resulted in endlessly proliferating talk about sex and in our conviction that the secret and truth of our very being lie in our sexual identity and behavior.[4] Our present quest for sexual "liberation" is no more than the ultimate victory of a discourse of sexuality which procures our consent to our own domination by means of a discipline of the body which we all too readily embrace ([9], pp. 151-59). While Foucault resists describing power as the "power of" any distinct social group by which it is consciously and purposively exercised, he often portrays medical science as facilitating the control both of individuals and of whole populations by its socially aggressive definitions of the body's significance.

Mary Douglas also sees the meaning of the body as culturally determined to a large extent. She finds in all cultures a human "drive to achieve consonance between social and physical and emotional experience" which finds expression in the use of the body as a natural symbol of the social order. The symbolic potentials of the body are in some ways culturally constant. To present the front rather than the back of one's body signifies respect; physical closeness signifies intimacy; the casting-off of physical waste products (spitting, urinating) is incompatible with formal discourse and may be used to interrupt it; and the more strongly classified and controlled is the social hierarchy, the more controlled the individual's bodily movements will be, even to the point of "etherealization" or the relative disembodiment of personal interactions ([7], pp. 100-101).

In cultures in which there is a strongly defined structuring of the roles of individuals and groups, controlled and formal behavior will also be highly valued ([7], p. 99). Conversely, in societies in which individuality and freedom are prized over and above social expectations, freedom of physical movement and expression — the individual's "control" over his or her own body — will also be accepted and valued. It is important to make explicit the implication, however, that even in ostensibly unrestricted societies, the significance of the body and its movements still follow social norms, are still ordered and even in a sense controlled by the social ethos.

Douglas discerns a movement in Western societies away from systems characterized by a high respect for social roles and structures, and the duties they present for individuals, to systems in which the sincerity and authenticity of the subject become more important than structures, and in which personal success eventually overrides respect for roles and duties ([7], p. 50). The latter sort of society, to which Douglas says "we" now belong, sees a demise of ritualism in public and private ("the celebration of Sunday dinner"), and a great informality of social and family life (the disappearance of rank according to age and sex, as reflected in the arrangement of living room chairs) ([7], p. 55). Children are educated to be interested in their own internal states and the feelings of others. But the "seeds of alienation" ([7], p. 190) are contained in the relocation of control to the personal system, and the lack of integration of the individual with the social body. We may infer that alienation from the social significance of one's own body will also result, so that individuals neither realize the social shaping of their embodied behavior nor take into account the social effects of their choices to execute their sincere and "autonomous" life-plans by means of embodied relationships. They may even see the body as, in Douglas's phrase, an "alien husk" from which to escape ([7], p. 191).

Despite a common emphasis on socialization of the body, Douglas and Foucault obviously differ in significant ways. First, Douglas sees the body in its physicality as in some sense a universal which is socially interpreted ([7], p. ivx), while Foucault edges toward the claim that the body is itself a social construction. Second, Douglas avoids Foucault's heavy, even cynical, association of social control with domination, leaving open in her cross-cultural studies the possibility that the body and its parts can be ordered to reinforce social relationships which are not necessarily repressive, or which are at least characterized by a solidarity in which the embodied individual immediately participates.

In her study of trance states ([7], pp. 104-10), Mary Douglas also paves the way to a recognition, fully achieved for instance in the work of Caroline Walker Bynum ([4], [3]), that Christianity, along with most or all other societies, sees the body (not only the spirit) as an avenue of transcendence and even of union with the divine. "Control, discipline, even torture of the flesh is, in medieval devotion, not so much the rejection of physicality as the elevation of it — a horrible yet delicious elevation — into a means of access to the divine" ([3], p. 182). Among the most universal bodily routes to the divinity are sex, food, and death, along with death's foretastes, pain and illness. Christianity has used all three.

The Body and Christian Society

While positive construals of the religious significance of sexual activity may have been scarce in Christian culture until the modern period, [5] permanent virginity as a religiously dedicated and ideal sexual identity was a distinctive contribution of early Christianity (1 Cor 7:8; this is Peter Brown's thesis [2]). Moreover, Bynum illustrates that the self-expressions of many mystics have strongly physical and indirectly sexual overtones ([4], p. 248; [3], p. 133). Food becomes a physical sharing in the divine life in the eucharistic meal ([4], pp. 252-53); in the sharing of food with the poor in imitation of God's mercy (Lk 6:36; Acts 6:1-6); in mystical and symbolic experiences of giving and receiving nurturance through feeding, even nursing ([4], pp. 269-76; [3], p. 133); and in the renunciation of food by fasting, complemented by the feast in celebration of divine grace and presence ([4], p. 250).

Likewise, Christianity is hardly alone among the world's religions in seeing death as a point of entry into a transcendent realm and of approach to God. Christians elaborate the religious significance of death in terms of last rites for the dying, funerary and burial practices, veneration of the dead and of their relics, martyrdom, resurrection, eternal life, eternal reward and punishment, and God's sharing in human death through the Cross of Christ. Anticipations of death in this life, often called "mortifications" of the body, include ascetic deprivation of the body and deliberate infliction of pain on it (including fasting); religious interpretations of illness as a trial, a gift, or a sign of sanctity; healing of illness, including the New Testament healing miracles and the religious ministries of healing which have existed throughout Christian tradition; and the actual bodily manifestation of the wounds which caused Christ's death (stigmata). Mystical experience also can include sensations of pain and of dying or of being near death or of passing through it. . . .

These examples serve to demonstrate that Christianity has been neither intransigently dualistic nor negative about the body. They also indicate that a positive, integrated approach to the body and soul, or body and mind, need not exclude — indeed may depend upon — an ordering of the body in relation to a social vision. But where

Foucault tends to portray social forces which determine the significance of the body as discourses of power-knowledge which serve regimes of domination, Douglas permits us to see that the background of social conditions within which we are embodied provides us with a framework for channeling, shaping, and disciplining our embodied experiences. Freedom never exists outside of some social vision; the communal vision which shapes bodily experience also brings the self's embodiment to consciousness, to expression, and to social agency.

Like other societies, Christianity both channels a social vision through the body, and defines community partly in terms of bodily experiences and roles. As current scholarship attests, the biblically authentic Christian social vision is characterized by inclusiveness and solidarity, especially toward enemies and toward marginalized and outcast persons and groups. The solidarity of the New Testament communities challenged social relations built on status, power, and economic dependency, even if it did not completely overturn them.[6] Inclusive solidarity as a defining feature of Jesus' kingdom preaching is familiar in the Sermon on the Mount's Beatitudes (Matt 5:1-12), and in Jesus' instruction to "love your enemies, do good to those who hate you" (Lk 6:27); in the parable of the Good Samaritan (Lk 10:30-37); in Jesus' association with sinners and outcasts; in his approach to women; in his sacrificial death. A representative restatement of the cultural challenge presented by Jesus and his first followers is offered by John Dominic Crossan. In Jesus' teaching, life, and death,

> the Kingdom of God is a community of radical or unbrokered equality in which individuals are in direct contact with one another and with God, unmediated by any established brokers or fixed locations ([6], p. 101).

Crossan uses Mary Douglas on the body as a microcosm of the social order to show how Jesus manifested social equality through practices of table fellowship, itinerancy, healing, the raising of Lazarus, and exorcisms. Jesus' healing miracles are of special relevance to medical practice. For Crossan, their significance does not consist in any intervention into the natural, physical order of "disease" but into the social world of "illness," in which disease often meant ritual uncleanness and social ostracization. Jesus' violation of the purity code by contact with a leper challenged both the body politic and the priestly authorities, impugning "the rights and prerogatives of society's boundary keepers and controllers"([6], p. 82). Jesus' healing miracles are important for their social significance, for their relevance to the new kingdom which includes the "marginalized and disenfranchised" ([6], p. 83), and refuses the traditional boundaries of order and exclusion symbolized in the disordered and thus excluded body of the sick. The Christian transformation of the social significance of the diseased body both symbolizes, and advances at the practical level an inclusive community in which traditional hierarchies are overturned. A particularly good example is Jesus' healing of the woman who had had a "flow of blood" for twelve years (Mark 5:25-34), since she was not only sick but female. She would have been especially stigmatized if the hemorrhage from which she suffered involved menstrual blood, making her ritually impure.

Peter Brown illumines ways in which the early churches shaped the sexual body to advance this same vision. Especially in its implications for gender relations and for social relations of unequal power in general, this reshaping too is relevant to medical practice. Brown contrasts the hierarchical household of the ancient world with egalitarian Christian communities which threatened the social order. Celibacy was sometimes practiced in the ancient world, but it never replaced marriage as the general ideal and cornerstone of the social welfare. When undertaken, it was often temporary (as in the case of the Vestal Virgins). In Roman society, the sexual act, the relation of human and wife, their marriage, the hierarchy of the household, and the government of the state, were not only analogous as concentric circles of order, but were dependent upon one another for their existence.

Although conservation of seed was thought to enhance the vitality and strength of a man, "eugenic sex," in which man and woman united their seed with full concentration and proper decorum, was a social duty and would have positive effects on the health, character, and even sex of the resulting child ([2], pp. 20-210). The concord of the couple in marriage elaborated their sexual cooperation, and was the foundation of the properly ordered household. While the early Roman ideal was unity in body and mind of the spouses, the married couple was seen by the beginning of the late antique period "less as a pair of equal lovers than as a reassuring microcosm of the social order" ([2], p. 17). This order was clearly not only hierarchical but patriarchal. It encompassed first of all the household and estate, where the husband cultivated the traits of active virility in his own body and deportment, and administered the bodies of wife, children, and slaves. The household mirrored the public order maintained by the governing classes.

Against this environment, Christian sexual renunciation may be seen, not as a mere repression of the body under the influence of dualistic philosophical and religious currents, but as a form of resistance to the hierarchical social order maintained through the reality and the symbolism of sex, marriage, and family. Perpetual virginity transformed the bodies of both men and women in their social significance, and enabled Christians (perhaps most especially women) "to break with the discreet discipline of the ancient city" ([2], p. 31). And beyond transforming the orders of personal relationships taken for granted in the ethos of the age, continence also broke with the continuity of history and of generations, announcing the eschatological advent of the Kingdom of God, and a "new creation" ([2], pp. 32, 64, 435).

Paul had a distinctive way of refracting Christian social cohesiveness through the body. The body is sanctified and an inauguration of the new age insofar as it is a "temple of the Holy Spirit" (1 Cor 6:19). The community of disciples as a whole is the material and historical presence of the body of Christ. The body of the believer participates in this communal identity to so great an extent that an act of sexual immorality will contaminate the very body of Christ (1 Cor 7:15). Corinth was a place where division based on status had fractured the community and introduced disorder into this transformed community. Some at Corinth apparently had taken the solution of embracing celibacy and totally dissolving the household. Paul himself recognized the radical effects of Christian baptism as an induction into a new social order (Gal 3:28). However, he resisted complete separatism from the pagan world, and emphasized the continuing validity of social bonds, including marriage and slavery.

While Paul's preference for celibacy may reflect a Stoic dualism of reason and passion to some extent, it also signifies a radical critique of the social order in which hierarchy reigned. His stated reasons for the preference are a suspicion neither of women (for he addresses both the wife and the husband) nor of the body, nor of sex itself.[7] Marriage should be avoided specifically to avoid "anxiety about worldly affairs" — the business and ordering of the household. Paul desires "to promote good order" but instead, that is, "to secure your undivided devotion to the Lord" (1 Cor 7:32-35). In other words, celibacy is for the sake of the transformed and transforming social order of the eschatological community, of which the body is a symbol.

Even in preferring celibacy ("I wish that all were as I myself am" (1 Cor 7:7), Paul does not make this sign of the new order into an entrance requirement ("But each has his own special gift from God, one of one kind and one of another" (1 Cor 7:7). The egalitarian solidarity of discipleship can also be at least partially reflected in marriage, even though Paul anticipates that it will in that state be more difficult to maintain. For instance, wife and husband "rule" equally over one another's bodies (1 Cor 7:4); neither partner is to divorce an unbelieving spouse who is willing to continue the relationship, though either may do so if the spouse is not (1 Cor 7:12-16); and Christians are exhorted to enact the transformative effects of mutual love even within the hierarchical household (Eph 5:21-6:9).[8]

Yet, as we have seen, Paul specifically contrasts the social ordering celibacy symbolizes to the social order of that household. In later Christianity, celibacy became an instrument of hierarchical control over believers, especially clergy and religious. Yet, following Brown's lead, we may say that permanent virginity for early Christians signs, not merely or simply the evils of the sexual body, but the solidarity of the kingdom which is radical and total. Involvement with sex, even sex "well-ordered" from a cultural point of view, will involve the disciple with a set of social relationships (organized around sex, gender, procreation, and family) in which it will be difficult to live out fully the equality, solidarity, compassion, and mercy among men and women, slave and free, and finally Jew and gentile (Gal 3:28) in which the kingdom of God is present.

Paul's representation of the sexual body as not fundamentally compliant with the norms of the social order is carried out in the early Christians' presentation of the body and its functions as in other ways subversive of power and hierarchy. Many disciplines of the Christian body have to do with eating or feeding in a way which symbolizes the unity of the community. For instance, Paul accuses those who maintain distinctions among rich and poor at the eucharistic table, by providing sumptuously for themselves while others go hungry, of "profaning the body and blood of the Lord" (1 Cor 11:27). Ministers to the needy were appointed in the community, and were charged with such duties as distribution of food to widows. Whether Jewish or Greek, the widows should be treated similarly (Acts 6:1-6). Concerning whether Christians should partake of meat that has been offered to idols, Paul acknowledges that idols have no real existence (1 Cor 8:4), and that food in and of itself does not establish one's relationship with God (1 Cor 8:8). Nonetheless, each should be concerned for the consciences of others in the community, and should not cause scandal to "weaker" members who may not yet have reached the same freeing knowledge (1 Cor 8:7; 10:28-29). "'Knowledge' puffs up, but love builds up" (1 Cor 8:1). Love as solidarity in community is symbolized by a control of the body which denies that the knowledgeable are "superior."

Symbolizations of the new order by means of bodily suffering and death pervade the gospels and epistles, and center on the death and resurrection of Jesus. We may add just a few examples of the appropriation of this unifying death in the Christian life. Paul, whom later historical sources attest was eventually martyred, sees his own imprisonments as a confirmation of his defense of the gospel and as a means of strengthening other members of Christ's body in their commitment to the faith (Phil 1:7, 14; see also Col 4:10; Eph 3:1; 4:1, 6:20). In his own name as "a prisoner for the Lord," Paul implores the church at Ephesus "to lead a life worthy of the calling to which you have been called, with all lowliness and meekness, with patience, forebearing one another in love, eager to maintain the unity of the Spirit in the bond of peace" (Eph 4:1-3). Paul rejects the bodily mark of circumcision because it is used to distinguish higher religious status, to set off the "glory" of those who belong from those who do not (Gal 6;12-15). Instead, he says, he bears on his own body "the marks of Jesus," possibly a reference to his having been beaten (Gal 6:7). Although Paul's death is not recounted in the New Testament, the Acts of the Apostles tells of other martyrdoms, including the stoning of Stephen (Acts 7:57-60), and the death of James at the hands of Herod (Acts 12:1-2). Stephen, like Jesus, dies praying for the forgiveness of his persecutors (Acts 7:60).

Overview and Recommendations

Certainly in the tradition, perhaps most of all in Augustine's writings, Christian control of the sexual body has come into alignment with dualistic and negative currents, leading Christians to see the body preeminently as a temptation to sin. This negativity is not only not required by, but is inconsistent with, New Testament symbolization of the body, especially the presence of God's reign in Jesus' birth, life, death, and resurrection; the Christian community as inclusive Body of Christ; the resurrection of the body as the full incorporation of the whole person into God's kingdom.

As we bring Christian views of the body toward medical practice, what perhaps is most in need of emphasis is the positive *social* significance of those views. A first significance of embodiment for a Christian ethics of medicine and healing is the importance of a stance of compassion toward the sick on the part of the care-givers. The point is not pity, but an empathic identification with the suffering of the other, which, to the extent humanly possible, reaches through boundaries of race, gender, class, and economic status. Only then can one serve, as did the Good Samaritan, as a "neighbor" to those who are injured and vulnerable.

A second significance proceeds partly from that identification; it is the realization that we too suffer and die, whether pain and mortality mark us already in profound ways or in temporarily subtle ones. With that realization comes the recognition of the vulnerability of every human being, and the need of everyone for redemptive inclusion in the unity of all being which the Christian eucharist signifies and of which the mystics of all religions have had a premonition. Doctors and patients are but provisionally set apart by the pain and supplication of the latter. A third significance proceeds both from compassion and from the universality of disease and death. That is the moral importance of a genuinely inclusive social practice of health care, which alleviates suffering, even while acknowledging the inevitability of death, and the interdependence of health and bodily life with other social, personal, and spiritual goods.

The social significance of embodiment for a Christian bioethics is neither a knowing priesthood of the medical professions, nor a resignation to human suffering as "God's will," nor an absolutization of the individual's "right to life," nor even the cultivation of altruistic virtues by members of care-giving professions. It is the challenge to create a community of solidarity in which suffering and death are healed and avoided when possible, and are recognized as constitutive of human selfhood even after they are not. In such a community, the suffering and dying self would not experience dependency as defilement, but as an extenuation and deepening of the self's social destiny. All persons in such a community might learn to take their own bodily vulnerability as an occasion for self-transcendence through compassion for the vulnerability of others and in openness to the sustaining communion of being which Christians symbolize as "resurrection life."

Notes

1. Thanks to Francis Elvey, S.J., Margaret Farley, Karen Lebacqz, Therese Lysaught, and James Nelson for very helpful critical comments on a first version of this essay.

2. Taylor perceptively explains why "authenticity" as "self-determining freedom" has to depend on "the understanding that independent of my will there is something noble, courageous, and hence significant in giving shape to my own life." Within the horizon of values against which moral authenticity takes place, some issues and values are more important than others, or "the very idea of self-choice falls into triviality and hence incoherence" ([19], p. 39).

3. I am grateful to Francis Elvey, S.J. for sharing with me his work in progress on the relevance of Foucault and Douglas to Christian conceptions of the body, which he applies to Thomas Aquinas's use of the body as a metaphor for society.

4. As Michael Foucault shows so well, a "controlling" discourse about sex all the better serves to accentuate it, to elevate sex as the secret of the self's identity, so that the long-run effect is guilty fascination or confessional self-display, rather than repression. Perhaps a Christian dualism about sex has ensured the repetition of social situations in which a normative discourse of strict sexual control has been accompanied by or broken out into anarchic practices of sexual perversion, especially by those in power — including the age-old rape and prostitution of women and sexual exploitation of children, the Victorian "double standard," and sexual abuse by clergy.

5. Take possibly Ephesians 5:23-32 on husbands and wives, and recall the sacramental status of marriage in at least some Christian communities, e.g., the Roman Catholic.

6. Several authors have recently made this argument, based on a social history approach to the distribution of power and status in the communities in which Christianity first arose. An example is Halvor Moxnes ([15]). This literature commonly draws on Moses Finley's description of client-patron relationships in first-century society ([18]).

7. Scholars widely agree that 1 Cor 7:1 ("It is well for a man not to touch a woman") is Paul's restatement of his opponents' position, to which he is about to reply.

8. The critical question is whether a transformation which still leaves the essential hierarchical structure intact is an adequate social adaptation or a betrayal of Kingdom solidarity ([16]).

Bibliography

[1] Ames, R. T.: "The Meaning of the Body in Classic Chinese Philosophy," in T. P. Kasulis et al. (eds.), *Self as Body in Asian Theory and Practice,* State University of New York Press, Albany, pp. 157-77.

[2] Brown, P.: 1988, *The Body and Society: Men, Women, and Sexual Renunciation in Early Christianity,* Columbia University Press, New York.

[3] Bynum, C. W.: 1991, *Fragmentation and Redemption: Essays on Gender and the Human Body in Medieval Religion,* Zone Books, New York.

[4] Bynum, C. W.: 1987, *Holy Feast and Holy Fast: The Religious Significance of Food to Medieval Women,* University of California Press, Berkeley, Los Angeles and London.
[5] Cahill, L. S., and Farley, M. A. (eds.): 1995, *Embodiment, Morality, and Medicine,* Kluwer Academic Publishers, Dordrecht.
[6] Crossan, J. D.: 1993, *Jesus: A Revolutionary Biography,* HarperCollins Publishers, New York.
[7] Douglas, M.: 1973, *Natural Symbols: Explorations in Cosmology,* Barrie & Jenkins, London.
[8] Finley, M. I.: 1973, *The Ancient Economy,* University of California Press, Berkeley and Los Angeles.
[9] Foucault, M.: 1978, *The History of Sexuality, Vol.1: An Introduction,* R. Hurley (trans.), Random House, New York.
[10] Kasulis, T. P.: 1993, 'Introduction', in T. P. Kasulis et al. (eds.), *Self as Body in Asian Theory and Practice,* State University of New York Press, Albany, pp. ix-xx.
[11] Lerner, G.: 1986, *The Creation of Patriarchy,* Oxford University Press, New York and Oxford.
[12] Martin, E.: 1987, *The Woman in the Body: A Cultural Analysis of Reproduction,* Beacon Press, Boston.
[13] Meeks, W. A.: 1993, *The Origins of Christian Morality: The First Two Centuries,* Yale University Press, New Haven and London.
[14] Merleau-Ponty, M.: 1962, *Phenomenology of Perception,* C. Smith (trans.), Routledge and Kegan Paul, London and Henley, N.J.
[15] Moxnes, H.: 1988, *The Economy of the Kingdom: Social Conflict and Economic Relations in Luke's Gospel,* Fortress Press, Philadelphia.
[16] Schüssler Fiorenza, E.: 1983, *In Memory of Her: A Feminist Theological Reconstruction of Christian Origins,* Crossroad Publishing Company, New York.
[17] Sheets-Johnstone, M. (ed.): 1993, *Giving the Body Its Due,* State University of New York Press, Albany.
[18] Sheets-Johnstone, M.: 1993, "The Materialization of the Body: A History of Western Medicine, A History in Progress," in M. Sheets-Johnstone (ed.): 1993, *Giving the Body Its Due,* State University of New York Press, Albany, pp. 132-58.
[19] Taylor, C.: 1991, *The Ethics of Authenticity,* Harvard University Press, Cambridge, Mass., and London.
[20] Turner, B. S.: 1984, *The Body and Society: Explorations in Social Theory,* Basil Blackwell, Oxford and New York.

56 Man as Patient

Robert Jenson

I

Man-as-patient, man as the physician professionally sees him, is an image with at least two sides. One side is determined by the physician's role as a technician of the behavioral sciences, the other by his role as a man dealing with his fellowmen. Let us begin by considering each side separately.

The patient lies — or stands, or sits — before the physician as a complex and malfunctioning system which the physician is called on — perhaps by the patient himself, perhaps not — to repair. In this respect, the physician's situation with respect to the patient is not decisively different from that of a systems engineer working on a rocket's malfunctioning fuel valves; indeed, the parts may well be spread out on a table in very similar fashion. It is important to note here that the physician's recognition of the moral and religious involvement of his patient, as factors which must be dealt with and supported for their health-giving value, does not transcend this picture. The physician is a technician of all the behavioral sciences, which include psychology and sociology. From the therapeutic point of view, recognition of "the whole man" complete with "inner man" is merely recognition of certain subsystems besides the chemical and organic subsystems. These subsystems, too, may need repair, or may be utilized as supporting mechanisms for repair of other subsystems.

As a consequence, the patient, as his title indi-

From *Studies in Man, Medicine and Theology,* vol. 1, *Man, Medicine and Theology.* Division for Mission in North America, Lutheran Church in America, 1967. Used by permission.

cates, is notably passive. The understanding on both sides is that the physician will do the thinking and the patient will obey. The good patient is precisely the one who behaves in accordance with this understanding. Indeed, the patient has in all probability "gone to the doctor" on purpose to be relieved of his responsibility: One "calls the doctor" at just those points in life where we formerly "called on the gods." Textbooks on the subject quite properly, therefore, speak of "patient management." The patient has abdicated just that active determination of his affairs which might otherwise make "management" an inappropriate word.

Thus man-as-patient is *manipulated* and *manipulable* man. Nor should this be taken too spiritually; the sheer physical and psychological manipulation to which the patient is subjected is of great importance to his situation. Man-as-patient — his guts, his genitalia, his fears, values and convictions, the wax in his ears — is suddenly bereft of all personal mystery. The patient must very really abandon himself to the physician in order to become a patient at all. There is, of course, a certain amount of ritual here which functions to save face for the patient: The physician's decrees are "medical *advice*" and the patient is always free to "call in another man" (as we always were to try another god). Such face-saving is needed because the relation of doctor and patient is also a *personal* relation. We turn next to this other side of the matter.

Despite the depersonalizing tendency of the patient's situation, the physician inescapably sees in the patient a man like himself. Indeed, it is precisely because the doctor sees in the patient a man in need of help that he exercises his technique on him. Their relation is a *human* relation. It may even become the "doctor-patient" relation, which, as the profession is well aware, can be explosively and even magically intimate. Even when the relation is much less than this, it is almost always sufficiently personal that the physician can never see the patient *only* as a reparable, manipulable object. Yesterday the patient was the physician's golf partner; tomorrow — both hope — he will be again. And even if the patient is a total stranger, he could have been a friend and may yet become one.

Is there any conflict between these two sides of the image of man-as-patient? Many physicians seem to believe that a clash does exist. Indeed, the medical profession seems sometimes to have a bad conscience about its inability to reconcile the conflict it feels here (or perhaps it has a bad conscience about *not* feeling any conflict where it supposes that it ought to). Issue after issue of the journals, whose substantive articles discuss the patient solely as a malfunctioning system, include editorials or more philosophical pieces lamenting a felt loss of "the human element" in medical practice and decrying an alleged tendency to practice medicine "merely" as a technology. This literature contrasts "technique" with "medical wisdom"; the "science" with the "art" of medicine. "Humanitarianism," it is said, "is failing to keep pace with the advancement of medical science." Young doctors are exhorted, in slightly despairing tones, to approach the patient as a "person" rather than a "case." Medicine suffers or — what comes to the same — thinks it suffers from a split in its image of man.

Yet, just as clear as the split is the presence of all the genuine humanity one could wish in actual discussions even of "patient management." In his practice, the physician somehow bridges the chasm which alarms him when he considers it abstractly.

This gives us the direction our further investigation of man-as-patient must take. Further understanding of the image of man-as-patient will be achieved by finding the origin of the apparent incoherence of the image. What *exactly* is there about seeing the patient as a manipulable object to be repaired which may seem to make it hard to see him as a *fellow*?

II

The first side of our preliminary evocation of man-as-patient reflects the physician's role as a technician of the biological and behavioral sciences, applying these sciences to the control of a particular part of nature. It reflects, therefore, the attitude toward nature which is intrinsic to technology, which one adopts in taking up the technological enterprise. It reflects this viewpoint on nature in the form of an image of man because man is the part of nature on which the physician exercises his technique.[1] There are several different ways of getting at the way in which medical technology leads to a particular image of man and in which this image may conflict with at least the traditional form of the image of man as a *fellow*-man. We will single out four (A-D following).

A

Medical technique is as old as the human race. But medical technique *as* a part of modern technology is part of something new in human history. Modern technology is new in that the knowledge by which it controls nature is a new kind of knowledge, the kind we call "science."

Scientific knowledge is knowledge wrought in the teeth of observation. Where the observed course of events does not correspond to the predictions made following a particular hypothesis, the hypothesis is altered. This principle may now seem obvious enough, but its consistent application is radically new in human culture and still achieved only by a tiny elite and by them only occasionally.

This radical procedure means that the prescriptions for the control of nature which the technologist draws from science are not like the magician's — the magician is the technologist of pre-scientific culture. The technologist's formulas actually work. If they do not they are withdrawn and replaced by others that will — unlike those of magic, to which success seems ultimately irrelevant.

Scientific technology, therefore, is successful technology. In addition, its success accelerates. Scientific knowledge is continuously self-correcting and so provides an ever-broadening base for its own progress and for the power of the technology based upon it.

Moreover, scientific knowledge is general. It does not suppose that the heavenly bodies are to be approached differently from the rocks on the shore, nor that a man is to be approached differently from an amoeba. This is so because science makes the wager of asserting propositions of the form "*Whenever* A, then B" or "In one hundred cases of A, eighty-five cases of B." Such propositions are overthrown by just one valid instance of A without B, or by one series of tests with a significant deviation from the predicted percentage of B's. Science makes this wager and seems to be winning it.

Thus scientific technology is universal technology. No part of reality is in principle exempt from the control it gives us. No awe holds back the technologist from proposing to establish mines on the moon. No barrier other than the reluctance of the proposed subjects stops us from breeding new varieties of men as we do of dogs.

The result of our technology's practicality and universality is that through it we do acquire vast control over nature. Our technology actually does transform the world and create for its masters a new image of nature. It creates a nature in the image of its informing spirit, in the image of the scientific ideal.

Science sees nature in the pattern "*Whenever* A, then B." Technology produces an image of nature which really conforms to this pattern. The nature transformed by technology is, therefore, a nature *without exceptions,* or with only predictable exceptions, which are thus no exceptions at all. Whatever is true of this nature is true of all of it.

It is precisely by the technological endeavor of the physician that *man* is incorporated into the technological image of nature. By the physician's taking up the technological enterprise with respect to man, man-as-patient becomes a part of that nature which brooks no exceptions. The language here is "In respect of . . . man is just like . . ."

But our traditional understanding of man has based its special regard for him on the conviction of his *exceptionality*: on the conviction that there is inherent in man's nature something which makes him radically different from all other creatures. (The dispute as to what that something might be need not concern us here.) We have believed men worthy of love and hate and fidelity, of all the personal bonds which we do not make with sticks or stones, because we have seen them as a different and "higher" kind of being. But man-as-patient is *defined* as *no exception.*

B

Technology, we have said, creates a version of nature after the pattern of the scientific ideal, after the pattern "Whenever A, then B." Now the practical translation of "Whenever A, then B" is "Whenever I do A, B will also happen." Technologized nature is nature which responds in this way to my orders. It is nature in which if I do A, B will follow; if I do C, D will follow; and in which the choice of doing A or C is my choice or someone else's. Technologized nature is manipulable nature.

Manipulable nature is radically demythologized nature. Pre-technological man lives in a nature whose forces and regularities controlled his destiny and set the pattern of his life. Therefore pre-technological man saw these forces as divine, and regarded those natural events in which they especially impinged on his life as revelations in which deity addressed him in reproach or promise. Water, air, the heavenly bodies — all were gods or demons. For technological man, the gods and demons are gone from nature, because he sees the powers of nature not as controlling him but as actually or potentially controlled by him. Consider for example, a flood. To pre-technological man it is a revelation of God's wrath. Technological man is, to be sure, as dead as any primitive if the waters close over him, and he may fear them just as intensely. But he does not find a revelation from above in the flood. He finds, rather, proof that the authorities have neglected to perform the "A" which would have prevented it and a reminder to vote for repair of this deficiency if he survives.

In technologized nature there are no divinities, no supernatural beings. The labors of the physician incorporate man into technologized nature. Thereby man is bereft of any claim to divinity. But that is the problem. For our traditional understanding of man has based the possibility of an attitude toward man appropriate only to him on his incipient divinity. "The spark of God in every man" has been the legitimation of our love and honor and fear for each other. Technologized man, here man-as-patient, has no such spark.

C

Traditionally, western man has found God "in the gaps." That is, we have introduced him as the explanation of those events in our experience which we could not otherwise explain, called on him for help in those situations where we could no longer help ourselves, and asked his mercy on the occasions when our morality lapsed. (The utterly unchristian character of this concept of God "in the gaps" is not our present concern.) Our life and world have been conceived of as fundamentally self-contained systems, suffering however from some gaps in the usually smooth series of cause and effect: the inexplicable recovery of an apparently doomed sufferer; the hopeless and undeserved financial crisis of a good man; the sudden failure of my normally good intentions. The traditional God of our society operates in exactly those gaps. He is the watchmaker who made and started the natural and historical processes in the first place and now from time to time intervenes with a miracle to keep the mechanism going on the occasions when it cannot keep going by itself.

The scientific and technological enterprises are inherently an assault upon the "God-in-the-gaps." For the whole point of these enterprises is the attempt to eliminate the gaps: to discover explanations for those events in our experience which we do not yet understand, and to extend our control to those circumstances of our lives not yet subject to our will. Science and technology simply are the labor of walling up God's erstwhile holes in the "gaps." It is, of course, well known that for every mystery which science clears up, it discovers ten others, and for every force of nature which technology tames, others yet more powerful are set loose. There are, and no doubt will be, plenty of gaps in our world. But it is the *attitude toward them* which one adopts in taking up the scientific and technological enterprises that is important. To do science *is* to see an unexplained event not as a mystery to be adored but as a puzzle to be solved. To do technology *is* to see the occurrences before which we are helpless not as fates to be pacified but as challenges to ingenuity. Involvement in these enterprises *is* a declaration of unbelief in the God-in-the-gaps and an installing of ourselves, with our intelligence and strength, in his place.

To the concept of God-in-the-gaps corresponded a concept of nature as inherently *gapped*, as, so to speak, fitted out with receptacles to receive God. As part of such a nature, man was thought of as having certain areas of his existence, such as sickness or moral crisis, where openness to God was built into him. The way one put this was to speak of man's "immortal soul." Moreover, man's openness to *man* was understood as part of his openness to God; man's openness to any other-than-he was conceived of as a function of his openness to *the* Other-than-he. It was thought of as a function of the "soul." Thus it, too, was *located* in man's nature, in, that is, the gaps in his nature.

Since man-as-patient is an image evoked, in part at least, by taking up the scientific and technological enterprises of gap-closing, man-as-patient lacks the built-in openness to God and other men on which we have traditionally relied as the basis of distinctive relations between men. We may say exactly the same thing this way: Traditional esteem for and love of man was esteem for man's supposedly built-in religiosity, his "immortal soul." Man-as-patient, like technologized man generally, lacks this organ.

D

Man-as-patient adopts this role by claiming to be sick, or in danger of becoming sick. The physician is, therefore, compelled to differentiate constantly between sick men and well men; even the physician who dislikes the distinction makes it all the time as he sends one man to the hospital and the other home, tries to inhibit one growth process and promote another. Thus man-as-patient always diverges somehow from what man *ought* to be. For "illness," after all, can only mean "a characteristic, of a certain man which that man's physician and he can try to alter and are determined to alter," and "health" can only mean "a characteristic of a certain man which he and his physician are content to leave." The analogy between the way in which a characteristic is determined to be a "fault" and the way in which another characteristic is determined to be an "illness" is obvious and close. Both determinations are *evaluations.* Man-as-patient is, therefore, defined by reference to a partial *ideal* of what man, in certain respects, *should* be like.

As an example, let us consider the case of a man with a stomach-ache which, after all due tests, proves to have "no organic basis." In these psychosomatic days consultations continue. In their course, the patient gives the physician to understand — without of course admitting that he does so — that he needs and wants his stomach-ache. Calling such a stomach-ache "illness" is not a matter of straightforward empirical labeling like calling an artifact in which one can sit a "chair." That it is an *evaluation* is shown by the position in which the physician now finds himself. He may let the patient continue with his stomach-ache, thus accepting that whether this condition is to be alleviated or not lies in the patient's free evaluating choice. Or he may set about to persuade the patient that his symptom is a "crutch" on which he *ought* not rely. Either way we find ourselves in the realm of values. Or to take an example from the other side, no twelfth-century doctor would have *wanted* to cure the ulcerative phenomena of the stigmatics — it would not even have occurred to him that these were the *kind* of thing one might set out to cure or not cure. The diagnostic handbooks are in fact codes of values.

Where does the physician get the standards by which he makes such evaluations? One can of course say that he uses the standards of his society, that he tries to cure whatever in his society is commonly regarded as illness. But this answer is incomplete. For the physician himself is a major influence in society's decision at this point. It often happens that the medical profession educates the public to regard as illness conditions formerly seen as "natural."

The tests do, of course, seem obvious enough: *Pain* is to be alleviated. *Disablement* is to be prevented or mitigated. Processes which would lead to the *death* of the patient are to be halted or slowed. Yet men in other cultures have sought pain and disablement as virtues and death as the fulfillment of life. That these are characteristics of life to be fought against is apparently not a self-evident universal truth. The comfortable, able and long-lived man is *one particular* ideal of man. Where does it come from? I suggest that it has been drawn from behavioral science's description of organic life: In all sufficiently complex organisms, pain is a stimulus to such activity as will, if successful, effect the cessation of the pain. All organisms seek maximum adaptation to their environments. And all organisms avoid and resist threats to the continuance of life. The picture of what man-as-patient ought to be is given by taking this *description* and making of it a *norm.*

It is inevitable that physicians will use behavioral science's description of man in this normative way. As the enterprise of forming hypotheses subject solely to confirmation or disconfirmation by the facts, science inherently avoids all moral or aesthetic judgment. Insofar, therefore, as medicine is a scientific technology, the physician must refrain in his work from moral or aesthetic evaluation. Yet evaluate he must. Where is he to turn for standards by which to evaluate? It must be remembered that we are not now speaking of the physician's own moral decisions with respect to the patient — here his resources are the same as anyone else's. (Though his problems are not. Bringing resources and problems together is the main task of these studies.) We are speaking of his evaluation of which characteristics of the patient are to be promoted and which inhibited by the exercise of his medical technique. The physician's obvious recourse is to turn to what is said about man by the science on which his technique is based and to treat this description as normative.

Making descriptions into norms is regular procedure in our culture. Wherever it is done, it amounts to a declaration that man as nature provides him is as he ought to be. Such a naturalistic ethos can be and often is noble and fine. But its picture of man excludes any sign of a need for man to become radically different from what he is; it excludes any sign of a need for man to rise above himself, to seek his true self in the future. So here: Man-as-patient rests complete in what he already is. But traditionally we have based our love for man exactly on what we *hoped* for from him.

III

In sum, taking up the technological enterprise with men as the objects, means renouncing the traditional basis for *understanding* why we shall have specifically personal bonds with each other. This is the reason why some feel an incongruity between two sides of the image of man-as-patient. It must be strongly emphasized that adopting the technological attitude toward a man does *not* make it impossible in fact to see and treat him as a fellow — this is proven by many physicians' notable success at doing both. But it does destroy the *image* of man-as-fellow which the tradition of our society provides us. The technological attitude renders implausible the *doctrine* that man, by reason of a reference beyond himself which is part of his very nature, is uniquely related to the divine and so is an exceptional kind of being to whom exceptional attitudes are appropriate — the doctrine by which our tradition has *understood* man as a fellow-man. So long as the image by which we see other men as our fellows is that provided by the tradition of our society, the total image of man-as-patient is incoherent. Whether this is bad or not depends on how important consistency is. Most physicians — like the rest of us — can doubtless continue their humane and concerned relation with their patients whether or not they have a rationale for doing this that is consistent with their other commitments. And yet it seems likely that sooner or later a crisis will occur.

What are the options? How can this incoherence be resolved, or, at least, lived with? An obvious and presumably much practiced option is strict compartmentalization. With one eye, the physician looks at the patient as the object of his technique. With the other eye, he sees in the patient the fellow-man of our traditional doctrines, the fellow-man whom he may serve and by whom he may be morally and spiritually enriched. And he simply refuses to worry about any possible incongruity. Despite the intended derogatory connotation of "compartmentalization," the short-range beneficence of this method should not be denied. Absolute consistency of attitudes is not possible anyway. And sometimes the cost of seeking it may be too high.

One way in which consistency could be purchased would be by denying the fellow-man side of the image of man-as-patient. The disaster here is not that the physician would thereby turn himself into a straight-out engineer — being an engineer is a fine thing. The disaster is that since the physician *cannot* cease to have men as his objects, he can take this option only by directly denying that his patients personally concern him: *i.e.*, by explicitly denying them special human worth. That this nihilist solution is possible, and what its practical consequences might be, has been demonstrated in the concentration camps of Nazi Germany.

The opposite way in which consistency could be purchased would be by ignoring the scientific origin of medical technique, by merely using the material results of scientific investigation without inner participation in the activity by which they are obtained. Just so the magician used poppy-juice to put people to sleep without knowing why it did so. Instead of a structure of testable theory, the magician had a structure of dreaming associations within which he "understood" the efficacy of the poppy. So also the physician could perhaps dissociate himself from the genuine scientific spirit and work within some other, specifically moral and spiritual framework of ideas, probably that of a political ideology. We can only imagine the pompous mumbo-jumbo which would result — and shudder.

There is another option. The physician may accept all sides of the image of man which his work evokes for him, accept them with their consequences — and *stand up to* the problem they pose. He may work with and for men who show no signs of being exceptions to the principles which describe the actions and relations of things in general, in whom he can find no spark of divinity nor built-in opening to God; yet who *nevertheless* demand to be lived for as would be appropriate to no other beings; who *nevertheless* in challenge and promise open to him the possibility of rising above what they and he are to a final mutual fulfillment of their life and his. What is special *in* man? Nothing, such a courageous physician will tell us — and yet he is to be confronted in an entirely special way. Is man divine? No, he will say — and yet in the commands and beseechings of my brother I am addressed by God. Does man open to a more perfect life beyond him? Not visibly — and yet one must set no limits to one's hopes for him. In sum, that men are unique and directed to some goal beyond themselves is not given in any factor *in their nature* — and yet we are to live with them in the faith that they are so directed.

The physician who from his special confrontation with his fellows, his confrontation with them as *patients,* spoke *so,* would speak an eminently sane and healing word. The great threat to a technological civilization is that men may become increasingly obscured from each other in their uniqueness as men. The cure is *not* retreat from or dilution of the technological enterprise. The cure is absolute clarity about and courage before the image of man evoked by the technological enterprise and before the question the image puts to us. Perhaps the physician, the man-technologist, is called to lead us to this clarity.

The question which our technological civilization calls us to stand up to is: How will you men live humanely *for* each other, without the illusion that in each other you meet semi-divinities or immortal souls? Perhaps the physician is the one specifically called to hear this question and speak it to the rest of us.

The believer is glad to hear this question. For the Christian proclamation shows man as a *creature:* i.e., one who in himself, in what he is and has, has no special hope beyond himself. But the Christian proclamation also shows man as one who nevertheless does live by what is beyond himself and by his own future possibility; who does this not by what he is in himself but *because God has addressed and addresses him,* because God has *spoken* to him and called him out of what he is and has in himself. To the question posed by the image of man-as-patient: Wherein is man special, if not in his nature? faith replies: Man is special and the appropriate partner of special, personal, relations not because of anything he is, but because of something that others than he — God and, thereupon, his fellows — have done and do to him, because they speak to him, address him. Because from outside him they call to him to *become* in some way different from what he is; they call him to a future goal beyond himself.

One more specification must be made. The *address* we are speaking of is in no way some sort of wordless or mystic speech. It is what traditional theology has called the "Law" and the "Gospel." The Law is the commands and promises with which our societies fill our ears and call us to be different from what we are (*i.e.,* call us forward into the future); the Gospel is the story which one human tells another about Jesus of Nazareth. And since the address we are speaking of is both the Law and the Gospel, it is by no means only those who hear the specifically Christian story — the Gospel — who are so addressed. By the "Law" we mean *all* the addresses which men make to each other; we call them "Law" because of the way in which all our speech to each other *obligates* us when we hear, and because of Christian faith's conviction that all our obligations are obligations to God. If it is being addressed by God which opens us up to each other, then the possibility and reality of actual humane behavior to each other is not at all limited to believers; for all men are in fact addressed by God.

Indeed, the voice of science itself, the obligating

address of the scientific community to each of its members as the work of research goes on, is Law, God's Law, for those who belong to this community. It is not merely that there is no conflict between involvement in the scientific and technological enterprise and being fellow-men to each other; involvement in the scientific enterprise can be itself the address which opens us and makes such personal existence possible. It may well be that a new humane ethos is arising from the very work of science and technology itself, if the humane involvement of those taken up in scientific-technological work can survive the loss of the old doctrines of *why* we should be fellow-men to each other. To these old doctrines — to the traditional image of the fellow-man — scientific technology is indeed fatal. It will be necessary either simply to *be* fellow-men to each other without any image by which to apprehend and understand each other as fellows, or to find that apprehension and understanding in some radically different way than we have traditionally done. I say "radically different" because it would be disastrous if we should simply invent some "scientific" substitute for the traditional doctrine of man. Attempts, for example, to use the uncertainty principle as the basis for a new exaltation of the "subject" are to be viewed with suspicion. For the "observer" with whom the uncertainty principle says we must reckon and the "fellow-men" whom I and my fellows are called to be to each other, are not the same at all, and pretending they are must pervert either the work of science or our human fellowship.

Whether or not, or for how long, it will be possible to live with and for each other as fellows without any doctrine of why we should do so, and without taking to pseudo-scientific ersatz doctrines of man's worth, is a point which it is wiser not to predict. But, to repeat, the believer is glad to hear the question posed by the technological enterprise. For the *knowledge* that — as opposed to the fact that — all men are addressed by God in the Law and that it is this that makes me and my fellow open to each other in a special way, is one of the benefits of that other more particular address of God by which faith lives, the Gospel. The situation of being called to live for my fellows without knowing why is one to which the Gospel can have something to say. And the temptation to cling to the traditional doctrine of man even after we can no longer wholly credit it, or to invent phony substitutes for it, is one from which the knowledge given by the Gospel can save us.

IV

The physician is the technologist who *cannot* be rid of men in all their humanity. Perhaps, therefore, he is the one called to make us fully understand what our technological civilization means for our vision of each other. Understanding this may be just what believers need if we are to see in man what the Gospel wants to point us to — see this clearly and in a way appropriate to our time and culture. The image of man-as-patient may be a hidden pivot of the present epoch in the history of the Gospel and in the history of our culture. If it is, the believing physician will play a decisive role both in his church and in his profession.

Notes

1. I use the term "part" because the physician's concern is not delimited by the boundaries of a *discipline.* The physician will use the results of, and if he is a research physician may himself pursue, any of the sciences that offer promise of help to his enterprise. His concern is delimited as concern for a *part* of nature in the most ordinary-language sense of "part."

57 Agency and an Interactional Model of Society

James M. Gustafson

The practical reasons that one could draw up for adhering to particular views of agency are not sufficient. At their worst they could become useful fictions, rationalizations for the sake of morality and a certain view of humanization. Philosophical or moral beliefs that are defended solely for their utility value deserve no more credence than religious beliefs so defended. The philosophical issues of action theory are the real issues. And one way in which they are distinguished is by looking at action from the agent's perspective on the one hand and the observer's on the other. Intentions as causes are always more persuasive from the agent's perspective. The reduction of intentions and volitions to the end stages of a particular causal sequence is more or less plausible from an observer's perspective; in retrospect, many intentions and actions are susceptible to more refined causal analysis than the agent is conscious of in the moment of choice.

As Midgley says, "Central factors in us *must* be accepted, and the right line of human conduct must lie somewhere within the range they allow."[1] This certainly would have to be admitted by even the most radical libertarians (not political libertarians but theorists of the "will"). Our intentions and choices, whether moral or otherwise, draw upon and give focus to our biological natures. Other factors must be accepted; at least they are not subject to radical revision and alteration in most persons under most circumstances. Cultural and social conditioning, while unpredictable to a degree in their effects, certainly predetermine the range of choices and actions under most circumstances. What we have become as a result of habituations and conscious commitments is a preselective reality that particularizes the limits and possibilities of action at a particular time. Similarly, the specific external location of our activity in both time and space limits and particularizes our human possibilities.

This is not to deny several important things. We can care for and develop our natural capacities so that more possibilities exist for us. This is a matter of choice and discipline. We need not be the prisoners of a given culture or society in the modern pluralistic and mobile world. The relativization of our "natural" cultures and societies occurs not only as a result of unintended exposures to different ones but also by deliberate effort to make contact with alternatives. We appear to have quite natural revulsions against repressive ways of life that have formed us; I take it that much of modern psychotherapy offers explanations of such resentments and individual rebellions. We need not resign ourselves to the limitations and possibilities of action that are prima facie apparent. We can act to alter those conditions so that the range of possibilities is amplified; we can choose to relate ourselves to other circumstances than those that immediately confront us.

In all of these possibilities, however, our agency is exercised to marshal and to direct realities that exist prior to our choices and actions. The scope of our "freedom" is not as vast as it is claimed to be from some points of view. Edwards, in his own eighteenth-century terms, makes a similar point. "[T]he will always follows the last dictate of understanding. But then the understanding must be taken in a large sense, as including the whole faculty of perception or apprehension, and not merely what is called reason or judgment."[2] Our freedom is the exercise of various capacities that are involved in human agency, capacities that earlier were called "faculties." Understanding, mo-

---

From James Gustafson, *Ethics from a Theocentric Perspective,* vol. 1, *Theology and Ethics* (Chicago: University of Chicago Press, 1981), pp. 289-93.

tives, desires, will, reason, and judgment are all involved. This view, it seems to me, does not denigrate humanity, and has the merit of more accurately portraying human agency. As Midgley so poignantly asks, "Why should not our excellence involve our whole nature?"[3]

Human accountability is not abolished from this point of view. To be sure, we can rightly indicate that persons have been held accountable in the past for more than they actually should have been. A great deal of misplaced guilt has been evoked by beliefs about the range of human freedom that are not defensible. Persons have been held morally accountable for events and effects for which they were only partially causally accountable. But one might argue that what we are held accountable for can be more complex and more particularized than can be included in a dialectic of freedom and nature, or freedom and destiny, when those are understood as specific and independent roles in the drama of life. We are accountable for the ways in which we bring our "natural" capacities to a focus of choice and action, for the assessment of our interrelations with other persons and other things in determining how we will exercise our powers, and for the understanding of the circumstances of our action. We are accountable for the ordering of our motives, drives, and desires, as well as for the consequences of our actions that are within our powers to control. We are accountable to ourselves, to the communities of which we are a part, and to those who are affected by our actions.

In contemporary moral philosophy it is almost axiomatic to say that we are to respect the rational autonomy of other agents; that we are to respect their freedom.[4] Certainly it is correct to respect their capacities for agency. But persons are more than their capacities for agency. We must also respect their bodily natures, and we have responsibilities to see that they are not deprived of necessities. We are to respect persons not merely as individuals but as "members one of another" in their communities. What any moralist means when he or she insists on respect for persons depends upon the image or view held of persons. A view can be more or less comprehensive, more or less complex. If persons are viewed as biological entities with an unique capacity for agency, what is respected is amplified beyond "rational autonomy." Indeed, when one sees how restricted is the range in which autonomy is exercised, and when one sees how the exercise of agency is dependent upon and limited by biological, social, cultural, and other conditions, respect only for autonomy can be viewed as denigrating.

It is my conviction that a reader can learn more about human agency from great novels than he or she can from philosophical treatises or scientific accounts of the subject. Novelists such as Jane Austen, George Eliot, and Tolstoy show with poignancy and detail how human agency and particular acts bring to focus many drives, many motives, and require assessments of complex circumstances. In novels that are perspicacious in their development of character and action, we see how choices are made in continuity with what persons had become as a result of their whole natures.

Man is an agent. But agency draws upon all that persons are; it is the capacity to exercise our powers in accordance with purposes and intentions to affect, either by overt action or by restraint, the subsequent course of events.

Our views of the nature of human beings are affected by the selection of a dominant metaphor or analogy for understanding social relations. Social theory in Western culture tends to be divided, in this respect, between an organic analogy and a contractual view of human interrelations. Of course there are combinations of these; the family emerges as a result both of a "contract" of marriage and the natural bonding between the couple and children. As a more or less natural (organic) unit, the family shapes our natural duties; parents do not make contracts with their children that define their obligations to them. In professional life and business transactions the contractual relationship is dominant; we consciously undertake obligations that are specified, and are bound to meet them.

Each of these, when driven to extremes or when used too exclusively, falsifies human experience and misconstrues human nature. The organic metaphor excessively highlights the processes of continuous mutual determination between persons, between groups, and in some instances, as in the extreme sociobiological views, between human beings and the rest of nature. It overcomes the dichotomy between body and "soul" by construing the activities of the intellect and other forms of human agency as necessary and determined outcomes of other processes. Only their ignorance, it would appear, keeps investigators from giving sufficient explanations of human activity, and that is being overcome. The individual is seen primarily as the outcome of the processes of life as a whole, and his or her "autonomy" is underestimated. In morality it is easy to claim, from this perspective, that the good of the whole body is of greater importance than the good of its individual parts. "Surgery," the denial of life and liberty to an individual "organ," is more readily justified.

The contractual model rests strongly on the primacy of individuals. Their being is implicitly if not explicitly judged to be of prior significance to the "whole." The agency of individuals has a more central role; society is seen to be more the result of the actions and choices of individuals, or of contractually bound groups, than as the outcome of "natural" processes. The distinctiveness of man among the animals is stressed more than the similarities and continuities. The autonomy of individuals is highly respected, and with this comes a moral stress on the respect for the autonomy and rights of individuals. In situations of conflict between the rights of individuals and benefits for a social group, the presumption is always in favor of the former. It is more difficult to make a case for restraints and denials of liberty and life for the sake of the well-being of a whole.

An interactional model of society takes into account what is valid in each of the other two models. It can account for the priority of society in the sense that we are the "products" of it to a large extent, and our initiatives are always in response to what exists and to the actions of others upon us. It recognizes that individuals and even most groups do not have the power to create or to recreate their larger societies. Novelty takes place within the developments in social life that are beyond the control of individual and corporate actions. Yet it recognizes the individual and corporate capacities for action. The processes of social change are not mechanically or organically construed; the exercise of powers does alter social orders and the course of historical events; it affects the development of culture. An interactional view provides no simple way of deciding in hard cases whether the individual's autonomy should be curbed for the sake of a larger good any more than it simply sustains the "good of the whole" over against the claims of individuals. Whether the moral weight rests primarily on the individual or particular groups over against the well-being of a larger community — a nation-state or the species — depends on valuations that are not determined by the model itself. Such critical choices, in any case, could not be universally predetermined in the abstract, or in very general terms. They are determined in relation to a particular set of circumstances and events. Societies are developing; their development is governed by a whole complex of processes of which particular events initiated by particular persons and groups are only a part. Multicausality, including human agency, must be taken into account in understanding individual, social, historical, and cultural developments.

Notes

1. Mary Midgley, *Beast and Man: The Roots of Human Nature* (Ithaca: Cornell University Press, 1978), p. 81.

2. Jonathan Edwards, *Freedom of the Will*, ed. Paul Ramsey (New Haven: Yale University Press, 1957), p. 148.

3. Midgley, *Beast and Man*, p. 204.

4. See, for example, Alan Donagan, *The Theory of Morality* (Chicago: University of Chicago Press, 1979), pp. 33-74.

58 The Basis of Medicine and Religion: Respect for Persons

David C. Thomasma

On the whole, the present age has lost respect for human life. Literature, music, and art reflect the fact that life is under assault. It is no wonder that mere survival is considered an exalted achievement in these times when human life can be ended before birth by being salinated in the mother's womb or can be born nutritionally brain-damaged and suffer from starvation, food additives, and a polluted environment. Even when human life survives all these assaults, it can be snuffed out in one of a hundred wars which break out all over the earth.

Against this admittedly negative scenario, the medical profession bravely asserts its commitment to respect human persons. Apart from religious organizations, the profession of health is one of the few effective international forces fostering the dignity and value of individual human beings. But because of its commitment to human life, healing, too, is under assault.

Within the profession, evidence exists of practices for economic gain, destruction of human dignity, and attacks on life. The profession also is under pressure from external sources to fulfill social aims for which it is ill-equipped[1] or to fulfill political purposes, such as the torture of prisoners, for which its commitments demand profound antipathy. Given these anti-life forces, it is all the more important that the healing profession renew its commitment to affirm the value of human life.

A close examination of the role of humanism in patient care reveals not only how current health professionals affirm this value, but also how religious-sponsored health care can develop its goals and values in the future. There is no need to retreat into the past; rather, health care leaders must continue to show courage and wisdom in implementing their convictions. This article will explore three generalizations about humanism in patient care: (1) that respect for persons is a guiding motive of both religion and the healing profession; (2) that ethical norms for the healing profession result from respect for persons; and (3) that religious affirmation can strengthen these ethical norms. This last point will emphasize the Catholic tradition.

Respect for Persons

The struggle for individual autonomy and recognition has been a long and hard one, and it is not yet completed. Both religion and medicine contain the seeds of that struggle, and both have played a major role in whatever success each has achieved. Religion and the profession of healing share the premise that human life is at once fragile and perfectible. Growth in virtue and health requires awareness of life's finitude and perfectibility and, at the same time, demands an affirmation that happiness and well-being are ideal aims for individuals. Such growth rests upon the altruistic assumption that human beings can help each other to improve. It is significant to note that the earliest priests were also medicine men.

The effects of virtue and health, happiness and well-being were virtually indistinguishable for all but the past 2,000 years, a relatively short part of the human lifespan. Respect for persons is a natural byproduct of the aims of happiness and well-being which are intrinsic to religion and the profession of healing. Respect for persons ascends the ladder of values as both religion and medicine concentrate on the individual.

As long as religion and medicine were both embodied in the person of the medicine man,

Reprinted with permission from *Linacre Quarterly,* vol. 47 (May 1984): 142-50. 850 Elm Grove Road, Elm Grove, WI 53122. Subscription rate: $20 per year; $5 per single issue.

their social and community aims were indistinguishable. For example, the Babylonians considered illness to be a direct consequence of sin, and healing included a confession of sins and infractions against community mores. But as early as 1500 B.C. Hindu physicians took an oath remarkably like the latter Hippocratic Oath in which respect for individual persons was coupled with a real sense of a profession, that is, a public commitment to care for individuals regardless of public mores.[2] Later, in Egypt and Greece the medical profession became sufficiently secure to divorce itself from religious aims. This action led the healing profession to concentrate on its moral commitments to individuals. The Hippocratic Oath clearly reveals this principle of individuation in its solemn promise not to harm the patient to whom one has professional obligations of care, confidentiality, and personal respect.[3]

The growth of respect for persons in religion was also linked to a principle of individuation, although its genesis was different. While anthropologists argue that a common feature of all religions was the respect for members of one's own tribe, universal respect for persons not in one's tribe or nation was long in coming. The theological movements of greatest import included the rise of universalism, demands for justice, and the distinction between creation and redemption concomitant with the emergence of the prophetic movement around 500 B.C.[5]

At the heart of prophetic universalism is the belief that the Creator made all human beings and called all to redemption. Exclusivism and tribal loyalties are not compatible with this conviction, and they are replaced with a belief in the inherent value of individuals which demands respect for all human persons. The growth of Christianity combined this vision with the Roman Empire's stoic view of natural rights.

Thus, professionalism in medicine coupled with the supranatural universalism of religion led to the principle of individuation; the value of respect for persons was firmly entrenched, even though actual behavior often was less than altruistic. Painting cultural progress in such broad strokes can be dangerous. Nevertheless, the picture painted above is relatively complete. Pedro Lain-Entralgo, in his excellent book *Doctor and Patient,* describes this relationship throughout history.[5] Although the rationale for the obligations in the relationship differs in Greek, Christian, and contemporary times, respect for individual persons underpins the relationship throughout these historical eras.[6] Similarly, respect for persons is at the heart of Judeo-Christian morality, which regards every human being as a child of God called to redemption.

Given this rich religious heritage, it is not surprising that Western political and philosophical thought underscores this same respect for persons. Each individual is regarded as having endowed rights that no individual or government can rescind. In addition to the philosophical movement which emphasized this theory of individual rights, moral philosophers have also highlighted this conviction. Kant held that persons should be treated, not as mere means, but as ends in themselves.[7] John Stuart Mill in *On Liberty* argued that the freedom of persons could not be infringed upon unless they were a danger to others or could not apprehend the negative consequences of their actions on others.

Norms for the Healing Professions

The principle of respect for persons offers norms of moral activity for the healing profession. Such respect is at the root of current guidelines on research and functions as the basis for clinical medicine. Of course, it continues to inform the ethical codes of the healing professions as well. Although this article is limited to an examination of the medical research guidelines and to reflections on clinical medicine, the norms which emerge from these reflections could lead to a rejuvenated code of ethics for the healing professions, a task which is outside the scope of this article.[9]

The Department of Health, Education, and Welfare (HEW) guidelines for human participation in medical research are based on the principle of the rights of subjects as human beings. Basic to the procedures following from this principle is the need for informed consent.[10] The requirement of informed consent is based on the conviction that persons are autonomous beings who, if their autonomy is diminished for some reason, must be protected. Thus respect for persons entails two ethical guidelines: "the requirement to acknowledge autonomy and the requirement to protect those with diminished autonomy."[11]

As the *Belmont Report* of the National Commission for the Protection of Human Subjects points out, respect for persons also entails a medical obligation to promote their well-being.[12] Hence, in addition to obtaining informed consent, medical research must compare risks and benefits to individual participants and must attempt, in scientific design, to maximize the benefit and minimize possible harm. Finally, respect for persons entails a principle of justice that demands that persons be treated fairly, without undue burdens. Thus, to perform all hypertension research only on poor black persons for the benefit of the whole population places an unjust burden on them as a class and diminishes their personal integrity.

Respect for persons leads to moral obligations in the health professions. The following norms for medical research flow from this principle:

1. *To recognize the autonomy of persons.* This norm rests not only on the principle of liberty proposed by Mill but also on the medical obligation to treat individuals as free agents so that they can be full partners in the research. The relationship of subject and researcher is promoted as a true human relationship.[13]

2. *To protect persons whose autonomy is impaired.* This norm is not simply a sequel to informed consent but follows as a professional obligation. It would be inappropriate to attempt to heal people while simultaneously diminishing their autonomy or taking advantage of their lack of it.

3. *To promote the well-being of persons.* This norm follows directly from the beneficent aim of medicine, i.e., the healing profession's obligation to benefit people exceeds the demands of justice. Caring for whole persons is a real professional obligation.

4. *To treat each person fairly.* This is a minimal norm of medical research. At the very least, healing requires that the person cannot be used for an experiment to benefit others unless the person also derives some benefit as an individual or as a member of a class.

Norms for Clinical Practice

These norms for medical research can be better understood by comparing them to similar norms for clinical medical practice. Apparently, many persons consent to research — even research that does not benefit them — in which the norms buttressing their individuality are not adequately applied. In studying the practical effects of the HEW guidelines, researchers found that most subjects tolerated lack of information and freedom in consent precisely because they did not want to impair their physician-patient relationship.[14] In other words, this clinical bond is so important and so primary that patients will suffer diminished personal autonomy and respect to maintain it.

Why is this clinical bond so important and what does its existence reveal about respect for persons? The clinical bond between the patient and the healing profession is based on a primary value: health. Persons who are healthy rank other values ahead of health. They see health, as have many philosophers from Aristotle to Dewey, as a condition for freedom and autonomy.[15] When persons become sick, however, they often rate health at the top of their list of values and rate other values, such as freedom and autonomy, secondary to the aim of healing.

Thus, when physicians and staff view persons only as patients, the sick individuals suffer from both a diminished state of health, and a diminished sense of autonomy. These individuals find themselves in an imbalanced relationship of almost childlike dependency on the healing profession. This feeling of dependency is perhaps the most irksome aspect of admission to a hospital.

The aim of the clinical bond between the patient and the healing profession is to restore health. This value is ranked highest in the patient's priorities and is affirmed by the healing professions. Professional obligations follow from this primary goal.

Clearly, respect for persons would be negated if treatment resulted in harm rather than healing. For this reason, the most ancient norm of medicine, expressed in the Hindu Oath and the Hippocratic Oath, is *primum non nocere* ("first of all, do no harm").[16] This norm is essentially beneficent. The health professional's obligation is primarily to the patient, even though other values of society may impinge on the clinical relationship. The clinical bond is so strong a relationship of obligation that Paul Ramsey calls it a canon or covenant of loyalty to distinguish its human faithfulness from lesser legal, contracted obligations.[17]

Two additional norms for clinical medicine also follow from the nature of the clinical bond.[18] The first of these is to respect the imbalanced relationship itself. The healing profession not only must fulfill its obligation to heal but also must recognize and help to restore those aspects which diminish the patient's personhood in the physician-patient relationship. Since the patient is no longer a fully autonomous and knowledgeable partner in this imbalanced relationship, the patient is in a diminished state as a person. Obligations inherent in such an imbalanced relationship include revealing the truth, supplying sufficient information for free decisions, and respecting the patient's right to refuse treatment.

The third norm of the clinical relationship is to treat each person as a class instance of the human race. This is really an obligation of justice. Since sick persons have an imbalanced relationship with the healing profession, promoting their well-being implies that all persons be treated equitably regardless of social standing and custom. The poor should receive the same care as the rich, blacks the same as whites, the aged the same as the young.

Respect for persons, then, is the guiding principle for the healing profession, in both research and clinical medicine. This respect is tailored to and modified by the healing relationship essential to medicine, from which its professional obligations flow.

Beyond Professionalism: Religion and Medicine

The previous section explained how respect for persons establishes professional obligations. This final section will discuss ways in which religious commitments reinforce professional obligations.

If respect for persons is the guiding motive of the healing profession, then medicine practiced for religious reasons can only strengthen this obligation. What medicine regards as professional obligations, religion views as human obligations. And it is this difference in viewpoints that constitutes any difference between professional and human obligations.

From a religious perspective, the respect due a human being arises from the fact that individuals are created by God and called to His salvation. No human person, regardless of how hopeless his or her life, may be abandoned. All persons are seen as sacramental, that is, extensions of God in human history. Each person is a created presence of God.

Hence the professional requirement to treat each person as a class instance of the human race means that, from a religious perspective, beyond the professional requirement of justice is a loving requirement of faith. One loves the person, not only as person but as a presence of God. As Jesus said, "Whatever you do for the least of these, you do to me." Thus, to justice is added mercy. From a religious perspective, those who have been ill-treated by society or by national mores deserve even better care than those who have not. St. Augustine's theological definition of justice, "to each according to his need," means that those in greater need of care should have more available.

There is a second point about the class instance norm. Professional obligations of justice and fairness do not address the deeper need of human beings to be loved as individuals. People want to be loved for their singularity, not because they belong to the race. As W. H. Auden says in his poem "Sept. 1, 1939," there is an "error bred in the bones of each woman and each man." What is that error? A craving not to be loved universally "but to be loved alone." Religion does not consider this desire an "error." Persons are to be respected not only through equitable treatment but by individual love for the qualities they portray. Indeed, the well-being of patients is often impeded by a lack of this individualized compassion.[19]

Religious concern for the imbalance inherent in the physician-patient relationship also transcends professional obligations. Seneca explains the role of love in the clinical relationship:

> Why is it that I owe something more to my physician and my teacher, and yet do not complete the payment of what is due to them? Because from

being physician and teacher they become friends, and we are under an obligation to them, not because of their skill, which they sell, but because of their kind and friendly goodwill.

If, therefore, a physician does nothing more than feel my pulse and put me on the list of those whom he visits on his rounds, instructing me what to do and what to avoid without any personal feeling, I owe him nothing more than his fee, because he does not see me as a friend but as a client. . . .

Why then are we so much indebted to these men? Not because what they have sold us is worth more than we paid for it, but because they have contributed something to us personally. A physician who gave me more attention than was necessary, because he was afraid for me, not for his professional reputation; who was not content to indicate remedies, but also applied them; who sat at my bedside among my anxious friends and hurried to me at times of crisis; for whom no service was too burdensome, none too distasteful to perform; who was not indifferent to my moans; to whom, although a host of others sent for him, I was always his chief concern; who took time for the others only when my illness permitted him.

Such a man has placed me under an obligation, not so much as a physician but as a friend.[20]

Finally the professional obligation to do no harm can be strengthened by a religious perspective, which goes beyond mere physical health. From a religious perspective, the well-being of patients requires genuine love of the patient as a person. Greater sympathy with the common condition of humankind, attention to family relationships, and the virtues of kindness, mercy, and charity result. Other needs besides just the physical are addressed.

The contrast between professional obligations and their religious affirmation can be understood by comparing the ways in which the prayer of Maimonides, a Jewish physician and philosopher in the Middle Ages, differs from the Oath of Hippocrates. The Oath clearly states professional obligations to individuals. But the Prayer of Maimonides moves beyond this professionalism to a profound sense of common humanity under the Father, to the religious task of healing as a work of God, and to love as the bond with patients:

I begin once more my daily work. Be Thou with me, Almighty, Father of Mercy, in all my efforts to heal the sick. For without thee, man is but a helpless creature. Grant that I may be filled with love for my art and for my fellow man. May the thirst for gain and the desire for fame be far from my heart. For these are the enemies of Pity and the ministers of Hate. Grant that I may be able to devote myself body and soul to the children who suffer from pain.

Preserve my strength, that I may be able to restore the strength of the rich and the poor, the good and the bad, the friend and the foe. Let me see in the sufferer the man alone. When wiser men teach me, let me be humble to learn; for the mind of man is so puny, and the art of healing is so vast. But when fools are ready to advise me or find fault with me, let me not listen to their folly. Let me be intent upon one thing, O Father of Mercy, to be always merciful to thy suffering children.

May there never rise in me the notion that I know enough, but give me strength and leisure and zeal to enlarge my knowledge. Our work is great, and the mind of man presses forward forever. Thou hast chosen me in thy grace, to watch over the life and death of thy creatures. I am about to fulfill my duties. Guide me in this immense work so that it may be of avail.

The sacramental character of individual persons, then, reinforces the norms of the healing profession by introducing love as the primary reason for promoting the well-being of human beings.

A close examination of the role of humanism in patient care, particularly the requirements to respect persons, can lead to setting the future goals of religious-sponsored health care institutions. Among the goals and standards already proposed by the Catholic Health Association, several deserve special attention in light of respect for persons.[21] First is that a Catholic healing organization must be committed to healing, especially by respecting each person's autonomy and providing hope to the weary. Second, in light of the imbalanced relationship of healing, the Catholic hospital must place special emphasis on justice for and love of the patient by working for the well-being of whole persons, whatever their religious convictions. Finally, the requirement of treating each person as an embodiment of the human race means that economic and organizational efficiency, however important, must not interfere with providing better care for the disenfranchised.

Because God loves each individual, each person's life is sacred. Catholic health care institutions must take absolute care to affirm and foster this sacredness. For a religious hospital, healing means not only curing but extending God's love to His creatures.

Notes

1. See Ivan Illich, *Medical Nemesis* (New York: Bantam Books, 1977).

2. The oath of Hindu physicians.

3. The Hippocratic Oath.

4. This universalism was especially evident in Zoroastrianism and Judaism. Among Jewish prophets, Second Isaiah is generally regarded as the first to formulate a universalism based upon a theology of creation.

5. Pedro Lain-Entralgo, *Doctor and Patient* (New York: McGraw-Hill, 1969).

6. The Greek relationship was described as one of friendship, the Christian as one of love, and the contemporary as one of comradeship. All of these presuppose respect for persons.

7. Immanual Kant, *Metaphysical Foundations of Morals,* ed. by C. J. Friedrich (New York: Modern Library Edition, 1965), pp. 140-87; R. S. Downie and Elizabeth Telfer, *Respect for Persons* (New York: Schocken, 1970), pp. 13-37. The authors argue that respect for persons in the Kantian formulation is the basic principle of all ethical theory.

8. John Stuart Mill, *On Liberty,* ed. by C. V. Shields (Indianapolis: Bobs-Merrill, 1956), pp. 114 ff.

9. Edmund D. Pellegrino, M.D., describes a way in which a new code of morality for the professions may be developed from the norms for clinical practice, both in a book-length manuscript co-authored with me and entitled "A Philosophical Basis of Medical Practice," in preparation at Oxford University Press, and in his "Toward a Reconstruction of Medical Morality," *Journal of Medicine and Philosophy,* March, 1979, pp. 32-56.

10. Dept. of Health, Education and Welfare, "Protection of Human Subjects," *Federal Register,* May 30, 1974, pp. 18914-18920; Rev. Kevin O'Rourke, "Fetal Experimentation: An Evaluation of the New Federal Norms," *Hospital Progress,* Sept., 1975, pp. 60-69.

11. National Commission for the Protection of Human Subjects, *Belmont Report: Ethical Principles and Guidelines for the Protection of Human Subjects of Research,* DHEW Publication No. OS 78-0012 (Washington, D.C.: DHEW, 1978), pp. 4-5.

12. Ibid., p. 6.

13. Alexander Capron, "Informed Consent in Catastrophic Disease Research and Treatment," reprinted in *Ethical Issues in Modern Medicine,* ed. by Hunt and Arras (Palo Alto, Calif.: Mayfield Publishing Co., 1977), pp. 253-64.

14. See, for example, a study of labor induction done by Bradford Gray and reported in his *Human Subjects in Medical Experimentation* (New York: Wiley, 1975), pp. 202-34.

15. Edmund D. Pellegrino, M.D., and I have tried to develop these norms for clinical practice from a philosophy of medical practice, a development differing from the one posed in this article.

16. Kudlein has illustrated how this norm was considered a general guideline for civic behavior during the Greek period. See "Medical Ethics and Popular Ethics in Greece and Rome," *Clio Medica,* 5, 1976, pp. 91-121. However, the use of this norm was part of the general context of *philia,* or friendship, prevailing as the explanation of the bond between physician and patient. See Lain-Entralgo, pp. 17-22.

17. Paul Ramsey, *The Patient as Person* (New Haven: Yale University Press, 1970), pp. 17-32.

18. These norms can also follow from a philosophy of medicine. See footnote 15.

19. To consider respect for persons as an end of human action, it is important to realize that a value is placed on persons for the qualities they portray. See Downie and Telfer, pp. 13-19.

20. Seneca, *De beneficiis,* VI, p. 16.

21. Catholic Health Association, The, *Evaluative Criteria for Catholic Health Care Facilities* (St. Louis: Catholic Health Assoc., 1979).

Part III

ISSUES IN MEDICAL ETHICS

Chapter Ten

CONTRACEPTION

The simple narrative of the first birth (Genesis 4:1) seems almost quaint today: "Now Adam knew Eve his wife, and she conceived and bore Cain, saying 'I have gotten a man by the help of the Lord.'" Since Genesis we humans have developed a wide variety of interventions into the natural processes of procreation. Already in Exodus we hear of the midwife, and more and more we have subdued the natural process of human begetting and have brought it more and more under our control, until today it is possible to intervene at a number of different points of the reproductive process, in a number of different ways, and for a number of different reasons.

The next few chapters provide a sampling of the theological reflection prompted by these new powers and an invitation to engage in such reflection yourself. This chapter deals specifically with the power to prevent conception.

Public discussion has focused on two principles in the consideration of contraceptive techniques, freedom and utility. This is not hard to demonstrate. The decision whether to use contraceptives or not is basically considered a private matter and protected from interference by one's right to privacy, by the right to do as one pleases as long as it doesn't impinge on another's equal freedom. When one's freedom is restricted or when there is publicly sanctioned advice about what to decide, the justification usually involves some calculation of risks and benefits, whether to the mother or the embryo or the society.

It is not surprising that freedom and utility are the principles which are publicly appealed to. The options in contemporary moral philosophy are often seen to be either formalism, with its Kantian heritage and its emphasis on freedom and autonomy, or utilitarianism with its pedigree in Mill and Bentham and its principle of the greatest good for the greatest number. The philosophers have not convinced us which principle is the right impartial principle, but they have evidently succeeded in convincing us that public moral discourse, including discourse about reproduction, must be limited and governed by principles we can and must hold on the basis of reason alone, specifically freedom and utility.

The strength of such an impartial perspective should not be neglected, especially in a pluralistic society; and a theological ethic need not disown impartial rationality. But for all the importance of freedom and utility when we deal with strangers, they provide little help in understanding the moral significance of the family or of being and becoming a parent (or not). The impartial principle of freedom tends to reduce such role relationships to contractual relationships between independent individuals; and utility tends to reduce them to instrumental relationships designed to achieve some extrinsic good. These impartial principles may need to be qualified by Christian convictions about freedom and about the good to be sought and done as well as supplemented by reflection about the significance of human sexuality and parenting — at least if we are to live with Christian integrity as well as impartial rationality. Our new powers over reproduction, including our power to prevent conception, demand theological reflection if we are to preserve Christian integrity in our exercise of human powers. That theological reflection involves a number of issues, many of them introduced before.

One issue is the relation of theological ethics to "natural" moral wisdom. The contrast is quite striking in this chapter between the claim of Paul VI in *Humanae Vitae* (selection 59) to be defending a "natural" morality and the effort of Karl Barth (selection 62) to articulate a distinctively Christian perspective *post Christum natum* (after the birth of Christ). Of course, the pope's account of "natural" morality is quite different from a Kantian emphasis on autonomy or a utilitarian emphasis on consequences. And the criticism of *Humanae Vitae* by Charles Curran (selection 60) depends in part on a different reading of "natural law"; Curran accuses the document of "physicalism," of taking biological law to be moral law and of prohibiting interference with nature.

Another issue is the meaning of respect for persons and their agency. Barth's essay makes significant appeals to "freedom," but it is hardly the conventional understanding of freedom as autonomy, as the capacity of a neutral agent to will what he will, unconstrained and uncoerced. Rather, it is the freedom given by God which recognizes that the Christian is not a law to himself (autonomous) but stands in and under the command of God. How should Christians think of freedom and of the respect due persons? The selection from Jim Gustafson in the previous chapter may prompt some questions here. Certainly it is theologically warranted to require respect for the capacities for agency, but is respect for persons identical to respect for their capacities for agency? Or, if persons are more than their capacities for agency, does respect for persons also require respect for their bodily natures? Again, does respect for persons entail respect for them not only as autonomous individuals but also as "members of one another," as members of communities, some of which at least are not of their own choosing? Answers to these questions will hardly resolve the moral question of contraception, but they will determine whether procreative decisions should be limited morally only by the requirement that they be made by consenting adults. If we assert the moral significance of our bodily natures and of the natural communities by which we are members of one another, there may be other moral requirements on procreative (and contraceptive) decisions than simply that they be made autonomously.

Consider, for example, our obligations to nurture and to sustain community. We live in a variety of communities, of course, but one can hardly consider procreative decisions without considering the community of marriage. *Humanae Vitae* calls attention to this community, to the mutual love which is to characterize it, and to the "unitive meaning" of sexual relations within it. To some readers, however, this very personal account of marriage stands in uneasy tension with the biological account of the "procreative meaning" of sexual relations. Some ask whether the "unitive meaning" should not take precedence over the biological and "procreative meaning" rather than being simply joined to it in "inseparable connection" in every act of sexual intercourse. Karl Barth, for example, asks whether the "marital fellowship" might sometimes be imperilled by the failure to use contraception.

Convictions about the sort of community that marriage is — and should be — will shape our disposition toward the children who might result from sexual intercourse. James Burtchaell argues (in selection 61) that part of what is at stake in thinking about contraception are competing conceptions of marriage. He invites us to consider Christian marriage as an exercise in adult education, as a school for virtue, and to think about our new powers over the beginnings of human life in that context.

Burtchaell's point may remind us that marriage and family, as communities in the context of other communities, are not simply "retreats" from the larger society but schools for service in it. And if that is so, then the question about contraception opens up questions of social ethics. In the selection from Charles Curran, for example, questions of population and of power are prominent. He retrieves the Catholic emphasis on the social nature of human existence to insist that the question of contraception be addressed not only in the context of the individual and the couple but also in the light of the social vision of the kingdom "always beyond our grasp." Contraceptive technologies, too, must be tested by and tied to considerations of economic and political justice, including justice for women.

One can hardly leave this point, however, without observing the concern of *Humanae Vitae* with the larger social consequences of the contraception revolution. Paul VI has been call a "prophet" for the prediction in *Humanae Vitae* of a "general lowering of morality" and of a sexism in which a woman is regarded and treated "as a mere instrument of selfish enjoyment."[1] A "contraceptive ethic" which divorces sexual intercourse not only from procreation but also from commitments of fidelity and responsibility for offspring is hardly in the interest of women or children or society.

Still another issue, which was examined in an earlier chapter, now bears concretely on this question. It is the issue of nature and its mastery. Is the normatively human to be found in nature or in mastery over nature? Is the natural process of procreation normative, or is it distinctively human procreation when it is controlled and planned, when the natural processes are brought under human control? Perhaps we are human precisely in being both children of nature and children of spirit, but what are the implications of that for reflection about birth control? Is the human sexual act ever simply "natural" or always "unnatural" insofar as it is formed by human intentions? Even the appeal to the "natural" is a form of human intentionality, and it is worth pondering *Humanae Vitae* as an attempt to protect not the "nature" of the act but the human and Christian significance of the act.

These questions are critically important not only to guide and direct the use (or nonuse) of contraceptive and other powers over procreation processes but also because unthinking use of contraceptives jeopardizes the quality of the sexual act by trivializing it, making it facile and insignificant. Theological reflection is necessary not only to limit our powers but also to preserve our capacities for expressing and gesturing our gratitude to God and our confidence in God with our sexuality. "It is," as Paul Ricoeur said, "probable that a rational use of contraception can only succeed where men are spiritually aroused to the need for maintaining the quality of sexual language."[2]

Notes

1. Janet E. Smith, "Paul VI as a Prophet," in Smith, ed., *Why "Humanae Vitae" Was Right: A Reader* (San Francisco: Ignatius Press, 1993), pp. 521-23.

2. Paul Ricoeur, quoted in "Sexuality and the Modern World: A Symposium," *Cross Currents* 14 (Spring 1964): 247.

Suggestions for Further Reading:

Cahill, Lisa. "Catholic Sexual Ethics and the Dignity of the Persons: A Double Message?" *Theological Studies* 60/1 (1989): 120-50.

Curran, Charles E., and Richard A. McCormick, eds. *Dialogue about Catholic Sexual Teaching* (New York: Paulist, 1993).

Dyck, Arthur J. "Ethics, Policy, and Population Debates," Chapter in *On Human Care* (Nashville: Abingdon Press, 1977), pp. 32-51.

Hamel, Ronald. "In the Name of God and Truth: The Catholic Ban on Sterilization," *Second Opinion* 19 (January 1994): 93-96.

Noonan, John T. *Contraception: A History of Its Treatment by the Catholic Theologians and Canonists*, enlarged edition (Cambridge, Mass.: Harvard University Press, 1986; original ed. 1965).

Potter, Ralph. "Religion, Politics, and Populations: A Time for Change," *Harvard Medical Alumni Bulletin*, 41 (1967): 14-21.

Spicker, Stuart F., et al. *The Contraceptive Ethos: Reproductive Rights and Responsibilities* (Dordrecht: Kluwer Academic Publishers, 1987).

Spitzer, W. O., and C. L. Saylor, eds. *Birth Control and the Christian: A Protestant Symposium on the Control of Human Reproduction* (Wheaton, Illinois: Tyndale, 1964).

Thielicke, Helmut. *The Ethics of Sex*. Translated by John W. Doberstein (New York: Harper and Row, 1964), pp. 200-225.

Veatch, Robert M., ed. *Population Policy and Ethics: The American Tradition* (New York: Irvington, 1997).

59 Of Human Life (*Humanae Vitae*)

Encyclical Letter of His Holiness on the Regulation of Birth

Paul VI

The Transmission of Life

The most serious duty of transmitting human life, for which married persons are the free and responsible collaborators of God the Creator, has always been a source of great joys to them, even if sometimes accompanied by not a few difficulties and by distress.

At all times the fulfillment of this duty has posed grave problems to the conscience of married persons, but, with the recent evolution of society, changes have taken place that give rise to new questions which the Church could not ignore, having to do with a matter which so closely touches upon the life and happiness of men. . . .

A Total Vision of Man

The problem of birth, like every other problem regarding human life, is to be considered, beyond partial perspectives — whether of the biological or psychological, demographic or sociological orders — in the light of an integral vision of man and of his vocation, not only his natural and earthly, but also his supernatural and eternal vocation. And since, in the attempt to justify artificial methods of birth control, many have appealed to the demands both of conjugal love and of "responsible parenthood" it is good to state very precisely the true concept of these two great realities of married life, referring principally to what was recently set forth in this regard, and in a highly authoritative form, by the Second Vatican Council in its pastoral constitution Gaudium et Spes (Constitution on the Church in the Modern World).

Conjugal love reveals its true nature and nobility when it is considered in its supreme origin, God, who is love,[1] "the Father, from whom every family in heaven and on earth is named."[2]

Marriage is not, then, the effect of chance or the product of evolution of unconscious natural forces; it is the wise institution of the Creator to realize in mankind His design of love. By means of the reciprocal personal gift of self, proper and exclusive to them, husband and wife tend towards the communion of their beings in view of mutual personal perfection, to collaborate with God in the generation and education of new lives.

For baptized persons, moreover, marriage invests the dignity of a sacramental sign of grace, inasmuch as it represents the union of Christ and of the Church.

Its Characteristics

Under this light, there clearly appear the characteristic marks and demands of conjugal love, and it is of supreme importance to have an exact idea of these.

This love is first of all fully human, that is to say, of the sense and of the spirit at the same time. It is not, then, a simple transport of instinct and sentiment, but also, and principally, an act of the free will, intended to endure and to grow by means of the joys and sorrows of daily life, in such a way that husband and wife become one only heart and one only soul, and together attain their human perfection.

Then, this love is total, that is to say, it is a very special form of personal friendship, in which husband and wife generously share everything, without undue reservations or selfish calculations. Whoever truly loves his marriage partner loves not only for what he receives, but for the partner's self,

From the St. Paul Editions, 1968. Used courtesy of the Daughters of St. Paul, 50 St. Paul's Ave., Boston MA 02130.

rejoicing that he can enrich his partner with the gift of himself.

Again, this love is faithful and exclusive until death. Thus in fact do bride and groom conceive it to be on the day when they freely and in full awareness assume the duty of the marriage bond. A fidelity, this, which can sometimes be difficult, but is always possible, always noble and meritorious, as no one can deny. The example of so many married persons down through the centuries shows, not only that fidelity is according to the nature of marriage, but also that it is a source of profound and lasting happiness and finally, this love is fecund for it is not exhausted by the communion between husband and wife, but is destined to continue, raising up new lives. "Marriage and conjugal love are by their nature ordained toward the begetting and educating of children. Children are really the supreme gift of marriage and contribute very substantially to the welfare of their parents."[3]

Responsible Parenthood

Hence conjugal love requires in husband and wife an awareness of their mission of "responsible parenthood," which today is rightly much insisted upon, and which also must be exactly understood. Consequently it is to be considered under different aspects which are legitimate and connected with one another.

In relation to the biological processes, responsible parenthood means the knowledge and respect of their functions; human intellect discovers in the power of giving life biological laws which are part of the human person.[4]

In relation to the tendencies of instinct or passion, responsible parenthood means that necessary dominion which reason and will must exercise over them.

In relation to physical, economic, psychological and social conditions, responsible parenthood is exercised, either by the deliberate and generous decision to raise a numerous family, or by the decision, made for grave motives and with due respect for the moral law, to avoid for the time being, or even for an indeterminate period, a new birth.

Responsible parenthood also and above all implies a more profound relationship to the objective moral order established by God, of which a right conscience is the faithful interpreter. The responsible exercise of parenthood implies, therefore, that husband and wife recognize fully their own duties towards God, towards themselves, towards the family and towards society, in a correct hierarchy of values.

In the task of transmitting life, therefore, they are not free to proceed completely at will, as if they could determine in a wholly autonomous way the honest path to follow; but they must conform their activity to the creative intention of God, expressed in the very nature of marriage and of its acts, and manifested by the constant teaching of the Church.[5]

Respect for the Nature and Purpose of the Marriage Act

These acts, by which husband and wife are united in chaste intimacy, and by means of which human life is transmitted, are, as the council recalled, "noble and worthy."[6] and they do not cease to be lawful if, for causes independent of the will of husband and wife, they are foreseen to be infecund, since they always remain ordained towards expressing and consolidating their union. In fact, as experience bears witness, not every conjugal act is followed by a new life. God has wisely disposed natural laws and rhythms of fecundity which, of themselves, cause a separation in the succession of births. Nonetheless the Church, calling men back to the observance of the norms of the natural law, as interpreted by its constant doctrine, teaches that each and every marriage act *(quilibet matrimonii usus)* must remain open to the transmission of life.[7]

Two Inseparable Aspects: Union and Procreation

That teaching, often set forth by the magisterium, is founded upon the inseparable connection, willed by God and unable to be broken by man on his own initiative, between the two meanings of the conjugal act: the unitive meaning and the procreative meaning. Indeed, by its intimate structure, the conjugal act, while most closely uniting husband

and wife, capacitates them for the generation of new lives, according to laws inscribed in the very being of man and of woman. By safeguarding both these essential aspects, the unitive and the procreative, the conjugal act preserves in its fullness the sense of true mutual love and its ordination towards man's most high calling to parenthood. We believe that the men of our day are particularly capable of seizing the deeply reasonable and human character of this fundamental principle.

Faithfulness to God's Design

It is in fact justly observed that a conjugal act imposed upon one's partner without regard for his or her condition and lawful desires is not a true act of love, and therefore denies an exigency of right moral order in the relationships between husband and wife. Hence, one who reflects well must also recognize that a reciprocal act of love, which jeopardizes the responsibility to transmit life which God the Creator, according to particular laws, inserted therein, is in contradiction with the design constitutive of marriage, and with the will of the Author of life. To use this divine gift destroying, even if only partially, its meaning and its purpose is to contradict the nature both of man and of woman and of their most intimate relationship and therefore it is to contradict also the plan of God and His will. On the other hand, to make use of the gift of conjugal love while respecting the laws of the generative process means to acknowledge oneself not to be the arbiter of the sources of human life, but rather the minister of the design established by the Creator. In fact, just as man does not have unlimited dominion over his body in general, so also, with particular reason, he has no such dominion over his generative faculties as such, because of their intrinsic ordination towards raising up life, of which God is the principle. "Human life is sacred," Pope John XXIII recalled; "from its very inception it reveals the creating hand of God."[8]

Illicit Ways of Regulating Birth

In conformity with these landmarks in the human and Christian vision of marriage, we must once again declare that the direct interruption of the generative process already begun, and, above all, directly willed and procured abortion, even if for therapeutic reasons, are to be absolutely excluded as licit means of regulating birth.[9]

Equally to be excluded, as the teaching authority of the Church has frequently declared, is direct sterilization, whether perpetual or temporary, whether of the man or of the woman.[10] Similarly excluded is every action which, either in anticipation of the conjugal act, or in its accomplishment, or in the development of its natural consequences, purposes, whether as an end or as a means, to render procreation impossible.[11]

To justify conjugal acts made intentionally infecund, one cannot invoke as valid reasons the lesser evil, or the fact that such acts would constitute a whole together with the fecund acts already performed or to follow later, and hence would share in one and the same moral goodness. In truth, if it is sometimes licit to tolerate a lesser evil in order to avoid a greater evil or to promote a greater good,[12] it is not licit, even for the gravest reasons, to do evil so that good may follow therefrom,[13] that is, to make into the object of a positive act of the will something which is intrinsically disorder, and hence unworthy of the human person, even when the intention is to safeguard or promote individual, family or social well-being. Consequently it is an error to think that a conjugal act which is deliberately made infecund and so is intrinsically dishonest could be made honest and right by the ensemble of a fecund conjugal life.

Licitness of Therapeutic Means

The Church, on the contrary, does not at all consider illicit the use of those therapeutic means truly necessary to cure diseases of the organism, even if an impediment to procreation, which may be foreseen, should result therefrom, provided such impediment is not, for whatever motive, directly willed.[14]

Licitness of Recourse to Infecund Periods

To this teaching of the Church on conjugal morals, the objection is made today, as we have elsewhere observed, that it is the prerogative of the human intellect to dominate the energies offered by irrational nature and to orientate them towards an end conformable to the good of man. Now, some may ask: in the present case, is it not reasonable in many circumstances to have resource to artificial birth control if, thereby, we secure the harmony and peace of the family, and better conditions for the education of the children already born? To this question it is necessary to reply with clarity: the Church is the first to praise and recommend the intervention of intelligence in a function which so closely associates the rational creature from his Creator; but she affirms that this must be done with respect for the order established by God.

If, then, there are serious motives to space out births, which derive from the physical or psychological conditions of husband and wife, or from external conditions, the Church teaches that it is then licit to take into account the natural rhythms immanent in the generative functions, for the use of marriage in the infecund periods only, and in this way to regulate birth without offending the moral principles which have been recalled earlier.[15]

The Church is coherent with herself when she considers recourse to the infecund periods to be licit, while at the same time condemning, as being always illicit, the use of means directly contrary to fecundation, even if such use is inspired by reasons which may appear honest and serious. In reality, there are essential differences between the two cases; in the former, the married couple make legitimate use of a natural disposition; in the latter, they impede the development of natural processes. It is true that, in the one and the other case, the married couple are concordant in the positive will of avoiding children for plausible reasons, seeking the certainty that offspring will not arrive; but it is also true that only in the former case are they able to renounce the use of marriage in the fecund periods when, for just motives, procreation is not desirable, while making use of it during infecund periods to manifest their affection and to safeguard their mutual fidelity. By so doing, they give proof of a truly and integrally honest love.

Grave Consequences of Methods of Artificial Birth Control

Upright men can even better convince themselves of the solid grounds on which the teaching of the Church in this field is based, if they care to reflect upon the consequences of methods of artificial birth control. Let them consider, first of all, how wide and easy a road would thus be opened up towards conjugal infidelity and the general lowering of morality. Not much experience is needed in order to know human weakness, and to understand that men — especially the young, who are so vulnerable on this point — have need of encouragement to be faithful to the moral law, so that they must not be offered some easy means of eluding its observance. It is also to be feared that the man, growing used to the employment of anticonceptive practices, may finally lose respect for the woman and, no longer caring for her physical and psychological equilibrium, may come to the point of considering her as a mere instrument of selfish enjoyment, and no longer as his respected and beloved companion.

Let it be considered also that a dangerous weapon would thus be placed in the hands of those public authorities who take no heed of moral exigencies. Who could blame a government for applying to the solution of the problems of the community those means acknowledged to be licit for married couples in the solution of a family problem? Who will stop rulers from favoring, from even imposing upon their peoples, if they were to consider it necessary, the method of contraception which they judge to be most efficacious? In such a way men, wishing to avoid individual, family, or social difficulties encountered in the observance of the divine law, would reach the point of placing at the mercy of the intervention of public authorities the most personal and most reserved sector of conjugal intimacy.

Consequently, if the mission of generating life is not to be exposed to the arbitrary will of men, one must necessarily recognize insurmountable limits to the possibility of man's domination over his own body and its functions; limits which no man, whether a private individual or one invested with authority, may licitly surpass. And such limits cannot be determined otherwise than by the respect due to the integrity of the human organism and its functions, according to the principles recalled earlier, and also according to the correct understanding of the "principle of totality" illustrated by our predecessor Pope Pius XII.[16]

The Church, Guarantor of True Human Values

It can be foreseen that this teaching will perhaps not be easily received by all: Too numerous are those voices — amplified by the modern means of propaganda — which are contrary to the voice of the Church. To tell the truth, the Church is not surprised to be made, like her divine founder, a "sign of contradiction,"[17] yet she does not because of this cease to proclaim with humble firmness the entire moral law, both natural and evangelical. Of such laws the Church was not the author, nor consequently can she be their arbiter; she is only their depositary and their interpreter, without ever being able to declare to be licit that which is not so by reason of its intimate and unchangeable opposition to the true good or man.

In defending conjugal morals in their integral wholeness, the Church knows that she contributes towards the establishment of a truly human civilization; she engages man not to abdicate from his own responsibility in order to rely on technical means; by that very fact she defends the dignity of man and wife. Faithful to both the teaching and the example of the Savior, she shows herself to be the sincere and disinterested friend of men, whom she wishes to help, even during their earthly sojourn, "to share as sons in the life of the living God, the Father of all men."[18]

Notes

1. Cf. I John 4:8.
2. Cf. Eph. 3:15.
3. Cf. Second Vatican Council, Pastoral constitution Gaudium et Spes, no. 50.
4. Cf. St. Thomas, Summa Theologia, I-II, q. 94, art 2.
5. Cf. Pastoral constitution Gaudium et Spes, nos. 50, 51.
6. Ibid., no. 49.
7. Cf. Pius XI, encyc. Casti Connubii, in *Acta Apostolicae Sedis* XXII (1930), p. 560; Pius XII, in AAS XLIII (1951), p. 843.
8. Cf. John XXIII, encyc. Mater et Magistra, in AAS LIII (1961), p. 447.
9. Cf. Catechismus Romanus Concilii Tridentini, part, II, Ch. VIII; Pius XI, encyc. Casti Connubii, in AAS XXII (1930), pp. 562-64; Pius XII, discorsi e Radiomessaggi, VI (1944), pp. 191-92; AAS XLIII (1951), pp. 842-43; pp. 857-59; John XXIII, encyc. Pacem in Terris, Apr. 1'1, 1963, in AAS LV (1963), pp. 259-60; Gaudium et Spes, no. 51.
10. Cf. Pius XI, encyc. Casti Connubii, in AAS XXII (1930), p. 565; decree on the Holy Office, Feb. 22, 1940, in AAS L. (1958), pp. 734-35.
11. Cf. Catechismus Romanus Concilii Tridentini, part. II, Ch. VIII; Pius XI, encyc. Casti Connubii, in AAS XXII (1930), pp. 559-61; Pius XII, AAS XLIII (1951), p. 853; AAS L (1958), pp. 734-35; John XXIII, encyc. Mater et Magistra, in AAS LIII (1961), p. 447.
12. Cf. Pius XII, alloc. To the National Congress of the Union of Catholic Jurists, Dec. 6, 1953, in AAS XLV (1953), pp. 798-99.
13. Cf. Rom. 3:8.
14. Cf. Pius XII, alloc. To Congress of the Italian Association of Urology, Oct. 8, 1953, in AAS XLV (1953), pp. 674-75; AAS L (1958), pp. 734-35.
15. Cf. Pius XII, AAS XLIII (1951), p. 846.
16. Cf. AAS XLV (1953), pp. 674-75; AAS XLVIII (1956), pp. 461-62.
17. Cf. Luke 2:34.
18. Cf. Paul VI, encyc. Populorum Progressio, March 26, 1967, no. 21.

60 The Contraceptive Revolution and the Human Condition

Charles E. Curran

The Council of the Society for Health and Human Values has determined that the most significant and far-reaching advance produced by the new biology is contraception. The purpose of this paper is to study from the perspective of moral theology or Christian ethics the phenomenon of contraception — the great revolution of the new biology — and to see what this tells us about new images of the human condition.[1]

I. The Contraception Revolution

The fact of the contraception revolution must be admitted by all. In 1976 only 7.7 percent of American married women were classified as fertile, not wanting to become pregnant, and nonusers of contraception in their marriage.[2] The changes brought about by contraception have been enormous. At the family level in all parts of the world the procreation of offspring can now be controlled by the marriage partners. No longer are sexual relationships necessarily connected with procreation. Family planning has replaced biological necessity as the way in which parents bring children into the world. Such family planning has above all freed the woman from the biological necessity of spending most of her life as a bearer and nurturer of children. The ability to plan, to limit the number of children, or even to have no children at all has already contributed much to the changing role of women in contemporary society. However, in parts of the world there is still some resistance to family planning and the use of contraception.

Effective contraceptive methods have made it possible at least in theory for the population of countries and of the world to be controlled. According to the "World Population Plan of Action" adopted by the World Population Congress meeting in Bucharest in 1974 under the auspices of the United Nations, if the world population growth continues at the rate of 2 percent, which has been occurring since 1950, there would be a doubling of the world population every thirty-five years.[3] There are different theories about the meaning and extent of the population problem, but at the very minimum all recognize the need for population control in some countries of the world. Effective and cheap contraceptive devices make the control of population much easier.

For individuals engaging in sexual relations contraception does away with the fear of pregnancy. It is difficult to correlate the exact relationship between sexual activity among young nonmarrieds and contraception, but the general wisdom maintains that contraception has definitely contributed to the fact that more unmarried people are sexually active today than ever before. A recent study shows a remarkable upsurge in premarital intercourse by unmarried teen-aged women living in metropolitan areas. A survey taken in 1971 indicated that 30 percent of these young unmarried women had sexual intercourse by the age nineteen. In 1976 the percentage rose to 43 percent. The last survey puts the figure at 50 percent.[4]

The term "revolution" is often abused in our media conscious age, but perhaps the word is justified in referring to the use of contraception and the resultant change brought about for individuals, for families, and for nations in dealing with the problem of human control over births. Effective contraceptive devices have given human beings control over the procreative aspect of sexual relationships and have contributed greatly to significant societal changes. However, the contraceptive revolution has not been without its

From *American Journal of Philosophy and Theology* 3 (May 1982): 42-59. Slightly abridged and edited from the original. Used by permission of the publisher and the author.

problems. There have been a number of significant debates in the area of contraception that can help us to evaluate better the whole question of contraception as an illustration of the ethical and human possibilities and dilemmas brought about by the new biology. The debates have centered on a number of issues — the morality of using contraception; the safety and side effects of contraceptive devices, especially the pill; the problems connected with population control; and the uses and abuses of the power of contraceptive technology.

The Morality of Contraception

The morality of using contraception as a means of family planning has been attacked primarily by the Roman Catholic Church. In 1968 Pope Paul VI reiterated the condemnation of artificial contraception in his encyclical *Humanae Vitae.* The Catholic Church, however, believes in responsible parenthood. Couples should bring into the world only those children that they can care for and educate properly. As early as 1951 Pope Pius XII acknowledged that medical, eugenic, economic, and social conditions can justify the desire to limit the size of one's family. But the official hierarchical Catholic teaching does not allow the use of any means that interfere with the natural act of sexual intercourse or with the sexual faculty. The God-given purpose of the sexual faculty is for the procreation and education of offspring and for the love union of the spouses. Every act of sexual intercourse must be open to this twofold finality. Human beings cannot directly interfere with the faculty or with the act so that the natural finality is frustrated.[5]

There are both practical and theoretical objections to this official teaching within Roman Catholicism. Archbishop John Quinn of San Francisco, president of the National Conference of Catholic Bishops, has recognized the serious pastoral problems existing in the American church on this issue. Quinn recently quoted statistics showing that 76.5 percent of American Catholic married women of child-bearing age use some form of contraception, and 94 percent of these were employing means condemned by the pope. Many theologians have disagreed with the conclusion and the reasoning proposed by the pope. Human beings do have the power and responsibility to interfere with the sexual faculty and act. The official Catholic teaching is often accused of a physicalism or biologism because the biological or physical structure of the act is made normative and cannot be interfered with.[6] I take this dissenting position.

Some Catholics and others have been advocating natural family planning whereby a couple determines the time of ovulation by an examination of the woman's cervical mucus and limits conjugal relations to the sterile time. Promoters of natural family planning (NFP) support this approach with many reasons — often using arguments proposed against other forms of contraception. Natural family planning capitalizes on the contemporary appreciation of the natural, which seeks to avoid additives and pills. NFP appeals to the highest aspect of the human — the love and discipline of the spouses — and is not merely a scientific technique. The method is totally safe and avoids many of the dangers often associated with the pill. NFP requires the joint cooperation of both spouses and does not put the burden of contraception on one — especially the woman.[7] There do seem to be many attractive aspects about NFP, but I personally see no moral problem in using other forms of contraception as a means of exercising responsible parenthood. Unfortunately, NFP does not appear to be effective where discipline, training, and high motivation are not present, so that its effectiveness with regard to population control is questionable.[8]

A related but different moral problem concerns the use of contraception by unmarried people. Although a surprising number of sexually active teenagers do not use contraception, still there can be no doubt that the availability of contraception has contributed to the growing frequency of extra and premarital sexual relations. In general the Judaeo-Christian tradition has historically condemned sexual relations outside the context of marriage. The vast majority of philosophical and theological ethicists seem to agree in insisting that sexual relations must be seen in the context of person relations. Casual and impersonal sex violates the human meaning of sexuality. Many, myself included, understand the full meaning of human sexuality in terms of the total commitment of one person to another in marriage. On the other hand, while maintaining that casual and impersonal sex and sex without full personal commitment are morally wrong, I and many others would urge people engaging in such sexual intercourse to use contraception as a way of avoiding conception. Such people obviously are not prepared to bring children into the world and educate them.

Safety and Side Effects

The question of safety and risk has been a constant worry for women and also a matter for frequent discussion in both the scientific and popular literature. An article in the *New York Times Magazine* in 1976 accepted the conclusion proposed by Professor Martin Vessey of Oxford, whose study group based their findings on the medical histories of 17,000 users of the pill. The benefits of the pill outweigh its disadvantages, but there are some qualifications. Pill users should be kept under general supervision by their doctors. They should limit the length of time they stay on the pill. After 35 years, since the adverse effects tend to increase, for example, the risk of a thromboembolic event, other methods of contraception are suggested.[9] . . .

The most intense study in the United States, conducted by the Kaiser-Permanente Medical Center at Walnut Creek, California, has involved more than sixteen thousand pill users over a period of ten years. The final report of this study, which will now cease because of its high cost (4.3 million dollars), is being readied for publication. Newspaper accounts report the findings that in a population of young, adult, white, middle-class women the risks of oral contraception use appear to be negligible. But the final word is not in, and women must weigh the pros and cons among the uncertainties. Smoking, long sun exposure, and having multiple sex partners increase the risks.[10]

However, there has been a continuing opposition to the use of contraceptive pills, especially from some feminist groups who view the risks connected with the pill as unacceptable and unnecessary. There are other forms of safe contraception which do not put such a burden on the woman.[11]

One can conclude there will probably never be a form of contraception which is absolutely safe with no negative side effects and no inconveniences. The woman using the pill now must make a prudential judgment based on the available information. However, one should remember that there are also risks in childbearing itself. . . .

There is one other "side effect" of the pill that should be mentioned, but with side effects understood in a broader way. This is the great rise in the rate of VD. In the mid-1950s there was a general feeling that VD was no longer a real problem in the United States. Federal appropriations for VD fell from a high of 17 million dollars to 3 million dollars in 1955. But in the late 1950s after the introduction of the pill the reported cases of infectious syphilis and gonorrhea began to rise. By the 1970s gonorrhea had become the number one of all the reportable communicable diseases in the United States. Similar growth in VD has been reported in other countries of the first world such as England, Canada, Australia, and Denmark.[12] One can legitimately assume that the use of the pill is causally related in some manner to the increase in VD because the pill (unlike the condom) does nothing to prevent the spread of VD. The linkage between the use of the pill and the rise of VD is another indication that there is no such thing as a contraceptive which is perfect from every perspective.

Population Control

The macro aspects of the contraception revolution involve especially the question of population control. Here, too, there has been much discussion in the last decades. Of primary importance is the very definition and understanding of the problem itself. I agree with the approach of Philip Hauser, who insists on a complex understanding of the problem, including four elements or even four crises. The population explosion refers to the growing number of people. The population implosion indicates the increasing concentration of people on relatively small portions of the earth's surface. The population displosion means the increasing heterogeneity of people who share the same geographical state as well as the same social, political, and economic conditions, as exemplified by current problems in Northern Ireland, in many African countries, and even in Canada. Finally, the technoplosion refers to the accelerated pace of technological innovation which has characterized our present era. Hauser maintains that the problems created or exacerbated by implosion and displosion will create more human misery during the remainder of this century than the problems produced by excessive fertility and growth.[13] However, we must not forget the long-range problems.

A fundamental ethical problem concerns the means used by government to control the growth of population. The moral values involved here are the freedom of the individual, justice, and the general welfare of the nation, including security and survival.[14] On a scale of government interference in a continuum from freedom to coercive policies, the following general approaches can be identified: education, motivation, and propaganda for population control together with provision of acceptable means of controlling fertility to all who want them; change of structures which affect demography; incentives offered to control population; coercive methods.[15]

In general I am opposed to coercive measures except as an absolutely last resort, but it is necessary to evaluate properly the role and meaning of freedom in these discussions about contraception and population control. Too often freedom in these matters can be poorly understood in an overly individualistic sense. Insistence on reproductive autonomy can forget the social dimensions of human sexuality and procreation. Sexuality and procreation involve a relationship to the human species. Precisely because of the social aspects of procreation the individual couple must give consideration to the broader question of overpopulation. The possibility of accepting coercion as a last resort, at least from a theoretical position, is based on this more social understanding of freedom and responsibility in the matter of marriage. However, in practice, the complexity of the population problem and the dangers of abuse argue against the acceptance of coercion.

The reasoning behind the official Catholic Church's teaching on procreation and its condemnation of artificial contraception is most instructive in this matter of freedom. The Catholic condemnation of artificial contraception rests on the assumption that the sexual faculty has a purpose and finality related to the species and including more than merely the individual or the couple. Freedom of the spouses is not the only ethical concern; the species must also be considered. The official Catholic approach is insightful in recognizing the need to consider more than the freedom of the spouses. Apart from the question of the means employed, the official Catholic position can and does support the need to control population if this is truly necessary for the human good. Catholic teaching in this and other related matters has never absolutized the freedom of the individual person but has constantly stressed the social nature of human existence. As mentioned above, I disagree with the aspect of official Catholic teaching which maintains that every single act must be open to procreation so that one cannot directly interfere with artificial means.

Contraception as Power

In the last few decades there has been a growing skepticism and criticism of science and technology. Much of the recent ferment surfaced again at the Conference on Faith, Science, and the Future sponsored by the World Council of Churches at the Massachusetts Institute of Technology in July 1979. One of the most significant divergencies in the conference, in the preparatory papers, and in meetings concerns the very meaning of science itself. Note that we are not talking about technology as applied science but rather about pure science itself. The one perspective, which has been typical of traditional Western understanding, sees science as an objective search for knowledge and a method for solving problems. The objectivity of science calls for the scientist to abandon all subjective prejudices and presuppositions and enter into give-and-take with fellow scientists in the objective and disinterested search for truth. The method of test and experiment facilitates this objective search. Yet there is no doubt that science itself can and has been abused. The tremendous cost of scientific research today means that pure science is subject to the industries and governments which support it. Likewise, the results of science and the technology it produces have been abused and put to wrong purposes. In this connection one can mention the question of atomic and nuclear weapons.[16]

A second view, often connected with a more radical perspective, sees science not so much as knowledge but as power. The sociology of knowledge reminds us that knowledge is always a function of practical interests. Science is power over nature and over people wielded by the strong against the weak. Science is what scientists do in the social situations in which they work. Science objectively exists only as a social reality and is closely related to economic and political interests. The objectivity and disinterestedness of science are a myth.[17]

Both positions seem to have some truth, but it is not necessary for us to become involved in a long discussion of the problem, since we are dealing with contraceptive technology, or applied science. All must recognize the connection between power and contraceptive technology. An examination of some of the debates in the matter of contraception shows that contraceptive technologies have constituted a power which has been used against the weak and the disadvantaged. Aspects of contraception as power have arisen vis-à-vis individual poor in this country, against women in general, and against the developing nations of the world.

First of all, contraception as power has been used against the poor in this country. Perhaps the best illustration has been the sterilization of people against their will. Headlines were created with the revelation that people in Virginia public institutions had been sterilized without their consent. Questions have also been raised about the free consent given by poor women to sterilizations when they did not truly understand the nature of the operation.[18] The dangers here are very real, and there have been many illustrations of such abuses of power without the truly informed consent of the persons involved.

Second, some feminists have maintained that women have been victimized by the pill. Men have used their dominant power to make sure that it is the woman who puts up with the risks of using the pill. While many look upon the pill as something which has brought about greater freedom for women, these feminists see the pill as another form of male oppression forcing the women to take all the risks involved in contraception. Feminists and others also resent the importance given to the psychological fears often mentioned as deterring the male from sterilization, even though male sterilization (vasectomy) is a much simpler medical procedure than female sterilization (tubal ligation). Contraception can become another form of male dominance.[19]

A third aspect of contraception as power is seen in the attitudes of many of the countries of the first world to the population problems in the developing nations. Too often official United States policy and the opinions of many Americans, especially before the 1974 United Nations Conference in Bucharest adopted its World Population Plan of Action, saw the solution of the overpopulation problem only in terms of a reduction of the birth rate through efficient, inexpensive, and readily available contraception. Population growth was seen as the cause of many other problems such as retarded economic growth, shortage of food resources, and pollution of the environment. One can readily recognize the temptation of employing a technological fix without realizing the complexity of the reality involved and above all without acknowledging the many problems created by the United States and other nations of the first world.

The complexity of the population problem is such that merely providing the means for individuals to control fertility is not enough. Other population factors are involved such as population distribution and structure, migration, mortality rates, and the role of women in society. Above all, the position of Americans with their unilateral approach to the population problems was suspect precisely because they failed to recognize the underlying problems to which the first world is contributing so much. Overconsumption by the first world creates just as many, if not more, problems than overpopulation by others. Above all the population question cannot be viewed apart from its interdependence with social phenomena such as economic change, environmental factors, and technological developments.[20]

There is some evidence to support the position that programs aimed at lowering fertility will not be successful unless they are accompanied by social and economic changes. To poverty-stricken mothers in American ghettos a child is a source of joy, hope, and contentment which cannot be had in any other ways.[21] India's programs for population control based on massive contraception and sterilization have been failures apparently because they did not recognize the interrelatedness of the population problem with other factors, especially the economic.[22] One can understand how the poorer nations of the world saw in the

American insistence on contraception and sterilization as the solution to the population problem another instance of the strong trying to hold on to their power and oppress the weak.

II. The Human Condition

What do this analysis of the contraceptive revolution and the ethical questions raised by it tell us about our image of the human condition? Our understanding of the human condition obviously influences our evaluation of contraceptive technology, but an analysis of the contraceptive revolution and its human and ethical ramifications also sheds some light on our appreciation of the human condition. Three different aspects of the human condition will be discussed — anthropology in general, human progress, and technological progress.

Anthropology

As might be expected, there have been and are different approaches to anthropology in the Christian tradition, and these differences continue to exist today. In general, one can distinguish more optimistic anthropologies and more pessimistic anthropologies. Harvey Cox with his emphasis on the secular city represented a more optimistic anthropology in his writings in the 1960s.[23] Cox did not deny the reality of sin, which in Christian theology has usually been the grounding for more pessimistic anthropology, but Cox attempted to reinterpret the very meaning of sin. The Christian tradition sees the primary sin of human beings as pride — the unwillingness to accept the limitations and dependency of our human condition. The good Christian thus becomes the individual who does not expect too much of oneself and is content to live within limitations. But today we need a doctrine of sin that will not encourage defense and dependency. We need an anthropology that will accentuate the responsibility that human beings must take for the cosmos and its future. An emphasis on guilt and forgiveness has made Christians look backward, but the gospel is a call to leave what is behind and open ourselves to the promises of the future. The primary sin is not pride but sloth — *acedia* — an abdication of our power and a failure to take responsibility for the world in which we live. Today the gospel calls the Christian to an adult stewardship, originality, inventiveness, and the control of the world. Even the sin of Adam and Eve was not pride but sloth. Self-doubt, hesitant activity, and dependency preceded that fatal nibble.[24]

Paul Ramsey, especially in his writings on the new biology, takes a more pessimistic view of anthropology and stresses that *hubris,* or pride, is the primary sin of human beings. Ramsey sees many ethical violations on the horizontal plane of human existence brought about by the new biology — coercive breeding or nonbreeding, injustices done to individuals or mishaps, the violation of the nature of human parenthood. All these ethical violations on the horizontal plane point to a fundamental flaw in the vertical dimension — *hubris,* or playing God. In attempts of the new biology to fabricate human beings, to prevent aging, to make cyborgs, to control intimate human moods and powers, Ramsey perceives the human desire to have limitless dominion over our lives — the fatal flaw of *hubris,* or the denial of our own creatureliness. Ramsey insists on the limitations of human wisdom as a guide for the rosy future portrayed by the messianic positivists. If our genetic planning policy is no better than our foreign policy or our urban policy, then we will truly be in trouble. Human beings must be willing to accept our finitude and our limitations, to say nothing of our sinfulness.[25]

My understanding of Christian anthropology is greatly influenced by what is logically the first step in any theological ethics — what has been called the stance, perspective, posture, or horizon of Christian ethics. The stance is the logically first step broad enough to encompass the entire matter of Christian ethics but also able to provide a perspective within which the field of moral theology can be viewed. As a stance for Christian ethics I proposed in *Personal Ethics* the need to see all human reality in terms of the fivefold Christian mysteries of creation, sin, incarnation, redemption, and resurrection destiny. In the light of this stance anthropology tends to find a balance between the extremes of Cox and Ramsey as mentioned above. Creation, incarnation, and redemption all point to human goodness and the power which is ours as God's gracious gift. However, creation also reminds us of our finitude and limitations; sin affects us without ever destroying our basic goodness and without totally escaping the reality of redemption; resurrection destiny as the fullness of the kingdom always lies beyond our attainment in this world.

Such a theoretical framework for anthropology, which recognizes the positive aspects of human existence but also cautions about continuing limitation, sinfulness, and incompleteness, is confirmed by our consideration of contraceptive technology and by developments in the new biology. Human beings through technology have a greater power and corresponding responsibility than we ever had before. With the new medical technology human beings are called upon to make decisions about life and death itself, e.g., pulling the plug on the respirator or deciding who will receive lifesaving technologies. But, on the other hand, finitude and sinfulness will always affect our human existence. Contraception has enhanced human responsibility and freed us from a determinism by the forces of nature, but biological or any other kind of technology cannot overcome our basic creatureliness. Likewise, the proclivity to abuse based on our continuing sinfulness must always be recognized. Contraception, despite its many contributions to human development, has also contributed somewhat to a depersonalization of human sexuality in some areas of human behavior. Technological contraceptive power has been used by the strong at the expense of the weak. A series of checks and balances on researchers, drug companies, and contraception programs of governments is an absolute necessity.

The recognition of the greater power and responsibility that human beings have achieved because of science, technology, and other developments has led some to describe the human being as a self-creator. In one sense the concept of the human person as a self-creator is not all that new. Thomas Aquinas grounded his anthropology in a similar concept. In the prologue to the second part of the *Summa Theologiae* which describes the ethical life, Aquinas briefly explains that he will now consider the human being who is an image of God precisely because the human being is endowed with intellect, free will, and the power of self-determination.[26] In contemporary theology Karl Rahner has emphasized the concept of the person as a self-creator. Such assertions must be properly understood. Rahner does not mean to deny all creaturely limitation, but he emphasizes that the human person truly creates and determines one's own self and subjectivity by one's free action. The German theologian stresses that the new aspect in this concept today is the fact that our transcendental self-manipulation can take on new historical and categorical forms because of our science and technology, especially in the biological area.[27] Rahner's emphasis on the subject is part of his transcendental approach, which can be criticized for not giving enough importance to the physical, social, political, and cosmic dimensions of human existence. However, Rahner would agree that we cannot speak of the human person as a self-creator understood in terms of one who makes something out of nothing. Human beings today, thanks to science and technology, have great power over our world, our environment, and even our bodies, but we can never deny our creaturely existence and limitations.

Intimately connected with the improper notion of the person as a self-creator is the ethical reductionism of seeing the human being only in terms of freedom. A proper human anthropology must recognize both our freedom and our limits. We are embodied spirits living in multiple relationships with others. As already pointed out in our discussion of contraceptive technology, a stress on individual freedom and autonomy has often failed to recognize that procreation involves us in a broader web of human relationships. Procreation can never be adequately considered only under the rubric of the freedom of the individual person or couple.

We do not exist in the world apart from our bodies, and to a certain extent we are limited by the givenness of our bodies. The official Catholic teaching condemns contraception as an unwarranted interference in the bodily structures of human existence. I do not agree with such a position, but I also do not agree with those who fail to recognize both the importance and the limitations of the bodily. Joseph Fletcher, for example, maintains that laboratory reproduction is more human than sexual reproduction precisely because it is more rational.[28] However, the bodily is a part of the human, and there are limitations connected with our body that we cannot forget.

Fatigue and pain are two readily experienced limitations with which we constantly live. In the discussion of contraceptive technologies the best illustration of bodily limitations is the problem with the safety and side effects of the pill. The complex hormonal systems of the human body cannot be interfered with at will. There are intricate relationships and connections that must be taken into account. The chemicals that prevent ovulation can and do have deleterious effects on other bodily organs and functions. These limitations of the complex bodily system are analogous to the limitations of the "eco-systems" in our cosmos. The ecological crisis has made us aware of these continuing material limitations of the cosmic world that we inhabit. By overstressing our dominion, our power, and our freedom to intervene in our natural world, we fail to give due importance to the limitations inherent in our bodies and in our cosmos. Yes, human beings have great power and responsibility, but we also have limits, and true responsibility calls for us to recognize these limits.

Human Progress

The question of human progress is ultimately connected with anthropology. What about human progress, especially in the light of the contraceptive revolution? Christian theology has taken a number of different approaches to human progress. In the early part of the twentieth century liberal Protestantism in general and the social gospel in particular emphasized human progress. Influenced by the theory of evolution and recent technological developments, these theologians accepted an evolutionary human progress, some even going so far as to accept the inevitability of such progress.[29]

Protestant liberalism was severely challenged by Karl Barth in Germany and by Reinhold Niebuhr in the United States. It was no coincidence that Barth's commentary on the Epistle to the Romans appeared in 1919,[30] and Niebuhr's *Moral Man and Immoral Society* was published in 1932.[31] The horror of the First World War burst the bubble of an optimistic progress which, according to the caricature, proclaimed that every day and in every way we were becoming better and better. The brutal reality of war contradicted the bland slogans of the social gospel — the fatherhood of God and the brotherhood of men. It is a sad commentary that the sharpest attack in the United States against the progressivism of liberal Protestantism was occasioned by the economic problems of the depression rather than by the war! But, whatever the occasions, the progressive and optimistic theology of the early part of the century was no longer acceptable in the light of the brutality of war and the harshness of the industrial revolution with its ever-widening gulf between the rich and the poor. The neoorthodoxy of Barth and the Christian realism of Niebuhr stressed the transcendence of God rather than immanence, placed heavy emphasis on human sinfulness, and insisted that the fullness of the kingdom lies beyond the world, or "beyond tragedy" as Niebuhr entitled one of his books of sermons.[32] The Second World War reinforced the mood of realism with its denial of dramatic human progress within history.

In the 1960s a change occurred which can be seen in the theology of secularity and the death of God theology.[33] Secularity was no longer something opposed to the gospel, but the gospel according to the theologians of secularity calls for us to accept secularity with all its hopes and promises. The older pessimistic theology no longer attracted universal support, especially in the light of the power and the responsibilities that were in the hands of human beings to shape their own future and the destiny of the world. There are those who said that the secular city theology was just a warmed-over version of the social gospel, but it captured the attention of many in the middle 1960s.[24]

Once again, however, human experience shifted. The great hopes of the early 1960s, as expressed for example in the inaugural address of John F. Kennedy in 1960 and Lyndon Johnson in 1964, were dashed against the stark realities of discrimination, war, and poverty. Many thought that the school desegregation decision of 1954 and the march on Selma marked the beginning of a new era in race relations, but the urban riots of the late 1960s reminded Americans of how deeply racism and poverty were engrained in our society. The 1960s began with great hopes of peace throughout the world, but the involvement in Vietnam disillusioned many Americans. On a worldwide basis the poverty problem indicated the structural problems of economic neocolonialism, because of which the first world was systematically keeping the developing world in the shackles of poverty. In the light of many of these developments the overly optimistic theology of the early 1960s was no longer convincing.

Changing attitudes to human progress from the 1960s to the present can be seen in the work of many theologians. Take, for example, Johannes Metz. In the early 1960s Metz put heavy emphasis on secularity and the world as history. This incarnational approach with its stress on history rather than on nature emphasized human freedom and responsibility in the world in which we live.[35] By the middle 1960s Metz's understanding of the problematic shifted from secularity to futurity, from an incarnational to an eschatological approach. Eschatology, futurity, and hope characterized the work of many theologians in this period. In this eschatology there was some continuity between the present and the future.[36] In the early 1970s a change emerged in Metz's development. The tone becomes more pessimistic as the aspect of suffering is added. The relationship of human beings to history now occurs through suffering, which is seen in the light of the dangerous memory of Jesus.[37] Finally in the later 1970s the eschatological element in Metz now emphasizes not the continuity but the discontinuity between the present and the future. Apocalyptic becomes a central theme in Metz, who strongly opposes an evolutionary and teleological view of eschatology which is often associated with the Western technological perspective.[38]

Thus we are confronted with the question: Is there truly human progress in history and how does it occur? Again, my theoretical approach is based on the stance or perspective. The goodness of creation, the incarnation, and the fact that redemption has already occurred argue for some continuity between the present and the future of the kingdom. However, human finitude, sinfulness, and resurrection destiny as future call for some discontinuity between the present and the future. The fullness of the kingdom is always beyond our grasp. Such a perspective has room for some truly human progress in history, but the negative aspects of finitude, sin, and eschatological incompleteness are limits against a naive, evolutionary, and too optimistic view of human progress. Such a perspective, especially when looking at history in the long view, does not expect to see any great or dramatic breakthrough in human progress. Yes, there can and will be some limited progress over time, but there will be no utopias existing in this world. My approach thus differs from both evolutionary progressivism and contemporary apocalypticism.

How does this theoretical view of human progress stand up in the light of experience in history? The interpretation of history is always risky. One can point to great deformations that have occurred in the development of history. Modern war with its nuclear weapons has become infinitely more destructive than earlier wars. However, I think there has been limited but significant historical advance in terms of truly human progress. A very basic ethical reality concerns the rights, dignity, and equality of human beings. Here one can note some true historical progress. Slavery is nowhere near as prevalent as it was at one time. Our society today is much more aware of the equal rights of women. Contemporary human beings have a greater area in which to exercise their freedom and responsibility in many aspects of human life. Democratic government has given individuals a greater participation in their government. The Declaration of Human Rights of the United Nations points to an ever-growing awareness on the international level of basic human rights. Without claiming any utopian or dramatic breakthroughs one can make an argument for some true but limited progress in history.

It seems as if theology has somewhat flip-flopped in its approach to human progress and has been too easily influenced by the immediate situations of the times. There will always be more optimistic and more pessimistic periods in human history, but a theological worldview must be supple enough to recognize these ups and downs without losing sight of the overall perspective which in my judgment recognizes some true but limited progress in the course of history. Struggle with penultimate victories somewhat outweighing penultimate defeats, will characterize our historical existence.

Technological Progress

What is the relationship between technological progress and truly human progress? One significant factor contributing to the optimistic understanding of human progress in the 1960s was technological progress. There can be no doubt that technology has made great progress. Human beings have come from the discovery of the wheel to the animal-drawn cart, to the steam engine, the automobile, the airplane, and the rocket ships that landed human beings on the moon. Technological developments seem to be ever progressive in the sense that new developments build on older discoveries and constantly move forward as illustrated in the case of transportation. However, the experience of the late 1960s and the 1970s caused many to take a quite critical look at technological progress.

First, technological progress is not the same as human progress. The apparently steady progressive thrust of technological progress is not true of human progress. Newer technology always builds on the old and improves on it, but look at other areas of human existence. Why do we still read Shakespeare, listen to Bach and Beethoven, admire the sculpture of ancient Greece and Rome, and recognize the artistry of Michelangelo or Raphael? Literature, art, drama, and music do not show this always-advancing progress which is true of science and technology. Human progress and technological progress are not the same precisely because the technological is only one small part of the human. Technology is never going to solve the great human problems of life and death, love and sharing, hope and endurance. Yet technology is not something evil or necessarily opposed to the human, but rather science and technology are the result of human creativity and therefore good. However, science and technology are also quite limited in terms of the truly and fully human. Since the human encompasses much more than the technological, humans at times must say no to the possibilities of technology.

Second, technological progress is not as unilaterally progressive and developmental as was supposed. Technological progress itself is ambiguous. Developments in transportation were used to illustrate the presumably always progressive nature of technological development, but later experience and reflection recall some negative aspects of such development. Think, for example, of the problem of air pollution or the flight from the cities occasioned by the mass use of automobiles. Technological advances, even apart from their relationship to the wider aspect of the human, are not without ambiguous side effects.

III. Conclusion

This paper has studied the contraceptive revolution and has analyzed the understanding of anthropology and of human and technological progress from the perspective of theological ethics. In light of all these considerations, some conclusions can now be drawn with regard to contraceptive technology and its relationship to the human.

First, contraceptive technology in general has been good for human beings. The effects of contraception in the matter of family planning and population control have been very beneficial. To free human beings from physical necessity and to give them greater control and responsibility enhances the reality of the human. The very term "responsible parenthood," accepted by just about all people today, calls attention to the human good which has been brought into being by contraceptive technology.

Second, contraceptive technology is a limited human good. Technology itself can never solve or even touch the deeper human questions and problems of life and death, loving concern, or egoism. Contraception can contribute to the well-being of spouses and of families. Population control can help nations and the whole world. However, the human problems and possibilities facing individuals, spouses, nations, and the world transcend the level of biological technologies or of all technologies combined. Recall the dangerously unilateral approach which viewed the problems of limiting population in the narrow terms of providing safe, cheap, and effective contraceptives and failed to recognize the many other aspects of the problem.

Third, this limited human good remains somewhat ambiguous. The best example of the ambiguity in contraceptive advances had been the dangers and side effects associated with the pill. There will undoubtedly never be a perfect contraceptive in the sense of something that is perfect from every single perspective — the hygienic, the eugenic, the aesthetic, etc. At the very minimum all existing contraceptive technologies seem to have some limitations and imperfections about them.

Fourth, contraception is a limited good which can be abused. While contraception has made it possible for people to practice responsible parenthood, it has also made it somewhat easier for others to engage in impersonal and irresponsible sexuality. Limited human goods are always subject to such abuse.

Fifth, contraceptive technology is susceptible to takeover by the strong at the expense of the weak. The poor in the country, women in general, and the poor nations of the world have all been victims of the contraceptive technology of the powerful. Thus contraceptive technology has been a good for human beings but a good that is somewhat limited, ambiguous, and vulnerable to takeover by the powerful at the expense of the weak. This assessment and understanding of contraceptive technology should provide us with a framework for judging the newer biological technologies that will come our way in the future.

Notes

1. This article was originally presented at the annual meeting of the Society for Health and Human Values in October 1980. Throughout the article contraception will be used in the strict sense to include both contraception and sterilization but *not* abortion.

2. Kathleen Ford, "Contraceptive Use in the United States, 1973-1976," *Family Planning Perspectives* 10 (1978): 264-69.

3. United Nations Economic and Social Council, "World Population Plan of Action," *World Population Conference* (October 2, 1974), E/5585, par. N. 3.

4. Melvin Zelnik and John F. Kantner, "Sexual Activity, Contraceptive Use and Pregnancy among Metropolitan Area Teenagers: 1971-1979," *Family Planning Perspectives* 12 (1980): 230-37.

5. For a summary of this hierarchical Catholic teaching, see Thomas J. O'Donnell, *Medicine and Christian Morality* (Staten Island, New York: Alba House, 1976), pp. 238-57.

6. Archbishop John R. Quinn, "New Context for Contraception Teaching," *Origins: N.C. Documentary Service* 10 (October 9, 1980): 263-67. For an overview of the discussion within Catholicism on the occasion of the encyclical *Humanae Vitae,* see William H. Shannon, *The Lively Debate: Response to Humanae Vitae* (New York: Sheed and Ward, 1970); Joseph A. Selling, "The Reaction to *Humanae Vitae:* A Study in Special and Fundamental Theology" (S.T.D. diss., Catholic University of Louvain, 1977).

7. Mary Shivanandan, *Natural Sex* (New York: Rawson, Wade Publishers, 1979).

8. World Health Organization, *Special Programme of Research, Development and Research Training in Human Reproduction,* 7th Annual Report, Geneva, November 1978. This report is quoted in Carl Djerassi, *The Politics of Contraception* (New York: W. W. Norton, 1980), pp. 9-10. For a defense of the effectiveness of NEP, see Shivanandan, *Natural Sex.*

9. Paul Vaughan, "The Pill Turns Twenty," *The New York Times Magazine,* June 13, 1976, pp. 9ff. The scientific source for *The New York Times Magazine* article is M. P. Vessey and R. Doll, "Is the Pill Safe Enough to Continue Using?" *Proceedings of the Royal Society of London,* vol. B. 195 (1976): 69-80.

10. *The Washington Post,* Tuesday, October 21, 1980, p. A7.

11. Barbara Seaman, *The Doctor's Case Against the Pill* (New York: Doubleday, 1980).

12. Louis Lasagna, *The VD Epidemic* (Philadelphia: Temple University Press, 1975), pp. 1-11.

13. Philip M. Hauser, "Population Criteria in Foreign Aid Programs," in *The Population Crisis and Moral Responsibility,* ed. J. Philip Wogaman (Washington: Public Affairs Press, 1973), pp. 233-39.

14. This is the conclusion of the Population Research Group of the Institute of Society, Ethics and the Life Sciences, which was charged by the Commission on Population Growth and the American Future to examine the relevant ethical values and principles. See *Population Policy and Ethics: The American Experience,* ed. Robert M. Veatch (New York: Irvington Publishers, 1977), especially pp. 477-84.

15. Robert M. Veatch, "An Ethical Analysis of Population Policy Proposals," in *Population Policy and Ethics,* pp. 445-75.

16. Robert Hanbury Brown, "The Nature of Science," in *Faith and Science in an Unjust World: Report of the World Council of Churches' Conference on Faith, Science and the Future,* vol. I, *Plenary Sessions,* ed. Roger L. Shinn (Philadelphia: Fortress Press, 1980), pp. 31-40.

17. Ruben Alves, "On the Eating Habits of Science," in *Faith and Science in an Unjust World,* pp. 41-43.

18. *The Washington Post,* February 23, 1980, p. A1. Patricia Donovan, "Sterilizing the Poor and Incompetent," *The Hastings Center Report* 6, 5 (October 1976): 7, 8; see also the symposium "Sterilization of the Re-

tarded: In Whose Interest?" *The Hastings Center Report* 8, 3 (June 1978): 28-41.

19. See Seaman, *The Doctor's Case Against the Pill.*

20. United Nations Economic and Social Council, "World Population Plan of Action," *World Population Conference* (October 2, 1974), E/5585, par. Nn. 20-67. For other authors who stressed the multidimensional aspects of the problem, see Donald P. Warwick, "Ethics and Population Control in Developing Countries," *The Hastings Center Report* 4, 3 (June 1974): 1-4; Peter J. Henriot, "Global Population in Perspective: Implications for U.S. Policy Response," *Theological Studies* 35 (1974): 48-70.

21. Arthur J. Dyck, "American Global Population Policy: An Ethical Analysis," *Linacre Quarterly* 42 (1975): 60.

22. John F. X. Harriott, "Bucharest and Beyond," *The Month* 7 (1974): 630.

23. Harvey Cox, *The Secular City: Secularization and Urbanization in Theological Perspective* (New York: Macmillan, 1965).

24. Harvey Cox, *On Not Leaving It to the Snake* (New York: Macmillan, 1967), pp. ix-xix.

25. Paul Ramsey, *Fabricated Man: The Ethics of Genetic Control* (New Haven: Yale University Press, 1970), especially pp. 90-96, 150-60.

26. Thomas Aquinas, *Summa Theologiae,* Ia-IIae, Prologue.

27. Karl Rahner, *Theological Investigations,* vol. IX, *Writings of 1965-1967,* I (New York: Herder and Herder, 1972), pp. 205-52.

28. Joseph Fletcher, "Ethical Aspects of Genetic Controls: Designed Genetic Changes in Man," *New England Journal of Medicine* 285 (September 30, 1971): 780-81; see also Fletcher, *The Ethics of Genetic Control: Ending Reproductive Roulette* (Garden City, New York: Doubleday Anchor Books, 1974).

29. For an overview of this period in Protestantism, see John Dillenberger and Claude Welch, *Protestant Christianity: Interpreted Through Its Development* (New York: Charles Scribner's Sons, 1954), pp. 160-254.

30. Karl Barth, *The Epistle to the Romans,* tr. from the 6th ed. by Edwyn C. Hoskyns (New York: Oxford University Press, 1968). For a study of Barth's ethics, see Robert E. Willis, *The Ethics of Karl Barth* (Leiden: E. J. Brill, 1971).

31. Reinhold Niebuhr, *Moral Man and Immoral Society* (New York: Charles Scribner's Sons, 1932); republished in 1960). For a recent evaluation of Niebuhr, see Ronald H. Stone, *Reinhold Niebuhr: Prophet to Politicians* (New York: Abingdon Press, 1972).

32. Reinhold Niebuhr, *Beyond Tragedy: Essays on the Christian Interpretation of History* (New York: Charles Scribner's Sons, 1937; republished in 1965).

33. As illustrations of this approach, see Harvey Cox, *The Secular City,* and Thomas J. J. Altizer and William Hamilton, *Radical Theology and the Death of God* (Indianapolis: Bobbs-Merrill Company, 1966).

34. *The Secular City Debate,* ed. Daniel Callahan (New York: Macmillan Company, 1966).

35. Johannes B. Metz, *Theology of the World* (New York: Seabury Press, 1973), part one, pp. 13-77. In the preface Metz indicates that the essays in this books were written between 1961 and 1967. Although Metz does not explicitly acknowledge any development in the preface, the reader can readily see the development in the book, with part one representing the incarnational stage. See Francis Fiorenza, "The Thought of J. B. Metz," *Philosophy Today* 10 (1966): 247-52.

36. Metz, "Chapter Three: An Eschatological View of the Church and the World," *Theology of the World,* pp. 81-97.

37. Johannes B. Metz, "The Future in the Memory of Suffering," *New Concilium* 76 (1972): 9-25; Metz, "The Future *Ex Memoria Passionis,*" in *Hope and the Future of Man,* ed. Ewert Cousins (Philadelphia: Fortress Press, 1972), pp. 117-31.

38. Johannes B. Metz, "For a Renewed Church before a Renewed Council: A Concept in Four Theses," in *Towards Vatican III: The Work That Needs to Be Done,* ed. David Tracy with Hans Küng and Johannes B. Metz (New York: Seabury, 1978), pp. 137-45. The suffering and apocalyptic themes are also found in his latest book containing articles published in the 1970s — Johannes Baptist Metz, *Faith in History and Society: Toward a Practical Fundamental Theology* (New York: Seabury, 1980).

61 "Human Life" and Human Love

James T. Burtchaell

The Pope's veto upon artificial contraception, some fear, may provoke schism within the Roman Catholic Church. Others disagree: the issue is not a crucial dogma, it is not at the epicenter of the Christian faith. But these more sanguine observers forget that schism never was the outcome of dogmatic disagreement. It grows out of anger. . . .

The public debate has already known bitter moments and acid words. Many Catholics, according to the polls, could not believe their ears, and are outraged. The Shepherd, who for his part surely anticipated some unhappy bleating from his flock, must have been startled at the barking, howling, and baying, and must wonder what sort of flock grazes in his pasture. Numerous and loud have been the bishops who have instantly demanded unqualified acceptance of *Humanae Vitae;* one is puzzled why similar loyalty oaths were not required after the same pope published *Populorum Progressio.* Many theologians — impressively many — reacted swiftly and dissented from the encyclical. I have felt it necessary to hesitate a while longer, for fear of speaking too rudely. Whenever a responsible and venerable world leader ignores the wisest and most professional advice he can obtain, and throws his full reputation and public respect into jeopardy for a policy he knows will fly in the face of popular sentiment and comfort, one takes pause before criticizing him. But in the end one cannot be abject for the sake of courtesy. And so — surely without rancor, and hopefully with some small measure of the great courage that Paul VI has himself displayed — I must now take public issue with an encyclical that I consider to be disappointingly inadequate and largely fallacious. . . .

Roman documents, it should be remembered, have taken different stands on contraception and on birth control. They are, after all, not exactly the same. Birth control is the more general term, since it includes both contraception and also infanticide before birth. Since abortion has traditionally been viewed by most Catholic divines as occult murder, it is regarded with no tolerance by Rome as a method of birth control. Contraception, an alternative mode of birth control, has been differently considered by Rome and in 1951 Pius XII executed a remarkable swerve in the course of recent tradition when he accepted contraception on principle, in his famous allocution to the Italian Midwives' Society: "There are serious motives, such as those often mentioned in the so-called medical, eugenic, economic and social 'indications,' that can exempt for a long time, perhaps even for the whole duration of the marriage, from the positive and obligatory carrying out of the act. From this it follows that observing the non-fertile periods alone can be lawful only under a moral aspect. Under the conditions mentioned it really is so."

Once the Pope admitted in principle that married couples might have good and wholesome reasons for controlling their own fertility, discussion narrowed to the single question of method. Pius approved only two methods of contraception: total abstinence and periodic abstinence (unfortunately called "rhythm"). All other methods he unflinchingly proscribed.

My own opinion on total abstinence between husband and wife is that it would generally be repugnant and offensive. There would, I reckon, be a few instances when this denial — even by mutual consent — of one of the most appropriate embodiments of marital commitment and affection would not be judged immoral. As for all other means of contraception — withdrawal, rhythm, artificial devices, anovulant pills, temporary or permanent sterilization — I can see no imposing intrinsic ethical difference between them. All are obviously artificial. Some require cultural sophistication (rhythm, pills), others involve a modicum of risk (sterilization), still others are unpleasant

From *Commonweal* 89, no. 7 (15 November 1968): 245-52. Slightly abridged and edited from the original. Used by permission.

(withdrawal, spermicides, devices). Catholic moralists have conventionally condemned all of them, and one ventures to suggest that much of their writing on the subject reads like treatises on sexual plumbing, with a devastatingly equivocal use of the term "unnatural."

Of all these methods I should be tempted to think of rhythm as the most unnatural of all, since it inhibits not only conception, but the expression of affection. It is, in my opinion, a base theology that would want intercourse to harmonize with the involuntary endocrine rhythm of ovulation and menstruation, while forsaking the greater spiritual and emotional ebbs and flows which should also govern sexual union. In the human species, especially, where coitus is freed from the estrous cycle, it is obviously open to personal meaning and depth quite independent of fertility. Different methods of contraception will be employed by couples in different circumstances. Medical advice and convenience will lead them to favor the surest and easiest means, although in certain instances they may have recourse to otherwise less preferable methods. All are artificial, of course, and artificiality in the biology of sexual intercourse need be no more loathsome than it is in synthetic fibers, vascular surgery, or musical composition.

According to the ethical model followed by *Humanae Vitae,* one must assign moral value to methods of contraception within the isolated context of a single event of coitus, rather than the full sequence and story of love and childbearing throughout the course of a marriage. The Pope parts company with his advisory commission, which reported: "The morality of sexual acts between married people takes its meaning first of all and specifically from the ordering of their actions in a fruitful married life, that is, one which is practiced with responsible, generous and prudent parenthood. It does not then depend upon the direct fecundity of each and every particular act."

The Pope rejects this view by stating simply that a single intercourse made intentionally infecund is intrinsically dishonest. But this begs the question. It is being argued precisely that the honesty of intercourse derives, not just from the individual act, but from the whole orientation of the marriage. There are certain features of intercourse which would always have to be present, like gentleness. Other features need to derive from the total sequence of sexual union, but are in no way attached to each event — conception would seem to be one such feature.

Consequently, it is difficult to follow the papal argument. I am unpersuaded that contraception is intrinsically immoral, and what is more, I doubt that the question can be answered on the narrow, single-intercourse basis which the encyclical has taken to be normative.

Primary End

Customary Catholic theology has claimed that the primary end of marriage and of sex is the begetting and rearing of children. Listed as secondary ends: the satisfaction of desire and mutual support. Contraception — so the argument runs — violates this primary purpose by frustrating procreation.

Few non-Catholics accept this outline. Fewer Catholics are anxious to defend it publicly. . . . The argument's greatest weakness, it seems to me, is that it bespeaks of a stud-farm theology. What does "primary end" mean? If it is supposed to mean that the act of intercourse is basically a biological act whose immediate orientation is aimed at procreation, all would agree. But the preponderance of Catholic writers seem to take "primary end" to mean "principal purpose," "most important goal," "chief finality." This is quite absurd. We could as well say that the "primary end" of the Nobel Prize Award Banquet is nutrition, that the "primary end" of the Mexico City Olympic Games is exercise, and that the "primary end" of Baptism is hygiene.

There are plenty of indications that a broader view exists among Catholics. Pius XI, in his encyclical letter on marriage in 1930, cites the traditional Augustinian "reproductive" formula, but later goes beyond it: "This inward molding of spouse to spouse, this eager striving to draw each other to fulfillment, can in the truest sense be called the primary purpose and explanation of marriage, as the *Roman Catechism* teaches. Marriage would thus be considered, not in the narrow sense as created for the procreation and education of offspring, but in the broad sense as the sharing, the familiarity, and the companionship of life in its fullness."

Pius XII laid similarly heavy emphasis on the personal dimension of sex when he spoke out sharply in 1951 against artificial insemination: "To reduce the cohabitation of married persons and the conjugal act to a mere organic function for the transmission of the germ of life would be to convert the domestic hearth, sanctuary of the family, into nothing more than a biological laboratory. . . . The conjugal act in its natural structure is a personal act, a simultaneous and immediate cooperation of the spouses which, by the very nature of the participants and the special character of the act, is the expression of that mutual self-giving which, in the words of Holy Scripture, effects the union 'in one flesh.' "

And just a few years back, the late Msgr. J. D. Conway, former president of the Canon Law Society of America, called for the old Augustinian formula to be dropped: "Canon 1013, which defines the purposes — the philosophical ends — of marriage, should be worded with greater delicacy. The primary purpose, procreation and education of children, clearly relegates to second rank the mutual love, happiness and welfare of the spouses. And these secondary purposes are further slighted by defining them as 'mutual aid and the remedy of concupiscence.' Even though law is not romantic it should be able to recognize in marriage something more human, positive, spiritual and amorous."

There is no reason why the Church should not produce a restatement which gives personal values their proper due. *Humanae Vitae* might have been that restatement. Conjugal love is a many-splendored thing. Christian theology has no choice but to confront it in all its fullness: what Daniel Sullivan has called "psychospiritual union and abandon, the total orgasm of the natural body and spirit."

Natural?

Another weak point in the standard Catholic formula is the undefined and ambiguous way it uses the notion "natural." Everyone agrees that it is good to be natural; what that might mean is more difficult to agree upon. The average European will think it natural to smoke, live gregariously in cities, and discuss politics and religion in the pub; the Peruvian Indian may do none of these, yet not think himself unnatural. A child of three may feel it natural to suck his thumb, as he may feel it natural at fifteen to masturbate; his parents will think both activities are unnatural and immature. Anthropologists tell us it is natural for all peoples to worship a deity; theologians find this suggestive of the supernatural. Manuals of medical ethics teach that progestational steroids (the Pill) are unnatural because they inhibit ovulation; Dr. Rock replies that they are as natural as vitamins. Catholic moralists have claimed it unnatural to misplace, trap, kill, or block the seed in intercourse, but have labeled the rhythm method natural. Not all Catholic parents would agree, as witness this letter to the editors in *Commonweal* in 1964:

"Our second child had shown us that the calendar approach to rhythm was ineffective in our case, and so my wife moved on to the more sophisticated paraphernalia of the rhythm system — thermometers, tapes, tubes and the like . . . We read and re-read the Catholic teaching on the natural law as it applied to marriage in general and to the Church's position on birth control in particular. Again and again the emphasis was found to be placed on what is 'natural'. And then we thought of the tapes and tubes and thermometers. This was natural?"

It seems hopeless to disentangle from this thicket of cross-purposes a working notion of "natural" that could serve the discussion of conjugal morality. For what it is worth, I should like to propose one from scratch.

Moral decisions in statecraft, economics, and jurisprudence are in constant flux, since the state, the economy, and the law are artificial institutions always on the move. There is something more perennial about the family. Marriage, it seems, has certain inbuilt requirements for success — requirements as complex as the intricate, constant makeup of man and woman. Though they have often failed to take the total view of marriage Catholics have rightly insisted that it has its ow ineluctable rules.

On the other hand, marital life is not automa cally controlled as is digestion; a life of love m be a life of free choice. Any appropriate notior "natural" will have to be correspondingly supple. There is perhaps no other human activity which so completely draws on the full range of forces in our nature: the will, the passions and affections, and the body. A restored vision of the "natural" would view the way in which these components of human nature are meant to respond to the conjugal situation: *What brings the personality of the spouses to full bloom, what promotes their growth to maturity, what brings husband, wife, and children to the highest pitch of happiness.*

Learning Generosity

It is unfortunate, not so much that the Pope has chosen to repeat such negative and unconvincing judgments on contraception, but that he continued to dwell almost exclusively upon the problem of method, without adequate attention to the far more crucial issue of motivation. Catholics have offered little insight into this more sensitive moral problem. Except for Pius XII's rather terse outline of reasonable causes, the conventional breeding theology has been about all we have had to give. On the other hand, I find the equally shrill and superficial sort of propaganda devised by those who promote contraception to be frighteningly deprived of any rich vision of marital growth in love. In any Dantesque view of the future, surely the canonist-moralists of the narrow tradition and the evangelists of the Planned Parenthood Federation will be consigned to each other's company.

My distress is that our quibbling over method fails to challenge the illusory motives which lead so many families to adopt contraception. This appears to be the case with individual couples, as also with entire peoples. In this country, for example, millions of families are pressed by medical urgency or financial crisis or similarly serious burdens that contraception can rightly relieve. And in numerous homes, births are timed to allow either for further self-growth in education, or for alternative forms of neighbor-service. But I would estimate that far more couples avoid or curtail children because they share the grudging national attitude that resents children as so many more drains on their generosity and budget. Bluntly: selfishness is perhaps the most frequent excuse for contraception in this rich county.

In this regard, one would fault the Pope for having said too little rather than too much. If a critic may be permitted to point out a passage in the encyclical which seems particularly well put, I would draw particular attention to the disappointingly brief remarks made in par. 9 about the characteristics of conjugal love: "This love is first of all fully human, that is to say, of the senses and of the spirit at the same time . . . This love is total, that is to say, it is a very special form of personal friendship, in which husband and wife generously share everything, without undue reservations or selfish calculations. . . . Again, this love is faithful and exclusive until death."

Here was the vein of thought that could have been worked so much more. It is here, in throwing up to his readers the awesome challenges of marriage, that the pontiff could have confronted the world with its increasingly contraceptive mentality. This is a point which needs making, needs shouting from the rooftops.

Someone is responsible for foisting on our world the fantastic idea that marriage is easy. The Catholic Church has, I think, tended to think it frighteningly difficult. It is always moving for a priest to face a young couple before the altar and guide them through the awesome oaths of total abandonment. Like six-year-olds promising in their prayers to "love God with my whole heart," the bride and groom speak in hyperbole. They could hardly be expected to imagine what are the deeps of "for better, for worse, for richer, for poorer, in sickness and in health, until death do us part." Their parents in the front pews have a good idea; the Church knows, and prays that the young man and woman will find the generosity to learn, and will learn the generosity.

Real love, to men and women born as we all are with a selfish streak, doesn't come easily at all. When Paul tells husbands to love their wives as Christ loved the Church and gave himself up for her, he is haunted by the symbol and measure of that cherishing: the crucifixion. Love, says the Song of Songs, is as mighty as death. It is a struggle to the death to give self away. It has to be learned so very slowly. Marriage is that great adventure in adult education, wherein parents have far more to learn and longer strides to make toward maturity then the children.

Growth in love — as all growth — means

stress and sacrifice. The Church has never tried to conceal this. She simply says that marriage is glorious if you accept the stress and sacrifice. It is hell if you try short-cuts. And there are all sorts of short-cuts offered these days.

Barbara Cadbury, for instance, returned from a good-cheer tour in Asia for the Planned Parenthood Federation, wrote enthusiastically in *Family Planning in East Asia* (Penguin, 1963) of the "courageous sense of realism" with which Japanese kill their children. But the government, she says, now feels "that abortion is, as a regular method of birth control, harmful to the individual despite its benefit to the nation." The individual harmed is presumably the individual killing, not the individual killed. (I am reminded of the complaint made by the Commandant of Auschwitz, that the excessive shipments of Jews to be gassed and cremated worked unreasonable hardship on the prison guards.) But Mrs. Cadbury's most telling remark is this: "No other country in the world has so rapidly passed from fertility-motivated habits to producing only desired and cherished children." The two million or so children each year who are not "desired and cherished" are cut out of the womb and thrown away.

The Catholic Church should see it just the other way around from Mrs. Cadbury. If a man and woman have brought to life in the womb a child who is not desired or cherished, their problem is not how to murder the child but how to learn to desire and cherish him. The Church would concede that it is often easier to kill your child than to love him. But to the Japanese parents and to Mrs. Cadbury she recommends the latter.

A young woman at whose marriage I had officiated came to me several months later to tell me that every night during intercourse she was seized with fear that she might conceive. They couldn't possibly, she cried, afford a baby yet. Knowing that her parents had given them a house and land, and that both husband and wife were working for good wages, I was rather surprised. As it turned out, they had gone heavily into debt to buy an oak living-room suite, a maple bedroom set, a dining room ensemble, kitchen appliances, and laundry equipment. The unfortunate couple had been sold a bill of goods — not by the furniture salesman, but by the rotten and damned culture that had so persuaded a man and his wife that a child came just below laundry equipment on their list of needs. Before the year was out they would come to loathe the oaken and maple boredom.

There are plenty of other examples which betray the radical disagreement between the Church and our culture regarding marriage. We are chided by the realists of the day for our intransigent stand against divorce. Once the marriage relationship is dead — especially when it is violently killed by adultery — it is false to pretend otherwise. The Church replies that the marriage bond is grounded, not on the love of the moment, but on oaths made in view of love. Obviously the oath without the love is misery. But it is the very function of forgiveness to restore that love and breathe into it an even steadier life than before. The Church never ignored the cold fact that adultery kills love; but she recommends resurrection instead of cremation. The Church should know something of forgiveness and its power. The only love-bond she has as Christ's bridge is one of her repentance and his forgiveness. Says Jean Guitton: "The remedy for the ills caused by love is a summons to progress in love. In other terms, love can cure the wounds it inflicts, on condition that it rises to greater heights."

The source which has taught me the most about marriage is the 19th chapter of the Gospel according to Matthew. The chapter records two interviews with Jesus. In the second, he is asked by a young man what he must do to possess eternal life. This was a standard question that any Jew would ask a rabbi and Jesus' answer at first is a very standard answer: "You must keep the Commandments." And he lists several of the very familiar commandments. The young man is pleased and replies that he has been observant since boyhood. Jesus then says that this is not enough. If he wants to go all the way, then he must sell everything, give it away, and follow after him. At this the young man is not so pleased because, as the evangelist points out, he has a great deal to sell. Somewhat disillusioned, he turns around and goes away. The point of the story is that he does not have eternal life even though he has kept the commandments from his youth.

Here Jesus is opposing to the religion of his day another type of faith which has no concrete terms or prior conditions. When a Jew purposely undertook the life of a Jew, he knew what he was undertaking. He was told in advance what were the terms of faith and he accepted them with eyes open. When a man accepted to follow Jesus, he had no idea what the terms were. Nothing specific was told him in advance except that he must surrender to whatever claims Jesus, through all of his neighbors, would put on him. The young man rightly recognized that this was far more frightening since there was no way of calculating how much he was giving away. And so . . . he relinquished eternal life. After he leaves the scene, the disciplines are somewhat nervous and they ask, "Well, if this is the way it is, who on earth could get into the Kingdom of Heaven?" and Jesus says it is not for everyone, it is a gift.

In the earlier part of the chapter, a very similar interview takes place. Jesus is asked what are the terms for divorce. In the religion of his day, people entered marriage knowing in advance what were the limits of endurance: what things a man could be expected to tolerate and what things he need not accept. Jesus insists that in marriage, as he conceives it, there are no terms; there is no divorce. The people go away shaking their heads. Once again the disciples are a little bit upset and they ask Jesus, "But if this is the way it is, who on earth could get married?" and he says, "It is not for everyone; it is a gift."

What I perceive from this chapter is that the unlimited surrender which a man very frighteningly makes to Jesus Christ in Baptism has as perhaps its closest imitation among men Christian marriage, wherein a man and a woman surrender to one another without terms. Jesus can say to a man in the crowd, "You! Follow me" and the man has no idea where that will lead. Just so, a man can say to a woman, "Follow me, with no idea where that will lead or what I will become." And the woman in her turn says to him, "And you follow me, not knowing where I will lead you." Marriage, like Baptism, begins in faith. It is a move based simply upon trust in a person — not a policy, a religion, a moral code, a set of requirements. It is an open-ended abandonment to an unpredictable person, who is known and cherished enough that one can make the surrender.

If this be so, then Christian marriage is not like all other marriages. Marriage is what you make of it and Christian marriage is a particular, voluntary form which Christians have fashioned for themselves. There are many other forms of marriage and we should not imagine that they are not legitimate. If in a certain culture it is accepted that a man has six wives, it is none of our business to constrain the man to discard five of them. If a man says to six women, "You are my wife," then they are indeed his wives. If in another culture it is understood that a man may exchange wives at whim, then it is none of our business to tell him he must marry for life. It is our calling to live our baptismal faith and our marriage faith before the eyes of all men and women so honestly and generously that the entire Christian commitment would in turn become their voluntary undertaking, also.

In fact, it is unfortunate that in our civil marriage ceremony, words are put into the mouths of men and women whereby they promise to one another things that they in no way intend to promise. In our society it is not understood that a man and a woman give themselves away for better, for worse, until death. They do not give themselves away unconditionally; they give themselves away indefinitely. Yet because our civil marriage form is descended from the Christian sacramental forms, couples are forced to say more than they mean.

Now if Christian marriage is a particular, extraordinary, peculiar way for a man and a woman to join together, then we must realize that it has particular obligations. The most important one is similar to the obligation to follow Jesus. When you tied yourself to a person, you cannot control your future. Every one of us has within himself an unbelievable potential for love and for generosity but we do not bring it out very willingly. It has to be torn out of us. And the thing about Christian marriage is that the surprises encountered demand a love and generosity from us that we can in no way calculate or control. If that be so, then the incalculability of the demands of children fits very closely into the generosity that a man and a woman share in marriage. If a man and a woman can and do calculate and hedge the major claims made upon their generosity in the course of their marriage, then I fear that it is less a marriage of faith, and it will not blossom into a marriage of love such as Christians can enjoy.

The Church should not be interested in breeding. A thoughtless priest said in the United States a few years ago that Catholics would put an end to religious discrimination in a generation or two by outproducing their contracepting opponents. Preachers have also suggested that the obligation to crowd heaven should stimulate Catholic parents to optimum production. Both statements breathe nonsense. Yet the Church has always had a smile for children, not because she is interested in population but because she is interested in love. And besides, she was once told that of such is the kingdom of heaven.

A first child, especially a boy-child, can easily be a threat to his father, for he seems to be a competitor for the wife's love that had been all his before. Similarly, each new child that swells the brood can seem a burden: the loaf must now be sliced just that much thinner. Faith sees another side to it. Bread may be sliced thinner, but love is sliced larger, and greater love sets about winning more bread. Every person, every parent is a fathomless well of love-potential. Children are not threats to love or competitors for it — they are new claims upon it, new tugs on the ungenerous heart to force it open further than it felt it could go. Children don't divide parents' love; they should invite it to multiply. Enormous resources of parent-love are let go stagnant in the heart's reservoirs for lack of children to make it gush and flow. Now obviously physical resources are not fathomless, and children must have bread. But in our age and culture, when parents feed their children cake and live in fear of a bread shortage, the Church weeps — and rightly so — that the children are starving in a famine of love.

One is so disappointed in the encyclical. One wishes the Pope had called parents to abandon themselves — in a way that would seem reckless to those without Christian faith — to their children as well as to one another. One wishes he had found a way to restore in husbands and wives so zestful an appetite for sons and daughters that when constrained to choose contraception for one strong motive or another, they would do so with reluctance and a sense of loss. Instead of grumbling that he has wrong-headedly forbidden artificial contraception, one regrets rather that he has not really preached to us the sort of good news that Matthew heard from Jesus.

If we have faith, we have hope. In this time of turmoil and contradiction, the Church will see its way through to a new and yet so very ancient understanding of what children do for their parents — of how they force them, in ways that surprise even themselves, to be greater men and women than they had planned. Jesus Christ has come to destroy all our plans — even those of parenthood.

62 Parents and Children

Karl Barth

Man can be father or mother. A husband and a wife can together become parents. Their relationship to their children in the light of the divine command must now occupy our attention. But first we must answer two unavoidable preliminary questions.

The first is posed by the fact that there are men who do not become parents. We are thinking of all those who broadly speaking might do so, and perhaps would like to do so, but either as bachelors or in childless marriage do not actually fulfil this possibility. What attitude are they to adopt to this lack? What has the divine command to say to them concerning it? In some degree they will all feel their childlessness to be a lack, a gap in the circle of what nature obviously intends for man, the absence of an important, desirable and hoped-for good. And those who have children and know what they owe to them will not try to dissuade them. The more grateful they are for the gift of children, so much the more intimately they will feel this lack with them. Parenthood is one of the most palpable illuminations and joys of life, and those to whom it is denied for different reasons have undoubtedly to bear the pain of loss. But we must not say more. If we can use the rather doubtful expression "happy parents," we must not infer that childlessness is a misfortune. And we must certainly not speak of an unfruitful marriage, for the fruitfulness of a marriage does not depend on whether it is fruitful in the physical sense. In the sphere of the New Testament message there is no necessity, no general command to continue the human race as such and therefore to procreate children. That this may happen, that the joy of parenthood should still have a place, that new generations may constantly follow those which precede, is all that can be said in the light of the fact which we must always take into fresh consideration, namely, that the kingdom of God comes and this world is passing away. *Post Christum natum* there can be no question of a divine law in virtue of which all these things must necessarily take place. On the contrary, it is one of the consolations of the coming kingdom and expiring time that this anxiety about posterity, that the burden of the postulate that we should and must bear children, heirs of our blood and name and honour and wealth, that the pressure and bitterness and tension of this question, if not the question itself, is removed from us all by the fact that the Son on whose birth alone everything seriously and ultimately depended has now been born and has now become our Brother. No one now has to be conceived and born. We need not expect any other than the One of whose coming we are certain because He is already come. Parenthood is now only to be understood as a free and in some sense optional gift of the goodness of God. It certainly cannot be a fault to be without children. . . .

The first point to be inferred as God's command to the childless is thus that they do not let themselves be misled about the matter. They must set their hope on God and therefore be comforted and cheerful. Their lack cannot be a true or final lack, for the Child who alone matters has been born for them too. And we must then continue that they may and must interpret their childlessness as something which specifically frees them for other tasks and cares and joys. To bring up children is a beautiful and promising thing, but the end and purpose of human life cannot and must not be sought in this, as all too happy parents would often have it, since the meaning of this activity is only earthly and temporary. One may and can and must live for God and one's fellows in a very different way. May not childlessness be an indication to those who are troubled by it that they should look all the more seriously to other and perhaps very obvious fields which might have lain fallow had there not been

From Karl Barth, *Church Dogmatics,* III/4, trans. A. T. Mackay et al. (Edinburgh: T&T Clark, 1961), pp. 265-76. Used by permission.

men and women without the desire or worry of bringing up children? And childless married couples in particular should feel the persuasion that as such they are all the more called and empowered to build up their life-companionship with particular care both outwardly and inwardly. Parenthood may be a consequence of marriage which is both joyful and rich in duties, but from a Christian point of view the true meaning and the primary aim of marriage is not to be an institution for the upbringing of children. On the contrary, children may be at least a serious threat to what man and wife should together mean in marriage for the surrounding world. From this point of view, childlessness can be a release and therefore a chance which those concerned ought to seize and exploit instead of merely grieving about it. And finally, should we not ask whether a man and his wife, and even those who are single, are any the less called to be elders, to fatherliness and motherliness, because they are not parents in the physical sense — elders who in regard to all young people have the same task as physical parents have toward their physical offspring? May there not be young persons in their locality whose physical parents may be dead, or for some reason do not fulfil their duty, so that they can help both them (and themselves) if they are willing directly or indirectly to fill the gap? Where the great message of divine comfort is not known and believed, such suggestions will be scorned as an offering of stones for bread. But where it is perceived and accepted, it is hard to see why the childless should not act upon one or other of these suggestions. The divine command, which is only the practical form of this comfort, will certainly draw them out of their grief and warn them to take some such action.

The second preliminary question to be considered is posed by the fact that, while it does not depend on the wishes of a man and woman if their sexual intercourse leads to the birth of a child and therefore to parenthood, they do have the technical possibility of so guiding their sexual activity that it does not have this consequence. Hence in regard to the prolongation of their existence in that of children they have at least this negative power of control. We allude to the problem of what is called birth control. From a Christian point of view, is the exercise of this control permissible, and if so may it sometimes be obligatory? . . .

Our starting point is again the fact that *post Christum natum* the propagation of the race ("Be fruitful, and multiply," Gen. 1:28) has ceased to be an unconditional command. It happens under God's long-suffering and patience, and is due to His mercy, that in these last days it may still take place. And it does actually do so with or without gratitude to the One who permits it. There may even be times and situations in which it will be the duty of the Christian community to awaken either a people or section of people which has grown tired of life, and despairs of the future, to the conscientious realisation that to avoid arbitrary decay they should make use of this merciful divine permission and seriously try to maintain the race. But a general necessity in this regard cannot be maintained on a Christian basis. . . .

From this standpoint, then, there can be no valid objection to birth control.

The matter is rather different, however, when we consider the problem of marital fellowship.

We must first insist that this life-fellowship as such, whether or not it includes parenthood, is a relationship which is sanctified by the command of God. We do not refer to sexual intercourse in itself and as such. Sexual intercourse performed for its own sake, whether within marriage or without, whether with or without birth control, is a nonhuman practice forbidden by the divine command. We say deliberately, however, that according to the command this life-fellowship as such, including its physical basis in sexual intercourse, has its own dignity and right irrespective of whether or not it includes parenthood. It was always crude to define marriage as an institution for the production of legitimate posterity. Even sexual intercourse may have a first essential meaning simply in the fact that it is integral to the completion of marital fellowship. From the standpoint of this fellowship, then, it may not be generally and necessarily required that it should be linked with the desire for or readiness for children. It may rather be that from the standpoint of this fellowship sexual intercourse should be performed in a way which implies that its meaning is simply the love relationship of the two partners and excludes the conception and birth of children.

At this point there does, of course, arise a question which in my judgment is the only one which weighs against the acceptability of birth control. Sexual intercourse as the physical completion of life-partnership in marriage can always be, not merely human action, but an offer of divine goodness made by the One who even in this last time does not will that it should be all up with us. Hence every act of intercourse which is technically obstructed or interrupted, or undertaken with no desire for children, or even refrained from on this ground, is a refusal of this divine offer, a renunciation of the widening and enriching of married fellowship which is divinely made possible by the fact that under the command of God this fellowship includes sexual intercourse. Can we really do this? Should we do so? Do we realise what it means? Does not a real unwillingness at this point involve an imperiling of marital fellowship, slight perhaps but possibly more serious, to the extent that the latter includes the possibility of this broadening? Can even sexual intercourse as the physical complement of marriage be perfect within its limits if it is thus burdened by reluctance in the face of this possibility, or even its deliberate refusal? Or can it be neglected through such reluctance without intimately threatening the whole structure of marriage? Those who basically affirm freedom for birth control cannot too severely put to themselves this practical question. The exercise of this freedom must have valid reasons if the gravity of this renunciation and the seriousness of this threat are to be dispelled, and what one does is therefore to be done with a clear conscience. By this question all frivolity and expediency are excluded. If married life includes sexual intercourse it means that the possibility of parenthood is a natural consequence. To be sure, the attempt to evade this consequence is not always the result of arbitrariness or sloth. Yet those who exclude this possibility and deliberately avoid this consequence must be asked whether they do so under the divine command and with a sense of responsibility to God, and not out of caprice. From this standpoint, therefore, a strong warning must be inserted which we must always consider. In the light of what marital fellowship demands, the use of this freedom may be something which the divine law strictly forbids. The fact remains, however, that even from this standpoint there can be no absolute denial of this freedom.

In favour of this essential freedom, we have to consider that not only the physical consummation of marriage in sexual intercourse as such, but within this the phenomena of procreation and conception, if they are not to elude the imperative of God's command, must be understood as a responsible action on the part of both those concerned. If marital fellowship, including sexual intercourse, has its own right and dignity, the same is true for the act of generation and conception. Just as the former is not merely an arrangement for the continuance of the species, so the latter are not to be regarded as merely the inevitable consequence of the physical intercourse which forms the climax of the fellowship. This means, however, that generation and conception are the effects of an action which is in its own particular way responsible. And as a responsible action it must and will be a choice and decision between Yes and No. Why should we not ask at this point concerning the divine command as though it were already known in this respect? Why should there not have to be a choice and decision at this point? With what right may it be said that these are not necessary here, but it is better to leave things to pot luck, i.e., to chance? It might be objected that they should be left to the rule of divine providence. Man should not interfere with this and therefore with the course of nature. With this, and therefore with "the course of nature" — this is the flaw in the reasoning. For surely the providence of God and the course of nature are not identical or even on the same level. Surely the former cannot be inferred from the latter! Surely the providence and will of God in the course of nature has in each case to be freshly discovered by the believer who hears and obeys His word, and apprehended and put into operation by him in personal responsibility, in the freedom of choice and decision. Surely the specific question: May I try to have a child? has in each case to be given a specific answer as he sets himself in the hands of the living God. Surely he is not allowed to dispense with rational reflection or to renounce an intelligent attitude at this point. The very opposite is the case. At this point especially intelligent reflection may and must constantly and particularly prevail, and nothing must be done except in responsible decision.

I gladly quote what Ernest Michel (*Ehe*, p.

189f.) says on this point: "Believing trust (in the government of providence) vouches also for the potential blessing given in the gift of children and adopts a responsible attitude with regard to the question of generation and conception, not a religiously masked naturalism. . . . To reveal its full potentiality as blessing, the blessing of children demands the responsible Yes of parents, just as every good gift of God is meant for the acceptance of the human being for whom it is intended, and only then is able to unfold its character as a gift and blessing. . . . We thus affirm birth control as a matter for responsible consideration. For it is part of the dignity of man that in responsibility he moulds nature intelligently to his purposes. It is hard to see why in the domain of sex he should simply accept the course of nature or even make it an ethical norm for himself."

The danger of such reflection and decision is obvious. We have already mentioned one of its forms. Broadly speaking, it may happen that in consequence of mistaken reflection an actual divine gift may be refused and a child who might have been the light and joy of its parents is not generated and conceived and does not come into existence. On the other hand, something may be affirmed which was not offered by God. Again in consequence of mistaken reflection, a child may be generated of whom it might well be said from the parents' standpoint that they would have been better without it. Thus the possibility of error exists on both sides. And both errors may mean an imperiling of marital and even sexual fellowship. Both may entail a divine judgment in some form. The danger of thus failing to do the will and command of God is no smaller, but also no greater, at this point than everywhere where responsible action and the venture of faith and obedience are required. The venture, however, is required at this point too. Hence it would be false to say that in view of the risk an unthinking *laissez faire* is better in this matter than action in free responsibility and decision.

It may be that in a given case the faith of a man and a woman will assume the form and character of a homely and courageous confidence in life. Thus the husband thinks that he is entitled to expect of his wife the ordeal of giving birth to children, and the wife believes that she may understand and accept this prospect not merely as a threat but also as a promise. Both of them believe that they are equal to the task imposed upon them with the possibility of generation and conception and therefore with that of the birth and existence of a child. When both together and each individually can believe this, then they ought to believe it, and therefore in all seriousness they should seek to have a child in the name of God, and what happens, even if they are mistaken, will at least happen in responsibility and therefore in a right relation to the divine command.

The idea of birth control can and should also and especially have this positive connotation. Birth control can also be the conscious and resolute refusal in faith of the possibility of refusing, i.e., the joyful willingness to have children and therefore to become parents. Undoubtedly it rests upon false ideas of the good old days to try to maintain that people were then so much more reckless with regard to procreation because they all had this confidence in life rooted in faith. Prudence, and a practice determined by it, were no less characteristic then than they are now. Yet in relation to the modern increase of carefulness in this direction, and the corresponding prevalence of birth control in the negative sense, the question arises why it is that to-day so many people obviously do not seem able to command this confidence in life. Changed social conditions are partly but not wholly responsible, for it was not among small farmers and workers that the modern habit arose and spread, but among the propertied middle and upper classes. It was, for example, an accompaniment of the high standard of living in modern America. A certain degeneration and impoverishment of faith rather than outward circumstances undoubtedly plays some part. And there can be no doubt that a positive choice and decision ought to be made far more often than they are today on the basis of this confidence in life grounded in faith.

Yet it is certainly not a Christian but a very heathen or even Jewish type of thought to try to make it an invariable rule that faith should self-evidently produce and exercise in all cases and circumstances this cheerful confidence in life. The fact may be that in certain circumstances a man cannot believe himself justified in expecting this of his wife. Indeed, various considerations regarding her physical and psychological health may forbid him to do so. There must be room for such considerations. Failure to take them into account was and is always to be described as male brutality. But the wife may also be forbidden to understand conception as a promise and therefore to desire it. And both may be prevented from believing that they can rightly assume responsibility for the birth and existence of a child. For both of them it may be impossible for one reason or another really to desire a child in the name of God and therefore in faith. It might also involve an imperiling of their marital fellowship if either or both were to do so in spite of these serious considerations. They must examine their consciences to be sure that these reasons are not merely pretexts of expediency and frivolity. But if their reasons stand this test, they ought not to desire a child (again at the risk of being mistaken), and what happens will happen in responsibility and therefore in a true relation to God's law.

Up to this point there is agreement today among all serious Christian moralists, whether doctors, theologians or ecclesiastics. It is accepted that, although the choice for or against generation and conception is not a matter for human caprice, it should not be left to chance and therefore lack the character of true decision, but must always be a matter of free obedience and therefore free consideration and decision. The disagreement that remains and cannot easily be overcome, especially between the Evangelical and Roman Catholic view, concerns the question how the negative decision, when taken in obedience to the divine command, is to be put into effect in harmony with this command and therefore in responsibility.

What is to happen when a man and woman actually believe they cannot accept the responsibility of generation and conception? Four possibilities arise: 1. the practice of complete sexual restraint; 2. sexual intercourse at periods when the woman cannot conceive; 3. *coitus interruptus;* and 4. the use of contraceptives. It must be said of all four, even of the first, let alone the second, (1) that in relation to the course of nature as such they have the character of human arrangement and control. To be consistent, those who on principle decline such a possibility must refuse all these possible courses of action. But if we cannot on principle refuse this possibility, we cannot basically and absolutely give one of these alternatives preference over another. Again, it must be said of all of them (2) that in each there is something painful, troublesome and we may say unnatural or artificial. Since it is a question of controlling the course of nature, and in this case its biological rhythm, this is not surprising. It is obvious that the negative decision in this matter must be paid for no less than the positive, and that the cost cannot be small either way, whichever possibility we choose on the negative side. The costliness is not in itself an argument against any of these four possibilities. If something preventive has to be done, then one of these four possibilities will be chosen in spite of their technical and therefore unnatural or artificial character and the painfulness inherent in each of them.

Sexual restraint or connubial asceticism, which was once the only possible course for Christians in the case of a negative decision, has been described in our times as at least the higher path and therefore to be recommended. The fact that it seems to be the most difficult and sometimes heroic makes it most impressive. It would be wrong to say that its practice is always impossible, and that it may not be obligatory for certain men in certain situations. Hence I do not think that it should be generally described as a terrible *tour de force* (so E. Brunner, *The Divine Imperative,* p. 369). But we must be clear that even this method is a matter of technique and therefore unnatural, artificial and painful. Where it is adopted we do not usually have to reckon seriously with injuries to the health of the two partners, but rather with undesirable psychological repressions which might have fatal consequences for the marital fellowship, which as such includes sexual intercourse. And what Paul says to married people in 1 Cor. 7:3f, and especially v. 5: "Defraud ye not one the other, except it be with consent for a time, that ye may give yourself to fasting and prayer; and come together again, that Satan tempt you not for your incontinency," hardly seems to point in this direction, although the reference is not, of course, to the problem of birth control. To strict but careful thinking this course cannot therefore claim to be the only possible solution to the problem.

In the second possibility, i.e., sexual intercourse at periods when there is no danger of conception, we have the great and so far the only concession which the Papacy can allow apart from the complete continency. The relevant clause in the Encyclical *Casti connubii* is put very guardedly and cautiously, but it is quite unmistakeable: *Neque contra naturae ordinem agere ii discendi sunt coniuges, qui iure suo recta et naturali ratione utuntur, etsi ob naturales sive temporis sive quorundam defectuum causas nova inde vita oriri non possit.* Apart from the main purpose of marriage (the procreation of children, as the Encyclical firmly maintains), there are also certain *secundarii fines* such as the *mutuum adiutorium* and *mutuus amor* of the married partners, which they may freely cultivate, so long as the *intrinseca natura* of the sexual act remains intact, its centrality is preserved and it takes place normally. T. Bovet (*Die Ehe*, p. 162) recommends his Roman Catholic readers to keep strictly to this injunction, "for it is especially important that they should be in harmony with their Church." They may thus adopt this course, and others with them who see in it a right and happy *via media.*: It is certainly feasible. Indeed, since it is distinct from the way of absolute asceticism on the one side, and obviously does less violence to the *intrinseca natura* of the sexual act on the other, it might well seem to be relatively the most feasible course of all. But we cannot take it too blithely. Why did not the papal pastor say expressly that the whole burden of the question whether we may exclude the possibility of procreation on our own judgment cannot be evaded even if we take this course, and that this question is really more serious than that with which he is clearly preoccupied, namely the normality or abnormality of the sexual act as such? And is not this, too, a painful course with its complicated technique and all the statistics and calculations which it involves? Indeed does the *natura intrinseca* of the sexual act really remain unaffected when its performance, although quite normal, is cramped by so much calculation which seems open to objection even from the medical standpoint, and by all the anxious considerations and obvious fears of the participants? What becomes of its spontaneity if it necessarily involves a constant glancing at the calendar of conception? And what becomes of its character as the joyful consummation of marital fellowship if its spontaneity is threatened in this way?

The simplest and perhaps the oldest and most popular method of preventing conception is that of *coitus interruptus* (*copula diminuata*). In a decree of the Holy Office, 22 Nov. 1922, Denz. 2240 note) the Roman Catholic Church forbids confessors spontaneously (*sponte sua*) and indiscriminately *(promiscue omnibus)* to advise this course, but according to the same text it does not seem to exclude it absolutely in individual cases, provided certain reservations are made by confessors. One cannot allege in objection to it the story of Onan the son of Judah (Gen. 38:7-10), because what is described as a sin worthy of death in that story does not consist in the substance of the act and therefore in what normally goes under this name today, but in his refusal to give adequate satisfaction to the Levirate law of marriage. We need not waste words, however, on the particularly unsatisfactory nature of this course. And there also seem to be medical objections to it on account of its psychological dangers. T. Bovet (*op. cit.*, p. 167) declares that for these reasons he must issue an emphatic warning against it, and that it can be harmlessly practised only for a time and by less sensitive married couples. In any event, we have always to reckon with the fact that it constitutes a special threat to marital fellowship.

It is obvious that with the fourth possibility, the use by man or woman of mechanical or chemical means of contraception, the technical and therefore unnatural or artificial character of the whole business is more immediately apparent than in the case of the previous alternatives. At this point, then, Roman Catholic moral and pastoral theology issues what is for the moment, at any rate in theory, an inflexible veto. The difficulty of the whole problem is again revealed in miniature by the fact that none of these means — assuming this fourth possibility is chosen — seems to be free from objection or even reliable, and that each of them is in some way suspect or even repellent. Some of them are even dangerous, so that they should not be used except on medical advice. And it is perfectly natural that even some who do not disallow birth control as such should feel a kind of instinctive or aesthetic repugnance to all the means suggested. The only thing is that they must not make their repugnance a law for others. Nor must it be supposed and asserted that at this point, where the artificiality is so apparent, we enter the sphere of what is evil and illegitimate. The use of these means is not evil just because they are so manifestly artificial. It is evil when it takes place for reasons of self-seeking, pleasure-seeking or expediency (cf. The statement of the Lambeth Conference 1930). The earlier courses are no less evil when they are adopted for these reasons. And the same holds good not only of these courses, or of birth control as a whole in its negative sense, but of the failure to exercise it if this is grounded in self-seeking, pleasure-seeking or expediency.

Among the various possibilities of negative birth control there is thus none to which, all things considered, an absolute and exclusive preference can be given, but there is also none which can be flatly rejected. Hence it is impossible to formulate any general rule facilitating choice among the four possibilities indicated. Does this mean that we can only conclude that in this matter each individual must choose and decide for himself in the freedom which faith confers? This is true enough. Yet we may still mention and seriously insist upon certain universal principles which must govern the choice made.

1. The choice will be correctly made if it is made, not without difficulty of course, yet with a clear and not an uneasy conscience, with the realisation that in the special responsibility in which one finds oneself it must take the form it does and may therefore do so. Whatever the outcome of the choice may be, if it is to be right it must be made in this freedom of obedience, i.e., it must be made and executed in faith, not in fear, doubt or dismay. As a human act it may, of course, be mistaken. And in any case it will be made only in transition through a more or less difficult set of problems. Hence it can be made — otherwise how could it be related to the freedom of faith? — in reliance upon God's forgiving grace and therefore upon the fifth petition of the Lord's Prayer. But this does not mean that here any more than elsewhere we may desire to sin with a view to forgiveness, and therefore act with a bad conscience. What we can desire only as conscious sin, and can therefore do only with a bad conscience, we ought not to desire and do at all either here or elsewhere.

2. If it is to be correct, the choice must in any case be made only in joint consideration and decision by the two partners. There must be no dictation, overreaching or deceit on either side, but they must both act in full freedom, i.e., they must both take the decision in the free responsibility of their faith and in such a way that they can be open with each other both before and after. Their resolve and its execution must be a communal task, a product of their whole life of fellowship in marriage, so that they can rejoice together in spite of all difficulties, and their solidarity can remain unbroken even though later they may have cause to regard the step as an error and therefore have to repent of it together. What the two partners will and do together will be well willed and done for all the unavoidable problems and the possibility of better information later.

3. The choice must be made with due regard to the fact that so far as possible the inevitable painfulness of each available course must be the burden of the husband and not of the wife. In this whole question of positive and negative birth control, and in all the various possibilities mentioned, it is the wife who is directly and primarily affected and concerned. Here if anywhere there is an opportunity intelligently to respect the order of the relationship of man and woman, and therefore to express the priority and demonstrate the masculinity of the man in such a matter that in every possible choice he takes into decisive account, first individually and then in common discussion and decision with his wife, the fact that biologically she is always in greater danger than he is, and that she must therefore bear the lighter burden, he himself the heavier. It is on this assumption that the decision must then be made which of the alternatives is to be adopted and which rejected. This does not mean that the wife may not be ready for sacrifice as her love requires. But if the husband does not take the initiative in surrendering his own wishes and shouldering the dangerous burden, there can be no genuine achievement in concert, the conscience of the two parties cannot be free, and the decision to adopt a particular course cannot be a good one. No doubt the problem of birth control is not immediately envisaged in 1 Pet. 3:7, but this text is a valid criterion for genuine answers to the problem: "Ye husbands, dwell with them according to knowledge, giving honour unto the wife, as unto the weaker vessel, and as being heirs together of the grace of life; that your prayers be not hindered."

Chapter Eleven

TECHNOLOGICAL REPRODUCTION

Until recently the story of human procreation was, for all of its wonder, a fairly commonplace story: Sexual intercourse sometimes resulted in a child; nothing else human beings did or could do resulted in a child; and the child that resulted was (by necessity) received as given. Technology has changed all that. There are technologies to prevent conception, technologies to accomplish it, and technologies to determine certain genetic characteristics of our offspring. The previous chapter focused on contraceptive technologies; subsequent chapters will examine genetic control and abortion; this chapter invites you to consider and evaluate the technologies that assist reproduction.

We are living in what John A. Robertson has called a "reproductive revolution."[1] One signal of it was the birth in 1978 of Louise Brown, the first child born alive who was conceived in a petri dish. In vitro fertilization (IVF), the technology used in the birth of Louise Brown, involves the removal of oocytes, their fertilization in vitro, and the implantation of resulting preembryos into the wall of the uterus. Louise was born with oocytes from her mother, semen from her father, and after fertilization she was implanted into the womb of the mother. The technology, however, can utilize donor oocytes, donor sperm, and a surrogate mother for gestation.

In the decades following the birth of Louise Brown other reproductive technologies have been developed, including GIFT, ZIFT, and ICSI. In gamete intrafallopian transfer (GIFT), after the oocytes are removed, a catheter is used to transfer them along with sperm into a woman's fallopian tube. In zygote intrafallopian transfer (ZIFT) the oocytes are inseminated in vitro but transferred as early preembryos into a woman's fallopian tube. Intracytoplasmic sperm injection (ICSI) utilizes surgery on a minute scale in order to insert a single sperm into the ooplasm of an oocyte and to achieve fertilization.

Artificial insemination (AI) is an older and simpler technology than IVF, utilizing a syringe to deposit sperm into a woman's uterus during the time of ovulation. It can use the sperm of either the husband (AIH) or a donor (AID), depositing it in either the wife or a surrogate mother.

Since 1978 the "reproductive revolution" has captured significant public and media attention. Headlines and talk-shows have chronicled the birth of Louise Brown, the experiences of surrogate mothers, the use of donated eggs by post-menopausal women, the disputes of divorcing couples over the custody of frozen embryos, and, of course, scandals like those of Dr. Cecil Jacobson, who used his own sperm in over sixty AID procedures, and Dr. Ricardo Asch, who allegedly took the eggs and embryos of some of the women in his infertility practice and used them without consent in the treatment of other women.

The technological control over procreation is not revolutionary because large numbers of children are born with the help of these technologies.[2] It is revolutionary because it requires a revisiting of some fundamental questions, questions about the significance of human sexual intercourse, about the responsibilities that attend human acts of begetting, about the meaning of becoming and being parents, about the appropriate disposition toward children. Issues of great human importance are at stake in the way we tell — and live — the story of our parenting.

These are not easy questions, of course, nor questions about which we may presume an easy "rational" consensus. In the absence of such a consensus, some have urged a policy of "procreative liberty."[3] According to such a view people have a right to reproduce (or not), and so, they also have a right to utilize technology to achieve their reproductive goals; moreover, this right is limited only by the duty not to harm others. With such a view, the meaning of "harm" is obviously important. Are persons harmed only if they are utilized in another's reproductive projects without their consent? Are the offspring of reproductive technologies only harmed if their lives are so full of suffering as to be worse than no life at all?[4]

Those who advocate "procreative liberty" continue to debate such questions, but they generally agree that what Robertson and others call "symbolic" harms should be disqualified from public relevance. "Symbolic" harms affect notions of right behavior which are taken to rest on particular religious or moral views not universally shared. They include, for example, concerns about the commodification of women or of children, concerns about the reduction of procreative behaviors to matters of physiology and matters for contract, concerns about the effect of reproductive technologies on our attitudes to human sexual intercourse and parenting.

Others, however, have insisted that these "symbolic" harms are of the greatest public relevance. Sometimes the argument is made that human beings are capable of a larger and richer rational consensus concerning procreation than the advocates of "procreative liberty" suppose. The claim in this case is that, while choice is an important value, it is not the only value relevant to procreation about which reasonable people can agree.

Sometimes the argument is made that the advocates of "procreative liberty" themselves assume a particular and "symbolic" account of human beings and their procreation. The claim in this case is that the advocates of "procreative liberty" are dependent upon dualistic accounts of human nature and of human procreation. "Procreative liberty," on this view, stands in that particular philosophical and rhetorical tradition which divides human nature into two, subject (or person) and object (or body), and which conceives of the true self, the person, as pure subjectivity standing over — and over against — the body and natural communities. The issue in this case is not whether a particular view of persons or of procreation is "symbolic" or not, for all accounts of persons and parenting are "symbolic"; there is no way of thinking and talking of human procreation which is "unencumbered with any metaphysical baggage."[5] The issue is rather what "symbols" for persons and their procreation are appropriate.

In either case, we can expect to find reminders that human beings are embodied creatures, that they are not in the body the way a taxi-driver is in the cab, or the way Descartes' ghost is presumably in the machine. And related to that, we can expect to find reminders that human beings are communal creatures, that they find themselves in relationships and with responsibilities not all of which are of their choosing.

If we were to think and talk about procreation in ways that honored embodiment and natural communities, what would we say? How should we guide and limit the new reproductive powers? If we were to reject the position that people have a right to use whatever reproductive technologies they choose, where would we draw the line? And why should we draw it there?

A line might be drawn prohibiting all reproductive technologies as "unnatural" and artificial. Few, however, accept the position that every technological intervention into natural processes is wrong; even the "Instruction on Respect for Human Life in Its Origin and on the Dignity of Procreation" (selection 63) observes, "These interventions are not to be rejected on the grounds that they are artificial." We may not be content with the slogan "It's not nice to fool with Mother Nature." The "Instruction" also says, however, that "what is technically possible is not for that very reason morally admissible." We should also reject the techno-logic that "if we can, we may." The issues raised in Chapter Seven about nature and its mastery are surely relevant here. Is technology simply a function of existing values, a way of getting what we already want — a child, say — or is that view of technology naive? Does it shape our values as much as it is a function of them? Might in vitro fertilization using donated oocytes shape and form our views of becoming and being parents as much as it is a function of the desire of some to become parents?

Should we, following the "Instruction," draw a line prohibiting reproductive technologies, on the basis of the respect due persons as embodied? As Paul Lauritzen's essay (selection 64) makes clear, both the "Instruction" and some feminists reject reproductive technologies on the basis of concerns about embodiment. If the "Instruction" worries particularly that these technologies commodify children and "disembody" procreation, some feminists worry that they commodify women, reducing them to reproductive machines. Lauritzen compares and contrasts these concerns, and although to some extent he shares them, he draws no line against reproductive technologies on the basis of them. Indeed, he suggests that — as Margaret Farley had said in an earlier chapter (selection 13) — for some individuals these technologies provide means to "mediate embodiment."

In the excerpt from Oliver O'Donovan's *Begotten or Made?* (selection 65) these concerns about embodiment lead to cautionary words rather than to a prohibition of IVF (at least as practiced by fairy-godmothers in fairy tales). O'Donovan draws a line instead against the utilization of donor seed. He does not insist that the procreative and unitive meaning of sexual intercourse be inseparably joined in every conjugal act, but he does insist that they have their context in marriage, in the embodied life-union of the couple. In that context he acknowledges that this technology can serve a "couple's quest for fruitfulness in their sexual embrace."

Janet Dickey McDowell (in selection 66) surveys some of the arguments against IVF, concluding that, while the technology is not inherently immoral, there are reasons to be cautious about donated ova and surrogacy. Still, she draws a line only against embryo banking, and she draws that line because it involves the deliberate creation of nascent life without any intention to care for it.

Where McDowell flashes an amber light, Sidney Callahan puts a stop light. In selection 67 she argues that reproductive technology may be used "if, and only if, it makes it possible for a normal, socially well-adjusted heterosexual couple to have a child they could not otherwise have owing to infertility," and she draws a clear line against employing third party donors or surrogate mothers. She displays the values in the cultural norm of joining the roles of genetic, gestational, and rearing parenting in one set of parents, and she argues that to separate these roles puts the dignity and well-being of the future child, the donor, the spouses, and our cultural ethos at risk.

Finally, in William F. May's analysis of surrogacy and especially the Baby M case (selection 68) there is an argument that a line must be drawn at least against the commercialization of these technologies. Commercial surrogacy — and sperm and ova vending — allows the practices (and symbols) of the marketplace to commodify women and children and to distort the meaning of parenting.

This chapter invites you to consider whether the concerns presented in these essays are merely "symbolic" concerns — or, if "symbolic," whether that disqualifies them from public discourse. You are being asked to consider whether we should think and talk about procreation in ways that honor embodiment and community. If our rhetoric were more appreciative of the embodied significance of procreation, would we be suspicious of reproductive acts void of an intention to care for the children who might result? Would we be suspicious of acts that deliberately separate procreation into something physiological and something contractual? You are being asked, in sum, to consider where we should draw the lines in the "reproductive revolution" — and why!

Notes

1. John A. Robertson, *Children of Choice: Freedom and the New Reproductive Technologies* (Princeton, N.J.: Princeton University Press, 1994), pp. 4-11.

2. In terms of numbers alone the most important issues in reproduction remain access to prenatal care and the reduction of infant mortality. The numbers, however, are not insignificant. The estimate of children born as a result of donor insemination in the U.S. every year is 20 to 30 thousand — of approximately three million births. In 1993 there were over five thousand deliveries from IVF (Society for Assisted Reproductive Technology, "Assisted Reproductive Technology in the United States and Canada: 1993 Results Generated for the American Society of Reproductive Medicine/Society for Assisted Reproductive Technology Registry," *Fertility and Sterility* 64 [1995]: 13-17.) Moreover, IVF has risen steadily — from 8,735 oocyte retrievals for IVF in 1987 to 27,443 oocyte retrievals reported in 1993 (Lynne S. Wilcox and James S. Marks, "Regulating Assisted Reproductive Technologies: Public Health, Consumer Protection, and Public Resources," *Women's Health Issues* 6, no. 3 [May/June 1966]: 175-80; 176).

3. Robertson, p. 3 *et passim;* see also United States Congress, Office of Technology Assessment, *Infertility: Medical and Social Choices* (Washington, D.C.: U.S. Government Printing Office, 1988), and The Ethics Committee of the American Fertility Society, *Ethical Considerations of Assisted Reproductive Technologies (Fertility and Sterility)* 62, no. 5 [Nov. 1994], Supplement 1). Bonnie Steinbock, "Regulating Assisted Reproductive Technologies: An Ethical Framework," *Women's Health Issues* 6, no. 3 (May/June 1996): 167-74, argues that "procreative liberty" is "a good starting place" but worries about "procreative liberty gone mad" (171). Gilbert C. Meilaender, *Body, Soul, and Bioethics* (Notre Dame: University of Notre Dame Press, 1995), pp. 61-88, is an important theological response to "procreative liberty." John A. Robertson, "Liberalism and the Limits of Procreative Liberty: A Response to My Critics," *Washington and Lee Law Review* 52, no. 1 (1995): 233-67, is a response to several of his earlier critics, including a reply to an earlier piece by Meilaender.

4. Cynthia B. Cohen, "'Give Me Children or I Shall Die!' New Reproductive Technologies and Harm to Children," *Hastings Center Report* 26, no. 2 (March-April 1996): 19-27, argues against John Robertson and other advocates of "reproductive liberty" who take this position, calling for attention to the effect of the new reproductive technologies on the children born of them.

5. Meilaender, p. 80.

Suggestions for Further Reading

Bouma, Hessel III, Douglas Diekema, Edward Langerak, Theodore Rottman, and Allen Verhey. *Christian Faith, Health, and Medical Practice* (Grand Rapids: William B. Eerdmans, 1989), pp. 176-204.

Braine, David. "The Human and Inhuman in Medicine: Review of Issues Concerning Reproductive Technology," in Luke Gormally, ed., *Moral Truth and Moral Tradition: Essays in Honor of Peter Geach and Elizabeth Anscombe* (Dublin: Four Courts Press, 1994).

Cahill, Lisa Sowle. *Sex, Gender, and Christian Ethics* (Cambridge: Cambridge University Press, 1996), pp. 217-57.

Cohen, Cynthia B. "Reproductive Technologies: Ethical Issues," in Warren T. Reich (ed.), *Encyclopedia of Bioethics* (revised edition: New York: Simon and Schuster Macmillan, 1995), vol. 4, pp. 2233-40.

———, (ed.). *New Ways of Making Babies: The Case of Egg Donation* (Bloomington: Indiana University Press, 1996).

Evans, Debra. *Without Moral Limits: Women, Reproduction, and the New Medical Technology* (Westchester, Illinois: Crossways, 1989).

Lauritzen, Paul. *Pursuing Parenthood: Ethical Issues in Assisted Reproduction* (Bloomington: Indiana University Press, 1993).

Meilaender, Gilbert C. *Body, Soul, and Bioethics* (Notre Dame: University of Notre Dame Press, 1995), pp. 61-105.

Overall, Christine (ed.) *The Future of Human Reproduction* (Toronto: Women's Press, 1989).

Ramsey, Paul. *Fabricated Man* (New Haven: Yale University Press, 1970).

Shannon, Thomas A., and Lisa Sowle Cahill. *Religion and Artificial Reproduction: An Inquiry into the Vatican "Instruction on Respect for Human Life in Its Origin and on the Dignity of Procreation"* (New York: Crossroad, 1988).

Smith, David H., and Judith A. Granbois. "New Technologies for Assisted Reproduction," in T. Sedgwick and P. Turner, eds., *The Crisis in Moral Teaching in the Episcopal Church* (Harrisburg, Penn.: Morehouse Publishing, 1992).

Smith, Harmon L., and Paul A. Lewis. "A Protestant View of New Reproductive Technologies," *Second Opinion* 14 (July 1990): 94-106.

"Symposium on the Warnock Report," *Ethics and Medicine* 1, no. 2 (1985).

Tiefel, Hans. "When Baby's Mother Is Also Grandma — and Sister," *Hastings Center Report* 15 (1985): 30-31.

Verhey, Allen. "Commodification, Commercialization, and Embodiment," *Women's Health Issues* 7, no. 3 (May/June 1997): 132-42.

63 Instruction on Respect for Human Life in Its Origin and on the Dignity of Procreation

Congregation for the Doctrine of the Faith

Foreword

The Congregation for the Doctrine of the Faith has been approached by various episcopal conferences or individual bishops, by theologians, doctors and scientists, concerning biomedical techniques which make it possible to intervene in the initial phase of the life of a human being and in the very process of procreation and their conformity with the principles of Catholic morality. The present instruction, which is the result of wide consultation and in particular of a careful evaluation of the declarations made by episcopates, does not intend to repeat all the church's teaching on the dignity of human life as it originates and on procreation, but to offer, in the light of the previous teaching of the magisterium, some specific replies to the main questions being asked in this regard.

The exposition is arranged as follows: An introduction will recall the fundamental principles of an anthropological and moral character which are necessary for a proper evaluation of the problems and for working out replies to those questions; the first part will have as its subject respect for the human being from the first moment of his or her existence; the second part will deal with the moral questions raised by technical interventions on human procreation; the third part will offer some orientations on the relationships between moral law and civil law in terms of the respect due to human embryos and fetuses and as regards the legitimacy of techniques of artificial procreation.

From *Origins,* vol. 16, no. 40 (March 19, 1987): 697-711. Used by permission.

Introduction

1. Biomedical Research and the Teaching of the Church

The gift of life which God the Creator and Father has entrusted to man calls him to appreciate the inestimable value of what he has been given and to take responsibility for it: this fundamental principle must be placed at the center of one's reflection in order to clarify and solve the moral problems raised by artificial interventions on life as it originates and on the processes of procreation.

Thanks to the progress of the biological and medical sciences, man has at his disposal even more effective therapeutic resources; but he can also acquire new powers, with unforeseeable consequences, over human life at its very beginning and in its first stages. Various procedures now make it possible to intervene not only in order to assist, but also to dominate the processes of procreation. These techniques can enable man to "take in hand his own destiny," but they also expose him "to the temptation to go beyond the limits of a reasonable dominion over nature."[1] They might constitute progress in the service of man, but they also involve serious risks. Many people are therefore expressing an urgent appeal that in interventions on procreation the values and rights of the human person be safeguarded. Requests for clarification and guidance are coming not only from the faithful, but also from those who recognize the church as "an expert in humanity"[2] with a mission to serve the "civilization of love"[3] and of life.

The church's magisterium does not intervene on the basis of a particular competence in the area of the experimental sciences; but having taken account of the data of research and technology, it intends to put forward, by virtue of its evangelical mission and apostolic duty, the moral teaching corresponding to the dignity of the person and to his or her integral vocation. It intends to do so by expounding the criteria of moral judgment as regards the applications of scientific research and technology, especially in relation to human life and its beginnings. These criteria are the respect, defense and promotion of man, his "primary and fundamental right" to life,[4] his dignity as a person who is endowed with a spiritual soul and with moral responsibility[5] and who is called to beatific communion with God.

The church's intervention in this field is inspired also by the love which she owes to man, helping him to recognize and respect his rights and duties. This love draws from the fount of Christ's love: As she contemplates the mystery of the incarnate word, the church also comes to understand the "mystery of man,"[6] by proclaiming the Gospel of salvation, she reveals to man his dignity and invites him to discover fully the truth of his own being. Thus the church once more puts forward the divine law in order to accomplish the work of truth and liberation.

For it is out of goodness — in order to indicate the path of life — that God gives human beings his commandments and the grace to observe them; and it is likewise out of goodness — in order to help them preserve along the same path — that God always offers to everyone his forgiveness. Christ has compassion on our weaknesses: He is our Creator and Redeemer. May his Spirit open men's hearts to the gift of God's peace and to an understanding of his precepts.

2. Science and Technology at the Service of the Human Process

God created man in his own image and likeness: "Male and female he created them" (Gn. 1:27), entrusting to them the task of "having dominion over the earth" (Gn. 1:28). Basic scientific research and applied research constitute a significant expression of this dominion of man over creation. Science and technology are valuable resources for man when placed at his service and when they promote his integral development for the benefit of all; but they cannot of themselves show the meaning of existence and of human progress. Being ordered to man, who initiates and develops them, they draw from the person and his moral values the indication of their purpose and the awareness of their limits.

It would on the one hand be illusory to claim that scientific research and its applications are morally neutral; on the other hand one cannot derive criteria for guidance from mere technical efficiency, from research's possible usefulness to some at the expense of others or, worse still, from prevailing ideologies. Thus science and technology require for their own intrinsic meaning an unconditional respect for the fundamental criteria of the moral law: That is to say, they must be at the service of the human person, of his inalienable rights and his true and integral good according to the design and will of God.[7]

The rapid development of technological discoveries gives greater urgency to this need to respect the criteria just mentioned: Science without conscience can only lead to man's ruin. "Our era needs such wisdom more than bygone ages if the discoveries made by man are to be further humanized. For the future of the world stands in peril unless wiser people are forthcoming."[8]

3. Anthropology and Procedures in the Biomedical Field

Which moral criteria must be applied in order to clarify the problems posed today in the field of biomedicine? The answer to this question presupposes a proper idea of the nature of the human person in his bodily dimension.

For it is only in keeping with his true nature that the human person can achieve self-realization as a "unified totality,"[9] and this nature is at the same time corporal and spiritual. By virtue of its substantial union with a spiritual soul, the human body cannot be considered as a mere complex of tissues, organs and functions, nor can it be evaluated in the same way as the body of animals; rather it is a constitutive part of the person who manifests and expresses himself through it.

The natural moral law expresses and lays down the purposes, rights and duties which are based upon the bodily and spiritual nature of the human person. Therefore this law cannot be thought of as simply a set of norms on the biological level; rather it must be defined as the rational order whereby man is called by the Creator to direct and regulate his life and actions and in particular to make use of his own body.[10]

A first consequence can be deduced from these principles: An intervention on the human body affects not only the tissues, the organs and their functions, but also involves the person himself on different levels. It involves, therefore, perhaps in an implicit but nonetheless real way, a moral significance and responsibility. Pope John Paul II forcefully reaffirmed this to the World Medical Association when he said:

"Each human person, in his absolutely unique singularity, is constituted not only by his spirit, but by his body as well. Thus, in the body and through the body, one touches the person himself in his concrete reality. To respect the dignity of man consequently amounts to safeguarding this identity of the man '*corpore et anima unus*,' as the Second Vatican Council says (*Gaudium et Spes*, 14.1). It is on the basis of this anthropological vision that one is to find the fundamental criteria for decision making in the case of procedures which are not strictly therapeutic, as, for example, those aimed at the improvement of the human biological condition."[11]

Applied biology and medicine work together for the integral good of human life when they come to the aid of a person stricken by illness and infirmity and when they respect his or her dignity as a creature of God. No biologist or doctor can reasonably claim, by virtue of his scientific competence, to be able to decide on people's origin and destiny. This norm must be applied in a particular way in the field of sexuality and procreation, in which man and woman actualize the fundamental values of love and life.

God, who is love and life, has inscribed in man and woman the vocation to share in a special way in his mystery of personal communion and in his work as Creator and Father.[12] For this reason marriage possesses specific goods and values in its union and in procreation which cannot be likened to those existing in lower forms of life. Such values and meanings are of the personal order and determine from the moral point of view the meaning and limits of artificial interventions on procreation and on the origin of human life. These interventions are not to be rejected on the grounds that they are artificial. As such, they bear witness to the possibilities of the art of medicine. But they must be given a moral evaluation in reference to the dignity of the human person, who is called to realize his vocation from God to the gift of love and the gift of life.

4. Fundamental Criteria for a Moral Judgment

The fundamental values connected with the techniques of artificial human procreation are two: the life of the human being called into existence and the special nature of the transmission of human life in marriage. The moral judgment on such methods of artificial procreation must therefore be formulated in reference to these values.

Physical life, with which the course of human life in the world begins, certainly does not itself contain the whole of a person's value nor does it represent the supreme good of man, who is called to eternal life. However it does constitute in a certain way the "fundamental" value of life precisely because upon this physical life all the other values of the person are based and developed.[13] The inviolability of the innocent human being's right to life "from the moment of conception until death"[14] is a sign and requirement of the very inviolability of the person to whom the Creator has given the gift of life.

By comparison with the transmission of other forms of life in the universe, the transmission of human life has a special character of its own, which derives from the special nature of the human person. "The transmission of human life is entrusted by nature to a personal and conscious act and as such is subject to the all-holy laws of God: immutable and inviolable laws which must be recognized and observed. For this reason one cannot use means and follow methods which could be licit in the transmission of life of plants and animals."[15]

Advances in technology have now made it possible to procreate apart from sexual relations through the meeting *in vitro* of the germ cells previously taken from the man and the woman. But what is technically possible is not for that very reason morally admissible. Rational reflection on the fundamental values of life and of human procreation is therefore indispensable for formulating a moral evaluation of such technological interventions on a human being from the first states of his development.

5. Teachings of the Magisterium

On its part, the magisterium of the church offers to human reason in this field too the light of revelation: The doctrine concerning man taught by the magisterium contains many elements which throw light on the problems being faced here.

From the moment of conception, the life of every human being is to be respected in the absolute way because man is the only creature on earth that God has "wished for himself"[16] and the spiritual soul of each man is "immediately created" by God;[17] his whole being bears the image of the Creator. Human life is sacred because from its beginning it involves "the creative action of God,"[18] and it remains forever in a special relationship with the Creator, who is its sole end.[19] God alone is the Lord of life from its beginning until its end: No one can in any circumstance claim for himself the right to destroy directly an innocent human being.[20]

Human procreation requires on the part of the spouses responsible collaboration with the fruitful love of God;[21] the gift of human life must be actualized in marriage through the specific and exclusive acts of husband and wife, in accordance with the laws inscribed in their persons and in their union.[22]

Respect for Human Embryos

Careful reflection on this reaching of the magisterium and on the evidence of reason, as mentioned above, enables us to respond to the numerous moral problems posed by technical interventions upon the human being in the first phases of his life and upon the processes of his conception.

1. What respect is due to the human embryo, taking into account his nature and identity?

The human being must be respected — as a person — from the very first instant of his existence.

The implementation of procedures of artificial fertilization has made possible various interventions upon embryos and human fetuses. The aims pursued are of various kinds: diagnostic and therapeutic, scientific and commercial. From all of this, serious problems arise. Can one speak of a right to experimentation upon human embryos for the purpose of scientific research? What norms or laws should be worked out with regard to this matter? The response to these problems presupposes a detailed reflection on the nature and specific identity — the word *status* is used — of the human embryo itself.

At the Second Vatican Council, the church for her part presented once again to modern man her constant and certain doctrine according to which: "Life once conceived, must be protected with the utmost care; abortion and infanticide are abominable crimes."[23] More recently, the Charter of the Rights of the Family, published by the Holy See, confirmed that "human life must be absolutely respected and protected from the moment of conception."[24]

This congregation is aware of the current debates concerning the beginning of human life concerning the individuality of the human being and concerning the identity of the human person. The congregation recalls the teachings found in the Declaration on Procured Abortion:

"From the time that the ovum is fertilized, a new life is begun which is neither that of the father nor of the mother; it is rather the life of a new human being with his own growth. It would never be made human if it were not human already. To this perpetual evidence . . . modern genetic science brings valuable confirmation. It has demonstrated that, from the first instant, the program is fixed as to what this living being will be: a man, this individual man with his characteristic aspects already well determined. Right from fertilization is begun the adventure of a human life, and each of its great capacities requires time . . . to find its place and to be in a position to act."[25]

This teaching remains valid and is further confirmed, if confirmation were needed, by recent findings of human biological science which recognize that in the zygote (the cell produced when the nuclei of the two gametes have fused) resulting from fertilization the biological identity of a new human individual is already constituted.

Certainly no experimental datum can be in itself sufficient to bring us to the recognition of a spiritual soul; nevertheless, the conclusions of science regarding the human embryo provide a valuable indication for discerning by the use of reason a personal presence at the moment of this first appearance of a human life: How could a human individual not be a human person? The magisterium has not expressly committed itself to an affirmation of a philosophical nature, but it constantly reaffirms the moral condemnation of any kind of procured abortion. This teaching has not been changed and is unchangeable.[26]

Thus the fruit of human generation from the first moment of its existence, that is to say, from the moment the zygote has formed, demands the unconditional respect that is morally due to the human being in his bodily and spiritual totality. The human being is to be respected and treated as a person from the moment of conception and therefore from that same moment his rights as a person must be recognized, among which in the first place is the inviolable right of every innocent human being to life.

This doctrinal reminder provides the fundamental criterion for the solution of the various problems posed by the development of the biomedical sciences in this field: Since the embryo must be treated as a person, it must also be defended in its integrity, tended and cared for, to the extent possible, in the same way as any other human being as far as medical assistance is concerned.

2. Is prenatal diagnosis morally licit?

If prenatal diagnosis represents the life and integrity of the embryo and the human fetus and is directed toward its safeguarding or healing as an individual, then the answer is affirmative.

For prenatal diagnosis makes it possible to know the condition of the embryo and of the fetus when still in the mother's womb. It permits or makes it possible to anticipate earlier and more effectively, certain therapeutic, medical or surgical procedures.

Such diagnosis is permissible, with the consent of the parents after they have been adequately informed, if the methods employed safeguard the life and integrity of the embryo and the mother, without subjecting them to disproportionate risks.[27] But this diagnosis is gravely opposed to the moral law when it is done with the thought of possibly inducing an abortion depending upon the results: A diagnosis which shows the existence of a malformation or a hereditary illness must not be the equivalent of a death sentence. Thus a woman would be committing a gravely illicit act if she were to request such a diagnosis with the deliberate intention of having an abortion should the results confirm the existence of a malformation or abnormality. The spouse or relatives or anyone else would similarly be acting in a manner contrary to the moral law if they were to counsel or impose such a diagnostic procedure on the expectant mother with the same intention of possibly proceeding to an abortion. So too the specialist would be guilty of illicit collaboration if, in conducting the diagnosis and in communicating its results, they were deliberately to contribute to establishing or favoring a link between prenatal diagnosis and abortion.

In conclusion, any directive or program of the civil and health authorities or of scientific organizations which in any way were to favor a link between prenatal diagnosis and abortion, or which were to go as far as directly to induce expectant mothers to submit to prenatal diagnosis planned for the purpose of eliminating fetuses which are affected by malformations or which are carriers of hereditary illness, is to be condemned as a violation of the unborn child's right to life and as an abuse to the prior rights and duties of the spouses.

3. Are therapeutic procedures carried out on the human embryo licit?

As with all medical interventions on patients, *one must uphold as licit procedures carried out on the human embryo which respect the life and integrity of the embryo and do not involve disproportionate risks for it, but are directed toward its healing, the improvement of its condition of health or its individual survival.*

Whatever the type of medical, surgical or other therapy, the free and informed consent of the parents is required, according to the deontological rules followed in the case of children. The application of this moral principle may call for delicate and particular precautions in the case of embryonic or fetal life.

The legitimacy and criteria of such procedures have been clearly stated by Pope John Paul II: "A strictly therapeutic intervention whose explicit objective is the healing of various maladies such as those stemming from chromosomal defects will, in principle, be considered desirable, provided it is directed to the true promotion of the personal well-being of the individual without doing harm to his integrity or worsening his conditions of life. Such an intervention would indeed fall within the logic of the Christian moral tradition."[28]

4. How is one to evaluate morally research and experimentation on human embryos and fetuses?

Medical research must refrain from operations on live embryos, unless there is a moral certainty of not causing harm to the life or integrity of the unborn child and the mother, and on condition that the parents have given their free and informed consent to the procedure. It follows that all research, even when limited to the simple observation of the embryo, would become illicit were it to involve risk to the embryo's physical integrity or life by reason of the methods used or the effects induced.

As regards experimentation, and presupposing the general distinction between experimentation for purposes which are not directly therapeutic and experimentation which is clearly therapeutic for the subject himself, in the case in point one must also distinguish between experimentation carried out on embryos which are still alive and experimentation carried out on embryos which are dead. *If the embryos are living, whether viable or not, they must be respected just like any other human person; experimentation on embryos which is not directly therapeutic is illicit.*[29]

No objective, even though noble in itself such as a foreseeable advantage to science, to other human beings or to society, can in any way justify experimentation on living human embryos or fetuses, whether viable or not, either inside or outside the mother's womb. The informed consent ordinarily required for clinical experimentation on adults cannot be granted by the parents, who may not freely dispose of the physical integrity or life of the unborn child. Moreover, experimentation on embryos and fetuses always involves risk, and indeed in most cases it involves the certain expectation of harm to their physical integrity or even their death.

To use human embryos or fetuses as the object or instrument of experimentation constitutes a crime against their dignity as human beings having a right to the same respect that is due to the child already born and to every human person.

The Charter of the Rights of the Family published by the Holy See affirms: "Respect for the dignity of the human being excludes all experimental manipulation or exploitation of the human embryo."[30] The practice of keeping alive human embryos *in vivo* or *in vitro* for experimental or commercial purposes is totally opposed to human dignity.

In the case of experimentation that is clearly therapeutic, namely, when it is a matter of experimental forms of therapy used for the benefit of the embryo itself in a final attempt to save its life and in the absence of other reliable forms of therapy, recourse to drugs or procedures not yet fully tested can be licit.[31]

The corpses of human embryos and fetuses, whether they have been deliberately aborted or not, must be respected just as the remains of other human beings. In particular, they cannot be subjected to mutilation or to autopsies if their death has not yet been verified and without the consent of the parents or of the mother. Furthermore, the moral requirements must be safeguarded that there be no complicity in deliberate abortion and that the risk of scandal be avoided. Also, in the case of dead fetuses, as for the corpses of adult persons, all commercial trafficking must be considered illicit and should be prohibited.

5. How is one to evaluate morally the use for research purposes of embryos obtained by fertilization "in vitro?"

Human embryos obtained *in vitro* are human beings and subjects with rights: Their dignity and right to life must be respected from the first moment of their existence. *It is immoral to produce human embryos destined to be exploited as disposable "biological material."*

In the usual practice of *in vitro* fertilization, not all of the embryos are transferred to the woman's body; some are destroyed. Just as the church condemns induced abortion, so she also forbids acts against the life of these human beings. *It is a duty to condemn the particular gravity of the voluntary destruction of human embryos obtained "in vitro" for the sole purpose of research, either by means of artificial insemination or by means of "twin fission."* By acting in this way the researcher usurps the place of God; and, even though he may be unaware of this, he sets himself up as the master of the destiny of others inasmuch as he arbitrarily chooses whom he will allow to live and whom he will send to death and kills defenseless human beings.

Methods of observation or experimentation which damage or impose grave and disproportionate risks upon embryos obtained *in vitro* are morally illicit for the same reasons. Every human being is to be respected for himself and cannot be reduced in worth to a pure and simple instrument for the advantage of others. *It is therefore not in conformity with the moral law deliberately to expose to death human embryos obtained "in vitro."* In consequence of the fact that they have been produced *in vitro*, those embryos which are not transferred into the body of the mother and are called "spare" are exposed to an absurd fate, with no possibility of their being offered safe means of survival which can be licitly pursued.

6. What judgment should be made on other procedures of manipulating embryos connected with the "techniques of human reproduction?"

Techniques of fertilization *in vitro* can open the way to other forms of biological and genetic manipulation of human embryos, such as attempts or plans for fertilization between human and animal gametes and the gestation of human embryos in the uterus of animals, or the hypothesis or project of constructing artificial uteruses for the human embryo. *These procedures are contrary to the human dignity proper to the embryo, and at the same time they are contrary to the right of every person to be conceived and to be born within marriage and from marriage.*[32] *Also, attempts or hypotheses for obtaining a human being without any connection with sexuality through "twin fission," cloning or parthenogenesis are to be considered contrary to the moral law, since they are in opposition to the dignity both of human procreation and of the conjugal union.*

The freezing of embryos, even when carried out in order to preserve the life of an embryo — cryopreservation — *constitutes an offense against the respect due to human beings* by exposing them to grave risks of death or harm to their physical integrity and depriving them, at least temporarily, of maternal shelter and gestation, thus placing them in a situation in which further offenses and manipulation are possible.

Certain attempts to influence chromosomic or genetic inheritance are not therapeutic, but are aimed at producing human beings selected according to sex or other predetermined qualities. These manipulations are contrary to the personal dignity of the human being and his or her integrity and identity. Therefore in no way can they be justified on the grounds of possible beneficial consequences for future humanity.[33] Every person must be respected for himself: In this consists the dignity and right of every human being from his or her beginning.

Interventions Upon Human Procreation

By *artificial procreation* or *artificial fertilization* are understood here the different technical procedures directed toward obtaining a human conception in a manner other than the sexual union of man and woman. This instruction deals with fertilization of an ovum in a test tube (*in vitro* fertilization) and artificial insemination through transfer into the woman's genital tracts of previously collected sperm.

A preliminary point for the moral evaluation of such technical procedures is constituted by the consideration of the circumstances and consequences which those procedures involve in relation to the respect due the human embryo. Development of the practice of *in vitro* fertilization has required innumerable fertilizations and destructions of human embryos. Even today, the usual practice presupposes a hyperovulation on the part of the woman: A number of ova are withdrawn, fertilized and then cultivated *in vitro* for some days. Usually not all are transferred into the genital tracts of the woman; some embryos, generally called "spare," are destroyed or frozen. On occasion, some of the implanted embryos are sacrificed for various eugenic, economic, or psychological reasons. Such deliberate destruction of human beings or their utilization for different purposes to the detriment of their integrity and life is contrary to the doctrine on procured abortion already recalled.

The connection between *in vitro* fertilization and the voluntary destruction of human embryos occurs too often. This is significant: Through these procedures, with apparently contrary purposes, life and death are subjected to the decision of man, who thus sets himself up as the giver of life and death by decree. This dynamic of violence and domination may remain unnoticed by those very individuals who, in wishing to utilize this procedure, become subject to it themselves. The facts recorded and the cold logic which links them must be taken into consideration for a moral judgment on *in vitro* fertilization and embryo transfer: The abortion mentality which has made this procedure possible thus leads, whether one wants it or not, to man's domination over the life and death of his fellow human beings and can lead to a system of radical eugenics.

Nevertheless, such abuses do not exempt one from a further and thorough ethical study of the techniques of artificial procreation considered in themselves, abstracting as far as possible from the destruction of embryos produced *in vitro*.

The present instruction will therefore take into consideration in the first place the problems posed by heterologous artificial fertilization, and subsequently those linked with homologous artificial fertilization.

Before formulating an ethical judgment on each of these procedures, the principles and values which determine the moral evaluation of each of them will be considered.

A. Heterologous Artificial Fertilization

1. Why must human procreation take place in marriage?

Every human being is always to be accepted as a gift and blessing of God. However, from the moral point of view a truly responsible procreation vis-à-vis the unborn child must be the fruit of marriage.

For human procreation has specific characteristics by virtue of the personal dignity of the parents and of the children: The procreation of a new person, whereby the man and the woman collaborate with the power of the Creator, must be the fruit and the sign of the mutual self-giving of the spouses, of their love and of their fidelity.[34] *The fidelity of the spouses in the unity of marriage involves reciprocal respect of their right to become a father and a mother only through each other.*

The child has the right to be conceived, carried in the womb, brought into the world and brought up within marriage: It is through the secure and recognized relationship to his own parents that the child can discover his own identity and achieve his own proper human development.

The parents find in their child a confirmation and completion of their reciprocal self-giving: The child is the living image of their love, the permanent sign of their conjugal union, the living and indissoluble concrete expression of their paternity and maternity.[35]

By reason of the vocation and social responsibilities of the person, the good of the children and of the parents contributes to the good of civil society; the vitality and stability of society require that children come into the world within a family and that the family be firmly based on marriage.

The tradition of the church and anthropological reflection recognize in marriage and in its indissoluble unity the only setting worthy of truly responsible procreation.

2. Does heterologous artificial fertilization conform to the dignity of the couple and to the truth of marriage?

Through *in vitro* fertilization and embryo transfer and heterologous artificial insemination, human conception is achieved through the fusion of gametes of at least one donor other than the spouses who are united in marriage. *Heterologous artificial fertilization is contrary to the unity of marriage, to the dignity of the spouses, to the vocation proper to parents, and to the child's right to be conceived and brought into the world in marriage and from marriage.*[36]

Respect for the unity of marriage and for conjugal fidelity demands that the child be conceived in marriage; the bond existing between husband and wife accords the spouses, in an objective and inalienable manner, the exclusive right to become father and mother solely through each other.[37] Recourse to the gametes of a third person in order to have sperm or ovum available constitutes a violation of the reciprocal commitment of the spouses and a grave lack in regard to the essential property of marriage which is its unity.

Heterologous artificial fertilization violates the rights of the child; it deprives him of his filial relationship with his parental origins and can hinder the maturing of his personal identity. Furthermore, it offends the common vocation of the spouses who are called to fatherhood and motherhood: It objectively deprives conjugal fruitfulness of its unity and integrity; it brings about and manifests a rupture between genetic parenthood, gestational parenthood and responsibility for upbringing. Such damage to the personal relationships within the family has repercussions on civil society: What threatens the unity and stability of the family is a source of dissension, disorder and injustice in the whole of social life.

These reasons lead to a negative moral judgment concerning heterologus artificial fertilization: Consequently, fertilization of a married women with the sperm of a donor different from her husband and fertilization with the husband's sperm of an ovum not coming from his wife are morally illicit. Furthermore, the artificial fertilization of a woman who is unmarried or a widow, whoever the donor may be, cannot be morally justified.

The desire to have a child and the love between spouses who long to obviate a sterility which cannot be overcome in any other way constitute understandable motivations; but subjectively good intentions do not render heterologous artificial fertilization conformable to the objective and inalienable properties of marriage or respectful of the rights of the child and of the spouses.

3. Is "surrogate" motherhood morally licit?

No, for the same reasons which lead one to reject heterologous artificial fertilization: For it is contrary to the unity of marriage and to the dignity of the procreation of the human person.

Surrogate motherhood represents an objective failure to meet the obligations of maternal love, of conjugal fidelity and of responsible motherhood; it offends the dignity and the right of the child to be conceived, carried in the womb, brought into the world and brought up by his own parents; it sets up, to the detriment of families, a division between the physical psychological and moral elements which constitute families.

B. Homologous Artificial Fertilization

Since heterologous artificial fertilization has been declared unacceptable, the question arises of how to evaluate morally the process of homologous artificial fertilization: *in vitro* fertilization and embryo transfer and artificial insemination between husband and wife. First a question of principle must be clarified.

4. What connection is required from the moral point of view between procreation and the conjugal act?

a) The church's teaching on marriage and human procreation affirms the "inseparable connection, willed by God and unable to be broken by man on his own initiative, between the two meanings of the conjugal act: the unitive meaning and the procreative meaning. Indeed, by its intimate structure the conjugal act, while most closely uniting husband and wife, capacitates them for the generation of new lives according to laws inscribed in the very being of man and of woman."[38] This principle, which is based upon the nature of marriage and the intimate connection of goods of marriage, has well-known consequences on the level of responsible fatherhood and motherhood. "By safeguarding both these essential aspects, the unitive and the procreative, the conjugal act preserves in its fullness the sense of true mutual love and its ordination toward man's exalted vocation to parenthood."[39]

The same doctrine concerning the link between the meanings of the conjugal act and between the goods of marriage throws light on the moral problem of homologous artificial fertilization, since "it is never permitted to separate these different aspects to such a degree as positively to exclude either the procreative intention or the conjugal relation."[40]

Contraception deliberately deprives the conjugal act of its openness to procreation and in this way brings about a voluntary dissociation of the ends of marriage. Homologous artificial fertilization, in seeking a procreation which is not the fruit of a specific act of conjugal union, objectively effects an analogous separation between the goods and the meanings of marriage.

Thus *fertilization is licitly sought when it is the result of a "conjugal act which is per se suitable for the generation of children, to which marriage is ordered by its nature and by which the spouses become one flesh."*[41] *But from the moral point of view procreation is deprived of its proper perfection when it is not desired as the fruit of the conjugal act, that is to say, of the specific act of the spouses' union.*

b) The moral value of the intimate link between the goods of marriage and between the meanings of the conjugal act is based upon the unity of the human being, a unity involving body and spiritual soul.[42] Spouses mutually express their personal love in the "language of the body," which clearly involves both "spousal meanings" and parental ones.[43] The conjugal act by which the couple mutually express their self-gift at the same time expresses openness to the gift of life. It is an act that is inseparably corporal and spiritual. It is in their bodies and through their bodies that the spouses consummate their marriage and are able to become father and mother. In order to respect the language of their bodies and their natural generosity, the conjugal union must take place with respect for its openness to procreation; and the procreation of a person must be the fruit and the result of married love. The origin of the human being thus follows from a procreation that is "linked to the union, not only biological but also spiritual, of the parents, made one by the bond of marriage."[44] Fertilization achieved outside of the bodies of the couple remains by this very fact deprived of the meanings and the values which are expressed in the language of the body and in the union of human persons.

c) Only respect for the link between the meanings of the conjugal act and respect for the unity of the human being make possible procreation in conformity with the dignity of the person. In his unique and irrepeatable origin, the child must be respected and recognized as equal in personal dignity to those who give him life. The human person must be accepted in his parents' act of union and love; the generation of a child must therefore be the fruit of that mutual giving[45] which is realized in the conjugal act wherein the spouses cooperate in the work of the Creator, who is love.[46]

In reality, the origin of a human person is the result of an act of giving. The one conceived must be the fruit of his parents' love. He cannot be desired or conceived as the product of an intervention of medical or biological techniques; that would be equivalent to reducing him to an object of scientific technology. No one may subject the coming of a child into the world to conditions of technical efficiency which are to be evaluated according to standards of control and dominion.

The moral relevance of the link between the meanings of the conjugal act and between the goods of marriage, as well as the unity of the human being and the dignity of his origin, demand that the procreation of a human person be brought about as the fruit of the conjugal act specific to the love between spouses. The link between procreation and the conjugal act is thus shown to be of great importance on the anthropological and moral planes, and it throws light on the positions of the magisterium with regard to homologous artificial fertilization.

5. Is homologous "in vitro" fertilization morally licit?

The answer to this question is strictly dependent on the principles just mentioned. Certainly one cannot ignore the legitimate aspirations of sterile couples. For some, recourse to homologous *in vitro* fertilization and embryo transfer appears to be the only way of fulfilling their sincere desire for a child. The question is asked whether the totality of conjugal life in such situations is not sufficient to ensure the dignity proper to human procreation. It is acknowledged that *in vitro* fertilization and embryo transfer certainly cannot supply for the absence of sexual relations[47] and cannot be preferred to the specific acts of conjugal union, given the risks involved for the child and the difficulties of the procedure. But it is asked whether, when there is no other way of overcoming the sterility which is a source of suffering, homologous *in vitro* fertilization may not constitute an aid, if not a form of therapy, whereby its moral licitness could be admitted.

The desire for a child — or at the very least an openness to the transmission of life — is a necessary prerequisite for the moral point of view for responsible human procreation. But this good intention is not sufficient for making a positive moral evaluation of *in vitro* fertilization between spouses. The process of *in vitro* fertilization and embryo transfer must be judged in itself and cannot borrow its definitive moral quality from the totality of conjugal life of which it becomes part nor from the conjugal acts which may precede or follow it.[48]

It has already been recalled that in the circumstances in which it is regularly practiced *in vitro* fertilization and embryo transfer involves the destruction of human beings, which is something contrary to the doctrine on the illicitness of abortion previously mentioned.[49] But even in a situation in which every precaution were taken to avoid the death of human embryos, homologous *in vitro* fertilization and embryo transfer dissociates from the conjugal act the actions which are directed to human fertilization. For this reason the very nature of homologous *in vitro* fertilization and embryo transfer also must be taken into account, even abstracting from the link with procured abortion.

Homologous *in vitro* fertilization and embryo transfer is brought about outside the bodies of the couple through actions of third parties whose competence and technical activity determine the success of the procedure. Such fertilization entrusts the life and identify of the embryo into the power of doctors and biologists and establishes the domination of technology over the origin and destiny of the human person. Such a relationship of domination is in itself contrary to the dignity and equality that must be common to parents and children.

Conception *in vitro* is the result of the technical action which presides over fertilization. *Such fertilization is neither in fact achieved nor positively willed as the expression and fruit of a specific act of the conjugal union. In homologous "in vitro" fertilization and embryo transfer, therefore, even if it is considered in the context of de facto existing sexual relations, the generation of the human person is objectively deprived of its proper perfection: namely, that of being the result and fruit of a conjugal act* in which the spouses can become "cooperators with God for giving life to a new person."[50]

The reasons enable us to understand why the act of conjugal love is considered in the teaching of the church as the only setting worthy of human procreation. For the same reasons the so-called "simple case," i.e., a homologous *in vitro* is free of any compromise with the abortive practice of destroying embryos and with masturbation, remains a technique which is morally illicit because it deprives human procreation of the dignity which is proper and connatural to it.

Certainly, homologous *in vitro* fertilization and embryo transfer fertilization is not marked by all that ethical negativity found in extraconjugal procreation; the family and marriage continue to constitute the setting for the birth and upbringing of the children. Nevertheless, in conformity with the traditional doctrine relating to the goods of marriage and the dignity of the person, *the church remains opposed from the moral point of view to homologous "in vitro" fertilization. Such fertilization is in itself illicit and in opposition to the dignity of procreation and of the conjugal union, even when everything is done to avoid the death of the human embryo.*

Although the manner in which human conception is achieved with *in vitro* fertilization and embryo transfer cannot be approved, every child which comes into the world must in any case be accepted as a living gift of the divine Goodness and must be brought up with love.

6. How is homologous artificial insemination to be evaluated from the moral point of view?

Homologous artificial insemination within marriage cannot be admitted except for those cases in which the technical means is not a substitute for the conjugal act but served to facilitate and to help so that the act attains its natural purpose.

The teaching of the magisterium on this point has already been stated.[51] This teaching is not just an expression of particular historical circumstances, but is based on the church's doctrine concerning the connection between the conjugal union and procreation and on a consideration of the personal nature of the conjugal act and of human procreation. "In its natural structure, the conjugal act is a personal action, a simultaneous and immediate cooperation on the part of the husband and wife, which by the very nature of the act is the expression of the mutual gift which, according to the words of Scripture, brings about union 'in one flesh.'"[52] Thus moral conscience "does not necessarily proscribe the use of certain artificial means destined solely either to the facilitating of the natural act or to ensuring that the natural act normally performed achieves its proper end."[53] If the technical means facilitates the conjugal act or helps it to reach its natural objectives, it can be morally acceptable. If, on the other hand, the procedure were to replace the conjugal act, it is morally illicit.

Artificial insemination as a substitute for the conjugal act is prohibited by reason of the voluntarily achieved dissociation of the two meanings of the conjugal act. Masturbation, through which the sperm is normally obtained, is another sign of this dissociation: Even when it is done for the purpose of procreation the act remains deprived of its unitive meaning: "It lacks the sexual relationship called for by the moral order, namely the relationship which realizes 'the full sense of mutual self-giving and human procreation in the context of true love.'"[54]

7. What moral criterion can be proposed with regard to medical intervention in human procreation?

The medical act must be evaluated not only with reference to its technical dimension, but also and above all in relation to its goal, which is the good of persons and their bodily and psychological health. The moral criteria for medical intervention in procreation are deduced from the dignity of human persons, of their sexuality and of their origin.

Medicine which seeks to be ordered to the integral good of the person must respect the specifically human values of sexuality.[55] *The doctor is at the service of persons and of human procreation. He does not have the authority to dispose of them or to decide their fate.* Medical intervention respects the dignity of persons when it seeks to assist the conjugal act either in order to facilitate its performance or in order to enable it to achieve its objective once it has been normally performed.[56]

On the other hand, it sometimes happens that a medical procedure technologically replaces the conjugal act in order to obtain a procreation which is neither its result nor its fruit. In this case the medical act is not, as it should be, at the service of conjugal union, but rather appropriates to itself the procreative function and thus contradicts the dignity and the inalienable rights of the spouses and of the child to be born.

The humanization of medicine, which is insisted upon today by everyone, requires respect for the integral dignity of the human person first of all in the act and at the moment in which the spouses transmit life to a new person. It is only logical therefore to address an urgent appeal to Catholic doctors and scientists that they bear exemplary witness to the respect due to the human embryo and to the dignity of procreation. The medical and nursing staff of Catholic hospitals and clinics are in a special way urged to do justice to the moral obligations which they have assumed, frequently also, as part of their contract. Those who are in charge of Catholic hospitals and clinics and who are often religious will take special care to safeguard and promote a diligent observance of the moral norms recalled in the present instruction.

8. The suffering caused by infertility in marriage.

The suffering of spouses who cannot have children or who are afraid of bringing a handicapped child into the world is a suffering that everyone must understand and properly evaluate.

On the part of the spouses, the desire for a child is natural: It expresses the vocation to fatherhood and motherhood inscribed in conjugal love. This desire can be even stronger if the couple is affected by sterility which appears incurable. Nevertheless, marriage does not confer upon spouses the right to have a child, but only the right to perform those natural acts which are per se ordered to procreation.[57]

A true and proper right to a child would be contrary to the child's dignity and nature. The child is not an object to which one has a right nor can he be considered as an object of ownership: Rather, a child is a gift, "the supreme gift"[58] *and the most gratuitous gift of marriage, and is a living testimony of the mutual giving of his parents. For this reason, the child has the right as already mentioned, to be the fruit of the specific act of the conjugal love of his parents; and he also has the right to be respected as a person from the moment of his conception.*

Nevertheless, whatever its cause or prognosis,

sterility is certainly a difficult trial. The community of believers is called to shed light upon and support the suffering of those who are unable to fulfill their legitimate aspiration to motherhood and fatherhood. Spouses who find themselves in this sad situation are called to find in it an opportunity for sharing in a particular way in the Lord's cross, the source of spiritual fruitfulness. Sterile couples must not forget that "even when procreation is not possible, conjugal life does not for this reason lose its value. Physical sterility in fact can be for spouses the occasion for other important services to the life of the human person, for example, adoption, various forms of educational work and assistance to other families and to poor or handicapped children."[59]

Many researchers are engaged in the fight against sterility. While fully safeguarding the dignity of human procreation, some have achieved results which previously seemed unattainable. Scientists therefore are to be encouraged to continue their research with the aim of preventing the causes of sterility and of being able to remedy them so that sterile couples will be able to procreate in full respect for their own personal dignity and that of the child to be born.

Moral and Civil Law

The Values and Moral Obligations that Civil Legislation Must Respect and Sanction in This Matter.

The inviolable right to life of every innocent human individual and the rights of the family and the institution of marriage constitute fundamental moral values because they concern the natural condition and integral vocation of the human person; at the same time they are constitutive elements of civil society and its order.

For this reason the new technological possibilities which have opened up in the field of biomedicine require the intervention of the political authorities and of the legislator, since an uncontrolled application of such techniques could lead to unforeseeable and damaging consequences for civil society. Recourse to the conscience of each individual and to the self-regulation of researchers cannot be sufficient for ensuring respect for personal rights and public order. If the legislator responsible for the common good were not watchful, he could be deprived of his prerogatives by researchers claiming to govern humanity in the name of the biological discoveries and the alleged "improvement" processes which they would draw from those discoveries. "Eugenism" and forms of discrimination between human beings could come to be legitimized: This would constitute an act of violence and a serious offense to the equality, dignity and fundamental rights of the human person.

The intervention of the public authority must be inspired by the rational principles which regulate the relationships between civil law and moral law. The task of the civil law is to ensure the common good of people through the recognition of and the defense of fundamental rights and through the promotion of peace and of public morality.[60] In no sphere of life can the civil law take the place of conscience or dictate norms concerning things which are outside its competence. It must sometimes tolerate, for the sake of public order, things which it cannot forbid without a greater evil resulting. However, the inalienable rights of the person must be recognized and respected by civil society and the political authority. These human rights depend neither on single individuals nor on parents; nor do they represent a concession made by society and the state: They pertain to human nature and are inherent in the person by virtue of the creative act from which the person took his or her origin.

Among such fundamental rights one should mention in this regard: a) every human being's right to life and physical integrity from the moment of conception until death; b) the rights of the family and of marriage as an institution and, in this area, the child's right to be conceived, brought into the world and brought up by his parents. To each of these two themes it is necessary here to give some further consideration.

In various states certain laws have authorized the direct suppression of innocents: The moment a positive law deprives a category of human beings of the protection which civil legislation must accord them, the state is denying the equality of all before the law. When the state does not place its power at the service of the rights of each citizen, and in particular of the more vulnerable, the very foundations of a state based on law are undermined. The political authority consequently cannot give approval to the calling of human beings into existence through procedures which would expose them to those very grave risks noted previously. The possible recognition by positive law and the political authorities of techniques of artificial transmission of life and the experimentation connected with it would widen the breach already opened by the legalization of abortion.

As a consequence of the respect and protection which must be ensured for the unborn child from the moment of his conception, the law must provide appropriate penal sanctions for every deliberate violation of the child's rights. The law cannot tolerate — indeed it must expressly forbid — that human beings, even at the embryonic stage, should be treated as objects of experimentation, be mutilated or destroyed with the excuse that they are superfluous or incapable of developing normally.

The political authority is bound to guarantee to the institution of the family, upon which society is based, the juridical protection to which it has a right. From the very fact that it is at the service of people, the political authority must also be at the service of the family. Civil law cannot grant approval to techniques of artificial procreation which, for the benefit of third parties (doctors, biologists, economic or governmental powers), take away what is a right inherent in the relationship between spouses; and therefore civil law cannot legalize the donation of gametes between persons who are not legitimately united in marriage.

Legislation must also prohibit, by virtue of the support which is due to the family, embryo banks, post-mortem insemination and "surrogate motherhood."

It is part of the duty of the public authority to ensure that the civil law is regulated according to the fundamental norms of the moral law in matters concerning human rights, human life and the institution of the family. Politicians must commit themselves, through their interventions upon public opinion, to securing in society the widest possible consensus on such essential points and to consolidating this consensus wherever it risks being weakened or is in danger of collapse.

In many countries the legalization of abortion and juridical tolerance of unmarried couples make it more difficult to secure respect for the fundamental rights recalled by this instruction. It is to be hoped that states will not become responsible for aggravating these socially damaging situations of injustice. It is rather to be hoped that nations and states will realize all the cultural, ideological and political implications connected with the techniques of artificial procreation and will find the wisdom and courage necessary for issuing laws which are more just and more respectful of human life and the institution of the family.

The civil legislation of many states confers an undue legitimation upon certain practices in the eyes of many today; it is seen to be incapable of guaranteeing that morality which is in conformity with the natural exigencies of the human person and with the "unwritten laws" etched by the Creator upon the human heart. All men of good will must commit themselves, particularly within their professional field and in the exercise of their civil rights, to ensuring the reform of morally unacceptable civil laws and the correction of illicit practices. In addition, "conscientious objection" vis-à-vis such laws must be supported and recognized. A movement of passive resistance to the legitimation of practices contrary to human life and dignity is beginning to make an ever sharper impression upon the moral conscience of many, especially among specialists in the biomedical sciences.

Conclusion

The spread of technologies of intervention in the processes of human procreation raises very serious moral problems in relation to the respect due to the human being from the moment of conception, to the dignity of the person, of his or her sexuality and of the transmission of life.

With this instruction the Congregation for the Doctrine of the Faith, in fulfilling its responsibility to promote and defend the church's teaching in so serious a matter, addresses a new and heartfelt invitation to all those who, by reason of their role and their commitment, can exercise a positive influence and ensure that in the family and in society due respect is accorded to life and love. It addresses this invitation to those responsible for the formation of consciences and of public opinion, to scientists and medical professionals, to jurists and politicians. It hopes that all will understand the incompatibility between recognition of the dignity of the human person and contempt for life and love, between faith in the living God and the claim to decide arbitrarily the origin and fate of a human being.

In particular, the Congregation for the Doctrine of the Faith addresses an invitation with confidence and encouragement to theologians, and above all to moralists, that they study more deeply and make ever more accessible to the faithful the contents of the teaching of the church's magisterium in the light of a valid anthropology in the matter of sexuality and marriage and in the context of the necessary interdisciplinary approach. Thus they will make it possible to understand ever more clearly the reasons for and the validity of this teaching. By defending man against the excesses of his own power, the church of God reminds him of the reasons for his true nobility; only in this way can the possibility of living and loving with that dignity and liberty which derive from respect for the truth be ensured for the men and women of tomorrow. The precise indications which are offered in the present instruction therefore are not meant to halt the effort of reflection, but rather to give it a renewed impulse in unrenounceable fidelity to the teaching of the church.

In the light of the truth about the gift of human life and in the light of the moral principles which flow from that truth, everyone is invited to act in the area of responsibility proper to each and, like the Good Samaritan, to recognize as a neighbor even the littlest among the children of men (cf. Lk. 10:29-37). Here Christ's words find a new and particular echo: "What you do to one of the least of my brethren, you do unto me" (Mt. 25:40).

During an audience granted to the undersigned perfect after the plenary session of the Congregation for the Doctrine of the Faith, the supreme pontiff, John Paul II, approved this instruction and ordered it to be published.

Given at Rome, from the Congregation for the Doctrine of the Faith, Feb. 22, 1987, the feast of the chair of St. Peter, the apostle.

Cardinal Joseph Ratzinger
Prefect

Archbishop Alberto Bovone
Secretary

Notes

1. Pope John Paul II, Discourse to those taking part in the 81st Congress of the Italian Society of Internal Medicine and the 82nd Congress of the Italian Society of General Surgery, Oct. 27, 1980: AAS 72 (1980) 1126.

2. Pope Paul VI, Discourse to the General Assembly of the United Nations, Oct. 4, 1965: AAS 57 (1965) 878; encyclical *Populorum Progressio,* 13: AAS 59 (1967) 263.

3. Ibid., Homily During the Mass Closing the Holy Year, Dec. 25, 1975: AAS 68 (1976) 145; Pope John Paul II, encyclical *Dives in Misericordia,* 30: AAS 72 (1980) 1224.

4. Pope John Paul II, Discourse to those taking part in the 35th General Assembly of the World Medical Association, Oct. 29, 1983: AAS 76 (1984) 390.

5. Cf. Declaration *Dignitatis Humanae,* 2.

6. Pastoral constitution *Gaudium et Spes,* 22; Pope John Paul II, encyclical *Redemptor Hominis,* 8: AAS 71 (1979) 270-272.

7. Cf. *Gaudium et Spes,* 35.

8. Ibid., 15; cf. also *Populorum Progressio,* 20: *Redemptor Hominis,* 15: Pope John Paul II, apostolic exhortation *Familiaris Consortio,* 11.

9. *Familiaris Consortio,* 11.

10. Cf. Pope Paul VI, encyclical *Humanae Vitae,* 10: AAS 60 (1986) 487-88.

11. Pope John Paul II, Discourse to the members of the 35th General Assembly of the World Medical Association, Oct. 29, 1983: AAS 76 (1984) 393.

12. Cf. *Familiaris Consortio,* 11, cf. also *Gaudium et Spes,* 50.

13. Congregation for the Doctrine of the Faith, Declaration on Procured Abortion, 9, AAS 66 (1974) 736-37.

14. Pope John Paul II, Discourse to those taking part in the 35th General Assembly of the World Medical Association, Oct. 29, 1983: AAS 76 (1984) 390.

15. Pope John XXIII, encyclical *Mater et Magistra,* III: AAS 53 (1961) 447.

16. *Gaudium et Spes,* 24.

17. Cf. Pope Pius XII, encyclical *Humani Generis:* AAS 42 (1950) 575; Pope Paul VI, *Professio Fidei:* AAS 60 (1968) 436.

18. *Mater et Magistra,* III; cf. Pope John Paul II, Discourse to priests participating in a Seminar on "Responsible Procreation," Sept. 17, 1983, *Insegnamenti di Giovanni Paolo II,* VI, 2 (1983) 562; "At the origin of each human person there is a creative act of God: No man comes into existence by chance; he is always the result of the creative love of God."

19. Cf. *Gaudium et Spes,* 24.

20. Cf. Pope Pius XII, Discourse to the St. Luke Medical-Biological Union, Nov. 12, 1944: *Discorsi e Radiomessaggi* VI (1944-1945) 191-92.

21. Cf. *Gaudium et Spes,* 50.

22. Cf. ibid., 51: "When it is a question of harmonizing married love with the responsible transmission of life, the moral character of one's behavior does not depend only on the good intention and the evaluation of the motives: The objective criteria must be used, criteria drawn from the nature of the human person and human acts, criteria which respect the total meaning of mutual self-giving and human procreation in the context of true love."

23. *Gaudium et Spes,* 51.

24. Holy See, Charter of the Rights of the Family, 4: *L'Osservatore Romano,* Nov. 25, 1983.

25. Congregation for the Doctrine of the Faith, Declaration on Procured Abortion, 12-13.

26. Cf. Pope Paul VI, Discourse to participants in the 23rd National Congress of Italian Catholic Jurists, Dec. 9, 1972: AAS 64 (1972) 777.

27. The obligation to avoid disproportionate risks involves an authentic respect for human beings and the uprightness of therapeutic intentions. It implies that the doctor "above all . . . must carefully evaluate the possible negative consequences which the necessary use of a particular exploratory technique may have upon the unborn child and avoid recourse to diagnostic procedures which do not offer sufficient guarantees of their honest purpose and substantial harmlessness. And if, as often happens in human choices, a degree of risk must be undertaken, he will take care to assure that it is justified by a truly urgent need for the diagnosis and by the importance of the results that can be achieved by it for the benefit of the unborn child himself." (Pope John Paul II, Discourse to participants in the Pro-Life Movement Congress, Dec. 3, 1982: *Insegnamenti di Giovanni Paolo II,* V, 3 [1982] 1512). This clarification concerning "proportionate risk" is also to be kept in mind in the following sections of the present instruction, whenever this term appears.

28. Pope John Paul II, Discourse to the participants in the 35th General Assembly of the World Medical Association, Oct. 29, 1983: AAS 76 (1984) 392.

29. Cf. Ibid., Address to a meeting of the Pontifical Academy of Sciences, Oct. 23, 1982: AAS 75 (1983) 37: "I condemn, in the most explicit and formal way, experimental manipulations of the human embryo, since the human being, from conception to death, cannot be exploited for any purpose whatever."

30. Charter of the Rights of the Family, 4b.

31. Cf. Pope John Paul II, Address to the participants in the Pro-Life Movement Congress, Dec. 3, 1982: *Insegnamenti di Giovanni Paolo II,* V, 3 (1982) 1511: "Any form of experimentation of the fetus that may damage its integrity or worsen its condition is unacceptable, except in the case of a final effort to save it from death." Congregation for the Doctrine of the Faith, Declaration on Euthanasia, 4: AAS 72 (1980) 550: "In the absence of other sufficient remedies, it is permitted, with the patient's consent, to have recourse to the means provided by the most advanced medical techniques, even if these means are still at the experimental stage and are not without a certain risk.

32. No one, before coming into existence, can claim a subjective right to begin to exist; nevertheless, it is legitimate to affirm the right of the child to have a fully human origin through conception in conformity with the personal nature of the human being. Life is a gift that must be bestowed in a manner worthy both of the subject receiving it and of the subjects transmitting it. This statement is to be borne in mind also for what will be explained concerning artificial human procreation.

33. Cf. Pope John Paul II, Discourse to those taking part in the 35th General Assembly of the World Medical Association, Oct. 29, 1983: AAS 76 (1984) 391.

34. Cf. *Gaudium et Spes,* 50.

35. Cf. *Familiaris Consortio,* 14.

36. Cf. Pope Pius XII, Discourse to those taking part in the Fourth International Congress of Catholic Doctors, Sept. 29, 1949: AAS 41 (1949) 559. According to the plan of the Creator, "a man leaves his father and his mother and cleaves to his wife, and they become one flesh" (Gn. 2:24). The unity of marriage, bound to the order of creation, is a truth accessible to natural reason. The church's tradition and magisterium frequently make reference to the Book of Genesis, both directly and through the passages of the New Testament that refer to it: Mt. 19:4-6; Mk. 10:5-8; Eph. 5:31. Cf. Athenagoras, *Legatio pro christianis,* 33: PG 6, 965-67; St. Chrysostom, *In Matthaeum homiliae,* LXII, 19, 1: PG 58 597; St. Leo the Great, *Epist. ad Rusticum,* 4: PL 54, 1204; Innocent III, Epist. *Gaudemus in Domino:* DS 778; Council of Lyons II, IV Session: DS 860; Council of Trent, XXIV Session: DS 1798, 1802; Pope Leo XIII, encyclical *Arcanum Divinae Sapientiae:* AAS 12 (1879-1880) 338-91: Pope Pius XI, encyclical *Casti Connubii:* AAS 22 (1930) 546-547; *Gaudium et Spes,* 48; *Familiaris Consortio,* 19; Code of Canon Law, Canon 1056.

37. Cf. Pope Pius XII, Discourse to those taking part

in the Fourth International Congress of Catholic Doctors, Sept. 29, 1949: AAS 41 (1949) 560; Discourse to those taking part in the Congress of the Italian Catholic Union of Midwives, Oct. 29, 1951: AAS 43 (1951) 850; Code of Canon Law, Canon 1134.

38. *Humanae Vitae,* 12.

39. Ibid.

40. Pope Pius XII, Discourse to those taking part in the Second Naples World Congress on Fertility and Human Sterility, May 19, 1956: AAS 48 (1956) 470.

41. Code of Canon Law, Canon 1061. According to this canon, the conjugal act is that by which the marriage is consummated if the couple "have performed (it) between themselves in a human manner."

42. Cf. *Gaudium et Spes,* 14.

43. Cf. Pope John Paul II, General Audience Jan. 16, 1980: *Insegnamenti di Giovanni Paolo II,* III, 1 (1980) 148-152.

44. Ibid. Discourse to those taking part in the 35th General Assembly of the World Medical Association, Oct. 29, 1983: AAS 76 (1984) 393.

45. Cf. *Gaudium et Spes,* 51.

46. Ibid., 50.

47. Cf. Pope Pius XII, Discourse to those taking part in the Fourth International Congress of Catholic Doctors, Sept. 29, 1949: AAS 41 (1949) 560: "It would be erroneous . . . to think that the possibility of resorting to this means (artificial fertilization) might render valid a marriage between persons unable to contract it because of the *impedimentum impotentiae.*"

48. A similar question was dealt with by Pope Paul VI, *Humanae Vitae,* 14.

49. Cf. *supra:* I, 1ff.

50. *Familiaris Consortio,* 14: AAS 74 (1982) 96.

51. Cf. Response of the Holy Office, March 17, 1897: DS 3323; Pope Pius XII, Discourse to those taking part in the Fourth International Congress of Catholic Doctors, Sept. 29, 1949: AAS 41 (1949) 560; Discourse to the Italian Catholic Union of Midwives, Oct. 29, 1951: AAS 43 (1951) 850; Discourse to those taking part in the Second Naples World Congress on Fertility and Human Sterility, May 19, 1956: AAS, 48 (1956) 471-73; Discourse to those taking part in the Seventh International Congress of the International Society of Hematology, Sept. 12, 1958: AAS 50 (1958) 733; *Mater et Magistra,* III.

52. Pope Pius XII, Discourse to the Italian Catholic Union of Midwives, Oct. 29, 1951: AAS 43 (1951) 850.

53. Ibid., Discourse to those taking part in the Fourth International Congress of Catholic Doctors, Sept. 29, 1949: AAS 41 (1949) 560.

54. Congregation for the Doctrine of the Faith, Declaration on Certain Questions Concerning Sexual Ethics, 9: AAS 68 (1976) 86, which quotes *Gaudium et Spes,* 51. Cf. Decree of the Holy Office, Aug. 2, 1929: AAS 21 (1929) 490; Pope Pius XII, Discourse to those taking part in the 26th Congress of the Italian Society of Urology, Oct. 8, 1953: AAS 45 (1953) 678.

55. Cf. Pope John XXIII, *Mater et Magistra,* III.

56. Cf. Pope Pius XII, Discourse to those taking part in the Fourth International Congress of Catholic Doctors, Sept. 29, 1949: AAS 41 (1949), 560.

57. Cf. Ibid., Discourse to those taking part in the Second Naples World Congress on Fertility and Human Sterility, May 19, 1956: AAS 48 (1956) 471-473.

58. *Gaudium et Spes,* 50.

59. *Familiaris Consortio,* 14.

60. Cf. *Dignitatis Humanae,* 7.

64 Whose Bodies? Which Selves? Appeals to Embodiment in Assessments of Reproductive Technology

Paul Lauritzen

Now men are far beyond the stage at which they expressed their envy of women's procreative power through couvade, transvestism, subincision. They are beyond merely giving spiritual birth in their baptismal-font wombs, beyond giving physical birth with their electronic fetal monitors, their forceps, their knives. Now they have laboratories. ([3], p. 314)

This passage from Gena Corea's book, *The Mother Machine* typifies the reaction of one important strand of feminist thought to the new technologies of reproduction and birth. It is fairly representative, for example, of the grave suspicion with which feminists associated with FINRRAGE (Feminists International Network of Resistance to Reproductive and Genetic Engineering) have greeted such possibilities as *in vitro* fertilization, embryo flushing and transfer, and gene therapy.

From Lisa Sowle Cahill and Margaret A. Farley, eds., *Embodiment, Morality, and Medicine* (Dordrecht: Kluwer Academic Publishers, 1995), pp. 113-26. Used with kind permission of Kluwer Academic Publishers.

According to this general line of thinking, the new reproductive technologies should be resisted because they concentrate power in the hands of a predominantly male and patriarchal medical establishment by disembodying procreation. By separating procreation from women's bodies, reproductive technology simultaneously reduces women to bodies, or body parts, and strips women of one traditional source of power, namely, the power to procreate. Hence Corea's warning. Previously men were denied direct control over the process of procreation; they might give birth symbolically or intervene medically in this process, but these were only simulacra of control. The existence of *in vitro* fertilization, however, and the distinct possibility of *in vitro* gestation turn resemblance into reality. Laboratory conception and gestation are a threat to women.

At the same time that FINRRAGE has mobilized to resist the new reproductive technologies, opposition has come from other quarters as well. The most substantial opposition has come from groups at the opposite end of the political spectrum, most notably the Roman Catholic Church. For example, the Catholic Church has also condemned *in vitro* fertilization, embryo flushing and transfer, and genetic engineering. Indeed, the Vatican has rejected virtually every application of the new reproductive technology (NRT), and, like FINRRAGE, the Vatican is worried about disembodiment. Thus, in the Vatican *Instruction* [2] on reproductive technology, we hear an echo of Corea's concern. We must take seriously the embodied nature of our existence, and failure to do so results in the reduction of a person to a product. So, for example, we find the Vatican insisting that "an intervention on the human body affects not only the tissues, the organs and their functions but also the person himself on different levels" ([2], p. 8).

This apparent convergence of two such different traditions of thought is interesting in itself. It is doubly so when, as in this volume, attention is focused on "how the realities of embodiment influence moral relationships in practical health care settings." Despite very serious differences between these traditions of thought — even on issues of embodiment — they agree in their rejection of reproductive technology, and they do so for reasons connected to worries about treating procreation as an out-of-the-body laboratory production. So examining how appeals to embodiment function in feminist and Vatican critiques of reproductive technology promises to be quite useful to the overall project of this volume. Moreover, if we attend to the similarities and differences between feminist appeals to embodiment and those of the Catholic Church, we may come to appreciate how the meaning of embodiment may vary from context to context. We may see, for example, how a religious appeal to embodiment in the Christian tradition takes quite a different form from an appeal to embodiment rooted in feminist thought, even if there are also substantial similarities between the two appeals.[1]

Feminist Opposition to Reproductive Technology

We can begin, then, with feminist opposition to reproductive technology. That one significant strand of feminist resistance is fueled by concerns about embodiment is clear. Yet, how precisely does the appeal to embodiment function in this particular feminist critique of reproductive technology? To answer that question, we can return to Gena Corea's work. According to Corea, reproductive technology is best understood in terms of two analogies that have implications for how we think about women's bodies and thus for how we think about, and treat, women. On the one hand, techniques for assisting human reproduction bear a striking resemblance to techniques used to facilitate reproduction in livestock. On the other hand, the commercial transactions frequently associated with reproductive technology bear a striking resemblance to those associated with sexual prostitution. Let us consider each of these analogies in turn.

Corea makes the comparison between reproductive technology in humans and scientific breeding of animals repeatedly and forcefully in her writings (see [3], [4], and [5]). Consider, she says, the techniques commonly used for breeding animals. Artificial insemination, superovulation, estrus synchronization, ova recovery, embryo evaluation, embryo transfer, and caesarean section are all available to animal breeders, just as they are to physicians of reproductive medicine [4]. Indeed, many applications of this technology used in infertility clinics have been adapted from their original use in the livestock breeding industry. This, says Corea, should give us pause because women have frequently been symbolically associated with animals in western thought, as "parts of nature to be controlled and subjugated" ([3], p. 313).

The point of the comparison between reproductive medicine and animal breeding is to invite an inspection of the attitudes that stand behind the practice of animal breeding. Once we see the attitudes driving animal reproduction, we may come to ask whether similar attitudes do not also drive reproductive medicine. And, as Corea shows, there is no mistaking the attitudes of animal breeders.

> When reproductive engineers manipulate the bodies of female animals today, they are clear, blunt and unapologetic about why they are doing it. They want to turn the females into machines for producing "superior" animals or into incubators for the embryos of more "valuable" females. They want, as one entrepreneur told me, to "manufacture embryos at a reduced cost." They aim to create beef cows yielding "quality carcasses of high cutability," and dairy cows producing more milk on the same amount of feed ([3], p. 312).

Or as a manager for Wall's Meat Company put it, this time in relation to the production of pork, "[t]he breeding sow should be thought of, and treated as, a valuable piece of machinery whose function is to pump out baby pigs like a sausage machine" ([4], p. 41).

Corea's point is clear: When the bodies of animals are treated in this fashion, when the animal is essentially reduced to its reproductive parts, the animal ceases to have any individuality or spiritual worth ([4], p. 39). The upshot of reproductive technology is thus that the animal is reduced to a reproductive commodity and nothing more. The worry is that we may come to think of women and their bodies in precisely the same terms.

This worry informs Corea's second analogy as well. If comparing reproductive medicine to livestock production is meant to highlight the possibility that employing reproductive technology may lead us to think about women's bodies as commodities, comparing reproductive medicine to prostitution is meant to highlight the fact that our society already conceptualizes women's bodies in market terms. Drawing on Andrea Dworkin's work, Corea shows that the reduction of women to commodities has already taken place. As Corea notes, our society already markets parts of women's bodies. Pornography is a thriving industry and sexual prostitution is widely perceived to be harmless and is thus tolerated as largely benign. But if women can sell vagina, rectum, and mouth, Corea asks, why not wombs, embryos, or eggs? Given how women are conceptualized in our society, the answer, of course, is that there is no reason to object to the marketing of women as reproductive commodities, and indeed, Corea says, that is precisely what we see with the development of a commercial surrogate mother industry and egg "donor" programs.

In fact, says Corea, we do not need to attend merely to the obvious comparison case, namely, surrogate motherhood. Talk to women who have been through *in vitro* fertilization programs. Quoting from an Australian study of women who had been treated in IVF programs, Corea draws attention to the dehumanizing aspects of the treatment.

> It [the IVF treatment] is embarrassing. You leave your pride on the hospital door when you walk in and pick it up when you leave. You feel like a piece of meat in a meat-works. But if you want a baby badly enough you'll do it ([5], p. 86).

Corea notes, for example, that many women report undergoing a process of emotional distancing during IVF. They attempt to separate mind from body and in fact come to feel disconnected from their bodies in ways that interfere with bodily love making with their partners. Here, Corea says, the comparison to prostitution is direct and disturbing.

> What kind of spiritual damage does it do to women when they emotionally separate their minds and bodies? . . . We have heard some prostitutes say that during intercourse with strangers who have rented the use of their bodies, they too separate their minds from their bodies as a means of self protection. We have heard some people with multiple personalities say that during extreme sexual abuse and torture in childhood, they split off into separate personalities in order to make what was happening to them endurable. In order to survive.
>
> What does it do to women in IVF "treatment" programs when, to varying extents, they separate their minds and bodies in order to make all the poking and prodding and embarrassments endurable? ([5], p. 86).

Corea is not the only feminist asking such questions, nor is she the only one to focus on the importance of embodiment to assessments of reproductive technology. Barbara Katz Rothman, for example, has made essentially the same point in her book, *Recreating Motherhood* [11].[2] In a chapter on the ways in which technological ideology shapes how we think about ourselves, Rothman summarizes one important line of resistance to technological thinking in terms that are strikingly similar to those set out above. "It is an objection," Rothman says, "to the notion of the world as a machine, the body as a machine, everything subject to hierarchical control, the world, ourselves, our bodies and our souls, ourselves and our children, divided, systematized, reduced" ([11], p. 54). Rothman's earlier work also focused on the effects of technology on conceptions of selfhood. In *The Tentative Pregnancy* [12], for example, she documents the effects of technologies of prenatal diagnosis on the experience of pregnancy, demonstrating that the existence of amniocentesis generates the same sort of emotional distancing, the same sort of splitting of the self, as Corea documents in regard to *in vitro* fertilization.

In fact, a careful reading of feminist responses to the technologies of reproductive medicine shows this to be a pervasive theme: reproductive technology encourages women to separate their selves from their bodies, and the resulting fragmentation leaves women vulnerable. Women become vulnerable because, with fragmentation, comes a willingness to treat women's bodies as biological machines that can be manipulated and controlled. Reproductive technology thus alienates women from their bodies and thereby strips them of an important source of personal fulfillment and power. As Margaret Farley puts it, "For many feminists the sundering of the power and process of reproduction from bodies of women constitutes a loss of major proportions. Hence, the notion of moving the whole process to the laboratory (using not only *in vitro* fertilization but artificial placentas *et al.*) is not one that receives much enthusiasm" ([7], p. 301).

Catholic Opposition to Reproductive Technology

If we turn now to the Vatican's response to reproductive technology, we see that the Catholic Church is also concerned about issues of embodiment. Consider, for example, the *Instruction* on reproductive technology issued by the Congregation for the Doctrine of the Faith in 1987, in which the position of the Church is set out at length. For our purposes, the introduction and the first two sections of this document are of particular interest, because the introduction sets out the basic moral considerations that are then applied in sections one and two to arrive at particular conclusions about reproductive technology. A careful reading of these three sections reveals that Vatican opposition to reproductive technology is supported by two lines of argument, both of which are rooted in concerns about embodiment. The first line of argument is set out in the introduction in terms of what the Vatican describes as "a proper idea of the nature of the human person in his bodily dimension" ([2], p. 8). The Congregation asks: What moral criteria must be used to assess reproductive technology? The first answer it gives is that any adequate criteria must recognize the bodily and spiritual unity of the person. In the Vatican's view, a person is a "unified totality," and thus it is wrong to treat a person in a way that reduces that person either to mere body or mere spirit. It is particularly important to keep this principle in mind, the Vatican says, when addressing ethical issues in medicine because there is a tendency in medicine to treat the body as "a mere complex of tissues, organs, and functions." Indeed, this is one of the central difficulties with reproductive medicine: it approaches human reproduction as if it were nothing more than the union of bodily parts, namely, of gametes. So one of the most serious problems with reproductive technology, the Vatican concludes, is precisely that it fails to treat the person as a unified whole. Instead, it treats the body in just the way the Vatican says it must not be treated, as a mere complex of tissues and organs. In other words, this technology treats our bodies functionally, the consequence of which is that persons get objectified and treated merely as means to an end. When this happens, technology is not simply assisting, but dominating the process of reproduction.

The second line of argument used to oppose interventions in the reproductive process is less obviously rooted in a concern about embodiment, but, once again, a careful reading of the text highlights the relevance of considerations of embodiment. This second line of reasoning is related to what the Vatican calls "the special nature of the transmission of human life in marriage." In the Vatican's view, since human procreation is the fruit of a "personal and conscious act," it is irreconcilably different from the transmission of life in other animals. It is intentional and purposive and therefore governed by laws. What laws? Laws, says the Vatican, given by God and "inscribed in the very being of man and woman."

As the language here suggests, the appeal is to a natural law conception of human nature, according to which we must understand the telos of human sexual life, marriage, and the family in order to discern the range of acceptable reproductive interventions. Moreover, the appeal is to a particular understanding of this telos, one in which intercourse, love, procreation, marriage, and the family belong together. In the Vatican's view, procreation is properly undertaken in the context of a loving monogamous marriage through an act of sexual intercourse. Here, then, is a second standard by which to assess interventions in the reproductive process. Any type of assisted reproduction that conforms to the procreative norm just articulated, i.e., any procreative attempt that includes sexual intercourse between partners in a loving monogamous marriage, helps facilitate the natural process of procreation and is therefore acceptable. Any intervention that fails to conform to the norm is a departure from the natural law with respect to human sexuality and is therefore morally problematic.

Two points are worth noting at this juncture. First, in rejecting reproductive technology as a violation of natural law, the Vatican is invoking the "inseparability thesis," set out in *Humanae Vitae*, and which supports Catholic opposition to contraception. Just as the Catholic Church condemns contraception because it separates what is never permitted to be separated by allowing for sex without procreation, so it condemns reproductive technology because it provides for the possibility of procreation without sex. This is important to note because many critics of the inseparability thesis have argued that, by insisting that each and every act of sexual intercourse must be open to procreation, the Vatican itself accepts a sort of "physicalist" understanding of sexuality that is incompatible with the holistic picture of the person as a "unified totality" of body and spirit that grounds the first line of argument against reproductive technology discussed above.

This observation suggests a second one. To say that reproductive technology separates procreation from sex is not equivalent to saying that reproductive technology disembodies procreation. So opposition to reproductive technology is not just opposition to those techniques, like IVF, that actually disembody conception, but opposition to how the body is used and viewed by reproductive technology generally. To be sure, the Vatican objection is not merely reducible to the consequentialist concern that all forms of reproductive technology move us toward the objectionable endpoint of extracorporeal gestation. Nevertheless, whether emphasis is placed upon the bodily and spiritual unity of a person, or upon the importance of keeping sex and procreation together, the Vatican is concerned that reproductive technology leads us to treat our bodies merely as a source of gametes, and that so treating our bodies is the first step to disembodying procreation altogether. We already have extracorporeal conception; can extracorporeal gestation be far behind? Ultimately, then, one important source of Vatican resistance to reproductive technology is that it encourages the disembodiment of procreation.

At this point it is worth noting that Vatican opposition to reproductive technology appears strikingly similar to feminist opposition to this technology, and that both groups couch their opposition in terms of the unfortunate consequences of disembodying procreation. Indeed the language of complaint is almost identical. Technological intervention in the process of procreation reduces reproduction to a production process in which humans are themselves reduced to products. Given the similarity of complaint, may we conclude that Vatican appeals to embodiment are essentially identical to feminist appeals to embodiment?

Janice Raymond [10] has argued that the answer to this question should be an emphatic and unequivocal "no!" The similarities, she says, are apparent only. In fact, according to Raymond, feminists should resist this equation, not only because it will be used by their opponents to discredit them as latter day Luddites, but because it is offensive to women. Linking fetalists — the term she uses for conservative religious opponents of reproductive technology — and feminists, she writes, "is an insult of the first order to women. It's tantamount to saying that behind every female idea or movement is male impetus, that women cannot stand on our own and create a woman-defined opposition to the NRTs for autonomous feminist reasons . . . " ([10], p. 60). "Feminists and fetalists," she says flatly, "are not aligned in any way" ([10], p. 65).

Raymond's total rejection of the similarities between Vatican opposition and feminist opposition is too extreme, but her argument is instructive nonetheless, for it demonstrates how an appeal to embodiment is inextricably tied to the context in which it is made. We therefore do well to take up her argument in some detail.

Raymond begins by noting that there are essentially two groups that have mounted substantial opposition to reproductive technology, feminists and the Roman Catholic Church, and that supporters of reproductive technology have an interest in trying to link feminist opposition to Catholic opposition as a way of discrediting both. Not only will advocates of reproductive technology adopt this "politics of guilt by association," but some conservative religious groups may attempt "to co-opt feminist language, ethics, and politics for their own cause" ([10], p. 60). So there may be a variety of reasons why individuals or groups might seek to conflate feminist opposition and Catholic opposition. Nevertheless, there are philosophical and political differences that make these traditions irreconcilable.

Raymond acknowledges that both the Catholic Church and feminists appeal to the language of embodiment in their critique of reproductive technology, but she says they "are talking about different bodies." ([10], p. 61). Feminists locate their appeal to embodiment within a context of opposition to violence against women, "Feminists," Raymond writes:

> are concerned about the ways in which the NRTs destroy a woman's bodily integrity and the totality of her personal and political existence. Many feminists criticize the way in which the 'technodocs' sever the biological processes of pregnancy and reproduction from the female body while at the same time making ever more invasive incursions into the female body for eggs, for implantation, for embryo transfers, and the like. Through such incursions, women can only come to be distanced from their autonomous bodily processes. And the net result of this is that women's bodies are perceived by themselves and others as a reproductive resource, as a field to be seeded, ploughed and ultimately harvested for the fruit of the womb. The feminist value of 'embodiment' translates to bodily integrity and the control of one's body. ([10], pp. 61-62)

By contrast, Raymond argues, Catholic opposition to disembodiment is located within a context of opposition to violence against fetuses. Consequently, in the Vatican *Instruction*, a document that, as we saw, appeals repeatedly to the language of embodiment, an entire section is devoted to a discussion of the effects of disembodied procreation on the fetus, but scarcely a word to the effects on women. "Nowhere," writes Raymonds about the Vatican *Instruction:*

> is there one mention of the 'disrespect' that is accorded to the woman's 'human life' by these technologies. One might expect that a document whose title purports to talk about the 'origin' of human life might at least mention women. But the so-called 'dignity of procreation' is applied in a general sense to the dignity of the human person and certainly not specifically to the dignity and integrity of the woman's body. . . . Nowhere is there any recognition that the body of the woman becomes an instrument in the technological procreative process and that this constitutes an assault against the dignity of women and a form of violence against women. The abstract inviolability of fetal life reigns supreme; the real and present violability of a woman's life, on which the new reproductive technologies depend for their very existence, is once more invisible ([10], pp. 63-64).

Moreover, Raymond argues, even when the Vatican is not focused exclusively on the bodies of fetuses, even when women's bodies come into view, the consequences of reproductive technology on women's bodies are seen against the backdrop of concern about sexuality, parenthood, or marriage, and not against a backdrop of concern about the bodily integrity of women, nor of concern that women have control of their bodies. So whereas feminist appeals to embodiment are rooted in a commitment to subverting "the entire fabric of sexual subordination and the ways in which that subordination has insured for men both sexual and reproductive access to women," Vatican appeals to embodiment are rooted in a pro-naturalist world view that embraces compulsory motherhood for women and thus subsumes ". . . the autonomy and independence of the woman to the 'interests' of the family . . ." ([10], p. 62).

Given the striking similarities that we noted above between feminist opposition to reproductive technology and Vatican opposition, is Raymond right? The answer is that Raymond is both partly right and partly wrong. Although Raymond is right to point out the very real differences between some of the feminist objections and some raised by the Catholic Church, she is wrong to dismiss as quickly as she does the mutual concern about disembodiment. To be sure, there are good reasons for feminists to be skeptical about Catholic opposition to reproductive technology. As we saw, the rather glaring omission of any explicit discussion of how reproductive technology affects women is one. Nevertheless, a healthy skepticism here does not justify Raymond's hasty dismissal of Vatican concerns about disembodiment.

For example, Raymond claims that while the Vatican uses the language of embodiment in criticizing reproductive technology, it is only concerned about women's body derivatively. That is, the Catholic Church is only concerned about women's bodies to the extent that these bodies serve the reproductive interest of men or are necessary to safeguarding the bodies of fetuses. She says, "for feminists, women are our bodies," and the unstated implication is that for the Catholic Church this is not true. If we look closely at the Vatican *Instruction*, however, we see nearly identical language, language that, I believe, is meant to express the same worry. Quoting Pope John Paul II, the Congregation for the Doctrine of the Faith endorses a claim that might well be summarized as, "touch the body, touch the person." "Each human person," we read, "in his absolutely unique singularity, is constituted not only by his spirit, but by his body as well. Thus, in the body and through the body, one touches the person himself in his concrete reality" ([2], p. 8). "Touch the body, touch the person" might well be substituted without loss of meaning for "women are our bodies."

Yet, if this comparison highlights the fact that Raymond states her case too strongly by claiming that the Vatican and feminists are not aligned in any way, it also reveals the truth of her observation that the context of appeals to embodiment is all important. Feminists apply the insight behind the aphorism "women are our bodies" from a context in which there is an explicit and unequivocal commitment to women's bodily integrity and to securing personal and political liberty for women. So feminists move directly from a concern about the disembodiment of procreation that appears to come with reproductive technology to an explicit discussion of how this technology affects women's bodies and thus women's hope for freedom and equality.

By contrast, the Catholic Church appeals to embodiment from within a context in which there has not traditionally been a significant commitment to women's equality. The upshot is that when the Vatican talks about embodiment, it is not typically speaking about women's bodies. So although "touch that person, touch the body" in fact articulates the same view of the human person as "women are our bodies," the former aphorism refers primarily to male bodies. Thus, when the Vatican turns to apply this insight in an assessment of reproductive technology, we should not be altogether surprised — though we may still be outraged — by the fact that it takes up the effects this technology has on the bodies of fetuses, but says nothing about its impact on the bodies of women.

Indeed, Raymond's emphatic repudiation of Vatican appeals to embodiment forces us to confront the fact that the Church's discussion of the effects of disembodiment takes place against the backdrop, not merely of an undistinguished record of commitment to the rights of women, but against a significant legacy of denigration of the body, women, and sexuality. Margaret Farley, for example, has pointed out that any appeal to embodiment within the Christian tradition must come to grips with the fact that the Christian tradition has frequently embraced a dualism that pits spirit against body, man against woman, reason against emotion, a dualism that has served to oppress women. "Body/spirit," Farley writes:

> is in many ways the basic dualism with which historical religions have struggled since late antiquity. Women, as we have already noted, have been associated with body, men with mind. Women's physiology has been interpreted as 'closer to nature' than men's in that many areas and functions of a woman's body seem to serve the human species as much or more than they serve the individual woman. Women's bodies, in this interpretation, are subject to a kind of fate — more so than men's. Women are immersed in 'matter,' in an inertness which has not its own agency. This is manifest not only in the determined rhythms of their bodily functions, but in a tendency to act from emotion rather than from reason, and in women's 'natural' work which is the caring for the bodies of children and men. ([7], p. 291)

Has the Church come to grips with this legacy in its appeal to embodiment in the *Instruction* on Reproductive Technology? Raymond has shown decisively that the answer to this question is "no." The lesson to be drawn here is that the Church's own best insights have been undermined by a continuing legacy of sexism and dualistic thinking. If the Vatican was not in fact blinkered by the regrettable bifurcation of reality that runs deep in the tradition, if instead the Vatican took seriously an incarnational theology that, in Carolyn Walker Bynum's words, treats the "body as locus, mot merely of pleasure but of personhood itself," ([1], p. 19) then the Vatican appeal to embodiment in the *Instruction* on Reproductive Technology would in fact commit it to attend seriously to women's bodily autonomy and to the threat posed to women's bodies by reproductive technology. It is regrettable that the *Instruction* does not do justice to the Church's own vision of the human person as "a unified totality" of body and spirit, but we should not dismiss the vision itself as sexist or misogynist for that reason.

If Raymond's juxtaposition of feminist criticism with Vatican criticism of reproductive technology helps us to see that any appeal to embodiment must be taken in context, and, if attending to the context of Vatican appeals to embodiment helps us to discern the shortcomings of Catholic opposition to reproductive technology, it is worth asking whether this juxtaposition does not also highlight the shortcomings of some feminist appeals to embodiment. I want in closing to suggest that it does and, indeed, to show how the Vatican *Instruction* might offer an important corrective to one strand of the feminist critique precisely at the point where the context of feminist appeals to embodiment undermines feminist insights.

To see once again that the comparison of feminist and Catholic opposition to reproductive technology is instructive, we may return to the analogy Gena Corea draws between sexual prostitution and the commodification of reproduction. We saw above that this comparison is made to highlight the dangers of an activity that appears to commodify women's bodies in a cultural context where women's bodies are already for sale in the marketplace. To explain the full force of this analogy, however, we must ask why sexual prostitution is morally problematic.[3] If feminism is committed to the bodily autonomy of women, why should women not be able to sell their bodies if they so choose? This is a difficult question for feminism, and it is instructive to see how one strand of feminist thought has answered this question. One answer to the question has essentially been to suggest that prostitution is so degrading and so dehumanizing, that no woman would choose to be a prostitute unless she were coerced.

It is this line of reasoning, for example, that Catherine MacKinnon has in mind when she writes that the fact that "... prostitution and modeling are structurally women's best economic options should give pause to those who would consider women's presence there a true act of free choice" ([9], p. 180). As MacKinnon points out, in other contexts, we readily acknowledge that people do degrading work for lack of better economic options, and we neither deny that the work is degrading nor deceive ourselves by thinking that the work is freely chosen. Indeed, even where a woman "chooses" prostitution in a context where she is not doing so, say, to feed herself or her children, we have good reason to suspect that other forms of coercion are at work. Perhaps self-esteem has been so undermined by a society that systematically devalues women that there is not a sufficient sense of self-worth to recognize the degradation of prostitution.

Thus, whether we are talking about economic coercion or other, perhaps less obvious forms of coercion, the important point is that this approach to prostitution challenges the presumption that prostitution is freely chosen. What MacKinnon says of pornography could also be said of prostitution. "I will leave you wondering . . . ," MacKinnon writes, "why it is that when a woman spreads her legs for a camera, she is assumed to be exercising free will" ([9], p. 180). Why is it, critics of prostitution might ask, that when a woman sells her body for money, she is assumed to be exercising free will? To reverse the presumption here is to take the view that sexual prostitution in itself could not possibly fulfill any legitimate interest for a person of self-respect. Hence, if a woman is selling her body, there is reason to suspect coercion.

I have argued elsewhere that this is in fact a powerful argument and that the critique of "liberal" conceptions of autonomy implicit in it is also significant (see [8]). For our purposes, it is important to see how the logic of this argument must be extended to reproductive technology if the comparison of assisted reproduction to sexual prostitution is to carry any weight. Take, for example, the argument that IVF turns a woman into a sort of reproductive prostitute. Part of the force of this argument comes from the suggestion that women are coerced into IVF, just as they are coerced into becoming prostitutes. Yet, if we consider the claim that to offer IVF to a childless woman is coercive, we discover that for this claim to be plausible we require a conviction comparable to the belief that eliminating prostitution could not conflict with any legitimate interest a woman of self-respect might have.

In one sense, of course, this is not true even of

prostitution. If a woman sells her body in order to feed herself or her children, she is obviously pursuing a legitimate interest. Nevertheless, the point opponents of prostitution and of reproductive technology wish to make is that there is nothing in the activity of selling one's body or in the procedures of assisted reproduction that is itself rewarding for women, and, consequently, if women choose either activity, the only explanation is that they have been coerced. The problem with pressing this line of argument, however, is that there is a more direct connection between assisted reproduction and the good of bearing and begetting a child than between prostitution and the good of feeding children. The upshot is that opponents of reproductive technology can only utilize this analogy with prostitution effectively, if they are simultaneously prepared to reject or devalue the importance of begetting and bearing children.

Unfortunately, when we examine the work of some who have opposed IVF on the grounds that it may be coercive, we see precisely this sort of skepticism about the value of children. For example, in an article entitled ' "Women Want It": *In Vitro* Fertilization and Women's Motivations for Participation,' Christine Crowe argues that women participate in IVF programs largely because they accept the dominant ideology of motherhood in Western culture, an ideology that includes the belief that biological motherhood is valuable. "IVF," Crowe writes, "relies upon women to perceive motherhood as desirable" ([6], pp. 547-48). Or consider Robyn Rowland's explanation of the pressures facing infertile women. Under the heading "pro-natalism and the experience of infertility," Rowland writes:

> To understand the impact of infertility, we need to understand that we live within a society which says that it is good to have children. That is, one which has pronatalist values. . . . The exclamations of wonder whenever we see something young, vulnerable, and cuddly such as a kitten are also reinforcing the desire for children ([13], p. 85).

Rowland is certainly correct that childless women face enormous pressure in Western societies, but does recognizing this fact, and the coercion that may come with it, also require rejecting any affirmation of children, as this passage appears to suggest?

Here we see how the context of feminist appeals to embodiment may also subvert the full significance of embodiment. To appeal to embodiment from within a context that emphasizes the way in which pregnancy, childbirth, and the care of children have been oppressive to women, poses the danger of neglecting the value of the decidedly embodied experience of pregnancy and the embodied goodness of children.

This is not to say that all, or even most, feminists who have opposed reproductive technology out of concerns over embodiment devalue children. Nor do I wish to deny that pregnancy is sometimes oppressive for women and perceived by women as such. Nor would I deny that having and rearing children can be unfulfilling or even disastrously burdensome. Still, those feminists who have categorically discounted the value to women of pregnancy and parenthood have not taken embodiment seriously enough. Given a preoccupation with combatting an ideology that sacralizes pregnancy and motherhood, it is easy to conflate the socially sanctioned belief that having children is desirable (and pregnancy uniquely fulfilling) with the very different proposition that women cannot be fulfilled unless they have children. Thus, in their eagerness to reject the latter claim, some feminists have been blinded to the fact that women may legitimately value carrying and caring for children. To celebrate is not to sacralize, and any view that fully embraced the importance of embodiment, could not but celebrate the experiences of bearing and rearing children.

In the final analysis, careful attention to Vatican and to feminist appeals to embodiment reveals striking differences that in turn highlight the shortcomings of both Vatican and some feminist opposition to reproductive technology. At the same time, however, we can see striking similarities. Both traditions of thought draw our attention to the potential dangers of disembodying procreation, and in doing so, both traditions properly highlight the importance of attention to issues of embodiment when reflecting morally on medicine. It is perhaps ironic, therefore, that, in assessing reproductive technology in light of the embodied character of human life, critics in both traditions go so wrong. For, surely, no adequate account of embodiment and reproductive technology would conclude that this technology always or necessarily violates the embodied quality of human procreation. On the contrary, for many infertile individuals, reproductive technology mediates embodiment, not the reverse (see [7]). That both Catholic opposition and some feminist opposition to reproductive technology appear blind to this fact demonstrates how important the context of appeals to embodiment can be.

John Carroll University
University Hts., Ohio, U.S.A.

Notes

1. For a fuller discussion of feminist and Catholic opposition to reproductive technology, see [8]. See also [14], [15].

2. It is important to note, however, that Rothman does not reach the same conclusions about reproductive technology as Corea, even though she shares Corea's worries about disembodiment.

3. In fact, I cannot hope to unpack this analogy fully here. To do so would require a complete analysis of the relationship between a prostitute and client, and an examination of that relationship compared to the relationship among infertile individuals, physicians, and gamete donors. I will focus only on the comparison between an infertile woman and a prostitute.

Bibliography

[1] Bynum, C. W.: 1991, *Fragmentation and Redemption,* Zone Books, New York.

[2] Congregation for the Doctrine of Faith: 1987, *Instruction on Respect for Human Life in Its Origin and on the Dignity of Procreation,* United States Catholic Conference, Washington.

[3] Corea, G.: 1985, *The Mother Machine,* Harper & Row, New York.

[4] Corea, G.: 1987, "The Reproductive Brothel," in G. Corea et al. (eds.), *Man-Made Women,* Indiana University Press, Bloomington, pp. 38-51.

[5] Corea, G.: 1988, "What the King Can Not See," in E. H. Baruch, A. F. D'Adamo, Jr. and J. Seager (eds.), *Embryos, Ethics, and Women's Rights,* Harrington Park Press, New York, pp. 77-93.

[6] Crowe, C.: 1985, "Women Want It: *In Vitro* Fertilization and Women's Motivations for Participation," *Women Studies International Forum* 8(6): 547-52.

[7] Farley, M.: 1985, "Feminist Theology and Bioethics," in B. H. Andolson, C. E. Gudorf, and M. D. Pellauer (eds.), *Women's Consciousness, Women's Conscience,* Harper and Row, San Francisco, pp. 285-305.

[8] Lauritzen, P.: 1993, *Pursuing Parenthood,* Indiana University Press, Bloomington.

[9] MacKinnon, C.: 1987, *Feminism Unmodified,* Harvard University Press, Cambridge, Mass.

[10] Raymond, J.: 1987, "Fetalists and Feminists: They are Not the Same," in P. Spallone and D. L. Steinberg (eds.), *Made to Order,* Pergamon, Oxford, pp. 58-66.

[11] Rothman, B. K.: 1989, *Recreating Motherhood,* W. W. Norton, New York.

[12] Rothman, B. K.: 1985, *The Tentative Pregnancy,* Viking Press, New York.

[13] Rowland, R.: 1987, "Women as Living Laboratories: The New Reproductive Technologies," in J. Figuerra-McDonough and R. C. Sarri (eds.), *The Trapped Woman,* Sage, Newbury Park, pp. 81-111.

[14] Ryan, M.: 1993, "Justice and Artificial Reproduction: A Catholic Feminist Analysis," Ph.D. dissertation, Yale University, New Haven, Conn.

[15] Ryan, M.: 1990, "The Argument for Unlimited Procreative Liberty: A Feminist Critique," *Hastings Center Report* 20(4): 6-12.

65 In a Glass Darkly

Oliver O'Donovan

Let me begin with a fairy tale. Once upon a time there lived in a forest a woodman and his wife, who longed for children and had none. One morning as she sat grieving over the loneliness of her home, the goodwife was surprised by a sudden apparition. A majestic and queenly figure stood in her kitchen, clothed from head to foot in glittering white and bearing a sparkling silver wand in her hand. 'I am your fairy godmother', she announced, 'I have come to propose a sensible solution to your difficulties.' The difficulties, she explained, had to do with an occluded oviduct; and what she proposed was what we in our world call *in vitro* fertilization with embryo replacement, except that in place of the length, difficulty, and uncertainty of the procedure which we know, all was to be made simple and certain by means of the magic wand. The woman responded to the plan with joy, and had no difficulty in persuading her husband to cooperate. Everything was done as the magic visitor proposed, and then she disappeared on her way to help some other needy godchildren, leaving the woodman and his wife to cope as best they might in the heart of the forest with an unexpected but far from unwelcome pregnancy.

And as the story goes on to tell, with more candour than is usual in fairy tales, that after she had gone the worthy pair began to question doubtfully, and to wonder at the ambiguity which attends all our encounters with the supernatural. Was the blessing so strangely bestowed upon them not qualified by a certain unwholesomeness, by that air of the disreputable which always clings to the practice of magic, try as we may to deny it, like a slight odour of decay? And was their visitor, unquestionably generous as her intentions were, not altogether too practical and busy a person to have acquired that simple translucent virtue which distinguishes the fairy godmother from the witch? In consenting to her plan, had they consented to something barbarous? and would they gain a child only to mourn the loss of their innocence — the very innocence which made them cherish the hope of children in the first place? Let us, while remaining strictly within the terms of the fairy story, and without presuming as yet to discuss what may take place in our less picturesque world, ask ourselves the questions which might have perplexed the woodman and his wife. Consider some of the doubts which could reasonably have occurred to them.

1. The first doubt, perhaps, would not have caused them prolonged anxiety. They might have thought that this procedure savoured of black magic rather than white because it did not *cure* the tubal blockage which was the cause of infertility, but merely *circumvented* it. That is to say: this magic strove to become compensatory rather than curative medicine. We have already confronted this question in discussing gamete donation; and we maintained that although compensatory medicine has less immediate claim upon our sympathies than curative medicine, there is no objection to it in principle. In the actual world the secondary status of compensatory medicine may properly have negative implications for IVF in a competition for scarce resources; but in a fairy story we assume that magic is an unlimited resource. It does not constitute an argument against the practice as such. It might, however, raise a second doubt . . .
2. Why was it necessary to adopt a compensatory approach to tubal infertility, instead of a curative one? Magic, after all, like scientific research, must be assumed to know no limits. If the fairy godmother had only concentrated her spells on the task of oviduct reconstruction, would she not have been able to cure the problem at source? Must we, then, not attribute her fascination with little glass phials

From Oliver O'Donovan, *Begotten or Made* (Oxford: Clarendon Press, 1984), pp. 66-86. Used by permission.

to a more sinister interest in projects of a frankly necromantic kind? To such a doubt we must concede this much justification at least: if at any time there was a straight choice to be made between two approaches to a problem, equally likely to be effective, one curative and one compensatory, it would be highly improper not to choose the cure, even if the other course offered gains for research not easily attainable otherwise. But the layman cannot judge whether this has ever been so, or could be so, with respect to oviduct reconstruction and *in vitro* fertilization. We should certainly not be in a hurry to assume that our scientific magic is capable of doing anything it sets its mind to. Failure to perfect techniques of oviduct reconstruction, which at present are limited, does not necessarily demonstrate a lack of will. There are, in fact, some striking examples of projects in this general field which have been assiduously pursued for some time with little success. And perhaps there is no need for the pious storyteller to attribute omnicompetence to magic spells in fairy tales either.

3. To be taken more seriously is a third doubt: that childlessness itself is not a pathological condition, and is therefore not suitable for medical magic, whether curative or compensatory. We should not employ medical means to compensate for non-medical disappointments. If I am too short to join the police force, too quickly winded to be selected for the Olympic team, or too forgetful to pass history examinations, it is not a matter for my doctor to deal with. Unless, that is, my failures are manifestly related to some physical pathology (I used to remember dates all right until I had glandular fever), or so exceptional as to place me right outside the normal conditions of healthy existence (I am so short of breath that I cannot stand up from my chair), and so constituting a pathology themselves.

Now, the difficulty with childlessness is that it is a matter of chance whether a child is conceived on any one occasion or not. It is possible in principle for a couple to remain childless for a long time without anything being wrong with either of them. We should object to the idea that medicine may be invoked to overcome simple contingency, especially in the begetting of children, where contingency, as I shall argue shortly, plays an important role. Furthermore, the variations in fertility between one person and another, or between different periods in one person's life, are not simply to be ironed out into a maximal norm; they are valuable and appropriate to us as a race, and contribute to our natural differentiation and diversification. We should object to the idea that medicine may be invoked merely to enhance fertility. Nevertheless, it is clearly the case that childlessness arises, among other ways, from pathologies. Tubal occlusion is an example of this. An organ which is incompetent to do what it is meant to do is *ipso facto* pathological, and a proper object of medical concern. So, then, when it is said that childlessness is not a pathological condition and should not be treated as though it were, we may agree, but with this proviso; that though childlessness as such is not a direct object of medical attention, a pathology underlying it may well be, and medicine may attempt to compensate for that pathology as well as cure it.

The appropriate question to raise (leaving our fairy godmother for the moment) is whether those who practice IVF techniques are alert to the distinction between pathological and merely contingent childlessness; and here, it would seem, there may be some ground for dissatisfaction. The category of 'idiopathic infertility' is used to embrace cases of a persistent failure to conceive where there is no obvious explanation of any kind, and it is commonly defined in terms of two years without conception in the absence of evidence of abnormal semen or tubal deficiency. This categorization itself is open to the charge of treating contingency as though it were pathology. The difficulty arises from the use of statistics to determine a failure to conceive as pathological. Statistics may, of course, have a perfectly proper role to play in defining pathological conditions. They will provide appropriate criteria, for example, to define male oligospermia: when a particular man has a quite abnormally low count of spermatozoa in the semen, then we are justified in thinking of his condition as a kind of pathology: his semen is no less manifestly incompetent to perform the task that it is meant for than a woman's blocked oviduct. But in the matter of achieving a pregnancy, statistics should be used with more caution. Pregnancy is not a condition of health, it is an event which depends on contingencies. It may be that a couple's stubborn childlessness is so abnormal statistically that the physician legitimately suspects a pathology which he cannot diagnose. But to suspect a pathology is not to prove one; and to dignify the case with the title 'idiopathic infertility' is merely to conceal the fact that it is the absence of an evident pathology rather than the presence of one that is puzzling. You cannot have a pathology which does not *belong* to either of the couple, but hovers between them, as it were, irresolutely. Although statistical abnormalities may entitle one to suspect a pathology, they do not entitle one to rule out the possibility that simple contingency alone is responsible. And in the 15 percent of cases in which pregnancy follows 'spontaneously', that is probably the truth of the matter. We would have every reason to object, then, if IVF were generally invoked to deal with 'idiopathic infertility'. We understand that this is not generally done at present — though not for any such scruples as we have just expressed.

4. A fourth doubt may assail the woodman and his wife, arising from the third. Granted that *in vitro* fertilization intends to treat pathology and not contingency, does it not have the effect of abolishing the contingency at the same time as it compensates for the pathology? If this is so, there will be a strong ground of objection to it (one which will not apply in the same way to some other means of compensating for infertility, such as artificial insemination). For the element of chance is one of the factors which most distinguish the act of begetting from the act of technique. In allowing something to randomness, we confess that, though we might, from a purely technical point of view, direct events, it is beyond our competence to direct them well. We commit ourselves to divine providence because we have reached the point at which we know we must stop making, and simply be. To say 'randomness', of course, is not to say 'providence'. Randomness is the inscrutable face which providence turns to us when we cannot trace its ways or guess its purpose. To accept the fact is to accept that we cannot plan for the best as God plans for the best, and that we cannot read his plans before the day he declares them. There are, to be sure, ways in which we reduce the degree of unpredictability indirectly, by choosing the time of intercourse carefully, for example, to fit in with natural rhythms of fertility. Yet for all that we may encourage conception to take place, its occurrence is not the direct object of our technique. We do not, in natural begetting, bring sperm and ovum together, and as it were, forcibly introduce them to each other. Thus we distinguish the act of begetting from those other acts in which we attempt to control the outcome directly, mastering with our hands or with our implements the material resistance which stands between the will and its proposed artefact.

But it is not the case that conception by *in vitro* fertilization abolishes contingency. It is true that it does so at one point: the actual fertilization of the ovum by the sperm is made the direct object of technique. There is therefore more difference between *in vitro* and *in vivo* than the mere difference of location that those phrases may suggest: there is a new, technical relationship to an event which has hitherto been subject only to indirect influences. But what is lost to contingency at the point of *fertilization* is not lost, but may even be enhanced, at the point of *implantation*. Implantation is still unpredictable and unmanipulable, an event which can only be encouraged, and not yet directly managed.

As one might expect, this very factor, which in our view goes some way to saving the humanity of the whole undertaking, is regarded by its practitioners as a technical imperfection to be overcome as soon as suitable means can be found. Since the early days of the practice it has been customary to reduce the element of unpredictability by replacing not one, but two or even three embryos in the womb, to increase the chance that one of them will implant. It is at least arguable that this does no further injury to the others than that which they might suffer in the course of nature anyway, for the fate of every new conceptus is doubtful. But it does reduce the doubtfulness which must attach to every *act* of embryo-replacement. It is easy to see why, from the administrative point of view, it is desirable to minimise the contingencies and maximise the rate of success at first attempt. Time, patience and resources are all consumed in repeated attempts which could be avoided. yet this observation, while making the practice of multiple replacement intelligible, does so in a way that rather strengthens than mitigates the force of the case against it; for it is precisely the integration of human fertilization into the general demands of an administrative system that more than anything else confirms its status as an act of 'making' rather than 'begetting'. The primary characteristic of a technological society is not the things it may *do* with the aid of machines, but the way it *thinks* of everything it does as a kind of mechanical production. Once begetting is acknowledged to be under the laws of time and motion efficiency, then its absorption into the world of productive technique is complete. The laws of operation cease to be the laws of natural procreation, aided discreetly by technical assistance; they become the laws of production, which swallow up all that is natural into their own world of artifice. That is why I think there is a great deal of symbolic importance in resisting multiple replacement of embryos. We should expect the practitioners to act inefficiently at this point, just as we expect researchers to act inefficiently when they are dealing with human subjects. Inefficiency is the worship they pay to the *humanum*, the human person and personal relationships, objects which cannot be subject to the laws which govern productive efficiency.

5. With this we come to the fifth doubt, which is the most serious of all the doubt which might assail our fairy-tale couple and demands the most protracted attention.

In my earlier discussions of transsexual surgery and gamete-donation I attempted to show that the issue of the making or begetting of children is correlated to another issue, the unity or separation of the procreative and relational goods of marriage. I argued that when procreation is not bound to the relational union established by the sexual bond, it becomes a chosen 'project' of the couple rather than a natural development of their common life. Sexual relationship, correspondingly, loses the seriousness which belongs to it because of our common need for a generation of children, and degenerates into merely a form of play. The document submitted to the Warnock Commission by the Catholic Bishops' Joint Committee on Bioethical Issues has made this point the basis of its objections to *in vitro* fertilization, and has argued the case with great eloquence.[2]

If in the course of natural procreation, the Committee maintains, the parents' hope for a child is fulfilled, then 'the child will be a gift embodying the parents' acts of personal . . . involvement with each other. Procreation will thus have been an extension of the parents' whole common life' (para. 21). But the same cannot be said of the child born as a result of *in vitro* fertilization, who will tend to be assigned 'to the same status as other objects of acquisition. The technical skills and decisions of the child's makers will have produced, they hope, a good product, a desirable acquisition' (para. 27). Although good parents 'will strive to assign the child his or her true status . . . they will be labouring against the real structure of the decisive choices and against the deep symbolism of all that was done to bring their child into being'. The 'structure of the decisive choices': that is what makes the decisive difference in the view of the Catholic Bishops' Committee.

> In procreation by sexual intercourse *one and the same act of choice* made by each spouse governs *both* the experienced and expressive sexual union *and* the procreation of the child. There is one intentional act. . . . But in IVF there are irreducibly separate acts of choice, all indispensible, and all the independent acts of different people. . . . Thus the IVF child comes into existence, not as a gift supervening on an act expressive of marital union . . . but rather in the manner of a product of a making (and indeed, typically, as the end-product of a process managed and carried out by persons other than his parents) [para. 24].

Within this argument we may notice two features. One is the principle that I have maintained, that procreation is safeguarded from degeneration by springing from a sexual relationship in which the child is not the immediate object of attention. The other is the further stipulation that these twin goods of marriage must be held together in *one intentional act* of sexual intercourse. The complaint against IVF is that there are 'separate acts of choice', that the unity of the procreative and the relational goods is not maintained in each single act. Now, it might seem that this further stipulation is merely a necessary clarification of what was implied in my principle. For the unity of procreative and relational goods will certainly be an empty thing if there is not some concrete expression of it. Anyone can agree, after all, that marriage should have both a relational good and a procreative one — and then pursue the two so distinctly that they become quite unrelated projects. And what other concrete point of unity can there be than the act of sexual intercourse, of its nature both procreative and relational? It is natural to assume, therefore, that the criticism of 'separate acts' maintained by the Catholic Bishops' Committee is the necessary corollary to our common concern.

Once we accept the 'one intentional act', however, certain other practices as well as IVF must fall under our disapproval. The Committee points out that their criticism applies also to Artificial Insemination (not simply to donor insemination, that is, which may be disapproved of quite apart from this doctrine, simply on the grounds of donor involvement, but to Artificial Insemination using the husband's semen). It does not say that their criticism could also apply to artificial contraception, which (in the eyes of some) is the Magna Carta of our modern separation of procreative and relational goods. There is nothing sinister about the document's silence on this point; indeed, it could be said to be the most responsible procedure in such a document not to raise issues which divide Christians, and indeed divide Catholics, if it is not germane to do so. In fact, the position maintained in the document does not necessarily imply a disapproval of artificial contraception, though it must tend to encourage such a disapproval. In the first place, the Committee explicitly denies that it objects to artificial intervention as such, and even suggests artificial procedures which would aid the act of intercourse to achieve its procreative goal without separating the acts. In the second place, it maintains the doctrine of the unity of the acts only to the point of saying that there must be no act with a procreative goal which does not also have a relational goal; it does not assert that there must be no intercourse for relationship alone without a procreative intent.

So, then, I mention contraception not in the mean and clever spirit of someone who thinks he has unmasked a hidden agenda in this Catholic document, but for two rather better reasons. Firstly, and incidentally, I wish to refute those who argue that the whole principle of the unity of relation to procreation was given away when we admitted artificial contraception. If even the Catholic Bishops can formulate the principle in a way that leaves the matter of contraception open, then the issue must be much more subtle than such objectors have supposed. Secondly, and more importantly, I mention it because there is an aspect of the contraception debate which affords an illuminating parallel for the question in hand. One of the arguments in favour of artificial contraception which Paul VI's famous encyclical mentioned, but did not answer, was that which he described as 'principle of totality', that is to say, the principle that the sexual life of a married couple should be viewed as a whole, not in terms of its distinct acts of intercourse. Fornication may take the form of a series of one-night stands (for that is its moral corruption, that the sexual act never leads beyond the occasion to establish a permanent bond of loyalty), but married love is entirely different. To break marriage down into a series of disconnected sexual acts is to falsify its true nature. As a whole, then, the married love of any couple should (barring serious reasons to the contrary) be both relation-building and procreative; the two ends of marriage are held together in the life of sexual partnership which the couple live together. But it is artificial to insist, as *Humanae Vitae* did, that 'each and every marriage act' must express the two goods equally. What was at issue in the matter of contraception was not the unity of procreation and relation as such, but the Moral Theological tradition known as 'strict act-analysis', which tends, in the eyes of its critics, to atomize certain human activities in ways that defy their inner structure.

Here, too, in the Catholics' argument against IVF, we have an instance of 'strict act-analysis'. They argue that the offensiveness of IVF and AIH resides in the "irreducibly separate acts of choice . . . the independent acts of different people', by which IVF procedure is carried through. To which we may reply that there are *distinct* acts of choice, which involve persons other than the couple, in any form of aided conception, including those forms of which the document approves. Whether they are *independent* acts of choice is precisely the question which requires moral insight. If they are indeed independent (and not subordinate to the couple's quest for fruitfulness in their sexual embrace) then they are certainly offensive. But that point cannot be settled simply by asserting that they are distinct. The question remains: is there a moral unity which holds together what happens at the hospital with what happens at home in bed? Can these procedures be understood appropriately as the couple's search for help within their sexual union (the total life-union of their bodies, that is, not a single sexual act)? And I have to confess that I do not see why not. News reports tell us that some IVF practitioners advise their Roman Catholic patients to have sexual intercourse following embryo-replacement, in order to respect the teaching of their church. It would seem to me that such advice might well be given to all patients, in order to help them form a correct view of what is, or should be, meant by the technique: not the making of a baby apart from the sexual embrace, but the aiding of the sexual embrace to achieve its proper goal of fruitfulness. Something of this kind, perhaps, is intended by another document submitted to the Warnock Commission, that from the Nationwide Festival of Light, which adds to its general approval of IVF and AIH when practised simply to aid childless marriages the caution: 'It should be stressed that we would envisage married couples continuing to enjoy normal sexual relations throughout their married life, despite the need for "assisted conception" techniques.' It should be stressed indeed, and not simply as a romantic afterthought, as though to suggest that the relationship may continue undisturbed while procreative enterprise proceeds in different ways, but as a fundamental point of reference which alone can make the procedure morally intelligible.

It may, of course, be wondered whether such subtleties are beyond the understanding of most couples who participate in the IVF programme, and whether such a practice can only have the effect of enforcing the widespread view of procreation as a project of the will. It may even be thought that the cultural influence of the practice is likely to be so bad that IVF should be discouraged for that reason alone. To such a suggestion perhaps we are in no position to put up a strong resistance. After all, the experience with contraception makes it highly plausible. It is possible that a wise society would understand IVF as a temptation; it is possible that a strong-willed society would resolve to put such a temptation aside. But this takes us beyond the scope of our fairy tale, in which no cultural consequences need be feared. These cultural questions are different from the question whether there is something intrinsically disordered about IVF. And to that question we have not found reason (speaking simply, of course, of IVF as practised by fairy-godmothers in fairy tales) to return a negative answer.

What, then, was achieved by discussing a fairy tale? It enabled us to concentrate our attention on an ideal, hypothetical simple-case IVF pregnancy, and so evaluate the procedure in the abstract. That is an important step in the moral discussion, but not one at which we can stop. Many current discussions seem content to stop there; but if we are to evaluate IVF as it really is, and not as it might be in a world of magic wands, we must take account of certain contextual features which are inseparable from it in reality. I shall speak of two such features in particular, which I think to be of central importance.

In the first place there is the inextricable involvement of clinical *in vitro* fertilization with nonclinical research on early human embryos. I say 'inextricable' although I am aware that some practitioners in this field insist on keeping these two questions distinct (as, of course, in conceptual abstraction they are). And I do not undervalue the restraint which some practitioners exercise in their research activities precisely in order to commend their work on its merits as clinical practice. Nevertheless, the distinction between this clinical practice and the research which supports it cannot be maintained with much plausibility for very long. We may accept two simple statements of fact from Dr. R. G. Edwards: 'Oocytes and embryos were grown during . . . early investigations without intention of replacing them in the uterus'; and: 'This preliminary period is by no means completed, even in hospitals and clinics where many pregnancies have already been established by IVF. Improved methods are needed to assess the normality of growth of the embryos, and to sustain or monitor their development without impairing the development of those which are to be replaced in the mother'.[3] In other words: IVF did depend on non-clinical embryo-research in order to become established; and it still does depend on non-clinical embryo-research in order to perfect its techniques. IVF is not the gift of a fairy-godmother; it is the gift of researchers. The suggestion that we can thank these researchers for their gift, make use of what they have achieved, and simultaneously declare all their research, past and future, to be illegitimate, is strikingly lacking both in consistency and realism. Our view of IVF, then, is necessarily determined by our view of non-clinical research on early embryos.

The second feature is the risk to the child who will be born; and in raising this issue it is necessary to specify rather carefully what kind of risk we are talking about and what its moral significance is. There may, in the first place, be risks of genetic or other defects which already arise in the course of natural procreation and which are replicated in artificial procreation. We may expect children born of IVF to show the same proportion of defects as children born in the course of nature; and such an event need not trouble us. There may, in the second place, be an *enhanced* risk of such defects, which is *indirectly* attributable to the IVF procedure. We may fear that more children may be born with inherited defects because the natural process of selection through foetal wastage is inhibited by the measures taken to ensure replacement. This will certainly trouble us, if it should turn out to be the case; but to what extent it will appear to be a decisive consideration will depend, no doubt, on the extent of the increment by which the natural risk is enhanced. It will be a matter of prudential judgement to decide whether this increment is compensated for by the great good of circumventing childlessness. I am speaking now about neither of these kinds of risk, but about risk *directly* attributable to the IVF procedure itself. Will there arise defects which are due, not to natural risk, not to the enhancement of natural risk indirectly, but directly to the procedure itself?

I do not claim to know, or even to suspect, the answer to that question. As I understand the situation, nobody knows the answer to it with certainty, even now. B. A. Liebermann and P. Dyer write of the 'as yet undetermined incidence of chromosomal and other diagnosable defects peculiar to *in vitro* fertilization'.[4] Experience with embryos frozen for a long period before replacement is still very limited. But even if somebody does now know the answer, or suspects that he knows it, and even if that answer is as favourable to IVF as could be hoped, it is still the case that nobody knew the answer when the procedure was inaugurated. And it is *the willingness to take these risks,* rather than the favourableness or unfavourableness of the outcome, which in my view gives the most decisive characterization to the whole enterprise.

The risk is usually justified by an argument that runs something like this: since there are risks associated with natural conception (which in some cases can be very high), why should we be more reluctant to incur risks from artificial conception than we are to incur those? Thus H. W. Jones maintains: 'This argument [i.e. the argument against risk-taking] could equally well be applied to a couple, the female of which is above the age of 35, where the expectation of an abnormality is measurable.'[5] And Gerald Elfstrom: 'Natural conception entails its attendant risks for the unborn without offering any clearcut benefit to it.'[6] We must not confuse this reply with another, which sounds very similar and, as I have said, raises no problems. It does not mean that artificial conception merely reproduces risks already attendant on natural conception. It means that we must be prepared to take new risks, uniquely related to artificial conception, because we have hitherto been prepared to take risks related to natural conception. The logic of the argument, it seems to me, is that we must lose all sense of difference between nature and artifice, between the constraints which are given to us as natural conditions for our lives, and the liabilities of projects which we have freely undertaken and might as freely not have undertaken. Thus Elfstrom revealingly concludes his argument: 'Both kinds of event [i.e. defective births arising from natural and artificial causes] result from human actions, and therefore both kinds of risk to the unborn may be avoided by human restraint.' That is the conclusion to which a technological society must certainly come. Even natural procreation is something which we may equally well undertake or not undertake, and it is subject to exactly the same cost-benefit calculus which we apply to all our projects. Thus having children 'naturally' is just another instrumental means chosen to realize a project which could, if it proved more efficient, equally well be realized by technical means. The whole of life, as I argued in the first lecture, comes to be interpreted in the light of technique.

We are faced with a choice, as Paul Ramsey rightly said in his reply to Elfstrom, in which 'no one can long halt between two opinions: one favouring artificiality as more human, delivering us from the "necessities" of nature, the other favouring the spontaneities of natural procreation'.[7] Like the people of Israel we must choose between Baal and Yahweh: but is it between the Baal of nature and the Yahweh of artifice (as an older generation of Old Testament critic liked to suggest) or between the Baal who may be manipulated by magic and the Yahweh who is sovereign Lord of man and creation? That, perhaps, is the fundamental form of our question. For the appearance of neutrality is only an appearance. Once we begin to justify the risks of artifice by analogy with the uncertainties of nature, we have put ourselves in a masterful position *vis-à-vis* the natural processes. The first step for any man to take in the understanding of divine providence, is to comprehend that God has evils at his disposal which he does not put at ours. Though he works good through war, death, disease, famine, and cruelty, it is not given to us to deploy these mysterious alchemies in hope that we may bring forth good from them. There is the world of difference between accepting the risk of a disabled child (where that risk is imposed upon us by nature) and ourselves imposing that risk in pursuit of our own purposes.

As we began with a fairy story, so let us end with a futuristic fable, set in the Europe of the twenty-first century, a Europe revolutionized by the diligent activities of the European Court of Human Rights. There were two persons disabled from birth, Jack and Jill, one born in the course of nature, the other as a result of *in vitro* fertilization. And it happened that when they reached years of discretion, the charitable society which was responsible for their support took the usual steps on their behalf. That is to say, it initiated wrongful-life suits against their parents, which was the customary means by which the society funded its charitable work out of the pockets of the parents' insurance companies. Jack accordingly filed his suit, charging his parents with negligence in omitting the usual precaution of amniocentesis and abortion, which would have spared him the curse of life and consciousness. Jill, however, proved unwilling to go along with what was asked of her. She said she loved her parents and did not want to sue them; and although it was explained many times that this was purely a legal and administrative matter which implied no breach of personal relationships, she stuck to her guns. Finally, when her charitable guardians pleaded with her that the care of such as she could never be funded if such sentimental feelings were always to be indulged, she proposed a compromise. She would do the unheard of thing, and sue the doctors responsible for her fertilization, alleging that her defects were due to IVF. And so it happened, to the consternation of the medical world and the pleasurable excitement of the legal one.

Of Jack you would hear no more, if it had not happened that his case was heard by a quixotic and idiosyncratic judge, one of those conservative old men of extensive antiquarian culture and a dislike of modern ways who do occasionally crop up in the legal profession though not as often as rumour would have it. And he dismissed what should have been a straightforward wrongful-life suit, invoking arguments that had been popular back in the twentieth century when such practices were strange and unfamiliar. He ruled that no one can sue for injury who is dependent upon the alleged injury for his standing to sue. Life is the presupposition of our ability to do anything else; therefore 'wrongful life' is a contradiction in terms, because a wrong can only be done to someone who already has life. One can sue one's mother he declared, for injuries sustained in the womb: one can sue her for smoking or drinking or taking drugs or driving without a seatbelt. But one cannot sue her either for conceiving one in the first place or for failing to terminate one's existence after one is conceived. And here he quoted some words from the ancient Book of Isaiah: 'Will the babe say to his father, "What are you begetting?" or to his mother, "What are you bringing to birth?"' (45:10). The parents of a child, the learned judge continued, were not responsible at law for the conferring of life upon the child in the same way that they might be responsible for other actions they performed. The law traditionally took the view that strictly speaking the ultimate author of a human life was not a parent, but a person or force that could not be made a defendant in court. It was altogether a paradoxical decision, and it would have remained a curiosity of the legal histories, struck down at the first opportunity by the appropriate review tribunal, had not a startling event occurred to perpetuate it.

The event was as follows: Jill's case came forward, and was heard by a judge of entirely modern sympathies, a lady of great subtlety and some wit, who immediately perceived the usefulness of the judgement in *Jack v. N and M* and used it as a precedent to dismiss Jill's case against her doctors. It had been elegantly demonstrated, she said, that one could not sue for wrongful life because life was the presupposition of the standing to sue. The learned judge had said, moreover, that the author of life cannot be made a defendant in any court. But in this case the medical team quite clearly occupied the position traditionally assigned to the author of life, by virtue of their having conferred existence upon the plaintiff *in vitro.* The argument, therefore, which protects the parent from prosecution for wrongful life, protects IVF doctors *a fortiori.* No one can sue the author of her existence; and if the parents, as relative authors, were thus protected, how much more the ultimate authors by whose acts existence is immediately conferred? And with exquisite appropriateness the judge concluded her judgment by capping the older judge's quotation with the words that come immediately before it: "Will the pot contend with the potter, or the earthenware with the hand that shaped it? Will the clay ask the potter what he is making? or his handiwork say to him 'You have no skill?'"

Can we resist this reasoning? Can we deny that risks taken in relation to a child's conception are risks for which the child can never properly hold anyone responsible? Can we deny, therefore, that the IVF practitioner, who takes these risks, not as a parent does, in renunciation to divine providence, but in calculation relating to his technical project, places himself in a quite unparalleled position *vis-à-vis* another human being? Is there another instance in our moral experience where someone may, in pursuit of a scheme of world-betterment, impose injuries upon another human being for which he cannot subsequently be held responsible? These paradoxes arise only because the beginning of a human being has come to be at the same time also a making; and that transformation has occurred, not, in my opinion, as a result of the separation of acts, but as a result of the taking of risks which place those who take them above the interrogation of those who suffer from them. I confess that I do not know how to think of an IVF child except (in some unclear but inescapable sense) as the *creature* of the doctors who assisted at her conception — which means, also, of the society to which the doctor belongs and for whom he acts.

If anyone finds this conception grotesque and self-evidently wrong, I congratulate him on his good habits of thought — but with a warning. Good habits of thought teach us to find the notion of one human being as the creature of another odd and repulsive; but habit alone will not protect a culture against the 'paradigm shift' in its perceptions which will occur when too much in what it observes and does is more obviously thought of in a new way. If our habits of thought continue to instruct us that the IVF child is radically equal to the doctors who produced her, then that is good — for the time being. But if we do not live and act in accordance with such conceptions, and if society welcomes more and more institutions and practices which implicitly deny them, then they will soon appear to be merely sentimental, the tatters and shreds which remind us of how we used once to clothe the world with intelligibility.

For myself, I do not *believe* that the doctor has become the child's creator. I do not believe it, though, as I have admitted, I do not know how to reconcile my unbelief with the obvious significance of *in vitro* fertilization. I can only confess, as a matter of Christian faith, that I believe in another and unique Creator who will not relinquish to others his place as the maker and preserver of mankind. To those who wish to make this confession with me let me put this closing question: should we not expect that a humanity which is so made will vindicate its maker, and his creatures, against every false claim to lordship?

Notes

1. J. F. Leeton and A. O. Trounson, in Edwards and Purdy, op. cit. pp. 325ff.
2. *In Vitro Fertilization: Morality and Public Policy* (Catholic Information Services, 1983).
3. R. G. Edwards and J. Purdy, eds., *Human Conception in Vitro* (Academic Press, 1982), p. 372.
4. Edwards and Purdy, p. 335.
5. Edwards and Purdy, p. 354.
6. *Hastings Center Report* 9, no. 2, p. 4.
7. Ibid., p. 21.

66 Ethical Implications of In Vitro Fertilization

Janet Dickey McDowell

. . . What should be the Christian response to IVF and associated techniques?

Some Christians believe that the response ought to be uniformly negative. The earliest and strongest objections to even limited employment of IVF came from within Christian traditions committed to the indivisibility of sexual union and reproduction. Those who oppose artificial forms of birth control (notably the Roman Catholic Church in its official statements) most often do so on the grounds that these forms deliberately sever a natural — that is biological — link between intercourse and procreation, a connection which ought not to be broken simply because to do so is unnatural. Their objection to IVF rests on the same premises. They contend that because IVF removes conception from its natural context, intercourse, it is impermissible. If sex without the potential for conception is wrong, then so, they say, is conception without sex.

These opponents to artificial birth control and IVF may be faulted at several points. Initially, one must question whether artificiality per se is reason enough to oppose a procedure like IVF. Kidney dialysis, respirators, even blood transfusions are also unnatural medical interventions, yet they are not opposed with the vigor of the Vatican's response to IVF. One may choose to distinguish between artificial birth control and a technique such as dialysis by pointing out that dialysis *supports* or *mimics* natural physiological function, whereas artificial birth control *thwarts* natural function. However, such a distinction would work against those who oppose IVF on grounds of its artificiality, for in fact it is far more analogous to dialysis, in that it also attempts to replace (by admittedly complex technological means) a deficient physiological function. Thus the Roman Catholic response to IVF appears inconsistent with its acceptance of other medical technologies.

A second difficulty with this most conservative rejection of IVF is that it presumes an absolute indivisibility of reproductive potential and the sexual expression of love in every single act of intercourse. The majority of Protestants (and a great many Roman Catholics who stand in tension with their tradition's stand on artificial birth control), while perceiving an important connection between reproduction and sexual love, do not assert that the reproductive purpose of sexuality needs to be served at all times. Instead, the unitive purpose of sexuality — its capacity to express love — is claimed as fundamental. Procreation will often be an outgrowth of a mature sexual relationship, but the temporary postponement of reproduction, or even a decision not to conceive children at all, is acceptable within this less naturalistic perspective.

This understanding of the values associated with intercourse would hold that love (as expressed in sexual activity) is preconditional to reproduction, and in that sense the two purposes remain linked. But because this view is less act-orientated, more concerned with the total relationship than with every instance of intercourse, there would be no reason to object to IVF. The fact that conception does not take place as the *direct* result of love made concrete through intercourse is less significant; provided that both love and the desire to procreate are elements of the couple's total relationship, IVF would not be problematic.

Other critics raise quite a different objection. They fear that IVF will encourage (by providing a means) an obsessive concern with having one's own child, a child genetically related to its parents. It is thought that those who choose to accept the discomfort, expense and inconvenience of IVF, rather than opting for adoption, may perceive parenthood too biologically. These critics are concerned that IVF candidates will fail to keep in mind that Christian parenthood is above all a moral commitment to nurture a child, not the contribution of ova or sperm.

It would seem, however, that this danger is not substantially greater for couples using IVF than for other couples. All parents are potentially prey to this sort of idolatry; a veiled worship of self and the continuation of self in future generations. Christian churches rightly ought to discourage all of its manifestations, whether in candidates for IVF or prospective parents who anticipate ordinary conception.

At the same time, it is important to remember that genetic inheritance is not incidental. A sense of lineage — connectedness to parents and grandparents and great-grandparents — while far from vital to successful family relationships, ought not to be discounted entirely. If only for very practical reasons, such as medical records, children often need to identify their genetic parents. Many contemporary adoptees testify to the psychological value of learning about those to whom one is bound by genetic ties. Additionally, a child resulting from the unique combination of the parents' reproductive cells — in a very real sense, their selves — may be a significant sign of their life together.

Kept in proper perspective, genetic parenthood is valuable. It would be unreasonable to deny couples unable to conceive without IVF the chance to experience such parenthood merely because the potential for misunderstanding exists. It is highly unlikely that Christians will ever totally disregard genetic parenthood. (Random child-swapping at birth or mandatory communal child care from very early ages would seem to be ways a community could curb a fixation on genetic parenthood. These have not, to my knowledge, been endorsed by any major Christian group.) Unless and until such a state of affairs comes about, it would be cruel to denounce as selfish or idolatrous those who desire to establish a genetically based family, even when a procedure like IVF is required.

Other objections to IVF have focused more narrowly on the technique itself. Some fear that fertilized ova created by the procedure may be destroyed or used for experimentation, rather than transferred to the uterus of the woman from whom they were obtained. Recovering and fertilizing several ova during IVF is very common; hormonal stimulation of the ovaries is a standard element of the procedure and frequently results in the production of more than one mature ovum.

Objections to possible destruction of or experimentation with fertilized ova stem from a contention that human life is worthy of moral respect (and even legal protection) from its origins in the fertilized ovum. To use fertilized ova for experimental purposes or to discard them would be, according to these critics, tantamount to abortion or human experimentation without consent.

This potentially serious reservation about IVF, however, is overcome by the particular procedure in use at the Eastern Virginia Medical School in Norfolk (the most "prolific" clinic in the U.S.). Where more than one ovum is recovered by the laparoscopy, all are exposed to sperm. Any which manifest successful cell division (and thus are "alive") are inserted into the woman's uterus and thus given an opportunity for implantation. None is used for experimental purposes or destroyed.

However, if a clinic chose to deviate from this procedure and retain some fertilized ova, the objections would be properly focused on the morality of destroying or experimenting with fertilized human ova, not on IVF itself. Setting aside the question of whether discarding a fertilized ovum *would* constitute abortion (and further, whether such abortion ought to be prohibited or discouraged), it is clear that this objection does not necessarily apply to present procedures, especially those used in U.S. clinics. Respect for human life at its very earliest stages is not inherently incompatible with in vitro fertilization and thus need not be the basis for opposing the technique.

It seems, then, that IVF is not inherently immoral. When employed to facilitate conception by loving couples, it is no more problematic than an artificial fallopian tube would be. The abuse of fertilized ova is not necessarily an element of the procedure, and those who would object on grounds of unnaturalness must be prepared to reject other medical interventions that bypass pathological conditions. Conceptions via IVF ought not simply to be tolerated; they should be celebrated, for they enable otherwise infertile couples to join in passing along the gift of life.

Nevertheless, future procedures relying in part on the IVF technique may pose moral dilemmas. Two in particular, embryo transfer (the insertion of a fertilized ovum into the uterus of a woman who did not provide the ovum) and ova and embryo banking (stockpiling frozen ova and fertilized ova), are being quietly attempted in Australia and perhaps elsewhere. Whereas IVF as currently practiced aids in the establishment of genetically connected families, these new applications run significant risks of confusing lineage, distorting traditional family structures, and/or depersonalizing human reproduction.

Defenders of ova and embryo banking argue that it need not be used in tandem with embryo transfer to a nondonor woman. They contend that frozen ova, fertilized or not, would merely be stored until such time as the donor chose to use them. Theoretically this would reduce the need for multiple surgeries to recover ova when implantation does not take place and the procedure must be repeated. This use of ova/embryo banks raises no objections not already discussed herein with regard to the basic IVF technique.

However, embryo transfer in combination with ova banking or embryo banking could be used in a variety of circumstances. For example, in the case of a woman with healthy ovaries but uterine disease (or the absence of a uterus) such that she could not carry a child, embryo transfer would make it possible for her to have her ovum removed, fertilized, then transferred to the uterus of another woman. This "genuine surrogate" would experience pregnancy and birth, and after birth the child would be surrendered to its genetic parents.

For another example, a woman with a healthy uterus who did not wish to have her own ovum fertilized (perhaps for eugenic reasons) could elect to have an ovum provided by an anonymous donor fertilized with her partner's sperm and then transferred to her uterus. Or she could choose to have an already fertilized ovum inserted. Using a donated unfertilized ovum would be strongly analogous to artificial insemination by an anonymous donor; employing the services of an embryo bank has been likened to very early adoption.

What objections might be raised to the genuine

surrogate application of IVF and embryo transfer? Primarily, one must be concerned with the attitude such a practice would engender toward the surrogate. Would she view herself merely as an incubator-for-hire, or be viewed in that light by those who employ her? Probably — perhaps even certainly. It would, in fact, be almost imperative for the surrogate to see herself in this way in order to maintain an emotional distance during pregnancy and thus be able to surrender the child at birth. She would have to guard zealously against viewing herself as a "mother," as more than a temporary "repository" for someone else's child. Do Christians wish to encourage women to perceive procreative capacities as mere services available for hire?

Further, an impersonal, businesslike attitude toward the surrogate on the part of the genetic parents seems crucial to a successful surrogate arrangement, unless the couple genuinely welcomes ongoing third-party involvement in their family life. The couple would seem to have only two choices: viewing the surrogate simply as a means to their reproductive end, or creating a new form of extended family. While the latter choice is not unthinkable (and perhaps not undesirable), the former is more likely. One must ask whether Christians wish to be the sort of people who treat one another in this way; the answer seems clearly negative. The kind of interactions among the primary parties necessary to make the genuine surrogate situation work are not those fostered by Christian values. It would be difficult (though not impossible) to structure a surrogate situation in such a way that people are fully respected as persons.

Ova banking is, as was suggested earlier, analogous to artificial insemination by donor (AID). Therefore qualms about AID — such as concern about psychological damage to the noncontributing partner, pseudo-adultery, confusion of the child's genetic inheritance, and devaluation of the anonymous donor — apply also to ova banking. Large numbers of people, many of them Christian, believe that the potential pitfalls of AID can be avoided through sensitive counseling and maximum participation by the male partner during the insemination process. The fact that embryo transfer would enable a woman to experience pregnancy and the birth of the child (conceived with an ovum not her own) would ensure in this case an even greater sense of full contribution to procreation by the partner whose genes are absent. Those who permit AID should welcome ova banking; those who find AID troublesome will view ova banking in a similar light.

In contrast to ova banking, embryo banking has some genuinely novel features — features which could well rule out its use. Fundamentally, objections to embryo banking stem from its deliberate creation of nascent life not desired by either genetic parent. While unintended conceptions do occur with some frequency as a result of intercourse, such conceptions are accidental — perhaps even tragic — and not normative. And many couples who conceive unintentionally do, upon reflection, welcome the child. But the anonymous contributors to a bank will never have such a change of heart. Presumably they will not even know whether their genetic offspring exist.

The analogy to adoption employed to defend the practice of anonymous embryo banking (and subsequent transfer) breaks down when one considers that it induces genetically broken families. The child will never have a chance to know biological kin. Adoption, in contrast, *copes with* broken biological relations; it does not create them. Such deliberate scrambling of lineage seems to serve only the purpose of allowing a couple to experience pregnancy and birth — a purpose that does not seem sufficiently important to warrant the possible confusion.

In summary, I have argued that IVF per se is not morally troublesome. It seems, in fact, to be a positive good in overcoming medical conditions that preclude procreation by some couples. However, other procedures relying on the IVF technique are less acceptable. Ova banking ought to be employed only with the same caution as AID. Genuine surrogate situations seem acceptable only under very rare circumstances that preserve respect for the surrogate. And the transfer of embryos provided by anonymous donors ought virtually to be prohibited altogether.

67 The Ethical Challenge of the New Reproductive Technology

Sidney Callahan

How should we ethically evaluate the new reproductive technologies developed to treat the increasing problem of human fertility? Our national debate over this troubling issue is just beginning. At this point, there are lacunae in law and regulatory procedures, while medical technological innovation and practice proceed without ethical consensus. This situation is due in part to the speed of recent developments, but we also find ourselves ethically perplexed because we, as a society, did not arrive at a consensus on the ethics of reproduction and responsible parenthood *before* the newest technologies appeared on the scene.

One obvious sign of the society's unresolved conflicts over the morality of reproduction can be found in the bitter debates over abortion and, to a lesser extent, contraception and contraceptive education in the schools. With no societal consensus on the ethical use of medical technology to plan, limit, or interrupt pregnancies, we are unprepared to evaluate the newest alternative reproductive technologies which *promote* conception and pregnancies. At the same time as we have seen rapid advances in regulating fertility, we have experienced an evolution in attitudes toward women, children, sexuality, and the family. These intersecting social developments have produced the pressing need to develop a new ethic of parenthood and responsible reproduction.[1] My focus here, however, is on the most recent challenge. How should we ethically assess the innovative array of techniques developed to overcome fertility — egg and sperm donations, surrogate mothers, in vitro fertilization, and embryo transplants?

Two Inadequate Approaches to Alternative Reproductive Technology

Two inadequate approaches to the ethical assessment of the new alternative reproductive technologies are mirror images of each other in the narrowness of their focus and the limitations of their analysis. On the one hand, a conservative approach adopts as a moral standard the biological integrity of the marital sexual act. The married couple's marital sexual and reproductive acts must not be tampered with for any reason, and sexual intercourse and procreation must remain united in each marital act so that "lovemaking and babymaking" are never separated. In this "act analysis," no technological intervention in the sexual act is countenanced or approved for any reason. Older arguments employed against artificial contraception are reiterated and applied to condemn any procedure separating functions which naturally occur together, and thus all reproduction by in vitro fertilization, artificial insemination, or third party surrogacy is deemed immoral. The only ethical stance toward new reproductive technologies would be to absolutely cease and desist; such procedures should come to a full stop.

At the other end of the ideological spectrum, another form of act analysis narrows its own focus to a person's desire for a child and the individual acts the person might perform in carrying out private arrangements for reproduction. As long as due process and informed consent by competent adults is guarded by proper contracts, any adult should be able to engage in any alternative reproductive procedure that technology can provide or that persons will sell or procure. This permissive

From Sidney Callahan, "The Ethical Challenge of the New Reproductive Technology," in John F. Monagle and David C. Thomasma, *Medical Ethics: A Guide for Health Professionals* (Rockville, Maryland: Aspen Publishers, Inc.) 1988, pp. 26-37. Used by permission.

stance is held to be justified on the basis of individual liberty, autonomy, reproductive privacy, and reproductive right. The burden of proof supposedly lies with those who would limit alternative reproductive technology, and in the name of liberty and individual autonomy, potential regulators are enjoined to show that concrete harmful consequences will result from a particular practice (if it is to be rejected). Of course, when there are as yet no existing consequences, it is impossible to *prove* harm will result. Indeed, even when there have been relevant cases (e.g., the AID children conceived by artificial insemination by donor), no long-term in-depth studies have been done. Therefore, the ethical response to alternative reproductive technologies is to proceed full steam ahead (with consideration given to due process and informed consent).

The premature ethical foreclosure implied in either of the above approaches to reproductive technologies is not adequate. An ethic based solely on the natural biological integrity of marital acts will not serve, because the mastery of nature through technological problem-solving is also completely natural to us — indeed, it is the glory of *homo sapiens*. Yet, because we are rational, we can also see that a fully permissive attitude toward reproductive technology presents serious problems as well. We are reminded that in the past, innovative uses of technology have resulted in ecological and ethical disasters. Abuses have been either fully intended, as with the Nazis, or inadvertent and accidental, as in countless innovative interventions, such as the use of diethylstilbestrol (DES) or thalidomide, which had bad side effects far outweighing the supposed advantages. There is a grain of truth in the warning that "control of nature" often ends up producing increased control (or oppression) of some people by other more powerful people. Technology itself has to be ethically assessed and rationally controlled. Faced with new reproductive technologies, we should not let the technological imperative (what can be done should be done), fueled in this case by people's desires, decide the question whether a course of action is right or good.

The Basis for Developing an Ethical Position

In the case of reproductive technology, ethical positions should emerge from a consideration of what will further the good of the potential child and the family, as well as provide appropriate social conditions for childrearing and strengthening our commitment to moral principles concerning individual responsibility in reproduction. We should move beyond a narrow focus on either biology or people's desires for children. In this serious matter, which involves children's lives and the social structure of our society, it is more prudent to consider first the values and goods safeguarded and protected at present by the operating norms of reproduction and childrearing before countenancing radical alterations. In matters of such serious collective import, the burden of proof should rightly be upon those who wish to experiment with the lives of others. (An ethical problem also arises in an overpopulated, impoverished world. However, since the main issue here concerns the use of reproductive technology, I think the correct statement of the ethical question is whether, or how far, present norms should be altered.)

One troubling tactic used by those urging the permissive acceptance of all new reproductive technologies is to base their arguments upon analogies from adoption or other childrearing arrangements that arise from divorce, death, desertion, or parental inadequacy. Much is made of the cases in which persons cope with single parenthood or successfully adapt to less-than-ideal situations. But the adequacy of "after the fact" crisis management does not justify planning beforehand to voluntarily replicate similar childrearing situations. Emergency solutions make poor operating norms. Even a child conceived through rape or incest might adapt and be glad to have been born, but surely it would be wrong to plan such conceptions beforehand on the grounds that the future child would rather exist than not or that the sexual abuser had no other means to reproduce. Similarly, and more to the point, heretofore we have not ethically or legally countenanced the practice of deliberately conceiving a child in order to give it to others for adoption, with or without payment. We have forbidden the selling of babies or, for that matter, the purchasing of bribes, sexual intercourse, or bodily organs. Certain cultural goods, safeguards, and values have been preserved by these existing norms. How can ethical guidelines for employing alternative reproductive methods strengthen rather than threaten our basic cultural values?

A Proposed Ethical Standard

It is ethically appropriate to use an alternative reproductive technology if, and only if, it makes it possible for a normal, socially well-adjusted heterosexual married couple to have a child that they could not otherwise have owing to infertility. Infertility does not seem strictly classifiable as a disease, but for a married couple it is clearly an unfortunate dysfunction or handicap, one which medicine may sometimes remedy. It seems wonderful, almost miraculous, that medical technology can often overcome a couple's infertility to restore normal function with techniques such as artificial insemination by husband (AIH), in vitro fertilization (IVF), or tubal ovum transfer methods. But holding to a proposed ethical standard of medical remediation and restoration of a married couple's average expectable fertility implies that medical professionals should not aim to alter or contravene what would otherwise exist as the normal conditions for procreation and childrearing.

A remedial standard based upon operating cultural norms requires that the genetic parents, the gestational parents, and the rearing parents be identical and that the parents be presently alive and well, in an appropriate time in their lifecycle, and possess average or adequate psychological and social resources for childrearing. Helping the severely retarded, the mentally ill, the genetically diseased, the destitute, the aged, or a widow with a dead spouse's sperm to have children they otherwise could not would be ethically unacceptable by this standard. It would also be unacceptable to alter average expectable conditions by efforts to produce multiple births or to select routinely for sex (the latter practice producing a whole host of other ethical problems which cannot be dealt with here). The power to intervene in such a crucial matter as the procreation of a new life makes the medical professionals or medical institutions involved into ethically responsible trustees of a potential child's future. As trustees, medical professionals would seem to have an ethical duty not to take risks on behalf of unconsenting others.

Medical professionals should be guided by a form of communal judgment influenced by cultural values and norms. What would most responsible would-be parents deem ethically appropriate reproductive behavior in a particular case? Physicians or other health care personnel can hardly, in good conscience, agree to and make possible irresponsible or ethically inappropriate reproductive acts affecting innocent new lives. Socially informed ethical judgments on behalf of the society are unavoidable. The fact that medical professionals and medical resources must be employed for remedial infertility treatments, which will produce direct social consequences, justifies using standards of judgment that take into account the general social good. Ethical standards which protect and strengthen positive outcomes for children, childrearing conditions, and cultural norms of responsible parenthood should be used to judge the appropriateness of a particular request for treatment of infertility.

The claim that an individual's right to reproduce would be violated if fertility treatments are not made available to any individual who requests them seems wrongheaded. A negative right not to be interfered with (e.g., the right to marry, which itself is not absolute) does not entail a positive right (e.g., that society is obligated to provide spouses). Moreover, as a society, we have already decided that when adequate childrearing conditions and the well-being of children are in the balance, social and professional intervention is justified. Adoption procedures, custodial decisions, and the child abuse laws involve rights and duties of professionals to make judgments on the fitness of parents. And as child abuse and resulting deaths regularly attest, it is far better to err on the side of safety than take risks. Should not medical professionals be similarly responsible in carrying out the interventions which will in essence give to a couple a baby to rear? If a couple seems within the normal range of average expectable parents, then remedial techniques that maintain the indenticalness of genetic, gestational, and rearing parentage, techniques such as AIH or IVF or tubal ovum transfer, would be ethically acceptable.

Employing third party donors or surrogate mothers is not, in my opinion, ever an ethically acceptable use of reproductive technologies. Procedures using donors or surrogates separate and variously recombine the source of sperm, eggs, embryos, gestational womb, and rearing parents. Such a separation — whether through artificial insemination by donor (AID), embryo transplants, or surrogate mothers — poses too many ethical and social risks to the dignity and well-being of the future child, the donor, individual spouses, the family as a whole, and our cultural ethos. To argue the case against third party donors, even for acceptable couples, we need to consider what values, goods, and safeguards have been inherent in the cultural norm: two heterosexual parents who are the genetic, gestational, and rearing parents of their child.

Many proponents of third party donors in alternative reproduction — for single men and women, homosexual couples, or infertile couples — ignore what happens *after* a baby is conceived, produced, or procured. Focusing on an individual or individual couples, the psychological and social dimensions of childrearing are separated from conception, gestation, and birth. Little account is taken of the fact that individuals live out their lifespan intergenerationally and in complex ecological and social systems.[2] No account is taken of the newest developments in family therapy and family system analysis. The assumption seems to be that why and how one gets a baby makes no difference in what happens afterwards. This may be true of hens or cows, but it is hardly true of complex, thinking, emoting, imaginative human beings functioning within social systems.

Another equally invalid line of argument cites the current trends toward the breakdown of the traditional family unit and jumps to the conclusion that since the nuclear family seems to be disintegrating anyway, and the society survives, why try to preserve the norms heretofore valued? Ominous cultural effects on children and women that correlate with the breakdown of the family are dismissed as having no application to individual cases.[3] But a growing body of psychological literature points to a less sanguine judgment. Having *two* rearing parents provides important advantages, and fathers play more of a role in the moral, social, and sexual-identity development of the child than has been recognized.[4]

Legitimizing and morally sanctioning third party or collaborative reproduction or assisting single or homosexual conceptions can contribute directly to the specific negative childrearing conditions in the culture which *do* harm individuals and the larger community. The culture's operating norms concerning the family provide irreplaceable goods and safeguards — particularly for women and their children — which we come to truly value as we see them attenuated. Arguments for limiting reproductive interventions to remediation with no third party interventions can best be made by considering what is at stake if we alter our norms. We put at risk the good of the family, the parents, the child, and the donor(s), as well as our sexual morality, with its focus on sexual responsibility.

The Family

The advantages and safeguards of having two heterosexual parents who are the genetic, gestational, and rearing parents are manifold and basic; this type of family was not accidentally selected for in biological and cultural evolution. Mammalian "in vivo" reproduction and primate parent-child bonding provide adaptive means for the protection, defense, and complex socialization of offspring. They far outperform reproduction by laying eggs that are then left floating in the sea or buried in the sand to take their chances with passing predators.[5] With the advent of long-living rational animals such as human beings, the basic primate models are broadened and deepened, with results in family units that include fathers and encompass additional kinship bonds.[6] Two heterosexual parents supported by kin and clan can engage in even more arduous parenting, including nurturing the young over an extended period. The nuclear family is founded on biology and may have originally evolved through natural selection, but it is as a cultural phenomenon, with its psychological and social effectiveness in generating responsibility, socialization, and deep altruistic bonds, that the family has achieved stability and universality.

Why has the nuclear family worked for so long

and held first place in the cultural competition?[7] The Western cultural ideal, gradually becoming less patriarchic as it comes to recognize the equality of women and children, has ensured far more than law, order, and social continuity. As the heterosexual members of a couple freely choose each other, they make a loving commitment to share the vicissitudes of life. Bonded in love and legal contract, they mutually exchange exclusive rights, giving each other emotional and economic priority. Love and sexuality often result in procreation, and the children then have a claim to equal parental care from both their father and mother. In addition, the extended families of both parents are important as supplemental supports for the couple, especially in cases of death or disaster.

No act analysis of one procreative period of time in a marriage can do justice to the fact that the reproductive couple exists as a unit within a family extended in time and kinship. Grandparents, grandchildren, aunts, cousins, and other relatives are important in family life for both pragmatic and psychological reasons. Individual identity is rooted in biologically based kinship and in small cooperating social units. The family is one remaining institution where status is given by birth, not earned or achieved. The irreversible bonds of kinship over time and through space produce rootedness and a sense of identity. Psychologically and socially the family provides emotional connections, social purpose, and meaning to life. Those individuals who do not marry and found families or who achieve membership in larger communities are still strongly connected to others through their families.[8] Each human being exists within a social envelope and must do so to flourish; the family is one of the most important elements in a human life. But as a cultural invention, why must a family be based upon biological kinship? Cannot any persons who declare themselves a family be a family?

While the internalized psychological image of a family and the intention to belong to a family are part of the foundations of a family, there is no denying the bond created by genetic kinship. One definition of the family is that a family consists of people who share genes. Sociobiologists have not exaggerated the importance of gene-sharing in human bonding.[9] In fact, the unwillingness of infertile couples to adopt and their struggles to have their own baby is testimony to the existence of what appears to be a strong innate urge to reproduce oneself. Culturally this is understood as the fusion of two genetic heritages, with the child situated within two lineages. Members of both lineages may be supportive, or one set of kin may by choice or chance be more important than the other, but having both sets provides important social resources. The child is heir to more than money or property when situated in a rooted kinship community.

The search by adopted children for their biological parents and possible siblings reveals the psychological need of humans to be situated and to know their origins.[10] When there is one or more third party donors — of sperm, eggs, or embryo — the child is cut off from either half or all of its genetic heritage. If deception is practiced concerning the child's origins, then both the child and the extended family will be wronged. Since family secrets are rarely kept completely, the delayed revelations produce disillusionment and distrust among those deceived. When a child and relatives are not lied to, the identity of the donor (or donors) becomes an issue for all concerned.

Parents and Spouses

Psychology has come to see genetic factors as more and more important in parent-child interactions and childrearing outcomes.[11] When rearing parents and genetic parents differ and the donor is unknown, there is a provocative void. If the donor is known and part of the rearing parents' family or social circle, there are other psychological problems and potential conflicts over who is the real parent and who has the primary rights and responsibilities. When the third party donor is also the surrogate mother, combining genetic and gestational parenthood, the social and legal problems can be profound. The much discussed Whitehead-Stern court struggle indicates the divisive chaos, struggle, and suffering that is possible in surrogate arrangements.

In the average expectable situation, two parents with equal genetic investment in the child are unified by their mutual relationship to the child. They are irreversibly connected and made kin to each other through the biological child they have procreated. Their love, commitment, and sexual bond has been made manifest in a new life. Their genetic link with the child, shared with their own family, produces a sense of family likeness and personal identification, leading to empathy and affective attunement. The child's genetic link to each spouse and his or her kin strengthens the marital bond. But the fact that the child is also a new and unique creation and a random fusion of the couple's genetic heritage gives enough distance to allow the child also to be seen as a separate other, with what has been called its "alien dignity as a human being" intact.[12] (Cloning oneself would be wrong for its egotistic intent and for the dehumanizing effects of trying to deny the uniqueness of identity.) The marital developments that occur during pregnancy also unite the couple and prepare them for the parental enterprise.[13] Since we are embodied creatures, the psychological bonds of caring and empathy are built upon the firm foundation of biological ties and bodily self-identity.

When technological intervention without donors, such as AIH or IVP or tubal ovum transfer, is used to correct infertility, the time, money, stress, and cooperative effort required to serve to test the unity of the couple and focus them upon their marital relationship and their mutual contribution to childbearing. The psychological bonding between them can transcend the stress caused by the less-than-ideal technological interventions in their sexual lives. The result of their joint effort will, as in natural pregnancy, be a baby they are equally invested in and equally related to. (In adoption, both parents also have an equal relationship to the child they are jointly rescuing.) Given the equal investment in their child, both parents are equally responsible for childrearing and support.

With third party genetic or gestational donors, however, the marital and biological unity is broken asunder. One parent will be related biologically to the child and the other parent will not. True, the nonrelated parent may give consent, but the consent, even if truly informed and uncoerced, can hardly equalize the imbalance. While there is certainly no real question of adultery in such a situation, nevertheless, the intruding third party donor, as in adultery, will inevitably have a psychological effect on the couple's life. Even if there is no jealousy or envy, the reproductive inadequacy of one partner has been made definite and reliance has been placed on an outsider's potency, genetic heritage, and superior reproductive capacity.[14]

Asymmetry in biological parental relationships within a family or household has always been problematic, from Cinderella to today's stepparents and reconstituted families. The most frequently cited cause of divorce in second marriages is the difficulty of dealing with another person's children.[15] Empathy, identification, a sense of kinship, and assurance of parental authority arise from family likeness and biological ties. In disturbed families under stress, one finds more incest, child abuse, and scapegoating when biological kinship is absent.[16] Biological ties become psychologically potent, because human beings fantasize in their intersubjective emotional interactions with one another and with their children. Parents' fantasies about a child's past and future do make a difference, as all students of child development or family dynamics will attest. Identical twins may even be treated very differently because parents project different fantasies upon them.[17] Third party donors and surrogates cannot be counted on to disappear from family consciousness even if legal contracts could control other ramifications or forbid actual interventions.

The Child

The most serious ethical problems in using third party donors in alternative reproduction concern the well-being of the potential child. A child conceived by new forms of collaborative reproduction is being made party to a social experiment without its consent. While no child is conceived by its own consent, a child not artificially produced is at least born in the same way as its parents and other persons normally have been. A child who has a donor or donors among its parents will be cut off from at least part of its genetic heritage and its kin in new ways. Even if there is no danger of transmitting unknown genetic disease or causing physiological harm to the child, the psychological relationship of the child to its parents is endangered, whether or not there is deception or secrecy about its origins.

It should be clear that adoption (which rescues a child already in existence) is very different ethically from planning to involve third party donors in procuring a child. An adopted child, while perhaps harboring resentment against its birth parent, must look at its rescuing adopters differently than a child would look at parents who have had it made to order. Treating the child like a commodity — something to be created for the pleasure of the parents — infringes the child's dignity. When one is begotten (not made), then one shares equally with one's parents in the ongoing transmission of the gift of life from generation to generation. The child procreated in the expectable way is a subsidiary gift arising from the prior marital relationship, not a product or project of the parental will.

Alternative reproductive techniques made available to single men and women or to homosexual couples will further endanger the child's status. Why should a child, at its creation, be treated as a property, a product, or a means to satisfy the wishes of adults? Even in natural reproduction, we now consider it ethically suspect to attempt to have a child not for its own sake, but because an adult wants to satisfy some personal need or desire.

Unfortunately, we are still saddled with residual ideologies that view children as a kind of personal property. Only gradually have we welcomed children as gifts — new lives given in trusteeship — and treated them as equal to adult persons in human dignity despite their dependency and their powerlessness.[18] Having a child for some extrinsic reason is now as generally unacceptable as marrying for money or some motive besides love and a desire for mutual happiness. Unfortunately, in the past some persons have wanted children to secure an inheritance, to prove sexual prowess, to procure a scapegoat, to gain revenge, to increase marital power, to secure social prestige, or to have someone of their own to love. The motives for conception influence the future relationship of the child to the parents. A couple absolutely and obsessively driven to have a child (as some couples become when faced with infertility) may not be prepared to rear the actual child once it is born. Being wanted and being well reared are not identical. Parental overinvestment in "gourmet children" can be psychologically difficult for a child.[19] Every child must achieve independence and a separate identity. Adolescent problems of anorexia, depression, and suicide have been seen as related to the dynamics of parent control.[20] Growing up and leaving home becomes a problem for children who have been used to fulfill parents.[21] The child who was wanted for all the wrong reasons is pressured to live up to parental dreams of the optimal baby or perfect child. Outright rejection of imperfect or nonoptimal babies contracted for by alternative reproductive technology is possible and should be a matter of grave concern.

In the course of a child's development, psychologists note that thinking and fantasizing about one's origins seems to be inevitable. A child with a "clouded genetic heritage" has a more difficult time achieving a secure personal identity.[22] Yet a secure identity, self-esteem, and a sense of autonomy and self-control are crucial in children's growth.[23] Parental control is overwhelming to children. If they know or believe their parents contracted to fabricate them rather than merely received them, they feel more reduced in power.

In alternative reproduction, the questions "Whose baby am I?" becomes inevitable.[13] "Why was my biological parent not more concerned with what would happen to the new life he or she helped to create?" The need to know about possible half-siblings and other kin may become urgent at some point in later development. From the child's point of view, the asymmetry of the relationship with the rearing parents is also a factor. Even if the Freudian psychoanalytic account of Oedipal family relationships is not correct in all its details, there still exist extremely complex fantasies and psychological currents that arise in the family triangle of mother, father, and child. Having two parents with whom one can safely identify, love, and leave behind is a great advantage. One's sexual origins and one's kin are important psychological realities to a child.

Donors and the Cultural Ethos

Procuring donors of sperm, eggs, embryos, or wombs is an essential component of collaborative reproduction. Yet encouraging persons to give, or worse to sell, their genetic or gestational capacity attacks a basic foundation of morality — that is, the taking of responsibility for the consequences of one's actions. Adult persons are held morally responsible for their words and deeds. In serious matters, such as sex and reproduction, which have irreversible lifetime consequences, we rightly hold persons to high standards of moral and legal responsibility. To counter the tendency or temptation toward sexual irresponsibility or parental neglect, Western culture has insisted that men and women be held accountable for their contribution to the creation of new life.

A donor, whether male or female, who takes part in collaborative reproduction does not assume personal responsibility for his or her momentous personal action engendering new life. In fact, the donor contracts (possibly with payment) to abdicate present and future personal responsibility. The donor is specifically enjoined not to carry through on what he or she initiates, but instead to hand over to physicians or others, often unknown others, the result of his or her reproductive capacity. The generative power to create a new life is by design ejected from consideration. This genetic generative capacity is not like a kidney (or any other organ), but is part of the basic identity that is received from one's own parents. When a person treats this capacity as trivial or sells the use of it, he or she breaks an implicit compact. Parental responsibility is an essential form of the natural responsibility human beings have to help each other, and it gives rise to moral claims not governed by specific contracts or commitments.[25]

Persons who abdicate parental responsibility also deprive their own parents of grandparenthood and any other of their descendants of knowledge of their kin. Future children from the donor, or other children of a surrogate mother, will never know their half brother or sister. To so disregard the reality of the biological integrity of our identity and allow donors to engage in contractual reproduction is to have a mistaken view of how human beings actually function — or should function.

If we succeed in isolating sexual and reproductive acts from long-term personal responsibility, this moral abdication will increase existing problems within the culture. Do we want to encourage women to be able to emotionally distance themselves from the child in their womb enough to give it up? Do we wish to sanction male detachment from their biological offspring? Already epidemics of divorce, illegitimate conceptions, and parental irresponsibility and failures are straining the family bonds and the firm commitment that are necessary for successful childrearing and the full development of individuals. If we legitimize the isolation of genetic, gestational, and social parentage and regularly allow reproduction to be governed by contract and purchase, our culture will become even more fragmented, rootless, and alienated.

One of the foundations of a responsible ethic concerning sexuality is to see sexual acts as personal acts involving the whole person. Lust is wrong because it disregards the whole person and his or her human dignity. Another person is reduced to a means of selfish pleasure, and if money is involved, exploitation of the needy can occur. So, too, it seems wrong to isolate and use a person's reproductive capacity apart from his or her personal life. When it is a woman donating her egg and gestational capacity, there is a grave danger of exploitation, as feminists have warned.[26] The physiological risks attending the drastic intervention in a woman's reproductive system needed for surrogacy or embryo transplants are considerable. But perhaps more important is that pregnancy is not simply a neutral organic experience, but a time of bonding of the mother to her child.

If a great deal of money is offered for surrogacy, needy women will be tempted to sell their bodies and suffer the emotional consequences — and the experience of prostitution leads one to expect that many of these women will then hand over the money to males. Feminists rightly protest that allowing women to be surrogates will in fact turn women into baby machines bought and regulated by those rich enough to pay.[27] From another perspective, a surrogate mother could also be seen as deliberately producing and selling her baby. What will these practices do to other children of the surrogate or, for that matter, other children in the society? Can children comprehend, without anxiety, the fact that mothers make babies and give them away for money? The great primordial reality of interdependency and mutual bonding represented by mother and child is attacked. Contracts and regulations can hardly stem the psychological and social harm alternative reproductive technologies make possible.

Conclusion

Our society faces a challenge to its traditional ethics of reproduction and family norms. The cultural norms, based upon biological predispositions, is for the genetic, gestational, and rearing parents to be identical and for the nuclear family to exist within an extended family kinship system. The family should be seen as an intergenerational institution having an ecological relationship with the larger society.

As the range of ethics has broadened to include a concern for the dignity, worth, and rights of women and children, so has our understanding of morally responsible parenthood been refined and developed. The parental enterprise is rightly seen as basically an altruistic one — children should not be viewed as a form of personal property or as a means to satisfy adult desires or fulfill adult needs. When making reproductive decisions, the good of the potential child, along with the general cultural conditions which further childrearing and family support systems, should take precedence over other considerations, such as biologically integral acts or individual desires.

I have argued for an ethical position that limits alternative reproductive techniques to remedying infertility in expectable parental conditions that preserve the cultural norm, which includes the identity of genetic, gestational, and rearing parents. Collaborative reproduction will not serve the good of the potential child or the family, nor will it meet the need of the culture for morally responsible reproductive behavior.

It seems a sign of cultural progress that children are highly valued and infertility is acknowledged as a misfortune. It is also wonderful that medical reproductive technology can remedy the handicap of infertility. But as medical professionals and people in general confront these innovative interventions, the ethical, psychological, and cultural dimensions of technological procedures cannot be discounted. For the good of the child, the donors, the family, and our society, certain ethical limits must be set. Not everything that can be done to satisfy individual reproductive desires should be done. As Ghandi said, "Means are ends in the making."[28] Collaborative reproduction using third parties comes at too high a price.

Notes

1. See Sidney Callahan, "An Ethical Analysis of Responsible Parenthood," in *Genetic Counseling: Facts, Values, and Norms.* Birth Defects: Original Article Series, vol. 15, no. 22 (New York: Alan R. Liss, 1979).

2. Barbara M. Newman and Philip R. Newman, *Development Through Life: A Psychosocial Approach* (Homewood, Ill.: The Dorsey Press, 1979); Lynn Hoffman, *Foundations of Family Therapy: A Conceptual Framework for Systems Change* (New York: Basic Books, 1981).

3. Daniel P. Moynihan, *Family and Nation* (New York: Harcourt Brace Jovanovich, 1986); Lenore J. Weitzman, *The Divorce Revolution* (New York: The Free Press, 1986).

4. The role of the father has been seen as critically important in both the female and male child's intellectual development, moral development, sex role identity, and future parenting; for a summary of relevant research, see Ross D. Parke, *Father* (Cambridge, Mass.: Harvard University Press, 1981) and Shirley M. H. Hanson and Frederick W. Bonett, *Dimensions of Fatherhood* (Beverly Hills, Calif.: Sage Publications, 1985).

5. See Jeanne Altman, "Sociobiological Perspectives on Parenthood," *Parenthood: A Psychodynamic Perspective* (New York: Guilford Press, 1984).

6. Kathleen Gough, "The Origin of the Family," *Journal of Marriage and the Family* (November 1971): 760-68. Peter J. Wilson, *Man the Promising Primate: The Conditions of Human Evolution* (New Haven, Conn.: Yale University Press, 1980).

7. George Peter Murdock, "The Universality of the Nuclear Family," in *A Modern Introduction to the Family,* ed. Norman W. Bell and Ezra F. Vogel (New York: The Free Press, 1968); Mary Jo Bane, *Here to Stay: American Families in the Twentieth Century* (New York: Basic Books, 1976).

8. Stephen P. Bank and Michael D. Kahn, *The Sibling Bond* (New York: Basic Books, 1982); Gunhild O. Hagestad, "The Aging Society as a Context for Family Life," *Daedalus: The Aging Society* (Winter 1986): 119-39.

9. E. O. Wilson, *Sociobiology* (Cambridge, Mass.: Harvard University Press, 1975).

10. Carol Nadelson, "The Absent Parent, Emotional Sequelae," in *Infertility: Medical, Emotional and Social Considerations,* ed. Miriam D. Mazor and Harriet F. Simons (New York: Human Sciences Press, 1984); Arthur D. Sorsky, Annette Baron, and Reuben Pannor,

"Identity Conflicts in Adoptees," in *New Directions in Childhood Psychopathology,* vol. 1 (New York: International Universities Press, 1982).

11. Twin studies and the recognition of inherited temperamental traits have followed studies showing a genetic component to alcoholism, manic-depression, schizophrenia, antisocial behavior, and I.Q. For a popular discussion of the findings in regard to schizophrenia and criminal behavior, see Sarnoff Mednick, "Crime in the Family Tree," *Psychology Today,* 19 (March 1985): 58-61. For a more general discussion by an anthropologist, see Melvin Konner, *The Tangled Wing: Biological Constraints on the Human Spirit* (New York: Holt, Rinehart & Winston, 1982).

12. Helmut Thielicke, *The Ethics of Sex* (New York: Harper & Row, 1964), pp. 32ff.

13. Aidan Macfarlane, *The Psychology of Childbirth* (Cambridge, Mass.: Harvard University Press, 1977); M. Greenberg, *The Birth of a Father* (New York: Continuum, 1985).

14. The difficulties of undergoing AID are described in Sharon Gibbons Collotta, "The Role of the Nurse in AID," in *Infertility;* see also R. Snowden, G. D. Mitchel, and E. M. Snowden, "Stigma and Stress in AID," in *Artificial Reproduction: A Social Investigation,* (London: George Allen & Unwin. 1983).

15. Brenda Maddox, *The Half Parent: Living with Other People's Children* (New York: M. Evans and Company, 1975); Renato Espinoza and Yvonne Newman, *Stepparenting: With Annotated Bibliography* (Rockville Md.: National Institute of Mental Health, Center for Studies of Child and Family Mental Health, 1979).

16. See "Explaining the Differences between Biological Father and Stepfather Incest," and "Social Factors in the Occurrence of Incestuous Abuse," in Diana E. H. Russell, *The Secret Trauma: Incest in the Lives of Girls and Women* (New York: Basic Books, 1986).

17. Daniel N. Stern, *The Interpersonal World of the Infant: A View from Psychoanalysis and Developmental Psychology* (New York: Basic Books, 1985).

18. There is the beginning of a philosophical reassessment of the status of children in Jeffrey Blustein, *Parents & Children: The Ethics of the Family* (Oxford: Oxford University Press, 1982), and in Onoroa O'Neill and William Ruddick, eds., *Having Children: Philosophical and Legal Reflections on Parenthood* (New York: Oxford University Press, 1979).

19. See "The Child as Surrogate Self" and "The Child as Status Symbol," in David Elkind, *The Hurried Child* (Reading, Mass.: Addison-Wesley, 1981).

20. Salvador Minuchin, Bernice L. Rosman, and Walter Baker, *Psychosomatic Families: Anorexia Nervosa in Context* (Cambridge, Mass.: Harvard University Press, 1978).

21. Jay Haley, *Leaving Home: The Therapy of Disturbed Young People* (New York: McGraw-Hill, 1980).

22. Betty J. Lifton, *Lost and Found: The Adoption Experience* (New York: Dial Press, 1979).

23. See "The Sense of Self," in Eleanor E. Maccoby, *Social Development: Psychological Growth and the Parent-Child Relationship* (New York: Harcourt Brace Jovanovich, 1980).

24. Lori Andrews, "Yours, Mine and Theirs," *Psychology Today* 18 (December 1984): 20-29.

25. Hans Jonas, *The Imperative of Responsibility: In Search of an Ethics for the Technological Age* (Chicago: University of Chicago Press, 1984).

26. Barbara Rothman, *The Tentative Pregnancy* (New York: Viking Press, 1986); H. Holmes, B. Hoskins, and M. Gross, *The Custom Made Child* (Clifton, N.J.: Humana Press, 1981).

27. Angela R. Holder, "Surrogate Motherhood: Babies for Fun and Profit," *Law, Medicine, and Health Care* 11 (June 1984): 115-17.

28. Mahatma Gandhi, *The Essential Gandhi* (New York: Random House, 1962).

68 The Gestated and Sold

William F. May

Many medical ordeals have resulted from advances in medical technology that have occurred without corresponding advances in our abilities to deal with the long-term results of applying that technology. In such "hard cases," the principal actors pay a huge price in suffering — Dax Coward, Karen Quinlan's parents, the principals in the Elizabeth Bouvia case and in the Baby Doe, Baby Fae, and Baby M cases, and the like. We call these *hard* cases, but we get inured to that term. "Hard" means that no matter which way people turn, they suffer. However they decide, they face numbness and tragedy. Moreover, the often intrusive attention which the media,[1] educators, and professional conferences impose compounds the tragedy. People who never expected or wanted celebrity suddenly find themselves isolated, spotlighted, and publicly tried in the media. They suffer all the indignities of a simultaneous public trial, carnival, and soap opera. Yet such cases raise important issues in public policy that require us to review and clarify our understanding of civilized life and, in this present case, to illuminate the generative and providential tasks of parenting upon which that life depends.

Dr. William Stern paid $20,000, half to a fertility center and the other half to Mary Beth Whitehead, who agreed to be artificially inseminated with sperm from Dr. Stern and to carry to term a baby, which Mrs. Whitehead would then turn over to Dr. Stern and his wife, Dr. Elizabeth Stern, to rear as their own. Mrs. Whitehead changed her mind and wanted the baby back. But, as a lawyer friend of mine put it, "A deal's a deal." The judge in the trial court in New Jersey awarded custody of the now famous Baby M to the baby's biological father.[2] Judge Harvey R. Sorkow denied visiting rights to Mary Beth Whitehead, and, "immediately after reading his decision to the press, . . . called the Sterns into his chambers so that Mrs. Stern could legally adopt the child."[3]

Let me concede two propositions at the outset on the issues raised by the Baby M case:

1. The problem of infertility ought to command our sympathy. A couple desiring to have a child touches us more than does a couple that thinks only about its stocks or the new house or car it wants to buy. We can be grateful that *in vitro* fertilization and other techniques help some infertile couples to have children. We can be glad that adoption agencies permit still others to take on the responsibilities of parenting.
2. The marketplace is a valuable mechanism for distributing money, merchandise, and services. It lets us exchange work for money and buy a huge variety of goods and services that gratify wants and needs. A society without a free marketplace rests upon command and obedience alone. It lacks dexterity; it is all thumbs. The marketplace is a splendid specialized mechanism in its place and sphere.

But, at the same time, the market's place and sphere is, and should be, limited. We do not believe that the market should sell everything. We live in different spheres, and different principles of distribution apply in different spheres. We do not believe, for example, that we should sell judges' decrees. We forbid the bribery of judges and juries because payoffs corrupt the very meaning of justice, which should be impartial, blind, unmoved by the sweet talk of money. We also do not believe that money should buy exemptions from the burden of military service in war. In the Civil War, some rich men bought commissions, and others hired poor men to fight for them. We blocked that sort of activity in World Wars I and II, but we slipped sideways into the practice in the

From William F. May, *The Patient's Ordeal* (Bloomington, Indiana: Indiana University Press, 1994), pp. 71-79. Used by permission.

Vietnam War, as disproportionate numbers of the poor, who could not pay for college exemptions, ended up with their names engraved on Bangladesh marble near the Lincoln Memorial. We believe further that we should not sell grades in school or prizes at sporting events and in artistic or intellectual competitions. We would corrupt the very substance and meaning of these awards and honors if we sold them on the open market to the highest bidder.

We also shy at letting a person sell body parts — an eye or a kidney — to another. A society demeans itself and its members and fails to solve its problems fittingly if it exploits the penurious to sell a part of themselves. The rich ought not solve their health care needs through the desperation of the poor.

Similarly we have thought it a bad idea to give the family *full* property rights in the body of a deceased member. The family has *quasi* property rights, in the sense that the responsibility to provide fitting and appropriate burial falls upon the family; but it cannot *sell* body parts or auction off a particularly notorious dead relative to the highest bidder — to a carnival, or to some other institution with a profit opportunity in mind.

The same restriction on the marketplace applies to adopting babies. We do not think it right to sell or auction infants or children as products or commodities.

In sum, what we have marked out here are a few of the territorial limits of the marketplace and the contractual exchanges upon which it depends. Michael Walzer calls these boundary points "blocked exchanges," beyond which one corrupts, demeans, and distorts the goods exchanged or acquired.[4]

In my judgment, the Baby M case ought to belong to one of these blocked exchanges. We misinterpret and corrupt the meaning of bearing and parenting a child when we pull them into the arena of a commercial transaction. And make no mistake about it: surrogate brokering grew into a substantial business. The *New York Times* on June 26, 1988 quoted Noel P. Keane, the lawyer who matched and arranged the contract between William Stern and Mary Beth Whitehead, as saying of his Infertility Center of New York, "We've had 238 children born, with 40 more on the way." His statement implies that his infertility center made some $2.5 million at $10,000 per transaction.

Judge Sorkow did seek to distinguish the Stern/Whitehead controversy from straightforward commerce in babies. First, he sought to decide in the "best interests of the child," the usual standard in an adoption or divorce proceeding. This attempt suggests that he would not simply decide the case on the evidence of money changing hands. He would assess the Sterns and the Whiteheads, to see which parents would provide the better home for the child. The judge conceded that Dr. Elizabeth Stern, a pediatrician, had, without benefit of outside professional judgment, diagnosed herself as suffering from multiple sclerosis, which she determined to be a risk to her bearing a child. She also had not sought out professional help to determine the implications of this condition for a pregnancy, and she had misrepresented her infertility. But Judge Sorkow found the Sterns, on the whole, to be "credible, sincere, and truthful people," whereas Mrs. Whitehead's behavior had convinced him that she had a "fundamental inability to speak the truth."[5] He concluded that the Sterns would make better parents than would the Whiteheads.

Some critics have argued that the rhetoric of the judge's appraisal (and that of court psychiatrists) reflected a marketplace bias in favor of the rich and a class bias in favor of professionals who know how to talk to other professionals, and against an agonized working-class mother who did not know how to behave plausibly toward lawyers, judges, and psychiatrists.

The New Jersey Supreme Court review of the case did not entirely agree with this criticism of the judge's decision. The court allowed custody of the child to remain with the father, since the evidence "clearly proved such custody to be in the best interests of the infant," but in other major particulars the court reversed the trial judge's decision. It found "the payment of money to a 'surrogate' mother illegal, perhaps criminal, and potentially degrading to women" and therefore voided "both the termination of the surrogate mother's parental rights and the adoption of the child by the wife/stepparent" and restored the "'surrogate' as the mother of the child. . . ."[6]

The state supreme court foresaw deeper issues in the precedent-setting features of this case. A court can easily condone a rescue operation to save one specific child. It is quite another matter to issue a decision that will enter the literature and establish precedent for future cases in a form that would let a woman sell her right to control her health care in the course of a pregnancy, that would effectively consign to another person decisions as to whether to abort or to carry to term a fetus, and that would regularize and normalize the commercial practice of surrogate motherhood. The further reason Judge Sorkow gave for this original decision carries particularly troubling consequences.

Judge Sorkow had a problem which he solved dubiously. His first reason (deciding in the child's "best interest") pulled the Baby M case toward the jurisdiction of family law governing adoption. That body of law allows a judge to decide a case on the basis of the "best interest" of the baby. But adoption law also prohibits selling babies. Judge Sorkow therefore had to pull the case out of the orbit of adoption law, since the Sterns paid $10,000 to Mrs. Whitehead and $10,000 to a lawyer-broker in the case. Sorkow's solution? He distinguished between a service and a product. William Stern was hiring Mrs. Whitehead to carry the baby, he was not buying the baby from her. The court could not charge him with buying the baby, because genetically he already owned the baby. Thus, Sorkow concluded, the transaction did not reduce the baby to a commodity. Stern bought only the services of the biological mother, not the product of those services. The product was already his.

Now, the actual terms of the contract make it clear that the judge's distinction flies in the face of the facts. The contract oriented relentlessly to the product, not the process. If the mother lost the child through a miscarriage before the fifth month of pregnancy, William Stern would pay her nothing; if she had a stillbirth, Dr. Stern would owe her only $1,000, not the $10,000. The full $10,000, in this one-sided contract and others like it, lies in escrow until the mother delivers the baby to its owner. Clearly the contract requires delivering a product. And when the mother delivers that child, the contract requires that she relinquish her rights as its genetic mother, her presumptive rights of custody over an already extant child. It is baby selling.

In addition to this *bad faith* in his reasoning, that is, the judge's pretense that the contract did not enforce a sale, his very distinction between a service performed and a product distorts the human meaning of giving birth to a child. This distinction reduces parenting to *manufacturing.* In manufacturing, we correctly distinguish between the process and the product of that process. Ordinarily, workers don't develop deep ties to the monkey wrenches or to the sump pumps they produce. It would be bad if they did. Sales would suffer: workers make products in order to sell them. Workers can take pride in their products, but they had better not agglutinate to them, or their company is in deep trouble. Indeed, they've got a problem if they don't move the product beyond the loading dock. An older language called workers "alienable" from the fruits of their labor. Producers of commodities hire marketers, experts in figuring out how to move the product into alien hands. Our alienable relations to things differ from our inalienable rights and the inalienable rights of children, by which I mean rights we cannot sell without assaulting and demeaning their and our innermost identities.

The judge clearly used the metaphor of manufacturing in settling the case. He discerned a clear-cut distinction between the service of processing a baby and the baby as a product. He assumes that the law can tidily separate the two. Dr. Stern pays for the process, not the product. Sorkow's metaphor reduces the woman's irreversible sale of her maternal rights to her child to a minor, easily negotiated detail.

The metaphor of manufacturing doesn't help in interpreting carrying and bearing a child. To detach that *process* from the child who emerges from the womb and to assume that one can sell the first without the sale affecting the second advances male obtuseness to a new height. Justice should be blind, but not stupid.

The metaphor of manufacturing overlooks altogether the reality of human bonding. We bond intensively. As indicated in the chapter on the retarded child, human beings biologically depend upon bonding between parents and the young to a degree that other animals do not. The opossum clings to the body of its mother, but the human baby cannot. It depends upon its mother to hold it. It needs the mother's active cradling, holding, cherishing, begun in the womb and carried forward into life for a time, and with an intensity unknown to any other creature. Human society depends heavily on the success of that bonding at every level from the womb through the wayward adventures of the child's education.

I would not want to claim that humans invariably bond. The substantial numbers of abortions and adoptions and the willingness of some women to put up their babies for sale prove the existence of many exceptions. These exceptions have persuaded the courts not to force a woman to carry a pregnancy to term or to keep and nurture a baby against her will. But at the same time, the propensity to bond works so powerfully that we call bonding not only usual but normal — so natural, indeed, that the state's enforcement of a commercial contract against Mrs. Whitehead's reconsidered wishes after bonding seems violent, not judicial.

These considerations lead me to oppose the type of proposal before the State Legislature of New York which would merely reform and regulate commercial contracts as they apply to surrogate motherhood, not eliminate them.[7] In particular, the legislature would require more fully developed informed consent on the part of both parties. (For example, the broker/lawyer in the Stern/Whitehead case hired psychiatrists to examine Mary Beth Whitehead. They reported to the broker/lawyer that she would probably not go through with the contract, but apparently the broker chose to withhold this information from Mrs. Whitehead and the Sterns. If the facts bear out this charge, the lawyer committed an appalling violation of his duties to clients: he withheld information crucial to them both in order to clinch the sale.) Second, the New York state law would insist on a prior court review to preclude such one-sided contracts as the Stern/Whitehead agreement.

This proposal to reform a commercial transaction does not go to the heart of the problem, however. To look at bearing a child as subject to a commercial contract distorts the event altogether. We should not regularize into law the separation of the genetic, gestational, and rearing tasks of parents except in rescue — that is, in adoption.

The alternative extreme of legislatively prohibiting surrogate motherhood creates a further set of difficulties, however. The state would find the prohibition difficult to enforce. Further, a law that criminalized the behavior of the mother, among other parties to a contract, might place the state in the awkward position of legislatively enforcing the natural human bonding between a mother and child by sending the mother to jail. Finally, an outright legislative prohibition of surrogacy might violate the constitutional right of privacy.

The Supreme Court of New Jersey has arrived at a more sensible solution to surrogate motherhood: it would not altogether prohibit such agreements, but, as it does in adoption, it would prohibit buying and selling children. A woman might still act as a surrogate mother, but not for hire. The law and the courts would discourage its commercialization in two ways: (1) by prohibiting the payment of a finder's fee, etc., to a third party, and (2), if money has changed hands between the two parties, by refusing to consider any contract or agreement legally enforceable. The full power of the state would not bear down to force the mother to give up her child, which is tantamount to saying that the exchange would come down once again to a gift. She would give the child as a gift, as she does in adoption.

Advocates of surrogate mothering argue that this policy would effectively eliminate the practice. It would knock out the commercial opportunity for a third party, with his prepared list of breeders, complete with pictures, psychological profiles, and IQ scores for each. Right and good! This elimination of a commercially interested third party might have the advantage of keeping legislation within the right-of-privacy clause of the U.S. Constitution, as the Supreme Court interprets it, while not denying altogether that special circumstances, which we cannot wholly anticipate, might make surrogacy defensible as a gift.

A member of the U.S. Congress drew an important boundary line recently when he said, "we want jurisdiction over the moneychangers in the temple; we do not want jurisdiction over the temple itself." The first part of his statement nicely marks out the territorial limits of the marketplace; the second, the equally important territorial limits of the state. As Samuel Johnson put the latter limits:

> How small of all that human hearts endure,
> That part which laws or kings can cause or cure.[8]

The state must both protect citizens against the marketplace but also, through its own self-restraint, respect the principle of the extraterritoriality of the person.

Undoubtedly, the Baby M case and others like it require public discussion as the society decides where it must draw its lines legally and morally. Surrogate motherhood is but one of many issues which advances in reproductive technology will pose for us. Increasingly, we will be tempted to reduce parenting to manufacturing. The term itself, "genetic engineering," speeds us along that road. Both negative eugenics, the art of eliminating deleterious genes and traits, and positive eugenics, the art of enhancing positive traits and capacities, tempt with the possibility of producing "designer genes." The agenda of negative and positive eugenics received a temporary setback when the Nazis embraced their goals in the 1930s. But in the next millennium, not unsavory totalitarians, but players in the marketplace will much more likely move us further in that direction. Fortunes will be there for the making by medical entrepreneurs who can grant the wishes of customers for superior children.

Few will deny the moral legitimacy of a disciplined negative eugenics that may help genetically blighted parents bear normal babies and thereby spare both parents and their children appalling ordeals. But the agenda of positive eugenics (enhancing memory, IQ scores, aggressiveness, and the like) would increasingly convert parenting into manufacturing. Moralist Francis Kane poses the long-range question: "Can anyone guarantee producing children according to our patent designs will be an act of self-giving love rather than vain self-display?"[9]

Clearly, we will not leave ourselves moral space for dealing with Kane's question if we discuss cases like Baby M in a form that distances ourselves from the behaviors scrutinized. As we play the roles of spectator and critic, we may fail to note our own subtle involvement in the behaviors examined and thus fail to prepare for the temptations ahead.

In these comments, for example, I have criticized the Baby M contract and the original judicial decision that supported it for treating a child as a product. But the temptation to treat a child as a product does not simply beset only the childless couple such as the Sterns or the judge who sides with them. Many parents yield to the temptation to treat their children as products when they live out their lives vicariously through the performance of their children. By midlife, parents see only too clearly the limits of their own lives, and they often press their children to conform to the idealized image of what the parents believe their child ought to become. They measure the child's performance against that image and signal rejection to the child when the child fails to live up to that standard or lives up to a different standard. Parents generally slip into thinking like a manufacturer or an engineer. They become relentlessly product-oriented.

Parents may need to recognize that marriage and parenting resemble dirt-farming more than engineering. Shakespeare once put it, crudely, "Caesar ploughed her and she cropped." In the changing seasons of married and family life, one turns the soil, broadcasts a little seed, prays for a little sun and rain, and hopes for the best.

Perhaps, then, the Baby M case delivers a message to all of us beyond the harsh judgments heaped on the deafened and beleaguered Sterns, Whitehead, and Judge Sorkow.

Parenting (even the sly parenting that mates furnish one another) includes two demands always in some tension with one another. On the one hand, parents need to affirm the *being* of the child; they need to accept the other as he is. As Frost said, home is where they have to take you in. Parenting requires accepting love. On the other hand, parents must also encourage and foster the *well-being* of the other, the child. They must promote the child's excellence. If they merely accept the other as he is, they may neglect the important business of his full growth and flourishing. Parenting requires transforming love.

Clearly, perhaps especially in a meritocratic society, we have tended one-sidedly toward transforming. We have fiercely demanded performance, accomplishment, and results. At our worst, we drive our ambition through our children like a stake through the heart. We behave like the ancient Gnostics who despised the given world. We reject the child for flawed achievements. We fall into the traps set by a society that insists on accomplishment in payment for acceptance. We increasingly define and seize upon our children as products. Medical technology simply enabled and lured the Sterns and Mary Beth Whitehead into acting out the parental assumptions of a one-sided modern culture. There, out in the open, in the glare of the klieg lights, the principals found themselves faced with a public ordeal. But, in the reflected light of that public ordeal, the double ordeal in all one-sided parenting was exposed.

Parents find it difficult to maintain an equilibrium between the two kinds of love. Accepting love, without transforming love, slides into indulgence and finally neglect. Transforming love, without accepting love, badgers and finally rejects. No wonder, then, that parenting leads so often to a sense of defeat — unless, in the divine comedy of things, parents discern an equilibrium of a different order, a transcendent parenting that embraces both their children and themselves in all their imperfections. This transcendent equilibrium goes by the name of justifying and sanctifying grace. God forgives but also empowers; God affirms but also transforms. That is the good news for parents behind the judgmental news that besets the Sterns and Whitehead and haunts us all.

Notes

1. Thomas William Mayo, in "Medical Decision Making During a Surrogate Pregnancy," *Houston Law Review* (Vol. 25, Number 3, May 1988), provides a roundup of the 34 reports on the Baby M case in *The New York Times* alone.

2. See *In Re* Baby "M," 217 N. J. Super. 313, 525, A.2d 1128, 1142-43 (N.J. Super. Ct. Ch. Div. 1987) Aff'd in part and rev'd in part, No. A-39-87 (N.J. to Feb. 3, 1988).

3. George J. Annas, "Baby M: Babies (and Justice) for Sale," *Hastings Center Report,* June 1987, p. 15.

4. See Michael Walzer, *Spheres of Justice* (New York: Basic Books, 1983), pp. 97, 100-103, 282-83, for a discussion of the moral importance of blocked exchanges in curbing the tyranny of money.

5. Annas, "Baby M . . . ," p. 14.

6. Excepts from the New Jersey Supreme Court decision "in the Matter of Baby M," *The New York Times,* February 4, 1988.

7. Apparently in the nine months following the Baby M trial court decision, some 70 bills bearing on surrogacy appeared before 27 state legislatures. See Paterson, "States Assess Surrogate Motherhood," *The New York Times,* Dec. 13, 1987, and Lori B. Andrews, "The Aftermath of Baby M: Proposed State Laws on Surrogate Motherhood," *Hastings Center Report,* Oct./Nov. 1987, pp. 31 and 38, as cited by Mayo, "Medical Decision Making . . . ," p. 603.

8. Samuel Johnson wrote the lines for Goldsmith's *Travellor,* cited by W. Jackson Bate, *Samuel Johnson* (New York: Harcourt Brace Jovanovich, 1975), p. 198.

9. Francis Kane, *The Evening Sun,* Baltimore, Thursday, October 5, 1989.

Chapter Twelve

GENETIC CONTROL

The Human Genome Project was launched in 1988; the project is scheduled to last fifteen years, to cost three billion dollars, and to achieve the goal of identifying and mapping the 100,000 genes and three billion little chemical bits that make up human DNA. Some greeted the project with great expectations of genetic diagnoses and therapies to come from the new information — and others were less hospitable to the project, anxious about "designer genes" and genetic ghettoes. Some talked about the human genome as though it were the Holy Grail, as though our fate was written not in the stars but in our genes, and as though knowledge of it would give us knowledge of the blueprint of our humanity. Others talked about the project as a Faustian bargain, as though this quest for knowledge and mastery were an arrogant denial of our humanity and fated us to inhumanity.

A decade after the project was inaugurated, scientists are ahead of schedule in their concordance of A's, C's, G's, and T's (the four molecules that are present in DNA — adenine, cytosine, guanine, and thymine) in human beings. The media regularly reports stories of the discovery of genes related to a host of diseases and conditions, among them breast cancer, prostate cancer, hemochromatosis, manic depression, homosexuality, and obesity. The progress has indeed been remarkable, but the progress has included a challenge to genetic determination and a new appreciation of the complexity of genetic inheritance. The formula of one gene for one disease works sometimes, to be sure. There is, for example, evidently a location on chromosome 4 which is linked to Huntington's disease. Even in this case, however, the variation in the expression of this genetic mutation is large; researchers have even found individuals with a mutation at that location on chromosome 4 who do not apparently suffer with Huntington's disease. This kind of discovery of one gene for one disease, however, seems not to be typical. There is, it seems, a complex interplay of genes with each other and with social and environmental factors. Triumphal reports about the discovery of a genetic location for manic depression, for example, have identified several different locations on several different chromosomes, and so far none of the results have been confirmed. The scientists themselves seem to be growing more suspicious of triumphal announcements that the genetic foundation of a complex disease or trait has been discovered.

With a lowering of voices shouting that genetic knowledge would save or damn us, there may be new opportunities for dialogue at the intersections of genetics and moral theology. M. Therese Lysaught insists (in selection 72) that for Christians knowledge of norms, identity, and the meaning of the "human" derives "from sources other than genetics, sources which serve to interpret genetic information rather than vice versa." The Report of the Church of Scotland, however, (in selection 73) hopes that genetic knowledge "can teach us that we are more inter-dependent than we thought." That would seem to corroborate a theme Lysaught takes to be based on those other "sources," but if genetic information can corroborate the Christian account of human nature, can it also challenge it? Granted that genetic information must always be interpreted (and from some particular standpoint), might it also prompt a reconsideration of the ways we have interpreted the meaning and significance of human life? It does seem to be the case, at any rate, that genetic knowledge and proposals for the use of that knowledge bring us inevitably to the consideration of some old and enduring — and religious — questions. The question of destiny, for example, was important to Paul Ramsey's response to the proposal of H. J. Muller (in selection 70), and it remains important at the intersection of genetics and moral theology. For what may we hope? And on what basis may we hope it? Or consider the question of human nature, central to the essay of Karl Rahner (in selection 71).

Genetic knowledge, of course, can be put to a variety of uses. One use of genetic knowledge serves the traditional medical objective of diagnosis. The number of diseases that can be diagnosed by means of genetic testing is growing rapidly, advanced regularly by the Human Genome Project. There are sometimes problems of accuracy, to be sure — hardly a new problem to diagnosis. And it should be noted that genetic testing frequently tests not for disease but for the probability of disease. It must also be remembered that genetic disorders can express themselves with a range of severity. Even so, genetic knowledge has already significantly contributed to the diagnostic capabilities of medicine.

Sometimes a genetic diagnosis can be joined to therapeutic interventions in order to forestall or limit the effects of the disease, even if it cannot be cured. For example, PKU (or phenylketonuria), a genetically based metabolic disease, can be detected in newborns by a simple test and, if detected, can be controlled by a special diet, forestalling and limiting the serious brain damage which would otherwise surely result. Indeed, the test for PKU is not simply made available to parents in consultation with their physician; it is routinely done in the PKU screening programs mandated by law.

A second example is the discovery of a genetic test for hemochromatosis, a common blood disorder causing the body to absorb too much iron, which in turn can cause damage to vital organs. The treatment in this case is, ironically, the ancient therapy of bloodletting. A proposal to mandate a screening program for hemochromatosis, however, has had to face several questions: Will people who test positive be at risk of being denied health insurance? Could they be at risk of being at a disadvantage when they look for work? Is genetic diagnosis really better than existing blood tests for the disease? Which is cheaper?

Genetic diagnosis, especially in the context of screening programs, raises issues concerning consent and confidentiality. May a genetic screen be made, for example, a condition of employment, or a requirement for the purchase of health insurance? Are people entitled to genetic information about prospective spouses? Moreover, if — as is often the case — a genetic diagnosis is not accompanied by therapeutic options for managing or treating the disease, a diagnosis can risk increasing anxiety rather than alleviating it. Worse than that, it can risk stigmatizing people. The Report of the Church of Scotland (selection 73) considers such issues.

Genetic knowledge can also be used therapeutically. The new appreciation of the complexity of genetics that has resulted from the Human Genome Project has also meant more modest expectations of the number and effectiveness of the genetic therapies that genetic knowledge can quickly provide. Even so, there have already been some stunningly successful therapeutic interventions with somatic gene therapy, most notably genetic therapy for ADA deficiency, a disease which robs youngsters of their immune system — and other genetic therapies are being developed. Somatic cell therapy, which does not affect the gametes, can be assessed in the same way that other therapies conventionally are, by a patient (or the patient's parents or guardian) weighing the risks and possible benefits to the patient. James Peterson (in selection 75) considers various ways of "drawing the line" to distinguish appropriate uses of genetic intervention from morally inappropriate. He argues against relying on the distinctions between "somatic" and "germ-line" therapies and between "cure" and "genetic enhancement," proposing a different set of criteria for "drawing the line."

Genetic knowledge can also, however, be put in the service of eugenic ends. Advances in reproductive science and technology have provided a remarkable control not only over whether to have a child but also over the sort of child we will have. The rapidly expanding knowledge of human genetics has made contraception, abortion, and reproductive technologies serviceable to eugenic ends.

The ability to diagnose the carriers of a number of genetic diseases has made it possible to calculate some of the genetic risks a particular couple would undertake for the sake of having a child. (David Schiedermayer contemplates his genetic inheritance in selection 69.) Such information can be used by prospective parents to make an informed decision about whether to take the known genetic risks in order to have a child. Paul Ramsey (selection 70, which dates from 1970) argues that people have "a genetic responsibility" to use contraceptive measures in order to avoid the risk of giving birth to "unduly defective individuals."

Suppose, however, that a couple chooses to circumvent the known risks by using artificial insemination with sperm from a donor or in vitro fertilization with ova from a donor. If donor gametes are used, what genetic characteristics of the donor(s) should be considered relevant? Race? Health? Intelligence? Should the purpose be to prevent the genetic risk to the child or to give the parents the sort of child they want or to improve the general gene pool? If we can improve the genetic endowment of our children or of the next generation by using donor seed, would "genetic responsibility" require such an alternative model of reproduction? Many years ago the Nobel Prize-winning geneticist H. J. Muller made precisely that recommendation, suggesting freezing and banking sperm from distinguished men in order to improve the genetic characteristics of the race. That proposal concerning our "genetic responsibility" was vigorously rejected by Ramsey in the selection below. You are invited by the selections in this chapter to consider this notion of "genetic responsibility" — to compare it perhaps to "reproductive liberty"; to ask surely to whom we are responsible, and for what; and to ponder how our response to God affects our sense of to whom and for what we are responsible genetically.

It is also possible, of course, to diagnose certain genetic diseases in the fetus prenatally. With amniocentesis (at 14-18 weeks of pregnancy), chorionic villi sampling (at 10-12 weeks), and the development of tests to identify fetal cells in maternal blood (at 7-8 weeks), it is becoming possible to diagnose many genetic conditions earlier and less invasively. With in vitro fertilization it is possible to make a genetic diagnosis before implantation. The genetic information provided can be used to decide whether to abort the fetus (or to implant the embryo). Hessel Bouma III (in selection 74) reflects on the real choices faced by real people in the context of their having and caring for children.

Prenatal diagnosis raises, of course, the question of abortion, and a fuller discussion of that topic must await the next chapter, but some questions are inevitable here. Should the severity of the genetic disease be relevant to the decision about abortion? Genetic conditions vary widely in their severity. Should the certainty of the prognosis be relevant? Down syndrome can be diagnosed with certainty, but the prognosis ranges from mild to profound mental retardation. Should the disappointment of parental preferences for certain genetic characteristics, say, for a male child, be sufficient reason for an abortion?

M. Therese Lysaught suggests that our attitudes toward children are at stake in these powers, and she worries that our society will become still less willing to provide support for "genetically defective" children when they are seen as "'products' of choice and not chance." Might health insurance programs refuse to pay for the care of an infant with Down syndrome whose condition could have been predicted and whose birth could have been prevented? Might government programs divert funds from the care of the genetically retarded to the education of "normal" and "gifted" children in order to encourage "genetic responsibility"? Such proposals are not only plausible but real.

Preimplantation diagnosis makes it increasingly plausible not only to avoid the birth of a "genetically defective" child but to select the embryo for implantation on the basis of certain genetic traits, to choose a little girl embryo, for example, rather than a little boy. The knowledge provided by the Human Genome Project will make such decisions considerably more informed. Indeed, it may become possible to intervene directly in the genes of our offspring in an effort to enhance their intelligence or their size or some other characteristic. Cloning, at least, seems to be a technical possibility after the birth of Dolly. The technical barriers to designing our children may well eventually be overcome. But are there moral barriers? Are there some limits, after all, to "reproductive liberty"? Is one limit that we ought not commodify our children?

There are many questions remaining, questions introduced in one way or another in earlier chapters which you might want to revisit: Is there a professional ethic? And is it relevant to questions of genetic control? What is the meaning of "health," specifically, in this context, "genetic health"? What should our disposition be toward nature, toward the mastery of nature? What is the meaning of "playing God," and may we do it? What is the moral significance of being a parent? And does genetic technology risk altering it?

There are questions also about social justice. It is worth also asking, as Lysaught does, whether the current health care system in the United States is capable of using the new information fairly. It is worth asking whether a society with a history of racism can be justly open to a screening program for the sickle-cell trait, or whether a society with a history of sexism can make fair use of a technology for sex selection.

In all of these questions it is important for members of believing communities to form and articulate their theological perspectives, not only in order to contribute to the public discussion at the intersection of genetics and ethics but to live their lives, to exercise their powers, and support other members of the community with religious integrity.

Suggestions for Further Reading

Cole-Turner, Ronald. *The New Genesis: Theology and the Genetic Revolution* (Louisville: Westminster John Knox Press, 1993).

Fletcher, John. *Coping with Genetic Disorders* (San Francisco: Harper and Row, 1982).

Gustafson, James M. *Intersections: Science, Theology, and Ethics* (Cleveland: Pilgrim Press, 1996).

Hubbard, Ruth, and Elijah Wald. "Exploding the Gene Myth: How Genetic Information is Produced and Manipulated by Scientists, Physicians, Employers, Insurance Companies, Educators, and Law Enforcers," *Second Opinion* 19 (April 1994): 76-84.

Kilner, John F., Rebecca D. Pentz, and Frank E. Young (eds.). *Genetic Ethics: Do the Ends Justify the Genes?* (Grand Rapids: William B. Eerdmans Publishing Co., 1997).

Lebacqz, Karen (ed.). *Genetics, Ethics, and Parenthood* (New York: Pilgrim Press, 1983).

Meilaender, Gilbert C. "Begetting and Cloning," *First Things* no. 74 (June/July 1997): 41-43.

Nelson, James Robert. *On the New Frontiers of Genetics and Religion* (Grand Rapids: William B. Eerdmans Publishing Co., 1994).

Parens, Erik. "The Goodness of Fragility: On the Prospect of Genetic Technologies Aimed at the Enhancement of Human Capacities," *Kennedy Institute of Ethics Journal* 5, no. 2 (1995): 141-53.

Peters, David A. "Risk Clarification, Genetic Screening, and Health Care: A Conflict Between Libertarian and Egalitarian Values," *CTNS Bulletin* 13 (Fall, 1993): 17-24.

Peters, Ted. "Patenting Life: Yes," and Richard D. Land and C. Ben Mitchell, "Patenting Life: No," *First Things* 63 (May 1996): 18-22.

Shinn, Roger. *The New Genetics: Challenges for Science, Faith, and Politics* (Wakefield, R.I.: Moyer Bell, 1996).

Verhey, Allen. "Theology after Dolly," *Christian Century,* March 19-26, 1997, pp. 285-86.

69 Mother and Father

David L. Schiedermayer

I inherited from you
the genes which promote easy tears
and crossing one's legs at the ankles
color blindness
(X-linked recessive)
male pattern baldness
(sex-influenced autosomal dominant)
early rising, myopia, shyness, high arches
(polygenetic multifactorial tendencies).

But I know I have 3 to 8 lethal genes
which if homozygous
would be fatal.
So believe me
I am thankful
for both of you.

From *House Calls, Rounds, and Healings* by David L. Schiedermayer, M.D.

70 Moral and Religious Implications of Genetic Control

Paul Ramsey

The Genetic Apocalypse and the End of Man

In order to analyze the moral implications of genetic control for western religions, it is necessary to lift up to view certain aspects of what it means to intend the world as a Christian or as a Jew. These also are modes of being human, and of how values are "otherwise known" in this world and ethical judgments made. On the assumption that it is a Christian *subject* who has come into the possession of all this genetic knowledge and who faces our genetic dilemma, what will be the attitude he takes toward eugenic proposals? Two ingredients are of chief importance. First, we have to contrast biblical or Christian eschatology with genetic eschatology, and observe how these practical proposals may change their hue when shifted from one ultimate philosophy of history to the other. This will be the matter of the present section of this chapter. Then, secondly (in the following section), we have to explore the bearing which the Christian understanding of the union between the personally unitive purpose and the procreative purpose of human sexual relations (sex as at once an act of love and an act of procreation) may have upon the question of the means to be used in genetic control.

The writings of H. J. Muller give the most vivid

From Paul Ramsey, *Fabricated Man* (New Haven: Yale University Press, 1970), pp. 22-59.

portrayal of the genetic cul-de-sac into which the human race is heading. He describes, in fact, a genetic apocalypse. His fellow geneticists can correct, if they must, the extremism of this vision. For the purpose of making clear, however, how one intends the world as a Christian, even in the face of such an apocalyptic account of the end toward which we are proceeding, or which is coming upon us, it is better to leave the vision unaltered and assume it to be a true account of the scientific facts.

Within a period of a few million years, according to Muller, provided that during this period our medical men have been able to continue to work with the kind of perfection they desire, "the then existing germ cells of what were once human beings would be a lot of hopeless, utterly diverse genetic monstrosities." Long before that, "the job of ministering to infirmities would come to consume all the energy that society could muster," leaving no surplus for general or higher cultural purposes.[1] People's time and energy would be mainly spent in an effort "to live carefully, to spare and prop up their own feebleness, to soothe their inner disharmonies and, in general, to doctor themselves as effectively as possible." Everyone will be an invalid, and everyone's accumulated internal disability would amount to lethality if he had to live under primitive conditions.[2] If any breakdown occurs in the complex hospital system that civilization will have become, mankind will be thrown back into a wretchedness with which his primitive beginnings cannot be compared.

> Our descendants' natural biological organization would in fact have disintegrated and have been replaced by complete disorder. Their only connection with mankind would then be the historical one that we ourselves had after all been their ancestors and sponsors, and the fact that their once-human material was still used for the purpose of converting it, artificially, into some semblance of man. However, it would in the end be far easier and more sensible to manufacture a complete man *de novo,* out of appropriately chosen raw materials, than to try to refashion into human form those pitiful relics which remained. For all of them would differ inordinately from one another, and each would present a whole series of most intricate research problems, before the treatments suitable for its own unique set of vagaries could be decided upon.[3]

It is unreasonable to expect medicine to keep up with the problem (especially because medical men themselves in that near, or distant, future will be subject to the same genetic decomposition); "at long last even the most sophisticated techniques available could no longer suffice to save men from their biological corruptions"[4] (and, again, I add to Muller's assumptions, medicine in that future could not be all that sophisticated, because of the genetic deterioration of the medical men who would be alive in the generation before the genetic *eschaton*).

Stripped of rhetoric, this means that, according to the genetic apocalypse, there shall come a time when *there will be none like us to come after us.* There have been other such scientific visions of the future. Whether this results from the pollution of our atmosphere and water by industrial refuse, or of the atmosphere by strontium 90, or from a collision of planets, the burning up of the earth, or the entropy of energy until our planet enters the eternal night of a universe run down, these scientific predictions — without exception — portray a planet no longer fit for human habitation, or a race of men no longer fit to live humanly. Because these are science-based apocalypses, the gruesome details of the "last days" can be filled in, and our imagination heightened in its apprehension of the truth concerning physical nature and the prospects of human history in the one dimension that is scientifically known to us. All these visions quite realistically teach that there will come a time when there will be none like us to come after us. It is as obvious as the ages are long that it is an infirm philosophy which teaches that "man can be courageous only so long as he knows he is survived by those who are like him, that [in *this* sense] he fulfils a role in something more permanent than himself."[5] Every scientific eschatology (with the single exception of the view that human history is eternal) places in jeopardy courage and all other values that are grounded in the future of the human generations. It does not matter whether the end comes early or late. Nor do the gruesome details do more than heighten the imagination. They do not add to the ultimate meaninglessness to which all human affairs were reduced when meaning came to rest in the temporal future (unless that future is foreknown to be eternal — and, if one thinks this through, it too is a melancholy prospect). All that can be said to the credit of the genetic apocalypse, or to the credit of any science-based eschatology, is that it makes *impressive* the truth that was already contained in the thought that men live in "one world."

Anyone who intends or perceives the world as a Christian will have to reply that he knew this all along, and that he has already taken into his system the idea that one day there will be none like us to come after us. Even gruesome details about what will happen in the "last days" are not missing from the Christian Apocalypse, even though admittedly these are not extrapolations from scientific facts or laws. The Revelation of St. John is still in the Bible; and even the so-called little apocalypse (Mark 13 and parallels) had this to say: "In those days shall be affliction, such as was not from the beginning of the creation which God created unto this time, neither shall be. . . . But in those days, after that tribulation, the sun shall be darkened, and the moon shall not give her light, and the stars of heaven shall fall, and the powers that are in heaven shall be shaken" (Mark 13:19, 24-25). Again, stripped of rhetoric, there will be none like us to come after us on this planet.

This means that Christian hope into, and through, the future depends not at all on denying the number or seriousness of the accumulating lethal mutations which Muller finds to be the case (let his fellow geneticists argue with him however they will).

Where genetics teaches that we are made out of genes and unto genes return, Genesis teaches that we are made out of the dust of the ground and unto dust we and all our seed return. Never has biblical faith and hope depended on denying or refusing to face any facts — either of history, or of physical or biological nature. No natural or historical "theodicy" was ever required to establish the providence of God, for this providence was not confined to the one dimension within which modern thought finds its limits.

It is as easy (and as difficult) to believe in God after Auschwitz, as it was after Sennacherib came down like a wolf on the fold to besiege and destroy the people of God. The Jews who chanted as they went to meet their cremation, "*Ani Ma'amin* . . ." — "I believe with unswerving faith in the coming of the Messiah" — uttered words appropriate to that earlier occasion, and to all temporal occasions. It is as easy (and as difficult) to believe in God after Mendel and Muller, as it was after Darwin or the dust of Genesis. Religious people have never denied, indeed they affirm, that God means to kill us all in the end, and in the end He is going to succeed. Anyone who intends the world as a Jew or as a Christian — to the measure in which this is his mode of being in the world — goes forth to meet the collision of planets or the running down of suns, and he exists toward a future that may contain a genetic apocalypse with his eye fixed on another *eschaton: "Ani Ma'amin* . . . " He may take the words literally, or they may imaginatively express his conviction that men live in "two cities" and not in one only. In no case need he deny whatever account science may give him of this city, this history, or this world, so long as science does not presume to turn itself into a theology by blitzing him into believing that it knows the one and only apocalypse.[6]

This does not mean a policy of inaction, or mere negative acceptance, of trends in history or in biology on the part of anyone who is a Christian knowing-*subject* of all that he knows about the world. Divine determination, properly understood, imposes no iron law of necessity, no more than does genetic determination. Only the ultimate *interpretation* of all the action that is going on is different, and significantly different. We shall have to ask what practical difference this makes as one man goes about responding (in all the action that comes upon him) to the action of the laws of genetics, while another goes about responding (in all the action coming upon mankind) to the action of God; or, as one gives answers to the ultimate untrustworthiness of the force behind genetic trends, while another answers with his life and choices to a trustworthiness beyond all real or seeming untrustworthy things.[7]

The differences are two — one pervasive and the other precise. In the first instance, one must notice the tone of assertive or declaratory optimism based on the ultimate and unrelieved pessimism that pervades the thought of some proponents of eugenics. The writings of H. J. Muller cannot be accounted for simply by the science of genetics, or even by the fact that his ethics is that of a man who intends the world as a scientist and who finds the whole dignity of man to consist in thought. As such, and in themselves, these things might be productive of more serenity, or serenity in action. But it is the whole creation, as it is known in genetics to be effectively present today and into the future, that Muller is fighting. No philosophy since Bertrand Russell's youthful essay[8] has been so self-consciously built upon the firm foundations of an unyielding despair. Mankind is doomed unless positive steps are taken to regulate our genetic endowment; and so horrendous is the genetic load that it often seems that Muller means to say that mankind is doomed no matter what steps are taken. Yet his optimism concerning the solutions he proposes is no less evident throughout; and all the more so, the more it is clear that his solutions (dependent as they are upon voluntary adoption) are unequal to the task. The author's language soars, he aspires higher, he challenges his contemporaries to nobler acts of genetic self-formation and improvement, all the more because of the abyss below. The abyss sets up such powerful wind currents that mankind seems destined to be drawn into it no matter how high we fly. These are some of the consequences of the fact that when all hope is gone, Muller hopes on *in despair.* An Abraham of genetic science, if one should arise, would be one who, when all hope is gone, hopes on *in faith,* and who therefore need neither fear the problem nor trust the solution of it too much.

The more precisely identifiable difference is the greater room there will be for an "ethics of means" in the outlook of anyone who is oriented upon the Christian *eschaton* and not upon the genetic cul-de-sac alone. Anyone who intends the world as a Christian or as a Jew knows along his pulses that he is not bound *to succeed* in preventing genetic deterioration, any more than he would be bound to retard entropy, or prevent planets from colliding with this earth or the sun from cooling. He is not under the necessity of *ensuring* that those who come after us will be like us, any more than he is bound to *ensure* that there will be those like us to come after us. He knows no such *absolute* command of nature or of nature's God. This does not mean that he will do nothing. But it does mean that as he goes about the urgent business of doing his duty in regard to future generations, he will not begin with the desired *end* and deduce his obligation exclusively from this end. He will not define *right* merely in terms of conduciveness to the good end; nor will he decide what *ought to be done* simply by calculating what actions are most likely to succeed in achieving the *absolutely imperative end* of genetic control or improvement.

The Christian knows no such absolutely imperative end that would justify any means. Therefore, as he goes about the urgent business of bringing his duty to people now alive more into line with his genetic duty to future generations, he will always have in mind the premise that there may be a number of things that might succeed better but would be intrinsically wrong means for him to adopt. Therefore, he has a larger place for an ethics of means that is not wholly dependent on the ends of action. He knows that there may be a great many actions that would be wrong to put forth in this world, no matter what good consequences are expected to follow from them — especially if these consequences are thought of simply along the line of temporal history where, according to the Christian, success is not promised mankind by either Scripture or sound reason. He will approach the question of genetic control with a category of "cruel and unusual means" that he is prohibited to employ just as he knows there are "cruel and unusual punishments" that are not to be employed in the penal code. He will ask, What are right means? no less than he asks, What are the proper objectives? And he will know in advance that any person, or any society or age, expecting ultimate success where ultimate success is not to be reached, is peculiarly apt to devise extreme and morally illegitimate means for getting there. This, he will know, can easily be the case if men go about making themselves the lords and creators of the future race of men. He will say, of course, of any historical and future-facing action in which he is morally obliged to engage: "Only the end can justify the means" (as Dean Acheson once said of foreign policy). However, because he is not wholly engaged in future-facing action or oriented upon the future consequences with the entirety of his being, he will immediately add (as Acheson did): "This is not to say that the end justified any means, or that some ends can justify anything."[9] An ethics of means not derived from, or dependent upon, the objectives of action is the immediate fruit of knowing that men have another end than the receding future contains.

The ethics which, as we have seen, governs genetic proposals says as much. A fruit of intending the world as a geneticist is an ethics whose means are determined by the values of free will and thought. This puts a considerable limit upon the actions which can be proposed for the prevention of the genetic apocalypse (which, if a correct prediction, belongs only to the *contents* of the science of genetics). Still, this is not a sufficient substance for the morality of action, or at least not all the substance a Christian will find to be valid. One who intends the world as a Christian will know man's dignity consists not only in thought or in his freedom, and he will find more elements in the nature of man which are deserving of respect and should be withheld from human handling or trespass. Specifically in connection with genetic proposals, he will know that there are more ways to violate man-womanhood than to violate the *freedom* of the parties; and that something voluntarily adopted can still be wrong. He will pay attention to this as he goes about using indifferent, permitted, or not immoral means to secure the *relatively* imperative ends of genetic control or improvement. To this ethics of means we turn in the next section.

The Covenant of Marriage and Right Means

In relation to genetic proposals, the most important element of Christian morality — and the most important ingredient that the Christian acknowledges to be deserving of respect in the nature of man — which needs to be brought into view is the teaching concerning *the union between* the two goods of human sexuality.

An act of sexual intercourse is at the same time an act of love and a procreative act. This does not mean that sexual intercourse always in fact nourishes love between the parties or always engenders a child. It simply means that it *tends*, of its own nature, toward the strengthening of love (the unitive or the communicative good), and toward the engendering of children (the procreative good). This will be the nature of human sexual relations, provided there is no obstruction to the realization of these natural ends (for example, infertility preventing procreation, or an infirm, infertile, or incurving heart that prevents the strengthening of the bonds of love).

Now, there has been much debate between Protestants and Roman Catholics concerning whether the unitive or the procreative good is primary, and concerning the hierarchical order or value-rank to be assigned these goods. I have shown elsewhere[10] that, contrary to popular belief, there is in the present day little or no essential difference between Roman Catholic and Protestant teachings on this point. The crucial question that remains is whether sexual intercourse as an act of love should ever be separated from sexual intercourse as a procreative act. This question remains to be decided, even if the unitive and procreative goods are equal in primacy, and even if it be said that the unitive end is the higher one. It still must be asked, Ought men and women ever to put entirely asunder what God joined together in the covenant of the generating generations of mankind? Assign the supreme importance to sexual intercourse as an act of personal love, and there still remains the question whether, in what sense, and in what manner, intercourse as an act of love should ever be divorced from sexual intercourse as in and of itself procreative.

Now, I will state as a premise of the following discussion that an ethics (whether proposed by nominal Christians or not) that *in principle*-sunders these two goods — regarding procreation as an aspect of biological nature to be subjected merely to the requirements of *technical* control while saying that the unitive purpose is the free, human, personal end of the matter — pays disrespect to the nature of human parenthood. *Human* parenthood is not the same as that of the animals God gave Adam complete dominion over. Such a viewpoint falls out of the bounds which limit the variety of Christian positions that may be taken up by, and debated among, people who undertake to intend the world as Christians.

It is important that these outer limits be carefully defined so that we see clearly the requirements of respect for the created nature of man-womanhood, and so that we do not rule out certain actions that have traditionally been excluded. Most Protestants, and nowadays a great many Catholics, endorse contraceptive devices which separate the sex *act* as an act of love from whatever tendency there may be in the act (at the time of the act, and in the sexual powers of the parties) toward the engendering of a child. But they do *not* separate the sphere or realm of their personal love from the sphere or realm of their procreation, nor do they distinguish between *the person* with whom the bond of love is nourished and *the person* with whom procreation may be brought into exercise. One has only to distinguish what is done in particular *acts* from what is intended, and done, in a whole series of acts of conjugal intercourse in order to see clearly that contraception need not be a radical attack upon what God joined together in the creation of man-womanhood. Where planned parenthood is not planned *un*parenthood, the husband and wife clearly do not tear their own one-flesh unity completely away from all positive response and obedience to the mystery of procreation — a power by which at a later time their own union originates the one flesh of a child.

Moreover, the fact that God joined together love and progeny (or the unitive and procreative purposes of sex and marriage) is held in honor, and not torn asunder, even when a couple for grave, or for what in their case is to them sufficient, reason adopt a lifelong policy of planned *un*parenthood. This possibility can no more be excluded by Protestant ethics than it is by Roman Catholic ethics, which teaches that under certain circumstances a couple may adopt a systematic and possibly lifelong policy of restricting their use of the unitive good to only such times as, it is believed, there is no tendency in the woman's sexual nature toward conception. The "grave reasons" permitting, or obliging this, have been extended in recent years (the original "reason" being extreme danger to a woman's life in childbirth) to include grave family financial difficulties (because the end is the procreation *and education* of the child). These "grave reasons" have been extended even to the point of allowing that the economy of the environing society and world overpopulation may be taken into account, by even the healthy and the wealthy, a sufficient reason for having fewer children or for having no more at all.[11] Once mankind's genetic dilemma is called to the attention of the Church and its moral theologians, I see no intrinsic reason why these categories of analysis may not be applied to allow ample room for voluntary eugenic decisions, either to have no children or to have fewer children, for the sake of future generations.

After all, Christian teachings have always held that by procreation one must perform his duty to the future generations of men; procreation has not been a matter of the selfish gratification of would-be parents. If the fact-situation disclosed by the science of genetics can prove that a given person cannot be the progenitor of healthy individuals (or at least not unduly defective individuals) in the next generations, then such a person's "right to have children" becomes his duty not to do so, or to have fewer children than he might want (since he never had any right to have children simply for his own sake). Protestant and Roman Catholic couples in practicing eugenic control over their own reproduction may (unless the latter's church changes its teaching about contraception in the wake of the Vatican Council) continue to say to one another: you in your way, and I in God's! In the turmoil over Pope Paul VI's encyclical *Humanae Vitae,* one Catholic couple says, in effect, to another: you in your way, I in the Church's or at least the Pope's. Still, it is clear that the Roman Catholic no less than the Protestant Christian could adopt a policy of lifelong non-parenthood, or less parentage, for eugenic reasons. Such married partners would still be saying by their actions that if either has a child, or if either has more children, this will be from their own one-flesh unity and not apart from it. Their response to what God joined together, and to the claim he placed upon human life when He ordained that procreation come from sexual love, would be expressed by their resolve to hold acts of procreation (even the procreation they have not, or have no more) within the sphere of acts of conjugal love, within the covenant of marriage. . . .

We have now to resume our examination of the various methods that have been proposed for the control or improvement of man's genetic inheritance, evaluating these in the light of the requirement that there be no complete, or radical, or "in principle" separation between the personally unitive and the procreative aspects of human sexual life. By this standard there would seem to be no objection to eugenically motivated birth control, if the facts are sufficient to show that genetic defects belong among those grave reasons that may warrant the systematic, even lifelong, prevention of conception. A husband and wife who decide to practice birth control for eugenic reasons are still resolved to hold acts of procreation (even the procreation they have not, or have no more) within the sphere of conjugal love.

This understanding of the moral limits upon methods that may properly be adopted in voluntary genetic control leads, I would argue, to the permissibility of artificial conception control (no less than to the permissibility of the so-called rhythm method) and to the endorsement of voluntary sterilization for eugenic reasons. I know that many of my fellow Christians do not agree with these conclusions. Yet it seems clear that both are open for choice as means (if the ends are important enough) — provided Christian ethics is no longer restricted to the analysis of individual *acts* and is concerned instead with the coincidence of the *spheres* of personal sexual love and of procreation (the spheres to which particular actions belong). Neither the husband (or wife) who practices artificial birth control nor the husband who decided to have a vasectomy is saying by the total course of his life anything other than that *if* either marriage partner has a child, or more children, it will be within their marriage-covenant, from their own one-flesh unity and not apart from it. In principle, they hold together, they do not put completely asunder, what God joined together — the sphere of procreation, even the procreation they have not or have no more, and the sphere in which they exchange acts that nurture their unity of life with one another. They honor the union between love and creation at the heart of God's act toward the world of his creatures, and they honor the image of this union in the union of love with procreativity in their own man-womanhood. Their morality is not oriented upon only the genetic consequences which are believed to justify any voluntary means; nor is it only an ethic of inner intention which is believed to make any sort of conduct right. They *do* something, and are constantly engaged in doing it. This gives their behavior a character that is derived neither wholly from the desired results nor from subjective intention. Through a whole course of life they actually unite their loving and their procreativity (which, incidental to this, they have not). So they do not do wrong. They do no wrong that good may come of it. They do right that good may come of it. (In this moral reasoning, the present writer can see no difference between the case for contraception and the case for voluntary contraceptive sterilization, except in not unimportant differences in the findings of fact that may warrant the one form of birth control or the other — and except for the fact that as yet sterilization is ordinarily irreversible. Even in terms of the more static formulations of the past, it should certainly be said that a vasectomy may be a far less serious invasion of nature than massive assault upon the woman's generative organism by means of contraceptive pills.) . . .

The notation to be made concerning genetic surgery, or the introduction of some anti-mutagent chemical intermediary, which will eliminate a genetic defect before it can be passed on through reproduction, is simple. Should the practice of such medical genetics become feasible at some time in the future, it will raise no moral questions at all — or at least none that are not already present in the practice of medicine generally. Morally, genetic medicine enabling a man and a woman to engender a child without some defective gene they carry would seem to be as permissible as treatment to cure infertility when one of the partners bears this defect. Any significant difference arises from the vastly greater complexity of the practice of genetic surgery and the seriousness of the consequences if, because of insufficient knowledge, an error is made. The cautionary word to be applied here is simply the moral warning against culpable ignorance. The science of genetics (and medical practice based on it) would be obliged both to be fully informed of the facts and to have a reasonable and well-examined expectation of doing more good than harm by eliminating the genetic defect in question. The seriousness of this consideration arises from the serious matter with which genetic surgery will be dealing. Still, the culpability of actions performed in unjustifiable ignorance cannot be invoked as a caution without allowing, at the same time, that in the practice of genetic medicine there doubtless will be errors made in inculpable ignorance. But genetic injuries of this order would be *tragic*, like birth injuries under certain circumstances. They would not entail *wrong*-doing; nor should applications of genetic science be stopped until all such eventualities are impossible. That would be an impossible demand, which no morality imposes.

The paradox is that the most unquestionably moral means of genetic control (direct medical action for the sake of the genotype by some "surgical" or chemical anti-mutagent before the genotype is produced) is technically the most difficult and distant in the future,[12] while a number of the means presently available (phenotypic breeding in or breeding out) are of quite questionable morality, and questionable for reasons that the voluntariness of the practice would not remove. . . .

H. J. Muller, of course, respects man's quality as a thinking animal; he would not violate his freedom, and he challenges men to noble action. This ethics, we have pointed out, is not to be found among the contents of the science of genetics, but is rather the necessary presupposition of man the geneticist and the fruit of intending the world with a scientific mind. Or, perhaps, Muller's humanism is a fruit of intending the world as a man within the community of men. Christian ethics, too, is not found among the contents of any natural science, nor can it be disproven by any of the facts that such sciences know. It is a fruit of intending the world as a Christian. (There is no conflict here between religion and science, but a conflict between two philosophies.) The Christian understands the *humanum* of man to include the body of his soul no less than the soul (mind) of his body. In particular, he holds in honor the union of the realm of personal love with the realm of procreativity in man-womanhood, which is the image of God's creation in the midst of His love. Since artificial insemination by means of semen from a nonhusband donor (AID) puts completely asunder what God joined together, this proposed method of genetic control or genetic improvement must be defined as an exercise of illicit dominion over man no less than the forcing of his free will would be. Not all dominion over man's own physical nature, of course, is wrong, but *this* would be — for reasons stated above.

In outline, Muller proposes that "germinal choice" be secured by giving eugenic direction to AID (Julian Huxley called this technique "preadoption" — it has already become a minority "institution" in our society). Muller also proposes that comparable techniques be developed and employed: "foster pregnancy" (artificial inovulation) and parthenogenesis (or stimulated asexual reproduction). The enormous difficulties in the way of perfecting punctiform genetic surgery or mutational direction by chemical intermediaries impel Muller to concentrate on presently available techniques of parental selection. Similarly, the apparently small gains for the race that can be secured by negative eugenics (because the genes will continue in great numbers as recessives in heterozygotes) impel him to advocate positive or progressive eugenics.[13] In positive genetics, one does not have to identify the genetic defects, or know that they do not add vigor in hybrids. One has only to identify the desired genotype (no small problem in itself!) and breed for it.

Muller rejects the following practices: choosing a donor who is likely to engender a child resembling the "adopting" father, using medical students (notoriously not of the highest intelligence) or barhops, using AID only when the husband is infertile or the carrier of grave genetic defect, and keeping the matter secret. Instead he proposes the selection of donors of the highest proven physical, mental, emotional, and moral traits, and he suggests that publicity be given to the practice so that more and more people may follow our genetic leaders by voluntarily deciding to bestow upon their "children" the very best genetic inheritance instead of their own precious genes.

In order for this practice to be most effective, Muller proposes that a system of deep-frozen semen banks be established and that records of phenotypes be kept and evaluated. At least twenty years should be allowed to elapse before the frozen semen is used, so that a sound judgment can be made upon the donor's capacities. The men who earn enduring esteem can thus be "manifolded" and "called upon to reappear age after age until the population in general has caught up with them."[14] It is an insufficient answer to this proposal to point out that in his 1935 book, *Out of the Night,* Muller stated that no intelligent and morally sensitive woman would refuse to bear a child of Lenin, while in later versions Lenin is omitted and Einstein, Pasteur, Descartes, Leonardo, and Lincoln are nominated.[15] Muller might well reply either by defending Lenin or by saying that not enough time had elapsed for sound judgment to be made on him.

To his fellow geneticists can be left the task of stating and demonstrating scientific and other socio-psychological objections, some of which follow: (1) the genes of a supposedly superior male may contain the injurious recessives which by artificial insemination would become widespread throughout the population instead of remaining in small proportion, as they now do;[16] (2) the validity of this proposal is not demonstrated by the present-day children of geniuses; (3) "it might turn out that parents who looked forward eagerly to having a Horowitz in the family would discover later that it was not so fine as they expected because he might have a temperament incompatible with that of a normal family," and "it is bad enough if we take responsibility only for the environment of our children; if we take responsibility for their genetic make-up, too, the guilt may become unbearable";[17] (4) we know nothing about the mutation rate that would continue in the frozen germ cells; (5) the IQ's of criminals would be raised,[18] (6) we could not have a "healthy society" because not many men would be "emotionally satisfied by children not their own."[19] Without debating these issues, my verdict upon the eugenic use of semen banks has been negative, in terms of the morality of means which Christian ethics must use as its standard of judgment.[20] . . .

Ends in View

Finally, we need to bring under scrutiny the ends or objectives of genetic control, and the choice to be made between negative eugenics (by breeding-out or by back-mutation) and progressive eugenics (by breeding-in or by positive direction of mutation).

H. J. Muller had supreme confidence that those pioneering spirits who lead the way in this generation in the employment of germinal selection can be trusted to choose, from a variety of choice-worthy genotypes (described to them by the keepers of the semen banks), the types that will be good for mankind to produce in greater numbers. "Can these critics," he asks, "really believe that the persons of unusual moral courage, progressive spirit, and eagerness to serve mankind, who will pioneer in germinal choice, and likewise those who in a more enlightened age will follow in the path thus laid down, will fail to recognize the fundamental human values?"[21] Muller expresses the guiding aims of particular eugenic decisions in quite general terms: "practically all peoples," he writes, "venerate creativity, wisdom, brotherliness, lovingkindness, perceptivity, expressivity, joy of life, fortitude, vigor, longevity."[22] Or again: "What is meant by superior is whatever is conducive to greater wisdom, cooperativeness, happiness, harmony of nature, or richness of potentialities."[23] This understanding of goals of eugenic decisions may be open to the objection that, in animal husbandry, one has to have very narrowly defined criteria governing the selection to be made. It is less open to the objection stated by Theodosius Dobzhansky: "Muller's implied assumption that there is, or can be *the* ideal human genotype which it is desirable to bestow upon everybody is not only unappealing but almost certainly wrong — it is human diversity that acted as a leaven of creative effort in the past and will so act in the future."[24] There is range enough, it would seem, in Muller's description of ideal man to permit a great variety of specific genotypes. The fact is that within these very general value assumptions, Muller counts on individual couples to pick the specific genotype they want to bestow on their "preadoptive" children.[25] Couples so enlightened as to resort in this and the next generation to germinal choice will not require a corps of axiologists or sociologists to tell them what are the most crying genetic needs of the man of today."[26] Thus, Muller is confident that a host of particular choices, made by people who have concrete options, can be laid, as it were, end to end with similar choices made by people in succeeding generations. The choices of the latter people will doubtless improve as their genetic inheritance improves, thus producing a continuity of choices in the ascending direction of genetic improvement (which was formerly the work of natural selection). This hope is only exceeded by Muller's certainty that, unless man assumes the direction of his genetic goals, the descent of the species is the sole alternative expectation.

Place beside this the objection, raised by Donald M. Mackay, based on the fact that the generation that first initiates genetic control cannot determine the goals that will be set by future generations — or establish any directional continuity. No one can prevent "the 'goal-setting' from drifting and oscillating as time goes on, under the influence of external or even internal factors." Suppose genotype X is chosen in a majority of instances in the first generation. No one can know "what kind of changes these men of type X would think desirable in their successors — and so on, into the future." If we cannot answer this question and establish a continuity from the beginning, then "to initiate such a process might show the reverse of responsibility, on any explication of the term." (Moreover, unless this question is answered and unless future answers to it are assured, then the process would be quite unlike animal husbandry.) "In short, to navigate by a landmark tied to your own ship's head is ultimately impossible."[27]

Now, how does one adjudicate between these opposing views? It is obvious that these judgments fall far outside the science of genetics itself. There may even be operative here a kind of ultimate determination of one man's individual mode of being in the world toward making man the creator and determiner of his own evolution, and, on the part of the other scientist, a personal determination away from that dizzy prospect. The present writer would say that in order to refuse to concede some degree of truth to Muller's opinion, one has to be a rather thoroughgoing relativist who denies to man any fundamental competence to make moral judgments. This is why, in addition to supporting genetically motivated conception control and voluntary sterilization, I have conceded that, if AID is not to be prohibited by law, it might morally be a better wrong to use AID with the intention of bestowing a better genetic inheritance upon a child than if it is used with complete anonymity in regard to the donor's genotypic qualities and only for the sake of securing a child as much like the putative parents as possible. In any case, the voluntariness of the genetic decisions made in any one generation, and through the generations, insures the *usus*, of Muller's proposal against such *abusus* as would forbid it *from the point of view of the ends only*, and would seem to render somewhat inconsequential such oscillation in goal-setting as might take place. Such oscillation in genetic decisions would be roughly comparable to oscillations in cultural decisions (taking place under the guidance of Muller's *jus gentium*) that may occur over the sweep of centuries; and the one would be no more and no less consequential than the other, while reciprocating strength to the other.

On the other side of this question, it must be acknowledged that this way of characterizing the goals to be set for positive human betterment does, despite its generality, describe the characteristics of a good geneticist, or the virtues of a good community of scientists, or at least the special values of man in the contemporary period. This is a science-based age, and an age of rapid social change in which men dream of inhabiting other planets after despoiling this one. It is an age in which "progressives" are in the saddle and ride mankind — ahead if not forward. In such an age it is natural enough that most of man's problems are defined in terms of "social lag" of one sort or another, and in terms of the laggard type of characters our genes continue to produce. Still, in the long view, mankind might be in the greatest peril if it succeeded in finding a way to increase its own momentum by selecting on a large scale for the special values of this present culture. In the long view, the race may have need of laggard types and traditional societies, who could take up the history of humanity again after the breakdown of the more momentous civilizations. If positive genetics gained its way, even under the aegis of a quite unexceptionable *jus gentium* setting the goals, would this not unavoidably take the form of genetically instituting some parochial *jus civilis*?

Partly because of the difficulties concerning goal-setting and because the negative goals would seem to be clearer, the present writer leans in the direction of approving preventive eugenics only. I do so also because the means to the ends of preventive genetics — whether these be the voluntary control of conception, or anti-mutagent surgery or chemicals — seem, at our present state of knowledge, to have the good effect of eliminating bad effects without as much danger of also producing an overflow of incalculable, unintended bad consequences. We may say with Hampton L. Carlson, "let us recommend preventive eugenics but proceed very cautiously in progressive eugenics. A firm scientific basis for the latter does not now exist."[28]

It must be admitted that the results on the total population of negative genetics may not be very effective in bringing about large-scale prevention of the deterioration of the gene pool. Nevertheless, faced by such pessimistic predictions, "it is well to remember that every defective individual that can be avoided represents a positive gain."[29] Also, if genetics can identify the *carriers* of genetic defects and thus we no longer need restrict preventive genetics to persons who are identifiably unfit themselves — if a qualitative control of reproduction can wisely be adopted by, and at the same time in the future back-mutation can be performed helpfully upon, a larger proportion of the population — then the results of preventive eugenics need not be so limited as it has been in the past. To sterilize *forcibly* all persons suffering from serious genetic defect would have hardly any influence on the proportion of that particular recessive gene in the population. But if carriers can be identified and if each heterozygous carrier has only half as many children as he would otherwise have, we would reduce the abnormal-gene frequency by fifty percent. This alone would greatly reduce the incidence of the defect in the next generation, and prevent untold future human misery.[30]

To make preventive eugenics more effective will require the development and widespread adoption of an "ethics of genetic duty." It is shocking to learn from the heredity clinics that have been established in recent years in more than a dozen cities in the United States, how many parents will accept grave risk of having defective children rather than remain childless. "When a husband and wife each carry a recessive deleterious gene similar to the one carried by the other, the chances of their having a defective child are one in four, with two children carriers of a single gene, but themselves without defect, and [only] the fourth child being neither a carrier nor defective. Couples in such a position, knowing that they have one chance in four of having a seriously defective child, and that two out of four of their children are likely to be carriers, still frequently take a chance that things will turn out all right."[31] This can only be called genetic imprudence, with the further notation that imprudence is gravely immoral.

In making genetic decisions to be effected by morally acceptable means, the benefits expected from a given course of action must be weighed against any risk (or loss of good) incurred. This is exactly the mode of moral reasoning used in deciding whether or not to use X rays in medical diagnosis, or radiation therapy in medical treatments. Should patients with cancerous growths, for whom (because of age and/or condition of health) the expectation of parenthood is quite small, be subjected to massive radiation therapy? The answer here is obviously affirmative. But how does one compare the detection of a case of tuberculosis by X-ray survey with genetic harm that will befall someone in generations to come? How compelling should the indication be before an unborn child is subjected to damage by a fluoroscopic examination of its mother?[32] Moral reasoning that applies the principle of prudence, or the principle of proportion between effects both of which arise from a single action, is notoriously inexact. Still, it is certain that it is *immoral* to be imprudent, and it is a dereliction of duty not to make this sort of appraisal as best one can, and to act upon the best knowledge one can secure.

It is hardly utopian to hope that with the dissemination of genetic knowledge there will arise increased concern about this problem, and among an increasing number of people a far greater moral sensitivity to their responsibilities to the future generations of mankind. Such an "ethics of genetic duty" was well stated by H. J. Muller: "Although it is a human right for people to have their infirmities cared for by every means that society can muster, they do not have the right knowingly to pass on to posterity such a load of infirmities of genetic or partly genetic origin as to cause an increase in the burden already being carried by the population."[33]

There is ample and well-established ground in Christian ethics for enlarging upon the theme of man's genetic responsibility. Having children was never regarded as a selfish prerogative. Instead, Christian teachings have always held that procreation is an act by which men and women are to perform their duty to future generations of men. If a given couple cannot be the progenitors of healthy individuals — at least not unduly defective individuals — or, if they are the carriers of serious defect, then such a couple's "right to have children" becomes their duty not to do so, or to have fewer children. The science of genetics may be able to inform them with certain knowledge of the fact-situation. That would be sufficient to place eugenic reasons among those serious causes justifying the systematic practice of lifelong *un*-parenthood, or of less parentage.

What is lacking is not the moral argument but a moral movement. The Christian churches have in the past been able to promote celibacy to the glory of God — men and women who for the supreme end of human existence "deny themselves" (if that is the term for it) both of the goods of marriage. These same Christian churches should be able to promote voluntary or "vocational" childlessness, or policies of restricted reproduction, for the sake of the children of generations to come. In place of Muller's "foster pregnancy," the churches could set before such couples alternatives that might be termed "foster parentage" — all the many ways in which human parental instincts may be fulfilled in couples who for mercy's sake have no children of their own. These persons would be called upon to "deny themselves" (if that is the term for it) one of the goods of marriage for the sake of that end itself. And they would honor the Creator of all human love and procreation, in that they would hold in incorruptible union the love that they have and the procreation they never have, or have no more.

Notes

1. H. J. Muller, "The Guidance of Human Evolution," in *Perspectives in Biology and Medicine* (Chicago: University of Chicago Press, 1959) 3 (Autumn 1959): 11.

2. H. J. Muller, "Our Load of Mutations," in *The American Journal of Human Genetics* 2 (June 1950): 146, 171.

3. Ibid., p. 146, Cf. Also Muller, "Should We Strengthen or Weaken our Genetic Heritage?" in Hudson Hoagland and Ralph W. Burhoe, eds., *Evolution and Man's Progress* (New York: Columbia University Press, 1962), p. 27. It does not seem a sufficient answer to all this to reply: "Norway rats . . . have been kept in laboratories since some time before 1840 and 1850. . . . But it does not follow that laboratory rats are decadent and unfit; nor does it follow that the 'welfare state' is making man decadent and unfit — to live in a welfare state!" (Theodosius Dobzhansky, *Mankind Evolving* [New Haven: Yale University Press, 1962], p. 326).

4. Muller, "Better Genes for Tomorrow," in Stuart Mudd, ed., *The Population Crisis and the Use of World Resources* (The Hague: Dr. W. Junk Publishers, 1964), p. 315.

5. Hannah Arendt, quoted in a *Worldview* editorial, Sept. 1958, p. 1.

6. In an article entitled, "Sex and People: A Critical Review" (*Religion and Life* 30 [Winter 1960-61]; 53-70), I sought to apply the edification found in Christian eschatology in refutation of certain genial viewpoints sometimes propounded by Christians on the basis of a doctrine of creation. These Christians hold that religious people *must* believe that God intends an abundant *earthly* life for every baby born, and that we would deny His providence if we doubt that world population control, combined with economic growthmanship, can finally succeed in fulfilling God's direction of human life to this end. Such a belief is secular progressivism with religious overtones. Taken seriously enough, it can lead, as easily as any other utopianism can, to the adoption of any means to that end, the control of the world's population. In essence, an independent morality of means, or righteousness in conduct, is collapsed into utilitarianism when the *eschaton* or man's supernatural end is replaced by any future *telos*.

7. The language of this paragraph reflects that of H. Richard Niebuhr, *The Responsible Self* (New York: Harper and Row, 1963).

8. "A Free Man's Worship." There is less posturing in Muller's despair, more in the optimism that floats over this despair, than in Russell.

9. "Ethics in International Relations Today," an address delivered at Amherst College, Dec. 9, 1964; quoted from *The New York Times*, Dec. 10, 1964.

10. "A Christian Approach to the Question of Sexual Relations Outside Marriage," in *The Journal of Religion* 45 (Apr. 1965): 100-18.

11. Gerald Kelley and John C. Ford, "Periodic Continence," in *Theological Studies* 23 (Dec. 1962): 590-624.

12. H. J. Muller, who favors phenotypic selection, describes the enormous difficulties in the way of perfecting methods of genotypic change in "Means and Aims in Human Genetic Betterment," in *The Control of Human Heredity and Evolution* (New York: Macmillan Co., 1965). In the advancement of science toward direction or change of the germ cells themselves, Muller believes "there may be in time a race between genetic surgery and robotics, and we may find that this old house will do no longer" (p. 109). I take him to mean that a new type of man may be as easily made as present man can be remade by direct action on his genes.

Neither, for Muller, is "utterly visionary." Since both robotics and the direction of mutation are visionary, however, Muller wants to proceed with parental selection by all the voluntary means presently available.

13. "As in most defensive operations, it is a dreary, frustrating business to have to run as fast as one can merely to stay in the same place. Nature did better for us. Why can we not do better for ourselves?" ("Guidance," p. 17). Thus, only progressive eugenics would be the equivalent of natural selection, which was phenotypic and preserved the genes of the strongest types.

14. "Guidance," p. 35.

15. Dobzhansky, p. 328; and Klein's comment in the discussion in *Man and His Future,* a Ciba Foundation Volume (London: J. and A. Churchill, 1963), p. 280.

16. J. Paul Scott in the discussion in *Evolution and Man's Progress,* p. 48.

17. R. S. Morison in ibid., p. 64.

18. Donald M. MacKay in the discussion in *Man and His Future,* p. 298.

19. John F. Brock in ibid., p. 287. Or that, in view of the incredible diversity of opinions expressed by the scientists, it is impossible to know what we should try to educate people to do in making genetic choices (Medawar in *Man and His Future,* p. 382).

20. There is an exceedingly profound and open-minded discussion of artificial insemination, from the point of view of a Lutheran ethics, in Helmut Thielicke's *The Ethics of Sex,* trans. John W. Doberstein (New York: Harper and Row, 1964), pp. 248-68.

21. "Better Genes for Tomorrow," p. 336.

22. "Genetic Progress by Voluntarily Conducted Germinal Choice," in *Man and His Future,* p. 260.

23. *The World View of Moderns,* University of Illinois 50th Anniversary Lecture Series (Urbana, Ill.: University of Illinois Press, 1958), p. 26. Without some consensus on the ultimate question of values, he points out elsewhere, all man's cultural activities, no less than his germinal choices, would be at cross-purposes ("Guidance," p. 19).

24. Bruce Wallace and Theodosius Dobzhansky, *Radiation, Genes, and Man* (New York: Henry Holt, 1959), p. 330.

25. "Couples desiring to have in their own families one or more children who are especially likely to embody their own ideals of worth will be afforded a wide range of choice. They will be assisted by records of the lives and characteristics of the donors and of their relatives, and by counsel from diverse specialists, but the final choice will be their own and their participation will be entirely voluntary" ("Means and Aims," p. 122).

26. Ibid., p. 118.

27. Donald M. MacKay in the discussion in *Man and His Future,* p. 286.

28. Hampton L. Carson, *Heredity and Human Life* (New York: Columbia University Press, 1963), p. 189.

29. Ibid., p. 188.

30. See James F. Crow, "Mechanisms and Trends in Human Evolution," in *Evolution and Man's Progress,* p. 18.

31. Frederick Osborn, "The Protection and Improvement of Man's Genetic Inheritance," in *The Population Crisis and the Use of World Resources,* pp. 308-9.

32. See Wallace and Dobzhansky, *Radiation,* pp. 184-85. Since these authors had just cogently stated (perhaps without knowing it) the "rule of double effect," I frankly do not understand their meaning in the following paragraph: "The importance one places on genetic damage depends, really, on the value one places on human life. If the importance of human life is absolute, if human life is infinitely precious, then the exact number of additional victims of genetic damage is not crucial. One death is as inadmissible as 100, 1,000, or 1,000,000. Infinity multiplied by any finite number is still infinity. Whoever claims that the number of genetic deaths is an important consideration in this problem claims that human life is of limited value" (p. 188). To the contrary, it is precisely because each human life has such value that it becomes important to take the numbers into account as one element in the proportion in situations where *not all can be saved.* Prudence is a matter of estimating the cost-benefit where infinite values (the lives of persons) are in conflict, where, e.g., persons in the present generation must be saved at the expense of persons in a future generation, or vice versa; and there is *no other alternative.*

33. H. J. Muller, *Man's Future Birthright* (University of New Hampshire, Feb., 1958), p. 18. See also Muller's "Guidance," p. 8.

71 The Problem of Genetic Manipulation

Karl Rahner

Man's finite nature implies that, however much he may conceivably (and even legitimately) submit his own self to planning, he is no less a being whose essence has been predetermined. He must accept this particular *existentiale* as well as the task of self-determination. We must now relate this fundamental anthropological and ethical insight to the concrete problem under discussion, and then draw the appropriate and necessary conclusions.

1. Man must freely accept his nature as being predetermined. For he has not called *himself* into existence. He has been projected into a particular world, and although his world is presented to him for his free acceptance or rejection, he has not *chosen* it himself. It is rather that the world confronts him as something which has been determined from another quarter, *before* he embarks on his own history as a free being. Consequently the world can never be 'worked over' to such an extent that man is eventually dealing only with material *he* has chosen and created. Even if it were exhaustively calculated and planned in advance by the parents, the very stuff which is the precondition of the test-tube baby's freedom is (as far as the baby *itself* is concerned — and this 'self' is what is decisive) something already decided by someone else, something alien, like the genes one receives according to natural conception at the present time. It is part of the test-tube child's freedom to ask why he is obliged to shape his whole lifelong history out of the particular material which his parents have so wisely and thoughtfully selected for him by means of technology and planning. The question still remains as to whether, having had one's 'good fortune' planned and predetermined, one really considers oneself to be 'fortunate'. Accepting this necessarily alien determination of one's own being *is* and *remains*, therefore, a fundamental task of man in his free moral existence. All this can be understood, by 'transcendental deduction', as a necessarily given factor of man's nature. Whenever the *amor fati* — *fatum* in the sense of what is uniquely committed to the individual — is no longer achieved, and wherever this *fatum* is no longer accepted confidently in patience and humility as the gift of an *incomprehensible* love, man is subject to total neurosis, to a basic fear concerning his destiny which weighs more heavily on him than all the things which, as a result of this fear, he tries to escape from. Man's fundamental guilt is the consequence of his freely refusing to accept this gift.

2. However, although this *existentiale* and what it implies (the task of free decision) exercises its sovereign influence in the ultimate ground of man's being, it must also take on a corresponding 'categorical', tangible form in time and space, lest, banished from man's existence, it should be forgotten and ultimately freely denied by him.

Now man is in a certain respect most free when he is not dealing with a 'thing' but calling into being another, freely responsible person. If he is not to conceal or fall short of his nature, man must be presented clearly with the dialectically opposite position of his freedom as a man. And in concrete terms that means that the freedom to determine another person must remain a clear-cut and radical destiny, which one has *not chosen* but *accepted.* Procreation in particular must not become an act of neurotic anxiety in the face of fate. The other person must remain the one who is both *made* and *accepted;* both an elevating influence, because he has been chosen, and a burden to be accepted and carried. If man, when confronted with his child, saw only what he had himself planned, he would not be looking at his own nature, nor would he experience his true self which is both free and the object of external determination. Genetic manipulation is the embodiment of the fear of

Chapter 14, "The Problem of Genetic Manipulation," from *Theological Investigations, Vol. IX: Writings of 1965-67* by Karl Rahner. Translated by Graham Harrison.

oneself, the fear of accepting one's self as the unknown quantity it is.

Someone might say that even genetic manipulation cannot really get rid of every indeterminate element in procreation and that therefore genetic manipulation does not run counter to what we have said. (In any case, surely certain 'eugenic precautions' are not really reprehensible?) In this case we must answer with another question: What, in actual fact, is the driving force behind genetic manipulation? What sort of person is driven to it? And the answer would be, in the first place, the *hate* of one's destiny; and secondly, it is the man who, at his innermost level, is in despair because he cannot *dispose* of existence. In genetic manipulation such a man clearly and unequivocally oversteps the boundary between legitimate eugenic precautions and the realm tyrannised by the desperate fear of destiny. Even in those cases where no precise boundary can be set, one can see that a particular action undoubtedly exceeds it. This is plain in the case in hand, since the concrete genetic manipulation is governed by the desire to banish the *fatum* from existence, at a particular point. To the extent that this intention does not quite succeed, it is contrary to the original desire, for this desire hates destiny and can only love — as the product of its own free action — what it has calculated and planned. It no longer desires to say 'I have gotten a man from the Lord' — from *God*, who cannot be manipulated and who must be concretely present in man's existence. The essence of this rather more theological conclusion can be seen just as clearly in the dimensions of concrete anthropology: *Does* man in the concrete — who is not a mere abstract concept — really wish, in accepting genetic manipulation, to accept what *cannot* be predetermined? Has he actually the courage to take a decision, the results of which are unforeseeable? Does he really want to enter into a future of open possibilities, full of both threatening and promising surprises? And if his will fails at this point, will he ever find it again in any other area of his existence? Or is he like a man who only wants to perform a particular function of his nature when it is too late for him to do otherwise, and who will thus not be really able to carry it out even then? These are the decisive questions.

3. Man has his own sphere of intimacy. Historically and sociologically its concrete form can vary considerably. But whether it is technologically possible to abolish it is not the point, for this sphere of intimacy *should* exist, and ought to be resolutely safeguarded. It forms the innermost region of freedom which man needs in order to be really self-determining. At whatever point anyone else is able and is permitted arbitrarily to invade another person's private area of free decision, freedom itself ceases to exist.

Man is right to designate the ultimate achievement of sexual union as belonging to this area of intimacy. For human sexuality, as a free activity both is and ought to be more than a merely biological function; namely, an activity of the whole human being: the appearance and realisation of personal love.[1] Now this personal love which is consummated sexually has within it an essential inner relation to the child, for the child is an embodiment of the abiding unity of the marriage-partners which is expressed in marital union. Genetic manipulation, however, does two things: it fundamentally separates the marital union from the procreation of a new person as this permanent embodiment of the unity of married love; and it transfers procreation, isolated and torn from its human matrix, to an area outside man's sphere of intimacy. It is this sphere of intimacy which is the proper context for sexual union, which itself implies the fundamental readiness of the marriage-partners to let their unity take the form of a child.

The fact that it is technologically *possible* to effect the changes involved in genetic manipulation while at the same time producing a new *human being* is no argument against the essential connectedness of the factors we have just referred to (the sphere of intimacy — the union of marital love — the child as the permanent form of this union). For the child produced by such a method is, in this sense, the child of the mother *and* of the donor. The latter refuses, however, to acknowledge his fatherhood in an act of personal love: he remains anonymous or at least does not wish to be the donor in respect of this particular mother; precisely through his anonymity he robs the child of the right and ability to fulfil the obligation of his existence, namely to accept himself as the child of these particular parents. Genetic manipulation of this sort is no more 'human', merely because it produces a human being, than a case of rape. The fact that a biological chain of cause-and-effect is not broken, even when the moral/human unity and the whole of really human meaningfulness receives a mortal blow (for the 'biological' side is intended to be an expression of this total meaningfulness), does nothing, in itself, to justify its own occurrence.

4. What we have just said is directed against the *desire* (which is at least implicit in genetic manipulation) to plan man totally; it runs counter to the nature of man in the sense we have outlined. Consequently saying 'No' to this desire is not dependent on the question of its feasibility, and it is both possible and permissible to ask the further question, whether this desire *could* be totally realised, and what would be the moral implication of a failure in the execution of these plans.[2]

Initially we should have to answer the first part of the question in the negative. It can confidently be said that it would be impossible, from the technological point of view, to implement a genetic manipulation involving *all* future human beings, because, however much apparatus and 'automation' one had at one's disposal, the fact that one would have to deal with each human being as an individual[3] would imply such a vast quantity of active 'manipulators' that it would take up, *per absurdum,* the whole of mankind's attention and energy. But what would be the moral significance of the impossibility of producing the *whole* of future mankind by genetic manipulation?

In the first place it does *not* mean — as we shall show more clearly *a posteriori* — that a *partial* genetic manipulation is morally admissible, i.e. on the grounds that in any case 'not much' will happen. The practical impossibility of overstepping a particular quantitative limit is by no means a reason for morally justifying any action within that limit. If everyone told lies, for instance, the telling of lies would have no effect, because no one would believe a liar any more. But that does not make a limited dose of lies a morally justifiable thing. Furthermore, if a *partial* genetic manipulation became normal practice, consciously recognised by society, it would create two new 'races' in mankind: the technologically manipulated, super-bred test-tube men who inevitably would have a special status in society, and the 'ordinary', unselected, mass-produced humans, procreated in the old way. But what new social tensions would arise from this, and at a time when racial discrimination and racial conflicts are laboriously being dismantled so that a gigantic, tightly-packed humanity can exist peacefully! Or is one to believe that this group of test-tube men, whose intelligence quotients would be clearly considerably higher from birth, would not aspire to such a unique position in society, and that the remaining herd of humanity (*without* 'pedigree') would obey them? But would the rest of mankind, remaining at least as intelligent, revolutionary and violent as *we* are, readily accept the leadership of pedigree test-tube men? All this would probably not happen provided that the number of genetically manipulated men were *very* small, and that for that very reason they could not lay claim to be the exclusive leaders of society. But in such a case the spokesmen of manipulation would not have achieved the very results they want, namely, to create mankind's elite of leaders, able to claim the right of leadership on account of their genetic qualifications. However, it must be declared immoral to plan to produce such conflict-laden material with its unforeseeable consequences. It constitutes a threat to man and to mankind.

5. Nowadays we are trying to extend and secure the individual's area of freedom. It is one of mankind's moral commissions. To pursue the practical possibility of genetically manipulating man is to threaten and encroach upon this free area. For it offers incalculable opportunities of man's manipulation — reaching to the very roots of his existence — *by organised society,* i.e. the state. This in turn subjects the state to the strong temptation of itself manipulating the genetic manipulation. And unless one adopts the radically false view (which is untenable from both the philosophical and the Christian standpoints) that what the state wants is automatically good and just, it must be acknowledged that, over and above the essential inner perversity of genetic manipulation, this gives the state the power of further immoral action in using it for its own purposes, to create men who suit its own predilections.

Let no-one say that *every* new and legitimate possibility always involved the temptation for man to misuse it, and that it is not thereby immoral, but must just be protected against abuse. The danger of misusing a newly created possibility may be taken into account *if* this new possibility is in itself justifiable and seems to be inevitable and required by man. But is this the case in genetic manipulation? What compelling aims does it have in view? That men should be able to grow a little older? But is that really desirable with the present size of world population, etc.? In any case, is this the right way — is it not the *only* way — to set about it? Or is the main aim that man should be genetically more intelligent and cultured? But is it true that higher intelligence is clearly correlated with a more highly developed humane sensitivity? Is the kind of intelligence which can be 'bred' in this way the kind we need today, i.e. the intelligence of wisdom, moral responsibility and selflessness? (For the other kind, the 'technical' kind of intelligence can be adequately increased by means of computers and cybernetics.) What is the point of genetic manipulation if not to extend the state's area of control and thus to diminish, instead of to increase, man's sphere of freedom? It would be wiser not to put weapons into the hands of one's aggressors.

6. In future man must develop a critical attitude toward the fascination exercised by every new possibility. Here, in general terms, we have a new moral commission.

Essentially it has always been possible to see that not everything which *can* be done, *ought* to be done.[4] The possibilities available to man in earlier days were, however, very stable, and as a result they had been tested countless times. The possibilities for evil (and they were relatively simple and clear-cut) were recognised promptly as such, since they were of common and general nature, e.g. that 'cheats never prosper', tyranny is eventually self-destructive, excessive indulgence destroys the ability to enjoy, etc. The situation was simple: one knew what one ought not to do because one had already experienced the fact that such things were not really lasting possibilities in the long run, although one could 'get away with it' for a time. But the past did teach a sound doctrine: one should *not* do everything one is *able* to do; there are times when the attraction of the possible must be resisted.

Nowadays the situation is different. New and practical possibilities are set before us in relatively rapid succession, and they have vast and far-reaching effects. It is a strange factor of the dialectic of the accelerating movement of our history that these new possibilities can be discovered more quickly than their ultimate effects can be ascertained by practical tests. This is why it is so vital for humanity to develop a resistance to the fascination of novel possibilities. Of course there are 'feedback' effects in the field of social morality too, and they put a brake on the lure of novelty: the latest attraction in the form of the mini-skirt becomes monotonous when everyone is wearing it; and if almost everyone adopts the policy of limiting the size of the family because of the demands it makes, a large family will suddenly become an 'attractive' possibility and even gain a new social prestige. But there is no guarantee that such feedback effects can be relied upon in social morality in every case. The irreparable catastrophe can already have taken place before any feedback has had time to take effect. In certain cases to create immunity from moral diseases requires more time than the disease itself allows.

Nowadays there are things with which one cannot have a preliminary run through, in order to gain experience for the next occasions and become wiser through trial and error. Or should one first of all arrange a 'trial run' for a total atomic war, for instance, before deciding to avoid a second one? Today we must be aware that a thing may have irreversible consequences. This is a fundamental conviction of Christianity's theology of history; in spite of the multifarious possible recombinations Christianity sees the course of history as being ultimately a one-way street. At all events, if the new humanity of the future is to survive, it must cultivate a sober and critical resistance to the fascination of novel possibilities.

Genetic manipulation seems to be, initially, a case in point. Are there any reasons against such a view? There could only be objections if there were considerable reasons *in favour* of genetic manipulation from other quarters. Like what, for instance? That we must bring the decline of intelligence and bodily health under control? But has anyone proved such a decline to be a fact? Or if it *is* partially the case, has it been shown that it could not be brought under control in another way? No such proofs are forthcoming.

7. There is another side to the fascination of novelty. The suggestion is that new possibilities will become actualities *all the same;* that nothing can resist them and that to offer any resistance is to be backing a loser; that one is being old-fash-

ioned and stick-in-the-mud by not joining forces with the heralds of the 'new age'. On the contrary, it is one of the fundamental duties of a genuinely moral and Christian man to endeavour to do precisely this: to be *absolutely* faithful to a thing in a situation where it seems hopelessly doomed to failure. The biological end of an individual is not the only death of which one must not be afraid. There are other kinds of apparent death which one must not fear. History is not made by those who try to foresee what is 'inevitable' so that they can jump on the cart of fate in good time, but by those who are prepared to take the ultimate risk of defeat. No one can say that genetic manipulation *inevitably* will come. The only person who 'knows' such a thing is the man who secretly *wishes* it to be so.

Is that kind of man a trustworthy prophet? Why should not mankind as a whole have to learn the lessons every individual has to learn in his own life if he is to survive, namely, the lessons of sacrifice and renunciation? After all we have said, the issue of sacrifice and renunciation is in this sense a 'rational' one and not the unreal fantasy of masochistic minds perversely obstructing their own progress. It is by no means certain that mankind will always be able to remain at the juvenile stage where it can only do the sort of 'mischief' which does not matter very much. That is surely another most valuable insight of our time. So then, if mankind as a whole must seek to learn the renunciation characteristic of maturity, it cannot be said that a rejection of genetic manipulation has 'no prospects' from the very beginning.

In conclusion let us recapitulate in order to understand the whole in the proper light. We do not claim that these observations against genetic manipulation are complete; rather they constitute an appeal to, and the inadequate objectifying of, a humane and Christian 'instinct' which can be discovered in the moral field. A moral awareness of this kind (which both is and does more than we have mentioned here) forms the context in which man has the courage to make decisions; thus a decision is also more than its rationale, because the act is always more than its theoretical foundation. This 'instinct' justifiably has the courage to say *Stat pro ratione voluntas* because such a confession need not necessarily be overcautious about making a decision. On the contrary it can claim to be the first really to make room for the possibility of genuine criticism and to bring to light the justification, implications and limitations of a real theoretical foundation. All theoretical reasoning always says (among other things), 'We do not *want* to manipulate man genetically'; but this will is meaningful in spite of the fact that it neither claims nor is obliged to be exhaustively analysable by theoretical reason; measured against the opposite will, *this* will is more deeply meaningful and more genuinely human. It must accept the risks involved in history and the unpredictable, in order to find out whether it is stronger than its converse, and whether it can endow its theoretical meaningfulness with the particular radiance which is the exclusive characteristic of *performed* reality. Modern man is faced with making this decision.

Of course, in saying this we have raised yet another problem. Right from the beginning, rejecting man's genetic manipulation is not a merely theoretical declaration but a deliberate act. Consequently this theoretical discussion cannot be supported conclusively by the general, formal authority of the Christian churches alone. And so, as in many other cases in moral theology, we are faced today with a new, additional question of great importance: How, in concrete terms, can such a rejection (of genetic manipulation) be established in modern society as society's *own* maxim, its own inner attitude and 'instinct', in the face of society's 'pluralism'? However, this particular problem of moral and pastoral theology is part of a wider issue[5] which cannot be pursued further within the limits of the present discussion.

Notes

1. Cf. The Pastoral Constitution of the Second Vatican Council, *Gaudium et Spes*, Nos. 47-52.

2. We need not go into the first part of the question in so far as the concrete details are concerned; that belongs to the field of natural science.

3. Here we can pass over the question as to whether it is possible or impossible to synthesise the hereditary material itself in large quantities.

4. Of course, in a real and most profound sense one cannot 'do' something which is really immoral, for evil, measured against the *whole* of reality (including man in

all his dimensions and God as well), is always impotent and ineffectual. Cf. Also B. Welte, *Über das Böse* (Freiburg, 1959).

5. Some pointers are given in K. Rahner, 'Reflections on Dialogue Within a Pluralistic Society', *Theological Investigations* VI (London and Baltimore, 1969), pp. 31-42.

72 From Clinic to Congregation: Religious Communities and Genetic Medicine[1]

M. Therese Lysaught

Although many factors drive genetic research, a fundamental impetus is one that undergirds medicine itself — the moral duty, obligation, conviction that we are to relieve human suffering, to cure human illness, when we have the capability and the moral freedom to do so. Fueled by this conviction and the massive federal funding on the Human Genome Project, the database of information about genetics and technologies tailored to this data grow at a phenomenal rate. Almost daily, newspapers announce the discovery or near-discovery of another new gene.

Essential to this impetus is a second conviction, one less familiar to conventional medicine — a belief that locates disease in an individual's genetic structure. Thus, as presidential task forces and policy analysts currently attempt to reform the external structure of health care delivery, a quieter, subtler reformation — or better, transformation — is already occurring within medicine; a metamorphosis to genetic medicine. A genetic approach to medicine not only redefines what constitutes "disease" and "health." When translated into the clinical setting, it shifts the traditional province of medicine from a crisis-management acute care model, which attends to problems as

From *Christian Scholar's Review* 23, no. 3 (March 1994): 329-48. Used by permission.

they become manifest, to a model of "predict and manage," which anticipates and seeks to forestall disease and illness through lifestyle and environmental management or genetic intervention.[2]

As this metamorphosis continues, individuals will more frequently find themselves immersed in a health care system that increasingly speaks the language of genetics. Many of these individuals will likely be some of the 145 million individuals who worship in one of the 358,000 religious congregations in the U.S.[3] As such, they will go from the offices of physicians and genetic counselors to the offices of clergy and pastors, seeking guidance on how to interpret the information they have received, how to locate the information in a context of belief that will give it meaning, how to envision and weigh the implications of various courses of action. They will want to know: "If I am at a high risk, should I have my fetus genetically screened?" "I have been told I possess the gene for X — what does this mean?" "Should I avoid having children?" "Will gene therapy change my daughter's identity?"

To begin the process of giving meaning to information about genetics, congregants and pastors might turn to theologians or chaplains who participate in the dialogue between religion and genetics.[4] However, in what little has been written to date, recent advice of those who represent religion in these discussions indicates a disheartening trend, evident in theoretical positions.

> Advances in genetics occasioned by the Human Genome Project call for Protestant and Roman Catholic theologians to *re-examine the adequacy of traditional interpretations* of creation, human nature, moral choices, and the relation of humanity to nature.[5] Posing these questions and suggesting that answers might be found in the notion of ongoing creativity could become significant *as religious leaders wake up to what is going on in research*. . . . The fear of the unknown future seems to be fueled by a desire to locate something unchanging within the material world, something that connects us with the eternal and unchanging God. . . . Should this religious disposition prevail, the present generation will be accused of "playing God," and theological arguments will be mustered to call for a halt to further genome research. If this happens our churches might find themselves in the embarrassing position of advocating ignorance over knowledge, of supporting the *status quo* in preference to transformation.[6]

This same trend is also evident in practical positions:

> Religious groups should *advocate* adequate access to reliable genetic information and counseling services, and appropriate training for genetic counselors.[7] Clergy are in a unique position to link the issues of [genetics] to religious or spiritual teachings and practices. This is part of their job. But clergy, no less than physicians and other hospital personnel, must be careful not to dictate . . . choices. Biases regarding what constitutes quality of life, especially, have no place. . . . Clergy should act as educators, not enforcers of rules. Autonomy and free will are closely related.[8]

Implicit — or not so implicit — in these statements is a shared conviction: religion is to be the handmaid of science. Religious groups and religious professionals are called to use their social influence to advance the cause of genetics. It is time, we are told, for religion to catch up, to "wake up," to scientific advances, progress, truth, and discoveries about the human condition. Religion — authoritarian, unreasoning, absolutist, and fear-driven — is portrayed as intellectually, epistemologically and ethically inferior to science, that value-neutral promoter of creativity, rational inquiry, and human progress. The "truths" discovered by science demand revision in religious beliefs.

Pastors who heed this one-sided counsel fail in their calling and fail their parishioners. Clearly, pastors and theologians should not simply reject genetics out of fear and ignorance; equally they ought not act as cheerleaders to advance the cause of genetics *qua* science and progress. Rather, clergy and theologians are called to engage their communities in processes of moral reflection and action, forging with congregants well-reasoned, theologically and scientifically informed frameworks for evaluating questions, challenges, and resources raised by genetics. These frameworks will, in different instances, lead congregants to abjure some particular genetic endeavors, to tread tentatively in the face of others, and to welcome still others. Moreover, when these frameworks offer viable alternatives to practices logically indicated by genetic technology, they will do so because they emerge out of and are translated into moral action, namely, liturgical and social practices which embody the framing convictions and create in the world ways of living with genetic differences and uncertainties. By modeling such alternatives, religious communities may well help society to "wake up" to the ideological and culturally-laden implications of certain genetic technologies; like religion, science too can be "fundamentalist."

But first, clergy need to attend to the problems faced by their parishioners as they move from clinic to congregation. In order to think and live faithfully in the face of genetic information, parishioners need: (1) a renewed understanding and experience of the religious community as a place of moral discourse and moral formation; (2) basic and up-to-date information about genetics, its history, its social context and function, its limits and its possibilities; and (3) ongoing dialogue on how new choices created and imposed by genetics and medicine bear on issues of major concern to the Christian faith. In the following, I will comment, albeit too briefly, on each of these.

I. Christian Communities as Places of Moral Discourse

Substantive moral discourse — which is by definition "public" — has become increasingly elusive in our culture.[9] The problem, it is claimed, is that the warrants used by most people for moral evaluation and decision-making — our particular identities and commitments, especially cultural beliefs and religious convictions — are personal, private, and incommensurate. So personal are they, in fact, that to evoke or invoke them often seems a novelty or a breach of the etiquette of public exchange. Worse, however, it is claimed that they are destructive of public tranquillity and cohesion by forestalling the possibility of communication, understanding, and consensus. Public life and its moral discourse is therefore rendered either as unfettered pluralism celebrated for its own sake or a thin, grey universalism which renders all difference invisible.

Over against these extremes stands the alternative of Christian communities — waning, it is true, but still viable. Members of Christian communities — although far from uniform — claim and are claimed by commonalities: a common activity of worship, a common language of faith, a common story of the Gospel, a common text of Scripture, common practices such as baptism, forgiveness, and prayer, common beliefs about the character of God and the world, the common task of discipleship. These commonalities resist the fragmentation and idiosyncracy of contemporary culture. They create a "public" forum by providing shared components for building a shared identity, a common moral framework. Such a framework supplies the context within which differences in individual experiences, identities, and understandings can be meaningfully discussed.

Moreover, these commonalities provide not only community but *content,* particular visions of human flourishing that shape contexts for interpretation. Members of Christian communities claim that embedded in their traditions and embodied in their practices are truths that provide premises for reasonable arguments: that God exists; that God's character is of a certain sort; that God intends certain ends for human beings and relates to human beings in certain ways. These are convictions which guide people's actions — even if tacitly — convictions by which people orient their lives, "in their worship, and in their living and their dying and their suffering and their caring for the suffering."[10]

While the nature of contemporary public philosophy renders it difficult to identify operative or tacit religious convictions in public moral reflection or integrate them where possibly indicated, Christian communities can provide models of what this integration might look like, as Allen Verhey has noted:

> In communities of faith, by some grace there is an effort to attend to God and to respond appropriately to God, to attend to all things as related to God and to respond in ways appropriate to their relations to God. There the tradition exists not merely as an archaic relic in an age of science and reason but as that which continues to evoke and to shape the loyalties and the identities of the community and its members, even as they make

> use of science and reason. . . . There people ask how religious convictions can guide and limit new medical powers.[11]

Although this is an ideal which few congregations meet, it is a challenge to which congregations are called.

But congregations provide not only the communal conditions of possibility and content for moral discourse and action; they also supply models of it. Many try to reduce religion to "themes" or "beliefs" or "principles" which can be applied to a situation apart from the agents involved or a communal worshipping context. But religious beliefs are neither self-evident nor self-interpreting. An ability to see and understand religious dimensions of life and events is forged over lifetimes and through communal and embodied practices. In this process, we learn from others. From the stories of Scripture and experiences of others, we learn how to see what God's grace looks like in events. From others in the tradition and in the community, we learn how — and how not — to understand the stories of Scripture and to correlate them with seemingly novel situations. From the successful and less-successful attempts of others to live faithfully, we learn what discipleship "looks like," not in 50 C.E. Palestine but in navigating contemporary culture. From others we learn how to forgive ourselves and others for inevitable moral failure. Others demonstrate how the rituals and practices of Christian life can sustain us in and through times of confusion.

None of this is easy, of course, nor will it always be successful; Christian communities are often known more for their error and politics than for being well-informed and well-intentioned. Like the moral life generally, moral discourse within Christian communities will not be tidy, will not supply easy, clear-cut answers. Moral discourse within Christian communities will most often focus not only on the "what to do" but also on questions of "why ought I do X?" or "how do I go on in the face of Y?" These questions now arise out of individuals' experiences of genetic medicine. In order adequately to deliberate on the "what," "why," and "how" of genetics, clergy and congregants need to understand the basics of genetics, the technologies it generates, and the social practices that are evolving from genetic capabilities.

II. Genetics and "Genetic Medicine"

In order to give a sense of the complexity of genetics, of the truly technically fascinating capabilities of genetic science, of the types of jargon and concepts individuals will encounter, of the processes that might seem, on first glance, to be morally dubious but that may in fact be functioning as moral red herrings (such as the ominous sounding "murine retroviral vectors"), I would next like to outline some of the fundamental concepts of genetics, technologies they have generated, and some of the issues raised. While this portrayal will be admittedly incomplete, in it I will try to display what currently serve as the three major components of genetic medicine: genetic testing, genetic therapy, and genetically-engineered pharmaceuticals.[12]

Like any scientific field, genetics has developed its own arcane language. Long before one can begin to interpret a bit of genetic information, one must understand the words and the grammar.[13] Although their meaning may be far from clear, the fundamental terms of genetics are by now familiar: chromosomes, DNA, genes. The nucleus of each cell in the human body (except the reproductive cells) contains 46 chromosomes — 23 pairs. One chromosome in each pair comes from each of an individual's parents. From cell to cell within a particular person's body, these chromosomes are essentially the same; slight variations can be introduced if mutations occur during the replication of a cell.

Chromosomes are composed of a substance called DNA — deoxyribonucleic acid — which is, in turn, composed of four molecules called nucleotides (adenosine, thymine, cytosine, and guanine), represented with the letters A-T-C-G. Thus, chromosomes are essentially very, very long chains of molecules of A, T, C, and G. The order in which these molecules appears within a given segment of DNA — . . . ATGCGCTAATGCCG-TAATCGTACGCGCGATGC . . . — is often referred to as a "code," for through an intricate process of translation of this sequence, DNA directs the production of every protein, enzyme, and cell in the human body. A DNA segment that contains the sequence or code for an entire molecule or product is called a "gene." There are an estimated 50,000 to 100,000 genes *in every human cell,* containing up to 6 *billion* nucleotides. Thus, a single chromosome could conceivably contain an average of 2,000 genes, while a single gene could conceivably contain an average of 60,000 nucleotides that must be sequenced in a particular order for the gene to function correctly, that is, to produce the proper protein.[14]

Aberrations in genetic structure are thought to cause approximately 3,000-5,000 diseases or physical conditions, including: enzyme deficiencies, familial hypercholesterolemia, Lesch-Nyhan syndrome, phenylketonuria, Gaucher disease, Hunter syndromes, sickle cell anemia, thalessemias, hormone production defects (such as absence of growth hormone), Tay-Sachs, Cystic Fibrosis, Huntington's disease. In conditions such as these, some alteration in the nucleotide sequence or in the location of the gene causes the body to produce either excessive amounts of some body proteins, dysfunctional versions of other proteins, or insufficient amounts of yet other proteins; the end result is disease. For example, diabetes is the result of the insufficient production and regulation of the protein insulin. Such conditions can be caused either by a single gene, a number of genes working in tandem, or through a combination of genetic, behavioral and environmental causes.

These fundamentals of genetics suggested the first procedure in the repertoire of genetic medicine: genetic testing or screening.[15] Genetic testing assays the chromosomes of adults and children, fetuses, and "pre-embryos" to determine possible gene variations which may correlate with diseases. The testing of children and adults has three stated objectives: (1) to suggest lifestyle changes that might forestall the manifestation of disease or to suggest ongoing monitoring of symptoms; (2) to help individuals or couples make decisions about whether or not to have children; and (3) to help individuals plan their futures. The testing of fetuses and "pre-embryos" presupposes the possibility of "therapeutic" abortion, although in some instances it is undertaken in order that parents can ready themselves for their child's condition.

Genetic testing is neither simple nor straightforward. Clinicians can only test for known genes; a clear report does not completely assure freedom from possible genetic disease. Even with known genes, however, as with all medical tests, false positives and false negatives can occur, both of which can be potentially devastating (especially to fetal patients). Since most conditions for which tests are available do not yet enjoy a cure or therapy, a positive test can also be potentially devastating. Moreover, a positive test does not necessarily indicate disease, but rather indicates the probability of contracting a disease or condition. Genetic regulation is not completely understood, and it is possible that other genes or environmental factors may modify the way a particular gene is expressed; thus, a condition may not occur, or its severity may vary.

Likewise, preconceptive testing also results only in probabilities. For example, if an individual possesses a gene for a genetically recessive condition, she must marry with an individual who also possesses a gene for the same condition, and then there is only a 25% chance that their offspring will manifest the condition. In cases where one parent possesses two recessive genes and manifests the condition, the likelihood rises only to 50%. For conditions that are autosomal dominant — i.e., only one "defective" gene is required for the expression of the disease, an example of which would be Huntington's disease — again there is only a 50% chance that a child will be afflicted. And again, in many cases the severity of the expression of the condition can vary, influenced by other genetic and environment factors.

Although the rhetoric surrounding the pursuit of genetic knowledge cites as its warrant the decrease of suffering, the increase of health and choices, and the conquest of disease, at this point genetics can do little more than diagnose, predict, identify. As mentioned, for most of the conditions it diagnoses, no cures and few therapies are possible. However, for some conditions correlated with the absence or underexpression of a particular gene, initial experiments in "gene therapy" have recently proved successful.

The first clinical trial in gene therapy was begun September 1990 at the National Institutes of Health, targeting a disease called severe combined immunodeficiency (SCID) or ADA deficiency.[16] Other remedies to ADA deficiency are available, but since they are not always effective, researchers hypothesized that ADA deficiency might be treated by gene therapy by removing an affected patient's bone marrow cells, inserting normal genes for the enzyme into them, and returning the treated cells to the patient's body, where they could grow and perhaps produce enough of the needed enzyme to degrade the toxic chemicals, thus restoring immune function.

In the first gene therapy experiment, the ADA gene was inserted into the DNA of the white blood cells by what is called a "murine retroviral vector," a genetically engineered mouse virus.[17] The procedure was successful: the transformed cells produced enough ADA to relieve the patient's severe immune deficiency even better than daily injections of the enzyme. The success of the ADA trials has led to the approval of seventeen further clinical trials of genetic therapy experimentation to test protocols for other conditions.[18]

This and similar approaches to genetic therapy are called *somatic* gene therapy, which works with the cells of an individual's body. An alternative approach is called *germline* or *gametic* gene therapy. In these procedures, technicians intervene in the genomes of either human gametes — sperm and ova — or of the cells of an early embryo. In somatic gene therapy, treatment affects only targeted cells in the patient's body, does not necessarily alter a person's genetic makeup, and functions like other therapies in that it needs to be periodically repeated; changes induced would not be passed on to children. Germline alteration, on the other hand, would produce genetic changes in all cells in the body (including an individual's reproductive cells), would introduce or remove characteristics on a permanent basis, and would not require repetitive interventions; these changes would be passed on to children.

To date, germline genetic intervention in humans is not technically possible, and the use of somatic gene therapy is extremely limited. In its somatic form, gene therapy differs little from other types of therapeutic interventions. Concerns about somatic genetic therapy are primarily questions of medical feasibility and risk of side effects: "What are the alternative methods of treatment? Is gene therapy likely to be more effective, less costly, safer, or otherwise more acceptable than available alternatives?" "How safe is the procedure? What are the data on short-term and long-term consequences?" "What are the side effects of the treatment and are they reversible or treatable?" These are, for the most part, practical questions.

"Germline" genetic intervention, however, raises very different questions, not only, or even primarily, medical, but ethical, philosophical, social and theological. Advocates of human germline intervention generally invoke three justifications. They argue that not all genetic defects can be corrected through somatic interventions. Secondly, they argue that germline genetic intervention could eliminate the need for repeated prenatal diagnosis and selective abortion in genetically at-risk families. Third, they argue that it could eliminate the need for repeated somatic gene therapy from generation to generation. Thus, their arguments draw on the warrants of freedom, necessity, and utility.[19] Further, some advocates extend these arguments to recommend not only *therapeutic* interventions but interventions to *enhance* an individual's (and their successor's) capabilities.

Those who oppose germline interventions likewise do so on a number of grounds. Opponents challenge the rhetoric of control that surrounds germline intervention. On the one hand, given our limited knowledge of genetic interactions, in developing these technologies, errors will occur, errors that are impossible to foresee and that may severely harm the future individuals involved. Again, given our limited knowledge of genetic interactions, it is not yet possible to foresee how changes in one part of an individual's genetic component may change the expression of another part. These changes may be perceived as benign, but we have yet to explore the meaning of so intentionally shaping the genetic component of a person's identity and personality. True "control" is not a possibility. But should it be desired? What is the relationship between my control exercised in the creation of another individual and the other's autonomy or freedom? Should we be exercising this kind of control over our progeny? On what grounds? Have we yet exhibited that we are capable of the kind of wisdom and humanity that would authorize this kind of paternalistic exercise? Can mere desire, want, or consumer taste provide sufficient guidance or authority?

A third piece of genetic medicine is genetically engineered pharmaceuticals. Just as geneticists can insert a gene into a cell and have it produce a specific protein in a patient's body, in some instances they can do this *in vitro*, synthetically producing large quantities of scarce biological compounds and receptor-selective drugs. Current examples of such genetically engineered pharmaceuticals would be insulin and growth hormone, among the dozen or so currently available. While the health benefits of many of these pharmaceuticals are readily apparent, this pharmaceutical armamentarium raises questions similar to those raised by somatic gene therapy, primarily questions of cost, access, and allocation of resources.

III. Contested Issues: Identity, Children, Power, Social Justice

Given the nature of genetic medicine, medical intervention in the lives of individuals will likely begin earlier and be more constant: they will be routinely screened as fetuses; any potential genetic condition will be monitored over the course of a lifetime; if indicated, genetic therapy might be attempted; as new genes are discovered, individuals may need to be screened again, perhaps on a regular basis; their fetuses will be screened; increasing number of pharmaceuticals will be produced through genetic techniques, and so on.

At present, however, individuals are for the most part confronted with simple genetic information — "your fetus possesses an extra chromosome" or "you possess a gene implicated in breast cancer" or "you possess the gene for Huntington's chorea." In spite of claims to neutrality and canons of "non-directiveness," such information tends to carry its own implications: "You should abort the fetus, spare it suffering, spare yourself the burden, and spare society the expense"; "We would advise prophylactic mastectomy"; or "You should get your affairs in order and inform your children; assisted suicide is available should you come near to losing your autonomy." While presented as "choices," these implications, and others like them, gather momentum toward social normativity and become increasingly "self-evident" (the choice of the "reasonable" person) as they are increasingly practiced.

These implications emerge out of a complex of anthropological, sociological and metaphysical commitments situated in a related structure of social practices. When, however, genetic information is considered in the context of community structured according to different practices and beliefs, the given implications are not quite as "self-evident." For those who consider genetic information in the context of a Christian community and its anthropological, theological, and sociological convictions and practices, alternative implications tend to emerge. In this section, I would like to consider four elements in a vision of human flourishing where the vision of genetic science and the vision of the Christian tradition differ: (1) identity; (2) children, strangers, and others; (3) control and power; and (4) social justice.

1. The Nature of Identity

Those who write on the ethical and religious dimensions of genetics frequently cite the statement by James D. Watson, co-discoverer of the double-helix shape of DNA and former director of the Human Genome Project, that the project's goal is "to find out what human being is."[20] This question is clearly a deeply religious one. At one seminar I attended on genetics, for example, we were informed that each individual has up to twenty defective genes in their genome; translation: everyone is defective. It seemed to be the biological version of original sin, with genetic therapy as the Pelagian savior. A related cohort are the genetic determinists, those who affirm that one's genome is one's destiny; here we meet the biological equivalent of predestination.

Many understand "what human being is" to be equivalent to the theological or philosophical concept of human nature. This raises two concerns: (1) that germline genetic interventions or human transgenic experiments might fundamentally alter what makes us human, might alter our "cerebral cortex and central nervous system capable of self-consciousness, enquiry, rational ordering and analysis, moral judgment and choice";[21] and (2) the implicit claim that, given the equation of the human genome with "what human being is" and human nature, the Human Genome Project will produce a genetic definition of the "normal" human being.

Both notions are thickly laden with particular convictions about what should be valued. The content of the "human" varies with history and culture. Likewise with the "normal." While it may be possible to determine an average or common genetic distribution, in many conversations a not so subtle shift occurs between notions of "normal" and notions of "*normative*." What if geneticists determine that part of the normal human genetic complement is a gene for adultery? Is it therefore normative? On what basis do or will we decide which characteristics are "human," "normal" and "undesirable"? What is to decide this? How quickly does "ideal" elide into "normal"? How do social structures and ideologies of "normalcy" reinforce each other?

Correlating religious doctrine and genetic science is a tricky affair. Here I will avoid discussing the epistemological issues and mention two practical problems. The most obvious problem is the one that has affected all attempts to discuss human nature: historically, socially, and culturally constructed concepts are read into nature or human biology, and human biology is then used as a warrant to provide an "objective" basis for a socially constructed belief or position. For example, Ronald Cole-Turner has attempted to correlate genetics and notions of free will and predestination:

> Correlations between genes and behavior, which will multiply as the genome project goes forward, are remarkably compatible with the more traditional view of original sin as a disordering of the will. According to this traditional view, it is not merely that the will struggles against an unruly body. The will itself is disordered and does not do what it wants to do. Paul's self-described "wretched man" (Romans 7:24) is consonant with the insight emerging from genetics. Our whole being, including the center of our personhood together with its will, is influenced by our genes. . . . Our genes carry the legacy of our evolution; and our personhood itself, including our capacities for consciousness, moral decision, and faith, arises from our genes as selected by evolution. Specific decisions and beliefs, of course, are not carried genetically. But our genes apparently do carry our individual inclination toward broad categories of attitude, religiosity, and behavior. . . . In time, we will come to see how our individual genotype influences not merely our eye color but our social attitudes, behaviors, and religious activities. . . . *Our souls are as different as our bodies.*[22]

Perhaps faith is a mutant version of reason.

A second problem arises when science is equated with objective, value-neutral, indisputable fact. Then, in trying to create a "fit" between a religious belief and a scientific position, the religious belief must give way. Again, Cole-Turner illustrates this:

> Christianity has assumed that all are morally and spiritually equal. *All* have sinned, all stand in need of grace, and all have the same degree of need and of capacity for salvation. All have the same moral capacity, and all are equally responsible for their behavior. Thanks to research in genetics, we are learning that this presumption of equality no longer holds. . . . We will learn how we vary in our capacity for moral and religious behaviors. . . . Needless to say, our theology must begin with a new axiom — namely, that we are all individual before God, with a unique set of genes and a unique set of moral and spiritual needs and capabilities. Salvation must be personalized as well as personal. Individual differences must be affirmed, not discriminated against. . . . [Thus] a growing awareness of our genetic individuality should prompt us to rethink the idea of redemption. . . . [O]ur genes, and not merely our life histories, affect the form of our redemption. In the future the doctrines of salvation and of the spiritual life will need to recognize individual variation.[23]

For Christians, normativity, identity and the meaning of the "human" derive from sources other than genetics, sources which serve to interpret genetic information rather than vice versa. Christians affirm through worship, practice, and story that identity is not determined by one's relationship to one's genome but rather by one's relationship to God and to God's cause. Through baptism, we are "born again," born into a new life and a new identity. Creation is not negated but is recreated; the identity derived from one's genetic component is now normed by the identity given through baptism, by being engrafted into the body of Christ in eucharist, by following a call to discipleship.

This approach to identity may help counter a number of disconcerting social trends. It will counter the myth of the genetic ideal by locating the description of an "ideal" life in relationship with God and community. It will counter the trend toward genetic uniformity by creating a framework that values and thereby prefers diversity ("We, though many, are one"). It will help remind us that "who we are" is only in small part constituted by our nature and genetic heritage: a good deal depends on "who is with us" through our growth and life, the conditions under which we grow, and "what we do" or "how we live" with our inheritance.

2. Attitudes Toward Children, Strangers and Others

Current genetic testing largely involves screening the genetic makeup of embryos and fetuses with the assumption that the genetically "defective" will be either aborted (if they are *in utero* or not implanted (if they are *in vitro*). Claims are beginning to be made that "couples have no obligation to produce genetically defective offspring" or that couples — or individuals — have a "right" to produce children free from genetic defects. Germline genetic interventions — both therapeutic and enhancing — are increasingly championed.

If genetic technologies make it increasingly easy to assay an embryo's genetic makeup, and individuals are persuaded to abort "undesirable" fetuses, it is conceivable that society will look less favorably on those who choose either not to have their children screened or who, in the light of screening, choose to bring these children to life. It is also conceivable that our utilitarian, bottom-line, efficiency-dominated society will be less and less likely to provide the financial and communal support for these children and their families when they are clearly "products" of choice and not chance. Decisions to give birth to imperfect children may become understood as "socially irresponsible." Abortions of the "defective" may even begin to be understood as "morally responsible," insofar as the autonomy of these defective fetuses may be compromised significantly, and they may be subjected to suffering.[24]

In the course of perfecting germline techniques, mistakes will be made which can produce lasting harms. What do we do then? If mistakes are introduced into an embryo's genetic makeup, two courses of action are open: simple destruction of "failures" or the killing/abortion of abnormal fetuses whose phenotypes do not correspond to initial expectations. Many scientists would understand the implanting of a "defective" blastocyst as a mistake and a waste of resources; they would prefer to have a "successful" outcome of the procedure. To proceed in the area of germline experimentation will entail the conscious acceptance that some embryos will be created solely as experimental material and others will necessarily be sacrificed for the sake of something else — science, others, etc. Not only is it questionable to use other, even potential, persons as means to an uncertain end, but it is questionable whether we should accept the assumption that genetically altered but defective embryos should be destroyed. What *is* the moral status of the "defective" unborn?

In the race of these technologies, Christians will need to revisit their theological understanding of children. This understanding will be informed by affirmations that life — and therefore children — are gifts.[25] This understanding of children will likewise be informed by the practice of baptism, in which parents give their children over to death that they may be born anew as *God's* children called to serve *God's* kingdom. God's purposes for our children — and for us through our children — may well be different from our purposes for our children and ourselves.

Congregations will need to examine as well the role children play in their common life, and the ways in which the life and social commitments of the community enable its members to welcome the other, the stranger, and those who are less perfect. Does the congregation integrate or marginalize those who are not "normal" or "successful" or "perfect" and thereby make it more difficult for parents to welcome a child who is different? These practices and beliefs, in conjunction with Christian commitments to serving the needy, the marginalized, the outcast, to welcoming the stranger in hospitality, provide resources for individuals faced with decisions to submit their fetuses to genetic testing.

3. Control and Power

Genetics is equipping us with powerful tools for determining our own future, as well as that of our children and our environment. Some are hopeful in the face of these new powers:

> God has put into our hands the possibility of what has so long been demanded by the great world religions, a change in man himself. . . . To succeed will be to begin a new and glorious stage in the history of what has been so defective a humanity.[26]

Others foresee in the powers of genetics the destruction of humanity, either by some alteration in the fundamental genetic basis of human nature or by a reduction of genetic diversity. The vehicle for this putative salvation or perdition is genetic technology. But the effects of technology need not be so apocalyptic to require serious consideration.

Technology, far from being a neutral tool amenable to human purposes, changes us as we use it. As Allen Verhey has noted, "although technologies are introduced as increasing our options, they can quickly become socially enforced. The automobile was introduced as an option to the horse, but try to ride a horse home on the interstate and you'll find yourself in trouble."[27] In a culture increasingly unable to engage in moral discourse, technological fixes become the remedy of choice for social problems. Moreover, technology may further exacerbate the social conditions which give rise to the problems. For example, the abortion pill — RU486 — may make abortion quicker and less painless, but by removing the symptom — unwanted pregnancy — it may well deflect attention from the underlying problem, namely, that 1.5 million American women and girls each year find themselves pregnant when they do not want to be and feel compelled to abort their children.

Most technological advances are heralded as methods for controlling the contingencies of nature and for increasing the range of human choices. Be it the problems of geography, pregnancy, or disease, technology is a vehicle for making nature amenable to human purposes. These questions of control are questions of power — power over those deemed "defective," power over our children, power over ourselves, power over nature. Power is also pursued under the auspices of the Human Genome Project, for by acquiring this knowledge some will inevitably be charged with power over others.

In contrast to both of these positions, in Scripture, creed and worship, Christians daily affirm different understandings of control and power. Davis' long-awaited transformation of humanity is affirmed to be ultimately an *eschatological* event; certainly, humanity can *change* humanity but not necessarily for the better. Christianity affirms that the remedy of the spiritual and moral defect that plagues humanity will be a matter of God's doing in God's time. Scripturally and theologically, there is an infinite qualitative difference between the transformation of humanity wrought by humanity and the transformation of humanity promised and wrought by God.

Christians are called to avoid worshiping the "false idol of technology."[28] But they are also called to be disciples, to pursue God's purposes in the world responsibly, such as healing the sick and attending to the sufferer. In these pursuits, Christians employ technology. To employ technology with integrity will require that clergy and congregations together reflect on the relationship between God's agency and human agency as well as the meanings and temptations of technology. Christian reflection on technology as such will entail Christian reflection on the relationship between humanity and nature. Are we stewards, co-creators, or "created co-creators"? At each step, when confronted with each new technology, Christians will need to ask themselves whether the kinds of power offered are compatible with the kind of power practiced by God and witnessed to in the Christian story of a God who redeemed humanity through suffering on a cross and whose power is made perfect in weakness.

This mention of "created co-creators" raises another issue. Discussion of genetic technologies and their attendant ethical analyses is often short-circuited by recourse to "bad axioms" or slogans, one of the most common of which is "playing God." Although often invoked, the meaning of this phrase has received scant treatment. C. Keith Boone reminds us that as with most bad axioms, although employed in the place of a sufficient argument, the slogan "playing God" points toward a kernel of truth that warrants closer inspection.[29]

In bioethics in general, agents are accused of "playing God" in situations involving decisions about who lives and who dies. Likewise in genetics, the slogan arises in two contexts, although primarily in the second — whether to abort genetically "defective" fetuses (i.e., who dies?) and regarding the manipulation of the germline, whether nonhuman or human (i.e., who — or sometimes, what — lives?). The ability to create potentially new life forms or new human individuality seems analogous to the power premised of God in the attribute "Creator."

There are a number of problems with the notion of "playing God." On the one hand, as Christians, we are called to "play God," to model ourselves as closely to God as possible. While the notion of "play" may, of course, carry more flippant connotations than the phrases "be obedient to" or "follow" or "to be disciples," we invariably look to God's character to find the essence of the human, the "imago dei." In discussions of genetics, the most frequently invoked divine characteristic is God's creativity, in which many find a call to and a model for our own creativity, identifying creativity as the "imago dei" and the essence of human being as "created co-creators."

The reason that the slogan "playing God" is unhelpful, then, is not that this activity of creativity is forbidden. Rather, the problem is that the God Christians are called to follow is a very different God. The slogan "playing God" reduces the identity of God to a single characteristic — e.g., the power to create — from a single biblical story found in the book of Genesis. The God imaged in "playing God" is the God of the Enlightenment, the same God who renders the modern "theodicy" question so problematic.[30] This god — omniscient, omnipotent, omnipresent, eternal, unchanging — is not the God known in and through Jesus Christ. The Enlightenment God emerges when "religion" is conceived generically, abstracted from its stories, histories, and particularities, presented as tolerant, universal, and nonoffensive for the purpose of "dialogue."

Christians, however, know that ultimately they cannot really play God. God's power to create ex nihilo and to make a new heaven and a new earth in the future is conceptually as well as practically unavailable to humanity. We constantly exercise our ability to create and recreate — new persons, new species, new conformations of nature. Yet no matter how proficient we become at manipulating created matter, the form of our creative endeavor will be qualitatively different from that we affirm of God.

Thus, while the slogan "playing God" fails to refute a particular endeavor, neither does the recognition of our call to be creative — our status as "created co-creators" — render a blanket sanction. The vision of God's creativity epitomized in the Genesis stories must be held in tension with other biblical images: suffering servant, resurrected savior, Body of Christ. The kernel of truth hidden in the slogan is thus quite different from the way the slogan is employed.

> In the Jewish and Christian traditions "playing God" is associated with pride and arrogance, the aping of divine power, or the attempt to gain salvation without the help of divinity. It is not the *use* of power and creativity that offends but rather attributing power to one's own resources. . . . "[P]laying God" is not, in this usage, an act against morality, but rather one against faith. . . . Yet these traditions might well morally object to . . . problems with human conceits about our ability to predict or control the outcomes of our actions.[31]

4. Social Justice

Basic primary health services are unavailable to large portions of the U.S. population (over 10%); the statistics for world health are even more dismal.[32] Yet the federal government has committed to spend \$3 billion over 15 years — \$200 million per year — on the Human Genome Project. Private concerns, including the biotechnology industry, have committed even more funds. Genetic biotech companies are making huge sums of money; their activity in the stock market has made millions more for other investors. Yet scientists are not unanimous in the scientific or medical merit of the Human Genome Project or its ability to meet its goals within its timeline or budget.

Is it just to allocate this magnitude of resources to genetics when it is well known that the primary cause of morbidity and mortality worldwide is poverty, when millions of people around the world have no access to the basics of modern medicine — sanitation, antibiotics, vaccines? It is estimated that only 5% of the genome contains genes correlated with disease conditions; is the investment in the Human Genome Project proportional to its health benefits? Allied to these questions are other questions of allocation, questions of the allocation of costs and benefits. Who pays the costs and reaps the benefits? Not necessarily the same persons. It has been argued that one sector of our population — that of the unborn — currently incurs a disproportionate burden of harm, insofar as some embryos are created solely for research purposes while others deemed inferior or "defective" are discarded. Moreover, given the emphasis on screening or altering nascent life, there will be an undue impact of these technologies on women (just as women already bear the bulk of the social cost of caring for those with genetic conditions).

The current structure of health care is grossly unjust. Because of limited access to health care among many populations — especially urban and poor — health problems become concentrated in these communities. For example, they experience higher infant mortality and decreased life expectancy. As gene therapy becomes more widely practiced, we can only expect that these injustices will be exacerbated. Somatic gene therapy will likely be expensive and available primarily to those whose health insurance will cover it, and the same is true for genetically-engineered pharmaceuticals. Enhancement programs would further compound these gross inequalities and discriminatory practices that constitute our culture, insofar as those with power and means will choose what characteristics will be valued, and those characteristics will undergird their own social power. This may well concentrate genetic problems and genetically-related diseases, conditions, and attributes in economically disadvantaged sectors of the populations exacerbating social class distinctions and likely racial distinctions as well.

In the face of these statistics, it is difficult to justify a blanket recommendation to "religious groups to advocate access to reliable genetic information and counseling services. . . ." When members of religious communities take what they know of God, identity, children, strangers, control and power, learned from their activities of worship and common life, into the world of their everyday activities, they will likely not turn into genetic lobbyists. Rather, activities of Christian social ministry in the age and culture of genetics will more likely resemble activities of Christian social ministry prior to the advent of genetics: welcoming and caring for the marginalized, the sick, the less than perfect; working for justice for those who are oppressed and voiceless; identifying attitudes and practices which exacerbate unjust social structures; living in ways consistent with their convictions, and supporting others in this difficult task.

IV. Conclusion

For those of us raised in a scientific culture, and even more for those of us trained as scientists, it is difficult not to be dazzled by the abilities and potential of genetics. Gene therapy seems to hold promise equal to that of penicillin. To understand the quiet, constant and microscopic activities of chromosomes, DNA, genes and their cross-generation effects, is to be awed, for some humbled, and for those who find pleasure in understanding, to be gratified.

But those who likewise know from recent history and personal experience the proclivities of human beings and Western culture, and who find themselves shaped by the stories, the convictions, the self-understandings of the Christian community, rightly pause — to learn more, to consider together, to discuss, to pray, to evaluate. The advent of genetic medicine does indeed call theologians, clergy, and lay persons as well to *re-examine* their interpretations of creation, human nature, moral choices, the character of God, and some interpretations may emerge as inadequate or ill-formed; some, however, will emerge with new power and relevance. Genetic medicine challenges us to renew the practice of moral discourse and to renew the congregation as the place where it occurs. Without such a practice or a place, congregants will be ill-equipped to live differently in the face of the powerful, often utilitarian, interpretations and implications presented to them by genetic medicine.

Notes

1. This paper originated out of two lectures, one to a meeting of the Christian Action Commission of the Reformed Church in America held at Hope College in Holland, Mich., and the other to members of Holy Trinity Lutheran Church, Glenview, Ill. I am grateful to my colleagues Dan Dugan and Ron Mahel for their helpful editorial comments.

2. See Jeff C. Goldsmith, "The Reshaping of Healthcare," *Healthcare Forum Journal* 35.3 and 4 (May/June and July/August 1992): 19-27 and 34-41.

3. Kenneth B. Bedell and Alice M. Jones, *Yearbook of American and Canadian Churches,* 1992 (Nashville: Abingdon, 1992). For more statistical information on religion in the U.S. see, *From Belief to Commitment: The Community Service Activities and Finances of Religious Congregations in the U.S.* (Washington: The Independent Sector, 1993).

4. Religious voices have been active in ethical discussions since the beginning of the genetic era. For a brief overview of this history see J. Robert Nelson, "The Role of Religions in the Analysis of the Ethical Issues of Human Gene Therapy," *Human Gene Therapy* 1 (1990): 43-48.

5. Theodore Frank Peters, "Theological Questions Raised by the Human Genome Initiative," (Unpublished Grant Proposal 1 RO1 HG00487 — 01, Submitted to the NIH/ELSI Program, 1990): 21, emphasis mine.

6. Ted F. Peters and Robert J. Russell, "The Human Genome Project: What Questions Does It Raise for Theology and Ethics?" *Midwest Medical Ethics* (Summer 1992): 12-17, emphasis mine. It is interesting, or more precisely, puzzling, to me that these fearful backward religionists who prefer ignorance to knowledge, are accused of "supporting the *status quo.*" One could marshall significant evidence to illustrate that the current *status quo* is defined by the technological imperative: if it can be done, it must be done. The current *status quo* is one that allows no limits to technological innovation — or "transformation" in Peters' words. It takes little moral courage to give science a blanket endorsement to keep on doing what it has been doing and what it wants to do. Aristotle defined courage as being afraid of the right thing in the right situation: it takes one with moral courage, who has sufficient creativity to envision possible negative outcomes, to challenge the *status quo* and muster good theological arguments which might weigh against a particular genetic endeavor.

7. J. Robert Nelson, "Summary Reflection Statement, June 1, 1992 — Genetics, Religion, and Ethics Project: The Institute of Religion and Baylor College of Medicine, The Texas Medical Center," *International Journal of Bioethics* 4.1 (March 1995): 20.

8. Laurel Arthur Burton, Suzanne B. Yellen, and Ellen Elpern, "Making Use of the Patient Self-Determination Act," *The Christian Century* 109:20 (June 17 — 24, 1992): 617. This passage comes out of a reflection on advance directives, but the general position is reflected in literature on genetics and, given the authors' premises, can be extrapolated to genetics. While my position also promotes clergy as "educators," the literature tends to suggest that clergy be "non-directive." However, as leaders, clergy are called to be directive — not biased, but directive. It is part of their job to marshal the best arguments and social/communal resources in support of theologically sound positions. It is also part of their job to practice true forgiveness, which is not equivalent with tolerance.

9. Most are familiar with Alasdair MacIntrye's description of the incoherent state of contemporary moral discourse and his diagnosis of the problem in the severing of moral frameworks from their communal, anthropological, and traditional correlates (*After Virtue* [Notre Dame, Ind.: University of Notre Dame, 1981]). H. Tristram Englehardt has proposed a moral framework coherent with specific anthropological and sociological structures of our culture, but rather than rectifying the chaos, it renders normative the impossibility of reasoned public moral discourse informed by particular commitments (*The Foundations of Bioethics* [New York: Oxford, 1986]).

10. Allen D. Verhey, "Talking of God — But with Whom?" *The Hastings Center Report* 20.4 (A Special Supplement, July/August 1990): 22.

11. Verhey, "Talking of God," p. 22.

12. In this paper, I am attempting to focus on the clinical manifestations of genetics — that which congregants will encounter. Consequently, I will not directly engage the issue that has probably received more attention than any other — the issue of the creation of new life forms. Initial antagonists in the debate were most heated about the ability of recombinant DNA techniques and transgenic experiments to create new species or to alter the "species essence" of humanity. Some were concerned about the impact of these activities on the ecological balance; these and questions of biodiversity remain central. These issues resulted in much theological reflection on nature and creation.

13. The importance of understanding language for

adequate interpretation is revealed by a recent Harris/March of Dimes survey. Respondents were asked if they approved or disapproved of gene therapy. 89% of those polled said they approved of gene therapy while 60% of the same pool confessed that they had heard almost nothing about the technique (*New York Times,* 9-29-92, B6). Not only must one understand this language, but one must be vigilant as well, insofar as the terms and phrases used often do a good bit of marketing. For example, the phrase *therapeutic abortion* adds a new procedure to the traditional armamentarium of therapy — i.e., ending a life. Likewise, both disease cure and enhancement are included under the rubric *gene therapy.* But enhancement is beyond the traditional jurisdiction of medicine and is difficult to warrant as "therapy."

14. The original objective of the Human Genome Project, the $3 billion, 15-year federally funded research project under the auspices of the National Institutes of Health, was to "map and sequence" the human genome. To "map" the human genome means to determine the location of the 100,000 genes on the chromosomes. To "sequence" the human genome means to determine the nucleotide sequence (the . . . ATGCGCTAATGCCGTAATAGCAG . . .) of each of those 100,000 genes. Since its initiation, the objective of the project has been scaled back to try to complete the "map" within the 15-year time frame.

15. Generally, genetic testing refers to the testing of an individual, and genetic screening refers to the mass testing of populations or groups.

16. See Charles Marwick, "As Number of Trials Increases, Gene Therapy Begins to Look Promising for Medicine's Future," *Journal of the American Medical Association* 267.21 (June 3, 1992); 2854-55. ADA deficiency, a relatively rare condition affecting about twenty people worldwide, usually causes death before the age of two years. Persons with this condition lack the enzyme adenosine deaminase (ADA), required to destroy toxic chemicals in white blood cells. Without it, white blood cells die and the immune system ceases to function. In ADA deficiency, the nucleotide sequence in the ADA gene is abnormal, usually caused by a mutation rather than inheritance. The mutation could be in the form of erroneous replacement of as little as one nucleotide by another or by the loss (or addition) of one or more nucleotides somewhere in the sequence. The altered sequence encodes an abnormal enzyme that does not function or causes insufficient production of ADA.

17. Retroviruses, like viruses, are essentially packets of DNA. They function by breaching a cell's external membrane, inserting their own DNA into the genomes of invaded cells, and reproducing themselves when the host cell reproduces. A mouse virus, however, does not exhibit pathological characteristics in human beings.

18. Over the next few years, one of the greatest areas of expansion in human gene therapy experimentation will probably be in the treatment of cancer. (See Natalie Angier, "Scientists Report Novel Therapy for Brain Tumors," *New York Times,* June 12, 1992, p. A12.) A novel and accidental protocol was reported in June 1992 for the treatment of brain tumors. Based on experiments with mice, researchers will inject genetically altered mouse skin cells into a patient's brain tumor. These cells have been designed to serve as virus factories, releasing steady pulses of harmless viruses into the surrounding tumor mass, where they can infect the tumor cells in the manner just described. Each of the viruses will carry a copy of a gene from a herpes virus which should make the infected tumor cells susceptible to a potent anti-herpes virus called ganciclovir. The viruses will be given a week to infect the tumor cells, and then the patient will be given ganciclovir, which should kill the tumor cells. What makes this experiment particularly remarkable is its specificity. The delivery viruses can only invade cells that divide. Brain cells do not divide, while tumor cells often reproduce at an expedited rate. Thus, the ganciclovir will only affect tumor cells and the normal brain tissue will not be harmed. In the fourteen mice on which this experiment was carried out, the brain tumors completely vanished in eleven and regressed significantly in the other three.

19. Allen Verhey has noted that the public debate surrounding the ethical dimensions of genetics has generally been limited to two issues: freedom and the weighing of risks and benefits (utility) ("The Morality of Genetic Engineering," *Christian Scholar's Review* 14 [1985]: 124-39). I think the current idiom for these two issues is choice and control. This focus engenders at least two problems. First, it masks the kind of assumptions that lie behind notions of freedom and utility — about the future; technology, nature, of our relationships to each other. Second, it shortcircuits reflection on more fundamental questions, namely, questions about "the sorts of persons we would be and become or about the kind of society we would be or become" (ibid., p. 126).

20. James D. Watson, quoted in *Science* 243 (January 13, 1989): 167.

21. G. R. Dunstan, "Gene Therapy, Human Nature,

and the Churches," *International Journal of Bioethics* 2.4 (October-December 1991): 236.

22. Ronald Cole-Turner, "Religion and the Human Genome," *Journal of Religion and Health* 31.2 (Summer 1992): 170-72.

23. "Religion and the Human Genome," pp. 171-72.

24. We can find evidence of this position in, again, Ronald Cole-Turner: "[W]hen it is a question of the genetic health of the unborn, in most genetic diseases there are only two medical interventions, pregnancy prevention and pregnancy termination. . . . Couples at risk who do not wish to forgo having offspring, and all other couples who are not screened, and conceive a child with a genetic defect, are left with the only remaining option: abortion" ("Religion and the Human Genome," p. 165). Clearly, bearing, welcoming and raising the child is not an option. He continues: "To do nothing (that is, to allow the pregnancy to continue) is to choose that a life of pain be allowed to continue to the point that the pain is experienced. It is to withdraw the only available act of mercy. But the only act we can offer is to terminate the prospects of an individual human life, precious to God even if destined to painful brevity" (ibid., 166). To be clear, Cole-Turner does not limit these statements only to genetic diseases that promise severe and unrelenting pain; they are general.

25. For fuller discussions of the meaning of children see Verhey, "Morality of Genetic Engineering," and Stanley Hauerwas, *Suffering Presence: Theological Reflections on Medicine, the Mentally Handicapped, and the Church* (Notre Dame, Ind.: University of Notre Dame Press, 1986); *Truthfulness and Tragedy.* (Notre Dame, Ind.: University of Notre Dame Press, 1977); and *Vision and Virtue* (Notre Dame, Ind.: University of Notre Dame Press, 1974).

Robert Davis, "What New Adam Lurks Inside the Gene Splice?" *New York Times,* March 15, 1987.

27. "Morality of Genetic Engineering," p. 134.

28. David A. Grimes, "Technological Follies: The Uncritical Acceptance of Medical Innovation," *Journal of American Medical Association* 269.23 (June 16, 1993): 3030-33.

29. C. Keith Boone, "Bad Axioms in Genetic Engineering," *The Hastings Center Report* (August/September 1988): 9-13.

30. See Stanley Hauerwas's discussion of this notion of God in *Naming the Silences: God, Medicine, and the Problems of Suffering* (Grand Rapids: Eerdmans, 1990).

31. Boone, "Bad Axioms," p. 10.

32. To quote from the Christian Medical Commission of the World Council of Churches: "In Asia, Africa, the Pacific and Latin America. . . . Seventy percent of the people live below the poverty line with little access to services like health, education, housing, land, food, and stable jobs. . . . In Brazil, for example, 6 million of the 10 million mentally ill are children, and 500,000 children die of malnutrition every year. Eighty-five percent of the 450 million people in the world who suffer from disability come from developing countries, which have only 2% of the resources to treat and care for disabilities" (*Healing and Wholeness: The Churches' Role in Health* [Geneva: Christian Medical Commission, 1990], pp. 24-25).

73 Genetics: The British Conversation and a Christian Response

Church of Scotland Board of Social Responsibility

The Clothier Report

In November 1989 the Government set up the Committee on the Ethics of Gene Therapy under the chairmanship of Sir Cecil Clothier. In January 1992 it produced the *Report of the Committee on the Ethics of Gene Therapy* ('The Clothier Report'). Among its main conclusions and recommendations, the Committee recommended 'that somatic cell gene therapy should, for the present, be conducted according to the discipline of research and governed by the exacting requirements which already apply in the United Kingdom to research involving human subjects' (chapter 8.5). The Committee found that 'Somatic cell gene therapy will be a new kind of treatment, but it does not represent a major departure from established practice, nor does it, in our view, pose new ethical challenges' (chapter 8.8). However, on the issue of germ line gene therapy, the Committee reported: 'we have concluded that there is insufficient knowledge to evaluate the risks to future generations. We recommend, therefore, that gene modification of the germ line should not yet be attempted.'

Emeritus Professor Margaret Stacey (formerly Professor of Sociology at the University of Warwick) was one of those invited by the subsequent Nuffield Committee to respond to its Report at the public Conference the Committee organised in London in March 1994. She also submitted comments on the Clothier Report. These comments were unpublished, but she supplied a copy to the Board of Social Responsibility Study Group, and gave permission for the Board to refer to them.

Professor Stacey warned: 'The social and cultural changes which may result from gene therapy have been ignored by the Committee. Consequently consideration of a range of ethical issues is omitted. In chapter 3 there is recognition that attitudes in future may change (3.2). However, there is no overt recognition that the introduction of genetic manipulation will itself inevitably change perceptions and beliefs about what is proper for individuals to ask others to do to them or their children. . . . The very concept of what it is to be a human being has already begun to be changed by prenatal diagnosis.'

She comments that: '. . . changes which may be wrought in beliefs and values are not referred to. Much innovative practice in human reproduction has already changed social values. The introduction of prenatal tests has modified expectations about childbirth and placed new responsibilities on mothers to avoid the delivery of an impaired neonate. . . . The new definitions required for parenthood embodied in the Human Fertilisation and Embryology Act show how far assisted reproduction has already changed social reality. Such changes have wider social and cultural consequences than for the relatively few infertile women and men to whom the procedures are applied. . . .'

As we have seen, it was the finding of the Clothier Committee that somatic cell gene therapy will be a new kind of treatment, but, in their view, 'it does not represent a major departure from established medical practice', nor does it 'pose new ethical challenges'.

Professor Stacey commented: 'Given the failure to examine the entire social and cultural area the claim that no new ethical principles are involved cannot be made. There is social science evidence to suggest that the use of prenatal diagnosis has changed a woman's experience of pregnancy and

---

From the Church of Scotland Board of Social Responsibility, *Human Genetics: A Christian Perspective,* edited by William Storrar and Iain Torrance, pp. 27-37, 59-63. Abridged and edited from the original. Used by permission.

initiated social and cultural changes about the meaning of motherhood, the acceptability of impaired children and adults. What the implication of these changes in the longer run may be has yet to be established; not all may be benign. . . .'

Professor Stacey concluded 'that the only conditions under which gene therapy could be permitted to proceed would be under carefully controlled conditions . . . social and cultural conditions must be satisfied as well as medical ones'. She recommended 'that the regulatory body should include social scientists as well as medical scientists and social workers or counsellors as well as medical practitioners. It should also include persons who have genetic disorders and members of ethnic minorities. At least half the committee should be composed of women, given the burden of treatment they would bear in the case of manipulation of embryos and also for the care of the impaired.'

The Nuffield Report

The *Nuffield Council on Bioethics* was set up in 1991 to consider the ethical issues provoked by the advances in biomedical research. It focused on the question of genetic screening for its first report, and in December 1993 it produced an excellent, authoritative and careful document entitled: *Genetic Screening: Ethical Issues.* It is worth reporting in some detail the range and conclusions of this report, before developing certain particular lines of criticism and comment. It addresses the crucial initial questions of consent and confidentiality.

The 'Nuffield Report' identified four initial issues in the area of genetic screening:

1. There may be a wide margin of error in assessing the risks affecting individuals and families.
2. The results of screening may raise issues of such importance for a family that it might well become difficult to apply the established principles of confidentiality between a physician and an individual patient.
3. A satisfactorily ethical handling of the new information yielded by screening might make considerable demands on professionals and health resources (this brings in questions of *appropriate* counselling and *informed* consent).
4. There is a danger of possible eugenic abuse.

The Report saw the need to create a broad framework of public understanding, in which the issues of proper consent, confidentiality and monitoring could be located.

In this identification of issues, we would highlight two aspects in particular: genetic knowledge is unusual, in that the information it provides seeps from one person to others (and it is this which raises different questions about confidentiality and what constitutes adequate — or informed — consent); and this knowledge (like any knowledge) is not simply a matter of 'cut and dried fact' which may be absorbed and assented to purely rationally, but requires a social context within which it is perceived as knowledge, and accepted and put to use. It is such a context which the Report calls for, by means of increased public awareness and education in genetics.

Consent

After an account of what genes are, and a description of current (1993) programmes of genetic screening, the Nuffield Report addresses the questions of providing information and obtaining consent (chapter 4). That is, it considers the information it considers people need to decide whether or not to accept screening, and the meaning and the implications of 'informed consent'. It notes that consenting to screening is different from consenting to treatment. With treatment, the individual initiates the process (seeks help). With screening, there is a process initiated (offered) by some other agent, to an individual who is apparently 'well'. Consenting to screening is different from consenting to treatment, as families are implicated when genetic information is discovered. These family members may not be in close touch, and may not have given consent to being screened. Informed consent also involves facing and thinking through unintended consequences: possibly protracted therapy; possibly termination of a pregnancy; possibly avoiding having further children. It is also the case that a test result may give no certain prediction, but a range of possibilities which have to be assessed.

To make a beginning, the Nuffield Report quotes the Department of Health's 1990 circular, *A Guide to Consent for Examination or Treatment.* This stipulates that patients are entitled to receive *sufficient* information to understand the proposed treatment, the possible *alternatives,* and the *risks.* Patients must be allowed to decide whether they will agree to the treatment, and they may refuse or withdraw consent at any time (Report, p. 31; Department of Health, NHS Management Executive, undated, chapter 1, paragraph 2). Building on this, the Report suggests that the kinds of information a person needs before consenting to being screened include:

1. How serious is the genetic condition which may be disclosed?
2. How variable are its effects?
3. What are the therapeutic options?
4. How is the disorder transmitted (dominant, recessive)?
5. What is the significance of being a carrier?
6. What is the reliability of the screening test?
7. The fact that screening may reveal unwanted information (paternity).

The implication of the Report, understandably enough, is that if one can provide this, one is providing *sufficient* information for *informed* consent. It allows that especially difficult questions emerge with the identification of late onset diseases like Huntington's disease or Alzheimer's disease. Is abortion an acceptable option when the probability of a late onset disease is identified? The Report notes that future screening programmes will have to provide a more precise understanding of 'late onset', and the implication is that this will then give sufficient information for informed consent. Our concern, as the Church, is to try to address these dilemmas at a more fundamental level. Information may only be received and make sense within a specific context. Within what context (culture) then will such information (of late onset disease, carrier status, etc.) make sense? How does a specifically Christian culture receive *this* kind of news? How does the possibility of being a carrier affect our self-understanding? Are we the kind of community which can give a welcome to the non-standard or disabled? Are we the kind of community which will reject those who will later develop disease? Such issues force the Church to ask what kind of community it is, and what is the understanding of hope which it brings to the world.

The Report underlines the importance of avoiding any hint of coercion in genetic screening programmes (p. 34). It notes (p. 35) that a review of routine screening for Down's syndrome in antenatal care indicated that the information provided was 'often not adequate and that women are not always sure of what tests they have undergone or what the results mean'.

The Report notes that in most pilot projects, written information has been supplemented by counseling. But, drawing on the results of two London trials to introduce genetic screening, it notes how difficult it was to convey adequate information to people who did not perceive a need for the knowledge that the test would supply (p. 36). It maintains that genetic matters are complex, but 'can be explained . . . by means of written material plus a brief discussion' (p. 36). It notes that counselling should be 'non-directive', but admits that in practice a dialogue which helps an individual is 'unlikely to remain completely neutral'. It suggests that counseling should include stress on: the voluntary nature of the screening, and the freedom and responsibility of the individual to decide; the importance of ensuring that the individual understands the purpose of the test and the significance of a positive result; an assurance of confidentiality coupled with a stress on the responsibility of individuals to inform partners and family members; an emphasis, at each stage, that consent to screening does not imply consent to any specific treatment or to the termination of a pregnancy. The Report also offers careful consideration of procedures to be adopted when attempting to gain informed consent from minors and the mentally ill or those with severe learning difficulties.

All of this chapter of the Nuffield Report is careful and conscientious. We note how it struggles to define adequate information, and to quantify it. We would suggest that part of the Report's difficulty is in thinking that 'information' is neutral, and that if you give enough information of the right kind, you reach 'adequacy'. Building on the Nuffield Report, we would suggest that one cannot bring about *consent* without producing *commitment*, and that one cannot produce commitment without arousing the *will*. The will is partially fuelled on 'fact' (physical data, statistics), but only partially. The Nuffield Report is right to stress the 'factual' side, as any responsible authority must endeavour to be truthful. But the will is also fuelled by *vision* (a creative, integrating understanding of how everything hangs together), which cannot be quantified. It would follow that we would want to suggest that 'adequacy' of information is not just a matter of quantity, but also of vision: it is information located within a context which has the power to sway the will.

The question then arises, with these new genetic questions, of the nature of the vision with which the statistics are received. As the Church, the community of those who respond to the self-giving life, death and resurrection of Christ, we have a distinctive and costly social vision. This must include a commitment to the vulnerable and the weak. Faced with new questions, new responsibilities and new dilemmas, the Church must re-examine its self-understanding. Is it really a community formed by the costly love of Christ?

The Church must be concerned not just with information and statistics, but with the impact on and consequences for the whole person when it considers the reception of any genetic/screening information. It must unleash its imagination to think of new ways of supporting those who are most in need. Our vision differs from that of Nuffield. A practical instance of this is the Board of Social Responsibility's new unit for severely disabled children at Springburn in Glasgow, called The Mallard.

Confidentiality

We turn to the way the Nuffield Report addresses the question of the results of genetic screening and the issues these raise for confidentiality (chapter 5 of the Report).

The Report suggests that after screening, an individual should normally be fully informed of the result. There may be difficulties, if screening produced results which are unwanted, unexpected and not covered by previous consent.

However, the Report sees more tractable difficulties where the screening of an individual produces results which seriously affect the interest of others. It notes that the perceived interests of members of the same family may sometimes clash. The writers of the Report reviewed existing case law, professional guidelines and current academic writing of the application of the principle of confidentiality where information arises which might be vital to the well-being or future of other family members (p. 42). The Report noted that 'in such clearly defined contexts, it may be appropriate to treat those family members as a "unit" and to place less emphasis on individual patient autonomy' (p. 43). This is an interesting comment, to which we will return later.

However, the approach taken to the problem by the Report is along more traditional lines. It allows that the accepted standards of confidentiality should be followed as far as possible. Where the application of such standards would result in grave damage to others, it suggests that health professionals should seek to persuade the individual to disclose the information. The report opens the idea that in exceptional cases, health professionals might be justified in disclosing genetic information to other family members, against the individual's wish. To cover such cases, the Report recommends that the appropriate professional bodies prepare guidelines (p. 53).

On what basis is this conclusion reached? The Report quotes Article 8(1) of the European Convention of Human Rights, which upholds the right of everyone to privacy in home, family life and correspondence (p. 44). The Report allows that there may be disagreement about the extent to which privacy is to be protected, but concedes that there is such a thing as privacy. Yet it goes on to refer to Article 8(2) of the European Convention, which provides that the individual's right to personal privacy may be overridden by legally introduced requirements to protect health or morals or the rights and freedoms of others (p. 45). Thus the Report acknowledges that a claim to privacy is not absolute. Others may claim to have a legitimate interest. The strength of that claim will vary: A relative for whom non-disclosure might lead to an unnecessary termination has a different claim from a query as to whether a prospective partner is likely in the long term to suffer from breast cancer (p. 45).

Similarly, the Report shows how confidentiality is protected by common law principles; the Data Protection Act 1984; and professional rules of conduct (the General Medical Council's guidelines). Yet none of these defend a confidentiality which is absolute: each provides for confidentiality to the individual to be overridden in exceptional cases where disclosure is in the public interest, or to prevent injury or other damage to the health of any person or persons.

Having established both that confidentiality is important and that it may be breached, the Report addresses the question of how to broker the exceptional cases. Against the suggestion that there be created a legally enforceable duty on the part of the individual to disclose information, or that doctors should be placed under a legal duty to reveal information, the Report attempts to develop the notion of the responsibility of the individual (p. 49); 'We adopt the view that a person acting responsibly would normally wish to communicate important genetic information to other family members.'

The Report allows that, exceptionally, an individual may withhold information from malice. Here it accepts that the individual's wishes may properly be overridden by a doctor (p. 50), and it recommends that professional bodies prepare guidelines (p. 53).

How are people to comment on this handling of the question of confidentiality? In our consideration of adequate information to produce informed consent, we suggested that the Report relied too much on a model of rationality alone. In this chapter, dealing with the issue of confidentially, we suggest the Report over relies on a model of private individualism.

It begins by noting the complexity of confidentiality, where others than the individual screened may have a legitimate interest in the result. But what is the understanding of humanity, the framework within which this question is complex? If you begin with a hard, post-Enlightenment understanding of the individual, then confidentiality will either be absolute (a basically Kantian stance), or up for utilitarian grabs (a basically Millian stance).

If people are to take genetic information seriously, it may be that the Churches can help us to unclench from individualism and have a different vision. We suggest that the discovery of genetic knowledge invites us, at least at certain levels, to unpick post-Enlightenment individualism. People are not such separate, isolated persons as they thought. This in turn leads to another question:

What kind of society are we that genetic information should be perceived as such a threat that we might want to hug it to ourselves? Are there alternative ways in which personhood may be protected, not by rules of privacy, but by a common vision of respect and mutual interdependence and help?

This is to build upon the instinct of the Report noted above, that it may be appropriate to treat family members as a 'unit', placing less emphasis on individual patient autonomy (p. 43). Having painted itself into a corner defending individualism, the Report attempts to extricate itself by appealing to the individual's sense of responsibility. It is not clear that this argument will work. Such a sharply defined individualism is not other-directed. By beginning where it does, the Report does not have a grammar which will lead it out of the problem it identifies: it has no bridge to lead it into the social solidarity it sees as a solution. By starting in a different place, and offering a different vision of community and inter-relatedness of people, which comes from our worship of the Trinitarian God, the Church may be able to show the way toward a more hospitable and responsive reception of genetic information, because we are committed to providing a context in which persons are genuinely valued and we are less afraid of others.

Stigmatisation

Chapter 8 of the Report addresses a third major ethical issue: the fear that genetic screening will lead to the *stigmatisation* of non-standard individuals. Stigmatisation is defined as 'branding, marking, or discrediting because of a particular characteristic' (p. 77). The stigmatisation of individuals is linked to *eugenics*; the belief 'that it is possible and desirable, through selective breeding and the elimination of undesirable individuals, to alter the hereditary qualities of a race or population' (p. 79).

The Report allows that 'there have always been

some negative social reactions to disability in all its forms' (p. 77). It goes on, somewhat helplessly, to point to a paradox in our modern society: on the one hand an effort is made 'to create an environment in which people with a disability are accepted into society and seen as having a worthwhile life'; on the other hand 'resources are spent on preventing their births'. It cites the fear that an emphasis on the genetic differences between ethnic groups could increase social discrimination (racism).

What may be done to avoid this? The Report may be aware of its vulnerability on this score. It suggests that proper educational programmes should reduce these dangers. 'A well-informed individual is less likely to feel stigmatised than a poorly-informed individual who has received little or no counseling' (p. 79). It continues, more effectively, 'it could be argued that, if we all found out our genetic variations, then there would be less concern about stigma.' Its major conclusion is that as a safeguard against eugenic abuse, the Report's recommendations on 'adequately informed consent, confidentiality and the central coordination and monitoring of genetic screening programmes' should be implemented (p. 81).

May we, as the Church, take this any further? We would suggest that stigmatisation is the downside of the celebration of rationalistic individualism. On that model of human action and society, it would be almost impossible to avoid (we tend to define ourselves by vilifying others).

Are there any other possibilities? If we have genetic knowledge (and we do), must we inevitably have stigmatisation, racism and eugenics? One line of response would be to confine genetic screening and engineering to the therapy of *serious* illnesses. A difficulty here is how to take account of the extent to which illnesses are socially constructed (as Margaret Stacey has reminded us). Another line of response would be to acknowledge more wholeheartedly the extent to which 'disability' is a social construct (Margaret Stacey tells us: 'What is disabling varies from one society to another depending on the nature of the society', in her comments on the *Report of the Committee on the Ethics of Gene Therapy*). There are cultures which prize sameness (all males over six foot, blond and blue-eyed). There are other cultures which glory in variety. Similarly, what is considered responsible, even what is considered expensive (in terms of the consumption of time and money), are socially defined. If genetic knowledge, rather than making us more competitive (possessive of the knowledge of 'our' genes), can teach us that we are more interdependent than we thought, we will all gain from it. This may be another avenue in which the Churches can take the lead. . . .

Traditionally the Church, through the work of the Board of Social Responsibility, has offered imaginative care to the disadvantaged and disabled. At a national level the Board offers residential care and ongoing respite care to families in a number of centres including Keith Lodge, Stonehaven, and the new purpose-built unit called The Mallard at Springburn, Glasgow. Such units care for young people with profound mental and physical problems. In Lanarkshire, the Cornerstone Project provides care in small groups for adults who would otherwise be hospitalised for the duration of their lives.

Underlying this care is the Christian view that all people are made in God's image, and are precious in his sight. The image of God is not distorted in the weak, the disabled or those suffering from genetic illness. Jürgen Moltmann has the view that there is really no such thing as 'the handicapped'. There are only people — people who have this or that difficulty, which makes the society of the strong and capable unjustly label them as 'handicapped'.

In the dilemmas of genetic screening and testing, Christians must offer people choices that are right for them. As genetic screening increases, there must be a concern that pressure will be brought to bear on parents not to have the children who are diagnosed before birth as suffering from disability. Maureen Ramsey points to this danger: 'So if a woman decides against prenatal screening or abortion when she is found to be carrying a foetus with a genetic defect, it becomes her shame, her guilt, her responsibility for the way the baby turns out. The end result becomes not her fate, but her fault' (*Genetic Counselling: Practice and Principles*, 1994, p. 253).

Parents may decide not to terminate a pregnancy, and such a decision may be contrary to the advice of professionals who may feel pressured by the financial restraints of the NHS. They may feel isolated at having a child who is regarded by others as 'a burden on society'. Such stigmatisation is anathema to Christians. Pastorally, parents making such a decision should receive support and confirmation, and continuing support as the child grows. We should not underestimate the anguish parents face in such circumstances. As one mother of a severely handicapped son (Professor Frances Young of Birmingham University) wrote for the Study Group: 'If I'd known in advance what our lives would hold I couldn't have faced it — his distress and my answering distress have at times been unbearable. But I thank God I was never faced with a decision about abortion. . . .'

Society in general is adopting a hypocritical approach to the disabled. While buildings and public places are rightly being altered and adapted for the use of the disabled, financial resources socially and medically are in danger of being diverted from their care. Lack of knowledge about certain conditions, particularly the less well publicised ones, can lead to a lack of understanding as to what restrictions in living the individual has.

Does the Church take seriously whether the disabled person can join other people around the communion table? Or are the physical restrictions too great? What of the embarrassment a carer may feel when a disabled person disturbs other worshippers? Whilst physical barriers can be removed, attitudes are more difficult to change.

For the Church the disabled must be more than objects of care. Frances Young speaks of disabled people belonging to society, not just through acceptance, but in being able to contribute. If they are truly to be persons, we must learn to receive from them.

Society can offer not only care to those who are disabled, but also the opportunity to influence decision-making on the care. Grampian Regional Council has implemented Sections 1 and 2 of the Disabled Persons Act. These give the disabled user of services the right to have an advocate or representative to speak on their behalf and help them in their dealings with staff, thus influencing decisions. Christians may feel this is a way of empowering and giving choice to disabled people.

The church must be sensitive to the fears of families about future care of loved ones and affirm the importance of adequate provision for them. The growing emphasis on care in the community, while it has a positive, imaginative and exciting side, also requires careful monitoring to ensure that proper funding and facilities are not only made available, but continue to be available.

Conclusion

The Board of Social Responsibility's aim in preparing this book has been to put human genetics in perspective. Contemporary developments and issues in human genetics have been set within an informed and balanced scientific perspective and a distinctive theological and pastoral perspective, all within the wider perspective of the public debate on bioethics. In a fast-changing discipline like human genetics, it is not possible to offer final conclusions. However, it is desirable to have such a responsible Christian perspective to offer the Church, and to offer our wider society guidance on an important topic that will increasingly affect all our lives. In this book, the Board of Social Responsibility has drawn attention to how future work should be undertaken to stimulate further thought and action by the Church. It is appropriate, then, that the last word should go to a Church member and close relative of a child with cystic fibrosis, who offered the Board of Social Responsibility Study Group on Human Genetics this personal testimony:

> You ask for comment on the 'predicament' of families facing cystic fibrosis, but there are two. There's the day-to-day predicament and, for want of a better word, the theological one.
>
> The day-to-day one is more easily defined and so unfairly allotted. It seems so cruel a burden on young parents. Grandparents and others might have shared it more when extended families were situated to give more mutual support. But we're hundreds of miles away, not up a close round the corner.
>
> We learn to welcome good intentions and kind words that go wrong because inevitably the well-wishers repeat each other. They so obviously wish they could remember just what was that more hopeful story about research they read in the papers; and they all say: 'There's so much more can be done nowadays.' Yes, but. . . . Besides, we feel guilty ourselves.

For me it's not just guilt — mixed with relief perhaps — that we can't be there to help with the physio and the daily worries. At long range it's easy to put the best gloss on things, always believing reassuring words on the phone about infections and minor illnesses, awkward enough with 'normal' children. We worry, and weep inwardly, but at our age our working and leisure lives or career prospects won't be overshadowed and possibly affected by the strains. But for the parents?

Maybe we subconsciously avoid long-term worries too. Like parents, we live in hope that medical progress already extending life expectation for CF sufferers will continue at its recent rate, even achieve the Great Breakthrough. But perhaps we secretly hope to opt out; to be gone before the troubles of CF childhood, mitigated by love and protective care, give way to the limitations and limited expectations of the teenage and young adult years.

I feel guilty about the extent to which grandparents can shut it out or switch it off. Even in insisting that we're treating all the family alike, we may help the pretence that they are all alike.

Yet I ought to believe that ultimately we are all alike, dependent on grace and with whatever equality of opportunity for eternity is consistent with what Paul says about predestination. I wish I did more firmly, and that may be a factor in feeling guilty about the theological predicament. It is because my faith isn't strong enough that it's not tested more?

Ought I to be railing against the Almighty, asking how unfairness fits into his perfect love, wondering how our girl will react to the Gospel miracles of healing? At the very least, should I not be setting out to do a Milton and justify the ways God to man? Instead there are different reactions amid the silent tears. A new insight into the power of love; a new sense of the uniqueness of human personality; a new scepticism about arguments for terminating a life once conceived. Perhaps also, amid unavoidable perplexity, a new revelation of the aptness of seeing God as our Father. Whatever else my grand-daughter is denied, I think (as I watch her parents cope) she will surely grasp the power of that metaphor, and also of the love of Mary for the child with so strange a destiny.

74 The Search for Shalom[1]

Hessel Bouma III

It is 1983. Mr. and Mrs. White are school teachers with two children, a 4-year-old daughter and a 3-year-old son, and are members of the local Lutheran church. Very ill as an infant, their son has been hospitalized twice, and tested for many things but without any definitive diagnosis. At wit's end and shooting in the dark, their pediatrician suggests, 'You know, I think we ought to test your son for CF (cystic fibrosis).[2] Just to rule it out, because I'm sure he doesn't have it.' The very next day the Whites travel with their children to the nearest large city where their son is tested. He tests positive! Before the news even sinks in, the clinicians suggest their daughter be tested also. She tests positive too! Years later, Mrs. White recalls that day as 'the worst day of our lives' and that the only initial information given them was 'Your children are going to die'.

Educated and resourceful, the Whites seek second opinions. Different tests confirm the CF diagnoses. Again, the results are presented coldly and negatively, though with a caveat, 'There are degrees of severity. We do not know how your children will do.' For the impending school year, Mr. and Mrs. White continue their teaching jobs but take their children out of preschool and arrange for Mrs. White's parents to care for them. At the end of the year, Mrs. White leaves her job

---

From Hessel Bouma III, "The Search for Shalom," in John F. Kilner, Rebecca D. Pentz, and Frank E. Young, eds., *Genetic Ethics: Do the Ends Justify the Genes?* The Center for Bioethics and Human Dignity.

to care for her children full time; Mr. White frets that he may never be able to change jobs lest they lose their health insurance coverage of the children. With the encouragement of a hospital social worker, they try out a CF support group but do not join since most of the group consists of people with similar, recently-diagnoses cases and a dominant woman whose daughter was so ill she never attended public school, was hospitalized regularly, and died at the age of seventeen. Their search for information in textbooks is similarly depressing — badly dated and showing CF patients with 'grotesque looking children'. One notable exception, however, is some very educational material from the Cystic Fibrosis Foundation. Ultimately they are referred to an elderly pulmonary specialist. Knowledgeable, patient, openly honest, the doctor restores their confidence, gives them realistic hope, and places them in contact with a group doing genetic research on cystic fibrosis. Within the year the children are participating in an enzyme study.

With strong parental support and good medical attention, both children are doing quite well. Mrs. White begins to see herself as a 'CF Mom', packing enzyme pills and medications in her children's lunches, writing notes to teachers about special concerns, filling out insurance forms *ad infinitum*, and patiently biting her lip as well-intentioned relatives and friends tell her, 'Maybe the doctors are wrong' or '[T]hey're going to outgrow it'. She continues to mull over the admonition of her pediatrician, 'Don't plan to have any more children'.

As the Whites' children continue to do well, Mr. and Mrs. White decide to try to have additional children, though only with prenatal diagnosis, to avoid having another child with cystic fibrosis. When Mrs. White becomes pregnant, CVS (chorionic villus sampling) at nine weeks reveals the fetus will have cystic fibrosis, and they abort the pregnancy. But two more pregnancies result in two healthy children after similar testing with CVS indicates that the fetuses will be carriers but not affected.

The Whites' children are now 17, 15, 9, and 7. The parents continue to ponder whether to tell the younger children they were tested for CF. Would their older children then ask, 'What if testing had been available with us? Would you have not allowed us to be born?' Asked whether they ever shared any of the initial diagnoses, thoughts of having additional children, or prenatal testing with their Lutheran pastor or congregation, the Whites respond, 'No'.

We join a second family in 1990. Mr. and Mrs. Smith are in their late twenties and run their own paint contracting company. Self-employed, they are uninsured. Having been raised in a dysfunctional family, Mrs. Smith left the church as a child, took drugs, and had an abortion as a sixteen-year-old. Ultimately committing her life to God, she is also committed to avoiding her family's previous mistakes. Shortly after their marriage, Mr. and Mrs. Smith become members of a large, full gospel, non-denominational church.

Mrs. Smith did not want a large family but always envisaged herself with one, maybe two children — boys. It turns out she has two daughters, now aged five and two. When she becomes pregnant again, she is devastated. Thoughts of putting three kids to bed at night and going grocery shopping with three children depress her. She does not want this baby and privately prays that she will lose it.

In the fourth month of her pregnancy, she agrees when her obstetrician suggests she have a maternal serum test. The test indicates she may have a 'problem pregnancy', perhaps a Down's syndrome baby. She and her husband are referred to a nearby hospital for an ultrasound. The friendly, outgoing technician performing the sonogram suddenly becomes really quiet, stops the procedure prematurely, and leaves the room. A few minutes later, the head of radiology enters, tells her to get dressed, and indicates that her doctor wants to see her. As she dresses, the radiologist takes Mr. Smith aside, telling him that the baby's head is four times larger than it should be and the stomach is outside of the abdomen. Later, in the doctor's office, the doctor tells them the baby does not have a chance but has a serious disorder (later identified as Trisomy 18[3]). He urges them to abort immediately, giving Mrs. Smith vaginal suppositories to take that same night in preparation for labour the next day.

However, Mrs. Smith responds, '[We] go to a church where we believe in miracles. We believe

God's still alive and he still cares about his people and he does things for them. He's active in their lives. [So] we thought we'd just pray and trust God and ask for a miracle'. From the doctor's office they go to her mother's home and tell her the news. Then they call their pastor who says, 'It's not my place to make this decision for you. You need to pray about it'. So the Smiths wait and ask the congregation to pray for them too.

When the Smiths inform the doctor and his staff of their decision not to end the pregnancy, they sense the staff are disapproving, curt, even full of ugly feelings and hate. But as the pregnancy progresses, the staff soften, begrudgingly appreciating the Smiths' commitment to their unborn child even at considerable inconvenience, expense, and substantial risk to Mrs. Smith's health.

> I felt guilty because I thought, 'I didn't even want him, and now he's sick and he's dying'. I was desperate. I loved him and I wanted him. I can't explain it. I thought, 'He's gotta live. He's just gotta live'. Then, too, it was the boy that I always wanted and didn't have. We're still not over it.

Through it all, the members of their church pray for them and support them, assuring that whatever happens, they will support them. The Smiths tentatively decide that they will abort if her life is in danger.

In her seventh month, on Christmas eve, Mrs. Smith goes into labour. When relatives and friends — including four associate ministers — from church hear, they come to the hospital and briefly visit throughout labour. As the time for delivery comes, the doctor arrives — the same doctor who had urged them to end the pregnancy — and the room is cleared. Through his own tears, the doctor delivers their son and lays him on his mother's chest. In the ensuing hour, relatives and friends gather with them and their dying son, looking at him, holding his hand, touching his face. He lives one hour. (No extraordinary or ordinary medical treatments were provided.) God has answered one of her most fervent prayers: he was born alive.

It is Mrs. Smith's mother who staunchly insists on a viewing and funeral. Through many tears, shared with many relatives and friends both within and outside the Christian community, the healing begins.

In retrospect, Mr. and Mrs. Smith remain grateful for a prenatal diagnosis which enabled them to prepare for the birth and death of their son. They are also profoundly grateful to their supporting church community, led by a senior pastor whose wife had experienced several miscarriages and had reluctantly ended another pregnancy under exceptional circumstances.

We again turn back the clock to 1990. A third set of parents, Mr. and Mrs. MacDonald, are both college educated. He is employed in the oil and gas industry, she as a sales representative for a major international business firm. When his firm fell on hard times, it ceased providing any health care benefits; so they are grateful for family health coverage through her employment. They are members of the local Catholic parish, though a recent change in priests has diminished their connections and commitments. They have one son who will be turning five shortly and Mrs. MacDonald is expecting their second child — a boy as identified on an otherwise uneventful ultrasound test. In March, Mrs. MacDonald goes into premature labour, which her doctor successfully stops. An amniocentesis the next day indicates that the fetus's lungs are insufficiently developed, so she takes ritodrine for four weeks. Upon C-section delivery, the obstetrician immediately notes Matthew has a partial cleft lip and club foot. Their pediatrician assures them, 'These are everyday problems. This is nothing.'

In ensuing weeks, Matthew has difficulty eating and gains no weight until put on cereal. At four months, a plastic surgeon operates to repair the cleft palate and an orthopedic surgeon corrects the right leg. But when Matthew is taken off the anesthetic, he ceases breathing and needs to be resuscitated and intubated. He is discharged after a ten-day hospitalization. By age of six month, Matthew is still not sitting up. When therapists cannot explain his developmental delay and therapy produces minimal advances, the pediatrician suspects cerebral palsy. An MRI and an EEG over a three-week period rule out cerebral palsy but do show inadequate myelination. The specialists muses, 'We just have to hope he catches up'.

By Matthew's first birthday, Mrs. MacDonald is depressed at the thought of giving him a birthday party, since he will not even know it. In desperation, she asks her pediatrician to initiate some chromosome tests. Three weeks later, when the results indicate there may be a problem with chromosome #5,[4] the pediatrician laments that he really does not trust that lab. They repeat the test. Three weeks later, the doctor informs them that Matthew has a piece missing from the middle portion of chromosome #5. It is extremely rare, it happens at conception, and, explains the doctor, he has never seen a little child with this particular problem. He says he does not know what prognosis to offer except that Mr. and Mrs. MacDonald are looking at severe handicaps, severe retardation, and severe hypotonia. Mr. MacDonald passes out.

Gradually the MacDonalds' lives change. Dad takes responsibility for their oldest son, mother for Matthew. Mrs. MacDonald undertakes to educate herself about chromosomal deletions. Matthew's health necessitates that he stay at home, so Mrs. MacDonald rarely ventures out except to work and to the medical library where the frequency of her visits necessitates monthly parking passes. By August, 1991, when she develops stomach pains, she is sure it is a well-earned ulcer. On the contrary, it turns out that she is pregnant despite being on the pill.

Her mother says, 'Pregnancy is always a cause for joy'. Mrs. MacDonald returns to her obstetrician and insists, 'Schedule a chromosome test'. Though chromosome tests had shown that neither she nor her husband have a chromosomal deletion, they feel they cannot have another child like Matthew. So a sample of chorionic villi are taken and sent for chromosomal analysis. Three weeks later the test results are in. Of twenty duplicate sample, nineteen show no problem, one is unclear. Unsatisfied that the risk is low enough, she insists on an early amniocentesis two weeks later. Three weeks later they are informed the chromosomes look fine and they have a little girl, whom they decide to name Christina.

As time passes, Mrs. MacDonald continues to bear the principal burden of caring for Matthew. Her amount of sleep decreases as her worries increase. Can she care for Matthew as well as Christina and her older son? She explores alternatives for Matthew. Finally a woman in the state capital who does placements for the state refers her — because they are Catholic — to a place in an adjacent state. It is a home called 'Holy Angels' run by an order of nuns known as 'Our Lady of Sorrows'. They provide continuous care for fifteen babies as well as teenagers and adults who, developmentally, are like one-to-four-year-old children. Very ambivalent about whether institutionalizing Matthew is the appropriate thing to do, the MacDonalds are greatly encouraged by an afternoon visit to 'Holy Angels'. Two weeks later, after reviewing Matthew's foot-thick medical files, the Catholic sisters promise to accept him several weeks before Christina is born.

The experiences of the Whites, Smiths, and MacDonalds illustrate a host of issues facing persons with genetic conditions today.[2] *To what extent will we allow our genetic heritage to determine who we fundamentally are?* Are the Whites who are carriers or affected with cystic fibrosis, is a baby Smith with Trisomy 18, or is Matthew MacDonald with a deletion of part of chromosome #5 fundamentally different from other human beings in any way that can possibly justify the stigmatization and ostracization associated with genetic conditions? What are the impacts of labelling on persons with genetic conditions or parents and relatives of someone with a genetic condition? How can the stigmatization and ostracization be eliminated, the labelling minimized, and the dignity of all persons, regardless of genetic identity, affirmed?

Should the presence of a genetic condition in a person affect the health care coverage, insurability, or employment of that individual? Mr. White and Mrs. MacDonald perceive themselves as locked into their present jobs so that health care coverage for their children will continue. Would losing or changing their jobs prevent them from obtaining group health insurance coverage with their new employers because their children have 'pre-existing conditions', or is current legislation now sufficient to protect them from this problem? Are the Whites' healthy children less likely to be considered for employment because they are identified as carriers of a genetic condition? Did the Smiths' lack of health insurance preclude diagnostic or treatment options for them? Could a health insurance carrier legitimately tell the Whites it will cover the CVS prenatal testing only if they agree to abort any fetus who will be affected with cystic fibrosis? On the average, persons like the two White children with cystic fibrosis average two weeks per year of hospitalization and annual medical care costs of $10-15,000. Institutionalized care such as Matthew MacDonald receives at 'Holy Angels' currently runs between $250-300 per day, or around $90-100,000 annually, paid for by Medicaid, state and federal funds, and Catholic charities (including vows of poverty taken by the Catholic sisters who run the home).

While some states (eleven at the last count) have enacted legislation to eliminate genetic discrimination, it is too soon to tell how effective these efforts are. Furthermore, the majority of states have yet to address these issues. There is a twofold challenge to society and religious communities here: to support health care reform and efforts to end discrimination in employment aimed at eradicating injustices and to contribute to organizations and individuals providing care for persons with genetic conditions.

For what purposes should genetic tests be developed and used? For example, should the Whites' oldest daughter have been tested pre-symptomatically? Should the potential spouses of all the White children be tested before marriage? Should the Smiths have undergone maternal serum testing if they were opposed to pregnancy termination? Should Mrs. MacDonald be permitted to insist on amniocentesis, with its slight risks, just because the CVS results were 95% rather than 100% conclusive?

Given the rapid pace of developments in genetics and the Human Genome Project, what is the prognosis for persons with genetic conditions? Genetic conditions may be quite variable. For example, CF may be characterized as sub-mild, mild, moderate, or severe. Can we accurately narrow the range of prognoses given to families with a genetic condition? Is it realistic for the Whites to hope for a cure for cystic fibrosis in the next few years? Do we pursue means of curing baby Smith's Trisomy 18 by removing the additional genetic material or curing Matthew MacDonald's partial deletion of chromosome #5 by adding the missing genes? Or do our best hopes lie in identifying and developing better treatments for symptoms and in delaying the development and progression of symptoms? Experience to date indicates that true cures for genetic conditions are years to decades away. For single-gene conditions, the development of new, innovative therapies is a realistic possibility but will require considerable time and resources. They are, therefore, more likely to be achieved for common genetic conditions than for rare ones. For many conditions, compassionate care and symptom management remain the most realistic hope.

Should genetic testing and counselling be regulated? Are there circumstances in which society should forbid genetic testing, e.g., for sex determination? May anyone do genetic testing and counselling, or should some measures of certification and quality control be required? The Whites, Smiths, and MacDonalds were all initially counselled by health care professionals untrained in genetic counselling; their initial experiences were deplorable and regrettable. In contrast, each is highly appreciative of the counselling they ultimately received from trained genetic counsellors. Are there genetics laboratories of dubious quality such as the MacDonalds apparently encountered? Or was their physician 'buying time' for a confirmation test from a second laboratory in light of the grim prognosis? May genetic counsellors, other health care practitioners, or religious leaders be directive (rather than non-directive) in their counselling? The Whites experienced directive counselling in both the testing of their oldest daughter and their pediatrician's admonition not to have more children. The Smiths experienced directive counselling from their obstetrician urging pregnancy termination almost immediately upon diagnosis.

Should the reproductive choices of persons who are carriers of or affected by a genetic condition be limited? If so, should these limits be placed by society, by one's religious tradition, voluntarily by the individual? Should the choice of whether or not to have another child by a couple at risk for a genetic condition be limited to pre-conception choices? Should the Whites be told, 'No more children'? Should they have to bear special penalties if they have another child with cystic fibrosis either intentionally as a result of taking the 24% risk of having another affected child or as a consequence of contraceptive failure? Is it morally irresponsible knowingly to bring into this world a child with significant genetic deficiencies?

Should pregnancy termination following maternal serum screening, sonograms, CVS, and/or amniocentesis be a regulated option? If pregnancy termination is not an allowable option, will society at large or a religious community in particular support a woman and her family in caring for an affected child? The Smiths found such support in their church; the MacDonalds found such support in 'Holy Angels'. If pregnancy termination is accepted, will society cease to care or in some ways curtail the treatments available for individuals already afflicted with a genetic disease? Will society limit its search for better treatments and cures for genetic diseases? Will women be coerced, subtly or overtly, to abort their unborn with certain genetic conditions, thereby causing women to become tentative about their pregnancies until everything is seen to be 'right'? If pregnancy termination were to be limited to severe genetic conditions, can a meaningful line be drawn between severe and less severe genetic conditions?[6]

Finally, virtually everyone with a genetic condition at one time or another wonders, 'Why me? What did I do to deserve this?' For members of religious traditions, the questions reflect a crisis of theodicy. If God is good, if God is omnipotent, then why am I suffering from this condition?[7]

How can religious traditions better address the issues of theodicy and assist members in their individual struggles with genetic conditions? The 'new genetics' poses difficult questions necessitating deeply personal and moral decisions. Unfortunately, most families appear to be like the Whites and the MacDonalds — very hesitant to involve members of their religious communities in their decisions, perhaps fearing superficial answers, rash judgment, and a lack of support. But there also are remarkable examples of religious communities such as the Smiths', who support people through their difficult decisions. There are other models as well, such as the 'Holy Angels', who provide exemplary, compassionate care.

This chapter represents a concerned effort on the part of many people both to appreciate genetic challenges and to appraise genetic possibilities. It emerges from a commitment

> to promote life, not death; health, not sickness,
> to suffer and counsel with those who suffer,
> to care compassionately when one cannot
> cure, and
> to be a part of God's presence in the valley of
> the shadow of death. . . .

in short to search for shalom.

Notes

1. This essay draws upon interviews of actual families published in Hessel Bouma III and Andy Lustig, eds., *Case Study Interviews* (Houston, TX: The Institute of Religion, 1992). The three accounts are all from the perspective of the families; only the names have been changed to provide a measure of anonymity. The interviews were conducted with Mrs. White, Mr. and Mrs. Smith, and Mrs. MacDonald and her mother. Readers should resist the temptation to generalize from these accounts about either specific genetic conditions or the responses by particular religious traditions.

2. Cystic fibrosis (CF) is the most common, fatal (current median life expectancy in late 20s), autosomal recessive disease in Caucasian populations. Approximately 1 in 25 Caucasians are carriers; between 1 in 2,000 and 1 in 3,000 are affected. The disease is characterized by a sodium and chloride salt imbalance, and thick mucus which contributes to chronic lung infections and pancreatic and digestive tract deficiencies. After decades of research, the CF gene was mapped to chromosome 7q31.2, cloned, and sequenced in 1989. Between 70 and 80% of persons with CF have a 3-base pair deletion which causes the cystic fibrosis transmembrane conductance regulator (the primary gene product) to lack one amino acid, phenylalanine, in the 508th position of 1,480 amino acids. Another approximately 500 different mutations in this gene have also now been described. Treatments consist of 'clap therapy' to loosen thick mucus, antibiotics, dietary enzymes, and psychosocial support. On the average, persons with CF spend two weeks/year hospitalized with average annual health care costs in the $10,000-15,000 range. For further information: Welsh, Michael J., Lap-Chee, Tsui, Boat, Thomas F. and Beaudet, Arthur L., 'Cystic fibrosis', in Scriver et al., eds., *The Metabolic and Molecular Basis of Inherited Disease* (New York, McGraw-Hill, Inc., 1995), pp. 3799-3876; U.S. Congress Office of Technology Assessment, 'Cystic Fibrosis and DNA Tests: Implications of Carrier Screening', OTA-BA-532 (Washington, DC, U.S. Government Printing Office, August 1992); *On-line Mendelian Inheritance*

in Man (http:www3.ncbi.nlm.nih.gov/Omim/); Cystic Fibrosis Foundation, 6931 Arlington Road, No. 200, Bethesda, MD, 20814.

3. Trisomy 18 is a genetic condition due to the presence of an abnormal number of chromosomes: three copies of chromosome #18 rather than the normal pair. It is due to a failure of the chromosomes to migrate appropriately (nondisjunction) to separate daughter cells during the formation of gametes. It appears to occur more frequently in the formation of eggs, correlates with increasing maternal age, and occurs approximately once in 5,000 liveborn infants. It is characterized by an abnormally small jaw, multiple malformations, severe failure to thrive, and an average life expectancy of approximately 6 months. For further information: Beaudet, Arthur L., Scriver, Charles R., Sly, William S. and Valie, David, 'Genetics, Biochemistry, and Molecular Basis of Variant Human Phenotypes', in *The Metabolic and Molecular Bases of Inherited Disease,* (New York: McGraw-Hill, Inc., 1995), pp. 66-68; Support Organization for Trisomy (SOFT) 18/13, c/o Barb Van Herreweghe, 2982 S. Union Street, Rochester, NY, 14624.

4. The deletion of a piece of a chromosome is usually quite rare and occurs randomly (unless it occurs in the formation of one parent's reproductive organs). The severity of any deletion is dependent upon the number of genes lost and how essential the lost genes are for normal functioning. Relatively simple diagnostic tests can identify gross deletions, but until the human genome map is completed, assessing how many genes are missing is difficult at best. Establishing any accurate prognosis is similarly problematical. For further information: Ledbetter, David H., and Ballabio, Andrea, 'Molecular cytogenetics of contiguous gene syndromes: Mechanisms and consequences of gene dosage imbalance', in *The Metabolic and Molecular Bases of Inherited Disease* (New York: McGraw-Hill, Inc., 1995), pp. 811-39; National Organization for Rare Disorders, P.O. Box 8923, New Fairfield, CT, 06812-8923.

5. Many of these issues have been identified as part of the Ethical, Legal, and Social Issues (ELSI) initiative of the Human Genome Project. See U.S. Department of Health and Human Services and U.S. Department of Energy, *Understanding Our Genetic Inheritance. The U.S. Human Genome Project: The First Five Years, 1991-1995.* (available from the National Technical Information Service, U.S. Department of Commerce, Springfield, Virginia, 22616). Cf. Genetics, Religion and Ethics Project, 'Summary Reflection Statement', *Human Gene Therapy* 3:525-27 (1992).

6. Several Christians have attempted to develop relevant criteria. For example, Bouma III, Hessel, Diekema, Douglas, Langerak, Edward, Rottman, Theodore, and Verhey, Allen, *Christian Faith, Health, and Medical Practice* (Grand Rapids: Eerdmans 1989), p. 227, discuss cases like Trisomy 18 and Tay-Sachs (in which the infant experiences a period of unrelenting pain and then dies). Cf. Jones, D. Gareth, *Brave New People* (Downers Grove, IL: InterVarsity, 1984), p. 178; and Wennberg, Robert, *Life in the Balance* (Grand Rapids: Eerdmans, 1985), pp. 142-43.

7. In the complete series of interviews from which the cases of the Whites, Smiths, and MacDonalds are taken, most families candidly described the struggles of their crisis. If families had a strong, good relationship with their religious community, they were far more willing to seek and accept advice and support from them. Christians, for example, commonly consult Smedes, Lewis B., *How Can It Be All Right When Everything Is All Wrong?* (San Francisco: Harper & Row, 1982); Biebel, David B., *If God is So Good, Why Do I Hurt So Bad?* (Colorado Springs: NavPress, 1989); Hauerwas, Stanley, *Naming the Silences: God, Medicine, and the Problem of Suffering* (Grand Rapids: Eerdmans, 1990).

75 Ethical Standards for Genetic Intervention

James C. Peterson, Ph.D.

The Bedouin in the Negev desert traditionally live in tents and move from place to place with their camels. Some camels can be quite curious. It is not surprising to find a camel sniffing under the edge of a tent, trying to discern what smells so interesting inside. One learns quickly that even if one does not mind a pair of large nostrils sniffling nearby, one needs to strike the muzzle with a sandal or hand directly, lest the whole camel soon be inside the tent. Camels seem much larger inside the tent than outside of it.

A commonly raised concern in discussions of genetics and ethics may be referred to as the 'camel's nose under the tent argument'. Sometimes it is called the slippery slope or the thin edge of the wedge. The concern is that taking certain acceptable steps may lead to a camel in the tent (or a thick end of a wedge, or a bottom of a slope) that one never intended. In terms of human genetic intervention, how do we use it where it serves well, without allowing it where it does not belong? Is there a way that we can consistently distinguish appropriate from inappropriate use?

Consider the case of panic disorder. About two percent of Americans sometimes find their heart suddenly racing. Many first assume that they are having a heart attack. They are overwhelmed with a feeling of utter terror, but without being afraid of anything in particular. In ten to fifty minutes the terror subsides, only to return when people least expect it. The attacks are distributed through families in a way that implies inherited susceptibility. Would it not be helpful to diagnose genetically the condition before the first attack, so that people could be warned? Would it not be a positive contribution to limit the attacks by pharmaceutical or someday even genetic intervention, if that could be done without adverse side effects? What would make such treatments fall within or outside appropriate intervention?

A Christian Context

Chapter 25 of the biblical book of Matthew — in which Jesus instructs his disciples on what to do in the time between his resurrection and his return at the last day of judgment — contains several themes directly applicable to our question. Today is still the in-between time about which Jesus spoke. Matthew 25 contains three stories. Each one raises issues that the next one answers. The first story is of ten maidens watching into the night for the coming of the bridegroom. The wait was so long that five of them ran out of oil for their lamps. While they were away buying more, the bridegroom came and they missed the wedding feast. The story reminds us always to be ready for the return of Jesus Christ. It could be before the completion of this sentence. On the other hand, it may be a long time. It has now been almost 2,000 years since Jesus gave people this warning. One must have both the foresight to prepare for the long haul (bringing enough oil) and the perseverance to endure. So what then are we supposed to do in the meantime?

The story that immediately follows answers that question. It tells of a master who left five talents with one servant, two with another, and one with a third, to each according to his ability. When the master returned he was pleased to see that the first and second servants had doubled their talents. The master was outraged, however, to discover that the third servant had simply buried the entrusted resource in order to return exactly what he had received. He had failed in his responsibility to multiply the resources the master had given to him. The first story in Matthew 25 warns that we should always be ready, but we may

From James C. Peterson, "Ethical Standards for Genetic Intervention," in John F. Kilner, Rebecca D. Pentz, and Frank E. Young, eds., *Genetic Ethics: Do the Ends Justify the Genes?* The Center for Bioethics and Human Dignity.

have to wait some time before the second coming. The second story tells us that the intervening time should be spent wisely in God's service, producing fruit from what he has entrusted to us. We are responsible to employ and multiply our God-given resources. In other words, we are to have our suitcases packed and ready to go, but not merely hang out at the airport.

So how should we put our God-given talents to work? What goals would God have us pursue? The next and last story in the chapter answers that question. It is a description of the final day of judgment. Those who belong to God's kingdom are separated from those who are not according to how they treated their neighbours. Those who fed the hungry and clothed the poor, cared for those who were sick and visited those in prison, are welcomed into God's kingdom. Those who did not are cast away. Good works do not earn a place in God's family; rather, they are characteristic of people who are in God's family. Such actions do not achieve salvation but they do reflect it. In the second chapter of Ephesians we read that we are 'saved by grace through faith, lest anyone should boast'. Sometimes neglected, the next sentence reads 'for we are his workmanship, created in Christ Jesus for good works'. These good works are a result of reconciliation with God, not the cause of salvation. Reconciliation with God is a free gift that, if fully received, will affect how one treats others. If one is being shaped by God as a child of God, one will come to care about what God cares about. God cares deeply about people.

The examples of expressing love for one's neighbour in these biblical passages address meeting physical and social needs such as feeding the hungry and caring for those who are sick. Apparently matter matters. In the first chapter of Genesis, Adam is described as made from the dust yet uniquely inbreathed with God's spirit. We human beings have a special calling, yet are of this earth. Being physical beings is not a bad thing. God created both this material world and our physical form and declared them 'good'. The physical is not our ultimate concern, but we should care about it because it is a part of God's creation and our stewardship.

Jesus lives this concern in his incarnation, teaching, and action. In the historic Christian tradition, Jesus is not only God among us but also the perfect example of what human beings are meant to be. Jesus came first and foremost to reconcile us with God, yet he also gave of himself in caring for people's physical concerns, sometimes to the point of utter physical exhaustion. In John he gives the commission that 'as the Father has sent him, so he now sends his disciples'.[1] We should actively care for people's physical concerns as he did.

Moreover, in all three of these sections of Matthew 25, errors of omission (not bringing enough oil, not multiplying talents, not caring for those in need) are treated as seriously as acts of commission. Pride is a serious danger, but so is sloth. Until the Lord returns, we are to do our best here. That includes our best effort to serve others, including addressing their physical needs.

This is only one chapter of the rich biblical tradition, but it is not an isolated one. Its themes are found throughout Scripture. They remind us to ask first, as we should of any potential tool, how human genetic intervention can best serve our neighbours. Asking that question is not trying to be God; it is following God's mandate to be of service.

Drawing the Line

Now remember the camel, which provides a great service to the Bedouin but does not belong in the tent. Usefulness in one context does not insure usefulness in another. Recognizing the potential service of human genetic intervention is not sufficient. We must ask under what circumstances it is possible to intervene without causing great harm. Thinking ahead is part of the mandate required of us, as illustrated in the story of the maidens and lamp oil in Matthew 25. How do we separate appropriate service of human genetic intervention from destructive use? The Parliamentary Assembly of the Council of Europe, the French National Ethics Committee, Canada's Royal Commission, and others have stated that genetic intervention is acceptable when it affects only the presenting patient. Such is called 'somatic cell therapy'. In contrast, 'germ-line therapy', a type of intervention which potentially affects future generations, would never be appropriate.[2] Others have argued that somatic therapy is the appropriate stopping point for pragmatic reasons. Germ-line intervention is not ruled out in principle; rather, it is ruled out until it is safe and reliable.[3]

However, the distinction between somatic and germ-line intervention is not the best place to draw the line between acceptable and harmful intervention. While the somatic/germ-line distinction is clear conceptually, in practice some somatic interventions will have germ-line effects. For example, a person who would not otherwise have been able to pass on a deleterious gene may be enabled to live to child-bearing age. The distinction misses the mark morally as well. If genetic surgery is safe and beneficial for one person, why not protect his or her children from having to endure the same genetic harm or repetitive somatic therapy?[4] The stakes of a mistake are greater, but so are the potential benefits. It is not possible to obtain informed consent from the future descendants, but neither is it for infants for whom we often act. When a child is born with a cleft palate, a largely inherited condition, we do not wait for the child to reach the age of eighteen for adult permission to do the needed surgery. Nor do we refuse to intervene because God sovereignly designed the child to be that way. We trust that God is pleased to work through us to improve the child's ability to speak and eat. If somatic therapy is warranted in some cases, germ-line extension of that change is probably so as well.[5]

The distinction between cure and enhancement does not provide a much better line.[6] First of all, it is a very difficult line to discern.[7] The distinction seems to fade the more closely it is analysed. All correction involves enhancing capacity. One who was blind is now able to see. One who was crippled is now able to walk. The difference between the two is that correction is limited to achieving 'normal' levels.[8] But what are normal levels?[9] Human characteristics generally fall within a range. Some people's vision is 20/60; others' is 20/10. If we correct to average in that range there will still be people who have better sight than average. With the lower abilities eliminated from the calculation by correction to the average, the average will increase. What was beyond normal will become normal. If we define correction as rescinding disease or disorder, what is disease?[10] Do we define disease as that which produces pain and suffering? If so, then childbirth and teething are diseases, for they are certainly painful. If disease is departure from the statistical norm, red hair and AB blood type would be diseases. If disease is departure from the statistical norm that the individual does not want, personal values would define disease differently from one person to the next. The syndrome of 'Drapetomania' was described in great detail in the *New Orleans Medical and Surgical Journal* in 1851.[11] According to the article's author, physician Samuel A. Cartwright, it is the disease that causes a slave to want to run away.

If we tie correction to today's average, why such loyalty to our current state? If we tie the norm to our pre-sin state, how do we know what that was? How is removing 'the effects of sin' any clearer than removing 'disease'? Even if one could discern our physical pre-fall state, why make that the final standard? To do so would require the assumption that pre-sin Adam was God's final intent for human physical form. Do we actually know that? Why consider Adam the pinnacle and not the starting point? God has created a world where acorns take decades to become fifty-foot oaks. It would be a bit disconcerting for squirrels and hikers if acorns sprang to mature size upon first contact with the ground. Our physical and spiritual lives are characterized by birth followed by a lifetime of growth, rather than instant maturity. God has chosen to design a world that works that way. We can never 'out-design' God. Is it not possible that God might sovereignly choose to develop further our design through us? The point is not to try to be God; it is to listen, prayerfully and thoughtfully, to what the one and only God would have us to do.

Five Standards

What would our Lord have us to do? It is much easier to raise questions than to make concrete proposals. However, as an alternative to the somatic/germ-line and cure/enhance criteria, I would propose the following five standards for recognizing if an intervention is appropriate. Any genetic intervention should be:

1) Incremental

Human genetic intervention should be incremental in degree and breadth of implementation. We are finite beings who do not begin to understand the interrelated complexity of our own bodies. The more I learn in genetic labs and clinics, the more I find myself humming the doxology. I am again and again awed at God's design in two senses. First I wonder at what I do see. One example is the 3,000 million base pairs of DNA in each cell of the human body, which would uncoil and stretch out to about two meters in a straight line. That is the proportional equivalent of stuffing thirty miles of fine fishing line into a plump blueberry, in such a way that the line could be unwound, copied, and restuffed at will. Secondly, I wonder at what I do not see or understand. At this point we do not even know what purpose most DNA serves. Only about ten percent of it is transcribed into mRNA for making proteins. What is the other ninety percent doing? It may be important for expression, structure, or some other function. At this point we do not know.

The pattern is consistent in human endeavours: more knowledge results in more awareness of what we do not know. One can learn a great deal about Thailand on a two-week visit, including some of its language, history, geography, and culture. Such new knowledge often reveals questions one would not have even thought of before. For that reason, growth in knowledge is not only fascinating and worthwhile. It is also humbling. When people as finite human beings are absolutely sure about anything, including genetics, they probably do not fully understand. The ones who most fully understand will rarely be absolutely sure (or at least so it seems). By pursuing genetic intervention incrementally, we can minimize the degree and extent of unexpected harms.

2) Choice-Expanding

We should also pursue only those interventions that enhance a person's options by freeing that individual from what is clearly destructive or by increasing the person's capability. Human development is immensely complex. Genetic intervention will more often be able to influence formation than determine it. Using that influence to enhance a person's bodily defenses against cancer or to increase incrementally one's aptitude for memorizing vocabulary, would not predestine the individual to a particular life. It would contribute to the range of options available for the individual's pursuit and achievement. In contrast, interventions that would limit the recipient — attempting to predestine the individual to a narrow end — would claim an arrogant authority over the recipient and show a lack of respect for him or her as a person. For example, it would not be appropriate for deaf parents to choose deafness for their child even if they preferred deaf culture to hearing culture. Deafness limits options. C. S. Lewis made this point for entire generations in *The Abolition of Man.* He argued that the first generation that would have the power so deeply to shape the next generation should not use it in a way to predestine the next generation's choices.[12] Each generation should be able to further or undo the last generation's contribution as they learn from its effects.

3) Parent-Directed

Genetic intervention decisions should be made primarily by the persons to be affected, or if that is not possible, by their parents.[13] Decentralizing choice in this way would first of all help to protect valuable diversity. Second, it would take into account what some have called the only empirically verifiable doctrine of Christianity, original sin. Only a generation ago the horrible crimes of the Holocaust were committed under the claim and cover of racial hygiene and eugenics. People will abuse any powerful technology if they are not held accountable. When one prefers sight to retinoblastoma, a genetically-based disease involving blindness, one is valuing a particular genetic endowment over another. That judgment is not nefarious. It is better to be able to see than not to be able to see. In contrast, the Nazi Germany claim of eugenics was horrifying on the following two counts, among others. First, the preferred genetic endowment was defined in terms of race — a characteristic which, even if clearly definable, would be irrelevant to well-being.[14] If genetic intervention decisions were made primarily by parents, no racial group would be in a position to use such choices destructively against another. Second, having other than the desired genetic endowment (or politics, or IQ, or health history . . .) was grounds in Nazi Germany for taking that person's life. However, a person's ongoing life and worth does not depend on genetic heritage. Persons should be protected and nurtured from their beginning, regardless of genetic endowment.[15] Parents are central to meeting that need and so are particularly well-suited to make genetic intervention decisions for their children.

4) Within Societal Boundaries

What if parents intend to make abusive or even simply foolish choices to the detriment of their own children? A fourth standard is that society should set minimal, broad limits for intervention. An example of such a constraint would be the first standard above — that any genetic intervention should be incremental. Living within some minimal societal limits is how we currently deal with education and medical care. Clearly recognized minimums are required of all parents, although they are free to satisfy such minimums in a variety of ways. Parents may home school their child or choose a private or public school, but as parents they are required to provide a basic education for their child. Children may go to a chiropractor or Chinese herbalist, but life-threatening conditions must be addressed or parents will answer to the state. There is no end of conflict at these intersections, but that is the nature of accountability in a sinful world.

5) By Acceptable Means

Means are often as important as ends. First, the form of genetic intervention should be as non-invasive as possible for all involved.[16] This is a difficult goal to achieve in some cases; making a change that would multiply throughout the body would probably require intervention at the earliest stages of pregnancy. Second, zero risk is impossible. We cannot achieve zero risk at the dentist's or driving to school, but it is reasonable to limit the risks we take to those proportionate to the intended benefits. Such a criterion is as applicable to genetic interventions as to other aspects of life.

While these five standards can help keep the camel's nose out of the tent by providing criteria to distinguish acceptable from unacceptable interventions, another version of the camel's nose or slippery slope argument remains unanswered.[17] Even if there is a clear conceptual difference between acceptable and unacceptable interventions, this conceptual difference may not be honoured in the real world, either in the choices of individuals or in the formation of social guidelines. Once we head in a certain direction we may run roughshod over appropriate stopping points.[18] This danger is exacerbated by the pervasive self-deception and distortion of individual and corporate judgment characteristic of our sinful state. The most powerful motivators for intervention might even be defensive in nature. If countries or individual parents see children other than their own receiving enhancement safely and to their economic advantage — e.g., through improvement in some aspect of intelligence — they will have a strong incentive to intervene similarly in their own children in order to remain competitive.[19]

If a corporation has invested millions in developing a genetic technology, it will promote its use to gain a financial return.[20] A good illustration of this is the recent direct marketing of cystic fibrosis carrier screening on British television.[21] Not only do standards for genetic intervention need to be developed, but also warranted confidence that such standards will be honoured. Otherwise, the long-term results could be more harmful than beneficial.

Genetic intervention will never yield a utopia.[22] Genetics cannot solve all physical concerns, nor is human life only physical. Published hopes that genetic intervention might deliver us from homelessness, alcoholism, criminality, divorce, and more, expect more than physical change can provide by itself.[23] But genetic intervention within the five standards suggested above can make life somewhat better for many people. If such is possible, we are responsible to our Lord as faithful stewards to pursue it. Even some instances of germ-line enhancement — ruled out by some — may fall within that God-honouring mandate. Being 'bright in the corner where we are', doing what we can to serve our neighbors, is part of our God-given commission and responsibility.

May we use the developing tool of genetic intervention wisely to that end.

Notes

1. John 17:18.

2. Parliamentary Assembly of the Council of Europe, "Recommendation 934 on genetic engineering," 1982. French National Ethics Committee, "Announcement on Gene Therapy," *Human Gene Therapy* 2 (1991): 329. Canadian Royal Commission, "*Proceed with Care: Final Report of the Royal Commission on New Reproductive Technologies,*" excerpted in *Human Gene Therapy* 5 (1994): 604. Wivel, Nelson A., and Walters, LeRoy, "Germ-line Gene Modification and Disease Prevention: Some Medical and Ethical Perspectives," *Science* 262 (22 October 1993): 533-38. Fletcher, John C., and Anderson, W. French, "Germ-line Gene Therapy: A New Stage of Debate," *Law, Medicine & Health Care* 20:1-2 (1992): 26-39.

3. Neel, James V., "Germ-Line Gene Therapy: Another View," *Human Gene Therapy* 4 (1993): 127-28.

4. Munro, Donald W., used the apt description of human genetic intervention as "microsurgery" in a speech entitled "Human Genetic Engineering, God's Gift?" at the Kepler Society, Boston, January 26, 1996.

5. Reichenbach, Bruce R., and Anderson, V. Elving, *On Behalf of God: A Christian Ethic for Biology* (Grand Rapids: Eerdmans, 1995), p. 186. Walters, LeRoy, "The Ethics of Human Germ-Line Genetic Intervention," in *Genes and Human Self-Knowledge: Historical and Philosophical Reflections on Modern Genetics,* edited by Weir, Robert F., Lawrence, Susan C., and Fales, Evan (Iowa City: University of Iowa Press, 1994), pp. 220-31.

6. For a detailed evaluation of the practical use and desirability of this distinction see Peterson, J., *An Ethical Analysis and Proposal for the Direction of Human Genetic Intervention* (Ann Arbor: UMI, 1992), order number 9237575 at 800-521-0600.

7. Murray, Thomas, "Assessing Genetic Technologies: Two Ethical Issues," *International Journal of Technology Assessment in Health Care* 10:4 (1994): 573-82. Bouma III, Hessel, Diekma, Douglas, Langerak, Edward, Rottman, Theodore, and Verhey, Allen, *Christian Faith, Health, and Medical Practice* (Grand Rapids: Eerdmans, 1989), p. 266.

8. Anderson, W. French, "Genetic Engineering and Our Humanness," *Human Gene Therapy* 5 (1994): 755-60.

9. Pettersson, Berg K., Riis, P., Tranoy, K. E., "Genetics in Democratic Societies," *Clinical Genetics* 48 (1995): 202.

10. Juengst, Eric Thomas, *The Concept of Genetic Disease and Theories of Medical Progress* (Ann Arbor: UMI 1985). Caplan, Arthur L., Englehardt, H. Tristram Jr., and McCartney, James, eds., *Concepts of Health and Disease: Interdisciplinary Perspectives* (Reading, Mass.: Addison-Wesley, 1981).

11. Cartwright, Samuel A., "Report on the Diseases and Physical Peculiarities of the Negro Race," *The New Orleans Medical and Surgical Journal* 7 (May 1851): 707-9.

12. Lewis, C. S., *The Abolition of Man* (New York: Macmillan, 1955).

13. Resnik, David, "Debunking the Slippery Slope Argument Against Human Germ-Line Gene Therapy," *The Journal of Medicine and Philosophy* 19 (1994): 35-37.

14. Hitler, Adolf, *Mein Kampf,* translated by Ludwig Lore (New York: Stackpole, 1939), p. 281. Seidelman, William E., "Mengele Medicus," *The Milbank Quarterly* 66:2 (1988): 223. Hohlfeld, Rainer, "Jenseits von Freiheit und Wurde: Kritische Anmerkungen zur gezielten genetischen Beeinflussung des Menschen," *Reformatio* 32 (May 1983): 220.

15. Jones, D. Gareth, and Telfer, Barbara, "Before I Was an Embryo, I Was a Pre-embryo: Or Was I?" *Bioethics* 9:1 (1995): 32-49.

16. Kass, Leon, *Toward a More Natural Science: Biology and Human Affairs* (New York: Free Press, 1985), p. 109. Ramsey, Paul, *Fabricated Man: The Ethics of Genetic Control* (New Haven: Yale University Press, 1970), pp. 89, 132-37.

17. Childress, James F., "Wedge Argument, Slippery Slope Argument, etc." in the *Westminster Dictionary of Christian Ethics,* edited by James F. Childress and John Macquarrie (Philadelphia: Westminster Press, 1986), p. 657.

18. Nelson, Hilde Lindemann, "Dethroning Choice: Analogy, Personhood, and the New Technologies," *Journal of Law, Medicine & Ethics* 23 (1995): 129-35.

19. Gardner, William, "Can Human Genetic Enhancement be Prohibited?" *The Journal of Medicine and Philosophy* 20 (1995): 65-84.

20. Editorial, "Capitalizing on the Genome," *Nature Genetics* 13:1 (May 1995): 1-5.

21. Harper, Peter S., "Direct Marketing of Cystic Fibrosis Carrier Screening: Commercial Push or Population Need?" *Journal of Medical Genetics* 32 (1995): 249-50.

22. Passmore, John, *The Perfectibility of Man* (New York: Charles Scribner's Sons, 1970).

23. Holtzman, Neil A., "Policy Implications of Genetic Technologies," *International Journal of Technology Assessment* 10:4 (1994): 570-71. Proctor, Robert N., "Genomics and Eugenics: How Fair is the Comparison?" pp. 76-93 in *Gene Mapping: Using Law and Ethics as Guides,* ed. Annas, George J., and Elias, Sherman (New York: Oxford University Press, 1992).

Chapter Thirteen

ABORTION

On January 22, 1973, the Supreme Court of the United States ruled in Roe v. Wade that state laws prohibiting abortion before a fetus is viable were unconstitutional. The court held that decisions about abortion were fundamentally private decisions, to be made in the context of conversations between a woman and her physician.

The public controversy about abortion did not begin with Roe v. Wade, and of course it did not end there either. But in the years since the ruling, the debate has become increasingly intractable. The arguments by both partisans in the debate, the advocates of a woman's right to control her own powers of reproduction and the advocates of a fetus's right to life, are familiar — and remain unpersuasive to the other side.

The argument has sometimes seemed deceptively simple, the questions at least readily identifiable, if not readily answerable. The one most important question has been frequently identified as the question of the status of the fetus. On the answer to that question all the law and the prophets with respect to abortion are sometimes presumed to hang. It is indeed an important question, and answers to it have important implications for abortion. On the one side are those who claim that the genetic uniqueness and completeness of a fertilized ovum should be enough to identify it as an individual member of the human species and so worthy of all the respect due any other human individual. On the other side are those who claim that the fetus does not have the necessary or sufficient attributes of human persons and so need be neither ascribed nor granted in practice the full rights of human persons, including the right to life. In between these two poles are developmental views of the fetus which regard some stage or stages of fetal development as morally significant and as demanding increasing respect and restraint. The question "Who counts as a person?" is relevant quite concretely to the discussion of abortion, and the earlier essays of Joseph Fletcher, Oliver O'Donovan, and Stanley Hauerwas should be read alongside the essays by the authors in this section.

The question is easily identified — but not easily answered. Roe v. Wade, for example, recognized that the moral status of the fetus was the point of controversy, but the court stood back and did not pretend to be wise enough to decide this issue. A frequent criticism of the reasoning of the court, however, is that although it acknowledged its inability to decide this "difficult" question, for all practical purposes it did decide it, ruling that before viability the fetus is simply not protectable by law. The court held that the legal status of the fetus may be distinguished from the moral status and that there was no precedent for holding that its legal status entitles it to the same protection of the law extended to persons. The point is not that the legal ruling of the court was right or wrong, but that it clearly distinguished legal from moral questions. That its legal holding was taken as moral license may provide an occasion to judge our society rather than the courts.

At any rate, the issue of the relation of law to morality, of public policy to the moral passions and projects that give one moral identity, is an issue which also demands attention. Christians may have reasons for ascribing a certain moral status to the fetus which can hardly be articulated in the courts or legislatures. Though Christians may sign and seal their trust in God's future by having and loving children, by resisting the "solution" of consigning even nascent life to the realm and powers of darkness, the convictions which evoke and sustain such behavior are not legally enforceable. The issue here is the relation of public policy and personal moral discernment, and many of the essays included make certain assumptions about it. It is related (but not identical) to questions about the relation of an impartial moral perspective and a candidly Christian perspective. Whatever one thinks about the relation of social policy and Christian morality, Christians should not permit their attention to be monopolized by the legal issues. They should not hesitate to articulate their fundamental convictions about human life, even though they may not be legally enforceable. If they do, they may lose the capacity to act with integrity themselves and may abandon society to a minimal account of morality in terms of legality.

One of the reasons the question of the status of the fetus has loomed so large is the public focus on autonomy as the relevant impartial principle. Public discussion has tended to make abortion an issue of the "rights" of individuals; then the only important questions are whether the fetus is an individual person or not and, if it is, what its rights are. A woman contemplating an abortion is sometimes considered as though she were simply exercising ownership rights over her own body, like a landlady with an undesirable tenant or pest. Partisans on both sides of the debate have relied heavily on the logic and language of individual autonomy and rights, but we should ask whether a focus on autonomy can do justice to the interdependence of people, whether it can attend both to the values which people freely choose and to the values of social relations and embodied existence which are not matters of choice, and whether it can appreciate the limitations on choice imposed by social arrangements and conditions.[1] Perhaps a religious perspective would qualify or challenge the focus on the autonomy of individuals with attention to human relatedness and vulnerability.

Some feminist perspectives, such as that of Beverly Wildung Harrison (selection 80), have relied on the logic and language of autonomy and rights, but others, like Sidney Callahan (selection 81), have called attention to human relatedness and vulnerability and to the limited choices some women contemplating an abortion have. The perspective on the situation changes not only in terms of how we see the fetus, but also in terms of how we see the woman. Is she an autonomous individual exercising ownership rights over her body? Or is she a character in a tragedy — a story in which evils have gathered and cannot all be avoided, a story in which goods have collided and cannot all be sought, a story wrought in part by a social context pervasively oppressive to women? Such a woman might understand abortion as violence, as a desperate violence inflicted not only upon an embryo but upon herself, but also as a tragic necessity. If such a challenge to a focus on autonomy is accepted, and if one sees the woman contemplating an abortion in this way, then opposition to abortion may perhaps be softened but surely must be joined by an effective support system — including financial, social, psychological, moral, and spiritual — for women and their children. If tragedy is acknowledged this side of the eschaton, then Christians may acknowledge that sometimes abortion may mournfully, repentantly, tearfully be indicated. But does tragedy fit with the Christian story? Do principles or values conflict genuinely or only apparently? If tragedy is acknowledged, then Christians are obliged to say what goods can weigh against the good of life and what indications there may be for abortion as a tragic choice. When thinking about the good of life, some of the earlier readings on "Life and Its Sanctity" (Chapter 4) might be examined again.

One of the points which comes across quite clearly in this section is that there is not only a division within our society on this issue, there is also a division within the Churches. Part of this division grows out of different understandings of the history of Christianity (cf. Maguire and Burtchaell, selection 76). That history is seen as oppressive by some like Beverly Wildung Harrison (selection 80), who indict the church for its past and present sexism. Thus the question of abortion raises the issues of how we understand the Christian past and what stance we then take towards that past. It is not simply the morality of abortion which is being disputed.

Finally, it may be observed that in Roe v. Wade the court presumed that the question of abortion would be a "medical decision" and that the professional integrity of physicians would restrict what the law could not prohibit. "Basic responsibility for [the decision to abort] must rest with the physician," it said.[2] That the court's legal ruling was taken as an entrepreneurial opportunity by some physicians may be reason to judge the profession rather than the ruling. At any rate, it raises again the question of a professional ethic and its relation to a Christian ethic. Is the profession simply the body of skills learned by training and accessible to consumers, or are there goods intrinsic to medicine as a practice and a profession, goods which can be violated when the skills are used for alien ends? And can those goods, if there be such, be nurtured or qualified by a Christian vision?

The issues identified for the reader's theological reflection include the relation of social policy recommendations to personal moral decisions; the relation of a professional ethic and a Christian ethic; the appropriate perspective on the situation involving the fetus, the woman, and their wider social context; the relevance and meaning and possible conflict of a number of principles, including autonomy, the sanctity of life, the protection of the vulnerable, and the liberation of the oppressed.

Notes

1. For a perceptive analysis and critique of the focus on autonomy see Helen John, SND, "Reflection on Autonomy and Abortion," in *Respect and Care in Medical Ethics*, ed. David Smith (Lanham, Md.: University Press of America, 1984).

2. Roe v. Wade, 410 U.S. 113(1973). See also *Biomedical-Ethical Issues: A Digest of Law and Policy Development* (United Ministries in Education, 1983), p. 16.

Suggestions for Further Reading

Blustein, Jeffrey, and Alan R. Fleischman. "The Pro-Life Maternal-Fetal Medicine Physician: A Problem of Integrity," *Hastings Center Report* 25 (January-February 1995): 22-26.

Cahill, Lisa Sowle. "Abortion, Sex and Gender: The Church's Public Voice," *America*, May 2, 1993, pp. 6-11.

Callahan, Sidney, and Daniel Callahan, eds. *Abortion: Understanding Differences* (New York: Plenum Press, 1984).

Heaney, Stephen J., ed. *Abortion: A New Generation of Catholic Responses* (Braintree, Mass.: Pope John Center, 1992).

Jung, Patricia Beattie, and Thomas A. Shannon. *Abortion and Catholicism: The American Debate* (New York: Crossroad, 1988).

Nolan, Kathleen. "What Makes an 'Other': Diversity, Disability, and the Softening of Our Hearts," *Second Opinion* 19 (October 1993): 116-19.

LaFleur, William R. *Liquid Life: Abortion and Buddhism in Japan* (Princeton, N.J.: Princeton University Press, 1992).

Rudy, Kathy. *Beyond Pro-Life and Pro-Choice: Moral Diversity in the Abortion Debate* (Boston: Beacon Press, 1995).

Simmons, Paul D. *Birth and Death: Bioethical Decision-Making* (Philadelphia: Westminster, 1983).

Tickle, Phyllis, ed. *Confessing Conscience: Churched Women on Abortion* (Nashville: Abingdon Press, 1990).

76 The Catholic Legacy and Abortion: A Debate

Daniel C. Maguire and
James T. Burtchaell, C.S.C.

In February of 1987 the theology department at the University of Notre Dame sponsored a major debate on abortion. The debaters in what was locally referred to as a "heavyweight bout" were James Tunstead Burtchaell, C.S.C., and Daniel C. Maguire. Father Burtchaell is a professor of theology at Notre Dame, a former provost of the university, and the author of *Rachel Weeping: The Case Against Abortion* and other books. Professor Maguire is a professor of theology at Marquette University, a past president of the Society of Christian Ethics, the author of *The Moral Choice* among other works, and an active critic of official Catholic teaching on abortion. The proposition Burtchaell and Maguire debated was: "*Recent developments and reflection provide authentic reasons to reconsider the virtually total Christian disapproval of abortion.*"

Daniel C. Maguire

In the 1980s, when the abortion issue has been most acrimonious and mischievous in church and state, honest debate is the only way to get this abortion bone out of the Catholic throat so that we can get on to more important pro-life issues.

There are more important pro-life issues. Forty-two thousand children die daily due to lack of basic nourishment and medicine. There are now some four tons of TNT stockpiled for every head on the planet. The number of heads on the planet may reach 8.5 billion by the year 2025, with 7 billion of them being in the third world. The problems of Ethiopia are but preview of the havoc of hunger to come unless reason and justice replace militarism and greed. Meanwhile, the arms race is poised to move into outer space, leaving the earth in a state of terminal peril.

Still, the abortion debate must get on. This debate between Burtchaell and myself is important, regardless of what Burtchaell and I say. This debate implies that the issue is debatable. If the absolute negative position on abortion were clear, there would be no need to debate it. There are no pro and con debates on the morality of rape. Abortion is an open question since, as John Connery, S.J., says, "not enough time has elapsed to provide a test of current opinions." Furthermore, Catholic bishops, while pressing for a no-abortion amendment to the Constitution, have said they are not trying to force Catholic dogma into law, but to appeal to the public on the basis of reason. It is precisely on the basis of reason that Protestants, Catholics, Jews, and others disagree, and so we must reason together about our agreements and disagreements. There is no one infallible view on abortion and we do well to debate the fallible.

It may disappoint some who come to feast on conflict that Burtchaell and I are not in total disagreement on abortion. We agree in three ways: First, both Burtchaell and I are pro-moral-choice on abortion. In his book, *Rachel Weeping*, Burtchaell writes: "Save for the rare, rare instance when it is a moral threat to a mother's life to carry her child to birth, there is no abortion that is not the unjust taking of another's life because it is a burden to one's own." Pronouncing this exception "rare, rare" is, of course, an empirical, first-world judgment. Bishop Francis Simons, former bishop of Indore, India, says such cases are not at all rare in the third world. Thus Burtchaell is approving of a lot of direct abortions. He has admitted a class that has many members. In so doing, he departs

From Daniel C. Maguire and James T. Burtchaell, C.S.C., "The Catholic Legacy & Abortion: A Debate," *Commonweal* 126 (20 November 1987): 657-72. Abridged and edited from the original. Used by permission.

from the Vatican theology of abortion as, of course, do I when the circumstances warrant it.

Second, neither Burtchaell nor I is pro-abortion. Indeed, only a sadist could be "pro-abortion." Abortion is a negative value at best. In Utopia, it would be almost uncalled for. This is a matter of common sense. One would not say of a woman who had a fulfilling family and professional life, that it was a pity she had not had an abortion to lend a touch of completion.

Third, both Burtchaell and I object to the idea of "abortion on demand." I object because the term is a sexist ellipsis. The phrase implies a verb, *demand,* and an object, *abortion,* but it tellingly omits the subject, *woman.* This is significant because woman is often missing in the conservative analysis of abortion. I further object to the expression "abortion on demand" because a woman should not have to demand that to which she has a moral right. Burtchaell, it would seem, is for un-abortion on demand imposed on women. There we do not agree, and so there are grounds for debate. Basically, Burtchaell and I differ because he stakes out a definitive and apodictic position on abortion before the witness of women has been heard and evaluated in Catholic theology.

This is a major problem in conservative Catholic theology on abortion. By saying that all abortions are immoral, a stinging judgment is delivered on one to two million American women and forty to fifty million women worldwide who decide each year for abortions. The absolutist position allows for only three judgments of these women: (1) They are evil since they knowingly choose objective evil. (2) They are ignorant, and are thus excused from subjective guilt. (3) They are excused by insanity. There is no gentle alternative. We should await the newly emerging witness of women on abortion before sealing off the issue in ways that indict all or most women who make these crisis choices. This is a call for modesty, not a call to justify all abortion decisions.

I also find Burtchaell ecumenically insensitive on this issue. He seems to take no account of the broad disagreement with his simplistic position found among mainstream Protestants. The General Board of the American Baptist churches, U.S.A., said in 1981 that the decision for abortion may be morally made "when all other possible alternatives will lead to greater destruction of human life and spirit." Abortion, they continued, must be a matter of "responsible, personal decision." The American Friends Service Committee said in 1970 that "it is far better to end an unwanted pregnancy than to encourage the evils resulting from forced pregnancy and childbirth." The General Convention of the Episcopal Church in 1982 listed serious threats to the mental or physical health of the woman, deformation of the fetus, and rape and incest as reasons making abortion "permissible." The General Assembly of the Presbyterian Church affirmed in 1983 the *Roe v. Wade* decision of the Supreme Court and said the "principle of inviolability can be applied" only when the fetus is viable. The General Synod of the United Church of Christ said "every woman must have the freedom of choice to follow her personal religious and moral convictions concerning the completion or termination of her pregnancy." They also called for public funding for abortion. The United Methodist Church in their General Conferences in both 1976 and 1984 listed a number of cases when "the path of a mature Christian judgment may indicate the advisability of abortion." The Lutheran Church in America, at its Biennial Convention in 1970, said that "on the basis of the evangelical ethic, a woman or couple may decide responsibly to seek an abortion."

A number of Jewish groups have offered similar witness, including the American Jewish Congress, B'nai B'rith Women, the Central Conference of American Rabbis, the Union of American Hebrew Congregations, and the National Council of Jewish Women. It is simplistic and arrogant to treat all of these relatives in faith as insensitive defenders of murder or irresponsible abortion. The Second Vatican Council said the ecumenical dialogue should "start with discussions concerning the application of the Gospel to moral questions." Such discussions have barely begun and Burtchaell and others would bar the door by brandishing obnoxious analogies that compare persons with nuanced views of abortion to defenders of the Nazi Holocaust and racism.

The heart of this debate is the question: is the anti-moral-choice position on abortion *the* Christian and Catholic view? Are the Catholic bishops correct when they refer to the "clear and constant" teaching of the church on abortion? My answer is negative to both questions. There is no "clear and constant" teaching on abortion, and Catholic moral theology and Christian ethics generally have been pro-moral-choice ever since we started looking at the circumstances of abortion. Since, as Teilhard de Chardin said, nothing is intelligible outside its history, let us look to the history of abortion theology in the Christian church. In doing this, I will often refer to the work of John Connery. I do this for several reasons. To begin with, he holds the most conservative position on abortion since he, unlike Burtchaell and me, allows *no* exceptions. Thus I cannot be accused of bringing in a witness who shares my position. More importantly, Connery's book, *Abortion: The Development of the Roman Catholic Perspective* (Loyola, 1977) is the most important modern Catholic book on abortion. Since its publication ten years ago, it has not had the influence it deserves. I do not say Connery would agree with all my interpretations of his work. I also do not say his book is all one needs for a historical study of this issue. However, Connery's anti-moral-choice conclusions are based on his ecclesiology, not on his historical research, and that research has pro-moral-choice implications that have not been mined.

Before treating the Jewish prelude to Christian thought on abortion, Connery advises us that "the Christian attitude toward abortion will be in general continuity with the tradition of the Jews of the pre-Christian and early Christian era."

No text in the Bible discusses abortion in the terms of our debate today. The only reference in the Hebrew Bible to abortion is in Exodus 21:22 which speaks of accidental abortion. Connery says the text shows that "the fetus did not have the same status as the mother in Hebrew Law." That is certainly true. The text also suggests that the key issue was the rights of the father to progeny; he could fine you for the misdeed, but he could not claim "an eye for an eye" as he could if a person such as the woman had been killed. Thus the biblical witness on abortion.

The Roman and Stoic position from which Christians would borrow freely, stressed the rights of the *paterfamilias* and that there was no soul until birth. The Jewish Talmud taught that the fetus was a part of the mother. The Mishnah says you can kill the fetus to save the mother since it is not a child until born. Josephus criticized abortion because it "diminishes the multitude." There is no evidence of a Christian revolution against these views or for them.

In the absence of scriptural support, the modern absolutists on abortion turn to the earliest Christian writers. What they find is that those few writers who mention abortion without elaboration were opposed to it, but not as homicide. No distinctively Christian position on abortion is in evidence. Indeed, there is no theology of abortion at all, according to Connery, since he says that does not begin on the subject until the thirteenth century. (I would place that beginning in the fifteenth century.) It violates historiography and the canons of literary criticism to say that *the* Christian viewpoint on abortion starts in the early church and floats clearly and constantly through the ages.

The Didache, discovered in 1875, was not a shaper of our tradition, but it is a favorite of the anti-moral-choice faction. It seems to be the product of an isolated Christian community in Syria and it draws on Jewish sources. It offers no textual evidence of discontinuity with Jewish views on abortion. Neither does *Pseudo Barnabas,* which also had Jewish roots. Athenagoras brought up abortion in his defense against cannibalism. This is not the setting of our debate. Clement of Alexandria opposed abortion as a cover-up for fornication. We do not know what views he held on other cases since he did no theological ethics on the subject. Cyprian was concerned about the case of a man kicking a woman in the stomach until she aborted. That is a bad idea, but it is not our debate. It is text-proofing and patristic fundamentalism to pretend these texts contain, even in germ, the modern negative absolute position on abortion.

Most important of the early writers is Tertullian. In his *Apologetica,* he seems to take the Jewish position on animation at birth. Elsewhere, he inclines to the Greek view that the fetus is ensouled when sufficiently formed *in utero.* Again, eclecticism and variety. Tertullian is important on another count. He addressed what we would call craniotomy and called it a "necessary cruelty." Connery concedes that Tertullian "does use expressions which might imply a justification of the procedure in his mind." It seems that the first primitive theology on abortion is open to moral choice.

A number of fourth- and fifth-century writers adopted the Greek idea of delayed animation. Early abortion in this view would not be homicide. Augustine said that the early fetus will perish like the sperm does. It will not rise with us at the resurrection of the dead. (Neither, he assures us, will the sperm, for which we can all be grateful.) The Council of Elvira's oft-cited canons may not refer to abortion at all, and the Council of Ancyra gives lesser punishments for abortion than for homicide. These documents influenced the Penitentials which dominated the moral scene from the sixth to the eleventh centuries.

In sum, let it be said that the sparse references to abortion in the first twelve hundred years of the Christian era are set in this context: (1) All occurred before the beginning of any formal theology on abortion. (2) They rose from a period of ignorance of the processes of generation, the ovum having been discovered only in the nineteenth century. (3) They came at a time of underpopulation. (4) They came in a time of notable sexism and negativity to sexuality. (5) Abortion was often condemned as a violation of the procreative nature of sex and not as murder. As Susan Teft Nicholson says, it is "misleading" in the terms of our public debate "to maintain that the Roman Catholic church has always condemned abortion." Sometimes abortion is called homicide, but so too are contraception and sterilization, suggesting that a dominant concern was sex used non-procreatively. It is fallacious and disingenuous to say that Christian teachers always condemned abortion without saying on what grounds they did so and without saying whether one accepts and argues from those same grounds today. At least the Vatican is consistent: it applies the natural law argument that sex is intrinsically procreative and rules out homosexuality, sterilization, and birth control.

The thirteenth was not the greatest of centuries for the theology of abortion. Small wonder Connery finds it "disappointing." Albert the Great revealed the central concern (which was for sex as necessarily procreative) by saying that sterilization is more damaging than abortion. Thomas Aquinas, in his entire *Summa*, has no articles on abortion at all. He only mentions the subject in answering two objections, one on accidental abortion and one on killing a woman to baptize her fetus. (Thomas said that was not to be done.) Elsewhere Thomas accepted the idea of delayed ensoulment. The thirteenth century did not share today's obsession with abortion.

Real analytical theological ethics of abortion began in the fifteenth century. Two Thomists set the tone for what would become common opinion into the eighteenth century. Antoninus, the archbishop of Florence, and John of Naples allowed early abortions of unanimated fetuses partly because of the perceived need for baptism and also for fear for the life of the woman from a late abortion, given the crude state of surgery then. These writers allowed probability as the basis for judgment whether or not the fetus was animated, giving the benefit of the doubt, in effect, to the woman. They did this even though they believed that baptism was necessary for salvation. This presaged the modern contention of scholars like Carole Tauer that the *dubium facti* of animation was equivalent to a *dubium juris,* in the language of later Probabilism, thus justifying some abortions as moral. The opinion approving direct early abortion became common in the church and was used in confessional practice.

The sixteenth century brought the influential Antoninus de Corduba into abortion theology. He said that if medicine of its nature is conductive to the health of the woman, even if it causes the abortion of an animated fetus, it may be used. The mother had a "prior right"; her health was more important than the life of the fetus. Thus bathing, bleeding, purgatives, or pain-killers could be used even though they were abortifacient. His language lacks the precision of early twentieth-century moral theology, but he clearly used a very broad reading of "saving the woman's life." It is hard to see the treatments he discusses as being a matter of life and death. Certainly, you could not kill a person just to save yourself from pain or to get your bowels moving. Corduba expanded the discussion.

Jesuit Thomas Sanchez, who died in the early seventeenth century, said all his contemporary theologians justified early abortions to save the woman. He introduced the idea which had much resonance that the fetus may be a quasi-aggressor. As Connery says: "Anyone who reads his text can hardly doubt that he is speaking of what later authors will call direct abortion." Catholic theology was struggling with the complexities of this issue and not succumbing to the panacea of a simplistic negative absolute.

After Sanchez, other theologians argued that the fetus is a kind of unjust aggressor at times . . . or that the fetus is not a formal but a material aggressor like an insane person, and that even causes like the woman's reputation might at times be enough to justify early, direct abortions. These Catholic theologians were allowed to debate the issue freely and they did not believe like men (they were all men) who possessed a factotum principle that would solve all or almost all abortion questions.

In the mid-nineteenth century, *Revue Théologique* published an essay in which it was argued that an abortion could be performed to save a woman four or five months pregnant if she would bleed to death without the abortion. The Holy Office had already declined to solve such a case even though several of its members favored the abortion. The Jesuit Ballerini of the Roman College justified therapeutic abortions by using a novel distinction between the acceleration of the birth with the resultant death of the fetus, and direct attacks on the fetus. Another Jesuit, Augustine Lehmkuhl who died in 1917, allowed the death of the animated fetus to save the life of the woman, and he called this a probable opinion. As was admitted at the time, this was direct abortion intended as a means. Lehmkuhl said the fetus could be assumed to have surrendered its right to life just as a person can give up a lifejacket to a friend.

The nineteenth-century debates on craniotomy also showed more flexibility than the anti-moral-choice partisans today. In 1869 the Sacred Penitentiary referred a questioner on a craniotomy case to the "well-tested and reliable authors" (*auctores probati:* a term that is usually mistranslated "approved authors") for an answer. This, in effect, invoked the tradition of Probabilism for what is virtually infanticide. Even two editors of the Vatican's *Acia Sanctae Sedis* defended direct killing through craniotomy, as did a number of other theologians.

At the end of the nineteenth century, the Vatican changed its mind on these matters and tried to impose cloture on theological discussion. Here, of course, we leave moral theology and philosophy and enter ecclesiology. The ecclesiological question is: do the Vatican dicasteries possess a supernatural talent to see through and beyond the empirical complexities of these issues and are they endowed with the exclusive power to reach beyond theology and philosophy to irrefragable absolutes that are immune to informed dissent? The primitive ecclesiology that affirms such tendentially magical power bears burdens of proof that cannot be met.

As these debates arrived into the twentieth century, we can see that they had not achieved a high level of clarity. Even the critical category "direct/indirect," which still dominates the conservative position today, was a greased pig that could not be tied down. In 1932, Gregorian University's Arthur Vermeersch marked out three different meanings of "direct/indirect," and the meanings have multiplied since Vermeersch. Those who say that the "clear and constant" Catholic teaching is that you may never directly terminate fetal life are standing on a loose philosophical plank. And it is a *philosophical* plank, not a given of faith.

The abortion debate in our day has taken on an intensity it never before had. It also has a new breadth for Catholics with Vatican II's recognition of the truly ecclesial nature of Protestant communions and with the arrival of laity and women into theology. It becomes even more inaccurate to speak of *the* Christian view. This is not to say that clerical theologians have not paid some dues on the issue. On the occasion of the Vatican attack on Charles Curran, hundreds of theologians internationally declared his work well within the perimeters of Catholic orthodoxy. He justifies abortion "to save human life" or for values "commensurate with human life." These commensurate values could be grave threats to the psychological health of the woman and extreme socio-economic conditions. Richard McCormick, who is widely seen as a moderate in moral theology, finds Curran's position "very close" to his own and adds that abortion can be justified by other values "consistent with our assessment of the values justifying the taking of extrauterine life." Now, as ever, there is no one Christian view of the morality of abortion.

The negative absolutists on abortion say that the personhood question has been settled by modern embryology. This is a strange departure since the tradition has always maintained that there is something transcendent about personhood, something spiritual called a "soul" by the ancients. The mystery here cannot be settled by a materialistic and scientific analysis. The efforts to do so reveals the theological emptiness of the absolutists.

What comes close to being "clear and constant" in the tradition is the theory of what is called "delayed animation," or "ensoulment." For nineteen hundred years, the early conceptum was not seen as a person. Opinions have run the full gamut from conception to puberty! The Greek view of ensoulment in forty to ninety days was dominant, but the jurist Baldus and some of the Louvain theologians like John Marcus said the rational soul did not arrive until birth.

Significantly, there were and are no funerals for miscarriages. The Holy Office in 1713 forbade baptism of a fetus that was not well formed. St. Alphonsus Liguori spoke as a traditionalist when he said: "Some are mistaken who say that the fetus is ensouled from the first moment of its conception, since the fetus is certainly not animated before it is formed." The prestigious *Catechism of the Council of Trent* said that if Jesus was animated at conception it was a miracle because "in the natural order, no body can be informed by a human soul except after the prescribed space of time." Dominican H. M. Héring said in 1951 that the theory of delayed animation still had strong Catholic support "especially among the philosophers, who are wont to investigate the matter more profoundly than the moralists and the canonists." As Professor Carol Tauer says, if one were to argue for the presence of a rational soul, "there is better positive argument available for animals like mature dolphins than there is for human zygotes, morulae, and blastocysts."

The most intelligent way to be anti-abortion is to look to the causes of unwanted pregnancies. Too often in the past we looked only at the woman with the crisis pregnancy, not to hear her, but to stone her, picket her, excommunicate her, and call our work pro-life. We should look rather to the causes that bring women to the clinic door and attack those rather than the woman.

I would list sexism as the first cause of unwanted pregnancies. Sexism is the belief that women are inferior, and how do you make love to an inferior? Carelessly and casually. This yields the hostile inseminator syndrome. It is hostility to enter a woman's body sexually taking no account of the fact that you may thereby be entering the next century. In terms of Christian hope, the implications may be eternal.

Poverty brings women to the clinic door, since poverty breeds chaos and despair and these breed unwanted pregnancies. In this light, the military budget can be seen as a major abortifacient in our society. The largely useless budget which sucks $35 million an hour, twenty-four hours a day out of our economic veins, causes social decay with its yield of unwanted pregnancies.

The surprised virgin syndrome leads to unwanted pregnancies. This is the inability to admit that the relationship is nearing the point where it could get sexual and that moral choices are called for. Counselors are told that "it just happened," but that is not candid since the onset of sexual ardor is noticeable.

The cult of romantic love produces unwanted pregnancies. The couple in the movie who tumble into bed for the final denouement are not to be interrupted for contraceptive indignities. The sacred exigencies of romantic love must be honored whatever the cost to the woman. And there are other social evils that contribute to unwanted pregnancies: the lack of sex education, the religious ban on contraception, and the negative attitudes toward sexuality that lead to eruptive sex.

Christians might best imitate the apostle Paul who, when he wrote to the sexually rambunctious Corinth, where abortion could have been no stranger, produced an epic song of love. The Judeo-Christian treasure houses a notion of love that could lead to more respectful relationships and more reverent sexual mores and fewer and fewer women at the clinic door.

As the abortion debate continues, I hope it would be freed from noxious and insulting analogies. The Holocaust imagery, used by Burtchaell and others, is repulsive in this context. It is offensive for Jewish people and other victims to be compared to blastocysts, embryos, and fetuses. It is especially galling when this is done by Catholics who, as a church, were not distinguished in their resistance to the real Holocaust. Slavery is another false analogue that equates pre-personal with personal life. And, once again, Catholics in this country were not in the forefront of the fight against slavery or for civil rights. Such analogies do not encourage the reasoned discourse that the problem of abortion needs.

James Tunstead Burtchaell

The men and women who first tried to follow the risen Jesus were Jews. They were not entirely unprepared for the moral demands this would make on them. The Christian road followed terrain already familiar to Jewish moral teaching. Infidelity was to be avoided in all its forms: adultery, incest, and idolatry. Believers were never to take crafty advantage of others, by perjury or sorcery or usury. And they were to restrain themselves from all violence, whether drunkenness, gossip, or murder. This ethical standard rests as firmly on rabbinical teaching as on the New Testament, which shows what a direct lineage there is from Hellenistic Judaism to early Christianity.

In the Sermon on the Mount Jesus invites his followers to go even further along this Way. It was not enough to spare your neighbor's life; you must not even hurl insults at him. If adultery was wrong, then so was lustful intent. And there was scant advantage from being a person of your sworn word if you were a chiseler whenever you were not under oath. Yet even this prophetic summons to a righteousness higher than that of the scribes and Pharisees would have found strong endorsement in many of the better synagogues around Judaea.

Christian moral doctrine showed its direct descent from Jewish ethics. It was ironic, then, that its great breakaway point of departure would be from one of the teachings Christians and Jews most closely shared. Both synagogue and church taught that authentic religion meant coming to the aid of women and children deprived of breadwinners, and of the indigent and the refugee aliens. Nothing could be more traditional for a Jew or more fundamental for a Christian than this ancient commitment to provide for the widow, the orphan, the pauper, the stranger. Yet it was precisely here that the young Christian community found a distinctive vigor and vision, and set forth from its mother's house on a moral journey of its own.

The alien and the pauper, the widow and the orphan, classic beneficiaries of preferential sustenance since Sinai, were suggestive to the Jesus people of four other forlorn categories that they must safeguard: the enemy and the slave, the wife and the infant — unborn or newborn.

The resident alien had to be guaranteed shelter, for he dwelt within the national enclosure of the land and trusted its people. But the Christian was bidden to go far beyond protecting the nearby alien. He was charged to cherish the distant enemy. He had heard it said that he must love his neighbor and hate his enemy. Jesus told him he must love his enemy even at the risk of receiving hatred from both his countrymen and his enemy. He was to set no more bounds to his bounty than the Father who lavished sunshine and rainfall on all fields alike. His pattern was the Lord Jesus who had loved to the death those who betrayed and denied and deserted and condemned and crucified him.

The poor were always a special charge on the Christian's conscience. But their endless needs suggested another, even more vulnerable, group. For those "in the Lord," no one was any longer to be demeaned as mere property of another. Even slaves had to be dealt with as brothers and sisters in the Lord.

Every man was to join in supporting the wives his fellow believers had left behind as widows. But now he was startled to be told that he no longer had a male's freedom of choice to dismiss his own wife. Jesus' rejection of divorce affected men and women differently, since only husbands had previously been free to reject their partners. Now women could no longer be chosen and then discarded by their men. Both alike must now be faithful throughout life, if they loved and married in the Lord.

There were four radical, prophetic imperatives that the new Christian faith set before those who would live in the Spirit and fire of Christ: four disconcerting duties that would distance them from Jews and Romans alike. First, the command to love their enemies struck down forever their exclusionary allegiance to a single race or nation. Second, the command to acknowledge slaves and masters as brothers and sisters condemned slavery to a long and sullen retreat, and ultimately to extinction. Third, the command that husbands and wives were to pledge an equal fidelity was a first yet crucial rejection of the corruption of men and women by their respective domination and acquiescence. These were thunderclaps of moral exclamation that bound the small and scrappy new fellowship to make the purpose of their lives the liberation of those most at a loss.

And there was a fourth point of radical conversation, for there was a fourth group of victims they had to embrace: Beyond the children orphaned by their parents' deaths were those still more helpless children whom their parents slew themselves.

Early Jewish law seems to have regarded the unborn as paternal property. A monetary indemnity was due to the father from anyone who caused his wife to abort. By the time of Jesus some Jewish circles were ready to see the fully formed fetus as a protectable human being. But abortion law was scanty and ambiguous. Roman law in the same era offered no protection against either abortion or infanticide, both of which were within the prerogatives of the male head-of-household. Neither tradition offered a protection for infants reliable enough to suit the first Christians, and they soon stated their own conviction which was to the point.

The most ancient Christian document we possess, besides the New Testament, is called *The Didache, The Instruction of the Twelve Apostles.* Already in this first-century catechism, the obligation to protect the unborn and the infant was included within the roster of essential moral duties:

> You shall not commit murder, you shall not commit adultery; you shall not prey upon boys; you shall not fornicate; you shall not deal in magic; you shall not practice sorcery; you shall not murder a child by abortion, or kill a newborn; you shall not covet your neighbor's goods . . . (*Didache 2:2-3).*

In a later passage the instruction describes what it calls "the way of death":

> It is the path of those who persecute the innocent, despise the truth, find their ease in lying . . . those who have no generosity for the poor, nor concern for the oppressed, nor any knowledge of who it was who made them; they are killers of children, destroyers of God's handiwork; they turn their backs on the needy and take advantage of the afflicted; they are cozy with the affluent but ruthless judges of the poor; sinners to the core. Children, may you be kept safe from it all! (5:2).

The Greek is as straightforward as my translation, bluntly choosing works like "kill" (*apokteinein*) and "murder" (*phoneuein*). Its word for abortion, *phthora,* means, literally, "destruction," and the one destroyed is called "child," *teknon,* the same gentle word used in the final sentence to address the readers themselves.

Shortly before or after the turn of the second century, the *Letter of Barnabas* repeats the *Didache's* injunction against abortion and infanticide in virtually the same words, and laments that they destroy small images of God (*Barnabas* 19:5: 20:2).

Early in the second century the Christian movement had achieved momentum enough to arouse antagonism in Roman society. Some of the most articulate writers of that age were apologists defending their fellow Christians against libel. And one of the slanders that outraged them most was the rumor that Christians slew infants to obtain blood for their eucharistic rites. It was a particularly galling lie, precisely because protection of the young had become such a Christian priority. These apologists did not conceal their contempt for the surrounding pagan society which was willing to destroy its young by choice. Minucius Felix, a Roman attorney of African origin, states the contrast angrily.

> There is a man I should now like to address, and that is the one who claims, or believes, that our initiations take place by means of the slaughter and blood of a baby. Do you think it possible to inflict fatal wounds on a baby so tender and tiny? That there could be anyone who would butcher a newborn babe, hardly yet a human being, who would shed and drain its blood? The only people capable of believing this is one capable of actually perpetrating it. And, in fact, it is a practice of yours, I observe, to expose your own children to birds and wild beasts, or at times to smother and strangle them — a pitiful way to die; and there

are women who swallow drugs to stifle in their womb the beginnings of a man on the way — committing infanticide even before they give birth to their infant (*Octavius* 30:1-2).

The same rumor was challenged by Athenagoras of Athens. How could Christians be accused of murder when they refused even to attend the circus events where humans perished as gladiators or as victims of wild beasts? Christians consider, he wrote, that even standing by and tolerating murder was much the same as murder itself. He then continues:

> We call it murder and say it will be accountable to God if women use instruments to procure abortion: how shall we be called murderers ourselves? The same person cannot regard that which a woman carries in her womb as a living creature, and therefore as an object of value to God, and then slay the creature that has come forth to the light of day (*Embassy for the Christians 35*).

Tertullian, perhaps the most eloquent of the second century apologists, repeatedly opposed the teaching of the Stoics that children are not yet alive in the womb, and that their soul is given them at birth. Arguing from philosophical more than biological grounds, he insisted that the body and soul grow together from the beginning.

> We have established the principle that all the natural potentialities of the soul with regard to sensation and intelligence are inherent in its very substance, as a result of the intrinsic nature of the soul. As the various stages of life pass, these powers develop, each in its own way, under the influence of circumstances, whether of education, environment, or of the supreme powers (*De Anima* 38:1; see also 37).

Abortion, he said, was not only homicide, it was parricide: the slaying of one's own flesh and blood.

> With us, murder is forbidden once for all. We are not free to destroy anyone conceived in the womb, while the blood is still being absorbed to build up the human being. To prevent the birth of a child is simply a swifter way to murder. It makes no difference whether one destroys a soul already born or interferes with it on its way to birth. It is a human being and one who will be a human being, for every fruit is there present in the seed (*Apologeticum* 9:8; see also 9:4-7).

Even in the case of a child whose uterine position makes birth impossible, when Tertullian would accept dismemberment to save the mother's life, he bluntly says the child is being "butchered by unavoidable savagery" (*De Anima* 25:4).

These are statements Christian apologists were making to outsiders. Among themselves, abortion continued to be reviled as a procedure unthinkable for believers. Clement of Alexandria, perhaps the leading theologian of the second century, wrote:

> If we would only control our lusts at the start, and if we would refrain from killing off the human race born or developing according to the divine plan, then our entire lives would be lived in harmony with nature as well. But women who resort to some sort of deadly abortion drug slay not only the embryo but, along with it, all human love [*philanthropia*] (*The Pedagogue* 96).

Early in the next century Hippolytus of Rome condemned bishop Callistus for his readiness to encourage marriage, legal or otherwise, between affluent women and lower-class or slave-class men. Such unions, he observed, had only tended to encourage abortion.

> Women who pass for believers began to resort to drugs to induce sterility, and to bind their abdomens tightly so as to abort the conceptus, because they did not want to have a child by a slave or lower-class type, for the sake of their family pride and their excessive wealth. Look what abuse of duty this lawless man has encouraged, by inciting them both to adultery and to murder. And after such outrageous activity they have the nerve to call themselves a Catholic church! (*Refutation of All Heresies* 9:12:25).

These forthright voices from the first and formative Christian years, all argued that the destruction of the child — unborn or newborn — is infamy for those who follow Christ.

Now I call your attention to five facts, five aspects of that early Christian conviction, which we should note and take to heart. First, the repudiation of abortion was not an isolated or esoteric doctrine. It formed part of an obligation by all believers to protect the four categories of people whom they now saw as peculiarly exposed to the whim and will of their fellow humans: the slave, the enemy, the wife, the infant — unborn or newborn. These were at great risk, as were the four traditional protégés: the poor, the alien, the widow, the orphan. And this fourfold obligation was preached across the full expanse of the church: from Carthage to Eqypt and up into Syria, then across Greece and in Rome.

Second, this was not a program simply for the more strenuous. It was presented as the imperative agenda for the church, the test for all discipleship. Believers were warned away from abortion as they were from adultery, murder, greed, and theft. The four Christian innovations were offered as the classic new signs of authenticity. If theirs was not a community where Jew and Gentile, man and woman, slave and free could show forth as one, then it failed to be Christian. That was their test.

Third, though these exhortations show a sensitive and compassionate sympathy for the victims, their principal moral concern is for the oppressors. It is the husband that bullies his wife whose person dwindles even more sadly than hers. The master or mistress who abuses the slave sustains an injury even greater than what the slave experiences. It is the mother who eliminates her son that Clement cares about, because she must destroy her *philanthropia* as well, her love for humankind, in order to do it. The disease of character that follows from exploitation of others was seen, in Christian perspective, to be more hideously incapacitating than the worst that befell victims. It could be a death far worse than death. Even when they enter the contemporary dispute over the ensoulment of the unborn, these writers dismiss it as a quibble when it comes to abortion: it is the same ruthless willingness to eliminate unwelcome others that shows itself in the slaying of the unborn, the newborn, or the parent. In truest Christian perspective, it is the oppressor who is destroyed.

Fourth, these writers knew well that any true protection of the helpless and exploited calls for a stable empowerment, so that those same people will not continue to be victimized. This means that the Christian moral agenda demands a price. Oppressors must give up their advantage. It little matters whether the advantage was seized purposefully or inherited unwittingly. There is suffering to be accepted by those in power if the disadvantaged and helpless are to be afforded true protection.

But there is a further sacrifice to be made. The victims must accept suffering as well. The price they must pay — if they are to be Christians — is that they must forgo resentment and hatred. Empowerment cannot be grasped as the means to take revenge or, still worse, as the way to begin to be an exploiter oneself. The victims must gaze directly upon those who have taken advantage of them, and recognize them as brothers and sisters who themselves may have been pressed by distress of one kind or another. So there is no moral accomplishment possible unless reconciliation extends the hand of fellowship across the battleline of suffering. There will be heavy and sometimes bitter things to accept if hatred is to be extinguished, and not merely aimed in a new direction.

Fifth, we must note that this was a rigorous duty presented to our Christian ancestors. The light was dazzling, and they often preferred to draw back into the cover of darkness. They and we have sinned against that light. Christians continued to relish and even to justify hatred against their enemies. They did not set the slaves free. Women were not welcomed into full and equal status. And parents continued to destroy their young.

Every person interested enough to follow this debate is aware that we live in an extraordinary age. Four great movements have stirred us round the world: (1) a movement for world peace that is more than a weariness of war; it is making bold and positive ventures towards the reduction of enmity and distrust; (2) a movement for the relief of bondage of every sort; freedom from slavery and from racial subjection, dignity for the worker, status for the migrant; (3) a movement for equality of women and a more integrated companionship with men, so that family and work can be humanized for each and for both together, and (4) a movement to rescue children from abortion, infanticide, infant mortality, and every sort of neglect and predatory danger.

In the trough of some of the most genocidal carnage and oppressive bondage and degradation of women and slaughter of innocent children, our era may be unusual in the readiness of some to listen to that bold and visionary Christian age whose teaching I have held up to your minds and memories.

Each of these movements is bent on empowerment. If the exploited do arise and claim their rightful places, will they take power like Spartacus or Robespierre or Pol Pot? Or will they take power like Mahatma Gandhi and Nelson Mandela . . . like Jesus? Christians may make the difference. This fourfold phalanx of conscience on the march is only partly Christian in origin. But I say that Christians will mean much to these movements of grace, and these movements must mean much to us.

We, possibly more than others, must immediately recognize that these various struggles are in alliance with each other. None can be pitted against another. The United States, for instance, must never imagine that enmity between nations will be subdued if our neighbors are in bondage to us. Enslavement and enmity must both vanish. Likewise, the movement of enhancement for women will never be furthered by making their children expendable. In America today abortion is said to involve a conflict of rights, a conflict of interests between women and their children. A Christian must hold suspect any human right which must be guaranteed by another human's elimination.

Another Christian contribution will be to tell all those who stand to lose power that it is in their highest interest to do so. For they have truly withered under the weight of their exploitative advantages. To say this to them with any credibility, we must first be utterly persuaded that oppressors suffer an even more tragic injury than their victims. Are you really ready to believe that the staff of Auschwitz perished in a worse tragedy than those they exterminated? Do you mourn more for the two thousand or so abortionists in America than for the eighteen million or so infants they have efficiently butchered? Were you more dismayed about Bull Connor than about Martin Luther King, Jr.? Or if you do believe that, can you say believably that you care for the mothers who destroy their unborn children, for they stand to lose even more than do their tragically destroyed offspring.

There is another characteristic Christian insight needed in the abortion struggle. We must see and say how often it is that women who victimize their children are themselves handicapped by never having enjoyed control over their own lives. They are victims . . . even though they are victims who destroy others.

How often it is that some helpless group is savaged by aggressors who have themselves been victims. They are survivors of outrage, and they now seek to relieve their stress and suffering by turning on others who are weaker still. Victims exploiting victims.

What is the background of parents who abuse and batter their children? A childhood of violence, incest, contempt. Victims lashing out at victims.

And who are aborting their daughters and sons today? Women and men who are alienated, abused, poor, who are at a loss to manage their own lives or intimacies. Victims destroyed, destroying victims.

Hate them — hate any victimizers — and you are simply cheering on the cycle of abuse and violence. Suppress your rage well enough to look closely and humanely at drug dealers, at rapists, at pathological prison guards, and you may see it there too: the same pathetic look of the battered spirit, preying on others wantonly.

Women who are desperate or autistic enough to destroy their children are among society's most abused victims. We owe them every help. But a truly compassionate support could never invite them to assuage their own anger by exterminating those more helpless still. It is by breaking the savage cycle of violence that victimization is laid to rest.

When you grasp the uplifted hand to prevent one injured person from striking out at another, you must do so in love, not in anger, for you are asking that person to absorb suffering rather than pass it on to another. And, to be a peacemaker, you must be as ready to sustain as you are to restrain. One must be more than just to accept injustice, yet deal out justice.

Our belief is in a Lord who was the innocent

victim of injustice. Yet he caught the impact of that injustice in his own body, his own self. He deadened it and refused to pass it on, he refused to let the hatred go on ricocheting through humankind. If we truly follow him we are committed to doing the same. And the truest test of that faith is whether we have the gumption to share it with others, with those who are treating others unjustly, but especially with people who are victims. We must prevail upon them to let us help them catch the impact of their distress in their own bodies, and in our own selves alongside theirs, without permitting the cycle of violence to carry on.

The fire of Pentecost rapidly enflamed the Christian community to a sense of what it was about. These Christians were in so many ways an observant Jewish movement: in their worship, their hopes, their moral way of life. But in two great matters they burst forth as men and women possessed by a new Spirit. They witnessed to the Resurrection: Jesus, at whose unjust execution they had been inert and disengaged, was risen to power as Messiah and Lord. That was the first great matter.

The second was like it. They too had been raised to unexpected power, and they stated with vehemence that they would no longer be passive before affliction. That determination was embodied in the entirely distinctive and innovative moral commitment to befriend the enemy, to embrother the slave, to raise up the wife, and to welcome the child. Their own lives were at stake, for these Christians believed that they would perish in their persons if they proved nonchalant about the suffering of any of these most vulnerable brothers and sisters. They rushed to their task, for many others' lives depended on them: the lives of those so powerful they could crush others without noticing; and the lives of their victims — unnoticed, undefended, even unnamed.

The revolt against abortion was no primitive and narrow dogma that a more sophisticated church has now outgrown. It was in the very center of the moral life by which the church first defined itself before the Lord and before the world. We have not yet approached it, and some speak of having surpassed it. Those first disciples who reverenced every unwanted child, born or unborn, would have been stupefied by the sight of their own children in the faith gainsaying this or any of that fourfold commitment. Were we to forswear the hated enemy, the enslaved laborer, the subjected woman, or the defenseless infant, and do that in his name, Christ would have died in vain.

In this debate we are asking whether recent developments and reflection give us authentic reasons to reconsider what the *Didache* and Athenagoras and Tertullian and our other ancestors in faith held to be essential. I say to you we have never had more reasons to reconsider their teaching. And I say that their teaching has never rung more defiantly as the prophetic call of Christ.

Maguire

John Courtney Murray used to say that disagreement is a rare achievement. We have achieved it in this debate. Burtchaell finds his position on abortion "in the very center of the moral life by which the church defined itself." The theological record does not support this simplistic contention.

Our differences are primarily methodological. Burtchaell designates the *Didache*, Athenagoras, Tertullian, and others as his "Scripture" since Scripture does not support his position. The difference is not that he goes to these texts and those of us who differ with him do not. The difference is that he finds in these texts what is not there. You cannot extract from words like *teknon* or *trucidatur* a revolution of consciousness on abortion. This kind of text-proofing and ignoring of the *Sitz im Leben* would not be tolerated in biblical exegesis.

What Burtchaell does is not good ethics. He wants to find an ideal in various disparate texts and leap from there to very practical conclusions in ethics that apply transculturally and transtemporally. James Gustafson and others have long warned of this temptation to avoid homework by rushing from perceived ideals to simple conclusions. Aquinas says that "human actions are good or bad according to their circumstances," and that moral life is marked by "*quasi infinitae diversitates.*" The tough part of ethics is the circumstantial analysis in which we confront these *diversi-*

tates. Burtchaell would spare us this by claiming to find an ideal that solves all (or almost all) abortion cases for all time.

Moral meaning does not just come from ideals. It is also housed in principles and it is incarnate in the circumstances of flesh and life. The moral decision is born at the interstices of all these sources of moral meaning. Burtchaell purveys a perceived ideal and then rushes to a conclusion that binds all kinds of people in all kinds of circumstances. I find in this approach the seeds of fanaticism. Even the old Penitentials that dominated Catholic thought for centuries were more capable of making distinctions where there were differences. They could allege that adultery was more serious than abortion. They tried for some sense of differentiation in their analysis of reality. Burtchaell fails here.

Burtchaell also assumes, what the Christian tradition did not, that the human embryo is a child, a baby, a person. Fifty-one percent of all abortions are done before the embryo has become a fetus. Even the Vatican, which is not shy in these matters, has not tried to settle the ensoulment question. Burtchaell is more dogmatic than the tradition which recognized doubt and gave the woman the benefit thereof.

Burtchaell would put all abortions, except the ones he approves of, in the category of butchery and murder. That makes forty to fifty million women butchers and murderesses every year. That is a sweeping judgment of a huge part of humanity, the feminine part, and the implications of that judgment, as I have said, are sexist.

In his opening statement, Burtchaell said many beautiful things beautifully. At times, I wished I could be entirely on his side. Our paths part when we come to the thorns of conflict situations where I find him guilty of oversimplification. Burtchaell dismisses Probabilism which theologians use to justify some abortions. The *doubt of fact* on embryonic and fetal personhood has been treated as a *doubt of law;* the basic assumptions of Probabilism were used even before the theory was formulated.

In conclusion, I return to my keynote positions that neither of us is pro-abortion. We would both like to see conditions which would make abortion less likely. We differ in our sense of the tragic possibility that those conditions are not always present.

Burtchaell

Professor Maguire points out that he does not read the Christian record as a constant support for the moral imperative against abortion. He is correct. The record of the church is no more honorable in its pursuit of that early commitment than it is in support of the early commitment to make slaves truly brothers and sisters. Nor would we want to use the history of the church to vindicate its failure to pursue its early insights regarding even companionship between women and men. On the contrary, there has been a great slumbering, denial, turning of the back on these convictions.

Professor Maguire also says that in Utopia abortion would be almost unnecessary. I do not think it is our task to frame ethics for Utopia. Nor do I think that Jesus was asking people to be just only when the world settled down to being just in return. Anyone who agrees to accept injustice without retaliating knows that she or he is not following a utopian ethic. *All* of these characteristically Christian moral imperatives require a readiness to do the good and lifegiving thing because one is determined to *do* justice, not merely because one can count on *receiving* justice.

"Are the many women who have committed abortion evil?" Professor Maguire asks. Are the many men who bullied them into it evil? Are the many men who aborted them evil? Those who have recounted their experiences to me deplore beyond anything else in their entire lives the destruction of their own children. I have known them to have carried this sadness for weeks, months . . . as long as sixty years. It was I who found myself trying to draw them away from the conviction that they must be evil, trying to draw them into a resolve that now they must turn and offer their lives to other helpless people who needed them. It was not I who was pointing the finger at them, but they who seemed to have sensed that people who do evil things to others wither. We all carry around the scars and handicaps and disablements of the advantage we have taken of others from time to time. I think it is entirely specious and sentimental to say: "So many have done it." So many have done a lot of things.

Lastly, I must disallow my opponent's use of Probabilism. Professor Maguire knows very well, for he is a well enough trained professor of ethics, that the tradition which developed the theology of Probabilism absolutely vetoed its use in any matter like abortion. Probabilism says that where there is confusion — legitimate, objective confusion — among goodminded people without a conflict of interest about the requirements of moral obligation, then you may follow a lenient course except when that more permissive choice might do harm to another, in which case you may not follow a probable opinion but must pursue the safer course. You may not go out and fire off your 30.06 rifle in the woods at every sound behind a bush. Indeed, when there is doubt, and when injury might follow, all benefit of doubt accrues to the potential victim. Therefore the doctrine of Probabilism would say: until the question of personhood of the unborn at various stages is resolved, all benefit of doubt goes to the potential victim.

77 Respect for Life in the Womb

Address to the Medical Association of Western Flanders (April 23, 1977)

Paul VI

Modern medicine is becoming more and more remote from the uninitiated because both its techniques and its language have become so complicated. At the same time, however, the high scientific level every physician should attain must not be allowed to overshadow or lessen that sense of the human reality and that attention to persons which have always characterized the medical profession and been the source of its greatness.

In the matter of medical ethics, we wish to insist once again on the foundation of everything else, namely, an unconditional respect for life from its very beginnings. It is important to understand why this principle, so essential to every civilization worthy of the name, is today being challenged and why we must firmly oppose what is being improperly termed a "liberalization."

The Catholic Church has always regarded abortion as an abominable crime because unqualified respect for even the very beginnings of life is a logical consequence of the mysteries of creation and redemption. In our Lord Jesus Christ every human being, even one whose physical life is utterly wretched, is called to the dignity of a child of God. That is what our faith teaches us.

Every Christian must draw the necessary con-

From *The Pope Speaks* 22 (Fall 1977): 281-82. Used courtesy of Our Sunday Visitor, Inc.

clusions from this premise and not let himself be blinded by what are claimed to be social or political necessities.

Still less may he excuse himself on the ground that he must respect the opinions of those who do not share his convictions for, in this area, the Christian faith simply casts a further, supernatural light on a moral attitude which is a universal and basic demand imposed by every rightly formed conscience and which is, therefore, legitimately regarded as a requirement of humanness itself, that is, of human nature in the philosophical sense of the term.

Every Christian must attribute the proper importance to this higher morality, this unwritten law which exists in the very heart of man and alone can provide a basis for an authentic social consensus and a legislation worthy of the name.

As doctors, moreover, as men and women who know the scientific and ethical norms of your profession, you have a special and very important role to play in informing and forming others, each of you according to your special competence, and in pointing out the serious errors on which propaganda for abortion is based. Who more than you are frequently in a position to denounce the manipulation of statistics, the overhasty claims in the area of biology and the disastrous physiological and psychological repercussions of abortion?

In encouraging you to fight on behalf of life, we do not forget — as we are sure you realize — the serious problems you face in the exercise of your profession. You need an enlightened conscience if you are to find practical solutions, often painful to implement, which will not sacrifice any of the values at stake. Is it not in this way that the role of physician, which is based on but involves more than technical competence, takes on its full dimension: the role, we mean, of being a person to whom nothing human is alien?

In your researches may you advance equally in knowledge and in awareness of your responsibilities! You can be sure that we lift up your intentions to the Lord, asking him to bless you, your families and all who come to seek your help.

78 A Protestant Ethical Approach

James M. Gustafson

In the ethics of abortion, the differences of opinion surface not only on the substantial moral question of whether it is permissible but also on the question of what is the proper method of moral reflection. The two questions are not entirely independent of each other, as this essay demonstrates. Catholics and Protestants have been divided on the question of method, as well as on the substantial moral judgment.

I. Salient Aspects of Traditional Catholic Arguments

Any Protestant moralist writing about abortion is necessarily indebted to the work of his Roman Catholic colleagues. Their work on this subject shows historical learning that is often absent among Protestants; it shows philosophical acumen exercised with great finesse once their starting principles are accepted; it shows command of the medical aspects of abortion beyond what one finds in cursory Protestant discussions; and it shows extraordinary seriousness about particular moral actions. Debt must also be acknowledged to the contemporary Protestant moralist who has learned most profoundly from the Catholics; namely Paul Ramsey, for his voluminous writing about problems of war and of medical ethics have introduced a note of intellectual rigor into Protestant ethics that was too often absent.

Every moral argument, no matter who makes it and what the issue at hand, must limit the factors that are brought into consideration. No one can handle all possible relevant bits of data, ranges of value, sources of insight, and pertinent principles in a manageable bit of discourse. What one admits to the statement of the moral issue in turn is crucial to the solutions given to it. The determination of which factors or principles are primary, or at least of greater importance than others, in the way one argues is also fairly decisive for the outcome of the argument. The traditional Catholic arguments about abortion can be characterized in part by the following delineations of the perspective from which they are made.[1]

First, the arguments are made by an *external judge.* They are written from the perspective of persons who claim the right to judge the past actions of others as morally right or wrong, or to tell others what future actions are morally right or wrong. To make the point differently, moral responsibility is ascribed to others for their actions, or it is prescribed or proscribed.

The perspective of the external judge can be distinguished from those of the persons who are more immediately involved in an abortion situation. It is clear, of course, that those involved, for example, physicians or mothers, might interpret their situations in terms that they have been taught by the external judges. Even if they do, however, the *position of personal responsibility* that physicians, mothers, and others have is different from that of the writer of a manual of moral theology, or of a priest who judges the moral rectitude of others and determines the penance that is to be required. To assume responsibility for an action is quite a different order of experience from ascribing responsibility to others for an action.[2] Physicians, mothers, and others are initiators of action, they are agents in the process of life who determine to a great extent what actually occurs. Their relationship to a situation involves their senses of accountability for consequences, their awareness of particular antecedents (for example, the conditions under which a pregnancy occurred), their sensibilities and emotions, their private past experiences and their private aspirations for the future, their personal commitments and loyalties.

Second, the arguments are made on a basically *juridical model.* The action is right or wrong depending on whether it conforms to or is contrary to a rule, a law, and the outcome of a moral argument. The rules or laws, of course, are defended on theological and philosophical grounds; they are not arbitrary fiats imposed by an authoritarian institution. Traditional authorities are cited; theological and philosophical principles are given to support these rules; the consequences of different possible courses of action are considered. The argument's principal terms and its logic, however, are directed toward the possibility of defining a morally right act and a morally wrong act. As with the civil law, there is a low tolerance for moral ambiguity. The advantages of this for the person whose behavior conforms to the outcome of the authoritative argument is that he probably can act with a "clear conscience," and he can justify his actions on the basis of authorities other than himself. His own responsibility for his actions, including its consequences, is decisively limited, for with reference to the juridical model of morality he has done what is determined by those whose authority he accepts to be correct. If the primary agents of action, mothers and physicians, for example, do not judge themselves only in the light of the rules, if they exercise the virtue of prudence, and the virtue of *epieikeia,* or equity in interpreting the law in a particular case, they are in a slightly different situation. Their own degree of responsibility is increased, and yet they have the advantage of the clarity of reflection that is given in the moral prescription.

The juridical model can be distinguished from others that view the justification for the moral rectitude of actions in different ways or that have different views of how moral judgments are to be made. Some persons have sought virtually to quantify the good and ill effects of courses of action, and as a result of this have suggested that action which assures the greatest good for the greatest number is right. Others have relied heavily on "moral sentiment" to be sensitive to the moral issues in a situation, and relied upon compassion, the sense of altruism, or the sense of moral indignation to determine the act. Some have relied upon insight and rational intuition to size up what is going on in a time and place and to discern what the proper human response ought to be. Or "love" has been asserted to have sufficient perspicacity and motivating power to enable one to perceive what is right in a situation. It has been cogently argued that morality develops out of experience, and that when laws become abstracted from experience, their informing and persuasive powers begin to evaporate.

Third, the traditional Catholic arguments largely confine the relevant data to *the physical.* The concern is with physical life, its sanctity and its preservation. Obviously, other aspects of human life depend upon the biological basis of the human body, and thus the primacy of this concern is valid. But on the whole, the arguments have not been extended to include concern for the emotional and spiritual well-being of the mother or the infant. The concern has been largely for the physical consequences of abortion.

Fourth, the arguments are limited by concerning themselves almost *exclusively with the physician and the patient* at the time of a particular pregnancy, isolating these two from the multiple relationships and responsibilities each has to and for others over long periods of time. The obvious basis for this is that the physician has to decide about abortions with individual patients as these patients come to him. But he also has responsibilities for the well-being of the whole of his society, and for the spiritual and moral well-being of the patient's family. It could be argued that there is no dissonance between what would be decided in a particular relationship between two people and what is good for society, but that is not self-evident. The focus on the mother's physical condition, and on her as a statistical instance of a general and uniform category of mothers, makes it difficult to consider this particular mother, her particular relationships, and her past spiritual as well as physical history. For example, arguments pertaining to "saving the life of the mother" do not admit as important evidence such factors as whether she is the mother of six other children dependent upon her, or no other children. In some other ways of discussing abortion such information might make a difference in the argument. I am suggesting that the time and space limits one uses to isolate what is "the case" have considerable effect on the way one argues.

Fifth, the traditional Catholic arguments are *rationalistic.* Obviously to make an argument one has to be rational, and to counter an argument one deems to be rationalistic he has to show what would be better reasons for arguing differently. What I refer to as rationalistic can be seen in the structure of many of the sections of the manuals of moral theology that deal with questions such as abortion, or the structure of manuals of medical ethics. One often finds brief assertions of "fundamental truths" which include definitions of terms used in these truths or in subsequent arguments. This might be followed by "basic principles" which will include distinctions between the kinds of law, principles pertaining to conscience, principles of action, a definition of the principle of double effect, and others. The principle of the sanctity or inviolability of human life is discussed at great length since its application is primary to particular cases.

One must recognize that any argument about abortion will use principles. But the rationalistic character of the arguments seems to reduce spiritual and personal individuality to abstract cases. The learning from historical experiences with their personal nuances seems to be squeezed out of the timeless abstractions. The sense of human compassion for suffering and the profound tragedy which is built into any situation in which the taking of life is morally plausible are gone. Individual instances must be typified in order to find what rubric they come under in the manual. While it is eminently clear that any discussion must abstract facts and principles from the vitality and complexity of lived experience, the degree of abstraction and the deductive reasoning of the traditional Catholic arguments remove the issues far from life. The alternative is not to wallow in feeling and visceral responses, nor is it to assume that one's deep involvement with the persons in a situation and one's awareness of the inexorable concreteness of their lives are sufficient to resolve the issues. But an approach which is more personal and experientially oriented is another possibility.

Sixth, the traditional perspective seeks to develop arguments that are based on *natural law,* and thus ought to be persuasive and binding on all men. Intentionally the particular historical standpoint and substance of the Christian message are subordinated to the natural law in the arguments. To be sure, arguments can be given for the consistency between the natural law and particular Christian affirmation; also anyone who would begin with particular Christian affirmations would have to show their viability on moral questions to those who did not share his religious outlook and convictions. To indicate that arguments from natural law can be distinguished from arguments that place particular historical aspects of Christian thought at a different point in the discussion is not to assert that the answer to questions about abortion can be found in "revelation," or that the use of human reason is less necessary. It is to suggest, however, that one's basic perspective toward life might be altered, and one's ordering of values might be different if the first-order affirmations dealt with God's will not only to preserve his creation, but to redeem it. One's attitude toward the persons involved might well be more tolerant, patient, loving, and forgiving, rather than judgmental. One might look for consistency between one's principles and the great themes of the Christian faith at a more central place in the discussion than the traditional Catholic arguments do. To predict that the outcome of the argument would be greatly different in every case would be folly, though it might very well be in some cases. Since theologically based moral arguments, like all others, are arguments made by human beings, many other factors than commonly held convictions enter into them.

These six points are meant to provide a descriptive delineation of salient aspects of traditional Catholic arguments. I have sought to indicate that alternative ways of working are possible with regard to each of them. To claim them to be insufficient or invalid without providing an alternative would be presumptuous. As a way of suggesting and exploring an alternative, I shall describe a situation, and indicate how I would go about making and justifying my moral judgment pertaining to it. In its basic structure it is in accord with the situations of persons who have sought me out for counsel, although for various reasons I have made a composite description.

II. A Discussion of a Human Choice

The pregnant woman is in her early twenties. She is a lapsed Catholic, with no significant religious affiliation at the present time, although she expresses some need for a "church." Her marriage was terminated by divorce; her husband was given custody of three children by that marriage. She had an affair with a man who "befriended" her, but there were no serious prospects for a marriage with him, and the affair has ended. Her family life was as disrupted and as tragic as that which is dramatically presented in Eugene O'Neill's *Long Day's Journey into Night.* Her alcoholic mother mistreated her children, coerced them into deceptive activity for her ends, and was given to periods of violence. Her father has been addicted to drugs, but has managed to continue in business, avoid incarceration, and provide a decent income for his family. The pregnant woman fled from home after high school to reside in a distant state, and has no significant contact with her parents or siblings. She has two or three friends.

Her pregnancy occurred when she was raped by her former husband and three other men after she had agreed to meet him to talk about their children. The rapes can only be described as acts of sadistic vengeance. She is unwilling to prefer charges against the men, since she believes it would be a further detriment to her children. She has no steady job, partially because of periodic gastro-intestinal illnesses, and has no other income. There are no known physiological difficulties which would jeopardize her life or that of the child. She is unusually intelligent and very articulate and is not hysterical about her situation. Termination of the pregnancy is a live option for her as a way to cope with one of many difficulties she faces.

The Christian Moralist's Responsible Relationship

In indicating that the position of writers of moral arguments about abortion in traditional Catholicism is that of an external judge, I did not wish to suggest that priests are not compassionate, understanding, and loving in their relationships to physicians and to mothers, nor did I intend to suggest that they overrule the liberty of conscience of others through authoritarian ecclesiastical sanctions. No doubt some have acted more like rigorous judges than loving pastors, but many have been patient, tolerant, loving, and aware of the limitations of any human authority. (This is not the place to raise the difficult problem of the magisterial authority of the Church, which logically could be raised here, an authority still used to threaten, coerce, and suspend dissident voices.) I do wish to suggest, however, that I believe the responsible relation of a Christian moralist to other persons precludes the primacy of the judgmental posture, either in the way we write or in the way we converse with others.

The moralist responding to this woman can establish one of a number of ways of relating to her in his conversations. The two extremes are obvious. On the one hand, he could determine that no physiological difficulties seem to be present in the pregnancy, and thus seek to enforce her compliance with the standard rule against abortions. The manuals would decide what right conduct is; her predicament would be defined so that factors that are important for others who respond to her are not pertinent to the decision about abortion. Both the moralist and the woman could defer further moral responsibility to the textbooks. On the other hand, he could take a highly permissive approach to the conversation. In reliance on a theory of morality that would minimize the objective moral considerations, and affirm that what a person feels is best is morally right, he could affirm consistently what her own dominant dispositions seemed to be, and let that determine the decision.

Somewhere between these is what I would delineate as a more responsible relationship than either of the two extremes. It would recognize that the moralist and the woman are in an interpersonal relationship; that is to say that as human beings they need to be open to each other, to have empathy for each other. Obviously the moralist, like any other counselor, is in a position to have more disclosed to him than he discloses of himself to the other, and he has professional competence that enables him to be relatively objective within the intersubjectivity of the relationship. But as a Christian moralist his obligation is first to be open and to understand the other, not to judge and to prescribe. He will recognize that his judgment and that of others who have informed him, while learned, mature, and hopefully sound, remains the judgment of a finite being with all the limitations of his perspective. He will, in a situation like this, acknowledge the liberty of her conscience, and will not immediately offer an authoritative answer to her question; indeed, the context of her question, and its nuances might make it a subtly different question than the one the textbooks answer. All this is not to say that he has nothing to contribute to the conversation. As a moralist he is to help her to objectify her situation, to see it from other perspectives than the one she comes with. He is to call to her attention not only alternative courses of action with some of the potential consequences of each (including the violation of civil law), but also the value of life and those values which would have to be higher in order to warrant the taking of life. He is to help her to understand her past, not as a way of excusing anything in the present, but as a way of gaining some objectivity toward the present. He is to find what constitutes her moral integrity and convictions, her desires and ends. He may find himself bringing these into the light of other ends which he deems to be important, or he may find himself inquiring whether potential courses of action are more or less in accord with the values and convictions she has. It is his obligation as a Christian moralist to bring the predicament into the light of as many subjective and objective considerations as his competence permits, including concerns for the wider moral order of the human community of which she is a part as this is sustained in civil laws.

Salient Facts in One Christian Moralist's Interpretation

The relationship of a moralist to a person who seeks conversation with him is by no means simple. Thus it is not easy to isolate what the salient facts of the predicament are, and to give a ready valence to each of them. Efforts at this analytical task are incumbent upon him, but he also *perceives* the person and the situation in some patterns or in a single whole pattern which already establish in his perception some of the relationships between the factors. He never confronts the salient facts as isolates, or as discrete entities that can be added arithmetically into a sum. The person confronts him not as isolable elements, and her experiences are not detached moments only chronologically related to each other. He does not respond to her any more than he responds to a portrait first of all as a series of colors, or a series of lines. He can in reflection discriminate between the colors and talk about the lines, but even then these are in particular relationships to each other in the portrait, and in his perception of it. He does not perceive the woman in pure objectivity, nor as she perceives her own predicament, though obviously he seeks to have his own perception informed by the actual predicament insofar as possible. Even in this, however, his perspective conditions how he "sees" and "feels" the relationships between factors that can be abstracted and isolated. This preface to a statement of salient facts is important, for it precludes both oversimplification and dogmatic analytical authority. He can never say to another person, "In comparable situations find out the answers to the following factual questions, and you will have an accurate picture of the predicament."

In the personal situation under discussion, it is clear that if medical factors alone were to be considered grounds for an abortion, none would be morally permissible. The woman had three pregnancies that came to full term, and the children were healthy. To the best of her knowledge there are no medical problems at the present time. Periodic gastro-intestinal illnesses, which might be relieved with better medical care, would not be sufficient medical grounds. Although the present pregnancy is disturbing for many reasons, including both the occasion on which the pregnancy occurred and the future social prospects for the woman and the child, in the judgment of the moralist the woman is able to cope with her situation without serious threat to her mental health. The medical factors, insofar as the moralist can grasp them, would not warrant a therapeutic abortion.

Legal factors potentially involved in this situation are serious. First, and most obvious, the woman resides in a state where abortion of pregnancies due to sexual crimes is not at present legally permissible. Since there are not sufficient grounds for a therapeutic abortion, a request to a physician would put him in legal jeopardy. Even if abortion was permissible because of the rapes, this woman was unwilling to report the rapes to the police since it involved her former husband and had potential implications for the care of her children. To report the rapes would involve the woman in court procedures which seem also to require time and energy that she needs to support herself financially. To seek an abortion on conscientious moral grounds would be to violate the law, and to implicate others in the violation. Not to press charges against the rapists is to protect them from prosecution. Disclosure of the rapes would make the abortion morally justifiable in the eyes of many, but it might lead to implications for her children. The legal factors are snarled and are complicated by social factors.

The moralist has to reckon with the financial plight of the woman. She is self-supporting, but her income is irregular. There are no savings. Application for welfare support might lead to the disclosure of matters she wishes to keep in confidence. If a legal abortion was possible, the physician would receive little or no remuneration from the patient. There are no funds in sight to finance an illegal abortion, and the medical risks involved in securing a quack rule that out as a viable prospect. The child, if not aborted, could be let out for adoption, and means might be found to give minimum support for the mother during pregnancy. If she should choose to keep the child, which is her moral right to do, there are no prospects for sufficient financial support, although with the recovery of her health the woman could join the work force and probably with her intelligence earn a modest income.

The spiritual and emotional factors involved are more difficult to assess. While the moralist is impressed with the relative calm with which the woman converses about her predicament, he is aware that this ability is probably the result of learning to cope with previous inhumane treatment and with events that led to no happy ending. Socially, she is sustained only by two or three friends, and these friendships could readily be disrupted by geographical mobility. She has no significant, explicit religious faith, and as a lapsed Catholic who views the Church and its priests as harsh taskmasters, she is unwilling to turn to it for spiritual and moral sustenance. She has a profound desire not merely to achieve a situation of equanimity, of absence of suffering and conflict, but also to achieve positive goals. Her mind is active, and she has read fairly widely; she expresses the aspiration to go to college, to become a teacher, or to engage in some other professional work, both for the sake of her self-fulfillment and for the contribution she can make to others. She has not been defeated by her past. She can articulate the possibility of keeping the child, and see the child as part of the world in which there would be some realization of goals, especially since she has been deprived of her other children. She has confidence, she has hope, and she seems to be able to love, though she wonders what else could happen to make her life any more difficult than it is. She carries something of a guilt load; the courts gave custody of her three children to her husband because of adultery charges against her. Yet, her interpretation of that marriage in her youth was that it freed her from her parental home, but the marriage itself was a "prison." She responds to the rapes more in horror than in hatred, but is too close to that experience to know its long-range impact on her.

The more readily identifiable moral factors are three, though in the ethical perspective of this paper, this constitutes an oversimple limitation of the "moral" and of the nature of moral responsibility. One is the inviolability of life, the sanctity of life. My opinion is that since the genotype is formed at conception, all the genetic potentialities of personal existence are there. Thus it is to be preserved unless reasons can be given that make an exception morally justifiable. A second is rape — not only a crime, but a morally evil deed. The sexual relations from which the pregnancy came were not only engaged in against the woman's will, but were in her judgment acts of retaliation and vengeance. The third is the relation of morality to the civil law. If abortion were considered to be morally justifiable, to have it done would be to break the civil law. It would be an act of conscientious objection to existing laws, and is susceptible to scrutiny by the moral arguments that pertain to the subject in itself.

All of these factors in isolated listing, and others that could be enumerated, do not add up to a moral decision. They are related to each other in particular ways, and the woman is related to her own ends, values, and to other beings. And the moralist's relationship is not that of a systems analyst sorting out and computing. His relationship is one of respect and concern for the person; it is colored by his perspective. It is necessary, then, to state what seem to be the factors that are present in the perspective of the moralist that influence his interpretation and judgment.

Salient Aspects of the Moralist's Perspective

The perception and the interpretation of the moralist are not a simple matter to discuss. It would be simpler if the author could reduce his perspective to: (a) theological and philosophical principles; (b) moral inferences drawn from these; and (c) rational application of these principles to a narrowly defined case. But more than belief, principles, and logic are involved in the moral decision. A basic perspective toward life accents certain values and shadows others. Attitudes, affections, and feelings of indignation against evil, compassion for suffering, and desire for restoration of wholeness color one's interpretation and judgment. Imagination, sensitivity, and empathy are all involved. For Christians, and many others presumably, love is at work, not merely as a word to be defined, and as a subject of propositions so that inferences can be drawn from it, but love as a human relationship, which can both move and inform the other virtues, including prudence and equity (to make a reference to St. Thomas). All of this does not mean that it is without objectivity.

The perspective of the Christian moralist is informed and directed by his fundamental trust that the forces of life seek the human good, that God is good, is love. This is a matter of trust and confidence, and not merely a matter of believing certain propositions to be true. (I believe certain statements about my wife to be true, including the statement that she wills and seeks my good, but the reasons for my trust in her cannot be described simply by such a statement.) Yet the way in which I state my convictions about this trust defines in part my moral perspective and my fundamental intentionality. (What I know *about* my wife sustains my trust in her, and in part sets the direction of our marriage.) Life, and particularly human life, is given to men by God's love: physical being dependent upon genetic continuity; the capacity of the human spirit for self-awareness, responsiveness, knowledge, and creativity; life together in human communities, in which we live and care for others and others live and care for us.

God wills the creation, preservation, reconciliation, and redemption of human life. Thus, one can infer, it is better to give and preserve life than to take it away; it is better to prevent its coming into being than to destroy it when it has come into being. But the purposes of God for life pertain to more than physical existence: there are conditions for human life that need delineation: physical health, possibilities for future good and meaning that engender and sustain hope, relationships of trust and love, freedom to respond and initiate and achieve, and many others. The love of God, and in response to it, the loves of men, are particularly sensitive to "the widow, the orphan, and the stranger in your midst," to the oppressed and the weak.

These brief and cryptic statements are the grounds for moral biases: life is to be preserved, the weak and the helpless are to be cared for especially, the moral requisite of trust, hope, love, freedom, justice, and others are to be met so that human life can be meaningful. The bias gives a direction, a fundamental intention that does not in itself resolve the darknesses beyond the reach of its light, the ambiguities of particular cases. It begins to order what preferences one would have under ideal conditions and under real conditions. One would prefer not to induce an abortion in this instance. There is consistency between this preference and the Christian moralist's faith and convictions. But one would prefer for conception to arise within love rather than hate, and one would prefer that there would be indications that the unknowable future were more favorably disposed to the human well-being of the mother and the child.

The perspective of the Christian moralist is informed and directed by his understanding of the nature of human life, as well as his convictions about God. Abbreviated statements of some convictions are sufficient here. These would be first, that moral life is a life of action, in which intentions, judgments, the exercise of bodily power and other forms of power and influence give direction to our responses to past events, and direction to future events themselves. Persons are active, responsive, creative, reflective, self-aware, initiating. The second would be that we can discern something of the order of relationships and activity that sustains, preserves, and develops our humanity. The child conceived in love, within a marriage (an order of love), within an order of society that maintains justice, is more likely to have a higher quality of life than one who is conceived in other conditions. The decision to seek an abortion is human, the act of abortion would be human, the relationships before, during, and after the abortion are human. The consequences are not fully predictable beyond the physical, and yet the human is more than perpetuation of the body. A moral order was violated in rape; are the human conditions present that would sustain and heal the humanity of the child and the mother in the future? The answer to that question is a finite, human answer, and how it will be answered by the mother and others deeply affects a most decisive act.

A third pertinent affirmation about human life is important: to be a creature is to be limited, and the good and the right are found within the conditions of limitation. Present acts respond to the conditions of past actions, conditions which are usually irrevocable, unalterable. Their consequences will be projected into the future and quickly become part of other actions and responses so that the actors in the present cannot fully know or determine the future. The limitations of knowledge, both of potentially verifiable facts and of good and evil, while no excuse for not knowing what can be known, nonetheless are present. Thus not only physical risk, but moral risk is fundamental to human action, and this risk in the life of this woman involves potential tragedy, suffering, and anguish. But her condition itself is the fruit both of events beyond her control (for example, the rapes) and events that have occurred because of choices (for example, earlier adultery). What many men find out about the dark side of existence through novels and dramas, she has experienced. Action is required within the limits; the good or the evil that is involved will be concrete, actual. Thus there is no abstract standard of conduct that can predetermine without moral ambiguity what the right action is in this predicament. Since predicaments like this have emerged before, however, one's conscientious moral interpretation can use those generalizations that have emerged out of the past for illumination, and for direction. They may present values or principles so universally valid that the present decision, if contrary to them, must be justified as a clear exception. Since action is specific, either the following of established rules, or the finding exceptions to them, refers to specifics. Specificity of good and evil is the human condition (I never know either in the abstract); choices are agonizingly specific. The moralist has the obligation conscientiously to assess the specific in the light of principles and arguments that pertain to it; the woman is entitled to see her predicament and potential courses of action in the light of as much distilled wisdom and experience as she can handle. Indeed, the principle of double effect (preferably multiple effects none of which are totally evil, and none of which are totally good) might assist in the reflection. But the choice remains in the realm of the finite, the limited, and the potentially wrong as well as right.

Pertinent Principles That Can Be Stipulated for Reflection

Neither the moralist nor the woman comes to a situation without some convictions and beliefs that begin to dissolve some of the complexity of the particularities into manageable terms. Perhaps the traditional Catholic arguments simply assume that one can begin with these convictions and principles, and need not immerse one's self in the tragic concreteness. The pertinent ones in this case have already been alluded to, but here they can be reduced to a simpler scheme.

1. Life is to be preserved rather than destroyed.
2. Those who cannot assert their own rights to life are especially to be protected.
3. There are exceptions to these rules.

Possible exceptions are:

a. "medical indications" that make therapeutic abortion morally viable. Condition not present here.

b. the pregnancy has occurred as a result of sexual crime. (I would grant this as a viable possible exception in every instance for reasons imbedded in the above discussion, if the woman herself were convinced that it was right. In other than detached academic discussions I would never dispatch an inquiry with a ready granting of the exception. If the woman sees the exception as valid, she has a right to more than a potentially legal justification for her decision; as a person she has the right to understand why it is an exception in her dreadful plight.)

c. the social and emotional conditions do not appear to be beneficial for the well-being of the mother and the child. (In particular circumstances, this may appear to be a justification, but I would not resort to it until possibilities for financial, social, and spiritual help have been explored.)

In the short-hand of principles this can be reduced to an inconsistency between on the one hand the first and second, and on the other hand 3.b. and perhaps 3.c. While I am called upon to give as many reasons for a decision between these two as I can, the choice can never be fully rationalized.

The Decision of the Moralist

My own decision is: (a) if I were in the woman's human predicament I believe I could morally justify an abortion, and thus: (b) I would affirm its moral propriety in this instance. Clearly logic alone is not the process by which a defense of this particular judgment can be given; clearly, the facts of the matter do not add up to a justification of abortion so that one can say "the situation determines everything." Nor is it a matter of some inspiration of the Spirit. It is a human decision, made in freedom, informed and governed by beliefs and values, as well as by attitudes and a fundamental perspective. It is a discernment of compassion for the woman, as well as of objective moral reflection. It may not be morally "right" in the eyes of others, and although we could indicate where the matters of dispute between us are in discourse, and perhaps even close the gap between opinions to some extent, argument about it would probably not be persuasive. The judgment is made with a sense of its limitations, which include the limitations of the one who decides (which might well result from his lack of courage, his pride, his slothfulness in thinking, and other perversities).[3]

Continuing Responsibilities of the Moralist

The responsibilities of the moralist, like the consequences for the woman, do not end at the moment a decision might be made in favor of an abortion. Some of them can be briefly indicated, since they have already been alluded to in the discussion. Since the moralist concurs in the decision, and since the decision was made in a relationship in which he accepts limited but real responsibility for the woman, he is obligated to continue his responsible relationship to her in ways consistent with the decision, and with her well-being. He cannot dismiss her to engage in subsequent implications of the decision on her own and to accept the consequences of such implications on her own. First, he is obligated to assist, if necessary, in finding competent medical care. In such a situation as the one described, with abortion laws as they now stand in most states, this is not necessarily an easy matter and not a trivial one. Second, financial resources are needed. To put her on her own in this regard would be to resign responsibility prematurely for a course of action in which the moralist concurred, and might jeopardize the woman's health and welfare. Third, the woman needs continuing social and moral support in her efforts to achieve her aspirations for relief from anguish and for a better human future. To deny continued support in this case is comparable to denying continued care and concern for the well-being of those who have large families as a result of a moral doctrine prohibiting contraception, or for children born out of wedlock, both reprehensible limitations of responsibility in my judgment. Fourth, the moralist is under obligation, if he is convinced of the propriety in this human situation of an abortion, to seek reform of abortion legislation which would remove the unjust legal barrier to what he believes to be morally appropriate. Other considerations must be brought to bear on the discussion of legal reform, such as the crucial matter of the legal and moral rights of the defenseless unborn persons, but it is consistent with the moral judgment in this case that the laws permit an action which is deemed to be morally approvable. To judge an action to be morally appropriate, and not to seek the alteration of legislation which would make such an action possible without penalties would be a serious inconsistency in the moralist's thinking and action. It would be comparable to approving conscientious objection to specific wars on moral grounds and not seeking to make such objection a legal possibility.

These points are made to indicate that the time and space limits of a moral issue extend beyond the focal point of a particular act. Indeed, the focal point has not been the abortion, but the well-being of the woman over a long range of time. If such a delineation of the situation is made, the responsibility of the moralist must be consonant in its dimensions with that. These points are made to reiterate an earlier one, then, namely that the delimitation which a moral issue receives from its discussants is a crucial factor in determining what data are significant and what the extent of responsibilities is.

III. The Location of This Discussion on the Current Map of Moral Theology

This essay began with a description of salient aspects of the traditional Catholic arguments. With reference to each of these, I have emphasized a different way of working. The discussion of this paper does not provide a totally different way of thinking about the matter; indeed, the concerns of traditional moral theology are brought into it.

In place of the external judge, the position of the persons who must assume responsibility for the decision has been stressed. This requires empathy with the woman and the physician who might become involved. But the moralist himself is responsible for his decision: if he offers recommendations he is responsible to all who accept and act upon them. If an abortion is induced, he shares moral responsibility for it. Moral decisions, however, are not made wallowing in sympathy and empathy. The element of disinterested objectivity is a necessity, something of the stance of the external judge or observer is involved. In a process of conversation with one who has the serious moral choice, however, the interpersonal relationship not only establishes the possibilities of open communication, but provides insight and understanding, and sensitizes the affections.

In place of the determination of an action as right or wrong by its conformity to a rule and its application, I have stressed the primacy of the person and human relationships and the concreteness of the choice within limited possibilities. There can be no guarantee of an objectively right action in the situation I have discussed, since there are several values which are objectively important, but which do not resolve themselves into a harmonious relation to each other. Since there is not a single overriding determination of what constitutes a right action, there can be no unambiguously right act.

Whereas the moral theology manuals generally limit discussion to the physical aspects of the human situation, I have set those in a wider context of human values, responsibilities, and aspirations. While this does not make the physical less serious, it sets it in relation to other matters of a morally serious nature, and thus qualifies the way one decides by complicating the values and factors to be taken into account.

I find it difficult in discussing possible abortions to limit the personal relationships as exclusively to the physician and the patient as do the manual discussions, and to limit the time span of experience to the fact of pregnancy and action pertaining to it alone. Most significantly in the instance discussed, the conditions under which the pregnancy occurred modify the discussion of the abortion.

The role of compassion and indignation, of attitudes and affections in the process of making a decision is affirmed in my discussion to a degree not admitted in traditional moral theology. Indeed, I indicated the importance of one's basic perspective, and the way in which one's perception of a situation is conditioned by this perspective. Situations cannot be reduced to discrete facts; one's response to them is determined in part by one's faith, basic intentions, and dispositions, as well as by analysis and the rational application of principles.

Although I have only sketched most briefly the theological convictions that inform the perspective, they perhaps have a more central place in the ways in which I proceed than is the case in traditional moral theology. I wish not to suggest that there is a deposit of revelation, supernaturally given, which I accept on authority as a basis of moral perspective; such a position is not the alternative to natural law. Ampler elaboration of this, however, is beyond the bounds of this paper.

Although the structure I have used as a model differs from that model used by the Roman Catholic manuals of moral theology, in a specific instance a Catholic moralist might reach a conclusion not strikingly dissimilar from my own in counseling the woman. He could do so by means of the classic Catholic doctrine of "good faith." As expounded by Alphonsus Liguori, a confessor is not to disturb the good faith of the penitent if he believes that telling the penitent he is committing a sin will not deter him from his course of action, but will merely put him in "bad faith," that is, in a state of mind where he is aware that what he is doing is opposed to the will of God. There are exceptions to this doctrine where the penitent must be informed of what is necessary to salvation, or where the common good is endangered by the proposed actions. These exceptions, however, do not seem applicable to the special kind of case I have outlined. Consequently, a Catholic moralist faced with a woman who believes she is doing what is right in seeking an abortion, and who in all probability would not be deterred by advice to the contrary, might well conclude that his responsibility was not to put the woman in bad faith.[4]

This Catholic approach to a particular case accords with mine in recognizing a principle of personal responsibility which the moralist must honor. He cannot coerce the person; in some sense each person must decide for himself. This approach differs from mine, however, in the analysis of the act of abortion, which is treated in a special sense as a sin. Elucidation of this difference would require extensive discussion of the relation of religion and morality in the two approaches, in the uses of the concept of sin, and other matters too large to be developed here. This Catholic approach also differs from mine in the limits it would impose on cooperation with the act by the counselor.

A Catholic moral theologian, if he approved of the outcome of the discussion presented here, might compliment it by indicating that it is an example of prudence informed by charity at work, or that it is an exercise in the virtue of *epikeia,* applying principles to particular cases. If such generosity were shown, I would not be adverse to being pleased, for it would indicate that some of the polarizations of contemporary moral theology between ethics of law and situational ethics are excessively drawn. I would also suggest, however, that there is a different valence given to prudence and equity, indeed, to the moral virtues, in the order of ethical analysis here than is the case in the treatises on medical ethics. There is a sense in which the present discussion subordinates law to virtue as points of reliance in making moral decisions.

Since there is no fixed position called "situation ethics," it would be futile to distinguish the approach taken here from what cannot be readily defined. I would say in general that in comparison with Paul Lehmann's ethics of the theonomous conscience,[5] with its confidence in a renewed sensitivity and imagination to perceive what God is doing in the world to make and keep human life human, the approach of this paper is more complex, and ultimately less certain about its answer. Further, the weight of responsibility for reflection and for action rests heavily upon the actor, since no perceptive powers I have enable me to overcome the distance between God and the action that I respond to. I cannot claim to perceive what *God* is doing. The polemical force with which Lehmann attacks "absolutist ethics" is foreign to this approach;[6] while I clearly believe that abstract principles and logic alone do not contain the dynamics of suffering and evil, or of love and good, their utility in bringing clarity to discussion is much treasured.

As the morally conscientious soldier fighting in a particular war is convinced that life can and ought to be taken, "justly" but also "mournfully,"[7] so the moralist can be convinced that the life of the defenseless fetus can be taken, less justly, but more mournfully.

Notes

1. The generalizations do not do injustice to the treatment of abortion in at least the following books: Thomas J. O'Donnell, S.J., *Morals in Medicine,* 2nd ed. (Westminster, Md.: Newman Press, 1960); Charles J. McFadden, O.S.A., *Medical Ethics,* 5th ed. (Philadelphia: F. A. Davis Co., 1961); John P. Kenny, O.P., *Principles of Medical Ethics,* 2nd ed. (Westminster, Md.: Newman Press, 1962); Gerald Kelley, S.J., *Medico-Moral Problems* (St. Louis: The Catholic Hospital Associations, 1985); Allan Keenan, O.F.M. and John Ryan, F.R.C.S.E., *Marriage: A Medical and Sacramental Study* (New York: Sheed and Ward, 1955). They apply also to manuals of moral theology that are more comprehensive than these which focus on medical care.

2. Albert Jonsen, S.J., in *Responsibility in Modern Religious Ethics* (Washington, D.C. Corpus Books, 1968), demonstrates the importance of the distinction made here. See pp. 36ff.

3. This procedure can be applied to cases other than pregnancy due to rape, obviously, and *might* lead to similar conclusions in instances of unwed girls, or older married women with large families, etc.

4. See Bernard Häring, "A Theological Evaluation," in *The Morality of Abortion: Legal and Historical Perspectives,* ed. John T. Noonan, Jr. (Cambridge, Mass.: Harvard University Press, 1970).

5. Paul Lehmann, *Ethics in a Christian Context* (New York: Harper & Row, 1964).

6. Ibid., pp. 124-32.

7. See Roland H. Bainton's discussions of the mournful mood of the just war theorists, in *Christian Attitudes Toward War and Peace* (New York: Abingdon Press, 1960), pp. 98, 112, 139, 145, and 221-22.

79 The Fetus as Parasite and Mushroom

Gilbert Meilaender

In one of the most widely anthologized of recent articles about abortion Judith Jarvis Thomson has provided a defense of abortion that, she contends, does not rely on denying human status of the fetus-to-be-aborted.[1] A great deal of the persuasive force of her arguments depends, I am inclined to think, on two analogies she uses. My purpose is to reflect on these analogies and to suggest that they are very strange indeed. The first of Thomson's analogies reflects an excessively individualistic notion of human personhood, a notion oblivious to the bonds that tie us to one another. The second expresses (but does not reflect upon) a person-body dualism. Together these analogies subtly distort the matter under discussion and manifest an insensitivity to the human character of birth and motherhood.

I will not try to argue here that all abortion is wrong nor even provide the beginnings of an argument to that effect. I will also not try to settle the difficult question of the point in time at which we have among us a new life, a new individual human being. These are important questions and necessary for any full-fledged treatment of abortion. They are not, however, my primary concern here. It is Thomson's images, not her arguments, upon which I focus.

Thomson herself grants for the sake of argument that the fetus is a person from the moment of conception (p. 48). Her concern is to suggest that opponents of abortion have tended to assume that, once this was established, the argument against abortion was finished. She, on the contrary, is puzzled about the move from the affirmation of the personhood of the fetus to the conclusion that the fetus can claim rights against the mother or that abortion is not morally permissible. She thinks that opponents of abortion pass over this problem much too quickly. In this she may well be correct, though it is worth noting even here that there is something a little strange about her case. If the fetus is a person — which we are granting for the sake of the discussion — then surely the burden of proof is on the side of those who deny that rights may properly be ascribed to it or who advocate taking its life. Thomson talks as if there were something unusual about this, whereas I should think it rather clear. It is not at all surprising that opponents of abortion should have assumed that persons have rights (and, most basically, a right to life), nor that they should have called upon others to protect these rights. It is not surprising that opponents of abortion should have confined their efforts largely to discussing when human life begins and to criticizing various proposed defenses of aborting such lives. To do that, of course, even to do it successfully, is not to show that no such defense is possible. But it is a perfectly understandable procedure if one assumes that — in the absence of forceful arguments to the contrary — one human life (even that of the fetus) is entitled to as much protection as another. That Thomson seems to distribute the burden of proof wrongly from the outset is itself cause for wonder.

The Fetus as Parasite

Suppose we grant that the fetus is a person, how then might we argue that abortion is, nevertheless, morally permissible? Thomson suggests that the mother's right to decide what happens to her body is stronger than the fetus's right to life — or, at least, that the mother is under no obligation to permit the fetus to continue to grow within her body. She grants, of course, that in some instances it would be morally reprehensible for the mother to abort the fetus. She speaks of Good Samaritans, Splendid Samaritans, and so forth. But these do

From Gilbert Meilaender, *The Limits of Love* (University Park: The Pennsylvania State University Press, 1987), pp. 48-59.

more than their duty. There is in no case an *obligation* not to abort or a justified rights-claim on the part of the fetus. At this point we may consider her first analogy: that of the unconscious violinist.

You are asked to suppose this case: There is a famous violinist suffering from a fatal ailment, and you alone have the right type of blood to help him. One night the Society of Music Lovers kidnaps you and plugs the violinist's circulatory system into yours. In this way the violinist can (for the amount of time needed to save his life) live off your system. Your kidneys can be used to extract poisons from his system as well as from yours. You wake up in the morning and find yourself in bed with the unconscious violinist, his system plugged into yours. And the question is whether it would be morally wrong for you or anyone else to unplug you, when such action would certainly mean the death of the violinist.

The force of the analogy is to present the opponent of abortion with a dilemma. If he says, "Once (innocent) life exists we should not directly take it," he seems committed to leaving himself plugged into the violinist for as long as necessary. If, on the other hand, he claims that the cases are markedly dissimilar in that he did not voluntarily consent to be plugged into the violinist, his case against abortion in certain kinds of situations (e.g., cases of rape) seem to collapse.

The one good thing I can think of to say for this analogy and the dilemma Thomson generates on the basis of it is that it may help us to see why abortion in cases of pregnancy resulting from rape *is* a very special and different matter. I am not, however, certain that Thomson always sees *why* this is so. She seems to think that rape is an exception *just as* pregnancy that required the mother to spend nine months in bed would be an exception (pp. 49f.). That she can run together pregnancy resulting from forcible intercourse with other cases is nothing short of remarkable. This shows that rape is an exception in her thinking only because it seems to impose a special burden for which the mother did not volunteer.

Thomson seems oblivious to what is surely more important than the fact the mother did not "invite" this fetus in — namely, the nature of the relationship in which the fetus was conceived, a relationship that strikes most of us as not only less than human but inhuman. This same blind spot is manifested later in her essay when Thomson suggests that a woman who became pregnant as a result of rape ought to carry the child to term if the pregnancy lasted only an hour (p. 60). In that case, the implication seems to be, the burden (though not volunteered for) would not be great enough to justify a refusal. Yet, even in such a case the relationship in which the fetus had been conceived would be one repugnant to our sense of humanity. The woman's body would have been forcibly used as a means for someone else's pleasure in a relationship devoid of genuine giving and receiving. Unless we think persons are not present in their bodies (as, we shall see, there is some reason to believe Thomson thinks), this means that not only the woman's body but her person has been used in an inhuman manner. One would, however, never guess any of this from Thomson's argument.

More important than this, however, is the way that analogy forces one to picture the fetus: as parasite. And, of course, there is no doubt that the fetus does for nine months live off the mother and make use of the mother's circulatory and waste-disposal systems. But shall we acquiesce in this picture of the fetus as parasite? Or shall we suggest that it subtly distorts the entire discussion? The latter seems to be the case.

There is, in the conception and growth of the fetus in its mother's womb, a striking act of creativity. This very same act witnesses as well to the self-spending that such creativity requires. That for nine months the child lives within (and, indeed, off) the mother provides a paradigm of human dependence and, we might also say, vicariousness. There is no human being who has not been so bound to others from the moment of his birth. For Thomson this is just so much biology, the relationship between mother and child being merely a biological one with no special human significance (p. 65). In her account, human significance seems to enter only when an act of will takes place, when the parent recognizes or acknowledges the child and thereby takes responsibility for it. Whatever it is that characterizes our humanity evidently has more relation to seeing ourselves as "isolated principles of will"[2] than as embodied creatures.

And yet, it is not impossible to think differently about the fact that the fetus lives off its mother.

We may see there a sign of what is truly human: an inescapable witness to the self-spending that human life requires and to the bonds of vicarious dependence that encompass the lives of us all. We may see there a sign — indeed, more than that, an embodiment — of the fact that we *do* live off others who never invited us to do so or granted us any rights thereto. And we may even find there an invitation to recognize that we cannot, without forfeiting our humanity, turn from the giving which is the other side of that receiving.

The first thing we notice, therefore, when we begin with Thomson to picture the fetus as parasite is the striking individualistic bias of this viewpoint. Vicariousness is to her simply a burden, not an essential part of creative human love. Perhaps then we ought to examine this picture of the fetus as parasite, reflect upon it a little more.

The womb is the natural environment of the fetus. We expect to find it there. We expect to find it nourished by and living off the mother. We expect, in short, that it will be dependent in this way. Yet, if we want to claim that there is moral significance to be discerned here — that here we may learn something about the proper shape of human life — we will have to say more than this. For could we not say much the same of any parasite that lives off its host? Is not the host its natural environment? Do we not expect to find the parasite dependent in this way? Will we not find both fetus living off mother and parasite living off host in nature? Why, then, should the cases be different?

"For most creatures," Annie Dillard writes, "being parasitized is a way of life."[3] We could, she suggests, write a "lives of the parasites" that would be a kind of "hellish hagiography," the devil's *summa theologica*.[4] Parasitism may, though I think it should not, be defined simply in terms of dependency. On this sort of definition "the essential criterion of parasitism is dependency, the loss of freedom to live an independent existence. . . ."[5] Such a definition may be too broad, however, since it might with some justification be taken to apply to almost anything in nature understood as an interconnected system. It is perhaps better to define parasitism more narrowly as "a type of symbiosis in which two different kinds of organism habitually associate with one another, to the detriment of one and the benefit of the other."[6] Annie Dillard's book is a gold mine of hair-raising descriptions of parasitism, if one is interested in examples. She writes at one point of an order of parasitic insects called "stylops."

> Stylops parasitize diverse other insects such as leaf hoppers, ants, bees, and wasps. The female spends her entire life inside the body of her host, with only the tip of her bean-shaped body protruding. She is a formless lump, having no wings, legs, eyes, or antennae; her vestigial mouth and anus are tiny, degenerate, and nonfunctional. She absorbs food — her host — through the skin of her abdomen, which is "inflated, white, and soft."[7]

Considering this and other like "natural" phenomena, Dillard is moved to ask: "Are my values then so diametrically opposed to those that nature preserves?" and "Is human culture with its values my only real home after all?"[8]

Perhaps the fetus in the mother's womb is just one more example of such parasitism. Why should we not picture it that way? The first thing that needs to be said is that we certainly can picture it that way. The second is that we need not do so. Nature provides us with countless examples of dependence. But nature's book must be read.

It is possible to think that some examples of dependence that nature presents us are corruptions or perversions of a principle that is rightly exemplified in others. Thus, the fact that the fetus lives off the mother while in her womb may be of enormous human significance and tell us much about what is appropriate to our natures. We may say with Marcel that "a family is not created or maintained as an entity without the exercise of a fundamental generosity."[9] That the parasite lives off the host demonstrates only that the principle of vicariousness can be distorted. Such an insight lay behind St. Augustine's privative theory of evil. When he says that evil has no independent existence and that it can exist only as a corruption of what is good, he is both giving us a reading of nature's book and asserting the priority of goodness.[10]

From this perspective, while granting that the fetus is in some respects like a parasite, we may come to see that the two are nevertheless quite different phenomena. They are ordered toward different ends. The analogy of the fetus as parasite fails to take note of the fact that parasitism is not a method of procreation. Creatures that are parasites have other — sometimes asexual — means of reproduction. To construct an analogy that invites us to picture the fetus as a parasite is, therefore, to misplace the phenomenon. Parasitism is different from procreation of one's kind. Furthermore, the fetus in the womb is moving toward a stage when it will attain a kind of independence relative to its earlier condition. But parasitism, on the other hand, "involves a gradual and progressive adaptation on the part of the parasite, and recovery of an independent status becomes increasingly difficult."[11] We may recall the stylops. The vicariousness of which the fetus provides a paradigm is strikingly creative — oriented not toward degenerative dependence but toward new life that will be able to give as it has received. Rightly ordered, vicariousness is meant to be creative and life-giving.

I have put the point in Augustinian terms. Augustine's belief, of course, had some theological roots. He knew and believed a story that spoke of nature as a good thing now corrupted. It gave him warrant, therefore, to expect that he might find in nature a relationship that could be exemplified in both good and bad ways. But we can also put the matter in slightly less theological terms. That the parasite lives off its host and the child off its mother are both natural in the sense that observation and inspection find both in nature. But in that sense, of course, nothing can be unnatural; whatever upon inspection we find simply *is* exhibited as part of nature, and corruption cannot exist. When we read nature's book, however, it is possible to say that some acts or conditions exemplify vicariousness in its natural — i.e., rightly ordered — state. Some sorts of dependence are appropriate to the sorts of creatures we are, even as some are corruptions of our nature.

We acknowledge this to be the case when we say that the womb of the mother is the natural environment of the fetus. It is quite appropriate for our natures that we should find the fetus there. Indeed, we think it of great human significance. How one proves to the skeptic that it *is* of such significance I am not at all sure. It is always possible to refuse to distinguish one example of vicariousness from another. It is possible to grant no significance to the fact that the dependence of the fetus is part of a creative act oriented toward new life. We certainly *can* think of individuals as isolated and refuse to grant that creation of new life has its origin in an act of self-spending that ought to be pronounced good. Therefore, I am uncertain how, in any strong sense, to prove what I have argued for. And yet, to think that it needs to be proven is already to imagine that we can think of human beings in isolation, apart from this relation of vicarious dependence. It is, in short, to imagine that we can think of them as other than human. We cannot, of course, prevent Thomson from adopting an angle of vision that pictures the fetus as if it were a parasite. But when she does this she is no longer discussing anything that we understand to be a human being. Hence, her analogy is subtly distorting. We cannot heed *both* it *and* her prior affirmation that she will grant from the outset that the fetus is a human being. The analogy asks us to picture the fetus as a parasite, and, though we can do that, we cannot do it while simultaneously thinking of the fetus as a human being.

When we see the parasite living off its host, we see a corrupt imitation of something that in itself exhibits right order; namely, the dependence of the fetus on its mother and the vicarious character of human life to which it witnesses. That we should find both in a world in which, as Augustine put it, pride perversely copies the work of love need not particularly surprise us. Thomson's picture of the fetus as parasite misses the human significance of vicarious dependence within love — and in so doing betrays the individualistic bias of her argument.

The Fetus as Mushroom

There is a later stage in Thomson's argument that also needs examination. In the course of broadening her defense of abortion to include within its scope many cases in which the mother willingly and knowingly risked pregnancy, she provides us with a new analogy. We are now asked to suppose that

> people-seeds drift about in the air like pollen, and if you open your windows, one may drift in and take root in your carpets or upholstery. You don't

> want children, so you fix up your windows with fine mesh screens, the very best you can buy. As can happen, however, and on very, very rare occasions does happen, one of the screens is defective, and a seed drifts in and takes root. (p. 59)

I label this picture "the fetus as mushroom" as a way of recalling that the imagery is scarcely original with Thomson. In his *De Cive,* Thomas Hobbes suggests that we "consider men as if but even now sprung out of the earth, and suddenly, like mushrooms, come to full maturity, without all kind of engagement to each other."[12] Part of the point of the analogy for Thomson is to suggest that parents may or may not, as they wish, take responsibility for children resulting from contraceptive failure. If, however, the opponent of abortion might wriggle a bit when claiming that cases of pregnancy resulting from rape differ in no special way from other pregnancies, surely we ought to wonder at least as much about an argument that suggests that pregnancy resulting from contraceptive failure is involuntary in a way similar to pregnancy resulting from rape.

But to focus on the analogy of fetus as mushroom: What angle of vision does it invite us to adopt? When the fetus is pictured this way, the biological relationship between mother (or parents) and child is of no special significance. It does not involve us personally in any important way, and we are essentially individuals isolated from one another. This is, I think, just one example of the very disembodied concept of a person that floats around Thomson's essay. There are strange dualisms scattered throughout it, not least of which is the talk about the mother's body as a house she owns. Indeed, we might say that here the analogies merge. Individualism and dualism feed one another as the fetus is conceived of both as parasite and mushroom.

Had Shakespeare known what Thomson knows we might have been bereft of some immortal lines. For, when Romeo creeps into Juliet's courtyard and she comes onto the balcony, Shakespeare places into Juliet's mouth the philosophy of Thomson and Hobbes:

> O Romeo, Romeo? Wherefore art thou Romeo?
> Deny thy father and refuse thy name!
> Or if thou wilt not, be but sworn my love,
> and I'll no longer be a Capulet.
> . . . .
> 'Tis but thy name that is my enemy.
> . . . .
> . . . O, be some other name![13]

But, of course, Shakespeare knows — and we are to know — that this philosophy is false. Juliet would have us pretend that we are "even now sprung out of the earth, and suddenly, like mushrooms, come to full maturity, without all kind of engagement to each other." It is not surprising that the story of one who believes that should be a tragedy. Romeo is a Montague and Juliet a Capulet. But is that not mere biology? Evidently not, for mere biology does not seem to have a part in the play. Romeo can no more deny his father or his name than Juliet can cease to be a Capulet. Their names help to fix their respective personal histories.

Thomson's picture of the fetus as mushroom would deny human, personal significance to a biological relationship that marks each of us. And here again we encounter the same problem in trying to adopt Thomson's angle of vision. We can think of creatures like the mushrooms her analogy suggest. But we cannot think of them in the terms her argument purports to grant: as human beings. For she has abstracted them from one of the relationships that importantly characterize our humanity.

My purpose in this chapter can, on the one hand, be construed very modestly indeed. I have merely tried to explain why it is that Thomson's defense of abortion appears to distort the issue almost beyond recognition. But, of course, the issues raised are really far from modest, and they involve questions beyond the scope of a single chapter.

The burden of my concern has been to ask how we are to discuss this issue. Thomson does not seem to me to discuss it in the terms she says she will grant. One does not know how she pictures a human being or what she thinks a person is. At times it seems that one cannot be a person unless some other person (how identified?) confers that status. At other times it seems that a person is a kind of disembodied, volitional agent. To subscribe to such view is, I believe, mistaken. But, then, how shall we discuss abortion? What shall we take Thomson to mean when she says she will assume that the fetus is a person? Her analogies seem to suggest that people are, in important ways, like parasites and mushrooms. Evidently she thinks it illuminating to picture human beings in that way. I confess that I do not. Thus, at least from certain perspectives, an argument like Thomson's must appear to be a sham, denying in its content what it professes to grant in its initial assumptions and thereby subtly leading the discussion astray.

Notes

1. Judith Jarvis Thomson, "A Defense of Abortion," *Philosophy and Public Affairs* 1 (Fall 1971): 47-66. Future references to this essay will be given by page number within parentheses in the body of the text.
2. The phrase is Iris Murdoch's in *The Sovereignty of Good* (London: Routledge and Kegan Paul, 1970), p. 48.
3. Annie Dillard, *Pilgrim at Tinker Creek* (New York: Harper's Magazine Press, 1974), p. 228.
4. Ibid., p. 229.
5. "Parasitology," in *The McGraw-Hill Encyclopedia of Science and Technology,* Volume 9 (New York: McGraw-Hill Books, 1971), p. 628.
6. "Parasitism," in *The Harper Encyclopedia of Science,* revised edition, ed. James R. Newman (New York: Harper and Row, 1967), p. 883.
7. Dillard, *Pilgrim at Tinker Creek,* p. 232.
8. Ibid., p. 176.
9. Gabriel Marcel, *Homo Viator* (New York: Harper Torchbooks, 1962), p. 87.
10. Augustine, *Concerning the City of God Against the Pagans,* trans. Henry Bettenson (New York: Penguin Books, 1972), XII, 3, 6.
11. "Parasitology," p. 628.
12. Thomas Hobbes, *Man and Citizen,* ed. Bernard Gert (Garden City, New York: Doubleday Anchor, 1972), VIII, 1. For similar imagery, cf. Lucretius, *De Rerum Natura,* V, pp. 783-825.
13. *Romeo and Juliet* II, ii, 35-38, 40, 44.

80 A Feminist-Liberation View of Abortion

Beverly Wildung Harrison

I describe my position as feminist liberation theological ethic of choice. I've written a long book on this subject [*Our Right to Choose: Toward a New Ethic of Abortion* (Boston: Beacon Press, 1983)]. When I published the book in 1983 my editor worried that I might regret the opening lines of the book, in which I say:

> The debate over abortion has moved outside the stream of "normal" political process and has pressed us into bitter social discourse. The disagreement about abortion is multifaceted and deep, and all participants contend that human lives are at stake. To be sure, morally sensitive people on both sides of the political controversy seek to minimize its vitriolic quality. Even so, a not insignificant number of persons opposed to legal abortion have moved beyond the "art" of politics as persuasion to coerce those who seek abortions. (p. 1)

Conversely, I point out that, prior to the legalization of abortion, many who were in favor of procreative choice — not to be confused with the moral choice for abortion — engaged in civil disobedience to assert what they believed to be their legitimate moral claims under a legal situation that was unjust. I tried to describe that the para-

From Beverly Wildung Harrison, "Third Presentation," *Church & Society* 80, no. 3 (January/February 1990): 60-71. Slightly abridged and edited from the original. Used by permission.

meters of the debate are serious and morally informed, and continued:

> Opponents of abortion share with many proponents an awareness, on some level, of this fundamental change in human history. The expectation that women's lives may, and even should, assume procreative choice is radically new. Nothing in our lives will remain unaffected by this movement toward procreative choice. Ancient ideas about women and the parameters of female existence were conditioned by the inevitability of procreation, even in cultures where fairly effective contraceptive controls existed. Those whose self-interest rests with the status quo have sensed the depth of change in human history implied by the emergence of a technology that assures procreative choice. Indeed, this awareness has much to do with the warlike zeal of the current controversy.
>
> We are only at the beginning of the public, political dispute over procreative choice in human history. If we do not obliterate ourselves with other life-destructive technologies in the meanwhile, the abortion debate probably will continue in one form or another for decades, perhaps for generations. This is because all of the intricate social systems that characterize human life — our institutions, mores, and customs and all the varied religious sacralization of these systems through all recorded history — have been shaped inherently *to control women's procreative power.* This control will not be relinquished without a struggle. (pp. 2-3)

Thus I threw down the gauntlet in terms of my own position. I have developed a complex position on two things: public policy with respect to abortion; and the act of, and the decision about, abortion, which I acknowledge to be morally and theologically more complex, and less certain, than my argument about public policy. One of the reasons I think my book has been rather marginalized and infrequently discussed in the debate, particularly in Christian circles, is because it is such a complicated argument, which I concede.

Three Audiences

I had three constituencies or audiences in mind as I wrote my book. As a professional Christian ethicist, a senior in terms of age and membership in the Society of Christian Ethics, I was persuaded by many women over the years that I was distinctly *required* (if not so much qualified) to answer the issue of the way in which, in the discourse of Christian ethics, misogyny is very much part and parcel of the theological and ethical debate about abortion. So I address a challenge to Christian religious ethicists, a challenge that is painful in my claims about the historically not-optimal grounds for Christian opposition to abortion.

Secondly, I address my work to moral philosophers — sometimes called secular moral philosophers (meaning only, of course, secular in the proper sense that they live in the laicized world, not in the clerical world). Many secular moral philosophers do exactly the same thing as Christian religious ethicists but have, I think, moved more rapidly to appreciate the claims of women's full dignity and moral agency. But they still have a liberal moral theory that I consider to be problematic.

The third audience that I address is women, and primarily two groups: women who are active in the reproductive rights organizations, and feminist activists.

I have long worked with groups such as Planned Parenthood, have long been a part of the Religious Coalition for Abortion Rights, and, more recently, have worked with more explicitly feminist groups such as the National Abortion Rights Action League. I have found that very often women were using two discourses — one appropriate to secular political debate in this society, and moral and theological discourses — but not understanding very clearly how they interacted. They were often, if I may say so, disposed to perceive abortion as what I recall as a liberal, single-issue shot. And of course abortion must not be viewed that way. I do not argue for abortion as a right, and I know now that happily much has changed in the last few years. I know of no reproductive rights organization using that language in its official materials.

I was also speaking to feminist activists — women who are specifically committed to enacting social policy that is supportive of the well-being of women; and particularly to feminist activists in the women's health movement of broadly based, and complicated, coalitions in this society. My message to these latter groups was about reformulating the debate to make clear that there are morally serious issues here, and that they must clearly differentiate legal and moral claims in this debate. Not that they can be ultimately separated; I do believe that the state has some responsibilities for the moral well-being of its citizens. Law has been described as "the moral tutor," and I hope we can do better than that. But law does set some limits in terms of mores and morality in society, although it has serious limits as well.

All moral traditions being liberal ones are primarily formulated, I believe, by a sort of secularism, which is somewhat dubious in that liberal political philosophy does not want the public debate to address the differing concepts we have of what a good community is. We can address what individual self-interest may be, we can legitimate that as part of the public discourse, but our particular liberalism is individualistic in a very precise sense in that it teaches us to think of these questions primarily in terms of what is good for persons — for individuals. I think it is part of our theological and moral mandate as Christians to insist that the issue of debate about the common good must become part of the common substance of the society. . . .

Theological and Moral Assumptions

The book has several theological and moral assumptions that are not widely shared in the Christian community. I think that is why it is easy to marginalize my argument and say that it is not really theological. I did not use theology as the entry point here. I used public moral discourse in the public debate as the entry point. But I do address the issue of theological and moral context. And I do so as liberation theologians do. Liberation theology is the source of much interest in our churches and in our theological institutions, but it is not well or widely understood, and so it puts me at some disadvantage.

One of my assumptions is that in every culture where Christianity has been the dominant religion there are always four theological ethical expressions. Some liberation theologians analyze this differently, but I will give you my particular version.

First, when a state has been also a predominantly Christian culture, there is the form of theology that I call *official state theology*: one that blends the understanding of divine calling and the vocation of the nation/state and sees the two as interacting and legitimating each other. The government of South Africa, for example, is a state that has an explicit Christian theology. It calls itself a Christian state; Marcos' Philippines did, as well. There are some governments that do this explicitly. We have a different tradition, but there also are powerful theological forces in this country arguing for a state-supported theology.

There is always also an *official theology in the churches,* called by different titles depending upon where you stand in relation to it. It is the theology of the leadership of the churches. When we look back at Christian history, it is Christian history read through the eyes of the elites of the Christian traditions — those whose text we have and remember. In the churches' present situation an official theology is struggling. It is being beckoned by the state to embrace the state and the state theology, and to do so — I will argue — in terms of the abortion issue.

The third manifestation of theology is what I will call *dissenting church theology.* Its present forms are chiefly liberal. Some forms of neo-orthodox theology are genuinely dissenting theologies but the problem, insofar as these theologies are highly individualistic and privatistic, is that they tend to present dissent [in the same ways]; in this case it is a dissent from the official position which is, of course, that which I would call patriarchal Christianity. The dissent is usually in terms of liberalism, appealing not to concerns for the social good but to the individual rights; therefore, frequently on the abortion issue the dissenting theologies are rather weak.

Liberation theologies derive from a different context. They are not necessarily church theologies; they are based upon a different understanding of divine agency, a different understanding of where the locus of the spirit lives and manifests itself in the world and in theologies that seek to serve marginalized communities, giving expression to the hope that is in them and the religious vision that is theirs. That is the theological framework in which I do my theology, and [in which] I want to be accountable. I want to be responsible in terms of church theology, including dissenting theology where I find much companionship. But I must tell you that my theology is done in order that women — fifty-one percent of humanity — should some day have a voice to name divine power and the nature of divine deliverance out of the fullness of our experience (as not all, but some, men have been able to do). Therefore, my accountability is quite different.

A Public Policy of Choices

With that as background, I want to describe the case I make for a public policy of choice and then elaborate on it in terms of moral decisions about choice. I argue — and this of course is contentious — that public policy about choice *must* be set with the recognition that a good society would be a society that minimizes coercion with respect to childbearing and reproduction. In a world with two thousand years of struggle, learning, and history, where we intend to be persons who value women's lives as profoundly as we value men's lives, we must recognize that if we were selecting rules for the good society, non-coercion in childbearing ought to be the intent of a good society. The minimalization of coercion in childbearing is fundamental to the reduction of violence in this society.

Next, I insist on the recognition of the full moral competence in the agency of women. This does not mean that women are morally superior or better. I certainly am not arguing, as I move into the specific decisions about abortions, that women don't make moral mistakes. I only observe in multifaceted ways, through the whole sweep of my argument, the extent to which female identity is associated with passivity, acquiescence, and sacrifice in the history of Christianity. Women are the exemplar Christians, or we are fallen women. And I argue that in the subtext about women is hidden this notion that women are only full moral agents when we conform to divine will as interpreted in patriarchal theology.

I also suggest that the question at stake with procreative choice is the question regarding the status of the pregnant woman in terms of full moral agency and the extent to which we must decide about whether or not pregnancy debilitates one and causes one to lose the standing of a moral agent. I also point out that the abortion dilemma must always be dealt with as it arises historically and concretely in women's lives. My book is about what it would be like if we Christians taught the history of abortion as the history of the struggle in women's lives to bring some coherence to the reproductive choice, rather than as a history of texts of the best remembered and most respected theologians (who, by the way, are important to me — but I do insist that on the subject of abortion they did not really give it much thought). They took over the general prohibitions to abortion because it always represented adultery. . . .

I ask that we look at the abortion dilemma, which is not a dilemma if you believe that the conceptus — the fertilized zygote — is a fully human person. It is a dilemma only in the sense that you have two fully existing persons whose interests may be at odds. If you think about it that way, you can always present the fetus as the most innocent, and in that model you naturally view abortion as always evil without looking at the circumstances.

Abortion arises in most cases because of a pregnancy that is distressing or unwanted; distressing because in the fundamental sense there are reasons for it to be unwanted. It arises in a number of situations that I will suggest. I am not giving privilege by mentioning coercion first. I do not want to argue my case on rape and incest, although I think rape and incest are heinous evils and I do not believe that coercion and childbearing should follow as the next social act on the victims. Pregnancy may be the result of coercion. It may be the result of no contraceptive precautions. Kristen Luker has written a book [*Taking a Chance: Abortion and the Decision Not to Contracept*] often used by the anti-abortion forces, and rightly so, because it's worrisome. She shows that there is a substantial population of young women out there who get pregnant repeatedly and use abortion rather casually and seem not to understand the issues at all. But we feminists look at that population and we know where those women came from. They came from being raised in a society in which they were never taught or never shaped by a profound message of female dignity and responsibility. Then, there are a few cases of contraceptive failure. Now, according to many anti-abortion protagonists in this society, that is really a very small minority. But it is not. Certainly no one who is responsible would dispute, I think, that well over half the abortions in this society are the result of contraceptive failure. Another situation is change of circumstances: the failure of a marriage, the collapse of one's economic underpinnings, all sorts of crises that can occur. This is the general typology of circumstances in which a woman may face an unwanted pregnancy.

Then there is a new and more difficult circumstance regarding genetic screening: because it is becoming almost mandatory now, women are frequently making discoveries about genetic disease or genetic atypicality (they are not the same thing). Gene disorders mean that your child will suffer from a deeply debilitating, painful physical demise and will die. Increasingly now, women and their partners have to decide what to do, sometimes within 48 hours after learning that their pregnancy is genetically atypical, and this is creating all sorts of difficulties.

Motherhood is an institution under attack from all sorts of sources. It is really tragic: we Christians are so preoccupied with abortion that we don't have time to think deeply about the total situation of procreative choice, which is worsening. I argue that the moral good is reproductive choice, the right of women to shape their lives in terms of their reproductive power in relation to the total scheme of the commitments, vocations, and values to which they are called, as others are called. We have to be very clear about sterilization abuse, which is still widespread although more subtle than it used to be; the limited advocacy of birth control technologies, what the embryologists are now suggesting that we think about in terms of the difference between contraceptive and contragestive technologies; poverty, certainly; and the high cost of child rearing — and you don't have to be poor to be daunted by the high cost not only of pregnancy and birth but of providing for children the rudiments of security in this society. There are innumerable other concerns in women's lives, including women's double and triple burdens, as forty percent of all children born in this society are raised by single mothers; that number is rapidly increasing and will continue to increase. The United Nations predicts that shortly the only abject poor in this world will be women and their dependent children. These projections are part of the historical situation. If we are going to be a church of justice and compassion, let's place our discussion in that context. . . .

Viability as a Criterion

I want to talk about the specific act of abortion. I address this to women deciding about abortion who have a responsibility to make that decision in relation to the others, their partners, husbands, lovers, and also other birth children, other members of the family, their roles in the community. They have a right to make that decision. But I argue that we must recognize, given all that we know about the intricate, intimate, physiological, spiritual, social process that is the coming to birth of a human being, that pre-embryos, embryos, and fetuses are involved. The reason science differentiates these terms is because there are differentiations in the process of coming to existence as a human being about which they must be clear if they are to do their work. (How theology and science are interrelated badly needs to be discussed.)

I understand that what Christians who argue that life begins at conception are really saying is that because conception is not an intentional human act we can understand it as the way God acts. I consider this the theology of the gaps: if human beings are not acting, then we can claim that God acts there. And that is not good enough in the modern world. We are part of nature. Our interventions shape and affect nature. Women's fertility has expanded. These things have changed constantly in history and we cannot use static notions. We have to, I argue, recognize that this is a process.

By what criteria are we saying that a particular form of human tissue, human genetic material, is a fully existent human person? It is a process. The criteria are debatable. (Anyone who says that they are not debatable, especially because God told us we can't think about it, is wrong. And we Presbyterians can turn ourselves into something we have never been, which is people who do not believe that the struggle for rational truth has any validity.) I propose viability as the appropriate criterion. Some of my readers begged me not to put that in my book. I have to put it there because it is what I believe. And that is what all of us should do on this issue. We should deliberate and think about these issues and we should stand for the best of the deliberations that we can make. So I named viability. They all said viability will become earlier because the conditions of pregnancy improve. Well, I took that risk, and in writing the new introduction to the second issue of the book, I am going to say that I still stand by that. . . .

In terms of this issue of viability, fetal life is not and could not be viable before the 23rd week of pregnancy, although most embryologists and Broadstein say reasonably the 26th week. Nor could a fetus have internal sensations, experience pain, be sensate in the usual sense. I argue that through this whole process a deciding woman should recognize that the further along she gets into the pregnancy, the weightier the moral reasons must be for ending the pregnancy. Obviously. Of course. But we live in a society in which the war over abortion is making it harder and harder for women to end pregnancies early.

Social Policy and Compromise

From my point of view, what can I consider the arena of compromise to be? I do not look for compromise in the fact that we will finally persuade each other specifically on how the individual choices about abortion should be resolved. I look for compromise at the level of social policy, and I have already said what it is. We must be committed to a society that enhances the dignity and full moral personhood of women. We must be committed to a society that attempts to reduce the resort to elective surgical abortion. We need a much broader social policy. We need in some ways to step back from the dilemma of abortion and treat it for what it is: a negative condition for stopping pregnancy when all else fails. We also need to spend far more energy talking about contraception and contragestion and the politics of making that available. Not to middle-stratum women — middle-stratum women will get abortions if they are criminalized again; you and I know that. . . .

We are at the point where we must ask ourselves seriously about contraception and contragestion. We must have those debates. And then we must also talk about services and availability for all women, because that is the issue. . . . There is an error in my book I did not catch. I said that 80 percent of all abortions were first trimester, and of course that is wrong. It is more like 93 percent in the first trimester. (Actually, some people now argue that it is 96 percent, but I think the number is going down because of the genetic testing issue.) In any case we really need to be committed to a social policy that reduces the point at which abortion is chosen, when it is chosen. There are many good moral reasons for this. Our commitment must be, therefore, to insist that unwanted pregnancy is not desirable, forcing women to bear children when they do not see that they have the resources to do so even when they don't want to. I argue that if we took the moral choice away from every man because he abused moral choice, no man would have any moral decision-making power in this society. Women do make choices — and we make bad choices. I am not trying to romanticize the female of the species. But we would optimize that choice and then would say that you also have an obligation to secure an abortion as rapidly as possible.

In Sweden they have moved from the typical abortion from twelve weeks to seven weeks — they have it down to seven weeks. With contragestives such as RU486 in France we could get it down to contragestion at the period of the early embryo. But the point is that Swedish society was behind that. We don't have to argue with women who make that choice, but we have to at least acknowledge that the state and the society give that discretion but urge its responsible condition, and abortions are available. They are not impediments to put in the way. The state can put all sorts of impediments in the way and by so doing does not prevent abortions as much as it makes them happen later. So I argue that until we talk seriously about public policy in the wider concrete context of women's lives, we cannot really talk about compromise. That's at the public policy level.

In terms of reconciliation among Christians, I believe as a liberation theologian that reconciliation is a gift of God, and I also believe that it is never fully embodied in our lifetime. I believe that we should all conduct our discourse within Christian community and in the wider public arena with great respect and effort to *hear,* which means presenting accurately what other people say. We also must recognize that we cannot artificially induce conditions of reconciliation. There are life and death issues at stake. The struggle that we are involved in is what this one little denomination — the Presbyterian Church — will do and how we shall stand. We are a divided people. And I believe that our positions must reflect that. They aren't going to be theologically optimal from any point of view. We have reached compromises. Others would like to force us to another set of compromises. We have to be honest about that. We are not in a position to decidedly affect public debate. But we are in a position to be who we are, a largely middle-stratum, sensitive, well-educated people with compassion who can help ameliorate the extremes of the debate but who also can insist that new concerns have to be faced in new ways. The status of the fetus and the dignity of women are new moral perspectives on the horizon.

81 Abortion and the Sexual Agenda: A Case for Pro-Life Feminism

Sidney Callahan

The abortion debate continues. In the latest and perhaps most crucial development, pro-life feminists are contesting pro-choice feminist claims that abortion rights are prerequisites for women's full development and social equality. The outcome of this debate may be decisive for the culture as a whole. Pro-life feminists, like myself, argue on good feminist principles that women can never achieve the fulfillment of feminist goals in a society permissive toward abortion.

These new arguments over abortion take place within liberal political circles. This round of intense intra-feminist conflict has spiraled beyond earlier right-versus-left abortion debates, which focused on "tragic choices," medical judgments, and legal compromises. Feminist theorists of the pro-choice position now put forth the demand for unrestricted abortion rights as a *moral imperative* and insist upon women's right to complete reproductive freedom. They morally justify the present situation and current abortion practices. Thus it is all the more important that pro-life feminists articulate their different feminist perspective.

These opposing arguments can best be seen when presented in turn. Perhaps the most highly developed feminist arguments for the morality and legality of abortion can be found in Beverly Wildung Harrison's *Our Right to Choose* (Beacon

From *Commonweal* 123 (April 25, 1986): 232-38. Used by permission.

Press, 1983) and Rosalind Pollack Petchesky's *Abortion and Woman's Choice* (Longman, 1984). Obviously it is difficult to do justice to these complex arguments, which draw on diverse strands of philosophy and social theory and are often interwoven in pro-choice feminists' own version of a "seamless garment." Yet the fundamental feminist case for the morality of abortion, encompassing the views of Harrison and Petchesky, can be analyzed in terms of four central moral claims: (1) the moral right to control one's own body; (2) the moral necessity of autonomy and choice in personal responsibility; (3) the moral claim for the contingent value of fetal life; (4) the moral right of women to true social equality.

1. The moral right to control one's own body.

Pro-choice feminism argues that a woman choosing an abortion is exercising a basic right of bodily integrity granted in our common law tradition. If she does not choose to be physically involved in the demands of pregnancy and birth, she should not be compelled to be so against her will. Just because it is *her* body which is involved, a woman should have the right to terminate any pregnancy, which at this point in medical history is tantamount to terminating fetal life. No one can be forced to donate an organ or submit to other invasive physical procedures for however good a cause. Thus no woman should be subjected to "compulsory pregnancy." And it should be noted that in pregnancy much more than a passive biological process is at stake.

From one perspective, the fetus is, as Petchesky says, a "biological parasite" taking resources from the woman's body. During pregnancy, a woman's whole life and energies will be actively involved in the nine-month process. Gestation and childbirth involve physical and psychological risks. After childbirth a woman will either be a mother who must undertake a twenty-year responsibility for childrearing, or face giving up her child for adoption or institutionalization. Since hers is the body, hers the risk, hers the burden, it is only just that she alone should be free to decide on pregnancy or abortion.

This moral claim to abortion, according to the pro-choice feminists, is especially valid in an individualistic society in which women cannot count on medical care or social support in pregnancy, childbirth, or child rearing. A moral abortion decision is never made in a social vacuum, but in the real-life society which exists here and now.

2. The moral necessity of autonomy and choice in personal responsibility.

Beyond the claim for individual *bodily* integrity, the pro-choice feminists claim that to be a full adult *morally*, a woman must be able to make responsible life commitments. To plan, choose, and exercise personal responsibility, one must have control of reproduction. A woman must be able to make yes-or-no decisions about a specific pregnancy, according to her present situation, resources, prior commitments, and life plan. Only with such reproductive freedom can a woman have the moral autonomy necessary to make mature commitments, in the area of family, work, or education.

Contraception provides a measure of personal control, but contraceptive failure or other chance events can too easily result in involuntary pregnancy. Only free access to abortion can provide the necessary guarantee. The chance biological process of an involuntary pregnancy should not be allowed to override all the other personal commitments and responsibilities a woman has: to others, to family, to work, to education, to her future development, health, or well-being. Without reproductive freedom, women's personal moral agency and human consciousness are subjected to biology and chance.

3. The moral claim for the contingent value of fetal life.

Pro-choice feminist exponents like Harrison and Petchesky claim that the value of fetal life is contingent upon the woman's free consent and subjective acceptance. The fetus must be invested with maternal valuing in order to become human. This process of "humanization" through personal consciousness and "sociality" can only be bestowed by the woman in whose body and psychosocial system a new life must mature. The meaning and value of fetal life are constructed by the woman; without this personal conferral there only exists a biological, physiological process. Thus fetal interests or fetal rights can never outweigh the woman's prior interest and rights. If a woman does not consent to invest her pregnancy with meaning or value, then the merely biological process can be freely terminated. Prior to her own free choice and conscious investment, a woman cannot be described as a "mother" nor can a "child" be said to exist.

Moreover, in cases of voluntary pregnancy, a woman can withdraw consent if fetal genetic defects or some other problem emerges at any time before birth. Late abortion should thus be granted without legal restrictions. Even the minimal qualifications and limitations on women embedded in *Roe v. Wade* are unacceptable — repressive remnants of patriarchal unwillingness to give power to women.

4. The moral right of women to full social equality.

Women have a moral right to full social equality. They should not be restricted or subordinated because of their sex. But this morally required equality cannot be realized without abortion's certain control of reproduction. Female social equality depends upon being able to compete and participate as freely as males can in the structures of educational and economic life. If a woman cannot control when and how she will be pregnant or rear children, she is at a distinct disadvantage, especially in our male-dominated world.

Psychological equality and well-being is also at stake. Women must enjoy the basic right of a person to the free exercise of heterosexual intercourse and full sexual expression, separated from procreation. No less than males, women should be able to be sexually active without the constantly inhibiting fear of pregnancy. Abortion is necessary for women's sexual fulfillment and the growth of uninhibited feminine self-confidence and ownership of their sexual powers.

But true sexual and reproductive freedom means freedom to procreate as well as to inhibit fertility. Pro-choice feminists are also worried that women's freedom to reproduce will be curtailed through the abuse of sterilization and needless hysterectomies. Besides the punitive tendencies of a male-dominated health care system, especially in response to repeated abortions or welfare pregnancies, there are other economic and social pressures inhibiting reproduction. Genuine reproductive freedom implies that day care, medical care, and financial support would be provided mothers, while fathers would take the full share in the burden and delights of raising children.

Many pro-choice feminists identify feminist ideals with communitarian, ecologically sensitive approaches to reshaping society. Following theorists like Sara Ruddick and Carol Gilligan, they link abortion rights with the growth of "maternal thinking" in our heretofore patriarchal society. Maternal thinking is loosely defined as a responsible commitment to the loving nurture of specific human beings as they actually exist in socially embedded interpersonal contexts. It is a moral perspective very different from the abstract, competitive, isolated, and principled rigidity so characteristic of patriarchy.

How does a pro-life feminist respond to these arguments? Pro-life feminists grant the good intentions of their pro-choice counterparts but protest that the pro-choice position is flawed, morally inadequate, and inconsistent with feminism's basic demands for justice. Pro-life feminists champion a more encompassing moral ideal. They recognize the claims of fetal life and offer a different perspective on what is good for women. The feminist vision is expanded and refocused.

1. From the moral right to control one's own body to a more inclusive ideal of justice.

The moral right to control one's own body does apply to cases of organ transplants, mastectomies, contraception, and sterilization; but it is not a conceptualization adequate for abortion. The abortion dilemma is caused by the fact that 266 days following a conception in one body, another body will emerge. One's own body no longer exists as a single unit but is engendering another organism's life. This dynamic passage from conception to birth is genetically ordered and universally found in the human species. Pregnancy is not like the growth of cancer or infestation by a biological parasite; it is the way every human being enters the world. Strained philosophical analogies fail to apply: having a baby is not like rescuing a drowning person, being hooked up to a famous violinist's artificial life-support system, donating organs for transplant — or anything else.

As embryology and fetology advance, it becomes clear that human development is a continuum. Just as astronomers are studying the first three minutes in the genesis of the universe, so the first moments, days, and weeks at the beginning of human life are the subject of increasing scientific attention. While neonatology pushes the definition of viability ever earlier, ultrasound and fetology expand the concept of the patient *in utero.* Within such a continuous growth process, it is hard to defend logically any demarcation point after conception as the point at which an immature form of human life is so different from the day before or the day after, that it can be morally or legally discounted as a non-person. Even the moment of birth can hardly differentiate a nine-month fetus from a newborn. It is not surprising that those who countenance late abortions are logically led to endorse selective infanticide.

The same legal tradition which in our society guarantees the right to control one's own body firmly recognizes the wrongfulness of harming other bodies, however immature, dependent, different looking, or powerless. The handicapped, the retarded, and newborns are legally protected from deliberate harm. Pro-life feminists reject the suppositions that would except the unborn from this protection.

After all, debates similar to those about the fetus were once conducted about feminine personhood. Just as women, or blacks, were considered too different, too underdeveloped, too "biological," to have souls or to possess legal rights, so the fetus is now seen as "merely" biological life, subsidiary to a person. A woman was once viewed as incorporated into the "one flesh" of her husband's person; she too was a form of bodily property. In all partriarchal unjust systems, lesser orders of human life are granted rights only when wanted, chosen, or invested with value by the powerful.

Fortunately, in the course of civilization there has been a gradual realization that justice demands the powerless and dependent to be protected against the uses of power wielded unilaterally. No human can be treated as a means to an end without consent. The fetus is an immature, dependent form of human life which only needs time and protection to develop. Surely, immaturity and dependence are not crimes.

In an effort to think about the essential requirements of a just society, philosophers like John Rawls recommend imagining yourself in an "original position," in which your position in the society to be created is hidden by a "veil of ignorance." You will have to weigh the possibility that any inequalities inherent in that society's practices may rebound upon you in the worst, as well as in the best, conceivable way. This thought experiment helps ensure justice for all.

Beverly Harrison argues that in such an envisioning of society everyone would institute abortion rights in order to guarantee that if one turned out to be a woman one would have reproductive freedom. But surely in the original position and behind the "veil of ignorance," you would have to contemplate the possibility of being the particular fetus to be aborted. Since everyone has passed through the fetal stage of development, it is false to refuse to imagine oneself in this state when thinking about a potential world in which justice would govern. Would it be just that an embryonic life — in half the cases, of course, a female life — be sacrificed to the right of a woman's control over her own body? A woman may be pregnant without consent and experience a great many penalties, but a fetus killed without consent pays the ultimate penalty.

It does not matter (*The Silent Scream* notwithstanding) whether the fetus being killed is fully conscious or feels pain. We do not sanction killing the innocent if it can be done painlessly or without the victim's awareness. Consciousness becomes important to the abortion debate because it is used as a criterion for the "personhood" so often seen as the prerequisite for legal protection. Yet certain philosophers set the standard of personhood so high that half the human race could not meet the criteria during most of their waking hours (let alone their sleeping ones). Sentience, self-consciousness, rational decision-making, social participation? Surely no infant or child under two, could qualify. Either our idea of person must be expanded or another criterion, such as human life itself, be employed to protect the weak in a just society. Pro-life feminists who defend the fetus empathetically identify with an immature state of growth passed through by themselves, their children, and everyone now alive.

It also seems a travesty of just procedures that a pregnant woman now, in effect, acts as sole judge of her own case, under the most stressful conditions. Yes, one can acknowledge that the pregnant woman will be subject to the potential burdens arising from a pregnancy, but it has never been thought right to have an interested party, especially the more powerful party, decide his or her own case when there may be a conflict of interest. If one considers the matter as a case of a powerful versus a powerless, silenced claimant, the pro-choice feminist argument can rightly be inverted: since hers is the body, hers the risk, and hers the greater burden, then how in fairness can a woman be the sole judge of the fetal right to life?

Human ambivalence, a bias toward self-interest, and emotional stress have always been recognized as endangering judgment. Freud declared that love and hate are so entwined that if instant thoughts could kill, we would all be dead in the bosom of our families. In the case of a woman's involuntary pregnancy, a complex, long-term solution requiring effort and energy has to compete with the immediate solution offered by a morning's visit to an abortion clinic. On the simple, perceptual plane, with imagination and thinking curtailed, the speed, ease, and privacy of abortion, combined with the small size of the embryo, tend to make early abortions seem less morally serious — even though speed, size, technical ease, and the private nature of an act have no moral standing.

As the most recent immigrants from non-personhood, feminists have traditionally fought for justice for themselves and the world. Women rally to feminism as a new and better way to live. Rejecting male aggression and destruction; feminists seek alternative, peaceful, ecologically sensitive means to resolve conflicts while respecting human potentiality. It is a chilling inconsistency to see pro-choice feminists demanding continued access to assembly-line, technological methods of fetal killing — the vacuum aspirator, prostaglandins, and dilation and evacuation. It is a betrayal of feminism, which has built the struggle for justice on the bedrock of women's empathy. After all, "maternal thinking" receives its name from a mother's unconditional acceptance and nurture of dependent, immature life. It is difficult to develop concern for women, children, the poor and the dispossessed — and to care about peace — and at the same time ignore fetal life.

2. From the necessity of autonomy and choice in personal responsibility to an expanded sense of responsibility.

A distorted idea of morality overemphasizes individual autonomy and active choice. Morality has often been viewed too exclusively as a matter of human agency and decisive action. In moral behavior persons must explicitly choose and aggressively exert their wills to intervene in the natural and social environments. The human will dominates the body, overcomes the given, breaks out of the material limits of nature. Thus if one does not choose to be pregnant or cannot rear a child, who must be given up for adoption, then better to abort the pregnancy. Willing, planning, choosing one's moral commitments through the contracting of one's individual resources becomes the premier model of moral responsibility.

But morality also consists of the good and worthy acceptance of the unexpected events that life presents. Responsiveness and response-ability to things unchosen are also instances of the highest human moral capacity. Morality is not confined to contracted agreements of isolated individuals. Yes, one is obligated by explicit contracts freely initiated, but human beings are also obligated by implicit compacts and involuntary relationships in which persons simply find themselves. To be embedded in a family, a neighborhood, a social system, brings moral obligations which were never entered into with informed consent.

Parent-child relationships are one instance of implicit moral obligations arising by virtue of our being part of the interdependent human community. A woman, involuntarily pregnant, has a moral obligation to the now-existing dependent fetus whether she explicitly consented to its existence or not. No pro-life feminist would dispute the forceful observations of pro-choice feminists about the extreme difficulties that bearing an unwanted child in our society can entail. But the stronger force of the fetal claim presses a woman to accept these burdens; the fetus possesses rights arising from its extreme need and the interdependency and unity of humankind. The woman's moral obligation arises both from her status as a human being embedded in the interdependent human community and her unique lifegiving female reproductive power. To follow the pro-choice feminist ideology of insistent individualistic autonomy and control is to betray a fundamental basis of the moral life.

3. From the moral claim of the contingent value of fetal life to the moral claim for the intrinsic value of human life.

The feminist pro-choice position which claims that the value of the fetus is contingent upon the pregnant woman's bestowal — or willed, conscious "construction" — of humanhood is seriously flawed. The inadequacies of this position flow from the erroneous premises (1) that human value and rights can be granted by individual will; (2) that the individual woman's consciousness can exist and operate in an *a priori* isolated fashion; and (3) that "mere" biological, genetic human life has little meaning. Pro-life feminism takes a very different stance to life and nature.

Human life from the beginning to the end of development *has* intrinsic value, which does not depend on meeting the selective criteria or tests set up by powerful others. A fundamental humanist assumption is at stake here. Either we are going to value embodied human life and humanity as a good thing, or take some variant of the nihilist position that assumes human life is just one more random occurrence in the universe such that each instance of human life must explicitly be justified to prove itself worthy to continue. When faced with a new life, or an involuntary pregnancy, there is a world of difference in whether one first asks, "Why continue?" or "Why not?" Where is the burden of proof going to rest? The concept of "compulsory pregnancy" is as distorted as labeling life "compulsory aging."

In a sound moral tradition, human rights arise from human needs, and it is the very nature of a right, or valid claim upon another, that it cannot be denied, conditionally delayed, or rescinded by more powerful others at their behest. It seems fallacious to hold that in the case of the fetus it is the pregnant woman alone who gives or removes its right to life and human status solely through her subjective conscious investment or "humanization." Surely no pregnant woman (or any other individual member of the species) has created her own human nature by an individually willed act of consciousness, nor for that matter been able to guarantee her own human rights. An individual woman and the unique individual embryonic life within her can only exist because of their participation in the genetic inheritance of the human species as a whole. Biological life should never be discounted. Membership in the species, or collective human family, is the basis for human solidarity, equality, and natural human rights.

4. The moral right of women to full social equality from a pro-life feminist perspective.

Pro-life feminists and pro-choice feminists are totally agreed on the moral right of women to the full social equality so far denied them. The disagreement between them concerns the definition of the desired goal and the best means to get there. Permissive abortion laws do not bring women reproductive freedom, social equality, sexual fulfillment, or full personal development.

Pragmatic failures of a pro-choice feminist position combined with a lack of moral vision are, in fact, causing disaffection among young women. Middle-aged pro-choice feminists blamed the "big chill" on the general conservative backlash. But they should look rather to their own elitist acceptance of male models of sex and to the sad picture they present of women's lives. Pitting women against their own offspring is not only morally offensive, it is psychologically and politically destructive. Women will never climb to equality and social empowerment over mounds of dead fetuses, numbering now in the millions. As long as most women choose to bear children, they stand to gain from the same constellation of attitudes and institutions that will also protect the fetus in the woman's womb — and they stand to lose from the cultural assumptions that support permissive abortion. Despite temporary conflicts of interest, feminine and fetal liberation are ultimately one and the same cause.

Women's rights and liberation are pragmatically linked to fetal rights because to obtain true equality, women need (1) more social support and changes in the structure of society, and (2) increased self-confidence, self-expectations, and self-esteem. Society in general, and men in particular, have to provide women more support in rearing the next generation, or our devastating feminization of poverty will continue. But if a woman claims the right to decide by herself whether the fetus becomes a child or not, what does this do to parental and communal responsibility? Why should men share responsibility for child support or childrearing if they cannot share in what is asserted to be the woman's sole decision? Furthermore, if explicit intentions and consciously accepted contracts are necessary for moral obligations, why should men be held responsible for what *they* do not voluntarily choose to happen? By pro-choice reasoning, a man who does not want to have a child, or whose contraceptive fails, can be exempted from the responsibilities of fatherhood and child support. Traditionally, many men have been laggards in assuming parental responsibility and support for their children; ironically, ready abortions often advocated as a response to male dereliction, legitimizes male irresponsibility and paves the way for even more male detatchment and lack of commitment.

For that matter, why should the state provide a system of day-care or child support, or require workplaces to accommodate women's maternity and the needs of childbearing? Permissive abortion, granted in the name of women's privacy and reproductive freedom, ratifies the view that pregnancies and children are a woman's private individual responsibility. More and more frequently, we hear some version of this old rationalization: if she refuses to get rid of it, it's her problem. A child becomes a product of the individual woman's freely chosen investment, a form of private property resulting from her own cost-benefit calculation. The larger community is relieved of moral responsibility.

With legal abortion freely available, a clear cultural message is given: conception and pregnancy are no longer serious moral matters. With abortion as an acceptable alternative, contraception is not as responsibly used; women take risks, often at the urging of male sexual partners. Repeat abortions increase, with all their psychological and medical repercussions. With more abortion there is more abortion. Behavior shapes thought as well as the other way around. One tends to justify morally what one has done; what becomes commonplace and institutionalized seems harmless. Habituation is a powerful psychological force. Psychologically it is also true that whatever is avoided becomes more threatening; in phobias it is the retreat from anxiety-producing events which reinforces future avoidance. Women begin to see themselves as too weak to cope with involuntary pregnancies. Finally, through the potency of social pressure and the force of inertia, it becomes more and more difficult, in fact almost unthinkable, *not* to use abortion to solve problem pregnancies. Abortion becomes no longer a choice but a "necessity."

But "necessity," beyond the organic failure and death of the body, is a dynamic social construction open to interpretation. The thrust of present feminist pro-choice arguments can only increase the justifiable indications for "necessary" abortion; every unwanted fetal handicap becomes more and more unacceptable. Repeatedly assured that in the name of reproductive freedom, women have a right to specify which pregnancies and which children they will accept, women justify sex selection, and abort unwanted females. Female infanticide, after all, is probably as old a custom as the human species possesses. Indeed, all kinds of selection of the fit and the favored for the good of the family and the tribe have always existed. Selective extinction is no new program.

There are far better goals for feminists to pursue. Pro-life feminists seek to expand and deepen the more communitarian, maternal elements of feminism — and move society from its male-dominated course. First and foremost, women have to insist upon a different, woman-centered approach to sex and reproduction. While Margaret Mead stressed the "womb envy" of males in other societies, it has been more or less repressed in our own.

In our male-dominated world, what men don't do, doesn't count. Pregnancy, childbirth, and nursing have been characterized as passive, debilitating, animal-like. The disease model of pregnancy and birth has been entrenched. This female disease or impairment, with its attendant "female troubles," naturally handicaps women in the "real" world of hunting, war, and the corporate fast track. Many pro-choice feminists, deliberately childless, adopt the male perspective when they cite the "basic injustice that women have to bear the babies," instead of seeing the injustice in the fact that men cannot. Women's biologically unique capacity and privilege has been denied, despised, and suppressed under male domination; unfortunately, many women have fallen for the phallic fallacy.

Childbirth often appears in pro-choice literature as a painful, traumatic, life-threatening experience. Yet giving birth is accurately seen as an arduous but normal exercise of life-giving power, a violent and ecstatic peak experience, which men can never know. Ironically, some pro-choice men and women think and talk of pregnancy and childbirth with the same repugnance that ancient ascetics displayed toward orgasms and sexual intercourse. The similarity may not be accidental. The obstetrician Niles Newton, herself a mother, has written of the extended threefold sexuality of women, who can experience orgasm, birth, and nursing as passionate pleasure-giving experiences. All of these are involuntary processes of the female body. Only orgasm, which males share, has been glorified as an involuntary function that is nature's great gift; the involuntary feminine processes of childbirth and nursing have been seen as bondage to biology.

Fully accepting our bodies as ourselves, what should women want? I think women will only flourish when there is a feminization of sexuality, very different from the current cultural trend toward masculinizing female sexuality. Women can never have the self-confidence and self-esteem they need to achieve feminist goals in society until a more holistic, feminine model of sexuality becomes the dominant cultural ethos. To say this affirms the view that men and women differ in the domain of sexual functioning, although they are more alike than different in other personality characteristics and competencies. For those of us committed to achieving sexual equality in the culture, it may be hard to accept the fact that sexual differences make it imperative to talk of distinct male and female models of sexuality. But if one wants to change sexual roles, one has to recognize pre-existing conditions. A great deal of evidence is accumulating which points to biological pressures for different male and female sexual functioning.

Males always and everywhere have been more physically aggressive and more likely to fuse sexuality with aggression and dominance. Females may be more variable in their sexuality, but since Masters and Johnson, we know that women have a greater capacity than men for repeated orgasm and a more tenuous path to arousal and orgasmic release. Most obviously, women also have a far greater sociobiological investment in the act of human reproduction. On the whole, women as compared to men possess a sexuality which is more complex, more intense, more extended in time, involving higher investment, risks, and psychosocial involvement.

Considering the differences in sexual functioning, it is not surprising that men and women in the same culture have often constructed different sexual ideals. In Western culture, since the nineteenth century at least, most women have espoused a version of sexual functioning in which sex acts are embedded within deep emotional bonds and secure long-term commitments. Within these committed "pair bonds" males assume parental obligation. In the idealized Victorian version of the Christian sexual ethic, culturally endorsed and maintained by women, the double standard was not countenanced. Men and women did not need to marry to be whole persons, but if they did engage in sexual functioning, they were to be equally chaste, faithful, responsible, loving, and parentally concerned. Many of the most influential women in the nineteenth-century women's movement preached and lived this sexual ethic, often by the side of exemplary feminist men. While the ideal has never been universally obtained, a culturally dominant demand for monogamy, self-control, and emotionally bonded and committed sex works well for women in every stage of their sexual life cycles. When love, chastity, fidelity, and commitment for better or worse are the ascendant cultural prerequisites for sexual functioning, young girls and women expect protection from rape and seduction, adult women justifiably demand male support in childrearing, and older women are more protected from abandonment as their biological attractions wane.

Of course, these feminine sexual ideals always coexisted in competition with another view. A more male-oriented model of erotic or amative sexuality endorses sexual permissiveness without long-term commitment or reproductive focus. Erotic sexuality emphasizes pleasure, play, passion, individual self-expression, and romantic games of courtship and conquest. It is assumed that a variety of partners and sexual experiences are necessary to stimulate romantic passion. This erotic model of the sexual life has often worked satisfactorily for men, both heterosexual and gay, and for certain cultural elites. But for the average woman, it is quite destructive. Women can only play the erotic game successfully when, like the "*Cosmopolitan* woman," they are young, physically attractive, economically powerful, and fulfilled enough in a career to be willing to sacrifice family life. Abortion is also required. As our society increasingly endorses this male-oriented, permissive view of sexuality, it is all too ready to give women abortion on demand. Abortion helps a woman's body be more like a man's. It has been observed that *Roe v. Wade* removed the last defense women possessed against male sexual demands.

Unfortunately, the modern feminist movement made a mistaken move at a critical juncture. Rightly rebelling against patriarchy, unequal education, restricted work opportunities, and women's downtrodden political status, feminists also rejected the nineteenth-century feminine sexual ethic. Amative, erotic, permissive sexuality (along with abortion rights) became symbolically identified with other struggles for social equality in education, work, and politics. This feminist mistake also turned off many potential recruits among women who could not deny the positive dimensions of their own traditional feminine roles, nor their allegiance to the older feminine sexual ethic of love and fidelity.

An ironic situation then arose in which many pro-choice feminists preach their own double standard. In the world of work and career, women are urged to grow up, to display mature self-discipline and self-control; they are told to persevere in long-term commitments, to cope with unexpected obstacles by learning to tough out the inevitable sufferings and setbacks entailed in life and work. But this mature ethic of commitment and self-discipline, recommended as the only way to progress in the world of work and personal achievement, is discounted in the domain of sexuality.

In pro-choice feminism, a permissive, erotic view of sexuality is assumed to be the only option. Sexual intercourse with a variety of partners is seen as "inevitable" from a young age and as a positive growth experience to be managed by access to contraception and abortion. Unfortunately, the pervasive cultural conviction that adolescents, or their elders, cannot exercise sexual self-control, undermines the responsible use of contraception. When a pregnancy occurs, the first abortion is viewed by some pro-choice circles as a *rite de passage*. Responsibly choosing an abortion supposedly ensures that a young woman will take charge of her own life, make her own decisions, and carefully practice contraception. But the social dynamics of a permissive, erotic model of sexuality, coupled with permissive laws, work toward repeat abortions. Instead of being empowered by their abortion choices, young women having abortions are confronting the debilitating reality of *not* bringing a baby into the world; *not* being able to count on a committed male partner; *not* accounting oneself strong enough, or the master of enough resources, to avoid killing the fetus. Young women are hardly going to develop the self-esteem, self-discipline, and self-confidence necessary to confront a male-dominated society through abortion.

The male-oriented sexual orientation has been harmful to women and children. It has helped bring us epidemics of venereal disease, infertility, pornography, sexual abuse, adolescent pregnancy, divorce, displaced older women, and abortion. Will these signals of something amiss stimulate pro-choice feminists to rethink what kind of sex ideal really serves women's best interests? While the erotic model cannot encompass commitment, the committed model can — happily encompass and encourage romance, passion, and playfulness. In fact, within the security of long-term commitments, women may be more likely to experience sexual pleasure and fulfillment.

The pro-life feminist position is not a return to the old feminine mystique. The espousal of "the eternal feminine" erred by viewing sexuality as so sacred that it cannot be humanly shaped at all. Woman's *whole* nature was supposed to be opposite man's, necessitating complementary and radically different social roles. Followed to its logical conclusion, such a view presumes that reproductive and sexual experience is necessary for human fulfillment. But as the early feminists insisted, no woman has to marry or engage in sexual intercourse to be fulfilled, nor does a woman have to give birth and raise children to be complete, nor must she stay home and function as an earth mother. But female sexuality does need to be deeply respected as a unique potential and trust. Since most contraceptives and sterilization procedures really do involve only the woman's body rather than destroying new life, they can be an acceptable and responsible moral option.

With sterilization available to accelerate the inevitable natural ending of fertility and childbearing, a woman confronts only a limited number of years in which she exercises her reproductive trust and may have to respond to an unplanned pregnancy. Responsible use of contraception can lower the probabilities even more. Yet abortion is not decreasing. The reason is the current permissive attitude embodied in the law, not the "hard cases" which constitute 3 percent of today's abortions. Since attitudes, the law, and behavior interact, pro-life feminists conclude that unless there is an enforced limitation of abortion, which currently confirms the sexual and social status quo, alternatives will never be developed. For women to get what they need in order to combine childbearing, education, and careers, society has to recognize that female bodies come with wombs. Women and their reproductive power, and the children women have, must be supported in new ways. Another and different round of feminist consciousness-raising is needed in which all of women's potential is accorded respect. This time, instead of humbly buying entrée by conforming to male lifestyles, women will demand that society accommodate itself to them.

New feminist efforts to rethink the meaning of sexuality, femininity, and reproduction are all the more vital as new techniques for artificial reproduction, surrogate motherhood, and the like present a whole new set of dilemmas. In the long run, the very long run, the abortion debate may be merely the opening round in a series of far-reaching struggles over the role of human sexuality and the ethics of reproduction. Significant changes in the culture, both positive and negative in outcome, may begin as local storms of controversy. We may be at one of those vaguely realized thresholds when we had best come to full attention. What kind of people are we going to be? Pro-life feminists pursue a vision for their sisters, daughters, and granddaughters. Will their great-granddaughters be grateful?

82 Liberation, Abortion, and Responsibility

Margaret A. Farley

The Present Impasse

When I was asked to write this article, it was suggested that I might want to assess the Roman Catholic church's position on abortion from my standpoint as a woman. It might also have been suggested that I evaluate the Women's Liberation position on abortion from my standpoint as a Roman Catholic. I have found it impossible to do either without falling into a recitation of concerns which anti-abortionists and pro-abortionists have presented to one another almost to the point of tedium. It occurred to me that it might be interesting, but on the whole unenlightening, to discuss rather the blurring of stereotypical positions when they are seen coming from concrete individuals who nonetheless stand in identifiable groups. I came finally to the conclusion that my own central concern now with the state of the abortion debate focuses on the present impasse between strong anti-abortionists (though clearly not equated with Roman Catholics, at least well represented by them) and strong pro-abortionists (though surely not equated with feminists, yet most significantly represented by them). It is an impasse not only in moral discourse, or in struggles between wants and beliefs, or in political battles for different sorts of laws (the battles are for the time being largely over on the legal front, and where they continue, they cannot be described as being at an impasse).[1] It is rather, an impasse in efforts either to mediate or to join issue between what are fundamentally opposing conscience claims, profoundly different experiences of moral obligation. If such an impasse remains unresolved for long, it seems to me that it can only contribute to a deepening moral anguish or a growing moral apathy, and to an overall societal fragmentation or self-deception.[2] One need not, perhaps, paint the picture so dramatically in order to recognize in it a cause for moral concern.

It is to be expected that in a genuinely pluralistic society there will at times emerge between different groups of persons contradictory experiences of moral obligation. Not only diversity but conflict will appear in regard to moral values. Intellectual convictions regarding moral action will produce opposing ethical arguments, but more than this, different and opposing experiences of obligation to action may bring persons in the practical order to painful cross purposes and attempts at mutually exclusive patterns of behavior.

Sophisticated forms of pluralism eliminate conflict by allowing diverse beliefs, ways of action, modes of decision, in so far as these do not seriously interfere with one another. One may (within some limits) worship as one wills, drink as one wills, speak as one wills, marry as one wills, beget children as one wills, because all of these are possible without preventing other persons from doing these and more things in other ways. Peaceful coexistence, in terms of responding to diverse experiences of moral obligation, is a highly developed pattern of social living. Conflict that would arise from infringement upon selves, property or action, is avoided by a society's acceptance of protective laws whose effectiveness depends in part on their ability to allow each member of society at least to follow his or her conscience (if not to pursue his or her every desire).

Some conscience calls (or experiences of moral obligation), however, are not so easily harmonized into patterns of coexistence. This is the case when moral obligations are perceived so differently that they demand of different persons actions that cannot be neatly relegated to a carefully apportioned private sphere. Thus, for example, opposing perceptions of obligations in relation to innocent third parties can constitute acute and seemingly unresolvable points of public conflict between private experiences of moral obligation. I take it that

From *Reflection* 71 (May 1974): 9-13. Used by permission.

such a situation obtains relative to the issue of abortion. On the one hand, some persons experience a profound and compelling obligation to alleviate situations which are oppressive and harmful to women. On the other hand, some persons experience an equally profound and compelling obligation to protect the lives of human fetuses.[3] In terms of their perceptions of the ways to respond to these obligations, these two groups of persons are led inevitably into public conflict. The goal of the one cannot be had if the goal of the other is to be achieved.

Given the nature of the experience of moral obligation (that is, its experience as an unconditional claim addressed to one's freedom), neither party to a dispute such as the one I have been describing (that is, one which involves concretely opposing courses of action) can simply retire to the sidelines. It would be a strange notion of conscience which would allow for passive acceptance of what is perceived as inherently harmful and unjust to third parties. Thus, those who understood restrictive abortion laws to be part of the overwhelming structures of oppression for women experienced themselves as obligated to work for liberalization of those laws. But those who understood abortion to be the taking of human life experienced no less an obligation to try to withstand the efforts of the others. And now, too, each of these groups of persons experiences a continuing obligation to secure the rights and welfare of either women or fetuses. The current legal status of the question does not settle the moral struggle which must continue between these groups. It is this struggle, however, which seems to me to be at an impasse — unresolved, and, without some advance in moral discourse, unresolvable. It can simply remain unresolved, of course (as long as in the realm of action there is at least no fighting in the streets — or in the hospitals and clinics), but the price of leaving a conflict which has been so large a concern for such large portions of society in a state of limbo may be, as I have suggested above, greater than it immediately appears to be. The conflict may never be resolved, but it seems to me crucial that we attempt to resolve the present impasse in which the conflict is caught. The only way open to such a resolution is precisely some advance in the moral discourse which engages the parties to the conflict.

The nature of the stalemate in moral discourse about abortion is suggested in the frequent observations that the opposing sides never really join issue. There is sometimes the implication given that this failure to come to terms with the opposite position is the result of malice, culpable insensitivity, or stupidity. On the contrary, it seems to me quite possible that it is a consequence of the very intensity of the experience of moral obligation which characterizes those on both sides of the question. The difficulty is that the objects which give rise to these experiences of obligation are not the same, and hence the focus of attention for anti-abortionists, who do not perceive themselves as against women, but rather for fetuses. Similarly, pro-abortionists do not understand themselves as against fetuses, but rather for women. The possibility that what each is for does indeed oppose what the other is for is perceived only in a defensive way. The strength of the concern which each side has for one object rather than the other does in fact, however, prevent each side from sharing the moral awareness of the other, and does in fact, also, make each the opponent of the other's concern.[4] Hence, there arise the mutual accusations that one side refuses to attend to the reality of the object with which the other side is concerned. The impasse is, indeed, a "passing in the night."

Conflicting experiences of moral obligation may be resolved by one person's being convinced by another that there is, after all, no justification for what was perceived as an obligation. It is not likely that either side in the abortion debate will soon be convinced in this way. Nor, I would argue, ought they to be. But past efforts have also persuaded me that there is little to be gained in simply calling on one side or the other to take into account the reality of the object with which the other is concerned. What might begin to break the impasse, however, is a decision by each to consider seriously the experience of the other precisely as a genuine experience of moral obligation. This would not entail a legitimizing of the experience of the other (for we can clearly have experiences of moral obligation which turn out to have been objectively unfounded, or consciences which turn out to have been mistaken), but only a recognition of it in the other as a moral experience which includes — at least for the other — a perceived obligation and hence a perceived responsibility.

Such a recognition may in itself expand the possibilities for sharing the moral awareness of an object hitherto seen only as a marginal concern in relation to the focal concern with which each side begins.

Areas of "Bad Faith"

The breaking of the impasse in the abortion debate may require yet another kind of dislodging, however. The "passing in the night" by the two groups in this debate has to some extent been maintained by the suspicion which each has harbored of the other's fundamental "bad faith" — "bad faith" in the Sartrean sense of self-deception, pretentiousness, hypocrisy, perhaps self-righteousness, and finally non-involvement. It may not be enough merely to recognize the "good faith" of the opponent's reported concern and experienced claim. It may be essential that each group take serious account of the opponent's charge against it of "bad faith." That is, it may be necessary that each consider in a self-critical way the possibility that it may itself be partially, and importantly, in "bad faith." The most immediate consequence of "bad faith" is not that one fails to understand an opponent's position; it is that one fails to understand and to disclose one's own position. It may be obvious, then, how self-recognition of areas of "bad faith" can help to clarify issues, discern points of convergence as well as clarify issues, discern points of convergence as well as divergence, work out morally acceptable compromises, or sustain energy to continue a prophetic stance. Let me show what I think might emerge and/or be left behind in the advancing debate were both sides to take such a recommendation seriously.

There are, it seems to me, at least three areas in the abortion debate where it is possible that both sides are to some extent in "bad faith." That is to say, there are three areas in which arguments are put forth which represent logical inconsistencies, abstractions from qualifying contexts, misapplication of principles, or rejection of verifiable counterevidence. These arguments at least appear to arise not from a failure of intellect, nor from malicious intent to deceive or confuse, but from some form of unwillingness to reflect fully on the data or reasoning at hand. The deficiencies in the arguments are in some way the result of irresponsibility, however slight or grave, however explicitly or implicitly conscious.[5]

The first of these areas is located within the debate regarding *the nature of the fetus.* On the one hand, it is difficult not to wonder about "bad faith" in a pro-abortion position which, in contradiction to persistent empirical evidence, rests its arguments wholly on the claim that the fetus is simply a part of the pregnant woman, a piece of tissue no more unique than an appendix. What is effective rhetorically is defective logically, however little weight one may wish to give to purely biological data. Arguments for total dependency in spite of some kind of autonomy of the fetus in relation to its mother seem in the long run more fruitful as well as more honest.[6] On the other hand, one must also wonder about "bad faith" in anti-abortion positions which admit no ambiguity, no uncertainty whatsoever, regarding the nature of the fetus, and thus argue for an absolute proscription of abortion. Such arguments belie the traditions to which they appeal and hide the important options which are able to be maintained within a position which unequivocally affirms the existence of human life from the time of conception.[7] They are all the more questionable as they seem to admit inconsistencies such as the simultaneous proscription of all direct abortion and the allowance of curettage after rape.[8] It seems clear that the conflict regarding abortion will neither be sustained in discourse nor ever advanced in thought or policy by opponents whose positions take the grounds of their own arguments with so little seriousness. On the contrary, a sober meeting of opponents in areas of recognized certainty and uncertainty may yet yield clarity, though disagreement, in moral appeal, and may yet yield helpful guidelines for a context of legal compromise.

The second area in which some amount of "bad faith" must at least be allowed as a possibility is the area in which consideration is given to *the needs and claims of women, of pregnant mothers, in regard to abortion.* The credibility of anti-abortionists is stretched considerably in this area, and that on several counts. (1) Present interpreters of the anti-abortion position allude very little to the anti-women aspects of the long tradition of anti-abortion arguments. Surely it could only help contemporary debate where they do point up the obscurities in a tradition where abortion appears almost always juxtaposed to largely inadequate views of human sexuality and marriage. Conditions conducive to abortion, if not arguments justifying it, have derived in some ways from these views. (2) While some proponents of the anti-abortion position have begun to see the need for alternate ways of dealing with problem pregnancies,[9] and have indeed made efforts to fill gaps in societal structures designed to care for women and children, few have sensed the kind of overall nature of the problem. One cannot help wondering about the increased credibility of anti-abortionists were their voices to be heard leading the challenge against cultural and societal frameworks which still give to women almost total responsibility for the rearing of children. (3) In their understandable concern to safeguard the independent reality of the fetus, anti-abortionists have too easily overlooked the nonetheless intimate relationship of mother and fetus. In order to understand anti-abortion principles one need not abstract from the experience of a mother who finds herself possessed by as well as possessing new life within her. "She feels it as at once an enrichment and an injury. . . . A new life is going to manifest itself and justify its own separate existence, she is proud of it; but she also feels herself tossed and driven, the plaything of obscure forces. It is especially noteworthy that the pregnant woman feels the immanence of her body at just the time when it is in transcendence: it turns upon itself in nausea and discomfort; it has ceased to exist for itself and thereupon becomes more sizable than ever before."[10] The recognition of the complexity as well as intimacy of this relationship may indeed not lead to the justification of abortion, but it is surely not irrelevant to the concrete moral context, and it surely must be taken into account when anti-abortionists consider the implications of a return to abortion laws which would depend upon coercion rather than moral suasion.

But pro-abortionists, too, must not consider themselves innocent of all possibility of "bad faith" in this area. In their very cry for attention to the plight of the mother, for consideration of her as subject and not only as object, they all too often objectify her by removing the relations of mutuality which are constitutive of subjectivity. Experiences of disrelation need not be denied in the recognition of possible experiences of mutuality between mother and fetus, or between mother and father. Tragedies of aloneness are not remedied by rigidifying them into paradigms for the understanding of womanhood and motherhood. When calls for liberation from oppressive situations and repressive laws turn to ideological claims which abstract from the fullness of human experience, their credibility must inevitably suffer. When distortive claims for self-sacrificial love are rightly rejected, but are replaced by counterclaims which recognize no covenant opportunities or responsibilities, the cause of women is not well served. One heavy burden gives way to another.

The third area for self-reflection regarding "bad faith" is the area in which *valuations are made of human life — whether of mother or fetus,* and in which *moral terms are assigned to the act of abortion.* Anti-abortionists appear at times to give absolute value to human life, to make absolute the prescription to preserve life. They have, then, frequently been faulted for the inconsistency of this position with other positions they may take regarding war and capital punishment, and with positions they fail to take regarding the desperate claims for life and human welfare by oppressed and forgotten peoples. Their credibility is further stretched by a reading of the history which has broadened then narrowed the possibilities for justified therapeutic abortion, and by a reading of the agonized casuistry which at times allows greater evils for the sake of purer consciences.[11] Finally, assignment of abortion to the category of murder may prove politically effective, but it does not accurately represent the carefully nuanced history of the anti-abortion tradition.[12]

Pro-abortionists, on the other hand, appear at times to consider human life so relative a value as to make response to it almost morally neutral. The more careful of feminist positions, however, find significance in the need to weigh values, to discern gradations of evil, and to regret the need for abortions at all.[13] "If it is not true that abortion is murder, it still cannot be considered in the same light as a mere contraceptive technique; an event has taken place that is a definite beginning, the progress of which is to be stopped."[14] Pro-abortion slogans, no less than anti-abortion ones, can benefit from carefulness of description vis-à-vis abortion and the methods of abortion.

New Levels of Moral Concern

We return, finally, to the obverse side of self-criticism. Recognition of the possibility of one's own "bad faith" enhances the possible recognition of genuine moral experience in the other. We need not fear that this will relativize all moral principles important to either side, or that it will dull the edges of a conflict which must grow more acute before it can begin to be resolved. If it succeeds in breaking the impasse in the moral debate, then new lines will need to be drawn, and new arguments will need to be given, and new obligations to action may need to be assumed. The line can no longer be, for example (at least in the moral realm, if not in the legal), between abortion on demand on the one side and absolute proscription of abortion on the other. Pro-abortionists must take seriously the recommendations now being offered for line-drawing in terms of the time of abortion, the method, the justifying reasons, possible alternatives, and shared decision-making.[15] Arguments for abortion can no longer give the impression that the highest form of feminine consciousness and the most comprehensive form of feminine liberty are to be found in the choice for abortion. And pro-abortionists must reflect soberly on the kind of moral leadership needed to avoid promoting alienation and spiritual as well as physical sterility. But so, too, must anti-abortionists consider seriously the need for new lines when the situation is one of violent disrelation or twofold danger of death or truly intolerable burden to the spirit or the body.[16] And so, too, must anti-abortionists take seriously their natural law position (if such is their source of appeal) and respect conscience wherever it appears, addressing it with reasons and not accusations. And so, finally, must anti-abortionists translate what has been a pastoral sensitivity for the individual person into the broader sphere of concern for change in centuries-laden structures of oppression. They, too must ask what kind of moral leadership is needed to change abortion-conducive societies and abortion-producing relationships.

Each side in the abortion debate must continue to submit its position to the structures whereby a pluralistic society attempts to mediate conflict through law or through a judicial system. Yet each must continue to make moral appeals to the other. Insofar as impasses in conflict are transcended, there may emerge greater clarity and modesty of claim along with stronger and more prophetic voices. There may also emerge the gradual recognition that the moral concerns in both the pro-abortion and anti-abortion positions lead finally to a kind of shared position that argues for a social context in which abortion becomes unnecessary. There is, after all, a "beyond abortion" position which must argue for values and structures that will liberate women, and men, and that will conduce to mutuality in child-rearing. Only through such a position can human life finally be valued, from its beginning to its end, wherever it is to be found.

Notes

1. They do, of course, continue. In fact, 200 abortion bills were introduced in state legislatures in 1973. Some of these aimed at regulating abortions in the second and third trimesters. Others attempted to clarify issues such as the place for consent of the husband, consent for a minor, conscientious objection for medical personnel and hospitals, etc. There is federal legislation pending regarding experimentation on fetuses, etc., as well as continuing efforts at the federal level to bring about a constitutional amendment.

2. There is evidence of this, for example, in the efforts of society to carry on "business as usual" in deciding questions regarding human genetics. The issue of abortion continues to sit in the middle of such decisions, but there is almost an agreed-upon silence about it, as if none were aware of the continuing diversion in its regard.

3. It would be inaccurate to insist that the only participants in the abortion debate are feminists and pro-life partisans, or that the only issues in the debate are ones which pit women against fetuses. Clearly, for example, the population issue has been an important one in the ongoing debate. Nonetheless, I would maintain that the impetus of the pro-abortion movement gained immeasurably with the growth of the Women's Liberation Movement, and that the poles of the debate have gradually come to mirror the issues raised by that movement.

4. Needless to say, not all partisans in the debate abstract thus from one another's position. The overall image which each side presents, however, is, I think, accurately described in these terms.

5. This does not contradict my assertion that the failure of one side to take account of the moral concern of the other can arise from the very intensity of the moral experience of each. "Bad faith" can be found in even the strongest and most sincere of moral positions. It does not vitiate moral concern, but it does in some way blind it.

6. See, for example, Jean MacRae, "A Feminist View of Abortion" *Proceedings of the Working Group on Women and Religion,* American Academy of Religion (1973), p. 113.

7. Noonan reads the history of Christianity's rejection of abortion as a gradual achievement of clarity and certainty. Nonetheless, the recurring "agnosticism on ensoulment" seems not yet transcended. Noonan, for example, cites the important role of the writings of Bernard Häring in settling the question. But Häring, a few years later, acknowledged a continuing degree of uncertainty. See John T. Noonan, "An Almost Absolute Value in History," in *The Morality of Abortion: Legal and Historical Perspectives* (Harvard, 1970), pp. 1-59. See also Bernard Häring, "A Theological Evaluation," in *The Morality of Abortion: Legal and Historical Perspectives,* p. 132. Paul Ramsey, too, admits a certain unclarity in this regard: "While my statement of the argument from genotype was a stronger one than Noonan's . . . my adherence to it was never full or certain." See Paul Ramsey, "Abortion: A Review Article," *The Thomist* XXXVII (January 1973): 188. Ramsey finally opts for the time of segmentation, or "the time at or after which it is settled whether there will be one or two or more distinct individuals," as the point at which human life begins.

It is never in question for anti-abortionists whether or not abortion is justified (it is not), but it is in question for some anti-abortionists whether justification is needed from the moment of conception or the time of implantation, segmentation, the development of brain impulses, etc.

8. Roman Catholic moral theologians still teach that for a time after rape, a woman may receive a D and C. This may have been founded originally on the belief that conception never takes place immediately after intercourse. The teaching has not been changed, however, even though such a belief is by no means always verifiable.

9. The important position and concern of birthright is a case in point.

10. Simone de Beauvoir, *The Second Sex* (Bantam, 1953), pp. 466-67.

11. This is the case when, in justifying abortion of an ectopic pregnancy, a tube must be removed in order to indirectly remove the fetus.

12. See Noonan, pp. 15, 23, 32, 35. It would be misleading to imply that in spite of different terminology, even different assessment of guilt entailed, the anti-abortion tradition within Christianity ever considered the obligation to prevent the killing of the fetus as anything other than an obligation of the highest order of seriousness.

13. See, for example, Sissela Bok, "Ethical Problems of Abortion," *The Hastings Center Studies* II (January 1974): 33-52.

14. S. de Beauvoir, p. 462.

15. See Bok, p. 52.

16. It seems necessary for anti-abortionists to admit such lines at least in the legal order. Even morally, however, serious grounds can be found, within an anti-abortion position, for such line-drawing.

Chapter Fourteen

CHOOSING DEATH AND LETTING DIE

In his "A Modern Psalm," the poet Robert Fraser reminds us that our medical technology has become one of our most powerful idols. The psalm begins:

> Medical science is my shepherd;
> I shall not want,
> It maketh me to lie down in hospital
> beds;
> It leadeth me beside the marvels of
> technology.

The poet ends by reminding us of the consequences of our idolatry:

> Surely coma and unconsciousness shall
> follow me
> all the days of my continued breathing;
> And I will dwell in the intensive care
> unit forever.

It is the case that medical technology can do great things for persons who are ill and who would die without its use. At the same time, this technology has become one of the ways in which we avoid facing our mortality. Our technology contributes to the illusion that we might live forever.

But we cannot! Once we realize this, idolatrous confidence in technology seems a creed ripe for doubt. Technology does not rescue us from our mortality, and it sometimes seems to deliver us not to our flourishing but to our suffering a lingering dying.

Then, to be sure, some turn back to technology as faithful savior to deliver us from such suffering. The technology may be as old as hemlock, but it promises a quick and painless death. The Hippocratic refusal to give a deadly drug even if asked for it is challenged by a compassion which simply wants to put a stop to suffering and arms itself with technology to do it.

An idolatrous confidence in technology and a fear of death or of suffering one's way to death (or both) form part of the context in which this culture struggles with issues of death and dying. The culture — and its conversations about choosing death and letting die — is also formed by an enthusiasm for autonomy. That autonomy, or personal freedom, is sometimes held to include "a right to die." But what does this "right to die" mean and entail? Is it a negative right, a right against having one's dying interfered with? Or is it a positive right, a right to intend one's own death and to receive assistance in "getting dead"? Does a "right to die" mean that the "right to life" is alienable, after all, in spite of *The Declaration of Independence*? Does it justify "consensual killing," voluntary euthanasia, physician-assisted suicide?

The culture is also formed by its appreciation of compassion. But what is compassion? And is it properly armed with artifice alone or with wisdom about life in a mortal body and about the human vulnerability to suffering? Is compassion a commitment to eliminate suffering, even if one has to eliminate the sufferer in order to do it? Can compassion kill? Or is compassion a commitment to be with the sufferer, to be present to share the burden of suffering, while it refuses to kill?

Some public accounts of freedom and compassion have rendered morally suspect the traditional distinctions between killing a patient and letting a patient die, between refusals of treatment and suicide. The meaning of a "right to die," the entailments of compassion, and this distinction between killing and letting die were large issues in the legal debate which led to the 1997 Supreme

Court decision, and they continue to be important issues in the continuing moral conversation about choosing death and letting die.

This chapter invites you to participate in that conversation. How should we think and speak about these issues as a society? as Christians? as caregivers? as mortal selves vulnerable to suffering? Many of the previous chapters in this volume, of course, are relevant to this conversation. This chapter might be read in the light of the earlier readings on "life and its sanctity," "death and its (in)dignity," "respect for persons and their agency," "care for patients and their suffering," and "nature and its mastery."

This chapter begins with an effort to articulate what may be regarded as the classic Christian tradition on these issues. Christian thinkers regarded life as a great good, but not as the greatest good. They regarded death as a great evil, but not as the greatest evil. The martyrs, for example, did not seek death, but they saw unfaithfulness as a greater evil. They did not intend either death or suffering, but they were willing to endure either for the sake of God's cause and their own integrity. Some Christians still bear witness to Christ by their choices about how they should live while they are dying, by their recognition of goods more weighty than their own ease and of duties more compelling than their own survival.

Thus thinkers working out of that tradition have no difficulty with the legitimacy of sometimes withholding and withdrawing medical interventions. They have claimed that we may sometimes allow to die but we may not aim at the person's death. Thus, it is permitted sometimes to withdraw medical treatment or to withhold a new treatment and allow a patient to die, but it is not permitted to kill the patient. James Bresnahan (selection 83) utilizes this distinction. John Paul II (selection 85) puts limits on our worship of technology. He argues that Christians are not obligated to submit to the latest medical intervention, that only ordinary remedies are required of us and when these are of no use in preventing death, they too may be forsworn. Gilbert Meilaender (selection 86) points to the intellectual justification of distinguishing between killing and allowing to die, by utilizing a distinction between what we aim at in our action and what the result(s) of our actions might be. All of these, in different ways, attempt to articulate the classic Christian tradition.

For better or for worse, however, the solutions of the past must face new questions today. First, the meaning of medical care for the dying is contested. Most persons agree that medical care may utilize antibiotics and ventilators. These are forms of medical care that may, in certain circumstances, when they are no longer necessary for care, be withdrawn. But what of liquids and nourishment that are given to a person intravenously or through a nasogastric tube? Are these forms of medical care that may be withdrawn, or are they a form of service, a giving of drink to the thirsty and food to the hungry, a service that we owe to all human beings, even and especially the dying? If we withdraw them, and no one can live for long without liquids and nourishment, must we see our action as aiming at or choosing the death of a person, or may we understand it in a different way as an acceptance of death?

As contentious as the withdrawal of liquids and nourishment once was and continues to be for some, it is not nearly as contentious as the issue of physician assisted suicide. The defense of physician assisted suicide generally relies upon two claims. The first concerns the autonomy of patients. If patients who are competent and terminally ill, and who are suffering greatly, ask for assistance in dying, then, some argue, we should not interfere if someone assists the patients in ending their lives. To interfere, so the argument goes, is to fail to respect their wishes, to fail to respect their autonomy.

The second claim rests upon a certain understanding of compassion. Persons who are suffering should have their suffering relieved; it is the compassionate thing to do. Persons who are terminally ill and who are suffering should have their suffering relieved, up to and including aiding them in taking their own lives. Compassion demands that we aid them in this fashion.

Richard McCormick (selection 89) disagrees. He fears the consequences of legalizing physician assisted suicide. He argues that arguments for physician-assisted suicide depend upon the absolutizing of autonomy and we are then left without any guidance about how we might use our autonomy. One of his fears is that if we focus exclusively upon autonomy, we make an idol of independence and we become intolerant of dependence. Gloria Maxson (selection 84) thinks that such intolerance is a very real threat to persons who are disabled.

McCormick also understands compassion differently. For him, physician assisted suicide is an act of isolation of the patient, a form of abandoning the patient, not an act of compassion. Compassion, he argues, leads to interdependence. Mark A. Duntley, Jr. (selection 87) agrees with McCormick about the importance of compassion, but he disagrees with the conclusion that assisted suicide can never be an act of compassion. Duntley observes that American physicians have undertreated pain and overtreated disease. He argues that a Christian account of compassion would insist on the moral importance of ongoing and covenantal relationships. He wants a health care system where such relationships are the norm and not the exception. Where such relationships are absent, he is critical of physician-assisted suicide, but where they are present, he suggests that compassion might lead to assistance in suicide.

Stanley Hauerwas (selection 90) also worries about the tendency of health care personnel to defer to decisions by patients presumed to be competent. He suggests that part of what is at stake here is a debate about the purposes of medicine. It is often said that medicine has two goals, to cure disease and to relieve suffering. Hauerwas suggests that medicine is for "caring when we cannot cure." Karen Lebacqz (selection 88), on the other hand, argues that even active euthanasia may be a form of care and thus may be morally justifiable, even if she worries about legalization.

As you reflect on these matters, think not only about your own dying or the dying of a loved one but also about what kinds of care you would want for yourself or your loved one. What would a good health system have? Does ours?

Suggestions for Further Reading

Foot, Phillippa. "Euthanasia," chapter in *Virtues and Vices* (Oxford: Basil Blackwell, 1978).

Glover, Jonathan. *Causing Death and Saving Lives* (London: Penguin, 1978).

Guroian, Vigen. *Life's Living Toward Dying: A Theological and Medical Ethical Study* (Grand Rapids: Wm. B. Eerdmans Publishing Co., 1996).

Hamel, Ronald P., and Edwin R. DuBose, eds. *Must We Suffer Our Way to Death: Cultural and Theological Perspectives on Death by Choice* (Dallas: Southern Methodist University Press, 1996).

Hamel, Ronald P., and M. Therese Lysaught. "Choosing Palliative Care: Do Religious Beliefs Make a Difference?" *Journal of Palliative Care* 10, no. 3 (1994): 61-65.

Hare, R. M. "Euthanasia: A Christian View," *Philosophical Exchange* 2 (Summer 1975).

Kilner, John F., Arlene B. Miller, and Edmund D. Pellegrino, eds. *Dignity and Dying: A Christian Appraisal* (Grand Rapids: Wm. B. Eerdmans Publishing Co., 1996).

Maguire, Daniel. *Death by Choice* (New York: Schocken, 1975).

Ramsey, Paul. *Ethics at the Edges of Life* (New Haven: Yale University Press, 1978), cf. pp. 143-335.

Schiedermayer, David. "Commuting to the Valley of the Shadow of Death: What My Patients Have Taught Me about Death — and Life — by Permitting Me to Be with Them at the End," *Christianity Today* 37 (October 4, 1993): 33-34.

Sulmasy, Daniel P. "Managed Care and Managed Death," *Archives of Internal Medicine* 155 (January 23, 1995): 133-36.

SUPPORT Investigators, "A Controlled Trial to Improve Outcomes for Seriously Ill Hospitalized Adults: The Study to Understand Prognoses and Preferences for Outcomes and Risks of Treatments (SUPPORT)," *JAMA* 274 (1995): 1591-98.

Vaux, Kenneth. *Death Ethics: Religious and Cultural Values in Prolonging and Ending Life* (Philadelphia: Trinity University Press, 1992).

Veatch, Robert M. *Death, Dying and the Biological Revolution: Our Last Quest for Responsibility* (New Haven: Yale University Press, 1976).

83 Catholic Spirituality and Medical Interventions in Dying

James F. Bresnahan, S.J.

Should Catholics in the United States prepare advance directives governing the kind of medical care they would want at the time of their dying? This question entails a fundamental but neglected issue of Catholic spirituality: How should Catholics and other Christians, and persons without formal religious affiliation too, prayerfully prepare for their dying within our contemporary high-technology medical culture? What attitudes and dispositions toward our inevitable dying should we seek to cultivate through prayer and reflection — given the power of modern technology to manage, delay and prolong that dying?

These questions require us to face the realities of our North American first-world culture, our way of resisting mortality and our frequently superstitious faith in technology. We must ask how we should respond to the prevailing preoccupation of many care-givers who emphasize aggressive use of cure-oriented medical treatment over the alternative medical treatment, comfort care, even when confronted with inevitable dying. How shall we respond, as well, to the proposals now being made legally to authorize assisted suicide or active euthanasia as a kind of technological "quick fix" for the kinds of suffering that accompany dying?

Finally, can we regard advance directives, the Living Will or Durable Agency for Health Care as practical measures to express these spiritual attitudes and dispositions toward dying that we have sought in prayer? Dare we regard legal provisions for specifying the kind of terminal care we want and do not want as "merely secular" and legalistic measures, perhaps even as irreligious temptations? Or can we make of such a document a personal spiritual testament?

Mandatory Information About Advance Directives.

All of us will be increasingly unable to avoid these questions. As of Dec. 1, 1991, all health care institutions receiving Medicare or Medicaid funds will be required by Federal law (the Danforth provision of the Omnibus Budget Reconciliation Act of 1990) to provide information on the law of the local jurisdiction enabling the patient to prepare advance directives for accepting or refusing medical care when the patient may have become incapable of personally authorizing or refusing a particular kind of care. This, in turn, will force all prudent physicians to discuss human dying and advance directives with their patients *before* they are admitted to a hospital or nursing facility — under penalty of finding their patients unduly alarmed or confused or even panicked by the information provided to them by the institution. The Federal law, therefore, forces us to deal with our North American disposition to avoid thinking about or discussing our dying and what it means for Christian believers to be cared for in a high-technology milieu.

The short answer to these questions about the religious meaning of human dying is familiar to all of us who are Catholics. We are to hold a crucifix. We are to pray to follow Christ in his dying. But this short answer does not reach far enough. We need to think through prayerfully all that this implies in the concrete for each one's dying under high-technology medical care. This was not necessary when medical treatment was comparatively impotent. It is necessary now.

Reprinted with permission of James F. Bresnahan and America Press, Inc., 106 West 56th Street, New York, NY 10019. Originally published in *America*'s June 29, 1991 issue.

Christian Dying as a Dying with and in Christ.

We are called by the empowering grace of Christ to live our lives, each of us uniquely, in the likeness of Jesus' own life among us. As Jesus lived for others, so must we. But following the way of Jesus leads "up to Jerusalem." Finally, that is to say, we are called, each one, to die our deaths in the likeness of Jesus' own dying.

Hence we must wrestle with the religious meaning of dying. It is fundamental to our understanding of our baptism, in which we are plunged into the dying of the Lord and also into His risen life. And this same calling is equally fundamental to our regular celebration of the Eucharist, in which we relive over and over again our union with Christ's life, death and Resurrection.

The late German Jesuit theologian, Karl Rahner, in his *Theology of Death*, elaborates this spirituality of Christian dying as a manifestation of our fundamental faith. Just as we receive and respond to the gift of living a life of love in Christ's likeness, so too are we to be drawn eventually to receive and enter into the grace of sharing in the dying of Christ. Our dying, like our living, is a work of freedom under grace. In our final attitude toward death, then, we are called and empowered to replicate Jesus' own free, redeeming self-surrender to the Father. As St. Paul insists, we are to fill up in our own bodies the suffering of Christ for His body, the church. By freely accepting our dying, we come to participate personally and finally in the fullness of that redemption which Christ has prepared for us in His own passion and dying.

Spirituality of Dying and Catholic Medical Ethics.

Our calling to make our dying a freely accepted fate, not just something forced upon us, is a major presupposition of current Catholic moral theology when it comes to making decisions about medical treatment in the face of death. Catholic ethicians such as Richard McCormick, S.J., John Paris, S.J., and Dennis Brodeur have eloquently expressed this moral theology in *America* (3/28/87). Less attention has been paid, however, to the roots of this moral theology in Catholic spirituality and dogmatics. Catholic moral theology rejects what Richard McCormick has called "medical vitalism," a clinging to biological existence at all costs, precisely because not only our living but also our dying is to be the object of our freedom. We are called to make decisions not only about preserving life and health but also about accepting our dying. We have to take a responsible moral stand about dying as well as living.

On the one hand, therefore, we reject the use of medical measures that are deliberately aimed at precipitating death, or that initiate a new lethal process to short-circuit a process of dying already underway from disease or injury. We rule out, therefore, the technological quick fix of lethal injection or deliberate overdose even though the subjective motivation of such acts may be to relieve suffering.

On the other hand, we affirm that measures needed to relieve suffering are always morally justified, and often morally demanded, even though death may occur sooner as a result of them — as long as we are not seeking to cause death but are trying prudently to measure the dose of analgesic to the needs of the suffering patient. And, though we reject deliberately planned, active euthanasia and assisted suicide, we strongly affirm that as death approaches we are allowed, sometimes even required, to refuse cure-oriented treatment that merely prolongs our dying.

The best Catholic moral theology thus requires us to strike a balance. We have a moral right and even in some circumstances the duty to reject "excessively burdensome" medical treatments even though death will follow from that decision. We may never simply reject our dying, and, finally, we must take responsibility for the way of our dying. The contemporary hospice movement (well described by William F. Carr in *America* 3/25/89) provides a practical expression of this moral theology of dying. This approach, of course, does not satisfy advocates of euthanasia and assisted suicide, for whom human autonomy is an absolute. At the other extreme, it is rejected as homicidal interference with God's providence by advocates of medical vitalism (who include a fringe of ultraconservative Catholics acting in the name of what they understand to be a "pro-life" ethic). Nonetheless, to many people in our society the well-known Catholic *via media* between precipitately causing death and hanging desperately onto mere biological existence appear to be utterly reasonable.

Within these moral boundaries, therefore, the Catholic moral theology of dying implies that each one of us is called to exercise responsible, discerning freedom in preparation for our dying. Each of us is to make a decision about the burdensomeness of proposed treatments and about the qualitative acceptability of the outcome of such treatments in our time of dying. Each of us must weigh burdens against benefits, not only for ourselves but for those we love and for our community. Graced freedom will be finally expressed by each one of us in our dying — Rahner's theological point. This implies that we will exercise spiritual discernment in preparing for and making this decision, a discernment that is rooted in prayerfully seeking to be ready to enter into Christ's dying when the time of death approaches for each of us.

Catholic Spirituality and Medical Ethics in Ecumenical Perspective.

This Catholic rejection of excessively burdensome treatment even though death follows has been widely influential in shaping a consensus in contemporary discussions of medical ethics. The basic human wisdom of this approach is widely shared not only by other Christians, but also by those of other religious convictions and of no religious affiliation. The reasonableness of being able to refuse excessively burdensome treatment and to respond affirmatively and adequately to the needs of those who suffer while refusing to precipitate death deliberately appeals to the moral experience of many persons involved in medical care-giving. Along with Catholics they endorse a hospice approach to dying that promises spiritual and psychological support as well as pain control rather than torturously prolonging the dying process in the name of cure. And they do so because they find a reasonable approach to dying too often absent in our medical culture — too few care-givers who are well trained in the hospice technique, too few who believe that it is really "respectable" medical care.

What resonance, we may ask, does the Catholic spirituality of dying evoke in those who agree with our moral theology but do not share our specific Catholic convictions about dying with Christ? The answer will be found in our shared moral experience, in the practical wisdom contained in this spirituality. That is, those who are not Catholic or even Christian, and who do not share the explicitly Catholic spirituality of dying, but who agree with our moral practice, do so because they recognize that human mortality must be met by something other than blind protest.

What resonates is the Catholic realism about dying as a normal event of human living. The spirituality of people who are not Catholic involves a fundamental piety about the struggle of the human person to come to terms not only with living but also with dying. All of us who seek to discern and decide about the role of medical treatment at the time of dying confront dimensions of human experience common to all persons of good will. We confront the mystery of suffering, of anticipatory grief, of seeking even in this extremity to care well for those we love and will leave behind. Each of us dies in relationship to others, with concern for those whom we seek to make loving even unto the end. The "secular" piety that accepts these realities need not find a thoroughly Catholic spirituality of dying wholly strange.

Some, of course, are puzzled at the readiness of Catholic moral theology to permit, though not to inflict, death, to forgo "life-prolonging" treatments when one reasonably judges them to be excessively burdensome — even though death results. The puzzle is solved by understanding that freely submitting to death can mean dying in Christ. While life and health are to be cherished as a gift of God, a Christian's dying is also the final gift of God's calling us to be conformed to Christ. Our dying is thus seen and accepted as the final gift of redemption in Christ. While persons who are not Christian will not ordinarily see their dying in these precise terms, many do experience a basic human need to exercise their autonomy by coming to terms with the ultimate limit of mortality.

Dying with Christ and Freely Dealing with Mortality.

Yet, for many, Karl Rahner's emphasis on graced freedom in entering into our dying with Christ presents a still deeper puzzle. How can we be "free" in this ultimate experience of limitation, of necessity, of unavoidable fate? Dying is what is inexorably imposed upon us by our mortal nature. We suffer death, and in faith we recognize that this reflects the mystery of human sinfulness that implicates us all — and Christ's redemptive transformation of the consequences of that sinfulness in his dying. But can we really claim to be free in what we do not, finally, control?

Christ suffered precisely this death of ours — He whom "the Father made sin though He was without sin." And Christ in his agony prayed to be delivered from the hour of His execution. Yet Jesus also states that He has come freely to "this hour." All four Gospel accounts of His passion and death underline Jesus' willing surrender of Himself in death into the hands of His Father "for us and for our salvation." So it must be possible for a follower of Jesus to join Christ's free self-surrender to dying.

In our culture generally, but especially in contemporary medical ethics, the exercise of human autonomy tends to be thought of almost exclusively as *control.* Patient autonomy is considered almost exclusively in terms of the patient's sharing control of diagnosis and treatment with the physician. Yet, in the patient/care-giver relationship there is always an element of free self-entrustment and submission to what is not and cannot be controlled. A patient's autonomy, therefore, contains an unavoidable dimension of submission, of willing self-surrender to the expert judgment and skill of the care-giver in the therapeutic alliance. Necessarily we exercise our freedom not only in controlling what is done to us but also *in submitting to it.*

In facing the advent of human dying, both patient and care-giver confront what cannot, in the end, be wholly controlled and manipulated. For all of us must die. The challenge is to live out the human meaning of this final event of life by an exercise of freedom that is not simply "in control." Pierre Teilhard de Chardin, the French Jesuit paleontologist and theologian, gives us insight into the spirituality that grasps this mystery of human freedom as not only active but also and necessarily passive.

Graced Freedom in Submission to Death.

In his *Divine Milieu,* Teilhard's primary concern was to encourage Christians to see their free initiative in worldly activity as creative, as truly a "building of the earth" which has permanent significance in the fullness of human redemption. But he insists that such a positive spiritual vision of human effort would be incomplete without recognizing and accepting what he calls God's "divinization of our passivities." We are to recognize both passivities of growth and passivities of diminishment as fundamental dimensions of the finite human sharing in God's creativity.

For Teilhard, therefore, the more ready we are to embrace our worldly tasks as our share in God's work of bringing the Body of Christ to completion, the more we must be ready to exercise graced freedom in accepting limitations, contradictions and disappointments in our activity. This acceptance is no less a freedom than the achievement of freedom through control. The final, decisive passivity of diminishment by which we enter the fullness of union with Christ is death. Ultimately, as humans drawn into the cosmic mystery of the Incarnation, we must be prepared to exercise our freedom in our dying, though this will not involve control, but submission, acceptance, self-surrender.

This spiritual understanding of the freedom in dying proposed by Rahner and Teilhard resonates with the common human experiences of loss and grief. We are always being trained by the crucial events of life to ask forgiveness of those we love for our defects in serving them in love, and we are being led constantly throughout our lives to that moment when we shall make our last concern the continued living in love of those whom we must leave behind. Over and over again I have seen those dying in hospitals far more concerned for the good of those they love and are living than for their own entry into the fearful experience of death. And I have seen those who practice a hospice approach to dying enable this kind of autonomy in the dying.

Those who are experienced in the hospice way of medical care of the dying become aware of the work of love toward those left behind that is inherent in human dying. The "life review," for instance, by which the dying person comes to terms with the meaning of his or her life by telling some personal history testifies to the deep meaning of our final struggle to express ourselves even in what is imposed upon us in our dying. The dying permit themselves to be loved and cared for by dear ones and care-givers. (Sadly, Dr. Timothy Quill's patient, described recently in *The New England Journal of Medicine,* apparently refused to do this.) The faithfulness of care-givers to one who is dying anticipates each one's own hope to be faithful to those left behind at the moment of death.

Advance Directives and the Meaning of Dying

What, then, does this Christian spirituality of death lead us to do in planning for our dying in a high-technology medical culture? In an advance directive we have a means of expressing the prayerful discernment that our spirituality seeks.

Advance directives that express our desire to take free responsibility for our dying include the Living Will and the Durable Power of Attorney (or Agency) for Health Care. These are legal documents explicitly authorized by the laws of many states but also possibly effective under common law in many other states that have not yet legislated their legal status. These documents record a person's wishes about which cure-oriented medical treatments a person refuses to have initiated or continued under specified circumstances when terminally ill but possibly incompetent, that is, unable any longer to express one's wishes. They focus our thoughts and prayers on our dying as it is likely to be in this culture.

The Living Will expresses for all concerned one's wishes about terminal care — but primarily it is addressed to the physicians who attend one's dying. The Durable Power of Attorney gives similar instructions about what end-stage care one wants, but it also appoints a specified person to act on one's behalf with care-givers to carry out these wishes. Some of the language in the widely noticed 1990 Cruzan decision of the U.S. Supreme Court implies that we have a 14th Amendment right to consent to or refuse medical care right up to the time of our death even when we may have become permanently incompetent. It is widely agreed that the case would have been resolved even under the strict evidentiary requirements of Missouri had Nancy Cruzan executed either a Living Will or a Durable Power of Attorney and indicated that she would not want medically engineered nutrition and hydration to prolong her dying in a permanent vegetative state.

Since the tendency of modern high-technology medicine is to persist in so-called "life-sustaining" treatments rather than shift to care that primarily aims to relieve suffering and enable the terminal patient to interact freely with loved ones and friends, these advance directives are needed to limit those kinds of medical intervention that merely prolong dying. If I am conscious, of course, I can instruct my physician directly and personally. But should I become unconscious or even partially impaired in my ability to instruct my doctor about treatments to be foregone, I will want to have taken responsibility for the impact of my dying on those around me. And since modern medical interventions can extend my dying even in an impaired or unconscious state, advance directives are more and more needed today. Constant progress in medical techniques not only prolongs functional living but also has the effect of unduly prolonging dying. Indeed, in my experience, the success of contemporary medicine in giving us "more time" often, if not always, brings with it the burden of a more difficult and frequently more painful dying.

Planning for Dying: Control or Submission?

In this medical culture, we need to explore the spiritual meaning of advance directives as an unavoidable challenge to our prayerful reflection and prudent planning. As Catholics we need to ask ourselves how we can use these legally formulated directives to express our faith convictions and commitments. And in this post-Vatican II era, as ecumenically minded Catholics we need to ask how our understanding of the ultimate meaning of such measures may coincide or conflict with that of non-Catholics with whom we live and work and die.

To take up a theme in contemporary Christian ethical discussions, the link between moral theology and Christian spirituality is narrative, the *story* of Jesus of Nazareth and its impact on our personal and communal story. In an advance directive I can give an account of how I wish my living and my dying to take its shape from the living and dying of Jesus.

The impact of Christ's life on our own hinges on discerning what one ought to do and to be. My prayerful reflection on Christ's dying should, first of all, shape decision-making about my own dying. What burdens do I find excessive for me, beyond bounds, or only acceptable if God gives special inspiration for that? How do I wish to avoid rashness and presumption should I become unable to express myself to my care-givers? What burdens do I refuse to see imposed on those whom I love? These points can be added to the standard forms of the Living Will or Durable Power of Attorney. Suffering will be given each of us, and grace will be given to bear it, but we must each take account of the possibilities of being ourselves, or having those we care about, made subject to excessive suffering.

Second, when engaged in confronting our own mortality, our spirituality can and should shape as well our individual and communal response to others in their suffering and dying. We are called to stand faithfully by those who are dying, to relieve their suffering in all ways possible when the dying person does not forbid us to do so. The greatest fear of the dying is abandonment by loved ones or care-givers. It is true that each of us enters an utterly lonely moment in dying, a moment in which one will echo Christ's own cry, "My God, my God, why have you forsaken me?" Yet as Christians we know that the presence of Mary and John at the foot of the cross models the behavior toward the dying that we should adopt. And we have considered St. Joseph the special saint of the dying because of our well-founded assumption that Jesus and Mary stayed by him in his dying.

Catholic piety and behavior in preparation for dying and in support of the dying requires stronger emphasis in preaching than it has now. Pastors should be reflecting and praying with their congregations for the purpose of enabling them to write a Living Will or Durable Power as a personal spiritual testament. And in general, the challenge of making advance directives such as a treatment ought to lead every Catholic parish to participate actively in the hospice movement.

Faithful and appropriate care of the dying and prayerful acceptance of our own dying effectively counter the tendencies of our time to deal inappropriately with dying — both superstitious devotion to an excessively aggressive use of technology to prolong dying and that despairing resort to the technological quick fix of induced death.

84 "Whose Life Is It, Anyway?" Ours, That's Whose!

Gloria Maxson

In this national year of the disabled, I take strong exception to the film *Whose Life Is It, Anyway?* for its underlying false premise; that the life of a disabled person could not be worth living, and should thus be "mercifully" terminated by suicide or euthanasia. As a chairbound victim of polio and arthritis, I strongly protest that the life I and my many disabled friends lead has genuine value in the sight of God — and humanity.

In the film, Richard Dreyfuss plays Ken, a young sculptor who has become a "quad" (quadriplegic — a person who is paralyzed in all four extremities) in a car accident, and decides in the initial period of trauma — never an auspicious time to make major decisions — that suicide is the only "rational" choice for a man severely disabled. In its one-sided argument in favor of Ken's death, the film denies the value of the lives we disabled persons live.

Whose Life Is It, Anyway? stacks the deck in favor of its position by failing to present the options available to a quadriplegic. It is shockingly untypical that Ken is kept for six months in intensive care before any rehabilitation is begun; actually, most quads have *completed* their rehabilitative training by that time. Glib doctors and social workers tell Ken he will "feel better" when his therapy starts — but it never does; nor is Ken ever taught to use such adaptive devices as reading machines and special typewriters. He is never introduced even to an electric wheelchair but is wheeled passively about, which deepens the sense of immobility and total dependency that makes him long for death.

What a difference an electric chair (covered by Medicare) has made in my own life! Gone is that awful sense of being preyed upon, the "sitting duck" syndrome that kept me weeping on the porch in driving rain, terrified to enter the house where I imagined that Something huge, mindless, nameless and malign awaited me. Now my husband says *I* am the Something mindless and malign as I careen at full tilt down our block, terrorizing the "fluffy old pussies" (Agatha Christie's phrase for little old ladies). I could have told the Ken character that if we can't have wings-at-our-heels, we can at least have wheels-at-our-hips. But no one tells him that or anything else that could alter his death wish.

Another inadequately treated aspect of Ken's trauma is his bitter sense of lost virility and conviction that he is "not a man anymore." Again, those around him fail to give him the insights provided by any good SCI (spinal cord injury) specialist, namely, that 70 per cent of quads can have normal genital intercourse, and that there are many other satisfying ways of making love, as the disabled veteran in *Coming Home* — a much more honest film — showed. No one examines Ken's sexuality to determine what sensory avenues are still open to him. Through those parts that confirm the popular assumptions about quadriplegics' sexuality, the man I saw the film with — himself a quad — kept muttering such things as: "There's more sex between the ears than between the extremities! As much warmth *north* of the Masters-Johnson line [the waistline] as *south* of it!"

We were both unnerved by Ken's insistence that death is "the only way out" since he is "dead already." The poet Robert Frost, and any of us "black-eyed ones" (Thomas Mann's phrase; the healthy-and-wealthy are "the blue-eyed ones"), could have told Ken that "the only way out is through," and to "learn what to make of a diminished thing." In the real world, any good doctor would have introduced Ken to SCI patients whose successful coping would have helped him navigate his dark passage back to life. But in the film no one helps him through the initial stages of grief and despair to self-acceptance. It is never explained to Ken that even a quadriplegic on dialysis, like himself, need not be hospitalized for life; with modern techniques and attendants, a person can live at home with the family and friends who can help him or her learn a new way of life based on "viable alternatives." All these tragic omissions strengthen Ken's case for taking his life — a case carefully manipulated by the film.

Although sculpting was Ken's life, he is not shown the many other ways his thwarted creativity could be expressed; only teaching is suggested, and he angrily rejects it. I, too, felt the awful anguish of losing my artistry with piano and guitar when my hands became crippled with arthritis. I could not have foreseen then, in the midst of my moist jeremiads, that one day I'd have an electric keyboard on which I could play melody with the two remaining, dancing fingers on my right hand, and automatic chords and rhythms with a dancing thumb on the left. Now, as I dash off "Für Elise," "Minuet in G" and "Turkish March," Beethoven no longer turns over in his grave, but sits bolt upright and bellows, "Ach Du Lieber, Meine Gloria — das ist gut!" I could not see that dark night of the soul, when all problems became "soul-sized," that I would be able to transfer my guitar skills to a large ukulele, and bawl out the same old ballads and naughty calypsos I did before. Furthermore, when I could no longer type at 90 wpm, or even handwrite, I didn't know I'd soon type with two fingers and find an orthopedic gripper that would enable me to write again, in so neat a hand my husband says it is "one of the graphic arts," and calls me "the Picasso of the ballpoint pen!"

As my friend and I viewed the film, we grew nervous on hearing the audience murmur assent to all the nihilisms about the disabled life, and remembered all the times people had said to us, "If I were you, I'd kill myself." It's just a small step from that to, "And why *don't* you?" In the audience, we sense a latent antagonism to our vulgar tenacity in preserving our lives, our precious "space" on this crowded planet — a space which may be hotly contested in the future, with elderly and ill-derly classed as expendables. Many films and plays still perpetuate the false notion that a disabled life is not worth living — a misperception that is still killing people, through suicide and misguided "mercy killings."

The film *Whose Life?* traffics in the current political mood that is dangerously cutting back vital aid to the severely disabled. At one point in the film, a character grumbles that "we are spending thousands on people like Ken, with little return, when with a few cents we could save Third World children!" How dare people force us to choose between our lives and those of Third World children! True, much money *is* wasted keeping Ken alive and hospitalized; for much less he could have been cared for at home, safely and with better results.

This film reflects the negative views about disability that are gaining wide acceptance in the many "wrongful life" suits against doctors for allowing babies born with defects to live. More hospitals now routinely offer parents of disabled babies the option of "mercy killing," even if the baby's defect is only deafness. A TV film told the story of a man who shot his quadriplegic brother on request, again reinforcing the misconception that a disabled life is worthless. *Whose Life?* purports to be an honest drama about an important social and ethical dilemma of our time, but in its shrinking from the moral obligation of treating the issue factually, the film is irresponsible. It was puzzling to hear such film critics as Gene Shalit of the "Today" show praise it as "life-affirming" — an enigmatic phrase, indeed, to use about a film that advocates suicide. To us of the black-eyed community, Mr. Shalit, "life-affirming" means body-retraining and body-retaining. Anything less is mere wordplay and sophistry.

As the film ended, my friend and I joined the crowd in the lobby to munch popcorn and chat, and received so many glances — some openly hostile — that we felt we might have to stand (sit) our ground or we'd be rushed and strung up between features! No matter what the public feels, *I* will never willingly relinquish a life that contains my husband, family, friends, a home, lobster thermidor, music and P. G. Wodehouse! Even in my handicapped childhood, I would have chosen to live. I read somewhere that all of nature's young things are valiant — they do not whine or bargain, but despite their wounds fight fiercely to live, and revel in being — and I know it is true. Perhaps I've "just compensated," as an atheistic college friend used to tell me. My reply is, "Yes, I have compensated — Christ is my compensation." For just as in my blinded early childhood I developed the "facial perception" that set every hair vibrating when someone is near, so now my nerve ends vibrate with the sense of that Presence who stands near but outside my harsh circumstances, and molds them into coherence and beauty.

Whose life is it, Ken? It's all of ours — and it should have been yours.

85 Euthanasia

Declaration of the Sacred Congregation for the Doctrine of the Faith (May 5, 1980)

John Paul II

The inherent rights and values of the human person hold an important place among the questions preoccupying the people of our day. Against this background the Second Vatican Council solemnly reaffirmed the eminent dignity of the human person and, especially, the person's right to life.

In keeping with this restatement the council denounced crimes against life, including "murder, genocide, abortion, euthanasia or willful self-destruction."[1]

More recently, the Sacred Congregation for the Doctrine of the Faith has reminded all followers of Christ of the Church's teaching on deliberate abortion.[2]

The same congregation now deems it opportune to set forth the Church's teaching on euthanasia.

It is true that on this point of doctrine recent popes have expounded principles which remain fully valid.[3]

On the other hand, recent medical advances have focused attention on new aspects of euthanasia which call for further explanation of the ethical norms.

In modern society, in which even the fundamental values of human life are frequently threat-

From *The Pope Speaks* 25 (Winter 1980): 289-96. Used courtesy of Our Sunday Visitor, Inc.

ened, cultural changes influence the way people view death and suffering.

Another point to be noted is the increasing ability of medical science to heal and to prolong life under certain conditions which, at times, raise questions of morality. Consequently, people living in these new circumstances ask anxious questions about the meaning of extreme old age and death.

They ask themselves, not unreasonably, whether or not they have the right to secure for themselves or their loved ones an "easy death" which shortens suffering and seems to them more in keeping with human dignity.

Purpose of the Document

On this subject a number of episcopal conferences have sent questions to the Sacred Congregation for the Doctrine of the Faith. The congregation has sought the views of experts on the various aspects of euthanasia and now intends this declaration as a reply to the inquiries of the bishops.

The statement will make it easier for them to present correct doctrine to the faithful committed to their care and will supply them with principles which they can communicate to civil authorities for their consideration in connection with this extremely serious problem.

The themes presented in this document are meant primarily for those who place their faith and hope in Jesus Christ, whose life, death and resurrection have given new meaning to the life and, especially, the death of Christians. As St. Paul says, "while we live we are responsible to the Lord, and when we die we die as His servants. Both in life and in death we are the Lord's."[4]

Among those who profess other religions, many are in agreement with us that faith in God as provident Creator and Lord of life — if indeed they share this faith — gives all human persons an eminent dignity and is their guarantee of respect.

Our hope is that this declaration will also win the assent of persons of good will who, though following divergent philosophies or ideologies, nevertheless have a keen awareness of the rights of the human person. In fact, these same rights have in recent years been the subject of declarations issued by international congresses.[5]

Since we are dealing here with fundamental rights inherent in every human person, it is evidently wrong to argue from religious pluralism or freedom of religion in order to deny the universal validity of these rights.

I The Value of Human Life

Human life is the basis of all values; it is the source and indispensable condition for every human activity and all society. While the majority of human beings regard life as sacred and maintain that no one can dispose of it at will, the followers of Christ see it as being something even more excellent: a loving gift from God, which they must preserve and render fruitful. This further consideration entails certain consequences:

1. No one may attack the life of an innocent person without thereby resisting the love of God for that person; without violating a fundamental right which can be neither lost nor alienated and, therefore, without committing an extremely serious crime.[6]
2. All human beings must live their lives in accordance with God's plan. Life is given to them as a possession which must bear fruit here on earth but which must wait for eternal life to achieve its full and absolute perfection.
3. Intentional death or suicide is just as wrong as is homicide. Such an action by a human being must be regarded as a rejection of God's supreme authority and loving plan.

In addition, suicide is often a rejection of love for oneself, a denial of the natural instinct to live and a flight from the duties of justice and charity one owes one's neighbors or various communities or human society as a whole.

At times, however, as everyone realizes, psychological factors may lessen or even completely eliminate responsibility.

Suicide must be carefully distinguished from the sacrifice of life in which men and women give their lives or endanger them for some noble cause such as the honor of God, the salvation of souls, or the service of the brethren.[7]

II Euthanasia

If we are to deal properly with the question of euthanasia, we must first explain carefully the meaning of our terms.

Etymologically, euthanasia meant, in antiquity, an *easy death,* that is, one free of severe pain. Nowadays, it is no longer this original meaning that comes to mind. Euthanasia refers, instead, of a medical intervention that lessens the suffering of illness or of the final agony, an intervention that at times carries with it the danger of terminating life prematurely.

Finally, the word euthanasia may also be used in a more limited sense to mean mercy killing, the purpose being to put a complete end to extreme suffering or to keep defective children, the incurably ill, or the mentally subnormal from living out a wretched and, perhaps, lengthy life that might impose an excessive burden on families or society.

We must make quite clear which of these meanings euthanasia is to have in the present document.

Euthanasia here means an action or omission that by its nature or by intention causes death with the purpose of putting an end to all suffering. Euthanasia is, therefore, a matter of intention and method.

We must firmly state once again that no one and nothing can, in any way, authorize the killing of an innocent human being, whether the latter be a fetus or embryo, or a child or an adult or an elderly person, or someone incurably ill or someone who is dying.

In addition, no one may ask for such a death-dealing action for oneself or for another for whom one is responsible, nor may one explicitly or implicitly consent to such an action. Nor may any authority legitimately command or permit it. For such an action is a violation of divine law, an offense against the dignity of the human person, a crime against life and an attack on the human race.

Always Objectively Wrong

It may be that long drawn out and almost unbearable pain, or some emotional or another reason, may convince individuals that they may legitimately ask for death for themselves or others. Although in these cases guilt may be diminished or completely lacking, such an error or judgment into which conscience may fall, perhaps in good faith, does not change the nature of the death-dealing action, which will always be impermissible.

The pleas of the very seriously ill as they beg at times to be put to death are hardly to be understood as conveying a real desire for euthanasia. They are almost always anguished pleas for help and love. What the sick need, in addition to medical care, is love: the warm human and supernatural affection in which all those around — parents and children, doctors and nurses — can and should enfold them.

III Meaning of Suffering

Death does not always come in wretched conditions and after almost intolerable suffering. Nor should we always be focusing our attention on very unusual cases. Many concordant testimonies persuade us to believe that nature itself has taken steps to ease separations at the moment of death, which would be extremely bitter if they involved a person in good health.

The length of an illness, advanced age, a state of loneliness and abandonment create psychological conditions in which it becomes easier to accept death.

We must admit, nonetheless, that death, often preceded or accompanied by severe and prolonged suffering, is an event that naturally causes anguish.

Bodily suffering is certainly an unavoidable part of the human condition. Viewed biologically, pain acts as an undeniably useful warning. But pain also affects the psychological life of the person, where its severity often outweighs its biological value and can become so intense that the person longs for its termination at any cost.

Suffering in the Plan of Salvation

According to Christian teaching, however, suffering, especially in the final moments of life, has a special place in God's plan of salvation. It is a sharing in the passion of Christ and unites the person with the redemptive sacrifice which Christ offered in obedience to the Father's will.

It is not surprising, then, that some Christians desire to use painkillers only in moderation so that they can deliberately accept at least a part of their suffering and thus consciously unite themselves with the crucified Christ.[8]

It would be imprudent, nonetheless, to impose this heroic response as a general norm. On the contrary, in the case of many sick people, human and Christian prudence urges the use of such medications as may alleviate or eliminate suffering, even though they cause secondary effects such as lethargy and diminished awareness.

In the case of persons who are unable to express themselves, it may legitimately be presumed that they want to take painkillers and have them administered according to the advice of the doctors.

Problems in the Use of Painkillers

The concentrated and protracted use of painkillers is not, however, without its difficulties, since habituation usually requires that the dosage be increased in order to maintain effectiveness. It is worth recalling here a statement of Pius XII that is still valid. A group of physicians had asked: "Is the removal of pain and consciousness by means of narcotics . . . permitted by religion and morality to both doctor and patient even at the approach of death and if one foresees that the use of narcotics will shorten life?" The pope answered: "Yes — provided that no other means exist and if, in the given circumstances, the action does not prevent the carrying out of other moral and religious duties."[9]

In this case, as is clear, death is by no means intended or sought, although the risk of it is being incurred for a good reason; the only intention is to diminish pain effectively by use of the painkillers available to medical science.

Painkillers which cause the sick to lose consciousness call for special attention, for it is important that people be able not only to satisfy moral obligations and family duties but also and especially to dispose themselves with full awareness for their meeting with Christ. Pius XII therefore warns: "The sick person should not, without serious reason, be deprived of consciousness."[10]

IV The Proportionate Use of Therapeutic Agents

In our day it is very important at the moment of death to safeguard the dignity of the person and the Christian meaning of life, in the face of a technological approach to death that can easily be abused. Some even speak of a "right to die." By this they mean, however, not a right of persons to inflict death on themselves at will by their own or another's hand, but rather a right to die peacefully and in a manner worthy of a human being and a Christian.

In this context the application of the healing art can sometimes raise questions.

In many cases the situation may be so complicated as to raise doubts about how to apply moral principles. In the last analysis, the decision rests with the conscience of the sick person or of those who have a right to act in the sick person's name or of the doctors, who must bear in mind the principles of morality and the several aspects of the case.

All have an obligation to care for their health or to seek such care from others. Those in charge of the sick must perform their task with care and apply the remedies that seem necessary or useful.

Does this mean that all possible remedies must be applied in every circumstance?

The Basis of Judgment

In the not too distant past moralists would have replied that the use of "extraordinary" means can never be obligatory. This reply is still valid in principle but it is, perhaps, less evident today because of its vagueness or because of rapid advances in the treatment of illness. For this reason some prefer to speak of "proportionate" and "disproportionate" means.

In any case, a correct judgment can be made regarding means, if the type of treatment, its degree of difficulty and danger, its expense, and the possibility of applying it are weighed against the results that can be expected, all this in the light of the sick person's condition and resources of body and spirit.

The following clarifications will facilitate the application of these general principles:

— If other remedies are lacking, it is permissible with the consent of the sick person, to use the most recent medical techniques, even if these are not yet fully tested and are not free of risk. The sick person who agrees to them can even give an example, thereby, of generous service to the human race.

— It is also licit to discontinue the use of these means as soon as results disappoint the hopes placed in them but, in making this decision, account should be taken of the legitimate desire of the sick person and his or her family as well as the opinion of truly expert physicians. The latter are better placed than anyone else for judging whether the expense of machinery and personnel is disproportionate to the foreseeable results and whether the medical techniques used will cause the sick person suffering or inconvenience greater than the benefits that may be derived from them.

Use Only of Ordinary Means

— It is always licit to be content with the ordinary remedies which medical science can supply. Therefore, no one may be obliged to submit to a type of cure which, though already in use, is not without risks or is excessively burdensome.

This rejection of a remedy is not to be compared to suicide; it is more justly to be regarded as a simple acceptance of the human condition or a desire to avoid the application of medical techniques that are disproportionate to the value of the anticipated results or, finally, a desire not to put a heavy burden on the family or the community.

— When death is imminent and cannot be prevented by remedies used, it is licit in conscience to decide to renounce treatments that can only yield a precarious and painful prolongation of life.

At the same time, however, ordinary treatment that is due to the sick in such cases may not be interrupted. There is no reason for the doctor to feel anxious in such cases as though he had not come to the aid of a person in danger.

The norms contained in this declaration are motivated by an intense desire to help human beings in a way that accords with the plan of the Creator. While life is to be regarded as God's gift, it also is true that death is unavoidable. We must be able, therefore, without in any way hastening the hour of death, to accept it with full consciousness of our responsibility and with full dignity, for death, indeed, puts an end to this earthly life but in doing so it opens the way to undying life.

All human beings, therefore, must properly dispose themselves for this event in the light of human values and Christians even more in the light of their faith.

Health Care Personnel and Death

Those engaged in health care should certainly omit no effort in applying the full skills of their art to the advantage of the sick and dying. They should also bear in mind, however, that there is another consolation such people need and need even more urgently: unlimited kindness and devoted charity. When service of this kind is rendered to human beings, it is also rendered to Christ himself, who said: "As often as you did it for one of my least brothers, you did it for me."[11]

Notes

1. *Pastoral Constitution on the Church in the World of Today,* no. 27 [TPSXI, 276].

2. Declaration on Abortion, November 18, 1874: AAS 66 (1974) 730-47; translated in TPS XIX, 250-62.

3. Pius XII, Address to the International Union of Societies of Catholic Women, September 11, 1947: AAS 39 (1947) 483; Address to the Italian Union of Catholic Midwives, October 29, 1951: AAS 43 (1951) 835-54; Address to the International Commission of Inquiry into Military Medicine, October 9, 1953: AAS (1953) 744-54; Address to the 11th Congress of the Italian Society of Anesthesiology, February 24, 1957: AAS (1957) 146. See also Pius XII, Address on the Question of Reanimation, November 24, 1957: AAS 49 (1957) 1027-33. Paul VI, Address to the Special United Nations Committee on Apartheid, May 22, 1974: AAS 66 (1974) 346. John Paul II, Address to the Bishops of the United States of America, October 5, 1979: AAS 71 (1979) 1225.

4. *Rom* 14, 8; see *Phil* 1, 20.

5. See, in particular, Recommendation 779 (1976) on the rights of the sick and dying, which was adopted by the Assembly of Deputies of the Council of Europe at its 27th regular meeting. See SIPECA, no. 1 (March, 1977), pp. 14-15.

6. We leave completely aside here the questions of the death penalty and of war. These involve special con-

siderations which fall outside of the scope of this declaration.

7. See *Jn* 15, 14.

8. See *Mt* 27, 34.

9. Address to the 11th Congress of the Italian Society of Anesthesiology, February 24, 1967: AAS 49 (1957) 147 [TPS b IV, 48].

10. Ibid.: AAS 59 (1957) 145 [TPS IV, 47]. See the same pope's address of September 9, 1958: AAS 50 (1958) 694.

11. *Mt* 25, 40.

86 Euthanasia and Christian Vision

Gilbert Meilaender

Every teacher has probably experienced, along with countless frustrations, moments in the classroom when something was said with perfect lucidity. I still recall one such moment three years ago when I was teaching a seminar dealing with ethical issues in death and dying. Knowing how difficult it can be to get students to consider these problems from within religious perspectives, I decided to force the issue at the outset by assigning as the first reading parts of those magnificent sections from Volume III/4 of Karl Barth's *Church Dogmatics* in which he discusses "Respect for Life" and "The Protection of Life." I gave the students little warning in advance, preferring to let the vigor and bombast of Barth's style have whatever effect it might.

The students, I must say in retrospect, probably thought more kindly of Barth (who had, after all, only written these sections) than of their teacher (who had assigned them to be read). But they good-naturedly went about doing the assignment, and our seminar had a worthwhile discussion — with students criticizing Barth and, even, sometimes defending him. However, neither criticism nor defense was really my goal. It was understanding — understanding of death and dying within a perspective steeped in centuries of Christian life and thought — that I was seeking. And at one

Reprinted by permission of the publisher from "Euthanasia and Christian Vision," *Thought* 57, December 1982 (New York: Fordham University Press, 1982), pp. 465-75.

moment, even in a moment of criticism, we achieved that understanding.

One young woman in the class, seeking to explain why Barth puzzled her so, put it quite simply: "What I really don't like about him is that he seems to think our lives are not our own." To which, after a moment of awed silence, I could only respond: "If you begin to see that about Barth, even if it gets under your skin and offends you deeply, then indeed you have begun to understand what he is saying."

In his discussion of "The Protection of Life," and in fact, within his specific discussion of euthanasia, Barth notes many of the difficult questions we might raise which seem to nudge us in the direction of approving euthanasia in certain tormenting cases. And then, rejecting these "tempting questions," he responds with his own typical flair. "All honour to the well-meaning humanitarianism of underlying motive! But that derivation is obviously from another book than that which we have thus far consulted."[1] In this brief essay I want to think about euthanasia not from the perspective of any "well-meaning humanitarianism" but from within the parameters of Christian belief — though, as we will see, one of the most important things to note is that, within those parameters, only what is consonant with Christian belief can be truly humane.[2]

The Paradigm Case

Determining what really qualified as euthanasia is no easy matter. Need the person "euthanatized" be suffering terribly? Or, at least, be near death? Suppose the person simply feels life is no longer worth living in a particular condition which may be deeply dissatisfying though not filled with suffering? Suppose the person's life is filled with suffering or seemingly devoid of meaning but he is unable to request euthanasia (because of a comatose condition, senility, etc.)? Or suppose the person is suffering greatly but steadfastly says he does not want to die? Suppose the "euthanatizer's" motive is not mercy but despair at the continued burden of caring for the person — will that qualify?

The list of questions needing clarification is endless once we start down this path. But I intend to get off the path at once by taking as our focus of attention a kind of paradigm case of what must surely count as euthanasia. If we can understand why *this* is morally wrong, much else will fall into place. James Rachels has suggested that "the clearest possible case of euthanasia" would be one having the following five features:[3]

(1) The person is deliberately killed.

(2) The person would have died soon anyway.

(3) The person was suffering terrible pain.

(4) The person asked to be killed.

(5) The motive of the killing was mercy — to provide the person with as good a death as possible under the circumstances.

Such a case is not simply "assisted suicide," since the case requires the presence of great suffering, the imminence of death in any case, and a motive of mercy. Furthermore, considering this sort of case sets aside arguments about voluntary and involuntary euthanasia and gives focus to our discussion.[4] If this case of voluntary euthanasia is permissible, other cases may also be (or may not). If this case is itself morally wrong, we are less likely to be able to argue for euthanasia in nonvoluntary and involuntary circumstances.

Aim and Result

One way of arguing that the paradigm case of euthanasia is morally permissible (perhaps even obligatory) is to claim that it does not differ in morally relevant ways from other acts which most of us approve. Consider a patient whose death is imminent, who is suffering terribly, and who may suddenly stop breathing and require resuscitation. We may think it best not to resuscitate such a person but simply to let him die. What could be the morally significant difference between such a "letting die" and simply giving this person a lethal injection which would have ended his life (and suffering) just as quickly? If it is morally right not to prolong his dying when he ceases breathing for a few moments, why is it morally wrong to kill him quickly and painlessly? Each act responds to the fact that death is imminent and recognizes that terrible suffering calls for relief. And the result in each case is the same: death.

In order to appreciate the important difference between these possibilities we must distinguish what we *aim* at in our action from the *result* of the action. Or, to paraphrase Charles Fried, we must distinguish between those actions which we invest with the personal involvement of purpose and those which merely "run through" our person.[5] This is a distinction which moral reflection can scarcely get along without. For example, if we fail to distinguish between aim and result we will be unable to see any difference between the self-sacrifice of a martyr and the suicide of a person weary of life. The result is the same for each: death. But the aim or purpose is quite different. Whereas the suicide aims at his death, the martyr aims at faithfulness to God (or loyalty of some other sort). Both martyr and suicide recognize in advance that the result of their choice and act will be death. But the martyr does not aim at death.

This distinction between aim and result is also helpful in explaining the moral difference between euthanatizing a suffering person near death and simply letting such a person die. Suppose this patient were to stop breathing, we were to reject the possibility of resuscitation, and then the person were suddenly to begin breathing again. Would we, simply because we had been willing to let this patient die, now proceed to smother him so that he would indeed die? Hardly. And the fact that we would not indicates that we did not *aim* at his death (in rejecting resuscitation), though his death could have been one *result* of what we did aim at (namely, proper care for him in his dying). By contrast, if we euthanatized such a person by giving him a lethal injection, we would indeed aim at his death; we would invest the act of aiming at his death with the personal involvement of our purpose.

A rejoinder: It is possible to grant the distinction between aim and result while still claiming that euthanasia in our paradigm case would be permissible (or obligatory). It may be true that there is a difference between allowing a patient to die and aiming at someone's death. But if the suffering of the dying person is truly intense and the person requests death, on what grounds could we refuse to assist him? If we refuse on the grounds that it would be wrong for us to aim at his death (which will certainly result soon anyway after more terrible suffering), are we not saying that we are unwilling to do him a great good if doing it requires that we dirty our hands in any way? To put the matter this way makes it seem that our real concern is with our own moral rectitude, not with the needs of the sufferer. It seems that we are so concerned about ourselves that in our eagerness to narrow the scope of our moral responsibility we have lost sight of the need and imperative to offer care.

This is, it should be obvious, what ethicists call a *consequentialist* rejoinder. It suggests that the good results (relieving the suffering) are sufficiently weighty to make the aim (of killing) morally permissible or obligatory. And, as far as I can tell, this rejoinder has become increasingly persuasive to large numbers of people.

Consequentialism may be described as that moral theory that holds that from the fact that some state of affairs *ought to be* it follows that we *ought to do* whatever is necessary to bring about that state of affairs. And, although teleological theories of morality are very ancient, consequentialism as a full-blown moral theory is traceable largely to Bentham and Mill in the late 18th and early 19th centuries. To remember this is instructive, since it is not implausible to suggest that such a moral theory would be most persuasive when Christendom had, in large measure, ceased to be Christian. Those who know themselves as creatures — not Creator — will recognize limits even upon their obligation to do good. As creatures we are to do all the good we can, but this means all the good we "morally can" — all the good we can within certain limits. It may be that the Creator *ought to do* whatever is necessary to bring about states of affairs which *ought to be*, but we stand under no such godlike imperative.[6]

One of the best ways to understand the remarkable appeal today of consequentialism as a moral theory is to see it as an ethic for those who (a) remain morally serious but (b) have ceased to believe in a God whose providential care will ultimately bring about whatever ought to be the case. If God is not there to accomplish what ought to be the case, we are the most likely candidates to shoulder the burden of that responsibility.[7] Conversely, it may be that we can make sense of distinguishing between two acts whose *result* is the same but whose *aim* is different only if we believe that our responsibilities (as creatures) are limited — that the responsibility for achieving certain results has been taken out of our hands (or, better, never given us in the first place). It ought to be the case that dying people not suffer terribly (indeed, that they not die). But, at least for Christians, it does not follow from that "ought to be" that we "ought to do" whatever is necessary — even euthanasia — to relieve them of that suffering.[8]

We are now in a position to see something important about the argument which claims that euthanasia (in the paradigm case) is permissible because it does not differ morally from cases of "letting die" which most of us approve. This argument often begins in a failure to distinguish aim and result; however, it is, as we have seen, difficult for moral theory to get along without this distinction. Seeing this, we recognize that the argument really becomes a claim that if the results are sufficiently good, any aim necessary to achieve them is permissible. And precisely at this turn in the argument, it may be difficult to keep "religion" and "morality" in those neat and separate compartments we have fashioned for them. At this point one steeped in Christian thought and committed to Christian life may wish to say with Barth: All honor to the well-meaning humanitarianism — and it is well-meaning. But the derivation — fit only for those who would, even if reluctantly, be "like God" — is obviously "derived from another book" than that which Christians are wont to consult.

Aim and Motive

If the distinction between aim and result makes it difficult to justify euthanasia in the paradigm case, another distinction may be more useful. We might suggest that the act of euthanatizing be redescribed in terms of the motive of mercy. We could describe the act not as killing but as relieving suffering. Or, rather than engaging in such wholesale redescription of the act, we might simply argue that our moral evaluation of the act cannot depend solely on its *aim* but must also consider its *motive.*

Consider the following illustration.[9] A condemned prisoner is in his cell only minutes before his scheduled execution. As he sits in fear and anguish, certain of his doom, another man who has managed to sneak into the prison shoots and kills him. This man is either (a) the father of children murdered by the prisoner, or (b) a close friend of the prisoner. In case (a) he shoots because he will not be satisfied simply to have the man executed. He desires that his own hand should bring about the prisoner's death. In case (b) the friend shoots because he wishes to spare his friend the terror and anguish of those last minutes, to deliver him from the indignity of the sheer animal fright he is undergoing.

Would it be proper to describe the father's act in (a) as an act of killing and the friend's in (b) as an act of relieving suffering? Although many people may be tempted to do so, it muddies rather than clarifies our analysis. If anything is clear in these cases, it is that both the vengeful father and the compassionate friend *aim* to kill though their *motives* are very different. Only by refusing to redescribe the aim of the act in terms of its motive do we keep the moral issue clearly before us. That issue is whether our moral evaluation of the act should depend solely on the agent's *aim* or whether that evaluation must also include the *motive.*

That the motive makes *some* difference almost everyone would agree. Few of us would be content to analyze the two cases simply as instances of "aiming to kill" without considering the quite different motives. The important question, however, is whether the praiseworthy motive of relieving suffering should so dominate our moral reflection that it leads us to term the act "right." I want to suggest that it should not, at least not within the parameters of Christian belief.

One might think that Christian emphasis on the overriding importance of love as a motive would suggest that whatever was done out of love was right. And, to be sure, Christians will often talk this way. Such talk, however, must be done against the background assumptions of Christian anthropology. Apart from that background of meaning we may doubt whether we have really understood the motive of love correctly. We need therefore to sketch in the background against which we can properly understand what loving care for a suffering person should be.[10]

Barth writes that human life "must always be regarded as a divine act of trust."[11] This means that all human life is "surrounded by a particular solemnity," which, if recognized, will lead us to "treat it with respect." At the same time, however, "life is no second God, and therefore the respect due to it cannot rival the reverence owed to God." One who knows this will seek to live life "within its appointed limits." Recognizing our life as a trust, we will be moved not by an "absolute will to live" but a will to live within these limits. Hence, when we understand ourselves as creatures, we will both value God's gift of life and recognize that the Giver himself constitutes the limit beyond which we ought not value the gift. "Temporal life is certainly not the highest of all goods. Just because it belongs to God, man may be forbidden to will its continuation at all costs." And at the same time, "if life is not the highest possession, then it is at least the highest and all-inclusive price" which human beings can pay. In short, life is a great good, but not the greatest (which is fidelity to God).

Death, the final enemy of life, must also be understood dialectically. The human mind can take and has quite naturally taken two equally plausible attitudes toward death.[12] We can regard death as of no consequence, heeding the Epicurean maxim that while we are alive death is not yet here, and when death is here we are no more. Thus the human being, in a majestic transcendence of the limits of earthly life, might seek to soar beyond the limits of finitude and find his good elsewhere. If death is of no consequence, we may seek it in exchange for some important good. Equally natural to the human mind is a seemingly opposite view — that death is the *summum malum,* the greatest evil to be avoided at all costs. Such a view, finding good only in earthly life, can find none in suffering and death.

The Christian mind, however, transcending what is "natural" and correcting it in light of the book it is accustomed to consult, has refused to take either of these quite plausible directions. Understood within the biblical narrative, death is an ambivalent phenomenon — too ambivalent to be seen only as the greatest of all evils, or as indifferent. Since the world narrated by the Bible begins in God and moves toward God, earthly life is his trust to be sustained faithfully and his gift to be valued and cared for. When life is seen from this perspective, we cannot say that death and suffering are of no consequence; on the contrary, we can even say with Barth that the human task in the face of suffering and death is not to accept but to offer "final resistance."[13] It is just as true, however, that death could never be the greatest evil. That title must be reserved for disobedience to and disbelief in God — a refusal to live within our appointed limits. So we can also repeat with Barth that "life is no second God."[14] We remember, after all, that Jesus goes to the cross in the name of obedience to his Father. We need not glorify or seek suffering, but we must be struck by the fact that a human being who is a willing sufferer stands squarely in the center of Christian piety. Jesus bears his suffering not because it is desirable but because the Father allots it to him within the limits of his earthly life. Death is — there is no way to put the matter simply — a great evil which God can turn to his good purposes. It is an evil which must ordinarily be resisted but which must also at some point be acknowledged. We can and ought to acknowledge what we do not and ought not seek. George Orwell, himself an "outsider," nicely summarized these background assumptions of Christian anthropology:

> The Christian attitude towards death is not that it is something to be welcomed, or that it is something to be met with stoical indifference, or that it is something to be avoided as long as possible; but that it is something profoundly tragic which has to be gone through with. A Christian, I suppose, if he were offered the chance of everlasting life on this earth would refuse it, but he would still feel that death is profoundly sad.[15]

This vision of the world, and of the meaning of life and death, has within Christendom given guidance to those reflecting on human suffering and dying. That moral guidance has amounted to the twofold proposition that, though we might properly cease to oppose death while aiming at other choiceworthy goods in life (hence, the possibility of martyrdom), we ought never aim at death as either our end or our means.

Against this background of belief we can better understand what *love* and *care* must be within a world construed in Christian terms. In *this* world no action which deliberately hastens death can be called "love." Not because the euthanatizer need have any evil motive. Indeed, as the case of the compassionate friend makes clear, the one who hastens death may seem to have a praiseworthy motive. Rather, such action cannot be loving because it cannot be part of the meaning of commitment to the well-being of another human being within the appointed limits of earthly life. The benevolence of the euthanatizer is enough like love to give us pause, to tempt us to call it love. And *perhaps* it may even be the closest those who feel themselves to bear full responsibility for relief of suffering and production of good in our world can come to love. But it is not the creaturely love which Christians praise, a love which can sometimes do no more than suffer as best we can with the sufferer.

Christian Love Enacted and Inculcated

Against this background — a background which pours meaning into words like "love" and "care" — we can contemplate the kind of case often considered in discussions of euthanasia.[16] A person may be in severe pain, certain to die within only a few days. Most of us would agree that further "lifesaving" treatment were not in order for such a person, that they would do no more than prolong his dying. Why, one may ask, do we not subject such a patient to useless treatments? Because, we reply, he is in agony and it would be wrong to prolong that agony needlessly. But now, if we face the facts honestly, we will admit that it takes this patient longer to die — and prolongs his suffering — if we simply withhold treatment than if we euthanatize him. Hence, there seems to be a contradiction within our reasoning. The motive for withholding treatment was a humanitarian one: relief of suffering. But in refusing to take the next step and euthanatize the patient we prolong his suffering and, thereby, belie our original motive. Hence the conclusion follows, quite contrary to the moral guidance embedded in the Christian vision of the world: Either we should keep this person alive as long as possible (and not pretend that our motive is the relief of suffering), or we should be willing to euthanatize him.

The argument gets much of its force from the seeming simplicity of the dilemma, but that simplicity is misleading. For, at least for Christian vision, the fundamental imperative is not "minimize suffering" but "maximize love and care." In that Christian world, in which death and suffering are great evils but not the greatest evil, love can never include in its meaning hastening a fellow human being toward (the evil of) death, nor can it mean a refusal to acknowledge death when it comes (as an evil but not the greatest evil). We can only know what the imperative "maximize love" means if we understand it against the background assumptions which make intelligible for Christians words like "love" and "care." The Christian mind has certainly not recommended that we seek suffering or call it an unqualified good, but it is an evil which, when endured faithfully, can be redemptive. William May has noted how parents in our time think that love for their children means, above all else, protecting those children from suffering. "As conscientious parents, they operate as though the powers that are decisive in the universe could not possibly do anything in and through the suffering of their children. . . . They take upon themselves the responsibilities of a savior-figure. . . ."[17] May sees clearly that "minimize suffering" and "maximize love" are not identical imperatives and do not offer the same direction for human action Perhaps the direction they give may often be the same, but at times — especially when we consider what it is proper to do for the irretrievably dying — we will discover how sharply they may differ.

I suggested above that we should not redescribe the *aim* of an act in terms of its *motive.* (We should not say that an act of killing a suffering person was simply an act of relieving suffering. We should say rather that we aimed at the death of the person in order to relieve his suffering. This keeps the moral issue more clearly before us.) But by now it will be evident that I have in fact gone some way toward redescribing the *motive* of the act in terms of its *aim.* (If the act is aimed at hastening the death of the suffering person, we should not see it as motivated by love.) Is this any better? The answer, I think, is "it depends."

It would not be better, it might even be worse, if my purpose were to deny any humanitarian motive to the person tempted to euthanatize a sufferer. Few people would find such a denial persuasive, and because we would not we are tempted to turn in the opposite direction and describe the act's aim in terms of its motive. We *do* recognize a difference between the vengeful father and the compassionate friend even though both aim to kill the condemned prisoner, and we want our moral judgments to be sufficiently nuanced to take account of these differences. The simple truth is that our evaluation of the act (described in terms of motive) often fall apart. In a world broken by sin and its consequences this should perhaps come as no surprise. Christians believe that we sinners — all of us — are not whole, and many of the stubborn problems of systematic ethical reflection testify to the truth of that belief. It is our lack of wholeness which is displayed in our inability to arrive at one judgment (or even one description) "whole and entire" of a single act. We find ourselves in a world in which people may sometimes seem to aim at doing evil from the best of motives (and think they must do so). And then we are tempted to elide aim and motive and call that evil at which they aim "good."

No amount of ethical reflection can heal this rift in our nature. From that predicament we will have to look for a deliverance greater than ethics can offer. However, here and now, in our broken world, we do better to take the aim of an act as our guiding light in describing and evaluating the act — and then evaluate the motive in light of this aim. This is better because moral reflection is not primarily a tool for fixing guilt and responsibility (in which case motive comes to the fore). It is, first and foremost, one of the ways in which we train ourselves and others to see the world rightly. We would be wrong to assert that no euthanatizer has or can have a humanitarian motive. But if we want not so much to fix praise or blame but to teach the meaning of the word "love," we are not wrong to say that love could never euthanatize. In the Christian world this is true. And in that world we know the right name for our own tendency to call those other, seemingly humanitarian, motives "love." The name for that tendency is *temptation.* We are being tempted to be "like God" when we toy with the possibility of defining our love — and the meaning of humanity — apart from the appointed limits of human life.

To redescribe the motive in terms of the act's aim, to attempt to *inculcate* a vision of the world in which love could never euthanatize, is therefore not only permissible but necessary for Christians. It is the only proper way to respond to the supposed dilemmas we are confronted with by reasoning which brackets Christian background assumptions from the outset. The Christian moral stance which emerges here is not a club with which to beat over the head those who disagree. It does not provide a superior vantage point from which to deny them any humanitarian motive in the ordinary sense. But it *is* a vision of what "humanity" and "humanitarian motives" should be. We may therefore say of those who disagree: "All honour to the well-meaning humanitarianism of underlying motive! But the derivation is obviously from another book than that which we have thus far consulted."

Notes

1. Karl Barth, *Church Dogmatics,* Vol. III/4, ed. G. W. Bromiley and T. F. Torrance (Edinburgh: T&T Clark, 1961), p. 425.

2. I will be exploring some of the *moral* issues involved in euthanasia without taking up *legal* problems which also arise. I do not assume any answer to the question, Should what is morally wrong be legally prohibited?

3. James Rachels, "Euthanasia," *Matters of Life and Death: New Introductory Essays in Moral Philosophy,* ed. Tom Regan (New York: Random House, 1980), p. 29.

4. Nonvoluntary euthanasia occurs when the person euthanatized is in a condition which makes it impossible for him to express a wish (e.g., senile, comatose). Involuntary euthanasia occurs when the person euthanatized expresses a desire *not* to be killed but is nevertheless euthanatized.

5. Charles Fried, *Right and Wrong* (Cambridge, Mass.: Harvard University Press, 1978), p. 27.

6. Cf. Joseph Butler, Dissertation "On the Nature of Virtue," appended to *The Analogy of Religion Natural and Revealed.* Morley's Universal Library edition (London: George Routledge & Sons, 1884), p. 301: "The fact then appears to be, that we are constituted so as to condemn falsehood, unprovoked violence, injustice, and to approve of benevolence to some preferably to others abstracted from all consideration, which conduct is likely to produce an overbalance of happiness or misery; and therefore, were the Author of Nature to propose nothing to Himself as an end but the production of happiness, were His moral character merely that of benevolence; yet ours is not so." In other words, though the Creator may be a consequentialist, creatures are not! For a contrary view, see Peter Geach, *The Virtues* (Cambridge: Cambridge University Press, 1977), pp. 95ff.

7. Whether this enlargement of the scope of our responsibility really works is another matter. Being responsible for everything may, for human beings, come quite close to being responsible for nothing. Charles Fried comments: "If, as consequentialism holds, we were indeed equally morally responsible for an infinite radiation of concentric circles originating from the center point of some action, then while it might look as if we were enlarging the scope of human responsibility and thus the significance of personality, the enlargement would be greater than we could support. . . . Total undifferentiated responsibility is the correlative of the morally overwhelming, undifferentiated plasma of happiness or pleasure" (*Right and Wrong*, pp. 34f.).

8. It is a hard, perhaps unanswerable, question whether there might ever be exceptions to this general standard for Christian conduct which I have enunciated. There might be a circumstance in which the pain of the sufferer was so terrible and unconquerable that one would want to consider an exception. To grant this possibility is not really to undermine the principle, since, as Charles Fried has noted, the "catastrophic" is a distinct moral concept, identifying an extreme situation in which the usual rules of morality do not apply (Right and Wrong, p. 10). We would be quite mistaken to build the whole of our morality on the basis of the catastrophic; in fact, it would then become the norm rather than the exception. One possible way to deal with such extreme circumstances without simply lapsing into consequentialist is to reason in a way analogous to Michael Walzer's reasoning about the rules of war in *Just and Unjust Wars* (New York: Basic Books, Inc., 1977). Walzer maintains the rules of war are binding even when they put us at a disadvantage, even when they may cost us victory. But he grants that there might be "extreme emergencies" in which we could break the rules; namely, when doing so was (a) morally necessary (i.e., the opponent was so evil — a Hitler — that it was morally imperative to defeat him) and (b) strategically necessary (no other way than violating the rules of war was available for defeating this opponent). Reasoning in an analogous way we might wonder whether the rule prohibiting euthanasia could be violated if (a) the suffering was so unbearable that the sufferer lost all capacity to bear that suffering with any sense of moral purpose or faithfulness to God; and (b) the pain was truly unconquerable. Whether such extreme circumstances ever occur is a question whose answer I cannot give. And even if such circumstances are possible, I remain uncertain about the force of this "thought experiment," which is offered tentatively.

9. This illustration is "inspired" by a different set of hypothetical cases offered by Paul Ramsey in "Some Rejoinders," *The Journal of Religious Ethics* 4 (Fall 1976): 204.

10. In what follows I draw upon my own formulations in two previous articles: "The Distinction Between Killing and Allowing to Die," *Theological Studies* 37 (September 1976): 467-70 and "Lutheran Theology and Bioethics: A Juxtaposition," *SPC Journal* 3 (1980): 25-30.

11. The passages cited in this paragraph may be found scattered throughout pages 336-42 and pages 401-2 of Vol. III/4 of *Church Dogmatics.*

12. For what follows cf. C. S. Lewis, *Miracles* (New York: Macmillan, 1947), pp. 129ff., and Paul Ramsey, *The Patient as Person* (New Haven and London: Yale University Press, 1970), pp. 144ff.

13. *Church Dogmatics,* III/4, p. 368.

14. Ibid., p. 342.

15. George Orwell, "The Meaning of a Poem," *My Country Right or Left,* 1940-1943. Volume II of *The Collected Essays, Journalism and Letters of George Orwell,* ed. Sonia Orwell and Ian Angus (New York: Harcourt Brace Jovanovich, 1968), p. 133.

16. For a strong statement of such a case see James Rachels, "Active and Passive Euthanasia," *New England Journal of Medicine* 292 (1975): 78-80.

17. William May, "The Metaphysical Plight of the Family," *Death Inside Out,* ed. Peter Steinfels and Robert M. Veatch (New York: Harper & Row, 1974), p. 51.

87 Covenantal Ethics and Care for the Dying

Mark A. Duntley, Jr.

Jack was dying of AIDS. Toward the end, in spite of huge doses of morphine, Jack's pain became almost unbearable. His mother, Louise, cared for him and watched him suffer. One day, as tears rolled from his eyes, Jack told Louise that he wanted to end his pain. He asked her if she would help him die when the time came. Reluctantly she agreed. But when the day arrived when Jack begged his mother to help him die, she could not bring herself to give him the pills they had set aside. Jack died three days later. Louise is both proud and ashamed of her inability to help her son die. But most of all, she wonders why health-care professionals cannot help dying people end their lives — and their suffering.

Louise is not alone in her wish. As medical technology gives more life-prolonging measures and as more people join the ranks of the elderly, the ultimate issue of individual choice — determining if, when and how to end one's own life — grows more urgent. The books *Last Wish*, by Betty Rollin, and *Final Exit*, by Derek Humphry, have become best-sellers in part because so many people fear a prolonged, painful death. Since such a death seems to be anything but good, it is understandable that many have come to believe that there are indeed times when the hopelessly suffering should be allowed to choose a quick and merciful death at the hands of a medical professional.

From Mark A. Duntley, Jr., "Covenantal Ethics and Care for the Dying," from *Christian Century* 108 (December 4, 1991): 1135-37. Used by permission.

> If wisdom be in suffering, O my lords!
> As you are great, be pitifully good:
> Who cannot condemn rashness in cold blood?
> To kill, I grant, is sin's extremist gust;
> But, in defence, by mercy, 'tis most just.
>
> Shakespeare

Recent innovations in biotechnological medicine have made patients more dependent upon medical professionals than ever. Ironically, however, patients today have more clout in determining their own treatment. For most of human history the healer — whether shaman, witch doctor, priest or physician — maintained almost complete control of treatment decisions. This legacy of paternalism in medicine has come under fire in our generation, as patients — and physicians — promote individual rights and patient autonomy. One recent poll found that almost two-thirds of Americans believe that a terminally ill patient has the right to stop treatment under any circumstances, even when facing imminent death. Patients' desires have become essential to treatment decisions — even in the face of death.

As moral and legal acceptance of withholding or withdrawing extraordinary medical treatment in terminal cases (passive euthanasia) increases, many suggest that administering a medication or treatment that will precipitate death (active euthanasia) may also be justifiable. Why should we be able to end the suffering of pets, yet not that of a loved one? A recent New York Times/CBS poll indicates that 53 percent of those surveyed approve of physician-assisted suicide.

> I will neither give a deadly drug to anybody if asked for it, nor will make a suggestion to this effect . . . In purity and holiness I will guard my life and my art.
>
> Hippocrates, The Hippocratic Oath

Yet many health-care professionals and physicians side with the American Medical Association in asserting that assisting in a patient's suicide betrays their pledge to heal, not kill, their patients. The AMA has asserted that "mercy killing" or the "intentional termination of the life of one human being by another" is wrong and very different from withholding or withdrawing "extraordinary means to prolong the life of the body when there is irrefutable evidence that biological death is imminent" (see Tom Beauchamp and James F. Childress, *Principles of Biomedical Ethics* [Oxford University Press, 1987]). Thus, while physicians have generally accepted forms of passive euthanasia for the terminally ill, most still believe that active euthanasia contradicts their professional responsibilities.

In recent years medical professionals have begun to admit that alleviating pain and suffering is a far more important healing task than that of prolonging life for the hopelessly ill. Pain management teams and new techniques for controlling pain have relieved many from living their final days in agony. This new treatment philosophy and the development of advanced pain-reduction therapies have led some health-care professionals to believe that only very few patients will desire help in committing suicide. Furthermore, although some physicians would consider assisting the suicide of special, individual cases, many oppose a social policy of sanctioning physician-assisted suicide, believing it would break down trust between physicians and patients. As Dr. Susan Tolle, director of the Center for Ethics at Oregon Health Sciences University, noted in the *Oregonian* (June 23, 1991), it would take only one wrongly administered lethal injection to "cause an uproar in the media leading to a backlash." Such a backlash could result in new, regressive restrictions on the treatment of the dying, thus prolonging the suffering of thousands of terminal patients.

> The quality of mercy is not strain'd,
> It droppeth as the gentle rain from heaven
> Upon the place beneath; it is twice bless'd;
> It blesseth him that gives and him that takes.
>
> Shakespeare

Ultimately, the crux of this matter lies deep in the essence of what it means to care for another human being. And at the heart of caring is the concept of mercy. Mercy or compassion toward the dying and suffering seems to be central to any philosophy of healing, and most certainly is the primary argument for the morality of euthanasia. If prolonging a painful or nonsentient existence can be cruel, then the responsibility to care for another human being may indeed require ending his or her struggle. The key issue is determining the circumstances in which physician-assisted suicide is indeed merciful treatment. Understanding mercy will help determine those circumstances.

Scriptures teach that mercy is inextricably tied to relationships, particularly covenantal relationships. One of the central meanings of covenant is complete commitment between the parties. The Old Testament shows the amazing ways God demonstrated a commitment to the covenant with the chosen people in forgiveness, in deliverance from enemies, in provision in the wilderness, etc. God bestows mercy (*chesed* and *rachamim*) on those within the covenantal relationship, and God's mercy is the fulfillment of a covenant based on love.

After the dedication of the temple, Solomon speaks of this integral relationship of covenant and mercy: "O Lord, God of Israel, there is no God like you in heaven above or on earth beneath, keeping covenant and mercy [*chesed*] for your servants who walk before you with all their heart, the covenant that you kept for your servant my father David as you declared to him; you promised with your mouth and have this day fulfilled with your hand" (1 Kings 8:23-24). Later in Israel's history, the prophet Hosea reminds the people that in spite of their infidelity and punishment, God's covenant would be renewed: "I will make for you a covenant on that day with the wild animals, the birds of the air, and the creeping things of the ground; and I will abolish the bow, the sword, and war from the land; and I will make you lie down in safety. And I will take you for my wife forever, I will take you for my wife in righteousness and in justice, in steadfast love, and in mercy [*rachamim*]" (Hos. 2:18-19). Mercy is available to Israel not because of the people's righteousness, but solely because of God's covenantal guarantee of faithfulness to them.

The Bible also sets forth God's mercy as a model for human beings to follow, and the key to obtaining mercy rests on covenantal relations. The covenant with God is the source of human covenants, and thus of mercy. Elizabeth Achtemeier points out that mercy is most evident within the closest ties of the family. "Where a family was, there was mercy. Where mercy was lacking, the familial ties were gone" (*Interpreter's Dictionary of the Bible* [Abingdon, 1962]). Mercy is also a part of the covenant relationship between the community and its dependents or the helpless, and is a sign of deep friendship and devotion. Before Jonathan sent David away with the knowledge that Saul intended to kill him, he spoke of the mercy their friendship required. " 'May the Lord be with you, as he has been with my father. If I am still alive, show me the mercy [*chesed*] of the Lord; but if I die, never cut off your mercy from my house, even if the Lord were to cut off every one of the enemies of David from the face of the earth.' Thus Jonathan made a covenant with the house of David" (1 Sam. 20:13b-16a). David later lived up to his covenant and showed mercy to Jonathan's crippled son, Mephibosheth. He restored the family land to Mephibosheth and invited him to eat with him at the royal table.

The New Testament tells of Jesus showing mercy to those around him, especially the sick and suffering. His deep compassion (*splagchnizomai* — literally, "to be moved in one's bowels") prompts him to act with mercy (*eleeo*), to heal the blind, feed the multitudes and even raise the dead. Achtemeier notes in the *Interpreter's Dictionary of the Bible* that Matthew has a recurrent theme concerning "the compassion and mercy which one member of the community owes to another." Indeed, their communal obligation is to love, aid and comfort each other. George Mendenhall suggests that the early Christians saw themselves as bound together in covenant, although this covenant is "a most free, creative reinterpretation of the older traditions" (*Interpreter's Dictionary of the Bible*).

If we appropriate the biblical standards of mercy, then we need to practice those standards in covenant relationships. Following are two famous cases of physician-assisted suicide that illustrate the difference between mercy in and outside of covenant.

The first is the case of 54-year-old Janet Adkins and Dr. Jack Kevorkian. In the early stages of Alzheimer's disease, Adkins decided she wanted to end her life in order to save herself and her family from the debilitating effects of the disease. From her home in Portland, Oregon, she contacted Kevorkian, a Michigan physician whom she had never met and asked him to help her end her life. He agreed, and she traveled to Michigan where he set up an intravenous system whereby she could push a button and receive a lethal injection in her arm. She died with the aid of this device in June 1990.

The second case is that of a 45-year-old leukemia patient, "Diane," and Dr. Timothy Quill ("Death and Dignity — A Case of Individualized Decision Making," *New England Journal of Medicine* [March 7, 1991]). Quill had been Diane's physician for eight years, and had informed her that the treatment of the disease had a 25 percent chance of success. However, Quill had written, Diane believed that she would "suffer unspeakably in the process," and she asked him to help her die. He provided her with barbiturates and instructions on how to use them, which she did in May 1990.

There is a significant ethical distinction between these two cases. While it is clear that both of these physicians believed they were acting mercifully, their respective relationships with their patients were quite dissimilar. Quill and Diane had a longstanding relationship characterized by mutual admiration and trust. Kevorkian and Adkins were virtual strangers. Quill could be merciful to Diane because he knew her and related to her as a friend. By all indications, Kevorkian and Janet Adkins did not know each other well enough for that.

Without an appropriate covenantal context for mercy, assisted suicide lacks moral force and sanction. Unfortunately, neither our health-care system nor our general attitude toward health-care providers encourages us to seek covenantal relationships with our physicians. On the one hand, the system tends to encourage technical specialization and cost management over physician-patient relationships. On the other hand, we tend to think of physicians as omniscient miracle workers who should always be able to cure us. As William F. May in his book *The Physician's Covenant* (Westminster, 1983) has so insightfully pointed out, our image of the physician as "fighter" (i.e., one who fights against disease and death) and the physician's self-image as that of "technician" (i.e., one who implements the powerful cures of modern biotechnology) can lead both patient and physician to view the relationship in merely contractual terms. Such a contractual relationship does not encourage the deep, personal connection of the healer and patient, and therefore does not lend itself to an easy determination of how best to care for the patient.

May asserts that the most basic relationship between physician and patient "rests in the image of the healer as covenanter, the central inclusive image for the whole." Covenantal relationships go beyond duty and obligation by centering on mutuality and enduring responsibility through affirmation and partnership. For those physicians and patients like Quill and Diane who have a covenantal rather than contractual relationship, assisted suicide can indeed become an experience of mercy and grace.

Karl Barth asserted, "The external dynamic of . . . covenant is that it rests on creation. In virtue of its being and nature, the creature is destined, prepared and equipped to be a partner of this covenant . . . thus the covenant is the goal of creation and creation, the way to the covenant" (*Church Dogmatics*). Deep personal relationships lie at the heart of divine and human mercy. As much as we want to codify rules about physician-assisted suicide and either outlaw it or define precisely when it is permissible, such an approach will not fit into a relational matrix.

In our current state of affairs, assisted-suicide cases will remain in an ethical gray area. Our challenge is to move beyond evaluating individual cases or searching for broad policies to reaffirming treasured truths about covenantal relationships built on trust and mutuality. In the realm of health care, this necessitates transforming our contractual system of "consumer ethics" into one based on personal relationships, mutual interest, the common good and "covenantal ethics." Such a transformation would not necessarily eliminate all the ethical dilemmas surrounding physician-assisted suicide, but it would much more adequately provide the covenantal context necessary for showing mercy to the dying.

88 Reflection

Karen Lebacqz

Since the question to which we respond is already quite delimited, let me add one more condition: not only is the person terminally ill and requesting termination of life, but she is in enduring and intractable pain that cannot be relieved short of being under heavy and constant doses of drugs. Under these conditions, to ask the question whether active euthanasia is ever permissible seems to me a bit absurd, if not obscene. The question should be inverted: is it ever permissible *not* to use active euthanasia for one who suffers so, with no hope of recovery? We would not hesitate to put an animal out of its misery. Why, then, would we not extend the same compassion to a human being?

No, make that: the same compassion to our mother or father, our brother, our child, our friend.[1] Surely if we care about another, as Nel Noddings so forcefully asserts, we would want to prevent that other's suffering.[2]

Of course, there are all the *practical* reasons for not doing so. How do we ensure that the person truly requests euthanasia? How do we measure enduring and intractable pain? Who will effect the active euthanasia, and how can it be administered in a way that reduces or eliminates the likelihood of abuse of the system? These are not unimportant questions. But in my view, they do not undermine the central moral issue, which has to do with caring, compassion, and prevention of suffering in the face of death.

Consider a woman dying of bone cancer, the

From Ron Hamel, ed., *Active Euthanasia, Religion, and the Public Debate* (Philadelphia: Trinity Press International), pp. 87-88. Used by permission.

mother of one of my friends. As the disease progresses, the pain worsens. To handle the pain, she is drugged constantly and sleeps more than 20 hours out of each day. Is it better to be so drugged than to be dead? Is it different? There was a time when Catholic moral theology did not allow painkillers to be used during childbirth, ostensibly because of the importance of being in possession of one's faculties in order to face God.[3] While today we might deem the refusal of painkillers during childbirth rather cruel, the underlying principle of being in possession of one's faculties as one faces death merits attention. I am not sure that it is better to be alive and permanently in a drugged state than to be dead. Minimally, this seems to be something over which human beings should be given some choice.

I have watched my own parents sign "living wills" in order to try to retain some choice over their ends. Would I really have the courage to refuse treatment on their behalf if that came to be necessary? I'm not sure I would, for although I would want to honor their wishes, I would also have a hard time letting go of those whom I love so much. Would I then have the courage to give them something to induce death if they requested it? Would I be moved by compassion for their suffering or by revulsion at the idea that I bring about death? The questions are not easy.

Or consider my own case. My paternal grandmother died in a diabetic coma. A diabetic coma is perhaps a better way to die than some other ways, and it can be deliberately induced. Diabetes may be, in that sense, a "convenient" disease. I do not know yet whether I have inherited late-onset diabetes. If I have, I may have some options that are not open to those without convenient diseases. If my body were ravaged by disease, my spirit weary from intractable pain, my death inevitable, and my soul ready to face God, I would want to have something available to me to end my life.

That is not a decision I would make easily or lightly. I know the cautions about euthanasia — the danger that it is only a temporary depression speaking, and not the "real" person; the possibility that the patient to be killed is not in fact terminally ill; the risk that social policy supporting voluntary euthanasia would too easily turn into involuntary euthanasia. These dangers I take seriously. I belong to no organizations that advocate voluntary euthanasia, for I find them too unguarded about such dangers.

Nonetheless, I think there are circumstances in which active euthanasia is *morally* justifiable. To say it is morally justifiable is not to say that it should become social policy; that is another matter. Moreover, the situation posed here is very limited; circumstances in which patients are terminally ill and have requested that their lives be terminated, along with the further qualification that they are in enduring and intractable pain.

To sum up, I love life. I want my parents to live forever. I wish my grandmother had not died. I resist my own aging and movement toward death. And yet I am also a Christian. I know that death is not the last word, not the greatest evil. Failure to live, to care, to enact justice, to be in proper relationship — those are greater evils. Death can serve evil or it can serve the values of life. As a way of bringing about death, active euthanasia can serve evil or it can serve the values of life. When it serves the values of life, it can be morally justified.

Notes

1. See Stanley Hauerwas, "My Uncle Charlie May Not Be Much of a Person but He's Still My Uncle Charlie," in *Truthfulness and Tragedy* (Notre Dame, Ind.: Notre Dame University Press, 1977).

2. Nel Noddings, *Caring: A Feminine Approach to Ethics and Moral Education* (Berkeley and Los Angeles: University of California Press, 1984), p. 32: "The mother as one-caring . . . wants first and most importantly to relieve her child's suffering."

3. How much misogyny entered that decision is beyond the scope of this piece.

89 Physician-Assisted Suicide: Flight from Compassion

Richard A. McCormick, S.J.

Most Americans (64 percent of those questioned this year by the *Boston Globe* and the Harvard School of Public Health) approve of physician-assisted suicide. It was somewhat surprising, therefore, that an initiative to legalize it was defeated in Washington State on November 5. The American Medical Association opposed Initiative 119, and its senior vice-president of medical education and science, M. Roy Schwarz, stated that the profession would not soon change its position. "Maybe in five or ten years, but not soon." Five or ten decades would be too soon, in my judgment. But Schwarz's prediction may be close to the mark. The medical profession is usually, and often enough properly, conservative on these matters, but one wonders how long it will hold out against proposals like Initiative 119, especially if these represent shifts in public opinion. Not long, I fear.

Initiative 119 was no surprise apparition. It represents the convergence and culmination of at least five cultural trends. If we understand these trends we should be much better able to deal with clones of 119 in the years ahead.

The absolutization of autonomy

The past 20 years or so have witnessed the flowering of patient autonomy as over against an earlier medical paternalism. Paternalism refers to a system in which treatment decisions are made against the patient's preferences or without the patient's knowledge and consent. It is now all but universally admitted, at least in Western circles, that individual decision-making regarding medical treatment is a necessary part of individual dignity. What is not so widely realized is that the current heavy emphasis on autonomy represents a reaction, and reactions have a way of becoming overreaction. In the religious sphere, a reaction against legalism can lead us into the dangers of antinomianism. When we try to stop being over authoritarian, we risk becoming anarchists.

I see two noxious offshoots of absolutizing autonomy. First, very little thought is then given to the values that ought to inform and guide the use of autonomy. Given such a vacuum, the sheer fact that a choice is the patient's tends to be viewed as the sole right-making characteristic of the choice. I call that absolutization. We have seen this approach in the way the pro-choice position on abortion is frequently presented. The fact that the choice is the woman's is regarded as the only right-making characteristic. But as Daniel Callahan notes, "There are good choices and there are bad choices." Unless we confront the features that make choices good or bad, autonomy alone tends to usurp that role. When it does, autonomy has become overstated and distorted. That overstatement translates into a total accommodation to the patient's values and wishes. If physician-assisted suicide is one of those wishes, well. . . .

The second concomitant of absolutizing autonomy is an intolerance of dependence on others. People abhor being dependent. Given the canonization of independence in our consciousness, "death with dignity" means: to die in *my way,* at *my time,* by *my hand.* Yet the Anglican Study Group was surely correct when it wrote in 1975:

> There is a movement of giving and receiving. At the beginning and at the end of life receiving predominates over and even excludes giving. But the value of human life does not depend only on its capacity to give. Love, *agape,* is the equal and unalterable regard for the value of other human beings independent of their particular characteristics. It extends to the helpless and hopeless, to those who have no value in their own eyes and seemingly none for society. Such neighbor-love is costly and sacrificial. It is easily destroyed. In the

From Richard McCormick, "Physician-Assisted Suicide: Flight from Compassion," *The Christian Century* 108 (December 4, 1991): 1132-34. Used by permission.

> giver it demands unlimited caring, in the recipient absolute trust. The question must be asked whether the practice of voluntary euthanasia is consistent with the fostering of such care and trust [*On Dying Well*, p. 22].

Have we forgotten this? I think so. Assisted suicide is a flight from compassion, not an expression of it. It should be suspect not because it is too hard, but because it is too easy. Have we forgotten that dependent old age is a call to cling to a power (God) beyond our control? I think so. Rejection of our own dependence means ultimately rejection of our interdependence and eventually of our very mortality. Once we have achieved that, we fail to see physician-assisted suicide for what it so often is: an act of isolation and abandonment.

The secularization of medicine

By "secularization" I mean the divorce of the profession of medicine from a moral tradition. Negatively, this refers to the fact that medicine is increasingly independent of the values that make health care a human service. Positively, it refers to the profession's growing preoccupation with factors that are peripheral to and distract from care (insurance premiums, business atmosphere, competition, accountability, structures, government controls, questions of liability and so on).

Quite practically, the secularization of the medical profession means that it is reduced to a business and physicians begin acting like businesspeople. As Dr. Edmund Pellegrino has observed, they claim the same rights as the businessperson — that is, to do business with whom they choose to. Medical knowledge is viewed as something that "belongs" to the physician and that can be dispensed on her own terms in the marketplace, and illness is seen as no different from any other need that requires a service.

When the medical profession is fully secularized, clinical judgments will also become secularized. And one important outcome of the secularization of clinical judgments is an overemphasis on autonomy. In this sense the absolutization of autonomy and the secularization of the medical profession are twin sisters.

The inadequate management of pain

Many people fear not death, but dying. And one thing they fear most about dying (we shall mention another below) is pain. Unfortunately, just about everything about physicians' treatment of pain is, well, painful. In a 1989 study conducted by Dr. Jamie H. Von Roenn of Northwestern University, some unsettling facts stood out. First, only one in ten physicians said they received good training in managing pain. A sign of this is that the National Cancer Institute spends only about one-fifth of 1 percent of its billion-dollar budget on pain research. Eighty-five percent of doctors surveyed stated that the majority of cancer patients are undermedicated. But Von Roenn estimated that if competently used, pain medicines could relieve the agony of 80 to 90 percent of cancer patients. Before pain can be controlled, it must be recognized. Yet in Von Roenn's findings, 60 percent of physicians admitted that the inability to assess pain remains a significant barrier to controlling pain. In brief, we have poor education, poor assessment and poor management.

Dr. Steven A. King, director of pain service in the department of psychiatry at the Maine Medical Center, put it forcefully:

> The pain associated with cancer can be managed successfully in the overwhelming majority of patients. Unfortunately, few medical schools and residency programs provide teaching on pain and its management and therefore many physicians are unaware of the wide array of treatment for cancer pain [*New York Times*, March 25, 1991].

If we had better education and better pain control, much of the perceived need for euthanasia would disappear.

The nutrition-hydration debate

Several prominent cases (such as those involving Paul Brophy in Massachusetts and Clarence Herbert in California) have propelled this problem onto center stage. This was especially true in the Nancy Cruzan case. People can now be maintained in a persistent vegetative states (PVS) for years by use of nasogastric tubes or gastrostomy tubes. But must or ought we do so? Few would argue for doing so when the patient has expressly declined such treatment while competent. But what about those who have not so expressed themselves? Here controversy has swirled around cases like that of Nancy Cruzan. Many ethicists and physicians are convinced that artificial nutrition and hydration are not required for persons diagnosed as irreversibly in a PVS. They base this view on the judgment that continuing in a PVS is not a benefit to the patient and therefore is not in the patient's best interests. This is my own conviction, and I wrote as much in support of Lester and Joyce Cruzan's decision to stop Nancy's gastrostomy feedings.

Others, however — a minority, I believe — view this decision in much more sinister terms. For example, some saw continuance in a PVS as a "great benefit" to Nancy Cruzan. A group of authors writing in *Issues of Law and Medicine* in 1987 stated: "In our judgment, feeding such [permanently unconscious] patients and providing them with fluids by means of tubes is *not* useless in the strict sense because it does bring to these patients a great benefit, namely, the preservation of their lives." The most recent statement espousing this view is by Bishop John J. Myers of Peoria, Illinois, in his Pastoral Instructions to health-care administrators. He argues that artificial nutrition-hydration efforts are not useless, since they "effectively deliver nutrients" to these patients, even though they do not reverse their vegetative state. To me, that judgment defines usefulness to the patient so narrowly that personal benefit is reduced to the maintenance of physiological functioning. Patient benefit is exhaustively defined by medical effectiveness alone. Other authors (such as Gilbert Meilaender of Oberlin) view the cessation of artificial nutrition-hydration from PVS patients as direct killing.

I cannot argue the case further here. My purpose is to note that the overwhelming majority of people I have polled on this matter do not want to be maintained indefinitely in a PVS because they do not regard this as a benefit to them. Indeed, they are appalled at the prospect. This is the second thing people fear about dying: the needless, heedless and aimless (as they see it) prolongation of the process. And this is where the nutrition-hydration question directly touches the issue of physician-assisted suicide. If our public policies are going to mandate nutrition-hydration treatments and prevent the discontinuance of them, people will easily view physician-assisted suicide as a preferable alternative. I am compelled to note here that certain fanatical fringes of the pro-life movement are counterproductive. By saying that Nancy Cruzan was "starved" and "killed" they will drive people to embrace physician-assisted suicide.

Closely connected with the nutrition-hydration discussion, indeed a part of it, is the distinction between killing and allowing to die. I realize that certain instances of allowing to die are irresponsible (and equivalent to killing); in some cases the distinction is hard to apply persuasively. But the distinction has served us well for many decades and it would be irresponsible to abandon it. Yet it is being fudged, not least by some courts that threaten with murder charges those who withdraw hopeless and dying patients from ventilators or other life supports. Judge Robert Muir did this at one point in the Karen Quinlan case. Those who removed Karen from the respirator, he said, would be subject to New Jersey's homicide laws. When judges confuse the removal of life supports with homicide, they make homicide look all the more acceptable. One way to soften resistance to the unacceptable is to confuse it with the acceptable.

The financial pressures of health care

No one needs to be told that there is great pressure on everyone, especially hospitals, to cut health-care costs. We are now spending 12 percent of the GNP for health care, more than any other nation in the world. Hospitals are pressured to cut costs by Health Maintenance Organizations and by Diagnostic Related Groups. Between 1980 and 1986, 414 hospitals closed, and an Arthur Anderson study predicts conservatively that 700 more will close by 1995. Acquisition decisions, hiring practices and incentive proposals are often closely tied to market forces.

Such economic pressures constitute a coercive atmosphere for the debilitated elderly and chronically ill. "Why must I hang on like this? Am I not a drain on my family and limited resources?" As Dr. Robert Bernhoft, a surgeon and president of Washington Physicians Against Initiative 119, put it: "These people [the elderly of limited means] are already under tremendous pressure to get out of the way." The next step is not a huge leap.

Dr. Peter McGough, an opponent of Initiative 119, states after the vote: "Saying No to assisted death is not enough. Now we have a responsibility to deal with the problems that brought out this concern." The five cultural trends described above indicate (even if they do not exhaust) the problems McGough was referring to. Failure to deal with them would invite a replay of Initiative 119 both in Washington and in other places.

90 Rational Suicide and Reasons for Living

Stanley Hauerwas

1. Suicide and the Ethics of Autonomy

There is a peculiar ambiguity concerning the morality of suicide in our society. Our commitment to the autonomy of the individual at least implies that suicide may not only be rational, but a "right."[1] Yet many continue to believe that anyone attempting suicide must be sick and therefore prevented from killing themselves. This ambiguity makes us hesitant even to analyze the morality of suicide because we fear we may discover that our society lacks any coherent moral policy or basis for preventing suicide.

Therefore the very idea of "rational suicide" is a bit threatening. We must all feel a slight twinge of concern about the book soon to be published by the British Voluntary Euthanasia Society that describes the various painless and foolproof methods of suicide. But it is by no means clear why we feel uncomfortable about having this kind of book widely distributed. As Nicholas Reed, the general secretary of the Society, suggests: suicide is "more and more seen as an acceptable way for a life to end, vastly preferable to some long, slow, painful death. We're simply helping in the fight for another human right — the right to die."[2]

We think there must be something wrong with this, but we are not sure what. I suspect our unease about these matters is part of the reason we wish to deny the existence of rational or autonomous suicide. If all potential suicides can be declared ill

From *Suffering Presence* by Stanley Hauerwas. © 1986 by University of Notre Dame Press, Notre Dame, IN. Reprinted by permission of the publisher.

by definition then we can prevent them ironically because the agent lacks autonomy. Therefore we intervene to prevent suicides in the name of autonomy which, if we were consistent, should require us to consider suicide a permissible moral act.

Once I was a participant in a seminar in medical ethics at one of our most prestigious medical schools. I was there to speak about suicide, but the week before the seminar had considered abortion. At that time I was told by these beginning medical students they decided it was their responsibility to perform an abortion if a woman requested it because a woman has the right to determine what she should do with her body — an ethical conclusion that they felt clearly justified on grounds of protecting the autonomy of the patient. Moreover this position, they argued, was appropriate if the professional dominance and paternalism of the medical profession was to be broken.

However, I asked them what they would do if they were attending in the Emergency Room and someone was brought in with slashed wrists with a suicide note pinned to their shirt front. First of all would they take the time to read the note to discover the state of the patient? Secondly would they say this is clearly not a medical matter and refuse to accept the patient? Or would they immediately begin to save the person's life? With the same unanimity concerning their responsibility to perform abortion they felt they must immediately begin trying to save the person's life.

The reason they gave to justify their intervention was that anyone taking their life must surely be sick. But it was not clear what kind of "sickness" was under consideration unless we define life itself as some kind of syndrome. Failing to make the case that all suicides must be sick they then suggested they must act to save such a person's life because it was their responsibility as doctors. But again I pressed them on what right they had to impose their role-related responsibilities on those who did not seek their services and, in fact, had clearly tried to avoid coming in contact with them. They then appealed to experience, citing cases when people have recovered from suicide attempts only to be thankful they had been helped. But again such appeals are not convincing since we can also point to the many who are not happy about being saved and soon make another attempt.

Our discussion began to be more and more frustrating for all involved, so a compromise was suggested. These future physicians felt the only solution was that when a suicide came to the Emergency Room the first time, the doctor's responsibility must always be to save their life. However if they came in a second time they could be allowed to die. That kind of solution, however, is not only morally unsatisfactory, but pragmatically difficult to institutionalize. What happens if each time the person is brought to the hospital they get a different physician?

I have told this story because I think it nicely illustrates the kind of difficulties we feel when we try to get a moral handle on suicide. We feel that Beauchamp and Childress are right that if a suicide is genuinely autonomous and there are no powerful utilitarian reasons or "reasons of human worth and dignity standing in the way, then we ought to allow the person to commit suicide, because we would otherwise be violating the person's autonomy."[3]

However, I want to suggest that this way of putting the matter, while completely consistent with an ethics of autonomy, is also deeply misleading. It is misleading not only because it reveals the insufficiency of autonomy either as a basis or ideal for the moral life[4] but also it simply fails to provide an appropriate account of why any of us decides or should decide to stay alive. Indeed it is odd even to think of our willingness to live as a decision. For example Beauchamp and Childress do not explain how anyone could take account of *all* relevant variables and future possibilities in considering suicide. Indeed that seems an odd condition for if we required it of even our most important decisions it would stop us from acting at all.

Yet by challenging this account I want clearly to distinguish my position from those who are intent to deny the possibility of rational suicide. I think that suicide can be and often is a rational decision of an "autonomous" agent, but I do not therefore think it is justified. It is extremely interesting, for example, that Augustine did not claim that suicide was irrational in criticizing the Stoic acceptance and even recommendation of suicide. Rather he pointed out that their acceptance of suicide belied their own understanding of the relation between evil and happiness and how a wise man thus should deal with adversity. Though the quote is long I think it worth providing the full text. Augustine says,

> There is a mighty force in the evils which compel a man, and, according to those philosophers, even a wise man, to rob himself of his existence as a man; although they say, and say with truth, that the first and greatest utterance of nature, as we may call it, is that a man should be reconciled to himself and for that reason should naturally shun death — that he should be his own friend, in that he should emphatically desire to continue as a living being and to remain alive in this combination of body and soul, and that this should be his aim. There is a mighty force in those evils which overpower this natural feeling which makes us employ all our strength in our endeavor to avoid death — which defeat this feeling so utterly that what was shunned is now wished and longed for, and, if it cannot come to him from some other source, is inflicted on a man by himself. There is a mighty force in those evils which make Fortitude a murderer — if indeed she is still to be called fortitude when she is so utterly vanquished by those evils that she not only cannot by her endurance keep guard over the man she has undertaken to govern and protect, but is herself compelled to go so far as to kill him. The wise man ought, indeed, to endure even death with a steadfastness, but a death that comes to him from outside himself. Whereas if he is compelled, as those philosophers say, to inflict it on himself, they must surely admit that these are not only evils, but intolerable evils, when they compel him to commit this crime.
>
> It follows from this that the life weighed down by such great and grievous ills, or at the mercy of such chances, would never be called happy, if the men who so term it, and who, when overcome by the growing weights of ills, surrender to adversity encompassing their own death — if these people would bring themselves to surrender to the truth, when overcome by sound reasoning, in their quest for the happy life, and would give up supposing that the ultimate, Supreme God is something to be enjoyed by them in this condition of mortality.[5]

The question is not, therefore, the question of whether suicide is "rational." Augustine knew well that the Stoics could provide outstanding examples of cool, unemotional, and rational suicide. He rather asks what kind of blessedness we should expect out of life. For Augustine the Stoic approval of suicide is an indication of the insufficient account they provided about what human existence should be about — namely they failed to see that the only happiness worth desiring is that which came from friendship with the true God. "Yet," he says, "these philosophers refuse to believe in this blessedness because they do not see it; and so they attempt to fabricate for themselves an utterly delusive happiness by means of a virtue whose falsity is in proportion to its arrogance."[6] So the issue is understood within a conception of life we think good and worthy.

2. The Grammar of Suicide

Before developing this line of reasoning, however, it should be pointed out that the discussion to this point has been trading on the assumption that we know what suicide is. Yet that is simply not the case. For as Beauchamp and Childress suggest, definitions of suicide such as "intentionally caused self-destruction not forced by the action of another person" are not nearly as unambiguous as they may at first seem. For example they point out when persons suffering from a terminal illness or mortal injury allow their death to occur we find ourselves reluctant to call that act "suicide," but if persons with a terminal illness take their life by active means we do refer to that act as one of suicide. Yet to only describe those acts that involved a direct action as suicide is misleading since we are not sure how we should describe cases where "a patient with a terminal condition might easily avoid dying for a long time but might choose to end his life immediately by not taking cheap and painless medication."[7]

Beauchamp and Childress suggest the reason we have difficulty deciding the meaning of suicide is that the term has an emotive meaning of disapproval that we prefer not to apply to certain kinds of ambiguous cases. The very logic of the term therefore tends to prejudice any pending moral analysis of the rightness or wrongness of suicide. As a means to try to deal with this problem they propose an "uncorrupted" definition of suicide as what occurs "if and only if one intentionally terminates one's own life — no matter what the conditions or precise nature of the intention or the causal route to death."[8]

As sympathetic as one must feel with their attempt to provide a clear and non-prejudicial account of suicide, however, the very idea of an "uncorrupted" definition of suicide distorts the very grammar of such notions. Beauchamp and Childress are quite right to point out that the notion itself cannot settle how and why suicide applies to certain kinds of behavior and not others. But what must be admitted, as Joseph Margolis has recently argued, is the culturally variable character of suicide. There are many competing views about the meaning and nature of suicide, "some religious, some not, some not even significantly so characterized. . . . There is no simple formula for designating, except trivially, an act of taking, or yielding, or making likely the end of, one's life that will count, universally as suicide. No, some selection of acts of this minimal sort will, in accord with an interpreting tradition, construe what was done as or as not suicide; and, so judging, the tradition will provide as well for the approval or condemnation of what was done. In short, suicide, like murder itself, is an act that can be specified only in a systematic way without a given tradition; and that specification itself depends on classifying the intention of the agent. We can say, therefore, that there is no minimal act of commission or omission that counts as suicide, except relative to some tradition; and, within particular traditions, the justifiability of particular suicides may yet be debatable."[9]

So the very way one understands "suicide" already involves moral judgments and requires argument. So I shall contend that if we rightly understand what life is about, suicide should be understood negatively and should not therefore be recommended as an alternative for anyone. This is not to deny that from certain perspectives suicide can be considered rational — as an institution, that is a way of characterizing a whole range of behavior, as well as an individual act. That it can be so understood, however, reveals how little the issue turns on the question of "rationality." We must rather ask whether the tradition through which we understand the meaning and nature of suicide is true.

3. Why Suicide Is Prohibited

I have argued elsewhere that suicide as an institution must be considered morally doubtful. That conclusion is based on the religious understanding that we should learn to regard our lives as gifts bestowed on us by a gracious Creator.[10] That such an appeal is explicitly religious is undeniable, but I would resist any suggestion that the religious nature of this appeal disqualifies it from public argument. Rather it is a reminder of Margolis' contention that any account of suicide necessarily draws on some tradition. Therefore my appeal to this kind of religious presupposition is but an explicit avowal of what any account of suicide must involve — though I certainly would not contend that the only basis for disapproving suicide is religious.

It is important, however, that the significance of the shift to the language of gift be properly appreciated. For it is a challenge to our normal presumptions about the way the prohibition of suicide is grounded in our "natural desire to live." Indeed it is not even clear to me that we have a "natural desire to live," or even if we do what its moral significance entails. The very phrase "natural desire to live," is fraught with ambiguity, but even worse it seems to suggest that when a person finds they no longer have such a desire there is no longer any reason for living.

In contrast the language of gift does not presuppose we have a "natural desires to live," but rather that our living is an obligation. It is an obligation that we at once owe our Creator and one another. For our creaturely status is but a reminder that our existence is not secured by our own power, but rather requires the constant care and trust in others. Our willingness to live in the face of suffering, pain, and sheer boredom of life is morally a service to one another as it is a sign that life can be endured as well as a source for joy and exuberance. Our obligation to sustain our lives even when they are threatened with or require living with a horrible disease is our way of being faithful to the trust that has sustained us in health and now in illness.[11] We take on a responsibility as sick people. That responsibility is simply to keep on living as it is our way of gesturing to those who care for us that we can be trusted and trust them even in our illness.

There is nothing about this position which entails that we must do everything we can do to keep ourselves alive under all conditions. Christians certainly do not believe that life is inherently sacred and therefore it must be sustained until the bitter end. Indeed the existence of the martyrs is a clear sign that Christians think the value of life can be overridden.[12] Indeed I think there is much to be said for distinguishing between preserving life and only prolonging death, but such a distinction does not turn on technical judgments about when we have in fact started dying, though it may involve such a judgment.[13] Rather the distinction is dependent on the inherited wisdom of a community that has some idea of what a "good death" entails.[14]

Such a death is one that allows us to remember the dead in a morally healthy way — that is, the manner of death does not prevent the living from remembering the manner and good of their life. To be sure we can train ourselves to remember a suicide as if the suicide said nothing about their life, but I think we would be unwise to do so. For to face the reality of a death by suicide is a reminder how often our community fails to offer the trust necessary to sustain our lives in health and illness. Suicide is not first a judgment about the agent, but a reminder that we have failed to embody as a community the commitment not to abandon one another. We fear being a burden for others, but even more to ourselves. Yet it is only by recognizing that in fact we are inescapably a burden that we face the reality and opportunity of living truthfully.

It is just such a commitment that medicine involves and why the physician's commitment to caring for the sick seems so distorted by an ethics of autonomy. Medicine is but a gesture, but an extremely significant gesture of a society, that while we all suffer from a condition that cannot be cured, nonetheless neither will we be abandoned. The task of medicine is to care even when it cannot cure.[15] The refusal to let an attempted suicide die is only our feeble, but real, attempt to remain a community of trust and care through the agency of medicine. Our prohibition and subsequent care of a suicide draws on our profoundest assumptions that each individual's life has a purpose beyond simply being "autonomous."

4. Reasons for Living and "Rational Suicide": An Example

However, the kind of religious appeals I have made as well as this kind of talk about "purpose" can easily be misleading. For it sounds as though suicide is religiously prohibited because people who believe in God really know what life is about. But that is not the case — at least in the usual sense a phrase such as "what life is about" is understood. Indeed the very reason that living is an obligation is that we are to go on living even though we are far from figuring out what life is about. Our reason for living is not that we are sure about the ultimate meaning of life, but rather that our lives have been touched by another and through that touch we believe we encounter the very being that graciously sustains our existence.

Indeed one of the problems with discussions of "rational suicide" is they seem to be determined by the assumption that the decision to live or to die turns on whether life, and more importantly, one's particular life, has meaning or purpose. Thus, Margolis, for example, suggests that a relatively neutral understanding of the issue raised by suicide is whether the deliberate taking of one's life in order simply to end it, not instrumentally for any ulterior purpose, can ever be rational or rationally justified. He suggests a rational suicide is when a person "aims overridingly at ending his own life and who, in a relevant sense, performs the act. The manner in which he suicides may be said to be by commission or omission, actively or passively, directly or indirectly, consciously or unconsciously, justifiably or reprehensibly — in accord with the classificatory distinctions of particular traditions."[16] According to Margolis such suicide is more likely to be justified if the person "decided that life was utterly meaningless" or "sincerely believed life to have no point at all."[17]

My difficulty with such a suggestion is that I have no idea what it would mean to know that life and in particular my life, was "utterly meaningless" or had "no point at all." In order to illustrate my difficulty about these matters let me call your attention to one of the better books about suicide — John Barth's *The Floating Opera.*[18] Barth's book consists of Todd Andrews' account of how one day in 1937 he decided to commit suicide. There was no particular reason that Andrews decided to commit suicide and that, we discover, is exactly the reason he decided to do so — namely, there is no reason for living or dying.

The protagonist has written the book to explain why he changed his mind and in the process we discover quite a bit about him. Most people would describe him as a cynic, but there is more to him than that. Andrews makes his living by practicing law in a small backwater town in the Chesapeake tidewater country. He became a lawyer because that is what his father wanted, but he is later stunned by his father's suicide. What bothered him was not that his father killed himself, but that he did so because he could not pay his debts due to the Depression.

Andrews has chosen to live free from any long-term commitments since the day in WWI when he killed a German sergeant with whom he had shared a foxhole through a terrible night of shelling. His lack of commitment extends even to his arrangement for living — he lives in a hotel room where he registers on a day to day basis. He has, however, been involved in a long-term affair with Jane Mack, his best friend's wife. Harrison Mack not only approved but actually arranged this as a further extension of their friendship. However by mutual agreement they have recently decided to end this form of their relation.[19] This is partly the result of the recent birth of Jeannie, who, even though her paternity remains unclear, has given the Macks a new sense of themselves as a couple.

Andrews also suffers from two diseases — subacute bacteriological endocarditis and chronic infection of the prostate. He was told thirty-five years ago that the former could kill him any time. The latter disease only caused him to cease living a wastrel's existence he had assumed during law school and begin what he claims is almost a saintly life. And indeed his life is in many ways exemplary, for he is a man who lives his life in accordance with those convictions he thinks most nearly true.

Even though he is not a professional philosopher, Andrews is a person with a definite philosophical bent. For years he had been working on notes, suitably filed in three peach baskets, for the writing of a Humean type *Inquiry* on the nature of causation. For if Hume was right that causes can only be inferred, then his task is to shorten as much as possible the leap between what we see and what we cannot see. That is, to get at the true reasons for our actions.[20]

This becomes particularly relevant if we are to understand Andrews' decision to commit suicide. He fully admits that there are abundant psychological reasons, for those inclined for such explanations, to explain his suicide — a motherless boyhood, his murder of the German sergeant, his father's hanging himself, his isolated adulthood, his ailing heart, his growing sexual impotency, injured vanity, frustrated ambition, boredom — the kinds of things psychoanalysts identify as "real" causes.[21] But for him the only reasons that interest him in dying are philosophical. These he states in five propositions which constitute his completed *Inquiry.* They simply are:

I. Nothing has intrinsic value. Things assume value only in terms of certain ends.
II. The reasons for which people attribute value to things are always ultimately arbitrary. That is, the ends in terms of which things assume value are themselves ultimately irrational.
III. There is, therefore, no ultimate "reason" for valuing anything.
IV. Living is action in some form. There is no reason for action in any form.
V. There is, then, no "reason" for living.[22]

And so Todd Andrews decided to kill himself one day in 1937.

However before doing so he decided to go see *The Original and Unparalleled Floating Opera,* a local minstrel show on a rundown showboat. The absurdity of the show matches perfectly Andrews' view of the absurdity of life. During the performance, Andrews goes to the ship's galley, turns on the gas only to be interrupted and saved by a workman who angrily calls him a damn fool — not because he tried to take his life, but because he could have blown up the ship.

More importantly, however, just as he is recovering, the Macks, who had also been attending the opera, rush into the galley with Jeannie who had suddenly taken sick and fainted. Though appealed to for help, Andrews suggests he is no good at such things and advises the Macks to rush to the hospital. However, the local doctor arrives and advises an alcohol rub reassuring everyone nothing is seriously wrong. In the emergency, however, and the concern Andrews felt about Jeannie, he discovers he no longer wants to commit suicide even though he could still easily jump into the Choptank river. For as he tells us, "something was different. Some qualitative change had occurred, instantly, down in the dining room. The fact is I had no reason to be concerned over little Jeannie, and yet my concern for that child was so intense, and had been so immediately forthcoming, that (I understood now) the first desperate sound of Jane's voice had snapped me out of a paralysis which there was no reason to terminate. No reason at all. Moreover, had I not, in abjuring my responsibility for Jeannie, for the first time in my life assumed it — for her, for her parents, and for myself? I was confused, and I refused to die that way. Things needed explaining; abstractions needed to be straightened out. To die now was simply out of the question, though I hated to spoil such a perfect day."[23]

Andrews suspects most philosophizing to be rationalization, but nonetheless his experience requires him to return to the propositions of his *Inquiry* to make a small revision of the fifth: V. There is then, no "reason" for living (or for suicide).[24] For now he tells us that he realized that even if values are only relative there are still relative values. "To realize that nothing has absolute value is surely overwhelming, but if one goes no further from that proposition than to become a saint, a cynic, or a suicide on principle, one hasn't gone far enough. If nothing makes any final difference, that fact makes no final difference either, and there is no more reason to commit suicide, say than not to, in the last analysis. Hamlet's question is, absolutely, meaningless. A narrow escape."[25]

The Christian prohibition of suicide is clearly based in our assumption that our lives are not ours to do with as we please. But that prohibition is but a reminder of the kind of commitments that make suicide which appears from certain perspectives and at particular times in our lives so rational, so wrong. It reminds us how important our commitment to be the kind of people who can care about a sick little girl and in the process learn to care for ourselves. That kind of lesson may not give life meaning, but it is certainly sufficient to help us muddle through with enough joy to sustain the important business of living.

Notes

1. For example, T. Beauchamp and J. Childress (*Principles of Biomedical Ethics* [New York: Oxford University Press, 1979], p. 90) suggest, "If the principle of autonomy is strongly relied upon for the justification of suicide, then it would seem that there is a right to commit suicide, so long as a person acts autonomously and does not seriously affect the interests of others."

2. "British 'Right to Die' Group Plans to Publish Manual on Suicide," *New York Times.*

3. T. Beauchamp and J. Childress, *Principles of Biomedical Ethics,* 93.

4. See F. Bergman, *On Being Free* (Notre Dame: University of Notre Dame Press, 1977); and G. Dworkin, "Moral Autonomy," in *Morals, Science, and Sociality,* ed. H. Engelhardt and D. Callahan (Hastings-on-Hudson, N.Y.: Hastings Center Publications, 1978).

5. Augustine, *The City of God,* trans. Henry Bettenson (Harmondsworth: Penguin, 1977), pp. 856-57.

6. Ibid., p. 857. Earlier Augustine had argued, "There were famous heroes who, though by the laws of war they could do violence to a conquered enemy, refused to do violence to themselves when conquered; though they had not the slightest fear of death, they chose to endure the enemy's domination rather than put themselves to death. They were fighting for their earthly country; the gods they worshipped were false; but their worship was genuine and they faithfully kept their oaths. Christians worship the true God and they yearn for a heavenly country; will they not have more reason to refrain from the crime of suicide, if God's providence subjects them for a time to their enemies for their probation or reformation. Their God does not abandon them in that humiliation, for he came from on high so humbly for their sake," pp. 35-36.

7. Beauchamp and Childress, *Principles of Biomedical Ethics,* p. 86.

8. Ibid., p. 87. Elsewhere Beauchamp provides a fuller account arguing suicide occurs when "a person intentionally brings about his or her own death in circumstances where others do not coerce him or her to the action, except in those cases where death is caused by conditions not specifically arranged by the agent for the purpose of bringing about his or her own death," T. Beauchamp, "Suicide," in *Matters of Life and Death,* ed. T. Regan (New York: Random House, 1980), p 77.

9. J. Margolis, *Negativities: The Limits of Life* (Columbus: Merriall, 1975), pp. 25-26.

10. S. Hauerwas, *Truthfulness and Tragedy* (Notre

Dame: University of Notre Dame Press, 1977), pp. 101-15.

11. See S. Hauerwas, "Reflections on Suffering, Death, and Medicine," *Ethics in Science and Medicine* 6 (1979): 229-37.

12. See S. Hauerwas, *Community of Character* (Notre Dame: University of Notre Dame Press, 1980).

13. S. Hauerwas, *Vision and Virtue* (Notre Dame: University of Notre Dame Press, 1974), pp. 166-86.

14. S. Hauerwas, "Religious Conceptions of Brain Death," in *Brain Death: Interrelated Medical and Social Issues*, ed. J. Korein (New York: New York Academy of Sciences, 1978), pp. 329-36.

15. S. Hauerwas, "Care," in *Encyclopedia of Bioethics*, ed. W. Reich (New York: Free Press, 1978), 1: 145-50.

16. Margolis, *Negativities*, p. 29.

17. Ibid., p. 24.

18. J. Barth, *The Floating Opera* (New York: Avon, 1956). For a similar approach from which I have learned much see H. Nielsen, "Margolis on Rational Suicide: An Argument for Case Studies in Ethics," *Ethics* 89, no. 4 (1979): 394-400. The fact that we must resort to example when considering such matters is an important indication how easily abstract discussions of the rightness or wrongness of suicide, for which there is no substitute and must certainly be done, can as easily mislead as they can help us clarify why the suicide is rightly understood in a negative manner. Seldom are any of us sure why it is we act and do not act as we do. We may say we would rather die than live with such and such disease, but how can we be so sure that is the reason? Beauchamp and Childress' suggestion that ideally a person contemplating suicide would consider all the variables is as much a formula for self-deception as one for self-knowledge. I suspect that is why Barth's book is so helpful — namely it is only by telling a story that we come to understand how the prohibition against suicide is meant to shape the self.

19. Andrews admits that this turn of affairs made him reconsider briefly his decision to commit suicide since the Macks might interpret his suicide as caused by their decision. But he says that this lasted only a moment since it occurred to him "What difference did it make to me how they interpreted my death? Nothing, absolutely, makes any difference. Nothing is ultimately important. And that, at least partly by my own choosing, that last act would be robbed of its real significance, would be interpreted in every way but the way I intended. This fact once realized, it seemed likely to me that here was a new significance, if possible even more genuine," Barth, *The Floating Opera*, p. 224.

20. The full title is actually *An Inquiry into the Circumstances Surrounding the Self-Destruction of Thomas F. Andrews, of Cambridge, Maryland, on Ground-Hog Day, 1930 (More Especially into the Causes Therefor).* Andrews tells us his aim is simply to learn why his father hanged himself. Andrews admits the real problem was one of "imperfect communication" between him and his father as he could find no adequate reason for his father's act. His *Inquiry*, however, became primarily a study of himself since he realized to understand imperfect communication requires perfect knowledge of each party. Andrews suggests at the end of the book if we have not understood his change of mind he is again cursed with imperfect communication — but the suggestion seems to be we have a better chance at communication than he had with his father as now at least we have Todd Andrews' story.

21. Barth, *The Floating Opera*, p. 224.

22. Ibid., pp. 238-43.

23. Ibid., p. 266.

24. Ibid., p. 270.

25. Ibid.

Chapter Fifteen

CARE OF NEONATES

The Long Dying of Baby Andrew is an account by Robert and Peggy Stinson of the birth and dying of their infant son in 1977. Baby Andrew was born at 24 weeks gestation, weighing 1 lb. 12 oz. He was taken to a neonatal intensive care unit, and all of the sophisticated resources of modern neonatal technology were used to keep him alive in spite of a multitude of medical problems, an uncertain prognosis for mental development, and the Stinson's wishes that "heroic" measures not be taken.

The Stinsons recounted this response to the neonatal unit's power to intervene in their child's dying:

> What threatened to be a simple, private horror has changed unexpectedly into something so altogether different, so altogether complicated that thoughts and feelings tangle hopelessly and give no guidance.
>
> Andrew is not our baby anymore — he's been taken over by a medical bureaucracy. The bureaucracy controls Andrew — access to Andrew, information about Andrew, decisions about what will happen to Andrew. It rolls inexorably onward, oblivious to our attempts to communicate, participate. . . .[1]

When Andrew finally died, Mrs. Stinson wrote in her journal, "Modern medicine makes possible a sad new epitaph: He died too late for grief."

The sophisticated medical technology of neonatal care sometimes enables a child not only to live but to flourish, but sometimes to live with no hope of human flourishing, sometimes to live with no hope of even human communication, sometimes only to suffer its way in a long dying towards death. The care of the newborn presents special medical and moral difficulties because diagnosis and prognosis are more obscure and uncertain and because neonates are mute about their preferences. Someone must make decisions about their care, but who and on what basis?

Those two questions — who should make decisions of this kind and what criteria should be used in making them — demand answers if we are to use our new powers in morally responsible ways.

Theological reflection concerning them is also required if we are to use these powers with Christian integrity and speak of them with Christian conviction.

Theologians have considered these issues, sometimes on the basis of an impartial perspective, sometimes on the basis of a candidly theological perspective. Once again, the question of the appropriate mode of moral reflection and the relation of Christian moral reflection to an impartial perspective are relevant. And again the application of even impartial principles will depend upon dispositions and biases shaped by one's fundamental convictions and loyalties.

It is recognized, for example, that an infant is not and has not ever been a rational autonomous individual, able to give free and informed consent. This is what necessitates a decision by someone else about care. But should the procedural decision about who should decide be based on "substituted judgment" — what the infant would be likely to decide if it were rational and autonomous — or the interdependency of members of communities, including and especially families?

Again, one's disposition toward medical technology subtly effects discernment in such cases. Is medical technology simply a value-free assortment of tools accessible to consumers who can decide either to use them to get what they want or, failing that, not to use them at all? Or is medical technology to be considered a part of medical practice and profession with its own ethos and commitment to benefit the patient, even a tiny patient? Is technology, including medical technology, not just the power of people over natural processes but necessarily also the power of some people, the medical community, for example, over other people, say, an infant's parents? Our answer to this will influence how we answer the first overriding question given above: Who is to make the decisions about the care and treatment of neonates? If we see neonatal technology as tied to a concern to benefit the patient, we may work to nurture a role for the physician in the decision-making process; whereas, if we see the technology as inevitably resulting in a power imbalance, we may work to restrain the role of the physician.

With respect to our second overarching question, what criteria are to be used in deciding on care and treatments of neonates, theological reflection may supply, support, qualify, or reject criteria advanced to guide the decision, whoever is to make it. The value of physical life, for example, can be given theological backing. But is life the only value — in the whole constellation of values which are involved in such decisions — which can be given theological backing? How, for example, should Christians think about suffering? May we choose suffering for another? How shall we weigh unavoidable suffering, if we do keep an infant alive, against unavoidable death, if we refrain from technological intervention? Can theological reflection help order the goods which cannot all be chosen? Can it help order the evils which cannot all be avoided? Can theological reflection help us to be truthful about the genuine conflict of genuine goods? Can it help us acknowledge tragic choices in the care of neonates?

These questions are particularly poignant when we turn to a discussion of how we should treat newborns who will never be fully functioning adults because of some congenital abnormalities but who might live to adulthood if they receive extensive medical treatment. How do we witness to the belief that they too are created in the image of God and need our care? How can theological reflection guide us about that case in their living and, sometimes tragically, in their dying?

Besides illuminating the questions of who should decide about the care of neonates and what criteria for deciding we ought to use in such cases, theological reflection may point us toward a third question, that of character: no matter who decides, what sort of person should they be? If parents make decisions about and for their infants, their decision will be made not only in terms of a rational application of a more of less abstract principle, but also in terms of their identity and integrity as parents. Then the question of a normative understanding of being a parent is reopened.

And if physicians decide, they will rely not only on technical skill in making diagnoses and prognoses but also on their understanding of the moral significance of their role. They will decide in ways that cohere with their self-understanding, that have integrity with their professional identity, that are faithful to their moral passions. So the question of a normative understanding of being a physician is reopened. What is the relation of character and conduct, of integrity and principles; and how should theological reflection or religious conviction qualify either?

Religious faith may at least remind us that we are talking not just about "defective neonates" but about our own children. It may remind us of ways other than technology to respond to their life and their death, to the threats to their flourishing and their sometimes long dying. A religious response to children and the loss of children may provide an important context in which to think about the appropriate technological, professional, parental, and social response to the demands of neonatal care.

Notes

1. Peggy Stinson and Robert Stinson, *The Long Dying of Baby Andrew* (Boston: Little, Brown, 1983).

Suggestions for Further Reading

Cohen, Libby G. *Before Their Time: Fetuses and Infants at Risk* (Washington, D.C.: American Association on Mental Retardation, 1990).

Guillemin, Jeanne, and Lynda Lytle Holmstrom. *Mixed*

Blessings: Intensive Care for Newborns (New York: Oxford University Press, 1986).

Gustaitis, Rasa. *A Time to Be Born, a Time to Die: Conflicts and Ethics in an Intensive Care Nursery* (Reading, Mass.: Addison Wesley, 1986).

Hauerwas, Stanley. "The Demands and the Limits of Care: On the Moral Dilemma of Neonatal Intensive Care," in *Truthfulness and Tragedy* by Stanley Hauerwas and Richard Bondi, (Notre Dame, Ind.: University of Notre Dame Press, 1977).

McCormick, Richard A. "To Save or Let Die: The Dilemma of Modern Medicine," *JAMA* 229 (1974): 172-76.

McMillan, Richard C., H. Tristram Engelhardt, Jr. and Stuart F. Spicker, eds. *Euthanasia and the Newborn: Conflicts Regarding Saving Lives* (Dordrecht: Kluwer, 1987).

Miller, Richard B. "Love and Death in a Pediatric Intensive Care Unit," *The Annual of the Society of Christian Ethics, with Cumulative Index,* 1996, Harlan Beckley, ed. (Washington, D.C.: Georgetown University Press, 1996).

Murray, Thomas H. and Arthur L. Caplan, eds. *Which Babies Shall Live: Humanistic Dimensions of the Care of Imperiled Newborns* (Clifton, N.J.: Humana Press, 1985).

Nolan, Kathleen, ed. "Imperiled Newborns," *Hastings Center Report* 17 (December 1987): 5-32.

Shelp, Earl E. *Born to Die? Deciding the Fate of Critically Ill Newborns* (New York: Free Press, 1986).

Smith, David H. "On Letting Some Babies Die," *Hastings Center Studies* 2 (May 1974): 37-46.

Weir, Robert F. *Selective Nontreatment of Handicapped Newborns: Moral Dilemmas in Neonatal Medicine* (New York: Oxford University Press, 1984).

91 Medicine and the Birth of Defective Children: Approaches of the Ancient World

Darrel W. Amundsen

So diverse are the varied strands of ancient Greek and Roman cultures that it is dangerous — indeed, probably irresponsible — to speak of any universal ancient attitudes and practices, unless significant qualifications are placed upon any assertions other than the most specific and limited. In attempting accurately to describe — or more correctly, to reconstruct — the response of people in antiquity to the defective newborn, it is necessary first to provide the broader context of values that informed, or actually formed, that response. And that broader context of values involves such issues as human worth, human dignity, the value of life, and human rights, inalienable and otherwise.

In the introduction to his very perspicacious monograph *Human Value: A Study in Ancient Philosophical Ethics,* John M. Rist maintains that the view that such rights as "the right to life, to have enough to eat, to live without fear of torture or degrading punishments, the right to work or to withhold one's labour," or any other rights, "are the universal property of men as such was virtually unknown in classical antiquity." He further asserts that classical antiquity had no theory "that all men are endowed at birth (or before) with a certain value . . . though some of its philosophers took certain steps toward such a theory."[1]

It is especially in the literature of political philosophy that theories of human value are developed. The most famous representative of this genre is Plato's *Republic,* which must be supplemented by the *Statesman* and the *Laws* to provide a thorough picture of Plato's conception of human value within the ideal state. Does the ideal state exist for its inhabitants, or do the latter exist for the sake of the state? It seems as though both are true in Plato's view. Private worth, which is possession of the virtues, will inevitably lead to the seeking of the public good. While personal worth or value is always manifest in one's social utility, and is thus contributory to the common good, Plato seems to hold that personal worth is the *telos* of the ideal state (as the best environment for growth in personal virtue), rather than that the state is the telos of personal value. But the relationship is transparently circular, cause and effect, means and end being inextricably interwoven.

Within Plato's ideal state, failure to contribute renders one worthless. And there are levels of worth; some people are superior to others. The Guardian class, of course, has an intrinsic value that exceeds that of slaves, whose only value is in their material contributions to the state. But slaves aside, even among the Guardian class there are grades of worth. Although Plato views men and women of the Guardian class as fully equal, the qualities of this class are starkly masculine, suggesting that the most virtuous (i.e., valuable) women are those who are most like men in their developed character. The children of superior adults clearly possess a potential worth that increases as they come closer to maturity. However, children's worth is not intrinsic but only potential, and children are valued in proportion to their approximation to the ideal adult. They must be malleable, disposed to virtue, and physically fit.

Plato's concern for healthy children is clearly seen in his marriage regulations. The maximum number of superior adults should couple with others of equal worth. The number of inferior types coupling with others of similar value should be kept at a minimum. Since adults who are too young or too old produce less vigorous children than do those who are of ideal age for procreation, people should be prevented from having children except during their ideal years for producing robust offspring.[2] Indeed, the purpose of marriage is first to produce children to ensure the continuity of the state, and second to improve human stock.[3]

In a society in which absolute value is always seen through the grid of social value, those who are physically defective, or at least those who are chronically ill, should not be kept alive by diet, drugs, and regimen, since such people will likely reproduce similarly wretched offspring and be of use neither to themselves nor to society.[4] Indeed, the only legitimate claim to medical care is the continued social usefulness of the one desiring care.

Aristotle's view of human value is expressed in a variety of his works, ranging from the biological to the political and ethical. He clearly postulates a hierarchy of worth within the species. Men with fully developed virtue(s) are most fully human, and thus of the greatest value both to themselves and to society. There are, of course, gradations within this group. All other humans are, by comparison, defective by nature or in their present state. Those who are defective by nature include especially those whom Aristotle calls "natural slaves," that is, individuals who have a capacity to acknowledge reason but not to conceptualize or to engage in rational activity. They are somewhat like domesticated animals: defective by nature. Also defective by nature, but having considerably greater range of capacity for virtue than natural slaves, are those women who themselves are not natural slaves. They are naturally defective by virtue of being women but yet, in unnatural or unusual circumstances, may demonstrate a kind of female excellence. But at the best they are defective males.

Quite distinct from natural slaves and women are children. Children may be natural slaves — a condition not immediately discernible — or female, and thus limited in potential. But all male children, except for those who prove to be natural slaves, are potentially virtuous men, therefore potentially fully human. Children, however, resemble natural slaves and animals more than they do virtuous men, because they lack the developed capacity for rational thought and behavior.

For both Plato and Aristotle, then, human

value is primarily social value and is determined by potentiality.[5]

Do the positions taken by Plato and Aristotle reflect the values of classical society? The answer to that question must be a highly qualified, yet hearty, affirmative; qualified, because there was a tremendous diversity of values in classical antiquity; a hearty affirmative for two reasons: (1) No pagan, whether philosopher or jurist, appears to have asked whether human beings have inherent value, or possess intrinsic rights, ontologically, irrespective of social value, legal status, age, sex, and so forth. (2) Connected with the first reason is a fundamental, though primitive and residual, principle that, as Thrasymachus expresses it, "justice is the will of the stronger." Rights are recognized only by their enforceability. It was against the idea that might makes right that various philosophers, including Plato and Aristotle, reacted. Power must be checked by justice, justice being essentially the definition and enforcement or rights. Rist observes that, "instead of starting with a consideration of human rights, or of basic rights, [the ancients] start with theories of power and of how power shall be tempered by justice. As their thought proceeds, they come to recognize that certain types of people, for various reasons, are in fact possessed of rights. . . . The moral problem is not viewed in terms of enlarging or protecting the rights of the weak, but of controlling and rationalizing the power of the strong."[6]

Rist's comments certainly appear valid when one considers the various legal systems of classical antiquity. Among the Greeks the exclusivistic atmosphere of the polis fostered a definition of rights focusing on citizens — more on males, who possessed the franchise, than on females, who did not. The rights of adult male citizens' dependents (wives, to a certain degree, and children) and human possessions (slaves) were essentially developed with a view to protecting the rights of the adult males on whom those persons depended or to whom they belonged. This prevailed even in the highly developed law of the Roman Empire, though its more cosmopolitan character is reflected in its extension of various, if limited, rights to a broader spectrum of society than had typically been the center of Greek attention. Yet the emphasis remains on the rights of the adult male citizen primarily, with a variety of rights defined for women (these rights essentially comprising limitations of their fathers' or husbands' power and authority), and even for slaves (slight limitations being placed on the absolute power of owners).

Human Value and Newborns

In part, some of the changes that we see during the early centuries of the empire were the result of what some have hailed as a growing humanitarianism, a by-product of a sentiment not of egalitarianism, but at least of the brotherhood of man, proclaimed by the Stoicism of this period. This found its way into the medical ethics of probably a minority of physicians in an ethic of respect for life that condemned both abortion and active (although not passive) euthanasia, and a broader sentiment of generosity and altruism, a philanthropy predicated upon the unexpressed and ill-defined feeling that somehow people have a value to which our compassion is owed.

Even this pagan humanitarianism, however, was not grounded on a principle of inherent value of life. A stand against abortion and active euthanasia by the probably Pythagorean author of the so-called Hippocratic Oath, and by such physicians as Scribonius Largus and Soranus, both of whom lived in the early empire, was based less upon an idea of inherent value or sanctity of life than on an abhorrence of a physician's using his art in actively terminating life (fetal or otherwise); and especially in the case of abortion, an enduring, if not always articulated principle that value is more potential than ontological.

The strongly held idea that human value is acquired rather than inherent was nearly pervasive in classical antiquity, even among those pagans who condemned abortion. It was so central to ancient conceptions of value that a fully developed principle of sanctity of human life was never achieved in pagan society. This is particularly easily demonstrated by considering the status of newborns and their treatment. Once more I quote John Rist:

> It was almost universally held in antiquity that a child has no intrinsic right to life in virtue of being born. What mattered was being adopted into a family or some other institution of society. Both

> Plato and Aristotle, as well as the Stoics, Epicurus, and presumably Plotinus, accept the morality of the exposure of infants . . . on eugenic or sometimes on purely economic grounds. . . . We see here further clear evidence of the ancient view that somehow value is acquired, either by the development of intelligence or by the acceptance into society. There is no reason to think that the philosophers made substantial advances on the assumptions of the general public in this regard.[7]

Rist is absolutely correct in this assertion. Some clarification, however, is necessary. It is misleading to say that in antiquity the attitude that "a child has no intrinsic right to life in virtue of being born" was "almost universal." There were indeed some pagans who did condemn exposure[8] of healthy children for any reason: is Rist referring to these by his qualifying "almost"? That would imply that such individuals condemned exposure of healthy infants on the grounds that there is an "intrinsic" right to life in virtue of being born. Or is Rist suggesting that there were some — that few permitted by his "almost" — who unequivocally condemned all infanticide, including exposure of healthy infants and the disposal of the defective? If there actually were any pagans in the second of these categories, they most certainly had not formulated an ethic of intrinsic human value, any more than had those who were in the first category. His "almost" cannot include any — even the most humanitarian — pagans, not even those were were adamant in condemning abortion.

Although Rist's first qualifier, the adverb *almost* can be misleading, his second qualifying phrase is more helpful, namely, that various philosophers accepted the morality of exposure of infants "on eugenic or sometimes on purely economic grounds." If we take the term *eugenic* in a broad sense, we can apply it to the disposal of defective infants, as distinct from the exposure of healthy infants for economic (or other non-eugenic) reasons. These two categories must be kept distinct if we are to understand the response of pagans in classical antiquity to defective infants.

First of all, it can be categorically asserted that there were no laws in classical antiquity, Greek or Roman, that prohibited the killing, by exposure or otherwise, of the defective newborn. Further, it is unlikely that there actually were any laws that classified exposure (as distinct from other forms of killing) of the healthy newborn as parricide or homicide, or prohibited the practice on other grounds, except, perhaps, in some limited regions or under unusual circumstances before the Christianization of the Roman Empire. If any such law or laws existed, there appears to have been little or no effort to enforce them.[9]

As already mentioned, there were some pagans who opposed the exposure of healthy infants. Aristotle implies in the *Politics* that there was in Greece some sentiment against exposure of healthy infants or traditions hostile to the practice, when he recommends that, if there are already too many children, abortion — before sensation *(prin aithēsin)*[10] — be practiced in those regions where "the regular customs hinder any of those born being exposed" *(ean hē takis tōn ethōn kōlyę mēden apotithesthai tōn gignomenōn)*.[11] The second-century B.C. historian Polybius criticizes the practice of child exposure, which he saw as one of the causes of the serious depopulation of Greece that occurred in the second century B.C., attributing the act to people's "pretentious extravagance, avarice and sloth."[12] The stoic philosopher Epictetus, who lived in the late first and early second centuries A.D., criticizes Epicurus for approving the exposure of children, saying that even a sheep or a wolf does not abandon its own offspring. His argument is that we ought not to be more foolish than sheep or more fierce than wolves, but rather should yield to our natural impulse to love our own offspring.[13] It is significant that he uses *stergein* here, the obvious word for having "natural affection," as distinct from other Greek words that are translated by the English word *love.*

Many of the examples of condemnation of child exposure found in classical authors are in descriptions of the practices of other cultures. The novelist Heliodorus (third century A.D.), in *An Ethiopian Romance* has an Ethiopian gymnosophist say that he found and reared an exposed girl "because for me it is not permissible to disregard an imperiled soul once it has taken on human form. This is a precept of our gymnosophists."[14] These attitudes were divergent enough from typical classical values that some authors were sufficiently intrigued to tickle their readers by relating such strange customs of exotic peoples. Others who decried various practices of their own societies describe the contrasting purity of other cultures. Tacitus, a contemporary of Epictetus, does both. He finds it remarkable that among the Germans it was regarded as shameful to kill any "lateborn" child, that is, an unwanted child.[15] He uses nearly an identical sentence when he attributes the same peculiarity to the Jews, a people whose customs he usually finds strange and obnoxious.[16]

That Jews of Tacitus' time regarded the killing of infants as a reprehensible act, violating sacred law, is evident from the writings of Philo Judaeus[17] and Josephus.[18] Relying on the writings of Hecataeus of Abdera (sixth/fifth centuries B.C.), Diodorus Siculus remarks that Moses required the Jews "to rear their children" *(teknoropohein)*,[19] and says virtually the same thing about the Egyptians, that is, that they are required "to raise all their children" *(ta gennōmena panta trephousin)*.[20] Oribasius (personal physician to Julian "the Apostate") maintains that Aristotle also attributed this same practice to the Egyptians *(to trephein panta ta ginomena)*.[21] And the geographer Strabo (first centuries B.C./A.D.) asserts that the Egyptians most zealously observe the custom of raising every child who is born *(to panta trephein ta gennōmena paidia)*.[22]

The expressed or implied motivations behind these condemnations of exposure differ. Epictetus obviously regards exposure as a violation of natural law. Polybius regards those who engaged in it as selfish and immoral. Tacitus says that the Germans held this practice (as well as any limitation of the number of their children) as *flagitium* (a disgraceful or shameful deed) and says of the Jews that they saw it as *nefas* (contrary to divine law, impious), a word much more charged with moral principle than that descriptive of German sentiment. Josephus maintains that it was forbidden by the Law, and Philo condemns it as murder, a perversion of natural law. Diodorus Siculus implies that the Jews were motivated to condemn the practice by a desire to increase their population, the motive specified by the same author for the Egyptians' forbidding the act. And Heliodorus' imaginary Ethiopian gymnosophist regarded it as morally wrong, at least for his exclusive group of gymnosophists.

The Killing of Defective Newborns

These instances of condemnation of child exposure, or of infanticide in the broader sense of the word, whether by some few Greeks or Romans or by exotic peoples, both Jews and pagans, can be taken to include the condemnation of the killing of the defective newborn, and not only the exposure of healthy infants. There is no qualifying phrase introduced by "except." The statements are generally quite specific and seem to imply that all that are born are raised, the word translated "raised" meaning "nourished," and the word translated "born" either the word commonly used for giving birth, or else the word for becoming or coming into existence. These phrases certainly would, on the surface, seem all-inclusive. Aristotle, you recall, recommends early abortion as a means of population control in the event that "regular customs hinder any of those born being exposed."[23] Such a statement seems inclusive, even in the English translation. But it most certainly is not, for it follows directly on this: "As to exposing or rearing the children born, let there be a law that no deformed child shall be reared" *(peri de apotheseōs kai trophēs ton gignomenōn estō nomos mēden pepērōmenon trephein)*.

Aristotle, writing in *Politics,* is describing "the best state." As we have just seen, in such a state he thinks there should be a law that no deformed child should be reared. While the practice of exposing or killing deformed infants was, as we shall see, common enough in classical antiquity, suggesting a law that would make it mandatory was not by any means typical. Quintus Curtius, writing in the first century A.D., thought it was worthy of note to inform his readers that at the time of Alexander the Great it was supposedly the custom in part of India not to permit parents to determine whether their children should be reared; the decision was in the hands of "those to whom the charge of the physical examination of children had been committed. If these have noted any who are conspicuous for defects or are crippled in some part of their limbs, they give orders to put them to death."[24] This sounds very similar to the well-known custom ascribed to the Spartans in Plutarch's *Life of Lycurgus:* "Offspring was not reared at the will of the father, but was taken and carried by him to a place . . . where the elders . . . officially examined the infant, and if it was well-built and sturdy, they ordered the father to rear it . . . but if it was ill-born and deformed, they sent it to . . . a chasm-like place at the foot of Mount Taÿgetus, in the conviction that the life of that which nature had not well-equipped at the very beginning for health and strength, was of no advantage, either to itself or to the state."[25]

The explanation given for this practice is a concern for eugenics. We can assume the same in the case of Aristotle's ideal state and the supposed custom in India. Another feature that they have in common is that the parents have no say in the matter. Both of these aspects are present in a passage from Plato's *Republic:* "The offspring of the inferior, and any of those of the other sort who are born defective, they will properly dispose of in secret, so that no one will know what has become of them."[26] This passage has been the focus of much controversy, with some scholars maintaining that it has nothing to do with exposure.[27] Irrespective of that debate, we need to step back for a moment and look at the vocabulary in these four passages used to describe the infants in question.

The child is described as *anapēron* (maimed, crippled) by Plato. Aristotle uses a related word, *pepērōmenon*, meaning essentially the same thing. The text of Quintus Curtius is somewhat corrupt, but the basic meaning is "defective" or "crippled." Plutarch uses two terms, the first of which, *agennes*, is quite unusual, having the meaning "unborn" or "uncreated," *perhaps* "grossly deformed"; the second, *amorphon*, means "misshapen" or "disfigured." Aside from the fact that the vocabulary is frustratingly imprecise, we should note that there appears to be nothing superstitious in the procedures or decision making described. The conditions are assumed to be natural defects, of no numinous or ominous character. The situation changes when we look at the Roman scene.

The first-century B.C. historian Dionysius of Halicarnassus attributes to Romulus, the legendary founder of Rome, the following law. Explaining how Romulus had made the city large and populous, Dionysius maintains that "he obliged the inhabitants to bring up all their male children and the first born of the females, and forbade them to destroy any children under three years of age unless they were maimed or monstrous from their very birth. These he did not forbid their parents to expose, provided they first showed them to their five nearest neighbors and these also approved."[28] Irrespective of the very questionable historicity of this "law," an important element is introduced. There are two different categories of defective infants here: *anapēron,* the same word Plato used, translated as "maimed," and *teras,* a noun denoting a sign or wonder, a marvel, a portent, or anything that serves as an omen, as, for instance, here a strange creature or monster. What is probably meant is a grossly deformed infant, perhaps the type implied by Plutarch's word *agennes.* The significant difference is that Plutarch's adjective is devoid of superstitious meaning, while the word *teras* is supernatural to the core. While the infant in Plutarch's account is probably no more or less grotesque than that in Dionysius', the response that each elicits is different, the response at least of the two authors as revealed in their choice of vocabulary.

Much more common in Roman than in Greek society was the occurrence of *prodigia* (in Greek, *terata*, plural of *teras*), unnatural and inexplicable events, such as the birth of a lamb with five legs, a human hermaphrodite, and the like. While some prodigia on record are so bizarre that their historicity must be discounted, many, perhaps most, are well within the realm of possibility, especially after exaggeration is subtracted from the account. A prodigium had enormous significance; it was itself a message from the supernatural powers, more often than not a warning, eliciting a communal fear and guilt in Roman society, particularly during the Republican period. The message had to be discerned by *haruspices* (soothsayers), the unnatural thing destroyed, and a *piaculum,* that is, an expiatory rite performed. Consider the following event, which occurred in 207 B.C., as recorded by the first-century B.C. historian Livy:

> Relieved of their religious scruples, men were troubled again by the report that at Frusino there had been born a child as large as a four-year-old, and not so much a wonder for size as because . . . it was uncertain whether male or female. In fact the soothsayers summoned from Etruria said it was a terrible and loathsome portent; it must be removed from Roman territory, far from contact

> with earth, and drowned in the sea. They put it alive into a chest, carried it out to sea and threw it overboard. The pontiffs likewise decreed that thrice nine maidens should sing a hymm as they marched through the city.[29]

Such events abound in the extant literature.[30] The motivations for the killing of such newborns are different from the primarily eugenic concerns of the other authors whom we have considered thus far. The response to prodigia is rooted in some very deep-seated fear, guilt, and shame that are only slightly evident in the response to the birth of sickly, maimed, or moderately deformed infants. The maimed, the deformed, and the monstrous constitute a continuum that can accommodate both superstitious and eugenic concerns. A law requiring the killing of deformed infants would include so-called monstrous births as well, motivated perhaps by both eugenic and superstitious responses. Such seem to underlie a law in the ancient Twelve Tables, a code thought to have been compiled in Rome in the fifth century B.C., to which Cicero alludes. This law required that a *puer ad deformitatem* be killed quickly.[31] While modern translators render this as "terribly deformed," that seems stronger than the Latin, which appears to accommodate the entire continuum described above.

The continuum broadens when we consider a passage in a treatise written by the first-century A.D. Stoic philosopher Seneca: "Mad dogs we knock on the head; the fierce and savage ox we slay; sickly sheep we put to the knife to keep them from infecting the flock; unnatural progeny we destroy; we drown even children who at birth are weakly and abnormal. Yet it is not anger, but reason that separates the harmful from the sound."[32] Here we see *portentosi,* that is, unnatural or monstrous births; *debiles,* that is, sickly or weak infants; and *monstrosi,* that is, deformed or abnormal newborns. We should note that Seneca is neither recommending nor condemning this practice. He simply gives it as an example, along with several others, of violence or ostensibly destructive activity, in which his society engaged as a matter of course, that did not involve anger or hatred but was motivated by a concern for individual or social good. The two sentences immediately preceding the section quoted say, "Does a man hate the members of his own body when he uses a knife upon them? There is no anger there, but the pitying desire to heal."

It should be clear that in Roman culture the killing of defective newborns was common, and was even apparently required in the case of those infants so grossly deformed or unusual as to appear to be *portentosi* or monstrous births. For Greece, however, we have seen only the anomalous conditions in Sparta and the "ideal" practices suggested by Aristotle and Plato. These really tell us little about conditions in Greek society during the classical period. There is, however, a passage in Plato's *Theaetetus* that is very revealing. The man whose name supplies the title for this dialogue has suggested that knowledge is nothing more than perception. Socrates wishes to subject this "brainchild" to examination to see whether it is worth rearing. Socrates had earlier warned him that that was precisely what he was going to do once Theaetetus gives birth to his idea:

> I suspect that you, as you yourself believe, are in pain because you are pregnant with something within you. Apply, then, to me, remembering that I am the son of a midwife and have myself a midwife's gifts, and do your best to answer the questions I ask as I ask them. And if, when I have examined any of the things you say, it should prove that I think it is a mere image and not real, and therefore quietly take it from you and throw it away, do not be angry as women are when they are deprived of their first offspring. For many, my dear friend, before this have got into such a state of mind towards me that they are actually ready to bite me, if I take some foolish notion away from them, and they do not believe that I do this in kindness.[33]

After Theaetetus elaborates his theory, Socrates says, "Shall we say that this is, so to speak, your newborn child and the result of midwifery? Or what shall we say?" Theaetetus replies, "We must say that, Socrates." Socrates then continues: "Well, we have at least managed to bring this forth, whatever it turns out to be; and not that it is born, we must in very truth perform the rite of running around with it in a circle — the circle of our argument — and see whether it may not turn out to be after all not worth rearing, but only a wind-egg, an imposture. But, perhaps, you think that any offspring of yours ought to be cared for and not put away; or will you bear to see it examined and not get angry if it is taken away from you, though it is your first-born?"[34] First of all, it is self-evident that the whole comparison would be sheer nonsense unless a custom prevailed of disposing of defective newborns, even defective first-borns, at least at Athens at that time. Second, we may note that mothers typically were angry when their first-born was taken from them. Apparently they were better able to cope with losing a defective infant if they already had at least one healthy child. Third, it is evident that the examination of a newborn infant was part of a midwife's responsibilities. There is relatively little attention given in ancient medical literature to the duties of midwives. However, Soranus, a physician who lived in Rome in the first and second centuries A.D., wrote a gynecological treatise — the best that has survived from antiquity — that was designed for midwives. A passage in this treatise is entitled "How to Recognize the Newborn That Is Worth Rearing." It reads:

> Now the midwife, having received the newborn, should first put it upon the earth, having examined beforehand whether the infant is male or female, and should make an announcement by signs as is the custom of women. She should also consider whether it is worth rearing or not. And the infant which is suited by nature for rearing will be distinguished by the fact that its mother has spent the period of pregnancy in good health, for conditions which require medical care, especially those of the body, also harm the fetus and enfeeble the foundations of its life. Second, by the fact that it has been born at the due time, best at the end of nine months, and if it so happens, later; but also after only seven months. Furthermore by the fact that when a woman puts it on the earth it immediately cries with proper vigor; for one that lives for some length of time without crying, or cries but weakly, is suspected of behaving so on account of some unfavorable condition. Also by the fact that it is perfect in all its parts, members and senses; that its ducts, namely of the ears, nose, pharynx, urethra, anus are free from obstruction; that the natural functions of every [member] are neither sluggish nor weak; that the joints bend and stretch; that it has due size and shape and is properly sensitive in every respect. This we may recognize from pressing the fingers against the surface of the body, for it is natural to suffer pain from everything that pricks or squeezes. And by conditions contrary to those mentioned, the infant not worth rearing is recognized.[35]

While this passage from Soranus gives concrete evidence for what was undoubtedly a common practice both in Greek and Roman cultures, it is not, strictly speaking, a medical pronouncement upon the decision-making processes involving the care of the defective newborn. It is written on the assumption that a defective infant is *eo ipso* not worth rearing. The question is simply how to determine most easily and efficiently which infants are worth rearing. Even this was a question seldom addressed by ancient medical authors. It was a midwife's concern — which is why we encounter this guidance in a gynecological treatise written for midwives. Not that medical authors, as well as natural philosophers, were uninterested in why some infants were born defective, and how to try to prevent this. Various intriguing suggestions were advanced and theories developed that are not germane to this study.

Two conclusions can now be drawn. One is that the *care* of defective newborns simply was not a medical concern in classical antiquity.[36] The second is that the morality of the killing of sickly or deformed newborns appears not to have been questioned, at least not in extant sources, either by nonmedical or by medical authors. Interestingly enough, Soranus, who was atypical of the ancient medical authors in condemning abortion, not only raises no objection to the rejection of defective newborns but also, as we have seen, quite dispassionately provides the criteria to be used by midwives in determining which newborns are worth rearing.

The Christian Principle of the Sanctity of Life

I have earlier asserted that the idea that human value is acquired rather than inherent was so central to ancient conceptions of value that a fully developed principle of the sanctity of human life, one that includes even the defective newborn, was never achieved in pagan antiquity. For apparently no pagan raised the question of whether human beings have inherent value, or possess intrinsic rights, ontologically, irrespective of social value, legal status, age, sex, and so forth. The first espousal of an idea of inherent human value in Western civilization depended on a belief that every human being was formed in the image of God. We shall return shortly to this principle of *imago Dei* as a basis for inherent human value.

It is unlikely, however, that the earliest Christians formulated a concise definition of human value based upon the concept of imago Dei. The condemnation of acts that would later be viewed as violations of the rights that accrue to a person as one formed in God's image were, in the earliest Christian literature, part of a broad moral indignation against those aspects of Greco-Roman culture which stand in the starkest contrast to the most basic principles of the gospel of love, mercy, compassion, and salvation from sin to holiness and purity. All aspects of pagan brutality and immorality were condemned; they seemed to early Christian apologists to be common and related features of a society that was viewed as corrupted to its very core by the disease of sin. Apologists condemned in the same breath gladiatorial shows, grossly cruel executions conducted as spectator sports, abortion, infanticide, and a broad and imaginative variety of sexual deviations. Some apologists saw abortion as a sexual crime, in that it was done to destroy the results of a sexual act that was lust when engaged in for a purpose other than procreation. Infanticide had the same motive as did exposure, except that the latter created a potential for another sexual sin, incest, since exposed children often ended up in brothels.[37]

So common, indeed universal, among Christians in the early centuries of Christianity was the condemnation of abortion and infanticide, including exposure,[38] that I shall only mention a few features. Some apologists point out that the practice of infanticide among the pagans is not surprising, in light of a tradition of the sacrifice of infants in various cults — a practice in which some cults still engaged, although it was strictly forbidden by law; and a practice, incidentally, of which early Christians were themselves slanderously accused. Further, these apologists claim, the pagan myths are full of tales of infanticide, which set a precedent of approbation. Further, some early church fathers contrast active infanticide with exposure, asserting that exposing a baby to cold, hunger, and carnivorous animals is more cruel than simply strangling it. But, they tell us, many pagans, thinking that it is impious to kill the infant with one's own hands, kill it by the less messy means of a slow death out of their sight.

None of the early Christian condemnations of infanticide make any reference to the condition of the baby, whether it is healthy or defective, or consider a possible eugenic motivation for the active or passive killing of a newborn. But while I asserted that the relatively rare instances of pagan condemnations of exposure would not have included the killing of the defective, I shall maintain even more categorically that early Christian condemnation of exposure and other forms of infanticide would have included any and every form of infanticide, active or passive, of newborns, whether they be healthy, sickly, or deformed.

There are three reasons that immediately come to mind for this attitude. The first, which I shall mention only in passing, is the significantly different attitude of Christianity to children generally. In classical society, even in its more humanitarian movements, children were essentially viewed as potential adults, their value residing in what they would become. We moderns, in a child-oriented society, generally do not appreciate just how revolutionary was Jesus' teaching that unless you become as little children you cannot enter the kingdom of God. Second, the social thrust of early Christianity was demonstrably and spectacularly oriented to helping the helpless, caring for the destitute, and succoring the deprived.

The third reason requires a little more space than the first two. I made reference earlier to the concept of people being created in God's image as ultimately providing the basis for a Christian theology of human value. I shall leave aside such questions as the relationship of image and likeness of God and the extent to which these concepts are entangled by patristic authors with the Platonic conception that likeness to God is the telos of human endeavor. The earliest Christian apologist who seems to imply the concept of imago Dei as a basis for the condemnation of abortion and infanticide is Clement of Alexandria (second century).[29] Even if the imago Dei may be defaced by human will, obstinacy, and sin, such could not be the case with the fetus and the newborn infant. Such an assertion obviously would include the sickly and deformed newborn. But what of the extreme end of the continuum of which I spoke earlier, the monstrous or grossly deformed?

Augustine, in the *City of God*,[40] comments on the tremendous diversity among people, enormous racial differences, and whole tribes of people who seem to us to be monstrous. He then says,

> If whole peoples have been monsters, we must explain the phenomenon as we explain the individual monsters who are born among us. God is the Creator of all; He knows best where and when and what is, or was, best for Him to create, since He deliberately fashioned the beauty of the whole out of both the similarity and dissimilarity of its parts. . . . I know men who were born with more than five fingers or toes, which is one of the slightest variations from the normal, but it would be a shame for anyone to be so silly as to suppose that, because he did not know why God did this, the Creator could make a mistake in regard to the number of fingers on a man's hand. Even in cases of greater variations, God knows what He is doing, and no one may rightly blame His work. . . . it would be impossible to list all the human offspring who have been very different from the parents from whom they were certainly born. Still, all these monsters undeniably owe their origin to Adam.[41]

Later in the same work, Augustine says that pagans mock the idea of the resurrection of the dead, referring to various physical defects as well as "all the human monstrosities that are born" and then asking, "What kind of resurrection will there be in cases like these?"[42] Augustine, in his *Enchiridion,* specifically addresses the question of the resurrection of the grossly deformed, or human "monstrosities":

> Concerning monsters which are born and live, however quickly they die, neither is resurrection to be denied them, nor is it to be believed that they will rise again as they are, but rather with an amended and perfected body. God forbid that the double-membered man recently born in the East — about whom most trustworthy brethren, who saw him, have reported, and Jerome the priest, of holy memory, left written mention — God forbid, I say, that we should think that at the resurrection there will be one such double man, and not rather two men, as would have been the case had twins been born. And so all other births which, as having some excess or some defect or because of some conspicuous deformity, are called monsters, will be brought again at the resurrection to the true form of human nature, so that one soul will have one body, and no bodies will cohere together, even those that were born in this condition, but each, apart, for himself, will have as his own those members whose sum makes the complete human body.[43]

The imago Dei, with its attendant value, rights, and responsibilities, attached in early Christian thought to the newborn, whether healthy or sickly, maimed, deformed, or monstrous, indeed to the whole continuum of the defective, in vivid contrast to the attitudes and practices of pagan antiquity. The Christian concept of imago Dei provided both the basis and the structure for the idea of inalienable rights and of intrinsic human value that has prevailed in Western society nearly until the present.

Notes

1. John M. Rist, *Human Value: A Study in Ancient Philosophical Ethics* (Leiden: E. J. Brill, 1982), p. 9.

2. Plato, in the *Republic,* recommends that women not bear children before age twenty (460E), but in *Laws* he sets the age at sixteen (785B). Aristotle recommends eighteen as the minimum age (*Politics* 1335a). Their concern is with eugenics.

3. Plato, *Laws* 773D, 783D-E.

4. Plato, *Republic* 407D-E, 410A.

5. For a discussion of Plato's and Aristotle's views on human value, see M. P. Golding and N. H. Golding, "Population Policy in Plato and Aristotle: Some Value Issues," *Arethusa* 8 (1968): 345-58; and Rist, *Human Value* (n. 1).

6. Rist, *Human Value* (n. 1), p. 131.

7. Ibid., pp. 141-42.

8. The prevalence of exposure in classical antiquity

has been debated by modern scholars. For some specialized studies see H. Bennett, "The Exposure of Infants in Ancient Rome," *Classical J.* 18 (1923): 341-51; H. Bolkestein, "The Exposure of Children at Athens and the ἐγχυτρίστριαι," *Classical Philol.* 17 (1922): 222-29; A. Cameron, "The Exposure of Children and Greek Ethics," *Classical Rev.* 46 (1932): 105-14; D. Engels, "The Problem of Female Infanticide in the Greco-Roman World," *Classical Philol.* 75 (1980): 112-20; R. H. Feen, "Abortion and Exposure in Ancient Greece: Assessing the Status of the Fetus and 'Newborn' from Classical Sources," in *Abortion and the Status of the Fetus,* ed. W. B. Bondeson and H. T. Engelhardt, Jr. (Dordrecht: D. Reidel, 1983), pp. 283-99; M. Radin, "Exposure of Infants in Roman Law and Practice," *Classical J.* 20 (1925): 337-42; and L. Van Hook, "The Exposure of Infants at Athens," *Trans. Amer. Philol. Soc.* 51 (1920): 134-45. Engels' assessment appears correct: "After careful analysis of the literacy evidence, earlier studies concerning the exposure of children (and any resultant infanticide) have established that the practice was of negligible importance in Greek and Roman society" (Engels, "Female Infanticide" [n. 8], 112). It has been popularly assumed that the exposure of female newborns was extremely common. Engels convincingly argues that the high level of female infanticide assumed for classical antiquity by some scholars would have produced demographic consequences of a catastrophic nature. It is, of course, important to bear in mind that exposure is an ambiguous word, and that very likely exposure, unless excessive, may well have affected the population relatively little since probably the majority of exposed infants were reared. Sometimes exposure is infanticide; sometimes it is simply abandonment.

9. J. W. Jones writes of ancient Greece generally that "neither Greek public opinion nor Greek law frowned on the practice [of exposure], if the exposure was not delayed beyond a few days after birth" (*The Law and Legal Theory of the Greeks* [Oxford: Clarendon, 1956], p. 288). Thebes, during the early centuries of the Christian era, may possibly be an exception, if Aelian (*Varia historia* 2.7) can be trusted (for which see Feen "Abortion and Exposure" [n.8], 289). Speaking only of Athens, A. R. W. Harrison says that while "there seems general agreement that there was probably no explicit enactment conferring the right to expose," nevertheless there is "no reason to doubt that the father had this absolute discretion and that the right of exposure was more than a purely formal one" (*The Law of Athens: The Family and Property* [Oxford: Clarendon, 1968], p. 71, and n. 1). Putting this in other terms, he says that an Athenian father's right to expose his child is "perhaps better expressed as the absence of a duty to introduce it into the family" (73), or "the right to expose should perhaps be thought of as the absence of a duty to rear" (74, and n. 2). The assertion made by the late-second century or early-third century A.D. physician-philosopher Sextus Empiricus, in his *Outlines of Pyrrhonism* 3.211, that "Solon gave the Athenians the law . . . by which he allowed each man to slay his own child" can be confidently rejected (Harrison, *The Law of Athens* [n. 9], p. 71, and n. 2). It can be categorically asserted that the Athenian father never "enjoyed a power remotely resembling the Roman father's *ius vitae ac necis*" (74), that is, "power of life and death" over his children. That power is, of course, the well-known Roman father's *patria potestas.* The question of the legality of exposure in Roman law is entangled in the complexity of the changing patria potestas during the imperial period as well as the development of laws governing the parental reclaiming of exposed children reared by others, either as free children or as slaves, and the sale of free newborns as slaves. The Roman father's authority to put his children to death appears not to have been rescinded until the reign of the first Christian emperor, Constantine, who in 318 promulgated a law concerning parricide, that is, the killing of parents and children (*Codex Justinianus* 9.17.1). In 374, Valentinian enacted a statute concerning homicide which made the killing of an infant a capital offense (*Codex Justinianus* 9.16.7). In the same year he issued another statute that seems unambiguously to forbid exposure of infants. It begins, "Unusquisque subolem suam nutriat. Quod is exponendam putaverit, animadversioni quae constituta est subiacebit" (Everyone should support his own offspring, and anyone who thinks that he can expose his child shall be subject to the penalty prescribed by law [*Codex Justinianus* 8.51.2]). While this seems clear enough, is the penalty referred to here that of Constantine's law of 318 concerning parricide, or is there an even earlier law to which this legislation of 374 has reference? This question is raised in great part by a statement made by the great Roman jurist Paul in his *Sententiae* (third century): "Necare videtur non tantum is qui partum praefocat, sed et is qui abicit et qui alimonia denegat et is qui publicis locis misericordiae causa exponit, quam ipse non habet" (Not only he who strangles a child is held to kill it, but also he who abandons it, or denies it food, as well as he who exposes it in a public place for the purpose of arousing the pity which he himself does not

feel. [The better manuscripts read *praefocat* = strangle; some read *perfocat* = smother. *Digest* 25.3.4]). Paul is here obviously defining *necare.* The exact significance of the passage for the right of the Roman father to kill his children — or to expose them — cannot be dogmatically asserted. For a discussion, see Radin, "Exposure of Infants" (n. 8). On *patria potestas,* see W. W. Buckland, *A Text-Book of Roman Law from Augustus to Justinian,* 2d ed. (Cambridge: Cambridge University Press, 1952), sec. 38.

10. On which see J. M. Oppenheimer, "When Sense and Life Begin: Background for a Remark in Aristotle's *Politics* (1335b24)," *Arethusa* 8 (1975): 331-43.

11. Aristotle, *Politics* 1335b, trans. H. Rackham (Cambridge, Mass.: Harvard University Press, 1932).

12. Polybius, *The Histories* 36.17, trans. W. Paton (Cambridge, Mass.: Harvard University Press, 1922-27).

13. Epictetus, *Discourses* 1.23.

14. Heliodorus, *An Ethiopian Romance,* trans. H. Thackeray (Ann Arbor: University of Michigan Press, 1957), p. 61.

15. Tacitus, *Germania* 19.

16. Tacitus, *The Histories* 5.5.

17. E. R. Goodenough, *The Jurisprudence of the Jewish Courts in Egypt: Legal Administration by the Jews under the Early Roman Empire as Described by Philo Judaeus* (Amsterdam: Philo, 1968), pp. 115-16.

18. Josephus, *Against Apion* 2.24.

19. Diodorus Siculus, *Library of History* 40.3, trans. C. H. Oldfather (Cambridge, Mass.: Harvard University Press, 1933-57).

20. Ibid., 1.80.

21. Oribasius, *Collectiones medicae,* ed. I. Reader (Amsterdam: Hakkert, 1928-33), 4: 99-100.

22. Strabo, *Georgraphy,* 172.5.

23. Aristotle, *Politics* (n. 11), 1335b.

24. Quintus Curtius, *History of Alexander* 9.1.25.

25. Plutarch, *The Parallel Lives: Life of Lycurgus* 16, trans. B. Perrin (Cambridge, Mass.: Harvard University Press, 1914-26).

26. Plato, *Republic,* 460C, trans. P. Shorey (Cambridge, Mass.: Harvard University Press, 1930-35).

27. See, for example, J. J. Mulhern, "Population and Plato's *Republic,*" *Arethusa* 8 (1975): 265-81.

28. Dionysius of Halicarnassus, *Roman Antiquities* 2.15, trans. E. Cary (Cambridge, Mass.: Harvard University Press, 1937-50).

29. Livy, *Histories* 37.27, trans. B. O. Foster, E. T. Sage, A. C. Schlesinger, and R. M. Geer (Cambridge, Mass.: Harvard University Press, 1919-59).

30. For an interesting discussion, see W. den Boer, "Prodigium and Morality," in his *Private Morality in Greece and Rome: Some Historical Aspects* (Leiden: E. J. Brill, 1979), pp. 93ff.

31. Cicero, *Laws* 3.8.

32. Seneca, *On Anger* 1.15, in *Moral Essays,* trans. J. W. Basore (Cambridge, Mass.: Harvard University Press, 1928-35).

33. Plato, *Theaetetus* 151B-C, trans. H. N. Fowler (Cambridge, Mass.: Harvard University Press, 1921).

34. Ibid., 160E, 161A.

35. Soranus, *Gynecology,* trans. Owsei Temkin (Baltimore: Johns Hopkins Press, 1956), pp. 79-80.

36. For an interesting discussion of the minor role of pediatrics in ancient medicine, see R. Etienne, "Ancient Medical Conscience and the Life of Children," *J. Psychohist,* 4 (1976-77): 127-61.

37. See, e.g., Justin Martyr, *The First Apology* 27; Tertullian, *Apology* 9; Clement of Alexandria, *Christ the Educator* 21; and Lactantius, *The Divine Institutes* 6.20.

38. See, e.g. Minucius Felix, *Octavius* 30; Justin Martyr, *The First Apology* 27; Lactantius *The Divine Institutes* 5.9; Tertullian, *Ad nationes.* 1.15; idem, *Apology* 9; idem, *The Didache* 2; *The Epistle of Barnabus* 19.5; and *The Epistle to Diognetus* 5-6. For a discussion, see I. Giordani, *The Social Message of the Early Fathers,* trans. A. Zizzamia (Boston: St. Paul Editions, 1977), pp. 243-52.

39. Rist, *Human Value* (n. 1), pp. 162-63.

40. Augustine, *City of God* 16.8.

41. Augustine, *City of God,* in *Writings of Saint Augustine,* various translators (Washington, D.C.: Catholic University of America Press, various dates), 7: 502-3.

42. Augustine, *City of God* 22.12, vol. 8, p. 459, in the edition cited in n. 41.

43. Augustine, *Enchiridion* 87, in *Writings of Saint Augustine* (n. 41), 4: 442-43.

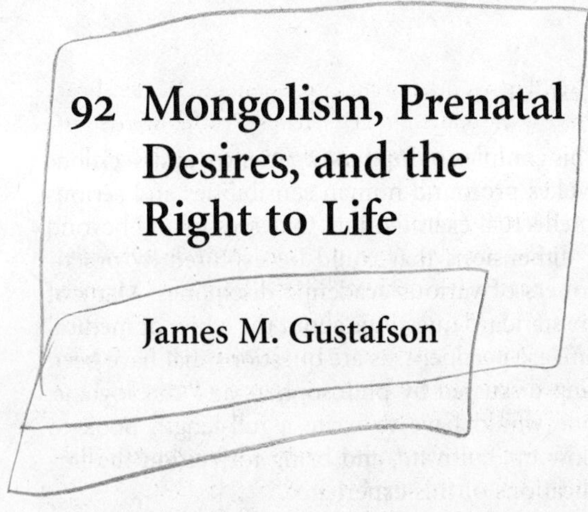

92 Mongolism, Prenatal Desires, and the Right to Life

James M. Gustafson

The Problem

The Family Setting

Mother, 34 years old, hospital nurse.
Father, 35 years old, lawyer.
Two normal children in the family.

In late fall of 1963, Mr. and Mrs. ________ gave birth to a premature baby boy. Soon after birth, the child was diagnosed as a "mongoloid" (Down's syndrome) with the added complication of an intestinal blockage (duodenal atresia). The latter could be corrected with an operation of quite normal risk. Without the operation, the child could not be fed and would die.

At the time of the birth Mrs. ________ overheard the doctor express his belief that the child was a mongol. She immediately indicated she did not want the child. The next day, in consultation with a physician, she maintained this position, refusing to give permission for the corrective operation on the intestinal block. Her husband supported her in this position, saying that his wife knew more about these things (i.e., mongoloid children) than he. The reason the mother gave for her position — "It would be unfair to the other children of the household to raise them with a mongoloid."

From *Perspectives in Biology and Medicine* 16 (Summer 1973): 529-57.

The physician explained to the parents that the degree of mental retardation cannot be predicted at birth — running from a very low mentality to borderline subnormal. As he said: "Mongolism, it should be stressed, is one of the milder forms of mental retardation. That is, mongols' IQs are generally in the 50-80 range, and sometimes a little higher. That is, they're almost always trainable. They can hold simple jobs. And they're famous for being happy children. They're perennially happy and usually a great joy." Without other complications, they can anticipate a long life.

Given the parents' decision, the hospital staff did not seek a court order to override the decision (see "Legal Setting" below). The child was put in a side room and, over an 11-day period, allowed to starve to death.

Following this episode, the parents undertook genetic counseling (chromosome studies) with regard to future possible pregnancies.

The Legal Setting

Since the possibility of a court order reversing the parents' decision naturally arose, the physician's opinion in this matter — and his decision not to seek such an order — is central. As he said: "In the situation in which the child has a known, serious mental abnormality, and would be a burden both to the parents financially and emotionally and perhaps to society, I think it's unlikely that the court would sustain an order to operate on the child against the parents' wishes." He went on to say: "I think one of the great difficulties, and I hope [this] will be part of the discussion relative to this child, is what happens in a family where a court order is used as the means of correcting a congenital abnormality. Does that child ever really become an accepted member of the family? And what are all of the feelings, particularly guilt and coercion feelings that the parents must have following that type of extraordinary force that's brought to bear upon them for making them accept a child that they did not wish to have?

Both doctors and nursing staff were firmly convinced that it was "clearly illegal" to hasten the child's death by the use of medication.

One of the doctors raised the further issue of

consent, saying: "Who has the right to decide for a child anyway? . . . The whole way we handle life and death is the reflection of the long-standing belief in this country that children don't have any rights, that they're not citizens, that their parents can decide to kill them or to let them live, as they choose."

The Hospital Setting

When posed the question of whether the case would have been taken to court had the child had a normal IQ, with the parents refusing permission for the intestinal operation, the near unanimous opinion of the doctors: "Yes, we would have tried to override their decision." Asked why, the doctors replied: "When a retarded child presents us with the same problem, a different value system comes in; and not only does the staff acquiesce in the parents' decision to let the child die, but it's probable that the courts would also. That is, there is a different standard. . . . There is this tendency to value life on the basis of intelligence. . . . [It's] a part of the American ethic."

The treatment of the child during the period of its dying was also interesting. One doctor commented on "putting the child in a side room." When asked about medication to hasten the death, he replied: "No one would ever do that. No one would ever think about it, because they feel uncomfortable about it. . . . A lot of the way we handle these things has to do with our own anxieties about death and our own desires to be separated from the decisions that we're making."

The nursing staff who had to tend to the child showed some resentment at this. One nurse said she had great difficulty just in entering the room and watching the child degenerate — she could "hardly bear to touch him." Another nurse, however, said: "I didn't mind coming to work. Because like I would rock him. And I think that kind of helped me some — to be able to sit there and hold him. And he was just a tiny little thing. He was really a very small baby. And he was cute. He had a cute little face to him, and it was easy to love him, you know?" And when the baby died, how did she feel? — "I was glad that it was over. It was an end for him."

Resolution

This complex of human experiences and decisions evokes profound human sensibilities and serious intellectual examination. One sees in and beyond it dimensions that could be explored by practitioners of various academic disciplines. Many of the standard questions about the ethics of medical care are pertinent, as are questions that have been long discussed by philosophers and theologians. One would have to write a full-length book to plow up, cultivate, and bring to fruition the implications of this experience.

I am convinced that, when we respond to a moral dilemma, the way in which we formulate the dilemma, the picture we draw of its salient features, is largely determinative of the choices we have. If the war in Vietnam is pictured as a struggle between the totalitarian forces of evil seeking to suppress all human values on the one side, and the forces of righteousness on the other, we have one sort of problem with limited choice. If, however, it is viewed as a struggle of oppressed people to throw off the shackles of colonialism and imperialism, we have another sort of problem. If it is pictured as more complex, the range of choices is wider, and the factors to be considered are more numerous. If the population problem is depicted as a race against imminent self-destruction of the human race, an ethics of survival seems to be legitimate and to deserve priority. If, however, the population problem is depicted more complexly, other values also determine policy, and our range of choices is broader.

One of the points under discussion in this medical case is how we should view it. What elements are in the accounts that the participants give to it? What elements were left out? What "values" did they seem to consider, and which did they seem to ignore? Perhaps if one made a different montage of the raw experience, one would have different choices and outcomes.

Whose picture is correct? It would not be difficult for one moral philosopher or theologian to present arguments that might undercut, if not demolish, the defenses made by the participants. Another moralist might make a strong defense of the decisions by assigning different degrees of importance to certain aspects of the case. The first might focus on the violation of individual rights, in this case the rights of the infant. The other might claim that the way of least possible suffering for the fewest persons over the longest range of time was the commendable outcome of the account as we have it. Both would be accounts drawn by external observers, not by active, participating agents. There is a tradition that says that ethical reflection by an ideal external observer can bring morally right answers. I have an observer's perspective, though not that of an "ideal observer." But I believe that it is both charitable and intellectually important to try to view the events as the major participants viewed them. The events remain closer to the confusions of the raw experience that way; the passions, feelings, and emotions have some echo of vitality remaining. The parents were not without feeling, the nurses not without anguish. The experiences could become a case in which *x* represents the rights of the infant to life, *y* represents the consequences of continued life as a mongoloid person, and *z* represents the consequences of his continued life for the family and the state. But such abstraction has a way of oversimplifying experience. One would "weigh" *x* against *y* and *z*. I cannot reproduce the drama even of the materials I have read, the interviews with doctors and nurses, and certainly even those are several long steps from the thoughts and feelings of the parents and the staff at that time. I shall, however, attempt to state the salient features of the dilemma for its participants; features that are each value laden and in part determinative of their decisions. In the process of doing that for the participants, I will indicate what reasons might justify their decisions. Following that I will draw a different picture of the experience, highlighting different values and principles, and show how this would lead to a different decision. Finally, I shall give the reasons why I, an observer, believe they, the participants, did the wrong thing. Their responsible and involved participation, one must remember, is very different from my detached reflection on documents and interviews almost a decade later.

The Mother's Decision

Our information about the mother's decision is secondhand. We cannot be certain that we have an accurate account of her reasons for not authorizing the surgery that could have saved the mongoloid infant's life. It is not my role to speculate whether her given reasons are her "real motives"; that would involve an assessment of her "unconscious." When she heard the child was probably a mongol, she "expressed some negative feeling" about it, and "did not want a retarded child." Because she was a nurse she understood what mongolism indicated. One reason beyond her feelings and wants is given: to raise a mongoloid child in the family would not be "fair" to the other children. That her decision was anguished we know from several sources.

For ethical reflection, three terms I have quoted are important: "negative feelings," "wants" or "desires," and "fair." We need to inquire about the status of each as a justification for her decision.

What moral weight can a negative feeling bear? On two quite different grounds, weight could be given to her feelings in an effort to sympathetically understand her decision. First, at the point of making a decision, there is always an element of the rightness or wrongness of the choice that defies full rational justification. When we see injustice being done, we have strong negative feelings; we do not need a sophisticated moral argument to tell us that the act is unjust. We "feel" that it is wrong. It might be said that the mother's "negative feeling" was evoked by an intuition that it would be wrong to save the infant's life, and that feeling is a reliable guide to conduct.

Second, her negative response to the diagnosis of mongolism suggests that she would not be capable of giving the child the affection and the care that it would require. The logic involved is an extrapolation from that moment to potential consequences for her continued relationship to the child in the future. The argument is familiar; it is common in the literature that supports abortion on request — "no unwanted child ought to be born." Why? Because unwanted children suffer from hostility and lack of affection from their mothers, and this is bad for them.

The second term is "wants" or "desires." The negative feelings are assumed to be an indication of her desires. We might infer that at some point she said, "I do not want a retarded child." The status of "wanting" is different, we might note, if it expresses a wish before the child is born, or if it expresses a desire that leads to the death of the infant after it is born. No normal pregnant woman would wish a retarded child. In this drama, however, it translates into: "I would rather not have the infant kept alive." Or, "I will not accept parental responsibilities for a retarded child." What is the status of a desire or a want as an ethical justification for an action? To discuss that fully would lead to an account of a vast literature. The crucial issue in this case is whether the existence of the infant lays a moral claim that supersedes the mother's desires.

If a solicitor of funds for the relief of refugees in Bengal requested a donation from her and she responded, "I do not want to give money for that cause," some persons would think her to be morally insensitive, but none could argue that the refugees in Bengal had a moral claim on her money which she was obligated to acknowledge. The existence of the infant lays a weightier claim on her than does a request for a donation. We would not say that the child's right to surgery, and thus to life, is wholly relative to, and therefore exclusively dependent upon, the mother's desires or wants.

Another illustration is closer to her situation than the request for a donation. A man asks a woman to marry him. Because she is asked, she is under no obligation to answer affirmatively. He might press claims upon her — they have expressed love for each other; or they have dated for a long time; he has developed his affection for her on the assumption that her responsiveness would lead to marriage. But none of these claims would be sufficient to overrule her desire not to marry him. Why? Two sorts of reasons might be given. One would refer to potential consequences: a marriage in which one partner does not desire the relationship leads to anxiety and suffering. To avoid needless suffering is obviously desirable. So in this case, it might be said that the mother's desire is to avoid needless suffering and anxiety: the undesirable consequences can be avoided by permitting the child to die.

The second sort of reason why a woman has no obligation to marry her suitor refers to her rights as an individual. A request for marriage does not constitute a moral obligation, since there is no prima facie claim by the suitor. The woman has a right to say no. Indeed, if the suitor sought to coerce her into marriage, everyone would assert that she has a right to refuse him. In our case, however, there are some differences. The infant is incapable of expressing a request or demand. Also, the relationship is different: the suitor is not dependent upon his girlfriend in some way that the infant is dependent upon his mother. Dependence functions in two different senses; the necessary conditions for the birth of the child were his conception and *in utero* nourishment — thus, in a sense the parents "caused" the child to come into being. And, apart from instituting adoption procedures, the parents are the only ones who can provide the necessary conditions for sustaining the child's life. The infant is dependent on them in the sense that he must rely upon their performance of certain acts in order to continue to exist. The ethical question to the mother is, Does the infant's physical life lay an unconditioned moral claim on the mother? She answered, implicitly, in the negative.

What backing might the negative answer be given? The most persuasive justification would come from an argument that there are no unconditioned moral claims upon one when those presumed claims go against one's desires and wants. The claims of another are relative to my desires, my wants. Neither the solicitor for Bengal relief nor the suitor has an unconditioned claim to make; in both cases a desire is sufficient grounds for denying such a claim. In our case, it would have to be argued that the two senses of dependence that the infant has on the mother are not sufficient conditions for a claim on her that would morally require the needed surgery. Since there are no unconditioned claims, and since the conditions in this drama are not sufficient to warrant a claim, the mother is justified in denying permission for the surgery.

We note here that in our culture there are two trends in the development of morality that run counter to each other: one is the trend that desires of the ego are the grounds for moral and legal claims. If a mother does not desire the fetus in her uterus, she has a right to an abortion. The other increasingly limits individual desires and wants. An employer might want to hire only white persons of German ancestry, but he has no right to do so.

The word "fair" appeals to quite different warrants. It would not be "fair" to the other children in the family to raise a mongoloid with them. In moral philosophy, fairness is either the same as justice or closely akin to it. Two traditional definitions of justice might show how fairness could be used in this case. One is "to each his due." The other children would not get what is due them because of the inordinate requirements of time, energy, and financial resources that would be required if the mongoloid child lived. Or, if they received what was due to them, there would not be sufficient time, energy, and other resources to attend to the particular needs of the mongoloid; his condition would require more than is due him. The other traditional definition is "equals shall be treated equally." In principle, all children in the family belong to a class of equals and should be treated equally. Whether the mongoloid belongs to that class of equals is in doubt. If he does, to treat him equally with the others would be unfair to him because of his particular needs. To treat him unequally would be unfair to the others.

Perhaps "fairness" did not imply "justice." Perhaps the mother was thinking about such consequences for the other children as the extra demands that would be made upon their patience, the time they would have to give the care of the child, the emotional problems they might have in coping with a retarded sibling, and the sense of shame they might have. These consequences also could be deemed to be unjust from her point of view. Since they had no accountability for the existence of the mongoloid, it was not fair to them that extra burdens be placed upon them.

To ask what was due the mongoloid infant raises harder issues. For the mother, he was not due surgical procedure that would sustain his life. He was "unequal" to her normal children, but the fact of his inequality does not necessarily imply that he has no right to live. This leads to a matter at the root of the mother's response which has to be dealt with separately.

She (and as we shall see, the doctors also) assumed that a factual distinction (between normal and mongoloid) makes the moral difference. Factual distinctions do make moral differences. A farmer who has no qualms about killing a runt pig would have moral scruples about killing a deformed infant. If the child had not been mongoloid and had an intestinal blockage, there would have been no question about permitting surgery to be done. The value of the infant is judged to be relative to a quality of its life that is predictable on the basis of the factual evidences of mongolism. Value is relative to quality: that is the justification. Given the absence of a certain quality, the value is not sufficient to maintain life; given absence of a quality, there is no right to physical life. (Questions about terminating life among very sick adults are parallel to this instance.)

What are the qualities, or what is *the* quality that is deficient in this infant? It is not the capacity for happiness, an end that Aristotle and others thought to be sufficient in itself. The mother and the doctors knew that mongoloids can be happy. It is not the capacity for pleasure, the end that the hedonistic utilitarians thought all men seek, for mongoloids can find pleasure in life. The clue is given when a physician says that the absence of the capacity for normal intelligence was crucial. He suggested that we live in a society in which intelligence is highly valued. Perhaps it is valued as a quality in itself, or as an end in itself by some, but probably there is a further point, namely that intelligence is necessary for productive contribution to one's own well-being and to that of others, but also others must contribute excessively to his care. The right of an infant, the value of his life, is relative to his intelligence; that is the most crucial factor in enabling or limiting his contribution to his own welfare and that of others. One has to defend such a point in terms of the sorts of contributions that would be praiseworthy and the sorts of costs that would be detrimental. The contribution of a sense of satisfaction to those who might enjoy caring for the mongoloid would not be sufficient. Indeed, a full defense would require a quantification of qualities, all based on predictions at the point of birth, that would count both for and against the child's life in a cost-benefit analysis.

The judgment that value is relative to qualities is not implausible. In our society we have traditionally valued the achiever more than the nonachievers. Some hospitals have sought to judge the qualities of the contributions of patients to society in determining who has access to scarce medical resources. A mongoloid is not valued as highly as a fine musician, an effective politician, a successful businessman, a civil rights leader whose actions have brought greater justice to the society, or a physician. To be sure, in other societies and at other times other qualities have been valued, but we judge by the qualities valued in our society and our time. Persons are rewarded according to their contributions to society. A defense of the mother's decision would have to be made on these grounds, with one further crucial step. That is, when the one necessary condition for productivity is deficient (with a high degree of certitude) at birth, there is no moral obligation to maintain that life. That the same reasoning would have been sufficient to justify overtly taking the infant's life seems not to have been the case. But that point emerges later in our discussion.

The reliance upon feelings, desires, fairness, and judgments of qualities of life makes sense to American middle-class white families, and anguished decisions can very well be settled in these terms. The choice made by the mother was not that of an unfeeling problem-solving machine, nor that of a rationalistic philosopher operating from these assumptions. It was a painful, conscientious decision, made apparently on these bases. One can ask, of course, whether her physicians should not have suggested other ways of perceiving and drawing the contours of the circumstances, other values and ends that she might consider. But that points to a subsequent topic.

The Father's Decision

The decision of the father is only a footnote to that of the mother. He consented to the choice of not operating on the infant, though he did seek precise information about mongolism and its consequences for the child. He was "willing to go along with the mother's wishes," he "understood her feelings, agreed with them," and was not in a position to make "the same intelligent decision that his wife was making."

Again we see that scientific evidence based on professional knowledge is determinative of a moral decision. The physician was forthright in indicating what the consequences would be of the course of action they were taking. The consequences of raising a mongoloid child were presumably judged to be more problematic than the death of the child.

The Decision of the Physicians

A number of points of reference in the contributions of the physicians to the case study enable us to formulate a constellation of values that determined their actions. After I have depicted that constellation, I shall analyze some of the points of reference to see how they can be defended.

The constellation can be stated summarily. The physicians felt no moral or legal obligation to save the life of a mongoloid infant by an ordinary surgical procedure when the parents did not desire that it should live. Thus, the infant was left to die. What would have been a serious but routine procedure was omitted in this instance on two conditions, both of which were judged to be necessary, but neither of which was sufficient in itself: the mongolism and the parents' desires. If the parents had desired for the mongoloid infant to be saved, the surgery would have been done. If the infant had not been mongoloid and the parents had refused permission for surgery to remove a bowel obstruction, the physicians would at least have argued against them and probably taken legal measures to override them. Thus, the value-laden points of reference appear to be the desires of the parents, the mongolism of the infant, the law, and choices about ordinary and extraordinary medical procedures.

One of the two most crucial points was the obligation the physicians felt to acquiesce to the desires of the parents. The choice of the parents not to operate was made on what the physicians judged to be adequate information: it was an act of informed consent on the part of the parents. There is no evidence that the physicians raised questions of a moral sort with the parents that they subsequently raised among themselves. For example, one physician later commented on the absence of rights for children in our society and in our legal system and on the role that the value of intelligence seems to have in judging worthiness of persons. These were matters, however, that the physicians did not feel obligated to raise with the distressed parents. The physicians acted on the principle that they are only to do procedures that the patient (or crucially in this case, the parents of the patient) wanted. There was no overriding right to life on the part of a mongoloid infant that led them to argue against the parents' desires or to seek a court order requiring the surgical procedure. They recognized the moral autonomy of the parents, and thus did not interfere; they accepted as a functioning principle that the parents have the right to decide whether an infant shall live.

Elaboration of the significance of parental autonomy is necessary in order to see the grounds on which it can be defended. First, the physicians apparently recognized that the conscientious parents were the moral supreme court. There are grounds for affirming the recognition of the moral autonomy of the principal persons in complex decisions. In this case, the principals were the parents; the infant did not have the capacities to express any desires or preferences he might have. The physicians said, implicitly, that the medical profession does not have a right to impose certain of its traditional values on persons if these are not conscientiously held by those persons.

There are similarities, but also differences, between this instance and that of a terminal patient. If the terminally ill patient expresses a desire not to have his life prolonged, physicians recognize his autonomy over his own body and thus feel under no obligation to sustain his life. Our case, however, would be more similar to one in which the terminally ill patient's family decided that no further procedures ought to be used to sustain life. No doubt there are many cases in which the patient is unable to express a preference due to his physical conditions, and in the light of persuasive medical and familial reasons the physician agrees not to sustain life. A difference between our case and that, however, has to be noted in order to isolate what seems to be the crucial point. In the case of the mongoloid infant, a decision is made at the beginning of his life and not at the end; the effect is to cut off a life which, given proper care, could be sustained for many years, rather than not sustaining a life which has no such prospects.

Several defenses might be made of their recognition of the parents' presumed rights in this case. The first is that parents have authority over their children until they reach an age of discretion, and in some respects until they reach legal maturity. Children do not have recognized rights over against parents in many respects. The crucial difference here, of course, is the claimed parental right in this case to determine that an infant shall not live. What grounds might there be for this? Those who claim the moral right to an abortion are claiming the right to determine whether a child shall live, and this claim is widely recognized both morally and legally. In this case we have an extension of the right to the point of birth. If there are sufficient grounds to indicate that the newborn child is significantly abnormal, the parents have the same right as they have when a severe genetic abnormality is detected prenatally on the basis of amniocentesis. Indeed, the physicians could argue that if a mother has a right to an abortion, she also has a right to determine whether a newborn infant shall continue to live. One is simply extending the time span and the circumstances under which this autonomy is recognized.

A second sort of defense might be made: that of the limits of professional competence and authority. The physicians could argue that in moral matters they have neither competence nor authority. Perhaps they would wish to distinguish between competence and authority. They have a competence to make a moral decision on the basis of their own moral and other values, but they have no authority to impose this upon their patients. Morals, they might argue, are subjective matters, and if anyone has competence in that area, it is philosophers, clergymen, and others who teach what is right and wrong. If the parents had no internalized values that militated against their decision, it is not in the province of the physicians to tell them what they ought to do. Indeed, in a morally pluralistic society, no one group or person has a right to impose his views on another. In this stronger argument for moral autonomy no physician would have any authority to impose his own moral values on any patient. A social role differentiation is noted: the medical profession has authority only in medical matters — not in moral matters. Indeed, they have an obligation to indicate what the medical alternatives are in order to have a decision made by informed consent, but insofar as moral values or principles are involved in decisions, they are not within their professional sphere.

An outsider might ask what is meant by authority. He might suggest that surely it is not the responsibility (or at least nor his primary responsibility) or the role of the physician to make moral decisions, and certainly not to enforce his decisions on others. Would he be violating his role if he did something less determinative than that, namely, in his counseling indicate to them what some of the moral considerations might be in choosing between medical alternatives? In our case the answer seems to be yes. If the principals desire moral counseling, they have the freedom to seek it from whomsoever they will. In his professional role he acknowledges that the recognition of the moral autonomy of the principals also assumes their moral self-sufficiency, that is, their capacities to make sound moral decisions without interference on his part, or the part of any other persons except insofar as the principals themselves seek such counsel. Indeed, in this case a good deal is made of the knowledgeabilty of the mother particularly, and this assumes that she is morally, as well as medically, knowledgeable. Or, if she is not, it is still not the physician's business to be her moral counselor.

The physicians also assumed in this case that the moral autonomy of the parents took precedence over the positive law. At least they felt no obligation to take recourse to the courts to save the life of this infant. On that issue we will reflect more when we discuss the legal point of reference.

Another sort of defense might be made. In the order of society, decisions should be left to the most intimate and smallest social unit involved. That is the right of such a unit, since the interposition of outside authority would be an infringement of its freedom. Also, since the family has to live with the consequences of the decision, it is the right of the parents to determine which potential consequences they find most desirable. The state, or the medical profession, has no right to interfere with the freedom of choice of the family. Again, in a formal way, the argument is familiar; the state has no right to interfere with the determination of what a woman wishes to do with her body, and thus antiabortion laws are infringements of her freedom. The determination of whether an infant shall be kept alive is simply an extension of the sphere of autonomy properly belonging to the smallest social unit involved.

In all the argument for moral autonomy, the medical fact that the infant is alive and can be kept alive does not make a crucial difference. The defense of the decision would have to be made in this way: if one grants moral autonomy to mothers to determine whether they will bring a fetus to birth, it is logical to assume that one will grant the same autonomy after birth, at least in instances where the infant is abnormal.

We have noted in our constellation of factors that the desire of the parents was a necessary but not a sufficient condition for the decisions of the physicians. If the infant had not been mongoloid, the physicians would not have so readily acquiesced to the parents' desires. Thus, we need to turn to the second necessary condition.

The second crucial point is that the infant was a mongoloid. The physicians would not have acceded to the parents' request as readily if the child had been normal; the parents would have authorized the surgical procedure if the child had been normal. Not every sort of abnormality would have led to the same decision on the part of the physicians. Their appeal was to the consequences of the abnormality of mongolism: the child would be a burden financially and emotionally to the parents. Since every child, regardless of his capacities for intelligent action, is a financial burden, and at least at times an emotional burden, it is clear that the physicians believed that the quantity or degree of burden in this case would exceed any benefits that might be forthcoming if the child were permitted to live. One can infer that a principle was operative, namely, that mongoloid infants have no inherent right to life; their right to life is conditional upon the willingness of their parents to accept them and care for them.

Previously we developed some of the reasons why a mongoloid infant was judged undesirable. Some of the same appeals to consequences entered into the decisions of the physicians. If we are to seek to develop reasons why the decisions might be judged to be morally correct, we must examine another point, namely, the operating definition of "abnormal" or "defective." There is no dissent to the medical judgment that the infant was mongoloid, though precise judgments about the seriousness of the child's defect were not possible at birth.

Our intention is to find as precisely as possible what principles or values might be invoked to claim that the "defectiveness" was sufficient to warrant not sustaining the life of this infant. As a procedure, we will begin with the most general appeals that might have been made to defend the physician's decision in this case. The most general principle would be that any infant who has any empirically verifiable degree of defect at birth has no right to life. No one would apply such a principle. Less general would be that all infants who are carriers of a genetic defect that would have potentially bad consequences for future generations have no right to life. A hemophiliac carrier would be a case in point. This principle would not be applicable, even if were invoked with approval, in this case.

Are the physicians prepared to claim that all genetically "abnormal" infants have no claim to life? I find no evidence that they would. Are they prepared to say that where the genetic abnormality affects the capacity for "happiness" the infant has no right to live? Such an appeal was not made in this case. It appears that "normal" in this case has reference to a capacity for a certain degree of intelligence.

A presumably detectable physical norm now functions as a norm in a moral sense, or as an ideal. The ideal cannot be specified in precise terms, but there is a vague judgment about the outer limits beyond which an infant is judged to be excessively far from the norm or ideal to deserve sustenance. Again, we come to the crucial role of an obvious sign of the lack of capacity for intelligence of a certain measurable sort in judging a defect to be intolerable. A further justification of this is made by an appeal to accepted social values, at least among middle- and upper-class persons in our society. Our society values intelligence; that value becomes the ideal norm from which abnormality or deficiencies are measured. Since the infant is judged not to be able to develop into an intelligent human being (and do all that "normal" intelligence enables a human being to do), his life is of insufficient value to override the desires of the parents not to have a retarded child.

Without specification of the limits to the sorts of cases to which it could be applied, the physicians would probably not wish to defend the notion that the values of a society determine the right to life. To do so would require that there be clear knowledge of who is valued in our society (we also value aggressive people, loving people, physically strong people, etc.), and in turn a procedure by which capacities for such qualities could be determined in infancy so that precise judgments could be made about what lives should be sustained. Some members of our society do not value black people; blackness would obviously be an insufficient basis for letting an infant die. Thus, in defense of their decision the physicians would have to appeal to "values generally held in our society." This creates a different problem of quantification: what percentage of dissent would count to deny a "general" holding of a value? They would also have to designate the limits to changes in socially held values beyond which they would not consent. If the parents belonged to a subculture that valued blue eyes more than it valued intelligence, and if they expressed a desire not to have a child because it had hazel eyes, the problem of the intestinal blockage would not have been a sufficient condition to refrain from the surgical procedure.

In sum, the ideal norm of the human that makes a difference in judging whether an infant has the right to life in this case is "the capacity for normal intelligence." For the good of the infant, for the sake of avoiding difficulties for the parents, and for the good of society, a significant deviation from normal intelligence, coupled with the appropriate parental desire, is sufficient to permit the infant to die.

A third point of reference was the law. The civil law and the courts figure in the decisions at two points. First, the physicians felt no obligation to seek a court order to save the life of the infant if the parents did not want it. Several possible inferences might be drawn from this. First, one can infer that the infant had no legal right to life; his legal right is conditional upon parental desires. Second, as indicated in the interviews, the physicians believed that the court would not insist upon the surgical procedure to save the infant since it was a mongoloid. Parental desires would override legal rights in such a case. And third (an explicit statement by the physician), if the infant's life had been saved as a result of a court order, there were doubts that it would have been "accepted" by the parents. Here is an implicit appeal to potential consequences: it is not beneficial for a child to be raised by parents who do not "accept" him. The assumption is that they could not change their attitudes.

If the infant had a legal right to life, this case presents an interesting instance of conscientious objection to law. The conscientious objector to military service claims that the power of the state to raise armies for the defense of what it judges to be the national interest is one that he conscientiously refrains from sharing. The common good, or the national interest, is not jeopardized by the granting of a special status to the objector because there are enough persons who do not object to man the military services. In this case, however, the function of the law is to protect the rights of individuals to life, and the physician-objector is claiming that he is under no obligation to seek the support of the legal system to sustain life even when he knows that it could be sustained. The evidence he has in hand (the parental desire and the diagnosis of mongolism) presumably provides sufficient moral grounds for his not complying with the law. From the standpoint of ethics, an appeal could be made to conscientious objection. If, however, the appropriate law does not qualify its claims in such a way as to *(a)* permit its nonapplicability in this case or *(b)* provide for exemption on grounds of conscientious objection, the objector is presumably willing to accept the consequences for his conscientious decision. This would be morally appropriate. The physician believed that the court would not insist on saving the infant's life, and thus he foresaw no great jeopardy to himself in following conscience rather than the law.

The second point at which the law figures is in the determination of how the infant should die. The decision not to induce death was made in part in the face of the illegality of overt euthanasia (in part, only, since also the hospital staff would "feel uncomfortable" about hastening the death). Once the end or purpose of action (or inaction) was judged to be morally justified, and judged likely to be free from legal censure, the physicians still felt obliged to achieve that purpose within means that would not be subject to legal sanctions. One can only speculate whether the physicians believed that a court that would not order an infant's life to be saved would in turn censure them for overtly taking the life, or whether the uncomfortable feelings of the hospital staff were more crucial in their decision. Their course of decisions could be interpreted as at one point not involving obligation to take recourse to the courts and at the other scrupulously obeying the law. It should be noted, however, that there is consistency of action on their part; in neither instance did they intervene in what was the "natural" course of developments. The moral justification to fail to intervene in the second moment had to be different from that in the first. In the first it provides the reasons for not saving a life; in the second, for not taking a life. This leads to the last aspect of the decisions of the physicians that I noted, namely, that choices were made between ordinary and extraordinary means of action.

There is no evidence in the interviews that the language of ordinary and extraordinary means of action was part of the vocabulary of the medical staff. It is, however, an honored and useful distinction in Catholic moral theology as it applies to medical care. The principle is that a physician is under no obligation to use extraordinary means to sustain life. The difficulty in the application of the principle is the choice of what falls under ordinary and what under extraordinary means. Under one set of circumstances a procedure may be judged ordinary, and under another extraordinary. The surgery required to remove the bowel obstruction in the infant was on the whole an ordinary procedure; there were no experimental aspects to it, and there were no unusual risks to the infant's life in having it done. If the infant had had no other genetic defects, there would have been no question about using it. The physicians could make a case that when the other defect was mongolism, the procedure would be an extraordinary one. The context of the judgment about ordinary and extraordinary was a wider one than the degree of risk to the life of the patient from surgery. It included his other defect, the desires of the family, the potential costs to the family and society, etc. No moralists, to my knowledge, would hold them culpable if the infant were so deformed that he would be labeled (nontechnically) a monstrosity. To heroically maintain the life of a monstrosity as long as one could would be most extraordinary. Thus, we return to whether the fact of mongolism and its consequences is a sufficient justification to judge the lifesaving procedure to be extraordinary in this instance. The physicians would argue that it is.

The infant was left to die with a minimum of care. No extraordinary means were used to maintain its life once the decision not to operate had been made. Was it extraordinary not to use even ordinary procedures to maintain the life of the infant once the decision not to operate had been made? The judgment clearly was in the negative. To do so would be to prolong a life that would not be saved in any case. At that point the infant was in a class of terminal patients, and the same justifications used for not prolonging the life of a terminal patient would apply here. Patients have a right to die, and physicians are under no moral obligation to sustain their lives when it is clear that they will not live for long. The crucial difference between a terminal cancer patient and this infant is that in the situation of the former, all procedures which might prolong life for a goodly length of time are likely to have been exhausted. In the case of the infant, the logic of obligations to terminal patients takes its course as a result of a decision not to act at all.

To induce death by some overt action is an extraordinary procedure. To justify overt action would require a justification of euthanasia. This case would be a good one from which to explore euthanasia from a moral point of view. Once a decision is made not to engage in a life-sustaining and lifesaving procedure, has not the crucial corner been turned? If that is a reasonable and moral thing to do, on what grounds would one argue that it is wrong to hasten death? Most obviously it is still illegal to do it, and next most obviously people have sensitive feelings about taking life. Further, it goes against the grain of the fundamental vocation of the medical profession to maintain life. But, of course, the decision not to operate also goes against that grain. If the first decision was justifiable, why was it not justifiable to hasten the death of the infant? We can only assume at this point traditional arguments against euthanasia would have been made.

The Decisions of the Nurses

The nurses, as the interviews indicated, are most important for their expressions of feelings, moral sensibilities, and frustrations. They demonstrate the importance of deeply held moral convictions and of profound compassion in determining human responses to ambiguous circumstances. If they had not known that the infant could have survived, the depth of their frustrations and feelings would have not been so great. Feelings they would have had, but they would have been compassion for an infant bound to die. The actual range of decision for them was clearly circumscribed by the role definitions in the medical professions; it was their duty to carry out the orders of the physicians. Even if they conscientiously believed that the orders they were executing were immoral, they could not radically reverse the course of events; they could not perform the required surgery. It was their lot to be the immediate participants in a sad event but to be powerless to alter its course.

It would be instructive to explore the reasons why the nurses felt frustrated, were deeply affected by their duties in this case. Moral convictions have their impact upon the feelings of persons as well as upon their rational decisions. A profound sense of vocation to relieve suffering and to preserve life no doubt lies behind their responses, as does a conviction about the sanctity of human life. For our purposes, however, we shall leave them with the observation that they are the instruments of the orders of the physicians. They have no right of conscientious objection, at least not in this set of circumstances.

Before turning to another evaluative description of the case, it is important to reiterate what was said in the beginning. The decisions by the principals were conscientious ones. The parents anguished. The physicians were informed by a sense of compassion in their consent to the parents' wishes; they did not wish to be party to potential suffering that was avoidable. Indeed, in the way in which they formulated the dilemma, they did what was reasonable to do. They chose the way of least possible suffering to the fewest persons over a long range of time, with one exception, namely, not taking the infant's life. By describing the dilemma from a somewhat different set of values, or giving different weight to different factors, another course of action would have been reasonable, and justified. The issue, it seems to me, is at the level of what is to be valued more highly, for one's very understanding of the problems he must solve are deeply affected by what one values most.

The Dilemma from a Different Moral Point of View

Wallace Stevens wrote in poetic form a subtle account of "Thirteen Ways of Looking at a Blackbird." Perhaps there are 13 ways of looking at this medical case. I shall attempt to look at it from only one more way. By describing the dilemma from a perspective that gives a different weight to some of the considerations that we have already exposed, one has a different picture, and different conclusions are called for. The moral integrity of any of the original participants is not challenged, not because of a radical relativism that says they have their points of view and I have mine, but out of respect for their conscientiousness. For several reasons, however, more consideration ought to have been given to two points. A difference in evaluative judgments would have made a difference of life or death for the infant, depending upon: (1) whether what one ought to do is determined by what one desires to do and (2) whether a mongoloid infant has a claim to life.

To restate the dilemma once again: If the parents had "desired" the mongoloid infant, the surgeons would have performed the operation that would have saved its life. If the infant had had a bowel obstruction that could be taken care of by an ordinary medical procedure, but had not been a mongoloid, the physicians would probably have insisted that the operation be performed.

Thus, one can recast the moral dilemma by giving a different weight to two things: the desires of the parents and the value or rights of a mongoloid infant. If the parents and the physicians believed strongly that there are things one ought to do even when one has no immediate positive feelings about doing them, no immediate strong desire to do them, the picture would have been different. If the parents and physicians believed that mongoloid children have intrinsic value, or have a right to life, or if they believed that mongolism is not sufficiently deviant from what is normatively human to merit death, the picture would have been different.

Thus, we can redraw the picture. To be sure, the parents are ambiguous about their feelings for a mongoloid infant, since it is normal to desire a normal infant rather than an abnormal infant. But (to avoid a discussion of abortion at this point) once an infant is born its independent existence provides independent value in itself, and those who brought it into being and those professionally responsible for its care have an obligation to sustain its life regardless of their negative or ambiguous feelings toward it. This probably would have been acknowledged by all concerned if the infant had not been mongoloid. For example, if the pregnancy had been accidental, and in this sense the child was not desired, and the infant had been normal, no one would have denied its right to exist once it was born, though some would while still *in utero,* and thus would have sought an abortion. If the mother refused to accept accountability for the infant, alternative means of caring for it would have been explored.

To be sure, a mongoloid infant is genetically defective, and raising and caring for it put burdens on the parents, the family, and the state beyond the burdens required to raise a normal infant. But a mongoloid infant is human, and thus has the intrinsic value of humanity and the rights of a human being. Further, given proper care, it can reach a point of significant fulfillment of its limited potentialities; it is capable of loving and responding to love; it is capable of realizing happiness; it can be trained to accept responsibility for itself within its capacities. Thus, the physicians and parents have an obligation to use all ordinary means to preserve its life. Indeed, the humanity of mentally defective children is recognized in our society by the fact that we do not permit their extermination and do have policies which provide, all too inadequately, for their care and nurture.

If our case had been interpreted in the light of moral beliefs that inform the previous two paragraphs, the only reasonable conclusion would be that the surgery ought to have been done.

The grounds for assigning the weights I have to these crucial points can be examined. First, with reference simply to common experience, we all have obligations to others, that are not contingent upon our immediate desires. When the registrar of my university indicates that senior grades have to be in by May 21, I have an obligation to read the exams, term papers, and senior essays in time to report the grades, regardless of my negative feelings toward those tasks or my preference to be doing something else. I have an obligation to my students, and to the university through its registrar, which I accepted when I assumed the social role of an instructor. The students have a claim on me; they have a right to expect me to fulfill my obligations to them and to the university. I might be excused from the obligation if I suddenly become too ill to fulfill it; my incapacity to fulfill it would be a temporarily excusing condition. But negative feelings toward that job, or toward my students, or a preference for writing a paper of my own at that time, would not constitute excusing conditions. I must consider, in determining what I do, the relationships that I have with others and the claims they have on me by virtue of those relationships.

In contrast to this case, it might be said that I have a contractual obligation to the university into which I freely entered. The situation of the parents is not the same. They have no legal contractual relationship with the infant, and thus their desires are not bound by obligations. Closer to their circumstances, then, might be other family relationships. I would argue that the fact that we brought our children into being lays a moral obligation on my wife and me to sustain and care for them to the best of our ability. They did not choose to be; and their very being is dependent, both causally and in other ways, upon us. In the relationships of dependence, there is a claim of them over against us. To be sure, it is a claim that also has its rewards and that we desire to fulfill within a relationship of love. But until they have reached an age when they can accept full accountability (or fuller accountability) for themselves, they have claims upon us by virtue of our being their parents, even when meeting those claims is to us financially costly, emotionally distressing, and in other ways not immediately desirable. Their claims are independent of our desires to fulfill them. Particular claims they might make can justifiably be turned down, and others can be negotiated, but the claim against us for their physical sustenance constitutes a moral obligation that we have to meet. That obligation is not conditioned by their IQ scores, whether they have cleft palates or perfectly formed faces, whether they are obedient or irritatingly independent, whether they are irritatingly obedient and passive or laudably self-determining. It is not conditioned by any predictions that might be made about whether they will become the persons we might desire that they become. The infant in our case has the same sort of claim, and thus the parents have a moral obligation to use all ordinary means to saves its life.

An objection might be made. Many of my fellow Christians would say that the obligation of the parents was to do that which is loving toward the infant. Not keeping the child alive was the loving thing to do with reference both to its interests and to the interests of the other members of the family. To respond to the objection, one needs first to establish the spongy character of the words "love" or "loving." They can absorb almost anything. Next one asks whether the loving character of an act is determined by feelings or by motives, or whether it is also judged by what is done. It is clear that I would argue for the latter. Indeed, the minimal conditions of a loving relationship include respect for the other, and certainly for the other's presumption of a right to live. I would, however, primarily make the case that the relationship of dependence grounds the claim, whether or not one feels loving toward the other.

The dependence relationship holds for the physicians as well as the parents in this case. The child's life depended utterly upon the capacity of the physicians to sustain it. The fact that an infant cannot articulate his claim is irrelevant. Physicians will struggle to save the life of a person who has attempted to commit suicide even when the patient might be in such a drugged condition that he cannot express his desire — a desire expressed already in his effort to take his life and overridden by the physician's action to save it. The claim of human life for preservation, even when such a person indicates a will not to live, presents a moral obligation to those who have the capacity to save it.

A different line of argument might be taken. If the decisions made were as reliant upon the desires of the parents as they appear to be, which is to say, if desire had a crucial role, what about the desire of the infant? The infant could not give informed consent to the nonintervention. One can hypothesize that every infant desires to live, and that even a defective child is likely to desire life rather than death when it reaches an age at which its desires can be articulated. Even if the right to live is contingent upon a desire, we can infer that the infant's desire would be for life. As a human being, he would have that desire, and thus it would constitute a claim on those whom he is dependent to fulfill it.

I have tried to make a persuasive case to indicate why the claim of the infant constitutes a moral obligation on the parents and the physicians to keep the child alive. The intrinsic value or rights of a human being are not qualified by any given person's intelligence or capacities for productivity, potential consequences of the sort that burden others. Rather, they are constituted by the very existence of the human being as one who is related to others and dependent upon others for his existence. The presumption is always in favor of sustaining life through ordinary means; the desires of persons that run counter to that presumption are not sufficient conditions for abrogating that right.

The power to determine whether the infant shall live or die is in the hands of others. Does the existence of such power carry with it the moral right to such determination? Long history of moral experience indicates not only that arguments have consistently been made against the judgment that the capacity to do something constitutes a right to do it, or put in more familiar terms, that might makes right. It also indicates that in historical situations where persons have claimed the right to determine who shall live because they have the power to do so, the consequences have hardly been beneficial to mankind. This, one acknowledges, is a "wedge" argument or a "camel's nose under the tent" argument. As such, its limits are clear. Given a culture in which humane values are regnant, it is not likely that the establishment of a principle that some persons under some circumstances claim the right to determine whether others shall live will be transformed into the principle that the right of a person to live is dependent upon his having the qualities approved by those who have the capacity to sustain or take his life. Yet while recognizing the sociological and historical limitations that exist in a humane society, one still must recognize the significance of a precedent. To cite an absurd example, what would happen if we lived in a society in which the existence of hazel eyes was considered a genetic defect by parents and physicians? The absurdity lies in the fact that no intelligent person would consider hazel eyes a genetic defect; the boundaries around the word *defect* are drawn by evidences better than eye color. But the precedent in principle remains; when one has established that the capacity to determine who shall live carries with it the right to determine who shall live, the line of discussion has shifted from a sharp presumption (of the right of all humans to live) to the softer, spongier determination of the qualities whose value will be determinative.

Often we cannot avoid using qualities and potential consequences in the determination of what might be justifiable exceptions to the presumption of the right to life on the part of any infant — indeed, any person. No moralist would insist that the physicians have an obligation to sustain the life of matter born from human parents that is judged to be a "monstrosity." Such divergence from the "normal" qualities presents no problem, and potential consequences for the continued existence surely enter into the decision. The physicians in our case believed that in the absence of a desire for the child on the part of the parents, mongolism was sufficiently removed from an ideal norm of the human that the infant had no overriding claim on them. We are in a sponge. Why would I draw the line on a different side of mongolism than the physicians did? While reasons can be given, one must recognize that there are intuitive elements, grounded in beliefs and profound feelings, that enter into particular judgments of this sort. I am not prepared to say that my respect for human life is "deeper," "profounder," or "stronger" than theirs. I am prepared to say that the way in which, and the reasons why, I respect life orient my judgment toward the other side of mongolism than theirs did.

First, the value that intelligence was given in this instance appears to me to be simplistic. Not all intelligent persons are socially commendable (choosing socially held values as the point of reference because one of the physicians did). Also, many persons of limited intelligence do things that are socially commendable, if only minimally providing the occasion for the expression of profound human affection and sympathy. There are many things we value about human life; that the assumption that one of them is the *sine qua non*, the necessary and sufficient condition for a life to be valued at all, oversimplifies human experience. If there is a *sine qua non*, it is physical life itself, for apart from it, all potentiality of providing benefits for oneself or for others is impossible. There are occasions on which other things are judged to be more valuable than physical life itself; we probably all would admire the person whose life is martyred for the sake of saving others. But the qualities or capacities we value exist in bundles, and not each as overriding in itself. The capacity for self-determination is valued, and on certain occasions we judge that it is worth dying, or taking life, for the sake of removing repressive limits imposed upon persons in that respect. But many free, self-determining persons are not very happy; indeed, often their anxiety increases with the enlargement of the range of things they must and can determine for themselves. Would we value a person exclusively because he is happy? Probably not, partly because his happiness has at least a mildly contagious effect on some other persons, and thus we value him because he makes others happy as well. To make one quality we value (short of physical life itself, and there are exceptions) determinative over all other qualities is to impoverish the richness and variety of human life. When we must use the sponge of qualities to determine exceptions to the presumption of the right to physical life, we need to face their variety, their complexity, the abrasiveness of one against the other, in the determination of action. In this case the potentialities of a mongoloid for satisfaction in life, for fulfilling his limited capacities, for happiness, for providing the occasions of meaningful (sometimes distressing and sometimes joyful) experience for others are sufficient so that no exception to the right to life should be made. Put differently, the anguish, suffering, embarrassment, expenses of family and state (I support the need for revision of social policy and practice) are not sufficiently negative to warrant that a mongoloid's life not be sustained by ordinary procedures.

Second, and harder to make persuasive, is that my view of human existence leads to a different assessment of the significance of suffering than appears to be operative in this case. The best argument to be made in support of the course of decisions as they occurred is that in the judgment of the principals involved, they were able to avoid more suffering and other costs for more people over a longer range of time than could have been avoided if the infant's life had been saved. To suggest a different evaluation of suffering is not to suggest that suffering is an unmitigated good, or that the acceptance of suffering when it could be avoided is a strategy that ought to be adopted for the good life, individually and collectively. Surely it is prudent and morally justifiable to avoid suffering if possible under most normal circumstances of life. But two questions would help to designate where a difference of opinion between myself and the principles in our drama can be located. One is, At what cost to others is it justifiable to avoid suffering for ourselves? On the basis of my previous exposition, I would argue that in this instance the avoidance of potential suffering at the cost of that life was not warranted. The moral claims of others upon me often involve emotional and financial stress, but that stress is not sufficient to warrant my ignoring the claims. The moral and legal claim of the government to the right to raise armies in defense of the national interest involves inconvenience, suffering, and even death for many; yet the fact that meeting that claim will cause an individual suffering is not sufficient ground to give conscientious objection. Indeed, we normally honor those who assume suffering for the sake of benefits to others.

The second question is, Does the suffering in prospect appear to be bearable for those who have to suffer? We recognize that the term "bearable" is a slippery slope and that fixing an answer to this question involves judgments that are always hypothetical. If, however, each person has a moral right to avoid all bearable inconvenience or suffering that appears to run counter to his immediate or long-range self-interest, there are many things necessary for the good of other individuals and for the common good that would not get done. In our case, there appear to be no evidences that the parents with assistance from other institutions would necessarily find the raising of a mongoloid child to bring suffering that they could not tolerate. Perhaps there is justifying evidence to which I do not have access, such as the possibility that the mother would be subject to severe mental illness if she had to take care of the child. But from the information I received, no convincing case could be made that the demands of raising the child would present intolerable and unbearable suffering to the family. That it would create greater anguish, greater inconvenience, and greater demands than raising a normal child would is clear. But that meeting these demands would cause greater suffering to this family than it does to thousands of others who raise mongoloid children seems not to be the case.

Finally, my view, grounded ultimately in religious convictions as well as moral beliefs, is that to be human is to have a vocation, a calling, and the calling of each of us is "to be for others" at least as much as "to be for ourselves." The weight that one places on "being for others" makes a difference in one's fundamental orientation toward all of his relationships, particularly when they conflict with his immediate self-interest. In the Torah we have that great commandment, rendered in the New English Bible as "you shall love your neighbor as a man like yourself" (Lev. 19:18). It is reiterated in the records we have of the words of Jesus, "Love your neighbor as yourself" (Matt. 22:39, and several other places). Saint Paul makes the point even stronger at one point: "Each of you must regard, not his own interests, but the other man's" (1 Cor. 10:24 NEB). And finally, the minimalist saying accredited both to Rabbi Hillel and to Jesus in different forms, "Do unto others as you would have others do unto you."

The point of the biblical citations is not to take recourse to dogmatic religious authority, as if these sayings come unmediated from the ultimate power and orderer of life. The point is to indicate a central trust in Judaism and Christianity which has nourished and sustained a fundamental moral outlook, namely, that we are "to be for others" at least as much as we are "to be for ourselves." The fact that this outlook has not been adhered to consistently by those who professed it does not count against it. It remains a vocation, a calling, a moral ideal, if not a moral obligation. The statement of such an outlook does not resolve all the particular problems of medical histories such as this one, but it shapes a bias, gives a weight, toward the well-being of the other against inconvenience or cost to oneself. In this case, I believe that all the rational inferences to be drawn from it, and all the emotive power that this calling evokes, lead to the conclusion that the ordinary surgical procedure should have been done, and the mongoloid infant's life saved.

93 The Death of Infant Doe: Jesus and the Neonates

Allen Verhey

I imagine it was a hot and sunny day, the kind of day when kids seem to have such boundless energy and grownups seem to wilt. The disciples, I suppose, were quite glad for the rest; at least they were a little peevish when women and children threatened to interrupt it. They rebuked them, the story in Mark 10 says. "Can't you see Jesus is an important person? What business do you have bothering him? Get back to your ovens, women! Return to your toys, children! Stay out of our way."

The disciples' response was conventional enough; surely understandable. Women and children were just not that important. They were numbered among the heathen and illiterate, with sinners and those who do not know the law, with slaves and property. They were not numbered at all when the members of the synagogue were counted. You needed ten *adult males* for a synagogue. Nine plus all the women and children of Galilee would not make a synagogue. Women and children just did not count for much. The disciples knew that and told them to go away.

Jesus gets angry too, but not with the women, not with the children. He gets angry with the disciples. He turns the conventional rules of pomp and protocol upside down. Those who don't count do count with him; he makes the last first! When will his disciples ever learn that? He says to them, "Let the children come to me. Do not hinder them.

From *The Reformed Journal* 32 (June 1982): 10-15. Used by permission. Revised by the author for this volume.

To them belongs the kingdom of God." The disciples must have been more than a little dumbfounded. Other strange behavior of this Galilean teacher had hardly prepared them for this.

There must have been babies there, and more than one dirty diaper, and Jesus takes them in his arms. There must have been toddlers and youngsters, curious and energetic, crying occasionally and interrupting often. "Women are meant to deal with them," the disciples thought, but Jesus blesses them. There must have been boys and girls, taking a break from playing tag and catch, and some who stood on the sidelines because of a limp or a disease or something else that made them unwelcome in the game, and Jesus lays his hands on them.

And as though all this is not enough, Jesus says, "If you want to enter the kingdom become like one of these children." People have speculated endlessly about how we are supposed to be like children. It is their *trust* some say; their *dependence* others say; their *joy* still others say; or their *simplicity.* There is perhaps some truth in each of those comparisons, but I really think they are beside the point. Jesus says in other places, "If any would be first of all, let him be last of all and the servant of all." And that's what he says here too. "Become like one of these children" means simply "become last — for such are first with me." That's the shocking thing. Jesus exalts the humble and humbles the exalted. He makes the last first. Those who don't count count with him. He blesses kids; dirty-diapered, sweaty, silly, obnoxious kids. He rebukes the disciples, impressed with their own importance and conventional prestige. And he makes it clear that to be his disciple, to welcome the kingdom, will mean to welcome, to serve and to help, these little children. Who is greatest in the kingdom? These little children and those who bless and serve them.

Soon after the death and resurrection of Jesus, that story was being told again and again in the young church. Pentecost had convinced the people of the church that Jesus continued to abide with them and that he continued to address them in their memory of what he had once said or done. Even as the church awaited the new creation, the redemption of their bodies and their adoption as sons, as Paul says, it was constantly informed and reformed by the stories about Jesus. Imagine, for example, Peter telling the story to settle the question of whether the children of believing parents should be baptized. Or Andrew telling the story in a slightly different way to exhort his hearers to a childlike faith. Or again, imagine some unknown preacher telling the story to protest the neglect and abandonment of children that was practiced in the Roman empire. The story found its way finally into Mark's gospel alongside sayings about marriage and riches to provide guidance for a Christian household.

The story continues to be told in the churches, of course. It is told in countless stained glass windows. We have all seen them. The only thing wrong with these windows is that the kids are too angelic. There are no runny noses or bruised knees or imperfections to be found in the stained glass representations of the story. The story has indeed become so familiar that we have to make an effort to stop and think about it, to contemplate what it would mean to make this story our story, to be informed and reformed by this story. I invite you to make that effort, specifically to think about what this story might mean for our care of neonates.

To do this there is another story that I want you to think about. It is a familiar story, too, the story of Infant Doe. It happened in Bloomington in 1982. Now Bloomington is a pleasant little city set in the lovely hills of southern Indiana. Bloomington Hospital is typical of hospitals in pleasant little cities; the daily human events of giving birth, suffering, and dying are attended to with the ordinary measure of professional competence and compassion. It seems unlikely that the story of birth, suffering, and death of a baby in Bloomington would capture national attention.

On April 9, 1982, a boy was born in Bloomington Hospital with Down's syndrome and esophageal atresia. Down's syndrome is a fairly common genetic defect which causes varying degrees of mental retardation and physical deformity. Esophageal atresia is a malformation of the esophagus, so that food taken orally cannot enter the stomach and instead causes choking.

The parents of this baby refused to consent to the surgical procedure necessary to correct the esophageal atresia. The obstetrician who had initially presented such "benign neglect" as one of the medical options supported the parents in that decision. A pediatrician who had been consulted to confirm the diagnosis dissented from such a course of "treatment." The Circuit Court in Bloomington and subsequently the Indiana Supreme Court in Indianapolis refused to override the parents' decision and to order the surgery to correct the esophagus of "Infant Doe." The baby lay in Bloomington Hospital for six days until his starving yielded to his death on April 15.

The obstetrician and the pediatrician disagreed not only about the recommended treatment but also about the chances for successful esophageal surgery, about the likelihood of other serious physical problems, and about the prognosis of retardation. The obstetrician, in presenting the options to the parents, said that the chances for successful surgery were about fifty-fifty, that other physical defects, including congenital heart disease, would subsequently have to be surgically corrected, and that the child would certainly be severely retarded. The pediatrician insisted that the likelihood of successful surgery was more like ninety percent, that there was no evidence of congenital heart disease, and that it was impossible to determine the severity of the retardation Infant Doe would have. The conflicting medical opinions and recommendations weighed heavily in the courts' decisions not to intervene, not to play either doctor or parent to the child.

The courts' hesitancy to pretend to either medical competence or parental compassion can be appreciated (especially by those schooled in something called "sphere sovereignty"). Moreover, the competence of the doctors and the compassion of the parents were widely attested. Still, the medical recommendation of the obstetrician and the decisions by the parents and by the justices were morally wrong — not just tragic, but wrong.

Decisions are tragic when goods come into conflict, when any decision brings in its train some wrong. This was not such a decision. The right decision would have been to do the surgery. I will undertake to defend that judgment in ways that are standard in medical ethics, in ways that rely on "impartial rationality" to formulate judgments and to solve dilemmas. One need not be a Christian to see that the decision not to treat Infant Doe was wrong. But I will also undertake to show that impartial rationality is inadequate, that it can provide only a minimal account of morality, and that when its minimalism is not acknowledged it can distort the moral life. Finally, because the conventional approach is inadequate, I will undertake another approach, a candidly Christian approach, an approach which owns the Christian story, including the story of Jesus and the children, as *our* story also in cases like Infant Doe's.

First, then, one need not be a Christian to see that the right decision would have been to perform the surgery to correct the esophagus so that Infant Doe could be fed. The impartial rational justification for saying this might be provided in a number of different ways. The most telling in my view is that if a "normal" child had been born with esophageal atresia, the surgery would have been performed — even if the obstetrician were right about the risks and the additional physical problems. The reason for "treating" Infant Doe differently was an irrelevant one, Infant Doe's Down's syndrome. (Furthermore, the obstetrician was simply wrong about the ability to predict so early the extent of retardation caused by Down's syndrome.)

Suppose that on April 9 two other babies were born in Bloomington. Suppose "Infant Smith" was born without Down's syndrome but with esophageal atresia. The consent to operate would surely have been given or ordered, and Infant Smith would probably be alive today. Suppose "Infant Jones" was born with Down's syndrome but without any life-threatening malformations of the esophagus. No consent to operate would have been necessary, and Infant Jones would probably be alive today. The difference between Infant Doe and Infant Smith, the difference between life and death, is that Infant Doe had Down's syndrome, nothing else. The difference between Infant Doe and Infant Jones, also the difference between life and death, is that Infant Doe had esophageal atresia in addition to Down's syndrome. If we ought to preserve and cherish the life of Infants Smith and Jones, then we ought also to have preserved and cherished the life of Infant Doe. The differences among these infants are irrelevant to the obligation to sustain their lives and to nurture their bodies and spirits.

This is not to deny that different conditions among infants may indicate different treatments or even in some cases the cessation of treatment. If a condition is terminal and if treatment would only prolong the child's dying and exacerbate his or her suffering, then treatment is not indicated. Anencephalic newborns are a clear case of legitimate neglect. There are tragic cases where a child's suffering from a disease and from the treatment of the disease is so profound as to put it outside the reach of human caring, let alone human curing. Such, however, was not the case with Infant Doe or other Down's syndrome youngsters. Down's syndrome is not a terminal condition; and if people who have it suffer more, it is not because surgery pains them more but because "normal" people can be cruel and spiteful. A Down's child can experience and delight in the reach and touch of human caring.

The neglect of Infant Doe was morally wrong. His death was caused by "natural causes," to be sure, but it was both possible and obligatory to interfere with those "natural causes." If a lifeguard neglected a drowning swimmer whom he recognized as his competition for his lover's affection, we would say he did wrong. That the drowned man died of "natural causes" would not prevent us from seeing the wrong done to him — or from invoking the category "murder." If the same lifeguard neglected a drowning wader whom he recognized as an infant with Down's syndrome, we should also say he did wrong. That the infant died of "natural causes" should not prevent us from seeing the wrong done to him — or from invoking the category "murder."

Someone may argue that "lifeguard" is a well-defined role with specific responsibilities and a tradition involving certain technical skills and moral virtues, and that the obligation to rescue the swimmer and the wader is really a role-obligation. Two replies might be made to this objection to our analogy. First, we might say that any person — lifeguard or not — who sees an infant stumble and fall face down in the water is obliged to attempt to rescue the child, Down's syndrome or not. The decision to neglect Infant Doe, by analogy, is simply morally wrong. The second reply is to acknowledge that "lifeguard" is a special role with special responsibilities and a tradition, and to insist that "physician" and "parent" are also such roles.

But here impartial rationality begins to fail us, for it tends to reduce role relations — for example, the relation of the doctors to Infant Doe or his parents or the relation of the parents to Infant Doe — to *contractual* arrangements between independent individuals. That is a minimal account of such roles at best, and when its minimalism is not acknowledged, it is an account which distorts the moral life and the covenants of which it is woven. The stance of impartial rationality cannot nurture any moral wisdom about these roles or sustain any moral traditions concerning them. And it is our confusion about these roles, our diminishing sense of a tradition concerning them, that accounts for the failure of a competent physician, compassionate parents, and duly humble justices to make the morally right decision with respect to the care of Infant Doe.

There are other inadequacies in the stance of impartial rationality which bore on the story of Infant Doe. The stance of impartial rationality tends to emphasize the procedural question, the question of who decides, rather than the substantive question of what should be decided. The first and final question in the care of Infant Doe was who should decide, and the answer was consistently that the parents should decide. I am not saying that that question or that answer is wrong, but I am saying that it provides only a minimal account of the moral issues, and that if its minimalism is forgotten or ignored, the moral life and particular moral issues can be distorted. I am saying that a fuller account of morality would focus as well on substantive questions — on the question of *what* should be decided — and on questions of character and virtue — on the question of *what* the person who decides should *be.*

Let me call attention to one other weakness (or inadequacy) of the approach of impartial rationality. This approach requires alienation from ourselves, from our own moral interests and loyalties, from our own histories and communities in order to adopt the impartial point of view. We are asked, nay, obliged, by this approach to view our own projects and passions as though we were objective outside observers. The stories which we own as our own, which provide our lives a narrative and which develop our own character, we are asked by this approach to disown — and for the sake of morality. Now, to be asked to pause occasionally and for the sake of analysis and judgment to view things as impartially as we can is in certain contexts not only legitimate but salutary, but neither physicians nor parents nor any Christian can finally live their moral lives like that with any integrity.

These remarks about the inadequacies of impartial rationality allow us to turn an important corner in this paper. My concern is not merely to make a moral judgment about the care of Infant Doe. The decision not to treat him was wrong, but the more interesting questions — and finally the more important questions, from my point of view — are, How could a competent physician, compassionate parents, and duly humble justices make such a decision? What stories and traditions make sense of such a decision? And how can the Christian story, explicitly the story of Jesus and the children, be brought to bear on such decisions? Can we begin to write a story of Jesus and the neonates? Let us examine briefly the stories and traditions of medicine, of parenting, and of society's attitude toward the handicapped.

The obstetrician, however competent and skillful he may have been, had apparently not been initiated into the tradition of medical care which insists that the practice of medicine involves more than techniques and skills, that it serves and embodies certain intrinsic goods. According to one witness to that tradition, the Hippocratic Oath, the end of medicine is "the benefit of the sick," not some extrinsic good like money or fame or the wishes of the medical "consumer."

The benefit of the sick does not stand as a motive for taking up certain ethically neutral skills. It does not identify an extrinsic good to be accomplished by means of ethically neutral technical means. Rather, the benefit of the sick is the *intrinsic* good of medicine. It governs the practice of medicine and entails certain standards which define medicine as a moral art. Medicine in this tradition intends to heal the sick, to protect and nurture health, to maintain and restore a measure of physical well-being. All the powers of medicine are guided and limited by those ends, and they may not be used to serve alien ends — and death is an alien end. In this sad world death will win its victories finally, but medicine which has identified with the tradition to which the Hippocratic Oath witnesses will not serve death or practice hospitality toward it. This tradition has its own stories, of course, stories about the great Hippocrates initiating his students into the art with an oath that they will indeed practice medicine for "the benefit of the sick," stories about dedicated physicians braving the elements or the opposition to help some sick scoundrel without worrying about the social utility of his patient or of his profession.

Medicine truly in the tradition formed and informed by such stories would and should have stood in the service of Infant Doe, the sick one, the patient, and braved the claims of any and all who wanted him dead. A physician initiated into such a tradition would not present the choice between possible life with Down's syndrome or certain death without esophageal surgery as an option to be contemplated, nor would he or she support the choice of death.

The obstetrician's failure to embody this tradition is symptomatic of our entire society's diminishing appreciation of this view of medicine and a growing confusion about the physician's role. These stories of medicine are today considered naive, sometimes foolish, both by physicians and by society. Properly impressed by modern medicine's technological accomplishments, we are tempted to view medicine as a collection of skills to get what we want, as a value-free enterprise which may be bought and sold to satisfy consumer desires, hired to do the autonomous bidding of the one who pays. Thus, a new model has taken over the understanding of medicine — that omnipresent model of the marketplace, where you get rich by supplying what the buyer wants.

The decision about Infant Doe is understandable, I think, within the marketplace model, but we are justifiably uncomfortable with this way of understanding medicine, for medical skills alone, removed from their original tradition, can make one either a good healer or a crafty murderer. The skills alone cannot provide the wisdom to make a morally right decision. Medicine formed by the model of the marketplace cannot and will not sustain the disposition of care and trust which have defined the characters of doctor and patient in the Hippocratic tradition. On the contrary, the marketplace model will end with medicine in the service of the rich and powerful, while the poor and weak watch and pray.

Infant Doe was too young to pray but not too young to groan with the rest of us "as we wait for . . . the redemption of our bodies" (Rom. 8:23).

That eschatological vision of Christianity — and the entire Christian story, including the story of Jesus and the children — provides a resource to support the fragile Hippocratic tradition of medicine, for it enlists us on the side of life and health in a world where death and evil still apparently reign. It makes us suspicious of and repentant for human capacities for pride and sloth with respect to medical technology. And it calls us to identify with and to serve especially the sick and the poor, the powerless and the despised, and all those who do not measure up to conventional standards.

A note must be added with respect to another community that evidently has the resources to support the fragile tradition of medicine — nurses. The nurses at Bloomington Hospital who were first charged with the "care" of Infant Doe refused to participate in his non-treatment masquerading as care. It violated the ends of nursing as they understood them; it compromised their integrity as members of a nursing community and as heirs of a medical tradition. The immediate consequence of their protest was not great: Infant Doe was simply moved from the nursery to a private room on a surgical floor. But a worthy tradition of medicine was represented and protected by their action. These nurses and others like them are a precious resource if the medical professions and society are to remember and relearn the medical moral tradition.

Our society is also confused about the role of parent. The parents of Infant Doe, however compassionate they may have been, had apparently not been initiated into a tradition of parental care which insists that parents have a duty not only to care *about* their children but to care *for* them, to tend to their physical, emotional, moral, and spiritual needs, not because they "measure-up," but because they are their children.

The parents' failure to represent this tradition is symptomatic of our society's growing confusion about parenting. The tradition has always been challenged by the contrary opinion (now usually unstated) that children are the property of parents to be disposed of as they wish, that children exist for the happiness of parents. Today, however, especially among the compassionate, the tradition is being challenged by a contrary opinion: the view that parents have the awesome responsibility to produce "perfect" children and to assure them a happy and successful life or at least the capacity to attain to and conform to the American ideal of "the good life."

All of us who are parents know we desire our children to be perfect. And all of us who are children know the pain that can be caused by that desire. The responsibility of making perfect children and making children perfect, which is now entering and forming a new model of medicine, will allow — or finally require — the abortion of the unborn who do not meet our standards and the neglect of newborns with diminished capacities to achieve *our* ideal of "the good life." Such a view of parenting will finally reduce our options to a perfect child or a dead child. The Infant Doe decision is understandable, I think, within a model of medicine that requires making perfect children and making children perfect, but that model will not and cannot coexist with the disposition of uncalculating nurturance and basic trust which have defined the relation of parent and child within the Christian story.

It is a commonplace to assert that the institution of the family is in crisis, but it can receive little support from conventional modern moral theory, whether utilitarian or formalist. Both have some power in dealing with our relation with strangers, but neither can deal adequately with the family or sustain it in a time of crisis. Family loyalties are an embarrassment to our calculations of "the greatest happiness for the greatest number" and to our assertions of autonomy. The tradition of the family — and experience in a family — reminds us both that "happiness" is not what it's all about and that we are not as independent, self-sufficient, and autonomous as we sometimes claim.

The fragile tradition of the family, too, may be and should be supported by the Christian story, for the Father's uncalculating nurturance is still the model from which to learn parenting. In the Christian vision the family is seen as a gift and a vocation, providing opportunities to learn to love the *im*perfect, the runny-nosed, and the just plain obnoxious. The story of a Lord who welcomed little children (along with the sick and women and sinners and all others who did not measure up) is a resource for that sort of uncalculating nurturance that can love the child who is there, that would and should insist on the support of others to enable that child to live and — within the limits of his condition and the world's fallenness — to flourish. Infant Doe's groans awaited not only "the redemption of our bodies" but "our adoption as sons." Parental nurturance formed and informed by the story of Jesus and the children would think it curious — at best — to be told that it was *optional* to do the surgery necessary for the child's life and flourishing, as though one has a choice whether to attend to those things necessary for one's child's life and flourishing or to neglect and starve one's child.

The fundamental point is this: although the parents were, by all accounts, compassionate individuals, love is *not* all you need — no matter what popular songs and popular preaching may tell us. Compassion exercised outside the moral tradition of parenting is quite capable of pitying and killing ("mercy-killing," some would call it) those who do not measure up to the perfection we want for and from our children. Joseph Fletcher — whom no one may accuse of not emphasizing love enough — has (in spite of himself) at least one moral rule: "No unwanted child should ever be born." Compassion by itself may be quite capable of formulating another rule: "No unwanted child need be fed."

The Indiana judges were properly hesitant to intervene in the private arena of medical and parental decisions about the appropriate care of "defective neonates" (a neologism to help us forget that it is our children we are talking about). As we have observed, the decision not to treat is sometimes perfectly legitimate and sometimes legitimately controverted. In such cases that decision is best left to the parents and to the advice of physicians. The decision not to treat Infant Doe, however, was immoral; yet the court did not have the resources to call it illegal.

In part the court could not judge the decision illegal because of the simple lack of law governing such cases. But it is also true that the predominant legal theory today, quite self-consciously impartial and rational, emphasizes autonomy and privacy and contract in ways which make it difficult to give legal support to the interdependencies of a family or to the moral traditions of certain roles in which there is no formal contract. I do not deny the moral importance of this legal theory or the pluralism it sponsors and sustains, but I do claim that it can give only a minimal account of the moral life, and also that society and the courts dangerously distort the moral life and endanger our life together when they reduce morality to such legality.

The courts might still have intervened in the case of Infant Doe if not for our confusion about the rights of the retarded and the otherwise handicapped and the rights of others to be free from contact with them. On the one hand, there is physical evidence everywhere — ramps, special bathrooms, barrier-free doorways — of legislation to integrate the handicapped into our social life. On the other hand, many such people remain segregated in institutions acknowledged to be inhumane; and in fact a 1981 Supreme Court decision, *Pennhurst v. Haldemann,* overturned a state court's order to close one such institution and to establish smaller facilities integrated into the state's residential communities.

Integration verses segregation, the rights of a minority versus the rights of a majority not to be confronted with them — it all has a dismally familiar ring. In the case of Infant Doe and others like him, integration would entail welcoming their life without celebrating or romanticizing their condition. It would mean recognizing their right to equal treatment by the law and by medicine. It would mean acknowledging that even if we call them "defective neonates" they remain our children and that attempts to cut off emotional and role relations with them are self-deceptive. And it would mean a willingness to pay the additional taxes necessary to support the care and nurturance of such children. Segregation, on the other hand, would mean a refusal to practice hospitality toward them or toward their lives, seceding from the obligations of community with them, and asserting our independence from them. The duly humble decision of the justices not to rule in the case is understandable in terms of the segregationist positions, and — however unwittingly — it strengthened that tradition for the future.

The Christian story — including the story of Jesus and the children — would support and sustain a tradition of including and welcoming society's outcasts, of serving and helping those who are last. If we keep telling the story of Jesus we may yet learn and live a life of joyful acceptance of people, including little people, who in other stories and other views don't count for much.

A competent physician, compassionate parents, and humble justices failed to make the right decision. The problem was not that the decision was extraordinarily difficult, a real moral dilemma. The problem was not that these people were mean-spirited or evil. The problem was rather that they had — however unwittingly or unconsciously — accepted the wrong models of medicine and parenting and relations with the handicapped. This is not altogether their fault: the traditions of caring and nurture and respect are fragile in contemporary culture. But those traditions have not completely broken down. Witness the statement of the pediatrician, "As a father and physician I can't make the decision to let the baby die." Witness the response of the nurses. Witness the offers to adopt Infant Doe.

Yet the traditions are weak. Babies are not even as fragile as the moral traditions that protect them. And the courts are apparently powerless to preserve those traditions. Infant Doe and all of us are dependent on moral traditions and communities, on covenants which can neither be reduced to contracts nor rendered legally enforceable means to legally enforceable ends.

Infant Doe now rests in peace. The sleep of many others is still disturbed by thoughts of his brief but real suffering and his calculated death. To judge these parents or these physicians will not ease our restlessness. But to resist the erosion of some ancient traditions about medicine and parenting and to establish a tradition of including the handicapped in our community is today part of our Christian vocation and our cultural mandate. Christians can, sometimes do, and should preserve and cherish a tradition about medicine that gives to doctors the worthy calling of healer, not the demeaning role of hired hand to do a consumer's bidding. Christians can, sometimes do, and should preserve and cherish a tradition about the family that gives parents the vocation of uncalculating nurturance and rescues them from the impossible obligation of making their children either perfect or "happy." Christians can, sometimes do, and should welcome and include those whom it is too much our impulse to shun and neglect.

Such medicine and such families and such a community may not always be "happy," but they will always be capable of being surprised by joy in caring for one they cannot cure. They will learn to tell and live a story of Jesus and the neonate. And when the groanings of all creation cease, they may hear, "As you did it to one of the least of these my brethren, you did it unto me."

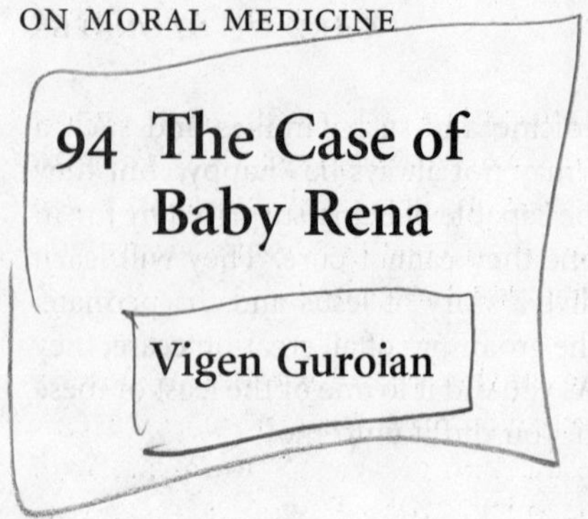

94 The Case of Baby Rena

Vigen Guroian

The God whose love is steadfast and whose mercy is abundant would never sanction euthanasia. However humanitarian or well-meaning the motives of those who advocate or practice euthanasia might be, they cannot justify what they do. In a Christian evaluation of the rightness or wrongness of euthanasia, the euthanizers' *aim* (i.e., their specific intent to bring about the death of an individual) is more important than their *motivation* (i.e., their desire to put an end to suffering). Or, to put it another way, the fact that euthanizers mean well is less important than the fact that the result of their "good intentions" is a person's death. While Christians might acknowledge the good intentions of those who in the name of humanitarianism practice euthanasia, we are constrained to condemn the act as sinful and wrong. The aim of euthanasia is contrary to everything God intends for us and has done for us in a fallen and sinful world, which, apart from his presence and saving activity, is a cosmic cemetery.[1]

There is a difference between a God-centered humanism and a naturalistic humanitarianism, and Christians must explain and emphasize that difference as a witness to an increasingly secular and utilitarian culture. To shed light on some of the important issues involved here, I want to take an extended look at the perplexing real-life case of a fourteen-month-old infant who died a painful and tragic death at a Washington, D.C., hospital.

From Vigen Guroian, *Life's Living Toward Dying* (Grand Rapids: Eerdmans, 1996), pp. 66-80.

The story of how "Baby Rena" met her death was reported in a two-part, front-page feature in the *Washington Post* in July of 1991.

> Murray Pollack, a physician at [Washington's] Children's Hospital, felt the time had come to change the rules. His 18-month old patient, Baby Rena, was dying, a victim of AIDS and heart disease. For six weeks, ever since her arrival at the intensive-care unit in late January, she had been breathing only with the help of a respirator. She was in so much pain that Pollack kept her constantly sedated. When nurses performed even the simplest procedure, such as weighing her, her blood pressure shot up and tears streamed down her face. But a tube in her throat made it impossible for her to utter a sound.[2]

Pollack had been called in to take the case after Baby Rena was brought to Children's Hospital on January 30. She died at the hospital on March 25. From the outset, Pollack judged that her case was probably "futile." In his view, keeping her on the respirator was not so much a life-saving measure as an intrusion into her dying process that intensified and prolonged her suffering. Pollack argued that he and the medical staff had "a responsibility to do what's best for Rena . . . and to give her the appropriate care — and that is not always giving her all care."[3] Pollack was not advocating mercy killing. Rather, he wanted those responsible for her care to "let go" — to let Rena die the death she was dying as well as possible — and in his judgment that called for removing her from intensive care and the respirator and providing medication to relieve her severe pain. Death would likely come sooner rather than later.

Children's Hospital requires the consent of parents or legal guardians to remove a minor from a respirator. Rena's mother had abandoned her at birth, making her a ward of the District government. She had been assigned foster parents, and while they had no legal standing in the decision, they strongly objected to Pollack's recommendations. They believed that God had told them "to take the child, and rear her in the nurture and admonition of God's word . . . and to battle the spirits of infirmity."[4] They demanded that her treatment "be motivated by a spiritual sense of obedience to God."[5] When the hospital sought the government's permission to take Rena off the respirator, the request was denied.

Baby Rena's foster parents, the pastor of their church, and their friends all played a significant role in determining the way in which she died. They all professed a Christian belief in the sanctity of life, and yet I cannot find a basis in my understanding of the Christian tradition to agree with either their reasoning or their judgment. Resources within the Christian faith lead me to believe that there are good reasons for drawing a distinction in health-care settings between directly killing people and allowing them to die. The former is euthanasia and is morally wrong; under certain circumstances, the latter is not. In fact, acquiescence in the face of an impending death may sometimes be required by Christian conscience. There are circumstances in which Christians are permitted — even duty bound — to let life ebb away in its natural course, so long as that course of action remains in accord with a corresponding duty to provide care that relieves pain and comforts the dying person.

Too often today, conscientious religious and nonreligious people alike lack the moral means to distinguish and accept such possibilities. This issue, like so many other moral controversies, tends to get framed in either/or terms: either one believes that everything possible must be done to save life or one supports euthanasia. The Baby Rena case illustrates how people get caught up in this sort of moral cul-de-sac. Religious and nonreligious antagonists tend to view one another's arguments as proof positive that they are far apart in worldview, but in fact they often stand on common ground: both their positions are rooted in secularity.

In defending a distinction between direct killing (euthanasia) and allowing to die; Paul Ramsey once observed that people in our society who hold opposite positions on euthanasia often end up defining it in the same way. Religious conviction does not seem to be a determining factor.

> The case for either of these points of view [favoring euthanasia or favoring efforts to save life at all costs] can be made only by discounting and rejecting the arguments for saving life qualifiedly but not always. In both cases, an ethics of only caring for the dying is reduced to the moral equivalent of euthanasia — in the one case, to oppose this ever, in the other case, to endorse it. Thus, the extremes meet, both medical scrupulosity and euthanasia, in rejecting the discriminating concepts of traditional medicine.[6]

Operating on the basis of a simple definition of God's sovereignty over life and an almost Manichaean identification of sickness and death with the demonic spirits, Baby Rena's foster parents were incapable of making a distinction between euthanasia and caring for Rena to the point of letting her die. Ramsey insisted that the traditional ethic (grounded in the belief that God is Creator, Lord of Life, and Redeemer) clearly holds that "letting life ebb away is *not* the same as actively encompassing a patient's life."[7] How is it that Baby Rena's foster parents, devoted religious people, failed to see and act on this important distinction? Why is it that they were held captive to the current popular meaning of euthanasia, to thinking in terms of the restrictive alternatives of either a utilitarian devaluation of life or an ethical vitalism that mystifies and absolutizes human life?

I think Alexander Schmemann had it basically right when he argued that the mark of secularism is the absence of God experienced in society and in people's lives. Vast numbers of people in our culture, religious and nonreligious alike, carry this mark of secularism in their understandings of God and the world, and this is nowhere more evident than in their attitudes toward death and dying.

Unconvinced of the existence of God or an afterlife, nonreligious secularists typically associate all value in life with human agency — human projects to eliminate suffering, injustice, and the like. They refuse to explain the world "in terms of an 'other world' of which no one knows anything, and life . . . in terms of a 'survival' about which no one has the slightest idea." Rejecting religious orthodoxies that ground the value of life in terms of death and an afterlife, they explain "death in terms of life."[8]

These nonreligious secularists may differ among themselves, however, about the scale of value on which human life ought to be measured. Some hold personal existence as the only concrete value and adhere to an ethical vitalism that insists on using every means possible in all circumstances to ward off personal death. Others reason from a utilitarian framework that the value of a life is qualified by the degree of good or happiness, pleasure or fulfillment that might reasonably be expected in it. On the basis of this quality-of-life principle, they argue that some lives might not be worth living, and hence that we might properly choose to end them through physician-assisted suicide or euthanasia.

Of late, increasing numbers of individuals are claiming the right and the competence to make such decisions.[9] In this regard, Dr. Jack Kevorkian is hardly exceptional. The medical ethicist Daniel Callahan has astutely pointed out the hubris of such claims and how they can lead to an outright denial of the distinction between killing and letting die. The argument for euthanasia and the legalization of physician-assisted suicide is basically "about the centrality and validity of control," says Callahan. "By making a denial of the distinction between killing and allowing to die central to the argument, the euthanasia movement has embodied the assumption, the conceit actually, that man is now wholly in control of everything, responsible for all life and all death.[10]

On the face of it, religious people like Baby Rena's foster parents who make the "other" spiritual world the measure of all value seem to be the opposite of nonreligious secularists. They profess to assign all ultimate decisions about life and death to God rather than human beings. And yet, significantly, both camps ground their reasoning in the presupposition that the world is essentially meaningless because God is absent from it. The nonreligious secularists simply remove God from the equation on the basis of either atheistic or agnostic presumptions; people like Baby Rena's foster parents — who I believe can be fairly characterized as religious secularists — effectively act as though God is restricted to a spiritual realm and is wholly absent from this fallen and sin-ridden world. From the standpoint of the classical Christian understanding of life and death, both camps inappropriately devalue the world by presuming that God is absent from it. The nonreligious secularists look only to human endeavor for meaning and single-mindedly seek to alleviate human suffering by whatever means possible, including the facilitation of death. The religious secularists look only to the spiritual realm for meaning and single-mindedly seek to preserve human life at all costs, on the grounds that such life is a gift from God that ought to be sustained at all costs, no matter what amount of physical suffering might be involved in the process of dying.

I believe that Baby Rena's foster parents made their decisions about her welfare on the basis of this kind of secular religious worldview. Their own description of their beliefs suggests that their religion is rooted in a metaphysical and moral dualism that radically separates physical existence (this world) from spiritual existence (the other world). This body-and-spirit dualism moved otherwise loving adults to insist that a small child's extreme physical pain be prolonged.

But what does it mean to care for the spiritual well-being of a loved one who is dying if that care does not include seriously taking account of the physical pain she endures and the imminence of her death?[11] During one conversation between the hospital staff and the parents, the foster father sketched three pictures, representing Rena's body, soul, and spirit. "We see that she had AIDS," he said. "It's real, because you can see it under the microscope." He went on to thank the hospital staff for working hard to meet her medical needs — the needs of her body. But he complained that they were ignoring her spiritual side. Pointing to the third sketch, he said, "It seems to me that until the hospital really addresses the spiritual area we won't be able to defeat these various spirits of infirmity, including AIDS, that we're fighting against here." He explained his belief that the decisions about Rena needed "to be motivated by a spiritual sense of obedience to God. It's most important to find out what God desires or what God wills for Rena." At one point, a hospital social worker said, "What you're saying is that you don't want to give up on the spiritual part even though we're giving up on the physician part." The father nodded his head. He recalled an earlier occasion on which Rena had rallied after the hospital staff had given up hope. "If we give up now, we won't fully understand. . . . We won't fully know that God's word is true."[12]

The foster father spoke of the need to discover what God wants as if that wasn't already evident at the level of Baby Rena's fleshly suffering and dying. What more could the parents possibly have been waiting for to reveal God's will in the situation? As Ramsey so aptly put it, "No Biblical theologian should take umbrage at the suggestion that a pronouncement of death is a medical question." Indeed, I would broaden that to say that no Christian should take umbrage at the suggestion that judgments about when death is imminent or further medical treatment is futile are properly medical determinations. "What personal life do we know except within the ambiance of a bodily existence?"[13] God does not need respirators to work miracles, but God entrusts determinations of whether we are biologically dying to our physicians whether they themselves trust in him or not. One writer of a letter to the editors of the *Washington Post* questioned the foster parents' identification of the will of God with doing everything possible to keep Rena alive:

> I hope that people reading the article on Baby Rena do not get the impression that keeping her on the respirator was the only decision that people with faith in God could have made. . . .
>
> Having faith [sometimes] requires people to voluntarily give control over a situation to God. Although giving up control is the key to doing God's will, you still need to figure out what it is that God wants you to do — that's the hard part.[14]

Preserving the Moral Distinction Between Killing and "Letting Die"

In his remarkable little book *The Patient as Person* Paul Ramsey ruminates,

> It may be that only in an age of faith when men know that dying cannot pass beyond God's love and care will men have the courage to apply limits [to lifesaving interventions in] medical practice. It may be that only upon the basis of faith in God can there be a conscionable category of "ceasing to oppose death," making room for caring for the dying. It may also be that only an age of faith is productive of absolute limits upon the taking of the lives of terminal patients, because of the alignment of many a human will with God's care for them here and now, and not only in the there and then of his providence.[15]

Baby Rena's foster parents were far more fixed on the "there and then" of God's providence than on any sort of effort to discern the alignment of the many human wills involved in her care with God's care. As I have been suggesting, this fixation on the "there and then" and a corresponding devaluation of the "here and now" belongs to a spiritualism and otherworldliness that are the symptom and product of secularism itself, not its opposite, as those who hold such religious views typically think. This is one area in which there is no practical difference between a secularized Christianity and modern fundamentalism. Nonreligious secularism is characteristically expressed in a desacralization of human life and the experienced world; Judeo-Christian religious secularism is characteristically expressed in the breakdown of the symbolic and sacramental structures in and by which individuals and communities experience God as both transcendent over the world and wholly manifest within it. Baby Rena's foster parents made repeated appeals to God and his law, but they were unable to imagine that God's encompassing love might permit a practical ethical distinction in the "here and now" between direct killing and letting die. They could not imagine that a merciful God would sanction allowing Baby Rena to die. The Orthodox Christian tradition, on the other hand, views this sort of allowing to die as not merely permissible but actually desirable in some cases, as we noted in Chapter 3 in our consideration of the prayer for the hastening of the dying process.

The articles in the *Washington Post* did not say whether Dr. Pollack was a religious man, but when I compare his proposals for Baby Rena's medical care with those of her foster parents, I believe that his proposals were more in keeping with the classical Christian conviction that in the here and now God's care should be aligned with human reason and judgment in decisions about when life is ebbing and need not be heroically extended. In making this judgment, I am simply comparing Pollack's plea that Baby Rena be allowed to die with the foster parents' insistence that her life be prolonged at all costs; I am not unqualifiedly endorsing Pollack's ethical reasoning, because I can't know fully what that reasoning entailed. The newspaper reports suggest that Pollack based his ethical judgment on a medical determination of the futility of additional treatment and a concern for the quality of the patient's remaining life. But there is nothing in the newspaper's description of Pollack's reasoning to indicate that he never considered euthanasia a possible solution to Baby Rena's plight or that it would have violated his ethical standards to have proposed such a course of action. For Christians, the distinction between killing and letting die is key.

Daniel Callahan provides a definition that is helpful in our efforts to make this distinction:

> "Letting die" is only possible if there is some underlying disease that will serve as the cause of death. Put me on a respirator now, when I am in good health, and nothing whatever will happen if it is turned off. I cannot be "allowed to die" by having a respirator turned off if I have healthy lungs. It is wholly different, however, if a doctor gives me a muscle-relaxing injection that will paralyze my lungs. Healthy or not, those lungs will cease to function and I will die. That is what it means to "kill" someone as distinguished from "letting" someone die. Put more formally, there must be an underlying fatal pathology if allowing to die is even possible. Killing, by contrast, provides its own fatal pathology. Nothing but the action of the doctor giving the lethal injection is necessary to bring about death.[16]

It has been argued that one need not appeal to faith in God to secure this distinction within medical ethics. This is essentially Callahan's own position.[17] But on this point I side with Ramsey. In the relatively rarefied atmosphere of medical ethics, it may be possible to establish principles and rules that secure a distinction between killing and letting die without recourse to the resources of the Christian tradition. But, as Ramsey suggests, it is becoming increasingly difficult to maintain this distinction as the moral force of biblical theism diminishes in our culture. Biblically rooted theism provides us with the conviction that God, the absolute source and sustainer of our being and our Redeemer, does not abandon us in death. As St. Paul says, "Neither death, nor life, . . . nor anything else in all creation, will be able to separate us from the love of God" (Rom. 8:38-39). Biblical theism has a vision of a *summum bonum* that supports making calibrated judgments about the kind and extent of the care we owe to those who are in the last stages of dying. But this vision is not predominant in our culture. The distinction between killing and letting die is not anchored in anything; not even appeals to the principle of trust between patient and physician or the doctor's Hippocratic oath seem sufficient.

We can find evidence of this problem in one of John Updike's short stories entitled "Killing." As the story opens, a young woman named Anne is sitting with her dying father in a nursing home. A series of strokes has left him unconscious, unable to swallow or communicate. Anne has made the decision that he should be kept in the nursing home rather than moved to a hospital where he would be fed intravenously. The hospital treatment might be able to extend his life, but it would not be able to change the fact that his condition is hopeless. Wherever he will lie, death will be near at hand. The attending physician has assured Anne that she has acted wisely, but she remains plagued with guilt. She cannot shake the thought that by leaving her father in the nursing home she has in effect ordered his execution. As Updike puts it, she "realized that her decision had been to kill her father. He could not swallow. He could not drink. Abandoned he must die.[18]

Most medical ethicists agree that in certain terminal cases, when intravenous feeding might actually contribute to pain or discomfort and needlessly slow the inevitable dying process, a decision like the one Anne authorizes is morally permissible.[19] But no one seems to have communicated this to Anne. She seems to be ignorant of the medical-ethical distinction between killing and letting die. There is no indication that she has been told why withholding intravenous feeding might be appropriate in her father's case. In the end, however, it is not really likely that such information and counseling would suffice to allay Anne's anguish. Denied essential supportive relationships, she is lacerated by her conflicting love for and revulsion at her bedridden, dying father. Like so many of her contemporaries, she has been cast into a situation for which she is ill prepared. While her sentiments run deep, her moral resources are threadbare and poorly defined. And, as is the case with so many other women in our society (in which this burden more often than not falls on women), she is alone in the time of crisis. She has been abandoned by an estranged husband, and her siblings are too busy and too distant to bother to help. Nor does she have a religious community in which she might voice her feelings of guilt and find forgiveness.

In "Killing," Updike ruthlessly unmasks the desolation of modern life that we try to cover with technology, therapeutic strategies, and euphemism. More important, through the compelling character of Anne he shows us how family members who are forced to make decisions about dying loved ones are often pushed to the precipice of total despair and an exhausted embrace of the thanatos syndrome. In Anne's case, an "irrational" love for her father, a lingering legacy of guilt from a largely moribund Christian past, and the unavailability of legal physician-assisted suicide or euthanasia combine to lead her to an otherwise reasonable and probably right decision. But one has to wonder how soon her character will be superseded in our literature by a "compassionate" and "heroic" daughter who has no qualms about authorizing euthanasia for her dying father.

Conclusion

In light of the tragic story of Baby Rena, there is one practical point that I would like to stress: biblical faith does make it possible for us to make reasonable moral judgments about when our primary obligation to a patient is not to do everything possible to extend her life but rather to care for her as if she is dying. There can come a time when we should no longer seek to cure the patient but should instead turn our efforts to providing care for her in order that her death be the best possible death. Informed by a true biblical faith, we will seek to navigate a course between an absolutistic ethical vitalism on the one hand and a utilitarian ethic of "quality of life," triage, and euthanasia on the other. In the concluding chapter we will turn to an exploration of some of the finer points of a biblically informed ethic of caring for the dying.

Notes

1. See Gilbert C. Meilaender, "Euthanasia and Christian Vision," pp. 655-62 in this volume.

2. Benjamin Weiser, "A Question of Letting Go," *Washington Post,* 14 July 1991, p. 1.

3, Benjamin Weiser, "While Child Suffered, Beliefs Clashed," *Washington Post,* 15 July 1991, p. 6.

4. Weiser, "A Question of Letting Go," p. 18.

5. Weiser, "While Child Suffered, Beliefs Clashed," p. 6.

6. Ramsey, *The Patient as Person* (New Haven: Yale University Press, 1970), p. 146.

7. Ramsey, *The Patient as Person,* p. 156.

8. Alexander Schmemann, *For the Life of the World: Sacraments and Orthodoxy* (Crestwood, N.Y.: St. Vladimir's Seminary Press, 1973), p. 98.

9. More than twenty years ago, Marya Mannes argued this way in *Last Rights* (New York: William Morrow, 1974). More recently, medical ethicist Margaret P. Battin has dismissed religious proscriptions of suicide and euthanasia and advocated a fundamental right of suicide (*Least Worst Death: Essays in Bioethics on the End of Life* [New York: Oxford University Press, 1994]).

10. Callahan, *What Kind of Life: The Limits of Medical Progress* (New York: Simon & Schuster, 1990), p. 242.

11. Kathleen M. Foley, a physician and professor at the Memorial Sloan-Kettering Cancer Center, has written extensively on the all-too-common failure to prescribe pain-reducing medicines and treatments to patients in advanced stages of cancer and other terminal illnesses. She argues that the growing interest in physician-assisted suicide might be more properly addressed if physicians and health-care providers were better educated in pain assessment and treatment and if patients and their families were better informed of their options. See, e.g., "The Relationship of Pain and Symptom Management to Patient Requests for Physician-Assisted Suicide," *Journal of Pain and Symptom Management* 5 (July 1991): 289-97.

Baby Rena's foster parents stood in the way of reducing her pain, but it is even more often the case that attending physicians allow their patients to suffer needlessly because they are not sufficiently well trained in assessing pain and supplying remedies. This judgment is supported by a recently published five-year study, the largest of its kind, which included the responses of over nine thousand patients in five teaching hospitals. The study was designed "to improve end-of-life decision making and reduce the frequency of a mechanically supported, painful, and prolonged death." The results were disappointing. "The phase I observation confirmed substantial shortcomings in care of seriously ill hospitalized adults. The phase II intervention failed to improve care or patient outcomes. Enhancing opportunities for more patient-physician communication, although advocated as the major method for improving outcomes," was found to be "inadequate to change established practices" ("A Controlled Trial to Improve Care for Seriously Ill Hospitalized Patients," *Journal of the American Medical Association* 274 [22/29 November 1995]: 1591). The report concluded, "We are left with a troubling situation. The picture we describe of the care of seriously ill or dying persons is not attractive. One would certainly prefer to envision that, when confronted with life-threatening illnesses, the patient and family would be included in discussions, realistic estimates of outcome would be valued, pain would be treated, and dying would not be prolonged. That is still a worthy vision" (p. 1597).

The *Washington Post* cited Joanne Lynn, the director of the Center to Improve Care of the Dying at George Washington University Medical Center as saying that "she was dumbfounded by the finding that more than one-third of the patients [in the study] died in pain. 'We would never tolerate rates like this for post-operative infections.' " In fact, the study revealed that "more than half of the patients who died were reported by their families in moderate or severe pain during most of their final three days of life." This figure is even more staggering given that the subjects of the report were a controlled group of patients who were supposed to benefit from the initiatives implemented by the study. The report stated that the most disturbing finding was that the measures that were meant "to improve care failed to have any discernible impact" (Don Colburn, *Washington Post,* 22 November 1995, p. 10).

I believe that to some extent it is inevitable that this study would be disappointing. The crisis in the ethos of medicine and medical care runs so deep that it cannot be resolved by procedure alone.

12. Weiser, "While Child Suffered, Beliefs Clashed," p. 6.

13. Ramsey, *The Patient as Person,* p. 61.

14. "The Agonizing Decisions Surrounding Baby Rena" (letter from Monica Michelizzi), *Washington Post,* 22 July 1991, p. 10.

15. Ramsey, *The Patient as Person,* p. 156.

16. Callahan, *The Troubled Dream of Life* (New York: Simon & Schuster, 1993), p. 77.

17. Callahan establishes this position in both *What Kind of Life* and *The Troubled Dream of Life.* See also chap. 2 of James F. Childress's *Priorities in Medical Ethics* (Philadelphia: Westminster Press, 1981).

18. Updike, "Killing," in *Trust Me* (New York: Fawcett Crest, 1987), p. 16. Updike describes the dying man as having parched lips and as exuding a putrid stench from his mouth. This is a realistic description of a patient who fails to receive the proper care in such a situation. To prevent dehydration and discomfort, caregivers must provide a regimen of oral hygiene and topical application of wetting agents or sipping fluids if the patient is conscious (see Joyce V. Zerwekh, "The Dehydration Question," *Nursing,* January 1983, pp. 47-51).

19. See Bonnie Steinbock, Joanne Lynn, James Childress, and Daniel Callahan, "Feeding the Dying Patient," *Hastings Center Report* 5 (October 1983): 13-22.

95 Tragedies and Medical Choices

Stephen E. Lammers

On June 29 Reitha Lakeberg gave birth by caesarean section to conjoined female twins. On August 29 the twins were surgically separated. The Lakeberg case, as it has come to be known, captures much of what is right and wrong about American medicine. A family is visited by a heartbreaking medical tragedy, and a powerful medical establishment tries, against almost insurmountable odds, to salvage something from the tragedy. In the background are troubling issues addressed in 30-second sound bites by ethicists who know that the case's complexities can't be adequately addressed under such constraints. What follows are my own slightly more extended reflections from within the Christian tradition. I readily acknowledge that there are others who are as reflective as I, and who also claim that tradition, who may see things differently.

Reitha Lakeberg knew relatively early in her pregnancy — some 12 to 13 weeks on — that she was carrying Siamese twins. She was advised to abort but chose not to. To comment on that decision would distract us from the issues I wish to consider here. The twin girls were joined in such a way that they shared at least two major organs. The structure of the liver was relatively normal; the structure of the heart abnormal. If the twins were separated, one of them would surely die because she would be without a heart. Further, even if surgeons managed to separate the twins without both dying, the chances were very slim that the surgery would be successful beyond that point, in part because the survivor would have an abnormal heart. After the children were born at Loyola Hospital outside Chicago the parents were advised that the children should be kept comfortable but that no surgical treatment should be sought. I do not know the reasoning of those who gave that advice, but I believe that advice was sound, especially in light of what followed.

The Lakebergs took the children to Philadelphia where they were advised that surgery was possible but that the chances for saving one of the children was slim. Indeed, the chances of success were given as "less than 1 percent" in one account. It was not clear whether "success" referred to having one child survive the surgery or, more important for our consideration, to the possibility of one child having anything resembling a normal life. This last issue is important for judging what occurred. The medical procedure that took place was not therapy in the usual sense; it was an experiment. It was not even an experiment in the sense that we could reasonably expect to learn something that could help other children, as we might, for example, with experiments performed on children with leukemia. This experiment had little chance of helping other children and very little chance of helping the survivor, if there were one. According to one newspaper report, not a single formerly conjoined twin who had an abnormal heart is alive, well, and in school today. Why then was the surgery performed? (As I write, the surviving twin, Angela, is holding her own.)

We can begin to perceive an answer to this question by first listening to the father, Ken Lakeberg, and then to one of the physicians defending the parents' decision to go ahead with the surgery. Likening the surgery to the lottery, Lakeberg asked rhetorically if it were not the case that everyone has an equal chance at winning the lottery. At the very least, I am bothered by this kind of imagery. The family may think that it would be great good fortune for one of their daughters to survive the surgery, but I question whether the fortunes of experimental surgery should have been the central point in their decision-making. The more important questions are, Who is the recipient of the potential benefits? and, Who is being subjected to the risks? More on that in a moment.

Important Questions to Lammers

From Stephen E. Lammers, "Tragedies and Medical Choices: The Lakeburg Twins," from *Christian Century* 110 (September 8-15, 1993): 845-46. Used by permission.

The physicians said some troubling things as well. One doctor was quoted as saying that it was the parents' right to decide whether to proceed with the surgery and that the physicians would not take this right away from them. It may well be that we cannot do better than to leave these tragic decisions to the parents. But Christians would at least want to ask what kind of right this is and what responsibilities are associated with it. Within the Christian tradition, parents try to be careful not to yield to the temptation to call their children their own, as though they were possessions. Christians understand that parents are stewards for God and that, while children are entrusted to parents, they ultimately belong to God. Naming the parents as decision-makers is not enough; we must also articulate how parents understand their decision-making power and what limits they place upon it.

In thinking about whether medical treatment should be undertaken, Christian tradition has raised concerns about the benefits and burdens to the patient. Are the potential benefits and burdens in some kind of balance? It is important to be clear about how we describe what we seek in these cases. There is no neutral description of the desired ends. If success is defined as the completion of the surgery with one survivor, regardless of how long that survivor lives or under what conditions, then we have one kind of success. In my view this is to draw the standard for success far too low. On the basis solely of the medical facts of the case, it would be unprecedented if the surviving daughter were to have anything resembling a normal childhood. The burdens of the surgery and the follow-up care will be great. It would not have been unreasonable to have concluded that the patient's potential burdens would be greater than her potential benefits, and to have forgone any "treatment" whatsoever.

Further, it is entirely possible that the physicians did not fully appreciate their role. Physicians are not people who simply do what they are asked to do by patients. If, for example, the parents had demanded that a particular child receive the single heart even though the designated child was clearly less likely to survive, would the parents' wishes have prevailed? Professionals cannot escape responsibility for their awesome powers simply by turning decisions over to others. They too should reflect on the limits of what they can do and on the limits of what they might seek. Further, they are obligated to give advice about how to proceed. Even if in the Lakeberg case the parents desired the surgery in the face of advice to the contrary, there was no obligation for the physicians to proceed.

The Lakeberg case raises troubling matters for society as well. The estimates of the cost of this surgery vary widely, but there is no doubt that it was extremely expensive. Medically much is possible; the issue, however, is not whether something can be done but whether it ought to be done. (Of course, this question has to be asked both for the good of the child involved and for society at large.) It is grimly ironic that we live in a society that permits a procedure such as the one performed in the Lakeberg case, but at the same time permits (and I use this term deliberately, since we can do otherwise) its infant-mortality rate to be one of the highest in the industrialized world. Such a state of affairs cannot be defended on any grounds.

Let no one misunderstand. The Lakeberg case involves tragedy that could not have been escaped either by operating or by forgoing the operation. All of the good that we would do, we cannot. All of the evils that we would avoid, we cannot. If one does not operate and allows the children to die, it is tragic. It is also tragic that one of the children died as a result of the surgery. Tragedy is central to this case. But the greatest tragedy is how the medical profession failed at a critical moment. The professionals were the persons with the most freedom of action, with the least coercive circumstances — the ones most able to evaluate what was at stake. To Amy, the deceased child, we can only say, "Rest in the peace of the Lord." To the Lakebergs, parents and children, "Godspeed!" Of the professionals, we can ask, "Next time, please do better."

96 Justice and Equal Treatment

Paul Ramsey

Let us consider one moral aspect of the practice of neglect: the question of justice. Some physicians who have reported that they let some babies die (perhaps hasten their dying) also report that they make such life or death decisions not only on the basis of the newborn's medical condition and prognosis, but on the basis of familial, social, and economic factors as well. If the marriage seems to be a strong one, an infant impaired to *x* degree may be treated, while an infant with the same impairment may not be treated if the marriage seems about to fall apart. Treatment may be given if the parents are wealthy; not, if they are poor.[1] Now, life may be unfair, as John Kennedy said; but to deliberately make medical care a function of inequities that exist at birth is evidently to add injustice to injury and fate.

Wiser and more righteous is the practice of Dr. Chester A. Swinyard of the New York University medical school's rehabilitation center. Upon the presentation to him of a defective newborn, he immediately tries to make clear to the mother the distinction between the question of ultimate custody of the child and questions concerning the care it needs. The mother must consent to operations, of course. But she is asked only to make judgments about the baby's care, while she is working through the problem of whether to accept the defective child as a substitute for her "lost child," i.e., the perfect baby she wanted. In the prism of the case, when the question is, Shall this open spine be closed? Shall a shunt be used to prevent further mental impairment? The mothers can usually answer correctly. In the case of spina bifida babies, Dr. Swinyard also reports very infrequent need of institutionalization or foster parents. That results from concentrating the mother's attention on what medical care requires, and not on lifelong burdens of custody.[2] One must entirely reject the contention of Duff and Campbell that parents, facing the prospect of oppressive burdens of care, are capable of making the most morally sensible decisions about the needs and rights of defective newborns. There is a Jewish teaching to the effect that only disinterested parties may, by even so innocuous a method as prayer, take any action which may lead to premature termination of life. Husband, children, family and those charged with the care of the patient may not pray for death.[3]

One can understand — even appreciate — the motives of a physician who considers an unhappy marriage or family poverty when weighing the tragedy facing one child against that facing another; and rations his help accordingly. Nevertheless, that surely is a species of injustice. Physicians are not appointed to remove all life's tragedy, least of all by lessening medical care now and letting infants die who for social reasons seem fated to have less care in the future than others. That's one way to remove every evening the human debris that has accumulated since morning.

There is a story that is going around — in fact I'm going around telling it — about how the pope, the chief rabbi of Jerusalem, and the general secretary of the World Council of Churches arrived in heaven the same day. Since they had been spiritual leaders here below and ecclesiastical figures to take notice of, they had some difficulty adjusting. Such was the equality there that everyone had to take his place and turn in the cafeteria line. After some muttering protest they fell into the customs of the place, until one day a little man dressed in a white coat came in and rushed to the head of the line. "Who's that?" asked the pope resentfully. "Oh, that's God," came the reply. "He thinks he's a doctor!"

If physicians are going to play God under the pretense of providing relief for the human condi-

---

From Paul Ramsey, *Ethics at the Edges of Life* (New Haven: Yale University Press, 1978), pp. 201-6.

tion, let us hope they play God as God plays God. Our God is no respecter of persons of good quality. Nor does he curtail his care for us because our parents are poor or have unhappy marriages, or because we are most in need of help. Again, a true humanism also leads to an "equality of life" standard.

A policy of selectively not treating severely defective infants appeals ultimately, it is true, to whatever constitutes the greatness and glory of humankind to give us a standard by which to determine the bottom line of life to be deemed worth living. Thus Joseph Fletcher proposed fifteen "positive human criteria" and five "negative human criteria" as an ensemble quality-of-life-index.[4] Then he reduced the number in an article entitled "Four Indicators of Humanhood — the Enquiry Matures."[5] There is no need for us to examine Fletcher's criteria — three of which seem to declare anyone who does not have a Western sense of time to be a non-person. Fletcher is simply a sign of our times. Many, more serious ethicists have joined in the search for "indicators of personhood." The fundamental question to be faced is whether the practice of medicine should be based on any such set of criteria (presuming they can be discovered and agreed upon).

To that question I want first to say that that's no way to play God as God plays God. That was not the bottom line of his providential care. When the prophet Jeremiah tells us, "Before I formed thee in the belly I knew thee; and before thou camest forth out of the womb I sanctified thee; and I ordained thee" (1:5), he does not mean to start us on a search for the "indicators of personhood" God was using or should have used before calling us by name. Neither did the psalmist when he cried, "Behold . . . The darkness and the light are both alike to thee. For thou has possessed my reins: thou hast covered me in my mother's womb. I will praise thee; for I am fearfully and wonderfully made: marvelous are thy works; and that my soul knoweth right well" (139:12b, 13, 14). No more did God, at the outset of his Egyptian rescue operation, look around for "indicators of peoplehood," choosing only those best qualified for national existence. "The Lord did not set his love upon you, nor choose you, because you were more in number than any people; for you were the fewest of all people. But because the Lord loved you, and because he would keep the oath he had sworn unto your father, hath the Lord brought you out with a mighty hand" (Deuteronomy 7:7, 8a).

Many of God's life and death decisions are inscrutable to us. People are born and die. Nations rise and fall. Doubtless God in his official governance does — or at least permits — lots of things (as the Irishman said) which he would never think of doing in a private capacity. Nor should we, who are not given dominion or co-regency over humankind. But there is no indication at all that God is a rationalist whose care is a function of indicators of our personhood, or of our achievement within those capacities. He makes his rain to fall upon the just and the unjust alike, and his sun to rise on the abnormal as well as the normal. Indeed, he has special care for the weak and the vulnerable among us earth people. He cares according to need, not capacity or merit.

These images and shadows of divine things are the foundation of Western medical care, together with that "Pythagorean manifesto,"[6] the Hippocratic oath. As *John* Fletcher has written:

> If we choose to be shaped by Judeo-Christian visions of the "createdness" of life within which every creature bears the image of God, we ought to care for the defective newborn as if our relation with the creator depended on the outcome. If we choose to be shaped by visions of the inherent dignity of each member of the human family, no matter what his or her predicament, we ought to care for this defenseless person as if the basis of our own dignity depended on the outcome.[7]

Care cannot fall short of universal equality.

Indicators of personhood may be of use in psychology, in educational theory, and in moral nurture, but to use such indices in the practice of medicine is a grave mistake. Even the search for such guidelines on which to base the care of defective newborn infants would launch neonatal medicine upon a trackless ocean of uncertainty, directly into arbitrary winds. Thus, one of the physicians at Yale-New Haven Hospital, explaining on television the newly announced policy of benign neglect of defective infants in that medical center, said that to have a life worth living a baby must be "lovable."[8] Millard S. Everett in his book

Ideal of Life writes that "no child should be admitted into the society of the living" who suffers "any physical or mental defect that would prevent marriage or would make others tolerate his company only from a sense of mercy. . . ."[9] Mercy me, to that we must say no. Medical criteria for care should remain physiological, as should also the signs by which physicians declare that a patient has died. Decisions to treat or not to treat should be the same for the normal and the abnormal alike. Searching for an index of personhood to use (comparing patient-persons, not treatments or treatment with no treatment) is rather like founding medical care on theological judgments about when God infuses the soul into the human organism.

Notes

1. In a published interview, Dr. Raymond S. Duff seems to me to be ambiguous on these points, even contradictory. On the one hand he says, "My guess is that neither social nor economic considerations influence the decisions we are talking about to any significant degree. I never felt that a troubled marriage or the economics of the family has really had a major influence. Parents may fight with one another but they still adhere to what they both consider is fair to the child." Yet two or three paragraphs later he reported the case of a couple who had to decide "how many lives would be wrecked: one of dubious value plus four others, *or* the one of dubious value. There was no real choice the family "felt" primarily because of space, money, time, and personal resources. That couple of modest means noted that the wealthy can "buy out" of the choice. Yet, again, a few paragraphs later, when asked whether there would be "a substantive difference in the number of infants allowed to die" if society was equipped with uniformly excellent, well-staffed custodial institutions, Dr. Duff replied, "I doubt it," citing "several parents who felt it is not right for their child to exist primarily to provide employment for others." He also distinguished the decision to "let die" in Yale-New Haven Hospital from the treatment accorded defective children in Nazi Germany by saying that in the current cases "family and physicians took into account not only the child's right (to live or to die) but the needs of the family and society, and, to some extent, future generations," protesting that "if we cannot trust these persons to do justice here, can anyone be trusted?" (Beverly Kelsey, "Shall These Children Live?": reprinted in the *Hastings Center Report* 5, no. 2).

The more technical and presumably well-considered article by Duff and Campbell is quite clear on these points ("Moral and Ethical Dilemmas in the Special-Care Nursery," *New England Journal of Medicine* 289, no. 17). There, the references to "the family economy," "siblings' rights to relief from the seemingly pointless, crushing burden," "the strains of the illness . . . believed to be threatening the marriage bonds and to be causing sibling behavioral disturbances," "fear that they and their other children would become socially enslaved, economically deprived, and permanently stigmatized, . . . [in] a state of 'chronic sorrow,' " stand without modulation, or without the claim that the family-physician decision was made simply for the sake of the defective child.

2. Swinyard's practice, as I understand it, is quite different from withholding prognosis of the child's condition. The parents of a child with meningomyelocele are not "simply told that the child needed an operation on the back as the first step in correcting several defects . . . while the activities of care proceeded at a brisk pace" (Duff and Campbell, "Moral and Ethical Dilemmas").

3. R. Chaim Palaggi, Chikekei Lev., I, Yoreh De'ah, no. 50.

4. "Medicine and the Nature of Man," in *The Teaching of Medical Ethics,* ed. Robert M. Veatch, Willard Gaylin, and Councilman Morgan; *Hastings Center Report* 2, no. 5 (November 1972): 1-4. See also the correspondence in vol. 3, no. 1 (February 1973), p. 13.

5. *Hastings Center Report* 4, no. 6 (December 1974): 4-7. These accordion concepts of "meaningful/meaningless," "humanhood," "relationships that can be considered human," and "man's ability to relate" (called, incorrectly, "minimal" criteria) are used throughout *Dying: Considerations Concerning the Passage from Life to Death,* an Interim Report by the Task Force on Human Life of the Anglican Church of Canada (Office of the General Secretary, 600 Jarvis Street, Toronto, Canada, June 1977; presented to the 1977 session of the Synod on August 11-18, 1977). Representing no official or authoritative views of the Anglican Church of Canada, the report proceeds to address our duties toward defective newborns as if they are "human-looking shapes" or at most "sentient" creatures: ". . . The only way to treat such defective infants humanly is not to treat them as human" (p. 14). A widening controversy over the report was reported in *The New York Times,*

July 28, 1977. The synod sent the report back to committee.

6. *Roe v. Wade,* 410, U.S. 113.

7. John Fletcher, "Abortion, Euthanasia, and Care of Defective Newborns," *New England Journal of Medicine* 292 (January 9, 1975): 75-78.

8. CBS News, January 2, 1973. In their landmark article ("Moral and Ethical Dilemmas") Drs. Raymond S. Duff and A. G. M. Campbell used the expression "meaningful humanhood." Dr. Duff in a subsequently published interview explained that criterion to mean "the capacity to love and be loved, to be independent, and to understand and plan for the future" (Beverly Kelsey, "Shall These Children Live?"). Asked whether a mongoloid child may have "meaningful humanhood," Dr. Duff seemed to hedge, leaving the decision to parents who "pay the fiddler to call the tune," while the physician and hospital policy need only sometimes decide "whether the family's God is fair to the child."

9. Cited by Daniel C. Maguire, *Death by Choice,* p. 7. Here Maguire indicates no disagreement with such criteria.

97 Our Religious Traditions and the Treatment of Infants

David H. Smith

I

The babies I want to discuss in this paper are not those that we call "normal" babies; rather, they are those that have problems and cause problems. They can only make the heart ache, and commentary written by outsiders can easily chafe the wounds. This may be especially true when the commentary is said to reflect the religious sensibilities or traditions of our people, for religion means to be about life and death and truth. We are sometimes outraged by religious claims and arguments, but usually that is because our expectations for religious insight and principle are so high. We chastise the goddess who has failed us. I understand my role to be to offer one ordering of religious perspectives on the care of impaired infants. Because the issues are so powerful and so complex, I shall strike at them in several different ways. I hope the result has a kind of unity or continuity, but I think it is more likely to be the coherence of a symphony rather than the logical tightness of a Euclidean proof. Indeed, I shall play several of the same notes that Professor Arras has struck in his discussion of this topic, but they are important notes, and my chord structure is rather different.

My general plan in the remarks that follow goes

This article appears in Thomas H. Murray and Arthur L. Caplan, eds., *Which Babies Shall Live?* (Clifton, N.J.: Humana Press, 1985). Used by permission of the Hastings Center and the author.

something like this. I shall begin by discussing some of the images or portraits of children and parents that rest in the consciousness of Western religious people. These portraits, I think, have informed our thinking about human relationships in profound ways. They provide some of the data from which theological moralists should begin their reflection. Of course, like all portraiture, they reflect the perspective of the painter; these are not value-neutral descriptions. Moreover, the "morals" of the incidents I am about to mention are not always clear and unambiguous. This ambiguity may well be part of their greatness, but it is also a limitation for purposes of moral analysis. The portraits are not a sufficient moral framework, nor even a sufficient basis for such thinking. Still, they are illuminating and constitutive of the life of our central traditions.

With these data spread out before us, I shall presume to extract some general principles from them. And I will apply these principles to some of the moral issues that may well have challenged many of us already.

II

At age 40 Isaac married Rebekah; their sons Esau and Jacob were born soon thereafter. "When the boys grew up, Esau was a skillful hunter, a man of the field, while Jacob was a quiet man, dwelling in tents. Isaac loved Esau, because he ate of his game; but Rebekah loved Jacob" (Genesis 25:27-28). Children here, and elsewhere in the Bible, have a kind of particularity, and parents respond to them with partiality. They like and dislike; they pick favorites. This human tendency, the stuff of great literature and soap-opera, is treated as an inevitable fact in the scriptural narratives.

In fact throughout our history the individuality of a child is related to the child's lineage. This is not always fortunate, however. In the book of Judges, Jephthah swears to kill the first person he sees on returning home if only the Lord will help him to triumph over the Ammonites. When he does come home victorious, "behold his daughter came out to meet him with timbrels and with dances; she was his only child; beside her he had neither son nor daughter." With her agreement he sacrifices her, "for I have opened my mouth to the Lord and I cannot take back my vow" (Judges 11:29f). We shall return to the question of parental vows shortly; for the moment I note that the fate of Jephthah's daughter is appropriately — if unhappily — determined by the behavior of her parent. Children are often victims in the biblical narratives and images (cf. Psalm 137:9 — "Happy shall be he who takes your [i.e., Babylonian] little ones and dashes them against the rock"). They are victims of a particularity, or peculiarity, over which they have no control. This is a not altogether happy or benevolent aspect of reality, in the biblical portraits.

This stress on particularity has not always been reflected in Western consciousness about children. In his rich study, *Centuries of Childhood*, Philippe Aries notes that hundreds of years passed before Western Europeans really discovered the special characteristics of childhood. Before the 17th century, he writes,

> No one thought of keeping a picture of a child if that child had either lived to grow to adulthood or had died in infancy. In the first case, childhood was simply an unimportant phase of which there was no need to keep any record; in the second case, that of the dead child, it was thought that the little thing which had disappeared so soon in life was not worthy of remembrance: there were far too many children whose survival was problematical. . . . One had several children in order to keep just a few. . . . People could not allow themselves to become too attached to something that was regarded as a probable loss.[1]

Increasingly, Aries observes, people began to realize that childhood was a special stage of life, valuable in its own right. This led to treating children as pets, to coddling, but increasingly to a notion that children had to be educated or disciplined so as to grow up into happy adults. Ultimately, however, only increased medical success as well as contraception has been able in the past 200 years to bring about a time in our society in which children are valued in and for themselves. Really taking particularity seriously was a long time coming.

This mention of education gets at another religious image of the child — the child as one whose future must be prepared for and whose character and education therefore matter. Beginning with the embryonic passover traditions in Exodus 12 and continuing right through the passover haggadah of the present time, Jewish life has always wanted to help the child situate himself as part of a people with a destiny, to have a sense of himself as part of a community with a past, present, and future. The great 20th-century Protestant theologian Karl Barth expresses this idea very well. Children, he says, "are not by nature their [parents'] property, subjects, servants or even pupils, but their apprentices, who are entrusted and subordinated to them in order that they might lead them into the way of life."[2] Jewish or Christian parenthood inevitably looks to the child's future with a vision of the good life.

Thirdly, and most centrally for our purposes, the religious images of childhood and parenting that we know are — as the quotation I just cited from Barth suggests — images of *limited* parental authority and dominion. When the baby Moses was three months old his mother put him in a basket and let him be taken over by others for his well-being (Exodus 2). At age twelve Jesus in the temple is not a very good boy, straying from his parents and telling them that he really has more important things to do than go home with the family. Mary and Joseph's authority over him is distinctly limited — indeed, if he is *the* paradigmatic child he vividly illustrates the ambivalence of parent/child relations, for he both is, and is not, *their* child.

This limitation of parental authority is nowhere more vivid than in the story of the binding (*akedah*) of Isaac by Abraham in Genesis 22. We are used to thinking of this story in terms of Isaac's loss of life, but of course it would have been Abraham's sacrifice in more ways than one. He is being asked to give up that which means the very most to him; it is a story of letting go. Abraham looks up and sees the ram and God explains, "now I know that you fear God, seeing you have not withheld your son, your only son, from me" (Genesis 22). Isaac's life is not, ultimately, Abraham's to dispose of as he may see fit, for Abraham would never have chosen this sacrifice. As a planning parent Abraham serves a master, and his parental power is limited.

This brings us to a fourth image of childhood that we find in our heritages. Elijah the Tishbite stays with a widow whose son dies. Elijah "stretched himself upon the child three times" and the child revived (1 Kings 17). The earliest history of Christianity tells the story of a boy named Eutychus (Lucky) who fell asleep in a third-story window while listening to a long sermon. He falls out of the window and dies, but Paul (the preacher) revives him with an embrace (Acts 20:8-12). Children are presented as having access to Jesus, and his contact with them in at least one version of the story is wonderfully physical and bodily: he takes them in his arms and blesses them (Mark 10:16 and parallels). It is not the child's personality alone, nor his future, but his body that is the focus of concern in these images. And for Christians this image is intensified even more in the extraordinary claim for an identification of God with the body of a crying, soiled, human baby. The *baby* Jesus is one of the two or three dominant Christian portraits.

Children in these images — and I have not pretended to give an encyclopedic account — are embodied human beings with a particular past and future. They create responsibilities for their parents. These parents, however, are not given complete dominion over their children, only a "slight seniority."[3]

III

These images do not of themselves lead us to moral conclusions. They only inform us; they require an ordering. I propose to use the notion of fidelity as an ordering principle. I shall assume that the great theme of Western religion is God's loyalty to us — loyalty responded to with betrayal and disobedience, occasionally with trust and love. A life of passionate devotion to God should involve compassionate loyalty to other persons: this is the central theme of Western religious morality. What does a faithful working out of the images I have sketched entail?

When we try to figure out how to be faithful to people, one thing these images push us to think about is the things that they live for, what — as we say — makes them tick. Thus when it comes time to shop for presents for a birthday or Christmas or Chanukah we look for presents that relate to the interests of a person. A set of records of Beethoven symphonies is marvelous for one person, a waste for someone else. Someone likes jewelry, someone else a set of golf clubs. People's interests or, as I would prefer to say, their loyalties vary. Loyalty to someone means respecting this kind of particularity. And the respect may go quite far; my love for my friend may well bring me to love what he loves, to care for those things that matter to him.

Usually we know something of a person's specificity from his or her explicitly stated preferences. We know that Dad likes to play golf because he says he does, and he says he doesn't care for classical music. In fact, however, this correlation between what people really are and who or what they say they are is not one to one. Many people *say* they like to do things which in fact it is clear that they do not much enjoy; anyone who has ever lived in a family can write a book about the various kinds of self-deception that human beings indulge in. Still, throughout most of our lives, we are willing to acknowledge that a person's decisions about his or her own life ought, at least, to have a preferred place. Medical decisions are no exception. Thus we support a right to refuse treatment and stress the importance of a requirement of informed consent.

The striking thing about babies, however, is that part of this stress on moral particularity cannot exist for them. They have never had a chance to care about or live for anything. They have not established a style of life or character. And some infants will never be able to do these things. It's not just that because of great defects some babies will never have the kind of personality that a normal person would have. It's rather that they have never got off the launching pad. The effect on our moral reasoning about them is that an important variable simply drops out of the picture. We see them as children whose individuality has not yet emerged.

They also begin with a minimal medical history. Their prognosis is at best uncertain. We don't know what degree of retardation a child with Down's syndrome will have, or how serious the deformity and hydrocephalus associated with myelomeningocele will turn out to be. Some premature babies have terrible and short lives; others do not. It is never possible to be absolutely sure of the outcome.

I draw from these facts the conclusions that for the most part we owe it to these babies to get them started. They are cursed by powers in their lineage over which no one has control. But the arguments of personal style and preference that might justify a decision for the death of an adult can never be applied directly to newborns, and it takes times to establish a kind of pattern of biological functioning such that we can extrapolate to future events and responses with some fairly good degree of plausibility.

A second thing that loyalty to another person means is interest in or concern for what he or she may become. Hence the power of the image of parent as educator. The idea perhaps is difficult. We think of people as set in their ways: "Oh, he could do it if he wanted to, but he will never skip Monday night football." And we tend to form and hold set pictures of people: he is punctual, she is stubborn, they are argumentative. It is true that the characters people have have a kind of constancy, but it is also true that people change and grow. Saints fall away, sinners convert, Prince Hal becomes Henry IV.

When we look into the future for our friends we find that we want many things for them. One of these is *happiness.* This is a notoriously hard term to define, and I am not capable of producing a statement that will instantly persuade everyone. But I think it obvious that happiness is something that we want for those we care about. We would describe as sick someone who wanted his child or spouse or parents to be *un*happy. Naturally I don't mean that we want happiness of any kind for them — we may well feel that some kinds of happiness are better than others. Certainly our religious traditions suggest the importance of piety before God as an ingredient in true happiness.

A second thing that we want for our friends is *excellence.* We hope that they will do something well. This something may be athletic, intellectual, or social. Some are good runners, others good thinkers, others are, as we say, good people. Yet however we define it, excellence is something that we want for our friends, and for religious persons it is associated with some kind of relation to God.

Given these goals the question becomes whether they are attainable. Seldom do we know the answer to this. This is particularly true with handicapped babies. We may be certain that they will *not* have the kinds of happiness or excellence that are open to normal children, *but this is scarcely the issue.* We are not trying to compare them with others, for not all children of God play the same role in the kingdom. Who of us would survive some great assize trying to decide if his own life, with all its defects, was worth living? The issue is, is some kind of happiness or excellence open to this child? As the custodians of their future we may act with hope. Our role is to help them know themselves and God, whatever their future may hold.

Related to this, I should mention that this stress on hope and the future is especially important when families are stretched and torn as they are in the cases we have been discussing. On the one hand, the parents need to stick with the child; on the other hand, the medical staff needs to stick with the family. Care is not an episodic or momentary thing. To be genuine it must involve a commitment to what is to come. Follow-up is very important. The uncertain character of the future is frightening, especially to parents whose dreams and expectations have been smashed. Loyal medical care for families in this situation, involves living through this uncertainty with them and, through one's presence, giving them hope.

Third, loyal care for persons involves care for their *bodies.* Children in the religious images are not just personalities, nor bundles of potentiality; they are living, struggling bodies. There are two aspects of this obvious point to which I wish to call attention. One of them is that the body has a kind of life of its own. It is not altogether malleable to human desire, whether we speak of the desire of its "owner" or of someone else. And health is comparably objective.

Let me put the issue a little differently. Bodies are not just things we have, they are things we *are.* The requirements of a healthy body can be generalized — they are not completely relative to cultural prejudices or values. And medical care involves care for bodies in a special way — not to the exclusion of everything else, not in some scientific way that excludes the caress and the cuddle — but oriented to the body all the same. My lawyer is a consultant on my rights, my tax man on my money, and my doctor on my body and its health. Medical care for a baby means making him comfortable.

A second important feature of bodies is that they change. Bodies pass through states, regardless of the desires of anyone. These include infancy, adolescence, middle age, aging, and dying. Proper forms of care should be adjusted to these various stages or moments in a life span. Pediatrics is not just medicine on small adults; we rightly use different terms to describe a highway accident to children, other adults, and the aged. Fidelity to a patient will always require optimal care, but as we change, so do the requirements of care. Throughout most of our lives medical loyalty to us means keeping us alive, but this ceases to be true at some point in our lives. Then we may actually speak of a need to die. Dr. Anna Fletcher has referred to a baby who was "trying to die."

Paul Ramsey has made this point with characteristic force. He says that the determination of when a person enters dying is a "medical" decision.[4] This means that there are changes in the ill person himself that determine what the right forms of treatment are. When a person starts to die our responsibilities shift. Ramsey's idea, which is rooted in religious images, is that a person's life trajectory at some point enters a dying phase. When that happens moral responsibility changes. Then the issue is, "Is he dying?" or, more generally, "What forms of treatment are optimal care for her in whatever time she has left?"

If the discernment of when someone begins to die — a determination that is relevant to the choice of appropriate forms of care — is a matter of what Eric Cassell has called the "healer's art," the substance of the point is best captured not in argument but in metaphor. A couple invite friends to dinner. Food and drink are pleasant; the conversation bubbles. The good host is hospitable and courteous to his guest, no matter what his shifts in mood. But there comes a time when the party "winds down" — a time to acknowledge that the evening is over. At that point, not easily determined by clock, conversation or basal metabolism, the good host does not press his guest to stay, but lets him go. Indeed he may have to *signal* that it is acceptable to leave. A good host will never be sure of his timing and will never kick out his guest. His jurisdiction over the guest is limited to taking care and permitting departure.

Analogously, loyalty to other persons involves

care for them of the best possible sort, and changing the forms of care as needs change. It means recognizing that a time comes when we can care for them no longer, only bid them Godspeed. We may, as it were, show them the door. But we should not kill a patient because that would be to betray him, to assume the kind of jurisdiction over his fate that is incompatible with being a good host. And we can never be sure of our timing.

Loyalty to the dying, in other words, is compatible with a choice of palliative clinical care and personal human support over life-extending technologies. It is of the greatest possible importance that this shift be seen as a shift to an alternative *medical* form of care and it is the great strength of the hospice movement to have refined and institutionalized these alternative forms of medical care. Loyalty to the dying not only tolerates but positively mandates this shift; making a guest stay longer than is good for him is very bad manners.

Many people will recognize the possibility that some children are born dying. This may be simply in virtue of prematurity. Thus I think we should simply comfort some newborns as they die. On the other hand, I have meant to suggest that any predictable defect, in particular retardation, is not a sufficient reason for saying a child is dying. It is especially important not to yield to pressure to come to a quick and efficient decision in order to spare people's feelings. It takes time to discern what is going on with a young and small patient's body.

This brings us to the last point I wish to make. *Loyalty to a defective baby requires involvement in a decision-making procedure of integrity and credibility.*

Some writers on medical ethics see this as the only issue. In the case of adults they stress the patient's right to die; for children they assert an absolute right of parents to make the decision. However, it is clear that in the biblical images of the gift of a child does not entitle parents to unlimited sovereignty over it. Abraham has to let go, despite his plans and hopes. Even if parents are the child's best proxy in virtue of their identification with it, their power should not be unchecked. There are other reasons for this. Parental judgment is finite and it is possible that the parent's identification and stake in the issue will produce excessive bias. Further, the communal nature of human existence implies that we do not live by ourselves; the family is not an island. Desertion of the family — and simply leaving the decision in their hands may amount to desertion — is a form of betrayal.

In effect I am saying that loyalty in these situations requires patience. There is no rushing the decision-making procedure, and no substitute for involvement of the physician throughout it. What is needed is a lot of talking among parents, physicians, nurses, and appropriately concerned others.

This is no panacea. Even a good process can go wrong or be misused. I can well understand — indeed I largely share — the impulse to establish minimal standards in the law. For in this area discretion abused is not just indiscreet; it is immoral. I do not think babies should be let go simply in virtue of Down's syndrome — as I hope I have suggested. But at the moment I cannot imagine a regulatory net or law that would ensure a discriminate result or that could be fine-tuned to the whole variety of cases we want to acknowledge. Thus I fall back on moral education and a process of listening, learning, and support.

In sum, loyalty is what the people of God owe defective babies. We owe them respect and hope, care and comfort for their body, fair play and due process. Sometimes this will mean we have to kiss them goodbye — but never without having made them welcome, never without a hug, and never without regret.

Notes

1. Philippe Aries, *Centuries of Childhood: A Social History of Family Life* (New York: Random House, 1965), p. 38.

2. Karl Barth, *Church Dogmatics,* III/4 (Edinburgh: T&T Clark, 1960), p. 243.

3. Ibid., p. 246.

4. Sometimes Ramsey suggests that it is a strictly objective and factual matter. This is mistaken. While there are clinical signs that one is dying (as there are of the onset of puberty), the actual discernment of the beginning of the process is largely a matter of art. Experience and skill are relevant to the determination, of course. Many of us (including some physicians) are tone

deaf to what is happening in the body of another. But there is no escaping the factor of judgment, of discerning perception. People's judgments will differ, to be sure, but this fact in no way proves the nonexistence of dying as a last stage of life.

98 The Retarded

William May

Offspring of the lower primates cling to the bodies of their mothers; marsupials hang on for dear life. But the human infant is unable to cling. The mother must hang onto as well as carry her young. This dependency upon the mother for the simple act of carrying, the precondition of so much else, makes the human infant rely heavily on bonding. A mother must actively cradle her child, cherish it, for it to flourish.

Bonding engenders loyalty to the being and well-being of another. In a sense, "loyalty" is too weak a term. It suggests a relation that depends upon the will of both parties. Bonding describes the way in which two people settle into one another's bone marrow and kidneys, imagination and bowels. Bonding does not demand a mystical merger of identity between two partners; but it establishes a tie so powerful that neither can undertake much without reckoning with the consequences for the being and well-being of the other.

Most attempts to identify the value of the retarded child neglect the process of parenting and bonding. Aspiring to abstraction, they proceed along lines implied in the title of a conference, "Natural Abilities and Perceived Worth." They impersonally consider measurable properties (such as intelligence) that distinguish the retarded and others from zebras, parsnips, and rocks. By "abstraction" I mean the kind of assessment of natural abilities that a professional or policy-maker might make in a hospital, a prison, or a high

From William May, *The Patient's Ordeal* (Bloomington: Indiana University Press), pp. 36-56. Used by permission.

school, an assessment cleanly distanced from a relation to the carrier of those capacities. From this lofty perspective, parental belief in worth may seem merely subjective, lacking in validity and valency.

This chapter explores, alternatively, the kind of valuing that goes on in the relation of parenting and bonding. It emphasizes a relational rather than a possessional view of the self. It explores the relationship *between* human beings for its clues to their being and value and our obligations to them, rather than assigning values according to the numbers scored. It looks to the dynamics of bonding between parents and their retarded child rather than to a distanced consideration of capacities possessed and performance attained.

Since no moral life can dodge adversity, this narrative about bonding will also have to deal with the great obstacles to bonding — both external and institutional, and internal and personal — which the parents of the retarded confront. While the parents of the retarded must overcome or circumvent these obstacles at their most difficult, such obstacles throw their shadows across all parenting, whatever the abilities of the child.

External Obstacles to Parenting

Most researchers have emphasized the obstacles institutions place in the way of early parenting and bonding, especially in the crucial hours and days immediately following birth. The modern nuclear family, we hear endlessly, suffers simultaneously from the absence of those community supports of family and friends that helped parents bond to their children in traditional societies and from the overbearing presence of the hospital and the medical staff at birth.

The celebrative atmosphere of home birth in traditional societies boosted the mother's growing attachment to the child. The excitement of other participants in the event aroused buoyancy and confidence in her. By contrast, the industrialized West has tended until recently to treat birth (even normal birth) "as an illness or an operation," and isolated it in an institution that often intimidates women.[1] The modern medical concern to prevent infection curtailed the physical contact between mother and child so crucial to bonding. Most normal births in the hospital condemned mothers and babies to several days of isolation and deprivation. As late as 1970, only 30 percent of mothers were permitted to touch their babies in the first days of life.

Hospitals have handled premature and abnormal babies even more antiseptically. These babies became "monstrous" in the literal sense of that term; that is, they became objects to see and point to but not to touch. Fittingly, the first director of a nursery for premature babies in this country, Martin Cooney, exhibited them at most major fairs and exhibitions in the United States from 1902 to 1940. Receipts from his *Kinderbrutanstalt* at the Chicago World Fair of 1932 ranked second only to ticket sales for fan dancer Sally Rand — someone else to see and point at but not touch. Cooney discovered, not surprisingly, that some of the mothers whose babies he sent out on exhibition did not want them back when, as they reached five pounds, he returned them. They had not bonded. Cooney's procedures, developed in the nursery of commerce, significantly shaped methods of newborn care in the United States — and not for premature babies only.

Recent critics have severely criticized medical professionals and institutions for disrupting bonding. Some of these critics have perhaps exaggerated. They gravely assumed that actions in the first few hours and days after birth irreversibly stamp the relationship of parents to their child. They have earnestly promised almost magical results from laying the baby across the mother's warm abdomen immediately after birth. Still, these critics have a point. Klaus and Kennell report that when early mother-child cuddling is lacking, breast-feeding fails more often, child-battering increases, and some statistical differences in I.Q. and language attainment show up as much as two years later.[2]

The additional care the retarded or handicapped baby needs compounds the problem. Increased professional and institutional interventions reduce the mother's contact with the baby during the sensitive period crucial to bonding. Psychologically, the mother and father need this contact. Every mother needs time to adjust to the appearance of her infant (often one to three days); the stark information that the child suffers from something wrong heightens fears. Often seeing and touching the child — even a deformed or retarded child — make it easier for parents to cope.

Changes in hospital practices since 1970 reflect a greater institutional respect for the parents' and babies' needs to touch and bond. Although aggressive medicine still dominates the intensive care unit for children, hospitals have shown more appreciation recently for the parents' need to know and touch and do the handling, nurturing, and sheltering their child needs. Professionals cannot neglect these activities and treat the child simply as a bundle of medical problems — containing so many grams of body weight, lab values, and deficits — and expect the child to come home to easy and natural parental embraces.

Internal Obstacles to Parenting

Probably the external, institutional obstacles to parenting and bonding would not loom so large if parents did not face even more formidable internal obstacles to bonding with their child. Parental emotions hinder bonding, whatever the institutional setting and whatever the child's status. The infant confronts its parents as a stranger, threatens to restrict their freedom, and makes them anxious about the future. The retarded child pushes each of these emotions to its extreme.

(1) Moral reflection that does not reckon with the experience of the child as a stranger misses the test that individuals face in parenting and bonding. Our deepest psychic response make us distrust and reject the stranger. This aversion showed on the day of our birth when we complained loudly about being ejected from the familiar comfort and warmth of the womb into a strange world. It appeared at seven months of age when we began to fear strangers and abandonment.[3] It continued at four years when we shied back behind our mother's skirts, as strangers leaned over, grinning, to tell us what a fine little boy or girl we were. And at ten we heard mysterious warnings not to go anywhere with strangers — strangers are tricky. Mother invested the stranger with an unspecified power to harm. Nor does adult life leave this aversion behind. Especially in this country, a country of immigrants, wave upon wave of strangers have made their way into established cities, neighborhoods, schools, unions, clubs, and businesses, assaulting the psyche and provoking patterns of recoil and aversion.

This disturbing experience of the strange stirs no less at the arrival of the newborn. In a sense, birth, especially first birth, confronts a young woman and man with the ultimate stranger, the newcomer, the absolute immigrant into this world. The young woman in *How Green Was My Valley* announces her pregnancy to her former boyfriend by saying, "We're going to have a little stranger." Something quintessentially new, and thus threatening, is coming into the world. The ceremonies of birth today, in an unfamiliar setting filled with masked officiants, reinforce the feeling of trepidation before the strange.

But the alien newcomer itself, more than the rites through which it arrives, unsettles the parents. How so? The human imagination contributes to the shock of alienation. In anticipation of their child's birth, parents tend to imagine greeting and holding a strapping, healthy baby, lustrous, smiling, and cooing at maternal care. They have already seen dozens of infants in supermarket strollers, or Gerber portraits of infants wrapped around jars on food shelves, or babies in Polaroid pictures, plump and fully human. This imaginative anticipation reduces the child-to-be to the familiar and manageable. The child will merely perpetuate, extend, and amplify the familiar world rather than push its parents into the novel and strange. The world-to-be will not shock or surprise. The present will overtake the future by way of peaceful annexation.

But the baby's arrival upsets the daydream. The mother discovers that the infant isn't herself cloned; it doesn't even resemble the father. She has borne a prune, a monkey, a strange looking thing. Further, it imposes its strange movements, its jarring demands, its noises at all hours; it turns one's life around rather than adds something to it. When it cries one wants to mother it, and yet it also makes the stomach nervously coil.

If the ordinary child intrudes itself as a stranger, the retarded child invades. It shatters all parental expectations. It converts the daydream into a nightmare. It presents the parents with a reality so alien to all their original hopes that the event confronts them with the force of death. The arrival of the retarded child kills the dream child and forces parents to grieve its loss.[4] This grief presents them with special difficulties in attaching themselves to the actual child, since we bond — to use the jargon of experts in the field — "monotropically." Close attachments form best to one child at a time. We cannot easily bond while mourning another. "We have noted in many parents who have lost one of a twin pair that they have found it difficult to mourn completely the baby who died and at the same time to feel attached to the survivor."[5] The death of the dream child ends the world that the mother and father trusted. They can only grudgingly embrace the new world that presents itself in the real child. Not all parents of retarded infants discover immediately that their child is retarded. Sometimes they bond to the child first and only subsequently discover mild to severe retardation. Such delayed recognition, however, does not wholly eliminate the trauma of coping as the newly discovered alien appears beneath the already accepted face.

In bonding and valuing the retarded, parents must first accept strangeness and overcome the aversion strangeness entails. The Enlightenment notion of the unity of humankind, which assumes universally shared characteristics, common properties, offers little help in reckoning with the strange. The Enlightenment, idealizing tolerance and benevolence, attempted to trivialize differences by measuring them on a scale of capacities and standards. It underestimated the stranger, who upsets my universe not because he differs from me in measurable ways but because, by existing, he shatters my rules and scales. The stranger creates a hemorrhage in my universe.

We do not bond, then, in a cozy assimilation or mystical merging of two beings. Like the love that precedes them (heterosexual love means, literally, love of the strange sex), parenting, bonding, and valuing require openness to the strange, learning devotion to the other set in strangeness. Nor does healthy bonding eliminate strangeness. Martin Buber observed that "othering" goes on in the I-Thou relationship. A relationship pales and dissolves when two beings take one another wholly for granted or presume too much on likeness. They no longer need to watch, listen, or attend to one another. Strangeness is the bracer in love. From the perspective of the biblical tradition, faith warrants openness to the stranger, not by the humane and liberal assertion that we must tolerate all men because, underneath, they are all alike, but because God himself, the primordial stranger, bonds to his creatures despite the abyss between them. Theologically, we must bond because of, not despite, strangeness.

(2) Parenting requires not only coping with the strange, but also losing a portion of one's freedom. Grief over the loss of freedom used to center in the institution of marriage itself. Today, however, both husband and wife work, allowing each to continue as part-time bachelors.

Having a child, more than marriage, makes the difference. Parents lost not only money (double salary), but time. The mother feels drawn to love the child, to care for it, to delight in it, but it also ties her down, takes her time. The baby turns out not to be a toy — it eats; it sleeps (at the beginning, 14 to 18 hours per day); it eliminates (at the outset, it urinates 18 times a day, defecates 4 to 7 times a day, and takes at least 8 diaper changes).

Parenting, in brief, poses the moral/metaphysical problem that *Huckleberry Finn* faced. The novel darkly suggests that love and freedom don't mix. Huck Finn runs away from his stifling hometown to freedom on the river. But, on the river, Huck meets up with Jim and bonds to him. His feeling for Jim makes him uneasy; it ties him down. Twain presents a gloomy vision; love and freedom diminish one another. Today, young people get out of the house and become sexually active and it tastes like freedom, but this freedom one day produces the event that suddenly and relentlessly ties them down. The growing bonds of love seem like bondage.

The retarded child intensifies this loss, certainly for those who keep the child home. Parenting inevitably curtails liberty, but ordinarily parents can view this loss as temporary. When their children grow up, parents hope to regain the freedom they have lost. But the retarded child does not fully grow up. Only the death of the parents — or the child — will end their responsibilities. Unless mildly retarded, the child can never take over full responsibility for his life; and he requires a much heavier investment of his parents' time in training. The retarded child's acquisition of those skills that other parents note in their children with some measure of gratification and relief — eating, dressing, personal hygiene, the mastery of social etiquette and rules governing work and play —

slows down to 2/2 time. The parents either adjust their own tempo accordingly or discover family life operating on two very different beats. Either way, spontaneity and freedom in family life diminish.

(3) Parenting expresses hope, but also stirs up anxiety about the future. Clearly, giving birth affirms the future. From the ancient Manichaeans forward, pessimists have always resisted bearing children. The Manichaeans loathed the material world, the body, sex, and the perpetuation of that world through progeny. The trappings of their mythology have withered, but the basic links between pessimism about the future and a great reluctance to have children still persist to this day: "the world is already overcrowded"; "I wouldn't want to go through that again"; "it would be wrong to bring children into the world."

A willingness to bear children shows optimism, but bearing a child also stirs up anxiety about what lies ahead. The affirmation contained in a child forces parents to scout the unknown on behalf of the precious but powerless. In ordinary parenting, apprehension about the future subsides as parents immerse themselves in daily demands and joys. But fear of the future always looms over the parents of the retarded. In the first stage, parents often suspect something, they know not what. (We fear most intensely, argued the existentialists, the evil not yet revealed.) When physicians name the problem, they give it some specificity, but ordinarily do not spell out its full ramifications. As the dreadful implications and complications of the original diagnosis unfold, parents begin to generalize about the future: whatever it is, it will be bad. Therefore, defensively, they turn to the present and do what they can, one day at a time. Sufficient unto the day is the evil thereof.

Nevertheless, the long-range future still disturbs. The severely impaired child tends to be the last child in a family. Its birth tends to have a contraceptive effect. The future also looks bleak at those moments when parents see retarded adults. As much as they feel that they have come to accept their retarded child and their own responsibilities, they discover that they cannot yet accept the adolescent and the adult-to-be. Helen Featherstone describes a visit to see older children. It poses for her as a parent all over again the confrontation with the strange. "The children had lost their otherworldly charm; they were not simply psychotic adolescents. The hopes of parents and teachers had faded along with their baby fat."[6] But even if one accepts the future adult-to-be, the bleak circumstances which that adult will face cannot help but disconcert. "Most of us, for all our hopes and dreams, are still fattening up our children for the inevitable institutional kill."[7]

Moments in Bonding

Bonding is a two-way street; parents and children interact. Although we can, at present, describe only crudely the experience of bonding from the baby's point of view, we can nevertheless see that the baby that self-confidently attaches itself to its mother is likely to behave in ways that arouse more affectionate and spontaneous maternal responses. Conversely, a child who has suffered traumatic institutional separation from its mother will react with anger, anxious possessiveness, or self-protective detachment. This obstructive behavior, in turn, produces negative responses from the mother that increase the child's anger, possessive clinging, or guarded apathy.[8] Further, the varying degrees of mental retardation, from profound to mild, make a difference in the obstacles parents face in bonding. A full treatment of bonding would have to take account of these differences.

Recent efforts to describe bonding with the retarded child sound very much like Kübler-Ross on death and dying; the sequence of anger, fear, denial, bargaining, and acceptance surfaces in the discussion. This approach has the advantage of letting the actual emotions of parents into the open. As in other crises to which her stages have applied, however, one wonders whether Kübler-Ross and those who follow her interpret these stages as descriptive or normative, chronological or concurrent, elective or compulsory.

An alternative scheme for interpreting bonding focuses less on specific emotional attitudes than on the magnitude of birth and the changes it calls for in parents' lives. Bearing a retarded child imposes upon parents an experience that corresponds structurally to those great turning points (and associated rites of passage) in traditional societies that transported people from one stage of life to another — birth, puberty, marriage, and death. The discussion of the Dax case makes it clear that these turning points included three "moments" or elements: (1) a break from the past; (2) a turbulent period of transition; and (3) entry into a new life and estate.[9] Whatever parenting a retarded child may entail emotionally for parents — fear, loneliness, resentment, and the like — it includes these three "moments." It wrenches them out of their former life, its assumptions and priorities; it produces a period of disorientation, confusion, and provisional adjustment; and, it is hoped, it ends in the parents' final attachment both to the child and to the circumstances that life with that child entails. In these respects, parenting resembles ancient rights of induction into the sacred. However, in the absence today of the definitive social rites that in traditional societies shaped and limited great crises and turning points, these "moments" do not follow in a tidy sequence. They overlap in the course of a profound sea change in the life and prospects of the parents.

Detachment from the Past

Detachment, at times, seems too mild a word; destruction more accurately tells the truth of the matter. The birth of a retarded child shatters one's world. "The world crumbled and fell around us," reports the mother of a Down's syndrome child.[10] "In one cataclysmic moment, our world had been shattered," another mother testifies.[11] Helen Featherstone, who has gathered evidence and also writes out of personal experience, states, "The shock of disability seems to obliterate the life that exists," and "threatens to define an ominous pattern for the new one."[12]

Trying to cope with the alien emphasizes this break with one's previous life. Routines, demands upon oneself and others, daily and long-range prospects change. The retarded child changes one's definitions of the important and the unimportant. The child alienates in that it estranges parents from their familiar world. Things look different — in the way parents view not only their own lives, but also the lives of their friends. Parents testify to their sense of isolation. This isolation shows up practically, but it also marks a deeper cultural isolation.

Practically, isolation begins in the hospital, where medical intervention often separates the mother not only from the child but from other mothers. It spreads as friends and relatives mumble or blurt in acknowledging the birth. (One mother reports that nothing unnerved her so much as her own mother's insistence that she institutionalize her child. Irony abounds in the advice the grandmother offered. She was attempting to mother her own daughter — to protect her from suffering. But the daughter found the advice troubling. It undermined her own ability to mother her retarded child. Her capacity to mother her child grew from the mothering she had received in childhood. But now her own mother seemed to say: "If you had been retarded, I would not have mothered you." The daughter kept her child but it disturbed other bonds.)

In time, the retarded child's special needs for care necessarily affect the family's daily routine and social life. Such needs not only throw out of balance parental efforts to give their several children equal attention, they also place early demands upon the other children as caregivers. Brothers and sisters sometimes feel cut off from their peers by their heavier responsibilities. The parent less engrossed in care also can grow to resent the special attention the retarded or the handicapped child receives. Not only is the child different, but the child's existence makes the marriage different. The primary caregiver, meanwhile, cannot help but compare her own plight (usually "her" — the world hasn't changed that much) with the lighter burdens of her contemporaries. One mother testifies that unhappiness alienates not only because others shun the unhappy but because the unhappy resent the others' happiness — especially when the fortunate take their happiness for granted.

Culturally, the birth of a retarded child cashiers not only the parents' social life but also their assumptions about prized American values: the American reliance on the wizardry of medicine, its orientation to youth as a symbol of promise, and its abhorrence of dependency. Americans have traditionally celebrated a technological triumphalism by assuming that all human problems will eventually yield to the organized assault of research and the strategic weapons generated by American research. But the parents quickly discover that medical research and the experts who wield the technologies which flow from it quickly reach their limits in helping a retarded child. A medical army marches in circles around their own tiny baby and its fateful problem. The physician cannot function heroically, but merely carries bad news. Medical magic that prolongs their child's life or patches up its other physical difficulties merely highlights medicine's inability to touch the fundamental cause of the parents' grief.

Further, the event heretically denies the conventional American attitude toward youth. As an immigrant people, Americans orient themselves more obsessively toward their children's performance than do members of more settled societies. In America, W. H. Auden once remarked, immigrant children live under the pressure to outstrip, in Great Britain, merely to live up to their parents.[13] The retarded child, however, cannot meet either demand. The child's severe impairment both shatters and yet fails to anesthetize them against the myths about youth. Parents suffer the discrepancy between myth and performance by feeling guilty for the child's shortfall. The American middle-class myth of producing the perfect child has always confused the process of manufacturing with giving birth. Americans take credit for the child as a product rather than rejoicing in it as a gift. In this atmosphere, the arrival of a retarded child signifies a personal failure rather than an imperfect gift. The child excommunicates its parents from the ordinary circle of nursery achievement. A child becomes "a dispiriting symbol of shared failure"[14] between husband and wife. The guilt and self-doubt compound the problem of attachment. As long as the child symbolizes failure, parents find it hard to love, hard to attach to, because in accepting the child, parents must ultimately learn to accept their discredited selves.

In yet another way, parents of the retarded feel isolated from the prevailing culture. Americans prize independence, both in their national and in their personal life. As a sinister obverse, they abhor dependency. Americans do not like to depend upon anyone personally and withdraw from those who threaten to depend, in turn, upon them. Europeans often complain that Americans, beneath their easy amiability, have little capacity for abiding friendship. Whether or not independence deserves praise, the failure to achieve it, either as a family or in any of its members, stigmatizes and isolates the family from others. The irremediable dependency of their severely or profoundly retarded child throws the family into a social plight that most others abhor and shun.

In a variety of ways, the retarded child disconnects its family from the culture at large. It is un-American; it makes aliens of parents, brothers, and sisters. For better or worse, they cannot participate immediately in the technological momentum, the orientation to youth, and the pride in independence that mark their peers. They become estranged in their own culture. Loyalty to this child requires a reconsidered relation to much else.

The parents and children suffer some of the pangs of detachment from their former life even when they choose to institutionalize the retarded child, though the form of their suffering differs. In this case, the child does not obtrude daily as a stranger in the home; rather, it belongs to a strange world, a specialized world of those similarly afflicted. Part of the task of accepting the child requires accepting the strange world to which it belongs. The parents reacquire some of their lost freedom by putting the child in an institution, but feelings of guilt and ambivalence often shadow that decision. Freedom does not come as a reward for the completion of the extended training tasks which parents customarily assume, but from deputizing others to discharge parental duties. In an important sense, parents affirm the future growth of their child by institutionalizing. The institution, after all, has resources for training beyond the reach and command of the nuclear family. But, at the same time, the decision to institutionalize requires parents to recognize the definitive outer limits to the child's potential. Hope loses its euphoria. Parents suffer at the same time an experience of loss resembling the original death which the discovery of retardation imposed. Bonding originally required the burial of the dream child and now institutionalization threatens with the burial of the actual child. However right the decision to institutionalize — and it can be very right indeed — the family faces with that decision its own subsequent coefficient of adversity.

Transition

In traditional societies, many perils accompany the passage from one estate to another (birth, puberty, marriage, war, peace, death). Such a passage often entails a suspension of ordinary activities associated with the old life. A potentially confusing period, it requires specialists (priest, warrior, shaman) to supervise and assist people through the transition rites associated with the great turning points in life.

Isolation and confusion can engulf parents with the arrival of the retarded infant. Professionals can err in opposite ways in handling this difficult transition. Out of compassion, caution, or their own aversion to pain, they may unduly prolong the transition by withholding the worst news. They dole it out to the parents in bits and pieces. Sometimes such compassion misses the mark. In the absence of candor, parents often generate worse fears. Anxiety feeds on uncertainty. Indeed, the transition period cannot end if parents fear that the future may hold even worse perils not yet revealed.

At the other extreme, professionals may fail to respect sufficiently the need for a transition. They may be unduly impatient with parents and unwilling to give adequate time to let parents assimilate bad news. They assume that parents should absorb the news and get on with the program. They do not realize that this kind of news both shocks and burns its way slowly into the mind. One doctor confesses, "It isn't okay to break the news, and support them for a week, and then give them an infant stimulation program and everything is fine. Some parents turn around very fast, and some turn around slowly. . . ."[15]

Parents usually need time to reorient themselves. Freud sensed the need for this time in any profound reconstruction of the self. When asked why the analyst could not simply tell the patient the truth about himself and be done with it, Freud remarked that the truth so delivered would sit like a parallel deposit in the mind, unassimilated.[16] Just so, parents of the retarded need to assimilate. They need some time to absorb the news that severs them from their former expectations, myths, and gratifications. They also need some time to enter into their new estate. The child (and their life with the child) carries its values, but its values strike with a force that transvalues rather than merely adds to the values which the parents already profess.

The specialists required in the period of transition include more than the obstetrician or the pediatrician whose repertoire of skills hardly begins to address the problems the child and the family face. The social worker, the nurse, the physical therapist, the special educator, the rabbi, minister, or priest, and other parents who have faced similar ordeals have important roles to play. The very recital of this list reminds us that our health care system and its schedule of rewards inadequately honor those who figure large in successful transition. Our third-party payment system rewards substantially those whose interventions hand to the parents their problem, but it provides much less adequate support to those who can give parents a helping hand with their problem. This disproportionate emphasis on acute care reduces too often the family's alternatives in care either to the expensive total institution or to the family's own limited, isolated resources. The system underfinances those supplementary services that might help make family care more tolerable and sustainable.

To assist a family wisely and enduringly, these various specialists must also help the family enlarge its sense of its own competence and resources. Eventually the family will need to review its positive assets. Such an inventory is difficult to undertake since the initial grief which the event provokes carries with it its own dark perception of the family's plight, a perception which impresses the grief-stricken as realistic. The serious accident along the highway or the discovery of the accident in one's genes both turns the world chilly and lowers one's sense of self-esteem. The victim suffers the double assault of despair and shame. Chaplains and other counselors have their work cut out for them. Admittedly, the lowering of self-esteem makes little rational sense (the self is not at fault), but, psychologically, the blow that exposes the sufferer in his vulnerability covers him with a sense of shameful resourcelessness. Thus the parents of the retarded and the handicapped and the accident victim need help in identifying those resources still theirs and in learning how to draw on them.

The chapter on the Dax case so emphasized the

patient's loss that it failed to underscore the importance of taking an inventory of what remains. This continuity of resources, however, does not soften the experience of break in identity or lessen the necessity of acquiring a new identity. The recovery of resources does not usually let one merely reassert one's old self intact as though nothing had intervened. Parents, for example, may need a reordered sense of themselves to recognize a now-valuable resource which they had previously relegated to the basement or the attic of their lives. Traits of character hardly required before the arrival of the retarded now loom large in helping the parents cope. And their gratifications also change. Accomplishments hardly noticed in the ordinary child now deserve a prize. One may still miss the allegro passages in rearing a child but the largo passages begin to acquire some subtlety for the retrained ear.

The term "transition" evokes the metaphor of a journey; and no pilgrim manages a difficult journey without some virtues that assist the passage. Loyalty heads the list of those virtues which a fully realized bonding requires: a double loyalty, to both the being and the well-being of the child. Parental loyalty, as noted later in this chapter, requires both. Neither loyalty is complete without the other. Both loyalties also require their own differing forms of the virtue of courage. Full pursuit of the child's well-being requires that "active" courage which Thomas Aquinas associated with "attack," the courage to overcome daunting obstacles which the parents of the retarded or the otherwise handicapped face in abundance. But loyal acceptance of the child's being, his existence as he is, requires that "passive" courage which Thomas associated with "endurance," the capacity to perdure in the midst of obstacles only some of which will yield to attack.

Bonding parents also require the virtue of justice, inasmuch as loyalty turns destructive without the constraint of justice. Left to itself, love responds without stint to the needs of another, but love diminishes into a sentiment less than just and, ultimately, less than loving if it fails to satisfy the legitimate claims of third parties. Specifically, love directed to the boundless needs of the retarded can sacrifice yet other members of the family. Justice requires some measure of equality in family life. However, equal treatment does not mean identical treatment. Justice defined as identical treatment blocks love's need to respond to specific needs. It foolishly misses the target when the differences between children in a family are great. Equal treatment in a family ought more appropriately to mean making an equal contribution to the good in the life of each member. This ideal lets the content of that contribution take different forms depending upon differing needs. It would remind sharply the retarded's parents of their equal but differing responsibilities to each of their children. Undoubtedly the sheer magnitude of the retarded's needs makes it difficult to accommodate tidily to the claims of justice in the distribution of love, but the claim of justice reminds parents that even as love does its best, it must also apportion at its best.

Other virtues must come into play, including a wisdom that distinguishes the important from the unimportant and the doable from the impossible. But whatever the virtues required along the way, bonding takes hold in the parents when the event they originally perceived as blank and intractable fate now seizes them as destiny, in which they imperfectly but humanly find their identity and calling.

Attachment

Healthy attachment presupposes a number of prenatal and immediate postnatal activities that support bonding. The mother, clearly, and the father in some instances also, can engage in: (a) prior to pregnancy, at least some touching of babies (even if only by babysitting); (b) during pregnancy, feeling the fetus kick (the perception of the fetus as a separate individual sometimes converts unwanted to more acceptable or wanted pregnancies); (c) witnessing birth (studies suggest that those who witness birth are more likely to bond to the child than those who do not); (d) immediate cuddling after birth (parents deprived of access to the baby during the so-called sensitive period, are inclined to be less attached; the baby "belongs," as it were, to someone else); (e) setting up a favorable institutional setting (homelike, if not at home, with professional staff assisting, rather than displacing, the mother); (f) reciprocally interacting (touch, eye-to-eye contact — the child can see at birth), talking (the neonate prefers the high-pitched female voice), entraining (a type of dance movement in the course of conversation between mother and child), smelling (by the fifth day a baby can tell its mother's breast pad), sensing (heat, and heartbeat) — to say nothing of absorbing the bacterial nasal flora and antibodies imparted with the mother's milk.[17]

We can interpret the proposal that final attachment to the retarded child resembles induction into the sacred in traditional societies either sentimentally or realistically. Sentimental testimony abounds. One parent professes, "I believe a brain-injured child is a gift from God. This child is a precious gift to the family."[18] Another parents avers, "The child we have is like an angel. Treat him well, he will put in a good word for us with God."[19] Medieval people sometimes referred to the retarded as "infants of the good God"[20] — and allowed them special freedom to roam. The fool, we know, enjoyed a measure of liberty in the royal court denied to others. This special elevation of the retarded reflects itself in the very word sometimes used to designate them: cretin. Although the word has now fallen into disuse or smacks of the pejorative, some suggest that it derives from the word "Christian." At one time, the retarded alone seemed to deserve the adjective "Christian" so often loosely (and wrongly) used to suggest innocence. Owing to their simplicity of mind, the retarded alone seemed incorruptible.

Such views verge on the sentimental. The phrase "gift of God" sometimes functions less as a theological assertion than as a claim about some inevitably good consequence that follows from the birth of a retarded child. It claims too much for the retarded's tonic impact on its family and society. It smacks too much, albeit poignantly, of the fervent rhetoric that one sometimes hears from AA and other support groups that need missionary zeal in order to sustain courage. Gifts from God — some retarded children surely may seem, but they are not inevitably so received or perceived. Taking responsibility for the retarded may deepen lives in some families. But suffering does not always ennoble. Heavy responsibilites can crush as well as strengthen their bearers.

Yet, parents and children do bond, and sometimes so deeply that the bonding powerfully transforms life. Another parent resorts to religious language: "A child like this is a sacrament." The parent thereby concedes that caring for an abnormal child makes one feel "outcast, doomed somehow not to be normal oneself," but acknowledges, at the same time, "an entirely different covenant with existence."[21] In another instance, the father of an autistic child rages against his lot and yet finally concedes: "Consciousness is like a free gift arising out of a bond that is tragic and good. But for him, I guess, and for us, the bond is what comes first."[22]

Words such as "tragic," "doomed," "outcast" still appear in the testimony, however. But the harshness of the experience no longer overwhelms. Parents and child have attached. Featherstone wryly acknowledges a negative sign of this bonding. "At the minimum and wintry level, acceptance may begin to bring the recognition that the child's hardship no longer represents the only obstacle to happiness."[23] Still, bonding can eventually bring rewards: the brother of a mildly retarded busboy reports taking stock of his deficient sibling. A stranger innocently asks him the rather conventional question — What does your brother do for a living? The young man, for the first time, does not answer preemptively by explaining that his brother, because retarded, works only as a menial in a restaurant. "Suddenly it struck me for the first time in the twenty-eight years of our lives together that mental slowness is not the sum of [my brother's] existence. He is a man who is married, holds down a job, pays taxes." So he returns to the question and simply tells the stranger, "He's in the restaurant business!"[24]

The literature on the retarded child usually closes with a discussion of "acceptance." However, acceptance does not describe the bonded parent without qualification. Attachment, at its deepest level, sets up a tension between acceptance of the child as it is and a quest for interventions that will improve his lot. Any human being bonded to the being and well-being of another does what he can and enlists the aid of others to serve its good. Simple acceptance alone hardly describes the parents' relationship to their child as they attempt what they can to foster their child's excellence and well-being. To that end, of course, they seek the services of the doctor and, eventually, the teacher — to stretch the child's capacities and to help it live up to them.

However, a compulsion to act can turn demonic, hammering the child with help that rejects the child as it is. It may also betray a profound self-rejection. The parent feels guilty about having produced a child with defects and attempts to atone by becoming a superparent. Sooner or later, the parent must reckon with and accept the child's limits. Otherwise, the effort to serve the child's excellence and well-being deteriorates into a battering and self-battering masked beneath the fair face of love.

Attachment needs both activism and acceptance. Religiously put: attachment becomes too quietistic if it slackens into mere acceptance of the child as it is. Love must will the well-being and not merely the being of the other. But, even worse, attachment lapses into a gnostic revulsion against the world if in the name of well-being it recoils from the child in its deprived state of being. One observer perceived the right balance between acceptance and intervention when he observed, "I admire the purpose and ingenuity with which parents and children forge a good life out of imperfect materials."[25] Attachment includes efforts at transformation, yes; but not as though all value rests in the transformation, as though the transformation must surpass the imperfect materials themselves for anything good to come of the life.

Valuing

We misunderstand valuing the retarded child if we place value wholly in the marketplace. By "marketplace" I mean a setting in which we treat the retarded child as a discrete item in the world, to be compared and weighted against other discrete items. In this setting, one asks what correlations appear between natural ability and perceived worth and then one tests out that worth by deciding on how many social resources (public and familiar) one will spend to support and enhance the retarded. What price, in effect, can the retarded command within the public and domestic economy? This question, so formulated, begs for an answer in the coin of utility.

This approach misses the issue in valuing not so much because it judges cruelly and ruthlessly (though it often does) but because it misses the even more cruel question which the retarded themselves pose. The retarded do not chiefly pose the question "What is the relative worth, or lack of it, of a child with my particular disabilities?" They ask, rather "What worth has a world that includes me in it?" Parents also face the latter, more encompassing, metaphysical question. This child, my child, not the child I hoped for, named, and registered for college in fancy, depresses for me utterly the world's worth. Herein lies the deep quarrel with God, the terrible envy and resentment of friends. Parents face not the problem of relative good in a marketplace of goods and preferences, but the problem of evil. The arrival of the deprived child raises the question of the worth of the world and the worthwhileness of life. The question deepens and darkens beyond the perceived worth of the child relative to other goods, to the worth of anything whatsoever. Nothing seems worth a candle. Do the powers that matter in life impoverish and crush, or do they bless?

Parents see the problem at this more metaphysical level because they suffer at this level. And, at least some of them, it would appear, have sought to respond at this level when they have confessed themselves to feel outcast and doomed and yet have reckoned with the child as establishing their "covenant with existence." Bonding to a child who renders questionable the value of existence reestablishes one's covenant with existence. Neither policy-makers nor professionals should deal with that testimony lightly.[26]

This covenant with existence demands devotion beyond the ordinary measure. Featherstone likens the plight of parents to the person who happens upon a drowning man. As the only person there, she can jump in and try to save him, or she can agonize on shore. "In the first case I am a hero; in the second, a coward. There is no way I can remain what I was before — an ordinary person."[27] But heroism alone does not sustain the covenant; the child also sustains the parents. That sustenance may be difficult to acknowledge without sounding as though one justifies the retardation. Yet some parents have acknowledged the deepening of their lives; they find themselves in retrospect a little kinder, a little gentler, a little more sensitive to the difficulties others face than they might otherwise have been.[28]

Because this is the case, valuing the retarded does not arbitrarily place a pricetag on an imperfect product that someone has manufactured. Valuing persons differs from inventing, fabricating, and marketing things. It discovers and honors what is already there; it does not merely impute; and therefore, reciprocally, this valuing, which opens to the value of the other, also imparts strength to those who do the valuing.

Values are not ideal demands alone; they also affirm and define strength and power. The Latin root for value — *valere* — from which we also derive valor and valid and convalescent — implies this affirmation. The convalescent whom illness has assaulted begins to grow again in strength. The valorous man or woman faces adversity strongly, stoutly, bravely, vigorously, and powerfully. The brave person exudes power in the face of odds.

Similarly, when we refer to values — to the value of the family, work, love, birth, and the retarded child — we talk, not about frothy matters that we imagine or invent, but about people, institutions, ideals, and demands that bear down upon us. They validate themselves, as it were, as stout, strong, vigorous, and powerful, prevailing upon us as worthy of response in our freedom. Values elicit commitments from which, in turn, strength and power derive.

An Epilogue on Policies and Quandaries

This essay has tried to put the problem of valuing the retarded in a relational setting. It has looked to the relationship between parents and child for its clue to moral claims and obligations. It has attended specifically to the process of bonding, as it honors and values another and as it generates loyalty and trust between those bonded. The path to bonding does not usually run smooth. Parents undergo an ordeal that beggars description except in the language reserved for induction into the sacred. The testimony of parents reminds me of the language that one associates with the relational thinkers. Kierkegaard spoke of fear and trembling in the God-relationship;[29] Heidegger reckoned with dread in the relationship to death;[30] Buber recognized that the "I" and the "Thou" remain strange to one another in the very midst of I-Thou address.[31] Relationship to the retarded at the deepest level requires a transformation that upsets, winnows, confuses, and turns around the self.

The use of this religious language also implies that the process of bonding affects more than psychological being; it affects us ontologically and morally; bonding gives a clue to the being and well-being of others, to one's obligation to them, and to one's own being and value in so honoring the tie.

This general approach departs from the prevailing tendency among moralists to resort exclusively to the notion of abstract rights and duties in dealing with the moral warrants for care of the retarded. Ethicists usually begin with natural capacities (such as intelligence) abstracted from the historical accidents of family, religion, education, and the like, and seek to determine what duties we owe to all human beings who possess and show these capacities. This approach has led, across the last century and a half, to establishing huge facilities designed to care for people who, by virtue of natural misfortune or historical accident, suffer abuse or neglect at the hands of their fellows or who need care of a kind which neither they nor their families nor their friends can offer. The support for these institutions — hospitals, mental hospitals, nursing homes, and workshops — comes largely from strangers (through taxation or philanthropic giving); further, they are manned by strangers, whose job it is to give help to strangers (to all persons whatsoever, irrespective of ties).

The approach taken in this essay differs (but only partly) from this prevailing view of rights and duties and its institutional results. The generation of a set of rights and duties to the retarded by abstractly considering natural abilities leads to moral minimalism and to a minimal discharge of those duties in huge institutions. Duties based on rights tend to diminish to whatever a socially undefined person can enforce against anybody. We write off additional obligations that grow from bonding as merely optional and preferential. These optional obligations enter into discussion of what the society owes creatures whose being and worth disclose themselves chiefly in the context of ties. The disquieting results of this minimalism are all about us in a rootless and libertarian post-Enlightenment society. We reduced our direct obligations toward the marginal and the deviant, and discharge those few obligations we acknowledge through the device of segregative institutions and isolative services. The retarded's right to these services and the shape we have given them result from a bondless consideration of natural abilities and worth. Meanwhile, the very scale and structure of the institutions themselves have made it more difficult to bond within their walls.

A more relational approach does not, however, argue for the dismantling of large-scale institutions. Criticism ought not obscure either the philanthropic impulse that often prompted their founding or the conscientious efforts of many of their managers and staff to calibrate their limited resources to real needs. Moreover, some versions of mainstreaming today set the needy free from segregated institutions only to abandon them to the *de facto* segregation of third-rate hotels or the streets and tunnels of a city. Care deteriorates from little to nothing.

At the policy level, a respect for the importance of bonding should encourage the reform rather than the dissolution of total institutions. It should highlight those various factors that foster and nurture small-scale community even in large institutional settings — architectual design, the layout of interior space, equipment, public and private rooms, and the strategic use of professional terms and volunteer groups. Further, a respect for bonding should encourage the society to provide some mildly or moderately retarded persons with more small-scale communities (surrogate families) as an alternative residential choice to either the large-scale institution or the family home. Such facilities would also lessen the trauma institutional residents face when the society mainstreams them (only too often a euphemism for drifting and crashing amongst the shoals and reefs of big-city life). Finally, it should also encourage more adequate public support to families to ease the burden of family care — more adequate training programs, respite houses that provide families with periodic relief from total care, and the mobilization of religious and other volunteer groups to supplement the nuclear family with some of those resources previously available only through the extended family.

Such strategic assistance to families helps at two points. It encourages more families to keep their children at home rather than commit them to institutions. It also lessens the traumas both the retarded and their families face if and as the society mainstreams more of the mildly or moderately retarded and thrusts them back into their homes. The family that receives back a deinstitutionalized child after having lived on its own needs help as it reabsorbs the child into the family.

Even though it might improve social policies and render less harsh the choices parents must make, a more relational approach will not solve all quandaries parents face: whether to institutionalize a child; what goods will best serve the well-being of a child; what balance to strike between the claims of the retarded child and those of other siblings, work, and marriage. Indeed, bonding often intensifies rather than solves problems in casuistry. The bonded agent must reckon with conflicting loyalties, not just competing preferences, when reaching a decision. He cannot, moreover, blunt the moral ache of the decision by resort to the marketplace device of calculating tradeoffs or balancing goods over evils. He must honor the tragic, or, as religious people may prefer, the divine comedic element in a moral decision. A decision to institutionalize does not merely add a debit to a balance. One persists in wishing otherwise, even when one chooses one's course. The brokenness, the incompleteness, the tragedy, the poignancy of a decision moves with us into the future — unless an ultimate perspective with more depth than a balance sheet lets us see things whole.

Finally, a relational approach cannot seriously claim to derive notions of worth wholly from the faulty testimony of those who bond to one another. If worth depends upon a human tie alone, the retarded child is wholly hostage to the erratic valuations of parents and caregivers, good, bad or indifferent. That is why Enlightenment moralists tried to establish a notion of worth irrespective of ties. Their minimalism sought to prevent worse fates. The external and internal obstacles to bonding and the awesome process of detachment, transition, and attachment must give one pause about placing authority for making ultimate judgments of worth in the hands of parents and others who face, many times unsuccessfully, that difficult ordeal. The battered child silences foolish sentimentality about the success rate of bonding. If value and the perception of value derive entirely from a relationship, then the powerless one within the relationship becomes wholly hostage to it. Parents cannot claim to be the sole or final arbiters of the value of their children. Frail and facing a process strewn with obstacles, parents do not always bond well or wisely. This consideration and caution partly led the theological tradition, when speaking relationally, to posit a God-relationship as encompassing, authorizing, judging, and forgiving all others. To testify, however, to that relationship with bonded conviction, one must suffer an induction into the sacred — of which the ordeals I have described in this essay offer a petty parable and sign.

Notes

1. For this and the following material on bonding, see Marshall A. Klaus and John H. Kennell, *Maternal-Infant Bonding* (St. Louis: C. V. Mosley, 1976), Chs. 1 and 3.

2. Ibid., p. 59.

3. Dr. Jerome Kagan has reported clinical evidence of these fears appearing at this age.

4. A. N. Solnit and M. H. Stark, "Mourning and the Birth of a Defective Child," *Psychoanalytic Study of the Child* 16 (1961): 523-37.

5. Klaus and Kennell, *Maternal-Infant Bonding*, p. 84.

6. Helen Featherstone, *A Difference in the Family* (New York: Basic Books, 1980), p. 25.

7. John Greenberg, *A Child Called Noah* (New York: Holt, Rinehart and Winston, 1972), p. 180.

8. For further details, see John Bowlby, *Attachment and Loss*, Vol. I (New York: Basic Books, 1969), p. 340.

9. See van Gennep, *Rites of Passage*, and Van der Leeuw, *Religion in Essence and Manifestation*, Vol. I, Part 2, Ch. 22, "Sacred Life."

10. J. Canning and C. Canning, *The Gift of Martha*, Children's Hospital Medical Center, cited by Helen Featherstone, *A Difference in the Family*, p. 220.

11. R. Massie and S. Massie, *Journey* (New York: Alfred A. Knopf, 1975), cited in Helen Featherstone, *A Difference in the Family*, p. 220.

12. Featherstone, *A Difference in the Family*, p. 220.

13. W. H. Auden offered this comment in personal conversation. I do not know whether he ever set it in print. This chapter on the retarded deals with the pressures that an immigrant nation's orientation to the achievement of its youth creates for the young; the chapter on the aged explores the corresponding neglect it encourages toward the elderly.

14. Featherstone, *A Difference in the Family*, p. 91.

15. Ibid., p. 188.

16. Sigmund Freud, *A General Introduction to Psychoanalysis* (New York: Permabooks, 1953). Freud writes: "What have we to do in order to bring what is unconscious in the patient into consciousness? At one time we thought that would be very simple; all we need to do would be to identify this unconscious matter and then tell the patient what it was. However, we know already that that was a shortsighted mistake. Our knowledge of what is unconscious in him is not equivalent to his knowledge of it; when we tell him what we know he does not assimilate it *in place of* his own unconscious thoughts, but *alongside* of them, and very little has been changed." Twenty-seventh lecture, "Transference," pp. 443-44.

17. Klaus and Kennel, *Maternal-Infant Bonding*, pp. 86-94.

18. Featherstone, *A Difference in the Family*, p. 281.

19. Ibid., p. 166.

20. Leo Kramer, *A History of the Care and Study of the Mentally Retarded* (Springfield, Ill.: Charles C. Thomas, 1964), p. 7.

21. Featherstone, *A Difference in the Family*, pp. 213-14.

22. Ibid., p. 237.

23. Ibid., p. 220.

24. Ibid., p. 176.

25. Ibid., p. 10.

26. For the author's attempt to deal with the issue of theodicy, see the concluding comment to the chapter on "Afflicting the Afflicted: Total Institutions" and the "Postscript" to this book, in addition to the chapter on the "Covenanter" in May, *The Physician's Covenant*, Ch. 4.

27. Featherstone, *A Difference in the Family*, p. 83.

28. See the "Postscript" for a further discussion of the reciprocities of giving and receiving that define covenanted lives.

29. Søren Kierkegaard, *Fear and Trembling*, tr. Walter Lowrie (New York: Doubleday & Co., 1954), pp. 146-47.

30. Heidegger elevated the phrase *Sein zum Tode* (being-toward-death) into one of the fundamental categories of existence in his *Sein und Zeit* (Tübingen: Max Niemeyer Verlag, 1957), eighth printing, pp. 235-67.

31. Martin Buber writes, "God is the Being that is directly, most nearly, and lastingly, over against us." *I and Thou* (New York: Charles Scribner's Sons, 1958), pp. 80-81.

99 Biblical Faith and the Loss of Children

Bruce C. Birch

Death always comes as an offense. Death is the end of life. For most of us life is good; death is the ultimate end of the touching, the sharing and the struggling together that make for wholeness. There has been much recent effort in the church to understand and deal with death, and we have been blessed by a great deal of helpful literature and attention in the communities of faith to the issues of death and dying.

There is something about the death of a child, however, which heightens the offense; we have not often faced that matter very directly in our churches. The death of a child is felt to be unacceptable. It seems unnatural. We can't use some of those bromides that we sometimes use to reassure ourselves; for example, "She lived a full life." Often a child's death becomes the occasion for a crisis of faith. Not only a matter of psychology of grief, a child's death is a challenge to our own deepest faith understandings. What kind of God would allow this to happen? What could faith possibly have to say to this experience?

These questions have been my own. In the fall of 1970 we were told that our daughter Christine had acute lymphocytic leukemia. This diagnosis came at the end of a difficult year for us. I had been fired from my first college teaching job because of antiwar activities. We had been unable to find a job and were forced to move out of our house. There was no place to go. We stored our furniture in a friend's basement and headed for parts unknown. I finally found a teaching job in August, one month before the beginning of school, and moved from Iowa, out on the plains where we had family close by, to South Carolina, a region of the country where we knew no one.

Six weeks after we arrived in South Carolina, we learned that our daughter had a potentially fatal illness. The nearest treatment center was in Atlanta, the Henrietta Eggleston Children's Hospital at Emory University. We traveled there to begin the arduous course of treatments which we hoped would put our daughter's disease into remission. A remission might have allowed her to receive the benefits of advancing medical knowledge in dealing with leukemia. But before Christine could be put into remission, she broke out in chicken pox, to which she had been exposed in the church nursery before we knew she had leukemia. Her diseased blood cells could not fight the infection and she went into shock. One month after the diagnosis, she died, on her third birthday. The precipitating cause of her death and its timing seemed cruel ironies.

We were filled with anger and grief. Where was God? Where was justice? Where was meaning? I can only share with you out of my own knowledge of the power of those questions — and my conviction that in the biblical tradition of the Christian faith, we do have some resources which help us, even in times of such loss.

We can begin by talking about the problem of God. God is the easiest hook on which to hang blame. Many instinctively feel that God must somehow be punishing them. "Why did God do this to me? I must have done something to deserve this." Unfortunately, that notion is reinforced by a good deal of popular religion; but the punisher God is not a helpful concept. It either produces guilt that is undeserved and unrelated to the situation, or it leads to angry rejection of God altogether.

This concept of a punisher God does sometimes appear in the Bible, however. In the Old Testament, particularly in Deuteronomy and in the Wisdom literature, we find a God who dispenses rewards and punishments for every human action, as if life could be reduced to such mechanical blessings and curses. But a corrective to this view also appears in the Bible; the entire Book of Job is a protest against it, sweeping away its irrelevant and monstrous blasphemy. Job is a righteous man who has suffered great and grievous loss. In the traditional story (chapters 1-2; 42:7 ff.) He is patient and long-suffering, and God finally restores everything to him. This traditional tale of the patient sufferer was surely known widely in the ancient world of Israel. That is not the total picture in the Book of Job, however. The author has split the old story in half, inserting into the middle of it, alongside the traditional picture of the patient Job, the hurt, angry and rebellious Job. This Job argues with the friends and challenges God. The friends say all the pious things: "God's purposes are too great for us. You must have deserved this, so accept it." But Job argues that all people, whether righteous or not, are vulnerable to suffering, and that a hidden, uncaring God is no help at all.

The Book of Job helps us to reject the notion of the punisher God as inadequate. It calls us to look further for a God who does care and who identifies with our pain. Perhaps the God who finally appears to Job in a whirlwind at the end of the book is a pointer toward a deity who at least engages and is present with those who suffer — but the Book of Job is not intended to give us easy answers to that struggle. By sweeping away glib responses to the problem of God in times of deep pain and suffering, the book points to our own struggles and our own engagement with an even wider biblical tradition in which there does appear a caring God who is central to our faith tradition. I want to describe three aspects of this divine image over against that of the punisher God.

The first is *God as hearer.* Over and over again in Scripture, we find lines like these: "I have heard their cries. Their cries have come to me. Their cries have fallen on my ears." Dorothee Sölle, in her important book *Suffering* (Fortress, 1975), suggests that the outcry is the beginning of healing. Israel knew the importance of expressing pain and despair to God, and in the midst of the community. Nowhere is this seen more eloquently than in the laments of the Psalter. We think of the Psalter as a book of praises, but the largest number of Psalms are songs of lamentation. One cannot read these laments without being impressed that Israel had a rather different concept of worship than we commonly do. The psalms are gutsy and honest; they don't pull any punches. They express despair: "Out of the depths have I cried to thee, O Lord" (Ps. 130). They express doubts: "My God, my God, why hast thou forsaken me?" (Ps. 22). They express anger and bitterness. The 137th Psalm, which begins, "By the waters of Babylon we sat down and wept," ends with lines so terrible in their expression of anger and bitterness that we almost never read them in public worship: "O daughter of Babylon, you devastator! . . . Happy shall he be who takes your little ones and dashes them against the rock!" Anger, bitterness, despair, doubt — it is all there, not because the tradition desires to affirm those expressions as ends in themselves but because if the pain is not exposed the healing cannot begin. These Psalms are often shocking to us because so much of our own worship tries to conceal our deepest wounds. Our own worship so often takes place at the level of the lowest common denominator of our corporate experience.

The role of the pastor as counselor can also serve to hide our deepest wounds from the wider community. I once was in a church in which someone expressed very deep hurt and anger during the time set aside for the sharing of concerns in the worship service — only to have the pastor remark at the end of the service, "Well, Fred, if you had brought that to me we could have talked about it without imposing on everyone else's worship experience." If the hurt is not exposed, the healing word cannot be spoken.

My wife and I found many in the church especially reluctant to deal with the death of a child. One can speak of one's recently deceased parent for years; it is not unusual and is widely acknowledged as healthy. But to speak of one's lost child is often to evoke responses like "Hasn't he gotten over that yet?" One of the most frequent pieces of advice given to people who lose small children is to have another child as soon as possible — as though that could mask the hurt or take away the loss. Out of our own experience we came to understand that the death of a child is threatening to all in a way that our own death as adults is not. Thus many prefer to hide their pain.

The Hebrews understood instinctively that such pain had to be shared. They believed God heard; if our cries were not expressed, then they could not come to God. Their response to pain and loss was dialogic. It was offered up to God in the belief that God cared and would respond. The interesting thing about the laments of the Psalter is that with one exception (Ps. 88), all the laments move toward praise. They begin with lines of despair and anguish such as "My God, my God, why hast thou forsaken me?" and move to expressions of confidence and trust. This was not because Israel thought God heard simply in order to grant our wishes. Israel knew that what we sometimes wish for in painful situations does not always take place — but it believed that God *would* respond. The Israelites ended their laments in praise, anticipating that out of God's response, new life could come from any crisis as God's gift, sometimes in unexpected ways.

This brings us to a second image of God which can aid us in times of loss: *God as life-giver.* Both the Hebrew Scripture and the New Testament know that God is the one who makes new life possible where only death seems to reign. It is important not to misunderstand this assertion. It does not remove the reality and the pain of death. That pain remains an offense. There are two great biblical symbols of God as life-giver out of the experience of death, which are also the great central symbols of salvation: the Exodus event in the Old Testament and the resurrection of Christ in the New Testament. Each of these central events witnesses to the faith conviction that life wins out over death, not because death is unreal or to be ignored or submerged but because God acts as the life-giver beyond death.

The deliverance from bondage in Egypt was a moment of birth for Israel as a people. They had come into being not out of their own efforts but as a result of God's gracious activity of deliverance. In bondage in Egypt and in the dramatic moment at the sea, death seemed to be the only possibility. Life came unexpectedly as God's gift, enabling a new future where none had seemed possible. To Israel this moment became a symbol of possibilities for new life beyond any experience of death. To be an Exodus people was not to live in a world without death; only God was without death. Exodus was a sign of God's gift of life despite death, beyond death, in the midst of death. One can give praise for life as God's gift even when the life of a child is ended prematurely, as was our daughter's. The three years of her life were a gift which her death cannot erase.

The resurrection symbol which is central to the Christian faith in the New Testament witness points to a message similar to that of Exodus. For the church, the resurrection has often lost its power because it is used to obscure the reality of death shown forth in the crucifixion. Our daughter's death came to us as a terrible offense and brought to us an immense sense of aloneness. No meaningful word could ever obscure that reality. It is present within me at this very moment. The disciples also knew the experience of pain and loss in Christ's crucifixion. The power of the resurrection is not in removing the offense of death but in saying, "This is not the final word." This is the good news which the community of faith is charged to carry to each new age.

The community of faith we knew in a house church in Iowa gathered around us again in Wichita, Kansas, to support us at the time of our daughter's death. Its members shared and received our sense of loss. With their support we chose to write a service of thanksgiving for Christine's life because we believed that her death could not be the final word, obscuring all that she had been in life. Her death could not be the final word for our lives either, and in the days after her death, church people helped us see the life that God makes possible beyond such painful moments.

Finally, I want to speak about *God as sufferer.* The biblical picture of God is of a God who suffers with us. This God not only hears and offers us the possibility of life-giving ways into the future; this God has shared our sufferings.

In the account of Moses' encounter with God in the burning bush, God says to Moses, "I have seen the affliction of my people, I have heard their cries. I know their sufferings" (Ex. 3:7). The Hebrew verb we translate as "know" is much broader than can be captured by any English word. It does not indicate "cognitive knowledge, knowledge in the head." Its meaning is closer to our verb "experience." It indicates interaction with and participation in the reality of that which is known. God's statement to Moses is one of the earliest points at which we can see the beginning of the tradition of a God who not only sees and hears from on high but who also chooses to enter into and experience our suffering with us.

The concept of the suffering God reaches a culmination in the crucifixion. There the divine Self shares our ultimate aloneness in pain and death in the form of the cross. Then God can say in the resurrection that death is not the final word, and say that not as a word from on high but as a word from our very midst. And we can better hear that word as meaningful.

We have been speaking of the problem of God. The Scriptures also address us at the point of affirming the life of a child. Our response to the death of a child often suggests that his or her death was more important than his or her life, however short. But Scripture is absolutely clear that all life is of God; all life should be valued as fully participating in God's creation.

One way the faith community can assist grieving parents is by honoring children in the first place. We need to examine our communities of faith in this regard. If we are attentive to the full personhood of our children, then when death tragically takes a child from our midst, we can celebrate the gift which has been among us and not just the life that might have been.

Finally, we must say a word about the role of the covenant community. It seems to me that the Scriptures uniformly witness to the importance of the corporate body of faith as the context of support in times of crisis. This was certainly our experience. In South Carolina, where we knew not a soul, people rose up to claim the privilege of ministering to our hurt. Even though we had no history with that community, we were part of the wider community of faith, and we received unqualified support. People also gathered to be with us in Kansas, where we went for our daughter's burial. If we had been alone, we might not have seen how important it was to affirm our daughter's life and not simply her death.

There seem to be three roles that the community of faith plays in such crises. First, the community helps to relieve the isolation suffered along with the anger and pain. A terrible sense of aloneness comes in the midst of such hardships; the community should surround us in those moments with a presence that it is a witness to the presence of God.

Second, the church should pass on and hold up symbols of our faith so that they are available to us in time of trauma as ways of seeing God's gift of life even beyond the offense of the moment. This function cannot be left until a crisis occurs. We have to labor constantly at the task of preparing people with the great symbol resources of our faith, in anticipation of the crises that come to us all.

We must know of Exodus and resurrection. We must learn of the God who hears, gives life to and suffers with us. In stories, hymns, liturgies and studies we equip ourselves with the resources of our faith. These resources will also help us bring the grief and pain out of the counselor's study and into the wider community, so that we all begin to draw on the faith symbols and words that speak to these experiences. We can then have recourse to those traditions when pain descends on us.

Finally, the community of faith mediates the healing word. The community helps to show us pathways into the future when we do not see them ourselves. It does this by receiving our pain and our loss, but also by refusing to believe that such pain and loss constitute the final word.

Out of these perspectives from Scripture and experience, has my daughter's death been made more acceptable? No! But is there a further word of meaning about her life and the life which goes forward for us? Through the grace of God and the support of the people of God, Yes!

Chapter Sixteen

THE PHYSICIAN-PATIENT RELATIONSHIP: ADVICE AND CONSENT

There is much talk in our society about how destructive relationships of dependency can be. Many people are concerned about the relationship between the patient and the physician because they see it as one of dependency. At the same time, others in our society are concerned because they see medicine becoming more and more impersonal and see the physician-patient relationship of the "good old days" becoming less and less possible.

What is at stake in these discussions? Those who take part in them often raise two points that appear to center upon the effect of technology on the physician-patient relationship. First, they claim that technology can lead to a depersonalization in that relationship: the patient becomes a "case" instead of a person. Second, they argue that the new technology that gives physicians power to cure disease also gives them a capacity to control patients. These observers of modern medicine argue that we must be protected from this new power of medical technology, or else physicians will use it to further encourage patient dependency.

As a response to the power imbalance between patients and physicians, some have suggested that physicians and patients should understand themselves as independent actors, each free to enter into or to leave the relationship. Recognition of the patient's freedom would act as a constraint upon the physician's power and would consequently boost the patient's own power. As the two actors approach each other with a greater degree of equality, many of the problems stemming from the original imbalance would be ameliorated.

Critics of this approach charge that it is false to the reality of illness and to the social reality within which people often find themselves. Particular patients often are disempowered by society because of attitudes toward race or gender or religion. Secondly, ill people are unfree; in fact, illness is experienced as a lack of freedom, at least initially. Thus the patient is, initially and almost by definition, dependent. Freedom and independence are important. Physicians may be trying to help their patients achieve more freedom and independence. Yet, society and illness can put limits on this help.

It is clear that one of the contested issues here is the authority of the physician. All agree that the physician has an authority of a certain kind, but there is a disagreement about the basis of that authority, what kind of authority it is, and the limits upon its legitimate exercise. We are familiar with a number of different models of authority in our culture. What might some of these models be?

In one model, people have authority by virtue of some skill they possess. Thus automobile mechanics have the skill that gives them the authority to make recommendations about what should be done to a car, but they may not impose their will. In another model, people have authority because they have been elected to public office or are responsible to elected officials.

Within the limits of law, these persons not only recommend, they also decide and can impose their will. We are all familiar with a third model too: the authority of the parent, who is assumed to have the child's best interest at heart and who can, again within limits, direct the child in certain ways. Corporate authority, based upon the assumption that those who invest and risk their money may decide how it is spent, provides yet another model. Consumers are the authority in the marketplace, deciding what will be produced by their choices. Finally, teachers are authorities in the transmission of knowledge. What can we learn from the models we have listed about the authority of the physician and his or her relationship to the patient?

Most of us would want the physician to have our best interest in mind, to be especially interested in our welfare — the kind of concern demanded of the parent-child model. Yet adult patients are not children; they ought to have more say in their treatment than do children in their upbringing, something that must be expressed by any model which emphasizes the independence of the patient. But we can learn from other models as well. Physicians have been given certain responsibilities and authority by public officials and they, and they alone, can perform certain actions for the public good. Rightfully, we expect them to live up to this public trust. Further, they have learned certain skills so that they — and we — may proceed on the basis of facts. Thus they have part of their authority because of their skill. Further, physicians not only make recommendations to patients about what should be done but they are expected to make decisions themselves and to teach the patient. This teaching takes place on two levels: first, there are basic facts about health and disease; and second the physician teaches what patients may expect, both of others and of themselves.

Daniel P. Sulmasy (selection 100) argues that our usual models of power and authority are inadequate, that we need to explore alternative ways of understanding the relationship between physicians and patients. Sulmasy would have us reflect on the possibility that physicians have unique roles with respect to the truth of our lives, not just the truths about our diseases.

It is this fact among others which makes truth telling in medicine so complicated. In the first place, truths about disease often are avoided, so say some physicians, in order to make it easier for the patient. But that very justification opens up a new area of inquiry. Do we avoid telling any truth that will be difficult for the patient, or are there truths that all ought to hear, including the truth that they will die? The question becomes even more troublesome when we recognize that Christians believe that suffering and death are not the last word about human life; consequently the prevention of suffering and the amelioration of the fear of death cannot stand by themselves as good reasons for evading the truth.

There is one further point to be made. Christians are called upon not simply to tell the truth but to build communities which will sustain truthfulness. What does this mean in the context of medicine? Does it change the question about telling the truth into something more complicated? Is it possible that some of the discussion about telling the truth stems from a fear about our inability to sustain truthfulness with the patient?

Thus far, the discussion of the relationship has focused upon the responsibilities of the physician. Are there obligations that are owed by the patient to the physician? For example, what about the patient's obligation to be truthful to the physician? Do patients have an obligation to follow the doctor's orders or at least inform the doctor if they are not going to do so? Physicians "practice" upon patients. Do patients have an obligation to make themselves available for this to novice medical practitioners so that the art of medicine may continue? Some writers suggest that patients teach their physicians. Is this part of what it means to be a patient? Further, is this something that the physician must remember in order to keep from becoming arrogant about the source of his/her knowledge?

Note that the more we discuss the mutual responsibilities of patients and physicians, the more we make it possible for both parties to acknowledge that each is indebted to the other for something that only the other can give. If that is the case, then both patients and physicians are dependent upon each other. And if that is the case, then the assumption of many that dependency is always to be avoided is called into question. Christians have a stake in this discussion. Is the very image of the independent actor who can make decisions apart from — indeed, even in opposition to — others, a seductive image to all of us in our culture, seductive in that it does not say enough about the relationship of the patient and the physician while pretending to say all?

Even to say, "physician and patient" is to limit our imagination somewhat. This is a limitation encouraged by a focus upon patient autonomy and physician paternalism in the literature of bioethics. In point of fact, as patients, we are rarely sick alone, without families and institutions (like churches) being involved. We also do not limit ourselves to physicians to be healed. We participate in HMO's; we go to hospitals and clinics. There we meet insurance people, admitting clerks, technicians, nurses and many others who help us receive our care or give it themselves.

These persons often are disempowered by the medical system. We depend upon them for our care and often we rely upon them as we struggle to determine what it is right to do. Ironically, often they are formally not noticed while being quite helpful to us in our difficulties.

Decisions in medicine often are struggles — not only between those involved in the process of deciding but also within us — to discover what ought to be done. The process may depend as much upon imagination as upon the available medical and other resources, as much upon who we think we are and what we wish to be as upon rational principles of right and wrong or the objective values of the goods to be accomplished or the evils to be avoided. Medical decisions are such that we are at stake, and this is why we have to think carefully about the context in which they take place. This chapter focuses upon part of that context, the relationship between the physician and the patient, and it invites the reader to struggle with the authors in these selections about that relationship.

Suggestions for Further Reading

Aquinas, Thomas. *Summa Theologica* 2.2 q. 110.

Barnard, David. "The Physician as Priest, Revisited," *Journal of Religion and Health* 24 (Winter 1985); 272-86.

Cassell, Eric J. *The Healer's Art* (Cambridge, Mass.: MIT Press, 1985).

Dyck, Arthur J. "Being a Physician and Being a Christian," *Second Opinion* 17 (October 1991): 135-38.

May, William F. *The Physician's Covenant: Images of the Healer in Medical Ethics* (Philadelphia: Westminster, 1983).

McCormick, Richard A. "Beyond Principlism Is Not Enough: A Theologian Reflects on the Real Challenge for U.S. Biomedical Ethics," in *A Matter of Principles? Ferment in U.S. Bioethics,* ed. Edwin R. DuBose et al. (Valley Forge, Penn.: Trinity International Press, 1994).

Pellegrino, Edmund D. "Self-Interest, the Physician's Duties, Medical Ethics," in *Duties to Others,* ed. Courtney S. Campbell and B. Andrew Lustig (Boston: Kluwer Academic Press, 1994).

Shelp, Earl E. *The Clinical Encounter: The Moral Fabric of the Patient-Physician Relationship* (Boston: Kluwer Academic, 1983).

Spiro, Howard M., ed., *Empathy and the Practice of Medicine* (New Haven: Yale University Press, 1993).

Thomasma, David C. "Autonomy and Trust in the Clinical Encounter: Reflections from a Theological Perspective," in *Theological Analyses of the Clinical Encounter,* ed. Gerald P. McKenny and Jonathan Sande (Dordrecht: Kluwer Academic Publishers, 1995).

Veatch, Robert M. *The Patient-Physician Relation: The Patient as Partner* (Bloomington, Ind.: Indiana University Press, 1991).

Zaner, Richard M. *Ethics and the Clinical Encounter* (Englewood Cliffs, N.J.: Prentice Hall, 1988).

100 *Exousia:* Healing with Authority in the Christian Tradition

Daniel P. Sulmasy

The contemporary Western world holds tenaciously to a demand for individual liberty which strands radically opposed to an ever increasing need for individuals to be dependent upon the expertise of others. Ironically, the banner of autonomy has been raised high at a moment in history characterized by profound interdependence in a complex, specialized, technological culture. Perhaps this conflict between the demand for independence and the demand for dependence is nowhere more readily apparent than it is in medicine.

It is easy, then, to see why the nature of authority should be such a thorny problem for contemporary society, and particularly for the practice of medicine. The many contemporary meanings of the word "authority" are perhaps reflective of the depth of the doubt about what authority actually is. This confusion is exemplified by the common observation that patients today often go to great lengths to get authoritative opinions regarding their various conditions, only to feel victimized because the very physicians who have rendered such opinions have treated them authoritatively.

Thus, the role of authority in the relationship between doctors and patients is usually understood as a struggle for power between doctors and patients. Power is generally understood as force of knowledge or force of will, and contemporary ethical arguments about authority in the doctor-patient relationship can usually be characterized as advocating either more or less power for either doctors or patients. But the central thesis of this essay is that, from a theological perspective, the whole basis of these arguments is wrongly conceived. The Judeo-Christian notion is best expressed by the Greek word for authority, *exousia.* The *exousia* to heal which Jesus gave his disciples (Mt. 10:1, Mk: 3:15; Lk. 9:1) has nothing to do with a struggle over knowledge and will between doctors and patients. To heal with *exousia* is to heal with an understanding that the only legitimate power (*dynamis*) expressed in the doctor-patient relationship is the *dynamis* of healing itself, and that this *dynamis* has a source which transcends and subsumes that relationship. A medical practice informed by *exousia* might negotiate a new course, avoiding the pitfalls of both unconstrained patient autonomy and physician paternalism. The perspective of *exousia* provides an alternative vision for medicine at a time when the fragmentation of an individualistic medical marketplace and the bureaucratic dehumanization of an unbridled medical technocracy threaten the integrity of the entire medical enterprise.

The Many Meanings of Authority

The meaning of authority is anything but clear. Kierkegaard's complaint about the "confusion involved in the fact that the concept of authority has been entirely forgotten in our confused age" [18] remains valid even today. To help set the many meanings of authority into a framework from which analysis can proceed, I will place these meanings under three basic headings. I will designate an appropriate preposition or article for each of these three uses of the word. Finally, I will define the three senses in which the adjectival form, "authoritative," is most closely associated with each meaning of the noun, "authority."

1. Authority as Control

The most typical meaning of authority refers to force of will or the ability of one person to control another's thoughts, words, or deeds. It can refer

From Gerald P. McKenny and Jonathan Sande, eds., *Theological Analyses of the Clinical Encounter* (Dordrecht: Kluwer Academic Publishers, 1994), pp. 85-104. Used with kind permission from Kluwer Academic Publishers.

either to the controlling power that a person actually possesses (e.g. — she is in a position of authority), or it can function as a noun designating the person who is in control, often in the plural (e.g. — she is wanted by the authorities). The typical preposition associated with this usage is "in." To be *in* authority is to have control. Using the word in this sense in a medical context one might say, "Doctors have too much authority." When the adjectival form, "authoritative," is used, it typically refers to an abuse of power or control (e.g. — that surgeon behaves authoritatively).

2. Authority as Expertise

The word "authority" is also frequently used when referring to knowledge, skills, precedents, and conclusive statements. It is especially used as a noun to refer to one who has such knowledge or skill. The typical article associated with this usage is "an." To be *an* authority is to possess knowledge and skills superior to others, often rendering the others dependent upon the authority for access to some good or service. Using the word in this sense in a medical context one might say, "Dr. Jones is an authority on ocular melanomas." When the adjective "authoritative" is used in this sense, it means that the opinion or answer is conclusive.

3. Authority as Warrant

A less common but by no means archaic use of the word refers either to the freedom granted by one who is in control, or to actions carried out with conviction. The preposition linked to this usage is "with." To act *with* authority is to act in the freedom granted one by someone else or to act with an apparent sense of legitimacy or conviction. In a medical context, using the word this way sounds unfamiliar. But one might say, for example, that "Dr. Smith practices with authority." When the adjective "authoritative" is used in this sense, its meaning can sometimes be approximated by the adjective "legitimate," sometimes by the adjective "genuine," and sometimes by both.

These three clusters seem to capture the families of meaning which come under the broad term "authority." They overlap, of course, and may exclude some marginal meanings of the term, but this classification ought to be sufficient for the purposes of this essay.

Authority, Hobbes, Locke, and Medicine

The use of the word "authority" in political philosophy depends heavily upon the English philosophers Thomas Hobbes and John Locke. This approach has been uncritically accepted by many as the primary means of understanding the role of authority in the doctor-patient relationship, particularly with respect to the concept of informed consent ([6], pp. 76-77; [8], pp. 44-47, 267-68; [10], pp. 13-14, 174-75, 369-73; [44], pp. 190-213). These authors use the word primarily in the first sense (authority as control). The word is also sometimes used in the second sense (authority as expertise), but generally with the assumption that expertise implies control (i.e. — to the extent that the doctor is *an* authority, the doctor is *in* authority). To understand the roots of this conception of authority, one must go to the sources.

For Hobbes, the questions surrounding authority begin with his convictions about human nature. "I put for a general inclination of all mankind a perpetual and restless desire of power after power, that ceaseth only in death" [*Leviathan*, Ch. XI]. Human beings, by nature, seek power, by which Hobbes means control. Liberty, for example, is simply the absence of external control [*Leviathan*, Ch. XIV]. Hobbes' convictions about ownership, coupled with his convictions about an innate human desire to control others and to be free from their control, defines what he means by authority. "He that owneth his words and actions is the AUTHOR: in which case the actor acteth by authority. . . . And as the right of possession is called dominion, so the right of doing any action is called AUTHORITY" [*Leviathan*, Ch. XVI]. Authority, then, is defined negatively: the absence of external control in the disposition of the actions and words one possesses. Finally, Hobbes is convinced that one will give up one's claims to authority only for greater gain, either by individual contract [*Leviathan*, Ch.XVI], or for the sake of self-preservation through participation in the commonwealth [*Leviathan*, Ch. XVIII]. Thus, the Hobbesian conception of authority essentially requires only two things: "effectively uncontested power and the right to rule" [19].

Locke's concept of authority is likewise connected to his concept of political power, which is described in terms of control. "It is impossible that the rules now on earth should make any benefit, or derive any the least shadow of authority from which is held to be the fountain of all power, 'Adam's private dominion and paternal jurisdiction'. . . ." [*Second Treatise on Government,* Ch. I]. Closely connected is Locke's concept of negative rights, which limit "the extent of the legislative power." Individuals are not to be interfered with, and others are given "power to make laws but by their own consent and by the authority received from them" [*Second Treatise on Government,* Ch. XI].

The key to understanding authority in contemporary political philosophy is to be aware of its Hobbesian/Lockean roots. Power, considered as the ability to control and be free from control of others, is the implicit assumption which dominates contemporary discussions of authority. Friedman, for instance, suggests that whether one considers authority as the ability to rule or influence (*in* authority), or the ability to inspire belief (*an* authority), it is always control which is at issue. He argues that one must surrender control by surrendering private judgment either in obeying a command or in accepting a premise on authority [14]. Similarly, Raz [36] admits that the contemporary notion of authority comes from a coercive concept of law. However, he suggests that authority be thought of primarily as a moral right to impose a duty, and only secondarily as a right to coerce others into compliance with these duties. But his bottom line is coercion, and the moral right to impose a duty must still be understood as control. Therefore, in contemporary political philosophy, authority is inevitably seen in conflict with autonomy [46].

Both the impetus for the dramatic new role of patient autonomy in medical decision making and the recent evolution of the doctrine of informed consent have depended upon a Hobbesian/Lockean conception of authority in the doctor-patient relationship. Flathman [12], for instance, paints a Hobbesian picture of doctors and patients. He sees two basic models of authority in the relationship:

1. a consensual model in which the physician is authorized to practice only so long as the physician's actions are congruent with the consensually agreed upon values of the community, and
2. a constrained conflict model in which there is no general consensus, and so physicians are placed *in* authority inasmuch as patients will do what physicians say despite their disagreement.

Flathman feels that the latter is more realistic. Patients reluctantly accept dependence upon experts because the price of not doing so is to give up the services the experts provide. Power dominates Flathman's discussion. Knowledge is power. Power is control. Therefore, as experts, physicians exert control through the power of their knowledge. And thus, life in the waiting room is inevitably solitary, poor, nasty, brutish, and short [cf. *Leviathan* Ch. XIII].

Veatch [43] is also influenced by Locke and Hobbes. He details how physicians do, in fact, act coercively, by controlling access to hospitals and drugs, committing suicidal or psychiatric patients to involuntary admissions, or administering required immunizations. Veatch accepts, however reluctantly, the necessity of giving such control to physicians. Physicians have the expertise to protect the healthy and the sane from the contagious and the psychotic. But while Veatch denies that there are any "value-free facts," he also claims to be able to distinguish facts from values in medical decision making. He insists that the authority of physicians be limited wherever possible to the technical arena, which is more factual than evaluative. He argues that the physicians should be *in* authority only to the extent that the physician is *an* authority. In effect, Veatch argues that patients own not only their bodies, but also the evaluative ideas they have about illness and treatment. Since medical decision making inevitably involves not only the patient's body but also all that the patient values, all medical authority properly belongs to the patient. Even though he thinks it is epistemologically impossible for a real physician to do so, Veatch's ideal physician would dispense "valueless," objective information about the body to patients, who must, regrettably, depend upon physicians for this information. Patients would then be independent in their decision-making. What is at stake in Veatch's theory is, of course, control. The authority of physicians is based on their technical expertise which defines, for Veatch, the moral limit of their control over patients. He writes, "No one in his right mind would conclude that those who are custodians of a particular value [knowledge of the body] should bear the responsibility for resolving disputes over the relation of that value with other values leading to one's integrated wholeness" [43]. Veatch worries that physicians, like Locke's princes, may overstep their prerogatives. Veatch's solution seems to be equally Lockean. He seems to urge patients, as Locke once urged the prince's subjects, "to get prerogative determined in those points wherein they found disadvantage from it" [*Second Treatise on Government,* Ch. XIV]. That is, Veatch seems to argue that the controlling authority of physicians can be to the disadvantage of patients and hurt them. Therefore, patients should seize control of those liberties traditionally given to doctors which have led to problems for patients. In declaring limitations on the doctor's latitude, Veatch could easily quote Locke and insist that no physician should complain about such a program of transferring control from physicians to patients, "because in so doing they [the patients] have not pulled anything from the prince [physician] that of right belong to him" [*Second Treatise on Government,* Ch. XIV].[1]

The Inadequacies of the Control Model

There are several underlying assumptions in the control model of authority which must be critically examined. These assumptions are foundational. They are so deeply embedded in the ethical theories which flow from them that they often escape attention. But an exposition of these assumptions seems necessary in order to explain some of the difficulties one faces in considering the concept of authority in contemporary medicine, and to look for fruitful alternatives.

Human Nature

First, these Hobbesian and Lockean theories of authority make implicit but striking assumptions about human nature. These assumptions about human nature are certainly not value-free. Notwithstanding Veatch's insistence that physicians be strictly limited to evaluative judgments about the body as such, the theories of both Flathman and Veatch begin with sweeping evaluative assumptions about the nature of the actors in the doctor-patient relationship. First, these theories assume that human beings constitutively seek personal liberty and control over others. Therefore, no one, whether a doctor or a patient or a Native American Chief, is worthy of trust. Second, these theories take the voluntary contract forged between equals to be the paradigmatic human ethical interaction. Therefore, as Hauerwas [16] has observed, these theories presuppose that "all relations that are less than fully 'voluntary' [are] morally suspect."

But such assumptions are largely untrue, particularly in the medical context. First, while acknowledging the reality of sin, it must be argued why one should accept the Hobbesian notion that the primary human drive is to control others and be free of their control. Christian belief, for example, suggests that the primary drive is to love and to be loved. In fact, most persons *can* name other persons that they can trust, and many would place their physicians on their list. Only the most distraught and disheartened say, in their alarm, that no one can be trusted [Ps. 115:2]. Those who cannot count their physicians among the trustworthy generally want another physician, because they understand the critical importance of trust in the doctor-patient relationship.

Second, the most paradigmatic human interactions are not voluntary contract interactions between equals, but involuntary relationships between unequals [4]. The most important human relationships are the ones over which people have no control. No amount of innovation in reproductive technology will ever allow people to choose their own biological parents. Each person enters this world helpless, completely dependent upon others. People have no power to declare themselves immortal or free of the possibility of disease. These conditions are out of human control. And it is precisely in the midst of this absence of control and in relation to the state of dependency which illness engenders that the ministrations of medicine are meted out.

Veatch notes the inadequacies of "raw contracting" as the moral basis of the relationship between doctors and patients, but he unfortunately merely replaces the notion of raw contracting with a boiled down form of contracting [43]. In so doing, he continues to cling to the notion that control is the basis of the doctor-patient relationship. But this view is contradicted by a reality which cannot be otherwise. The doctor-patient relationship is predicated firmly on the fact of illness, which entails the loss of control.

Finally, the increasing interdependence which constitutes our contemporary social relationships, particularly in the medical arena, ought to provide a clue that human beings are not inherently atomistic, but inherently social and interdependent. As Aquinas put it, "man has a natural inclination to know the trust about God and to live in society" [*Summa Theologiae* I, II, q. 94, art. 2.c]. It would seem obvious this is neither Veatch or Flatham's view of human nature.

Human beings are flawed, of course, and often fail to live out their potential. But a judgment that human beings are naturally selfish and that any behavior which appears to be goodness is really self-interest merely begs the question. Nor is this a matter which can be settled by experience. Experience teaches us only the following: some doctors are mostly good, and some doctors are mostly bad. It will remain an axiomatic choice, a faith assumption, to decide whether the fragile vessel of the physician is a glass half empty or a glass half full. The assumption of the Roman Catholic tradition of Christianity is optimistic: grace can build upon the reasonableness of human nature. Other Christian traditions are not so optimistic about the state of human beings outside of grace, but are at least optimistic to the extent that they believe in the power of grace to fill the fragile human vessel. In contrast to the Hobbesian assumption, Christian belief points to an open possibility that human beings can be better than they are now. Neither physicians nor anyone else will ever be better unless this possibility can be assumed.

An HMO with Only One Member?

The second problem with the control model is that it assumes an intersubjectivist morality for medicine. It assumes that all moral truth in medicine resides in the subjectivity of the autonomous individual. But since individual patients need other individuals called doctors when they seek healing, this poses a problem. More than one subjectivity is involved once a person enters a human relationship. How is one to settle differences if neither has a greater claim to be in the right? The only possible solution under the assumptions of the control model is to construct an *intersubjective* morality, either by contract or consensus. But since such intersubjectivity is never quite objectivity ([22], p. 22), the project is doomed to fail.

Veatch [43] and Engelhardt [8, 9] appear to argue along the following lines. They begin with the assumption that each individual is his or her own moral authority. As Flathman argues [12], when there is complete consensus on what the good is for medicine, there is no need for any external authority in medicine. But Veatch and Engelhardt both agree that such an intersubjective consensus does not exist. Therefore, they conclude that patients and doctors whose views overlap ought to seek each other out, forming voluntary communities of intersubjective agreement in medical morals in which authority can function.

The problems with this view are significant. Taken to its logical conclusion, the theory implies that each person ought to become his or her own personal Health Maintenance Organization (HMO). If there truly is no source of authority (conceived of as control) other than oneself, and conflict is inevitable because human nature implies a need to control others and to be free from their control, then each individual would ideally be his or her own personal health care system, in complete control of his or her own care and free from the control of doctors. Ideally, one supposes, all medical information about one's own body could be processed and analyzed by a computer which would be programmed to provide the treatment one selected from a range of options.

But such a view is far from reality and not ideal for anyone. Medicine is an intrinsically interpersonal enterprise. A purely rational computer medicine could never truly *care* for patients. Care requires persons. Yet Veatch's ideal of value free information given to completely autonomous patients who are free to decide what to do with that information in light of their own subjective values can only be realized by a machine. No one of right mind would want to be cared for by a health care system which merely objectively provided information about the body and paid no attention to the value of the whole person. There is even emerging evidence that the doctor-patient relationship is itself part of the therapeutic effect [38]. In addition, medicine seems to require (at least in those important cases where people seek out doctors) the presence of another. Self-diagnosis and self-treatment are always dangerous, even for experts. Finally, it seems that medicine is not just an interpersonal interaction between two individuals. It is an inherently communal enterprise. Without a prior commitment of professionals to share knowledge with each other, a system of one-person HMOs, if ever started, would soon grow into an absurd system of isolated, proprietary medical data banks, limited by the narrow experiences of individuals who functioned as their own doctors. The Hobbesian would then face a dilemma. Since medical knowledge is control, and control is what the Hobbesian desires, to share his medical knowledge would be to relinquish precious control over others. In addition, sharing implies accepting information from others, and to do so would be to acknowledge their control over his life, and this too would be unacceptable to the Hobbesian. On the other hand, not to share might lead like-minded persons to be equally stingy, and then he would risk dying from a curable sickness that he would not have the knowledge to treat. Thus he would neither be able to share nor not share. The Hobbesian view cannot be sustained in the limit.

Now a Hobbesian might not concede that there is a problem with his assumptions. Painfully, the Hobbesian might say, the above ideal of private, value-free computer medicine is simply not possible, even though it really *is* what everyone would want. Therefore a Hobbesian patient would reluctantly compromise for the sake of personal interests and accept dependence on medical professionals, but only to the least degree compatible with the patient's interests in pleasure, health, and longevity.

But the counter-argument here is standard. If the real justification for accepting the control of others were the maximization of one's own best interests as one defines them, then the only consistent position would be to lie about one's acceptance of the controlling influence of others in order to gain the benefits offered by contract, but then to do as one pleases in order to escape the control enjoyed by the contract. For example, suppose that a Hobbesian smoker were to join an HMO which forbade smoking in order to eliminate the costs of caring for smoking-related diseases, thereby saving money for everyone in the HMO. The Hobbesian who loves to smoke might promise not to smoke in order to join this HMO and save money. But his actions would be most consistent with the underlying justification of the Hobbesian theory (i.e., self interest), if he smoked whenever he could do so without getting caught. It is easy to see that once this process became generalized, the very basis for the compromise reached by the social contract would be destroyed. Thus the Hobbesian HMO, whether with one member or many, results in a *reductio ad absurdum.*

Medical Monasticism

As Finnis points out, groups can coordinate action to a common purpose or goal either through unanimity or authority ([11], pp. 231-33). But if there is no unanimity, and if the Hobbesian view is absurd, where can one look for a theory of authority in medicine?

MacIntyre notes that when groups cannot achieve what they must by acting as individuals, practices spring up to achieve those goals. Practices are not forms of political or organizational power, but organized, rule-governed enterprises requiring judgments about how to best understand particular cases or reformulate the rules in the light of particular cases [24]. Medicine, of course, is a practice. And practices are inherently prescriptive. The doctor is said to *prescribe* therapy. To make a prescriptive statements such as, "x ought to be done" is to make "a claim which by the very use of the words implies a greater authority behind it than the expression of feelings or choices" ([24], pp. 51-52). This is true no matter how much one may claim to "own" these feelings or choices.

MacIntyre [24] realistically surveys the contemporary West, in constant rebellion against all forms of tradition and authority, deeply divided and unable to form a consensus about anything, and wonders only why it has taken so long for society to come to the impasse now faced by medicine: the demand for absolute autonomy in the face of its increasing impossibility. In the dissolution of the culture he sees only a profession which has become, "not quite a craftsman's guild, not quite a trade union of skilled workers, not quite anything." He despairs of the possibility of ever achieving enough agreement on the nature and goals of medicine to ever have a true professional practice again. His only positive solution is the possibility of achieving small communities of patients and doctors with a common vision — a vision in which the Western world would be dotted with a series of HMOs operating as medical monasteries in these new Dark Ages. The West only awaits a "new St. Benedict" ([24], p. 263) who will be the founder of these medical communities.

But this view is ultimately also unsatisfactory. MacIntyre is right in calling medicine a practice and right that the institution of medicine is currently threatened by contemporary views of authority. But the practice of medicine still retains enough internal coherence to remain a unified practice. The bodies of atheists and of Christians remain, after all, fundamentally the same. While their ultimate moral views remain radically different, it is hard to see, in the end, how the proposals of Engelhardt ([8], pp. 336-69), Veatch [43], and MacIntyre [24], really differ, except that they vary in the extent to which each thinks that a series of distinct medico-moral communities is a goal to strive for or a state of affairs for which one might reluctantly settle.

Authority, Sociology, and Medicine

Political philosophy is not the only contemporary discipline with important views about authority in the doctor-patient relationship. Sociologists have a view of this relationship as well. The sociological view, however, shares important similarities with the view of political philosophy. The sociological understanding of authority is largely derived from the seminal work of Max Weber, who defined authority as the power to issue commands that will be obeyed ([45], p. 152). As in the work of Hobbes, conflict and control are the essential features for Weber. He did distinguish *Macht*, "the probability that one actor . . . will be in a position to carry out his own will despite resistance," from *Herrschaft*, "the probability that a command with a specific content will be obeyed by a given group of persons." But *Herrschaft* is still conceived of as one will controlling another will. It is simply a less overtly violent imposition of one will upon another. Weber distinguishes three types of justification offered for authority other than simple *Macht:* rational grounds, traditional grounds, and charismatic grounds ([45], pp. 324-52). But it seems, as Hauerwas has noted, that even Weber's typological tryptic "fails to clarify what it means to acknowledge an authority as legitimate" [16].

Talcott Parsons has addressed the issue of authority in the doctor-patient relationship forthrightly ([30], pp. 441-42, 464-65). While not referring to Weber directly in this regard, it is clear that Parsons also assumes a model of authority based on relationships of power. Parsons suggests a "social control" model based on the advantages to society of giving physicians control over individual patients. This theory results from Parsons' empirical observations. Yet his conclusions are undeniable *interpretations* of his empirical observations and cannot simply be unquestioningly accepted as factual. And even if it is the case that the interpretation of Parsons is true (namely, that doctors really do act as authority figures exerting social control over the ill), it cannot therefore be concluded that this is the way things *ought* to be. This would represent a genuine example of the "Naturalistic Fallacy"; a true violation of the fact/value distinction. The fact/value distinction requires that moral claims not be justified solely on the basis of factual claims ([5], pp. 336-79). On the strength of this principle, even if Parsons were correct in the judgment that physicians used authority to control patients, this would not imply that an interpretation of medical authority based on social control theory is morally correct.

These interpretations of authority as control, based on either sociological theories or the theories of political philosophy or both, are pervasive in the literature of medical ethics. Countless discussions of the conflict between autonomy and beneficence have essentially been based upon this interpretation. It has almost begun to seem as if the fundamental task for medical ethics is to find the proper balance of authority in the power relationship between physicians and patients, with beneficence interpreted to mean authority for doctors, and autonomy interpreted to mean authority for patient. For instance, in their book on informed consent, Faden and Beauchamp acknowledge that "the issue of proper authority for decisionmaking is an implicit theme throughout this volume. In health care, professionals and patients alike see the authority for one decision as properly the professional's and authority for other decisions as properly the patient's" ([10], pp. 13-14). Empirical researchers have used this schema in part, perhaps, because it is amenable to quantification on scales generated by survey instruments and seems to capture at least some of the reality of the interactions between doctors and patients. I myself have fallen into this trap [41], but I am now convinced that the model so constrains the rich reality of the doctor-patient relationship that it is inadequate. A solution is not to be sought by accepting the basic correctness of the model and merely suggesting a shift from "unquestioning acceptance of physician authority, as embodied in the Parsonian model" to a "more egalitarian bargaining" state [20]. The problem lies with the Hobbesian assumptions of the sociological model itself.

Exousia, Dynamis, and Healing

When Jesus sent his disciples out into the world, he gave them "power and authority to overcome all demons and to cure diseases. He sent them forth to proclaim the reign of God and heal the afflicted" [Lk. 9:1-2; cf. Mt. 10:1 and Mk. 3:15]. In this passage, it is important to note that Luke attributes to Jesus a distinction between the power that heals (*dynamis* in the Greek) from the authority (*exousia*) to heal. This is a distinction which is made with remarkable consistency throughout the writings of the New Testament [1, 13, 15, 27]. In making this distinction, it would seem that Scripture is suggesting that neither force of will nor the power of expertise is at issue in a discussion of the authority to heal. This is a perspective which is remarkably different from any account of authority and healing based on Hobbesian/Lockean political philosophy or sociology.

In relation to healing, *dynamis* is the power of healing itself. It was *dynamis* that Jesus felt go out of him when the woman with the hemorrhage touched his cloak and was cured [Mk. 5:30]. *Dynamis* is the pure power to heal. *Dynamis* is power *for*, not power *over* others. In a neo-Platonic sense, *dynamis* is self-diffusive. It has nothing to do with force of will. *Dynamis* goes out from Jesus without his willing it.

Dynamis is also used to characterize expertise. Thus, Simon Magus, the magician, was said to have the *dynamis* to heal [Acts 8:9-25]. But *dynamis* is clearly distinguished from *exousia.* When Simon Magus eventually came to faith, he realized the insufficiency of mere *dynamis.* He also wanted the authority (*exousia*) to impose hands. But the apostles would not grant him that. The very fact that he wanted to buy *exousia* was an indication to them that he was unworthy. And when the Pharisees wanted to know how Jesus had the *dynamis* to forgive sin [Mk. 2:1-12], he avoided the word *dynamis* in his reply. He said, instead, that he had the *exousia* to both heal and forgive sin. He proceeded to demonstrate both.

Exousia presumes *dynamis,* but not vice-versa. In Greek usage *exousia* was an illusion if not backed by real *dynamis* [13]. *Exousia* meant "the warrant or the right to do something" [24]. Thus, *exousia* is really closest in meaning to the third definition of authority set forth at the beginning of this essay. *Exousia* denoted an inner sense, and even a "moral power" in Stoic thought [13]. In the New Testament, *exousia* refers to the rule of God in nature and in the spiritual world, and especially the freedom which is given to Jesus and which he gives to the apostles [13]. While *exousia* is exercised with respect to sickness, the elements, and demons, Jesus specifically rejects any political application of *exousia* [1]. His kingdom, as he tells Pilate, is not of this world [Jn. 18:36]. *Exousia* is intrinsically related to the *Logos.* Nothing takes place apart from the *exousia* of Jesus. It is the freedom given to the community which orients itself to the Word made flesh. Hence, it can never be used arbitrarily [13].

New Testament *exousia* cannot be bestowed or produced. It emerges in practice. It is not more Weberian charismatic authority, which can be used for either good or for evil. *Exousia* rests upon a practical and convincing insight into the Good, the True, and the Beautiful. It springs forth out of tradition. It becomes manifest upon recognition by the community ([15], p. 17). Hence, the magician who already had the *dynamis* to heal cannot buy *exousia* [Acts 8:9-25]. God rebukes those who misuse power as raw *dynamis* and deny the *exousia* of God [cf. Is. 5:8-9]. *Exousia* comes with experience, and is characterized by wisdom, equanimity, talent, charisma, and selflessness ([15], p. 17). William Osler himself could scarcely have done a better job of describing the virtues of a good physician. A physician might have the *dynamis* of actually being *an* authority, but without *exousia,* that physician will never heal *with* authority.

Exousia and Virtue

The Greek terms *dynamis* and *exousia* correspond to the Latin terms *potestas* and *auctoritas,* respectively. The Romans used *potestas* to describe the rule of Nero and Caligula, but *auctoritas* to describe the rule of Caesar and Augustus ([15], p. 52). The Western concept of rights as powers, a concept which strongly influences contemporary discussions of medical ethics, developed around the concept of *potestas* ([9], p. 61). Originally, *auctoritas* or authority had a meaning similar to that of *exousia.* But as discussed above, authority assumed a definition based on the concept of power in the writings of Hobbes and Locke. Since then, it seems that the distinction between power and authority (*potestas* and *auctoritas; dynamis* and *exousia*) has nearly vanished from Western writing. Consequently, contemporary writings about authority in the doctor-patient relationship have been largely oriented either to assert the traditional power of the doctor over the patient or to defend a revolt in which the patient's power is asserted over against the doctor's power.

Exousia represents, to some extent, a *tertium quid* in this examination of the relationship between doctors and patients. In the New Testament understanding, authority does not originate from either the patient or from the doctor. "Like everything human, the measure of excellence in authority is its ordination to God and its success in ordaining its subjects to God" [28].

Exousia is not itself a virtue. It is not an Aristotelian mean in the sense of being the just equilibrium point between the opposed poles of excessive control for either the doctor or the patient. *Exousia* is both an orientation to virtue and the fruit of the vine. *Exousia* results from the recognition by both the doctor and the patient that their relationship is not oriented to one or another of two individual human beings, but to a "third thing" (i.e., to God).

Exousia is an orientation to a *telos.* It is the recognition of the *telos* and the subordination of all related activities to the *telos.* As such, *exousia* is both orientation to virtue and the possibility of virtue. Without a *telos,* there is no virtue. To speak of virtue is to presume the authority of an excellence towards which virtuous activities are oriented. Virtue demands the recognition of authority. And, once one acknowledges an authentic *telos,* one's actions are expected to be virtuous.

Exousia may be likened to grace. One does not earn or own *exousia.* Yet, it can be expressed and it can be recognized. But it cannot emerge unless its divine source has been recognized. And unless it bears fruit in virtuous life and points beyond itself, any claim to *exousia* is disingenuous.

To practice medicine with *exousia* is to ordain one's practice to the good of the patient and to ordain one's practice for the good of the patient to the glory of God. In this way, the *dynamis* to heal, which is already given in nature and in human reason, not only becomes actual but has a context and an ultimate orientation, emerging from God and leading back to God. *Exousia* therefore demands the virtues of practice: wisdom, equanimity, selflessness, trustworthiness, concern, and fidelity. The role of the doctor is defined by an oath to practice in keeping with the virtues demanded by God's free gift of the *exousia* to care for the needs of the sick. A physician practices *with* authority to the extent that this oath is upheld [39].

Virtue is also expected of the patient, but healing is never withheld because a patient does not live up to the perfect fulfillment of these virtues. The patient must also realize that the grace of healing is mediated through flawed and fragile human beings who may not live up to the virtues demanded by *exousia.* The virtues of the patient concern the stewardship of the body, which is given as a gift by God. Patients can be asked to care for their bodies, to avoid what is harmful to their bodies, to be compliant with prescriptions, and to be honest historians. But even the good of the body must be subordinated to the *telos*, which transcends the body itself.

The Wisdom of Ben Sira

The deuterocanonical text of Ben Sira (the Book of Sirach or Ecclesiasticus) is included in the wisdom literature of the Roman Catholic Scriptures and is referred to 82 times in the Jewish Talmud ([37], pp. 17-20). The physician's poem from this text [38:1-15] helps to provide insights into the view of authority in the healing relationship within the Judeo-Christian tradition.

In ancient Hebrew thought, healing was traditionally reserved for God alone. To make a claim to be able to heal, then, was to ascribe to oneself qualities traditionally reserved for God alone, thus making oneself God's equal. This was an abomination. It was among the worst of all sins. It was the practice of magic and darkness associated with the enemies of God: the herbs and spells and incantations of idolaters [40].

But the rational medicine of the Greeks was not only wiser and more efficacious than the medicine of Babylon and Egypt, it made a claim to a rational basis for practice not associated with idolatry. Jews could contemplate availing themselves of the services of these Hippocratic physicians, then, if there were some theological way to reconcile this new rational medicine with the traditional understanding that healing came from the Almighty, not from human beings. Such a theological understanding is expressed in the physician's poem from the Wisdom of Ben Sira (ca. 175 B.C.). This understanding gave Hellenized Jews, for the first time in the history of Israel, an opportunity to practice medicine and ask for the assistance of physicians when sick [40].

While the poem does not use the words for power or authority directly in describing the relationship between doctor and patient, either in the original Hebrew or in the Greek translation written by Ben Sira's grandson, the themes raised by the poem deal quite explicitly with the topic. "From God the doctor has his wisdom," the poem insists. God endows the earth with all the healing herbs the doctor uses. The pure *dynamis* for healing comes originally from God, but it is through the doctor that "God's creative work continues without cease in its efficacy on the surface of the earth." Yet *dynamis* is not enough. The *exousia* to heal must also come from God. The first verse of the poem admonishes the patient to honor the physician not only because his services are "essential" (i.e., that he has *dynamis*), but also because it was God "who established his profession" (i.e., gave him *exousia*).

The orientation of medicine to God is made clear. Both the doctor and the patient are explicitly urged to pray. The physician does not falsely arrogate to himself powers over the patient which properly belong to God. And the patient does not insist on power and rights over and against the physician. Their relationship is a covenant of trust between doctor and patient authorized by the orientation of that covenant to the overarching covenant between God and all of God's people [40]. This view harmonizes with that of contemporary Christian theologians who characterize the doctor-patient relationship as a covenant [26, 35]. Power is not thought of as force of will, but as the actual possibility of healing. Authority is not force of will or the possession of specialized knowledge, but the mutual recognition by both the healer and the healed of the ultimate source of the power to heal and the ultimate source of the warrant to heal. To claim to heal by one's own force of knowledge or will is arrogant. To offer healing as a contract implies ownership of what belongs properly to God, and is thus intolerable. It is only by practicing under both covenants, with the *exousia* which God gives and which demands so much of the doctor, that the *dynamis* of expertise can become an actual act of healing for the patient.

Exousia, Freedom, and Service

The Scriptural perspective which governs the conception of authority covered by the term *exousia* also offers an understanding of the relationship between freedom and authority which differs from contemporary usage. This perspective emphasizes the relationship of loving service to the concept of freedom as well as to the concept of authority. This perspective is highly relevant to discussions of the doctor-patient relationship.

Gunneweg and Schmithals write that the true authority of *exousia* "arises out of freedom and is based upon the possibility of rendering help as a servant" ([15], p. 21). During his final meal with his disciples, a dispute arises among them as to who is the greatest. Jesus admonishes them not to "lord it over" other people, but to fulfill what it means when it is said that those who have *exousia* over people are called their benefactors. Those in positions of true *exousia* must be servants, in imitation of Jesus, who stood among the disciples as one who serves [Lk. 22:24-30]. Similarly, in the Gospel of John, Jesus urges the disciples to follow his example of service and wash each other's feet [Jn. 13:1-17]. Henri Nouwen, implicitly writing with an understanding of authority as *exousia*, asserts that compassion is the substance of legitimate authority ([29], pp. 40-43).

Exousia implies that authority is an assertion of the other in freedom. It is not mere *dynamis*, which is really indifferent to the will of the other, nor is it a coercive use of power, which is the assertion of personal will against the will of the other [28]. *Exousia* is authority which addresses human freedom and human reason. *Exousia* is authority which assumes a mutual orientation towards a *tertium quid*. *Exousia* is always at the service of others and their freedom. "An earthly authority which does not point beyond itself becomes demonic and will show itself as arbitrary, naked power" [28]. The life of Joseph Mengele provides a chilling example of what can happen when a medical professional distorts the authority of the profession far beyond the legitimacy and genuineness of *exousia*.

The concept of *exousia* captures a sense of human freedom which seems to have been overlooked by the Hobbesian perspective on authority, whether presented in the form of political philosophy or sociology. Hannah Arendt has written that "authority implies an obedience in which men retain their freedom" [3]. Such a statement must seem paradoxical in a culture which considers obedience and freedom as opposites. What kind of freedom is there which does not preclude obedience?

The freedom of *exousia* is the freedom which comes with liberation from self-preoccupation. It is the freedom which only loving service can bring. It is also the free acceptance of human nature with all its inherent limits, including death. It is liberation from the punishment of Sisyphus, condemned to the eternal trial of attempting to make those limits disappear [28]. It is therefore liberation from both the entrepreneurial approach to medicine often assumed by physicians and the consumerist approach to medicine often assumed by patients. Because the doctor does not own the authority to heal, the doctor cannot put healing up for sale on the market. Because the patient cannot purchase immortality, the patient need not expend all his or her human resources on a grandiose death-denying delusion.

The virtuous doctor, then, will practice with *exousia*, recognizing that healing is authorized by God, who also gives the possibility of healing in the resources of the earth and in the resourcefulness of human reason and imagination. In the covenant which exists between God and the healer, the physician must assume the virtues demanded by *exousia*, placing healing power at the service of others and at the service of their freedom. This means recognizing the dignity and freedom of the patient, and demands, in turn, a covenant between doctor and patient. *Exousia* implies the concept of authority to which Hauerwas referred when he wrote that it is not derived from knowledge or expertise, but from mastery of the practical moral skills involved in the physician's commitment to care for and never abandon the ill and the dying [16]. Likewise, to coerce, manipulate, or ignore the patient is incompatible with the spirit of practicing with *exousia*. Informed consent, then, assumes importance not as the patient's autonomous authorization of the physician's actions, but as the mutual recognition of the gifts of freedom and healing which only God bestows. Authority does not reside with the patient as something to be given to the doctor. Nor is authority something that resides with the doctor as something to be exercised over the patient. Rather, it is the result of the mutual recognition of the dignity of both doctor and patient, each reverencing the life of God in the other.

Exousia, Mystery, and Healing

God is a holy mystery, and the awesome presence of God in the doctor-patient relationship ought never be ignored. But God's mystery ought never be invoked as a stopgap for our knowledge; a mere concept to define the limits of human science. When medical authority is considered only as a control (practicing *in* authority), or when medical authority is considered only as the power of knowledge and expertise (practicing as *an* authority), the fundamental mystery of God's place in the healing relationship is obscured. But when medicine is practiced *with* authority (*exousia*), the holy mystery of God's healing presence opens out before both the doctor and the patient.

Robert Burt has complained that the increasing use of the courts to settle medical cases of ethical concern in advance of any anticipated actions by physicians and patients accepts the false presumptions that medical decision making is certain when it is not, and that direct conversation between the doctor and patient is to be avoided when it ought not. Patients, doctors, and hospitals turn instead "to the last bastion of unquestionable authority in our society: the Judge, the embodiment of the Law" [7]. In going to the courts, they fail to recognize both the ontological and moral ambiguity of those cases which fall at the "edges of life." They seek certitude and security where there is only uncertainty and insecurity. They seek control in situations which are fundamentally out of their control.

But the patient and doctor who recognize *exousia* know that the physician's authority is not called into question when there is no control and there is no knowledge. Those who base their authority on control and knowledge will experience these cases as threats. But *exousia* commits both doctor and patient to a recognition of the fundamental mystery of God's presence in the covenant between them. *Exousia* commits both to a recognition of the mysteries of death and limitation. The foundation of *exousia* is the transcendent, which is revealed in the immanence of sickness and death. In the midst of the powerlessness and confusion wrought by illness and death, faith and reverence replace desperation and delusion. Control slips away from one *in* authority. Expertise slips away from *an* authority. The power and the authority belong to God alone.

Exousia, Medicine, and the Secular City

MacIntyre [24] despairs of the possibility of any kind of moral consensus regarding either what constitutes the good or how various goods ought to be related to one another. He argues that the concept of a profession is inherently linked to the concept of authority. He concludes that the vitality of all professions has been irrevocably destroyed because the concept of authority has lost all meaning in the wake of the loss of moral consensus.

This despair has been challenged by Pellegrino [31]. He notes that the recognition of the legitimacy of the claims of patients to act as moral agents in the doctor-patient relationship is a positive good which ought to be sustained and strengthened. But he also cautions that both patient and physician must be seen as moral agents. Physicians cannot become mere instruments of the patient's autonomous choices.

The view offered here, through the scriptural concept of *exousia,* would seem to obviate these difficulties by transforming the discussion from a debate about power for doctors and patients into a search for that *tertium quid* to which both can point as the source of authority. Paternalism is the mistaken view that authority has to do with knowledge and control which properly belong to the medical profession. "Autonomism" is the mistaken view that authority has to do with control which properly belongs to the patient, but which the patient grants to the physician only because the patient lacks the knowledge. The way of *exousia* is the "third way."

MacIntyre is certainly correct in his assessment that there is no moral consensus, let alone any religious consensus, in the Western world. One might therefore argue that the scriptural notion of *exousia* would be helpful only if one accepted MacIntyre's vision of small communities in which patients and staff shared the Judeo-Christian faith and its conception of the authority to heal. But a great many people would want no part of such communities, either because they have no faith or because their faith does not include the concept of *exousia.*

Does this imply that the concept of *exousia* is irrelevant in a pluralistic society? Does medicine have no unifying goal other than to maximize personal liberty to the extent that others are not harmed? Is total fragmentation of the profession inevitable?

I would suggest that the profession itself will ultimately resist fragmentation into distinct medico-moral practices. Granted, in the wake of intense specialization and sub-specialization, it might no longer be possible in a certain sense to talk of a single medical profession. Nonetheless, there seems to be enough unity inherent in the professional activities of contemporary Western physicians to resist fragmentation into little philosophically or religiously distinct professions. The interdependence of medical knowledge, the uniformity of the initial education, the fundamental belief in rational medicine based on scientific evidence, and the oath that physicians take to put this knowledge at the service of patients are critical unifying elements for the profession. Despite the many centrifugal forces which threaten contemporary medical practice, the fact of illness and the act of profession might still form, as Pellegrino points out [32], a secular basis for a *tertium quid* of the sort that could serve as a source of *exousia* for the relationship between doctor and patient. These would constitute integral constituents of the healing relationship, transcending the power concerns of both doctor and the patient. Beneficence and autonomy might cease to be considered antithetical. Pellegrino and Thomasma locate a *telos* intrinsic to the practice of medicine: the good of the patient. This forms the basis, on secular grounds alone, of a new model for the doctor-patient relationship: beneficence in trust [34]. It requires a trusting relationship between doctor and patient not unlike the religious concept of a covenant. It demands virtue of both doctors and patients. Such a model of the healing relationship does not have the power of a truly Judeo-Christian model like the one developed in this paper, but it certainly has secular credibility. And even a secular notion of *exousia* would certainly provide a helpful alternative to the twin vices of physician paternalism and patient "autonomism."

A Clinical Example

To illustrate, in a preliminary and sketchy fashion, how the adoption of a view of medical authority as *exousia* might affect the practice even of secular medicine, I will offer the following example.

Suppose a patient, dying of metastatic lung cancer, is placed on a morphine drip by his doctor to treat his severe pain. Suppose that this patient, quite medically sophisticated, begins to manipulate the drip rate on his own intravenous pump.

A doctor who conceived of authority as power might perceive this patient's behavior as a threat to the authority of the doctors and nurses. If somewhat enlightened, she might interpret this as a manipulative behavior in which the patient was acting out because of fear of death. Her reaction to this behavior would probably be to reassert control by "setting limits" so that the patient would understand the boundaries of proper patient behavior. She might, mercifully, increase the drip rate, but tell the patient that he could only ask for a change in drip rate once per nursing shift, and that he would be carefully watched so that he did not increase the rate on his own. Since he lacked the knowledge (power) to safely adjust the rate, she would insist that control of the morphine dose must be the prerogative of the doctor. If he objected, mutual anger and stalemate might ensue.

On the other hand, if the doctor conceived of authority as *exousia*, she might behave differently. She might ask herself, and the patient, what the *telos* was at this stage of illness and in their doctor-patient relationship. She might ask how they could work towards the overall *telos* of medicine (the good of the patient) in this situation, and how the patient saw his ability to control the rate of the morphine drip fitting into that *telos*. They might agree that the power of the drug (a power which belongs to neither of them) could be better expressed in the service of that *telos* if the patient actually could manipulate the dose of morphine within certain bounds of safety. Thus, the goal both shared could be achieved and the power of medicine more fully expressed in the setting of their mutually trusting relationship.

One can only speculate that it was such an exchange which must have given rise to the wonderful new development of Patient Controlled Analgesia (PCA), in which the patient is given a baseline infusion rate of narcotic but can give additional drug boluses (limited by safety concerns) as necessary to relieve pain not relieved by the baseline infusion. The sum of the boluses required are then used to calculate adjustments in the baseline rate [42].

Some might object that the use of PCA for such a patient merely illustrates an effective redistribution of power and control from doctor to patient, but this interpretation would miss the point. Certainly it is not patient power or doctor power which is at stake here. The things that matter are mutual trust, shared goals, and the expression of a power which belongs not to the doctor or to the patient, but to Humankind or to Nature or to God (or to all three). Certainly it is not control, but loss of control which is the dominant theme in such a situation. To engage in a struggle for control over the rate of morphine infusion as an expression of continued personal control in the face of the overwhelming reality of the patient's imminent, ineluctable death would be absurd for both doctor and patient. The wise physician recognizes the dignity and freedom of her patient even in these final moments, and both doctor and patient ordain their freedom to the common goal of alleviating suffering even in the face of their mutual powerlessness to prevent death. Thus would a wise physician practice *with* authority, in the spirit of *exousia.*

Conclusion

Contemporary discussions of authority in the doctor-patient relationship have largely been based on either sociological or political models. Both of these models assume that authority means control or expertise or both. Under such models, the notion of authority in the doctor-patient relationship has been viewed as a struggle for power between doctors and patients. This perhaps has generated some of the difficulties now confronting medicine, where many physicians continue to exert paternalistic control over patients, while many patients now practice medical consumerism. The New Testament view of authority, *exousia*, provides an alternative view which suggests that the authority to heal is neither a possession of the physician nor of the patient, but a free gift from God. *Exousia* is the warrant to heal. *Exousia* requires virtue from both doctor and patient in a covenant relationship, subsumed under the greater covenant between God and all God's people. The notion of *exousia* also points to a way for secular medicine to move beyond the contradictions of medical authority conceived of as knowledge and control. Perhaps a recovery of the notion of *exousia* can help medicine escape from a spirit of antagonism which is increasingly making the experiences of both going to the doctor and of practicing medicine unsatisfactory for both doctors and patients.

Acknowledgments

I am grateful to Dr. Edmund D. Pellegrino for his thoughtful review of a draft of this manuscript and to the Charles E. Culpeper Foundation for their generous support of my work.

Center for Clinical Bioethics
Georgetown University Medical Center
Washington, D.C., U.S.A.

Notes

1. It is of interest that while Locke was trained as a physician, he never saw any patients professionally.

Bibliography

[1] Amiot, F., and Galopin, P. M.: 1973, 'Authority,' in X. Leon-Dufour (ed.), *Dictionary of Biblical Theology,* 2nd ed., Seabury Press, New York, pp. 36-39.

[2] Aquinas, St. Thomas: 1966, *Summa Theologiae,* vol. 28, Blackfriars edition, T. Gilly, O.P. (ed.), McGraw-Hill, New York.

[3] Arendt, H.: 1968, 'What Is Authority?', in *Between Past and Future,* Penguin Press, Harmondsworth, Middlesex, England, pp. 91-141.

[4] Baier, A. C.: 1987, 'The Need For More Than Justice,' in M. Hanen and K. Nielsen (eds.), 'Science, Ethics, and Feminism', *Canadian Journal of Philosophy* 13 (Suppl.), 41-56.

[5] Beauchamp, T. L.: 1982, *Philosophical Ethics,* New York, McGraw-Hill.

[6] Beauchamp, T. L., and Childress, J. F.: 1989, *Principles of Biomedical Ethics,* Oxford University Press, New York.

[7] Burt, R. A.: 1988, 'Uncertainty and Medical Author-

ity in the World of Jay Katz,' *Law, Medicine, and Health Care* 16, 190-96.

[8] Engelhardt, H. T.: 1986, *The Foundations of Bioethics,* Oxford University Press, New York.

[9] Engelhardt, H. T.: 1991, *Secular Humanism: The Search for a Common Morality,* Trinity Press International, Philadelphia.

[10] Faden, R. R., and Beauchamp, T. L.: 1986, *A History and Theory of Informed Consent,* Oxford University Press, New York.

[11] Finnis, J.: 1980, *Natural Law, Natural Rights,* Clarendon Press, Oxford, England.

[12] Flathman, R.: 1982, 'Power, Authority, and Rights in Medicine,' in G. J. Agich (ed.), *Responsibility in Health Care,* D. Reidel, Dordrecht, the Netherlands, pp. 105-25.

[13] Foerster, W.F.: 1964, 'Exousia,' in G. Kittel and G. Friedrich (eds.), *Theological Dictionary of the New Testament,* vol. II, Eerdmans, Grand Rapids, pp. 562-75.

[14] Friedman, R.B.: 1991, 'On the Concept of Authority in Political Philosophy,' in J. Raz (ed.), *Authority,* New York, University Press, pp. 56-91.

[15] Gunneweg, A. H. J., and Achmithals, W.: 1982, *Authority,* J. E. Steely (trans.), Abingdon Press, Nashville, Tennessee.

[16] Hauerwas, S.: 1982, 'Authority and the Profession of Medicine,' in G. J. Agich (ed.), *Responsibility in Health Care,* D. Reidel, Dordrecht, the Netherlands, pp. 83-104.

[17] Hobbes, T.: 1651 (1946), *Leviathan, or the Matter, Forme, and Power of a Commonwealth, Ecclesiastical and Civil,* M. Oakshott (ed.), Basil Blackwell, Oxford, England.

[18] Kierkegaard, S.: 1955, *On Authority and Revelation: The Book of Adler,* W. Lowrie (trans.), Princeton University Press, Princeton, New Jersey, p. XVI.

[19] Ladenson, R.: 1991, 'In Defense of a Hobbesian Conception of Law,' in J. Raz (ed.), *Authority,* New York, University Press, New York, pp. 32-55.

[20] Lavin, B., Haug, M., Belgrave, L. K., and Breslau, N.: 1987, 'Change in Student Physicians' Views on Authority Relationships with Patients,' *Journal of Health and Social Behavior* 28, 258-72.

[21] Locke, J.: 1690 (1988), 'An Essay Concerning the True Original Extent and End of Civil Government,' in *Two Treatises of Government,* P. Laslett (ed.), Cambridge University Press, New York, pp. 256-428.

[22] Mackie, J. L.: 1977, *Ethics: Inventing Right and Wrong,* Penguin Books, Harmondsworth, Middlesex, England.

[23] MacIntyre, A.: 1967, *Secularization and Moral Change,* Oxford University Press, London, England.

[24] MacIntyre, A.: 1977, 'Patients as Agents,' in S. F. Spicker, and H. T. Englehardt (eds.), *Philosophical Medical Ethics: Its Nature and Significance,* D. Reidel, Dordrecht, the Netherlands, pp. 197-212.

[25] MacIntyre, A.: 1984, *After Virtue,* University of Notre Dame Press, Notre Dame, Indiana.

[26] May, W. F.: 1983, *The Physician's Covenant,* Westminster Press, Philadelphia.

[27] Molinski, W.: 1975, 'Authority,' in K. Rahner (ed.), *The Concise Sacramentum Mundi,* Seabury Press, New York, pp. 60-65.

[28] Myers, A. C. (ed.): 1987, *The Eerdmans Bible Dictionary,* Eerdmans, Grand Rapids, Michigan, pp. 108, 844-45.

[29] Nouwen, H. J.: 1972, *The Wounded Healer,* Doubleday, Garden City, New York.

[30] Parsons, T.: 1951, *The Social System,* The Free Press, Glencoe, Illinois.

[31] Pellegrino, E. D.: 'Moral Agency and Professional Ethics: Some Notes on the Transformation of the Physician-Patient Encounter,' in S. F. Spicker, and H. T. Engelhardt (eds.), *Philosophical Medical Ethics: Its Nature and Significance,* D. Reidel, Dordrecht, the Netherlands, pp. 213-20.

[32] Pellegrino, E. D.: 1979, 'Towards a Reconstruction of Medical Morality: The Primacy of Act of Profession and the Fact of Illness,' *Journal of Medicine and Philosophy* 4(1), 32-56.

[33] Pellegrino, E. D., and Thomasma, D. C.: 1981, *A Philosophical Basis of Medical Practice,* Oxford University Press, New York.

[34] Pellegrino, E. D., and Thomasma, D. C.: 1989, *For the Patient's Good: Towards the Restoration of Beneficence in Medical Ethics,* Oxford University Press, New York.

[35] Ramsey, P.: 1970, *The Patient as Person,* Yale University Press, New Haven, pp. xi-xviii.

[36] Raz, J.: 1991, 'Introduction,' in J. Raz (ed.), *Authority,* New York University Press, New York, pp. 1-19.

[37] Skehan, P. A., and DiLella, A. A.: 1987, *The Wisdom of Ben Sira,* Anchor Bible Series, vol. 39, Doubleday, New York.

[38] Suchman, A. L., and Matthews, D. A.: 1988, 'What Makes the Doctor-Patient Relationship Therapeutic? Exploring the Connexional Dimension of Medical Care,' *Annals of Internal Medicine* 108, 125-30.

[39] Sulmasy, D. P.: 1989, 'By Whose Authority: Emerging Issues in Medical Ethics,' *Theological Studies* 50, 95-119.

[40] Sulmasy, D. P.: 1989, 'The Covenant Within the Covenant: Doctors and Patients in Sirach 38:1-15,' *Linacre Quarterly* 55(4), 14-24.

[41] Sulmasy, D. P., Geller, G., Levine, D. M., and Faden, R.: 1990, 'Medical House Officers' Knowledge, Confidence, and Attitudes Regarding Medical Ethics,' *Archives of Internal Medicine* 150, 2509-13.

[42] Tansen, A., Hartvig, P., Fagerlund, C., and Dahlstrom, B.: 1982, 'Patient-controlled Analgesic Therapy: Part II. Individual Analgesic Demand and Plasma Concentrations of Pethidine and Post-operative Pain,' *Clinical Pharmacokinetics* 7, 164-75.

[43] Veatch, R. M.: 1982, 'Medical Authority and Professional Medical Authority: The Nature of Authority in Medicine for Decisions by Lay Persons and Professionals,' in G. J. Agich (ed.), *Responsibility in Health Care,* D. Reidel, Dordrecht, the Netherlands, pp. 127-37.

[44] Veatch, R.; 1981, *A Theory of Medical Ethics,* Basic Books, New York.

[45] Weber, M.: 1947 (1968), *Theory of Social and Economic Organizations,* A. M. Anderson and T. Parsons (trans.), Free Press, New York.

[46] Wolff, R. P.: 1991, 'The Conflict Between Authority and Autonomy,' in J. Raz (ed.), *Authority,* New York University Press, New York, pp. 20-31.

101 Honor Thy Patient

David Schiedermayer

A sixty-two-year-old recently retired man who was a foreman at a local paper mill sees his physician, complaining of abdominal pain and weight loss. He has a barium enema, and an apple core lesion highly suspicious for cancer is found in his colon. By agreement of his physician and his wife, he is not informed of the results of the x-ray, and is scheduled for exploratory surgery. The cancer is found to be widespread. There are large metastatic deposits in his liver and mesentery (fat in intestines). Again, he is not informed of the findings.

He has a rapid downhill clinical course. All of his visitors, including his eight-year-old grandson, are cautioned "not to tell" him his diagnosis. He is dead in four months.

I was the eight-year-old grandson. This man who died of colon cancer without ever officially knowing his diagnosis was my paternal grandfather. When he died in the early 1960s, many physicians withheld bad news from patients, and metastatic colon cancer is certainly bad news. There were several problems, however, with not telling my grandfather he had cancer. First, he was not given the chance to be involved (and he was the kind of man who would have wanted to be involved) in his own health care. Second, when he needed abdominal surgery, he was not really informed enough to consent to the procedure. Third, when he later became incompetent, no one knew his preferences regarding various types of

---

From David Schiedermayer, *Putting the Soul Back in Medicine: Reflections on Compassion and Ethics* (Grand Rapids: Baker Book House, 1994), pp. 36-49. Used by permission.

treatments. His physician did not maliciously withhold the news of his cancer; on the contrary, the physician thought he was being kind and caring. He thought the information would actually harm my grandfather. "Not telling" was the standard of care until quite recently. In this chapter I will examine "not telling" in its historical and biblical contexts and in the doctor-patient relationship of the 1990s.

Informed Consent: A Brief History

Informed consent has its historical underpinnings in English common law on battery, which forbids harmful or offensive nonconsensual touching. No special exceptions were made for medical care, except in emergency situations. The modern American judicial expression of informed consent was that of Judge Cardoza in 1914: "Every human being of adult years and sound mind has a right to determine what shall be done with his own body; and a surgeon who performs an operation without his patient's consent commits an assault for which he is liable for damages."[1] A competent patient can refuse any treatment.

In the latter half of this century, the courts began to marry the provider's traditional duty to secure consent with a new affirmative obligation of disclosure, perhaps best understood as a duty to warn, resulting in a new legal doctrine of "informed consent." This doctrine was first stated in a 1957 California decision, *Salgo v. Leland Stanford, Jr., Stanford University Board of Trustees.* The judicial development of informed consent was prompted, in part, by revelations of Nazi physician atrocities during World War II and the Nuremburg Code (1946-1949) which states the "voluntary consent of the human subject is absolutely essential . . . the person involved should have sufficient knowledge and comprehension of the elements of the [experiment] involved as to enable him to make an understanding and enlightened decision [regarding participation]." The code specifies that these elements are "the nature, duration, and purpose of the experiment; the method and means by which it is to be conducted; all inconveniences and hazards reasonably to be expected; and the effects upon his health or person which may possibly come from his participation in the experiment."[2]

Some of these elements have been incorporated into the current doctrine of informed consent, which requires the doctor to discuss the following:

1. the diagnosis of the disease and prognosis if untreated
2. the treatments which might improve the prognosis
3. information on alternative treatments

Adequate informed consent involves some sort of effort on the part of the physician to assure comprehension by the patient. It is measured by the effective transfer of information that would allow reasonable persons to make prudent choices on their own behalf. It is important to note that informed consent requires far more than a signature on the bottom of a list of complications. "Such recitations," the President's Commission for the Study of Ethical Problems in Medicine and Biomedical and Behavioral Research notes, "can be so overwhelming that patients are unable to distinguish truly significant information and to make sound decisions."[3] Rather, informed consent attempts to bring a conversational imperative to the often relatively silent world of the doctor and patient.

Why Physicians Resist Informed Consent

The members of the president's commission stated that their ultimate question was, "How can a fuller, shared understanding by patient and professional of their common enterprise be promoted, so that patients can participate, on an informed basis and to the extent they care to do so, in making decisions about their health care?"[4]

Implicit in the phrasing of this question is the commission's concern that some physicians are not really obtaining "informed consent." Why have physicians so disliked the concept?

As Jay Katz, M.D., writes convincingly in his book *The Silent World of Doctor and Patient:*

> Had they [physicians] appreciated that even the doctrine's [informed consent] modest appeal to patient self-determination represented a radical break with medical practices, as transmitted from teacher to student during more than two thou-

> sand years of recorded medical history, they might have been less embarrassed by standing so unpreparedly . . . before this new obligation.
>
> They might perhaps have realized that their silence had been until most recently [the last twenty-five years] a historical necessity, dictated not only by the inadequacy of medical knowledge but also by physicians' incapacity to discriminate between therapeutic effectiveness based on their actual physical interventions, and benefits that must be ascribed to other causes. They might also have argued that the practice of silence was part of a long and venerable tradition that deserved not to be dismissed lightly. They might at least have pleaded for time, because before they could embrace the unaccustomed obligation to talk with their patients, many problems required extensive study. None of this happened. Instead, passive-aggressive defensiveness, acrimony, and confusion have marked the early history of the age of informed consent. The physician-patient dialogue, now a mixture of proffered and withheld information, has become even more opaque; surely it is not based on the idea of shared decision making.[5]

While the goal of informed consent may seem laudable, it is one which many physicians resist instinctively on several levels and for several reasons. First, as Katz notes, the idea of informed consent is a new concept, and "the art is long." Second, it is foreign to traditional medical practice and values, which are parentalistic. Third, it is a legal concept, not a medical one. As Leon Kass, M.D. puts it, "Physicians who have long taken for granted their benevolent intentions toward their patients and prided themselves on their ability to judge the just-right thing to do in the circumstances, will not see the need for, and will bridle at . . . lawyers who insist on establishing a patient's bill of rights or laying down an explicit contract between the so-called consumers and providers of health services."[6] Sider and Clements have listed the following ten problems with an informed consent, autonomy-based medical ethic:[7]

1. Such an ethic focuses on who is to choose rather than on what is chosen.
2. The assumption is that information is always a positive good and that obtaining informed consent is the physician's primary moral task.
3. The wishes of family members and physicians are considered morally irrelevant.
4. The implication is that egotism is more dependable than altruism for health care decisions.
5. The excessive emphasis on patient choice alone splits facts from values, medical science from medical ethics, and clinical thinking from moral reasoning.
6. Autonomy is considered more important than beneficence, and elaborate justifications are necessary to treat the patient for the patient's good without consent.
7. The framework assumes that a political (or legal) model is the most appropriate for the physician-patient relationship.
8. The patient preference ethic tends to confuse medical values with the individual physician's personal values.
9. The fundamental task of medical ethics in this system is to justify legal coercion.
10. Physicians risk demoralization and deprofessionalization if medical therapeutics is grounded in subjectivist preferences.

While these objections are important and have some merit, they polarize the discussion into an autonomy-beneficence dichotomy, and we are left fighting about whether the doctor or the patient knows best. This is a no-win battle; each knows *different* things. The doctor knows the diagnosis, prognosis, and treatment; the patient knows his or her preferences, pain, and suffering. In the real world, we need to talk to each other and come to a mutual understanding. We need to balance unbridled autonomy, which is perhaps better called selfishness, with the legitimate need to make one's own medical decisions as a patient. What do we know about the physician-patient dialogue?

Studies in Silence

According to Katz, while doctors and patients have always conversed, doctors have not employed words to invite patient participation in sharing the burdens of treatment decisions. As a simple illustration, he points to physicians' historical practice of silence when the patient has a fatal disease like my grandfather's, and asks, "If [physicians think] remaining life can be shortened and made insufferable by words, can it not just as easily be made insufferable by silence?"[8]

Katz's argument against silence in this setting is supported by new scientific information that patients want to know their diagnoses and prognoses even if they have fatal diseases. For example, burn patients whose survival is unprecedented and patients with inoperable cancer are not harmed by being informed of their prognoses.

Many patients also want to discuss the option of cardiopulmonary resuscitation (CPR). Surprisingly high numbers of patients haven't been asked if they want CPR, and many people would refuse it if asked. In a landmark study, Bedell and Delbanco reported that only 19 percent of the 154 patients who had been resuscitated in their hospital in 1981 had been asked earlier if they wanted to have CPR if it became necessary.[9] Eighty-six percent of the patients in their study were competent, and nearly all the physicians involved said they favored participation of patients in these decisions "at least sometimes." In almost a fifth of the cases, the families were consulted instead of the patients, although these patients were just as likely to be competent.

If their physicians had talked to these patients they would have been surprised. Of the twenty-four competent patients who survived to discharge, eight stated they had not desired CPR and wouldn't want it again, but only one of the sixteen physicians caring for these patients suspected the patient felt this way. In an accompanying editorial in the *New England Journal of Medicine,* Marcia Angell, M.D. suggests physicians ask their fully competent patient the following three questions:[10]

1. Do you wish to be fully informed of medical findings and consulted on all major decisions?
2. If so, do you have any objections to having your family informed as well as yourself?
3. If you do not wish to be fully informed, would you like to designate a family member or someone else to be informed in your stead?

By and large, Angell says, sick people have much the same interest as healthy people in participating in decisions which affect them, and most patients probably would want their families informed as well. However, nothing should be taken for granted. "What does the patient want? Ask him," she concludes.

The Doctor-Patient Relationship

Despite the problems both doctor and patient may have with the marriage of the concepts "informed" and "consent," informed consent is still the ideal because it can help doctors and patients talk with each other. Physicians need to see beyond the patients' "rights" to informed consent, and beyond physicians' "duty" to inform their patients to what is essentially a Christian imperative: Honor thy patient. Honor thy patient by talking to him or her as a person, as Jesus talked to people he encountered. Ethically valid consent is a process of shared decision making based on mutual respect and participation, an approach which characterizes the Christian's attitudes toward relationships. Jesus put it this way in Matthew 22:39-40: "You shall love your neighbor as yourself. On these two commandments [loving the Lord with your whole heart, soul, and mind, and loving your neighbor as yourself] depend the whole Law and the Prophets (NASB)."

The concept of informed consent at its deepest level — mutual love and respect — is in line with Jesus' teachings. While Jesus referred to religious law here, there is a sense in which the meaning of the civil law of informed consent also depends on these commandments, for otherwise it is a "useless ritual involving the recital of the contents of a form," in the words of the president's commission. Furthermore, in the actual clinical situations where the legal doctrine of informed consent is most difficult to enforce — those that involve the incompetent adult, the retarded child, the newborn, the unborn — it is precisely this mutual respect and honor for the other which enables physicians to care for patients in a manner which "fulfills the law."

I will address these clinical situations later in this chapter. For now let us turn to the common, "easy" situation of a doctor's relationship with a competent patient. This doctor-patient accommodation has been described by Dr. Mark Siegler:

The nature of the patient involved — his personality, character, attitudes, and values — and the factors which led him to seek a medical encounter with this particular physician — are central components to the process. Similarly, the personality, character, attitude, values, and technical skills of the physician affect the accommodation. Further, the quality of the interaction between patient and physician — the chemistry of the interaction — modifies the process. Of course, the nature of the medical problem, including its type, acuteness, gravity, and its potential for remediation, will be a major determinant of whether a physician-patient accommodation is achieved. For example, the entire process will be modified profoundly and telescoped if the patient is acutely or critically ill and alternative medical resources are unavailable. Finally, other considerations which may affect the achievement of a physician-patient accommodation include clinical setting, e.g., a hospital, doctor's office, or the patient's home; the organization of the medical service, HMO, or fee-for-service; and also, occasionally, the claims of other relevant third-party interests such as those of family, insurers, or the state.[11]

In each medical encounter, at each point, the patient and physician can arrive at a joint decision in which the physician agrees to care for the patient and the patient agrees to be treated by the physician. A physician is not obligated to enter a physician-patient relationship if he believes that he is unable to help the patient, or if he believes that even if he could help the patient he could do so only by sacrificing his own standards of what it means to be a good and responsible physician — in other words, if the relationship would result in an action the physician considers illegal or immoral.

In some situations, the physician will be largely in control, as in this case: A twenty-nine-year-old man is severely injured in an automobile accident. He is admitted to the emergency room, and it is apparent he is critically ill. There is no other emergency room in the area. The physician on call begins caring for him immediately.

In other situations, such as the following, the patient will be largely in control: A fifty-three-year-old man with well-controlled hypertension is experiencing impotence from his antihypertensive medication. His physician explains the risks of changing medications. The patient understands that another medication may not be as effective as the current one, but the patient strongly requests the change. His physician agrees to try another drug.

The particular balance of responsibility may change with time and circumstances. It is not an easy relationship, not even when both physician and patient are open and sensitive. Physicians and other health professionals can share decision-making power with many of their patients, but there is a problem: how can physicians share decision-making power with noncompliant or incapacitated patients?

Noncompliance and the Case of Mrs. Sarah T.

Sarah T. was a forty-five-year-old white woman who had uncontrolled diabetes mellitus. She first came to see me in 1981 with severe retinopathy and a dorsal foot ulcer six by eight centimeters around and four centimeters in depth. The tendons of her foot were visible in the wound, and an x-ray showed underlying osteomyelitis. Extensive skin grafting covered the wound, but the bone stayed infected despite long-term antibiotics. She required frequent hospitalization for foot ulcers. In the hospital on a diet, her blood sugars were normal to low. Once home, her blood sugars rose again to the 400 range and her insulin dosage had to be increased again. Dozens of clinic visits followed over the next four years. Her eye disease worsened; she had new foot ulcers. When I made a house call, I found an eight-pack of Pepsi and a bag of Snickers bars (the big ones) in her refrigerator. I again discussed diet and adjusted her insulin dose upward. One night the emergency room called: Sarah T. had gas gangrene. The surgeons amputated both legs above the knees. She survived and was confined to a wheelchair.

One day she phoned me complaining of neck tightness. I notified the paramedics, and in the emergency room her electrocardiogram showed a large anterior wall myocardial infarction. She was admitted to the coronary care unit in congestive heart failure. The cardiologist said she needed a

Swan-Ganz catheter to monitor her cardiac pressures. I talked with Sarah T. She was frightened. I assumed she was worried about her recent heart attack and her difficulty with breathing, but she told me her real fear: needles. She was desperately afraid of needles and did not want the Swan because of the large needle.

Sarah T. and I often had difficulty arriving at a satisfactory physician-patient relationship, because she was afraid I would stop caring for her if she told me the truth. She felt guilty about her diet; I felt guilty that I couldn't help her more and that her diabetes was hurting her so much. I can honestly say I would not have abandoned her, because although I was not achieving my medical "goals," I felt I was still able to help her through the various acute illnesses she encountered.

Physicians often suspect (as I did with Sarah T.) that their patients are noncompliant, and it should come as no surprise to caregivers that imperfection in diets, exercise, or medication are common. According to an extensive review, up to 50 percent of patients with hypertension fail to follow referral advice; over 50 percent drop out of care in one year; and only about two-thirds of those who remain under care consume enough medication to adequately control their blood pressure. Noncompliance for short-term regimens is as high as 92 percent in careful studies. The problem cuts across all socioeconomic and educational boundaries; 50 percent of all patients for whom some appropriate therapy is prescribed fail to receive full benefit through inadequate adherence to treatment. Health professionals are notoriously noncompliant patients. Doctors, nurses, and allied health professionals often fail to take medicine properly.

Every clinician knows there are no pat answers for reaching a satisfactory doctor-patient relationship with non-compliant patients. These are some of our most "difficult" patients, because we cannot reach a true agreement easily. Working with such patients requires the qualities of mercy and patience. Physicians are imperfect imitators of God, who bears with us (and doesn't abandon us) through all our failures.

The Physician-Patient Relationship When the Patient Is Incapacitated

There are several groups of incapacitated patients. First there are those "informed incapacitated" patients who may be elderly with mild dementia who are able to understand at one time but not another and whose capacity may vary from morning to night. Second are those who have been previously capacitated but are now incapacitated. Third are those who will never have decision-making capacity, such as the profoundly mentally retarded. Finally, there are those who lack capacity but have the potential to have decision-making capacity, like minor children or the unborn.

When physicians care for incapacitated patients, they assume more of the decision-making power. Advanced directives, in the form of living wills or durable powers of attorney, represent the wishes of once-decisional patients, so such directives enable patients to share some of the decision-making power even when they become incapacitated.[12] The following case illustrates the use of an advanced directive: A sixty-two-year-old man is admitted to the hospital after suffering a cardiac arrest. The patient is in a coma as a result of prolonged anoxia during the resuscitation. The patient has a living will, which states, "If I have an incurable injury I direct the life-sustaining procedures be withheld or withdrawn and that I be permitted to die naturally."

The patient's condition worsens and he develops acute renal failure. His physicians discuss dialysis with his wife. On the basis of knowing him and his stated wishes, she thinks he would refuse dialysis in his present condition. She asks his physicians not to dialyze him, and they agree.

Although a direct doctor-patient agreement with an incapacitated patient, like this patient in anoxic coma, is often impossible to achieve, a legitimate understanding can often be reached between the doctor and those who speak for the patient. While a decisional patient may refuse any treatment, the ability of the incapacitated person's "spokesperson" to refuse lifesaving treatment is properly somewhat more limited. As in this case, it must be based on what the patient would prefer *were he able to converse.*

Conclusion

As clinicians in the 1990s, many of us realize that we no longer want to live in a silent world; we wish to communicate and share our difficult decisions. Like patients, we are dissatisfied with a medical ethic that promulgates health-professional estrangement and patient isolation. The health-professional-patient relationship, a model of shared information and mutual consent, is a model which enables us to treat patients as human beings. This relationship also allows us to free the patient to accept (or reject) our advice.

There are problems with obtaining informed consent, respecting free will, and forging a health-professional-patient accommodation; these acts are intellectually challenging, emotionally trying, and time consuming for all involved. It was easier the old way. But my grandfather would be pleased that we are beginning to try to honor our patients as ourselves.

Notes

1. Schloendorff vs. Society of New York Hospital, 211 N.Y. 125, 105 N.E. 92, 95 (1914).

2. W. L. Prosser, *Handbook of the Law of Torts*, 4th ed. (St. Paul: West Publishing Company, 1971), #10 at 36, #32 at 165, cited in *President's Commission for the Study of Ethical Problems in Medicine and Biomedical and Behavioral Research*, Vol. 1: 20-1.

3. Ibid.: 28.

4. Ibid.: 31.

5. J. Katz, *The Silent World of Doctor and Patient* (New York: Free Press, 1984), See also Jay Katz, "Disclosure and Consent: In Search of Their Roots," in *Genetics and the Law II*, eds. Aubrey Milansky and George J. Annas (New York: Plenum Press, 1980): 124.

6. L. Kass, "Ethical Dilemmas in the Care of the Ill: What Is the Physician's Service?" *Journal of the American Medical Association* 244 (1980): 1811-16.

7. R. C. Sider and C. D. Clements, "The New Medical Ethics: A Second Opinion," *Archives of Internal Medicine* 145 (1985): 2169-71.

8. J. Katz, *The Silent World:* 20.

9. S. E. Bedell and T. L. Delbanco, "Choices about Cardiopulmonary Resuscitation in the Hospital: When Do Physicians Talk to Patients?" *New England Journal of Medicine* 310 (1984): 1089-93.

10. M. Angell, "Respecting the Autonomy of Competent Patients," ibid.: 1115-16.

11. M. Siegler, "Searching for Moral Certainty in Medicine: A Proposal for a New Model of the Doctor-Patient Encounter," *Bulletin of the New York Academy of Medicine* 57 (1981): 56-69.

12. L. Emanuel, "Advance Directives: What Have We Learned So Far?" *The Journal of Clinical Ethics*, 4(1993): 8-16.

102 Thorn-in-the-Flesh Decision Making: A Christian Overview of the Ethics of Treatment

Richard J. Mouw

The ethical perspectives which get employed in medical ethical discussions often seem rather narrow in scope. Sometimes the methodology seems closely linked to a "values clarification" approach, in which the people involved are encouraged to get clearer about the value commitments with which they operate. Or, ethical issues are introduced within a framework of a kind of "systems analysis," and the questions are put in this way: How can we plug our values into the procedures of medical care? How can we best fit the ethical component into the system of medical decision making?

From a Christian point of view there is something deeply unsatisfactory about these ways of dealing with the issues. This sense of dissatisfaction was expressed to me recently by a medical professional who had been involved in a discussion of ethical issues at a seminar in the hospital where she works. At this seminar she experienced a profound frustration: "I just don't know where to *begin* in bringing my own beliefs to bear on that discussion. I felt like those questions were very important to me, but I also felt that I had to come at those questions in a very different way!"

This experience of frustration is based — or so I judge — on a proper assessment of typical discussions of medical ethics. Very often those discussions move on to casuistry before getting clear about the principles which must inform casuistical deliberation. Nor can the moral principles proper to medical decision making be arrived at merely by explicating our intuitions or by systematizing our hunches. Medical ethical discussion must be rooted in a broad-ranging, self-conscious awareness of the larger moral and more-than-moral contexts in which medical questions arise.

Take, for example, the systems-analysis approach to which I have already alluded. This approach seems to work on the following model. There is a system of medical decision making that encompasses various diagnostic, prognostic, and therapeutic options. This system is taken as a given. The question then is asked whether this system or set of procedures and options is fully adequate without some ethical components being added to it. The view that the system by itself is inadequate seems to be what Ivan Illich has in mind when he complains that in a highly "medicalized" culture "medical ethics have been secreted into a specialized department that brings theory into line with actual practice" (*Medical Nemesis: The Expropriation of Health* [New York: Bantam, 1977], p. 40). Illich's own view calls for an evaluative critique of that system of medical care itself; he is convinced that the basic assumptions of our medicalized society must be called into question. Whatever our own assessment may be of the details of Illich's critique, he does seem to be correct in insisting that we must be sensitive to the basic presuppositions which shape the discussion of medical ethics.

We must recognize the limitations of the medical perspective by looking at the ways in which formulations of that perspective relate to other kinds of concerns, including ethical concerns. But lest that sound like a self-serving statement coming from an ethicist, let me go one step further. We must also recognize the limitations of the ethical perspective by looking at the ways in which formulations of *that* perspective relate to other kinds of concerns, concerns which range more broadly than the issues of ethical rightness and wrongness.

Medical ethics as an area of scholarly and professional inquiry must be tamed — put into its proper place — by the recognition that neither

Used by permission of the author.

medical nor ethical nor medical ethical discussion is adequate for dealing with the issues which arise in the context of medical decision making. My basic contention here will not be shocking to Calvinists. Medical ethics must itself function within the context of a larger world-and-life view. As Christians we cannot discuss a perplexing medical dilemma for very long without sensing the need to discuss our views of human nature, our perspectives on the society in which we live, and our concepts of health and healing and human well-being and eternal destiny.

For as long as any of us can remember there have been groups around that have reminded us of the role of basic presuppositions in dealing with medical issues. Jehovah's Witnesses have refused blood transfusions; Christian Scientists have rejected conventional definitions of "disease" and "cure"; Seventh Day Adventists have questioned accepted traditions regarding nutrition; the Old Reformed have eschewed preventative medicine. Few of us are convinced by the exegetical and theological cases which these groups offer in defense of their departures from conventional medical wisdom. But, like Ivan Illich's more recent heterodoxies, they do remind us of a *level* of critical concern which we must attempt to maintain — a reminder that has also been reinforced by recent interest in Chinese acupuncture, "indigenous" medicine, the hospice movement, and other phenomena.

Some rather harsh recent criticisms of medical orthodoxy have alleged that there are perverse psychological, social, political and economic forces which have shaped the attitudes and patterns at work in medical decision making. These criticisms have a direct bearing on a consideration of the processes of medical treatment. Elisabeth Kübler-Ross and others have argued that the alleged "objectivity" of medical practitioners is often a cover-up for the insecurity and fear in the presence of suffering and death on the part of those professionals. Others have argued that the medical care professions are tainted by sexism, racism, classism, ageism, and elitism.

As I have said, these latter considerations — which we might think of as having to do with, roughly speaking, the sociology of medicine — bear very directly on the ethics of treatment. It is not necessary here to decide the degree to which these sociological criticisms of medical orthodoxy are correct. But we can allow the sensitivities from which they stem to inform our own discussion. At the very least this means that we ought not construe the treatment process in too narrow a fashion. There is, for example, a distressing tendency in much of the literature dealing with the ethics of treatment to focus almost exclusively on the physician-patient relationship, as if these were the only two roles which have an important place in medical treatment. The fact is that the treatment process encompasses many relationships involving a number of different roles: for example, the relationship between physician and nurse, nurse and patient, physician and family, clergy and patient.

How should we as Christians view these relationships in the context of the treatment process? In a 1956 article published in the A.M.A. *Archives of Internal Medicine*, Thomas Szasz and Marc Hollender distinguished among three basic models of the physician-patient relationship in the hope of showing "that certain philosophical preconceptions associated with the notions of 'disease,' 'treatment,' and 'cure' have a profound bearing on both the theory and practice of medicine." Their first model is that of "Activity-Passivity," which they judge to be the oldest model operating in medical care. Here the physician is viewed as active, the patient as acted upon. "Treatment" takes place irrespective of the patient's contribution and regardless of the outcome. There is a similarity here between the patient and a helpless infant, on the one hand, and between physician and parent, on the other."

The second model is that of "Guidance-Cooperation." Here the patient takes on a more active role than in the previous model. But the decision-making power resides with the physician. The physician "guides"; the patient "cooperates." If the earlier model can be likened to the relationship between parent and helpless infant, this one more closely parallels that between parent and adolescent child.

The third model is given the label of "Mutual Participation," and it is based on "the postulate that equality among human beings is desirable." Patient and physician have roughly equal power, they are mutually interdependent, and they search for decisions which will be satisfactory to both parties.

Several observations are necessary concerning the intentions of Szasz and Hollender in presenting these models. First, they make it clear that no one single model is adequate to all situations involving medical decisions. For example, the Activity-Passivity model may be quite appropriate to a situation where a physician must treat a comatose patient. Second, Szasz and Hollender obviously do think that the third model, Mutual Participation, is the ideal to be strived for. They tell us that "in an evolutionary sense, the pattern of mutual participation is more highly developed than the other two models of doctor-patient relationship." And third, we must highlight the fact that Szasz and Hollender are presenting these models as ways of sorting out different patterns or distributions of power and authority in medical decision making. In the first model, all power resides with the physician; in the second, the patient at least has the right or power to consent to the physician's decision; in the third, power is distributed along egalitarian lines.

I want to comment further on some of these matters. But before doing so, I must briefly observe that Szasz and Hollender themselves manifest the syndrome, which I mentioned earlier, of discussing the treatment process as if it were exclusively an affair between *physician* and patient. I will attempt to remedy that pattern by referring more generally to the relationship between medical professional and patient.

I daresay that many of us in the Christian community would never think of attempting to understand the relationship between medical professional and patient along the lines suggested by the third model proposed by Szasz and Hollender. Nor would we find the first model, that of Activity-Passivity, to be appropriate, except in unusual circumstances. Most of us would take the second model, in which the patient cooperates with the expert guidance of the professional, as quite proper — even the ideal way of viewing medical situations. But of course it is precisely the notion of the "expertise" of the professional which is under attack from the perspective of the egalitarian.

The denial of the expertise of the medical professional comes in two forms today. First, there are those who hold to a pluralistic or relativistic view of medical theory. They reject the notion of a "neutral" or "objective" medical science. Medical theories and technologies are shaped by cultural perspectives, and their formation and formulation are guided by culturally embedded understandings of such things as "health," "disease," and "cure." The Navajo medicine man, the faith healer, the Eastern guru, the shaman, the surgeon from Cincinnati, the practitioner of acupuncture — each is rooted in a different form of social organization embodying a different normative understanding of human nature. To evaluate these perspectives in terms of "primitive" or "modern" or "advanced" is already to be adopting a given cultural archimedian point. There can be no question of whether one system is better than another; each is simply different from the rest. Or, if comparative evaluations *can* be made, they cannot be made superficially; they must be based on an assessment of the larger cultural context from which given perspectives and technologies derive their meaning and effectiveness.

There are important and fascinating issues here — issues which bear directly on questions in the philosophy of science and epistemology. But the second form of the challenge to medical expertise has closer links to medical ethics and the sociology of medicine, so we will look at that version more closely.

The second way in which people challenge the expertise of the medical professional focuses on the role of what are considered to be significant nonmedical factors in medical decision making. Those who issue this kind of challenge may or may not have sympathies with the first form of challenge. Nonetheless they are inclined to view situations of medical decision making in such a way that careful attention is given to various nonmedical features of those situations. The medical professional may be viewed as having some degree of expertise with regard to medical science and technology; but it is argued that the benefits of medical expertise are outweighed by the professional's lack of expertise regarding other, more important, factors at work in situations of medical decision making. Sometimes it is even suggested that medical professionals manifest a systematic bias regarding these nonmedical factors, a bias which distorts and perverts their appeals to medical expertise. For example, a feminist writing under a pseudonym and describing herself as a "fat Radical Ther-

I disagree

apist" (Aldebaran, "Fat Liberation," in *Love, Therapy and Politics,* ed. Hogie Wyckoff [New York: Grove Press, 1976], pp. 197-212) has argued that the medical establishment and the insurance companies have conspired to suppress and distort accurate information regarding fatness and health. In the course of making her case she refers to "the mystification of medical knowledge which has oppressed fat people for so long," and she alleges that "the hostility of doctors toward fat people is well-documented." This oppression, she suggests, is especially directed toward women: the medical and mental health professions are committed to the ideals of "beauty, poise and health." In foisting these ideals on women in the name of medical "objectivity" they force many people into lives of "anxiety, self-hatred, and, ultimately, more failure."

This line is argument is an extreme case in point for a pattern of thinking which others are inclined to pursue in more modest tones: the medical professions are organized along lines which promote insensitivity to what it means to be a woman, a black, a homosexual, a ghetto-dweller. Yet characteristics of this sort are crucial elements in medical situations. A patient possessing such characteristics is in fact the "expert" regarding the medical situation in which he or she is involved. Prescriptions concerning what is "best" for a person in that situation must be made from the point of view of the patient.

It should be obvious from the little that I have said about this line of criticism of medical professionals that this is an area of discussion where a number of different dynamics are at work. Some critics attribute to medical professionals a systematic bias against certain groups of people; others view medical orthodoxy as a manifestation of a perverse ideology; still others limit themselves to pointing out certain widespread social and psychological insensitivities associated with medical practice.

But underlying some of the criticisms in this area are assumptions which are closely related to the third model described by Szasz and Hollender, the egalitarian model. This does seem to me to be what is going on in Ivan Illich's critique of what he considers our "medicalized society." I offer as evidence the concluding paragraph of his book, *Medical Nemesis:*

> Man's consciously lived fragility, individuality, and relatedness make the experience of pain, of sickness, and of death an integral part of his life. The ability to cope with this trio autonomously is fundamental to his health. As he becomes dependent on the management of his intimacy, he renounces his autonomy and his health *must* decline. The true miracle of modern medicine is diabolical. It consists in making not only individuals but whole populations survive on inhumanly low levels of personal health. Medical nemesis is the negative feedback of a social organization that set out to improve and equalize the opportunity for each man to cope in autonomy and ended by destroying it.

Here we have a clear example of someone who pits human "autonomy" against the "dependency" fostered by medical orthodoxy. According to Illich, the most significant factors at work in a situation of medical decision making are these: as a fragile individual, the questions of how I am going to cope with *my* pain, *my* sickness, *my* death, are an integral part of my life. The autonomous exercise of my ability to cope with these matters is central to my own health. "Health" is not something which can be defined in purely physiological terms, such that a professional intervention on my behalf, an intervention over which I have no control and which brings about a certain state of physiological equilibrium, can make me "healthy." Health *includes* my autonomous coping with my own pain and sickness. Any medical care system which attempts to bypass my active involvement in the decisions which affect these most intimate matters in my life is, as Illich puts it, diabolical: it inevitably reduces my personal health; it makes me dependent on its own alleged expertise. The fact is that the professional is attempting to manage a situation in which I alone may be the true expert; for I alone am qualified to decide how my pain, my sickness, and my death will function in my life plan.

I must confess that my own response to this line of argument is an ambivalent one. Let me first explain the negative side of my reaction. As an orthodox Calvinist I bristle when I hear the word "autonomy." I cut my own theological and philosophical teeth on the writings of Carl Henry, Cornelius Van Til and Herman Dooyeweerd, and I learned my lessons well. "Autonomy" means "self-legislating"; an autonomous agent makes his or her own laws. And from a biblical perspective this simply will not do. People are not their own law-makers; they cannot produce their own norms for living. The plea for autonomy is a vain boast, a boast which echoes the arrogance of the serpent in Genesis 3: "when you eat of [the fruit of the tree] your eyes will be opened, and you will be like God."

This is not to say that the word "autonomy," whenever it is used, always means something devilish. Even some orthodox Calvinists have been known to speak of the need for an "autonomous Christian school system" — by which they mean a school system whose direction is not decided by a government or a church but which sets its own course. I do not know whether Illich himself means to use the term in a way that I would consider to be completely perverse. But I do know that sinful autonomy — the prideful desire to set one's own course, thereby refusing to recognize God's sovereign rule — is a very real tendency in the human heart. And it is a tendency which manifests itself in all areas of living and decision making, including those areas having to do with medicine and health. So it is never silly for us to raise the question whether we are hearing echoes from the Garden in contemporary pleas on behalf of autonomous decision making.

But even when we are sure that a given plea for autonomy is diabolical in nature, that does not decide the matter. Even the serpent of Genesis 3 must be given his due. We know that the serpent always lies, that he is always wrong; but we must take pains to discern the nature of his error in a given context. The Bible makes it clear that while the serpent was thoroughly evil, he was not thoroughly stupid. Genesis 3 begins, after all, with the observation that "the serpent was more subtle than any other wild creature that the Lord God had made." The serpent's lie was in fact a perversion of the truth. He was trading on a subtlety. In tempting Eve, the serpent told her that she could become "like God." Now that is not just a simple falsehood — it is a perversion of the truth. In Genesis 1 we learn that Adam and Eve were in fact created in the image and likeness of God. There is a perfectly proper sense in which human beings are "like God." We are God-imagers. The serpent in Genesis 3 was twisting the truth into a falsehood. He was telling a God-imager that she should become a God-pretender; he was encouraging someone who was already made in the image of God to try to *be* a god. In doing so the serpent was trading on a subtlety: he was, as I have already said, twisting the truth.

Now, what does all of this have to do with Ivan Illich's plea for autonomy? I want to suggest that even if we were convinced that Illich was encouraging persons to be autonomous in the straightforwardly sinful sense of Genesis 3, he still might not be *all* wrong. He might be twisting the truth. And then it would be our job to see the truth that might reside in his perversion of the truth.

Let me try to illustrate my contention here by going through a few lines of Illich's paragraph again, but this time substituting references to the image of God for his uses of the concept of autonomy.

> Man's consciously lived fragility, individuality, and relatedness make the experience of pain, of sickness, and death an integral part of his life. The ability to cope with this trio in a God-imaging manner is fundamental to his health. As he becomes dependent on the management of his intimacy, he renounces the divine image and his health *must* decline. . . .

I am of the opinion that this formulation does not sound so off-base to Christian ears. To be healthy in a Christian sense is to be capable of exercising God-given capacities; it is to be able to fulfill one's calling. If conventional medical practice creates the kind of dependency that reduces this capacity in a patient then it would seem that we must say Christian things about that medical practice which are as harsh as the things being said by Illich and others.

But there is an important "if" in what I just said: "*if* conventional medical practice" reduces God-imaging activity. . . . The important question here is, *Does* it?

A fully adequate answer to this question would, of course, require the sifting of much empirical data. But we can get at the question in a slightly different way by expanding it in this manner: Does it *necessarily?* That is, given the fact that conventional medical practice creates certain kinds of dependencies in patients, are these dependencies necessarily detrimental to God-imaging?

Dependency as such is not a bad thing, viewed from a Christian perspective. Indeed, in a rather basic and crucial way, human beings are radically dependent upon God. Nor is dependency upon the *expertise* of others a bad thing, since the God on whom we are dependent is overwhelmingly expert about everything. Is it, then, that dependency upon the expertise of other *human beings* is something to be avoided? I think not. The notions of individual callings and mutual service suggest that different human beings will develop different kinds of expertise, and that we each must respect the gifts of others and rely on others for guidance in different areas of life. We might put the point this way with reference to medical expertise: dependence on the expert guidance of medical professionals is good and proper if that dependence is an image-promoting dependence. Similarly, expert medical guidance is a good thing for a professional to provide, if that guidance is image promoting.

This way of putting the case is neither trivial nor misleading. The apostle Peter instructs believers to "be subject for the Lord's sake to every human institution" (1 Peter 2:13); and although the immediate context of his remarks seems to be political in nature, I do not think that we violate the spirit of this instruction when we apply it to patterns of authority in other spheres of life. But if this legitimately applies to subjection to medical authority, we must also draw parallels between what the Bible says about the proper exercise of political authority and the proper exercise of authority in the medical sphere. Romans 13 makes it clear that God calls rulers to serve as his ministers, rewarding those who perform good works and punishing evildoers. Similarly, if we extend this pattern of biblical teaching to medical practice, those who would exercise medical authority must minister to those under their care.

If the desire to exercise sinful autonomy is to be condemned in the patient, it must also be condemned in the medical professional. In neither case may a person act like a "self-legislator," pretending that he or she is the sole source or reference point for decision-making norms. Patient and professional alike stand *coram deo,* before the face of God.

But of course the situation is complicated by the fact that not all human beings agree about matters pertaining to the relationship of people to God. Some people, both professionals and patients, do not believe in God. And even among Christians there is much diversity in beliefs concerning what it means to live before the face of God. Even under the best conditions possible in a sinful society, some degree of conflict is to be expected.

The professional-patient relationship can be characterized by four possible distributions of belief and unbelief: Christian professional and Christian patient; Christian professional and non-Christian patient; non-Christian professional and Christian patient; non-Christian professional and non-Christian patient. For our purposes here, let us concentrate on the roles of Christian professional and Christian patient under some of these distributions.

Consider first the role of the Christian patient. I am convinced that the Christian patient ought to have a strong interest in being knowledgeably involved in basic decisions regarding his or her medical treatment. This flies in the face of the attitudes of many professionals, especially in the pre-Kübler-Ross era. For example, in a 1961 study of physicians' attitudes toward "truth telling" in cancer cases (reprinted in *Moral Problems in Medicine,* pp. 109-16), Donald Oken reported that many physicians favored a policy "as little as possible in the most general terms consistent with maintaining cooperation in treatment. . . . Questioning by the patient almost invariably is disregarded and considered a plea for reassurance unless persistent, and intuitively perceived as 'a real wish to know.' Even then it may be ignored. The vast majority of these doctors . . . approach the issue with the view that disclosure should be avoided unless there are positive indications, rather than the reverse."

The language used here is clearly that of power and control. The professional controls information about the patient's condition, dispensing it only when it is judged to be in the "real" interests of the patient to do so. From a biblical point of view, this attitude seems to be clearly unsatisfactory. In almost every case there are prima facie reasonable grounds for thinking that it *is* in the best interests of the Christian patient to struggle knowledgeably with the issues of pain, suffering, and death. In 2 Corinthians 12, the apostle Paul describes his own struggles before the Lord regarding his "thorn in the flesh"; three times he bargained with God in the hope of having the affliction removed. Whether his bargaining process was characterized by emotional maturity and stability is not revealed. But it is obvious that his struggle had an important spiritual outcome, namely, the recognition that God's power could be made perfect in his own weakness. This episode, along with the account of King Hezekiah's negotiations with the Lord regarding the time of his own death, reveals, I think, a biblical pattern for viewing the role of suffering in the life of the believer: we must allow pain, suffering, and the expectation of death — even though these are usually very agonizing factors to confront — to visit us as sanctifying forces in our lives. No medical professional has the unqualified right to deny us these struggles by withholding information from us. Perhaps there are extenuating circumstances in which information may be withheld from a Christian patient, but the bias must clearly be in favor of truth telling, even if such disclosures require educating the patient regarding complex medical analyses. There is, I suggest, a Christian "right to know" about the facts concerning one's physical condition.

But what of the role of the Christian professional in situations in which there is real or potential conflict between professional judgment and the wishes and beliefs of the patient? There is an increasing body of medical and legal literature which argues strongly for the rights of patients to refuse life-saving treatment or even to commit what we might think of as "active suicide." For example, Norman Cantor comes to this conclusion in a 1973 *Rutgers Law Review* article after reviewing a wide variety of medical and legal considerations. He suggests that professional deference to the desires of the patient in refusing treatment must be based on a "sensitivity toward personal interests in bodily integrity and self-determination."

I'm not sure exactly what Cantor means by "bodily integrity," but his appeal to the importance of "self-determination" is clearly related to the "autonomy" theme which we have already discussed. My own hunch is that we as Christians can arrive at a similar conclusion to Cantor's by traveling quite a different route.

It is unfortunate that the phrase "playing God" is often used to describe a pattern whereby professionals override the wishes and desires of a patient in prescribing certain kinds of treatment. This is unfortunate because the biblical God in important respects does not himself "play God" in this manner. The God of the Scriptures is patient with unbelief and sin. He does not override the human will in some tyrannical fashion in order to bring people into conformity with his plans. Even the Canons of the Synod of Dort — which many consider to be the harshest of Calvinist documents — insist that God "does not treat men as senseless stocks and blocks, nor take away their will and its properties, or do violence thereto." The Canons then go on to use the language of "wooing" or courtship to describe God's electing procedures, and they regularly treat the unsaved as being *allowed* by God to remain in the condition of unbelief which they *themselves* have chosen. The biblical God does not "play God" by manipulating people with a disregard to their own choices and convictions.

The Christian professional must imitate God's patience with sinners, refusing to coerce, but choosing instead of invite, to persuade, to educate, and to reason — all of which presupposes a respect for the sincerely held convictions and desires of others. The patient's right to know must be supplemented by the professional's right to attempt to persuade.

In a profoundly Christian sense, medical decision making is a "thorny" business; our decisions must be wrestled with in a world that is presently full of thorns. And our struggles are complicated by the fact that these thorns come in several varieties, from the point of view of theological taxonomy. There are, first of all, the thorns of the curse: "Cursed is the ground because of you; in toil you shall eat of it all the days of your life; thorns and thistles it shall bring forth to you" (Genesis 3:17-18). Surrounded by these thorns, human beings issue forth the groans of their physical suffering, they chafe under the yoke of a host of oppressors, and they are drenched with the sweat of their own labors — sensing in all of this that they are made of dust, and to dust they shall return.

But if we survey the thorn-infested landscape of the fallen world with the eyes of faith, we can also discern the thorns of our redemption. Those thorns, which drew blood when pressed into the Savior's brow, were worn as a crown of victory over the cursedness of the creation: for "he was wounded for our transgressions, he was bruised for our iniquities; upon him was the chastisement that made us whole, and with his stripes we are healed" (Isaiah 53:5). And because of the thorns which were worn on Calvary, we can carry the thorns which become embedded in our own flesh as thorns of sanctification, knowing that in our own weakness, we are made strong in the power of God (2 Corinthians 12:10).

A thorny business indeed. And it is made no easier by the difficulties at times of sorting out the thorns of our cursedness from the thorns of our sanctification. When do I resign myself to suffering and disease and when do I pray confidently for the removal of a thorn lodged in my flesh? In a given encounter with pain, into which garden is the Savior leading me: the Garden of Gethsemane or the garden which surrounds the empty tomb?

The Christian, whether as patient or professional, must face these questions in their complexity and troublesomeness: not in the loneliness of a pretended human autonomy, but with the responsibility of a God-imager, called to share in the exercise of dominion over all that the Lord has placed in the world. In the present age, this necessitates thorn-in-the-flesh decision making. But it is decision making that must take place in the context of the kind of community described so well by Father Henri Nouwen in his excellent little book, *The Wounded Healer* (New York: Doubleday, 1972, p. 96):

> A Christian community is . . . A healing community not because wounds are cured and pains are alleviated, but because wounds and pains become openings or occasions for a new vision. Mutual confession then becomes a mutual deepening of hope, and sharing weakness becomes a reminder to one and all of the coming strength.

103 The Truthfulness of a Physician

Helmut Thielicke

It is impossible to make lying even a subject of ethical discussion, if the person who tells the lie is acting on the maxim that the purpose of his speaking alone determines the truth or falsity of what he says. Voltaire has something to this effect in his letter of October 21, 1736, to Thiriot: "Lying is a vice only when it effects evil; it is a great virtue when it accomplishes good. So be more virtuous than ever! One must lie like the devil, not timorously or only occasionally, but confidently and constantly. Lie, my friend, lie."[1] Lying can be the subject of ethical discussion only when we are clear on two points.

In the first place, we must acknowledge that there is genuine conflict between truth and love, between truth and practical necessity. A well-known example used by such diverse writers as F. H. R. Frank,[2] Fichte,[3] and N. H. Søe,[4] involves the question of what one should do when a critically ill woman asks about her dying child, and there is a strong possibility that a full disclosure of the truth will kill the mother. For our present purposes the important thing is not to resolve the conflict but simply to point out that a real conflict exists.

As a matter of fact, the three authors cited give very different answers, in accordance with radically different criteria. Søe thinks that the duty of love takes priority; as a test he commends the consideration that if I withhold the truth from

From Helmut Thielicke, *Theological Ethics,* vol. 1, ed. William H. Lazareth (Philadelphia: Fortress, 1966), pp. 520-21, 551-66.

someone, he will come to know this later on when the situation changes, and will then lose all confidence in me. Frank says that the truth should not be withheld because the death of the child is from God, and God can spare the mother any harmful consequences of the disclosure. Fichte says abruptly: "If the woman die of the truth, then let her die!" Though the solutions differ so widely, they are all at one in seeing that what is required here is decision rather than casuistic calculation.

A real conflict always raises the question of compromise, namely, which of the two colliding postulates should be given priority over the other. In certain circumstances, therefore, there is in fact a relation between the truth and a specific situation, a relation which I cannot overlook.

The second point on which we must be clear is that there is a relation between "truth and the person" as well as between "truth and the situation." A statement may be objectively correct and still not be "true," if the one who utters it is not qualified to do so. When a schoolboy writes in his essay that Goethe is the greatest of all poets, this may be correct, but as stated by these lips or by this pen it is not "true." That is doubtless what Nietzsche meant when he said that "a toothless mouth no longer has the right to the truth."

In this connection we may also remember Kierkegaard's comparison. When, at the end of a life devoted to the pursuit of knowledge, Faust asserts, "I now see that we can know nothing," this conclusion, formulated at the end of his development, is qualitatively very different from the same statement taken over by a student in his first semester to justify his indolence. What is "correct" about the utterance in both cases is too trivial to deserve being called "truth." Correctness becomes truth only when it is so related to existence as to become the confessional expression of existence, its self-declaration. This is why proverbial truths, when uttered by school children or indolent freshmen, do not stand under the sign of truth. They are characterized either by "precocity" or by trickery, and in either case by an element of mendacity which is the very opposite of truth. . . .

We shall proceed by analyzing closely a typical situation which can reliably serve to illustrate a larger complex of questions. To illustrate the conflict between the duty of sparing others and the duty of telling the truth, we shall examine here the problem of the physician at the bed of his patient. We shall begin with certain basic insights which either were expressed in our earlier deliberations or may be deduced from them.

We have stated that truth is not adequately defined simply in terms of the agreement between a statement and objective reality. On the contrary, it became clear to us that, if we are to define a statement as true, account must also be taken of the sphere within which that statement is made. In fulfilling my duty to tell the truth I cannot abstract myself from the situation in which I speak.

It is also clear, however, that truth depends on the person who does the speaking. Naturally this is not true of the statements of exact science.[5] But it does apply to truths which belong to the human and personal sphere. I can communicate only that which I have and am. I can state a truth only in the act of confessing, i.e., only as I am myself related to the truth in question.

He who himself lives in untruth covertly changes even the objective truths which he happens to speak into untruths. What is formally true, true in form, can be falsified by what it is that actually dwells in this form. Pornographic literature, for example, may contain objectively correct statements concerning erotic and sexual processes.[6] Yet in pornography the parcels of truth are integrated into a perverse system of values and thus become unequivocal lies. Pornography falsifies the place of sex in humanity. It depersonalizes, biologizes, and psychologizes it. Out of the "true" stones of individual processes it makes a perverted mosaic. It uses "truths" but tells lies. It does so because the pornographer, although he uses correct and in some sense "true" details, is not personally related to the truth of the whole. In his own person he has missed its real meaning and purpose. So it is that the untruth of the person makes the statement to be untrue.

An analogous process may be seen in the temptation of Jesus in the wilderness. The tempter appeals to the words of Holy Scripture. He thus appeals to "truths," to things which are correct in detail. But on the lips of the satanic liar these become lies because they are spoken in the context of a false relationship. To use an arithmetical figure, these individual truths are set within a bracket before which there stands a minus sign.

The negative thus robs them of their positive value as truths. The devil who so uses them is falsehood in person. Hence that which is originally correct becomes false; the truth becomes a lie.

The general statement of Luther that it is "the person who makes the works"[7] may here be reformulated to the effect that it is the person who makes the statement true or false. Only he who is subject to truth tells the truth. The liar always lies, even when he uses truth. Either way, man is always making confession of the ultimate relationship in which he stands. Confession is the only way in which "human" truth can be stated.

These preliminary but very basic observations, which in part take up and develop points already made, will serve then to introduce us to the specific problem of this section: What should the physician do when his patient is incurably ill or at the point of death? Does he owe his patient the truth or should be practice deception?[8]

It is obvious that this situation creates a genuine conflict. In the weakened condition of those who are seriously ill, information concerning the gravity of the sickness may come as a shock and really prove fatal. If we assume that there is still a slight hope of improvement, this prospect may be shattered by the imparting of such information, whereas the encouragement afforded the patient by a positive, though untrue, diagnosis of his condition may in fact spark his will to recover, and thus snatch him back from the critical point.

To recognize this possibility is to come directly up against a fundamental fact in the whole problem of truth. In certain circumstances truth is not just the sum and substance of a correct determination and delineation of the facts. On the contrary, the statement of a very questionable truth can itself conceivably bring into being facts which were not really present at the moment they were proclaimed in the name of truth, facts which could not at that time have comprised the content of a "true" statement. This is what happens, for example, in "fortune-telling." Here the significance of the pronouncement is not objectively to state something, but magically to bring it to pass. In other words, the prognosis in fortune-telling, while it does not state an existing truth concerning the future (since to do so would be to presuppose the existence of the future itself), it often does make the stated facts true. It causes them, as it were, to become true. This may happen, for example, when the one who is under the influence of such a prognosis actually reckons with the facts contained in it, whether by looking forward hopefully to something which is welcome, or by allowing some fearful prospect to gain magical power over him, like a tree which has such power over someone learning to ride a bicycle that he is magnetically attracted by it.

Only when we grasp this point do we appreciate the full severity of the problem by which we are confronted. If there is some chance that the optimistic, though dubious, prognosis of the doctor may become true, ought he not to risk it? Ought he not to tread the narrow and slippery ridge which separates truth from falsehood?

How then is the doctor to decide between the constructive lie and the destructive truth? The deception of patients has, in fact, made its way into the stronghold of medical practice to some extent under the rubric of "suggestion therapy." We need only think of the saline injections given in lieu of a drug which has to be withheld, like morphine. Psychosomatic interaction may make it imperative that certain psychical preconditions be created in order to make somatic effects possible. These preconditions are impossible unless wool is pulled, as it were, over the eyes of the psyche, i.e., unless it is decided. This is undoubtedly a working rule of the doctor's art which the patient, without any loss of confidence, will regard as justified once he is in condition again to make appropriate judgments. Indeed the deception is practiced precisely in order to bring the patient to this condition. In the situation of the patient it certainly does not amount to a lie, because it does not affect the person in the central core of his being, as it would if he were misled about his proximity to death, or if during a long siege of cancer he were deceived into neglecting important internal or external matters which he would have wanted to care for had he been given a more realistic appraisal of his situation.[9]

Then too in the latter case concealment of the true situation is inevitably followed by a chain reaction of further deceptions, so that finally we have, not a single structure of lies, but a whole colony of such structures. A pact of secrecy and deception must be sworn by a whole group of nurses, attendants, relatives, and friends. To avoid the terrible collapse of these finely spun illusions, and the attendant shock and radical collapse of confidence which must go with it, the deception is sometimes sustained even in the very last stages of the illness by means of narcotics, a chemically induced kind of personal irresponsibility.

These examples show that the concept of a "working rule of the doctor's art" cannot be a blanket authorization for all the various deceptions which, rightly or wrongly, are advanced as being necessary for medical reasons. The line between what is permissible and what is impermissible is very difficult to determine. Indeed this cannot be done a priori. There are, however, certain indications that this line does not lie merely at the point where the deception relates to the issue of life and death. This is shown, for example, by the therapeutically as well as morally dubious mock operations which are sometimes performed on neurotics under the category of "suggestion therapy."[10]

In our further discussion of this medical conflict between telling the truth and sparing the patient we shall now apply to the situation of the physician what we have laid down concerning the dependence of the truth that we speak on the truth that we are as persons. We may begin with the negative proposition that the untruth in which a person, in this case the doctor, may find himself can show itself at the sickbed of one who is on the point of death, or very likely to die, in the following forms.

The physician may be motivated by fear in respect of the dying person or his relatives. The anguish, the psychologically understandable reluctance, which keeps him from "shattering" the other person with a grave pronouncement, leads to out and out lying if in fact it triumphs over the truth. For in this case the motive is not to spare the other; it is to spare oneself. Hence the doctor does not merely speak untruth; he speaks out of untruth, i.e., out of a situation which is itself untrue. In appearance he seems to be impelled by the motive of a love which desires to spare; in fact, however, he is impelled by the very opposite.

It is again the untruth of the person which is involved when the doctor fears that he may have to share these last moments with a patient who is incurably ill and knows it. In others words, the doctor is afraid that he will have to disclose the secret of his own failure. This particular fear is twofold.

In the first place, there is the natural and understandable defensive reaction against the fact that in every visit and consultation and treatment he must publicly demonstrate the limits of his ability, and perhaps even his human failure. Any concession to this defensive reaction is obviously a concession to untruth. What is involved here is not only an untruth of speech but also an untruth of being. The reaction is not merely psychological but also philosophical. It is based on the fact that the doctor does not clearly understand the fundamental relation between medical treatment and the nature which is treated, between medical ability and its limits, between the courage to act and the humility to surrender. It is based too on ignorance of the fact that sickness and death are not just a fate which befalls a man but a task to be taken up — by doctor and patient together. When the doctor is not clear about these basic questions he stands in a false and illusory relationship to the fundamental realities of existence. It is no wonder, then, that what he says on the basis of this untruth should also be untrue.

In the second place, and closely related to what has just been said, there is the fear that in face of death, and of the mystery of life therein declared, he can only betray his complete "inner" helplessness, and so be forced to give a false hope instead of saying something which conveys real help, enlightenment, and "knowledge." Not to know the truth about death always means lying in face of death. If the physician has not himself faced the mystery of death, he must evade the dying. None of us can give more than he himself has.

Having stated the matter negatively, we may now put it in positive terms and say that the doctor is in the truth, first, if he himself has a relation to death, or, more accurately, if he has the true relation to death, i.e., if he knows the Lord of life and death. The man who is clear about the basic realities of life and death, who has faced up to these realities, will also be able to find the word of truth. There are no routine statements which can fill the gap when this existential condition is not met. Truth is constitutively linked with the confession of that which we have come to know in our own existence.

Second, the doctor is in the truth if he sees the

"true man" in the other person. This "true man" is characterized by the fact that he is not merely the activating center of certain vital functions, a physiological "it," a bundle of woes which must be spared as many pains and disturbances as possible. On the contrary, his life between birth and death is one of decision and responsibility; in face of the borderline situation of death he is thus summoned to win his life, or to lose it, to hold on or to fail, in short, to face the basic realities of his existence. Only when the physician respects this situation does he stand in a relation of truth to the other person. If he does not, the relation is one of falsehood, whether he actually tells lies or merely follows the evasive tactic of silence.

Third, the doctor is in the truth if he respects the truth of illness and of the fact that man must die, i.e., if he does not regard sickness merely as a physiological and somatic event but realizes that man, the whole man, is sick. He must note well the terminology of the sufferer, which more often than not says quite specifically "I am sick," rather than just that "something is wrong with" this or that particular part of the anatomy; and he must know the reason for such phraseology. The patient's use of the first person means that man is the subject of his illness. Sickness is not a calamity which befalls him, reducing him to the level of an object. We need not call upon psychosomatic medicine — which is of course very emphatic, determined, and perhaps even extreme on this score — to find medical men who appreciate this point and who interpret the phenomenon of illness along these lines even from the medical standpoint.

This understanding means that being sick is a matter of the whole person. Consequently the truth of sickness can be grasped only when it is regarded not as a hostile force from without, but as a component part of man himself with which man must grapple and come to terms as he does with himself.

For the doctor this means that he must be ready to help the patient to accept illness, and in certain instances its incurability, and also death, and to understand these things as a task to be tackled. The truth of sickness and death is not perceived if we simply allow the instinct of self-preservation to dominate the field, and hence take a purely negative attitude toward illness. There is of course an unnatural element in it which must be combated. Yet illness also has about it a providential aspect which is to be accepted and brought into harmony with the person.

The struggle which is demanded of the patient in face of sickness and death can never be an externally oriented insistence that this cannot and must not happen to me. It must be rather an inwardly oriented struggle with oneself, a struggle for an answer to the question who and what this person is who is thus stricken, how to deal with the new demands that such a blow brings, how through endurance and acceptance it can be made meaningful and hence differentiated from an accidental calamity. The question is not merely why did this have to happen to me, but for what purpose.

Fourth, the doctor is thus in the truth to the degree that he knows the truth, i.e., to the degree that he knows the meaning and purpose of the blow and lives it out in his own life. Only according to the measure of his relation to this truth can he give true information on the actual situation of the patient in respect of the blow that has befallen him. Where the doctor is not related to this truth, or where the relationship is a negative one, he will be forced to lie, and at the same time to resort to the false excuse that he does so out of a desire to spare the patient, that he is acting out of a love which is here in conflict with the duty of truth. In face of death there can be no openness and honesty unless at least one of the two parties, doctor or patient, knows the meaning of that which is about to happen. In such a case, however, experience repeatedly confirms the fact that the truth makes free (John 8:32), and that fear of the unknown gives way to peace. Truth and peace indeed belong together. . . .

Now that we have stated the basic points — but not before! — we can turn to the pedagogical question of how in the borderline situation of incurable illness or death those who know the "truth" can impart it to the patient. If we tackle this question too soon, we fail to see the existential problem of the physician, which is the main point at issue, and treat the matter instead as one simply of tactics or technique. Something which touches the very roots of our understanding of man is thus reduced to a matter of simple working rules.

Even here, however, we again do only partial

justice to the situation if the final result of our wisdom is only the recommendation of a certain method or technique, or if we speak merely of the required tact and necessary sympathy. For here too the problems are not just psychological but existential.

We come up against this problem when we ask why a certain method is needed at all. There are obviously some truths which can be communicated by means of a method which is wholly factual and not at all psychological. The question as to the truth of the Pythagorean theorem requires proof, and hence also a method of "proving" it, whereas the truth about death clearly demands a method of "communication" which embraces the human element.

Obviously this must mean that this particular truth is not one I can just blurt out at any time. The physician may come right out with it, of course, when he is dealing with a colleague who is called in as consultant; to him he can discreetly communicate the realization that there is nothing more to be done. In relation to the patient, however, such directness of communication is not possible. Whereas the colleague who takes part in a medical consultation can receive such news with factual objectivity, or with emotion but of a very different kind, for the patient himself it could entail a fatal shock.

The fact that the same truth can have such very different effects on different individuals is clear indication of the fact that in respect of this kind of truth — as distinct from that of the Pythagorean theorem! — men can have very different relationships to it. We may formulate the distinction as follows. Relationship to the Pythagorean theorem is timeless and hence unhistorical; that which relates to this truth is the abstract understanding which is independent of situations and of a particular existence. Relationship to the truth of death and of whatever else befalls me, however, is historical. This truth becomes free only in concrete encounters with the blows that strike, in the conflict and experienced problems of life. It is a truth which in the course of things either comes to light or is increasingly obscured. Its corollary, then, is either a developing knowledge or a hardening ignorance.

The development of this knowledge is expressed in the concept of "enlightenment" or "wisdom," that which lies at the end of the process. Wisdom is not something that can be imparted at any moment, like the Pythagorean theorem. It has its own time, its own hour and moment. To the degree that it is the object of wisdom, therefore, the truth cannot be taken over from others, like the truths of mathematics, or even like certain communicated facts, e.g., of history. Truth can only be appropriated. It can be attained to only in the process of growth. It becomes free only as I am confronted with it, only as these confrontations actually take place in my life. A child can, of course, repeat the sayings of Plato or of Paul concerning death. He can even bring to them a measure of intellectual apprehension. But he cannot "appropriate" them because he has not yet been confronted by death or by our "being unto death." He must simply wait upon this knowledge until it is released within him.

But this means that we have departed from the purely psychological level of how to tell the patient and have pressed on to the heart of the matter itself, namely, the truth which is to be communicated. The truth at issue here is the truth of death, not the fact that a certain concrete event is about to take place, but the truth about death itself: the truth that we must die, we must depart this life, and that our life has a goal (Ps. 39:4-6).

This is a truth which I cannot communicate to the one concerned in a direct way, or at any time whatever, as I might communicate truth to a colleague who is not personally involved. The inability to do so obviously means that in practice I must to some extent withhold and conceal the truth, giving it only slowly and in small doses. Am I lying, then, when I do this?

We can make headway with this question only if we distinguish sharply between the psychological and the existential standpoints involved in the situation. The psychological answer to the question why a direct and unmitigated communication is impossible is that the suddenness of the communication (since it could presumably take place "at any time") does not befit the psychical state of the patient and could produce quite a shock. The existential answer is that such a communication would not be in keeping with the nature of this truth. By its very nature, the truth about life and death is a developing and ripening truth; it is not timeless and hence accessible at any time. The communication of this truth must consequently include that process in the course of which the truth can become free and the physician can contribute to its becoming free. Our concern here is with a truth to which we must be led, a truth which is not a presupposition but a goal.

For this reason it is not a lie, nor is it sabotage of the truth, if the doctor is at first very slow and hesitant about communicating, if he steers clear of the subject of death in order to approach the patient from a wholly different angle and prepare him for the real theme of his situation. Whether the physician lies or not does not depend on whether he momentarily avoids the situation or directly acknowledges it. It depends rather on whether he regards his first momentary denial as the initial or preliminary stage of that process which ultimately leads to the truth, a process into and through which he is determined to lead his patient *or* whether the denial is final, made with the intention of "sparing" the patient to the very end any certainty as to his condition, so that he can finally be conjured over the last threshold in a state of unconsciousness, with the help of narcotics as a chemical means of concealment.

In the latter case the method can only be the expression of a particular matter, the actual relationship to death. In terms of the specific relationship in question, it is held that beyond death there is nothing but unconscious nothingness. Hence it is deemed appropriate on this side of the threshold too to induce unconsciousness. A man's life has no specific significance since it bears no relation to anything beyond itself which could force him to make certain basic decisions. As a result, the last phase of a man's life is filled up entirely with the wounded and hence anguished impulse of self-preservation. Since man is helpless in face of death to forestall that lethal attack upon his instinct to survive, the only remaining possibility is to put an end to those final torments which it causes. Logically, then, the acute problem is one not of existence but of chemistry. The question of death has been reduced to zero.

If, on the other hand, the doctor is resolved to lead the patient into that process of disclosure, into that borderline theme of existence, then his action is not out of keeping with the truth even if in the first instance he conceals rather than reveals. The doctor does honor to the truth by making himself a companion of the patient in this entire process, and by therewith deciding to communicate with him in face of the ultimate reality. . . .

We are thus confronted by an important and basic fact of human existence which we now observe in many different connections. Man's special prerogative of being endowed with personal freedom is wholly ambivalent. It is oriented toward genuine responsibility before the divine Thou, toward man's relationship with God; but on the dark side it also possesses the other possibility of using a gift of grace to evade the claim of that which is sent and ordained by God.

We have said that the truth of death really becomes free only when I can speak in the first person: "I die." And we have tried to explain this statement in terms of its negative counterpart. Only when the death at issue is my death does it cease to be a general and hence only half-true phenomenon and become a personal event in which I experience the mystery of my existence. Thus death is something that must grow upon me. In the words of Ranier Maria Rilke, it must grow "in me."

It was in this sense that Karl Holl, when he lay on his death bed and the doctor wanted to help him over the last hour with narcotics, stated in reply, "I will not be robbed of *my death!*" It goes without saying that what moved him in this desire to remain conscious was not the curiosity of a scientist wanting to observe the extinction of life "from within," but the mystery of existence, to which one's own death belongs and which is experienced in this personal and intimate way. Because love, the meaning of life, and human extremity all reach their end and climax in death, it is here that the real substance of life first becomes fully apparent. A person really comes to know himself at death. This is why death is not merely physical or natural but quite "personal." Its truth is revealed fully only when "*I* die."

It is important to bear in mind this fact that the truth about death is something which "grows" in life. It is not something that we always have at our disposal and can communicate at any time. It is also important to realize that in this process of growth there is always a gap between knowledge of "death in general" and knowledge of "my own death" in particular.

Now the relation to death — or lack of relation

— in which the patient stands is something which cannot be known in advance. Consequently the character of the disclosures which the doctor must make is linked with the situation, with the person addressed, with the doctor's own knowledge of death, and in all of these with that particular form of truth which is involved in man's "being unto death." Certainly the fact that this truth is one which grows and develops must be expressed also in the character of the communication made to the person who is incurably ill or on the point of death. This communication must itself be a gradual disclosure, a preparatory leading of the patient into a discovery of his own.

On these grounds compromise — the merely temporary compromise! — between the postulate of "sparing" the patient, i.e., the postulate of a gradual process, on the one side, and factual diagnostic truth, on the other, is perfectly legitimate. This must be said even though the suspension of factual truth remains a genuine burden for the conscience which is constantly at war with itself and always tempted to yield to illusion. Even in this case the rift in the structure of the world is too obvious to miss, namely, the divergence and conflict between the different forms of truth. If the peace with God which prevailed at the beginning were still extant, there would be no conflict as there is now between the privilege of going home and the necessity of departing. There would be no painful severing of ties, because there would really be only one tie. And we would not be wandering between two worlds, existing in a state of cleavage. But then no "preparatory leading" would be needed, and consequently no compromise such as that involved in the suspension of factual truth. Thus in the depths of every human situation we discover evidence of the fact that our world is a fallen world still awaiting its redemption.

In conclusion, may we repeat the decisive point of all we have been saying. No man can bring another to what he himself does not have. No man can liberate in another a truth which he himself does not share. The final issue is not the psychological technique used in such disclosures nor the problem of formal factual truth, i.e., the agreement between what the doctor says and the actual state of things at a given moment. What is ultimately at stake is the appeal to the fact that the physician is himself a human being who must come to truth and to maturity. This is his task.

There is much talk about the patient being a person, a whole man who is to be treated therapeutically in his personal being, in his humanity, and whose illness is not to be regarded as a somatic or biological accident, something which has merely come upon him. All this is true. But it is equally true — and unfortunately this has not been seen with the same clarity — that the physician too is a person, a whole man, and that his skillful deeds of diagnosis and therapy are not merely a matter of technique, but are expressive of his humanity, which is herewith challenged to its very foundations.

Notes

1. The quotation from Voltaire's *Oeuvres Complètes* (Paris, 1818), XXXI, 446, is cited in Victor von Cathrein, *Moralphilosophie* (Leipzig, 1924), II, 90, n. 8.

2. See F. H. R. Frank, *System der christlichen Sittlichkeit* (Erlangen: Deichert, 1884), I, 421.

3. This question was put to Fichte by H. Steffens, according to H. Martensen, *Christian Ethics* (Special Part, First Division: Individual Ethics), trans. William Affleck (4th ed.; Edinburgh: T&T Clark, n.d.), p. 217.

4. See N. H. Søe, *Christliche Ethik* (Munich: Kaiser, 1949), pp. 277-78.

5. See Kierkegaard's "Reflections on Christianity and Natural Science," in his *Eine Literarische Anzeige,* trans. Emanuel Hirsch (Düsseldorf: Diederichs, 1959), pp. 125-29.

6. This is true even of the various Kinsey reports, which stand on the three-corner frontier of zoology, pornography, and anthropology.

7. *WA* 39^{I}, 283.

8. The same question could of course be put to the pastor, but for reasons of method which will emerge later the example of the physician is more suited to our present purposes, since it forces us to consider how the situation of illness works out in terms of a variety of philosophical positions.

9. This example is suggested by Richard Siebeck, *Medizin in Bewegung* (Stuttgart, 1949).

10. The case reported by Jones, for all the humor of its outcome, nonetheless illustrates the point. A very wealthy and pampered woman, severely neurotic, constantly complained about headaches caused by the sofa

in her head. Various remedies were tried but without success. Finally a mock operation was performed. When the patient awakened from the anesthetic, back in her room with her head generously wrapped in bandages, she noticed on her night stand a tiny doll-house size sofa. Looking at it but a moment she said merely, "My sofa was green." Arthur Jones, "Arzt und Lüge," *Universitas* X (1949): 1198f.

104 The Physician-Patient Relationship

Bernard Häring

The doctor-patient tie is a covenant of persons. In times of serious illness and in the total ordering of the medical profession, the contribution of the doctor can never be severed from personal concern. The privacy and intimate reactions of the ailing person transcend by far the impersonal basis of many other relationships. While the seller-buyer contract is founded on commutative justice, the relationship between doctor and patient is distinguished and characterized by such personal attitudes as fidelity, reverence, respect, truthfulness and mutual trust. If the doctor wants to do justice to the patient by caring for his total health and helping him to accept his illness and discover its personal meaning, he must regard the sick human being in his uniqueness, with inviolable personal rights and expectations. He must also take into account the patient's relationship to God, his fellowmen and society, particularly his family.

A physician's fidelity and responsibility towards his patient entail a correlative responsibility towards his fellowmen and society, although it is not always simple to reconcile the interests of the patient with those of society. At times the dilemma of medical ethics seems insoluble because of the need to consider the patient on the one hand, as a distinct individual, and on the other, as a constituent member of a society which sets claims upon him. The physician's resolution not to depart from the concept of the patient as a person is decisive ethically; such a stance necessarily includes his essential relationships and responsibili-

From Bernard Häring, *Medical Ethics* (South Bend: Fides, 1973), pp. 199-205. Used by permission.

ties to his fellowmen. In this frame of reference, the doctor does not violate the fidelity of his covenant if he fails to accede to a patient's selfish and irresponsible wishes but acts according to the best interests and personal calling of the patient. In grave cases, after having exhausted all means of persuading a patient to responsible action, the physician may be compelled to protect the just expectations and rights of his fellow-citizens and of society even against the patient's will.

I have already mentioned the importance of an atmosphere of truthfulness and trust in the crucial matter of the doctor's deportment when faced by the prospect of a patient's death. Only if we understand fully the import of these qualities in the covenant between physician and patient can we realize the attitude proper to a doctor as death approaches. On the other hand, we have also seen how a guarded truthfulness in this extreme situation influences the patient-physician relationship in the matter of therapy. Truthfulness and trust from both patient and doctor are needed, but it is chiefly the veracity and trustworthiness of the physician that condition responsiveness and confidence in the patient.

The significance of the covenant of trust linking doctor and patient becomes most critical in the matter of confidentiality. Professional secrecy is an essential component of the medical ethos. The oath of Hippocrates says: 'If it be what should not be noised abroad I will keep silence thereon.' The American Medical Association code declares: 'Confidence . . . should never be revealed unless the law requires it or it is necessary to protect the welfare of individuals or communities.'

In almost all countries, the law requires that contagious diseases be reported. Such a request is absolutely justified by the common good in spite of the fact that it may be most unpleasant for the diseased person. Beyond the legal obligation and on the grounds of his medical ethos, the doctor will evince concern that other persons be not unnecessarily exposed to the danger of contagion. Even in highly developed countries, the general population is not yet sufficiently protected against contamination by communicable diseases, open tuberculosis for instance. The immediate family should be informed of proper methods of protecting itself and friends. Care should be taken that contagious persons do not use any public facilities as long as they constitute a considerable threat as 'carriers'.[1]

It is first of all the patient's obligation to show responsibility towards the people with whom he lives. The doctor or, where available, the social worker or member of the community medical team, ought to explain to him the situation and the consequences of irresponsible behavior. The adult patient should then be expected to act responsibly, but if he cannot, or if he proves unwilling to do so, the physician must assume his part of the responsibility in keeping with the principle of subsidiarity, so as to protect the patient and society.[2]

In cases where the physician cannot motivate or convince the patient of his duty to communicate what he should, the doctor himself becomes accountable. But before informing others because of special responsibilities, the doctor has to ponder well all the values at stake. There are situations, for example, in cases of venereal disease, when even though others may be exposed to some danger or damage, it may be better to keep silent than to make use of information which has been obtained professionally, with the inevitable risk of diminishing the patient's trust. It is not just the relationship of this one patient to this one doctor that is in jeopardy. One doctor's imprudent use of confidence, should it come to the knowledge of others, can impair the relationship of many doctors with their patients. Only when there is serious danger for others is the doctor allowed or obliged to speak when a patient refuses to fulfil an obvious obligation to make known his infectious disease.

Every patient should be aware that when he reveals his condition to a physician, the doctor can never be a willing accomplice to crime by an unjustified silence. Secrecy can never become a taboo. Observance or non-observance must always be judged with respect to the welfare of the patient and of all other persons involved. The saying, 'The sabbath was made for man and not man for the sabbath' applies also to secrecy. . . .

A trust-inspiring relationship between physician and patient demands, according to the situation, reliable information relative to the extent of risk attendant on certain treatments to be taken by the patient. It is understood that the doctor will first decide which treatment is most suitable so that he will not propose indifferently a number of possibilities which the patient himself would have to examine in order to find out which would best serve him. In most cases, it is incumbent on the physician to decide on the desirability of a treatment, but whenever a certain procedure or operation entails considerable risk, he will inform the patient adequately in view of the total situation of his health. Were the disclosure of such information to constitute a risk of grave harm to the patient, the doctor will renounce doing so directly. Instead he may choose to inform members of the family and await the final decision from them.

The physician will refrain from using new and yet unproven medication or therapeutic means when a better or equally good prospect with lesser risk is available. Similarly, the doctor will not prefer a very expensive treatment to a relatively less expensive one if both serve the same purpose unless the patient or his family, after accurate information, explicitly indicate preference for the more costly method. Whenever there is question of using very expensive treatments with no real prospect of success, the physician should not burden the patient or his family with a decision since they would not enjoy the full freedom of spirit to say 'no' although they might be resentful of the idea. He should unilaterally decide to renounce such a course of action; it would be against the physician-patient covenant to impose on the patient's family extremely high expenses for a treatment which holds no promise of substantial help.

The physician's responsibility is particularly great when he resorts to medication or treatment which can cause moral danger to the patient. The concept of full human health serving as a basis for ethical considerations obliges him to include in his diagnostic efforts all the elements of his patient's particular endowment and character, such as for instance, *abulia* or weakness of the will. He may have to renounce hormonal treatments which can stimulate sexual desire beyond the patient's capacity for self-control.

Should a therapist consider hypnosis as a part of treatment, he has then to inform the patient honestly and seek his permission. No one ever entrusts himself so totally to possible manipulation by a therapist without making an explicit judgment that the therapist is worthy of this great moral trust. The therapist must also ask himself whether such a procedure will truly serve his patient in terms of promoting his moral freedom.

Particular caution is to be exercised in the use of sedatives and other drugs likely to constitute for certain individual patients a danger of addiction. Especially serious in consequence would be to risk such treatment when a patient has previously manifested a propensity towards drug addiction.

The hormonal control of pregnancy in the case of unmarried women, especially of young girls, poses serious moral problems for the doctor. He can often foresee that his prescription will be a further step toward moral laxity. On the other hand, his refusal to prescribe may well result in an abortion in the case of an undesired pregnancy. His decision needs serious reflection. If by medical arguments he cannot change the patient's attitude, then a realistic approach may avoid the greater danger. Where law makes the permission of the patients mandatory, the doctor will not resort to any subterfuge. Even where there is no legal interdiction to the treatment of a minor without parental permission, the doctor will not forget his responsibility towards the family. He will consult the parents to the extent he can without abdicating his own responsibility.

Notes

1. R. Arnoldt, 'Seuchenhygienisch bedenkliche Verschwiegenheit bei ansteckungsfähiger Lungentuberkulose,' *Praxis der Pneumologie* 22 (1968): 176-82.

2. Cf.: Henry A. Davidson, 'Professional Secrecy,' in *Ethical Issues in Medicine,* ed. E. F. Torrey (Boston: Little, Brown and Co., 1968), p. 193.

105 Teacher

William F. May

Among several images one could use to describe the healer, the covenantal image alone demands that healers teach their patients. Other images — those of parent, technician, fighter, and contractor — may do so incidentally, but at best they usually generate ambivalence toward the teaching function.

The parental image tends to reduce patients to dependent children, stricken sheep. Compassionate care and vicarious decision-making rather than candid instruction characterize the professional's task. Only too often, parentalist healers, like Dostoevsky's Grand Inquisitor, have a low estimate of their charges and want to protect them from that turmoil which knowledge and freedom entail.

The location of many teaching hospitals and residency training programs in the inner city tends further to convince young professionals that preventive medicine and the teaching it requires are activities of low yield. Residents complain that patients often come in only when their diseases flare. Preventive medicine seems beside the point. Destructive habits so grip the patient as to make rehabilitation or stable chronic care difficult to sustain. After treatment, patients go back into the streets and fall into the same injurious habits again. They forget appointments; they don't comply with a regimen. Patients will say: "I don't know what medicines I take. It's in the chart. Read the chart." But the resident knows that the chart records what the physician prescribed, not what the patient is taking, if anything. Further, patients fear the truth or fail to assimilate it, or accept it but selectively. Some pounce on the bad news and panic; others dissolve the bad news in a blurry confusion and ignore the importance of compliance. In response, physicians retreat into a limited parentalist mode, making decisions on behalf of the patient in the sanctuary of the hospital, knowing that the world beyond the hospital walls will shortly defeat their childlike charges. Thus, early in their education physicians come to expect very little from patients. Cynicism, despair, and sometimes resentment infect the exhausted resident.

And yet — even parentalism offers some moral warrant for teaching one's patients. The parent, after all, is committed to the being and well-being of the child, and the good parent recognizes education as an important ingredient in the child's flourishing. The main thrust of the image, however, condescends too much to encourage persistent teaching. Give what care you can to hurting charges and let it go at that.

To the degree that practitioners think of themselves only as contractors dispensing technical services they will also tend to depreciate the place of teaching in therapy. Contracted for and paid on a piecework basis, whether by the consumer personally or by a third-party payment system, the therapist offers discrete, itemizable services rather than taking continuous responsibility for the patient's improvement in self-care and health maintenance. Teaching takes time; it reduces the number of patients the physician can see; it complicates the question of patient management and exposes the physician to the possibility of making personal as well as technical errors. Both the specialist and the generalist can draw back from teaching the patient — the specialist offering encoded information to the attending physician, and the attending physician sometimes reneging on the task by defining himself or herself chiefly as the orchestrator of technical services. And yet the contractualist model retains a fragment of the teaching responsibility, to the degree that the seller of services accepts responsibility to inform the buyer about the services and the product offered for sale. Further, Health Maintenance Organiza-

---

tions (HMOs) draw up contracts with their patients that give professional financial incentives to teach better.

The military model hardly emphasizes the physician as teacher. It conjoins the technical and contractual models with an adversarial setting to produce the mercenary who fights against disease and death. The patient has fallen victim to invasive powers. Amateurs mucking about with weapons that they hardly understand will only blow themselves up. A little knowledge is a dangerous thing. The expert in biological warfare should decide which drugs best counter the intricacies of the enemy's attack, its time, its place, and its force. Besides, under the conditions of battle, with the physician fighting on behalf of a thousand little principalities, explaining wastes time.

Both the economics of medicine and the structure of medical education reinforce the tendency of physicians, who live by the technical-contractualist-military models, to neglect teaching. The third-party payment system rewards physicians for discrete, piecework services to the sick. It does not reward them for teaching patients how to maintain their health or even for securing high levels of compliance with the doctor's regimen. Not surprisingly, a President's Committee on Health Care Education reported for 1973 that only one half of one percent of annual health care expenditures went for health education.[1] While HMOs make a good-faith effort to redirect the economic incentives toward preventive medicine, the high turnover rates of patient subscribers in HMOs (30 percent per year) do not suggest that those organizations have succeeded in giving the professional much financial incentive to practice pedagogically persuasive preventive medicine.[2]

Neither medical school education nor residency training programs prepare physicians adequately for teaching. Professional education prepares them as depositories of information, not sharers of what they know. "Medicine is the only graduate school to rely on multiple choice examinations," complains one academic physician.[3] Sadly enough, this subarticulate standard of testing fails to challenge the student to organize and teach effectively, or even to retain what he or she knows. According to a study of a second-year class at a distinguished medical school, the half-life of a retained factual item is about three weeks; 90 percent of factual items retained for true-false examinations have taken flight by graduation.[4]

Cumulatively, a professional education that centers in the mere acquisition of factual information converts education itself from a public trust to privately held property. The student soon assumes that he or she has acquired knowledge as a private stockpile of goods to be sold wholly as the certified possessor sees it. The information that lab tests, X-rays, and biopsies yield belongs to the professional rather than to the patient whose destiny they foretell. And patients often submit to this view. They would feel as shy about reading the physician's workup of their case — while he or she is out of the office — as about reading any other papers or letters on the desk. Such information seems like private property, for the physician alone to divulge. Thus the very terms of professional education and clinical training and practice combine to obscure the communal origins of professional education and the duty to share generously what one knows.

The quarrel in medicine over whether physicians should teach their patients is not new; it dates back to the classical world. The "rough empirics" in ancient Greece (who, familiar with treatments but not with the scientific reasons for their success, practiced largely on slaves) used to ridicule the more scientifically oriented physicians (who, practicing largely on free men and their families, sought to teach their patients). The scientific physicians complained that the empirics offered little more than what Láin Entralgo has called a veterinary practice on men. But the empirics argued that patients don't want to become doctors, they want to be cured.

Modern technicians have argued *a fortiori* that the knowledge base of medicine has grown so complicated as to make the effort to teach patients today even more futile than in ancient Greece. Physicians do not share a common scientific understanding with even their most educated patients. The knowledge explosion has produced in our time a fallout of ignorance. And since knowledge confers power, the ignorant, to the extent of their ignorance, become powerless. For better or for worse, patients can only submit themselves to the superior knowledge, authority, good intentions, and technical ingenuity of the doctor. . . .

The covenantal image for the health care practitioner pushes the profession unequivocally in the direction of teaching. To the degree that physicians and institutions accept a covenantal responsibility for the being and well-being of their patients — above and beyond the delivery of technical services — they must engage in the delicate business of transforming their patients' habits. The prevention of disease, the recovery from a siege of illness, and the successful coping with chronic conditions require, in one form or another, the reconstruction of life-styles. Whenever healers engage in these activities, they transform rather than merely transact. They do not simply offer services to satisfy the wants and wishes of people as they are; they engage in transforming commitments, priorities, and life rhythms.

But any professional effort to transform patients flirts with danger. It can quickly deteriorate into a puritanical officiousness — a runaway parentalism — unless teaching becomes its chief instrument. Teaching offers one of the few ways in which one can engage in transformation while respecting the patient's intelligence and power of self-determination. Good teaching depends not only upon a direct grasp of one's subject, a desire to share it, and some verbal facility, it also requires a kind of moral imagination that permits one to enter into the life circumstances of the learner: to reckon with the difficulties the learner faces in acquiring, assimilating, and acting on what he or she needs to know. Good teachers do not attempt to transform their students by bending them against their will, or by charming them out of their faculties, or by managing them behind their backs. Rather, they help them see their lives and their habits in a new light and thereby aid them in unlocking a freedom to perform in new ways.

Teaching has a place in medical practice across a broad spectrum of activities. Obviously, preventive, rehabilitative, chronic, and terminal care include a teaching component. Since the educational task of the physician shows least obviously in those activities in which physicians intervene most, this brief tour of the horizon ought to begin with the physician's efforts to cure.

Acute Care Medicine

Except for the most aggressive of interventions, therapy requires some measure of cooperation from the patient. But noncompliance rates range from 30 to 60 percent of patients, and even higher in those cases in which patients suffer no painful symptoms.[5] Those percentages are extraordinarily high. A clinical drug test would probably disappoint if it failed to help 30 to 60 percent of patients treated. No obstacle looms quite so large as noncompliance in impeding effective intervention.

Strategies for enhancing compliance depend upon improving the physician's prowess as a teacher. One study shows that rates of compliance doubled from 29 to 54 percent depending upon whether instructors provided low or high levels of instruction.[6] "Words are to a prescription what a preamble is to a constitution," as Láin Entralgo, the Spanish historian of medicine, once argued. The Preamble to the Constitution of the United States ("We the people of the United States in order to form a more perfect union . . . ") provides a clarifying context that makes sense and provides purpose for the laws that follow. Without that preamble, the fundamental law of the land just sits there, opaque, arbitrary, and perhaps relatively unintelligible to subsequent generations. Even God provided a context for his commands. Before issuing the Ten Commandments, Scripture reports, God announced and explained to the Israelites the grounds for their obedience: "I am the LORD your God, who brought you out of the land of Egypt, out of the house of bondage" (Ex. 20:2). The reminder about these deeds explains the commandments that follow: "You shall have no other gods before me. You shall not . . . " When physicians issue prescriptions wordlessly, opaquely, without an earnest effort to clarify and persuade, they do not play God; they usurp another kind of privilege, high-handed, arrogant, and ultimately obtuse. One thinks of Kierkegaard's characterization of the demonic state in *The Concept of Dread*.[7] He describes it as "shutupness," a dreadful taciturnity, unrevealing, unhelpful, withdrawn, and cruelly destructive to those who need a healing word.

Every profession depends upon an esoteric body of knowledge, encoded by specialists and relatively inaccessible to the layperson. What has been carefully encoded needs decoding; and that process requires adept teaching. Not surprisingly, then, the literature on compliance emphasizes those strategies prized by the good teacher. Physicians must teach early in the game (one of the most stubborn obstacles to compliance springs from the patient's conviction that the original diagnosis itself is wrong);[8] they must teach clearly in nontechnical language (decoding); they produce better results when they offer the explanation in both oral and written form; and whatever they say, they must organize well. They have to allow for a period of time in the course of which the patient internalizes the news. Doctors partly condemn the learning capacity of their patients because they fail to appreciate the patient's need for repetition and for time to assimilate the diagnostic and prognostic news, which is sometimes difficult to bear. Information simply unloaded on the patient sits like a parallel deposit in the mind; unassimilated and inert.

Compliance rates also improve when the physician teaches not only the patient but the patient's family. Efforts at weight loss or control of hypertension and arthritis, and recovery programs after heart attacks, show better results when the family actively supports the program.[9] Problems of compliance in these areas raise questions about the place of teaching in preventive and rehabilitative medicine.

Preventive Medicine

Physicians and the public at large, until recently, have held preventive medicine in low esteem. Hygeia, the goddess of health, has never been a match for the god of healing. Asclepius always appears in full feather, the quintessentially male, TV-spectacular agent of interventionist medicine. Since the discovery of penicillin and the antibiotics, money for research and health delivery has gone largely to acute care. Expenditures in the name of Asclepius rose 800 percent in the two decades following World War II.[10] The third-party system, under public and private insurance programs, has tilted in almost every detail toward curative medicine. The fraction of funds going into health education has remained constant and minuscule (about one half of one percent) while the portion of the GNP devoted to health care has risen astronomically during the period 1940-1981.[11] Yet, during this same period — except for the success of antibiotics, mind-control drugs, and some surgical procedures — the actual advances in acute care have not been all that striking. The life expectancy of fifty-year-old males during two decades rose only 8 months despite the most generous expenditure of funds and talent on acute care in world history.[12]

The goddess Hygeia symbolizes the condition of health rather than the activity of healing: the steadfast rule of reason in body care rather than the rule of ingenuity in body repair; the balanced classical concern for dietetrics and gymnastics rather than the more occult appeals to special nostrums, insights, and powers. But, alas, Hygeia has always been, and ever will be, a dull gray goddess, without box-office draw or fund-raising appeal. W. Hutchinson saw the structural problem with a steady eye when he wrote:

> The system of remuneration makes the physician's income dependent upon the amount of sickness. Our system's philosophy might be condensed in the motto "millions for the care and not one cent for prevention." It seems to me that the weakness of our system lies in this one fact, that it gives [physicians] such exceedingly little opportunity for what has been called the practice of preventive medicine.[13]

Hutchinson wrote these lines in 1886.

The obstacles to the development of preventive medicine do not come entirely from physicians — either from their economic self-interest or from a special perception of role that discourages good teaching. Four types of patients, even under the best of circumstances, make the task of preventive medicine a slow boring through hard wood (Max Weber's phrase about another difficult vocation — politics). Patients of the first type assume their own de facto immortality. Someday they will die, but not yet. Disease and death for the moment remain abstract, deferrable, and remote. They feel the medicine of immortality already within them. They do not need preventive medicine. Patients of the second type seem less given to denial. They go to the doctor and listen to all the explanations. But the doctor discovers on the next visit that none of it sinks in. A kind of selective interferon seems at work, blocking out what the doctor has to say. The patient has internalized nothing.

At the opposite extreme are those patients given to what Robert Jay Lifton, in another connection, called nuclearism. Such persons solve the problem of threat by cozying up to the source of danger. Contact with the forbidden, the destructive, magnifies their life. The actor Slim Pickens, in the film *Dr. Strangelove,* portrays a country colonel who straddles a nuclear bomb and rides it ecstatically to his own destruction. Nuclearists feel drawn to the pull of the cigarette, the regular swell of liquor in the head, the helmetless ride on a motorcycle at high speed, the pressure cooker of a job, the brinkmanship with the psyche that goes with drugs and sleep deprivation. Recklessness in all its forms acquires a kind of demonic force that makes all the cautionary advice and counsel of preventive medicine seem beside the point and demeaning.

Finally, there are the hypochondriacs. Like the nuclearists, they preoccupy themselves with danger, but in this case they let danger provide them with an excuse for diminishing their life. Hypochondriacs see trouble on every side, risk at every corner, poison in the very food they eat, the blast of cancer in the sun, a dangerous depletion in every psychic exertion, and the potential for terminal disease in the most transient colony of germs to which they play host. Such persons frustrate preventive medicine. Health alone unhealthily obsesses them, miniaturizes their life, makes them too fearful to exude that health which a life well expended on matters of greater moment sometimes fosters. Encountering patients such as these in their daily experience must dampen physicians' hopes for preventive medicine. So much advice falls on stony ground.

Still, the rate of death due to heart attack and stroke has declined rapidly in recent years, and the evidence does not suggest that open-heart surgery, resuscitation techniques, and other improved interventions have made the difference in the huge decline. Rather, changes in diet (especially reduced salt intake), regular exercise, reductions in weight, drug compliance for control of hypertension, and other essentially preventive measures seem to account for the improvements in health. This progress hardly results from the teaching efforts of physicians alone. Deeper cultural changes are at work. The magisterial authority of the media and the networking of patient groups play their part in improving self-care. But it would be passing strange for physicians to withdraw from preventive work simply because others as well help to provide it.

The skepticism doctors often betray toward preventive work may result partly from their failure to be imaginative about the social setting in which it should take place. They too readily generalize from their own one-on-one curative work and take for granted the individual tutorial (a little too private to be fully effective) as the only appropriate setting for their teaching. As alternatives to the tutorial in the physician's office, society offers the even more private and isolating spot commercials on television, the bus advertisements, the newspaper columns, or the individual pamphlets distributed by the American Heart Association and American Cancer Society. Physicians largely ignore the fact that most teaching takes place in public classrooms — from the three R's to AA. Other, more communal, strategies for educating patients deserve attention.

The chief of clinical services in student health at a large Midwestern university saw just such an opportunity for communal preventive medicine at his campus. Ordinarily, jobs in student health are dull. (Either students seem radiantly healthy and need nothing medical that is more technically complicated than antibiotics and a good night's respite from the dormitory, or they are too sick to remain in school — in which case also the physician does not get to handle an interesting case. Psychiatrists, of course, are an exception in that they get to take care of young students just separated from home whose emotional problems respond best to treatment *in situ.*) But this young physician — not a psychiatrist — chose a career in student health because he was interested in preventive medicine and, given that interest, he explained, a university campus offered a splendid opportunity. In its preventive program, his clinic did a health profile of each student on arrival, including a projection of life expectancy on the basis of current habits and a second projection on the basis of an alternative set of habits. Then the clinic, taking advantage of a computer analysis and classification of problems, pulled the potentially hypertensive, the obese, et al., into a classroom where the health care practitioners taught and worked at their problems collectively.

The program had four advantages over conventional preventive efforts: it picked up patients at a relatively early age; it pulled them into a setting that kept them feeling normal and let them respond normally to their obligations; it provided them with a support group of fellows with a similar problem, thus overcoming the discouraging isolation that young people with special problems feel; and finally, the classroom provided for economies of scale as compared with conventional, expensive tutorial contact with a professional. When a visitor to the campus asked why a similarly motivated health care team could not work with other institutions — such as corporations, unions, service organizations, and churches — the young physician reported that his own group in student health was on the verge of signing a contract with the local Presbyterian church.

A few health care groups have similarly allied themselves with religious communities, but on the whole, the helping professions have not thought through the ways in which they might link with so-called intermediate institutions to offer services directed to prevention and rehabilitation. The dominant model of health care defined by the delivery of services in a freestanding hospital or in a private office has — in addition to its other disadvantages — emphasized the individual at the expense of the communal, and the manipulative at the expense of the cognitive in the task of healing.

Rehabilitative and Chronic Care

In preventive medicine, the physician faces the difficult task of persuading patients that they face real threats to their health. In rehabilitative medicine, few patients can doubt for long the reality of the assault. The patient has just suffered a massive blow to body confidence. An accident maims or disfigures and imposes a catastrophic change on the patient's very self-perception — his or her movement and looks. A coronary suddenly throws the mainspring of life itself into terrible disarray. A stroke slurs speech, renders useless one side of the body, confuses memory and vision, and depresses the spirit. A burn scorches the skin and tightens movement, leaving the victim like a countryside charred and crippled by the firestorm of war; and kidney failure poisons every river in the system, subjecting the victim to impotence and depression.

Patients pass through three states: (1) their life brutally changes and they plunge into shock, numbness, and grief; (2) they suffer a period of perilous transition; until at length (3) they make their way into a new life under the terms and conditions of their disability. The entire process compares structurally with the great rites of passage in traditional societies.

Similarly, the ritual "turn points" in traditional societies — the events associated with puberty, marriage, birth, death, seedtime, sickness, and war — included three moments, all of them important to a successful passage. The first moment imposed a radical separation of the participant from his or her past life. Young people undergoing a puberty rite suffered, at the outset, perhaps segregation, a whipping, a tattooing, or the pulling of a tooth. The mutilation visibly signified a death to one's former life. Second, the novitiate underwent a period of transition, with its appropriate regimen and ordeal under the tutelage of specialists. Third, the candidate eventually entered into a new estate. One could not view this new identity as something added on to one's previous life by way of peaceful annexation. A radical alteration had occurred, affecting habits, demands, regimen, and core identity. The relation between old and new resembled a kind of death and resurrection. Calendars reflect this sacral dimension as they order and measure time before and after the event.

Similarly, in the case of personal catastrophe, we measure time before and after — the accident, the heart attack, the stroke, the operation, or the birth of the retarded child.

The role of the modern healer both resembles and differs from that of the religious specialist who presides over traditional rites of passage. First, the healer does not, like the traditional priest, make the first "moment" occur. But he or she has special knowledge of what has taken place and of its convulsive impact on the patient. If the healer served as the attending physician in the case, he or she helped set a limit to its destructive consequences. That special knowledge and service provides a basis for the second role as tutor and guide during the transition period. Or, by referral, the healer helps legitimate those who will take over rehabilitative therapy. Depending on the severity of the accident or the disease, the patient will need to engage in a drastic reconstruction of habits. One must perhaps learn all over again how to walk, exercise, eat, rest, and pace oneself in daily work.

In addition to helping in the reconstruction of skills, the healer has to reckon with the psychological perils of the transitional period. The sufferer, to be sure, cannot doubt the reality of the problem; the heart attack overwhelms, palpably, beyond compare, but all outsize events, whether good or bad, have their own kind of unreality. "Has this really happened to me? It hardly seems possible. It won't be there when I wake up in the morning." Alternatively, the patient descends into despair — another kind of unreality that obscures the resources of both therapy and the gathering inner resources that the passage of time places at the patient's own disposal. Or again, the patient passes beyond the confusion and disorientation of the original assault into the ordered procedures of the institution that has provided treatment, but this alien order still seems unreal because so patently not his or her own.

When the patient begins tentatively, almost experimentally, to take hold of the rehabilitating regimen, then the person may move suddenly out of numbness, despair, and confusion and be inclined to overestimate touchingly and pathetically the speed of recovery — expecting rapid strides back into the old familiar world — only to experience a setback, physical and psychological, that signals a far more protracted period of recovery. And then, still later, there is the discovery that one recovers not only slowly but incompletely. The patient will never become again the person he or she once was, "as good as new," but a different human being, permanently limited in one way or another, and inwardly altered by this ordeal.

And yet a third stage eventually comes when the patient reenters the world, a world itself not quite the same, shadowed in some ways, poignantly heightened in others, as skills once taken for granted now seem almost miraculous, and as sounds and smells hitherto unnoticed seem a grace note in life. Friendships and family bonds stretch and rearrange — in some cases deepen, in others tragically weaken — until at length one's powerful link with the attending physician, physical therapist, or occupational therapist, one's mentor and guide, as it were, ends.

The company of those who serve as tutors to patients may include not only the attending physician and nurse but also physical therapists, occupational therapists, workers on various outpatient services, and, last but hardly least, other patients who have themselves survived a similar ordeal. . . .

The physician's general neglect of teaching increases the burden on other health care professionals. This substitution sometimes seems an improvement. Training programs in other fields usually emphasize the professional's responsibility to teach not only in rehabilitation but in preventive, curative, and chronic care. But when the physician defaults from teaching and hands on the patient to persons with less clout, the legitimation of authority sometimes suffers. The physician needs to lay the groundwork for what follows even if he or she does not execute in every detail the therapeutic regimen.

Nurses particularly find themselves in a delicate position, in dealing with acute-care cases, if they must teach the patient — yet the physician retains full authority over disclosure and neglects the responsibilities that go with that authority. Since the nurse sees the patient constantly while the physician ducks in and out, the emotional strain of failing to level with the patient and the patient's family falls on the nurse's shoulders. Other professionals need the legitimation of authority and direction and technical guidance that the physician can provide, and the physician needs the kind of information that only those who have day-to-day contact with the patient can furnish.

Selected former patients, organized and unorganized, also serve a teaching function. Admittedly, the company of other patients in a similar plight has its risks. They sometimes exhibit a tedious missionary zeal, a paternal officiousness that seeks to dominate through greater experience, a half-baked professionalism or a strained cheerfulness. Leaders of support groups usually try to weed out those former patients who have failed to effect successful passage through the illness (sometimes for reasons not at all related to their ordeal). But even those who have reconstructed their life despite catastrophe can depress the newly arrived patient, as they soberly remind that person of the severe handicaps he or she must eventually accept. The pitfalls await, yet the active mentoring performed by former alcoholics, burn victims, heart attack and cancer patients remind us, in an age that tends to reduce healing to the limited alternatives of professional care or self-care, that instruction often goes on among a company of peers.

Terminal Care and the Question of Style

The forms of medical care covered so far — curative, preventive, and rehabilitative — demand that the physician teach; terminal care, less obviously so. Teaching seems irrelevant to the ultimate crisis. Indeed, the truth itself appears, at best, out of place; at worst, crushing. In the last chapter, I argued for the truth, but the truth in the context of fidelity. In this context, the truth expands beyond true assertions to the professional's more extended vocation as a teacher. The issue of terminal care now returns us again to the further question of the teacher's style. Clearly, teaching in medical crisis differs from ordinary academic instruction. The teacher deals with a profoundly troubled listener. The news the teacher brings can devastate. One must be wise and tactful in how one tells the truth.

The delicacy of crisis and terminal care forces a further look at the language used in communicating with patients. Our resources in language fall into several categories: (1) direct, immediate, blunt talk; (2) circumlocution or double-talk; (3) silence; and (4) discourse that proceeds — partly, at least — by way of indirection.

Silence, of course, can lead to sharing, but also to evasion. The technical nature of the medical vocabulary provides plenty of opportunities for a second form of evasion — elusive double-talk. Evasion is more difficult to achieve than it appears. Body language and countenance blurt out more than words reveal. Even though physicians manage information, family members cannot do so deftly. The face betrays what the tongue cannot say. So the patient lives with the knowledge, without benefit of whatever additional help the physician might offer. We may deny death but cannot avoid it.

The last decade has seen a huge reaction against the response of silence. Death courses have outenrolled their competitors in elective offerings at American colleges. Dr. Kübler-Ross achieved celebrity with her book *On Death and Dying.* Broadway has brought forth several plays on the subject. Direct talk on the subject abounds. Too often, however, we assume (especially as Americans) that we can only tell the truth directly, immediately, bluntly. Such talk seems the only alternative to evasive silence or circumlocution. On the subject of sex, for example, we assume that the only alternative to the repressions of the Victorian Age is the tiresome, gabby, explicit discussions of sex imposed upon our adolescents from junior high forward.

However, we can also talk *indirectly* on the weighty subjects of death, religion, and love. Obviously, gabby bluntness in the presence of one dying is wholly inappropriate. It reckons in no way with the solemnity of the event. The physician owes the truth, but not all patients want the truth in exhaustive clinical detail. In such cases, we can surely find some alternatives to blunt talk other than double-talk, a condescending cheerfulness, or a frightening silence.

Perhaps examples of what I mean by indirection will suffice. One doctor reports[14] that many patients brought up the question of their own death in an indirect form: some asked him, for example, whether he thought they should buy a house, marry, or undergo plastic surgery. The doctor realized that the answer "Yes — surely, go ahead" in a big cheerful voice evaded. On the other hand, the answer "No" stopped discussion. He found it important to tell them that he recognized the importance of the question. From that point on, he could discuss with them their uncertainties, anxieties, and fears. The doctor and the patient could share. The doctor need not dwell on the subject for long; after its acknowledgment, he could proceed to the details of daily life without the change of subject becoming an evasion.

We can achieve indirection in another way. Although it sometimes imposes too much to approach the subject frontally under the immediate pressure of its presence, we can achieve indirection if we discuss death in advance of a crisis. Rabbis, priests, or ministers who suddenly feel tongue-tied and irrelevant in the sickroom get what they deserve if they have not worked through the problem with their people in a series of sermons or in work sessions with lay groups. Words too blunt and inappropriate in the crisis itself may, if spoken earlier, provide an indirect basis for sharing burdens. Physicians may similarly discover that the truth shared earlier provides a basis for weathering subsequent events without having to impose it suddenly in a later crisis.

Professionals should not use the option of indirect language as an excuse for delivering signals so remote as to evade or mislead. At its best, indirect discourse verbally respects rather than avoids reality. A kind of double respect comes into play: respect both for the solemnity of the event and for the distance that the patient chooses to maintain in his or her relationship to the event. A man who knew that he had cancer once said to his middle-aged son, a writer on the subject of death and dying, "Go easy, Don." The man knew he had cancer. But at the same time, he wanted to establish the distance he wished to maintain between himself and his son, and the imminent event of his death. He did not want his son to favor him with seminar-length discussions on the subject. Only a fool would not have respected this request. Some distancing and indirection occurs in our relationship to death.

The language of indirection treats death decorously as a sacred event. Indirection often best suits our approach to the sacred. The Jews did not attempt to look directly on Yahweh's face. They dared not approach God casually and directly. But they also could not avoid God's presence. Jews could hold their ground before their Lord in a relation that was genuine but indirect. So also, we need not dwell directly on the subject of death interminably or avoid it by a condescending cheerfulness wholly inappropriate to the event. Still, two human beings can acknowledge death, if ever so indirectly, and hold their ground before it until parted. . . .

Teaching Among Professional Colleagues

Throughout this chapter the emphasis has fallen on teaching the patient. Only a fraction of physicians, however, deal with patients. Others function as specialists who abet the work of their colleagues with patients. Such specialists must teach their attending colleagues — discreetly. In the course of delivering technical information, specialists engage in a kind of continuing education. This delicate relationship to colleagues generates opposing moral dangers. Specialists can display, on the one hand, a too-officious, judgmental, and pompous style that condescends toward the generalist and, on the other hand, an obsequiousness that fails in candor, often for the sake of referrals. Particularly specialists at university tertiary care centers face important moral and political issues of style as they relate to outlying practitioners. A kind of town-gown tension can grow up between two sets of professionals. The staff at a teaching hospital must teach in such a way as to empower rather than humiliate their colleagues who have responsibility for primary care. Otherwise, the mediocre and defensive practitioner may fail to refer for fear of exposing his or her own inadequacies. This outcome produces not only inconvenient business consequences for the specialist but also more than inconvenient results for future patients who fall into the hands of inadequate caretakers.

Some of the dangers that go with the pomp of hierarchy would abate if the specialist remembered his or her professional debt to the generalist. To be sure, the specialist normally instructs and advises the general practitioner, but often the teaching role is reversed. The specialist needs to learn from, and sometimes to be corrected by, the generalist. The specialist requires, in the first place, the proper flow of information. Further, in case of ambiguous symptoms the specialist sometimes needs to be protected from the tendency to pull a diagnosis in the direction of his or her own particular field of expertise. The generalist alone may possess both the information and the broader perspective crucial to developing the correct differential diagnosis.

Notes

1. Carter L. Marshall, "Prevention and Health Education," in *Maxcy-Rosenau Public Health and Preventive Medicine,* 11th ed., ed. by John M. Last et al. (Appleton-Century-Crofts, 1980), pp. 1114-15.

2. Duncan Neuhauser, "Don't Teach Preventive Medicine: A Contrary View," *Public Health Reports* 97 (May-June 1982): 222.

3. Ibid., p. 221.

4. Ibid.

5. Marshall Becker and Lois Maiman, "Strategies for Enhancing Patient Compliance," *Journal for Community Health* 6 (Winter 1980): 113.

6. Ibid., p. 114.

7. Søren Kierkegaard, *The Concept of Dread,* tr. by Walter Lowrie (Princeton University Press, 1944), pp. 110-15.

8. Becker and Maiman, "Strategies for Enhancing Patient Compliance," p. 119.

9. Ibid., pp. 127-29.

10. Marshall, "Prevention and Health Education," p. 1114.

11. Daniel R. Waldo (ed.), *Health Care Financing Trends* 3, No. 1 (June 1982): 2.

12. Marshall, "Prevention and Health Education," p. 1114.

13. W. Hutchinson, "Health Insurance, On Our Financial Relation to the Public," *Journal of the American Medical Association* 7 (Oct. 30, 1886): 447-81. Quoted by Duncan Neuhauser, "Don't Teach Preventive Medicine," p. 222.

14. Samuel L. Feder, "Attitudes of Patients with Advanced Malignancy," in *Death and Dying: Attitudes of Patient and Doctor,* Symposium No. 11, Group for the Advancement of Psychiatry (New York: Mental Health Materials Center, 1965), p. 619.

106 Empowerment in the Clinical Setting

Karen Lebacqz

In *Professional Ethics: Power and Paradox* [17], I proposed that the power of the professional person is morally relevant to determining what should be done in the practice setting and that justice or empowerment of the client becomes a central norm for professional practice.[1] The time has now come to see what justice as empowerment means for the clinical setting. The task is particularly crucial in light of Kapp's recent definition of empowerment as advocating for oneself and participating maximally in one's own significant decisions ([14], p. 5). Under this definition, to choose dependence upon others is to "forego" empowerment ([14], p. 6). I will explore below the adequacy of this definition.

Just as we learn about justice by exploring experiences of injustice [16], so we may learn about empowerment by exploring disempowerment. Disempowerment, and therefore empowerment, within the clinical setting will differ from setting to setting and from population to population. I will examine two populations: those who begin with power and become disempowered in the clinical setting, and those who begin from a position of relative powerlessness and experience the clinical setting from that perspective.

From Karen Lebacqz, "Empowerment in the Clinical Setting," in Gerald P. McKenny and Jonathan Sande, eds., *Theological Analysis of the Clinical Encounter* (Dordrecht: Kluwer Academic Publishers, 1994), pp. 133-47. Used with kind permission from Kluwer Academic Publishers.

The Disempowerment of the Powerful

Hans Jonas once argued that the ideal research subject is a doctor: the doctor is best positioned to understand the risks and implications of the research, and to give a truly voluntary and informed consent [13]. In short, the doctor as subject is most likely to be empowered in the research setting. Similarly, the doctor as patient is most likely to be empowered in the clinical setting. By looking at the disempowerment experienced by those most likely to retain power in the clinical setting, we begin to develop a sense of what constitutes disempowerment and therefore what would constitute empowerment. So we begin with those who experience no language, cultural, knowledge, or sexual barriers to empowerment.

Yet even white, male, well-educated doctors, when they become patients, experience disempowerment in the clinical setting. The film "The Doctor," based on *A Taste of My Own Medicine* by Ed Rosenbaum [22] and just released at the time of writing this essay, demonstrates precisely this disempowerment. Here is a physician, a surgeon, accustomed to ordering people around in the hospital who must now wait in line, fill out forms by the hour, be told "sorry, the doctor is late today," and undergo any number of forms of indignity experienced routinely by patients.

A similar story is told in Oliver Sacks' delightful treatise *A Leg to Stand On* [24]. Sacks broke his leg in a climbing accident. Not only was the leg broken; Sacks also lost all sense of feeling in his leg, and all ability to move or exercise voluntary control over it. He lost "proprioception," the sense of owning one's own limbs and having command over them. Ironically, proprioception is one of the foci of Sack's work as a neurologist. Thus, his story is the story of a man who moves not only from the status of physician to the status of patient, but indeed, to the very kind of patient that he himself treats. He thus learned to see from the "inside" what his patients had tried to communicate to him.

Two Miseries, Two Empowerments

To be a patient — at least under critical circumstances — is to live in an altered world. It is almost as though one has entered the "twilight zone." Perceptions are distorted, time and space appear different, even everyday conversation can loom threateningly: "'Execution tomorrow,' said the clerk in Admissions. I knew it must have been, 'Operation tomorrow,' but the feeling of execution overwhelmed what he said" ([24], p. 46).

Illness takes place on two levels. Sacks calls it "two miseries." One is the physical disability, the "organically determined erosion of being and space" ([24], p. 158). The other he calls the "moral" dimension associated with "the reduced stationless status of a patient, and, in particular, conflict with and surrender to 'them' — 'them' being the surgeon, the whole system, the institution. . . ." ([24], p. 158).

Illness is not just a matter of physical disability. The clinical setting involves also, and even more importantly, a change in one's structural and sociological status. One becomes a "patient."

Even the most powerful of patients therefore feel disempowered in two ways. First, they have lost some ability previously possessed — in Sacks' case, the ability to walk and even to feel his own leg. Loss of ability is annoying at best, frightening at worst: "I found myself . . . scared and confounded to the roots of my being" ([24], p. 79). This is the first "misery" with which the patient deals, and it is often overwhelming in itself, undermining one's ability to deal normally with the world.

But patients have also lost normal status in the world. For Sacks, and for many others, it is the role of patient as much as physical disability itself that inflicts misery and requires empowerment. "I felt morally helpless, paralyzed, contracted, confined — and not just contracted, but contorted as well, into roles and postures of abjection" ([24], p. 158). For example, Sacks asked for spinal rather than general anesthesia, and his request was denied. He writes, "I felt curiously helpless . . . and I thought, Is *this* what 'being a patient' means?" Sociologists have described the "sick role" or status of patient. From the inside, this status is often a feeling of diminishment. Sacks calls himself a "man reduced, and dependent" ([24], p. 133).

The role of patient is reinforced by institutional structures and practices: "we were set apart, we patients in white nightgowns, and avoided clearly, though unconsciously, like lepers" ([24], p. 163). As Alan Goldman puts it in his examination of professional ethics,

> life in hospitals . . . continues to be filled with needless rituals suggestive of patient passivity, dependence, and impotence. The institutional setting is still structured in such a way as to block the exercise of rights at least partially accepted intellectually. . . . Patients are rarely permitted to see their charts; pills are almost literally shoved into their mouths. . . . Often newly admitted patients perfectly capable of walking are taken to their rooms in wheelchairs, an apt symbol of the helpless pose they are made to assume from the time of their entrance into this alien and authoritarian setting ([10], pp. 224-25).

Ultimately, suggests Sacks, he indeed became an "invalid": in-valid ([24], p. 164). Sacks resisted the patient role at every step. Yet he recognized that both he and the surgeon were, in a sense, "forced to play roles — he the role of the All-knowing Specialist, I the role of the Know-nothing Patient" ([24], p. 105).

If illness is composed of two miseries, then recovery will require two empowerments. "Now we needed a double recovery — a physical recovery, and a spiritual movement *to* health" ([24], p. 164). The patient needs physical healing — in Sacks' case, surgery and physical therapy so that he could once again walk, run, jump, and do things that his body had "forgotten" how to do. But as much as the physical healing, the patient needs recovery from the abject, reduced, dependent status of patient.

Both miseries are disempowering. But it is the "contortion" into roles and postures of abjection that is the core of the power gap between physician and patient. Such contortion need not accompany physical deterioration. Different structures reduce the second "misery."

Nor is such contortion necessarily diminished when physical healing takes place. Too often, we assume that once health is restored, the patient automatically becomes a non-patient and experiences restored moral status. In my experience, this is not true. Effects of dependent status can linger, making future contacts difficult and undermining patients' sense of their own worth and being. While the patient may literally move outside the hospital or clinic and cease being a patient in a technical sense, the psycho-sociological effects of dependent patienthood may remain. Moreover, during the time of clinical care, the dependent status of patient can adversely affect medical treatment.

What can be done to empower patients? The loss of function, the physical disability, is the initial presenting problem. The best the medical team can do in the face of it is to try to heal. But is the loss of status, the diminished sense of personhood that often accompanies being a patient, also necessary? Must there be two miseries? Is there a way to reduce the second misery, to hasten recovery from it, and to empower the patient who experiences it? Using Sacks' experience, we can examine the disempowerment of the powerful and suggest how different structures and responses might empower the patient.

The Central Role of Communication

The clinical context begins with communication. Disempowerment begins with failures of communication. One of the most disempowering things that happens in the clinical context is shutting down the patient's words.

In Sacks' case, this began with his first attempts to share what had happened. "They wanted to know the 'salient facts' and I wanted to tell them everything — the entire story" ([24], p. 47). Something had *happened* to Sacks. It was his story. He wanted to tell it. And he wanted to be heard. So from the first "intake" interview in which Sacks tried to tell the "entire" story and the medical team asked for the "salient facts," things went awry.

Failure to communicate went far beyond this first incident. Sacks knew that something was wrong with his leg because he had lost all feeling in it. He waited (and waited and waited!) for the surgeon to come in order to raise his concerns. The surgeon finally appeared, only to state briskly, "there's nothing to worry about" and disappear before Sacks could say more than "but . . ." Sacks was given no *time* to communicate.

As the days went by and the leg failed to respond to physiotherapy, Sacks became desperate to communicate his concern: "Desperately now, I wanted communication, and reassurance" ([24], p. 88). Above all, he recognized a need to communicate to the surgeon and have the surgeon understand. While he wanted reassurance, he was prepared to accept the truth if no reassurance could be given: "I should respect whatever he said so long as it was frank and showed respect for me, for my dignity as a man" ([24], p. 93).

When the surgeon came, he neither looked at Sacks nor spoke to him, but turned to the nurse and said, "Well, Sister, and how is the patient now?" ([24], p. 104). Rather than respect and frankness, Sacks was treated as a nonentity. He was not even addressed by the surgeon, but talked about as if he were not there. Sacks was given no *respect* for himself as a communicator; all the communication was with those around him. Using Kapp's definition of empowerment as advocating for oneself and participating "maximally" in one's own significant decisions, Sacks was clearly disempowered.

Sacks persisted in raising his concern and tried, falteringly, to tell the physician what was wrong:

> It's . . . it's . . . I don't seem to be able to contract the quadriceps . . . and, er . . the muscle doesn't seem to have any tone. And . . . and . . . I have difficulty locating the position of the leg ([24], p. 104).

I have quoted this speech as Sacks describes it. If it is an accurate representation of what he said, this fact alone is significant. Sacks is a literary man. He writes eloquently, powerfully.[2] It is difficult to imagine him at a loss for words, or stumbling over his words. Yet, confronted with the power of the physician, and in his own dependent state as patient, stumble is apparently what he did. He seems to have stammered, acted hesitant and evidenced confusion.

There may be an important lesson here for empowerment in the clinical context. Few medical people realize how dis-empowering the very context is. Patients generally feel inadequate in their descriptions of what is wrong. They hesitate, stumble, try to find the right words. Nothing seems to come out right. The patient who stumbles over her words is not necessarily stupid, but may simply be experiencing, as Sacks did, a diminishment of her capacity to verbalize.

I went to my physician complaining of pain in my hip joint. He asked me to stand and turn in certain ways, and then declared flatly that it could not be my *joint* which was hurting. It must be the *tendon*, not the joint. To him, this technicality and diagnostic accuracy is very important. To me, only the pain that makes it hard for me to climb stairs is important. I do not care whether the pain originates in the joint, technically speaking, or in the tendon. I care only about what can be done to alleviate it, since I live in a house full of stairs. But his focus on the technicalities made it difficult for me to persist in my query. I had been told that I was *wrong*. I felt inadequate and unable to communicate. I gave up, and no treatment was forthcoming.

Sacks suggests that there is among doctors, "in acute hospitals at least, a presumption of stupidity in their patients" ([24], p. 171). Whether all doctors do in fact consider their patients stupid, in acute or other contexts, failures to communicate often have the subtle effect of giving the patient a sense that she or he is not only stupid but also not worthy of the physician's time and effort.

Failure to hear the patient's story, impatience to get to salient facts, lack of time to listen, failure to address the patient at all, focusing on technicalities or calling the patient's understanding wrong — all these are disempowering in the clinical context. The patient who has been treated this way often gives up on the effort to communicate.

Many feel keenly their "ex-communication" ([24], p. 110). Not only have they been shut out from the healthy world literally — stuck in the hospital, wrapped in white gowns, and avoided by healthy people — but they are now shut out symbolically by failure to communicate, to listen, to honor their perspective. "As a patient in the hospital I felt both anguish and asphyxia — the anguish of being confronted with dissolution, and asphyxia because I would not be heard" ([24], p. 209). Thus does Sacks describe the life-killing effect of having communication shut off.

Lack of communication is not the only thing that is disempowering in the clinical context. Being denied a legitimate request (e.g. for spinal rather than general anesthesia), being forced to wear unattractive hospital gowns that strip one's individuality, being shunted from department to department like a sack of potatoes — all these and many other routine aspects of clinical care also take power away from patients. But many of these ills would be compensated by careful communication that leaves patients feeling as though they have been treated as persons, as though they can advocate for themselves and participate maximally in decisions. As Sacks puts it, he would have been content with whatever he was told, so long as it was told with respect.

The Liberating Word

If failures of communication are the beginning of disempowerment, then communication can be the beginning of empowerment: "The postures, the passivity of the patient, last as long as the doctor orders. . . ." ([24], p. 133). Sacks points to the importance of the liberating word on several occasions. In order to heal, to regain use of his leg, he had to walk. Rehabilitation is based on action. Yet the action was birthed not just by himself, but by others: "I had to *do* it, give birth to the New Act, but others were needed to deliver me, and *say*, 'Do it!' " ([24], p. 182). He calls this speaking the essential role of the teacher or therapist. It is a form of midwifery. Only as others granted permission could he find the way to do something new.

Once he missed a memorial service that he would have liked to attend, and lamented to the nurse that he was unable to go. "Why not?" she queried. By challenging the limitations he had set for himself, she removed them: "The moment she spoke and said, 'Why not?' a great barrier disappeared. . . . Whatever it was, I was liberated by her words" ([24], p. 184).

Words of support ("do it") and words of challenge ("why can't you?") can both be liberating. Both can set the patient free to take a new step in the healing process and to claim skills and territory that the patient has not been able to claim by herself.

Empathy

But communication goes far beyond words. When Sacks was first injured, a young surgeon danced into his room, and leaped on the bed-side table. This surgeon had once had a broken leg, and showed Sacks the scars from surgery. "He didn't talk like a text-book. He scarcely talked at all — he acted. He leapt and danced and showed me his wounds, showing me at the same time his perfect recovery" ([24], p. 44). This visit made Sacks feel "immeasurably better." Here, he encountered someone who had been through it and could demonstrate that there is light at the end of the tunnel. Later, another surgeon came to see Sacks, and Sacks felt that he could communicate with this man. "*I've been through this myself*," said the surgeon. "I had a broken leg. . . . *I know what it's like*" ([24], p. 183). The empathy that comes from experience communicates and empowers.

Empathy gives authority to speak: "So when Mr. Amundsen said that the time had come to graduate, and give up one crutch, he spoke with authority — the only real authority, that of experience and understanding" ([24], p. 183). Sacks reflects on his own change as a physician because of what he went through as a patient, "Now I *knew*, for I had experienced myself. And now I could truly begin to understand my patients" ([24], p. 202). At the end of the film "The Doctor," the protagonist puts all his physician-in-training through the experience of being a patient in the hospital. Sacks suggests that there is an "absolute and categorical difference" between a doctor who knows and one who does not, and that this difference is because of the personal experience of "descending to the very depths of disease and dissolution" ([24], p. 203).

There is here, then, an important epistemological question that related to empowerment. One who knows what the patient suffers and can truly hear the patient can empower the patient. But how does one "know" what the patient suffers? Those who have been through a similar experience have readiest access to empathy. This suggests that, where possible, medical care teams should include at least one care-giver who has experienced what the patient suffers. Where this is not possible, groups of patients with similar problems might be assembled. Patients often feel more secure about their position and more enabled to question medical practice when they are with a group that shares their experience.

Art and Religion

Sacks found several other things empowering as well. When he was rebuffed by the surgeon who told him that his concerns were "nothing," he felt as though he had entered a scotoma, "a hole in reality itself" ([24], p. 109). "In this limbo, this dark night," he writes, "I could not turn to science.

Faced with a reality, which reason could not solve, I turned to art and religion for comfort. . . ." ([24], p. 114). Two additional sources of empowerment, then, are art and religion.

A friend loaned Sacks a tape recorder with only one tape: Mendelssohn's violin concerto. "Something happened" to Sacks from the first playing of the music. The music appeared to reveal the creative and animating principle of the world, his leg. "The sense of hopelessness, of interminable darkness, lifted" ([24], p. 119). When he first tried to walk on crutches, he was unable to do so until suddenly the music began to play in his mind, and then he found that he could move to the rhythm.

In his own medical practice, Sacks finds that music can "center" his patients. It appears to restore a sense of the inner self that has been lost through neurological injury or disease ([24], p. 219). Because healing and empowerment involve both physical rhythms of the body and also the "center" of the self, music might be a powerful tool for empowerment. "Music," writes Sacks, "was a divine message and messenger of life. It was quintessentially quick — the 'quickening art,' as Kant has called it. . . ." ([24], p. 148). This makes me wonder what would happen if our hospitals provided not television sets but stereos equipped with the great masterpieces of music from the centuries!

Art is not the only response to realities which reason cannot solve "Science and reason could not talk of 'nothingness,' of 'hell,' or 'limbo': or of 'spiritual night.' They had no place for 'absence, darkness, death.' Yet these were the overwhelming realities of this time" ([24], p. 114). In order to find a language adequate to describe his experiences, Sacks turned to religion. The patient who faces dissolution of her world needs a language adequate to give voice to that dissolution and to provide a framework within which it can be understood, accepted, and overcome. The language of science and reason is often too sterile for this task. The language of science and reason is often too sterile for this task. The language of religion, precisely because it is often poetic [5] and mysterious, is adequate to the task.

Sacks gives eloquent expression to the power of religious language when he writes, "In a sense my experience had been a religious one — I had certainly thought of the leg as exiled, God-forsaken, when it was 'lost' and, when it was restored, restored in a transcendental way" ([24], p. 190). While he admits that his experience was also a "riveting scientific and cognitive" experience, it had transcended the limits of science and cognition. A language beyond science was needed.

Moreover, it is not only the *language* of religion that is empowering. Sacks went home for a night to see his family. While there, he attended synagogue. Here he experienced, "inexpressible joy": "Behind my family I felt embraced by a community and, behind this, by the beauty of old traditions, and, behind this, by the ultimate, eternal joy of the law" ([24], p. 189). Religion is not just a language. It is a community, a set of laws and rituals, a sense of belonging to something larger and more grounding than one's own family or personal universe. All of these things have empowering possibility. They also suggest that Kapp's definition of empowerment is too individualistic and based too much on an autonomy model. Empowerment includes community and connection; it includes strengthening and honoring relationships.

Summary

What Sacks needed was "a leg to stand on." He needed it in two senses: the literal, physical healing of his limb, and the symbolic, "moral" healing of his status in the world. Because there were two miseries, two empowerments — two "legs" — were needed. The second leg is social and spiritual. Although the empowering possibilities of physical healing should not be underestimated, neither should the need for the second leg be neglected. It has to do with the meaning system of the patient, with hope and fear, with anxiety and joy, with community and solidarity. It is a leg composed of the liberating word, the communication that comes from empathy, the centering power of music and art, the adequacy of religious language and the solidity of religious ritual and community.

The Disempowerment of the Powerless

Oliver Sacks was one of the lucky ones. White, male, well-educated, a physician to boot, he was in a position to be as powerful as any patient can be. The mere fact that one so powerful experienced two "miseries" and needed two empowerments gives us many clues as to what happens in the clinical setting. But it does not cover the situation of those who are not powerful at the outset. What about those who suffer language, educational, racial, or sexual barriers when confronting the medical establishment?[3] The experiences of patients who are female, non-white, poor, not well educated, or in some other way less powerful than the white physician suggest some additional dimensions of disempowerment and therefore of empowerment. Those who begin in a more powerless position have many more barriers to empowerment. For them, it will take not only a change in communication, a bit more thoughtfulness, or a little music to give them back their moral status and sense of wholeness. For them, it will take nothing short of a change in the system.

Consent and Rationality

Consider, for example, the case of Maria Diaz, whose doctors recommended tubal ligation while she was in the last stages of a difficult labor. "I told them I would not accept that. I kept saying no and the doctors kept telling me that this was for my own good" ([7], p. 108). Maria Diaz never agreed to be sterilized and signed no consent forms for the procedure; but she was sterilized during caesarian section. Later, she and other Hispanic women brought a suit against U.S.C.-L.A. medical center where the procedure was performed. In a subsequent study, Dreifus and her colleagues found that nine of 23 physicians interviewed had either witnessed coercion or worked under conditions that border on coercion: "hard-selling, dispensing of misinformation, approaching women during labor, offering sterilization at a time of stress, on-the-job racism" ([7], 1. 116).

Maria Diaz was disempowered in two ways. First, she was treated not simply without her consent but against her explicit will. In spite of her constant advocacy for herself, she did not participate even minimally in a very significant decision. Using Kapp's definition, she was disempowered.

But she was disempowered in another way as well. Sterilization is a life-changing operation with earth-shattering ramifications for women from "machismo" cultures. In "machismo" culture, a man's stature may be measured by the number of children he sires. He may divorce or abandon a woman who cannot bear children. Indeed, this is what happened to Lupe Acosta, whose common-law husband of eight years left her after she was sterilized against her will ([7], p. 107). She ended up on welfare, experiencing not only medical disempowerment, but social and economic disempowerment as well. A decision to refuse sterilization that may not seem "sensible" or "rational" in one culture may be very sensible in another. Empowerment in this context would require sensitivity to such cross-cultural issues, and recognition of the devastating consequences of what might seem a "sensible" decision in white North American culture.

Oliver Sacks may not have been told everything that he wanted to know, and may not have had the kind of communication that he desired. But at no time did he experience the kind of disempowerment that these poor, multi-parous women with language and cultural barriers experienced. He was not treated *against* his will, nor was a foreign rationality imposed on him.

Medical Harm

Practices such as forced sterilization would be condemned as unjust by most observers. Harder to uncover are the injustices, the disempowerments, built into ordinary, routine medical practice. Here, there are two levels on which we must look for disempowerment and therefore for empowerment. In Sacks' case, the primary disempowerment came with the social *role* of patient — with losing control, being ignored, and not having social power.[4] But for many women, these social concomitants of the role of patient are only part of the picture. Medical practice historically has contributed not only to this second "misery" for women, but also to the first "misery," the phenomenon of physical disintegration itself.

Feminists and concerned women over the years have exposed a range of obstetrical and gynecological practices that actually *endanger* women's health. Unnecessary hysterectomies [15], use of the Dalkon shield [6], clitoridectomies [4, 23] — any number of practices with serious deleterious impact on women's health have been "routine" or common at one time in our history. For example, a number of studies have documented the movement from child-birth to the "delivery" of children in obstetrical units [11, 29]. Historical evidence suggests that midwifery was safer than obstetrics at the time when the (largely male) medical professionals pushed out the (largely female) midwives. Many women have objected to the health risks presented for both mother and child by routine obstetrical practices. Ethel, who bore 16 children, puts it plainly:

> I had all mine at home except the last six. . . . [I]t was easier to have them at home than to have them at the hospital. . . . They'd take me to the hospital and they'd strap me down. I'd like to never have the baby! When I was home, you know, I'd walk till the pains got so bad that I had to lay down then I'd lay down and have the baby. Without any anesthetic and never no stitches or nothing, because they waited till time. Now they cut you, you know, and they don't give you time to have it. . . . That's what ruins women's health ([3], p. 229).

That such practices actually are dangerous has been argued by several commentators [21, 25].

In this context, empowerment for women includes having control over one's own body and important medical decisions. The dimension of decision-making that Kapp lifts up remains important. But empowerment also includes better health care practices that do not endanger women or children.

In a study of court cases, Miles and August found that when the patient was a man, the court constructed his preferences for treatment in 75% of cases and allowed those preferences to be determining. But when the patient was a woman, the court constructed her preferences in only 14% of cases, and her preferences were not determinative of treatment decisions. Miles and August conclude that "women are disadvantaged in having their moral agency taken less seriously than that of men" ([20], p. 92). If Sacks had difficulty being heard and treated as a moral agent, imagine what he might have faced had he been a woman instead of a man. Thus, on the level of the second "misery," which Sacks calls the moral level, women are not treated equally with men. Empowerment in such a case means not having a double standard: both male and female patients should be treated with attention to their own expressed preferences as well as to their familial connections.

But it is not only the second level of "misery" on which women are not treated equally. Ayanian and Epstein found that "women who are hospitalized for coronary heart disease undergo fewer major diagnostic and therapeutic procedures than men" ([2], p. 221). Steingart et al. argue that it is "disturbing" to find that women report more cardiac disability before infraction than do men, but are less likely to receive treatments known (in men) to lessen symptoms and improve functional capacity ([26], p. 230). Just as Miles and August found that women's statements of not wanting to be kept alive were dismissed as "emotional" rather than "rational" desires, so it is possible that women's complaints of chest pain may not be taken as seriously as men's. Empowerment for women in the clinical setting clearly begins with having our voices honored and appropriate interventions utilized.

Empathy and the Non-treatment of Women's Issues

Another subtle form of disempowerment is the non-treatment of or non-focus on women's issues. Coronary artery disease is the leading cause of death in women ([26], p. 226). Yet our common image of "heart attack" is an image of a middle-aged professional man, not an image of a woman. The studies just cited make clear that there is much we do not know about how to treat heart disease in women. We have focused on men's needs, but not on women's.

Similarly, more women die *each year* of breast cancer than men died of AIDS in the first *ten years* of the epidemic [30]. It is estimated that one out of every three women will get cancer during their lifetime, and the breast cancer incidence rate has increased 32% in the last decade [27]. Yet, there is neither the commitment of funds for research and development of new treatments and interventions nor the commitment of public energies and attention to breast cancer that we currently experience for AIDS. Empowerment means *attending* to women's issues, and making them a priority for clinical research and treatment.

The reasons for the relative lack of attention to

issues so central to women's lives are complex. Lack of women physicians and researchers may be an important contributing factor. A history of exclusion of women from top ranks of the medical profession leaves its legacy. Walsh concludes her historical study of the discrimination against women in the medical profession with these cautioning words: "There is an interrelationship between discrimination against women as medical students and physicians and against women as patients — resulting in the present lack of research on breast cancer, excessive rates of hysterectomies and surgery on women . . . and generally deficient health care for women" ([28], pp. 281-82).

Lack of women physicians not only influences choices about research and clinical emphasis; it also influences the possibilities for empathy, so important in Sacks' experience of healing. What male physician can truly empathize with the birth pains of a woman patient, or with what it means to a woman to lose a breast to surgery? If empathy is important for empowerment, then women will experience less empowerment than men when they are treated in a system that does not encourage women physicians. Similarly, white caregivers have difficulty empathizing with women and men of color; the well-to-do will not even imagine some problems experienced by those who are economically disadvantaged; and so on. Empowerment in the clinical context will require a change in the system that encourages different care-providers.

Problems of Access

While the focus of this essay is on empowerment *within* the clinical setting, some of the most important empowerment issues for those who are relatively powerless have to do with access *to* the clinical setting. Ectopic pregnancy is now the leading cause of maternal death among African-American women [19]. But in 1982 there were 44,000 women in New York state identified as at "high risk" who became pregnant, had no health insurance, and were not eligible for Medicaid ([19], p. 58). Without health insurance or the means to pay, these women do not get *into* the clinical setting. Their empowerment must begin outside that setting, with changes in political, social, and economic policies, Medicaid eligibility, and access to health care. Similarly, for older women, changes in Medicare to allow access to needed health care is critical.

While problems of access raise larger social and political issues, there are some things that can be done within the clinical setting to address these problems. For instance, would women who are eligible for Medicaid be able to find a physician who accepts Medicaid patients? "The worst medical problems I've had really," says Ethel, a poor mountain woman with 12 living children, "has been since I been on welfare. Trying to see the kinds of doctors that's needed for the children and myself, and they don't take the card — needing to see specialists, and the specialists don't take the card" ([3], p. 231). At the same time that we are experiencing the "feminization of poverty," with women increasingly among the poor who must depend on Medicaid, we are also experiencing a time in which ob-gyns, who specialize in women's diseases and reproductive processes, have the lowest rate of Medicaid participation of all primary care physicians ([19], p. 57). Women who cannot get into the health care system at all are doubly disempowered.

Empowerment in this context means the willingness of clinical care providers to "take the card" and deal with the government red tape, the bureaucratic form-filling, and the loss of income represented by accepting those patients. If more physicians "took the card" and had to deal with these inconveniences, perhaps we would see a faster move toward a more equitable system of access for the poor, many of whom are women.

Alternative Structures

Under these circumstances, it is no wonder that many women and other relatively powerless people have felt that empowerment cannot happen within the system. Empowerment means not only advocating for oneself and participating in significant decisions, but receiving care from a radically re-oriented system.

Some have moved to establishing alternative health care systems. One such organization was called "Jane" [1, 12]. Run by women on a nonhierarchical basis, "Jane" helped women get access to safe abortion during the time that abortions were largely illegal in the United States. "Jane" was part of a larger movement that involved teaching women about their bodies, their sexuality, and their own medical care [8, 9]. Alternative clinics were set up where women were trained to do their own vaginal examinations and to monitor their gynecological health. These organizations were empowering for women because they gave women knowledge, allowed women to help each other in non-hierarchical structure, and kept control of important bodily processes largely in the hands of women themselves. They strengthened relationships among women patients and providers, and tried to deal with issues that were central from the perspective and rationality of women of different cultures.

But alternative structures outside the system are not the only solution. Recognizing the rise of breast cancer and the crucial place of mammograms in diagnosis and early treatment, the Medical Center of Central Massachusetts set out to discover why women were so reluctant to come in for mammograms and whether something could be done about it. They asked women to talk about what keeps them from having mammograms. Among the factors that keep women away, they found these:

1. lack of child-care;
2. cold and unattractive hospital gowns;
3. lack of privacy;
4. inadequately trained technicians, with resulting pain and discomfort;
5. lengthy waiting time between testing and results.

The mammography unit was redesigned to address these problems: it now provides child-care, privacy, specially trained technicians, attractive and warm clothing, immediate test results, and so on. Such structural changes provide empowerment not just for individual patients, but for the entire class of patients and ultimately for society as a whole.

Summary

The lesson to be learned from those who are relatively powerless is that we need changes in the system, not just changes of attitude in a few care-providers. More thoughtful listening, a willingness to hear the "whole" story and not just the "salient facts" will still be important. But it is the system that must be scrutinized for how it disempowers those who are already powerless, and how it could be made more empowering instead.

Empowerment in the clinical setting will require allowing patients to be their own advocates and to participate in significant decision-making. It will require not treating patients against their will, nor assuming that one culture's "rationality" makes sense for all cultures. It will require honoring those forms of rationality, such as art and religion, that offer a language "beyond" reason and science, a language that may be more appropriate to the patient's needs. It will require recognizing the network of community and relationships that affect patients' lives and decisions. But above all, it will require changing the system so that those who are relatively powerless have access to health care, for without that access, all talk of empowerment within the clinical setting is void.

Pacific School of Religion
Berkeley, California
U.S.A.

Notes

1. The definition of justice and dimensions of justice as empowerment are further explored in *Six Theories of Justice* [18] and *Justice in an Unjust World* [16].

2. I have also heard him speak publicly and found his address strong.

3. Precisely because these patients are already relatively powerless in the system, they are less likely to write books about their experiences than are the more powerful who become patients.

4. Loss of control and autonomy is a typically male problem; feminist literature suggests that loss of relationship might be more problematic for women.

Bibliography

[1] Addelson, K. P.: 1986, 'Moral Revolution,' in M. Pearsall (ed.), *Women and Values: Readings in Recent Feminist Philosophy,* Wadsworth, Belmont, CA, pp. 291-309.

[2] Ayanian, J. Z., and Epstein, A. M.: 1991, 'Differences in the Use of Procedures between Women and Men Hospitalized for Coronary Heart Disease,' *New England Journal of Medicine* 325(4): 221-30 (July 25).

[3] Baker, D.: 1977, 'The Class Factor: Mountain Women Speak Out on Women's Health,' in C. Dreifus (ed.), *Seizing Our Bodies*, Random House, NY, pp. 223-32.

[4] Barker-Benfield, G. J.: 1977, 'Sexual Surgery in Late-Nineteenth Century America,' in C. Dreifus (ed.), *Seizing our Bodies*, Random House, NY, pp. 13-41.

[5] Brueggemann, W.: 1989, *Finally Comes the Poet: Daring Speech for Proclamation*, Fortress Press, Minneapolis.

[6] Dowie, M., and Johnston, T.: 1977, 'A Case of Corporate Malpractice and the Dalkon Shield,' in C. Dreifus (ed.), *Seizing Our Bodies*, Random House, NY, pp. 86-104.

[7] Dreifus, C.: 1977, 'Sterilizing the Poor,' in C. Dreifus (ed.), *Seizing Our Bodies*, Random House, NY, pp. 105-20.

[8] Frankfort, E.: 1977, 'Vaginal Politics,' in C. Dreifus (ed.), *Seizing Our Bodies*, Random House, NY, pp. 263-70.

[9] Fruchter, R. G., et al.: 1977, 'The Women's Health Movement: Where Are We Now?,' in C. Dreifus (ed.), *Seizing Our Bodies*, Random House, NY, pp. 271-78.

[10] Goldman, A. H.: 1980, *The Moral Foundations of Professional Ethics*, Rowman and Littlefield, Totowa, NJ.

[11] Haire, D.: 1972, *The Cultural Warping of Childbirth*, International Childbirth Education Association, Seattle.

[12] 'Jane': 1990, 'Just Call "Jane",' in M. G. Fried (ed.), *From Abortion to Reproductive Freedom: Transforming a Movement*, South End Press, Boston.

[13] Jonas, H.: 1970, 'Philosophical Reflections on Human Experimentation,' in P. Freund (ed.), *Experimentation with Human Subjects*, George Braziller, NY, pp. 1-31.

[14] Kapp, M. B.: 1989, 'Medical Empowerment of the Elderly,' *Hastings Center Report* 19(4), (July-August).

[15] Larned, D.: 1977, 'The Epidemic in Unnecessary Hysterectomy,' in C. Dreifus (ed.), *Seizing Our Bodies*, Random House, NY, pp. 195-208.

[16] Lebacqz, K.: 1987: *Justice in an Unjust World: Foundations for a Christian Approach to Justice*, Augsburg Publishing House, Minneapolis, MN.

[17] Lebacqz, K.: 1985, *Professional Ethics: Power and Paradox*, Abingdon Press, Nashville, TN.

[18] Lebacqz, K.: 1986, *Six Theories of Justice: Perspectives from Philosophical and Theological Ethics*, Augsburg Publishing House, Minneapolis, MN.

[19] McBarnette, L.: 1988, 'Women and Poverty: The Effects on Reproductive Status,' in C. A. Perales and L. S. Young (eds.), *Too Little, Too Late: Dealing with the Health Needs of Women in Poverty*, Harrington Park Press, New York.

[20] Miles, S. H., and August, A.: 1990, "Courts, Gender and 'The Right to Die'," *Law, Medicine, and Health Care* 18 (102): 85-95 (Spring/Summer).

[21] Rich, A.: 1986, *Of Woman Born: Motherhood as Experience and Institution*, W. W. Norton, NY.

[22] Rosenbaum, E.: 1988, *A Taste of My Own Medicine*; now published as *The Doctor*, Ivy Books, NY.

[23] Rothman, B. K.: 1979, 'Women, Health and Medicine,' in J. Freeman (ed.), *Women: A Feminist Perspective*, 2nd ed., Mayfield Publishing Co., Palo Alto, CA.

[24] Sacks, O.: 1984, *A Leg to Stand On*, Harper and Row, NY.

[25] Sarah, R.: 1988, 'Power, Certainty, and the Fear of Death,' in E. H. Baruch, A. F. D'Adamo, and J. Seager (eds.), *Embryos, Ethics, and Women's Rights: Exploring the New Reproductive Technologies*, Harrington Park Press, New York.

[26] Steingart, R. M., et al.: 1991, 'Sex Differences in the Management of Coronary Artery Disease,' *New England Journal of Medicine* 325(4) (July 25), 226-30.

[27] Steingraber, S.: 1991, 'Lifestyles Don't Kill. Carcinogens in Air, Food, and Water Do,' in M. Stocker (ed.), *Cancer as a Woman's Issue: Scratching the Surface*, Third Side Press, Chicago.

[28] Walsh, M. R.: 1977, *'Doctors Wanted: No Women Need Apply': Sexual Barriers in the Medical Profession, 1835-1975*, Yale University Press, New Haven.

[29] Wertz, R. W., and Wertz, D. C.: 1977, *Lying-In: A History of Childbirth in America*, The Free Press, NY.

[30] Winnow, J.: 1991, 'Lesbians' Evolving Health Care: Our Lives Depend on It,' in M. Stocker (ed.), *Cancer as a Woman's Issue: Scratching the Surface*, Third Side Press, Chicago.

Chapter Seventeen

PSYCHIATRIC CARE: PROFESSIONAL COMMITMENTS AND SOCIETAL RESPONSIBILITIES

Psychiatry is formed of two Greek words, *psyche* (soul) and *iatreia* (healing). The derivation itself raises again the issue of the first chapter of this anthology, the relation of religion to medicine, in this case the relation of religion to the knowledge and skills of psychiatric medicine. The Churches have regarded the "cure of souls" as part of their task for a very long time;[1] today, however, a psychiatrist, a "soul healer," is a specially trained physician, not a cleric. How should be think of the relation of Christianity to contemporary mental health care?

The issue is complicated, of course, not only by the diversity within Christianity but by the diversity among the practitioners of the "cure of souls." Besides psychiatrists, contemporary practitioners include psychologists, who are not medical doctors but Ph.D.s in psychology with at least a year of supervised practice, psychiatric social workers, counselors of various kinds, family therapists, pastoral counselors, and still others. These practitioners of the "cure of souls" have different training, of course, but there are also diverse assumptions, therapies, and loyalties at work in contemporary "soul healing." A psychologist working on the biochemical bases of schizophrenia may have very little in common with a colleague studying small-group behavior. A psychiatrist utilizing drugs to alter mood, behavior, or mental functioning may have little interest in psychotherapeutic analysis. A therapist utilizing behavior modification techniques may have little sympathy for logotherapy or gestalt therapy or hypnotherapy or psychodrama or transactional analysis or EST or the primal scream. The disciples of Freud may have a polemical relation with the disciples of Jung or Rogers or Skinner or Frankel.

The diversity among therapists extends also to their attitudes toward religion. Freud saw religion as a form of mental illness, as an "obsessional neurosis," as "a system of wishful illusions."[2] Carl Jung, on the other hand, regarded religion as necessary for mental health, because "it is the role of religion to give a meaning to the life of man."[3] There remain differences of opinion among therapists about whether religion is pathological or therapeutic.[4]

People of faith have different opinions of scientific psychiatry, too. Some would wholly reject secular psychiatric knowledge and skills in favor of the religious practices of prayer, confession, absolution, and even exorcism. Others would test the religious practices of their communities by their therapeutic benefits, regarding their own religion as instrumental to happiness or peace of mind. Some regard psychiatric medicine and religion as independent and mutually irrelevant. And still others refuse any of these options, neither rejecting psychiatric knowledge and skill nor reducing religion to merely another therapeutic tool, but attempting to challenge and qualify certain assumptions, to consider the goals and means of particular therapies, and to nurture and order certain loyalties on the basis of theological reflection.

The first two selections in this chapter may be regarded as attempts to address the relation of contemporary mental health care and religion. Seward Hiltner, one of the most prominent theologians at the intersection of religion and mental health care, announces in an opening disclaimer (in selection 107) that human goods must not be reduced to mental health, but one may ask whether his position so emphasizes the contributions of religion to mental health that he interprets and tests religion by its therapeutic effectiveness. The selection from the eminent child psychiatrist Robert Coles protests both against the "secular idolatry" of psychology and psychiatry and against clergy who surrender the practices of believing communities in their efforts to be effective therapists, adopting the ends and means and language of psychology.

The essay by Ian S. Evison (selection 109) revisits the question of the relation of medicine to ethics, here the relation of psychiatric medicine to ethics. He uses Robert Lifton and Thomas Szasz to display contrasting accounts of that relation. Robert Lifton denies the possibility of a "value-free" psychiatry and urges it and its practitioners to enlist in "the struggle of life against the forces of death." Thomas Szasz insists that psychiatry be "value-neutral" and that it achieve value-neutrality by respecting the autonomy of patients. Evison traces Lifton's view to Romanticism and communitarianism, and he traces Szasz's perspective to the Enlightenment and laissez-faire individualism.

Evison himself attempts to articulate a position between Lifton and Szasz by calling psychiatry and its practitioners to pursue "the admittedly ethical but limited goal of basic human functioning." On his view, psychiatry should (unlike Lifton) bracket the larger, richer, and more particular visions of individual and social good but reject (unlike Szasz) the pretence of value-neutrality; he regards his position as a form of "public theology." It is worth pausing to ask whether Evison is successful in his effort to articulate a "public theology" that could guide and limit the powers of psychiatric medicine. Lifton might respond that such a psychiatry would inevitably get coopted by the "forces of death" in a culture like Nazi Germany[5] — or our own — especially if the standard of "adequate functioning" would seem to presume some account of what a person is "for." We know what a watch is for, of course, and so we have reasonable standards for judging whether a watch is functioning adequately, and particular theologies have some ideas about what human beings are "for," but can a "public theology" judge whether a person is functioning adequately? What do you think?

The contrast between Lifton and Szasz also retrieves other issues developed earlier in this book. Consider, for example, what each says about the "profession" and its integrity. Or consider their accounts of "mental health" and "illness." Or consider their accounts of suffering and of freedom. Each of these issues has implications for the practice of the "cure of souls" today.

The moral issues in psychiatric medicine are many and varied. They include, for example, issues of confidentiality; transference and countertransference (including erotic attraction between patient and analyst); involuntary commitment; the use (and abuse) of behavior modification techniques, psychosurgery, psychopharmacology, and psychoanalysis; the conventional reliance upon informed consent when a patient's cognitive ability or autonomy is compromised; and access to mental health services. Each of these issues is comprised, of course, of more concrete questions.

Consider, for example, some of the questions raised by psychopharmacology. Antipsychotic, antidepressant, and antianxiety drugs have made a dramatic difference in the lives of many patients, relieving some of the disabling symptoms of mental illness. They have also prompted, however, some moral questions.

There is, for example, the question of "to whom" these drugs should be given, and specifically whether consent is either necessary or sufficient. Competent patients have a right to refuse treatment, but these drugs are frequently prescribed for patients whose ability to process information (and to trust their caregivers) is impaired. Psychotic patients, for example, may be paranoid, suspicious of the drugs they are asked to take. Indeed, as one study has shown, the more severely psychotic patients, those who need the drug more, are more likely to refuse treatment than the less severely psychotic patients.[6] If the refusal to consent to medication results in a danger to the patient or to others, may the medication be given without consent? How great does the danger have to be? Does life have to be at risk? Or is a risk to some other good sufficient justification for temporarily forcing medication? There are reasons, perhaps, not to count consent as a necessary condition for medication, and the possibility of addiction to some of these drugs is reason enough to reject consent as sufficient condition for prescription.

There is also the question of "by whom" these drugs are prescribed. Of course, the prescription is written by a psychiatrist, but at whose request? Upon whose recommendation? This is a question, then, of whom the therapist serves: Whose agent is the therapist? To whom is the therapist finally loyal? The spouse? The parents? The state? The military? The prison warden? The teacher? The mental health care institution? The patient? And if the patient, the patient as autonomous choice-maker or the patient as an embodied and communal (and currently dysfunctional) self? The therapist can often experience conflicting responsibilities, feeling like a double agent.

The question of "for what end" is related to the above discussion. Presumably, the end, the purpose, of the medication (or any other intervention) would be the mental health of the patient. But what is "mental health"? Freedom from anxiety and guilt? A sense of self-control? Adequate functioning? Appropriate social behavior?[7] Some critics worry that the "end" is really the imposition of "orthodox" behaviors in a community, silencing dissent and eliminating "social deviancy," or the efficient preservation of control in a prison, a classroom, or a mental health care institution. They worry, moreover, that some of the definitions of "mental health" can function as rationalizations to license such abuses of psychiatric powers. Paul S. Appelbaum suggests (in selection 110) that the goal of at least some who advocated a policy of deinstitutionalization, which psychopharmaceuticals made plausible, was the reduction of the population (and the costs) of state mental institutions rather than a concern about the mental health of the residents.

Questions of means include the traditional medical concerns about the side effects of these drugs and about the wisdom of alternative treatments. The side effects are indeed significant. Patients using antipsychotic drugs, for example, frequently feel sedated, uncomfortable, and slowed; and many such patients become noncompliant. Moreover, these patients experience additional difficulties in social interaction. The debate about "deinstitutionalization" is in part a debate about the wisdom of alternative treatments.

As Paul Applebaum tells the story of the triumph (and the tragedy) of "deinstitutionalization," it is worth revisiting the issue of our attitudes toward technology. Did we expect too much from the psychopharmaceuticals? Surely, these drugs have been of great help to many. But have the extravagant expectations of both physicians and the public conspired with the interests of pharmaceutical and insurance agencies (whether public or private) to create a situation in which these drugs are too casually prescribed and expected to eliminate both suffering and the need to be present to the suffering?

Since Applebaum and others call for some reversal in the policy of deinstitutionalization, it is worth considering again some of the issues prompted by "total institutions," and the selection by William F. May in this chapter (selection 111) does that splendidly.

The Christian response to deinstitutionalization includes, however, not only contributions to the public discussion about state institutions but also reflection about the Christian community's responsibility to be hospitable and supportive to the mentally ill persons. Brett Webb-Mitchell suggests ways Christian communities can support and empower deinstitutionalized people — and reasons why the Churches should (selection 112). As he reminds us, it is important to acknowledge the responsibility to care even when we cannot cure. The "cure of souls" is frequently beyond our reach, but Christian integrity may well be at stake in the willingness still to care.

Edmund Pellegrino focuses on the importance of confidentiality in psychotherapeutic relationships (selection 113). Finally, selection 114 displays the effort of one Christian mental health care center to articulate a Christian vision and mission for its work and institution life.

Notes

1. John T. McNeill, *A History of the Cure of Souls* (Garden City, N.Y.: Harper & Brothers, 1951).

2. Sigmund Freud, *The Future of an Illusion* (Garden City, N.Y.: Doubleday, 1961; first published in 1927), pp. 71-72.

3. Carl Jung, ed. *Man and His Symbols* (London: Aldus Books, 1964), p. 89. Gordon Allport, like Jung,

considered religion a potentially important contributor to mental health; see, e.g., *The Individual and His Religion* (New York: Macmillan, 1950).

4. See, for example, the debate between Allen Bergin and Albert Ellis; Allen E. Bergin, "Psychotherapy and Religious Values," *Journal of Consulting and Clinical Psychology* 48 (1980): 95-100; Albert Ellis, "Psychotherapy and Atheistic Values: A Response to A. E. Bergin's 'Psychotherapy and Atheistic Values,'" ibid., pp. 635-39; Bergin, "Religious and Humanistic Values: A Reply to Ellis and Walls," ibid., pp. 642-45. See also David B. Larson and Susan S. Larson, "Religious Commitment and Health: Valuing the Relationship," *Second Opinion* 17, no. 1 (July 1991): 27-40, which combines an autobiographical account of David Larson's confrontation with a prejudice against religion in his psychiatric training with a survey of the empirical research on the contribution of religion to mental health.

5. Besides the books mentioned in Evison's bibliography, Robert J. Lifton is also the author of *The Nazi Doctors* (New York: Basic Books, 1985).

6. Stephen R. Marder, Andrew Mebane, Ching-Piao Chien, William J. Winslade, Elizabeth Swann, and Theodore Van Putten, "A Comparison of Patients Who Refuse and Consent to Neuroleptic Treatment," *American Journal of Psychiatry* 140, no. 4 (1983): 470-72.

7. See C. Daniel Batson, Patricia Schoenrade, and W. Larry Ventis, *Religion and the Individual: A Social Psychological Perspective* (New York: Oxford, 1993), pp. 230-92, for a discussion of seven different conceptions of mental health and the relationship of religious commitment to each of the seven conceptions.

Suggestions for Further Reading

Aden, Leroy, and David G. Benner (eds.). *Counseling and the Human Predicament: A Study of Sin, Guilt and Forgiveness* (Grand Rapids: Baker Book House, 1989).

Bhugra, Dinesh. *Psychiatry and Religion: Context, Consensus and Controversies,* (London: Routledge, 1996).

Bloch, Sidney, and Paul Chodoff (eds.). *Psychiatric Ethics* (second edition; Oxford: Oxford University Press, 1991).

Browning, Don S., Thomas Jobe, and Ian S. Evison (eds.). *Religions and Ethical Factors in Psychiatric Practice* (Chicago: Nelson-Hall, 1990).

Burt Robert. *Taking Care of Strangers: The Rule of Law in Doctor-patient Relations* (New York: Free Press, 1979).

Jones, James William. *Contemporary Psychoanalysis and Religion: Transference and Transcendence* (New Haven: Yale University Press, 1991).

Kopelman, Loretta, and John C. Moskop (eds.). *Ethics and Mental Retardation* (Dordrecht, the Netherlands: D. Reidel, 1984).

Numbers, Ronald L., and Janet S. Numbers. "Religious Insanity: History of a Diagnosis," *Second Opinion* 3 (1986): 56-77.

Robinson, Lillian H. (ed.). *Psychiatry and Religion: Overlapping Concerns* (Washington, D.C.: American Psychiatric Association Press, 1986).

Shafranske, Edward P. *Religion and the Clinical Practice of Psychology* (Washington, D.C.: American Psychological Association, 1996).

Szasz, Thomas. *The Theology of Medicine: The Political-Philosophical Foundations of Medical Ethics* (Baton Rouge: Louisiana State University Press, 1977).

Tillich, Paul. *The Meaning of Health: Essays in Existentialism, Psychoanalysis, and Religion* (Chicago: Exploration Press, 1984).

Wallace, Edwin R., IV. "Reflection on the Relationship between Psychoanalysis and Christianity," *Pastoral Psychology* 31, no. 4 (Summer, 1983): 215-43.

107 Some Contributions of Religion to Mental Health

Seward Hiltner

Mental hygiene teaches something to religion and the church. But religion and the church make contributions to mental health whose full significance is not always realized. "There is no integration which compares with that which comes from religious faith or a religious goal," says Dr. Earl D. Bond.[1] "I am convinced that the Christian religion is one of the most valuable and potent influences that we possess for producing that harmony and peace of mind . . . needed to bring health and power to a large proportion of nervous patients," reports Dr. J. A. Hadfield.[2]

Fortunately we are not wholly dependent upon the personal testimony of scientists for our conviction that religion does have a constructive influence for health in the widest and deepest sense. Such quotations as these, which could be multiplied, perform the service, however, of indicating how we may look for the kind of contribution which religion in practice makes to health. . . .

In approaching the contributions which religion makes to mental health in a practical sense, we must accept two points as preliminaries. The first is that religion is not interested merely in health. Theologians would say that health, even considered in the modern sense as relating to body, mind and spirit, is not the same as salvation because health is "temporal" or in time, and salvation is "eternal" or beyond time. As George A. Buttrick puts it in reference to prayer, for example, "The integration wrought by prayer goes far beyond health of body and 'mind' — as it must to be convincing, for all men must die."[3] Assertions of this kind are true in the basic sense in which they are intended. It is also true that Kagawa in the slums of Tokyo spent his physical health, — yet that which he enhanced can hardly be completely circumscribed under the idea of health. Christianity says there are other things than health which man should seek. But it does not say that one should seek ill-health. . . .

The second introductory point we must make is that not all interpretations (and living out) of religion, of Christianity, are healthy, in the sense of health of the whole personality. We have not spoken of "healthful" or "unhealthful" religion. This is because use of the latter words would imply a discussion of the relative soundness of something before the individual got hold of it (or before it got hold of him.) It is certainly true that healthful and unhealthful religions exist. We believe that a religion glorifying the state as a substitute for the Christian God is possessed of, to say the least, unhealthful tendencies. We believe that a group which, wittingly or not, emphasizes but one aspect of the nature of God to the exclusion of all others is unhealthful, as for instance sentimental groups which say that because God forgives, he never judges. Yet our concern will not basically be with the healthfulness or unhealthfulness of religions; that has been well written about in other places.[4]

What we must also recognize is that a Christianity sound in ideas can be so interpreted by an individual that its total influence upon his personality may be progressive or regressive, healthy or unhealthy.[5] This fact has always been recognized by the church in some measure. As early as Cyprian's time, and probably earlier, we find church leaders counseling against those who went out to seek martyrdom. Heinrich Suso, the great mystic of the Middle Ages, was refused canonization because he had "punished" himself too much and too severely. Thus the basic impulse to sacrifice for the sake of the Christian cause was recognized as sound, but the church had to be sure it was "for the Christian cause" and not for something else of which even the individual might be

---

From Seward Hiltner, *Religion and Health* (New York: Macmillan, 1943), pp. 22-35, 41. Slightly abridged and edited from the original. Used by permission of the Hiltner family.

unaware. Catholic theology in particular has paid a good deal of attention to such matters.

But in recent years we have been aided to more basic standards for judging whether or not an individual is interpreting his religion soundly. A few suggestions about the criteria for distinguishing healthy from unhealthy religion are in order at this point. We suggest six criteria.

A healthy interpretation of religion must be related to the whole personality. To put it one way, it cannot profess to deal only with the soul or spirit and neglect the mind and body. There are still people who believe that because Christianity deals with the eternal and the hereafter it has no relevance to the state of things today. There are literalists who are concerned with salvation of the "soul" to the neglect of the individual's total welfare, which includes neglect of what is, from our point of view, his spiritual welfare. Much moralistic interpretation of religion belongs in this class. One might of course point out kinds of religion which emphasize the body out of proportion to the mind and spirit, and even some which emphasize the mind out of proportion to the body and spirit. But the danger of confusing the soul with the personality is more common in Christianity. That indicates both its high state and its great danger. The thing that we are forced to call the total personality is that to which our interpretation of religion must be related.

Religion must grow up intellectually and emotionally along with other aspects of the personality. This is not done by interpreting religion after the Alice in Wonderland fashion, believing seven impossible things before breakfast. If religion sometimes means dealing with the impossible, it is never *because* it is impossible. The great lawyer, Clarence Darrow, used to make annual trips to the Chicago Theological Seminary to discuss religion with the students. With his keen mind, he would nevertheless spend these sessions explaining why he did not believe in a religion that none of his hearers had believed in since their earliest childhood. An interpretation of religion which insists on remaining at a childhood level can only be rejected. There is no more point in "disbelieving" in a childish conception of God than there would be in disbelieving in what such concepts as "earth" or "art" meant to one as a child. There is no point in disbelieving in the existence of one's father merely because the early belief in the father's omnipotence has changed with the growth of the personality. Religious ideas and feelings must grow up.

Emotional interpretations of religion must be non-substantive. Religion, for example, which replaces the need for earthly friends by supplying heavenly friends may be more healthy than no religion at all, but it is still rather far down the scale. Religion brings something which nothing else can bring; it is not a substitute for relaxation, for work, for clear thinking, for making autonomous decisions, or for suffering. It is not an automatic solver of problems. In the basic sense it does aid in the solution of problems, but not as a substitute for hard work, clear thought or courageous decision. It strengthens the resources with which problems may be solved, though it may at times heighten the urgency of the problems.

Religion must be interpreted in a non-compulsive manner. There are some types of individual attitudes which are often incorrectly praised as fine religious outlooks. One of these is submissiveness, which is essentially a strategy of trying to get what we want by making the other fellow sorry for us. Mental hygiene has told us enough about the dangers of the model child to indicate where the danger lies. Power-getting through the institutions of religion is also sometimes, though not so frequently, mistaken for a sound religious outlook. There is the church worker who expresses his craving to lead or to boss only in church activities because there he does not expect to meet with the open rejection of his ambition which he would find elsewhere unless it were curbed by social interests.

More subtle than either of these compulsive ways in which religion may be used is trying to coerce others into loving us. Love and security are fundamental needs. The only proper way in which to get them is first to give them, as they are first given us in childhood. If the child is not given them, he will — indeed he must — try somehow to get them. Parents who have themselves been frustrated in receiving affection and basic psychological and spiritual security may not be able to receive spontaneous affection from their children because they cannot give it; and they may use coercive methods without any awareness of what they are doing. They may bribe, threaten, appeal to pity or to duty — and all of these techniques may be bound up with religion. Where religion is interpreted in this way, the soundest of Christian ideas will be badly warped. The compulsive element lies in the fact that, although the strategy is self-defeating, under the circumstances it seems impossible to do anything else. This is the spiritual vicious circle at work, and it scarcely makes for a healthy interpretation of religion.

Religion must be interpreted in an outgoing manner. It must have a social as well as a divine object. "Emotional atheists" are usually people who feel so defensive about themselves, who have so little real regard or affection for what they feel themselves to be, that they cannot possibly have regard or reverence for anything outside themselves. Love and regard (which are akin to reverence in the high Christian sense) are not quantities; and in their deepest respects are not to be compared with energy concepts. For one cannot love others (or God) more as he loves (or has regard for) himself less. Without some self-affirmation there can be little affirmation of others or of God which is not spurious.[6] Religion is sometimes interpreted in such highly individualistic terms that it has no real social reference. To call religion "what man does with his solitariness," as A. N. Whitehead does, is one thing which in a deep sense is true.[7] To say that religion has no social reference is quite another, as is the common attempt to separate a mythical "individual" from a "social" gospel. Religion will furnish no technical answers to questions of social organization, politics, and the like; but it will have reference to change in social organization as much as it will to the basic concerns for the status of others represented in all welfare movements. Religion must be interpreted in an outgoing manner.

There are other ways of approaching the standards by which healthy and unhealthy interpretations of religion may be judged. Those which are exploitative are unhealthy. Those which condemn the sinner as well as the sin are unhealthy; those which insist that the sinner is always more and greater than the sin are healthy. Those which are sentimental are unhealthy; as are those which are purely rationalistic or voluntaristic. Religion is not all idea, not all will. Those religions which make the personality equivalent to consciousness are unhealthy; those which see the whole personality as something both greater and deeper are not. Those which refuse to face the potentialities for evil in men as well as in man are unhealthy; but so are those which refuse to recognize the potentialities for creation and for good.

These criteria are not purely those of mental hygiene, nor yet of religion. They represent the infusion of mental hygiene discoveries into the pattern of critical Christian thinking. Without first accepting some basic Christian notions, it would be difficult to accept them all. It is beyond our scope to go much into their background; yet their character is sufficiently self-authenticating for us to recognize the validity of most of them even as they are stated. The fact that mental hygiene reinforces most of them indicates only the increased necessity for religion and mental hygiene to work cooperatively together.

It is useless, however, to consider the contributions which religion makes to health without this prior attention to the relative healthiness or unhealthiness of the interpretations of religion. Religious ideas themselves are important; and various criteria, including those of healthfulness or unhealthfulness, may be used to evaluate them. One idea is not as good as another. But there has rarely been any danger of forgetting the importance of the emotional interpretation. Hence this introduction.

If we suppose that a person has a healthy emotional interpretation of religion, in what ways specifically does his religious life support and enhance the health of his whole personality? Though it is valuable to put our question in this way, we should not forget that none of us have "perfect" interpretations of religion. What we do is to share certain insights into the nature of reality and our relationship to it. We are speaking, then, as much of religious outlooks and practices that may be used for improving health as of simple examination of the influence of fine religious insights that are already present.

Religion can help us to integrate our lives around the reality in the universe which is both rational and meaningful — the only worshipful reality. We have already hinted that a lack of reverence or regard for what we mean when we say "God" is a kind of blocking of natural trends toward socialization, and that it is caused by a feeling of lack of psychological safety and security within ourselves, however unconscious this feeling may be. If a person is tied up in knots inside himself, will power will not get him out. But if religion can give him a vision of something in the universe that he can actually trust, whose counterpart is within him, he is on the road to finding himself. In such a person's background we usually find that he has not been able to trust — that his mother, for example, sometimes slapped him and sometimes gave him a stick of candy when he disobeyed instead of being consistent about his emotional education. How can such a person be other than tied up in knots? Of course he may take religion and tie it up inside himself along with everything else. But if he gets any vision of that meaningful reality which does protect and bring safety and security, it may help him so that he will look for the evidences of security and affection that exist all about him and even in himself.

In the second place, religion may help to get a person away from egocentricity, infantilism, and the avoidance of responsibility. We know today that most stages in the development of the emotional life are accompanied by more pain than we later remember. Once the transition is made — for example, from the gang period to adolescence — the rewards of growth and new responsibility normally outweigh the pains. But in some persons the pains are so great as to retard the progress, and in none of us is the process entirely smooth or complete. And it is so easy to relapse into infantilism or avoidance of responsibility about some things that are especially important. Here religion may enter. Suppose that one's particular infantilism is to ridicule the prevalence of great social needs, to feel at least that paying attention to them is none of one's own business. And suppose that such a person somehow gets a vision that the brotherhood of man is the other side of the coin of the fatherhood of God? His social conscience can no longer be so dull or so dulled.

If we had a text, it would be this story from Luke:[8] "When a foul spirit goes out of a man, it roams through deserts in search of rest, and when it finds none, it says, 'I will go back to my house that I left.' And it goes and finds it unoccupied, cleaned and in order. Then it goes and gets seven other spirits more wicked than itself, and they go in and live there, and in the end the man is worse off than he was before." The search for health cannot be merely negative. Mental hygiene cannot be merely a process of chasing out evil spirits. For if the devils are chased out and nothing constructive takes their place, the person may indeed be worse off than before. Never take away a man's crutch unless you can say, "Take up thy bed and walk." And religion can say this, metaphorically speaking. Healthy religion ought to furnish the constructive occupant of the house. The evil spirits must be driven out, to use the ancient language, but that is only half the story. Health in our usage is not merely negative — it is also positive; but it cannot be truly positive unless the perspective and the insights of religion are a part of it.

There are two ways to reach a goal. The first is by keeping one's eyes fixed on the goal and ignoring the obstacles. This should be known as the cracked-shin method. The other is by keeping one's eyes on the obstacles and failing to look at the goal. We may call this the wander-in-circles method. Neither is adequate in itself. The great contribution of mental hygiene to religion is the pointing out of the real nature of the obstacles; the great contribution of religion to mental hygiene is the vision of the goal.

Healthy religion makes a person less dependent upon mere cultural standards, upon keeping up unconsciously with the Joneses. We live in a culture in which a man's worth is too often judged by his skill in competition, and especially in economic competition. The spiritual danger arises at the point where a man has no other standard of judgment of his own worth than that which this cultural pattern, as one example, can give him. We know of the suicides that followed the beginnings of the depression in 1929. Though there were individual factors involved, we could see in the lives of such persons the confusion of their success in competition with their very selves. They had no concept of themselves except that which they accepted from their culture; hence they had no resources when the crisis came. We are not implying that personal worth should be independent of what one does, but that one should have standards in reaching an estimate of one's personal worth which go deeper than that of keeping up with the Joneses. If religion gives anything at all, it is this. What but this can give magnificent courage to our brother religionists and others who are being persecuted in many lands? This is what we mean by the religious statement that every man is a child of God. There is something in the nature of the universe that in itself gives life meaning and value. We call recognition of this freedom, but it is not merely freedom of the will. We would do better to call it freedom of the whole personality.

We thought once that "human nature" was what we saw in people around us and in ourselves, that is, that our culture was the only possible expression of inherent "human nature." Those sciences which have contributed to mental hygiene, and in this case anthropology in particular, have shown us how false this is. Through the comparative study of different cultures, we have seen that inherent human nature is a great deal more flexible than anyone fully realized even a half-century ago.[9] Such conclusions suggest an additional reason why religion is not simply something to reinforce the prohibitions or commands laid upon the individual by the prevailing environment. Underlying assumptions become more necessary than ever. Science can make clear to us what the prevailing assumptions are, and that these are not the only possible ones; but only religion can furnish the kind of assumptions needed to transform the unsatisfactory elements in our own culture. Religion can speak of what life ought to be as well as pass judgment on what it is.

We know, too, that religion may actually have a marked influence upon the processes of healing. With mental and spiritual symptoms this scarcely needs proof. But there is also some evidence that religion has an influence upon bodily symptoms and processes.

Worship is a religious method that helps to develop healthy persons, though this is of course not the only aim of worship. Worship ought to and does mean many things; but prominent among them is the sense that an individual thereby becomes one of a community on the level of aspiration. He bows before that which he reverences, not so much to honor it as because it is natural to do so, and he thereby gets a sense of "communion" with all mankind. All high religions believe that this community is not artificial or merely sociological, but that it goes deep into the nature of reality. Worship is, then, a discovery in some measure of the reality of that community. It makes a great difference what one worships. We know now why the early Christians could not worship the symbols of the Roman Empire. For only in religions of the quality of Christianity and Judaism do we find a God who is truly worshipful. Worship itself is a natural activity of man, one of the motivating forces toward which is the desire for fellowship and communion; but it makes a great difference what one worships. For religion cannot be satisfied with reverence of that which is not worshipful, and cannot be interested merely in an integration of personality around ideals that are temporarily successful or efficient but that in the long run are destructive. The integration that brings real health must in the long run be one that corresponds with the nature of the highest reality of which we are aware.

Still another contribution that religion can make to health is in developing what has been called "tension capacity." Children want what they want when they want it. As adults we have to learn that the fulfilment of some needs or wishes must be postponed or even renounced. Thus we must learn to live in situations that would ordinarily produce tension without being tense. This is an inner achievement. No one else can do it for us. This emphasis on self-discipline (which does not mean bowing the head in defeat) rather than discipline from outside is an essential part of all healthy religion. Such religion can help us attain it.

Finally, religion appreciates and helps us to face what may be called the irreducible mystery of life. Fortunately life is not all a mystery; and religion performs a poor service to health if it tries, as has often been done, to create a mystery where none exists, or to seek allegiance by claiming a special hold on mystery. But when all that is said, much of life and experience is still a mystery. One may ignore or deny the mystery, which is blind. Or one may think only of the day when it may be past, which is romantic. Or one may work as the scientist does to make the mystery intelligible at specific points, which is praiseworthy, of course, so far as it goes. But some mystery still remains. Religion first of all faces this mystery as such. At its best, the mystery is never reverenced. We do not worship God because we have no idea of what He is. But the mystery is there.

In the ordinary experiences of life we know that problems must be faced as problems, not evaded or ignored. If one is to have health of spirit as well as of body and mind, on must apply the same principle in this cosmic realm. Emerson said of the great historian, Gibbon, "That man Gibbon had no shrine." A man with no consciousness of the mystery within his existence is ignoring or evading a problem. The proper attitude is, of course, not to magnify the mystery nor to worship it, but to face it as such. . . .

We have been able only to suggest some of the contributions which religion can and does make to health. We believe that these contributions are among the most significant, though not the only, functions of religion. In so far as religion helps persons to face realities, and especially realities which are actually or potentially evil, and provides strength or wisdom or courage to deal with them — it leads toward health as well as toward Christian character. Not all religion, not all Christianity, and not all interpretations of sound Christian ideas accomplish this; and one of our first steps in attempting to make the Christian contribution to mental health larger is to recognize this fact. Armed with some comprehension of what kinds of religious interpretations and practices tend to make for health and which do not, we are in a position to consider both the general and the specific contributions of religion to health.

Notes

1. Earl D. Bond, M.D., quoted in "Aims," Commission on Religion and Health, Federal Council of Churches.

2. J. A. Hadfield, M.D., "The Psychology of Power" in *The Spirit*, ed. by B. H. Streeter, The Macmillan Co., 1919, p. 110. Quoted by George A. Buttrick in *Prayer*, Abingdon-Cokesbury, 1942, p. 50.

3. Ibid., p. 51.

4. See for instance Charles T. Holman, *The Religion of a Healthy Mind*, N.Y., Round Table Press, 1940.

5. See Carroll A. Wise, *Religion in Illness and Health*, N.Y., Harper and Bros., 1942.

6. See Erich Fromm, "Selfishness and Self-Love," *Psychiatry*, November, 1939.

7. A. N. Whitehead, *Religion in the Making*, N.Y., The Macmillan Co., 1926.

8. Luke 11:24-26.

9. See for example Ruth Benedict, *Patterns of Culture*, Boston, Houghton Mifflin Co., 1934.

108 Psychology as Faith

Robert Coles

At various moments in these columns I have made snide references to the secular idolatry which it has been the fate of psychology and psychiatry to become for so many of us. My wife and our sons have suggested I spell out some of my thoughts on this subject, hence this essay. I must say that I speak as one of the gullible, the susceptible, the all too readily devotional — having put in years of teaching in medicine and pediatrics, in psychiatry and child psychiatry, in psychoanalysis, and done so with an eagerness and zeal and self-assurance, if not self-importance, I have yet to shake off, no matter these words, and others I'll write before I go to meet my Maker. "Once smitten, for life smitten," as a teacher of mine in high school used to say, and how we mocked his arrogant determinism, we who were so sure that no one or nothing would get its teeth into us unless we rationally and with utterly independent judgment had decided that such be the case.

In fact, I think we need to know why that teacher's observation does so commonly turn out to be true — the intellectual and psychological, and not least, social and economic "investment," so to speak, we make in what amounts to a way of thinking, as well as a career. The issue, as always, is pride, the sin of sins. To be a psychiatrist in America today, one says with all the risks of even more pride, of narcissism, is to take a substantial risk with one's spiritual future, as Anna Freud obliquely declared in one of her books (*Normality and Pathology in Childhood*). There she rendered

From Robert Coles, *Harvard Diary: Reflections on the Sacred and the Secular* (New York: Crossroad), pp. 92-94. Used with permission of the Crossroad Publishing Company.

a chronicle of the unblinking credulity accorded any and every psychoanalytic assumption, however tentatively posited; and as she said more bluntly to a few of us at Yale Medical School in a meeting both instructive and unsettling during the mid-1970s: "I do not understand why so many people want us to tell them the answers to everything that happens in life! We have enough trouble figuring out the few riddles we are equipped to investigate!"

Well, of course, she *did* understand only too well what has happened, especially in America: the mind as a constant preoccupation for many people who are basically agnostic, and who regard themselves as the ultimate, if passing, reality — which preoccupation constitutes a socially and historically conditioned boost to the egoism or narcissism we all must confront in ourselves. The result is everywhere apparent: parents who don't dare bring up their children, from infancy on, without recourse to one expert's book, then another's; students who are mesmerized by talk of psychological "stages" and "phases" and "behavioral patterns" and "complexes"; grown-up people who constantly talk of an "identity crisis" or a "mid-life crisis"; elderly men and women who worry about "the emotional aspects of old age," and those attending them at home or in the hospital who aim at becoming versed in steering the "dying" through *their* "stages" or "phases"; newspaper columnists, if not gurus, and their counterparts on television who have something to say about every single human predicament — the bottom line being, always, a consultation with a "therapist"; and worst of all, the everyday language of our given culture, saturated with psychological expressions, if not banalities, to the point that a Woody Allen movie strikes one not as exaggeration, caricature, or satire, but as documentary realism.

Especially sad and disedifying is the preoccupation of all too many clergy with the dubious blandishments of contemporary psychology and psychiatry. I do not mean to say there is no value in understanding what psychoanalytic studies, and others done in this century by medical and psychological investigators, have to offer any of us who spend time with our fellow human beings — in the home, in school, at work, and certainly, in the various places visited by ministers and priests. The issue is the further step not a few of today's clergy have taken — whereby "pastoral counseling," for instance, becomes their major ideological absorption and the use of the language of psychology their major source of self-satisfaction. Surely we are in danger of losing our religious faith when the chief satisfaction of our lives consists of an endless attribution of psychological nomenclature to all who happen to come our way.

I am tired, for instance, of the unwarranted, undeserved acquiescence some ministers (and alas, recently, priests as well) show to various "experts" who tell them about important "relationships" (talking about psychological jargon) and about "mental health" (whatever *that* is) and about the supposed "value" of religion (the height of condescension) in a person's so-called "psychic economy." I am tired of watching ministers or priests mouth psychiatric pieties, when "hard praying" (as I used to hear it put in the rural South) is what the particular human being may want, and yes, urgently require. I am tired of all the "value-free" declarations in the name of what is called "social science"; tired, too, of the complexities, ambiguities, and paradoxes of our moral life being swept into yet another "developmental scheme," with "stages" geared to ages.

As Walker Percy reminded us, and we ought to keep reminding ourselves, one can "get all A's and flunk life" — meaning one can answer some psychological theorist's hypothetical moral scenarios brilliantly in a given office or research setting, and then go into this world of sin and drive a car like an arrogant murderer, or push ahead in dozens of other ways that any moment may provide.

Back in the 1930s a host of brilliant people, including psychiatrists, psychologists, physicians, and alas, philosophers, ministers, and priests made their various accommodations, if not scandalous agreements of support, with the Nazis. Those highly educated ones might have scored well in some psychological theorist's "scale" of moral development; might have obtained good results in a Rorschach test, in a TAT test; might have mastered the Minnesota Multi-Phasic examinations; might have gotten top scores in our SAT tests given prospective college students; might have been pronounced in possession of "stable personalities" by an examining psychiatrist — all too "stable," they were, all too in resonance with that much touted "reality principle," namely Hitler's murderous authority.

Dietrich Bonhoeffer was a singular person indeed, and when he blasted psychology and psychiatry, as he did in his prison letters, we ought to take sharp notice. (We ought to take sharp notice, too, of efforts to stifle criticism of aspects of psychology or psychiatry. When such criticism gets called "resistance," or a mark of a "problem" — then an ideology is at work; agree with us or be banished!) Bonhoeffer, it seems, was prophetic not only with respect to his nation's tragedy in the 1930s and early 1940s, but also with respect to the continuing threats which certain aspects of 20th-century Western thinking pose to people of religious faith.

June 1984

109 Between the Priestly Doctor and the Myth of Mental Illness

Ian S. Evison

What should be the relationship of psychiatry to social ethics? Should psychiatry seek to be value neutral, to base its judgments wholly on scientific criteria? Or should psychiatry — must psychiatry inevitably — seek to promote a determinate view of the good person and the good society? Psychiatry has struggled with this problem since the beginnings of the profession in North America in the nineteenth century. Psychiatry has found itself involved in each great social conflict in the past century and a half. Before the Civil War, psychiatrists discussed whether *drapetomania,* slaves running away from their masters, was a mental disease (Cartwright 1851, 707). During the suffragette campaigns of the late nineteenth century psychiatrists discussed whether the discontent of women was a form of "nervousness" that might be remedied by a "rest cure" (Gilman [1892] 1980). During the Vietnam war, psychiatrists discussed how to cure the "inappropriate" reluctance of soldiers to go into battle (Bloch 1969). And during recent revisions in the standard diagnostic manual, the DSM-III psychiatrists have classified smoking as an illness and no longer refer to homosexuality as an illness.

During some periods, psychiatry has been confident that it finally has disentangled itself from social ethics, yet retrospectively it is hard to say that this was so. What is notable is the correlation

From Don S. Browning et al., eds., *Religious and Ethical Factors in Psychiatric Practice* (Chicago: Nelson-Hall, 1990), pp. 131-57.

between periods when psychiatry has been confident about its ethical neutrality, and periods when the nation has been complacent about the ethical virtue of existing social arrangements. Since every movement from abortion to women's liberation has turned up new insights about the ethical presuppositions of psychiatric diagnosis, the conclusion is unavoidable that the entanglement of psychiatry with ethics is permanent.

Yet it is an empty victory simply to force upon psychiatry the realization that judgments concerning mental illness have an ethical core. For psychiatry has at the same time a need to establish itself as independent of ethical entanglement. Nor is this drive based simply on Cartesian anxiety concerning relativism inherited from Western philosophic traditions (Bernstein 1983, 16-17). It also arises from the concrete exigencies of practice. Reliable and responsible ways to make difficult decisions need to be found.

Is there a third option beyond both the improbable claim to be ethically neutral and the impractical suggestion that psychiatry resign itself to relativism? Will psychiatry drown in indeterminacy if it lets go of the claim to be purely scientific? My aim in this paper is to describe such a "third option." To establish it, I propose to use practical theology and its reflection on the affirmations of ultimate concern of a community in terms of their implications for the goals, norms, and means of practice. In particular, I hope to show that, although the basic orienting goals of psychiatric practice cannot be determined by empirical technical reasoning, this does not mean that the ends must remain indeterminate: our choices concerning ultimate ends (*theo*) can be informed, if not determined, by reasoned discussion (*logy*). In this reasoned discussion, theological ethics plays a central role (Tracy 1977, 88).

A way to balance the ethical dependence and independence of psychiatry — I will argue — is to see the orienting goal of psychiatry as a minimum one of promoting "basic human functioning." A psychiatry that understood itself as in service of such a basic goal would be free from broader agendas of personal and social reform, and yet would have a solid base from which to develop limited self-critical and social-critical roles.

This paper is organized in three sections. In each I will bring into conversation representatives of the two tendencies in psychiatry that I have identified: Robert Lifton and Thomas Szasz, as representatives of activism and value-neutrality respectively. In the first section, I will sketch out an interpretation of the history of psychiatry broad enough to show how the historical arguments made by Lifton and Szasz are not simply contradictory, but rather are part of a larger whole. In the second, I will use the conversation between Lifton and Szasz to bring out the orienting world views of each. And in the third, I will add my own voice to the conversation as a mediation, arguing that each is partly right and that the profession of psychiatry should understand itself as serving the limited ethical end of *basic human functioning.*

The Social and Historical Context

The history of psychiatry has most often been written as an account of developing technologies of treatment; however, this view does not do justice to the complexity of the relationship of the professions to culture. The issues at stake are not narrowly technical. Lifton and Szasz each see part of this. The first task is to place their differing insights within a single larger history of the professions.

The psychiatrist who will serve in this paper as an example of activist psychiatry, Robert Lifton, found precedence for his ethically committed vision in the derivation of the word *professional.* Speaking of the struggle between ethically committed and ethically neutral visions of the professions, Lifton commented:

> One source of perspective on that struggle was a return to the root idea of profession, the idea of what it means to profess. Indeed, an examination of the evolution of these two words could provide something close to a cultural history of the West. The prefix "pro" means forward, toward the front, forth, out, or into a public position. "Fess" derives from the Latin *fateri* or *fass*, meaning to confess, own, acknowledge. To profess (or be professed), then, originally meant a personal form of out-front public acknowledgment. And that which was acknowledged or "confessed" always (until the sixteenth century) had to do with religion: with taking the vows of a religious order or de-

claring one's religious faith. But as society became secularized, the word came to mean "to make claim to have knowledge of an art or science" or "to declare oneself expert or proficient in" an enterprise of any kind. (Lifton 1976, 165-66).

There is truth in Lifton's observation of the religious origins of the professions. Law and medicine arose in the twelfth and thirteenth centuries as specialties among the clergy (Ullman 1975; Berman 1985). We can still see the faint religious imprint in the fact that the word *professional* carries connotations of responsibility and seriousness as well as technical competence, and in the respect that people in the professions, especially in the "learned professions" of ministry, medicine, and law, command in areas far beyond their technical competencies.

Yet one must be careful. Lifton concluded that the idea of ethical neutrality is a later addition and a by-product of secularization. This is not so. The independence of the professions, if not their ethical neutrality in the modern sense, is as old as the dependence of the professions on the religious substance of the culture. The independence of the profession is rooted in the relationships of independence and dependence implicit in the covenanting between Yahweh and the people of Israel and in the covenanting of feudal lords and vassals in which suzerainty relationships were reaffirmed — relationships in which the vassals provided services to the lords in return for privileges. The professions by analogy were in service of God and society but had independent domains in which they were entitled to exercise stewardship.

This heritage has been mediated to us through the figures of the Protestant Reformation who translated the substance of the medieval understanding of the relationships of the professions to society by the concepts of *calling* and *vocation*. In the call is the origin of both a special dependence upon God of the one called the legitimation of certain independent actions. The pervasive influence of these ideas has become well-known through Weber's *The Protestant Ethic and the Spirit of Capitalism*. Calvin's own summary in the *Institutes* captures the essentials:

> The Lord bids each one of us in all life's actions to look to his calling. For he knows with what great restlessness human nature flames, with what fickleness it is born hither and thither, how its ambition longs to embrace various things at once. Therefore, lest through our stupidity and rashness everything be turned topsy-turvy, he has named these various kinds of living "callings." Therefore each individual has his own post so that he may not heedlessly wander about throughout life. Now, so necessary is this distinction that all our actions are judged by it, often indeed far otherwise than in the judgment of human and philosophical reason. No deed is considered more noble, even among philosophers, than to free one's country from tyranny. Yet a private citizen who lays his hand upon a tyrant is openly condemned by the heavenly judge. (Bk. 3, ch. 10, sec. 6)

Secular occupations are "from God," and they imply a responsibility to society as a whole, yet not — as Calvin took pains to explain — an unlimited license to political activity. Also, contrary to the thesis that ethical neutrality is a by-product of secularization, it should be noted that Calvin gave solidly theological reasons for the independence from politics of people in secular callings.

In fact, so strong are Calvin's theological arguments against political involvement that one might ask whether he was condemning it completely. Within the concept of a "vocation" or a "profession" there is always a dialectic between involvement and detachment, and while Calvin stressed the detachment side of the dialectic, he did not destroy the dialectic itself. Calvin's statements against political involvement must be seen against the background of the debacle of the peasant's revolt in Munster in 1535, which raised the fear that the Reformation might lead to complete anarchy (Williams 1975, 378-81). When Calvin said cautionary things about political involvement by Christians, he was concerned that if involvement could be structured and limited, the possibility for both religious and political reform would be destroyed. He did not proscribe all political activity but only the questioning of the ultimate grounding or political organization of society.

The religious substance of the concept of calling in the professions dissipated with the rise of professional schools associated with universities in Paris, Berlin, and Bologna, and the general secularization of European culture in the seventeenth and eighteenth centuries. This resulted not in the loss of the wider responsibility of the professions, but rather in a transformation of it. For example, the privilege of wearing an academic robe implied a responsibility to the wider cultural heritage, transmitting, transforming, and applying the ethos of the culture in an evolving situation (Adams 1986, 269).

The rise of the professional associate in Anglo-Saxon cultures caused an important development in the dialectic of professional involvement in and independence from the wider culture. Thomas Hobbes called voluntary associations of all sorts "worms in the entrails of the sovereign": they made possible organized dissent by providing independent centers of legitimation and authority. Yet the ultimate decision of our political system has been to allow and encourage such associations. They have been important vehicles for mediation and for making politically effective the involved yet detached nature of groups in society (Adams 1986, 276). The professional association is a further development in which voluntary associations representing professions receive quasi-governmental powers within certain spheres. In its special status, the professional association repeats the same dual identity: it is a private group, yet corresponding with its special privileges it has a special responsibility to society as a whole.

Although to be "professional" has always meant to have special technical knowledge (as the priest knowing the liturgy), this knowledge did not become what we think of as technical knowledge — empirically based and supported by massive technology — until comparatively recently. Nor was it seen as the exclusive source of legitimacy. A number of factors, including the explosive growth of science and technology in the later nineteenth and early twentieth centuries, contributed to an expanded understanding of a profession as a group of people defined by their technical ability to perform a task or provide a service. In fact this definition eclipsed the understanding of the broader cultural involvement of professions.

In Germany, the consolidation of the unified state and the concomitant development of a rationalized bureaucracy led to the understanding of the professions as serving particular limited duties in a larger structure. In England, development of laissez-faire mercantilism gave rise to an understanding of professionals as independent business people who dealt with clients on the basis of freely negotiated contracts. Thomas Szasz finds precedence for his views of value-neutrality in this era:

> Doctors and patients have come a long way since the nineteenth century, but we had better think twice before we conclude it has all been progress. It is of more than passing interest to note, in this connection, one of the definitions of the word *profession* in the *Oxford English Dictionary.* "A profession in our country," wrote a British gentleman named Maurice in 1829, "is expressly that kind of business which deals with men as men, and is thus distinguished from a Trade, which deals primarily for the external wants or occasions of men." Until recently, this criterion applied particularly to the practice of medicine and law, the relations between practitioners and their clients being based on mutual respect and trust and of course, the studied avoidance of coercion. (Szasz 1987, 129)

While there are problems with this interpretation, Szasz is correct to turn to the era of the rise of British mercantilism for the antecedents to his views, including his opinion that the professional has no social roles aside from the services to individuals rendered in fulfillment of contracts (all other activities being without contract and hence, in his view, coercive).

The American professions were massively influenced by their German and British counterparts in the latter nineteenth and early twentieth centuries. The foreign impulses toward functionalism combined with domestic impulses, most notably the increasing pluralization of society that was occurring with massive immigration. Paul Starr has noted that the multiplication of nonstandard medical practitioners and the protection to incompetence provided by the anonymity of urban life led the medical establishment to assert a right to a monopoly on care (Starr 1982, 18). Further, in the increasingly pluralistic environment, ways were needed to serve people that were not dependent on commonality of culture or even language between professional and client. In medicine the triumph of the functional view was market by the publishing of the Flexner report in 1910, *Medical Education in the United States and Canada,* and the reorganization of the AMA in 1901.

The history of psychiatry in the later nineteenth and early twentieth centuries is both an example of these developments and a reaction against them. James Luther Adams, speaking from an acquaintance with Erikson and Fromm, said that "the appearance of the psychiatrist is itself a sign of the demand for professional men who are capable of a wider competence than is suggested by the term 'specialty of function.'" Yet Adams immediately questioned whether "the average psychiatrist has the professional training that fits him for his dealing with the basic questions of ethos having to do with the very meaning of life" (Adams 1986, 273). While the development of psychiatry can be interpreted as a reaction against the functionalization of medicine, it is also an example of it. The development of psychiatry testifies to the continued concern of the medical profession for something more than the narrowly functional, and it is also an extension of the functional view into new areas.

While it is tempting to interpret the history of the professions as one of inexorable increase in technical competence and functionalism, and to project this inexorable increase into the future (Ramsey 1970, xvi), this view is simplistic. It suggests that the only ethical challenge of the professions is to decide how to use new technologies. The complexity of the ethical challenge was highlighted at a recent conference in honor of the Flexner report ("Flexner and the 1990's: Medical Education in the 20th Century," University of Illinois at Chicago, June 10-11, 1986). The picture of medicine that emerged was one in which the technology of medicine would continue to develop, but in which the development of medicine as a whole would not be technology driven. It was pointed out that, in spite of popular views to the contrary, no "cures" to major diseases have been discovered since the polio vaccine in the 1950s and that researchers on the major "killer diseases" of cancer and heart disease hardly speak in terms of discovering "cures."

Psychiatrists have realized that the high hopes for "cures" to the major mental illnesses that accompanied the introduction of antipsychotic drugs and the resulting sharp reductions in population of mental institutions in the late fifties were inflated (Freedom et al. 1975, 1921). The mentally ill homeless today on the nation's streets are a guilty reminder that deinstitutionalization was not cure, and even has led some to question whether it is correct to speak of "cures" to mental illnesses at all.

The impulses towards functionalism in medicine that characterized the "Flexner Era" seem to be spent. If they are, it will mean that economic and social factors will drive medicine as much as technological ones. Social and preventive medicine will attain new prominence. It will mean also a new rapprochement between technical reasoning about means of accomplishing specific ends, and practical moral reasoning about how it is good to live.

Works that search out the historical conditioning and the ethical presuppositions of science have multiplied in recent decades (e.g., Kuhn 1970). While these works perform the hermeneutical task of showing the ethical and religious components of "scientific" ideas, few take the additional step of critically showing how the ethical or religious ideas can be evaluated. This is a crucial omission, since one of the reasons that professions in the late nineteenth century began to claim to be "value-free" was that they despaired of the possibility of ethical discussion in a pluralistic society. The insight that our ideas must depend on ethical presuppositions without the demonstration that our practices can depend on them is a counsel of despair. It leaves only the options of fideism and nihilism.

Having provided a broad cultural interpretation of the changing fortunes of the ethical dimension of the professions, I must immediately point out that one cannot go directly from an undertaking of the ethical dimension to practical decisions about what is to be done. The cultural situation is only one factor impinging on practice. The institutional roles of psychiatrists are evolving. Patient populations and the economics of psychiatric practice are changing. The technological base is developing. Yet, it is perhaps in such a complex situation that higher-level orienting perspectives for this profession become the most important.

The Contemporary Debate between Activist and Value-Neutral Psychiatry: Robert Lifton vs. Thomas Szasz

Two contrasting visions for psychiatry have in recent years fought for dominance: ethical commitment and ethical neutrality. To explore these positions and to help develop a mediating option I will bring representatives of these two tendencies into conversation in this section: Robert Lifton on the side of activist psychiatry and ethical commitments, and Thomas Szasz on the side of value neutrality. Although these two figures are alienated from much of contemporary psychiatry, they represent ideal types who embody significant tendencies in the profession.

Within psychiatry there is a significant undercurrent of belief that tends toward the view that "neuroses of society" produce individual neuroses and therefore psychiatrists must to some extent take responsibility for "treating" society as well as the individual. The implications of this activist view would enlarge psychiatry to almost priestly dimensions, giving the profession a role in writing ethical prescriptions for the good society. On the other hand, some believe that social problems will be generated as long as individuals are unregenerated. Taken to its extreme, this view implies that the only route to changing society is through changing individuals, and further, that one should only work to change individuals in the sense of seeking to restore or promote an ethically neutral quality of health. Most psychiatrists avoid both these extremes and claim that their concern is with something much less grandiose than whether ultimately society causes individual problems or individuals cause social problems. Yet, in order to explore the issues that exist between the activist and the value-neutral positions, I have not chosen people who represent this middle view. Like the doctor who waited for her patients to get sicker so that diagnosis would be easier, I have chosen, rather, two extreme cases. Although my purpose in this section is to point out the philosophical issues between the different prescriptions for change in the psychiatric profession, I do not mean to imply that the position of either Lifton or Szasz is without empirical grounding or that the existence of a philosophic dimension to their thought ipso facto brings into question its validity.

Robert Lifton

Robert Lifton has become known as a psychohistorian. Many of his books have been studies of individuals caught up in the dynamics of history. If one looks at how he interprets the actions of a specific person, it is easy to see the connection between the judgments he makes and his much broader views about human action and responsibility. His broader philosophical and ethical commitments and his related thoughts about the role of psychiatry are exemplified in his involvement in the defense of Patty Hearst.

Patty Hearst appeared to Lifton as a bland wisp of a woman caught up in terrorism. For him the analogy to the victims of Chinese brainwashing during the Korean war was clear. The *New York Times* reported his testimony:

> Prisoners of the Chinese, he said, were cut off from their past to make them reliant on their captors. Dr. Lifton said that in Miss Hearst's case the bank robberies cut her ties to the past. But he also said that "there was no ideological conversion" although her compliance with orders was "absolute."
>
> Finally, the prisoners returning to Hong Kong seemed to be confused and to want to indicate some remaining tie to the behavior and thought pattern set by their treatment, Dr. Lifton said.
>
> It was in that connection that he sought to explain another thing that has been a problem for Miss Hearst's defense: the clenched fist salute she repeatedly gave immediately after her arrest.
>
> "That is the sort of thing that I described as the last act of compliance among those coming back from China." (February 28, 1976, p. 32)

Lifton clearly believes that his ideas about people caught up in the dynamics of history could lead to insights of more general applicability:

> In my work . . . I found that studying an extreme situation such as that facing the survivors of the atomic bomb can lead to insights about everyday death, about ordinary people facing what Kurt Vonnegut has called "plain old death." Our psychological ideas about death have become so stereotyped, so limited and impoverished, that exposure to a holocaust like Hiroshima, or My Lai,

> or the entire American involvement in Indochina, forces us to develop new ideas and hypotheses that begin to account for some reactions we observe. (Lifton 1976, 29)

At the furthest reaches of generality these "new ideas and hypotheses" imply that the best way to understand human action generally is *as caught up in history.* As Lifton expressed it, the theme of death and the continuity of life became in his later work his controlling image (Lifton 1976, 61). This image became a "new paradigm" for understanding life (Lifton, 1976, 60).

Lifton asserted that, whereas in Freud's day the major psychological dynamics were repression and release of sexual energy, today the major dynamics are better understood in terms of the struggle of life against the forces of death (Lifton 1973, 20). He quoted Camus's character, the plague doctor, Dr. Rieux: "The task of life is to construct an art of living in times of catastrophe in order to be reborn by fighting openly against the death instinct at work in our history" (Lifton 1976, 116). Yet in stark contrast to the view of Camus, the struggle against the death instinct was not for Lifton a struggle of will, but of impersonal forces of life and death. The forces of life arise out of a mythic zone, which, quoting Eliade, he described as "the zone of the sacred, the zone of the absolute reality" (Lifton 1976, 145). The true principle of life is a principle of Protean transformation (Lifton 1961, 316). If Lifton thought the individual will has any significance, he did not discuss it. When he described the My Lai massacre there were no actors present, only embodiments of social forces. There was no massacre, only an "atrocity-producing situation," a combination of elements that were "inevitably genocidal" (Lifton 1973, 109).

> In all, it is not too much to say that the illusions surrounding an aberrant American quest for immortalizing glory, virtue, power, control, influence, and know-how are directly responsible for the more focused My Lai illusion. (Lifton 1973, 66)

Likewise, Patty Hearst is a tragic figure because "given who she was and what had happened to her, there was really no other path she could have taken" (Lifton as quoted by Szasz 1976a, 11).

In this understanding, the task of the doctor and of the good person generally becomes more the cure of a sick society than the cure of individuals:

> As a giver of forms the insurgent survivor must perforce become a leader. Dr. Rieux, the central figure of *The Plague,* is called upon to provide both medical and spiritual therapy. His antagonist is not only the plague itself, but the more general evil the plague stands for — "the feeling of suffocation from which we all suffered and the atmosphere of dread and exile in which we lived." (Lifton 1976, 120)

The role of a professional is to pro-fess. Doctors who claimed to be ethically neutral but provide "curative" treatment for soldiers who refuse to fight in an unjust war were for Lifton paradigmatic examples of those who would use the forces of life for the purposes of death.

Psychotherapy must be more than a means of curing the individual. When Lifton led group therapy sessions for Vietnam veterans, their aim was not so much to help individuals as to create new social arrangements and rejuvenate old ones.

> The rap groups have been one small expression . . . of a much larger cultural struggle . . . toward creating animating institutions. Whether these emerge from existing institutions significantly modified or as "alternative institutions," they can serve the important function of providing new ways of being a professional and of working with professionals. (Lifton 1976, 161)

Like the stone the builders discarded, the Vietnam veterans became the cornerstone of the new society. "I want to raise the question of the significance of an important change undergone by a relatively small group of men for a larger change in human consciousness now sought from many sides" (Lifton 1976, 21).

Is this psychology or social philosophy? It is hard to say at what point this line is crossed, but it is also hard to avoid the resonances of this with such clear exemplars of social philosophy as John Winthrop's "City on a Hill." The Massachusetts Bay Colony, like the veterans' rap groups, was created as an "animating institution." It was created to regenerate Europe "weighted down with the weight of death." Both Lifton and Winthrop assumed that in a regenerated society individuals would be regenerated. Both ran into problems when this did not happen.

Looked at in historical perspective, Lifton's rap groups continue the communitarian theme in American social philosophy, which has been renewed in a myriad of forms from Brook Farm through the Owenite communities, the social settlement movement, the Pullman Community, the Great Society programs, and the communes of the sixties. In each there was the assumption that in the society was the salvation of the individual, and that the way to rejuvenate society was to create model institutions. All of these experiments ran into trouble over the fact that even in the most regenerate of social arrangements some people remained stubbornly unregenerate.

It is intriguing how Lifton, like many American communitarians, shares features with romanticism and its responses to Enlightenment rationalism. His reference to the Middle Ages as a time before rationalism (for Lifton before professionalism) had vitiated ability of the will to act with conviction, is reminiscent of romantic nostalgia for that era exemplified by Novalis's *Christianity and Europe* of 1799. Yet like Balzac in *The Quest for the Absolute,* Lifton does not denigrate the scientists but rather enlarges their role to almost priestly dimensions. The way Lifton emphasizes reason as symbol-making in the mythic realm, in contrast to discursive reason, also closely parallels the distinction Kant made and Coleridge developed between Understanding and Reason (*Verstand* and *Vernunft*). Further in common with romanticism, Lifton is deeply conscious that there is a dark and destructive side to what lies beyond consciousness (as shown in Schopenhauer's *The World as Will and Idea,* 1818). Patty Hearst is a tragic figure, not because of the terrible consequences of her choices but because she is helpless before forces greater than herself. Most basically, there is the affinity at the level of anthropology: for the romantics, the Enlightenment had made people the masters of their own fates at the price of emphasizing what Wordsworth termed the "inferior faculties" of reason, and at the price of cutting them off from access to the dimension of truth itself, the "principles of truth" (Baumer 1973, 203). Like Schopenhauer and Coleridge in their rebellions against Lockean and Humean empiricism, Lifton breaks out of rationalism at the price of reducing the function of the will to that of receptivity to the forces of the universe, thus losing a conceptual place for choice in his thought.

Thomas Szasz

Thomas Szasz is a perceptive critic of Lifton because his basic affinities of thought are precisely opposite. He agrees with Lifton that psychiatry hides its dependence on ethical presuppositions, but his view of what should be done about the problem is precisely opposite. Whereas Lifton proposes that psychiatry should become explicit about its ethical commitments, Szasz believes that any hope for psychiatry — and on the question of whether there is hope he has become ever more doubtful — rests in reestablishing psychiatry on a value-neutral basis. This opposition between Lifton and Szasz arises from diverse sources, starting with the fact that each takes different practical problems in professional practice as symptomatic of the problems of psychiatry in general, and ending with the fact that each draws upon a different stream of social thought and a different philosophic tradition. Whereas Lifton's orientation was towards communitarian tradition of American social thought, and to romanticism, Szasz's orientation is towards individuals and the Enlightenment.

The task of sketching out the philosophic dimensions of Szasz's thought is both easier and harder than it was for Lifton. It is easier in that, while Lifton is rarely explicit or even conscious of how he draws on wider cultural resources, Szasz is both conscious and explicit. There is no need to conjecture about which philosophers he is indebted to. He tells us: Locke, Hume, and Mill (Szasz 1987, 354-55). However, the philosophic dimensions of Szasz's thought are also harder to trace than those of Lifton because, in spite of his voluminous writings, he rarely elaborates his own constructive proposals. Never an optimist, in recent years he has become bleakly cynical about the possibilities for change in psychiatry or society.

It is thus necessary to review the thinking of Szasz in two stages, first, to summarize his criticism of our representative of activist psychiatry, Lifton, and second, to review Szasz's constructive position from such hints of it as can be found in the nooks and crannies of his work.

Whereas Lifton developed his position by reflecting on the role of psychiatrists in such world-transforming dynamics as war, Szasz began to develop his position by reflecting on the role of psychiatrists in involuntary hospitalization of mental patients and, slightly later on, what he decided was the mirror problem, the role of psychiatrists as court witnesses. His observation was that involuntary hospitalization had become a means by which society or a person's family could control behavior that was bothersome but not illegal. Likewise, the insanity defense became a means whereby a person could be excused for actions that were illegal. Both practices make end runs around fundamental principles of democratic government — that a person can be deprived of liberty only by a finding of criminal guilt in a public trial, and that a person who performs a criminal act will be held accountable.

Especially at the time he wrote his original work on the myth of mental illness, Szasz was making observations on which there was broad, if not universal, accord both in the psychiatric profession and in the general public. What was controversial about Szasz's position was his generalizations of his more limited observations.

He arrived at his sweeping conclusion that mental illness is a "myth" by roughly this chain of reasoning: hospitalization for mental diseases has been subject to abuse, whereas hospitalization for physical diseases has not. Hence is it logical to look for the cause of the abuse in the distinction between mental and bodily diseases. What is the distinction? Szasz noticed that there is a fundamental difference between saying that someone has mental disease and saying she has liver disease. This distinction is revealed in the nuance of language. When it is said that a person's liver is diseased, the presumption is that an examination of the liver could be made and some physical anomaly found; the same cannot be said concerning a mental disease. It might be possible to perform an operation on a person's brain and find a physical anomaly there, but then it would not be mental disease but brain disease. In fact, it is in the space between mind disease and brain disease that Szasz located the possibilities for abuse. To say that a person has a "diseased mind" is, he argued, like saying there is a disease in the body politic. It is a metaphor expressing disapproval of actions that we judge to be wrong.

> Illnesses of the body reflect a general consensus on the definition of health. However, the behavior which people come to criticize and view as mental illness is simply a disagreement on whether or not such a behavior should be permitted. (Szasz 1983, 218)

Nor does it change the metaphorical nature of the judgment that a relationship can at times be established between mental diseases and physical diseases.

When a psychiatrist says that someone is mentally "ill," she is making a value judgment. Yet psychiatrists claim to make purely empirical judgments:

> [I hold] that contemporary psychotherapists deal with problems of living, rather than mental illnesses, and their cures stand in opposition to a currently prevalent claim according to which mental illness is just as "real" and "objective" as bodily illness. This is a confusing claim since it is never known exactly what is meant by such words as "real" or "objective." I suspect, however, that what is intended by the proponents of this view is to create the idea in the popular mind that mental illness is some sort of disease entity, like an infection or a malignancy. . . . In my opinion, there is not a shred of evidence to support this idea. (Szasz 1960, 116)

For psychiatrists and their patients to act as though mental disease is real disease is a double impersonation in which a patient pretends to be sick and a psychiatrist pretends to give treatment.

Szasz pointed out that belief in mental illness, or at least acting as if one believed in mental illness, can function as belief in myth — hence his well-known claim that mental illness is mythical. From this follow his radical normative claims about the practices of psychiatry: since they are based on claims concerning "mythical" illnesses, neither involuntary hospitalization nor the insanity defense are ever legitimate, and psychiatry can be made legitimate, if at all, only by reestablishing it on a value-free foundation.

In saying this, Szasz does not intend to argue that the phenomena referred to as mental illness do not exist. "While I have argued that mental illnesses do not exist, I obviously do not imply that the social and psychological occurrences to which this label is currently attached also do not exist" (Szasz 1960, 11). His point rather is anthropological (Szasz 1983, 207, 227). He wishes to "criticize and counter a contemporary tendency to deny the moral aspects of psychiatry (and psychotherapy) and to substitute for them allegedly value-free medical considerations" (Szasz 1960, 116). "The problem with the medical model is that it disguises moral matters as medical" (Szasz 1983, 221).

How is morality disguised as medicine? Supposedly mental disease causes a person to lose the capacity of moral responsibility, much as multiple sclerosis causes loss of muscle control. In actuality the direction of the logic is precisely the reverse:

> Critical consideration of the connections between mental illness and responsibility thus points to a relationship of profound negation: as death negates life, insanity negates responsibility. It is not so much, as is commonly believed, that insanity diminishes or annuls the mentally ill person's capacity for responsibility; instead it is rather that our idea of insanity itself negates our concept of responsibility. Although it appears as if nonresponsibility were a condition separate from insanity but sometimes caused by it . . . in fact nonresponsibility and insanity are essentially synonymous. (Szasz 1983, 269)

The problem caused by the negation of responsibility is not only, or even primarily, injustice to individuals; at a more profound level the harm is that all are diminished as human beings.

The logic of determinism does not — Szasz argues — admit of distinctions. If one chooses to view life according to the logic of determinism, all free will becomes an illusion. Szasz quotes Freud:

> Many people, as is well known, contest the assumption of complete psychical determinism by appealing to a special feeling of conviction that there is free will. This feeling of conviction exists; and it does not give way before a belief of determinism. (However) . . . what is left free by one side receives its motivation from the other side, from the unconscious; and in this way determinism in the physical sphere is still carried out without a gap. (Szasz 1987, 243)

While psychiatrists may often think, like Freud, that they free people to love and to work, they instead promote a view of the human as determined. While claiming to extend the sphere of reason in human life, psychiatry extinguishes it in a revived doctrine of predestination.

Thomas Szasz's response to Lifton's testimony in the Hearst case began with this broadside:

> Dr. Robert Jay Lifton, professor of psychiatry at Yale University, testified (as he was quoted as saying in the *New York Times*) that Patty Hearst "came under the category that I wrote about in my book of the obviously confused about what had happened to her." In the style characteristic of the courtroom psychiatrist, he thus makes Hearst into a "case" about whose conduct he, the brainwashing expert, knows more than does the "patient" herself. Such psychiatric self-flattery is acquired at the expense of the patient's self-esteem, not to mention, in this case, her father's money. (Szasz 1976a, 11)

Lifton discussed a metaphorical disease, brainwashing, as if it were a literal disease and so transformed a discussion of whether what Hearst did was right or wrong into a discussion of whether she was sick or healthy. Szasz commented:

> The crucial question becomes: What is "brainwashing"? Are there, as the term implies, two kinds of brains: washed and unwashed? How do we know which is which?
>
> Actually, it's all quite simple. Like many dramatic terms, "brainwashing" is a metaphor. A person can no more wash another's brain with coercion or conversation than he can make him bleed with a cutting remark.
>
> If there is no such thing as brainwashing, what does this metaphor stand for? It stands for one of the most universal human experiences and events, namely for one person influencing another. However we do not call all types of personal or psy-

> chological influences "brainwashing." We reserve this term for influences of which we disapprove. (Szasz 1976, 11)

In spite of this pointed criticism, Szasz was less concerned with the specifics of Lifton's testimony than with the principle that psychiatrists have no role in the courtroom. Such a role subverts the political system. This same criticism applied equally to Lifton's conclusion that My Lai was "an atrocity-producing situation," and to any conclusion that a person's actions are caused by social forces. Lifton was able to uncover the "fact" that actions are determined because he had assumed it.

However, Szasz's position was not simply a psychiatric version of law-and-order politics. His point was more fundamental: it is dangerous to excuse someone on the basis of lack of moral responsibility. This danger is evident if we note the affinity between how Lifton excused Patty Hearst's actions and how her father dismissed them — just as he dismissed the views of Patty's mother and of women in general as childlike (Weed 1976).

Another plausible psychological interpretation of Patty's "conversion" to that of her captors was that she wanted to force her father to take her seriously. If this was so, Lifton's "defense" that she was not responsible for her action was a cruel extension of her father's and society's sexism. As Szasz has said:

> That this psychiatric-psychoanalytic view on responsibility encourages lay people to be irresponsible and physicians to be paternalistic is obvious and requires no further comment. Perhaps because it is less obvious, people often do not realize that relieving a person of his responsibility is tantamount to relieving him, partly or entirely, of his humanity as well. The person who claims that he, not his brother, is responsible for his brother's welfare and happiness, stabs at the very heart of his brother as a person. (Szasz 1987, 245)

The insight has not been lost on oppressed groups that it is a short step from being excused on the basis of not being responsible for one's actions, to being dismissed as not fully human.

What has Szasz accomplished with his critique? Although he has not proven that action is free, he has refuted the opposing position advocated by Lifton. Thus, he has made two important contributions. First, he has shown, from a different, less sympathetic angle, what was said in my earlier discussion of Lifton's position: that in building his position Lifton must have drawn from sources other than empirical observation. I would not say that this fact invalidates Lifton's position, but I do agree heartily that Lifton did something other than deduce conclusions from evidence. However, I would put the case more positively, saying that in Lifton's position there is an interplay between empirical and philosophical perspectives. This does not mean that the involvement of psychiatrists in the judicial process, which Lifton advocates, is completely illegitimate, but we do need a discussion of whether such hybrid practical moral conclusions have grounds for legitimacy.

The second way in which Szasz's critique advances the discussion is to suggest the need for a second look at Szasz's own position. If he has not proven that actions are free on the basis of deductions from empirical evidence, then what is the source of this conclusion? It emerges that there is just as much of a dialectic between empirical observations and world view for Szasz as there is for Lifton. Whereas the communitarian stream of social thought and romanticism inform Lifton's work, individualism and Enlightenment rationalism mediated through laissez-faire perspectives inform Szasz.

It remains to investigate Szasz's own constructive position. Although this position appears only infrequently in his work, and hardly at all in his most recent publications, it is decisively important if we are to understand the commitments which lie behind his critiques. He presents himself as wanting simply to establish the truth by exposing falsehood, yet he is guided in decisive ways in his pursuit of these goals by broader visions of the good person and the good society.

Szasz's observation that specific actions are not determined shades into a more general conclusion: the world is a place in which actions are free.

> Man's actions represent free choices for which he is responsible, but for which he may rhetorically seek to avoid responsibility, most prominently

> through attributing behavior to literal and/or figurative gods. The traditional Judeo-Christian monotheistic god would be an example of the former, while physicians might be classified as the latter.
>
> The crucial moral characteristic of the human condition is the dual experience of freedom of the will and personal responsibility. (Szasz 1983, 23-24)

Szasz seems blind to the fact that the *will* is "mythical" in the same sense he argued *mind* or *mental illness* to be. Luckily for him this does not mean that *free will* is necessarily an illegitimate concept, but only that it is philosophically rather than empirically based, and is connected with a broader philosophical point of view.

Szasz's understanding of action as free is connected with his understanding of the struggle of reason against irrationalism.

> Man's awareness of himself and of the world about him seems to be a steadily expanding one, bringing in its wake an ever larger burden of understanding. . . . This burden then, is to be expected and must not be misinterpreted. Our only rational means of lightening it is more understanding, and appropriate action based on such understanding. The main alternative lies in action as though the burden were not what in fact we perceive it to be and taking refuge in an outmoded theological view of man. (Szasz 1960, 177)

The hero of this world view is the person who takes on the burden of understanding, aware of her limits, content with the slow gains of reason, and steadfastly refusing blandishment of the "theological view of man" and its successors. For Lifton, the paradigmatic examples of human wrongdoing are the psychiatrists who use the forces of life to promote war. But for Szasz, the chief examples are the psychiatrists who are the successors to the historic opponents of free will: the theologians and priests.

Recently Szasz has become so cynical about the alliance of psychiatry and medicine with the forces of determinism and irrationalism that he rarely mentions his ideals for psychiatry. However, he did indicate his vision for the profession in his early works. In *The Ethics of Psychoanalysis* Szasz proposed a vision of psychiatry that he called "autonomous psychotherapy."

> I chose this expression [autonomous psychotherapy] to indicate the paramount aim of this procedure: preservation and expansion of the client's autonomy. To emphasize the nature of the therapeutic method, rather than its aim, the procedure could also be called "contractual psychotherapy"; the analyst-analysand relationship is determined neither by the patient's "therapeutic needs" nor by the analyst's "therapeutic ambition," but rather by an explicit and mutually accepted set of promises and expectations, which I call "the contract." (Szasz 1965, 7)

The contract for Szasz was not one feature of therapy, but rather its essence. The ability to keep a contract became for him both the goal of therapy and the definition of health:

> In large part, the analysis of the analytic situation is the analysis of the contract. A contractual agreement, by its very nature, may be broken in one of two ways: by underfulfilling or by overfulfilling one's obligations. These two types of contract violation correspond, roughly, to the characterological postures of the person who exploits and the one who allows himself to be exploited. To an extent, the former is typical of the so-called oral-demanding, or greedy, individual or of the sadist, and the latter, of the so-called mature, or generous person or of the masochist. (Szasz 1965, 191)

The ability to give fair measure — the ultimate commercial virtue — is the norm of health. Self-sacrifice — except as it is required to precisely fulfill contractual obligations — is not only a questionable good; it is positively a vice. By this extension of his logic, Szasz revealed that "ethically neutral" is not ethical neutrality. If Szasz wants psychiatrists to stand above the fray of moral disagreements, and above the efforts to improve society, it is so as to be more visible as a beacon pointing beyond them:

> Perhaps the relationship between the modern psychotherapist and his patient is a beacon that ever-increasing numbers of men will find themselves

> forced to follow, lest they become spiritually enslaved or physically destroyed. (Szasz 1961, 310)

"Autonomous" psychotherapy produces the prototype of the good person and the psychotherapeutic relationship is the norm of all relationships.

Szasz's image of the good person was also an image of the good society, since he presumed, as all advocates of *laissez-faire* must to remain consistent, that there is a preestablished harmony of interests:

> In a modern society, based more on contract that on status, the autonomous personality will be socially more competent and useful than his heteronomous counterpart. Moreover, and very significantly, autonomy is the only positive freedom whose realization does not injure others. (Szasz 1965, 22)

If only each person would act autonomously, the best result would be achieved for all. To accept the notion that one person can hurt another by pursuit of self-interest is, Szasz concluded, like accepting the notion that "a sadist is one who refuses to hurt a masochist" (Szasz 165,23).

This is the Enlightenment as it filtered through Locke, Hume, and Mill, and even more directly into the American experience through Emerson. The standard of good becomes the good inside, and doing anything other than realizing this is betrayal:

> Nothing is at last sacred but the integrity of our own mind. . . . On my saying, "What have I to do with the sacredness of traditions, if I live wholly from within?" my friend suggested — "But these impulses may be from below, not from above." I replied, "They do not seem to me to be such, but if I am the devil's child, I will live then from the devil." No law can be sacred to me but that of my nature. (Emerson 1899, 47-48)

When developed to this point, autonomy is more than a good. It has swallowed up the good.

The social ideal of *laissez-faire* individualism has traveled a crooked course from the eighteenth century, when it was the battle cry of the middle class against aristocratic privilege, to the nineteenth century, when it reversed its meaning to become the battle cry of the robber barons against social legislation. The dictum that each is entitled to the fruits of his labors came to mean whoever has got it must deserve it. Emerson's "Self-Reliance" became William Graham Sumner's succinct answer to the question of what social classes owe to each other: nothing (Sumner [1883] 1986). Not only is social activism not morally obligatory, it is a disruption of social laws, what Szasz called "coercion," and what Sumner called "social meddling." Whereas Lifton's ideal of the professional was someone who professes, Szasz's ideal is of a professional who at all costs avoids doing so.

Lifton's and Szasz's views of the relation of professionalism to ethics are two parts of an earlier dual concept. Robert Lifton's understanding of the professions, as committed to sustaining and transforming the ethical vision of culture, is a distant relative of the view that callings are from God and of the understanding expressed in such customs as the wearing of academic robes by professionals. Thomas Szasz's understanding of the professions as independent from ethics is similarly related to theological understandings of the independence of those who practice a calling within an appointed domain of stewardship. There is a family resemblance between Calvin's view that we each serve God best by sticking to our individual callings, and Szasz's view that society profits most when each person sticks to a policy of noninterference.

Furthermore, these differing views of the professions are rooted in differences in basic anthropology. In *The Nature and Destiny of Man,* Reinhold Niebuhr has shown how romantic understandings of the human as determined and rationalist understandings of the human as free are by-products of the breakup of classic theological understandings of the human as self-transcending. This basic theological understanding originates in an Augustinian concept of the human as made in the image of God. Paul Tillich, also drawing heavily on this Augustinian heritage, described determinism and free will as a basic polar opposition in the ontological structure of the human. As Tillich described it, free will and determinism, or freedom and destiny, exist in dialectical relationship. Destiny is a structured aspect of myself and my environment that makes me who I am. It is the concreteness out of which decisions arise. Freedom, on the other hand, is the structure of destiny made real (Tillich 1951, 182-86).

Yet this view contains a danger. To say that two divergent tendencies in the understanding of the relationship of ethics to the professions are the "broken halves" of a classic theological understanding of calling or vocation points prematurely to a normative solution. Even if the two tendencies were once held together in classical theological formulations, this does not mean that they can be, or should be, again. It still needs to be argued that those theological concepts meet contemporary demands, particularly the demand that they be compatible with radical pluralism.

The reasons for this go beyond the fact that arguments based on the authority of a particular religious tradition are unlikely to succeed in a public forum. There are theological objections to any proposal that replaces the present with the past. History moves forward, not only chronologically but also theologically. Lifton and Szasz have done more than move away from theological understandings of vocation; they have advanced those understandings — and have done so for compelling reasons. Given this, can classic traditions of reflection still serve as guides?

Solution

Can a theological concept help guide our understanding of the relationship between ethics and the professions? In the 1820s, de Tocqueville observed that in America a distinguishing feature of public life was the way theological, and explicitly Christian, presuppositions guided public discourse: "Christianity reigns without obstacles, by universal consent; consequently, everything in the moral field is certain and fixed, although the world of politics is given over to argument and experiment" (*Democracy in America* [1835, 1840] 1969, 292, as quoted in Bellah 1986, 80).

Yet, in spite of what de Tocqueville said, the question of the proper role of such concepts is perennial. A generation ago John Dewey, John Courtney Murray, and Walter Lippman all argued the need for a public philosophy which, if it were not quite a public theology, would be at least informed by particular cultural traditions. As Bruce Kuklick has argued, neither Lippman nor Dewey quite managed to do public philosophy without doing public theology (Bellah 1986, 82), and, of course, Murray did not argue that one should try. Although Lippman, Dewey, and Murray disagreed on the substance of a public theology, Murray's statement of the need for one speaks for all three.

> And if this country is to be overthrown from within or from without, I would suggest that it will not be overthrown by Communism. It will be overthrown because it will have made an impossible experiment. It will have undertaken to establish a technological order of most marvelous intricacy, which will have been constructed and will operate without relations to true political ends; and this technological order will hang, as it were, suspended over a moral confusion; and this moral confusion will itself be suspended over a spiritual vacuum. This would be the real danger resulting from a type of fallacious, fictitious, fragile unity that could be created among us. ("Return to Tribalism," *Catholic Mind,* January 1962, as cited in Neuhaus 1984, 84)

The issue has surfaced again recently, first in Solzhenitsyn's Harvard speech, and then in Richard Neuhaus's *The Naked Public Square.* Yet there remains the suspicion that those who have been most strident in their criticisms have not understood fully the legitimate claims of pluralism. This is certainly true for Solzhenitsyn, whose own view of public life is both theocentric and Christocentric.

There is a group who would argue that "public theology" is an oxymoron. Or, rather, there are two groups who have historically opposed the concept of a public theology. Channing first observed that the extreme secularists and the extreme religionists come together to support the notion that if an issue is not resolvable by narrowly empirical means, then it is not amenable to rational discussion at all (Channing 1849, vol. 3 66). William James similarly observed the affinities between narrow empiricists and supernaturalists (James [1902] 1925, 19).

Does theology have a place in public discussion? Szasz stressed the human capacity for choice; Lifton stressed what lies outside the human choice. Each criticized religion for including in its understanding of the human that part of the dual understanding that he excluded. Tillich commented that in the contradiction between free will and determinism, reason looks into its abyss. Whether to view the human as a creature of reason or as a creature of vitality cannot be decided by theoretical reason or reduced to narrowly empirical terms.

A characteristic of classic theological understandings of the human is that they have held together free and determined aspects of the human spirit. Even when the human capacity for choice has been emphasized least, voluntaristic elements have been retained in theological discussion. There has rarely, if ever, been a time without general agreement that human beings must be recognized as responsible. This has not been simply a political necessity of a ruling power. It has also been an insight held most tenaciously when the church was most oppressed. The reason for this is one that Szasz accurately recognized: to be "understood" in the sense of being held to be not responsible is also to be dismissed, or regarded as not fully human.

In affinity with Lifton, an appreciation of the limitations of the will has also been part of classic theological understandings. The human capacity for choice is limited first by physical limitations and by habit, but more profoundly we are limited by internal divisions of the will that the apostle Paul referred to when he said, "what I would, that I do not; but what I hate, that I do" (Romans 7:15).

Whatever the ultimate foundations of religious truth, a proximate norm for it must be that it accord with common human experience. The further limits of religious truth may be beyond rational discussion; yet there exists an arena of discourse that is authentically theological, but about which broadly empirical public discussions and evaluations are possible.

While no imposition of the understandings of a particular religious tradition can or should be made, it may be possible for the concept of the professions to be renewed by allowing itself to be instructed by both tendencies of the classic theological concept of calling. Such an understanding of the professions would borrow its form from the theological concept; yet its content would be independently justifiable as a mediation between such poles of thinking as are represented by Lifton and Szasz.

Psychiatry should not seek either to "base itself wholly on science" or to serve expansive visions of individual and social good, but should rather serve the admittedly ethical but limited goal of *basic human functioning.* Basic functioning is a basement concept on which can be built the more expansive ideas of virtue. It contains a rudimentary view of what it is to be a good person, but only in the minimal sense of a person whose actions could be discussed as good or bad. It is a goal defined formally as that norm which, when violated, brings into question the humanness of an action, not its morality, and materially as the community consensus refined by reflection and critique.

A psychiatry which served the goal of basic human functioning would not claim to be based purely on science, but it would still be scientific in a number of respects. It would include reasoning about how to achieve the end of adequate functioning, and about whether a person corresponds to the minimum concept of adequate functioning. Furthermore, it would retain the asceticism often characteristic of science in that it would hold itself back from direct participation in debates about more complete understandings of the nature of the good person and the good society. Psychiatry has been accused of a poverty of ends. In the understanding I am proposing, psychiatry would make this fault a virtue, taking a "vow of poverty" concerning ends, practicing an ascetic attitude concerning larger visions of individual and social good, and making use of only that which is necessary for practicing its own vocation.

Yet this understanding of psychiatry could also be instructed by Lifton's side of the concept of calling. It could say, when asked to treat a soldier who would not fight, that it could serve the larger end of combat effectiveness of the unit only by serving the narrower end of basic functioning. To the extent that soldiers who were capable of basic functioning still chose not to fight, psychiatry would have no role in convincing them to change their minds. Likewise, psychiatry could not say anything about the metaphysical validity of religious beliefs, but would be able to say that particular religious practices undermined the capacity for basic functioning. Thus, although such a psychiatry could not follow Lifton in his larger demand that psychiatry help build the good society, it could contribute to a social good greater than the sum of its contribution to the adequate functioning of individuals.

Such an understanding of the role of psychiatry as serving a limited but authentically moral end, is in keeping with its position as a profession. A profession organizing itself into a voluntary association, such as the American Psychiatric Association, occupies a mediating function in society (Adams 1986, 268). Unlike a political party or a religious denomination, a professional association has a fiduciary responsibility to society as whole. Because of the fact that it is a private organization, not directly regulated by the government, and yet has a larger public role, one could argue that it rightfully should be conservative in the ends it chooses to serve. Such an end as adequate functioning is one that would allow psychiatry to serve both its narrower and its larger roles in society.

In the specific case of Patty Hearst, psychiatry would be able to testify concerning how her actions corresponded to a norm of adequate functioning. However, it could not make the kinds of global claims that Lifton made at the trial. It would need to recognize that in entering the courtroom it had entered an area beyond its fiduciary responsibility. Such a position in fact corresponds to the emerging self-understanding of the profession. The American Psychiatric Association has endorsed the position that psychiatrists should not be allowed to testify about "'ultimate issues' such as whether or not the defendant was, in their judgment, 'sane' or 'insane,' 'responsible' or not. . . ." (American Psychiatric Association 1982, 13). Even Szasz has suggested that within such bounds there may be a place for psychiatric testimony (Szasz 1983, 146).

The suggestion I make that adequate functioning become the governing norm of mental health has precedent in the American context. Richard Cabot, in a 1908 article entitled "An American Type of Psychotherapy," proposed a moral component to psychiatry that could be established on the basis of a broad social consensus; this is not altogether different from the concept of adequate functioning I propose (Cabot 1908, 7). His proposal did not win the day then, but may bear reconsidering now.

Notes

Adams, James L. 1986. *Voluntary Associations: Socio-cultural Analyses and Theological Interpretation.* Chicago: Exploration Press.

American Medical Association. 1983. "The Insanity Defense in Criminal Trials and Limitations of Psychiatric Testimony." Report G of the Board of Trustees.

American Psychiatrist Association. 1982. *American Psychiatric Association Statement on the Insanity Defense.*

Baumer, Franklin L. 1973. "Romanticism." In *Dictionary of the History of Ideas,* pp. 198-204. New York: Scribner's.

Bellah, Robert N. 1986. "Public Philosophy and Public Theology in America Today." In *Civil Religion and Political Theology,* ed. Leroy S. Rouner. Notre Dame: University of Notre Dame Press.

Berman, Harold. 1985. *Law and Revolution: The Formation of the Western Legal Tradition.* Cambridge, Mass.: Harvard University Press.

Bernstein, Richard J. 1983. *Beyond Objectivism and Relativism.* Philadelphia: University of Pennsylvania Press.

Bloch, H. Spencer. 1969. "Army Clinical Psychiatry in the Combat Zone — 1967-1968." *American Journal of Psychiatry* 126, 3 (September): 289-98.

Cabot, Richard C. 1908. "The American Type of Psychotherapy." *Psychotherapy* 1, 1:5-13.

Calvin, John. 1966. *The Institutes of the Christian Religion* (1559). Volume 1. Philadelphia: Westminster Press.

Cartwright, Samuel A. 1851. "Report on the Diseases and Physical Peculiarities of the Negro Race." *New Orleans Medical and Surgical Journal,* May, pp. 691-715.

Channing, William E. 1949. *The Works of William E. Channing.* Boston: George G. Channing.

Emerson, Ralph Waldo. 1899. *Essays: First Series.* Philadelphia: Henry Alemus.

Flexner, Abraham. 1910. *Medical Education in the United States and Canada.* Bulletin no. 4. New York: Carnegie Foundation for the Advancement of Teaching.

Freedman, Alfred M., Harold I. Kaplan, and Benjamin J. Sadock, eds. 1975. *Comprehensive Textbook of Psychiatry.* Second edition. Baltimore: Williams and Wilkins.

Gamwell, Franklin I. "Religion and Reason in American Politics." *Journal of Law and Religion* 2:325-42.

Gilman, Charlotte Perkins. 1892. "The Yellow Wallpaper." *New England Magazine*, January, pp. 3-20.

———. 1980. *The Charlotte Perkins Gilman Reader.* New York: Pantheon Books.

Ingleby, David, ed. 1980. *Critical Psychiatry: The Politics of Mental Health.* New York: Pantheon.

James, William. 1922. *Pragmatism: A New Name for Some Old Ways of Thinking.* London: Longmans, Green and Co.

———. 1925. *The Varieties of Religious Experience* (1902). New York: Longmans, Green and Co.

Kuhn, Thomas. 1970. *The Structure of Scientific Revolutions.* Chicago: University of Chicago Press.

Kuklick, Bruce. 1977. *The Rise of American Philosophy.* New Haven: Yale University Press.

Laor, Nathaniel. 1982. "Szasz, Feuchtersleben, and the History of Psychiatry."*Psychiatry* (November): 316-24.

———. 1984. "The Autonomy of the Mentally Ill: A Case Study in Individualistic Ethics." *Philosophy of Social Science* 14:331-49.

Lifton, Robert Jay. 1961. *Thought Reform and the Psychology of Totalism: A Study of Brainwashing in China.* New York: Norton.

———. 1961. *History and Human Survival.* New York: Random House.

———. 1967. *Boundaries: Psychological Man in Revolution.* New York: Random House.

———. 1973. *Home from the War: Vietnam Veterans, Neither Victims nor Executioners.* New York: Simon and Schuster.

———. 1976. *The Life of the Self: Toward a New Psychology.* New York: Simon and Schuster.

———. 1979. *The Broken Connection: On Death and the Continuity of Life.* New York: Simon and Schuster.

Maxim, Jerrold S. 1986. *The New Psychiatry.* New York: Mentor.

Neuhaus, Richard. 1984. *The Naked Public Square: Religion and Democracy in America.* Grand Rapids: Eerdmans.

Niebuhr, Reinhold. 1941. *The Nature and Destiny of Man: A Christian Interpretation,* Volumes 1 and 2. New York: Scribner's.

Ramsey, Paul. 1970. *The Patient as Person.* New Haven: Yale University Press.

Rouner, Leroy, ed. 1986. *Civil Religion and Political Theology.* Notre Dame: University of Notre Dame Press.

Schleiermacher, Friedrich. 1966. *Brief Outline on the Study of Theology.* Richmond, VA: John Knox Press.

Starr, Paul. 1982. *The Social Transformation of American Medicine.* New York: Basic Books.

Sumner, William Graham. 1986. *What Social Classes Owe to Each Other* (1883). Caldwell, ID: Caxton Printers.

Szasz, Thomas. 1957. "Commitment of the Mentally Ill: Treatment or Social Restraint?" *Journal of Nervous and Mental Diseases* 125:293-307.

———. 1960. "The Myth of Mental Illness." *American Psychologist* 115:113-18.

———. 1961. *The Myth of Mental Illness: Foundations of a Theory of Personal Conduct.* New York: Harper and Row.

———. 1963. *Law, Liberty, and Psychiatry: An Inquiry into the Social Uses of Mental Health Practices.* New York: Macmillan.

———. 1965. *The Ethics of Psychoanalysis: The Theory and Method of Autonomous Psychotherapy.* New York and London: Basic Books.

———. 1973. *The Manufacture of Madness: A Comparative Study of the Inquisition and the Mental Health Movement.* Frogmore, St. Albans: Granada Publishing Ltd.

———. 1976a. "Mercenary Psychiatry." *New Republic* March 13, pp. 10-12.

———. 1976b. "Some Call It Brainwashing." *New Republic,* March 6, pp. 10-13.

———. 1977. *The Theology of Medicine: The Political-Philosophical Foundations of Medical Ethics.* Baton Rouge: Louisiana State University Press.

———. 1978. *The Myth of Psychotherapy. Mental Healing as Religion, Rhetoric, and Repression.* Garden City, NY: Anchor Press.

———. 1983. *Thomas Szasz: Primary Values and Major Contentions,* ed. Richard E. Vatz and Lee S. Weinberg. Buffalo: Prometheus Books.

———. 1987. *Insanity: The Idea and Its Consequences.* New York: Wiley.

Tillich, Paul. 1951. *Systematic Theology: Volume I.* Chicago: University of Chicago Press.

Tocqueville, Alexis de. 1969. *Democracy in America.* 1835, 1840. New York: Doubleday Anchor.

Tracy, David. 1977. "Revisionist Practical Theology and the Meaning of Public Discourse." *Pastoral Psychology* 26, 2 (Winter): 83-94.

Ullman, Walter. 1975. *Law and Politics in the Middle Ages.* Ithaca, NY: Cornell University Press.

Weed, Steven. 1976. *My Search for Patty Hearst.* New York: Crown.

Williams, George. 1975. *The Radical Reformation.* Philadelphia: Westminster Press.

110 Crazy in the Streets

Paul S. Appelbaum

They are an inescapable presence in urban America. In New York City they live in subway tunnels and on steam grates, and die in cardboard boxes on windswept street corners. The Los Angeles City Council has opened its chambers to them, allowing them to seek refuge from the Southern California winter on its hard marble floors. Pioneer Square in Seattle, Lafayette Park in Washington, the old downtown in Atlanta have all become places of refuge for these pitiable figures, so hard to tell apart: clothes tattered, skins stained by the streets, backs bent in a perpetual search for something edible, smokable, or tradable that may have found its way to the pavement below.

Riddled by psychotic illnesses, abandoned by the systems that once pledged to care for them as long as they needed care, they are the deinstitutionalized mentally ill, the detritus of the latest fashion in mental-health policy. The lucky ones live in board-and-care homes where they can be assured of their next meal; perhaps they have a place to go a few hours a week for support, coffee, even an effort at restoring their productive capacity. Those less fortunate live in our public places, existing on the beneficence of their fellow men and God. It is extraordinary how quickly we have become immune to their presence. Where we might once have felt compassion, revulsion, or fear, now we feel almost nothing at all.

There are times, of course, when the reality of the deinstitutionalized breaks through our defenses. Three days after the Statue of Liberty extravaganza in the New York harbor last July, in

---

Reprinted from *Commentary,* May 1987, by permission;

the shadow of the icon of huddled masses, a psychotic man ran amok on the Staten Island ferry, slashing at enemies in a war entirely of his own imagining. Two victims died. Investigations ensued. For a moment we became aware of the world of shelters and emergency rooms, a world where even those willing to accept help and clearly in need of it are turned away because the state has deliberately dismantled the system where they might once have received care. Briefly, the curious wondered, how did this come to be?

Like its victims, the policy of deinstitutionalization has been taken for granted. It is difficult to recall that mentally ill persons ever were treated differently. Yet the process that came to be called deinstitutionalization (no one knows when the term was coined) only began in the mid-1950's, and did not move into high gear until a decade later. Although the term itself suggests a unitary policy, deinstitutionalization has had complex roots, and at different times has sought diverse goals. Its failure, however, was all but preordained by several of the forces that gave it birth. Any attempt to correct the debacle that has attended the contraction — some might say implosion — of our public mental-health systems will require an understanding of those forces.

II

The idea that the states bear some responsibility for the care of the mentally ill was not immediately obvious to the founders of this country. Through the colonial and federalist periods, care of psychotic and other dependent persons was the responsibility of local communities. They responded then as many of them do today. Almshouses and jails were overrun with the mentally ill, who, though thrown together with the criminal, tubercular, and mendicant, were often treated with a cruelty visited on none of the others.

Change came in the second quarter of the 19th century. New interest was stimulated among a small number of physicians in a system of treatment of the mentally ill begun in a Quaker hospital in England and called "moral" care. The name — with its ironic allusion to the immorality that had governed most other efforts to deal with the mentally ill — denoted a therapeutic system based on the radical idea that the mentally ill were more like us than unlike. If they were treated with kindness, encouraged to establish order in their lives, given the opportunity to work at productive trades, and provided with models of behavior, their mental illnesses might dissipate.

The belief that the mentally ill could be treated, and thus need not be relegated to the cellars of local jails, was championed by Dorothea Dix, a spinster Sunday-school teacher from Massachusetts, who traversed the country, cataloguing the barbarities inflicted on mentally ill persons and petitioning legislatures to establish facilities where moral treatment might be applied. Her efforts and those of others resulted in the creation of a network of state-operated hospitals. As the states assumed ever wider responsibility for the mentally ill, the hospitals grew in size, absorbing the denizens of the jails and poorhouses.

In the wake of the Civil War, as the burdens created by waves of immigration stood unrelieved by increases in funding, the public hospitals surrendered the goal of active treatment. They continued to expand, but changed into enormous holding units, to which the mentally ill were sent and from which many never emerged. Once again sliding to the bottom of the list of social priorities, the mentally ill were often treated with brutality. At best, they suffered from benign indifference to anything more than their needs for shelter and food.

Such had been the condition of public mental hospitals for nearly eighty years as World War II came to a close. Periodic efforts at reform had left them largely untouched. Over one-half million patients languished in their wards, accounting for half of the occupants of hospital beds in the country. The state hospitals had swelled to bloated proportions. Pilgrim State Hospital on Long Island, New York's largest, held nearly 20,000 patients. St. Elizabeth's in Washington, D.C., the only mental hospital operated directly by the federal government, had its own railroad and post office. Most facilities, located away from major population centers, used patients to work large farms on their grounds, thus defraying a good part of the costs of running the institution.

A new generation of psychiatrists, returning from the war, began to express their disquiet with the system as it was. They had seen how rapid-treatment models in hospitals close to the front and the introduction of group therapy had drastically cut the morbidity of psychiatric conditions evident earlier in World War I. With the belief that patients need not spend their lives sitting idly in smoky, locked wards, they determined to tackle a situation which Albert Deutsch had described as the "shame of the states."

These psychiatrists and their disciples, emphasizing the desirability of preparing patients for return to the community, began to introduce reforms into the state systems. Wards that had been locked for nearly a century were opened; male and female patients were allowed to mix. Active treatment programs were begun, and many patients, particularly elderly ones, were screened prior to admission, with efforts made to divert them where possible to more appropriate settings. The effects soon became evident. More than a century of inexorable growth in state-hospital populations began to reverse itself in 1955, when the number of residents peaked at just over 558,000. The first phase of deinstitutionalization was under way.

A second factor was introduced at this point. In 1952, French scientists searching for a better antihistamine discovered chlorpromazine, the first medication with the power to mute and even reverse the symptoms of psychosis. Introduced in this country in 1954 under the trade name Thorazine (elsewhere the medication was called Largactil, a name that better conveys the enormous hope that accompanied its debut), the drug rapidly and permanently altered the treatment of severe mental illness. The ineffective treatments of the past, from bleedings and purgings, cold baths and whirling chairs, to barbiturates and lobotomies, were supplanted by a genuinely effective medication. Thorazine's limitations and side-effects would become better known in the future; for now the emphasis was on its ability to suppress the most flagrant symptoms of psychosis.

Patients bedeviled by hallucinatory voices and ridden by irrational fears, who previously could have been managed only in inpatient units, now became tractable. They still suffered from schizophrenia, still manifested the blunted emotions, confused thinking, odd postures that the disease inflicts. But the symptoms which had made it impossible for them to live outside the hospital could, in many cases, be controlled.

Psychiatrists still argue over whether the new ideas of hospital and community treatment or the introduction of Thorazine provided the initial push that lowered state-hospital censuses. The truth is that both factors probably played a role, with the medications allowing the new psychiatric enthusiasm for community-based care to be applied to a larger group of patients than might otherwise have been the case. The effects of the first stage of deinstitutionalization can be seen in the figures for patients resident in state psychiatric facilities. By 1965 that number had decreased gradually but steadily to 475,000.

III

Until the mid-1960's, deinstitutionalization had been a pragmatic innovation; its driving force was the conviction that some patients could be treated and maintained in the community. Although large-scale studies supporting this belief were lacking, psychiatrists' everyday experiences confirmed its validity. Further, control of the process of discharging patients was solidly in the hands of mental-health professionals. By the end of the first decade of deinstitutionalization, however, the process was in the midst of being transformed.

What had begun as an empirical venture was now about to become a movement. Deinstitutionalization was captured by the proponents of a variety of ideologists, who sensed its value for their causes. Although their underlying philosophies were often at odds, they agreed on what seemed a simple statement of mission: all patients should be treated in the community or in short-term facilities. The state hospitals should be closed.

Some of the earliest advocates of this position were themselves psychiatrists. Unlike their predecessors, who first let light and air into the back wards, these practitioners were not content to whittle away at the number of patients in state hospitals. They sought systemic changes. The pragmatism of the psychiatrists, persuaded on their return from the war that many patients could be treated without long-term hospitalization, was transmuted into a rigid credo. No patient should be confined in a massive state facility, it was now declared. All treatment should take place in the community.

These advocates, who saw themselves as part of a new subspecialty of community psychiatry, were heavily influenced by the sociologists of institutional life, notably Erving Goffman, the author of *Asylums.* The book, based on a year of observing patients and staff at St. Elizabeth's Hospital in Washington, D.C., catalogued the ways, subtle and blatant, in which patients were forced by the demands of a large institution into an unthinking conformity of behavior and thought. The rules that constrained their behavior, Goffman wrote, derived not from a consideration of therapeutic needs, but from the desires of hospital staff members to simplify their own tasks. From Goffman's work a new syndrome was defined — "institutionalism": the progressive loss of functional abilities caused by the denial of opportunities to make choices for oneself, and leading to a state of chronic dependency. Robbed of their ability to function on their own, state-hospital patients had no alternative but to remain in an environment in which their lives were directed by others.

Community psychiatry embellished Goffman's charges. Articles in professional journals began to allege that the chronic disability accompanying psychiatric illnesses, particularly schizophrenia, was not a result of the disease process itself, but an effect of archaic treatment methods in which patients were uprooted from their own communities. With the attachments of a lifetime severed, often irretrievably, patients lost the incentive and then the will to maintain their abilities to relate to others and function in social environments. Thus, state hospitals, in addition to subjecting patients to abominable physical conditions — the stuff of exposés since the 1860's — were exacerbating and embedding the very symptoms they purported to treat. The only way to prevent the development of a new generation of dysfunctional chronic patients was to close the hospitals.

Of course, alternative places of treatment would have to be created. In 1963, the new community psychiatrists persuaded a President already interested in mental-health issues and a receptive Congress that, with a new approach, chronicity could be averted. The consensus that emerged was embodied in the Community Mental Health Center Act of 1963. With seed money from the federal government, the law encouraged the development of outpatient clinics in every area of the country. Ultimately, it was hoped, no citizen would live outside one of the 2,000 designated "catchment areas" in which community-based treatment could be provided.

Psychiatric proponents of closing the state hospitals found unlikely allies in a group of civil-libertarian attorneys who were now turning their attention to the mentally ill. Fresh from victories in the civil-rights movement, and armed with potent new constitutional interpretations that restricted the power of the state to infringe personal liberties, these lawyers sought the dismantling of state hospitals as the first step in eliminating all coercive treatment of the mentally ill. They sought this end not simply because they believed that encouraging autonomy reduced chronicity, as the community psychiatrists claimed, but because in their own hierarchy of values individual autonomy was paramount.

Mentally ill persons seemed particularly appropriate targets for a crusade against governmental power, for the state was depriving them of liberty — with ostensibly benevolent aims, yet in conditions that belied the goal of treatment. It appeared to these critics that ultimately the state was concerned most with maintaining imbalances of power that favored the privileged classes and with suppressing dissent. By confining and discrediting the more obstreperous members of the lower classes, the mental-health system served as a pillar of the ruling elite.

Critiques of this sort were not rare in the late 1960's, when skepticism of established power was, for many, a prerequisite of intellectual discourse. Its application to psychiatry was encouraged, however, by the writings of iconoclastic psychiatrists like Thomas Szasz, who maintained that mental illness was a "myth," perpetuated only as a mechanism for social control, and R. D. Laing, whose books touted the value of the psychotic experience for elevating one's perceptions of the meaning of life. Additional academic support for Szasz's views came from sociologists known as labeling theorists who believed that deviance was a creation of the person with the power so to name it.

Whereas the community psychiatrists initially sought to achieve their ends through a legislative reconstruction of the mental-health system, the civil-libertarian attorneys favored the judicial route. They attacked the major mechanism for entry into the public mental-health system, the statutes governing involuntary commitment. These laws, they charged, were unconstitutionally broad in allowing any mentally ill person in need of treatment to be hospitalized against his will. Surely individual liberty could not legitimately be abridged in the absence of a substantial threat to a person's life or to the life of others. In addition, they alleged that the wording of the statutes, many little changed for one hundred years, was impermissibly vague; particularly problematic for the civil libertarians were the definitions of mental illness and the circumstances that rendered one committable.

In an era of judicial activism, many courts, both federal and state, agreed. Involuntary commitment came to be limited to persons exhibiting danger to themselves or others; strict, criminal-law-style procedures came to be required, including judicial hearings with legal representation. As the trend in the courts became apparent, many legislatures altered their statutes in anticipation of decisions in their own jurisdictions, or in emulation of California, where civil libertarians won legislative approval of a tightened statute even without the threat of court action.

The final common pathway of this complex set of interests led through the state legislatures. Although concerns about better treatment for chronic patients and the enhancement of individual liberty were not foreign here, more mundane concerns made themselves felt as well. The old state mental hospitals took up a significant proportion of most state budgets, in some jurisdictions the largest single allocation. Advocates of closing the old facilities were not reticent in claiming enormous cost savings if patients were transferred to community-based care. And even if real costs remained constant, the availability of new federal entitlement programs such as Supplemental Security Income and Medicaid, to which outpatients but not inpatients would have access, promised a shift in the cost of supporting these people from the states to the federal government.

In many states, this was the final straw. The possibility that patients could be cared for in the community at less expense, perhaps with better results, and certainly with greater liberty, was an irresistible attraction. Deinstitutionalization was too valuable a tool of social policy to remain a discretionary option of state-hospital psychiatrists. It now became an avowed goal of the states. Quotas were set for reductions in state-hospital populations; timetables were drawn up for the closure of facilities. Individual discretion in the release of patients was overridden by legislative and administrative fiat. Patients were to be released at all costs. New admissions were to be discouraged, in some cases prohibited. In the words of Joseph Morrissey, if the first phase of deinstitutionalization reflected an opening of the back door, the second phase was marked by a closing of the front door.

Thus did deinstitutionalization assume the form in which we know it today.

IV

If a decrease in patient population is the sole measure for gauging the outcome of deinstitutionalization, the success of the policy is unquestionable. From 1965 to 1975, in-patient populations in state hospitals fell from 475,000 to 193,000. By 1980, the figure was 137,000, and today all indications are that the number is even smaller. Relatively few of the state hospitals closed. The majority shrank from bustling colonies with thousands of patients to enclaves of a few hundred patients, clustered in a few buildings in largely abandoned campuses.

Yet by the mid-1970's professionals in the field and policy analysts had begun to ask whether the underlying goals espoused by the advocates of deinstitutionalization were really being met. Are the majority of the mentally ill, by whatever measure one chooses to apply, better off now than before the depopulation of the state hospitals? The inescapable answer is that they are not.

A large part of the reason for the movement's failure stems from its overly optimistic belief in the ability of many mentally ill persons to function on their own, without the much-maligned structure of state-hospitals care. Rather than liberating patients from the constraints of institutional life, the movement to reduce the role of state hospitals merely shifted the locus of their regimented existence. Indeed, *trans*institutionalization may be a better term to describe the process that occurred. It is estimated that 750,000 chronic mentally ill persons now live in nursing homes, a figure nearly 50 percent higher than the state-hospital population as its 1955 apogee. Additional hundreds of thousands live in board-and-care homes or other group residences. Many of these facilities, particularly the nursing homes, have locked wards nearly indistinguishable from the old state hospitals. They are, in psychiatrist H. Richard Lamb's evocative phrase, the asylums in the community.

Many of the mentally ill, of course, have drifted away entirely from any form of care. Given the freedom to choose, they have chosen to live on the streets; according to various estimates they comprise between 40 and 60 percent of homeless persons. They filter into overcrowded shelters — as Juan Gonzalez did before becoming the agent of his fantasies on the Staten Island ferry — where they may experience fleeting contact with mental-health personnel. The lack of external structure is reflected in their internal disorganization. Whatever chance they had to wire together their shattered egos has been lost.

What of the hopes of the community psychiatrists that liberating patients from state hospitals would prevent the development of the chronic dependency which stigmatizes the mentally ill and inhibits their reintegration into the community? They learned a sad lesson suspected by many of their colleagues all along. The withdrawal, apathy, bizarre thinking, and oddities of behavior which Goffman and his students attributed to "institutionalism" appear even in the populations maintained outside of institutions. They are the effects of the underlying psychiatric illnesses, usually schizophrenia, not of the efforts to treat those conditions. And contrary to the claims of the labeling theorists, it is the peculiar behavior of severely psychotic persons, not the fact that they were once hospitalized and "labeled" ill, that stigmatizes and isolates them in the community. Studies of discharged patients demonstrate that those who continue to display the signs of their illnesses and disrupt the lives of others are the ones who suffer social discrimination.

To some extent, the community psychiatrists never had a chance to test their theories. The community mental-health centers in which they envisioned care taking place were, for the most part, never built. Fewer than half of the projected 2,000 centers reached operation. Of those that did, many turned from the severely ill to more desirable patients, less disturbed, easier to treat, more gratifying, and above all, as federal subsidies were phased out, able to pay for their own care. A few model programs, working with a selected group of cooperative patients, are all the community psychiatrists have to show for their dreams. But the evidence suggests that even optimal levels of community care cannot enable many mentally ill persons to live on their own.

The goals of the civil libertarians, except in the narrowest sense, have fared little better. If one conceives that liberty is enhanced merely by the release of patients from the hospitals to the streets, then perhaps one might glean satisfaction from the course of deinstitutionalization to date. But if individual autonomy implies the ability to make reasoned choices in the context of a coherent plan for one's life, then one must conclude that few of the deinstitutionalized have achieved autonomy. One study found fewer than half the residents of a large board-and-care home with a desire to change anything at all about their lives, no matter how unrealistic their objectives might be. If the facade of autonomy has been expanded, the reality has suffered.

Finally, and with fitting irony, not even the hope that deinstitutionalization would save money has been realized. It was originally anticipated that the closing of state hospitals would allow the transfer of their budgetary allocations to community facilities. But state hospitals proved difficult to close. As many hospitals existed in 1980 as in 1955, despite a fourfold reduction in patients. Even with current, broad definitions of who can survive in the community, tens of thousands of patients nationwide continue to require institutional care, often long-term. They are so regressed, self-destructive, violent, or otherwise disruptive that no community can tolerate them in its midst. Moreover, the communities that derive jobs from the facilities have fought hard to preserve them. As censuses have fallen, per-capita costs of care have increased, pushed up even further by pressure to improve the level of care for those who remain. Many costs for the treatment of outpatients have been redistributed, with the federal and local governments bearing heavier burdens; but no one has ever demonstrated overall savings. Even as the quality of life for many mentally ill persons has fallen, state mental-health budgets have continued to expand.

V

Both the failure of deinstitutionalization and our seeming paralysis in correcting it stem from the same source: the transformation of deinstitutionalization from a pragmatic enterprise to an ideological crusade. The goal of the first phase of the process — to treat in the community all mentally ill persons who did not require full-time supervision and might do equally well or better in alternate settings — was hardly objectionable. Had state-hospital populations been reduced in a deliberate manner, with patients released no faster than treatment, housing, and rehabilitative facilities became available in the community, the visions of psychiatry's Young Turks of the 1950's might well have been realized.

Once the release of state-hospital patients became a matter of faith, however, this individualized approach was thrown to the winds. In the Manichaean view that soon predominated, confinement in state hospitals came to be seen as invariably bad. Freedom was always preferred, both for its own sake and because it had a desirable, albeit mysterious therapeutic value. Further, we came to doubt our own benevolent impulses, yielding to those who claimed that any effort to act for the welfare of others was illegitimate and doomed to end with their oppression. Thus, although we may now recognize the failure of deinstitutionalization, we as a society have been unable to reverse course; these same ideologies continue to dominate our policies not by the power of logic but by the force of habit.

It is time to rethink these presuppositions. That freedom *per se* will not cure mental illness is evident from the abject condition of so many of the deinstitutionalized. More difficult to deal with is the belief that even if the lives of hundreds of thousands of mentally ill persons have been made objectively more miserable by the emptying of our state hospitals, we have no right to deprive people of liberty, even for their own benefit. In the currently fashionable jargon of bioethics, the value of autonomy always trumps the value of beneficence.

Interestingly, this position is now being challenged by a number of our leading public philosophers, who have called attention to its neglected costs. Robert Burt of the Yale Law School and Daniel Callahan of the Hastings Center, for example, have taken aim at the belief that the freedom to do as we please should be our primary societal value. This emphasis on individual autonomy, they point out, has come to mean that in making our choices, as long as we do not actively infringe on the prerogatives of others, we face no obligation to consider them and their needs. The result has been the creation of an atomistic community in which, relieved of the duty to care for others, we pursue our goals in disregard of the suffering that surrounds us. This lack of an obligation to care for others has been transmuted in some cases into an actual duty to ignore their suffering, lest we act in such a way as to limit their autonomy.

Although Burt and Callahan have not addressed themselves to mental-health policy *per se*, there is no better illustration of their thesis. The right to liberty has become an excuse for failing to address, even failing to recognize, the needs of the thousands of abandoned men and women we sweep by in our streets, in our parks, and in the train and bus stations where they gather for warmth. We have persuaded ourselves that it is better to ignore them — that we have an obligation to ignore them — because their autonomy would be endangered by our concern.

But the impulse to act for the benefit of others is the adhesive substance that binds human communities together. A value system that loosens those bonds by glorifying individual autonomy threatens the cohesion of the polity. Nobody wants to live in a society characterized by unrestrained intervention (even with benevolent intent), but that does not mean we must reject altogether the notion that doing good for others, despite their reluctance, is morally appropriate under some conditions.

Meaningful autonomy does not consist merely in the ability to make choices for oneself. Witness the psychotic ex-patients on the streets, who withdraw into rarely used doorways, rigidly still for hours at a time, hoping, like chameleons on the forest floor, that immobility will help them fade into the grimy urban background, bringing safety and temporary peace from the world which they envision as a terrifying series of threats. Can the choices they make, limited as they are to the selection of a doorway for the day, be called a significant embodiment of human autonomy? Or is the behavior rather to be understood on the level of a simple reflex — autonomous only in a strictly formal sense?

Far from impinging on their autonomy, treatment of such psychotics, even coercive treatment, would not only hold out some hope of mitigating their condition but might simultaneously increase their capacity for more sophisticated autonomous choices. To adopt the typological scheme of the philosopher Bruce Miller, patients might thereby be enabled to move from mere freedom of action to choices that reflect congruence with personal values, effective rational deliberation, and moral reflection. Our intervention, though depriving them of the right to autonomy in the short term, may enhance that quality in the long run. In such circumstances, benevolence and autonomy are no longer antagonistic principles.

VI

Deinstitutionalization is a remnant of a different era in our political life, one in which we sought broadly-framed solutions to human problems that have defied man's creativity for millennia. In the 1960's and 70's we declared war on poverty, and we determined to wipe out injustice and bigotry; government, we believed, had the tools and resources to accomplish these ends; all that was needed was the will.

This set of beliefs, applied to the mentally ill, allowed us to ignore the failure of a century-and-a-half of mental-health reform in this country, in the conviction that this time we had the answer. The problem, as it was defined, was the system of large state hospitals. Like a cancer, it could be easily excised. And the will was there.

Unfortunately, the analysis was wrong. The problems of severe mental illness have proved resistant to unitary solutions. For some patients, discharge from the state hospitals was a blessing. For all too many others, it was the ultimate curse. Far from a panacea, the policy created as many problems as it solved, perhaps more. To be sure, it is never easy to admit that massive social initiatives have been misconceived. The time has come, however, to lay deinstitutionalization to rest.

It would not be difficult to outline a reasonable program to restore some sense to the care of the mentally ill; moderate expansion of beds in state facilities, especially for the most severely ill patients; good community-based services for those patients — and their number is not small — who could prosper outside of an institution with proper supports; and greater authority for the state to detain and treat the severely mentally ill for their own benefit, even if they pose no immediate threat to their lives or those of others.

Deinstitutionalization has been a tragedy, but it need not be an irreversible one.

111 Afflicting the Afflicted: Total Institutions

William May

This chapter will examine institutions as symbols of death, not those institutions and movements that obviously traffic in killing — war, concentration camps, revolutionary terrorism — but rather our health care institutions, which, though devoted to the fight against death, often become its instrument and symbol. Our total institutions reflect primordial images for sickness and death, images of hiding and devouring prominent in folklore, literature, dream life, and ritual behavior.[1]

Traditional societies interpreted sickness as the soul's departure from the body; and death as the soul's irreversible journey to a hidden realm. The enfeebled condition of the sick man or woman suggested that the animating principle, that is, the soul, had obviously vacated the body and retired to an invisible place, inaccessible to ordinary folk. Only the shaman could heal by tracking after and retrieving the soul, a feat which the healer accomplished by going into an ecstatic trance. He left his own body to fetch back the soul of the afflicted.

On death, when, at length, the soul departed for good, the body of the deceased turned into a shroud, a mask; that is, it now hid rather than revealed the soul that once animated it. Fittingly, funeral rites must shroud the shroud, that is, wrap up the body, and hide it away permanently in the ground. This final ritual of hiding carried the weight of a religious duty with which none could interfere. Thus Sophocles' King Creon horrified Antigone by refusing to let her bury her traitorous brother's body. No crime could place a man's body beyond the dignity of burial. Polyneices' corpse should not remain exposed to view where men could stare at it. Antigone had an indefectible duty to hide it from sight.

Sickness and death additionally suggest the image of devouring. To this day, we associate some diseases with eating. We call tuberculosis "consumption"; the malignant tumor feeds off its host; high fever burns and consumes. "Eating, devouring, hunger, death, and maw go together," writes Erich Neumann, "and we still speak, just like the primitive, of 'death's maw,' a 'devouring war,' a 'consuming disease.' "[2]

Total Institutions and the Temptation to Hide the Sick, the Aged, the Imprisoned, and the Mentally Ill

Increasingly, in the modern world, we have placed the sick, the aged, the criminal, and the mentally impaired and disturbed in total institutions, thereby segregating them from the society at large. Some 80 percent of Americans will eventually die not in the home, but in a total institution. The nursing home industry has expanded rapidly in recent decades, and special regions of the country have turned into huge territorial nursing homes where we hide the aged and they hide from us. It used to be said that children should be seen but not heard. Now we imply to many of the aged that they should be neither seen nor heard. Long before their death, we bury them in the folds of the total institution, hidden, out of sight and out of mind, until we are called upon, finally, to bury them again.

Similarly, mental hospitals and penal institutions subliminally associate with the oblivion of death. " 'The prisoner,' a Sing Sing chaplain observed, 'was taught to consider himself dead to all without the prison walls."[3] A warden in 1826 prohibited contacts with the outside world, saying, "while confined here . . . you are to be literally buried from the world."[4] Such strictures on communication with the outside world have lessened today, but, still, prisoners call themselves the

From William May, *The Patient's Ordeal* (Bloomington, Indiana University Press), 1994, pp. 142-55. Used by permission.

forgotten men. Our society has insisted on the thick walls of prisons and other institutions not only to keep inmates in but also to keep the world out. The walls say two things to an inmate: do not expect to *escape* from here, but also do not really expect others to visit you here. The society preaches the same message to many of the mentally disturbed and the chronically ill when it consigns them to institutional bins where they sometimes receive minimal, custodial care until their final disappearance.

This colonization of the distressed occurs for all the understandable reasons that obtain in a highly differentiated society with its specialized functions and services. The seriously distressed or disabled often overload the already burdened nuclear family. American society has not offered enough assists to family caregivers to provide them with some respite and relief. Institutions, moreover, can deliver important technical services that only mobilized professional resources can offer. I am not a Luddite who would urge that we smash the bureaucracies, that we "total" the total institutions or recklessly "deinstitutionalize" their residents. When we cast out the mentally disturbed from the huge custodial institutions where they were formerly incarcerated and recolonize them in third-rate hotels unattended, they go off their medication and end up in the streets. The heartless 1980s made that clear.

Yet we need to acknowledge candidly the suffering that our efforts to heal impose, the ordeals which the residents of our institutions face, partly gratuitous and eliminable, partly ineradicable, if we would offer what we can compassionately and effectively.

Some nursing homes have provided particularly cynical, even scandalous care; the mentally disturbed often receive notoriously poor treatment of their physical ailments. One harassed hospital administrator in New York City spoke with particular bitterness: apparently, he said, the emotionally disturbed are miraculously endowed with immunity to disease once committed to a mental hospital. For, in the New York City hospitals with which he is familiar, the insane never seem to come down with cancer, gall bladder trouble, or pulmonary or heart conditions serious enough to treat.

Although such neglect is remediable, institutionalization, whether good or bad, often tends to afflict the afflicted more subtly, by depriving them of community. The existentialists used to define being human as "being present" to others and letting others be present to oneself. Institutionalization often not only deprives the inmate of the opportunity to be present to the community but also relieves the larger society of the need to be present to the aged and distressed.

Although one would not want to do without the technical services that our health bureaucracies offer, they can exact a high price by imposing upon residents a kind of premature burial. The institution forces upon them a loss of name, identity, companionship, and acclaim — an extremity of deprivation of which the ordinary citizen has a foretaste in his complaints about the anonymous and impersonal conditions of modern life. To this degree, the nursing home for the poor, the prison, and the chronic care hospital serve as destination and symbol for a society at large that already operates to deprive its citizens of significance. Many people have suffered a loss of community long before their institutionalization. Indeed, the institution may in fact provide them with more community than they have enjoyed for years.

The Hospital and Death as Devourer

While disease wracks his body, the acutely ill patient often has a more general sense of being exhausted and consumed by a world that has depleted all his personal resources. In the recent Western past, when a member of the middle class suffered a breakdown in health he sought respite in the sanctuary of the home, where the doctor visited him. This pattern of care prevailed for the middle and upper classes through the nineteenth and early twentieth centuries. Treatment for the poor differed. The poor went to the teaching hospitals, where, in exchange for medical services, they sometimes signed over to the staff their cadavers for research purposes. Thus the hospital acquired, especially for the poor, associations as an institution that not only serves, but consumes the body.

Today, care for the seriously ill among the middle and upper classes has moved to the hospitals, thus giving other members of society a taste of the earlier plight of the indigent. Despite its indisputable technological advantages over the home, the hospital exacts a high price both psychologically and financially. Psychologically, it gnaws — with its alien machines, rhythms, language, and routines — at that identity which a person previously maintained in the outside world. The patient must surrender his customary *control* of his world not only to the disease but to those who fight against it. His capacity for *savoring* his world is also numbed by the disease and by those procedures imposed upon him in the fight against it — diet, drugs, X-rays, surgery, nausea-inducing therapy, and sleeping potions. Finally, his capacity for *communicating* with his world erodes as he loses his social role. Just as disease rips him out of his usual place in the community and makes him feel less secure in his dealings with fellows, the procedures of the hospital remind him acutely of this loss by placing him in the hands of professionals — the nurse and the doctor — precisely those who seem unassailably secure in their own identities.

The financial trauma patients face makes it difficult to think of the hospital as sanctuary. Not only disease but medical expenses devour the patient, and if not the patient, the patient's family. Current systems of national health care, while distributing costs somewhat, have caused the total social expense of medicine to rocket to nearly 12 percent of the gross national product without increasing commensurately, as compared with other developed nations, the quality of health care. Nothing quite matches inflation for producing a sense that one's world is a devouring world; and no item has matched health care in the inventory of rising costs.

Chronic, even more than acute, care centers have acquired associations with death as devourer. Erving Goffman has worked out this theme in his long essay on asylums, a term which covers prisons, mental hospitals, monasteries, and the like, places where "a large number of like-situated individuals, cut off from the wider society for an appreciable period of time, together lead an enclosed, formally administered round of life."[5] Such an institution devours in the sense that it can deprive systematically the sick, the deviant, and the aged of their former identities.

> The recruit comes into the establishment with a conception of himself made possible by certain stable social arrangements in his home world. Upon entrance, he is immediately stripped of the support provided by these arrangements. In the accurate language of some of our oldest institutions, he begins a series of abasements, degradations, humiliations, and profanations of self. His self is systematically, if often unintentionally, mortified. . . .[6]

Goffman particularly attends to admission rites and procedures. The act of taking off one's old clothes and donning new garments impresses symbolically upon the inmate the price he must pay for entering into the total institution: the surrender of his old personal identity and autonomy and the acquisition of a new identity oriented to the authority of the professional staff and to the aims and purposes and the smooth operation of the institution. (The metaphor of changing clothes, of course, dates all the way back to the Benedictine Rule, and behind that to the letters of the Apostle Paul, and, still earlier, to rites of passage in primitive societies. It tells the prospective candidate that his new life demands devouring of the old, though in the case of the asylum inmate the new identity itself often leads eventually to the oblivion of death.)

The word "total" refers not simply to the comprehensive way in which the institution organizes all activities — eating, sleeping, working, leisure, and therapy sessions — but also to the strategies by which the institution invades the interior life of its inmates. In civilian life, Goffman observes, institutions usually claim the resident's overt behavior alone, releasing to the individual the question of his private attitude toward the organization. But in total institutions, the staff can legitimately busy itself with the resident's interior reactions to authority through a process that Goffman calls "looping." The resident finds to his dismay that his protective response to an assault upon his dignity itself collapses back into the situation and provides the staff with reasons for yet further controls; ". . . he cannot defend himself in the usual way by establishing distance between the mortifying situation and himself."[7] The all-monitoring eye of the supervisor surveys both his inner and his outer life and organizes the prison of his therapy.

The Motives for Institutionalization

However sensitively run, total institutions can exact from their residents a price, as they impose upon the segregated the ordeals of banishment and deprivation. What explanations can we offer for their attraction, above and beyond the original philanthropic impulses that founded them and the technical services they orchestrate? (I set aside in answer to this question the motives for entering the handsomely designed and expensive three-tier retirement centers to which the affluent elderly often move themselves.)

Philip Slater, a sociologist, offers the rawest explanation of their appeal in America. He argues that Americans are tempted to solve their problems by resorting to what he calls "the toilet assumption." We behave as though the most efficient and sanitary way of solving a problem is to avoid it by voiding it. To argue the depth of this tendency in the American character, Slater offered a revisionist view (in the *Pursuit of Loneliness*) on the motives of immigrants who settled this country. Our celebratory histories to the contrary, Americans were not the most heroic of Europe's millions. Rather, they were self-selectively those most inclined to solve the problems of an ancient continent and aging relatives by escaping from them. Americans have endlessly repeated this strategy of abandonment: as an immigrant people became a migratory people, moving from the East across the plains to the West; then, as a migratory people became a mobile people, leaving small towns in order to "make it" in the city; and then, after making our cities uninhabitable, fleeing from the city to the suburbs; and, finally, retreating from the tedium of the suburbs to the weekend retreat in the country. Slater sees in this ruthlessness the work of the toilet assumption — the American tendency to dispose of problems by flushing them.[8]

But why are we so drawn to the toilet assumption? Slater's attempt to explain it as a special character defect of those who migrated to America is historically dubious. Most immigrants did not come to the United States in order to flush the problems of their native countries. Certainly not the blacks, and probably not most of the whites. In his essay *Going to America*, Terry Colman notes that English absentee landlords in the late 1840s sought to get rid of huge numbers of Irish peasants on their estates by shipping them off to America. The practice was commonly known as "shoveling out."[9] It would appear that some of our forebears were not the flushers as much as the flushed.

Furthermore, if Michel Foucault's *Madness and Civilization* can be credited, Europeans in the Classical period of the seventeenth and eighteenth centuries already exhibited the tendency to solve problems by banishing a defiled population to a special institution. In this respect, the Age of Reason differed from the earlier medieval and renaissance worlds. Medieval society, according to Foucault, except for its treatment of lepers (and religious minorities), incarcerated its own members for reasons of deviancy much less often than did the reputedly more tolerant Age of Reason. Renaissance society let the mad and the indigent mingle in the society at large. But by the seventeenth and eighteenth centuries, rulers incarcerated the idle, the poor, the insane, and the criminal without distinction in lazar houses.

The religious ritual of confession, Foucault believes, helped shape and reflected the more generous, earlier medieval attitude toward deviancy. Confession concedes the fact of human imperfection, but also implies some confidence that evil can be let out into the open without engulfing those who pray. But classical Europe, with its proud celebration of human reason, "felt a shame in the presence of the inhuman"[10] that the earlier ages did not experience. After the seventeenth century, Western society increasingly assumed that one can handle evil only by banishing it. Put another way: an age that aspires to total autonomy admits with more difficulty the dependent, the defective, and the irrational into its life. These imperfect members of society represent a negativity so threatening and absolute that a society pretending to autonomy can only put them out of sight.

Foucault knew that this impulse to banish did not spring from crude brutality. He recognized the philanthropic element in the move to sequester: "Interest in cure and expulsion coincide."[11] But it took David Rothman's *The Discovery of the Asylum* to show the intimate historical connection between the impulse to rehabilitate and the compulsion to segregate. The American historian documented the drastic change that occurred in the

1820s and afterward in the United States in the handling of crime, madness, and indigency. Until the early nineteenth century, Americans either whipped, pilloried, drove out of town, or hanged their criminals. Jails served as little more than temporary lockups until the penal system decided on the appropriate punishment. Not until the 1820s did this country adopt the strategy of building, and isolating criminals in, huge penitentiaries.

Similar changes occurred about the same time in the handling of the indigent and the insane. Until the 1820s, welfare funds largely supported families or surrogate families to take care of the poor. But increasingly in the nineteenth century, America constructed, and incarcerated the poor in, its great workhouses. Similarly, the country moved the mad from the attic and the hovel at the edge of town to the insane asylum.

Reformers made these changes for the philanthropic purpose of removing stricken populations from the evil influences of the society at large to the protected environment of the penitentiary or the asylum, where, under carefully controlled conditions (including isolation, work, discipline, and obedience under the authority of professionals), the distressed had a chance to recover. By the end of the Civil War, however, these massive, standardized facilities deteriorated into institutional bins, manned by professionals and subprofessional staff and filled with racial minorities.

In the medieval church, as a priest and his assistants dragged a leper out of the church with backward step and committed him to the lazar house, they would say to him: "And howsoever thou mayest be apart from the church and the company of the Sound, yet art thou not apart from the grace of God."[12] In the last one hundred years, our implied ritual address to the mad, the aged, and the criminal has been: "And howsoever thou mayest be apart from the community and the company of the Sound, yet art thou not apart from the ministrations of the Professional."

Thus rationalism, philanthropy, and professionalism intertwine with banishment and deprivation.

In my judgment, however, both Slater's attempt to locate the toilet assumption uniquely in the American immigrant experience and Foucault's effort to blame the impulse to banish exclusively on classical rationalism fail to persuade. Solving problems by dodging them dates back at least to the parable of the Good Samaritan. "Passing by on the other side" tempted ancient priests and levites as well as the modern middle class as a way of achieving some distance from the distressed. The impulses both to sequester and to devour spring from within humankind and not just idiosyncratically from careerist Americans or eighteenth-century rationalists.

We underestimate, moreover, the real power of these impulses within us in adopting too moralistic a view of their origin — in assuming that they issue from a gratuitous ruthlessness or complacency. Our neglect of the indigent does not result solely from the fact that we are too smug or too engrossed in our own riches to bother with them. If we examine our excuses for neglect,[13] including our reasons for institutionalization, we discover not so much smugness but anxiety, not self-assurance but a sense of harassment, not riches but a feeling of bankruptcy. The statement "I am too busy to care for her now" often betrays a free-floating anxiety: "I am riddled with concern about my own affairs. I can't break free from the grip of my own needs. They hold me in a vise. Maybe next year will be different. But this year is impossible."

Or again, the question "What can I do?" often blurts out no more than one's own despair: "I have nothing for the real needs of another because what I have doesn't satisfy my own. What help could I possibly offer him? It is better to avoid him. To face him would be too depressing. He would remind me of the emptiness of my own fate." Many a man avoids a visit to the bed of a dying friend for reason of the latter dread. He knows he has nothing to say that will help. He feels resourceless before his friend's imminent death and his own. He himself is in need, and a face-to-face meeting with his friend would remind him of his own exigency.

Not all expediency in our treatment of the distressed springs from gross callousness; rather, we are busily engaged in obscuring from view our own poverty: both hiding from ourselves and hiding our selves. We consign to oblivion the maimed, the disfigured, and the decrepit, because we have already condemned to oblivion a portion of ourselves. To address them in their needs would require us to permit ourselves to be addressed in our needs. But we recoil from accepting the depths of our own neediness. The hidden away threaten us with what we have already hidden away from ourselves. For some such reason, we prefer, even at great expense, to remove them from sight. And what better way to place them in the shadows and to obscure our own neediness, than to hand them over to professionals whose métier it is to make a show of strength, experience, and competence in handling a given subdivision of the distressed? Thus the exigent provide an opportunity for the community to exhibit its precedence and power over them.

A Concluding Comment

Three major and differing political reactions have emerged in interpreting the problems raised in this essay — conservative, reformist, and revolutionary. These reactions require comment in the light of the religious tradition that engages me as a theologian.

The modern, pragmatic, libertarian conservative would find in David Rothman's account of the emergence and decline of the asylum vindication for his skepticism about reform. The degeneration of the asylum provides but another sad tale of reform gone to seed. In the brief period of forty years, institutions with utopian aspirations deteriorated into dumping grounds for the desperate. Why bother, Mr. Reformer? Spare me your plans and save me some change.

Hobbes and his latter-day descendants among conservatives would darken this particular historical lesson into a comprehensive pessimism. Our institutions can do little more than keep human misery in check because of the murderous appetites to which human beings are subject. The impulses to sequester and devour derive from human nature; they are not just a cultural accident. Hobbes provided the anthropological foundations for this claim by observing: animals hunger only with the hunger of the moment, but man, like Satan, hungers and thirsts *infinitely.* His boundless, devouring hunger makes man "the most predatory, the most cunning, the strongest, and the most dangerous animal."[14] Moreover, Hobbes linked, by implication, this activity of devouring with the further impulse to sequester when he argued that men characteristically differ from animals in their "striving after honor and positions of honor, after precedence over others and recognition of this precedence by others, ambition, pride, and the passion for fame."[15] One man's glory demands another man's eclipse. When we aspire to step forward into the light, we betray the underside of this aspiration in our readiness to see others overshadowed by our illumination. Man's boundless craving, and specifically his appetite for honor and precedence, generates that enmity among humankind which justifies, in Hobbes's estimate, his characterization of the state of nature as "solitary, poor, nasty, brutish, and short." Thus, devouring and overshadowing connect, and our fears that others will devour and surpass us reinforce these murderous impulses. Hobbes resolved our sorry plight by arguing that we must accept our irrevocable duties of obedience to the state and its agencies, which, albeit oppressive, exercise a monopoly over the power of death and thereby keep terror within limits.

In their differing ways, both conservative skepticism and Hobbesian pessimism justify the *status quo* or the *status quo ante* for those institutions that consume, consign to oblivion, or oppress. Hobbes warns, in effect, leave well enough alone. Things are bad, but could be worse. Neither the skeptic nor the Hobbesian conservative appreciates the very real differences institutions (and public institutions) can make, not just in maintaining order, but in aspiring to the good. Without some sense of the distinctions between better and worse and the ineliminable and the reformable, one leaves very little room for improving the lot of the needy, ourselves included.

At the opposite end of the political spectrum, utopian reformers and revolutionaries tend to locate death in our institutional life alone. They see individuals and groups as relatively innocent victims of an oppressive social order. The reformer does battle with social evils, discrete and episodic, in the hope of making things better. But the revolutionary views the specter of overtaxed clinics in ghetto neighborhoods, rotting vegetables in wards, infected blood in banks, and foul overcrowding in jails as symptoms of a generally discredited social and political structure. The system serves the excellors and the devourers rather than the failed and the deprived. Since, however, individuals and groups are relatively innocent victims of the system, reformers and revolutionaries believe that humankind possesses the moral resources either for the piecemeal improvement of the system (the reformer's aim) or for the total displacement of the current system by one superior to it (the revolutionary's hope).

The positions of Hobbesian conservatives and of revolutionaries, like many other opposites, ultimately resemble one another. Both parties think too globally. The conservative wholly justifies and the revolutionary wholly repudiates institutions as they are. As such, they fail to distinguish sufficiently between varied total institutions, better and worse, and to discriminate among varied proposals for their discrete improvement. The chapters in this volume [*The Patient's Ordeal*] on the institutionalized retarded and on the aged attempt to show some of those qualities of total institutions that make them both indispensable and praiseworthy and the workers and residents within them deserving of our admiration. Thus, while I have emphasized in this chapter the ordeals which institutionalization imposes, I have not done so with the intent of repudiating the institutions. They impose some ordeals intrinsically and inevitably and others gratuitously. Wise reforms will eliminate the gratuitous, reduce to a minimum the inevitable, improve the necessary, and reserve institutionalization to as small a population as possible.

What response can one make theologically to these contending general assessments of institutions in our time? Reinhold Niebuhr offered the most influential theological response during the period under review. Niebuhr faulted the Hobbesian pessimists for locating destructiveness exclusively within the murderous impulses of humankind and for dealing too kindly with its institutional manifestations. However, Niebuhr also criticized the reformers and the revolutionary optimists for locating oppression exclusively in the social system and for exculpating individuals and groups as its relatively innocent victims. Niebuhr urged, instead, a more complex anthropology that sought to do justice both to the human and institutional capacity for good and to the individual and social capacity for destructiveness.

While salutary, Niebuhr's theological response did not address the more metaphysical question that underlies the social debates of our time. Both parties to the political debate, despite their differences, share in common a somewhat gloomy metaphysical vision. They both tend to define their politics by the experience of death and destruction alone. Conservatives justify institutions and revolutionaries justify their overthrowal in reaction to a negativity rather than to the experience of some positive, nurturant power which may offer hope of rebirth and thus authorizes their action. The fear of death and destruction keeps the conservative defensive about institutions; the hatred of death often provokes the revolutionary to attack them.

Fear supplies the hydraulic fluid and pressure that make the system work for the Hobbesian conservative. Inasmuch as institutions derive their power from the fear of death, we cannot expect them to dispense with this fear. Leviathan — and all its attendant institutions — deserves a monopoly over the power of death for fear of that even more murderous state of affairs that afflicts us in a state of nature without its ministrations.

Correspondingly, the hatred of death usually provides revolutionaries and often reformers with their life's meaning and vocation. Such activists may rightly see the evils of the system, but wrongly define their vocation by that perception alone. Evil serves them as that absolute which authorizes their activities and shapes their plans for a new or better society. They seek relentlessly to eliminate the negative from human life as their passion and calling.

Perhaps the eighteenth-century European and nineteenth-century American experiments with total institutions teach a somewhat different lesson. They emphasize that an ethic defined by resistance alone usually imposes on others what it seeks to depose. The total institution failed partly because it operated reflexively against negativities, the absolute negativities of madness, crime, dependency, and decrepitude. Society assumed that the negative absolutely must be eliminated (through the ministrations of the professional) and, when it cannot be eliminated, it must be sequestered or eliminated by being sequestered.

It may be less pernicious to assume that the negative is not absolute and therefore that its elimination is not the precondition of a truly human existence. Once conservatives, reformers, and revolutionaries no longer treat negativities as absolutes, then the conservative may be less tempted to justify institutional repression and reformers less tempted to lay upon professionals the fatal charge to eliminate negativity or to banish ruthlessly its host. This deflation of evil, moreover, need not lead to quietism or complacency. Action against evil does not require that we inflate it absolutely.

Where, however, does one find theological warrant for this alternative vision of the metaphysical setting in which social action takes place? In my own efforts to puzzle over this problem as a Christian theologian, I have found myself drawn to the passages about the "suffering servant" in Isaiah. Remarkably enough, the text locates God's servant in the very arena of death that we have been exploring. He exposed himself to deprivation and oblivion. "He was despised and rejected by men; a man of sorrows and acquainted with grief, and as one from whom men hide their faces, he was despised, and we esteemed him not" (Isaiah 53:3). The passage furthermore does not suggest that this move into the site of deprivation and death engulfs him. Though "he was cut off from the land of the living" and though he "poured out his soul to death," his resources do not thereby deplete or thin out. Quite the contrary: in and through his outpouring of service, the will of the Lord actually prospers in his hand. God's servant "suffers" — not simply as tortured, but as determinedly subject to the will of God. God may will him to places where he must endure. But his suffering resembles more "suffer the little children to come unto me" than "look what suffering I have endured for your sake, ungrateful woman!" He suffers but also suffers as an attending to, a following, a tracking after the powerful will that creates, preserves, and upholds in love. Therefore, the passage suggests a peculiarly intimate connection between love's flourishing and his own dying.[16]

The assertion of any such link between dying and prospering contrasts starkly with our ordinary conception of social action. In traditional social action, we assume some kind of dualistic battle in which either we gradually prevail over death (in which case death diminishes) or we find our resources gradually thinned out by death (in which case we diminish). But this passage suggests that the suffering servant makes his own dying, that is, his own laying down of his life, an essential ingredient in that life which he shares with the community. "By his stripes we are healed."

Christians have traditionally drawn a moral implication from this passage. A community that professes such a servant as savior cannot avoid going into places marked by rejection, pain, and oblivion. In failing to do so, the community would defect from its own mission in the God from whom no secret places are hid.

Concretely, such a savior demands of the churches that they not leave health care exclusively in the hands of the bureaucracies and their professional staffs which serve as the current chief instruments of a society's sequestering. The churches must find ways to open themselves up to loving the institutionalized needy: (1) to provide supplemental services above and beyond those that the bureaucracies can provide; (2) to criticize bureaucracies for their failure to provide what they ought to provide and thereby to assist in their improvement; (3) to encourage the development of alternative delivery systems where appropriate; and (4) to provide the community at large with sufficient contact with the plight of the deprived and the forlorn so as to effect a more favorable ethos in the society toward them and the ordeals that beset them.

But a moralistic reading of the passage from Isaiah does not cut through to the nerve of the problem. The problem we face consists not simply of other people's suffering but of our own. We avoid the failures of others because we cannot bear to see our own failures reflected in their faces; we deprive the needy because we absorbingly attempt to overcome our own limitless sense of deprivation; and rarely are we so tempted to impose pain on others as when we are hellbent on relieving it, convinced of the absolute righteousness of our cause and the indispensability of our contribution in promoting that cause.

Thus the final word spoken in Isaiah 53 must address our own metaphysical plight.

If the anointed of God has exposed himself to deprivation and oblivion, then men and women need fear no longer that the death and failure that they know in themselves can separate them from God. Those powers they fear as absolute have been rendered of no account, either as they appear in them or as they beset their fellow creatures.

This position of metaphysical optimism differs from the vision of the conservative who elevates the powers of darkness and disorder into a divine figure of chaos which institutions must grimly contain; and it differs from the pessimism of the revolutionary whose cause derives its inspiration from the repressive institutional negativity that he seeks to overcome. The act of dying for others penetrates, rather than sidesteps or merely reacts to, the negative. Death looms as one of the principalities and powers, to be sure, but a creature for all of that, incapable of separating human beings from the substance of self-expending love. As this love takes hold of men and women, they suffer rebirth, perhaps in blood and fire, perhaps in water, but, in any event, reconnected to creative, nurturant, and donative love.

This vision of the human plight should not undercut the motive for works of mercy and relief among people and the reformation of defective institutions. Quite the contrary, it should enable them, for it deprives the negative of its ultimacy and therefore its power to paralyze, dominate, and distort. It relieves men and women of the burden of messianism. They need no longer repress the negative in themselves, or impose it on others, or obsess on it in their enemies, or protect themselves from it through the shield of the professional. They can freely perform whatever acts of kindness they can and even receive such acts from others, as a limited sign of a huge mercy which their own works have not produced.

Notes

1. For a discussion of death as a "Hider-Goddess," see Edgar Herzog, *Psyche and Death, Archaic Myths and Modern Dreams in Analytical Psychology* (London: Hodder and Stoughton, 1966). Hermann Güntert's language studies of the Indo-Germanic (and pre-Indo-Germanic) period lead Herzog to state (p. 39) that a "mysterious hiding and shrouding has been experienced as the first essential character-trait of the numinous, hidden power of death in early times."

2. Erich Neumann, *The Origins and History of Consciousness* (Princeton, NJ: Princeton University Press, First Princeton/Bollingen Paperback Printing, 1970). For further explorations of death as devourer, see Richard and Eva Blum, *Health and Healing in Rural Greece* (Stanford, CA: Stanford University Press, 1965), p. 129, and Herzog, *Psyche and Death*, Ch. 4, "The Death Demon as Dog and Wolf."

3. David J. Rothman, *The Discovery of the Asylum* (Boston: Little, Brown and Co., 1971), p. 95.

4. Ibid.

5. Erving Goffman, *Asylums* (Garden City, NY: Anchor Books, 1961), p. xiii.

6. Ibid., p. 14.

7. Ibid., p. 36.

8. Philip Elliot Slater, *The Pursuit of Loneliness* (Boston: Beacon Press, 1976), pp. 21-23.

9. Terry Colman, *Going to America* (New York: Random House, 1972), p. 216.

10. Michel Foucault, *Madness and Civilization* (New York: Random House, Vintage Books, 1973), p. 68.

11. Ibid., p. 7.

12. Ibid., p. 6.

13. See William F. May, *A Catalogue of Sins* (New York: Holt, Rinehart, and Winston, 1967), Ch. 6, for a fuller treatment of the sin of neglect.

14. Leo Strauss, *The Political Philosophy of Hobbes* (Oxford: The Clarendon Press, 1936), p. 9.

15. Ibid., p. 11.

16. The now-deceased Professor Arthur C. McGill of Harvard Divinity School offered the best examination of this topic in an as yet unpublished paper on "Identity and Death," in the care of the literary executor of his estate, Professor David Cain, Mary Washington College.

112 Welcoming Unexpected Guests to the Banquet

Brett Webb-Mitchell

The focus of this article is the challenge of discovering the place of people with disabilities in the life of a congregation or parish. The article's message is appropriate for such occasions of the church's life as Christian Family Sunday in May, or Access Sunday, or Ability Awareness Sunday, in which the gifts of all people, including those with disabilities, are emphasized. The names are fictitious due to confidentiality.

It is a cool summer morning in the hills surrounding Montreat, North Carolina, as parents gather together to share something they have in common: a child with a disabling condition. The topic of discussion for this gathering has to do with how their individual congregations first responded to the presence of their child with a disability. The parents' responses echoed one another as they told of congregations who, though scared at first, learned to at least accept that the couple had a child with a disabling condition. Most of the parents learned how to work with their churches so that their child had a place in Sunday school, youth groups, and worship. Karen, whose two children have cerebral palsy and developmental problems, shared that her congregation has grown to accept her children and involve them in the life of the church. But Joy, whose son has Down's syndrome, said that the support was fragile at best. She handles the fragile support by no longer expecting much from the church but expecting much from God to care for her and her family.

From Brett Webb-Mitchell, "Welcoming Unexpected Guests to the Banquet," *Journal for Preachers* 16, no. 3 (1993):15-19. Used by permission.

Other parents of children with disability and adults with disabilities have experienced the church's fragile support. Many people with disabling conditions are angry at their church for what feels like a lack of caring support, a feeling that carries over to their relationship with God. Some people with disabilities feel that "if a healthy child is a perfect miracle of God, who created the imperfect child?"[1] For the writer Bern Ikeler, the whole family questioned and cried to the Creator: "What is happening to us?" Born with cerebral palsy, Bern's birth was the death of the family's dream child. Unlike a child's physical death, a disability is a death that happens hundreds of times each day, as the child is unable to do what "normal" children could do.[2]

It isn't only those intimately connected with a person's disabling conditions who have felt the fragility of support. Church leaders have also admitted that their support is fragile. Many say they don't know what to say or do for the family of the person with a disability. Continually afraid of saying something offensive at the wrong time, offering help not needed, some choose to say and do nothing at all. Practical signs of support are absent, the comforting words of care needing to be expressed are rarely heard, and the gift of being present in the challenging times in a disabled person's life is withheld.

This reaction is not isolated to churches. We live in a society which has created a mistaken belief that shapes our collective perception, or misperception, of disabled people. We have been lured to believe that having a disabling condition means one is less than fully human, regardless of what combination of gifts and talents a person might have; people focus on one's physical, mental, or sensory limitations. The person with a disabling condition is a provocative, painful sign of our own mortal condition and something that we'd rather deny than accept.[3] As the theologian Stanley Hauerwas writes, the natural response to the misperceived stereotype that people with a disabling condition are in pain is to get away from the person as quickly as possible.[4] Such pain, or illusion of pain, is a threat to our communities.

Misperception of people with disabling conditions in congregations is not an individual problem, but is a dark, knotted disturbing thread that runs throughout the richly textured fabric of congregational life. The challenge for the church is to rightly perceive that some people have physical, mental, or sensory conditions that naturally impose real limitations in terms of what some can and cannot do in life. Members of Christ's community are to look *through* and *beyond* one's abilities or disabilities into the heart of the other person as we come to be with another person, whether in times of exuberant celebration or righteous anger. We are called to live with one another as a sign of God's grace.

The gospel message affirms this message of grace in Jesus' call to love God with our whole being, and to love one's neighbor as ourselves (Matt. 22:39). Overt exclusion of another person in God's family, regardless of one's abilities or limitations, hurts and offends everyone in the body of Christ. Jesus emphasized that Christians share a spiritual bond of loving care with one another that transcends our own previous, natural kinship network. Jesus points to the existence of a spiritually ordered community of neighbors, where we view ourselves as selves-embedded-in-community, rather than disconnected individuals living in the selfish and unjust order of the scarcity paradigm.

The anthropologist Richard Katz wrote that the scarcity paradigm assumes we live in a world of scarce, nonrenewable resources, and only those who are rich or powerful enough may accumulate and control the distribution of these resources. Such resources include items like oil, water, and health care provisions for people with disabilities.[5] Whatever truth there may be in a scarcity of natural resources, the paradigm can be used to distort important elements of human life. Some, for example, perceive love as a scarce resource, fearful that they may squander it in the wrong places, thus using it all with no love left in reserve for an emergency. They are not aware that this is backward thinking as, in reality, the more we share love with one another, the more we have of it.[6] The scarcity paradigm is a justified description of our contemporary American culture, and from such cultural pressures, none of us are exempt, including those of us who consider ourselves members of Christ's body.

Juxtaposed with the scarcity paradigm as applied to culture is the alternative spiritually ordered community of caring love found in Jesus' vivid description of God's kingdom. Throughout the gospel accounts, Jesus keeps pointing his disciples to the powerful reality of God's kingdom, the embodiment of a paradigm of abundance. The theologian Lesslie Newbigin suggests that the church on earth, called into existence by God in Christ, is a signpost on the arduous journey of faith, pointing the faithful followers of Jesus to the eventual, glorious destination.[7] Yet Jesus' vision of God's kingdom is more than our final destination. Instead, it is a different lens on reality, a new spiritually ordered lifestyle that we should be committed to living out in this time and place. The Church is called by God in Christ to live life on earth with an eye on this kingdom whenever we pray the Lord's prayer: "Thy kingdom come, Thy will be done, on earth as it is in heaven" (Matt. 6:10, RSV).

In telling his followers about God's kingdom, Jesus used many parables, metaphors, and analogies. One powerful parable that reveals the inclusive nature of God's kingdom is found in the parable of the "Great Banquet Feast" (Luke 14:15-24, NIV). In this parable, Jesus takes the Old Testament image of the messianic banquet, which is prepared and hosted by Yahweh, surrounded by the leaders and prophets of the children of Israel, and uses this banquet as metaphor for God's kingdom, with God as the host and Jesus as the servant.

To summarize the story, the host has invited three prominent, wealthy men, and probably their families, to come to a large banquet he has prepared, but they all refuse him: they are all too busy with their ordinary lives to take time to accept the gracious invitation of the host to this most delicious love feast. The claim of God, the host, upon their lives was crowded out by things of this world. The host, angry at such a response, tells the servant, "Go out at once into the streets and lanes of the town and bring in the poor and maimed and blind and lame" (vs. 21). This most likely included the outcasts of Jewish society, like those people from the leper colonies, those who sat at the city gates and begged for money, and those who stole from others along the dark alleyways of Jerusalem to support themselves. At first, many probably stalled because they did not feel worthy and, in feeling unworthy, declined the invitation. The host then tells the servant to *compel* the people to come "that my house may be filled" (vs. 23).

In verse 24, the host is telling the servant the theological point of the story: None of those who were first invited will taste my dinner. But this isn't by God's choice to exclude them, for the invited guests excluded themselves from the banquet. Instead, these vacancies have been filled by those seen as the most unlikely, unworthy, unexpecting guests at this feast: the poor, disabled outcasts of Jewish society. By turning to these rejected, disabled citizens, those who hid along the highways and the hedges, God transforms them from unwanted social outcasts to wanted, honored, though unexpected guests in God's kingdom.

Are those who are disabled in this story symbolic of only those who are obviously disabled in our time and place? I think not. Those who are disabled in this story represent all humankind. The people who are disabled represent all who come before God every Sunday, all too aware of wounds and brokenness, filled with the painful knowledge that God knows the sinful condition of their lives, aware of their human limitations and inadequacies, yet who still dare to come and share in the love feast presented before us by the Creator, our all-forgiving host.

This simple yet profound parable of God's kingdom has important theological implications that may enable congregations to learn how to invite, welcome, and accept all who wish to enter the church, regardless of their abilities or limitations. To begin with, we need to remember that the good news of this story is that the invitation to God's banquet table is not based upon our human good works, nor dependent upon our money or fame. Instead, the invitation to this banquet is the gift of salvation extended through God's gift of grace. We are invited because God first loved us. The only way one can remain outside and away from the banquet is by consciously turning down the invitation. The New Testament theologian Joseph Fitzmyer writes, while we cannot save ourselves, we can very well damn ourselves.[8]

This idea of grace runs contrary to the implied message of the scarcity paradigm that suggests that such love and attention are limited resources. The scarcity paradigm is overtly and covertly communicated to many people with disabling conditions and their families. Many leaders in congregations determine whether disabled persons may attend worship or other activities by asking the narrow question, "What can they *do* in worship?" as if God values us only for what we can do, not for who we are.

Nowhere in Scripture is it written that one has to be able to *do* certain things in order to worship God, or that one must have a specific I.Q., or behave in a socially appropriate fashion. It has been said by many who worship with those who have been labeled severely or profoundly mentally retarded that the greatest gift they give is the understanding that God valued and enjoys *who* we are, as children of God's, rather than what we *do*. What one finally gets out of worship is, most likely, between the "invited guest" and the "host" of the banquet.

Another important lesson is the realization that God's banquet table is big enough for all who are invited to sit at it and enjoy the meal. There is no sense in the parable that the banquet room was not big enough or overly crowded. There was so much space left over at one point that the servant was sent out a second time to bring in more people. Each person has a special place at God's table at this love feast. No one is shunted away from the feast.

This lesson from God's banquet table runs contrary to some congregations which may resemble a family reunion. When I grew up, dinners at the family reunions were in two different rooms. In the dining room was the adult table, with china, crystal, the best silver on an Irish linen tablecloth, with a floral bouquet, and candles in the center. Meanwhile, the kitchen was the room for the children with a rickety card table, folding chairs, plastic-ware, and no flowers. This room was child proof.

Many churches have opted for this family reunion paradigm for worship. Some churches have set aside a separate chapel, sometimes called the "Weeping Chapel," located off the main sanctuary for those with disabilities to sit in along with nursing mothers and their crying, babbling babies. Others, like those with hearing impairment, are tired of feeling closed out of the hearing-centered parish during worship and have established their own churches for the "deaf community" in their denominations. This parable raises a question for our churches: Is this banquet table symbolic of our gathering, willing to welcome all who wish to enter?

The final lesson is remembering that each person who was invited and came to the banquet had this one, essential characteristic in common: they probably had never seen themselves as members of a community of love. Each person had seen themselves as disconnected individuals, with long-forgotten family connections, isolated from the Jewish community. They were hiding in the alleyways because they were lonely outcasts.

Being brought together through the host's gracious invitation, gathered around a common table, they began to see that they were more or less like the other invited guests: they saw other poor strangers transformed, unexpectedly, into invited honored guests. Who would have thought that the one with leprosy, the outlaw, the disenfranchised, the undervalued, would be God's welcomed guests? All it took was accepting the invitation to come to God's feast.

What is moving in this story is that not one of these people could ever repay the host in kind, for none of these individuals had ever tasted or seen such splendor as was found at this feast. They simply accepted God's invitation to "taste my banquet." And in accepting this invitation, their lives were forever changed.

The challenge for the church is to break away from the dominant culture's misperceptions which keep those who have a disabling condition on the disenfranchised, undervalued margins of our society. Jesus' parable establishes a vision of God's kingdom that gives those who are disabled a place not only close to God's heart in God's kingdom, but more importantly, the realization that the one with a disabling condition has an invaluable place in the living body of Christ. But Jesus' parable calls for nothing less than a conversion of the church's collective heart in inviting and welcoming all who wish to worship God. To God, people with disabling conditions are not just another special-interest social-action task force and project for our churches. This is more than social posturing; this is kingdom of God ethics ruling.[9] People who, by the way, have some real limitations and unique gifts, have been invited to have a seat at the finest meal at God's love feast.

The reason that Jesus told the parable is so that we have a practical, concrete vision of the loving nature of God's kingdom in our churches. Such love, writes social critic Wendell Berry, is never abstract: "It does not adhere to the universe of the planet or the nation or the institution or the profession, but to the singular sparrows of the street, the lilies of the field, 'the least of these my brothers and sisters.' "[10]

Jesus is calling the church to live its life according to this alternative vision of God's kingdom. We are to move over on the pews and discover that God wants all who wish to enter our sanctuaries to worship God to be free to do so. Christ's body is made of those who think they are able and those whom we have labeled, "disabled," who appear less fortunate, broken, and wounded. We need these "unexpected guests" to be invited in order to be reminded that it is God in Christ alone who can heal the wounds deep within, and mend the broken hearts, because we are God's children. God's banquet table is a place for all Christians, upholding the common good of all members of Christ's body, on earth as it is in heaven.

Notes

1. Helen Featherstone, *There's a Difference in the Family* (New York: Penguin Books, 1980).

2. Bernard Ikeler, *Parenting Your Disabled Child* (Philadelphia: Westminster Press, 1986).

3. Ernest Becker, *The Denial of Death* (New York: Free Press, 1973).

4. Stanley Hauerwas, *Naming the Silences* (Grand Rapids: Wm. B. Eerdmans Publishing Co., 1990).

5. Richard Katz, "Empowerment and Synergy: Expanding the Community's Healing Resources." Unpublished manuscript (Cambridge, Mass.: Harvard University, 1984), p. 1.

6. This perception of love came from conversation with Stanley Hauerwas.

7. Lesslie Newbigin, *Sign of the Kingdom* (Grand Rapids: Wm. B. Eerdmans Publishing Co., 1980).

8. Joseph Fitzmyer, *Anchor Bible Commentary Series: The Gospel According to Luke X-XXIV* (New York: Doubleday, 1985).

9. John Howard Yoder, *The Priestly Kingdom* (Notre Dame: University of Notre Dame Press, 1984).

10. Wendell Berry, *Home Economics* (San Francisco: North Point Press, 1987).

113 Secrets of the Couch and the Grave: The Anne Sexton Case

Edmund D. Pellegrino

The dead have no right of redress. The biographer, for better or worse, has the last word.

—Ronald Steel

Introduction

In 1991, Diane Wood Middlebrook,[1] a professor of English at Stanford University, published a biography of the poet Anne Sexton in which, among other things, she used as source material some 300 tapes of Sexton's psychotherapeutic sessions with her psychiatrist, Dr. Martin Orne. After some years of reluctance and with the concurrence of Sexton's daughter and literary executor, Linda Gray Sexton, Orne released the tapes to Professor Middlebrook. Middlebrook's picture of Sexton drew heavily on the tapes, supplemented by scrapbooks, letters, photos, clippings, unpublished poems, and hospital records.

The book was met by a storm of immediate controversy and an extraordinary spate of reviews and commentaries in the popular press.[2-8] The book was praised for carrying out the presumed wishes of the poet to share her sufferings for the benefit of those similarly afflicted, for providing insight into the connections between psychosis and creativity, for destigmatizing emotional illness, for its witness against paternalism, and for underscoring the need for psychiatric treatment. The critics, on the other hand, were severe in their condemnation of Dr. Orne's violation of the ethics of confidentiality, of the adverse impact of the revelations on members of Sexton's family who did not share the enthusiasm of other members for opening the tapes to public scrutiny, and of the dubiety about claims that others might possibly gain benefit from revelations of Sexton's sexual aberrations, constant emotional turmoil, and eventual suicide. One detailed legal analysis found that Dr. Orne and, to a lesser extent, Linda Sexton committed infractions of the laws of torts, contract, and fiduciary relationships.[9] Others deem the whole controversy a teapot tempest inspired by fear of frank discussions of sex, by antifeminist bias, and outmoded notions of the rights of the dead. In any case, they argued, this appeared to be a "victimless" crime.

Given the ubiquity and seeming instability of the public for salacious details of the biographies of artists and celebrities, one would have thought such revelations would occasion scant commentary: the plethora of comments and book reviews was, therefore, surprising.[10] What was unusual was the question of violation of confidentiality by the psychotherapist. A similar ethical issue was raised by recent revelations about the life of Chairman Mao by his personal physician.[11] The legal issues aside, a number of serious questions of professional ethics are raised by the book. The central issue is the ethical propriety of release of the tapes and their use by the biographer. But there were also questions about the ethical infraction of Sexton's second psychiatrist, who had sexual relations with her, the associated question of the responsibility of the first psychiatrist to report that fact, and the possible responsibility of the third psychiatrist for Sexton's suicide and its possible relationship to her terminating Sexton's treatment because of frustration with Sexton's behavior as a patient.[12]

This essay focuses only on the central issue of confidentiality. The second psychiatrist's conduct in having sexual relations with his patient during therapy — and charging for those sessions! — is beyond ethical defense. As to the first psychiatrist's obligation to report his knowledge of the second

From Edmund D. Pellegrino, *Cambridge Quarterly of Healthcare Ethics* 5, no. 2 (Spring 1996): 189-203. Reprinted with the permission of Cambridge University Press.

psychiatrist's sexual misbehavior, there is some evidence that he tried to do so, although perhaps tardily. The details of the third psychiatrist's treatment of Ms. Sexton and its relationship to her suicide are far too problematic for consideration without more information than is available at this writing.

I will examine the confidentiality issue in a series of questions: What is the nature of confidentiality in general? How does it differ in psychotherapeutic relationships? When, if ever, may confidentiality be breached? Does it belong solely to the patient, or is it shared by family, friends, and others who might be hurt by revelations of secrets? Does the public have a right to know all the details of the lives of public personages? Do psychiatric patients have a special claim on knowledge of the psychotherapy of other persons similarly afflicted? Does the moral right of confidentiality extend beyond the couch to the grave? Do dead persons have a claim on their psychiatrist, and, if so, for how long?

On the way to examining these questions, I will examine the ethical propriety of the conduct of Anne Sexton's psychiatrist, her daughter and executor, Linda, and her biographer, Professor Middlebrook. My purpose is not so much to pass judgment as to provide an ethical framework against which such judgments might be made. I will use the details in the biography, but only parenthetically, to illustrate the ways in which Sexton's biographer, literary executor, and therapist justified their release of the tapes.

Some Facts About the Biography

There is little real question about the sincerity of the motivations of Anne Sexton's psychiatrist, daughter, and biographer to act in her interest, to do so in an ethically justifiable way that might help others, and to fulfill Anne Sexton's wishes. The question is whether, in fact, they achieved these ends and by what ethical criteria we might judge their actions.

At the outset, it should be clear that Professor Middlebrook's biography is not a piece of sensationalizing semifiction like so many psychobiographies of famous people these days. Middlebrook attempts a sober, factual, and sympathetic narrative adhering to the facts available to her. Her subject was an unusually complex, disturbed, suicidal, and remarkably gifted woman. Middlebrook quite accurately characterizes Sexton as, among other things: ". . . a suburban housewife, . . . a New England WASP, . . . half-cracked, . . . intimate, confessional, . . . insistently female, [and] . . . a serious, disciplined artist whose work had been admired from the beginning by distinguished peers."[13]

If there is sensation in the biography, it is because the subject was a source of sensation. The revelations of adultery, alcohol and drug abuse, probable incest and sexual abuse, the torments of feelings of inadequacy, the acting and posturing, the conscious attempt to fashion a public persona — all of this belonged to Sexton's life and was accurately portrayed. In the face of all her emotional sufferings, Sexton produced a highly regarded body of poetry, won a Pulitzer Prize, and became a professor at Boston University. Her success notwithstanding, her emotional distress was not allayed, and she committed suicide at age 45 after many years of inpatient and outpatient psychotherapy.

It is against the background reality of this complicated life narrative that I shall consider some of the ethical aspects of confidentiality in psychotherapy and psychobiography.

Moral Basis for Keeping Confidences

What Is the Nature of the Obligation?

The moral right to protection of secrets and the corresponding duty of others not to reveal them is fundamental in human relationships. Both are rooted in the respect owed other persons and in the trust essential to interpersonal transactions. Without these, we would lose the benefits of intimacy, counseling, and advice on matters of personal interest that we may wish to share with selected persons. We would also be vulnerable to harm from information broadcast about us that others chance upon.

Violations of confidence are violations of our person inasmuch as our innermost thoughts, personal experiences, promises, foibles, or vices are parts of our person. We may yield them voluntarily to some and withhold them from others as we choose. Confidences are possessions entrusted to others over which those who receive them have stewardship but not ownership. This applies to confidences one person tells us about her/himself or about someone else. To voluntarily accept such confidences is to enter a trust covenant. If we are not willing to keep the promise of confidentiality, we must not accept the information in the first place.

Sometimes we stumble fortuitously upon secrets about other persons without the opportunity to refuse the information. Even then, there is an implicit obligation not to reveal what we learn even though we did not voluntarily promise to keep what we learned secret. This is true also of confidences others confide in us before we know what we are being told is a secret. Under these circumstances, there is an additional problem of deciding what should or should not be revealed. The obligation to protect secrets is indirect, but is binding regardless of whether the intermediary informer has failed to swear us to confidentiality. No matter how we come into possession of secrets, we are bound to treat them with circumspection and safeguard them from revelation to others. The gravity of this obligation is in direct proportion to the harm to the person or her/his reputation that would accrue if the confidence were violated.

The obligation to protect confidences is related to, but not identical with, the protection of a person's privacy. Privacy centers on the moral right to be free of the invasion of our physical or emotional lives by those who have no permission to do so. Privacy derives from our nature as rational creatures capable of fashioning our own identity, and making choices about how much of ourselves to conceal or reveal to others. We violate privacy when we search out information about others by reading their mail, eavesdropping, wiretapping a phone, etc. In violations of privacy, we do not ask or invite the sharing of a secret. We steal the secret and, thus, take a part of a person's identity from him/her. This is an act of moral theft because privacy invasions involve the acquisition of secrets to which we have not been given privileged access in the first place.

What Is Special About Confidentiality in Psychotherapy?

The duty to protect confidences takes on special urgency and special stricture in therapeutic relationships among physicians, psychotherapists, and all who have privileged access to the patient or to the patient's records. This access is a necessity if the patient is to be helped. She/he must reveal details of her/his innermost private life that would ordinarily be closed to family members and intimate friends. The patient must disclose this information in a state of vulnerability at a time when the capacity and the resolve to make judicious decisions is compromised.

The patient is dependent upon the therapist, who, in turn, elicits the patient's confidence and trust as intrinsic to fulfillment of the therapeutic role. It is this trust that motivates the patient to reveal confidences. Receiving confidences, the physician implicitly promises to safeguard what is revealed and to use it only for the purposes for which it was revealed. Through this covenant of trust, the patient's expectation is that he/she will retain control over the release of what has been disclosed. To release the physician from the promise, the patient must give morally valid consent, that is, consent that is informed, competent, and made without coercion.

These realities pertain to every kind of therapeutic relationship, but they are especially true in psychiatry. There the innermost details of a patient's most personal and intimate life are, of necessity, laid bare. The vulnerability of the patient is heightened many times by the volatile and unpredictable chemistry of transference and countertransference.[14, 15] The chemistry of transference is unique for each relationship. It determines what is explored and what will be revealed. That chemistry makes the probability of truly informed consent problematic at best. What is revealed in a psychotherapeutic session may be highly detrimental to the patient's job and social and familial relationships. In the case of the forensic psychiatrist, what is disclosed can contribute to conviction of a crime or even the death penalty. Here, the serious question arises of whether it is ever possible to separate the psychiatrist as therapist from the psychiatrist as technical legal expert.[16]

Psychiatrists and other physicians are familiar with the obligation to preserve confidences found in the Oath of Hippocrates, and in the statements on Medical Ethics of the American Medical Association and the American Psychiatric Association.[17] It is the probable infraction of these traditional injunctions against disclosing confidences that has generated much of the debate over the release of the tapes of Anne Sexton's therapeutic sessions. Few would quarrel with the validity of the *prima facie* obligation to protect what is revealed in a therapeutic session.[18] What is at issue is when, if ever, such confidences can be revealed and under what conditions.

When Confidences May Be Disclosed

In the matter of confidentiality, the language of the Hippocratic Oath is open to at least two interpretations. It says ". . . whatever in connection with my professional practice, or not in connection with it, I see or hear in the life of men which ought not to be spoken abroad, I will not divulge as reckoning that all such should be kept secret."[19] Some take this to mean that whatever is observed or heard must be kept secret always; others take it to mean that what must be kept secret is what *ought not* to be told, implying that some things ought to be told. This latter interpretation grants the physician discretion in judging what ought to be revealed. No further elaboration of what might constitute the limits of the duty of confidence is provided, however.

The same ambiguity persists in the treatment of confidences in modern codes. Thus, the International Code of Medical Ethics (1949) speaks of "absolute secrecy." The Declaration of Geneva (1968) goes further: "I will respect the secrets which are confided to me even after the person has died." The British Medical Association, likewise, holds that the patient's death does not absolve the doctor from the obligation of secrecy. The AMA Principles of 1980 call for preservation of confidences ". . . within the constraints of law," thus opening the way for conflict between what is morally a *prima facie* obligation and what law may dictate.

It is increasingly difficult to protect confidentiality in the complicated, fragmented, and team-oriented healthcare system of today. Confidential information is no longer confined to the physician. Patient care today makes it necessary to share information about the patient with many others who need to speak to the patient or read his/her chart if they are to fulfill their professional responsibilities. Many of these persons have only brief, intermittent, and superficial personal contact with the patient. Others, like pathologists, radiologists, or imaging specialists, may never enter personally into the patient-physician relationship at all. This is especially true of third party payers, utilization reviewers, medical students, or social workers. Usually, the patient has little suspicion about the number or identity of these persons, many of whom, in small communities, will easily be able to identify the patient.[20] No patient could give anything more than implicit or tacit consent to the vast array of persons who, for a variety of reasons, may become party to the most intimate details of that patient's life.

Yet the complexity of modern medicine and the multiplication of persons who may have access to privileged information (and who may not handle it with discretion) do not make the concept of confidentiality a "deception" as Siegler suggests.[21] In psychiatric practice, for example, separate charts can be prepared, and kept under lock and key, for the more sensitive material. To be sure, the way modern medicine is practiced compounds the difficulties. But, the difficulties cannot eradicate so fundamental an obligation. It is dangerous to patient welfare to minimize the obligation of maintaining confidentiality. Rather, it is essential to reaffirm its moral significance despite the difficulties and to take the measures required to protect professional secrets as much as possible. The burden of proof certainly must be borne by any psychiatrist who chooses to breach confidentiality.

To reveal a confidence is a violation of the *prima facie* principles of beneficence, respect for persons, promise keeping, and trust. However, justice is also a *prima facie* obligation. Justice may require that we override one obligation to satisfy another. Justice is an underdeveloped concept in the Hippocratic ethic which is so strongly focused on the patient-physician dyad.[22] This deficiency also characterizes most of the codes that have been patterned upon the Hippocratic ethic for 2,500 years.

The contemporary predominance of the principle of self-determination in medical ethics strongly affirms the patient as the central factor in medical ethics. But, like confidentiality, self-determination itself is a *prima facie,* not an absolute, principle. Freedom and autonomy are to be limited if they result in compromise of the freedom of other persons. This is the first principle of Mill's *On Liberty,*[23] which is at the conceptual heart of the idea of personal freedom. Mill's second principle allows individuals to be subject to social coercion if respecting their freedom results in violation of some socially definable obligation to another, or to fulfill rightful expectations others may have of us.

Under both of Mill's stipulations, confidentiality — which can be interpreted as a means of self-governance and, therefore, of personal liberty — is itself subject to limitation. There are circumstances under which promises to safeguard confidentiality would not be valid and under which there would be a positive obligation in the interests of justice to violate the patient's normal claim to confidentiality. This is true of the obligation to preserve confidentiality in general, and in the medical relationship in particular. What are these conditions, and did they exist in the Sexton case?

Conditions for Ethical Disclosure of Confidences

Disclosure of confidences may be voluntary or involuntary. When they are voluntary, the patient releases the physician, hospital, or other persons from obligation by giving morally valid consent. He/she may still withhold certain aspects of his/her record, particularly in psychiatric illnesses. But even with voluntary consent, patients must be made aware of the uses to which the confidential information is to be put. They must be warned of any dangers in granting consent and of the harmful uses to which knowledge of their personal lives may be subject. The physician must release only what is essential for the purpose — informing a consultant, a family member, or supplying data for insurance purposes or a court proceeding.

A morally valid consent to release confidential information should be explicit and demonstrable by some form of concrete evidence, like a signed and witnessed statement. To assure the proper handling of case histories, some have suggested a living will to protect psychiatric case files specifically. The stringency of those conditions is in direct proportion to the gravity and potential dangers in release of the information in question. When the patient is not competent to give consent, a morally valid surrogate takes his/her place — one who knows the patient's values, and has no conflicts of interest in release of the information. The surrogate is under moral compulsion to act as the patient would have desired.

Under certain circumstances, confidences must be breached, nonvoluntarily or involuntarily, over the objections of patients or their valid surrogates. Some clear examples are the reporting of child abuse, gunshot wounds, tuberculosis, or venereal diseases. These actions are required by both law and morality on the principle of protection of the public good.

More debatable are instances of involuntary release of confidential information for the benefit of the patient. A physician may find his patient depressed, suicidal, or alcohol addicted. The patient may refuse to be treated and want the information kept confidential, yet the physician might ask a psychiatrist colleague to see the patient over the patient's objection. A psychiatrist might be informed by a spouse of her husband's drinking, abuse of medication, dangerous driving, etc., on the condition that the information be kept secret.[24] To withhold this information from the patient is deceptive and undermines trust. But to reveal it may disrupt relationships with a well-intentioned spouse or friend. The uncertainties are compounded when we realize that the information we are told in secret even when well intentioned, may be erroneous or unrelated to the patient's problem.

An argument can be made that most secrets of this type should be told to the patient and the information should be disclosed. Informants should be told their information is likely to be revealed. Occasionally, secrecy may be justified.[25] But if this is the case, a heavy burden of proof rests with the physician to show that, on balance, omission of disclosure is a beneficent act.

Violations of confidence are justified when there is foreseeable harm that is serious, probably, and definable to an identifiable third party or parties. The Tarasoff case[26] is a well-known example involving a patient who confided to his psychologist his intention to kill his girlfriend. The psychologist failed to warn the victim or the police. He was sued by the family when the patient killed the woman.

The majority opinion of the California Supreme Court held that the therapist had an obligation to protect the victim. A minority of the justices, however, assessed the harm differently, arguing against disclosure on grounds that confidence in psychotherapists would be undermined. As a result, patients would not seek to be treated or would withhold knowledge about their violent tendencies, thus reducing the chance for treatment and increasing the likelihood of violence.

The differences of ascertaining the seriousness of threats to harm others, their frequency, and the lack of quantifying measures are concerns for conscientious therapists. But the arguments of the judicial minority and therapists notwithstanding, it is difficult to see how a therapist in possession of knowledge that might prevent serious harm or death to others could be excused from an obligation of disclosure. Obviously, there needs to be a reasonable probability that harm would occur. Also, a due proportionality must exist between the harm done by breaking the confidence and the harm of not doing so. Clearly, there will be gradations in the obligation to disclose information based on the amount of harm, the number of people at risk, and the patient's right to confidentiality. Some balance must be struck among these factors.

Some of the difficulties of finding a balance are illustrated in cases of known seropositivity to the HIV virus. The patient's spouse or identified sexual partner(s) should be told after the patient has been given a chance to do so, but refuses or fails to do so. When there are multiple partners whose identity would be difficult to ascertain, the obligation of disclosure is mitigated. On the other hand, disclosure is mandatory when a health professional suffers a needle prick in fulfillment of her/his duties to patients. The health worker is entitled to the chance for early treatment if the patient whose blood was involved was HIV positive, and relief of anxiety if the patient was negative. Indeed, this is an instance in which, out of justice for the health worker, mandatory testing would be morally defensible if a patient did not know his/her HIV serology or refused to reveal it.[27]

In short, there is no justification to conceal knowledge of the possibility of exposure to a uniformly fatal disease like AIDS in the name of either autonomy or confidentiality if harm to an identifiable other person is a possibility. This is likewise the case when a patient's job entails responsibility for the welfare and lives of others. The therapist who is aware of substance abuse, psychological disorder, epilepsy, etc., in a truck driver, airline pilot, or locomotive engineer is under obligation to reveal that knowledge to appropriate persons.

Obviously, no simple formula will resolve the tensions between the *prima facie* obligations to preserve confidences on the one hand, and to serve justice and beneficence on the other. The difficulties do not excuse therapists from a serious effort to engage in some form of moral calculus involving degree and probability of harm to the patient from disclosure or to others from concealment, the number of people involved, and the reliability of the data in question. Such an analysis will certainly not guarantee moral certitude. But it will set some limits on the *prima facie* obligation to guard confidences and the conditions that might warrant violation of this serious moral proscription.

Confidentiality and the Sexton Tapes

Anne Sexton's psychiatrist, Dr. Martin Orne, initiated the taping sessions as an aid to therapy because Sexton often could not remember from one session to the next.[28] With the taping sessions Orne felt he could maintain continuity across sessions and sustain therapeutic progress. He also felt the tapes helped Sexton's poetic efforts, which he had suggested and encouraged as part of her therapy early in their association.

Anne Sexton made no mention of these tapes in her otherwise detailed will. Only four tapes were found in her papers at her death. Sexton's biographer, Diane Middlebrook, seems sure from what she learned about Sexton that she would not have held back the tapes that were then in the possession of Dr. Orne. Middlebrook bases her presumption of permission on her appraisal that Sexton did not have a strong sense of privacy and was considered exhibitionistic and lacking in reserve. From this, she concludes that Sexton would have found meaning in her suffering only by communicating it with other.[29]

Similarly, Dr. Orne, after several years of reluctance, agreed to release the tapes to Middlebrook because he felt they could help others afflicted like Anne Sexton. He did not have explicit permission to do so, but inferred from his intimate knowledge of Sexton's personality that she would want them released if they could relieve suffering of others. Thus, he became Middlebrook's willing collaborator in her use of the tapes he had recorded.

The reasons for release of the tapes and material therein asserted by Martin Orne, Linda Sexton, and Diane Middlebrook do not square very well with the reasons outlined earlier in this essay for breaching confidences ethically. No identifiable third parties would have been harmed in a definable way by keeping the confidence. However, there was potential harm to others in making the revelations, that is, members of the family who did not entirely share Linda Sexton's confidence that Anne Sexton would have wanted the material released. Other patients under psychotherapy with Orne or other psychiatrists could identify with Sexton and be depressed by her suicide. Furthermore, it is not known how many patients or potential patients had their trust in psychotherapy undermined by knowing their analyses might one day be revealed.

The two major reasons given for release of the tapes were that Anne, herself, would have wanted the tapes made public (a right of disclosure) and that if the tapes were released, some good might come to other patients in psychotherapy or, more distantly, that a better understanding of literary creativity might be obtained.

There is insufficient evidence that Sexton did give, or would have given, permission for the use of the information contained in her taped therapy sessions. The evidence to which Dr. Orne and Linda Sexton appeal in their argument that permission would have been granted is entirely presumptive. It is based in the facts that Sexton was a "confessional" poet (and, by this simple fact, would have wanted to confess all), that she was exhibitionistic, and that her therapy appeared in her poetry anyway.

It must be pointed out that Sexton was ambiguous even about her exhibitionism. She took great pains to present herself as she wanted to be perceived by her public. She admitted, "I can be deeply personal, but I'm not being personal about myself."[30] Further, it is not at all clear how much of Dr. Orne's assumption of consent is the result of the transference — counter transference dynamic. Some have suggested he was motivated by a desire to share in his patient's limelight.[31, 32] They ask why he did not destroy the tapes at Anne's death, a practice some psychiatrists regard as mandatory with highly sensitive material. It is unfair to attribute selfish motives to Dr. Orne, but it is also unfair to assume they were not possible in a relationship as complicated as any relationship with Anne Sexton seems destined to have been.

Similar allegations of self-interest have been leveled against Linda Saxton. It has been suggested that she may have been sexually abused by her mother and may have suffered emotional trauma from her mother's psychological aberrances. The urge to recount traumatic childhood experiences of this kind and to work out feelings of victimization are realities that cannot be totally ignored. Again, it would be unfair to impute such motives to Linda, but equally unfair to her mother not to consider them at all.

The upshot of the matter is that the evidence for Anne Sexton's consent is based primarily on assumptions and inferences. This kind of evidence is indirect and open to alternative explanations. There does not appear to be enough solid evidence to justify breaching confidences of such sensitive material as the tapes contained. Certainly, the conditions of confidentiality do not seem to be present.

But what about the putative good for others that Orne, Middlebrook, Linda Sexton, and Maxine Kumin, Anne's poet friend, all put forth as justification for release? What might some of those presumptive goods be?

There is little or no evidence that intimate knowledge of another person's psychosocial and sexual torments are, in themselves, therapeutic or prophylactic for others similarly afflicted. Because the outcome in this case was suicide, harm might just as arguably occur. One could reasonably argue that some benefit could accrue to students of psychiatry from a study of Martin Orne's method of therapy or the intricacies of Ms. Sexton's case. If Sexton had, in fact, intended the tapes for such use, there could be little quarrel with their release. They would be used by a limited audience with some social claim or knowledge of psychoanalytic procedure. The identity of the patient would be concealed. In any case, justification for use of the tapes for residents in psychiatry does not translate easily into their release to a biographer or to the general public.

Some might argue that any insight we might gather into the connections between the creative poetic life and the interstices of Anne Sexton's psychosexual life would tell us something about the mysteries of artistic creativity. Erica Jong argues that we must understand all we can about the artist's surrender to her subject matter.[33] But Freud, himself, warned us against this kind of psychologism. In his own analysis of the creative life of Leonardo daVinci, he said, "We have to admit that the nature of artistic attainment is psychoanalytically inaccessible to us."[34] The perilousness of such analyses is further illustrated in Peter Gay's compendious biography of Freud.[35] Gay points out that Freud attributed all of Leonardo's artistic attainments and presumed homosexuality to a childhood fantasy involving a vulture. Freud, himself, was the victim of the German mistranslation of the Italian word for "kite" or "hawk." The kite has a very different symbolic significance from that constructed by Freud for the "vulture." In any case, as Barzun points out, psychobiographical constructs are notoriously deceptive, especially about sexual matters.[36]

Equally precarious as an argument for releasing the tapes is the claim that, as a literary figure, Anne Sexton was "in the public domain." There is no justifiable moral claim to confidential information on the part of the general public to intimate details of a celebrity's life unless the public has some very good reason to be informed. Knowledge of the serious psychiatric pathology of a public official could be in the public interest. The First Amendment right to free flow of information, however, is not an automatic right to access to intimate details of the lives of public figures that would serve no purpose beyond feeding salacious interests. Anne Sexton's poetry is in the public domain, not her psychiatric case file. To grant any sort of moral claim to so nebulous an entity as the public domain is to give sanction to the all too common temptation of the media and the public for psychological voyeurism.

Moreover, we hardly need to encourage the current obsessive fixation on the sex lives of public figures. It helps little to understand writing, sculpting, painting, or composing to know about every convolution in the emotional life of the artist. Freud, himself, is more prudent in these matters than some of his disciples: "It behooves us," he said, "to be very careful not to forget that, after all, we are dealing with analogies and that it is dangerous to drag them out of the region where they have originated and have matured."[37] Would it change the artistic achievements of Dante, Shakespeare, or T. S. Eliot, or help us to understand their genius better to have access to their therapeutic sessions if these were available? Would it help anyone to write poetry like theirs?

To Whom Does the Right of Confidentiality Belong?

Even in the absence of the possibility of informed consent, the obligation of confidentiality could be abrogated legitimately by a morally valid surrogate under certain circumstances, that is, if a previously competent patient becomes incompetent, or, as in the case of Anne Sexton, the patient dies. (We will examine postmortem confidentiality a little later.) To be a morally valid surrogate requires that the surrogate him/herself be competent, be charged with stewardship of the confidential information, and have no obvious conflict of interest in its release.

We have already dealt with the problematic nature of delegated authority by Anne Sexton to her psychiatrist and/or her daughter during her life. Whether either would qualify as a "morally valid" surrogate must remain an open question. Certainly the possibility of real conflicts of threats cannot be ruled out by people so intimately involved as Sexton's psychiatrist, daughter, and biographer.

Two problems arise when we examine the question of surrogacy. First of all, in the foreword to

Middlebrook's book, Dr. Orne makes quite a point of how much his audiotaping contributed to Sexton's therapy, to his discovery of her poetic talent, and to his suggestion that her progress was undercut by her subsequent psychotherapists. He refers to the undermining of Anne's relationship with her husband, who was necessary to her mental health. He complains that he was not allowed to see Sexton intermittently, as was his wont, and he even suggests that all of this contributed to her suicide. The final paragraph of his foreword is especially revealing:[28]

> . . . although I felt obliged not to interfere with the guidelines that had been established for Anne's treatment in the last years of her life. Anne called to say that she would be in Philadelphia and that she hoped she could see me. I expected to see her, but she never made it. Sadly, in therapy, had Anne been encouraged to hold onto the vital supports that had helped her build the innovative career that meant so much to her and others, it is my view that Anne Sexton would be alive today.

This is, no doubt, a heartfelt but a very grave indictment of Orne's colleagues. Without indulging in psychoanalysis at a distance, one cannot help but wonder what role his own emotional state played in Dr. Orne's decision to release the tapes.

From the Couch to the Grave

One might argue that the death of Anne Sexton relieved her surrogates of all obligations, because the dead cannot be harmed. This ignores the real harm that can be done to the memory of a dead person. A person does not lose all identity or dignity after death. Death does not eradicate covenants and promises made in good faith during life. If this were so, wills would be meaningless. In fact, we do show respect for the body of the dead person. We respect their wishes about distribution of their mental possessions or bodily parts. Is not the person's intimate life worthy of at least equal respect?

Some have called the allegations of breach of confidentiality a "victimless crime," because the dead cannot be harmed physically or emotionally. On this view, there seems to be no substance to the requirement of codes of medical ethics that hold the physician to confidentiality after the patient's death. Jefferson held this view when he said, "The dead have no rights. They are nothing and nothing cannot own something." Ecclesiastes puts it this way: "For the living know that they shall die but the dead know not anything, neither have they anymore a reward; for the memory of them is forgotten" (Ecclesiastes 9:15). Erica Jong, commenting on the Sexton case, takes the same view.[39]

Yet this flies in the face of the fact that, in most cultures, the dead are respected and revered; their memory is a sacred heritage, meaningful to families, friends, and nations. Memory of the dead is something not to be dishonored. Indeed, many families struggle to refurbish the reputation of deceased members whom they deem to have been unjustly judged during life, sometimes centuries after they died. Moreover, few would say that they are totally indifferent to what posterity thinks of them. Indeed, those who deny an afterlife are often most insistent that their genuine immortality lies in the way future generations will judge them. Cicero puts it well: "The life of the dead consists in being presented in the minds of the living."

Perhaps the wisest attitude to the rights of the dead is captured by Confucius: "If we treat the dead as if they were wholly dead, it shows want of affection; if we treat them as wholly alive, it shows want of sense." This is a little more practical than the ancient adage "*De mortuis nil nisi bonum.*" Sometimes truth, justice, and history require that we set the record straight and reveal the evil that humans do as well as the good.

This does not mean that confidentiality cannot be overridden after death; rather, despite death, it remains a *prima facie* obligation. We must judge when to override the confidentiality of the dead by the same ethical criteria we use to make judgments about release of confidences about living people. Revealing confidences about the dead when doing so would restore justice to them or to another person, refurbish their or another person's reputation, straighten out claims on estates or authorship, or verify important points of history is a mandatory breach of confidentiality. None of these justifications, however, seems to have been present in the release of the Anne Sexton tapes.

Who Owns Secrets?

Throughout this discussion, I have emphasized the moral claim of confidentiality during life and even after death of a patient undergoing psychotherapy. But, a further question is the degree to which others who are mentioned or affected by the release of confidences also have a claim on confidentiality. All members of Sexton's family did not agree that release of the tapes was a good thing.[40] There is information about the lives of Sexton's father and mother that could be damaging to their memories. Other family members could be offended by what was made public about Anne.

Generally speaking, the right of confidentiality extends to those about whom a secret is told, as well as those who reveal the secret. Whatever secrets we chance upon concerning intimate parts of other people's lives imposes the obligation of stewardship, even if we did not seek out that stewardship. The same ethical criteria apply to safeguarding and releasing secrets about others as apply to the secrets we tell others in confidence.

Finally, what about the rights to disclosure? To whom does the right of disclosure belong in psychotherapeutic relationships? Certainly, the patient has the primary right to disclose what he/she deems fit for disclosure. But is this right absolute? As mentioned earlier, this right is abrogated if grave harm to others occurs as a result of secrecy. What happens when the patient wishes to disclose but the therapist does not? Some have argued that the therapist must maintain such absolute hold on confidentiality that neither the patient nor the family can request him/her to reveal confidences; only the patient can reveal those confidences.[41] Here we confront the recurrent conflict between absolute patient autonomy and absolute physician authority. As I have tried to show elsewhere,[42] this calls for a judicious balancing of benevolence and autonomy that cannot be detailed here.

A Few Words About Psychobiography

This discussion has centered primarily on the ethics of the psychiatric relationship. Little has been said of the obligations of biographers. It can be argued that, by definition, biography involves some invasions of a living or dead person's privacy. Biographers, therefore, cannot be accused *ipso facto* and *en masse* of unethical invasions of privacy. Yet the precise limit of the invasions they are permitted is an ethical question that has not yet been carefully examined. Suffice it to say that the use of tapes of psychotherapeutic sessions is sufficiently usual to permit raising privacy as well as confidentiality questions. One can easily imagine future cases of this type, that, given the ubiquity and technical ingenuity of modern audio and visual recording devices, are certain to occur. What will the information highway do to even the confidentiality of a psychotherapeutic session?

Often those with literary interests and capabilities are understandably impatient with the difficult and not always definitive methodology of ethical analysis. There is even a suggestion that literature and ethics are examples of the "right-brain/left-brain polarity" that irrevocably divides art and reason. But the imaginative and the rational dimensions of human existence cannot be so neatly separated. Good ethics should not, and cannot, destroy genuine art; nor can or should art, however great, obliterate ethics or substitute for it. Gauguin's conduct toward his family remains despicable. The beauty of his paintings does not redeem the kind of life he led.

Certainly, biography is an important and often socially useful enterprise. Society and our culture would lose much if we did not have critical studies of the lives of other persons in our own time and in times past. But a question remains about the degree to which physicians, and psychotherapists in particular, should provide material for the biographer. In the Sexton case, Willard Gaylin is firm in his insistence that Dr. Orne should not have been Middlebrook's "research assistant." He goes further and claims that physicians have no "obligation to history."[43] Clearly, the ethics of biography, the way confidential material is discovered and revealed, and the part physicians might play in either deserves study.

Conclusion

Anne Sexton's case is important in itself, but also for the precedent it establishes. To be sure, there are, and have been, numerous postmortem revelations of the intimacies of artists' lives. Indeed, this is almost the rule of late 20th-century biography, particularly when it comes to the sexual persona. These revelations seem not to have had the ethical scrutiny they deserve. Once the criteria for maintaining confidentiality are loosened, especially in a widely publicized case like Sexton's, a logical gradient is established in the direction of further loosening of the traditional bonds of confidentiality. Gradually, the concept of confidentiality can become so diluted as to be meaningless. The ethically defensible boundaries that should protect confidentiality can become so flexible that they lose their restraining influence. As a result, one of the pediments upon which the covenant of trust, central to any therapeutic relationship, is based, can be irreparably damaged, to the peril of the patient and the profession.

What I have tried to show is that, far from being a "decrepit" concept, confidentiality remains a vital element in all human relationships, especially those of a psychotherapeutic nature. The obligation to protect confidences has a strong moral foundation in the ethics of liberty, autonomy, and privacy. It is a *prima facie* obligation, but not an absolute obligation. It may be overridden in certain specific circumstances. These circumstances are applicable to the living as to the dead, and they bind surrogates as well as therapists. The whole subject of confidentiality, especially in pursuit of the art of biography, deserves closer empirical and ethical examination. The tendency to see confidentiality as outmoded is seriously in error. Rather, its complexities should stimulate us to a more careful analysis of its limits in unusual cases like Anne Sexton's.

The Sexton biography should serve to sensitize all of us — therapists, patients, and biographers — to the serious and complex nature of the moral covenant that entrusts us with private life of our fellow human beings — living or dead.

The doctors should fear arrogance
more than cardiac arrest.
If they are too proud,
and some are,
then they leave home on horseback.
But God returns them on foot.

Anne Sexton, "Doctors"

Notes

1. Middlebrook, D. W. *Anne Sexton, A Biography.* Boston, Massachusetts: Houghton Mifflin, 1991.

2. Ablow, K. R. Whose life is it, anyway? Keeping confidences shared in psychotherapy. *Washington Post Health* 1991; 7:9, 24.

3. Burnam, J. F. Secrets about patients. *New England Journal of Medicine* 1991; 24:1130-3.

4. Chaffin, D. S., Goldstein, R. L. The Anne Sexton case: protecting confidentiality? [Letter and Reply]. *Psychiatric Annals* 1992; 22:586-7.

5. Eisenberg, C. Confidentiality in psychotherapy — the case of Anne Sexton [Review of Middlebrook biography] *New England Journal of Medicine* 1991; 325:1451.

6. Goldstein, R. L. Psychiatric poetic license? Postmortem disclosure of confidential information in the Anne Sexton case. *Psychiatric Annals* 1992; 22:341-8.

7. Kibel, H. B., Bloom, V. Sexton's psychiatrist violated ethics. *New York Times* 1991; Sep 8:A26 (col. 1).

8. Stone, A. A. Confidentiality in psychotherapy — the case of Anne Sexton. *New England Journal of Medicine* 1991; 325:1450-1.

9. Carton, S. The Poet, the bibliographer, and the shrink: psychiatrist-patient confidentiality and the Anne Sexton biography. *University of Miami Entertainment and Sports Law Review* 1993; 10:117-64.

10. At this writing, there are 36 published book reviews. Surprisingly, little or nothing has been said by ethicists on this case.

11. Zhisui, L. *The Private Life of Chairman Mao* [Trans. H-C Tai]. New York: Random House, 1994.

12. See note 8. Stone. 1991; 325:1450.

13. See note 1. Middlebrook. 1191:xix.

14. Langs, R. *The Bi-Personal Field.* New York: Jason Aronson, 1976.

15. Tiefer, L. Personal perspective: the neurotic need of psychotherapists to exploit their patient's problems. *Los Angeles Times* 1991; June 21:M1.

16. Pellegrino, E. D. Societal duty and moral complicity: the physician's dilemma of divided loyalty. *International Journal of Law and Psychiatry* 1993; 16:371-91.

17. American Psychiatric Association. *The Principles of Medical Ethics with Annotations Especially Applicable to Psychiatry.* Washington, DC: American Psychiatric Association, 1989; Section IV.

18. Beauchamp, T. L., Childress, J. F. *Principles of Bioethics,* 3rd ed. New York: Oxford University Press, 1989: 335-41.

19. Hippocrates. *Hippocrates,* Vol. I [Trans. W. H. S. Jones]. Boston: Loeb Classical Library, Harvard University Press, 1972; 289-302.

20. Weiss, B. D. Confidentiality expectations of patients, physicians, and medical students. *Journal of the American Medical Association* 1982; 247:2695-7.

21. Siegler, M. Confidentiality in medicine — a decrepit concept. *New England Journal of Medicine* 1982; 307:1518-21.

22. Pellegrino, E. D. Toward an expanded medical ethics: the Hippocratic ethic revisited. In: Bulger, R. J., ed. *Hippocrates Revisited.* New York: MEDCOM Press, 1973: 133-47.

23. Mills, J. S. *On Liberty* [edited with an introduction by E. Rappaport]. Indianapolis, Indiana: Hackett Publishing Company, 1978: 73-91.

24. See note 3. Burnam. 1991; 24:1130-3.

25. See note 3. Burnam. 1991; 24:1130-3.

26. *Tarasoff v. Regents of the University of California.* California Supreme Court 17, California Reports 3rd Series, 425, July 1, 1976.

27. Pellegrino, E. D. HIV infection and the ethics of clinical care. *The Journal of Legal Medicine* 1989; 10:29-46.

28. Orne, M. Sexton tapes. *New York Times* 1991; July 23:A21.

29. See note 1. Middlebrook. 1991: xxii-iii.

30. See note 1. Middlebrook. 1991: 158.

31. See note 8. Stone. 1991; 325: 1451.

32. See note 15. Tiefer. 1991; June 21:M1.

33. Jong, E. Anne Sexton's river of words. *New York Times* 1991; Aug 17:A21, A17.

34. Freud, S. *Leonardo daVinci: A Study in Psychosexuality* [trans. A. A. Brill]. New York: Random House, 1947: 130.

35. Barzun, J. *Clio and the Doctors.* Chicago University Press, 1974:42-5.

36. Barzun, J. *Clio and the Doctors.* Chicago University Press, 1974:42-5.

37. Freud, S. *Civilization and Its Discontents* [trans. J. Riviere]. Michigan: Anchor Books. 1958:103-4.

38. See note 1. Middlebrook. 1991: xviii.

39. See note 33. Jong. 1991; Aug 17: A21, A17.

40. Stocker, C. The late poet's sister and nieces are battling to tell their slice of the family's story. *Boston Globe* 1991: Aug 13: A20 (col. 1).

41. Weissberg, J. A. The poet's art mined, the patient's anguish. *New York Times* 1991; July 26: A26.

42. Pellegrino, E. D. Patient and physician autonomy: conflicting rights and obligations in the physician-patient relationship. *The Journal of Contemporary Health, Law, and Policy* 1994; 10:47-68.

43. As quoted in Stanley, A. Poet told all; therapist provides the record. *New York Times* 1991; July 15: C13.

114 Pine Rest Christian Hospital Mission Statement

Pine Rest Christian Hospital is called to express the healing ministry of Jesus Christ by providing mental health services with professional excellence and Christian integrity.

Foundational Affirmations

We affirm our heritage. Pine Rest Christian Hospital was established in 1910 to provide Christian care and professional treatment to mentally ill persons. Science and technology have changed a great deal since 1910, and so have methods for treating mental illness, **but the mission and vocation of Pine Rest have remained the same: to express the healing ministry of Jesus Christ by providing mental health services with professional excellence and Christian integrity.**

We affirm our calling to express the healing ministry of Jesus. It is in the Bible that we learn of that ministry and hear that call. As compassion was at the center of Jesus' ministry, **so we pledge ourselves to care.** As Jesus' compassion reached out to all, **so we pledge ourselves to openness and hospitality** in our services to patients, families, and communities. As Christ made known and real the victory of God over sickness and suffering by his works of healing and his words of blessing, **so we pledge ourselves,** as recipients of his healing grace, **to our best efforts to heal, to relieve, to teach, to help to cope.** And as Christ is present to those who hurt, **so we pledge ourselves,** even when our best efforts fail, **still to care** and never simply to abandon the patient. We celebrate the gifts that each member of our staff brings to the care of our patients.

Pine Rest Christian Hospital, Cutlerville, Michigan.

We affirm our commitment to professional excellence in this healing ministry. The professional focus of the healing ministry of Pine Rest is mental health care. We do not understand mental health so broadly that it becomes identical to happiness nor so narrowly that it requires the identification of a biological cause. Rather, we interpret mental health to include the capacities God intends human persons to have in order to function well cognitively, emotionally, behaviorally, relationally, and spiritually.

We pledge ourselves to professional excellence, which we understand to include **both the technical excellence** established by well-qualified personnel and sustained by continuous quality improvement **and the moral excellence** which belongs to the best traditions of mental health care professionals, the commitment to patients and their good and the recognition that their good is realized in community.

We affirm our commitment to Christian integrity in this healing ministry. By its narrative of God's work and word, and especially by its account of Jesus' person and ministry, Scripture provides for us an identity that nurtures and sustains our care and requires of us faithfulness. Faithfulness to Jesus, who cared for sinners and healed them, **requires of us a readiness not to condemn or to judge but to heal and to care for others.** Therapy and health education are never value-neutral, and Jesus' compassion was never morally indifferent. So, faithfulness to Jesus and genuine care for patients **requires of us a recognition that some behaviors and some attitudes impede the movement of patients toward wholeness.** While respecting, protecting, and even strengthening the freedom to choose, we will consider with our patients the impact of choices upon their physical, psychological, social, and spiritual well-being.

We celebrate Scripture as the revelation of God and of God's cause. It does not provide a medical text or a ready answer to every moral dilemma, but it does provide the remembrance of a Lord who is the Truth and so a reminder that the Truth is not simply our possession. Faithfulness to Scripture, therefore, calls us from any proud contentment with what we think we know and from any slothful acceptance of half-truths or self-deceptions; **it calls us to patient and humble biblical inquiry and scientific investigation,** confident that all truth finally comes from God and finally points to God. We will struggle to integrate faith and therapy, spiritual disciplines and the best clinical practices.

Scripture provides a narrative of God in relationship to God's people and of God's people in relationship to each other. Faithfulness to Scripture, therefore, requires therapy to recognize that human beings and human well-being are relational. **We pledge ourselves to support and nurture the communities that support and nurture persons,** and families and churches and schools, of course, are the most important of these.

Since Jesus cared for the poor and preached good news to them, faithfulness requires that we strive to care for the poor and for those unable to meet the full cost of services. There are limits, of course, to our resources, but with the contributions of staff, volunteers, board members, and constituents, and with careful and creative management of resources, **we pledge ourselves to a continuing concern for the care of the poor,** lest their hurt be ignored and their cries muted.

Practical Guidelines

For the Care of Patients:

1. Our mission points us toward the care of patients. Expressing the healing ministry of Jesus requires care. Both Christian integrity and professional excellence demand commitment to the patient's well-being.
2. Because we care, we strive to heal, to restore patients to mental health, to effective cognitive, affective, relational, and spiritual functioning, to restore them to self-control and community, to enable them — within the limits of their condition and our resources — to flourish. And when we cannot completely restore mental health, we still are called to care, to be present to the suffering, and never to simply abandon them to their hurt.
3. Because we care, we will respect the patient's integrity and community. Attention will be given to the whole person as the image of God and to the complex interaction of the many dimensions of a patient's well-being, including the physical, emotional, social, moral, and spiritual. Such care enlists the patient in a partnership of therapy and utilizes the gifts and resources of the patient in his or her own recovery.
4. Such care also enlists the gifts and skills of every member of the staff. We recognize as part of the care owed patients not only the skills of a multi-disciplinary clinical staff, including pastoral care, but also the gift of prayer, not only therapy but also the provision and maintenance of a pleasant environment, of comfortable rooms, of appealing food, of courteous and efficient admitting and appointment procedures.
5. The privileged access to a patient's privacy and vulnerability, provided in trust for the sake of therapy, will not be used for any other purpose than the patient's well-being. Caring requires confidentiality. Confidentiality does not exist for the sake of the hospital or its clinical staff, but for the sake of the patient and the patient's therapy. Of course, information that the patient or another person is at serious risk of significant harm must be divulged; the patient's well-being requires it. And there are some times when care for the patient as a member of a family or of a community can override the respect due the patient's privacy and confidentiality. However, the patient must always remain the primary and final focus of care.
6. Care requires continuity. Continuity requires not only thoughtful assignment of clinical staff to the patient within Pine Rest programs but also good communication between Pine Rest and the persons or agencies who refer patients or to whom patients are referred.
7. Given finite resources and the limits imposed by third-party payers, hard choices must be faced. Our commitment to each patient will

require efforts to provide the best care within the limits imposed by insurance programs, creative new models of care, which can be provided effectively within those limits, and sometimes to insist that the patient continue in care past the limits imposed by insurance carriers. Pine Rest will work to establish a reputation both for professional creativity in response to such limitations and for Christian and professional commitment to the patient's well-being in spite of them.

For Moral Commitments in Therapy Contexts:

1. Our commitment to the patient and to the patient's well-being involves and invokes a readiness to speak a Christian word on the giving and taking of human life, on the making and keeping of covenants and promises, on sexuality and its expressions. Our calling is not to moral indifference. We will neither hide nor abandon our moral commitments; we will silence neither the voice of the Christian tradition nor the counselor's moral convictions nor the still small voice of the patient's conscience.
2. Therapy situations sometimes present tragic choices, choices where evils gather and cannot all be avoided. In such cases — when, for example, abortion is considered to preserve from other real harms, or divorce, to preserve a marriage partner from abuse — then we will not celebrate the evil, but we will invoke the resources of faith for courage to help make morally ambiguous choices and for a sense of forgiveness also for tragic choices.
3. Christian therapists are neither external judges of their patients nor proxy decision-makers for their patients. Our commitments to God and to the neighbor who is a patient require us to respect and to nurture the capacity of the patient to hear and to give reasons for moral choice, and they enlist us in the patient's struggle to compose a life story that can be owned by the patient and told with integrity.

For Governance:

1. All positions of governance or leadership at Pine Rest have a special responsibility to sustain and nurture the capacity to fulfill its mission.
2. All such positions of the hospital have a special responsibility to sustain and to nurture the sense of "calling" of every member of Pine Rest Christian Hospital's healing community and a sense of genuine participation in the mission of Pine Rest. No one is to be regarded merely as "a hireling."
3. All such positions have also a special responsibility to sustain and to nurture the community's conversation about the mission of Pine Rest and communal discernment about its implications.
4. The leadership of Pine Rest should construe their role as service and their task to be empowering all to work with joy and within community.
5. Those in positions of governance should faithfully and honestly represent the institution to constituents and external agencies.

For Hiring and Promotions:

1. Ideal candidates for any position and/or promotion would have the following four characteristics:

   a. An ability and a willingness to own the calling of Pine Rest as their own. The ideal candidate professes the Christian faith.

   b. A moral and professional excellence fitting to the position for which they are applying. The ideal candidate possesses moral virtues and strength of character.

   c. A technical excellence appropriate to the position for which they are applying. The ideal candidate is well-trained for the position and possesses demonstrable competence in the skills and knowledge relevant to the tasks required by the position.

   d. Special qualifications important to Pine Rest's fulfillment of its calling. For example, Pine Rest shall take affirmative steps to assure that minorities and females are included in the workforce and treated equally and fairly in all employment matters.
2. Real candidates, of course, may not have all four qualifications or all four with the same excellence. Pine Rest will search for the ideal candidate and not decide prematurely to settle

for a candidate who is less than the ideal. In some instances, one of the four qualifications may be judged more important than the others; when this is so, the special considerations which would require or warrant giving special weight to one of these qualifications should be identified and discussed in advance.

3. Under no circumstances should anyone be hired or promoted who is unable or unwilling to support the mission of Pine Rest. The leadership of Pine Rest (including board members, executive officers, and those making personnel decisions) has the responsibility to assure that no appointment compromises the ability of the hospital to fulfill its mission with Christian integrity.

For Relations with Other Organizations:

1. Pine Rest treasures and honors its relationship to the churches and its supporting constituency. It is responsible to them to be authentic in its mission, faithful to its calling. It should provide services to enhance and complement the pastoral care and educational role of churches and to provide a reliable referral agency for the churches.
2. Pine Rest acknowledges its responsibilities to those who refer patients. Good communication with them is important also to the care of the patient. For example, progress reports should be communicated regularly and discharge reports should be sent promptly.
3. Pine Rest acknowledges a responsibility to provide programs in mental health education and mental health maintenance for churches, schools, corporations, and other community organizations.
4. Joint ventures with other Christian institutions and programs will be evaluated in terms of whether such ventures enhance the capacity of Pine Rest to pursue its mission. Particular questions will include whether the venture compromises or enhances the professional excellence with which Pine Rest can provide services and the ability of Pine Rest to serve the mental health care needs of the poor.
5. Joint ventures with other institutions or programs will also need to be evaluated in terms of the effect on the Christian integrity of Pine Rest. Such joint ventures may be pursued for the sake of professional excellence and service to the community, especially the poor, but special care must be taken to protect and preserve the Christian identity and the institutional autonomy of Pine Rest itself.

For Staff Relationships:

1. Because with different gifts and skills we share a common mission, each has the responsibility to encourage and to nurture the ability of others to make their distinctive contribution and to utilize their gifts as good stewards. Each bears responsibility for courtesy and collegiality with co-workers.
2. Because that common mission is an expression of Christ's ministry, our relationships with each other should be consistent with his works and words. Racism and sexism are not consistent with the ministry of Jesus. Patience and kindness are.
3. Because we would attend to the whole program and treat those who entrust themselves to our care with respect for the multi-dimensional complexity of human persons and human problems, we affirm a multi-disciplinary staff of care-givers.
4. Leadership is necessary; good leadership can be identified as that which respects and nurtures the diversity of gifts and skills of other members of the multi-disciplinary staff and the different perspectives on the patient's problem and therapy which they bring. Leadership does not license arbitrary dominance over others or muting the voices of those with different skills and perspective.
5. "Role players" are also necessary; good team play can be identified as that which contributes one's own special skills and competence to care without boasting about one's own gifts or discipline and without either denying or envying the gifts and skills of others.

For the Care of the Poor:

1. To express the healing ministry of Christ is to express the healing ministry of the one "anointed to preach good news to the poor."

Care of the poor has been an historic part of the mission of Pine Rest, and it remains an essential mark of our faithfulness to our calling. Therefore, Pine Rest must continue its efforts to provide mental health services for the poor.

2. Pine Rest should continue to solicit the help of the churches for this ministry to the poor. It should mobilize the resources of constituents and staff to continue this work.
3. The recognition of finite resources requires both the careful stewardship of those resources and creativity with them in order to support and sustain programs intended to provide mental health services for the poor,
4. Some satellite programs should serve communities of poverty. The educational and preventative programs of Pine Rest should include initiatives among the poor.
5. The mental health of the poor depends on many things besides the provision of mental health services. Pine Rest should be a public advocate for the poor, for their security, for their opportunities to escape from poverty, for training programs, and naturally, for their access to mental health services.

Chapter Eighteen

RESEARCH AND EXPERIMENTATION

After the Second World War the world was horrified to learn that Nazi physicians had conducted experiments upon human beings against their will. Jews, gypsies, and others were subjected to painful and often lethal experiments, frequently for the sake of information useful to the war effort. People were outraged that physicians had taken part in these experiments. Physicians are supposed to have the special interest of patients in mind, but these doctors used the patients as means to achieve the interests of others. The Nuremberg Tribunal condemned the behavior of these physicians, and it set as the first principle of the Nuremberg Code that the voluntary consent of people is absolutely required before they may be made subject to a scientific experiment.

It is easy enough, perhaps, to believe Nazis and other fascists capable of unethical experimentation on human subjects, but it is harder to believe that *we* would be capable of it. Yet, beginning in 1932 and continuing for forty years (or twenty-five years after the Nuremberg Code was published) the U.S. Public Health Service sponsored a study of the natural history of syphilis in untreated black men in Tuskegee, Alabama. The men involved in this study were not told the purpose of the study; they were not even given a truthful diagnosis; and, after penicillin was discovered, they were not offered that treatment for their disease.[1]

Many other real-life horror stories of unethical experimentation with human subjects could be told.[2] They take their place in our cultural tradition alongside the fictional horror stories of the "mad scientist." Perhaps it is easy enough for us to believe that a "mad scientist" could be capable of unethical experiments, but none of us are mad scientists. Before we grow too self-confident, however, we should consider another morally dubious experiment.

Stanley Milgram, a social psychologist at Yale University, conducted some experiments to investigate obedience to authority.[3] In soliciting volunteers, however, he reported that the purpose of the experiment was to test the effect of punishment on learning. When a volunteer came to the laboratory, he or she was met by two people, an actor posing as another volunteer and "the experimenter." The actor was designated "learner" and the real volunteer was designated "teacher." The actor/learner was strapped into a chair, and the volunteer/teacher was told to test the learner's ability to memorize a random set of words. When the learner got a word wrong, the teacher was to prod the learner by administering an electric shock, increasing the severity for each wrong answer until, beyond 375 volts (marked "danger: severe shock"), 450 volts (marked "XXX") was reached. The actor/learner was not in fact ever shocked, but the volunteer/teacher did not know that. When the actor/learner screamed in apparent pain, or when he demanded that the experiment be stopped, if the volunteer/teacher hesitated, the experimenter would direct the volunteer/teacher to continue and to increase the voltage. The result was stunning; in most variations on the protocol nearly two-thirds of the volunteers ignored the protests of the learner and obeyed the commands of the experimenter, administering shocks up to 450 volts (frequently thinking that they had killed the learner).

This stunning result is enough, perhaps, to disturb our complacency that "we" would never endanger a human being in an unethical experiment. One may ask, however, whether the Milgram experiment itself was immoral. The "volunteers" were deliberately deceived. They gave no informed consent to the real experiment. Moreover, the experiment risked real harm to its subjects. Even if the injury was to their self-esteem, even if it was the truth that hurt, the "volunteers" had not solicited that self-discovery, that truth, and had not voluntarily accepted that risk.

Is there an explanation for the behavior of these volunteers? Or of Milgram? One variation in the protocol had a suggestively different outcome. In this variation the lab-coated experimenter was called away from the experiment and he authorized an "ordinary man" to conduct the experiment. Compliance with the commands of this "ordinary man" without the mantle of science fell from two-thirds to one-fifth. Why did that make such a difference? Robert Burt answers that the mantle of science, the impersonal ethos of a scientific experiment, had overwhelmed the humanity of both the volunteers and of Milgram.

In common with his subjects, once Milgram had conceived himself as participating in a scientific experiment and saw his subjects through the prism of this ethos, he suppressed both any empathic response to their pain and any inhibitions that might come from feeling personally responsible for their pain. Milgram and his subjects acted similarly.[4]

With the authority of science commanding them, people were willing to do what they would otherwise find morally objectionable. The demands of science, the necessity of research, can obliterate our reluctance to harm another human being. Milgram and his experiment should obliterate the complacency that any of us are immune from a readiness to violate human beings in experimentation when "science requires it."

The best protection for each of us may be to think hard about the questions raised by experimentation and to articulate some binding convictions with respect to it. This chapter invites you to do just that.

Among the questions raised by experimentation upon human beings, one — surely not the least significant — is the role of the physician. We expect physicians to be committed to the "benefit of the sick," as the Hippocratic Oath put it long ago. And, in order to benefit the sick, we expect physicians to acquire knowledge. Indeed, one of the reasons the sick entrust themselves to the care of physicians is precisely that they know better the workings of the body and of medicines. Research is important to the care of the sick. Without research — as is still too often the case — unproven treatments are introduced with great fanfare but without proven efficacy. Rigorous experiments limit the harm to patients of untested therapies. Even so, a conflict is always possible between the need to advance knowledge so that many patients may be benefitted and protected and the need to benefit and protect this patient. In situations of conflict, to whom or to what is a physician finally loyal?

Modern science and technology have given physicians enormous power over patients; that power can be abused when physicians simply use patients for their own purpose, even when it is a noble purpose like the acquisition of knowledge to help other patients. Patients frequently depend upon their physicians; sometimes they acquiesce to a physician's request out of fear of losing care or because they trust the physician's commitment to their well-being. And sometimes, to be sure, they urge their physicians to try "the latest" thing, before it has been proven safe or effective.

The issue is only exacerbated by the fragmentation of medical care. Numerous commentators have noted the fragmentation of modern medical care. Specialist after specialist sees the patient, and often it is unclear who is in charge of the case. Experimentation increases that fragmentation of care — and the potential for divided identities and loyalties among the physicians/researchers. If the responsibility to benefit and protect the patient above all others is no longer professed by all involved with the patient, or if that responsibility is too diffuse among the caretakers, how can the patient/subject be protected?

One response here is simply to underscore the responsibility of at least one physician to protect this particular patient, to be the advocate for this particular patient's well-being. As important as this proposal may be, many have regarded it as insufficient or as unnecessarily paternalistic, proposing instead, like the Nuremberg Code, that the free and informed consent of the research subject is "absolutely essential." Then, all patients/subjects would know what was being proposed and have the opportunity to accept or refuse participation in the research.

Thus two moral imperatives confront one another. The first might be framed, "Give no untested therapy," while the second might read, "No testing without consent." These two demands are the starting point for the discussion. They are captured nicely in Edmund Pellegrino's attention to the moral "necessity" and the moral "danger" of experimentation (in selection 116). If experimentation is to go forward, it will be important to ask about the meaning and application of the consent requirement.

The profound essay by the Jewish philosopher Hans Jonas (selection 117) is a classic piece on human experimentation and the "conscription" of consent; it is worth pausing over in consideration of the meaning and sufficiency of "free and informed consent."

Consider also, however, along with Charles E. Curran (in selection 118) the necessity and moral danger of experimentation on those who are unable to give consent, on children (and mentally retarded patients and the mentally ill). Parents or guardians make many decisions about their lives and about their care; may they also give consent to research involving them? Critics of such a proposal have protested against relaxation of a strict application of the Nuremberg standard, arguing that, although we may volunteer ourselves to take certain risks for the sake of learning something that will benefit others, we may not volunteer another to take such risks — and certainly not one whom we are charged to protect.[5]

On the other hand, critics of such a strict application of the Nuremberg standard have argued that such experimentation is necessary to test the safety and effectiveness of treatments for children (and mentally retarded persons and mentally ill patients) — whether the treatments are traditional, innovative, or investigational. Unless we involve some of them in controlled tests, we turn them into "therapeutic orphans."[6]

Some have sought to negotiate this conflict by following the Helsinki Declaration,[7] which allows research upon children and others who are legally incompetent only when a parent or guardian consents and "only to the extent that medical research is justified by its potential diagnostic or therapeutic value for the patient." The Helsinki Declaration insists that, if the research is not intended to benefit the patient, then "the subjects should be volunteers." Critics of this solution, however, have observed at least two problems: Calling a study "therapeutic" can be misleading, hiding significant risks and burdens and suggesting (an unproven) safety and efficacy. Moreover, the Helsinki Declaration seems to prohibit important studies on children that are safe but not directly beneficial to the child (for example, investigations of normal development or of the natural history of a pediatric disease for which there is not yet an effective therapy).

Charles Curran defends yet another option, the option favored by U.S. regulations: to allow parents and guardians to consent to research on children (and other incompetents) if the research is likely to benefit them in ways that outweigh the risks to them; or if the research does not inflict unwarranted risks or harms. Curran himself, however, complains about the failure to distinguish clearly those risks and harms which are acceptable and which are not. An agreement with this option may mask quite different accounts of the risks that are regarded as acceptable. What do you think?

Two variations on the question of the use of children are included here. Thomas Nairn takes up the very interesting cross-cultural question of the use of children from another country in an HIV vaccine experimentation. The second variation, if it may be called that, is the question of research on human embryos. The NIH Human Embryo Research Panel did not regard embryos as the smallest and most vulnerable of our children, but it did insist that they warrant "serious moral consideration." (The summary of their report is provided in selection 120.) The Ramsey Colloquium found the report and its recommendations "morally repugnant" (selection 121), not denying that important things could be learned by research on embryos, but denying that they could be learned morally by the sort of research the NIH panel thought acceptable.

Questions about the meaning and application of the consent requirement have also surfaced when experiments have been conducted on those whose ability to give genuinely free consent is questionable, on prisoners, for example, or on those for whom access to care is contingent upon participation in an experimental protocol.

A related question is the question of distributive justice, "Who will reap the benefits and who will bear the burdens of experimentation? And is such distribution of benefits and burdens fair?" If we are not candid about this question, poor people in the wards and clinics of teaching hospitals will be the ones who bear the risks of experimentation while the middle and upper classes will benefit from the research. In a study of the side-effects of oral contraceptives, for example, seventy-six women (mostly poor Mexican-Americans) who sought care from a San Antonio clinic to prevent pregnancy were given placebos (without their knowledge or consent to a research protocol involving placebos).[8] Hans Jonas (in selection 117) suggests an alternative approach to the "conscription" of volunteers and to the distribution of risks and benefits; he proposes to start experiments with those whose knowledge and commitments make consent to participation in an experiment unquestionably informed and free, that is, with the researchers themselves.

The benefits of research also raise questions of distributive justice. Feminists and people of color have observed that, especially in the choice of problems to be studied, scientific research in this country shows a bias in favor of white males.[9]

Institutional Review Boards are the committees within institutions which approve (or not) proposals for research involving human subjects. It seems clear that it has been salutary to require investigators to win the approval of a group of peers and community members rather than relying on their own judgment about whether an experiment is ethical or not; even so, questions can be raised about whether Institutional Review Boards provide sufficient protection against unethical experimentation. Do they, for example, by their membership share a bias that can effect not only the choice of problems to be studied but also the choice of methods used in data gathering? Are they, perhaps, biased toward approval by their relations with colleagues or by their interest in the scientific and economic success of their institutions? Are they, perhaps, like Milgram and his teacher/ subjects, blinded by the "scientific ethos" and the necessity of research? (You might imagine yourself a member of an Institutional Review Board and consider both what kinds of questions you would ask and what kinds of standards you would use.)

There are other important questions, of course. We have not mentioned genetic research or reproductive research or behavioral research, issues which overlap with the topics of other chapters in this book. We hope, however, that the selections remind you that, if knowledge is power, that power can be used unjustly, and that, if the price of gaining knowledge is costly, those costs can be distributed unfairly.

Notes

1. James Jones, *Bad Blood: The Tuskegee Syphilis Experiment* (New York: Free Press, 1981).

2. See, e.g., Benjamin Freedman, "Research, Unethical," in Warren T. Reich (ed.), *Encyclopedia of Bioethics* (revised edition; New York: Simon & Schuster Macmillan, 1995), vol. 4, pp. 2258-61.

3. Stanley Milgram, *Obedience to Authority* (New York: Harper and Row, 1974).

4. Robert A. Burt, *Taking Care of Strangers: The Rule of Law in Doctor-Patient Relations* (New York: The Free Press, 1979), p. 89.

5. See, e.g., Paul Ramsey, *The Patient as Person: Explorations in Medical Ethics* (New Haven: Yale University Press, 1970).

6. See, e.g., Richard A. McCormick, "Proxy Consent in the Experimental Situation," *Perspectives in Biology and Medicine* 18, no. 1, pp. 2-20.

7. The World Medical Association's Declaration of Helsinki was written in 1964 (and subsequently revised three times). See Warren Reich (ed.), *Encyclopedia of Bioethics* (revised edition; New York: Simon and Schuster Macmillan, 1995), vol. 5, pp. 2765-67.

8. Robert M. Veatch, "'Experimental' Pregnancy," *Hastings Center Report* 1 (June 1971): 2-3.

9. See, e.g., Rita Arditti, Pat Brennan, and Steve Cavrak (eds.), *Science and Liberation* (Boston: South End Press, 1980).

Suggestions for Further Reading

Annas, George J., and Michael A. Grodin. *The Nazi Doctors and the Nuremberg Code: Human Rights in Human Experimentation* (New York: Oxford University Press, 1992).

Campbell, Courtney. "Awe Diminished," *Hastings Center Report* 25, no 1 (January-February, 1995): 44-45.

Caplan, Arthur L. (ed.). *When Medicine Went Mad: Bio-*

ethics and the Holocaust (Totowa, N.J.: Humana Press, 1992).

Carney, Frederick S. "A Moral Analysis of Human Experimentation," *Perkins Journal* 39, no. 1 (January 1986): 24-33.

Childress, James F. "Love and Justice in Christian Biomedical Ethics," in Earl E. Shelp (ed.), *Theology and Bioethics* (Dordrecht, The Netherlands: D. Reidel, 1985), pp. 225-43.

Jones, H. James. *Bad Blood: The Tuskegee Syphilis Experiment,* 2nd edition (New York: The Free Press, 1996).

Lebacqz, Karen. "Controlled Clinical Trials: Some Ethical Issues," *Controlled Clinical Trials,* May 1980, pp. 29-36.

Levine, Robert J. *Ethics and Regulation of Clinical Research,* 2nd edition (Baltimore: Urban and Schwarzenberg, 1986).

McNeill, Paul M. *The Ethics and Politics of Human Experimentation* (Cambridge: Cambridge University Press, 1993).

Meilaender, Gilbert C. *Body, Soul, and Bioethics* (Notre Dame: University of Notre Dame Press, 1995), pp. 89-105.

Post, Stephen G. "Nazi Data and the Rights of Jews," *Journal of Law and Religion* 6, no. 2 (1988): 429-33.

Ramsey, Paul. *The Patient as Person* (New Haven: Yale University Press, 1970).

———. *The Ethics of Fetal Research* (New Haven: Yale University Press, 1975).

Spicker, Stuart F. (ed.). *The Use of Human Beings in Research: with Special Reference to Clinical Trials* (Boston: Kluwer Academic Publishers, 1988).

Vanderpol, Harold Y. *The Ethics of Research Involving Human Subjects* (Frederick, Md.: University Publishing Group, 1996).

Veatch, Robert M. *The Patient as Partner: A Theory of Human-Experimentation Ethics* (Bloomington: Indiana University Press, 1987).

Walters, LeRoy. "Some Ethical Issues in Research Involving Human Subjects," *Perspectives in Biology and Medicine* (Winter 1977): 193-211.

115 Vivisection

C. S. Lewis

It is the rarest thing in the world to hear a rational discussion of vivisection. Those who disapprove of it are commonly accused of 'sentimentality', and very often their arguments justify the accusation. They paint pictures of pretty little dogs on dissection tables. But the other side lies open to exactly the same charge. They also often defend the practice by drawing pictures of suffering women and children whose pain can be relieved (we are assured) only by the fruits of vivisection. The one appeal, quite as clearly as the other, is addressed to emotion, to the particular emotion we call pity. And neither appeal proves anything. If the thing is right — and if right at all, it is a duty — then pity for the animal is one of the temptations we must resist in order to perform that duty. If the thing is wrong, then pity for human suffering is precisely the temptation which will most probably lure us into doing that wrong thing. But the real question — whether it is right or wrong — remains meanwhile just where it was.

A rational discussion of this subject begins by inquiring whether pain is, or is not, an evil. If it is not, then the case against vivisection falls. But then so does the case for vivisection. If it is not defended on the ground that it reduces human suffering, on what ground can it be defended? And if pain is not an evil, why should human suffering be reduced? We must therefore assume as a basis for the whole discussion that pain is an evil, otherwise there is nothing to be discussed.

Now if pain is an evil then the infliction of pain, considered in itself, must clearly be an evil act. But there are such things as necessary evils. Some acts which would be bad, simply in themselves, may be excusable and even laudable when they are necessary means to a greater good. In saying that the infliction of pain, simply in itself, is bad, we are not saying that pain ought never to be inflicted. Most of us think that it can rightly be inflicted for a good purpose — as in dentistry or just and reformatory punishment. The point is that it always requires justification. On the man whom we find inflicting pain rests the burden of showing why an act which in itself would be simply bad is, in those particular circumstances, good. If we find a man giving pleasure it is for us to prove (if we criticise him) that his action is wrong. But if we find a man inflicting pain it is for him to prove that his action is right. If he cannot, he is a wicked man.

Now vivisection can only be defended by showing it to be right that one species should suffer in order that another species should be happier. And here we come to the parting of the ways. The Christian defender and the ordinary 'scientific' (i.e., naturalistic) defender of vivisection have to take quite different lines.

The Christian defender, especially in the Latin countries, is very apt to say that we are entitled to do anything we please to animals because they 'have no souls'. But what does this mean? If it means that animals have no consciousness, then how is this known? They certainly behave as if they had, or at least the higher animals do. I myself am inclined to think that far fewer animals than is supposed have what we should recognise as consciousness. But that is only an opinion. Unless we know on other grounds that vivisection is right we must not take the moral risk of tormenting them on a mere opinion. On the other hand, the statement that they 'have no souls' may mean that they have no moral responsibilities and are not immortal. But the absence of 'soul' in that sense makes the infliction of pain upon them not easier but harder to justify For it means that animals cannot deserve pain, nor profit morally by the discipline of pain, nor be recompensed by happiness in another life for suffering in this. Thus all the factors which render pain more tolerable or make it less totally evil in the case of human beings will be lacking in the beasts. 'Soullessness', in so far as it is relevant to the question at all, is an argument against vivisection.

The only rational line for the Christian vivisectionist to take is to say that the superiority of man over beast is a real objective fact, guaranteed by Revelation, and that the propriety of sacrificing beast to man is a logical consequence. We are 'worth more than many sparrows',[1] and in saying this we are not merely expressing a natural preference for our own species simply because it is our own but conforming to a hierarchical order created by God and really present in the universe whether anyone acknowledges it or not. The position may not be satisfactory. We may fail to see how a benevolent Deity could wish us to draw such conclusions from the hierarchical order He has created. We may find it difficult to formulate a human right of tormenting beasts in terms which would not equally imply an angelic right of tormenting men. And we may feel that though objective superiority is rightly claimed by man, yet that very superiority ought partly to *consist in* not behaving like a vivisector: that we ought to prove ourselves better than the beasts precisely by the fact of acknowledging duties to them which they do not acknowledge to us. But on all these questions different opinions can be honestly held. If on grounds of our real, divinely ordained, superiority a Christian pathologist thinks it right to vivisect, and does so with scrupulous care to avoid the least dram or scruple of unnecessary pain, in a trembling awe at the responsibility which he assumes, and with a vivid sense of the high mode in which human life must be lived if it is to justify the sacrifices made for it, then (whether we agree with him or not) we can respect his point of view.

But of course the vast majority of vivisectors have no such theological background. They are most of them naturalistic and Darwinian. Now here, surely, we come up against a very alarming fact. The very same people who will most contemptuously brush aside any consideration of animal suffering if it stands in the way of 'research' will also, in another context, most vehemently deny that there is any radical difference between man and the other animals. On the naturalistic view the beasts are at bottom just the same *sort* of thing as ourselves. Man is simply the cleverest of the anthropoids. All the grounds on which a Christian might defend vivisection are thus cut from under our feet. We sacrifice other species to our own not because our own has any objective metaphysical privilege over others, but simply because it is ours. It may be very natural to have this loyalty to our own species, but let us hear no more from the naturalists about the 'sentimentality' of anti-vivisectionists. If loyalty to our own species, preference for man simply because we are men, is not a sentiment, then what is? It may be a good sentiment or a bad one. But a sentiment it certainly is. Try to base it on logic and see what happens!

But the most sinister thing about modern vivisection is this. If a mere sentiment justifies cruelty, why stop at a sentiment for the whole human race? There is also a sentiment for the white man against the black, for a *Herrenvolk* against the non-Aryans, for 'civilized' or 'progressive' peoples against 'savage' or 'backward' peoples. Finally, for our own country, party, or class against others. Once the old Christian idea of a total difference in kind between man and beast has been abandoned, then no argument for experiments on animals can be found which is not also an argument for experiments on inferior men. If we cut up beasts simply because they cannot prevent us and because we are backing our own side in the struggle for existence, it is only logical to cut up imbeciles, criminals, enemies, or capitalists for the same reason. Indeed, experiments on men have already begun. We all hear that Nazi scientists have done them. We all suspect that our own scientists may begin to do so, in secret, at any moment.

The alarming thing is that the vivisectors have won the first round. In the nineteenth and eighteenth century a man was not stamped as a 'crank' for protesting against vivisection. Lewis Carroll protests, if I remember his famous letter correctly, on the very same ground which I have just used.[2] Dr. Johnson — a man whose mind had as much *iron* in it as any man's — protested in a note on *Cymbeline* which is worth quoting in full. In Act I, scene v, the Queen explains to the Doctor that she wants poisons to experiment on 'such creatures as We count not worth the hanging, — but none human.'[3] The Doctor replies: 'Your Highness / Shall from this practice but make hard your heart.'[4] Johnson comments: 'The thought would probably have been more amplified, had our author lived to be shocked with such experiments as have been published in later times, by a race of men that have practised tortures without pity, and related them without shame, and are yet suffered to erect their heads among human beings.'[5]

The words are his, not mine, and in truth we hardly dare in these days to use such calmly stern language. The reason why we do not dare is that the other side has in fact won. And though cruelty even to beasts is an important matter, their victory is symptomatic of matters more important still. The victory of vivisection marks a great advance in the triumph of ruthless, non-moral utilitarianism over the old world of ethical law; a triumph in which we, as well as animals, are already the victims, and of which Dachau and Hiroshima mark the more recent achievements. In justifying cruelty to animals we put ourselves also on the animal level. We choose the jungle and must abide by our choice.

You will notice I have spent no time in discussing what actually goes on in the laboratories. We shall be told, of course, that there is surprisingly little cruelty. That is a question with which, at present, I have nothing to do. We must first decide what should be allowed; after that it is for the police to discover what is already being done.

Notes

1. Matthew x. 31.
2. 'Vivisection as a Sign of the Times', *The Works of Lewis Carroll,* ed. Roger Lancelyn Green (London, 1965), pp. 1089-92. See also 'Some Popular Fallacies about Vivisection', *ibid.*, pp. 1092-1100.
3. Shakespeare, *Cymbeline,* I, v. 19-20.
4. Ibid., 23.
5. *Johnson on Shakespeare: Essays and Notes Selected and Set Forth with an Introduction by Sir Walter Raleigh* (London, 1908), p. 181.

116 The Necessity, Promise, and Dangers of Human Experimentation

Edmund D. Pellegrino

"In every field of twentieth-century development there comes a point of technical perfection beyond which man finds himself in the shadow of his own creations."[1]

New technologies by their very nature must challenge existing social values and institutions. The opening up of new options for human action must call the old ones into question. As man gains control of the process of change, he is forced to decision on the ends to which he will direct his own future.[2]

Characteristically, the enthusiasm for innovation far outstrips the conscious decision-making essential to the humanization of technologic advances. Society is inevitably forced to a more conscious choice between what *can be* done and what *should be* done. It is also required to reexamine the dominant assumption that human happiness will be had if only we can apply more technical knowledge to human problems.

The tensions are exquisitely epitomized in modern medicine which owes its prodigious advances to the avid absorption of technology. For here, in the most human of sciences, technology has forced two profound transformations, the consequences of which are still to be understood. First, the physician is called upon increasingly to be a scientist as well as a helper of the patient, and second, medicine itself promises to become increasingly an instrument of applied biology and sociology.

These two trends are altering the traditional character of the relationship of the physician to the person and to society. They impart the features of a technological transaction to what must remain an intensely human relationship and they intrude the features of a public and social transaction into what must also be a personal and individual confrontation. These transformations challenge the ethical codes and values as well as the decision-making mechanisms which have served medicine for so long.

Human experimentation is a special case of this conflict of technological possibility and human values. Indeed, it is the paradigm of the larger question of how man deals with the value decisions induced by technologic progress and the powers it confers. Examination of the questions raised by the use of human beings to advance the technology of medicine and biology can illumine the larger question of how best to institutionalize and socialize the decisions which will determine if new technologies are truly to serve human ends. It is within this larger frame that we must examine the necessity, promise and problems of human experimentation.

Emergence of the Physician as Scientist

Medicine has advanced through most of its history by careful observation of largely uncontrolled and fortuitous clinical events. Through rigorous reasoning and careful attention to the rule of evidence, the natural history of diseases was formulated from these observations. Our vast storehouse of clinical wisdom was collected in this way by consummate clinicians from Hippocrates to Sydenham and Osler to the present day. Such experiments as occurred were the "experiments" of nature, perceptible as such to only the most astute clinicians. Deliberate and controlled modification of the clinical situation as part of an orderly advance of knowledge was virtually unknown.

As long as the acquisition of knowledge re-

From *Experiments with Man: Report of an Ecumenical Consultation,* World Council of Churches Studies no. 6, ed. Hans-Ruedi Weber (New York: Friendship Press, 1969), pp. 31-56. Published by the World Council of Churches and used by permission.

mained thus essentially observational, the physician did not face a conflict in values or functions. But, as soon as the spirit of experimental science becomes a part of medicine, the doctor is faced with serious conflicts in his role as helper of other humans in distress. Experimental science means the collection of verifiable, quantifiable data in a controlled way and usually to test an hypothesis derived from prior observations and reasoning. In clinical medicine, this requires that the patient become a subject as well as a patient and the doctor must simultaneously be a scientist as well as a helper. In addition to being an ailing person, the patient becomes a complex experimental system in which multiple variables must be controlled and manipulated if valid information is to be derived.

The patient-subject and physician-helper dichotomies are an irremediable complexity of human experimentation and the distinctions between them must not be blurred out. They imply an essential tension in values and a paradox of function and roles for both doctor and patient. Individual good is necessarily counterpoised against the common good; scientific values are placed against personal and human values; and, even the rights of future generations are potentially compromised by the rights of those living today. The expectations of society can only be fulfilled by a critical ordering of these conflicting values in such a way that experimentation on humans can be used to advance the good of man without violating his humanity in the process.

Levels of Human Experimentation

There is a continuum of ways in which humans may participate in the acquisition of useful medical knowledge, each associated with ethical questions of differing complexity. Recognizing the arbitrary nature of such divisions, it is nonetheless essential to break the continuum into a few categories.

First, is the level of unconscious and unintentional experiment which is part of everyday medical practice. Each patient possesses a personal and physiological uniqueness which is the admiration and the frustration of every clinician. Even routine treatment can become an experimental venture, since the variables are never the same and the outcome always in doubt.

A major function of scientific medicine is to reduce this form of experimentation to an absolute minimum and to make ordinary clinical decisions as rational as possible. Much of what we accept as standard practice has not been subjected to the same scrutiny accorded a new procedure. The ethically sensitive physician will keep this fact always before him and remember that the rights of his patients can be as much compromised by propagation of an accepted but untested procedure as by a new one. A clinician contributes much to medical progress if he demonstrates the dangers or inadequacies of an accepted procedure.

A second level of medical research, not necessarily experimental, is the observational alluded to above as the major source of medical advances in the past. The collation of clinical observations from charts, examination of patients, autopsy material, epidemiologic studies, tests on blood and body fluids obtained in the normal course of clinical management are examples of this type of research.

The ethical problems here are relatively simple. They involve such matters as how much additional discomfort one can ask a patient to undergo to obtain extra samples of blood, whether it is proper to impose extra days of hospitalization and expense necessary for a clinical study, whether data obtained in one situation can be used for another purpose, etc. These are important ethical questions which are not given the consideration they deserve. The dangers to the patient, however, are usually minor and the invasion of personal rights is minimal. Hence, the ethical issues are generally resolvable by a weighing of benefits and risks.

The third level of research is human experimentation properly speaking. It involves the conscious manipulation of the patient's clinical situation, altering some aspect of his management to gather information, answer some specific question or devise a new treatment. Here, the rules of scientific procedure and evidence can come squarely into conflict with the rights of the patient. Such experimentation is usually of three types:

(a) therapeutic research aimed at some benefit to the patient himself, trial of a new drug or operative procedure.

(b) experimentation designed to answer physiological or clinical questions about a disease process with results only remotely of benefit to the patient.

(c) physiological observations, assessment of drug effects on normal volunteer subjects with no personal benefit accruing to the subject, but of potential value in the general advance of medicine.

In type (a) the patient is a patient primarily and a subject secondarily. In type (b) he is a subject primarily and in type (c) the subject is not a patient at all unless something goes awry with the experiment.

There is a fourth level of experimentation which derives from the possibilities inherent in genetic engineering and it will be discussed later.

It might be well to illustrate more specifically some of the distinctions between these different levels of medical research by alluding to hypertension. In this disorder, we are interested in the nature of elevation of the blood pressure beyond certain norms set for a given population of a specific age and sex.

At the observational level of research we can study hypertension by a variety of simple non-injurious manoeuvres — measurement of the blood pressure, study of family history, life span, autopsy findings and cause of death, blood chemical findings, etc. Except for the potential invasions of privacy inherent in the use of certain details of the patient's life, there is little threat to personal rights. Much useful information has been gathered in this way on the natural history of high blood pressure.

Another level of investigation would involve attempts by drugs or operative procedures to treat the elevated blood pressure in the hope of preventing damage to heart, brain and kidney. Here, all the ethical problems of drug trials would be faced. There is potentiality of benefit to the patient, but also possibility of harm in the use of an untried drug whose toxic effects are as yet unknown.

A more complex problem is the study of the disorders of function of heart, brain or kidney in patients with hypertension. To do this, the patient is subjected to manipulations and studies which have no promise of immediate benefit to him, but would add to our knowledge of the disease. They might be helpful to others at a future date. These manipulations, like cardiac catheterization, kidney function studies of cerebral blood flow measurement carry certain risks and discomforts and, hence, pose certain threats to the rights of the patient. Even more difficult ethically is the situation in which these same studies are performed on normal volunteers with the hope of providing information of ultimate benefit to those with hypertension.

The most difficult level of research involving manipulation of genetic chemistry is still only a very remote possibility in hypertension. Yet, we do know that there is a high incidence of hypertension in certain families and, hence, some genetic defect as yet undescribed probably exists. If the biochemical genetic defect were to be described, we would wish to eradicate this defect in the fetus during pregnancy by appropriate chemical alteration of the genetic material. Even more appropriate would be prevention of the defect by altering the genetic constitution of the germ cells of mother or father, or both. The dangers of such experimentation are not at all clear. The total effects of manipulation of so delicate and so vital a mechanism as the gene and its subunits are so complex that they cannot be accurately assessed in advance.

To these legitimate forms of experimentation we can add examples of two spurious varieties — pseudo-research and unrecognized experimentation. A physician would be engaged in the former if he "tried out" a new drug on twenty-five patients in his practice, without controls of any kind and then drew conclusions on its effectiveness. The latter kind is more common. It involves, for example, accepting a new preparation or procedure for routine use in one's practice before it had received adequate evaluation for effectiveness and danger.

The Necessity of Human Experimentation

Human experimentation in practice usually poses a mixture of these several levels of ethical complexity. Each raises special questions which in the actual situation are closely intermingled and difficult to dissect free of each other. The complexities of the ethical problems and their analysis cannot vitiate the importance of continuing to develop the scientific and experimental basis of medical practice. For, lacking this, we would be compelled to indulge in unrecognized experimentation or what is worse, a variety of pseudo-research, which gives the benediction of validity to unsubstantiated conclusions.

There can be no substitute for observations in humans to obtain reliable information ultimately to be used in treating human disease. Animal experiments, comparative physiology, artificial organ systems and computer models are all useful preliminary adjuncts to prevent the premature initiation of human experimentation or the pursuit of a trivial problem. The human response to a drug or an operation must finally be assessed and in this assessment scientific and moral probity must both be preserved.

This being the case, the focal issue is a more precise definition of the conditions under which human experimentation is legitimate and the extent to which the individual can be permitted to yield up some of his rights as a person for potential benefits to himself and his fellows. This is the ground upon which physicians, moralists, lawyers, theologians and others can meet to resolve the conflicts inherent in the use of humans for individual and social good.

There are certain values essential to the moral health of the individual and of society which cannot be sacrificed without peril — the right of privacy and dignity, of informed consent, of freedom to participate in any experiment, of veracity on the part of the investigator and of justice which guarantees redress and compensation to the subject of an ill-advised or immoral experiment. The Nazi example of unprincipled experimentation on humans in the name of science or the state is still fresh in our minds and stands for ever as the extreme denial of those personal rights we must guard at all cost. A more absolute repudiation of the physician's role as helper cannot be imagined.

Yet, even the rights we regard as absolutes must be placed within a social context. Here, we have the classical ethical problem of a potential conflict of two values, both classified as good and impinging upon each other. Resolution cannot be achieved by exalting one or by complete abnegation of the other. Instead, we are compelled to a critical ordering of individual and social good to each other. This is the central ethical requirement in making human experimentation serve truly human ends. In a highly organized and complex society all rights are interdependent and few are absolute. Each right must be operationally and situationally conditioned by the social matrix within which it occurs.

We can now examine some of the dangers to personal rights which are inherent in human experimentation. Which of these can be yielded up, for what reasons, to what extent and under what scientific, social and ethical controls? Some rights endangered in all types of human experimentation are: the rights of privacy, of consent and disclosure, of life and of redress for wrong.

Dangers to the Rights of Privacy

Every person has the right to choose what parts of his interior life and personality he will expose to others and under what conditions. This right is fundamental to his dignity and integrity as a person; his social effectiveness and emotional health depend upon it. Protection of this right is a mandate in medical and other professional ethical codes. Without it the person cannot confidently enter transactions with lawyer, physician or psychologist.

The right to privacy is so intrinsic to human dignity and freedom that we can violate it only for the highest social and public purposes. In the interests of public health and safety we already permit some invasions of the right to privacy as in census-taking, registering for a passport and professional licensure. As the dependence of society upon an individual increases, even more infringement on privacy is tolerated as in security clearances, for national defense, and in law enforcement and the certification of pilots and operators of public vehicles.

In human experimentation, too, there are gradations of permissible forfeiture of the right to privacy. Clinical records, laboratory tests, x-rays, interviews, results and details of operations and sundry other data collected in the ordinary care of patients are universally used to advance medical knowledge and teaching. As long as anonymity is preserved, there is only a small danger to privacy in such activities. The use of such data is implicit and is sanctioned by society and in every teaching hospital.

The problem is more complex where more specific identifying data are essential to the research such as photographs, family background and other intimate personal data. Certain examinations may be undertaken for research purposes unrelated to the needs of the patient and thus expose him to revelations he would not sanction. Specimens of blood or body secretions, biopsies or x-rays examined for research purposes unrelated to treatment constitute potential violations of privacy. The danger to privacy is still quite indirect in these situations.

The really serious threat to privacy, however, lies in behavioural research in which the patient's own beliefs and emotional responses are the subject of study.[3] The social utility of such research is hardly contestable in a world beset by individual and national social maladjustments. While the social benefits are great, the threats to privacy are equally great and sometimes very subtle. The gadgetry of an electronic age — microphones, tapes, concealed cameras, one-way mirrors, computer storage and retrieval of data, as well as behaviour-modifying drugs and hypnosis — all provide serious temptations even to the scrupulous investigator. Irresponsibly used, these devices can frustrate the subject's freedom to decide what he shall reveal, to whom and for what purpose.

Even the more traditional research tools, like the interview, the psychological test, the observation and interpretation of behaviour by others often leads to unwitting revelations by the patient. In many studies deception is an essential part of the protocol and is deliberately used to unmask the subject's deeper attitudes, beliefs and fears. Unconscious or subtle deception, coercion and exploitation of the subject are constant threats and these are accentuated when the data are stored and recalled later for uses different than those originally intended. Moreover, long-term storage of data makes them available to investigators who did not make the original agreement with the subject and can unwittingly violate privacy.

The ethical accommodation between the social benefits of behavioural research and the threats it poses to privacy centre on the issues of consent and confidentiality. Under conditions which guarantee understanding and free assent by the patient, the right to privacy can be forfeited for social benefit. We shall speak of the intricacies of consent more specifically later.

The assurance of confidentiality is a minimum requirement if the right to privacy is to be licitly invaded. Confidentiality must be protected as fully as the aims of the research will permit. Whenever possible the research design must incorporate anonymity. Even more important is the assumption by the responsible investigator of the personal duty to safeguard the information he collects from present and future uses which might violate privacy. Highly personal data must not be made available to other investigators without prior consent of the subject. Personal indentifications with research data should be destroyed as soon as the purposes of the research have been attained.

There may well be situations in which the public interest in certain data transcends the individual right to privacy. Such situations should be unusual and the decision to violate confidentiality in such instances must be made only after the most careful deliberation and only with some definite expression of social sanction.

There is promise that part of the ethical problem of confidentiality created by electronics can be ameliorated by this same means. Newer methods of data retrieval built on special codes or even the specific voice pattern of the investigator might well be used to protect privileged data against improper use.

Public anxiety about the misuse of privileged information of all kinds is mounting. If the merits of behavioural research are to be preserved, the investigator must provide a very clear statement of his ethical code underscoring the importance of personal privacy and the conditions for its prevention. The alternative is a restrictive public response inimical to research as well as the public good.

The Right of Consent and the Responsibility of Disclosure

In a democratic society, the right to integrity of the psychological sphere contained in the notion of privacy is paralleled by the right to bodily integrity. The right to determine what shall be done with one's own body is a fundamental posit of human personality. Every medical intervention, experimental or therapeutic, carries some risk of bodily injury or discomfort and, hence, every medical intervention potentially threatens this human right no matter how promising it might be for the individual or society.

The ethical safeguards against loss of the right of privacy as well as bodily integrity reside in the investigator's obligation to obtain the consent of the subject and to disclose the information requisite to that consent. This is a complicated and vexatious subject which will engage most people who think about human experimentation. I will emphasize only a few points which, as a physician, I consider fundamental.

Consent has a variety of definitions. The most useful operational condition for consent in my opinion is the agreement on the part of the subject, the investigator and subsequent reviewers that the subject has been afforded maximum opportunity to determine what shall be done to him in every kind of medical transaction, experimental or therapeutic. In short, the subject must be a partner in the decision and the final determinant of whether he participates and under what conditions. For consent to be valid it must be free of coercion and comprehending of the dangers and alternatives as well as the benefits of the proposed intervention. Absolutely stated then, no procedure can be justified which does not achieve agreement by a subject who is free and informed.

An overly rigid and literal interpretation of this principle would impede experimentation to the detriment of both the individual and society. We face again the intersection of a fundamental human right with the need to "invade" that right in a controlled way in order to advance knowledge for the benefit of all. The right must be protected maximally while impediments to legitimate research are minimized.

An extensive array of dangers to freedom of consent is subtly intermingled in any clinical investigation. These centre usually on hidden duress or the difficulty of communicating the investigator's knowledge to a layman so that the latter can make a truly informed decision.

Obviously, in certain situations free and knowledgeable consent is impossible in infants, young children, the aged, the feeble, the unconscious or the mentally retarded. Here, consent must be delegated to some other person or agency who can act as advocate on behalf of the subject. The greatest care must be exerted in experimentation with these groups. Social utility can too easily be adduced as a reason for performing an experiment. Prior social sanction by some of the mechanisms to be described later is an absolute necessity.

Concealed coercion, often unrecognized by the physician or his subject, is a more subtle but more frequent danger to be guarded against assiduously. We have but to consider the effects on consent of such factors as the excessive awe of the unsophisticated for science, the overwhelming zeal of the investigator and his need to advance himself academically, the disproportion in technical information between investigator and subject, the peculiar susceptibility of students, prisoners, and underprivileged or the fear of loss of regard among one's peers by not "volunteering." Misplaced efforts to protect the patient from "anxiety" or to "spare" him complicated explanations can become unrecognized justifications for feeble and superficial attempts at "consent." Then, too, there are the legalistic few who use a signed permission as a substitute for full and adequate explanation.

Free consent is impossible without the chance to weigh the risks involved, the alternatives to a given intervention, the benefits to be derived and discomforts to be borne. The responsibility for disclosure of all significant information affecting the subject's well-being rests firmly on the physician investigator. Zeal for the experiment can too easily obfuscate this duty and the temptation to easy consent is an ever present threat. Even where deception is part of the experimental design as in drug trials, responsibility for disclosure still remains. The subject must be told that certain information is being withheld and its general nature identified, e.g., that some patients will get a placebo and others a drug and that he may be in either group.

I wish to express a strong personal bias in favor of total or near-total disclosure. In my own experiences, I have found few patients who did not prefer candour if delicately handled, to deception, however slight or well-meaning. Without adequate disclosure consent becomes a meaningless justification for medical interventions and an insult to the dignity of a free person.

Even prior to valid consent is the question of whether it is morally proper to ask the patient to run the risk at all. If the subject is a greviously ill patient and the new procedure or observations are designed to help him even remotely, a crude cost-benefit analysis is usually possible. Weighing knowledge of the disease, its prognosis, the utility of standard methods of treatment, patient and doctor can jointly arrive at a valid decision to run the risks. Most medical advances, including the much discussed organ replacement procedures, involve such decisions. If all the dimensions of consent are scrupulously attended to, such research need not violate the rights of the person though it may raise other social questions.

But, the really delicate situation is the one in which the experiment is designed to gain knowledge of potential benefit to others, but not to the subject as in non-therapeutic research on volunteers. Here, the issues of morality are more complex. When a normal volunteer allows himself to be infected with hepatitis virus or the malarial parasite, takes a new drug or undergoes cardiac catheterization, he exposes himself to considerable risk and discomfort with no benefit to himself.

While such experiments are necessary for the good of all, they do most sharply juxtapose the individual and social good. In such circumstances, the investigator must rigidly respect the right of the subject to full disclosure, including the fact the information obtained may be of dubious or even trivial significance. The advance of science is too freely used as a justification for such experiments especially when uninformed subjects are used. Man can legitimately be a means to helping other men, but not a means to the mere advancement of science.

The voluntary exposure of the subject to some hazards under such circumstances appears to be justifiable. Subject and investigator are on the frontiers of exploration just as much as if they were embarking on a voyage into space. Our current system of morality permits the voluntary risking of life in battle, or in emergencies to save another's life. Is not a similar principle involved in human experimentation for the potential benefit of mankind? Provided the volunteer is not foolhardy or psychotic or under duress and the investigator has devised a significant experiment with appropriate safeguards, experiments on normal volunteers for the general good are consistent with the values we hold as individuals and as a society.

In any kind of human experimentation, with patients or well volunteers, attempts to weigh risks against benefits in arriving at consent become meaningless if the research question is trivial, the control inadequate or the investigator incompetent. The investigator cannot ask himself too often whether the experiment is worth doing, whether it has already been done adequately or whether his methods will answer the question at issue. As one reviews experimental protocols involving human subjects, it becomes only too apparent that this is an oft-neglected dimension of morality. More surveillance over experimental design is necessary if we wish to reduce our vulnerability to informed public criticism. It is certainly immoral to ask a subject to run even the slightest risk to obtain information that is redundant or trivial.

It is appropriate at this juncture as we consider the matter of consent to note some of the very powerful, but often sublimated pressures which modulate the investigator's behaviour as he seeks to obtain the consent of his subject. The clinical investigator is an academic physician whose advancement is contingent upon the quality of research he produces. His drives to make significant discoveries, to design and effect "elegant" experiments and to mimic the rigor of the physical scientist can obfuscate the small light of conscience under a cloud of justifications. The scientist, after all, shares with other humans the drives for power, glory and preferments.

Indeed, there is some basis for the fear of some humanists that scientific investigations in humans may constitute the most acute form of human "hubris." Current widespread discussion of the necessity for ethical criteria and social sanctions for human investigations should result in reasonable constraints on these subtle temptations peculiar to the physician-scientist.

The Right of Life — A Specific Challenge

The most fundamental of human rights, the right to life, may be endangered in human experiments although this danger is usually remote. The ethical questions in these instances focus on the right of disposition of one's own body and life. The traditional limitations of this right imposed on the investigator and the subject have long been the subject of much consideration and will not be reviewed here.

There is, however, a new and specific challenge to this right which is inherent in the current experiments and therapeutic procedures involving organ replacement. A diseased vital organ in one person is replaced by one removed from another person supposedly dead. By this act, in the case of heart transplantation, for example, one person gains the privilege of life and the donor loses it. The matter is complicated by the fact that technical success is enhanced by maintaining organ viability which may mean sustaining "life" in the donor by artificial means.

The crucial danger lies in the temptation to "update" the moment of death to ensure better results for the recipient with the resultant danger of removing a vital organ from a donor still "alive." Thus, some surgeons have even suggested that in cardiac transplantation the heart of the donor should be "beating" for best results.[4] The ethical issues are clearly dependent upon a more generally accepted definition of death than is now available.

On this point some physicians are willing to define death in terms of a configuration of objective observations.[5] They base the diagnosis on such things as: total unawareness of external stimuli, absence of spontaneous muscular movements or breathing for one hour, absence of eye movements, swallowing, yawning or vocalization and loss of all tendon reflexes. When these observations are repeated in 24 hours death is diagnosed and all measures are discontinued. Other physicians, as in the "Sydney Declaration," prefer to leave the diagnosis to the "clinical judgment" of the physician and are disinclined to a more specific definition.[6]

All authorities are, however, increasingly in agreement that death is a gradual process in which there are successive steps of increasing reversibility or stripping away of boundary conditions.[7] The ethician here must depend upon the physician's expert testimony and the physician must combine ethical and scientific judgements in providing his answer. The matter is of more than academic interest since cardiac transplantation is becoming more widespread and, in one hospital at least, approaches the cost of an ordinary surgical procedure.[8]

I am of the opinion that a more specific and objectively stated definition of death is necessary for moral and legal purposes. A definition is needed which can receive social sanction and which can be used to define the boundaries of invasion of the right to life which society will permit. More importantly, it is an absolute requisite if certain types of experimentation and new forms of therapy are to be made morally tolerable. Any such definition will still need applicability in an individual case and here the physician's clinical judgement is brought into play. His burden is still a fearful one, but he can make the decision within a specific and objective framework, continually redefined and clarified by new knowledge.

The Right of Redress for Patient and Investigator

A society which expects to reap the benefits of new technologies should sanction experimentation explicitly enough to protect the subject and the investigator against liabilities they may incur even in morally acceptable and carefully planned experimentation. The subject is in justice entitled to compensation for injury or disability he may suffer in experiments designed to benefit others. The investigator has the right to be protected against legal actions or damage to his reputation from alleged or actual injury to the subject in valid experimental situations.

Legitimate investigators are becoming increasingly sensitive to mounting public sensitivity and may be dissuaded from morally proper and important studies by fear of legal action. The investigator must not be allowed to bear the responsibility for advancing the general good alone. Hospitals, research institutions, and universities must provide legal and insurance protection to the participants in legitimate research. Many technical, legal and economic issues are raised but the moral requisite for compensation seems indisputable.

Stresses on the Physician-Patient Relationship

The absorption of effective technologies into medicine and the emergence of the physician as scientist have induced stresses in the most important features of the medical transaction — its intensely personal nature. Until the emergence of scientific medicine, the physician's behaviour was dictated solely by the good of his individual patient and this was above all other considerations. The whole thrust of traditional codes of medical ethics has been to protect this right.

Clinical investigation dilutes the physician's responsibilities. His duties to science and society become admixed with his mandate to be the helper, advocate and protector of the patient. Some hold that it is unreasonable to expect the same physician to be both scientist and helper.[8] One physician, it is asserted, should be assigned the cure of the patient and another the care of the experiment.

This suggestion would introduce another danger to the physician-patient relationship — that of divided responsibility. The physician in charge of the care of the patient needs the fullest understanding of the experimental protocol. Without it, he cannot act in the patient's best interest which sometimes is better served by continuing the experiment and sometimes by discontinuance. The patient will be better protected when responsibility for his care and for the experimental protocol are in the same hands. Our efforts must be directed more strenuously to preparing clinical investigators for double responsibilities as helpers and scientists. By institutionalizing the policies governing research on humans and by providing surveillance by professionals and laymen, the subtle dangers of a double responsibility can be minimized but not entirely eliminated.

The team nature of most clinical investigations is an additional factor tending to dilute responsibility. Many persons — physicians, nurses, technicians, basic scientists and non-professionals — may be involved in carrying out some part of the experimental procedure. How do we allocate responsibility equitably when something goes awry with the experiment? There must be a leader of the experimental team who can assume responsibility for its actions. It is difficult to conceive how this peculiar combination of responsibilities can be optimally fulfilled by other than a single physician — one capable of clinical judgement, scientific expertise and ethical consciousness.

There are two additional violations of the trust implicit in the physician-patient transaction which may occur. One of these is pseudo-research, in which a physician attempts to evaluate some new drug or procedure in his own practice without controls, experimental design or means for objective evaluation. The other is to be found in the unrecognized research which accompanies the use of long-accepted procedures or new diagnostic methods which have never been properly evaluated. In both instances the patient is unwittingly the participant in an experiment which can serve no useful purpose and which may be useless, costly or even risky. These two spheres of "research" can hardly be dignified as scientific but they do represent a neglected realm of medical morality upon which each practitioner should periodically examine himself.

Medicine as Social and Applied Biology

We have dealt up to now with the dangers to certain individual human rights which grow out of our efforts to make medicine a more rational discipline through experimentation. More complex threats are faced when we begin to apply the potentialities of modern biology on a large scale for social purposes which may transcend individual rights. The range of possibilities grows each day as discoveries succeed each other in genetics, the behavioural sciences, immunology and sex and population biology. We can consider here only a few illustrative situations to epitomize the varieties of ethical questions we must confront even now.

Among the possibilities opened up by modern biology, manipulation of the genetic material by chemical or mechanical means is the most spectacular. It offers man the possibility of predetermining the number, kind, quality, and behaviour of present and future generations. The species for the first time could determine its own evolution. We must deal then, with compromise of the rights of the unborn or of future generations whom we shall never meet. Consent in the usual sense is meaningless.

Genetic engineering, that is, manipulation of the genetic material by chemical or physical means may be "primary" or "secondary," each type with different ethical dimensions. In the "secondary" variety some genetically induced metabolic or structural abnormality in an unborn fetus could be modified or corrected during intrauterine life for example. The experimental subject — the fetus — cannot consent but the parents can at least act as its advocates and can enjoy the privilege of free and informed consent on its behalf. Such genetic manipulation, if it can be made to yield predictable results, might be a very useful tool. It would pose the same problems as other types of experimentation in which a valid therapeutic goal is sought. A cost-benefit analysis would at least be possible since the results would be immediate enough to be studied in one generation.

A more exquisite threat to human rights is posed in "primary" genetic engineering. Here, the genetic material of individuals or groups might be manipulated in order to produce some ideal or more desirable human being in future generations. New and unparalleled freedom is thus open to the race, but new constraints would be imposed on future individuals who would have no opportunity to participate in the decision. The temptations in such human engineering are enormous for utopians all of whom have a favourite plan for the improvement of the species. We can hardly deny that the recorded behaviour of the human race is susceptible to improvement. But unfortunately, the scientific and moral deterrents to the use of genetic engineering as a solution to man's problems are formidable.

First, genetic engineering, while much talked of, is still barely a promise. Then, the predictability of a given genetic manipulation has yet to be appraised. Thirdly, we have no way of guaranteeing the wisdom of our genetic engineers.

More disturbing are the moral questions involved in usurping the rights of the unborn and imposing upon them our own version of the good life — a version our young people everywhere are already rejecting. Man's wisdom to determine the ends to which his new powers will be directed is highly questionable.

Granting the limitations of our scientific knowledge of genetic engineering, we already have potent methods of altering the number and distribution of humans. The principles of human eugenics have been known for some time. Long-term contraception is a reality. Sperm banks and thus controlled fertilization are already a possibility. The reproductive process is being brought under explicit control so that the right to procreate might be limited to those with the most favorable confluence of genes. To ensure the emergence of this "genetic aristocracy," the reproductive function might even be separated from marriage and the family. The more effective these methods become the more urgent will be the pressures to apply them.

The control of human behaviour by psychologic, pharmacologic and electronic means constitutes the penultimate threat to human freedom. It is possible experimentally to modify behaviour, change anger to pacificity, aggression to submission and increase intellectual productivity. Such potent instruments for good and evil are perhaps more dangerous than an atomic bomb. Annihilation might be preferable to certain kinds of manipulation which could divest man of the things which make him human, and uniquely a person.

The ethical questions in behavioural manipulation are of the most fundamental sort. How much diversity in personality and behaviour will society tolerate? Are the social virtues of the termitary or the ant hill sufficient to outweigh the less directed, but hazardous play of personal choices? What indeed is mind, personality and spirit? Are these realms as inviolate as we thought? Or, are they too as manipulable as the body, for what appear to be socially desirable goals?

There is little doubt that man will explore these and other potentialities inherent in the new biology. When he does so man will undoubtedly turn to the physician as the agent through whom to apply his new technology. As the physician of the future increasingly delegates his technical functions to non-physicians, he will be drawn into a new role as a practitioner of social biology. The public will expect him to assume this role, since he has traditionally dealt with man in the totality of his existential experiences.

This role as an applied biologist will immerse the physician more deeply in ethical problems than ever before. He will be required to answer for himself as a person, and for his patients such frustrating questions as: Who shall be permitted to procreate to ensure a "better" species? Who shall determine the desirable characteristics of future humans? What physical and behavioural characteristics should be bred in and which ones bred out? How many males do we need and how many females? Who will make the policy decisions?

These are not fanciful questions given the present directions of biological investigations. A collision course seems inevitable between the physician's responsibility to protect individual and personal rights and the possible goals society may select from the expanding armamentarium of the new biology. As a practitioner of social biology the doctor will be compelled to re-examine all the assumptions which underlie his traditional relationship with the patient. If relevant guidelines are to be developed a deeper discourse than has hitherto been the case will be demanded in medical ethics. Presumptuous indeed would be the physician or the profession which attempted to solve these dilemmas alone. Medicine must enter into continuing and respectful conversations with the social and humane disciplines — law, theology, philosophy, political science. The doctor will remain the expert witness in matters medical, but his policy decisions must be modulated within a broader social frame than he has ever experienced before.

Some Implications in Philosophy and Theology

It would be inappropriate before an audience of theologians to dilate at length on some of the deeper but more important implications in human experimentation and the new biology. Yet, it may be useful as a clinician to make two points which I feel are particularly relevant.

First, it is clear that answers to the new questions posed in medical ethics must be based in a renewed inquiry into the metaphysics and ontology of man. This is the central problem of modern philosophy. We cannot hope for a final "definition" of man, but we can expect a continuing refurbishment of what we think he is and what his destiny should be. Medical thinking has been too exclusively normative and not enough ontological in its perspectives.[9]

Secondly, a few words on charity are essential. We have throughout this essay emphasized the rights of the person as they have emerged in the philosophy of the western world. The language of rights necessarily imposes certain limitations on our actions. These limitations can be ameliorated in theological discourse which deals with the possibilities of surrender of these rights voluntarily and out of love for one's fellows. Indeed, there are imaginable instances in which participation as a subject in human experiments can be regarded as a duty as well as a charitable act. It is for the physician to define the promise and dangers of experimentation in man; it is for the ethician to dissect the intersecting rights of person and society; it is for the theologian to temper their findings with the theology of charity and of duty.

Some Educational Implications

To function within the matrix I have described and to deal effectively with the newer dimensions of medical ethics the education of physicians will require considerable modification. With such powerful tools at his disposal, the doctor's ethical sensibilities and perceptions really become critical determinants of whether man will indeed fall under "the shadow of his own creations."

The physician's acts grow finally out of his personal conception of what he thinks man is and society should be. Medical education, at least in the United States, is largely technical, pragmatic and geared to the development of competence — all essential and ethically defensible goals. But, they are not sufficient to meet the ethical questions physicians face even today, to say nothing of tomorrow's problems. Too many clinical faculty members eschew discussion of critical, ethical and philosophical issues or feel that they can be pragmatically resolved. The antispeculative bias of medical education has served it well, but not sufficiently.

Fortunately, students themselves are generating pressures for freer discussion of these matters and I am certain that their interest will make medical education more responsive to social and ethical issues. Educators are examining a variety of ways to introduce ethical and social perspectives into medical education. I should like to enumerate a few of my personal preferences in this regard.

(a) "Courses" in medical ethics have been notoriously nonproductive for today's students, who are disinclined to abstract discussions. Such courses might have validity as electives in depth after a student has seen the problems in concrete situations.

(b) The most effective means of eliciting student interest in ethical issues is to discuss them in the clinical situation, at the "bedside" and as part of his daily clinical experience. Interdisciplinary conferences, built around a specific patient with whom the student has worked, have proved in my personal experiences to be well received. This requires that theologians, philosophers and lawyers be willing to enter the clinical situation, participate in a concrete dialogue and make their points in a "give and take" atmosphere. It also requires too that clinical teachers be themselves better prepared for ethical discourse.

(c) A more formal education in ethics and philosophy should be afforded for small numbers of students who may wish to specialize in the newer questions posed by medical advances. We need a core of individuals educated in medicine and philosophy or the relevant disciplines to do scholarly work in this field, be teachers for the rest of us and provide a more effective liaison with the other university disciplines.

(d) Admission committees must seek out more applicants with a sincere interest in the social responsibilities of medicine. Premedical scientific preparation will continue to be important. But, an orientation to the social sciences and the humanities is as significant for most of tomorrow's doctors.

(e) Obviously we cannot wait solely for a new generation to improve the perceptions of physicians to these questions. Efforts along the lines I have outlined above, are urgently needed to bring the practising physician into closer contact with the social and ethical effects of his daily medical arts.

Social and Institutional Control of Experimentation

My major purpose has been to fulfil my assignment to outline the necessity and dangers of human experimentation. *Clearly,* human experimentation is a necessity; *clearly,* it threatens certain individual rights; *clearly,* in permitting it, society sanctions certain graded limitations on the absolute rights of individuals for the good of all. What mechanisms can we elaborate to assure that the partial invasion of human rights is carried out in conformity with our system of moral values and in a rational and balanced way?

I do not believe, as some of my colleagues have argued, that the stewardship can be assigned solely to the physician investigator. To do so would encourage an increasingly restrictive public policy which would restrain the responsible investigator and impede the development of judicious social sanctions for therapeutics as well as experimental medical arts.

Instead, I see the physician acting as an indispensable part of a socialized and institutionalized system, the totality of which is directed to reasonable control of the delicate ethical algebra involved in human experimentation. Let us examine briefly, the several levels of responsibility and control in this system.

1. The physician is the final instrument for attaining health aspirations of society. In human experimentation he must combine ethical science and ethical behaviour. The first safeguard, then, is his adherence to the ethics of good science which in itself can reinforce other social and institutional means for protecting the rights of patients. I refer to the mandates of good science — personal competence, careful formulation of the questions, careful design of the experiment, reliable observation, honesty in reporting results, willingness to expose one's work to peer criticism and surveillance, and willingness to explain it to the public.

Good scientific ethics will prevent the initiation of frivolous or faulty protocol. It must be combined with the strictest attention to ethical behaviour in the traditional professional sense. Medical ethical codes have recently been expanded and refined to deal more explicitly with the questions of human experimentation. They are not immutable guides but statements of ideals to be preserved. To be living documents they need constantly to be refurbished in the light of new technologies and the evolution of ethical and legal thought.

To this groundwork of unassailable scientific and professional ethics, the physician must add humanity and compassion in dealing with his subject as both work their way through the intricacies of consent, disclosure and the conduct of the experiment.

2. The next level of control is the assumption by each institution of its corporate ethical responsibility for the conduct of all research within its walls. Ethical review committees, as now required by the United States Public Health Service, must be the instruments of institutional guarantee for the rights of patients studied in universities and hospitals.

These committees have two clear functions — Firstly, the values of the community in which they reside. Thus, they define operationally the degree to which certain rights can be invaded for the common good and under what conditions. Secondly, they provide a first point of appeal for the patient who is wronged. Such committees must separate out morally trivial experiments from those which significantly threaten personal rights. In the review of protocols such committees could make on-the-spot decisions in cases of doubt within a certain measure of freedom from strict adherence to any particular code.

The membership of such committees should be widely representative, consisting of physicians and other health professionals, lawyers, theologians, and members of the educated public. They should be chosen for their sensitivity and empathy for both the patient and investigator. They must utilize relevant scientific information and enjoy some sophistication in the psychology and sociology of decision making.

Such committees must appreciate their own moral responsibilities. The members necessarily share some of the investigator's responsibilities. Careless review of a proposal is morally indefensible. The committee members thereby become abettors of an injustice and are morally and legally culpable if they do not carry out their work conscientiously.

3. The highest level of control should reside in a national or governmental body which sets the policies and the moral climate within which local committees and individuals work. This body should set long-range policies, anticipate dangers and maintain proper balance between the concern for human rights and for legitimate scientific investigation. This group could act as the advocate of cultural values at the national level. It should provide social sanctions for experimentation and the legal machinery for protecting the subject and the investigator from the risks they incur. It could serve as an appeal mechanism for unusual cases or when a new technology introduces new ethical dimensions.

Lastly, a potent means of control for the whole process lies in the non-regulatory but highly essential dialogue between ethicians, physicians, sociologists, and theologians on the ontological bases for the rights of man. After all, the entire process of decision making rests on a proper metaphysic of man. This, too, must undergo continuing development and refinement as biology and medicine reveal new insights into body, mind, and spirit.

Responsibility exerted at each of these levels would provide a matrix for reasonable and just decision making which could simultaneously advance the social good and protect the precious rights and dignity of the individual human person.

Society, the Individual and Medicine

Our age is characterized by the most strenuous effort thus far to expand man's experiences as a free individual and a social being. A crisis between these values is inevitable, but it must not be resolved as an antinomy of individual *versus* society. Indeed, as Teilhard de Chardin has so admirably suggested, the interdependence and convergence of human life which he envisioned can presage an even more precious kind of individual life: "The socialization whose hour seems to have sounded for mankind does not by any means signify the ending of the era of the individual on Earth, but far more its beginning."[10]

Medicine, posited between the sciences and the humanities, is one of man's most potent instruments for enlarging both his individual and his social being. To serve this purpose, medicine must respond to the current challenges by creating a new unity of its scientific, ethical and social perspectives. If it does, it might become the genius of that new humanism the world so desperately needs to make technology ever the servant of human purpose.

Notes

1. P. Gascar, "Putting Technology in its Place," *World Health,* March 1968, 50.

2. E. G. Mesthene, "How Technology Will Shape the Future," *Science* 161 (12 July 1968): 135-43.

3. O. M. Ruebhausen and O. G. Brim, "Privacy and Behavioral Research," *Columbia Law Review* 65 (November 1965): 1184 ff.

4. Harold M. Schmeck, Jr., "Symposium Hears Transplant Plea," *New York Times,* 9 September 1968, 23.

5. Robert Reinhold, "Harvard Panel Asks Definition of Death Based on Brain," *New York Times,* 5 August 1968, 1, 35.

6. The Declaration of Sydney, *Medical Journal of Australia,* 24 August 1968, 364.

7. M. Polanyi, "Life's Irreducible Structure," *Science* 160 (21 June 1968): 1308-12.

8. O. Guttentag, "The Physician's Point of View," *Science* 117 (1953): 207-10.

9. E. D. Pellegrino, "Medicine, Philosophy and Man's Infirmity." *Conditio Humana, Festschrift for Professor Erwin Straus* (Springer Verlag, October 1966), pp. 272-84.

10. P. Teilhard de Chardin, *The Future of Man* (New York: Harper and Row, 1964), p. 47.

117 Philosophical Reflections on Experimenting with Human Subjects

Hans Jonas

Experimenting with human subjects is going on in many fields of scientific and technological progress. It is designed to replace the over-all instruction by natural, occasional experience with the selective information from artificial, systematic experiment which physical science has found so effective in dealing with inanimate nature. Of the new experimentation with man, medical is surely the most legitimate; psychological, the most dubious; biological (still to come), the most dangerous. I have chosen here to deal with the first only, where the case *for* it is strongest and the task of adjudicating conflicting claims hardest. . . .

I. The Peculiarity of Human Experimentation

Experimentation was originally sanctioned by natural science. There it is performed on inanimate objects, and this raises no moral problems. But as soon as animate, feeling beings become the subjects of experiment, as they do in the life sciences and especially in medical research, this innocence of the search for knowledge is lost and

Reprinted by permission of *Daedalus,* Journal of the American Academy of the Arts and Sciences, from the issue entitled "Ethical Aspects of Experimentation with Human Subjects," Spring 1969, Vol. 98, No. 2.

questions of conscience arise. The depth of which moral and religious sensibilities can become aroused over these questions is shown by the vivisection issue. Human experimentation must sharpen the issue as it involves ultimate questions of personal dignity and sacrosanctity. One profound difference between the human experiment and the physical (beside that between animate and inanimate, feeling and unfeeling nature) is this: The physical experiment employs small-scale, artificially devised substitutes for that about which knowledge is to be obtained, and the experimenter extrapolates from these models and simulated conditions to nature at large. Something deputizes for the "real thing" — balls, rolling down an inclined plane for sun and planets, electric discharges from a condenser for real lightning, and so on. For the most part, no such substitution is possible in the biological sphere. We must operate on the original itself, the real thing in the fullest sense, and perhaps affect it irreversibly. No simulacrum can take its place. Especially in the human sphere, experimentation loses entirely the advantage of the clear division between vicarious model and true object. Up to a point, animals may fulfill the proxy role of the classical physical experiment. But in the end man himself must furnish knowledge about himself, and the comfortable separation of noncommittal experiment and definitive action vanishes. An experiment in education affects the lives of its subjects, perhaps a whole generation of schoolchildren. Human experimentation for whatever purpose is always *also* a responsible, nonexperimental, definitive dealing with the subject himself. And not even the noblest purpose abrogates the obligations this involves.

This is the root of the problem with which we are faced: Can both that purpose and this obligation be satisfied? If not, what would be a just compromise? Which side should give way to the other? The question is inherently philosophical as it concerns not merely pragmatic difficulties and their arbitration, but a genuine conflict of values involving principles of a high order. May I put the conflict in these terms? On principle, it is felt, human beings *ought not* to be dealt with in that way (the "guinea pig" protest); on the other hand, such dealings are increasingly urged on us by considerations, in turn appealing to principle, that claim to override those objections. Such a claim must be carefully assessed, especially when it is swept along by a mighty tide. Putting the matter thus, we have already made one important assumption rooted in our "Western" cultural tradition: The prohibitive rule is, to that way of thinking, the primary and axiomatic one; the permissive counter-rule, as qualifying the first, is secondary and stands in need of justification. We must justify the infringement of a primary inviolability, which needs no justification itself; and the justification of its infringement must be by values and needs of a dignity commensurate with those to be sacrificed. . . .

II. "Individual Versus Society" as the Conceptual Framework

The setting for the conflict most consistently invoked in the literature is the polarity of individual versus society — the possible tension between the individual good and the common good, between private and public welfare. . . . I have grave doubts about the adequacy of this frame of reference, but I will go along with it part of the way. It does apply to some extent, and it has the advantage of being familiar. We concede, as a matter of course, to the common good some pragmatically determined measure of precedence over the individual good. In terms of rights, we let some of the basic rights of the individual be overruled by the acknowledged rights of society — as a matter of right and moral justness and not of mere force or dire necessity (much as such necessity may be adduced in defense of that right). But in making that concession, we require a careful clarification of what the needs, interests, and rights of society are, for society — as distinct from any plurality of individuals — is an abstraction and, as such, is subject to our definition, while the individual is the primary concrete, prior to all definition, and his basic good is more or less known. Thus the unknown in our problem is the so-called common or public good and its potentially superior claims, to which the individual good must or might sometimes be sacrificed, in circumstances that in turn must also be counted among the unknowns of our question. Note that in putting the matter in this way — that is, in asking about the right of society to individual sacrifice — the consent of the sacrificial subject is no necessary part of the *basic* question.

"Consent," however, is the other most consistently emphasized and examined concept in discussions of this issue. This attention betrays a feeling that the "social" angle is not fully satisfactory. If society has a right, its exercise is not contingent on volunteering. On the other hand, if volunteering is fully genuine, no public right to the volunteered act need be construed. There is a difference between the moral or emotional appeal of a cause that elicits volunteering and a right that demands compliance — for example, with particular reference to the social sphere, between the *moral claim* of a common good and society's *right* to that good and to the means of its realization. A moral claim cannot be met without consent; a right can do without it. Where consent is present anyway, the distinction may become immaterial. But the awareness of the many ambiguities besetting the "consent" actually available and used in medical research[1] prompts recourse to the idea of a public right conceived independently of (and valid prior to) consent; and, vice versa, the awareness of the problematic nature of such a right makes even its advocates still insist on the idea of consent with all its ambiguities: an uneasy situation either way.

Nor does it help much to replace the language of "rights" by that of "interests" and then argue the sheer cumulative weight of the interest of the many over against those of the few or the single individual. "Interests" range all the way from the most marginal and optional to the most vital and imperative, and only those sanctioned by particular importance and merit will be admitted to court in such a calculus — which simply brings us back to the question of right or moral claim. Moreover, the appeal to numbers is dangerous. Is the number of those afflicted with a particular disease great enough to warrant violating the interests of the non-afflicted? Since the number of the latter is usually so much greater, the argument can actually turn around to the contention that the cumulative weight of interest is on *their* side. Finally, it may well be the case that the individual's interest in his own inviolability is itself a public interest, such that its publicly condoned violation, irrespective of numbers, violates the interest of all. In that case, its protection in *each* instance would be a paramount interest, and the comparison of numbers will not avail.

These are some of the difficulties hidden in the conceptual framework indicated by the terms "society-individual," "interest," and "rights." But we also spoke of a moral call, and this points to another dimension — not indeed divorced from the social sphere, but transcending it. And there is something even beyond that: true sacrifice from highest devotion, for which there are no laws or rules except that it must be absolutely free. "No one has the right to choose martyrs for science" was a statement repeatedly quoted in the November, 1967, *Daedalus* conference. But no scientist can be prevented from making himself a martyr for his science. At all times, dedicated explorers, thinkers, and artists have immolated themselves on the altar of their vocation, and creative genius most often pays the price of happiness, health, and life for its own consummation. But no one, not even society, has the shred of a right to expect and ask these things in the normal course of events. They come to the rest of us as a *gratia gratis data.*

III. The Sacrificial Theme

Yet we must face the somber truth that the *ultima ratio* of communal life is and has always been the compulsory, vicarious sacrifice of individual lives. The primordial sacrificial situation is that of outright human sacrifices in early communities. These were not acts of blood-lust or gleeful savagery; they were the solemn execution of a supreme, sacral necessity. One of the fellowship of men had to die so that all could live, the earth be fertile, the cycle of nature renewed. The victim often was not a captured enemy, but a select member of the group: "The king must die." If there was cruelty here, it was not that of men, but that of the gods, or rather of the stern order of things, which was believed to exact that price for the bounty of life. To assure it for the community, and to assure it ever again, the awesome *quid pro quo* had to be paid over again.

Far should it be from us to belittle, from the height of our enlightened knowledge, the majesty of the underlying conception. The particular *causal* views that prompted our ancestors have long since been relegated to the realm of superstition. But in moments of national danger we still send the flower of our young manhood to offer their lives for the continued life of the community, and if it is a just war, we see them go forth as consecrated and strangely ennobled by a sacrificial role. Nor do we make their going forth depend on their own will and consent, much as we may desire and foster these. We conscript them according to law. We conscript the best and feel morally disturbed if the draft, either by design or in effect, works so that mainly the disadvantaged, socially less useful, more expendable, make up those whose lives are to buy ours. No rational persuasion of the pragmatic necessity here at work can do away with the feeling, a mixture of gratitude and guilt, that the sphere of the sacred is touched with the vicarious offering of life for life. Quite apart from these dramatic occasions, there is, it appears, a persistent and constitutive aspect of human immolation to the very being and prospering of human society — an immolation in terms of life and happiness, imposed or voluntary, of few for many. What Goethe has said of the rise of Christianity may well apply to the nature of civilization in general: "*Opfer fallen hier, / Weder Lamm noch Stier, / Aber Menschenopfer unerhoert.*"[2] We can never rest comfortably in the belief that the soil from which our satisfactions sprout is not watered with the blood of martyrs. But a troubled conscience compels us, the undeserving beneficiaries, to ask: Who is to be martyred? In the service of what cause and by whose choice?

Not for a moment do I wish to suggest that medical experimentation on human subjects, sick or healthy, is to be likened to primeval human sacrifices. Yet something sacrificial is involved in the selective abrogation of personal inviolability and the ritualized exposure to gratuitous risk of health and life, justified by a presumed greater, social good. My examples from the sphere of stark sacrifice were intended to sharpen the issues implied in that context and to set them off clearly from the kinds of obligations and constraints imposed on the citizen in the normal course of things or generally demanded of the individual in exchange for the advantages of civil society.

IV. The "Social Contract" Theme

The first thing to say in such a setting-off is that the sacrificial area is not covered by what is called the "social contract." This fiction of political theory, premised on the primacy of the individual, was designed to supply a rationale for the *limitation* of individual freedom and power required for the existence of the body politic, whose existence in turn is for the benefit of the individuals. The principle of these limitations is that their *general* observance profits all, and that therefore the individual observer, assuring this general observance for his part, profits by it himself. I observe property rights because their general observance assures my own; I observe traffic rules because their general observance assures my own safety; and so on. The obligations here are mutual and general; no one is singled out for special sacrifice. Moreover, for the most part, *qua* limitations of my liberty, the laws thus deducible from the hypothetical "social contract" enjoin me from certain actions rather than obligate me to positive actions (as did the laws of feudal society). Even where the latter is the case, as in the duty to pay taxes, the rationale is that I am myself a beneficiary of the services financed through these payments. Even the contributions levied by the welfare state, though not originally contemplated in the liberal version of the social contract theory, can be interpreted as a personal insurance policy of one sort or another — be it against the contingency of my own indigence, be it against the dangers of disaffection from the laws in consequence of widespread unrelieved destitution, be it even against the disadvantages of a diminished consumer market. Thus, by some stretch, such contributions can still be subsumed under the principle of enlightened self-interest. But no complete abrogation of self-interest at any time is in the terms of the social contract, and so pure sacrifice falls outside it. Under the putative terms of the contract alone, I cannot be required to die for the public good. . . .

But in time of war our society itself supersedes the nice balance of the social contract with an almost absolute precedence of public necessities over individual rights. In this and similar emergencies, the sacrosanctity of the individual is abrogated, and what for all practical purposes amounts to a near-totalitarian, quasi-communist state of affairs is *temporarily* permitted to prevail. In such situations, the community is conceded the right to make calls on its members, or certain of its members, entirely different in magnitude and kind from the calls normally allowed. It is deemed right that a part of the population bears a disproportionate burden of risk of a disproportionate gravity; and it is deemed right that the rest of the community accepts this sacrifice, whether voluntary or enforced, and reaps its benefits — difficult as we find it to justify this acceptance and this benefit by any normal ethical categories. We justify it transethically, as it were, by the supreme collective emergency, formalized, for example, by the declaration of a state of war.

Medical experimentation on human subjects falls somewhere between this overpowering case and the normal transactions of the social contract. On the one hand, no comparable extreme issue of social survival is (by and large) at stake. And no comparable extreme sacrifice or foreseeable risk is (by and large) asked. On the other hand, what is asked goes decidedly beyond, even runs counter to, what it is otherwise deemed fair to let the individual sign over of his person to the benefit of the "common good." Indeed, our sensitivity to the kind of intrusion and use involved is such that only an end of transcendent value or overriding urgency can make it arguable and possibly acceptable in our eyes.

V. Health as a Public Good

The cause invoked is health and, in its more critical aspect, life itself — clearly superlative goods that the physician serves directly by curing and the researcher indirectly by the knowledge gained through his experiments. There is no question about the good served nor about the evil fought — disease and premature death. But a good to whom and an evil to whom? Here the issue tends to become somewhat clouded. In the attempt to give experimentation the proper dignity (on the problematic view that a value becomes greater by being "social" instead of merely individual), the health in question or the disease in question is somehow predicated on the social whole, as if it were society that, in the persons of its members, enjoyed the one and suffered the other. For the purposes of our problem, public interest can then be pitted against private interest, the common good against the individual good. Indeed, I have found health called a national resource, which of course it is, but surely not in the first place.

In trying to resolve some of the complexities and ambiguities lurking in these conceptualizations, I have pondered a particular statement, made in the form of a question, which I found in the *Proceedings* of the earlier *Daedalus* conference: "Can society afford to discard the tissues and organs of the hopelessly unconscious patient when they could be used to restore the otherwise hopelessly ill, but still salvageable individual?" And somewhat later: "A strong case can be made that society can ill afford to discard the tissues and organs of the hopelessly unconscious patient; they are greatly needed for study and experimental trial to help those who can be salvaged."[3] I hasten to add that any suspicion of callousness that the "commodity" language these statements may suggest is immediately dispelled by the name of the speaker, Dr. Henry K. Beecher, for whose humanity and moral sensibility there can be nothing but admiration. But the use, in all innocence, of this language gives food for thought. Let me, for a moment, take the question literally. "Discarding" implies proprietary rights — nobody can discard what does not belong to him in the first place. Does society then own my body? "Salvaging" implies the same and, moreover, a use-value to the owner. Is the life-extension of certain individuals then a public interest? "Affording" implies a critically vital level of such an interest — that is, of the loss or gain involved. And "society" itself — what is it? When does a need, an aim, an obligation become social? Let us reflect on some of these terms.

VI. What Society Can Afford

"Can Society afford . . . ?" Afford what? To let people die intact, thereby withholding something from other people who desperately need it, who in consequence will have to die too? These other, unfortunate people indeed cannot afford not to have a kidney, heart, or other organ of the dying patient, on which they depend for an extension of their lease on life; but does that give them a right to it? And does it oblige society to procure it for them? What is it that *society* can or cannot afford — leaving aside for the moment the question of what it has a *right* to? It surely can afford to lose members through death; more than that, it is built on the balance of death and birth decreed by the order of life. This is too general, of course, for our question, but perhaps it is well to remember. The specific question seems to be whether society can afford to let some people die whose death might be deferred by particular means if these were authorized by society. Again, if it is merely a question of what society can or cannot afford, rather than of what it ought or ought not to do, the answer must be: Of course, it can. If cancer, heart disease, and other organic, noncontagious ills, especially those tending to strike the old more than the young, continue to exact their toll at the normal rate of incidence (including the toll of private anguish and misery), society can go on flourishing in every way.

Here, by contrast, are some examples of what, in sober truth, society cannot afford. It cannot afford to let an epidemic rage unchecked; a persistent excess of deaths over births, but neither — we might add — too great an excess of births over deaths; too low an average life expectancy even if demographically balanced by fertility, but neither too great a longevity with the necessitated correlative dearth of youth in the social body; a debilitating state of general health; and things of this kind. These are plain cases where the whole condition of society is critically affected, and the public interest can make its imperative claims. The Black Death of the Middle Ages was a *public* calamity of the acute kind; the life-sapping ravages of endemic malaria or sleeping sickness in certain areas are a public calamity of the chronic kind. Such situations a society as a whole can truly not "afford," and they may call for extraordinary remedies, including, perhaps, the invasion of private sacrosanctities.

This is not entirely a matter of numbers and numerical ratios. Society, in a subtler sense, cannot "afford" a single miscarriage of justice, a single inequity in the dispensation of its laws, the violation of the rights of even the tiniest minority, because these undermine the moral basis on which society's existence rests. Nor can it, for a similar reason, afford the absence or atrophy in its midst of compassion and of the effort to alleviate suffering — be it widespread or rare — one form of which is the effort to conquer disease of any kind, whether "socially" significant (by reason of number) or not. And in short, society cannot afford the absence among its members of *virtue* with its readiness for sacrifice beyond defined duty. Since its presence — that is to say, that of personal idealism — is a matter of grace and not of decree, we have the paradox that society depends for its existence on intangibles of nothing less than a religious order, for which it can hope, but which it cannot enforce. All the more must it protect this most precious capital from abuse.

For what objectives connected with the medio-biological sphere should this reserve be drawn upon — for example, in the form of accepting, soliciting, perhaps even imposing the submission of human subjects to experimentation? We postulate that this must be not just a worthy cause, as any promotion of the health of anybody doubtlessly is, but a cause qualifying for transcendent social sanction. Here one thinks first of those cases critically affecting the whole condition, present and future, of the community we have illustrated. Something equivalent to what in the political sphere is called "clear and present danger" may be invoked and a state of emergency proclaimed, thereby suspending certain otherwise inviolable prohibitions and taboos. We may observe that averting a disaster always carries greater weight than promoting a good. Extraordinary danger excuses extraordinary means. This covers human experimentation, which we would like to count, as far as possible, among the extraordinary rather than the ordinary means of serving the common good under public auspices. Naturally, since foresight and responsibility for the future are of the essence of institutional society, averting disaster extends into long-term prevention, although the lesser urgency will warrant less sweeping licenses.

VII. Society and the Cause of Progress

Much weaker is the case where it is a matter not of saving but of improving society. Much of medical research falls into this category. As stated before, a permanent death rate from heart failure or cancer does not threaten society. So long as certain statistical ratios are maintained, the incidence of disease and of disease-induced mortality is not (in the strict sense) a "social" misfortune. I hasten to add that it is not therefore less of a human misfortune, and the call for relief issuing with silent eloquence from each victim and all potential victims is of no lesser dignity. But it is misleading to equate the fundamentally human response to it with what is owed to society: it is owed by man to man — and it is thereby owed by society to the individuals as soon as the adequate ministering to these concerns outgrows (as it progressively does) the scope of private spontaneity and is made a public mandate. It is thus that society assumes responsibility for medical care, research, old age, and innumerable other things not originally of the public realm (in the original "social contract"), and they become duties toward "society" (rather than directly toward one's fellow man) by the fact that they are socially operated.

Indeed, we expect from organized society no longer mere protection against harm and the securing of the conditions of our preservation, but active and constant improvement in all the domains of life: the waging of the battle against nature, the enhancement of the human estate — in short, the promotion of progress. This is an expansive goal, one far surpassing the disaster norm of our previous reflections. It lacks the urgency of the latter, but has the nobility of the free, forward thrust. It surely is worth sacrifices. It is not at all a question of what society can afford, but of what it is committed to, beyond all necessity, by our mandate. Its trusteeship has become an established, ongoing, institutionalized business of the body politic. As eager beneficiaries of its gains, we now owe to "society," as its chief agent, our individual contributions toward its *continued pursuit.* I emphasize "continued pursuit." Maintaining the existing level requires no more than the orthodox means of taxation and enforcement of professional standards that raise no problems. The more optional goal of pushing forward is also more exacting. We have this syndrome: Progress is by our choosing an acknowledged interest of society, in which we have a stake in various degrees; science is a necessary instrument of progress; research is a necessary instrument of science; and in medical science experimentation on human subjects is a necessary instrument of research. Therefore, human experimentation has come to be a societal interest.

The destination of research is essentially melioristic. It does not serve the preservation of the existing good from which I profit myself and to which I am obligated. Unless the present state is intolerable, the melioristic goal is in a sense gratuitous, and this not only from the vantage point of the present. Our descendants have a right to be left an unplundered planet; they do not have a right to new miracle cures. We have sinned against them, if by our doing we have destroyed their inheritance — which we are doing at full blast; we have not sinned against them, if by the time they come around arthritis has not yet been conquered (unless by sheer neglect). And generally, in the matter of progress, as humanity had no claim on a Newton, a Michelangelo, or a St. Francis to appear, and no right to the blessings of their unscheduled deeds, so progress, with all our methodical labor for it, cannot be budgeted in advance and its fruits received as a due. Its coming-about at all and its turning out for good (of which we can never be sure) must rather be regarded as something akin to grace.

VIII. The Melioristic Goal, Medical Research, and Individual Duty

Nowhere is the melioristic goal more inherent than in medicine. To the physician, it is not gratuitous. He is committed to curing and thus to improving the power to cure. Gratuitous we called it (outside disaster conditions) as a *social* goal, but noble at the same time. Both the nobility and the gratuitousness must influence the manner in which self-sacrifice for it is elicited, and even its free offer accepted. Freedom is certainly the first condition to be observed here. The surrender of one's body to medical experimentation is entirely outside the enforceable "social contract."

Or can it be construed to fall within its terms — namely, as repayment for benefits from past experimentation that I have enjoyed myself? But I am indebted for these benefits not to society, but to the past "martyrs," to whom society is indebted itself, and society has no right to call in my personal debt by way of adding new to its own. Moreover, gratitude is not an enforceable social obligation; it anyway does not mean that I must emulate the deed. Most of all, if it was wrong to exact such sacrifice in the first place, it does not become right to exact it again with the plea of the profit it has brought me. If, however, it was not exacted, but entirely free, as it ought to have been, then it should remain so, and its precedence must not be used as a social pressure on others for doing the same under the sign of duty.

Indeed, we must look outside the sphere of the social contract, outside the whole realm of public rights and duties, for the motivations and norms by which we can expect ever again the upwelling of a will to give what nobody — neither society, nor fellow man, nor posterity — is entitled to. There are such dimensions in man with trans-social well-springs of conduct, and I have already pointed to the paradox, or mystery, that society cannot prosper without them, that it must draw on them, but cannot command them.

What about the moral law as such a transcendent motivation of conduct? It goes considerably beyond the public law of the social contract. The latter, we saw, is founded on the rule of enlightened self-interest: *Do ut des* — I give so that I be given to. The law of individual conscience asks more. Under the Golden Rule, for example, I am required to give as I wish to be given to under like circumstances, but not in order that I be given to and not in expectation of return. Reciprocity, essential to the social law, is not a condition of the moral law. One subtle "expectation" and "self-interest," but of the moral order itself, may even then be in my mind: I prefer the environment of a moral society and can expect to contribute to the general morality by my own example. But even if I should always be the dupe, the Golden Rule holds. (If the social law breaks faith with me, I am released from its claim.)

IX. Moral Law and Transmoral Dedication

Can I, then, be called upon to offer myself for medical experimentation in the name of the moral law? *Prima facie,* the Golden Rule seems to apply. I should wish, were I dying of a disease, that enough volunteers in the past had provided enough knowledge through the gift of their bodies that I could now be saved. I should wish, were I desperately in need of a transplant, that the dying patient next door had agreed to a definition of death by which his organs would become available to me in the freshest possible condition. I surely should also wish, were I drowning, that somebody would risk his life, even sacrifice his life, for mine.

But the last example reminds us that only the negative form of the Golden Rule ("Do not do unto others what you do not want done unto yourself") is fully prescriptive. The positive form ("Do unto others as you would wish them to do unto you"), in whose compass our issue falls, points to an infinite, open horizon where prescriptive force soon ceases. We may well say of somebody that he ought to have come to the succor of B, to have shared with him in his need, and the like. But we may not say that he ought to have given his life for him. To have done so would be praiseworthy; not to have done so is not blameworthy. It cannot be asked of him; if he fails to do so, he reneges on no duty. But *he* may say of himself, and only he, that he ought to have given his life. *This* "ought" is strictly between him and himself, or between him and God; no outside party — fellow man or society — can appropriate its voice. It can humbly receive the supererogatory gifts from the free enactment of it.

We must, in other words, distinguish between moral obligation and the much larger sphere of moral value. (This, incidentally, shows up the error in the widely held view of value theory that the higher a value, the stronger its claim and the greater the duty to realize it. The highest are in the region beyond duty and claim.) The ethical dimension far exceeds that of the moral law and reaches into the sublime solitude of dedication and ultimate commitment, away from all reckoning and rule — in short, into the sphere of the *holy.* From there alone can the offer of self-sacrifice genuinely spring, and this — its source — must be honored religiously. How? The first duty here falling on the research community, when it enlists and uses this source, is the safeguarding of true authenticity and spontaneity.

X. The "Conscription" of Consent

But here we must realize that the mere issuing of the appeal, the calling for volunteers, with the moral and social pressures it inevitably generates, amounts even under the most meticulous rules of consent to a sort of *conscripting*. And some soliciting is necessarily involved. This was in part meant by the earlier remark that in this area sin and guilt can perhaps not be wholly avoided. And this is why "consent," surely a non-negotiable minimum requirement, is not the full answer to the problem. Granting then that soliciting and therefore some degree of conscripting are part of the situation, who may conscript and who may be conscripted? Or less harshly expressed: Who should issue appeals and to whom?

The naturally qualified issuer of the appeal is the research scientist himself, collectively the main carrier of the impulse and the one with the technical competence to judge. But his being very much an interested party (with vested interests, indeed, not purely in the public good, but in the scientific enterprise as such, in "his" project, and even in his career) makes him also suspect. The ineradicable dialectic of this situation — a delicate incompatibility problem — calls for particular controls by the research community and by public authority that we need not discuss. They can mitigate, but not eliminate the problem. We have to live with the ambiguity, the treacherous impurity of everything human.

XI. Self-Recruitment of the Community

To whom should the appeal be addressed? The natural issuer of the call is also the first natural addressee: the physician-researcher himself and the scientific confraternity at large. With such a coincidence — indeed, the noble tradition with which the whole business of human experimentation started — almost all of the associated legal, ethical, and metaphysical problems vanish. If it is full, autonomous identification of the subject with the purpose that is required for the dignifying of his serving as a subject — here it is; if strongest motivation — here it is; if fullest understanding — here it is; if freest decision — here it is; if greatest integration with the person's total, chosen pursuit — here it is. With the fact of self-solicitation the issue of consent in all its insoluble equivocality is bypassed *per se*. Not even the condition that the particular purpose be truly important and the project reasonably promising, which must hold in any solicitation of others, need be satisfied here. By himself, the scientist is free to obey his obsession, to play his hunch, to wager on chance, to follow the lure of ambition. It is all part of the "divine madness" that somehow animates the ceaseless pressing against frontiers. For the rest of society, which has a deep-seated disposition to look with reverence and awe upon the guardians of the mysteries of life, the profession assumes with this proof of its devotion the role of a self-chosen, consecrated fraternity, not unlike the monastic orders of the past, and this would come nearest to the actual, religious origins of the art of healing. . . .

XII. "Identification" as the Principle of Recruitment in General

If the properties we adduced as the particular qualifications of the members of the scientific fraternity itself are taken as general criteria of selection, then one should look for additional subjects where a maximum of identification, understanding, and spontaneity can be expected — that is, among the most highly motivated, the most highly educated, and the least "captive" members of the community. From this naturally scarce resource, a descending order of permissibility leads to greater abundance and ease of supply, whose use should become proportionately more hesitant as the exculpating criteria are relaxed. An inversion of normal "market" behavior is demanded here — namely, to accept the lowest quotation last (and excused only by the greatest pressure of need); to pay the highest price first.

The ruling principle in our considerations is that the "wrong" of reification can only be made "right" by such authentic identification with the cause that it is the subject's as well as the researcher's cause — whereby his role in its service is not just permitted by him, but *willed*. That sovereign will of his which embraces the end as his own restores his personhood to the otherwise depersonalizing context. To be valid it must be autonomous and informed. The latter condition can, outside the research community, only be fulfilled by degrees; but the higher the degree of the understanding regarding the purpose and the technique, the more valid becomes the endorsement of the will. A margin of mere trust inevitably remains. Ultimately, the appeal for volunteers should seek this free and generous endorsement, the appropriation of the research purpose into the person's own scheme of ends. Thus, the appeal is in truth addressed to the one, mysterious, and sacred source of any such generosity of the will — "devotion," whose forms and objects of commitment are various and may invest different motivations in different individuals. The following, for instance, may be responsive to the "call" we are discussing: compassion with human suffering, zeal for humanity, reverence for the Golden Rule, enthusiasm for progress, homage to the cause of knowledge, even longing for sacrificial justification (do not call that "masochism," please). On all these, I say, it is defensible and right to draw when the research objective is worthy enough; and it is a prime duty of the research community (especially in view of what we called the "margin of trust") to see that this sacred source is never abused for frivolous ends. For a less than adequate cause, not even the freest, unsolicited offer should be accepted.

XIII. The Rule of the "Descending Order" and Its Counter-Utility Sense

We have laid down what must seem to be a forbidding rule to the number-hungry research industry. Having faith in the transcendent potential of man, I do not fear that the "source" will ever fail a society that does not destroy it — and only such a one is worthy of the blessings of progress. But "elitistic" the rule is (as is the enterprise of progress itself), and elites are by nature small. The combined attribute of motivation and information, plus the absence of external pressures, tends to be socially so circumscribed that strict adherence to the rule might numerically starve the research process. This is why I spoke of a descending order of permissibility, which is itself permissive, but where the realization that it is a *descending* order is not without pragmatic import. Departing from the august norm, the appeal must needs shift from idealism to docility, from high-mindedness to compliance, from judgment to trust. Consent spreads over the whole spectrum. I will not go into the casuistics of this penumbral area. I merely indicate the principle of the order of preference: The poorer in knowledge, motivation, and freedom of decision (and that, alas, means the more readily available in terms of numbers and possible manipulation), the more sparingly and indeed reluctantly should the reservoir be used, and the more compelling must therefore become the countervailing justification.

Let us note that this is the opposite of a social utility standard, the reverse of the order by "availability and expendability": The most valuable and scarcest, the least expendable elements of the social organism, are to be the first candidates for risk and sacrifice. It is the standard of *noblesse oblige;* and with all its counterutility and seeming "wastefulness," we feel a rightness about it and perhaps even a higher "utility," for the soul of the community lives by this spirit.[4] It is also the opposite of what the day-to-day interests of research clamor for, and for the scientific community to honor it will mean that it will have to fight a strong temptation to go by routine to the readiest sources of supply — the suggestible, the ignorant, the dependent, the "captive" in various senses.[5] I do not believe that heightened resistance here must cripple research, which cannot be permitted; but it may indeed slow it down by the smaller numbers fed into experimentation in consequence. This price — a possibly slower rate of progress — may have to be paid for the preservation of the most precious capital of higher communal life.

XIV. Experimentation on Patients

So far we have been speaking on the tacit assumption that the subjects of experimentation are recruited from among the healthy. To the question "Who is conscriptable?" the spontaneous answer is: Least and last of all the sick — the most available of all as they are under treatment and observation anyway. That the afflicted should not be called upon to bear additional burden and risk, that they are society's special trust and the physician's trust in particular — these are elementary responses of our moral sense. Yet the very destination of medical research, the conquest of disease, requires at the crucial stage trial and verification on precisely the sufferers from the disease, and their total exemption would defeat the purpose itself. In acknowledging this inescapable necessity, we enter the most sensitive area of the whole complex, the one most keenly felt and most searchingly discussed by the practitioners themselves. No wonder, it touches the heart of the doctor-patient relation, putting its most solemn obligations to the test. There is nothing new in what I have to say about the ethics of the doctor-patient relation, but for the purpose of confronting it with the issue of experimentation some of the oldest verities must be recalled.

A. The Fundamental Privilege of the Sick

In the course of treatment, the physician is obligated to the patient and to no one else. He is not the agent of society, nor of the interests of medical science, nor of the patient's family, nor of his co-sufferers, or future sufferers from the same disease. The patient alone counts when he is under the physician's care. By the simple law of bilateral contract (analogous, for example, to the relation of lawyer to client and its "conflict of interest" rule), the physician is bound not to let any other interest interfere with that of the patient in being cured. But manifestly more sublime norms than contractual ones are involved. We may speak of a sacred trust; strictly by its terms, the doctor is, as it were, alone with his patient and God.

There is one normal exception to this — that is, to the doctor's not being the agent of society vis-à-vis the patient, but the trustee of his interests alone: the quarantining of the contagious sick. This is plainly not for the patient's interest, but for that of others threatened by him. (In vaccination, we have a combination of both: protection of the individual and others.) But preventing the patient from causing harm to others is not the same as exploiting him for the advantage of others. And there is, of course, the abnormal exception of collective catastrophe, the analogue to a state of war. The physician who desperately battles a raging epidemic is under a unique dispensation that suspends in a nonspecifiable way some of the strictures of normal practice, including possibly those against experimental liberties with his patients. No rules can be devised for the waiving of rules in extremities. And as with the famous shipwreck examples of ethical theory, the less said about it the better. But what is allowable there and may later be passed over in forgiving silence cannot serve as a precedent. We are concerned with non-extreme, non-emergency conditions where the voice of principle can be heard and claims can be adjudicated free from duress. We have conceded that there are such claims, and that if there is to be medical advance at all, not even the superlative privilege of the suffering and the sick can be kept wholly intact from the intrusion of its needs. About this least palatable, most disquieting part of our subject, I have to offer only groping, inconclusive remarks.

B. The Principle of "Identification" Applied to Patients

On the whole, the same principles would seem to hold here as are found to hold with "normal subjects": motivation, identification, understanding on the part of the subject. But it is clear that these conditions are peculiarly difficult to satisfy with regard to a patient. His physical state, psychic preoccupation, dependent relation to the doctor, the submissive attitude induced by treatment — everything connected with his condition and situation makes the sick person inherently less of a sovereign person than the healthy one. Spontaneity of self-offering has almost to be ruled out; consent is marred by lower resistance or captive circumstance, and so on. In fact, all the factors that make the patient, as a category, particularly accessible and welcome for experimentation at the same time compromise the quality of the responding affirmation that must morally redeem the making use of them. This, in addition to the primacy of the physician's duty, puts a heightened onus on the physician-researcher to limit his undue power to the most important and defensible research objectives and, of course, to keep persuasion at a minimum.

Still, with all the disabilities noted, there is scope among patients for observing the rule of the "descending order of permissibility" that we have laid down for normal subjects, in vexing inversion of the utility order of quantitative abundance and qualitative "expendability." By the principle of this order, those patients who most identify with and are cognizant of the cause of research — members of the medical profession (who after all are sometimes patients themselves) — come first; the highly motivated and educated, also least dependent, among the lay patients come next; and so on down the line. An added consideration here is seriousness of condition, which again operates in inverse proportion. Here the profession must fight the tempting sophistry that the hopeless case is expendable (because in prospect already expended) and therefore especially usable; and generally the attitude that the poorer the chances of the patient the more justifiable his recruitment for experimentation (other than for his own benefit). The opposite is true.

C. Nondisclosure as a Borderline Case

Then there is the case where ignorance of the subject, sometimes even of the experiment, is of the essence of the experiment (the "double blind"-control group-placebo syndrome). It is said to be a necessary element of the scientific process. Whatever may be said about its ethics in regard to normal subjects, especially volunteers, it is an outright betrayal of trust in regard to the patient who believes that he is receiving treatment. Only supreme importance of the objective can exonerate it, without making it less of a transgression. The patient is definitely wronged even when not harmed. And ethics apart, the practice of such deception holds the danger of undermining the faith in the *bona fides* of treatment, the beneficial intent of the physician — the very basis of the doctor-patient relationship. In every respect, it follows that concealed experiment on patients — that is, experiment under the guise of treatment — should be the rarest exception, at best, if it cannot be wholly avoided.

This has still the merit of a borderline problem. The same is not true of the other case of necessary ignorance of the subject — that of the unconscious patient. Drafting him for nontherapeutic experiments is simply and unqualifiedly impermissible; progress or not, he must never be used, on the inflexible principle that utter helplessness demands utter protection.

When preparing this paper, I filled pages with a casuistics of this harrowing field, but then scrapped most of it, realizing my dilettante status. The shadings are endless, and only the physician-researcher can discern them properly as the cases arise. Into his lap the decision is thrown. The philosophical rule, once it has admitted into itself the idea of a sliding scale, cannot really specify its own application. It can only impress on the practitioner a general maxim or attitude for the exercise of his judgment and conscience in the concrete occasions of his work. In our case, I am afraid, it means making life more difficult for him.

It will also be noted that, somewhat at variance with the emphasis in the literature, I have not dwelt on the element of "risk" and very little on that of "consent." Discussion of the first is beyond the layman's competence; the emphasis on the second has been lessened because of its equivocal character. It is a truism to say that one should strive to minimize the risk and to maximize the consent. The more demanding concept of "identification," which I have used, includes "consent" in its maximal or authentic form, and the assumption of risk is its privilege.

XV. No Experiments on Patients Unrelated to Their Own Disease

Although my ponderings have, on the whole, yielded points of view rather than definite prescriptions, premises rather than conclusions, they have led me to a few unequivocal yeses and noes. The first is the emphatic rule that patients should be experimented upon, if at all, *only* with reference to *their disease.* Never should there be added to the gratuitousness of the experiment as such the gratuitousness of service to an unrelated cause. This follows simply from what we have found to be the *only* excuse for infracting the special exemption of the sick at all — namely, that the scientific war on disease cannot accomplish its goal without drawing the sufferers from disease into the investigative process. If under this excuse they become subjects of experiment, they do so *because,* and only because, of *their* disease.

This is the fundamental and self-sufficient consideration. That the patient cannot possibly benefit from the unrelated experiment therapeutically, while he might from experiment related to his condition, is also true, but lies beyond the problem area of pure experiment. I am in any case discussing nontherapeutic experimentation only, where *ex hypothesi* the patient does not benefit. Experiment as part of therapy — that is, directed toward helping the subject himself — is a different matter altogether and raises its own problems, but hardly philosophical ones. As long as a doctor can say, even if only in his own thought: "There is no known cure for your condition (or: You have responded to none); but there is promise in a new treatment still under investigation, not quite tested yet as to effectiveness and safety; you will be taking a chance, but all things considered, I judge it in your best interest to let me try it on you" — as long as he can speak thus, he speaks as the patient's physician and may err, but does not transform the patient into a subject of experimentation. Introduction of an untried therapy into treatment where the tried ones have failed is not "experimentation on the patient."

Generally, and almost needless to say, with all the rules of the book, there is something "experimental" (because tentative) about every individual treatment, beginning with the diagnosis itself; and he would be a poor doctor who would not learn from every case for the benefit of future cases, and a poor member of the profession who would not make any new insights gained from his treatments available to the profession at large. Thus, knowledge may be advanced in the treatment of any patient, and the interest of the medical art and all sufferers from the same affliction as well as the patient himself may be served if something happens to be learned from his case. But this gain to knowledge and future therapy is incidental to the *bona fide* service to the present patient. He has the right to expect that the doctor does nothing to him just in order to learn.

In that case, the doctor's imaginary speech would run, for instance, like this: "There is nothing more I can do for you. But you can do something for me. Speaking no longer as your physician but on behalf of medical science, we could learn a great deal about future cases of this kind if you would permit me to perform certain experiments on you. It is understood that you yourself would not benefit from any knowledge we might gain; but future patients would." This statement would express the purely experimental situation, assumedly here with the subject's concurrence and with all cards on the table. In Alexander Bickel's words: "It is a different situation when the doctor is no longer trying to make [the patient] well, but is trying to find out how to make others well in the future."[6]

But even in the second case, that of the nontherapeutic experiment where the patient does not benefit, at least the patient's own disease is enlisted in the cause of fighting that disease, even if only in others. It is yet another thing to say or think: "Since you are here — in the hospital with its facilities — anyway, under our care and observation anyway, away from your job (or, perhaps, doomed) anyway, we wish to profit from your being available for some other research of great interest we are presently engaged in." From the standpoint of merely medical ethics, which has only to consider risk, consent, and the worth of the objective, there may be no cardinal difference between this case and the last one. I hope that the medical reader will not think I am making too fine a point when I say that from the standpoint of the subject and his dignity there is a cardinal difference that crosses the line between the permissible and the impermissible, and this by the same principle of "identification" I have been invoking all along. Whatever the rights and wrongs of any experimentation on any patient — in the one case, at least that residue of identification is left him that it is his own affliction by which he can contribute to the conquest of that affliction, his own kind of suffering which he helps to alleviate in others; and so in a sense it is his own cause. It is totally indefensible to rob the unfortunate of this intimacy with the purpose and make his misfortune a convenience for the furtherance of alien concerns. The observance of this rule is essential, I think, to at least attenuate the wrong that nontherapeutic experimenting on patients commits in any case.

XVI. Conclusion

There would now have to be said something about nonmedical experiments on human subjects, notably psychological and genetic, of which I have not lost sight. But I must leave this for another occasion. I wish only to say in conclusion that if some of the practical implications of my reasonings are felt to work out toward a slower rate of progress, this should not cause too great dismay. Let us not forget that progress is an optional goal, not an unconditional commitment, and that its tempo in particular, compulsive as it may become, has nothing sacred about it. Let us also remember that a slower progress in the conquest of disease would not threaten society, grievous as it is to those who have to deplore that their particular disease be not yet conquered, but that society would indeed be threatened by the erosion of those moral values whose loss, possibly caused by too ruthless a pursuit of scientific progress, would make its most dazzling triumphs not worth having. Let us finally remember that it cannot be the aim of progress to abolish the lot of mortality. Of some ill or other, each of us will die. Our mortal condition is upon us with its harshness but also its wisdom — because without it there would not be the eternally renewed promise of the freshness, immediacy, and eagerness of youth; nor would there be for any of us the incentive to number our days and make them count. With all our striving to wrest from our mortality what we can, we should bear its burden with patience and dignity.

Notes

1. Cf. M. H. Pappworth, "Ethical Issues in Experimental Medicine" in D. R. Cutler (editor), *Updating Life and Death* (Boston, 1969), pp. 64-69.

2. *Die Braut von Korinth:* "Victims do fall here, / Neither lamb nor steer, / Nay, but human offerings untold."

3. *Proceedings of the Conference on the Ethical Aspects of Experimentation on Human Subjects,* November 3-4, 1967 (Boston, Mass.), pp. 50-51.

4. Socially, everyone is expendable relatively — that is, in different degrees; religiously, no one is expendable absolutely: The "image of God" is in all. If it can be enhanced, then not by anyone being expended, but by someone expending himself.

5. This refers to captives of circumstances, not of justice. Prison inmates are, with respect to our problem, in a special class. If we hold to some idea of guilt, and to the supposition that our judicial system is not entirely at fault, they may be held to stand in a special debt to society, and their offer to serve — from whatever motive — may be accepted with a minimum of qualms as a means of reparation.

6. *Proceedings,* p. 33. To spell out the difference between the two cases: In the first case, the patient himself is meant to be the beneficiary of the experiment, and directly so; the "subject" of the experiment is at the same time its object, its end. It is performed not for gaining knowledge, but for helping him — and helping him in the *act* of performing it, even if by its results it also contributes to a broader testing process currently under way. It is in fact part of the treatment itself and an "experiment" only in the loose sense of being untried and highly tentative. But whatever the degree of uncertainty, the motivating anticipation (the wage, if you like) is for success, and success here means the subject's own good. To a pure experiment, by contrast, undertaken to gain knowledge, the difference of success and failure is not germane, only that of conclusiveness and inconclusiveness. The "negative" result has as much to teach as the "positive." Also, the true experiment is an act distinct from the uses later made of the findings. And, most important, the subject experimented on is distinct from the eventual beneficiaries of those findings: He lets himself be used as a means toward an end external to himself (even if he should at some later time happen to be among the beneficiaries himself). With respect to his own present needs and his own good, the act is gratuitous.

118 Ethical Considerations in Human Experimentation: Experimentation Involving Children

Charles E. Curran

It will be helpful to discuss in particular a significant and prismatic case of human experimentation — the use of children in nontherapeutic experimentation. The discussion will not descend to the level of proposing guidelines — for example, it will not even discuss the exact age of what is meant by children who are unable to give consent.

There has been a great divergence in the literature and proposed guidelines about the ethics of using children in medical experimentation understood in the strict sense. Many researchers have proposed the need to use children but have also recognized the role of proper safeguards. Louis Lasagna, a professor of medicine and experimental therapeutics, accepts the use of children and even justifies the famous experiment of the Willowbrook School in New York.[1] Franz J. Ingelfinger, an editor of the *New England Journal of Medicine,* argues against the absolute position of the World Medical Association statement that does not allow experimentation on children under any circumstances.[2] Charles Lowe, M.D., and associates point out all the advantages that have accrued through experimentation on children and accept its necessity but also recognize the need for some ethical restrictions which might very well prevent our obtaining some of the knowledge and technological progress which we could have obtained under the looser restrictions of the past.[3] The proposed Health, Education, and Welfare Department (HEW) guidelines also begin with the assumption that experimentation on children is necessary for medical advances for the good of other children. These guidelines conclude that substantial risk with children is never acceptable but that some risk is justified with the ultimate determination to be made by review committees.[4]

Some researchers have proposed that not even the parents should be allowed to consent to possibly risky research on their children. Henry K. Beecher and William J. Curran conclude that children under 14 may be involved in medical experimentation only when there is no discernible risk.[5] As might be expected, some philosophical and religious ethicists tend to be more reluctant or even opposed to the use of children in medical experimentation, but again this does not hold true of all ethicists. Paul Ramsey, basing his argument on the canon of loyalty by which the parent is related to the child, opposes any medical experimentation with children because the primary ethical consideration is not the risk or degree of risk but the offense of touching, which would be involved in any experimentation.[6] William F. May supports the same conclusion, since proxy consent by the parents in such cases involves a contradiction — it necessarily requires one to treat a child or other incompetent individual as a moral agent, something that a child or another incompetent actually is not.[7]

Richard A. McCormick disagrees with Ramsey and comes to a conclusion similar to Beecher's in allowing experimentation where there is no discernible risk (although he at times speaks of no notable disadvantages and accepts the concept of low risk if it means no realistic risk), undue discomfort, or inconvenience.[8] McCormick bases his conclusion on the fact that such an act is something that one ought to do for other members of the human community and is not merely a work of supererogation which would never be justified by proxy consent. Elsewhere McCormick rightly points out that his conclusion is quite similar to the one I have proposed on this question.[9]

In the light of further considerations, I have

From the *Duquesne Law Review* 13 (Summer 1975): 837-40. Used by permission.

changed my earlier position, which, in reaction to Paul Ramsey's approach, proposed that experimentation on children is acceptable when there is no discernible risk.[10] Now I am willing to accept some risk, discomfort, or inconvenience. Theology and ethics have always had difficulty in dealing with children, primarily because of their inability to consent freely — the hallmark of the adult human. For example, Catholic theology at one time excluded children who died without baptism from the fullness of eternal life because they were unable to have baptism of desire. Recall, however, that in the ethical considerations I insisted that consent was not the only consideration, for consent itself must always be properly ordered.

McCormick and others claim that the HEW guidelines are utilitarian, but I do not think that conclusion is necessarily accurate. Unlike McCormick, I would see the individual human being in more relational terms rather than as an individual with certain basic human tendencies or human goods which are equally basic and self-evidently attractive and against which one must never directly choose.[11] A more relational understanding would not see all these goods as equally basic and of equal value. Likewise, without unduly subordinating the individual or others, this view recognizes that in our relational existence with others we are often exposed to some risk which is not for our benefit — and this is so for children too. In a less complex and relational world, a child would be better off growing up in an environment where there is no air pollution, but other values are decisive in the choice of where the family lives, even though this redounds only secondarily to the good of the child and definitely causes some harm to the child. One might argue that even here the decision is made for the good of the child, but consider another example. I believe that individual children in some circumstances should undergo the inconvenience of busing in order to achieve the racial integration of schools — which is proximately and primarily for the good of others and only very indirectly redounds to the good of the individual child.

A more relational understanding recognizes that children are often exposed by parents and others to some risk or inconvenience which is not primarily and directly for their own benefit. I agree with McCormick and Lowe and associates that it is necessary here to distinguish two kinds of obligations.[12] A person may freely expose oneself to a greater risk than the parent can take with the child. The parent can, however, expose the child to some risk, low risk or slight risk for the good of others. My primary difficulty with the HEW guidelines is the failure to spell out what is meant by the some risk which is forbidden. As practical guidelines these would be much more helpful and less open to abuse if they would offer a more explicit understanding of what is meant by some risk and thereby give more detailed guidelines for the final decision to be made by review committees.

Although I would accept the ethical validity of parents giving proxy consent for experimentation which exposes their child to low risk, some risk, or slight risk (or discomfort or inconvenience), I still recognize the absolute need for practical vigilance in all areas of such experimentation. Above all, children should never be used in experimentation unless there is no other way to achieve the purpose of the experiment.

Notes

1. Lasagna, "Special Subjects in Human Experimentation," in *Reflections on Medical Experimentation in Humans,* ed. P. Freund (New York: George Braziller, 1970), p. 271.

2. Ingelfinger, "Ethics of Experiments on Children," *New England Journal of Medicine* 288 (1973): 791.

3. Lowe, Alexander, and Mishkin, "Nontherapeutic Research on Children: An Ethical Dilemma," *Journal of Pediatrics* 84 (1974): 468.

4. 38 Fed. Reg. 31, 740-42 (1973).

5. Curran & Beecher, "Experimentation in Children: A Reexamination of Legal Ethical Principles," *Journal of the American Medical Association* 210 (1969): 77-82.

6. See P. Ramsey, *The Patient as Person* (New Haven: Yale University Press, 1970), pp. 1-58.

7. May, "Experimenting on Human Subjects," *Linacre Quarterly* 41 (1974): 238-50.

8. McCormick, "Proxy Consent in the Experimentation Situation," in *Love and Society,* ed. J. Johnson & D. Smith (n.p., 1974), pp. 221-24 (hereinafter cited as McCormick).

9. McCormick, "Notes on Moral Theology," *Theological Studies* 36 (1975): 77, 117-28.

10. C. Curran, *Politics, Medicine and Christian Ethics* (Philadelphia: Fortress, 1973), pp. 132-35.

11. McCormick, "Proxy Consent," p. 218.

12. McCormick's thesis is that one may give proxy consent where it is a case of what the person ought to do but not if it is a work of charity that one could freely do for others. His explanation of this in terms of the parents deciding to allow the child to die (by withholding extraordinary means) seems weak, for ethicists do not usually claim that the child or person ought to die but that one *can* decide not to use extraordinary means.

119 The Use of Zairian Children in HIV Vaccine Experimentation

A Cross-Cultural Study in Medical Ethics

Thomas A. Nairn

I. The Situation

In April of 1991, John Crewdson, a reporter for the *Chicago Tribune,* began a series of articles about three deaths which had occurred in Paris as a result of an AIDS vaccine experiment conducted by Dr. Daniel Zagury, a immunologist of the Institut Jean Godinot of the Université Pierre et Marie Curie.[1] Although all three of the victims had been infected with the HIV virus prior to the experimentation, the deaths resulted from acute necrosis, a vaccinia disease.

The articles tell of an investigation by the National Institutes of Health (NIH) and its Office for Protection from Research Risks (OPRR) into the research of Dr. Zagury. The NIH was concerned with the work of a French researcher because Zagury had been a collaborator with Robert Gallo of the National Cancer Institute (NIC) since 1984 when a Materials Transfer Agreement was executed between the NCI and Dr. Zagury.[2] Even more problematical was the transfer to Dr. Zagury by Dr. Bernard Moss of the National Institute of

From *The Annual of the Society of Christian Ethics* (Baltimore: Georgetown University Press, 1993). Used by permission.

Allergy and Infectious Diseases of a recombinant vaccinia strain into which Moss had inserted HIV envelope proteins.[3] It was apparent that this was the vaccinia strain that had been used in the experiments that occasioned the three deaths. Thus the NIH investigation was into possible noncompliance with the Department of Health and Human Service's regulations for the Protection of Human Research Subjects.

The investigation extended into several of Zagury's research projects. In addition to the phase I trial with 28 seropositive patients at the Hôpital Saint Antoine in Paris, these experiments included several studies which occurred in Zaire: immunotherapy on two Zairian subjects with advanced AIDS, a phase I vaccinia study on nine HIV-seronegative Zairian children, a similar study on 45 HIV-seronegative volunteers from Zaire's military with some civilians, and a fourth study (taking 4-5 years) analyzing blood samples from HIV seropositive members of the Zairian military.[4] These experiments were in addition to a variety of *in vitro* and animal experiments that Zagury had previously conducted.

For the purposes of this paper, I will concentrate on the phase I vaccinia study on Zairian children in order to address some of the biomedical issues involved when one conducts research in a cross-cultural setting. Although I will touch upon a variety of questions that this experimental protocol raises,[5] I will concentrate on (1) the understanding of informed consent in the use of *children* in such a phase I study and (2) the use of children *of a different culture* in such a study. Rather than being two different questions, they might be better understood as two foci of the same ethical question.

Beginning in November of 1986, Dr. Zagury conducted a phase I vaccine trial involving ten seronegative individuals. One of the ten was Zagury himself, but the other nine experimental subjects were Zairian children ranging in age from two to twelve. All the children's fathers had already died of AIDS, and all of their mothers had tested positive for the HIV virus. The children themselves, however, were all seronegative and had no additional risk for contracting the virus than others living in sub-Saharan Africa.[6] The experimental protocol was reviewed by an ethics committee in Zaire[7] but none in France. In his series of articles, Crewdson maintains that there were eleven children in this group, including a six-year-old girl, a five-year-old boy and two three-year-old girls. He also contends that a month later, another eleven Zairian children were inoculated, including a twenty-two-month-old baby.[8]

Although some of the OPRR reports question the ethical justification for enrolling children in such a phase I trial,[9] Zagury himself defended this decision. In a letter to Charles McCarthy, the Director of the OPRR, Zagury stated that the use of children was in accord with French (if not American) law, as long as there was the written consent of the parents. He quoted specifically from the Huriet law.[10] He steadfastly maintained that the mothers of all the children had signed consent forms.

In the same letter, he maintained that his motivation for these tests was compassion. He stated:

> I should stress that in our action we profited by compassionately allowing for the participation of the children. Their fathers had died of AIDS; and their mothers, wasting away because of the same disease, begged us to do something for their children. This inoculation, evidently good, did not bring them either clinical or human harm. All the children came through the experiment well. Rather than harm, our action proved to be a source of comfort and hope for their families.[11]

In this letter and elsewhere[12] he continued to emphasize that all children developed no immediate or later complications from the immunization. He concluded his report by suggesting that the NIH itself had resorted to a sort of ethical imperialism, narrowly focusing on the supposed moral superiority of its own policies and procedures and not being sensitive to the importance of the work which had been done?

> We deplore the entire action of the OPRR arising from the allegations, which it did not attempt to substantiate, made by the journalist John Crewdson, whose motives, which are very often alien to this profession, . . . were not examined by the OPRR.
>
> We regard it as deplorable that in a matter like AIDS we should mire ourselves in procedures that have nothing to do with the disease and are

fraught with errors that are serious and dangerous for everyone, which hinder and destabilize the researchers who are entirely committed to their work, and above all, the sufferers, who should not be forgotten.[13]

II. Background

As noted above, Zagury defended his work by maintaining the general ethical appropriateness of his experimental protocol and by noting that the motivation for his inclusion of Zairian children was compassion, thereby providing "a source of comfort and hope." One must therefore begin this study by asking about the nature of Zagury's research itself.

A. The Development of an AIDS Vaccine

Since the discovery of the HIV virus, there have been many attempts to develop a vaccine against infection, reprsenting an entire spectrum of approaches: the use of killed-virus preparations, nonpathogenic variants of the virus, virus subunits, anti-idiotypes, and a variety of genetically engineered recombinant viruses utilizing subunits of the HIV virus.[14] The genetic engineering approach "appears to be a major choice to be considered seriously."[15] This is precisely the sort of vaccine developed by Moss and tested by Zagury.

Yet, there have also been obvious problems with the development of any vaccine. Animal studies are almost impossible. Only members of the great ape family, that group most closely related to humans, have been reported to be susceptible to infection from the HIV virus.[16] Most of these species are endangered or threatened, and the chimpanzee remains the most suitable model by means of which to study the disease. Yet even this animal model is problematic. Aside from the high cost of using and keeping these animals, no chimpanzee has yet developed the clinical syndrome of AIDS even though infected.[17] One can therefore question their ultimate benefit in such studies.

Human research has also been hampered by multiple problems. These include the nature of the spread of the disease, the prolonged period from infection to display of symptoms, the fact that the virus frequently mutates even within the same individual, and the current reality that the very "definition of protective immunity against initial infection with HIV remains unknown."[18]

One needs to understand these facts in evaluating the study of Dr. Zagury, both as regards its possibilities and also as regards its limits. There is no downplaying the importance of developing the vaccine. Yet one must investigate Zagury's understanding of the purpose of his experiments as opposed to what his African subjects might have understood. Finally, one must ascertain the ethical implications not only of the use of Africans in such experimentation but especially that of African children.

B. The Nature of a Phase I Vaccine Study

Traditionally, experimental trials occur in three phases:

> A phase I trial involves testing a small group of subjects (members of AIDS risk groups or others) to evaluate the short-term safety and immunogenicity of the vaccine;
>
> a phase II trial determines the ideal dose and spacing of the vaccine through larger safety and immunogenicity trials; and
>
> a phase III trial determines the actual protection against HIV infection through large scale efficacy trials involving as many as 1,000 to 2,000 subjects. A phase III trial would be randomized, double-blind, and controlled.[19]

Thus, phase I trials are typically conducted at the beginning of a study, utilize small numbers of subjects, and evaluate the effects, including possible toxic side effects, of given experimental agents upon the subjects.[20] The purpose of a phase I study is therefore not to test the success of a drug's long-range immunogenic activity on a class of subjects. In a report on his study of the children, Zagury himself concluded:

> We suggest that this approach be considered as a prototype candidate vaccine against AIDS. However, whether the above described immune state against HIV confers protection against AIDS has

> to be established. Indeed, an estimation of the efficacy of a vaccine for protection against AIDS can only be achieved after a large scale clinical trial in a group of volunteers with a high risk of natural infection and followed for an adequate period of time.[21]

It is difficult to maintain that those taking part in such a phase I trial are not exposed to risks. The very fact that three patients died in the Saint Antoine experiment from a reaction to the vaccinia attest to this point. In addition to the possible risks inherent to the initial administration of any viral vaccine preparation, there is also the possibility that because of a partial tolerance developed in the phase I study, a subject may not be able effectively to use a possible AIDS vaccine developed in the future.[22]

Given these considerations, there are certain ethical limits within which these studies ought to be undertaken. While some maintain that phase I studies should utilize only animal subjects, most admit that such a principle is too restrictive. This may be especially true in dealing with the HIV virus. Nevertheless, having acknowledged that the participation of human subjects in phase I vaccine studies can be ethical, can one justify the use of Africans in such tests? For many, this raises the specter of racism such as that associated with the Tuskegee Syphilis Study.[23] Thus, it has been stated that "when a new vaccine is first given trial in a primitive African tribe, one needs to go no further. The investigator feels insecure and unsafe with the material and wants to get his quick answer from a group in whom consent is impossible, information is totally lacking, and the backlash is insignificant."[24] Consequently, according to a statement issued by the Consultation on Criteria for International Testing of Candidate HIV Vaccines sponsored by the World Health Organization's Global Programme on AIDS in 1989: "In general, initial Phase I trials should be conducted in the country of origin of the vaccine. Phase I results, including those that indicate toxicity which prevents further trials of the vaccine, should be made public."[25]

Yet, this analysis seems too simplistic. There can be reasons for such testing of African adults. Among the reasons are the high incidence of the infection on the continent,[26] its probable benefit for Africans in general, and — more controversial — because of the reduction of high-risk behaviors among high-risk groups in countries such as the U.S., the incidence of HIV infection is declining in these countries. Researchers are facing the possibility "that longer phase III trials of AIDS vaccine may have to be done in groups in the United States who are traditionally less compliant or in populations of certain foreign countries where the incidence of infection is still high."[27] Accordingly, the use of Africans may likely lead to speedier and more accurate trials.

Acknowledging the potential ethical difficulties inherent in a French researcher using African subjects in a phase I vaccine study, I would like to bracket these questions for the sake of the present study. One can potentially justify the use of human subjects for phase I vaccine studies, as opposed to animal or *in vitro* studies. One might even justify, though with greater hesitancy, the use of adults from another nation or culture in such studies. I will now concentrate on the use of children, especially children of a different culture and race, in such a phase I study.

III. Anthropology and the Ethics of Experimentation on Zairian Children

In the case described above, a French experimenter is being investigated by a U.S. government agency for research conducted on Zairian children. Such a case demands some sort of cross-cultural analysis. Yet, when one enters such an international and multicultural arena, ambiguities multiply.

There has been an ongoing debate among both experimenters and ethicists when faced with the situation of experimenting on subjects from a different culture. One way of formulating the central question of this debate has been: "Should ethical standards be substantially the same everywhere, or is it inevitable that they differ from region to region, reflecting local beliefs and custom? . . . Underlying these concerns is the fundamental issue of whether ethical standards are relative, to be weighed against competing claims and modified accordingly, or whether, like scientific standards, they are absolute?"[28] Much ink has been spilt over this question, defending a spectrum of points of view.

While this question is important, one does not necessarily have to answer it in order to acknowledge the ambiguities present when dealing with ethical issues involving persons from a different culture. Still less does acknowledging the insights of anthropology detract from the ethical nature of such an investigation. Both anthropology and ethics can become tools in analyzing the morality of the experiment described above. In making this move, one acknowledges that anthropology does have something to say, in either a broad or limited manner, to the ethicists evaluating a situation such as this phase I vaccine experiment. For example, reading the account given by Dr. Zagury, even in the most positive light, one might properly ask the anthropologist whether what Zagury claimed he understood as occurring between him and the mothers would be at all similar to what mothers of these children understood as occurring.

One insight of anthropology, which can assist the ethicist here, is that of the notion of a health care system. As articulated by Arthur Kleinman:

> Patients and healers are basic components of such systems and thus are embedded in specific configurations of cultural means and social relationships. They cannot be understood apart from this context. Illness and healing also are part of the system of health care. Within that system, they are articulated as culturally constituted experiences and activities, respectively. In the context of culture, the study of patients and healers, and illness and healing, must, therefore, start with an analysis of health care systems.[29]

The interaction between Dr. Zagury and the Zairian mothers and their children represents the interplay between two different and possibly antagonistic health care systems. One system constructs reality by means of symbols dependent upon the scientific method and "professionalism,"[30] a system which would also be at home with a Western philosophical understanding of concepts such as autonomy, informed consent, and substituted judgment. The other might be understood more in terms of a "folk system."[31] If this is correct, one confronts two questions: (1) whether and how the notion of experiment, and especially "phase I experiment," easily understood within the scientific-professional health care system, might be understood within a "folk" health care system, especially when Dr. Zagury himself seemed to have spoken to the mothers in terms of "comfort and hope"; and (2) how the related concepts of informed consent and proxy consent for those without capacity to competently make their own judgments can be understood once these concepts are separated from the broad Western tradition that has given them meaning.

In attempting to answer these questions, I will first analyze the traditionally Western concepts of informed consent and substituted judgment in order to question the morality of Zagury's experiment from a broadly European/North American perspective. I will then attempt to ask these questions from an African perspective in order to investigate the issues involved when confronting culturally different health care systems.

IV. Experimentation with Children: Western Style

From its beginnings in the last century, the discipline of experimental medicine has acknowledged the tension between the experimenter as scientist and the experimenter as physician dedicated to the health of the subject.[32] Recent decades have witnessed the development of a variety of codes of ethics regarding human experimentation, most importantly the Nuremberg Code of 1947 and, more recently, the Declaration of Helsinki of 1964 (amended in 1975, 1983, and 1989). These codes, and others like them, recognize that experiments on human subjects must be undertaken within a certain ethical and legal context. They have stressed the dignity and rights of the individual and derived from this, the necessity of informed and voluntary nature of any consent to becoming a subject of experimentation. This area of informed and voluntary consent is problematic when the subject is a child.

A. Human Autonomy and the Nature of Informed Consent

The Western liberal tradition in general and especially the Anglo-American system of common law have placed a great deal of emphasis on the concept of autonomy. The understanding of individual choice and freedom has developed in terms of this notion of autonomy.[33] U.S. courts, for example, have consistently ruled against anything that they have considered to be an infringement upon a person's autonomy by others, including even the person's family. Recently, in the famous Cruzan case, the U.S. Supreme Court cited favorably a 1891 judgment stating that "no right is held more sacred, or is more carefully guarded, by the common law, than the right of every individual to the possession and control of his own person, free from all restraint or interference of others, unless by clear and unquestionable authority of law."[34]

When the understanding of autonomy is used to refer to actions, certain generally accepted components of autonomous action emerge. Faden and Beauchamp, for example, describe such action as follows: "X acts autonomously only if X acts (1) intentionally, (2) with understanding, and (3) without controlling influences."[35] While each of these elements are themselves open to further interpretation, one can begin to see the relation between the notion of autonomy and that of informed consent. Such consent is seen as necessary both to protect the dignity of the subject and to help ensure that the person is treated as an end and not merely as a means to another person's end. Thus the Nuremberg Code demands that for one to consent to participate in any research, that person must "(1) be so situated as to be able to exercise free power of choice; (2) have the legal capacity to give consent; (3) have sufficient . . . comprehension to made an enlightened decision; and (4) have sufficient knowledge on which to decide."[36]

However, if the exercise of informed consent is situated in a context of competency and sufficient comprehension, a further question arises regarding the manner in which one may protect the rights of one judged not competent of exercising this autonomy. If the subject in question had at one time been deemed competent, one may have recourse to some form of transmitted judgment, by which that individual's previously expressed desires may be made known. A problem ensues, however, when the subject has never been in a position to exercise autonomous judgment.

B. Autonomy, Consent, and Experimentation with Children

Attempts to deal with this problem have focused around the understanding of what is in the "best interest" of the individual. Although concrete judgments of "best interest" differ, the notion itself, as that element that protects one's rights and dignity from unreasonable claims by others, is preserved both in law and in ethics. It is the same notion of dignity that imposes upon adults, and especially upon a child's parents, the duty to protect the child: "For their part, children have a right as persons to freedom from conditions that might impair the full development of their human capacities, especially their autonomy."[37]

As framed in U.S. law,[38] a child as a minor legally requires a parent's or guardian's permission to participate in research, even though he or she may be old enough to be of sufficient capacity to understand the nature of research and thereby able to consent to his or her own participation in the research project.[39] By demanding parental permission, the law does not thereby give parents absolute discretion regarding proxy consent. Traditionally there have been two limits on proxy consent for a minor, (1) the "best interest" judgment already discussed and (2) the understanding of a "reasonable person" or a "reasonable parent."[40] Thus, for example, there are certain medical procedures, such as a blood transfusion, that must be performed upon a child even if the procedure is against a parent's religious beliefs.

Even these concepts have been open to debate, however, and there is a spectrum of points of view regarding what constitutes the "best interest" of a child and consequently what forms of experimentation to which a "reasonable parent" would give proxy consent. The classic expression of this debate has been that between Paul Ramsey and Richard McCormick.[41] Ramsey has argued that any experimentation on a child which does not directly benefit the child is not ethically permissible. Parents simply do not have the right to give such proxy consent:

> It is better to say of the consent-requirement or of the ethics of consent that this basically means that the *power* of proxy consent is not a *right*; that if men are in some sense capable of granting con-

> sent by proxy they should not for that reason do so; and that no one ought to consent for a child to be made the subject of medical investigations primarily for the accumulation of scientific knowledge, except in the face of epidemic conditions that bring upon the individual child proportionately the same or likely greater dangers. . . . A parent's decisive concern is for the care and protection of the child, to whom he owes the highest fiduciary loyalty, even when he also appreciates the benefits to come to others from the investigation and might submit his own person to experiment in order to obtain them.[42]

For Ramsey, any permission for nontherapeutic experimentation is necessarily treating the child not as an end but merely as a means to another's end and is thus a breach of the parent's fiduciary trust.

McCormick, on the other hand, uses the concept of sociality to argue that there are certain forms of experimentation in which a child ought to participate and for which a parent ought to give consent, even if there is no direct benefit to the child. If there is reason why adults are not able to participate in a particular experiment, if there is only "minimal risk" to the child, and if the experiment would contribute to benefits for others, then proxy consent is moral.[43] McCormick takes this position because there are things "that the child *ought*, simply as a human being, to choose."[44] It should be noted, however, that the language used in McCormick's argument contains terms such as "minimal risk," "no discernible risk," and "no notable inconvenience."[45] Thus McCormick's position by no means gives a parent carte blanche for proxy consent.

C. Zagury's Experiment

If one were to judge the ethics of Zagury's experimental protocol solely on the basis of the Western tradition of autonomy, informed consent, and proxy consent for minors, one would probably describe the research as unethical. One reaches this conclusion by recourse to both considerations discussed above. Regarding the issue of proxy consent, although the experimenter paid attention to the procedural details involved in obtaining signed "informed consent" forms, it is quite dubious whether he ever really obtained the mothers' informed consent. A signed consent form must not be equated with informed consent. Rather, the criteria for informed consent, which the tradition (especially as enshrined in the Nuremberg Code) demands, include sufficient knowledge, comprehension, capacity, and ability to exercise free choice. Zagury might have followed the protocol that demands that the proper forms be obtained, but it is by no means evident that the criteria for obtaining true informed consent were fulfilled.

An even more basic ethical question, however, is why a researcher would use children in a phase I study such as that described above. It does not seem that Zagury received special information by using children that he would not have received by using only adult subjects. Despite his protests to the contrary, children were put at risk without a concomitant benefit either to themselves or to other children. Given Zagury's seeming inability to explain the need for children in a phase I experimental protocol, one must have strong doubts regarding the morality of such experimentation.

V. Experimentation with Children Revisited: An African Perspective

These conclusions regarding the morality of Zagury's research solely from the point of view of the Western ethical tradition does not complete our task. A valid question remains regarding how Zagury's work might have been understood by those from whom he obtained consent. The discussion in this section will be more suggestive than definitive for two reasons. First, given the nature of the relation between anthropology and ethics, it seems more appropriate to conduct this investigation as a series of questions that can guide the ethicist rather than offer definite conclusions. Second, since Dr. Zagury has refused to release information about the children he used as subjects, it is difficult to reach particular conclusions, especially in the section on consent.

We have seen how anthropology can help to provide a context within which the ethicist may ask even more basic questions. From this discussion, one sees how the ethical norms that proscribe certain forms of experimentation on children arise from a particular Western point of view, which places a high value on autonomy. How does an experimenter translate this concern into a Zairian context with its own particular understanding of personhood and of childhood?

A helpful tool may be the distinction developed by anthropologist Richard Shweder between "egocentric-contractual" understandings of the person and "sociocentric-organic" understandings. While the former expresses

> features of the context-dependent, occasion-bound concept of the person: (1) no attempt to distinguish the individual from the station she or he occupies; (2) the view that obligations and rights are differentially apportioned by role, group, and so on; (3) a disinclination to ascribe intrinsic moral worth to people merely because they are people.[46]

Anthropologists who hold this distinction suggest, for example, that our notion of autonomy is not the result of a quasi-metaphysical discovery of the way things really are nor an inductive generalization. Rather it is a "creation of the collective imagination" of the West.[47] It "fits" into our way of seeing the world, but there is no reason why it must be accepted by a member of a sociocentric-organic culture. Shweder further explains:

> To members of sociocentric-organic cultures the concept of the autonomous individual, free to choose and mind his or her own business, must feel alien, a bizarre idea cutting the self off from the interdependent whole, dooming it to a life of isolation and loneliness.[48]

A. Personhood and Childhood in Zaire

The Zairian person is constituted by means of a web of relations, incorporating lineage, clan, and tribe. An ethicist may properly ask how the ethical principle of respect for persons, enshrined in Western tradition, might play itself out within a sociocentric-organic context. What would the very process of decision-making look like? For example, someone from a sociocentric-organic culture would very likely take exception to a Western framing of the notion of human rights in terms of noninterference. Such noninterference would itself be construed as immoral.

In Africa, the very reason given for having children differs from those usually given in the West. As Kilbride and Kilbride note, "the parent . . . literally has children for the group."[49] Considerable importance is attached to having children, not only for the parents but especially for the clan. At the same time, there is what a Westerner might see as ambivalence regarding the child. On the one hand, the child is not yet seen as a person. On the other hand, the young child is linked to the divine. Pierre Erny notes:

> To say that a small child is "water" is equivalent to saying that he is not yet a person, that he has no social meaning yet. "He is not solid yet," . . . and he is put in the category of things. Belonging still to the cosmos, he must grow tough before he asserts himself as a social being, and this process involves many dangers.[50]

Within this context, one understands the process of maturing in a different light. Willy De Craemer, for example, portrays a dynamic notion of person in which a child grows into personhood: "becoming a person is seen developmentally — as a state that is progressively achieved through stages, and by degrees, including ancestorhood."[51] Personhood, furthermore, becomes something that some individuals may never attain.

Certain situations that seem to go counter to our own Western sensibilities may seem quite normal to an African. In discussing the decisions of the Akamba tribe of Africa, for example, John Kilner relates:

> Whereas in the United States we tend to value the young more highly than the old because they are more productive economically, these Akamba espouse a more relational view of life. Life, they insist, is more than atomistic sums of individual economic contributions; it is the social fabric of interpersonal relations. The older a person becomes, the more intricately interwoven that person becomes in the lives of others, and the greater the damage done if that person is removed. At the same time, the older person has wisdom — a perspective on life that comes only with age — which is considered to be a particularly important social resource.[52]

I am not trying to suggest, however, that in certain African cultures children are expendable. Precisely because a child is not yet integrated into society, the child is seen as linked to the divine and to the other world.[53] The death of an infant is often interpreted as a curse to the family or clan from the spirits of the dead.[54]

This investigation seems to indicate that in whatever way a child is seen in Zaire, he or she is *not* viewed in the way typically understood in the West. The child is in a process of becoming related to its parents, clan, tribe, and society, in a process of becoming a person. At the same time, it is seen as already linked to God and to the cosmos. Prior to asking the relevance of this understanding for ethics, it may be helpful to also raise the question of what proxy consent might look like in Zaire.

B. The Question of Proxy Consent

The distinction between egocentric-contractual and sociocentric-organic cultures also affects the understanding of the nature of consent. To repeat a question raised earlier, what is the likelihood that what Zagury claims he understood as occurring between him and the mothers is similar to what the mothers of these children understood as occurring? Since traditional societies attach importance to one's answering questions in terms of the authority's expectations, there is a high probability that signing such a form was merely a form of deference, signing because an authority desired it rather than as an act of freedom and knowledge.

One may next ask whether the *mothers* of the children were even the proper people from whom to obtain proxy consent. This question is itself multifaceted, eventually raising a final question regarding the very nature and possibility of proxy consent in an African context. At one level, one must ask regarding the nature of kinship and responsibility in Zairian clans and tribes. In Zaire, tribes may be matrilinear or patrilinear. Information regarding the particular tribes and clans of the children who served as subjects is not available. Yet this knowledge is quite important in assessing the suitability of any consent given. For example, it is at least somewhat likely that members of one of the dominant tribes in Zaire, the Kasai, were among the experimental subjects. As a patrilinear tribe, a parental uncle of these children may have been much more significant than the mother in any decision to consent to experimentation.

This line of reasoning, however, leads to still another set of questions. We have already mentioned that in a sociocentric-organic culture, the relation between person and society must be seen differently from that understood in the West. John Janzen has described the social components in medical decision-making in Zaire as involving the sufferer, the specialist or professional, kinship factions, and nonkinship factions. This is further complicated by various supportive and antagonistic relationships between the sufferer and other members of the kinship and nonkinship factions and similar relationships between the other members of the kinship and nonkinship factions themselves.[55] It is this nexus of complicated relationships that forms the Zairian culture and from which the person cannot be extricated. Thus there are many legitimators of decisions, extending to kin, clan, tribe, and even to ancestors.

Janzen refers to these kinship groups that mediate between the sufferer and the specialist as "therapy management groups."[56] Our Western understanding of privacy and the authority of the specialist are antithetical to this kinship organization. Therapy is usually performed in the presence of the sufferer's kin. The relationship between the specialist and the therapy management group is an egalitarian one. In fact, the group often amends or even rejects the specialist's suggestion for therapy.[57] It is also common for the second and third parties in the management group to take the dominant role in decision-making, with the sufferer accepting a passive role.[58]

For therapy to be effective, there must be consensus among members of the therapy management group, though the scope of participation among kin is partly determined by the significance of the problem. Routine therapeutic questions focus the decision-making around few persons. Crisis situations, however, demand extensive consultation and participation. Disagreement within a management group can itself precipitate a crisis, until agreed-upon norms and relationships can be re-established.

Thus, in a Zairian context, "consent" necessarily means more than that of an individual and definitely more than one other individual serving as "proxy." This seems prima facie to run counter to Western values regarding experimentation, enshrined, for example, in the Helsinki Declaration, which states: "Concern for the interests of the subject must always prevail over the interests of science and society."[59] Nevertheless, if what was said above is true, it is impossible to delineate how the interests of a Zairian individual conflict with those of his or her kin, clan, or tribe. As O. O. Ajayi states, it is difficult for an African "to see how the interests of the subject conflict with the interest of the society except, of course, if the society is not his own."[60] If the above is correct, the very notion of *proxy* consent is meaningless in a Zairian context. Important decisions simply cannot be made by an individual and must involve the family, clan, and possibly even the tribe.

VI. Conclusion: The Ethics of Dr. Zagury's Experiment

It may seem to some that this foray into anthropology has been irrelevant, complicating matters so much that no ethical decision can be made, or thrown ethics into a sea of cultural relativism. On the contrary, I believe that such a detour ultimately proves to be clarifying. I believe that one may come to four conclusions regarding the ethics of Zagury's research protocol.

1. Dr. Zagury's claim that the experiment was performed out of compassion seems to be contradicted by the fact that it was a phase I vaccine experiment. Phase I research, *ipso facto,* exposes experimental subjects to risk, with any direct benefit to a seronegative person being accidental. One does not yet know enough about the proposed vaccine to ascertain that it would be beneficial. Furthermore, the burden of proof rests upon Zagury to demonstrate the necessity of using seronegative children. To date he has never given any reason for this choice.

2. Ethicists representing a variety of points of view within the Western philosophical tradition would judge Zagury's research protocol unethical for two reasons. On the one hand, even though the experimenter obtained signed consent forms, it is not obvious that he received free and informed consent. Even more basically, however, given his seeming inability to explain the necessity of using children in a phase I study, great ethical difficulties arise from the very fact that he used children in a phase I study.

3. When these same facts are viewed from an African point of view, however, some ambiguity arises. Can one both respect the person of the child and also respect a culture which might have fewer difficulties in allowing a child to participate in an experiment that would in turn have benefit for the society as a whole? If one takes seriously the sociocentric-organic nature of Zairian culture, a negative answer to this question is not automatic.

In fact, the question itself lays bare a difficulty inherent in some ways in which bioethics has been understood. Often this notion of ethics has become too closely equated with a rather literal adherence to published codes. Thus Zagury was concerned that the mothers of the children sign consent forms. Yet, at the same time he seems to have been oblivious to the values that provide the justification for the norms themselves.

Several contemporary, usually Catholic, ethicists, generally grouped together under the term of proportionalists, suggest that at times "it is necessary to contemplate true departures from norms as well as unusual applications of them."[61] It seems to me that nowhere is this more clearly the case than when one is working in a cross-cultural context. In such a situation, it is important to know what the rules are, but even more important to know the values that the rules are trying to protect. It becomes crucial to have an attitude both respectful and critical, acknowledging that some basic moral understandings that we use as guides may look quite different when applied in cross-cultural situations.

Yet, in trying to respect the values of another culture and the way those values are protected by norms and rules, it is equally important to understand the interrelation among the norms and values of a culture. Thus one must not stop by merely asking how the culture sees decision-making in general. Respect for the culture would seem to demand a general respect for decisions made by kinship groups and the acceptance not only of the presence but also the authority of such forms of decision-making.

4. This leads to my fourth conclusion. A researcher should not pick and choose which elements of a culture he or she accepts based upon

the way in which it will help or hinder the research. "Cross-cultural sensitivity" does not give an experimenter license to bend and break norms of professional conduct merely for the sake of research. In fact, the opposite is probably more true. While an ethical researcher would avoid the extremes of playing loose with the rules and never going beyond the strict norm, she or he would at least be tentative and self-critical regarding the necessary superiority of his or her ethical stance. Such an experimenter would attempt to be true to his or her own conscience while being at the same time respectful of the culture of those who are the experimental subjects. Experimental protocols may need to pass two ethical tests, a general ethical test of respect for persons and a more specific test of how true respect may be obtained in a particular culture.

This specific ethical test would not abandon basic values but rather ask how such values are to be enfleshed in culturally different contexts. Often this may mean that protocols that appear to run counter to expressed norms may, upon closer analysis, reveal better ways of protecting the values in question. On occasion, however, a true impasse might arise because of a genuine clash of values themselves. At such times, the experimenter may very well find it ethically necessary to abandon a particular experiment in a particular culture. Such cross-cultural sensitivity may benefit not only the subjects of the experimentation but the ethical person who is the experimenter as well.

Notes

1. John Crewdson, "Three Deaths in AIDS Vaccine Tests," *Chicago Tribune,* 14 April 1991, pp. 1, 16-17; "U.S. Health Agency Will Probe 3 Deaths from AIDS Vaccine Tests," *Chicago Tribune,* 26 April 1991, p. 14; "After 3 Die in Tests, France Bans AIDS Vaccine," *Chicago Tribune* 16 June 1991, pp. 1, 10; "Secret AIDS Tests on African Kids Detailed," *Chicago Tribune,* 17 July 1991, pp. 1-2.

2. Saul Rosen and Alison Wichman, memorandum to F. William Dommel, Jr., Director, Division of Human Subjects Protections, OPRR, 5 October 1990, p. 2. The memoranda and letters cited in this essay are on file with the author.

3. William C. Eby, memorandum to F. William Dommel, 14 March 1991, p. 2. Crewdson explains: "Moss's idea was to use the vaccina virus as a delivery system for the AIDS virus gene. Since his vaccinia recombinant contained only a part of the AIDS virus, recipients were in no danger of getting AIDS. But their immune systems might generate antibodies to the protein produced by the inserted gene that would protect them against the later infection with AIDS." Crewdson, "Secret AIDS tests on African Kids Detailed," pp. 1-2. Dr. Moss maintains that the vaccine was intended for use only in animals and that "he gave no authorization for administration to humans." See Rosen/Wichman memorandum, p. 4.

4. Eby memorandum, pp. 1-4.

5. It is interesting to note that several reports to the OPRR cite possible violations of ethical principles but do not necessarily include the use of children among them. The violations most often mentioned were the use of Moss's recombinant vaccinia strain on humans, though it was only to be used for *in vitro* or animal experimentation and enrolling subjects at the Hôpital Saint Antoine who were already receiving AZT, thus deviating from the approved protocol. See, for example, the Eby memorandum, p. 6; Priscilla A. Campbell, Report to the OPRR, 15 March 1991, pp. 2-3. I will not deal with these questions in this paper.

6. Rosen/Wichman memorandum, p. 4.

7. This committee was organized at the request of Dr. Zagury who had been advised to do so by Dr. Robert Gallo. See Rosen/Wichman memorandum, pp. 4-5.

8. "Secret AIDS Tests on African Kids Detailed," p. 2. Furthermore, there is an unconfirmed report that at least three of these children have already died in Kinshasa, Zaire. See *Africa Faith and Justice Network Update,* 13 February 1992.

9. See, for example, the Rosen/Wichman memorandum, p. 4.

10. "La loi Huriet en précise les modalités: 'le consentement signé des parents à cette vaccination.'" Daniel Zagury and Odie Picard, letter to Charles McCarthy, 21 June 1991, p. 5. Zagury also emphasized that the first person in the world to be vaccinated by Louis Pasteur was an eight-year-old French child.

11. Zagury/Picard letter to McCarthy, p. 5.

12. Daniel Zagury, reply to the OPRR's Interim Report, delivered through his attorney, Bernard Dartevelle, 15 July 1991, p. 14.

13. Ibid., p. 19.

14. Peter J. Fischinger, et al., "Toward a Vaccine Against AIDS: Rationale and Current Progress," *The*

Mount Sinai Journal of Medicine 53, 8 (December 1986): 639-40.

15. Ibid., 640.

16. Robert H. Purcell, "Animal Models for the Development of a Vaccine for the Acquired Immunodeficiency Syndrome," in Anthony Fauci, moderator, "Development and Evaluation of a Vaccine for Human Immunodeficiency Virus (HIV) Infection," *Annals of Internal Medicine* 10, 5 (March 1989): 382.

17. Ibid.

18. Anthony S. Fauci, "Vaccine for Human Immunodeficiency Virus Infection," in ibid., 373-74.

19. See Nicholas A. Cristakis, "The Ethical Design of an AIDS Vaccine Trial in Africa," *Hastings Center Report* 18, 3 (June/July 1988): 32.

20. See David Byar, "Design Considerations for AIDS Trials," *New England Journal of Medicine* 323, 19 (8 November 1990): 1343.

21. Daniel Zagury, et al., "A Group Specific Anamnestic Immune Reaction Against HIV-1 Induced by a Candidate Vaccine Against AIDS," *Nature* 332, 21 (April 1988): 730. It is interesting to note that nowhere in this article does Zagury mention that the subjects of this study were children.

22. See Joan P. Porter, et al., "Ethical Considerations in AIDS Vaccine Testing," *IRB: A Review of Human Subjects Research* (May/June 1989): 2. This essay was quoted in Carol Levine, Report to the Office for Protection from Research Risks, 14 March 1991, p. 5.

23. See, for example, James Jones, *Bad Blood: The Tuskegee Syphillis Experiment* (New York: The Free Press, 1981). See also Patricia A. King, "The Dangers of Difference," *Hastings Center Report* 22, 6 (November-December 1992): 35-38.

24. Francis D. Moore, "Therapeutic Innovation: Ethical Boundaries in the Initial Clinical Trials of New Drugs and Surgical Procedures," *Daedalus* 98, 2 (Spring 1969): 520. While this is undoubtedly an overstatement regarding the study I am investigating, it is of interest that an unidentified source close to Zagury claimed that they conducted the trial there because "[i]t was easier to get official permission [in Zaire] than in France." See Cristakis, "The Ethical Design of an AIDS Vaccine Trial," 31.

25. Quoted in Levine, Report to the Office for Protection from Research Risks, p. 2.

26. Of the 10 million people who have been infected with the HIV virus world-wide, 6.5 million live in Sub-Saharan Africa. In many African cities, more than 10% of all young adults are infected. Between 20 and 30% of pregnant women are infected, and 40% of the children born to these women will have developed AIDS perinatally. See Roy M. Anderson and Robert M. May, "Understanding the AIDS Pandemic," *Scientific American* 266, 5 (May 1992): 59. See also Erik Eckholm, "AIDS, Fatally Steady in the U.S., Accelerates Worldwide," *New York Times*, 28 June 1992, E5.

27. Fauci, "Vaccine for Human Immunodeficiency Virus Infection," 374.

28. Marcia Angell, "Ethical Imperialism? Ethics in International Collaborative Clinical Research," *New England Journal of Medicine* 319, 16 (20 October 1988): 1081.

29. Arthur Kleinman, *Patients and Healers in the Context of Culture: An Exploration of the Borderland between Anthropology, Medicine, and Psychiatry* (Berkeley: University of California Press, 1980), pp. 24-25.

30. See ibid., pp. 53-59.

31. Ibid., pp. 59-60. For a description of an African "folk" system, see John M. Janzen, "Health, Religion, and Medicine in Central and Southern African Traditions," in *Healing and Restoring: Health and Medicine in the World's Religious Traditions*, ed. Lawrence Sullivan (New York: Macmillan Publishing Company, 1989), pp. 225-54. See also John M. Janzen, *The Quest for Therapy in Lower Zaire* (Berkeley, University of California Press, 1978).

32. See, for example, one of the earliest books on experimental medicine: Claude Bernard, *An Introduction to the Study of Experimental Medicine* (1857): "It is our duty and our right to perform an experiment on man whenever it can save his life, cure him or gain him some personal benefit. The principle of medical and surgical morality, therefore, consists in never performing on man an experiment which might be harmful to him to any extent, even though the result might be highly advantageous to science, i.e., to the health of others." Trans. Henry Copley Greene (New York: The Macmillan Company, 1927), p. 101.

33. See, for example, Ruth R. Faden and Tom L. Beauchamp, *A History of Informed Consent* (Oxford: Oxford University Press, 1986), pp. 7-9.

34. U. S. Supreme Court, "Cruzan v. Director, Missouri Department of Health," *Origins* 20 (5 July 1990): 128. The Court continues, "This notion of bodily integrity has been embodied in the requirement that informed consent is generally required for medical treatment."

35. Faden and Beauchamp, *A History of Informed Consent*, p. 238.

36. The Nuremberg Code, quoted in Karen Lebacqz and Robert J. Levine, "Informed Consent in Human Research: Ethical and Legal Aspects," in *Encyclopedia of Bioethics* (New York: The Free Press, 1978), p. 757.

37. Robert Proulx Heaney and Charles J. Dougherty, *Research for Health Professionals* (Ames: University of Iowa Press, 1988), p. 224.

38. Code of Federal Regulations, 45 CFR 46, revised March 8, 1983.

39. See Dennis M. Maloney, *Protection of Human Research Subjects: A Practical Guide to Federal Laws and Regulations* (New York: Plenum Press, 1984), p. 315.

40. See J. K. Mason, *Medico-Legal Aspects of Reproduction and Parenthood* (Brookfield, Vermont: Gower Publishing Company, 1990), pp. 283-90.

41. See Paul Ramsey, *The Patient as Person* (New Haven: Yale University Press, 1970), pp. 1-58; Richard A. McCormick, "Sharing in Sociality: Children and Experimentation," in *How Brave a New World?* (Garden City, New York: Doubleday and Co., 1981), pp. 87-98. It is interesting to note that the National Commission for the Protection of Human Subjects of Biomedical and Behavioral Research framed its own discussion of recommendations for the protection of children around this same debate. See *Research Involving Children: Report and Recommendations* (Washington, D.C.: U.S. Government Printing Office, 1977), pp. 95-104.

42. Ramsey, *The Patient as Person,* p. 25.

43. McCormick, "Sharing in Sociality," pp. 89-90.

44. Ibid., p. 89.

45. Ibid., p. 95.

46. Richard A. Shweder, *Thinking Through Cultures* (Cambridge, Mass.: Harvard University Press, 1991), p. 151.

47. Ibid., p. 153.

48. Ibid., p. 154.

49. Philip L. Kilbride and Janet C. Kilbride, *Changing Family Life in East Africa: Women and Children at Risk* (University Park: The Pennsylvania State University Press, 1990), p. 85.

50. Pierre Erny, *Childhood and Cosmos: The Social Psychology of the Black African Child* (Rockville, Maryland: Media Intellectics Corporation, 1973), pp. 166-67.

51. Willy De Craemer, "A Cross-cultural Perspective on Personhood," *Millbank Memorial Fund Quarterly/Health and Society* 61, 1 (1983): 24.

52. John F. Kilner, "Who Shall Be Saved? An African Answer," *Hastings Center Report* 14, 3 (June 1984): 19.

53. Erny, *Childhood and Cosmos,* pp. 82-85.

54. Kilbride and Kilbride, *Changing Family Life in East Africa,* p. 116.

55. Janzen speaks of this as the "triangle of truth." See Janzen, *The Quest for Therapy in Lower Zaire,* p. 145; for a discussion of these various components, see pp. 139-50.

56. Ibid., p. xviii.

57. Ibid., p. 142.

58. This is true even when the sufferer is an educated adult, whether male or female. See ibid., p. 90.

59. The Helsinki Declaration, in *Handbook of Declarations* (Paris: World Medical Association, 1992), 17C, p. 2, #5.

60. O. O. Ajayi, "Taboos and Clinical Research in West Africa," *Journal of Medical Ethics* 6 (1980): 61. See also Cristakis, "The Ethical Design of an AIDS Vaccine Trial in Africa," p. 35.

61. Lisa Cahill, *Between the Sexes: Foundations for a Christian Ethics of Sexuality* (Philadelphia: Fortress Press, 1985), p. 148. See also Richard Gula, *What Are They Saying About Moral Norms?* (New York: Paulist Press, 1982).

120 Major Conclusions and Recommendations from the Final Report of the NIH Human Embryo Research Panel

Guiding Considerations

The Panel concluded that certain areas of research involving the preimplantation human embryo are acceptable for Federal funding within a framework of stringent guidelines. Three overarching considerations led the Panel to this conclusion:

- the promises of the human benefit from the research is significant;
- the preimplantation human embryo warrants serious moral consideration as a developing form of human life, but it does not have the same moral status as infants and children because of the absence of developmental individuation, the lack of even the possibility of sentience and most other qualities considered relevant to the moral status of persons, and the very high rate of natural mortality at this stage; and,
- Federal funding of such research would provide consistent ethical and scientific review at the national level to an area of research that has been ongoing in the private sector without such review and public scrutiny.

Definition

"Preimplantation human embryo" is defined by the Panel as a fertilized ovum in vitro that has never been transferred to or implanted in a uterus. This includes a fertilized ovum that has been flushed from a woman before implantation in the uterus. This procedure, which is both infrequent and poses special risks, is included because it is one potential source of embryos.

General Principles

The following general principles should govern Federally funded research involving the preimplantation human embryo:

- The research must be conducted by scientifically qualified individuals in an appropriate research setting.
- The research must consist of a valid research design and promise significant scientific or clinical benefit.
- The research goals cannot be otherwise accomplished by using animals or unfertilized gametes. In addition, where applicable, adequate prior animal studies must have been conducted.
- The number of embryos required for the research must be kept to the minimum consistent with scientific criteria for validity.
- Donors of gametes or embryos must have given informed consent with regard to the nature and purpose of the specific research being undertaken.
- There must be no purchase or sale of gametes or embryos used in research. Reasonable compensation in clinical studies should be permissible to defray a subject's expenses, over and above the costs of drugs and procedures required for standard treatment, provided that no compensation or financial inducements of any sort are offered in exchange for the donation of gametes or embryos, and so long as the level of compensation is in accordance with Federal regulations governing human subjects

From the Final Report of the NIH Human Embryo Research Panel, September 27, 1994.

research and that it is consistent with general compensation practice for other federally-funded experimental protocols.

- Research protocols and consent forms must be reviewed and approved by an appropriate Institutional Review Board, and for the immediate future an ad hoc review process which extends beyond the existing review process to be established by the NIH and operated for a period of at least three years.
- There must be equitable selection of donors of gametes and embryos and efforts must be made to ensure that benefits and risks are fairly distributed among subgroups of the population.
- Out of respect for the special character of the preimplantation human embryo, research involving preimplantation embryos should be limited to the shortest time period consistent with the goals of each research proposal, and for the present, research involving human embryos should not be permitted beyond the time of the usual appearance of the primitive streak in vivo (14 days). An exception to this is made for research protocols with the goal of reliably identifying in the laboratory the appearance of the primitive streak.

Fertilization of Oocytes for Research

With regard to the difficult issue of whether it is ethically acceptable to fertilize oocytes expressly for research purposes, the Panel concluded that studies that require the fertilization of oocytes are needed to answer crucial questions in reproductive medicine and that it would therefore be unwise to prohibit the fertilization and study of oocytes for research purposes altogether. However, because the preimplantation human embryo merits respect as a developing form of human life, the Panel recommends that the deliberate fertilization for research purposes be allowed only under two conditions (examples of research that might meet these two conditions are provided in the Panel report). Those conditions are:

- when the research by its very nature cannot otherwise be validly conducted.
- when a compelling case can be made that this is necessary for the validity of a study that is potentially of outstanding scientific and therapeutic value. Because of their concern that attempts might be made to create embryos for reasons that relate solely to the scarcity of embryos remaining from infertility programs and because of their interest in preventing the creation of embryos for any but the most compelling reasons, Panel members believe that special scrutiny during the review process is warranted for research that may meet the second condition.

Parthenogenesis

The Panel was asked to consider the acceptability of Federal funding of research involving the parthenogenesis, the activation of eggs to begin cleavage and development without fertilization (activated eggs are called parthenotes). Human parthenotes are not developmentally viable, and they do not represent a form of asexual reproduction. Because research on parthenotes might provide information on the specific role of the egg mechanisms in activating and sustaining early development, without generating a human embryo, as well as shed light on problems arising during oocyte development that promote a type of ovarian tumor formation, the Panel recommends that research proposals involving parthenogenesis be considered ethically acceptable on condition that they adhere to the general principles and that under no circumstances is transfer of parthenogenetically activated oocytes permitted.

Sources of Gametes and Embryos

With regard to sources of gametes and embryos — which could include women in IVF programs, healthy volunteers, women undergoing pelvic surgery, women and girls who have died, and aborted fetuses — the Panel concluded that the following were acceptable sources of gametes and/or embryos provided all other conditions regarding consent, risk/benefit, and limits on commercialization are met:

- Women/couples in IVF programs. Great care must be taken to ensure that there is no undue, or even subtle, pressure to donate. The voluntary nature of such donations is essential, and under no circumstances should individuals who do not wish to donate their gametes ever feel pressured to do so.

- Women undergoing scheduled pelvic surgery, as long as no additional risks are imposed. Researchers must explain any changes from standard surgical procedures and, if hormonal stimulation is used, the risks of such drugs.
- Women who are not scheduled to undergo a surgical procedure, but only for research that involves transfer of the resulting embryo for the purpose of establishing a pregnancy.
- Women who have died, but only for research that does not involve transfer and as long as the woman had not expressly objected to such use of her oocytes and that appropriate consent is obtained. Consenting donors, or next of kin proxy, should be clearly and specifically aware that the organ being donated is the ovary and that it might be used in research that could involve the fertilization of any oocytes derived from it.

The Panel concluded that the following sources were unacceptable for Federally funded research:

- Women who are not scheduled to undergo a surgical procedure, unless the research is for the purpose of establishing a pregnancy.
- Oocytes obtained from aborted fetuses for research that involves transfer. The use of fetal oocytes in research that does not involve transfer also should not be supported until the ethical implications are more fully explored and addressed.

Review and Oversight

Because of the sensitive nature of research involving the preimplantation human embryo, all such research proposals submitted to the NIH for funding or that are proposed for conduct in the NIH intramural research program should be subject for a period of at least three years to an additional review at the national level by an ad hoc body created with discretionary authority of the Director of NIH. When the ad hoc review body ceases to exist, all such research proposals should continue to be specially monitored by the NIH councils and the NIH Office for Protection from Research Risks. This monitoring would include a commitment by the councils to pay particular attention to the protocols as they are presented for approval, in order to ensure that the local Institutional Review Board and NIH study section have correctly applied the guidelines adopted by the Director of NIH.

Categories of Research

Consistent with its mandate, the Panel considered specific areas of research in terms of acceptability for Federal funding. The Panel was charged to classify types of embryo research into three categories: (1) acceptable for federal funding; (2) warranting additional review; and (3) unacceptable for federal funding.

Acceptable for Federal Funding

A research proposal is presumed acceptable if it is in accordance with the general and specific guidelines recommended by the Panel and unless it has been placed in the warranting additional review or unacceptable categories. Examples of acceptable research include, but are not limited to, the following:

- Studies aimed at improving the likelihood of a successful outcome for a pregnancy.
- Research on the process of fertilization.
- Studies on egg activation and the relative role of paternally-derived and maternally-derived genetic material in embryo development (parthenogenesis without transfer).
- Studies in oocyte maturation or freezing followed by fertilization to determine developmental and chromosomal normality.
- Research involving preimplantation genetic diagnosis, with and without transfer.
- Research involving the development of embryonic stem cells but only with embryos resulting from IVF treatment or clinical research that have been donated with the consent of the progenitors.
- Nuclear transplantation into an enucleated,

fertilized or unfertilized (but activated) egg, without transfer, for research that aims to circumvent or correct an inherited cytoplasmic defect. [A narrow majority of the Panel believed such research should be acceptable for Federal funding. Nearly as many thought that the ethical implications of research involving the transplantation of a nucleus, whether transfer was contemplated or not, needed further study before the research could be considered acceptable for Federal funding.]

- Research involving the use of existing embryos where one of the progenitors was an anonymous gamete source who received monetary compensation. In order to determine whether the exception might apply, special attention must be given during the review process to ensure that payment has not been provided for the embryo itself and that all other proposed guidelines are met. (This exception would apply only to embryos already in existence at the time at which this report is accepted by the Advisory Committee to the Director, NIH, should such acceptance occur.)
- A request to fertilize ova when a compelling case can be made that this is needed for the validity of a study that is potentially of outstanding scientific and therapeutic value. Special attention is warranted for such research because of concern that attempts might be made to create embryos for reasons that relate solely to the scarcity of embryos remaining from infertility programs and because of the Panel's interest in preventing the creation of embryos for any but the most compelling reasons.

Warrants Additional Review

Research in this category is of a particularly sensitive nature. The Panel did not make a determination for the acceptability of these proposals and recommends that there be a presumption against funding such research for the foreseeable future. This presumption could be overcome only by an extraordinary showing of scientific or therapeutic merit together with explicit consideration of the ethical issues and social consequences. The Panel recommends that such research proposals be funded only after review by a broad-based ad hoc body created at the discretion of the Director, NIH, or by some other formal review process.

- Research between the appearance of the primitive streak and the beginning of neural tube closure.
- Cloning by blastomere separation or blastocyst splitting without transfer.
- Nuclear transplantation into an enucleated, fertilized or unfertilized (but activated) egg, with transfer, with the aim of circumventing or correcting an inherited cytoplasmic defect.
- Research involving the development of embryonic stem cells from embryos fertilized expressly for this purpose. [Decided by a narrow majority of members. A number of members felt that the research was acceptable for Federal funding and some believed that such research should be considered unacceptable for Federal funding].
- Research that uses fetal oocytes for fertilization without transfer. [Decided by a narrow majority of members. A number of members believed that such research should be placed in the unacceptable category.]

Unacceptable for Federal Funding

The Panel was guided by four ethical considerations in determining the types of research that should be unacceptable for Federal funding: the potential adverse consequences of the research for liveborn children, women, and men; the respect due the preimplantation embryo; concern for public sensitivities on highly controversial research proposals; and, concern for the meaning of humanness, parenthood, and the succession of generation. Throughout its report the Panel balanced these concerns against the scientific promise and the clinical and therapeutic value of proposed research, particularly as it might contribute to the well-being of women, children, and men. For the types of research considered unacceptable, the Panel determined that the scientific and therapeutic value was low or questionable, or that animal studies did not warrant progressing to human research. Even if claims were made for their scientific or therapeutic value, the Panel believed that serious ethical concerns would counsel against Federal funding of such research. Such unacceptable research includes:

- Cloning of human preimplantation embryos by separating blastomeres or dividing blastocysts (induced twinning), followed by transfer in utero.
- Studies designed to transplant embryonic or adult nuclei into an enucleated egg, including nuclear cloning, in order to duplicate a genome or to increase the number of embryos with the same genotype, with transfer.
- Research beyond the onset of closure of the neural tube.
- Research involving the fertilization of fetal oocytes with transfer.
- Preimplantation genetic diagnosis for sex selection except for sex-linked genetic diseases.
- Development of human-nonhuman and human-human chimeras with or without transfer.
- Cross-species fertilization except for clinical tests of the ability of sperm to penetrate eggs.
- Attempted transfer of parthenogenetically activated human eggs.
- Attempted transfer of human embryos into nonhuman animals for gestation.
- Transfer of human embryos for extrauterine or abdominal pregnancy.

121 The Inhuman Use of Human Beings

A Statement on Embryo Research by the Ramsey Colloquium

A panel of nineteen experts appointed by the National Institutes of Health has recommended government funding for conceiving human embryos in the laboratory for the sole purpose of using them as materials for research. After carefully studying the Report on the Human Embryo Research Panel, we conclude that this recommendation is morally repugnant, entails grave injustice to innocent human beings, and constitutes an assault upon the foundational ideas of human dignity and rights essential to a free and decent society. The arguments offered by the Panel are more ideological and self-interested than scientific; the actions recommended by the Panel cross the threshold into a world of apparently limitless technological manipulation and manufacture of human life. The Panel claims to draw a "clear line" against experiments that almost everyone would deem abhorrent. In fact it does not draw such a line and, by virtue of its own logic, it cannot draw such a line. The recommendation, if adopted, will be a fateful step for humanity from which it may be impossible to turn back.

All of us have a stake in the questions raised. In a society such as ours, these questions cannot be, they must not be, decided by a committee of

---

From *First Things* no. 49 (January 1995): 17-21. Used by permission.

experts. We urge a comprehensive public debate and intense congressional scrutiny regarding the proposals emanating from the NIH. The research recommended by the Panel should not be funded by the government. It should not be done at all. It should be prohibited by law. In what follows we attempt to explain how we have reached this conclusion.

We are confident that most people, to the extent that they are aware of the Panel's recommendation, experience an immediate and strong revulsion. This is not to be dismissed as an irrational reaction. It signals a deep, intuitive awareness of lines that must not be crossed if we are to maintain our sometimes fragile hold upon our own humanity.

For instance, the *Washington Post's* editorial response to the Panel's proposal declared flatly that "The creation of human embryos specifically for research that will destroy them is unconscionable." The acids of moral relativism have not advanced so far in our culture as to destroy completely the capacity to know and say that *some things are simply not to be countenanced,* much less approved and funded by the government. The editorial goes on to distinguish the present question from that of abortion. "To suggest that support for abortion rights equals support for such [embryo] experimentation is to buy abortion opponents' view that permitting abortion means erasing society's ability to make distinctions." The question of creating, using, and destroying human embryos cannot be separated entirely from the question of abortion, but the two questions can and should be distinguished. We hope that most people, whatever their views on the legalization of abortion, will be moved to take a stand at this new line that must not be crossed.

The ominously new thing in the Panel's Report is that embryonic human life should be treated simply as research material to be used and discarded — and should even be brought into being solely for that purpose. The Report readily acknowledges that the embryos to be used are instances of human life. It does not hesitate to answer the question of when a new human life begins. Indeed, indisputable scientific evidence leaves no choice: a new human life begins at conception (or, as the Report usually prefers, "fertilization"). The Report speaks of the embryo from the earliest moment as "developing human life." We are at various points told that the very early embryo deserves "serious moral consideration," "moral respect," "profound respect," and "some added measure of respect beyond that accorded animal subjects."

Honesty requires that we speak not simply of human life but of a human being. Skin and intestinal tissue, even eggs and sperm, are human life. But, unlike such instances of human life, the embryo from the earliest moment has the active capacity to articulate itself into what everyone acknowledges is a human being. The embryo is a being; that is to say, it is an integral whole with actual existence. The being is human; it will not articulate itself into some other kind of animal. Any being that is human is a human being. If it is objected that, at five days or fifteen days, the embryo does not look like a human being, it must be pointed out that this is precisely what a human being looks like — and what each of us looked like — at five or fifteen days of development. Clarity of language is essential to clarity of thought.

The question is, whether the government should permit and fund the production of human beings — completely innocent and powerless human beings — to be used as material for scientific research. After answering the question in the affirmative, the Report then considers which human beings can be so used and which cannot. It is one of the most treasured maxims of our civilization that human beings are always to be treated as ends and never merely as means. In a partial dissent from the Report, Professor Patricia A. King, a member of the Panel, writes, "The fertilization of human oocytes [female eggs] for research purposes is unnerving because human life is being created solely for human *use.* I do not believe that this society has developed the conceptual frameworks necessary to guide us down this slope. . . . At the very least, we should proceed with extreme caution." The conclusion that properly follows from her fully justified anxiety is that we should proceed not at all. Regrettably, the other members of the Panel appear not to have shared even the anxiety.

In weighing the question of which human beings can be used as a means to the ends of scientific progress and which cannot, the Report says the decision must rest on a "multi-factorial" judgment. By this is meant that no one principle or line of reasoning will support the conclusion that the Panel reaches. The Report's use of "multi-factorial" judgment is tantamount to suggesting that an accumulation of doubtful arguments will produce a convincing conclusion. In the course of reaching its "multi-factorial" judgment, the Panel entangles itself in philosophical, moral, and even scientific confusions. We are sorry to report that, in some of its arguments, the Panel invites the charge of being more than a little disingenuous.

In order to decide which human embryos are usable and which are "protectable" from such use, the Report leans very heavily on the concept of "personhood." The question is switched from "When does the life of a human begin?" to "When does a human being become a person?" Persons are protectable; nonpersons are those who are deemed to be something less than persons and are not protectable. But the only reason they are not protectable is that they will not be protected. Although they are obviously protectable in the sense that we are capable of protecting them, they are designated "not protectable" because we have decided not to protect them. And we decide not to protect them because they are not persons. Whether they are persons, and therefore protectable, depends upon their possessing certain qualities that we associate with persons and think worth protecting. Here and elsewhere in the Report, the reader is struck by a large measure of circularity in the Panel's reasoning.

The question is not whether the embryo is protectable but whether it is in need of protection. The Report says that "the commencement of protectability is not an all or nothing matter, but results from a being's increasing possession of qualities that make respecting it (and hence limiting others' liberty in relation to it) more compelling." In other words, moral standing develops as the human being develops, and "personhood" is an award we bestow for performance. The principle espoused by the Report leads to the suggestion that our obligation to afford protection to a human being is in inverse proportion to his or her need for protection. Put differently, those who are fully and undoubtedly persons are protectable because they are, by and large, able to protect themselves.

It is not traditional in ethical discourse to discuss what "life" or "forms of life" or "developing forms of life" are entitled to respect and protection. Living human beings are so entitled. The classical conviction of our culture has been that, contrary to the Report, it is "an all or nothing matter." We are implicated in the fate of all; every human being is inviolable. It has taken society much blood and struggle to overcome what Professor King calls the "conceptual frameworks" whereby the powerful justified excluding various categories of the powerless from moral parity. The Panel's use of "personhood" is such a conceptual framework, and it applies to both the born and unborn.

The concept of personhood has a complicated history in theology, philosophy, and law. Personhood is certainly not a scientific concept. As used by the Panel, it is an ideological concept, an idea in the service of a program aimed at changing dramatically our civilization's understanding of human life and community. In this Report, personhood is a status that we bestow. We who have received that status decide who will be admitted to, and who will be excluded from, the circle of those who are recognized as persons and are therefore entitled to respect and protection. We are told that protectability increases with an "increasing possession of qualities" that we find compelling. It follows that protectability decreases with the decreasing possession of such qualities.

From their writings and public statements, we know that some members of the Panel do not flinch from the ominous implications of that principle for those who have lost their "compelling" qualities, especially at the end of the life spectrum. As a more complete explanation of its ethical reasoning, the Report cites an article by Professor Ronald Green, himself a member of the Panel, "Toward a Copernican Revolution in Our Thinking About Life's Beginning and Life's End." It is indeed a revolution that is proposed by Professor Green and by the Human Embryo Research Panel. The cited article asserts that there are no "qualities existing *out there*" in any human being requiring us to respect him or her as a person. Whether to grant or deny "personhood" (and hence the right not to be harmed or killed) is, we are told, "the outcome of a very active and complex process of decision on our part." In the current language of the academy, personhood is entirely a "social construct." Whether someone is too young or too old, too retarded or too sick, too troublesome or too useless to be entitled to personhood is determined by a "decision on our part." The American people have not been consulted about, and certainly have not consented to, this "Copernican Revolution" in our understanding of human dignity and human rights.

The revolution is necessary, however, in order to license, morally and legally, the research that the Panel recommends. The "conceptual frameworks" of the Report's extended ethical and philosophical reflection obscure rather than illumine the questions at hand. As already indicated, the question is not the difference between human beings and other animals. Similarly, the Report makes much of the "preimplantation embryo" (implantation in the womb usually begins with the sixth day and is completed by the fourteenth day after conception). A "greater measure of respect" is due the embryo after the fourteenth day, says the Panel. This is gravely misleading. In question are not preimplantation embryos but *unimplanted* embryos — embroys produced with the intention that they will *not* be implanted and can therefore be kept alive and experimented upon as long as they are scientifically useful.

There are additional obfuscations. The Report makes much of the "twinning" factor. An early embryo is said not to be "individuated" because in a very small minority of cases the embryo may "twin" into two or more human beings. The ethical significance of this possibility is elusive. The fact that in rare instances an embryo may divide is no justification whatever for deliberately producing human embryos for the purpose of experimentation that will destroy them. Moreover, the Report repeatedly points to the "potential" of the embryo for further development as an indicator of whether or not it is "protectable." Here the circularity of reasoning is particularly blatant: A human being is not protectable in the early stages of development because, the Report claims, it has no potential for further development. But in the case of the embryo produced in the laboratory it has no potential for further development for the sole reason that researchers will not protect it. Because they wish to use it, they do not protect it; because they do not protect it, its natural potential for development is destroyed; because it thus "has no potential," it is declared "not protectable."

The monumental questions raised by this report — Who shall live and who shall die? Who belongs to the community and the commonly protected? How do we distinguish between human beings and laboratory animals? — demand much more serious thinking than is offered by the Human Embryo Research Panel.

The Panel claims to have established clear lines and clear time limits regarding what it is permissible to do with human embryos. The claim is false, and it seems that the panelists know that it is false. The Report says that research with these living human beings "should not be permitted beyond the time of the usual appearance of the primitive streak in vivo (14 days)." (The primitive streak is a groove that develops along the midline of the embryonic disc and its appearance is viewed as one of several milestones in the embryo's continuous development.) But this time limit is clearly arbitrary and chosen as a pragmatic compromise, as the transcript of the Panel's deliberations makes clear.

The panelists all know that development is continuous and it offers no such bright natural line to those who would "ascribe personhood." Moreover, this "time limit" is by no means firm, as is evident in the Report's assertion that it should serve "at the present time," and "for the foreseeable future." Some technically possible and scientifically interesting experiments "warrant additional review," while others are deemed "unacceptable for federal funding" because the desired experiments can at present be done with laboratory animals and because of "concern for public sensitivities on highly controversial research proposals." At the present time. For the foreseeable future.

For example, producing genetically identical individuals to be born at different times, freezing an embryonic human being who is genetically identical to a born child in order to serve as a latter source for organ and tissue transplantation, cloning an existing human being, and making "carbon copies" of an existing embryo — these and other projects are declared to be "inappropriate." It is not clear that the Report opposes the doing of these things; it simply does not recommend, at present, federal funding for doing them. But in the logic of the Report, there is no reason *in principle* why these things should not be done or why they should not be funded by the government.

"Throughout its deliberations," we are told, "the Panel relied on the principle that research involving preimplantation embryos is acceptable public policy only if the research promises significant scientific and therapeutic benefits." But a principle that says something should not be done unless there are strong motives for doing it is no principle at all. The claim to have set limits is vitiated by the repeated assertion that exceptions can be made for "serious and compelling reasons." The "Copernican Revolution" is nothing less than the abandonment of any and all principled limits. If it is for "serious and compelling reasons," scientists can do whatever they decided to do with human beings who are declared to be "unprotectable." And they can get government funding for doing it, within the limits of "public sensitivities." There is no reason, in principle, why such license would be confined to very small and very young human beings.

Of course the Panel believes that its recommendations are supported by "serious and compelling reasons" having to do with gains in scientific knowledge and therapeutic benefits. We do not doubt that lethal experiments on powerless and unconsenting human beings might result in findings of scientific interest. As for therapeutic benefits, the Report holds out the promise of improved success with in vitro fertilization, new contraceptive techniques, new prospects for genetic screening, the production of cell lines for use in tissue transplantation, and, more vaguely, treatment of cancer and other diseases.

In fact, the Report seems too reticent in its discussion of possible "benefits" from the research it proposes. In a time when the entire human genome is being mapped, when the age is rising at which many women first become mothers, when, consequently, there is increased anxiety about the risk of genetic diseases, when harvesting parts from the embryo and fetus may have therapeutic uses for older human beings, when care for the handicapped and defective is viewed by many as excessively burdensome, and when it seems technically possible to produce custom-made babies — in such a time it is not surprising that people might be tempted to agree that the Panel's recommendations are supported by "serious and compelling reasons." The Report explicitly encourages funding for "preimplantation genetic screening," and the laboratory testing of artificially fertilized embryos before they are placed in the womb. The normalizing of in vitro fertilization and the universalizing of genetic screening in order to eliminate the unfit and advance eugenic goals are part of a "brave new world" clearly advanced by the proposals of the Human Embryo Research Panel.

Is this the future we want? Who should decide? That brings us to the makeup and role of the Panel itself.

"Americans hold widely different views on the question of the moral value of prenatal life at its various stages," the Report notes. "It is not the role of those who help form public policy to decide which of these views is correct. Instead, public policy represents an effort to arrive at a reasonable accommodation to diverse interests." The Panel says it eschews the task of adopting a particular philosophy or settling arguments that it describes as "metaphysically complex and controverted." In fact, however, in order to legitimate morally what it recommends, the Panel does adopt a particular philosophy that it believes cuts through the complexities and controversies. That philosophy is ordinarily called utilitarianism. It is a primitive and unreflective version of utilitarianism, to be sure, but the message is unequivocal: the end justifies the means. If there are "serious and compelling reasons," it would seem that the end would justify any means. Certainly it justifies producing, using, and destroying human beings who are valued only for their utility as tools serving the purposes of scientific research. The Panel's is not a "multi-factorial" judgment. There is ultimately only one factor: scientific utility.

While claiming not to impose a moral judgment or philosophy, the Panel imposes a moral judgment and philosophy. At the same time, while apparently only offering advice to the NIH, the Panel has in effect arrogated to itself the work of our elected representatives. It is the task of politicians and legislatures "to arrive at a reasonable accommodation to diverse interests." A panel of experts might inform political deliberation by displaying the full range of facts, arguments, and considerations that legislators should take into account in making decisions. This Panel could not do that, however. While the Panel heard testimony from those who do not share its crassly utilitarian philosophy, such diversity was not included in the Panel itself. As explained by the chairman at the Panel's first meeting, it was thought inappropriate to include any members who oppose the research in question. Thus the Panel was able to arrive at a "reasonable accommodation" of the "widely different views" on the questions at hand by conveniently eliminating different views.

Additionally troubling is the fact that members of the Panel are themselves doing the very research for which they are recommending federal funding. An ethics advisory panel certainly must take testimony from scientists involved in the research under consideration. In this case, however, it would seem that members of an advisory panel are recommending federal grants for their own work. This is ordinarily not called advising but lobbying. Congress should examine closely the apparent conflict of interest involved.

Our concern is with the philosophy and moral reasoning embraced by the Panel. Our conviction — and, we are confident, the conviction of almost all Americans — is that the ominous questions engaged must not be decided by one-sided committees of the National Institutes of Health. What affects all should, through our representative process, be decided by all. The proposal that some human beings should be declared "not protectable" affects all of us. The proposal that human beings should be treated merely as means rather than ends is revolutionary, but it is not new. Such "conceptual frameworks" have a terrifying history, not least in this bloodiest of centuries.

The production of human beings for the purpose of experiments that will destroy them should be prohibited by law. The use of human beings for experiments that will do them harm and to which they have not given their consent should be prohibited by law. It matters not how young or how small, how old or how powerless, such human beings may be. Some nations ban or severely restrict the research proposed by the Panel (e.g., Norway, Germany, Austria, Australia). In the shadow of the unspeakable horror of Nazism, the Nuremberg Code declared, "No experiment should be conducted where there is an a priori reason to believe that death or disabling injury will occur." And the 1975 Helsinki Declaration of the World Medical Association affirms, "Concern for the interests of the subject must always prevail over the interest of science and society."

It is objected that a ban would not be enforceable. If so, how can anyone believe that the proposed regulation by NIH would be enforceable? The research recommended by the Panel is now being done under various auspices, with or without government funding. Driven by scientific curiosity and hubris, reinforced by the prospect of great commercial gain and a belief that it will produce benefits for society, such research probably cannot be stopped altogether. But the necessity of a law does not depend on its being universally effective. What must be made illegal and declared morally odious is any research that subjects human beings to scientific experimentation that will certainly result in their grave injury or death.

The shamelessly partisan and conceptually confused Report of the Human Embryo Research Panel should be unambiguously rejected. Limits that are "for the present time" and "for the foreseeable future" limit nothing. They are but unconvincing reassurances that scientists are going carefully where they should not be permitted to go at all. If the course recommended by the Panel is approved, the foreseeable future is ominously clear: it is a return to the past when people contrived "conceptual frameworks" for excluding categories of human beings, born and unborn, from our common humanity.

Chapter Nineteen

ALLOCATION AND DISTRIBUTION

The doctor in George Bernard Shaw's "The Doctor's Dilemma" had enough elixir to help only one patient. Who was it to be? The good man Blenkinsop or the rotten artist Dubedat? The doctor finds it a hard choice: "Blenkinsop's an honest decent man; but is he any use? Dubedat's a rotten blackguard; but he's a genuine source of pretty and pleasant and good things." Catching the drift of these remarks, the doctor's companion attempts to form from them a universal principle: "Suppose you had this choice put before you: either to go through life and find all the pictures bad but all the men and women good, or to go through life and find all the pictures good and all the men and women rotten. Which would you choose?"

The doctor's dilemma has been repeated many different times since then and with many different medical resources. When penicillin was first discovered and proven effective, hard choices had to be made about who would receive it. When hemodialysis was first clinically used, hard choices had to be made about who would receive the treatment. Organs for transplant do not match the demand or need for them, and hard choices are necessary concerning who will receive the available organs. Time and energy are also held in finite supply, and the limits on these resources, too, create dilemmas for doctors.

One suggestion in response to such hard choices is to increase the supply. Produce more elixir. Manufacture more penicillin. Make enough kidney dialysis units to treat everyone in need. Secure more organs for transplant. Train more doctors.

Such a response, however, does not eliminate "the doctor's dilemma" with respect to developing technologies — for example, a totally implantable artificial heart — and increasing the supply requires a resource which is itself in short supply, money. Medical care is costly, and becoming costlier still. There are a number of reasons for increasing medical costs, not the least significant of which is the increasingly sophisticated technology of medical care. The bill for the care of baby Andrew Stinson (the premature infant mentioned in the introduction to Chapter 15) was $104,403.20, for example. Today that bill would be something like $220,000. It is little wonder that the percentage of our gross national product that we spend on health care has climbed above 14 percent. The point is that even if we did secure more organs for transplant, perhaps by moving from a policy of organ donation to a policy of routine organ harvesting, it would not eliminate all limiting factors of scarcity; we would still have to find the money to pay the medical expenses for each transplant. If the transplants were unsupported by public monies, than only the rich would have access to such medical care, and the policy of organ acquisition, which in theory would allow more organ transplants, would end up serving only the rich. Is that fair allocation? If transplant surgery were paid for with public funds, the public would quickly encounter the problem of scarcity of funds and hard choices concerning allocation.

The decision to provide resources to meet the problems of scarcity in medical care thus creates hard choices for a society, for to allocate funds to organ procurement and transplant means to have less for the critical care of hemophiliac, diabetic, and neonatal patients. Suppose we increased funding for all critical care; then we would have less for the care of retarded and handicapped patients, less for medical research, less for preventive medicine, less for providing access to a primary care physician for indigent persons. Or suppose we increased funding for health-related needs, suppose we let the percentage of our gross national product spent on these needs move up to seventeen, nineteen, even twenty percent; then we would have less to spend on education, on security, on providing access to music and art and the humanities. Suppose you had this choice put before you: to go through life either to find all the men and women and children with the best health care available but ignorant of Shakespeare and Picasso and Mozart, or to find all the men and women and children knowledgeable and appreciative of the great artistic traditions but at risk of death should disease strike. Which would you choose?

How can or should public policy choices be made? Is the principle of justice enough? If so, what is justice and what does it require? If not, what vision of the sort of society we should be and become must supplement it, and how can it be justified? Again, what bearing does cost-effectiveness have? Preventive medicine is often more cost-effective than crisis intervention. Should we, therefore, take resources from crisis intervention and put them into preventive medicine? But what if the sort of society we want to effect is not just a relatively healthy society but also a society in which the cries of the sick and helpless are heard and answered? Health Maintenance Organizations (HMOs) and managed care are attempts to contain costs, but what if they mean that patients go home sicker than they might otherwise? What if HMOs and managed care make it more difficult for hospitals to shift costs to cover the care of the indigent and therefore hospitals no longer care for the poor?

Hospitals have been forced into business competition with each other in order to survive. Cost containment is a worthy goal, but must it be joined to the pursuit of equitable access to health care or some form of guaranteed ordinary care if it is to be worthy social policy? David Schiedermayer's parody of the Hippocratic Oath (selection 122) reminds us of how those issues affect the physician on a daily basis. What Schiedermayer's parody does not address directly is the quality of that care. If the quality of care declines under managed care, will that be good social policy? Who will bear the burden of managed care, the poor through reduced access, all of us through reduced quality, those who care for us at home (usually women) when we used to be cared for at the hospital, or some combination of the above?

The doctor's dilemmas and the social policy questions usually take up most of our time and energy in discussions of allocation. But the churches are involved in this matter, too. Many hospitals were founded by churches as a signal of their loyalty to Christ the healer and a gesture of their care for the sick and helpless. Now the churches may have cause to reassert their interest in medicine, to assure the care of the poor and to witness to society of their Lord and of their responsibilities. But churches and church members have limited resources, too. How can we rank health care and hunger relief and evangelism and securing justice and other needs all as part of the one mission of the one God? These are hard choices and costly choices for churches, too.

The essays below get to these issues — and more besides. Gene Outka's piece (selection 123) is justly classified as a classic — not only because if is so often cited in the literature but also because it utilizes classic Protestant patterns of moral reflection, presupposing individualism, reflecting on the relation of love as the fundamental Christian principle and justice as the fundamental social principle, formulating standards for social policy makers, here the goal of equal access to health care. B. Andrew Lustig's piece (selection 124) is also concerned with social policy and with defending the claim to a right to health care. His argument is a classic Catholic one, not only because he appeals to papal pronouncements but more because he presupposes a more communal understanding of society and utilizes arguments to identify certain basic goods not only as goods chosen by individuals but as communal goods. It is interesting to compare these two articles, to consider, for example, the differences between a right to equal access and a right to ordinary health care, or the differences in their treatment of individual responsibility for health, and to trace those differences, if possible, to the different perspectives of the authors.

Teresa Meldonado gives us a first-person account (selection 128) of what it means to be poor and to be seeking health care in this country. Her essay is one to read while reflecting on B. Andrew Lustig's account of the "preferential option for the poor."

John Kilner (in selection 126) raises the issue of medical care for the elderly in our society, considering proposals to limit their care at times when resources are scarce. L. Gregory Jones (in selection 127) raises a challenge to all attempts to ration resources in our society. Jones's response is to argue that issues of personal and professional identity are more important than any proposed solution based upon economic principles.

This chapter brings up issues about which all citizens can and should reflect. What difference does it make to reflect on these questions as Christians, in our various communities? What might these communities be saying and doing about how health care is distributed in our society? It is to that ongoing reflection that we invite you as we come to the close of this book.

Shalom!

Suggestions for Further Reading

Calabresi, Guido, and Philip Bobbitt. *Tragic Choices* (New York: Norton, 1978).

Campbell, Courtney S. "Spirituality in Health-Care Reform," *Journal of Religion and Health* 34 (Winter, 1995): 277-85.

Childress, James F. "Fairness in the Allocation and Delivery of Health Care: The Case of Organ Transplantation," in *A Time to Be Born and a Time to Die*, ed. B. Kogan (Hawthorne, N.Y.: Aldine de Gruyter, 1991).

Churchill, Larry R. *Rationing Health Care in America: Perceptions and Principles of Justice* (Notre Dame, Ind.: University of Notre Dame Press, 1987).

Crigger, Bette Jane, ed. "The Place of Ethics in Health Care Reform," *Hastings Center Report* 24 (May-June 1994): 7-12.

Dougherty, Charles J. *Back to Reform: Values, Markets and the Health Care System* (New York: Oxford University Press, 1996).

Keane, Philip S. *Health Care Reform: A Catholic View* (New York: Paulist Press, 1993).

May, William F. *Testing the Medical Covenant: Active Euthanasia and Health Care Reform* (Grand Rapids: Wm. B. Eerdmans, 1996).

Meulen, H. J., et al. "What Do We Owe the Elderly? Allocating Social and Health Care Resources," *Hastings Center Report,* 24: Supplement, March-April 1994.

Schiedermayer, David. "Healing the Health-care System: How Should Christ's Mandate that We Care for "the Least of These" Guide Our National Debate on Health-care Reform?" *Christianity Today* 37 (October 25, 1993): 16-17.

Zoloth-Dorfman, Laurie. "First, Make Meaning: An Ethics of Encounter for Health Care Reform," *Tikkun* 8 (July-August 1993): 23-26.

122 "The Corporate Physician's Oath"

David Schiedermayer

I swear by Humana and Columbia HCA and Cigna and Prudential and FHP and Wellpoint and HMO and PPO and IPA, making them my witnesses, that I will fulfill according to my ability this oath and this covenant:

To hold the one who has taught me this business as equal to my corporation president, and to live my life in partnership with him or her, and if he or she is in need of capital to give him or her some of mine, and to regard his or her offspring as equal to my colleagues and to teach them this business — if they desire to learn it — for a fee and under contract; to give a share of my practice management techniques and computer systems and all other business acumen to my children and the children of those who have taught me, and to students who have signed the contract and have taken an oath according to Medicare law, but to no one else.

I will apply dietetic measures for the benefit of the obese, the alcoholic, the smoker, and the drug addict, but in this culture and in this political climate I will seldom be able to keep them from self-harm and injustice.

I will neither give a deadly drug to anybody if asked for it, nor will I make a suggestion to that effect (depending on the outcome of Oregon's Ballot Measure 16). As an internist I will not do an abortion, leaving that to the obstetricians. In fear of malpractice I will guard my life and my business.

I will not use the knife, but I will try to learn some form of endoscopy.

Into whatever clinics I may enter, I will come for the benefit of the members, required to remain clear of all except capitated care for the indigent.

Things which I may see or hear in the course of treatment, or even outside of treatment regarding the life of human beings, things which one should never divulge outside, I will report to government commissions, immigration officials, hospital administrators, or use in my book.

If I fulfill this oath and do not violate it, may it be granted to me to enjoy life and business, being able to retire at age 50 in the sunbelt. If I transgress it and swear falsely, may Milwaukee be my lot.

Used with permission of the author. An earlier version was published as "The Hippocratic Oath — Corporate Version," in the *New England Journal of Medicine,* Jan. 2, 1986, p. 62.

123 Social Justice and Equal Access to Health Care

Gene Outka

I want to consider the following questions. Is it possible to understand and to justify morally a societal goal which increasing numbers of people, including Americans, accept as normative? The goal is: the assurance of comprehensive health services for every person irrespective of income or geographic location. Indeed, the goal now has almost the status of a platitude. Currently in the United States politicians in various camps give it at least verbal endorsement.[1] I do not propose to examine the possible sociological determinants in this emergent consensus. I hope to show that whatever these determinants are, one may offer a plausible case in defense of the goal on reasonable grounds. To demonstrate why appeals to the goal get so successfully under our skins, I shall have recourse to a set of conceptions of social justice. Some of the standard conceptions, found in a number of writings on justice, will do.[2] By reflecting on them it seems to me a prima facie case can be established, namely, that every person in the entire resident population should have equal access to health care delivery.

The case is prima facie only. I wish to set aside as far as possible a related question which comes readily enough to mind. In the world of "suboptimal alternatives," with the constraints for example which impinge on the government as it makes decisions about resource allocation, what is one to say? What criteria should be employed? Paul Ramsey, in *The Patient as Person*, thinks that the large question of how to choose between medical and other societal priorities is "almost, if not altogether, incorrigible to moral reasoning."[3] Whether it is or not is a matter which must be ignored for the present. One may simply observe in passing that choices are unavoidable nonetheless, as Ramsey acknowledges, even where the government allows them to be made by default, so that in some instances they are determined largely by which private pressure groups prove to be dominant. In any event, there is virtue in taking up one complicated question at a time and we need to get the thrust of the case for equal access before us. It is enough to observe now that Americans attach an obviously high priority to organized health care. National health expenditures for the fiscal year 1972 were $83.4 billion.[4] Even if such an enormous sum is not entirely adequate, we may still ask: how are we to justify spending whatever we do in accordance as far as possible with the goal of equal access? The answer I propose involves distinguishing various conceptions of social justice and trying to show which of these apply or fail to apply to health care considerations. Only toward the end of the paper will some institutional implications be given more than passing attention, and then in a strictly programmatic way.

Another sort of query should be noted as we begin. What stake does someone in religious ethics have in this discussion? For the reasonable case envisaged is offered after all in the public forum. If the issue is how to justify morally the societal goal which seems so obvious to so many, whether or not they are religious believers, does the religious ethicist then simply participate qua citizen? Here I think we should be wary of simplifying formulae. Why for example should a Jew or a Christian not welcome wide support for a societal goal which he or she can affirm and reaffirm, or reflect only on instances where such support is not forthcoming? If a number of ethical schemes, both religious and humanist, converge in their acceptance of the goal of equal access to health care, so be it. Secularists can join forces with believers, at least at some levels or points, without implying there must be unanimity on every moral issue. Yet

---

it also seems too simple if one claims to wear only the citizen's hat when making the case in question. At least I should admit that a commitment to the basic normative principle which in Christian writings is often called *agape* may influence the account to follow in ways large and small.[5] For example, someone with such a commitment will quite naturally take a special interest in appeals to the generic characteristics all persons share rather than the idiosyncratic attainments which distinguish persons from one another, and in the playing down of desert considerations. As I shall try to show, such appeals are centrally relevant to the case for equal access. And they are nicely in line with the normative pressures agapeic considerations typically exert.

One issue of theoretical importance in religious ethics also emerges in connection with this last point. The approach in this paper may throw a little indirect light on the traditional question, especially prominent in Christian ethics, of how love and justice are related. To distinguish different conceptions of social justice will put us in a better position, I think, to recognize that often it is ambiguous to ask about "*the* relation." There may be different relations to different conceptions. For the conceptions themselves may sometimes produce discordant indications, or turn out to be incommensurable, or reflect, when different ones are seized upon, rival moral points of view. I shall note several of these relations as we proceed.

Which then among the standard conceptions of social justice appear to be particularly relevant or irrelevant? Let us consider the following five:

I. To each according to his merit or desert.
II. To each according to his societal contribution.
III. To each according to his contribution in satisfying whatever is freely desired by others in the open marketplace of supply and demand.
IV. To each according to his needs.
V. Similar treatment for similar cases.

In general I shall argue that the first three of these are less relevant because of certain distinctive features which health crises possess. I shall focus on crises here not because I think preventive care is unimportant (the opposite is true), but because the crisis situation shows most clearly the special significance we attach to medical treatment as an institutionalized activity or social practice, and the basic purpose we suppose it to have.

I

To each according to his merit or desert. Meritarian conceptions, above all perhaps, are grading ones: advantages are allocated in accordance with amounts of energy expended or kinds of results achieved. What is judged is particular conduct which distinguishes persons from one another and not only the fact that all the parties are human beings. Sometimes a competitive aspect looms large.

In certain contexts it is illuminating to distinguish between efforts and achievements. In the case of efforts one characteristically focuses on the individual: rewards are based on the pains one takes. Some have supposed, for example, that entry into the kingdom of heaven is linked more directly to energy displayed and fidelity shown than to successful results attained.

To assess achievements is to weight actual performance and productive contributions. The academic prize is awarded to the student with the highest gradepoint average, regardless of the amount of midnight oil he or she burned in preparing for the examinations. Sometimes we may exclaim, "it's just not fair," when person X writes a brilliant paper with little effort while we are forced to devote more time with less impressive results. But then our complaint may be directed against differences in innate ability and talent which no expenditure of effort altogether removes.

After the difference between effort and achievement, and related distinctions, have been acknowledged, what should be stressed I think is the general importance of meritarian or desert criteria in the thinking of most people about justice. These criteria may serve to illuminate a number of disputes about the justice of various practices and institutional arrangements in our society. It may help to explain, for instance, the resentment among the working class against the welfare system. However wrongheaded or self-deceptive the resentment often is, particularly when directed toward those who want to work but for various reasons beyond their control cannot, at its better moments it involves in effect an appeal to desert considerations. "Something for nothing" is repudiated as unjust; benefits should be proportional (or at least related) to costs; those who can make an effort should do so, whatever the degree of their training or significance of their contribution to society; and so on. So, too, persons deserve to have what they have labored for; unless they infringe on the works of others their efforts and achievements are justly theirs.

Occasionally the appeal to desert extends to a wholesale rejection of other considerations as grounds for just claims. The most conspicuous target is need. Consider this statement by Ayn Rand.

> A morality that holds *need* as a claim, holds emptiness — nonexistence — as its standard of value; it rewards an absence, a defect: weakness, inability, incompetence, suffering, disease, disaster, the lack, the fault, the flaw — the *zero.*
>
> Who provides the account to pay these claims? Those who are cursed for being non-zeros, each to the extent of his distance from that ideal. Since all values are the product of virtues, the degree of your virtue is used as the measure of your penalty; the degree of your faults is used as the measure of your gain. Your code declares that the rational man must sacrifice himself to the irrational, the independent man to parasites, the honest man to the dishonest, the man of justice to the unjust, the productive man to thieving loafers, the man of integrity to compromising knaves, the man of self-esteem to sniveling neurotics. Do you wonder at the meanness of soul in those you see around you? The man who achieves these virtues will not accept your moral code; the man who accepts your moral code will not achieve these virtues.[6]

I have noted elsewhere[7] that *agape,* while it characteristically plays down, need not formally disallow attention to considerations falling under merit or desert; for the case of merit as well as need it may be possible, the quotation above notwithstanding, to reason solely from egalitarian premises. A major reason such attention is warranted concerns what was called there the differential exercise of an equal liberty. That is, one may fittingly revere another's moral capacities and thus the efforts he makes as well as the ends he seeks. Such reverence may lead one to weight expenditure of energy and specific achievements. I would simply hold now (1) that the idea of justice is not exhaustively characterized by the notion of desert, even if one agrees that the latter plays an important role; and (2) that the notion of desert is especially ill-suited to play an important role in the determination of policies which should govern a system of health care.

Why is it so ill-suited? Here we encounter some of the distinctive features which it seems to me health crises possess. Let me put it in this way. Health crises seem non-meritarian because they occur so often for reason beyond our control or power to predict. They frequently fall without discrimination on the (according-to-merit) just and unjust, i.e., the virtuous and the wicked, the industrious and the slothful alike.

While we may believe that virtues and vices cannot depend upon natural contingencies, we are bound to admit, it seems, that many health crises do. It makes sense therefore to say that we are equal in being randomly susceptible to these crises. Even those who ascribe a prominent role to desert acknowledge that justice has also properly to do with pleas of "But I could not help it."[8] One seeks to distinguish such cases from those acknowledged to be praiseworthy or blameworthy. Then it seems unfair as well as unkind to discriminate among those who suffer health crises on the basis of their personal deserts. For it would be odd to maintain that a newborn child deserves his hemophilia or the tumor afflicting her spine.

These considerations help to explain why the following rough distinction is often made. Bernard Williams, for example, in his discussion of "equality in unequal circumstances," identifies two different sorts of inequality, inequality of merit and inequality of need, and two corresponding goods, those earned by effort and those demanded by need.[9] Medical treatment in the event of illness is located under the umbrella of need. He concludes: "Leaving aside preventive medicine, the proper ground of distribution of medical care is ill health: this is a necessary truth."[10] An irrational state of affairs is held to obtain if those whose needs are the same are treated unequally, when needs are the ground of the treatment. One might put the point this way. When people are equal in the relevant respects —

in this case when their needs are the same and occur in a context of random, undeserved susceptibility — that by itself is a good reason for treating them equally.[11]

In many societies, however, a second necessary condition for the receipt of medical treatment exists de facto: the possession of money. This is not the place to consider the general question of when inequalities in wealth may be regarded as just. It is enough to note that one can plausibly appeal to all of the conceptions of justice we are embarked in sorting out. A person may be thought to be entitled to a higher income when he works more, contributes more, risks more, and not simply when he needs more. We may think it fair that the industrious should have more money than the slothful and the surgeon more than the tobacconist. The difficulty comes in the misfit between the reasons for differential incomes and the reasons for receiving medical treatment. The former may include a pluralistic set of claims in which different notions of justice must be meshed. The latter are more monistically focused on needs, and the other notions not accorded a similar relevance. Yet money may nonetheless remain as a causally necessary condition for receiving medical treatment. It may be the power to secure what one needs. The senses in which health crises are distinctive may then be insufficiently determinative for the policies which govern the actual availability of treatment. The nearly automatic links between income, prestige, and the receipt of comparatively higher quality medical treatment should then be subjected to critical scrutiny. For unequal treatment of the rich ill and the poor ill is unjust if, again, needs rather than differential income constitute the ground of such treatment.

Suppose one agrees that it is important to recognize the misfit between the reasons for differential incomes and the reasons for receiving medical treatment, and that therefore income as such should not govern the actual availability of treatment. One may still ask whether the case so far relies excessively on "pure" instances where desert considerations are admittedly out of place. That there are such pure instances, tumors afflicting the spine, hemophilia, and so on, is not denied. Yet it is an exaggeration if we go on and regard all health crises as utterly unconnected with desert. Note for example that Williams leaves aside preventive medicine. And if in a cool hour we examine the statistics, we find that a vast number of deaths occur each year due to causes not always beyond our control, e.g., automobile accidents, drugs, alcohol, tobacco, obesity, and so on. In some final reckoning it seems that many persons (though crucially, not all) have an effect on, and arguably a responsibility for, their own medical needs. Consider the following bidders for emergency care: (1) a person with a heart attack who is seriously overweight; (2) a football hero who has suffered a concussion; (3) a man with lung cancer who has smoked cigarettes for forty years; (4) a 60-year-old man who has always taken excellent care of himself and is suddenly stricken with leukemia; (5) a three-year-old girl who has swallowed poison left out carelessly by her parents; (6) a 14-year-old boy who has been beaten without provocation by a gang and suffers brain damage and recurrent attacks of uncontrollable terror; (7) a college student who has slashed his wrists (and not for the first time) from a psychological need for attention; (8) a woman raised in the ghetto who is found unconscious due to an overdose of heroin.

These cases help to show why the whole subject of medical treatment is so crucial and so perplexing. They attest to some melancholy elements in human experience. People suffer in varying ratios the effects of their natural and undeserved vulnerabilities, the irresponsibility and brutality of others, and their own desires and weaknesses. In some final reckoning then desert considerations seem not irrelevant to many health crises. The practical applicability of this admission, however, in the instance of health care delivery, appears limited. We may agree that it underscores the importance of preventive health care by stressing the influence we sometimes have over our medical needs. But if we try to foster such care by increasing the penalties for neglect, we normally confine ourselves to calculations about incentives. At the risk of being denounced in some quarters as censorious and puritanical, perhaps we should for example levy far higher taxes on alcohol and tobacco and pump the dollars directly into health care programs rather than (say) into highway building. Yet these steps would by no means lead necessarily to a demand that we correlate in some strict way a demonstrated effort to be temperate with the receipt of privileged medical treatment as a reward. Would it be feasible to allocate the additional tax monies to the man with leukemia before the overweight man suffering a heart attack on the ground of a difference in desert? At the point of emergency care at least, it seems impracticable for the doctor to discriminate between these cases, to make meritarian judgments at the point of catastrophe. And the number of persons who are in need of medical treatment for reasons utterly beyond their control remains a datum with tenacious relevance. There are those who suffer the ravages of a tornado, are handicapped by a genetic defect, beaten without provocation, etc. A commitment to the basic purpose of medical care and to the institutions for achieving it involves the recognition of this persistent state of affairs.

II

To each according to his social contribution. This conception gives moral primacy to notions such as the public interest, the common good, the welfare of the community, or the greatest good of the greatest number. Here one judges the social consequences of particular conduct. The formula can be construed in at least two ways.[12] It may refer to the interest of the social group considered collectively, where the group has some independent life all its own. The group's welfare is the decisive criterion for determining what constitutes any member's proper share. Or the common good may refer only to an aggregation of distinct individuals and considered distributively.

Either version accords such a primacy to what is socially advantageous as to be unacceptable not only to defenders of need, but also, it would seem, of desert. For the criteria of effort and achievement are often conceived along rather individualistic lines. The pains an agent takes or the results he brings about deserve recompense, whether or not the public interest is directly served. No automatic harmony then is necessarily assumed between his just share as individually earned and his proper share from the vantage point of the common good. Moreover, the test of social advantage *simpliciter* obviously threatens the agapeic concern with some minimal consideration due each person which is never to be disregarded for the sake of long-range social benefits. No one should be considered as *merely* a means or instrument.

The relevance of the canon of social productiveness to health crises may accordingly also be challenged. Indeed, such crises may cut against it in that they occur more frequently to those whose comparative contribution to the general welfare is less, e.g., the aged, the disabled, children.

Consider for example Paul Ramsey's persuasive critique of social and economic criteria for the allocation of a single scarce medical resource. He begins by recounting the imponderables which faced the widely-discussed "public committee" at the Swedish Hospital in Seattle when it deliberated in the early 1960's. The sparse resource in this case was the kidney machine. The committee was charged with the responsibility of selecting among patients suffering chronic renal failure those who were to receive dialysis. Its criteria were broadly social and economic. Considerations weighed included age, sex, marital status, number of dependents, income, net worth, educational background, occupation, past performance and future potential. The application of such criteria proved to be exceedingly problematic. Should someone with six children always have priority over an artist or composer? Were those who arranged matters so that their families would not burden society to be penalized in effect for being provident? And so on. Two critics of the committee found "a disturbing picture of the bourgeoisie sparing the bourgeoisie" and observed that "the Pacific Northwest is no place for a Henry David Thoreau with bad kidneys."[13]

The mistake, Ramsey believes, is to introduce criteria of social worthiness in the first place. In those situations of choice where not all can be saved and yet all need not die, "the equal right of every human being to live, and not relative personal or social worth, should be the ruling principle."[14] The principle leads to a criterion of "random choice among equals" expressed by a lottery scheme or a practice of "first-come, first-served." Several reasons stand behind Ramsey's defense of the criterion of random choice. First, a religious belief in the equality of persons before God leads intelligibly to a refusal to choose between those who are dying in any way other than random patient selection. Otherwise their equal value as human beings is threatened. Second, a moral primacy is ascribed to survival over other (perhaps superior) interests persons may have, in that it is the condition of everything else. ". . . Life is a value incommensurate with all others, and so not negotiable by bartering one man's worth against another's."[15]) Third, the entire enterprise of estimating a person's social worth is viewed with final skepticism. ". . . We have no way of knowing how really and truly to estimate a man's societal worth or his worth to others or to himself in unfocused social situations in the ordinary lives of men in their communities."[16] This statement, incidentally, appears to allow something other than randomness in *focused* social situations; when say, a President or Prime Minister and the owner of the local bar rush for the last place in the bomb shelter, and the knowledge of the former can save many lives. In any event, I have been concerned with a restricted point to which Ramsey's discussion brings illustrative support. The canon of social productiveness is notoriously difficult to apply as a workable criterion for distributing medical services to those who need them.

One may go further. A system of health care delivery which treats people on the basis of the medical care required may often go against (at least narrowly conceived) calculations of societal advantage. For example, the health care needs of people tend to rise during that period of their lives, signaled by retirement, when their incomes and social productivity are declining. More generally:

> Some 40 to 50 percent of the American people — the aged, children, the dependent poor, and those with some significant chronic disability are in categories requiring relatively large amounts of medical care but with inadequate resources to purchase such care.[17]

If one agrees, for whatever reasons, with the agapeic judgment that each person should be regarded as irreducibly valuable, then one cannot succumb to a social productiveness criterion of human worth. Interests are to be equally considered even when people have ceased to be, or are not yet, or perhaps never will be, public assets.

III

To each according to his contribution in satisfying whatever is freely desired by others in the open marketplace of supply and demand. Here we have a test which, though similar to the preceding one, concentrates on what is desired de facto by certain segments of the community rather than the community as a whole, and on the relative scarcity of the service rendered. It is tantamount to the canon of supply and demand as espoused by various laissez-faire theoreticians.[18] Rewards should be given to those who by virtue of special skill, prescience, risk-taking, and the like discern what is desired and are able to take the requisite steps to bring satisfaction. A surgeon, it may be argued, contributes more than a nurse because of the greater training and skill required, burdens borne, and effective care provided, and should be compensated accordingly. So too perhaps, a star quarterback on a pro-football team should be remunerated even more highly because of the rare athletic prowess needed, hazards involved, and widespread demand to watch him play.

This formula does not then call for the weighing of the value of various contributions, and tends to conflate needs and wants under a notion of desires. It also assumes that a prominent part is assigned to consumer free-choice. The consumer should be at liberty to express his preferences, and to select from a variety of competing goods and services. Those who resist many changes currently proposed in the organization and financing of health care delivery in the U.S.A. — such as national health insurance — often do so by appealing to some variant of this formula.

Yet it seems health crises are often of overriding importance when they occur. They appear therefore not satisfactorily accommodated to the context of a free marketplace where consumers may freely choose among alternative goods and services.

To clarify what is at stake in the above contention, let us examine an opposing case. Robert M. Sade, M.D., published an article in *The New England Journal of Medicine* entitled "Medical Care as a Right: A Refutation" (1971). He attacks programs of national health insurance in the name of a person's right to select one's own values, determine how they may be realized, and dispose of them if one chooses without coercion from other men. The values in question are construed as economic ones in the context of supply and demand. So we read:

> In a free society, man exercises his right to sustain his own life by producing economic values in the form of goods and services that he is, or should be, free to exchange with other men who are similarly free to trade with him or not. The economic values produced, however, are not given as gifts by nature, but exist only by virtue of the thought and effort of individual men. Goods and services are thus owned as a consequence of the right to sustain life by one's own physical and mental effort.[19]

Sade compares the situation of the physician to that of the baker. The one who produces a loaf of bread should as owner have the power to dispose of his own product. It is immoral simply to expropriate the bread without the baker's permission. Similarly, "medical care is neither a right nor a privilege: it is a service that is provided by doctors and others to people who wish to purchase it."[20] Any coercive regulation of professional practices by the society at large is held to be analogous to taking the bread from the baker without his consent. Such regulation violates the freedom of the physician over his own services and will lead inevitably to provider-apathy.

The analogy surely misleads. To assume that doctors autonomously produce goods and services in a fashion closely akin to a baker is grossly oversimplified. The baker may himself rely on the agricultural produce of others, yet there is a crucial difference in the degree of dependence. Modern physicians depend on the achievements of medical technology and the entire scientific base underlying it, all of which is made possible by a host of persons whose salaries are often notably less. Moreover, the amount of taxpayer support for medical research and education is too enormous to make any such unqualified case for provider-autonomy plausible.

However conceptually clouded Sade's article may be, its stress on a free exchange of goods and services reflects one historically influential rationale for much American medical practice. And he applies it not only to physicians but also to patients or "consumers."

> The question is whether the decision of how to allocate the consumer's dollar should belong to the consumer or to the state. It has already been shown that the choice of how a doctor's services should be rendered belongs only to the doctor: in the same way the choice of whether to buy a doctor's service rather than some other commodity or service belongs to the consumer as a logical consequence of the right to his own life.[21]

This account is misguided, I think, because it ignores the overriding importance which is so often attached to health crises. When lumps appear on someone's neck, it usually makes little sense to talk of choosing whether to buy a doctor's service rather than a color television set. References to just trade-offs suddenly seem out of place. No compensation suffices, since the penalties may differ so much.

There is even a further restriction on consumer choice. One's knowledge in these circumstances is comparatively so limited. The physician makes most of the decisions: about diagnosis, treatment, hospitalization, number of return visits, and so on. In brief:

> The consumer knows very little about the medical services he is buying — probably less than about any other service he purchases. . . . While [he] can still play a role in policing the market, that role is much more limited in the field of health care than in almost any other area of private economic activity.[22]

For much of the way, then, an appeal to supply and demand and consumer choice is not quite fitting. It neglects the issue of the value of various contributions. And it fails to allow for the recognition that medical treatments may be overridingly desired. In contexts of catastrophe at any rate, when life itself is threatened, most persons (other than those who are apathetic or seek to escape from the terrifying prospects) cannot take medical care to be merely one option among others.

IV

To each according to his needs. The concept of needs is sometimes taken to apply to an entire range of interests which concern a person's "psycho-physical existence."[23] On this wide usage, to attribute a need to someone is to say that the person lacks what is thought to conduce to his or her "welfare" — understood in both a physiological sense (e.g., for food, drink, shelter, and health) and a psychological one (e.g., for continuous human affection and support).

Yet even in the case of such a wide usage, what the person lacks is typically assumed to be basic. Attention is restricted to recurrent considerations rather than to every possible individual whim or frivolous pursuit. So one is not surprised to meet with the contention that a preferable rendering of this formula would be: "to each according to his essential needs."[24] This contention seems to me well taken. It implies, for one thing, that basic needs are distinguishable from felt needs or wants. For the latter may encompass expressions of personal preference unrelated to considerations of survival or subsistence, and sometimes artificially generated by circumstances of rising affluence in the society at large.

Essential needs are also typically assumed to be given rather than acquired. They are not constituted by any action for which the person is responsible by virtue of his or her distinctively greater effort. It is almost as if the designation "innocent" may be linked illuminatingly to need, as retribution, punishment, and so on, are to desert, and in complex ways, to freedom. Thus essential needs are likewise distinguishable from deserts. Where needs are unequal, one thinks of them as fortuitously distributed; as part, perhaps, of a kind of "natural lottery."[25] So very often the advantages of health and the burdens of illness, for example, strike one as arbitrary effects of the lottery. It seems wrong to say that a newborn child deserves as a reward all of his faculties when he has done nothing in particular which distinguishes him from another newborn who comes into the world deprived of one or more of them. Similarly, though crudely, many religious believers do not look on natural events as personal deserts. They are not inclined to pronounce sentences such as "That evil person with incurable cancer got what he deserved." They are disposed instead to search for some distinction between what they may call the conditions of finitude on the one hand and sin and moral evil on the other. If the distinction is "ultimately" invalid, in this life it seems inscrutably so. Here and now it may be usefully drawn. Inequalities in the need for medical treatment are taken, it appears, to reflect the conditions of finitude more than anything else.

One can even go on to argue that among our basic or essential needs, the case of medical treatment is conspicuous in the following sense. While food and shelter are not matters about which we are at liberty to please ourselves, they are at least predictable. We can plan, for instance, to store up food and fuel for the winter. It may be held that responsibility increases along with the power to predict. If so, then many health crises seem peculiarly random and uncontrollable. Cancer, given the present state of knowledge at any rate, is a contingent disaster, whereas hunger is a steady threat. Who will need serious medical care, and when, is then perhaps a classic example of uncertainty.

Finally, and more theoretically, it is often observed that a need-conception of justice comes closest to charity or *agape*.[26] I think there are indeed crucial overlaps.[27] To cite several of them: the equal consideration *agape* enjoins has to do in the first instance with those generic endowments which people share, the characteristics of a person qua human existent. Needs, as we have seen, likewise concern those things essential to the life and welfare of men considered simply as men.[28] They are not based on particular conduct alone, on those idiosyncratic attainments which contribute to someone's being such-and-such a kind of person. Yet a certain sort of inequality is recognized, for needs differ in divergent circumstances and so treatments must if benefits are to be equalized. *Agape* too allows for a distinction between equal consideration and identical treatment. The aim of equalizing benefits is implied by the injunction to consider the interests of each party equally. This may require differential treatments of differing interests.

Overlaps such as these will doubtless strike some as so extensive that it may be asked whether *agape* and a need-conception of justice are virtually equivalent. I think not. One contrast was pointed out before. The differential treatment enjoined by *agape* is more complex and goes deeper. In the case of *agape*, attention may be appropriately given to varying *efforts* as well as to unequal *needs.* More generally one may say that agapeic considerations extend to all of the psychological nuances and contextual details of individual persons and their circumstances. Imaginative concern is enjoined for concrete human beings: for what someone is uniquely, for what he or she — as a matter of personal history and distinctive identity — wants, feels, thinks, celebrates, and endures. The attempt to establish and enhance mutual affection between individual persons is taken likewise to be fitting. Conceptions of social justice, including "to each according to his essential needs," tend to be more restrictive; they call attention to considerations which obtain for a number of persons, to impersonally specified criteria for assessing collective policies and practices. *Agape* involves more, even if one supposes never less.

Other differences could be noted. What is important now however is the recognition that, in matters of health care in particular, *agape* and a need-conception of justice are conjoined in a number of relevant respects. At least this is so for those who think that, again, justice has properly to do with pleas of "But I could not help it." It seeks to distinguish such cases from those acknowledged to be praiseworthy or blameworthy. The formula "to each according to his needs" is one cogent way of identifying the moral relevance of these pleas. To ignore them may be thought to be unfair as well as unkind when they arise from the deprivation of some essential need. The move to confine the notion of justice wholly to desert considerations is thereby resisted as well. Hence we may say that sometimes "questions of social justice arise just because people are unequal in ways they can do very little to change and . . . only by attending to these inequalities can one be said to be giving their interests equal consideration."[29]

V

Similar treatment for similar cases. This conception is perhaps the most familiar of all. Certainly it is the most formal and inclusive one. It is frequently taken as an elementary appeal to consistency and linked to the universalizability test. One should not make an arbitrary exception on one's own behalf, but rather should apply impartially whatever standards one accepts. The conception can be fruitfully applied to health care questions and I shall assume its relevance. Yet as literally interpreted, it is necessary but not sufficient. For rightly or not, it is often held to be as compatible with no positive treatment whatever as with active promotion of other people's interests, as long as all are equally and impartially included. Its exponents sometimes assume such active promotion without demonstrating clearly how this is built into the conception itself. Moreover, it may obscure a distinction which we have seen agapists and others make: between equal consideration and identical treatment. Needs may differ and so treatments must, if benefits are to be equalized.

I have placed this conception at the end of the list partly because it moves us, despite its formality, toward practice. Let me suggest briefly how it does so. Suppose first of all one agrees with the case so far offered. Suppose, that is, it has been shown convincingly that a need-conception of justice applies with greater relevance than the earlier three when one reflects about the basic purpose of medical care. To treat one class of people differently from another because of income or geographic location should therefore be ruled out, because such reasons are irrelevant. (The irrelevance is conceptual, rather than always, unfortunately, causal.) In short, all persons should have equal access, "as needed, without financial, geographic, or other barriers, to the whole spectrum of health services."[30]

Suppose however, secondly, that the goal of equal access collides on some occasions with the realities of finite medical resources and needs which prove to be insatiable. That such collisions occur in fact it would be idle to deny. And it is here that the practical bearing of the formula of similar treatment for similar cases should be noticed. Let us recall Williams's conclusion: "the proper ground of distribution of medical care is ill health: this is a necessary truth." While I agree with the essentials of his argument — for all the reasons above — I would prefer, for practical purposes, a slightly more modest formulation. Illness is the proper ground for the *receipt* of medical care. However, the *distribution* of medical care in less-than-optimal circumstances requires us to face the collisions. I would argue that in such circumstances the formula of similar treatment for similar cases may be construed so as to guide actual choices in the way most compatible with the goal of equal access. The formula's allowance of no positive treatment whatever may justify exclusion of entire classes of cases from a priority list. Yet it forbids doing so for irrelevant or arbitrary reasons. So (1) if we accept the case for equal access, but (2) if we simply cannot, physically cannot, treat all who are in need, it seems more just to discriminate by virtue of categories of illness, for example, rather than between the rich ill and poor ill. All persons with a certain rare, non-communicable disease would not receive priority, let us say, where the costs were inordinate, the prospects for rehabilitation remote, and for the sake of equalized benefits to many more. Or with Ramsey we may urge a policy of random patient selection when one must decide between claimants for a medical treatment unavailable to all. Or we may acknowledge that any notion of "comprehensive benefits" to which persons should have equal access is subject to practical restrictions which will vary from society to society depending on resources at a given time. Even in a country as affluent as the United States there will surely always be items excluded, e.g., perhaps over-the-counter drugs, some teenage orthodontia, cosmetic surgery, and the like.[31] Here too the formula of similar treatment for similar cases may serve to modify the application of a need-conception of justice in order to address the insatiability-problem and limit frivolous use. In all of the foregoing instances of restriction, however, the relevant feature remains the illness, discomfort, etc. itself. The goal of equal access then retains its prima facie authoritativeness. It is imperfectly realized rather than disregarded.

VI

These latter comments lead on to the question of institutional implications. I cannot aim here of course for the specificity rightly sought by policy-makers. My endeavor has been conceptual elucidation. While the ethicist needs to be apprised about the facts, he or she does not, qua ethicist, don the mantle of the policy-expert. In any case, only rarely does anyone do both things equally well. Yet cross-fertilization is extremely desirable. For experts should not be isolated from the wider assumptions their recommendations may reflect. I shall merely list some of the topics which would have to be discussed at length if we were to get clear about the implications. Examples will be limited to the current situation in the United States.

Anyone who accepts the case for equal access will naturally be concerned about de facto disparities in the availability of medical treatment. Let us consider two relevant indictments of current American practice. They appear in the writings not only of those who attack indiscriminately a system seen to be governed only by the appetite for profit and power, but also of those who denounce in less sweeping terms and espouse more cautiously reformist positions. The first shortcoming has to do with the maldistribution of supply. Per capita ratios of physicians to populations served vary, sometimes notoriously, between affluent suburbs and rural and inner city areas. This problem is exacerbated by the distressing data concerning the greater health needs of the poor. Chronic disease, frequency and duration of hospitalization, psychiatric disorders, infant death rates, etc. — these occur in significantly larger proportions to lower income members of American society.[32] A further complication is that "the distribution of health insurance coverage is badly skewed. Practically all the rich have insurance. But among the poor, about two-thirds have none. As a result, among people aged 25 to 64 who die, some 45 to 50 per cent have neither hospital nor surgical coverage."[33] This last point connects with a second shortcoming frequently cited. Even those who are otherwise economically independent may be shattered by the high cost of a "catastrophic illness."[34]

Proposals for institutional reforms designed to overcome such disparities are bound to be taken seriously by any defender of equal access. What he or she will be disposed to press for, of course, is the removal of any double standard or "two class" system of care. The viable procedures for bringing this about are not obvious, and comparisons with certain other societies (for relevant alternative

Proposed answers

models) are drawn now with perhaps less confidence.[35] One set of commonly discussed proposals includes (1) incentive subsidies to physicians, hospitals, and medical centers to provide services in regions of poverty (to overcome in part the unwillingness — to which no unique culpability need be ascribed — of many providers and their spouses to work and live in grim surroundings); (2) licensure controls to avoid comparatively excessive concentrations of physicians in regions of affluence; (3) a period of time (say, two years) in an underserved area as a requirement for licensing; (4) redistribution facilities which allow for population shifts.

A second set of proposals is linked with health insurance itself. While I cannot venture into the intricacies of medical economics or comment on the various bills for national health insurance presently inundating Congress, it may be instructive to take brief note of one proposal in which, once more, the defender of equal access is bound to take an interest (even if he or she finally rejects it on certain practical grounds). The precise details of the proposal are unimportant for our purposes.[36] Consider this crude sketch. Each citizen is (in effect) issued a card by the government. Whenever "legitimate" medical expenses (however determined for a given society) exceed, say, 10 percent of his or her annual taxable income, the card may be presented so that additional costs incurred will be paid for out of general tax revenues. The reasons urged on behalf of this sort of arrangement include the following. In the case of medical care there is warrant for proportionately equalizing what is spent from anyone's total taxable income. This warrant reflects the conditions, discussed earlier, of the natural lottery. Insofar as the advantages of health and the burdens of illness are random and undeserved, we may find it in our common interest to share risks. A fixed percentage of income attests to the misfit, also mentioned previously, between the reasons for differential total income and the reasons for receiving medical treatment. If money remains a causally necessary condition for receiving medical treatment, then a way must be found to place it in the hands of those who need it. The card is one such means. It is designed effectively to equalize purchasing power. In this way it seems to accord nicely with the goal of equal access. On the other side, the requirement of initial out-of-pocket expenses — sufficiently large in comparison to average family expenditures on health care — is designed to discourage frivolous use and foster awareness that medical care is a benefit not to be simply taken as a matter of course. It also safeguards against an excessively large tax burden while providing universal protection against the often disastrous costs of serious illnesses. Whether 10 percent is too great a chunk for the very poor to pay, and whether by itself the proposal will feed price inflation and neglect of preventive medicine are questions which would have to be answered.

Another kind of possible institutional reform will also greatly interest the defender of equal access. This has to do with the "design of health care systems" or "care settings." The prevalent setting in American society has always been "fee-for-service." It is left up to each person to obtain the requisite care and to pay for it as he or she goes along. Because costs for medical treatment have accelerated at such an alarming rate, and because the sheer diffusion of energy and effort so characteristic of American medical practice leaves more and more people dissatisfied, alternatives for fee-for-service have been considered of late with unprecedented seriousness. The alternative care setting most widely discussed is prepaid practice, and specifically the "health maintenance organization" (HMO). Here one finds "an organized system of care which accepts the responsibility to provide or otherwise assure comprehensive care to a defined population for a fixed periodic payment per person or per family. . . ."[37] The best-known HMO is the Kaiser-Permanente Medical Care Program.[38] Does the HMO serve to realize the goal of equal access more fully? One line of argument in its favor is this. It is plausible to think that equal access will be fostered by the more economical care setting. HMO's are held to be less costly per capita in at least two respects: hospitalization rates are much below the national average; and less often noted, physician manpower is as well. To be sure, one should be sensitive to the corruptions in each type of setting. While fee-for-service has resulted in a suspiciously high number of surgeries (twice as many per capita in the United States as in Great Britain), the HMO physician may more frequently permit the patient's needs to be overridden by the organization's pressure to economize. It may also be more difficult in an HMO setting to provide for close personal relations between a particular physician and a particular patient (something commended, of course, on all sides). After such corruptions are allowed for, the data seem encouraging to such an extent that a defender of equal access will certainly support the repeal of any law which limits the development of prepaid practice, to approve of "front-aid" subsidies for HMO's to increase their number overall and achieve a more equitable distribution throughout the country, and so on. At a minimum, each care setting should be available in every region. If we assume a common freedom to choose between them, each may help to guard against the peculiar temptations to which the other is exposed.

To assess in any serious way proposals for institutional reform such as the above is beyond the scope of this paper. We would eventually be led, for example, into the question of whether it is consistent for the rich to pay more than the poor for the same treatment when, again, needs rather than income constitute the ground of the treatment,[39] and from there into the tangled subject of the "ethics of redistribution" in general.[40] Other complex issues deserve to be considered as well, e.g., the criteria for allocation of limited resources,[41] and how conceptions of justice apply to the providers of health care.[42]

Those committed to self-conscious moral and religious reflection about subjects in medicine have concentrated, perhaps unduly, on issues about care of individual patients (as death approaches, for instance). These issues plainly warrant the most careful consideration. One would like to see in addition, however, more attention paid to social questions in medical ethics. To attend to them is not necessarily to leave behind all of the matters which reach deeply into the human condition. Any detailed case for institutional reforms, for example, will be enriched if the proponent asks soberly whether certain conflicts and certain perplexities allow for more than partial improvements and provisional resolutions. Can public and private interests ever be made fully to coincide by legislative and administrative means? Will the commitment of a physician to an individual patient and the commitment of the legislator to the "common good" ever be harmonized in every case? Our anxiety may be too intractable. Our fear of illness and of dying may be so pronounced and immediate that we will seize the nearly automatic connections between privilege, wealth, and power if we can. We will do everything possible to have our kidney machines even if the charts make it clear that many more would benefit from mandatory immunization at a fraction of the cost. And our capacity for taking in rival points of view may be too limited. Once we have witnessed tangible suffering, we cannot just return with ease to public policies aimed at statistical patients. Those who believe that justice is the preeminent virtue of institutions and that a case can be convincingly made on behalf of justice for equal access to health care would do well to ponder such conflicts and perplexities. Our reforms might then seem, to ourselves and to others, less abstract and jargon-filled in formulation and less sanguine and piecemeal in substance. They would reflect a greater awareness of what we have to confront.

Notes

1. See, e.g., Richard M. Nixon, "President's Message on Health Care System," Document no. 92-261 (March 2, 1972), House of Representatives, Washington, D.C.: and Edward M. Kennedy, *In Critical Condition: The Crisis in America's Health Care* (New York: Simon and Schuster, 1972).

2. These writings include Hugo A. Bedau, "Radical Egalitarianism," in *Justice and Equality*, ed. Hugo A. Bedau (Englewood Cliffs, N.J.: Prentice-Hall, 1971); John Hospers, *Human Conduct* (New York: Harcourt, Brace and World, 1961); J. R. Lucas, "Justice," *Philosophy* 47 (July 1972): 229-48; C. Perelman, *The Idea of Justice and the Problem of Argument*, trans. J. Petrie (London: Routledge and Kegan Paul, 1963); Nicholas Rescher, *Distributive Justice* (Indianapolis: Bobbs-Merrill, 1966); John A. Ryan, *Distributive Justice* (New York: Macmillan, 1916); and Gregory Vlastos, "Justice and Equality," in *Social Justice*, ed. Richard B. Brandt (Englewood Cliffs, N.J.: Prentice-Hall, 1962).

3. Paul Ramsey, *The Patient as Person* (New Haven: Yale University Press, 1970), p. 240.

4. Nancy Hicks, "Nation's Doctors Move to Police Medical Care," *New York Times*, 28 October 1973, p. 52.

5. See Gene Outka, *Agape: An Ethical Analysis* (New Haven: Yale University Press, 1972).

6. Ayn Rand, *Atlas Shrugged* (New York: Signet, 1957), p. 958.

7. Outka, *Agape,* pp. 89-90, 165-67.

8. Lucas, "Justice," p. 321.

9. Bernard A. O. Williams, "The Idea of Equality," in *Justice and Equality,* ed. Bedau, pp. 126-37.

10. Williams, "The Idea of Equality," p. 127.

11. See also Thomas Nagel, "Equal Treatment and Compensatory Discrimination," *Philosophy and Public Affairs* 2 (Summer 1973): 354.

12. Rescher, *Distributive Justice,* pp. 79-80.

13. Quoted in Ramsey, *Patient as Person,* p. 248.

14. Ibid., p. 256.

15. Ibid.

16. Ibid.

17. Anne R. Somers, *Health Care in Transition: Directions for the Future* (Chicago: Hospital Research and Educational Trust, 1971), p. 20.

18. See Rescher, *Distributive Justice,* pp. 80-81.

19. Robert M. Sade, "Medical Care as a Right: A Refutation," *New England Journal of Medicine* 285 (December 1971): 1289.

20. Ibid.

21. Ibid., p. 1291.

22. Charles L. Schultze et al., *Setting National Priorities: The 1973 Budget* (Washington, D.C.: The Brookings Institution, 1972), pp. 214-15.

23. Outka, *Agape,* pp. 264-65.

24. Perelman, *The Idea of Justice,* p. 22.

25. See John Rawls, *A Theory of Justice* (Cambridge, Mass.: Harvard University Press, 1971), p. 104.

26. See, e.g., Perelman, *The Idea of Justice,* p. 23.

27. See Outka, *Agape,* pp. 91-92, 309-12.

28. See also A. M. Honoré, "Social Justice," in *Essays in Legal Philosophy,* ed. Robert S. Summers (Oxford: Basil Blackwell, 1968).

29. Stanley I. Benn, "Egalitarianism and the Equal Consideration of Interests," in *Justice and Equality,* ed. Bedau, 1964.

30. Anne R. Somers and Herman M. Somers, "The Organization and Financing of Health Care: Issues and Directions for the Future," *American Journal of Orthopsychiatry* 42 (January 1972): 122.

31. Anne R. Somers and Herman M. Somers, "Major Issues in National Health Insurance," *Milbank Memorial Fund Quarterly* 50 (April 1972): 182.

32. James Z. Appel, "Health Care Delivery," in *The Health of Americans,* ed. Boisfeuillet Jones (Englewood Cliffs, N.J.: Prentice-Hall, 1970); and William N. Hubbard, "Health Knowledge," in *The Health of Americans,* ed. Jones.

33. Somers, *Health Care in Transition,* p. 46.

34. See some eloquent examples in Kennedy, *In Critical Condition.*

35. See Odin Anderson, *Health Care: Can There Be Equity? The United States, Sweden and England* (New York: Wiley, 1973).

36. For one much-discussed version, see Martin S. Feldstein, "A New Approach to National Health Insurance," *The Public Interest* 23 (Spring 1971).

37. Anne R. Somers, ed., *The Kaiser-Permanente Medical Care Program* (New York: The Commonwealth Fund, 1971), p. v.

38. See also Sidney R. Garfield, "Prevention of Dissipation of Health Services Resources," *American Journal of Public Health* 61 (1971).

39. Andrew Ward, "The Idea of Equality Reconsidered," *Philosophy* 48 (January 1973).

40. See, e.g., Stanley I. Benn and Richard S. Peters, *The Principles of Political Thought* (New York: The Free Press, 1965), pp. 155-78; and Bertrand de Jouvenel, *The Ethics of Redistribution* (Cambridge: Cambridge University Press, 1952).

41. The issue of priorities is at least threefold: (1) between improved medical care and other social needs, e.g., to restrain auto accidents and pollution; (2) between different sorts of medical treatments for different illnesses, e.g., prevention vs. crisis intervention and exotic treatments; (3) between persons all of whom need a single scarce resource and not all can have it, e.g., Ramsey's discussion of how to decide among those who are to receive dialysis. Moreover, (1) can be subdivided between (a) improved medical care and other social needs which affect health directly, e.g., drug addiction, auto accidents, and pollution; (b) improved medical care and other social needs which serve the overall aim of community-survival, e.g., a common defense. In the case of (2), one would like to see far more careful discussion of some general criteria which might be employed, e.g., numbers affected, degree of contagion, prospects for rehabilitation, and so on.

42. What sorts of appeals to justice might be cogently made to warrant, for instance, the differentially high income physicians receive? Here are three possibilities: (1) the greater skill and responsibility involved should be rewarded proportionately, i.e., one should attend to considerations of *desert;* (2) there should be *compensation* for the money invested for education and facilities

in order to restore circumstances of approximate equality (this argument, while a common one in medical circles, would need to consider that medical education is received in part at public expense and that the modern physician is the highest paid professional in the country); (3) the difference should benefit the least advantaged more than an alternative arrangement where disparities are less. We prefer a society where the medical profession flourishes and everyone has a longer life expectancy to one where everyone is poverty-stricken with a shorter life expectancy ("splendidly equalized destitution"). Yet how are we to ascertain the minimum degree of differential income required for the least advantaged members of the society to be better off?

Discussions of "justice and the interests of providers" are, I think, badly needed. Physicians in the United States have suffered a decline in prestige for various reasons, e.g., the way many used Medicare to support and increase their own incomes. Yet one should endeavor to assess their interests fairly. A concern for professional autonomy is clearly important, though one may ask whether adequate attention has been paid to the distinction between the imposition of cost-controls from outside and interference with professional medical judgments. One may affirm the former, it seems, and still reject — energetically — the latter.

124 Reform and Rationing: Reflections on Health Care in Light of Catholic Social Teaching[1]

B. Andrew Lustig

Introduction

In this essay, I analyze two issues at the forefront of recent policy discussion — health care reform and health care rationing — in light of Roman Catholic social teaching. It is important, as I begin, to identify and critique a position often deemed to be the conventional wisdom on the place of religion in policy debates. Many would assert that the claims of particular religious communities are irrelevant or unnecessary to the formulation and justification of public policy in a secular and pluralistic society. However, their easy dismissal of religious voices can be questioned on two grounds. First, they assume, with little or no argument, that the claims of religious communities cannot be justified in more general terms. If such common ground were indeed absent, it would seemingly follow that religious communities could not fully participate in policy formation because of constitutional concerns regarding the separation of church and state. However, this first assumption is demonstrably false. The facts of

From Earl E. Shelp, *Secular Bioethics in Theological Perspective* (Dordrecht: Kluwer Academic Publishers, 1996), pp. 31-50. Used with kind permission from Kluwer Academic Publishers.

overlapping consensus, despite the varied theological, philosophical, and political viewpoints of those who achieve practical agreement, play a pivotal role in legislative pronouncements and judicial reasoning. Shared moral and legal conclusions on particular issues and common policy conclusions on appropriate societal remedies are possible despite the lack of agreement about the first principles at work in particular perspectives, whether religiously informed or not. Second, the tendency to disqualify the claims of religious communities from debates on public policy confuses the *process* of public discussion and debate, where the views of particular communities may exercise legitimate influence, with the *warrants* for and *justification* of policy choices, where parochial appeals are inappropriate.

The present essay is offered as an exercise meant to illustrate, through the lens of debates on health care reform and rationing, how Roman Catholicism has engaged the problematic of particularism in public debate and discussion. The essay falls naturally into three parts. After this brief introduction, I consider, in Part I, the theological warrants in modern Catholic social teaching on the nature and scope of health care as a positive right. In Part II, I consider the legitimacy of health care rationing in light of Catholic social principles that constrain health care as an individual entitlement according to the requirements of the common good. In Part III, I assess the relevance of Catholic arguments on health care reform and rationing to the broader secular debate on those issues. I conclude by suggesting that the Roman Catholic approach, while sharing affinities with consensus principles that can be developed on other grounds, also brings a distinctive perspective to issues of health care policy.

I. Health Care in Catholic Social Teaching

In Catholic social teaching since Vatican II, access to health care is seen as a positive right, i.e., a justified entitlement claimable by individuals against society. The warrants for that position are expressly theological, involving a number of themes and principles that, while interconnected, can be analyzed separately. The first is an appeal to the dignity of the individual made in the image of God. The second is an understanding of the common good, which in contrast to secular liberal understandings, presents an organic vision of society with duties incumbent on institutions according to the purposes of society as established by God. The third theme, which is developed in the modern encyclical literature as an extension of the traditional emphasis upon the common good, is the regulative ideal of social justice. Social justice is a specific notion that enjoins institutions and, increasingly, governments to guarantee the basic material concomitants of individual dignity. The fourth theme involves an appeal to the principle of subsidiarity, first enunciated by Pius XI, which speaks to the intrinsic and instrumental value of meeting the basic needs of persons at the lowest or least centralized level of association and authority possible. Finally, certain Catholic writers have emphasized distributive justice as a decisive appeal that functions, in important respects, independently of the general institutional focus expressed in the language of social justice. Each of these themes or principles merits careful attention.

In Catholic social teaching, every individual has dignity because he or she is made in the image and likeness of God (Genesis 1:26) and has been redeemed by Christ (Ephesians 1:10). By the time of John XXIII, the material conditions required by individual dignity have been enumerated into a list of specific individual rights, including the right to health care, which must be safeguarded by responsible institutions. John says in *Pacem in Terris*:

> . . . we see that every man has the right to life, to bodily integrity, and to the means which are necessary and suitable for the proper development of life. These means are primarily food, clothing, shelter, rest, *medical care*, and finally the necessary social services [emphasis mine]. Therefore, a human being also has the right to security in cases of sickness, inability to work, widowhood, old age, unemployment, or in any other case in which he is deprived of the means of subsistence through no fault of his own ([5], p. 167).

In John's successor, Paul VI, one finds a renewed emphasis on a theme central to the writings of Pius XI, namely, that "material well-being is not simply instrumental in value. It is not a means of a dignified life. It is, rather, *integral* to the standard of all moral value, human dignity" ([8], p. 79).

Throughout this discussion, one is struck by the general nature of papal pronouncements about what individual dignity requires. That level of generality is not surprising. The encyclicals are statements of theological and moral vision rather than policy recommendations. They provide more than a mere statement of ideals but less than a blueprint for specific choice and action. Nonetheless, the expressly theological basis of human dignity provides, albeit in quite general terms, a different and richer context for understanding the usual arguments about liberty and equality in secular debates about the right to medical care. In Catholic social teaching, although individuals are endowed with freedom, theirs is a freedom to be exercised in community. The latter emphasis is surely to be expected, given the trinitarian nature of the God whom Christians worship and in whose image they are made. That trinitarian understanding has specific moral implications. In the words of one commentator:

> . . . our trinitarian theology becomes a radical challenge to community. How can Christians say they believe in God if they are unwilling to put together structures that build human community and meet fundamental human needs? How can someone really claim to believe in the triune God and not feel a sense of outrage about the quarter of the U.S. population which lacks or is inadequately supplied with such a basic good as health care coverage? If we believe in the triune God as the very ground of community, the problem of our health care system is not just an ethical or economic or political problem. The problem is ultimately a religious or theological problem ([10], p. 105).

In light of the belief in God as Trinity, and in contrast to the polarities one often finds in secular debates about positive rights, Catholic social teaching elevates neither liberty nor equality to a position of unchallenged priority. Rather than seeing either value as trumping the other, Catholic teaching, especially since the time of John XXIII, presents liberty and equality as mutually accommodating principles.

The notion of the common good is a second characteristic emphasis in recent Catholic social teaching. Again, this appeal, much like the theological grounding for arguments about individual dignity, offers an alternative to those secular versions of political theory that emphasize liberty as either a side-constraint or as a primary positive value. Unlike approaches that begin (and often end) with an emphasis upon individualism, the common good is fundamentally social and institutional in its focus. It stresses human dependence and interdependence. However, the common good should not be interpreted as a Roman Catholic analogue to a utilitarian calculus. Rather, the common good is the "set of social conditions which facilitate the realization of personal goods by individuals" ([8], p. 64). The common good

> insists on the conditions and institutions . . . necessary for human cooperation and the achievement of shared objectives as decisive normative elements in the social situation, elements which individualism is both unable to account for in theory and likely to neglect in practice ([11], p. 102).

The common good need not be viewed as being in necessary tension with the rights of individuals, at least in encyclicals since the time of John XXIII. Rather, the common good functions in two important senses: first, it is invoked to temper and correct the inequities often associated with secular individualism; and second, it incorporates guarantees for personal rights and duties ([12], pp. 429-36). Still, in contrast to individualistic theories, a fundamentally social understanding infuses Catholic social thought. This social perspective is especially evident in Catholic teaching on the nature and scope of property, with implications for a number of positive rights, including the entitlement to health care. Theologically, men and women are imagers of a trinitarian God. Practically, this suggests that the claims of individuals to resources are limited by the claims of others for the satisfaction of basic needs. In hard cases, where choice is inevitable, John Paul II characterizes the conclusions of the tradition as follows:

> Christian tradition has never upheld [private property] as absolute or untouchable. On the contrary, it has always understood this right within

> the broader context of the right common to all to use the goods of the whole of creation: the right to private property is subordinated to the right to common use, to the fact that goods are meant for everyone ([9], # 43).

In this emphasis on property in common as a regulative notion, the common good emerges as fundamental. Individual rights and duties are seen as constitutive of the common good, but there are no absolute or unmediated claims to private ownership of property. Unlike perspectives that begin with the distinction between private and public resources as the unassailable datum from which moral analysis proceeds, the Catholic tradition does not deem individual ownership to be sacrosanct. Rather, common access according to use remains the relevant criterion according to which social arrangements and practices must be assessed, especially in the circumstances of a developed economy.

As a third theme, the Catholic tradition has emphasized, since its enunciation by Pius XI in *Quadragesimo Anno,* the so-called principle of subsidiarity. In one respect, this principle can be seen as following logically from the idea of the common good ([I], p. 132). Drew Christiansen describes subsidiarity as "another dimension" of the common good; subsidiarity, then, involves "the notion that responsibility is rightly exercised at the smallest appropriate level" ([3], pp. 46-47). Thus, problems that can be addressed by the small-scale initiatives of individuals or voluntary associations should be handled at those levels. Matters that can be solved by lower levels of governmental involvement (city rather than state, state rather than federal) should also be addressed at the lowest level possible to achieve effective results. As a functional corollary of the common good, such a prudential concern with efficiency is quite appropriate. Subsidiarity implies that "the first responsibility in meeting human needs rests with the free and competent individual, then with the local group" ([I], p. 132). Moreover, there is essential, not only instrumental, value in the moral involvement of individuals in the interpersonal forms of association that subsidiarity commends as a functional aspect of the common good. The common good, as I noted, involves the good of persons. Subsidiarity, as an expression of the common good, involves the intrinsic value of direct and immediate forms of the individual's responsibility to others.

However, since the papacy of John XXIII, there has been an increasing emphasis in the Church's social teaching on the necessity of governmental involvement in meeting the basic needs of persons. The principle of subsidiarity, then, bears two implications for health care reform proposals. As Keane observes:

> . . . Catholic social teaching on subsidiarity . . . can tell us two important things. First, we really do need to find a health care system which offers us some balance between private management and public management. . . . Second, in view of the increasingly complex character of health care delivery, it is only to be expected (and clearly "catholic") that more and more government management of health care will in fact be necessary. Thus we ought not to be afraid on religious/moral grounds of the fact that many of the major health care reform proposals which are being discussed in the United States today are calling for a significantly increased level of government involvement, at least in the financing of health care. In the end, Catholic social teaching may well help us to decide which of the current reform proposals seem best, by challenging us to consider carefully which proposal best mixes subsidiarity and socialization in our current health care context ([10], pp. 149-50).

To be sure, given the complex features of modern social and economic life, the links between property in common and the common good cannot be understood literally. Thus, since the time of Pius XI, the common good is usually linked with another idea characteristic of recent social teaching, viz. social justice. Pius XI invokes the notion of social justice as a "conceptual tool by which moral reasoning takes into account the fact that relationships between persons have an institutional or structural dimension" ([8], p. 54). In contrast to atomistic understandings of individual rights, Pius emphasizes social justice as a regulative institutional principle. As societies develop, as medicine progresses, institutions, especially at the governmental level, are morally required to mediate the claims of human dignity and to shape the content of human rights, including the right to medical care.

Another emphasis in recent Catholic social teaching has been the so-called "preferential option for the poor." Although this option is sometimes invoked as a separate appeal, it can be viewed as a practical implication of the three broader themes discussed above: the positive rights of individuals, the common good, and social justice. In service to these values, institutions are required to respond to those inequities between and among individuals that particularly threaten the dignity of the most disadvantaged in society. Whether one views the preferential option for the poor as an implication of more fundamental values, or as having independent standing, the practical results at the level of social policy, about health care and other social goods, are likely to be the same.

Finally, some recent perspectives have emphasized the need to invoke distributive justice as an appeal that functions somewhat independently of the more general focus of social justice. Philip Keane is representative of this trend, especially in relation to arguments about health care reform. Although Keane is sympathetic to the broad critique of health care institutions afforded by the language of social justice, he is skeptical about the precision it affords regarding the practical questions associated with health care reform and rationing. Thus he says:

> . . . reform of the structures of society so that society can more effectively deliver health care still depends on society's having a clearer focus on just what health care goods it ought to be delivering to people. Thus, while the social structures question, like the equality question, is a pivotal aspect of all justice including health care justice, my judgment is that the distribution question (i.e., What health care benefits must we provide?) is the most central of all the justice questions which relate to health care ([10], p. 138).

Keane continues in a cautious vein:

> If we focus too much on social justice, the risk is that we will emphasize the structures necessary to furnish health care instead of first focusing on the human need of real persons to have real health care crises adequately addressed. Such emphasis on structures without a prior commitment to genuine human needs can raise all the fears of complex bureaucracies without really substantial goals ([10], p. 139).

For these reasons, Keane believes that the principle of distributive justice should assume moral priority in debates about reform and rationing. In developing this claim, he appeals to the work of Protestant theologian Gene Outka on the requirements of distributive justice in health care [13]. Outka views health care needs as discontinuous from other basic needs. According to Outka, medical needs are randomly distributed, to significant degree "unmerited," often catastrophic, and to a great extent unpredictable. Outka therefore sees critical health care emergencies as having an immediacy and urgency that distinguishes them from other sorts of deprivation. Given that distinctiveness, Outka concludes that "similar treatment for similar cases," based on a criterion of medical need, is the fairest canon of distributive justice among various alternatives that have been proposed for health care delivery. Keane characterizes Outka's conclusions in this way:

> . . . with careful reflection and dialogue, we should determine those health care needs which we as a society must meet as a minimum standard, and then provide those needs for everyone, regardless of merit, usefulness, economic ability, etc. Such an approach means that there will be some possible health services which will not be provided because they are not truly needs or because they are beyond our capacity as a society of mortals who must face the fact of death ([10], p. 142).

II. Two Recent Catholic Documents on Health Care

I now turn my attention to two recent Catholic documents that focus specifically on health care, one the U.S. Bishops' "Resolution on Health Care Reform," the other a moral analysis of health care rationing by the Catholic Hospital Association entitled *With Justice for All?* I have several reasons for analyzing these documents in some detail: first, to discuss the warrants at work in their arguments; second, to scrutinize and critique several conceptual and practical tensions in their respective recommendations for public policy; and finally, to use the documents as points of reference for Part III's brief overview of the relevance of theologically based arguments to secular policy debates.

A. The U.S. Bishops' Resolution on Health Care Reform

The recent "Resolution on Health Care Reform" by the U.S. Roman Catholic bishops provides the occasion for a closer look at the way that basic principles of Catholic social teaching on the right to health care have been brought to bear on general issues of health care reform. In its introduction, the resolution identifies the fundamental problems that beset present health-care delivery: excessive costs, lack of access for many Americans, and questions about the quality of the care provided. The bishops address the document to the "Catholic community" *and* to "the leaders of our nation" ([15], p. 98). The document, although at times expressly theological, also attempts to speak to the broader public, primarily through its appeals to human dignity, which can be justified for both theological and non-theological reasons, and by its expressions of concern about the plight of those presently underserved by the U.S. health care system.

The resolution appeals to the recent tradition by rooting its approach to health care in the three fundamental themes I discussed in Part I. First, "[e]very person has a right to adequate health care. This right flows from the sanctity of human life and the dignity that belongs to all human persons, who are made in the image of God." Health care is a "basic human right, an essential safeguard of human life and dignity." Moreover, the bishops' call for reform is rooted in "the priorities of social justice and the principle of the common good." In light of these fundamental values, the bishops judge that "existing patterns of health care in the United States do not meet the minimal standard of social justice and the common good." Indeed, "the current health care system is so inequitable, and the disparities between rich and poor and those with access and those without are so great, that it is clearly unjust" ([15], p. 99).

The bishops also appeal to a preferential option for the poor as a particular implication of the common good. Pointing out that the "burdens of the system are not shared equally," the bishops conclude that we must "measure our health system in terms of how it affects the weak and disadvantaged." Fundamental reform must be especially concerned with "the impact of national health policies on the poor and the vulnerable." In this context, the bishops quote with approval a recent ecumenical statement on the common good; to wit:

> More than anything else, the call to the common good is a reminder that we are one human family, whatever our differences of race, gender, ethnicity, or economic status. In our vision of the common good, a crucial moral test is how the weakest are faring. We give special priority to the poor and vulnerable since those with the greatest needs and burdens have first claim on our common efforts. In protecting the lives and promoting the dignity of the poor and vulnerable, we strengthen all of society ([15], p. 98).

As a final appeal in Section I of the Resolution, the bishops invoke the prudential notion of "stewardship." The cost of present health care in the United States "strains the private economy and leaves too few resources for housing, education, and other economic and social needs." In response, "[s]tewardship demands that we address the duplication, waste and other factors that make our system so expensive" ([15], p. 99).

The practical focus of Section II of the bishops' resolution raises the same cluster of thematic concerns in more focused fashion. In this section, the bishops set forth eight practical criteria by which to judge the moral adequacy of proposals for reform. The criteria are as follows: (1) respect for life, (2) priority concern for the poor, (3) universal access, (4) comprehensive benefits, (5) pluralism, (6) quality, (7) cost containment and controls, and (8) equitable financing. Given the brevity of the resolution, these criteria are not adequately developed, but as a whole, they emerge as practical expressions of the fundamental theological values that inform the Catholic tradition on health care. At the same time, because the bishops clearly intend these criteria as useful guides for assessing public policy, it is important to note certain conceptual and practical tensions between and among the various criteria. For purposes of the present discussion, I will focus on the first four.

Overall, the criteria are based on considerations of human dignity that are theologically based: thus, "reform of the health care system which is truly fundamental and enduring must be rooted in values which reflect the essential dignity of each person, ensure that basic human rights are protected, and recognize the unique needs and claims of the poor" ([15], p. 100).

The first principle, respect for life, speaks to the need for any reform proposal to "preserve and enhance the sanctity and dignity of human life from conception to natural death" ([15], p. 100). Nonetheless, "sanctity of life" does not, of itself, shed light upon *how* to proceed in cases when "hard choices" involving allocation of resources must be made between and among individuals, all of whom might at least marginally benefit from continued provision of care. Moreover, the relevance of this first principle to certain "hard cases" (including abortion and the status of persistently vegetative patients) is unclear, since the grounding of "personhood" claims in these instances may depend on theological understandings of "ensoulment" or capacities to "image" God that are not available as warrants for secular policy.

The second principle — priority concern for the poor — implies, according to the resolution, that any reform proposal should be judged as to "whether it gives special priority to meeting the most pressing health care needs of the poor and underserved, ensuring that they receive quality health services" ([15], p. 100). Here the difference between according the "preferential option for the poor" independent weight or interpreting it as a particular implication of the common good may significantly affect how one assesses a particular reform proposal. While it is doubtless true that working correlations between overall indices of poverty and poorer health can be drawn, it is not the case that for any particular indigent individual, health outcomes will necessarily be correlated with access to health care. Indeed, there are strong arguments, doubtless of a more prophetic sort, that reform of health care as a discrete sector may be one of the least effective ways of improving the *general* health outcomes of the poor as a class. Overall poverty, not simply limited access to medical care, may be a far more relevant determinant of health than the bishops' second criterion suggests.

With regard to medical care, then, the preferential option for the poor will require greater attention to a definition of the "poor" for whom preference is to be shown — those who are "generally poor," according to most indices, or those who are "medically indigent." To the extent that the unclarity persists, the relevance of the criterion for any particular patient, as compared with its relevance as a working generalization about classes of persons, will not be obvious. Indeed, for any particular patient, the first criterion, "respect for life," might suggest that general indices of poverty, in contrast to criteria relating specifically to medical need or medical indigence, may discriminate unfairly against a needy patient who would not (at least initially) qualify according to the former indices.

By contrast, if the "preferential option for the poor" does not have independent weight but instead is seen as a particular application or implication of the common good, then determinations of medical indigence or medical need might proceed apace with difficult judgments about basic social goods other than medical care. On this account of the preferential option, the common good might be invoked as a systematic consideration to limit the availability of resources for particular individuals as the result of prior social choices, independent of individual circumstances of need. In this scenario, one might then be able to distinguish circumstances that are admittedly unfortunate from those that are unfair ([4], pp. 342ff.).

According to the bishops' third criterion, any morally acceptable proposal must provide "universal access to comprehensive health care for every person living in the United States." A number of practical questions arise here. How shall the system be reformed in order to provide genuinely universal access to comprehensive benefits? What implications might this principle have for conscripted medical service to presently underserved areas, especially in rural America? Alternatively, if one relies on market mechanisms and incentives to expand access and availability, how will such competitive economics work to ensure entitlement on a universal basis? In addition, should citizenship be morally decisive in determining access to available services? The wording of this criterion would suggest that health care coverage be limited to those within the United States but also that all persons within U.S. borders (not only citizens) be provided care. Practically, this may pose significant difficulties, since the costs of such care, indiscriminately provided, may undercut the willingness and/or ability of taxpayers to fund a basic level of health care for all.

The fourth criterion offers a benchmark of "comprehensive benefits" for any morally acceptable reform proposal. Comprehensive benefits include those "sufficient to maintain and promote good health, to provide preventive care, to treat disease, injury, and disability appropriately and to care for persons who are chronically ill or dying" ([15], p. 100). Again, the choices and tradeoffs required among these various goods might well conflict with the focus on particular individuals seemingly implied in such principles as "respect for life" or "universal access." Health care "sufficient to maintain and promote good health" for a given individual may be, in effect, a black hole, since that person's needs, according to the fourth criterion, might swallow an inordinate amount of resources to which others with lesser needs might otherwise have access. Moreover, as noted above, medical services may be fairly low among overall indices for health. Thus criteria for "health care" reform, if invoked without sufficient attention to the multifactorial nature of good health as an outcome, may be coopted by tendencies already present in technology-driven medicine to misallocate funds that could be better spent on primary or preventive care. Finally, only "caring for" those who are chronically ill or dying might involve a number of rationing choices that, while supported on grounds of the common good or social justice, fail to comport with the individual focus of other criteria.

As noted above, Section II of the resolution sets forth a number of other practical criteria for assessing reform proposals, which, while interesting, emerge as fairly "commonsensical" in tone. By contrast, Section III lists four "essential priorities" that the bishops urge upon their readers in applying their eight criteria of assessment: (1) priority concern for the poor and universal access; (2) respect for human life and human dignity; (3) pursuing the common good and preserving pluralism; and (4) restraining costs ([15], pp. 100-101). Although each of these priorities merits scrutiny in its own right, I will focus on key tensions generated by the bishops' discussion of the first and third priorities.

In their discussion of the first priority — concern for the poor and universal access — the bishops voice strong support for "measures to ensure true universal access and rapid steps to improve the health care of the poor and underserved" ([15], p. 100). In light of that commitment, they "do not support a two-tiered health system since separate health care coverage for the poor usually results in poor health care. Linking the health care of poor and working class families to the health care of those with greater resources is probably the best assurance of comprehensive benefits and quality care" ([15], pp. 100-101). Nonetheless, in discussing their third priority — preserving pluralism — the bishops emphasize the following:

> We believe the debate can be advanced by a continuing focus on the common good and a healthy respect for genuine pluralism. A reformed system must encourage the creative and renewed involvement of both the public and private sectors. . . . It must also respect the religious and ethical values of both individuals and institutions involved in the health care system ([15], p. 101).

While it is true that both priorities, as normative generalizations, may help frame policy discussions on health care reform, the potential for tensions between a commitment to a single-tiered system and a respect for pluralism of individuals and institutions is, as a matter of practical policy choice, enormous. Moreover, in light of the theological convictions central to the broader Catholic discussion of health care, considerations of individual liberty and dignity, as well as of the common good, might reasonably lead to a different practical conclusion; viz., that two tiers of health care delivery are both morally appropriate and practically preferable, so long as universal access to comprehensive basic care is assured. Consider, for example, basic education as a useful analogy to health care: a tax-based commitment to education for all citizens does not prevent individual parents from paying for alternative "basic" schooling for their children. It is not obvious, at least without a great deal more argument than the bishops provide, that health care should be viewed differently. Nor is it obvious, in light of the general theological warrants analyzed in Part I of this essay, that the common good would necessarily dictate the priority of equality over liberty in the delivery of health care.

The bishops' tendency to ignore or underemphasize conceptual and practical tensions among criteria and normative priorities is instructive for several reasons. First, it indicates that the bishops often conflate hortatory and pragmatic concerns in their discussion. Second, it suggests that a great deal more by way of careful, practically oriented, argument will be necessary before their assessment criteria and normative priorities can be viewed as significant contributions to the policy debate. Third, as I will conclude in Part III, the conceptual and practical tensions in the bishops' discussion will require the discriminating reader to identify the various modes of moral discourse at work in their recommendations in order to appreciate the different ways that Catholic themes and principles may be relevant to secular discussions.

B. The Ethics of Health Care Rationing

In Part I we discussed a number of relevant theologically grounded principles in Catholic social teaching on health care. We have seen how the bishops' resolution addresses general issues of health care reform. I turn now to a consideration of how Catholic themes and principles may function in judgments about the legitimacy of health care rationing. Here, because I am considering rationing along the lines developed by the Health Services Commission in Oregon, a brief review of the Oregon plan is in order.

1. The Oregon Model of Health Care Rationing

In 1989, the Oregon State legislature passed the Oregon Basic Health Services Act. The Act established a Health Services Commission, which was charged to develop a "priority list of health services, ranging from the most important to the least important for the entire Medicaid population." The purpose of the Act was to permit expansion of Medicaid coverage to all Oregonians up to 100 percent of the federal poverty level, and to do so by covering only those services judged to be of sufficient importance or priority. In effect, rather than providing extensive medical coverage for only some of the poor, Oregon chose to provide limited coverage to *every* poor person, as measured by the federal poverty standard.

The most recent version of the Oregon list ranks about 700 medical procedures according to their effectiveness. Depending on how many procedures can be financed from the Medicaid budget, the state will draw a line — paying for every procedure above the line but none below. Initially, Oregon has agreed to underwrite the first 568 procedures — thereby excluding, for example, treatment of common colds and infectious mononucleosis.

There are a number of important features to the Oregon proposal that require attention. First, the Oregon Basic Health Services Act of 1989, if its proponents are to be believed, was meant not as an effort to institutionalize rationing of health care for the poor, but to begin a *process* that will, if successful, establish a unified system of setting health care priorities that will eventually cover the vast majority of Oregon's citizens. There are three separate bills that comprise the approach. The Basic Health Benefits Act expands coverage and access by extending Medicaid eligibility to Oregonians below the federal poverty line. Priorities will be set for preferentially funding services that are judged to be the most effective in contributing to length and quality of life. If funding restrictions occur, procedures with the least potential for benefit will not be offered. The Act will establish statewide managed care through prepaid plans and other mechanisms designed to contain costs while ensuring access and coordination of care. A second Senate bill, the State Health Risk Pool Act, would establish a Medicaid Insurance Pool program for "medical uninsurables," that is, persons who do not qualify for Medicaid and who cannot now qualify for coverage because of preexisting conditions. The Act sets out the ways that state and private insurers will subsidize the pool. Finally, the so-called Health Insurance

Partnership Act, if passed, will mandate that four years after the implementation of the Basic Act, employers must provide health benefits that can be purchased through the state insurance pool. The benefits package offered by employers must offer coverage equal to or greater than that provided in the Medicaid benefits package. Any employer who does not provide insurance to all permanent employees and their dependents by a specified date will be taxed at a rate that approximates what would otherwise be the employer's contribution toward insurance.

2. *With Justice for All? The Ethics of Health Care Rationing*

Beyond the general development of health care as a right constrained by common good requirements in the encyclicals, there has also been a recent focused discussion of health care rationing offered by the Catholic Health Association (CHA). The CHA document, *With Justice for All? The Ethics of Health Care Rationing,* provides the most focused analysis to date of health care rationing, in light of Catholic principles.

Chapter Three of *With Justice for All?* on "The Public Policy Context" develops eight criteria for assessing the "ethics of rationing." These criteria can be summarized as follows. First, the need for health care rationing must be demonstrable. Second, health rationing must be oriented toward the common good. Third, a basic level of health care must be available to all. Fourth, rationing of health care should apply to all. Fifth, rationing should result from an open and participatory process. Sixth, the health care of disadvantaged persons has an ethical priority. Seventh, rationing must be free of wrongful discrimination. Finally, the social and economic effects of health care rationing must be monitored ([2], pp. x-xi).

Several of these criteria might, at first glance, appear to justify Oregon-like efforts to devise acceptable strategies for Medicaid rationing, while others would seem to disallow such selectively targeted efforts. Although the need for rationing may be "demonstrable," given the rise in health care inflation and the lack of coverage for so many uninsured and underinsured persons, Catholic principles would appear to dictate rationing as a last rather than a first or even intermediate resort. Thus easy or early recourse to rationing as the only practical solution to issues of cost, quality of care, and access may undercut prior efforts to eliminate inefficiencies and waste. Nonetheless, if Oregon's priority-setting is the first step in a more comprehensive process that will lead to systematic scrutiny of the efficacy and cost-effectiveness of medical services, Medicaid "rationing" may work in tandem with practical efforts toward more comprehensive reform.

Moreover, Oregon's plan, again if seen as a first step toward more systematic reform, seems, relative to the status quo, to be oriented toward the common good. As the CHA document notes:

> Clinical medicine must always be oriented to the best interests of every individual patient. However, public policy choices governing the distribution of health care services beyond the level determined to be each person's right must consider the common good. An ethically acceptable rationing scheme must limit expensive medical services, when necessary, in a way that is fair to all ([2], p. 21).

Again, assuming the best case scenario for the eventual passage of all three bills, Oregon's priority-setting will define for the vast majority of all state residents, beginning with the Medicaid population, what the right to basic care means. Rather than rhetoric, the scope of the entitlement to basic care will be specified. Every poor person, and ultimately all those who, while not poor, are uninsured or uninsurable, will be able to claim a meaningful entitlement. That willingness to set priorities — denying access to low-rated services and procedures while expanding access to cost-effective and efficacious care — appears at least in principle to be oriented to the common good. So too, assuming that the Oregon Medicaid experiment is in fact a first step toward comprehensive reform, the Basic Health Services Act will do much to help establish a basic level of health care for all who are presently marginalized — the poor, the uninsured, the underinsured.

However, Oregon-like proposals are problematic in light of two other criteria set forth in the CHA document. According to the fourth criterion, rationing should apply to all: "Those who construct and implement a health care rationing system are likely better to understand its effects on others if they, too, are required to live within the limitations they construct" ([2], p. 22). And again:

> Only when rationing applies to all can it be the occasion for sharing a common hardship rather than an occasion for deepening the gaps between wealthy and poor, old and young, healthy and sick, and among racial groups. Equity in rationing would suffer if a significant minority of the public obtained their care outside the health care system while acquiescing to limitations on services for those who were economically less secure ([2], p. 23).

This suggestion — that rationing should apply to all — is a criterion obviously at odds with our usual assumptions about two tiers of health care delivery being an inevitable part of health care in the United States. Given the general Catholic discussion of private property and its limits, this criterion is perhaps unsurprising, and indeed, there are two points that might be mustered in its defense. First, the criterion challenges us to reconsider our working assumptions about two tiers of health care. A casual acceptance of two tiers of health care delivery, in respect of the freedom of those better off to obtain more expensive care, may undercut the sense of solidarity that the common good emphasizes. Second, even if the criterion is not implemented, it may encourage us to consider our mutual responsibilities for one another; by so doing, it might serve to broaden the package of basic services that are seen as sufficiently comprehensive, by most citizens, to make "buying out" of basic coverage less appealing. Indeed, in contrast to the U.S. bishops' call for a single tier of health care, the CHA document discusses a first approximation of satisfying this criterion in a realistic footnote:

> Practically speaking, this criterion could be satisfied if those "buying out" of a rationed health care system constituted a very small percentage of Americans. If too many choose to "buy out," the rationed system would be disproportionately composed of the economically disadvantaged and would be more likely to decline in scope and quality. A large proportion of Americans "buying out" would also send a strong political signal that the rationed system is insufficiently comprehensive or seriously deficient in other respects ([2], p. 22).

Still, the criterion that rationing should apply to all, even granting the realism expressed in the above footnote, suggests that the Catholic Health Association would deem the present exclusion of certain large groups — especially the Medicare population — as unacceptable, even on prudential grounds. So long as some groups are deemed to be "untouchable" relative to general standards of rationing that apply to other large populations, there emerges a perception, at the very least, of serious inequity that fails to comport to recent Catholic social teaching on property. After all, a large percentage of Medicare coverage draws upon common resources, as with Medicaid. To be sure, there are differences in the initial moral appeals that were made in creating Medicare and Medicaid as legal entitlements: Medicare was, to large extent, seen as a merit-based entitlement due the elderly poor for their years of service, while Medicaid was perceived as an entitlement based on grounds of charity. Nonetheless, though I cannot develop a full argument here, I have concluded elsewhere that Catholic social teaching places moral priority on property in common, based upon use criteria according to need [12]. Consequently, arbitrary exclusion of the Medicare population from the scope of rationing would seem to require something more than prudential judgments to be morally compelling in light of Catholic social principles.

A final criterion might also call Oregon's process into question, the criterion that "the health care of disadvantaged persons has an ethical priority." As with the bishops' resolution, it is difficult to specify the target of this principle; i.e., are we speaking of those generally indigent, or the medically indigent? Although these groups overlap, the principle might well be applied differently, depending upon how that determination is made. One way to consider the issue would be to pose it in Rawlsian terms: does the impact of the Oregon Basic Health Services Act make the worst off better or worse off as a group? On the one hand, the basic Act does not seem to require much from better-off Oregonians. Providers will be reimbursed more for their services. Unless and until taxes rise to expand coverage for Medicaid (which appears quite unlikely), businesses and taxpayers will not pay much more. Moreover, those who are privately covered will continue to enjoy benefits, with tax-subsidized insurance, not available to their poorer Oregonian neighbors. Neither of these results seems in accord with the Catholic emphasis upon the common good and the need for a broader understanding of social justice.

On the other hand, if the Basic Health Benefits Act ultimately functions in tandem with the other two bills, extension of the priority setting beyond the Medicaid population will do much, as a comprehensive strategy, to improve the lot of all who would gain access, finally, to a meaningful entitlement to basic care. If one reads the future more optimistically, benefits to those presently disadvantaged by gaps in coverage would emerge, and this CHA criterion would be more clearly satisfied.

III. The Relevance of Catholic Principles to the Secular Debate

In Part I, I discussed the principles of Catholic social thought on medical care as an individual right, but one constrained by considerations of the common good, as well as of social and distributive justice. In Part II, I assessed two recent Catholic documents — one on health care reform, the other on rationing. In this section, I will conclude by posing a series of related questions about how, or whether, a particular theological understanding — here the Catholic tradition on health care — can have resonance with and relevance to the formation and justification of secular policy? What good might a specifically Catholic perspective do in our public discussion of the nature and scope of health care as a right? How might a Catholic perspective further the public debate on such a large and controversial issue as health care rationing?

To revisit an earlier point: we should not assume, at least without argument, that a particular religious voice is irrelevant to policy choices simply because we insist on finding secular and pluralistic warrants for policy formulation. A more full-blooded reading of secular pluralism would celebrate, rather than discourage, the vibrancy of various voices in the public dialogue about difficult issues. James Gustafson reminds us that moral discourse, whether theologically inspired or not, may function in a number of ways. He discusses four "modes" of moral discourse — what he calls ethical discourse, prophetic discourse, narrative discourse, and policy discourse. Each of these. he suggests, is at some level necessary to the moral deliberations of particular communities and society at large but none is, of itself, sufficient [6].

These days, of course, "ethical discourse" may be the mode most familiar to us — the so-called "Georgetown mantra" of principles, the appeals to various rights, the vocabularies of consequentialism and deontology. Ethics is an important language, for it serves to frame our reflections as we justify choices in a pluralistic society where a common narrative cannot be assumed. But ethics, according to Gustafson, tends to be micro-focused, small in scale, working within the status quo, not concerned, much of the time, with the larger cultural or social picture. Ethical discourse may also be rather dry, often trading on technical or legal niceties. Ethics may talk more about the patient's right to refuse treatment than it does about the cultural worship of medical technology that may pose such a quandary in the first place. Ethics may speak exhaustively (and exhaustingly) about the autonomy of individuals in making their own decisions even as it gives short shrift to the discussion of the individual's responsibilities to the larger society.

Prophetic discourse, by contrast, is often passionate in its sweeping indictment of larger cultural trends and social sins. Such discourse makes up in vision what it lacks in precision. It forces us to notice the forest through the trees, to see those large-scale background features that the ethical mode in the foreground often tends to underplay.

The discourse of narrative is the language of story, the story that shapes a community — in the Christian tradition, the centrality of the good news, the complexity of the parables, the attitudes and ethos shaped by the story the community tells, the faithfulness of the community to its own shaping narrative. Narrative is not the language of argument, of precise moral reasoning, of premises and conclusions. Narrative is more full-blooded, less skeletal. The bare bones of argument so dear to secular philosophers are covered with the flesh and blood of tradition. Narrative, before all else, is about inspiration, about the formation of character. We are shaped by the stories that we tell.

Finally, there is policy discourse. Policy discourse, rather than focusing on ideal theories or grand conceptions, usually functions within the constraints of history and culture. It works with the values already embedded in the choices that we have made. It seldom, if ever, is prophetic; its horizon is limited. It generally asks not, "What is the good or the right choice?" but, within a range of alternatives, "What is the reasonably good and feasible choice?"

It is useful, in light of Gustafson's distinctions, to consider in which mode or modes Catholic social teaching belongs in debates about health care reform and rationing. With all the appropriate caveats in place concerning the differences between the formation and the justification of public policy in a secular pluralistic society, Roman Catholic discussions of health care might contribute to policy formation in a number of different, perhaps complementary, ways. As ethical discourse, Catholic thought might call us to achieve a better balance between the language of "rights" and "obligations." Individuals have rights, but the language of the common good provides a useful counter to the usual stridency of rights language. As prophetic discourse, the Catholic understanding of the limits on private property might call into question the unexamined assumptions of a secular society about the seemingly sacrosanct status of individual acquisition and private property. Moreover, the CHA criterion that rationing should apply to all — however impracticable it may be — might force us to reconsider our status quo assumptions about separate and unequal forms of care.

So too, the Catholic voice, by emphasizing certain themes in the Christian story — especially the universalizing tendency of Christian love — might invite broader reflections about what we owe one another and how we are responsible to one another for the meeting of our basic needs. In addition, the richer narrative voice would surely reinforce distinctive emphases in Catholic institutions, perhaps about the sorts of services that they will or will not ration. Finally, the Catholic policy voice, proclaimed by the bishops in their resolution and by the CHA in its statement on rationing, will challenge Catholics, and perhaps others, to consider their own best moral instincts and values, especially those already embedded in earlier policy choices about expanding access and improving care, as exemplified by the passage of Medicare and Medicaid.

None of these modes of moral discourse, as I have suggested, is likely to provide, in itself, a specifically "Roman Catholic" warrant for secular social policy or public choices on health care reform. Indeed, in the two documents that I analyzed in Part II, the mixture of modes is quite striking, even as it leaves one uncertain about how to interpret the authority of particular conclusions. However, because Roman Catholic social ethics continues to invoke natural law categories of reflection, one would not expect Catholic policy discourse to be unique (although on some issues it will retain a distinctive cast). After all, the strength of natural law, in principle, is its availability as a source of natural moral insight to persons of good will. Yet it is worth remarking, as I close, that the persuasiveness of natural law in Catholic arguments has been quite variable, even to those still somewhat sympathetic to that methodology. As Bryan Hehir observes, recent Catholic policy statements argued in natural law terms have been received more favorably on general matters of social ethics than on specific issues in bioethics and sexual ethics. For example, in their pastoral letters in the 1980s on the economy and war and peace, the U.S. Catholic bishops invoked a recognizable version of natural law. In Hehir's judgment:

> Even though such a position is not well known or widely used in American academic or social policy debate, the positions of the bishops catalyzed a broad public discussion and found support beyond the boundaries of the Catholic community. [Moreover] [(t]he bishops' philosophical perspective often found more support than the specific policy conclusions they drew from it ([7], p. 357).

By contrast, on particular biomedical and sexual issues, "it has been very difficult to get a hearing for either the philosophical foundation or the conclusions espoused by the bishops" ([7], p. 357).

The reasons for that difference in reception are complex, but they involve, most crucially, the way that general principles and particular policy conclusions are distinguished or conflated in social ethics and bioethics respectively. The counsels of prudence usually feature more prominently in social teaching than in the strict moral conclusions traditionally reached on sexual and bioethical issues, primarily, as Hehir notes, because the latter involve judgments about "intrinsically evil acts" ([7], p. 358). To be sure, the recent stance taken by the U.S. bishops against support for any package of basic health care benefits that includes abortion exemplifies a point of intersection between two ordinarily distinct approaches. Indeed, the policy arguments required to sustain that position will offer an instructive challenge for Catholics who wish to speak appropriately in the policy mode. While one would clearly expect religious values to be invoked as focal elements of prophetic or narrative discourse, policy arguments, on abortion and other issues, require nonparochial, i.e., public, reasons. This, indeed, remains the central drama of being a public church: to witness by persuasion as well as by example, to speak to similarities as well as differences, to discover and celebrate those commonalities of experience and reflection that allow religious values, albeit indirectly, to work their leaven upon the world.

Institute of Religion/Center for Ethics
Texas Medical Center

Note

1. Significant sections of this essay closely parallel my analysis of recent Catholic documents on health care in "The Common Good in a Secular Society," *The Journal of Medicine and Philosophy* 18 (1993): 569-87.

Bibliography

1. Ashley, B. M. and O'Rourke, K. D., 1978, *Health Care Ethics,* Catholic Hospital Association, St. Louis.

2. Catholic Hospital Association (CHA), 1991, *With Justice for All? The Ethics of Health Care Rationing,* St. Louis, Mo.

3. Christiansen, D., 1991, "The Great Divide," *Linacre Quarterly* 58 (May), 40-50.

4. Engelhardt, H. T., 1986, *The Foundations of Bioethics,* Oxford University Press, New York.

5. Gremillion, J. (ed.), 1976, *The Gospel of Peace and Justice: Catholic Social Teaching Since Pope John,* Orbis Books, Maryknoll, New York.

6. Gustafson, J., 1990, "Moral Discourse About Medicine: A Variety of Forms," *The Journal of Medicine and Philosophy* 15 (April): 125-42.

7. Hehir, J. B., 1992, "Policy Arguments in a Public Church: Catholic Social Ethics and Bioethics," *The Journal of Medicine and Philosophy* 17 (June): 347-64.

8. Hollenbach, D., 1979, *Claims in Conflict: Retrieving and Renewing the Catholic Human Rights Tradition,* Paulist Press, New York.

9. John Paul II, 1981, *On Human Work,* United States Catholic Conference Office of Publishing Services, Washington, D.C.

10. Keane, P., 1993, *Health Care Reform: A Catholic View,* Paulist Press, New York.

11. Langan, J., 1986, "Common Good," in James Childress and John Macquarrie (eds.), *The Westminster Dictionary of Christian Ethics,* Westminster Press, Philadelphia, p. 102.

12. Lustig, B. A., 1990, "Property and Justice in the Modern Encyclical Literature," *Harvard Theological Review* 83, 415-46.

13. Outka, G., 1974, "Social Justice and Equal Access to Health Care," *The Journal of Religious Ethics* 2 (Spring), 11-32.

14. Treacy, G. C. (ed.), 1939, *Five Great Encyclicals,* Paulist Press, New York.

15. United States Bishops, 1993, "Resolution on Health Care Reform," *Origins* 23, 98-102.

125 Sanctity and Scarcity: The Makings of Tragedy

Allen Verhey

Crisis is common to medicine. Coping with tragedy comes with the territory. But crises and tragedies come in different forms. The kind of crisis routinely handled by medicine is the medical emergency, but the crisis confronting medicine today is more financial than medical. The form of tragedy familiar to medicine is "the sad story," for people can tell very sad stories indeed of or with their bodies. But the form of tragedy facing medicine in its financial crisis was familiar to Sophocles as a story in which "goods collide and evils gather."

As Sophocles knew, the really important issues in such cases are the issues of identity, of character, and of virtue, and it is not too much to claim that the financial crisis of medicine is an identity crisis for medicine. Medicine needs to address questions of public policy, doubtless, but no public policy "solution" will substitute for professional integrity. Authentic tragedies, after all, do not admit of being remedied — by public policy or by anything else human. They can, however, be endured by strength of character, by virtue. Our children may yet have a legacy of medical care in which they may take human delight as well as technological pride.

Medicine has always been best equipped to respond to the medical crisis. A fascinating and terrifying collection of technologies is quickly and skillfully brought to bear in such a crisis. Pumps make strange soft sounds. Other machines command our attention with little bleeping noises, while the blinking lights of still others demand our concentration. Even those like me who are uninitiated in such mysteries and cannot decipher any meaning in the sounds and lights find it hard to turn from them or to look past them. When we do, of course, we encounter not just technology but tragedy, the sad stories people tell of their bodies. The machines both point us toward tragedy and hide it from us. But anyone with eyes to see will finally see tragedy beyond the blinking lights; anyone with ears to hear will finally hear its sighs above the bleeping sounds.

The appropriate human and Christian response to this sort of tragedy has always been sympathy and care. All human beings, after all, even (or especially) those in crisis, those whose stories are sad stories, are the objects of God's unbounded love. Thus, as Gandhi said, "in that which is most basic, . . . the value of each life, we are all equal." That is all — but all of that — that I mean by "sanctity."

Some human beings have made it their business — no, more than their business, their *profession*, their avowed and public identity — to respond to such sad stories, to the stories of massive heart attacks and tumors growing slowly but surely or to the medical emergencies in the narratives of disaster and catastrophe, with the sympathy and care appropriate to a person's "sanctity." For centuries such sympathy and care were almost helpless in the face of tragedy. Medicine's duty was to care when there was no cure, when patients were "overmastered by their diseases." Everyone acknowledged the tragedy, but they also acknowledged that nothing could be done in the crisis.

Since Francis Bacon, who first insisted that to call any disease incurable "gives a legal sanction as it were to neglect and inattention, and exempts ignorance from discredit," medical science and technology have gradually developed to the point that we are not quite so helpless and hopeless in the medical emergency. Medicine has learned to care, if not more intensely, then at least more effectually. Moved by compassion for those who suffer, prompted by a sense of the sanctity of the life in crisis, medicine has learned to intervene in some sad stories of human suffering and premature dying, so that — sometimes at least — the sad story has a happy ending after all.

From *The Reformed Journal* 35 (February 1985): 10-14. Used by permission.

The very success of medicine, however, has led to another form of crisis and reminded it of another form of tragedy. The new crisis is not medical but financial: we simply do not have the resources to do all we can do and all we want to do for all patients. That is what I mean by "scarcity." It is "scarcity" which makes allocation necessary; if we do not have the resources to do all we can do and want to do for all patients, then we must limit what we will do for at least some patients.

I need hardly pause to demonstrate "scarcity." The United States now spends more than 10 percent of its gross national product on health care. Perhaps we can and will spend still more, but there is a limit. We value other things as well as health — education, other human services for the indigent and the elderly, the environment. There is a limit, and establishing that limit and then enforcing it will require decisions about allocation, about rationing the goods and services that we can provide. Public policy will decide what public resources will be allocated to health care and what to other social goods, and public policy will also decide what resources within health care funds will be allocated to medical research, to preventive medicine, to crisis medicine, etc. And these decisions will necessitate other decisions within medical care about who will receive the scarce vaccine, the scarce artificial heart, the scarce bed.

If it is "scarcity" which makes allocation decisions necessary, it is "sanctity" which makes them tragic. For when the goods or services to be allocated are goods or services on which life or health may depend and when the unbounded love of God for each one requires that we regard each life as of equal value, then the necessary allocation decision is necessarily tragic.

The notion of tragedy here is not just the "sad story," but the Sophoclean sort in which goods collide and evils gather. Because goods collide, to choose one good is to choose against another good, and, of course, we should never choose against the good. Because evils gather, they cannot all be avoided, but, of course, we should never choose the evil. The financial crisis of medicine requires tragic choices of this sort, and medicine must learn to live with and to cope with this sort of tragedy as well.

Medicine is not unacquainted with tragedy of the Sophoclean sort, however, and its own experience may provide valuable lessons for enduring its financial crisis. Not all the sad stories of medical crises, after all, have happy endings. Sometimes medicine's interventions preserve a patient's life, but it is a life either full of pain or empty of a capacity for human relationships. The tragic consequences of medical choices frequently require choosing one good over another, rejecting one evil while accepting another.

Two lessons emerge from such tragic choices that are relevant to allocation decisions. The first thing we learn is that tragic choices are always a consequence of our finitude, of the fact that we are not gods, that our mortality is indefeasible, and that our resources, while considerable, are still finite. The point of this is obvious: medicine and medical technology do not and cannot provide an escape either from our mortality or from the finitude of our resources. Medicine does not and cannot eliminate tragedy of the Sophoclean sort.

This is obvious, I say, but we have not been disposed to acknowledge the obvious. Perhaps our enthusiasm for medicine and medical technology as a response to the sad story has blinded us to its limits. Perhaps because medicine reminds us so vividly of tragedy, we have used it ironically and self-deceptively to hide and deny tragedy and the limits imposed by our mortality and the finitude of our resources. We have been disposed to fight against our own mortality — but some, and finally all, of us *are* "overmastered by our diseases," in spite of Bacon. We have been disposed to promise "everything for everyone" when it comes to allocation — but our limited resources forbid our fulfilling that promise. Doctors and nurses may not deny the tragic truth about our world or the tragic limits of medicine either to their patients or to themselves.

The truthfulness necessary to acknowledge tragedy and the humility necessary to cope with it can be sustained by piety, for piety knows it is God, not medicine, who brings a new age. For all its benefits, medicine has yet to deliver us, and will not deliver us, from our finitude and to our flourishing. The final victory over disease and death, pain and tears, is a divine victory, not a technological one. Such truthfulness and humility, nurtured by piety, might make it possible to lower the expectations and demands laid against medicine and to sustain a medical character identified less with the technological wizard than with the professional covenanted to care in the midst of tragedy, to care even when she cannot — or may not — cure.

If the first thing we learn from tragic choices in the case of dying patients is that we cannot successfully and may not truthfully deny our finitude, the second thing we learn is that the choice to use medical technology — or the refusal to use it even when we can — can be irremediably ambiguous. To claim to "solve" these problems, to arrive at some unambiguously "right" answer, makes one a comic character in the midst of tragedy, demonstrating either that one does not understand the limits of medicine (not to mention the limits of philosophy and theology) or that one lacks an appropriately awful sense of sanctity. When medical technology is being used to sustain a life, but a life either full of pain or empty of a capacity for human relationships, it may be morally appropriate to withdraw the medical technology — but it is not simply "good." A person should not choose either death or a lingering dying for someone else — but choose one must. The choice is not right or wrong, but right *and* wrong; not good or bad, but good *and* bad. The choice is tragic and irremediably ambiguous.

Goods, genuine goods, come into conflict, genuine conflict. Evils gather and cannot all be avoided. The ambiguity is hard, but it can be endured. It becomes destructive only when we refuse to recognize our choices for what they are, when, for example, we call death a "good," or when we refuse to acknowledge each other and ourselves for what we are: loved by God. In what is most basic, life itself, we are all equal, but finite and mortal, tragic figures in need finally of God's grace and God's future. Piety can help sustain such truthfulness and nurture the confidence in God's final triumph and forgiveness necessary to endure it and to make the necessary even though ambiguous choices.

The financial crisis now confronts medicine with such tragic choices in its allocation decisions. Allocation decisions, of course, are not new in medicine. What nurse has not experienced the finitude of her own resources for helping? Who will receive care when a dying patient needs someone to talk to, when a patient with a heart condition needs constant monitoring, and too many others need more care than can be provided? What doctor has not put off one patient for the sake of another? What hospital administrator has not faced hard and tragic choices constrained because funds to purchase equipment and to operate medical units are finite? The financial crisis has only made such choices more public, more frequent, and more urgent. Medicine's response to its financial crisis, if what it has learned from the care of dying patients is true, will not be a response that denies or avoids moral ambiguity. Many proffered responses, however, attempt to do exactly that.

In allocation decisions there are two strategies for denying tragedy: one is to deny sanctity; the other is to deny scarcity. Both strategies are illustrated in the response to the crisis of kidney dialysis. In 1961 a committee at the Seattle Artificial Kidney Center was formed to select those patients who would receive treatment when not all could. It allocated the scarce medical treatment to those whom it considered the most deserving; it denied sanctity, denied the equal value of each of the lives of the medically acceptable candidates. Most of the criticism of this committee focused on the denial of what we called "sanctity." Paul Freund, for example, argued that "in a matter of choosing for life or death, not involving specific wrongdoing, no one should assume the responsibility of judging *comparative* worthiness to live on the basis of unfocused criteria of virtue and social worthiness." Such a strategy was and remains morally unacceptable.

The next strategy was to deny *scarcity,* to provide almost universal funding for kidney dialysis, in order to acknowledge and affirm sanctity. The strategy was, of course, self-deceptive, for a policy which promises kidney dialysis for everyone distinguishes those dying from renal failure from those dying from other diseases. There are limits, and the tragedy of the necessary allocation decisions cannot be hidden or denied for long.

In any context of scarce resources, of course, the notion of distributive justice is applicable, and decisions which violate that principle are not only tragic but wrong. To provide ordinary health care to the wealthy because they can pay or to the nice because we like them or to the promising because of their social utility while we withhold it from the poor, the outcast, and the handicapped is not only tragic but unjust. Just what justice requires in the distribution of health care is, of course, a much debated and very debatable topic. Without attempting to enter fully into that discussion, let me simply propose Charles Fried's conclusion that justice requires that all citizens be entitled to "a decent minimum of health care," without supplying his argument or spelling out what "a decent minimum" might be. This seems to be the position recommended for future public policy by the president's commission in its report, "Securing Access to Health Care." The authors of the report retreated from the "equal access — equal care" goal of the last twenty years. They recognized scarcity, that there simply are not the resources to do all we can do and would like to do for all patients. They accepted — because in recognizing scarcity, they had to accept — the notion of "two-track care."

My point is not that this is wrong. Public policy must deal with scarcity and in dealing with scarcity the claims of justice are properly adamant. My point is that such a policy does not "solve" or remove tragedy. Physicians and nurses commit themselves to provide not a decent minimum of health care to their patients, but to offer their *best* efforts with their *best* tools. To provide the best care for all is impossible; there are limits to our resources. To provide "a decent minimum" for all patients may be possible, and it is required by justice. But not to provide the best care for any patient is not, therefore, "good." It remains tragic.

Some health planners have urged a policy of cost containment that decided whether to create a new technology or to keep an existing one available based on its cost-effectiveness. Preventive medicine is ordinarily favored above critical care on this basis because it is generally cheaper and results in better health for more people. There is some wisdom here — and some folly. But it does not solve the tragedy. Physicians and nurses are not committed to the health of some distant patient, some statistical patient, or society as a patient; they are committed to the life and the flourishing of the patient on the table or in the bed in front of them. And society signals its compassion by allocating resources to those in the midst of suffering, not those who are prospective sufferers. To provide the best care for all is impossible; there *are* limits to our resources. To be concerned about cost-effectiveness is a legitimate concern. But not to provide a costly but genuine therapy is not therefore "good." It remains tragic.

The constraints of justice and cost containment are just that for medicine: they are constraints, not virtues. Public policy based on such considerations will set the limits within which medicine can act with integrity. But medicine must act with integrity within those constraints. That is important to say, for the financial crisis in medicine has created an identity crisis. Rival and alien definitions are being used to understand medicine and to shape its response to the financial crisis. The rational and impartial perspectives of justice and utility are legitimate, but they threaten to alienate medicine from itself, from its own moral interests and loyalties, from the projects and passions which give it moral character. How medicine deals with its financial crisis will determine the character of our children's medicine. Medicine must reassert an identity of care in the midst of tragedy, of care even when it cannot — or may not — cure. The definition of medicine must continue to center on caring, intensive caring, for the patient in crisis, but it will have to acknowledge truthfully that its story is a tragic story. Medicine will have to make allocation decisions, and how it makes those decisions will express its sense of itself, its values, integrity, and character. The questions answered by allocation decisions are: "What is medicine?" and "What shall it become?"

In this crisis some are suggesting that medicine be defined by that quintessentially American story of the marketplace, where you get rich by supplying what the buyer wants. Then medicine is simply a commodity, that collection of skills to get what we want, a value-free enterprise which may be bought and sold to satisfy consumer desires, hired to do the autonomous bidding of the one who pays. But we are all uncomfortable with the marketplace definition of medicine, for such medicine cannot and will not sustain the dispositions of care and trust which have sometimes defined the characters of doctor and patient. Marketplace medicine will become a medicine in the service of the rich and powerful, while the poor and weak watch and pray.

If medicine is true to itself as a profession prompted by and practiced in care for those in tragedy, born and nurtured by its sense of the sanctity of the life in crisis, then it cannot and will not regard the marketplace definition as its definition. Piety provides a resource to support this fragile identity, for it acknowledges that we are enlisted on the side of life and health in a world where death and evil still apparently reign, and it owns a story, told elegantly by the physician Luke, of good news to the poor, to the sick, to the despised.

In response to the financial crisis and in rejecting a pure market allocation of medical resources, medicine may honor and applaud proposals for guaranteeing access to "a decent minimum" and for assessing cost-effectiveness. But medicine may not identify with the impartial perspective which prompts these proposals. Medicine should not allow itself to become an agent of public or economic policy, even good public or economic policy. It must preserve its own identity, its own integrity, even when that requires acknowledging the moral ambiguity of abiding by the constraints public policy and an impartial perspective may impose.

I suggest that it is not only medical integrity which is at stake but the success of the public policies as well. A lively sense of medicine's professional identity and its awful sense of the sanctity of all lives in crisis may keep a two-track medical delivery system from becoming a two-class system. At least such a medicine will constantly remind the rest of us not only of scarcity but also of sanctity, of the tragedy and the moral ambiguity of allocation decisions where life and health are at stake.

A lively sense of medicine's professional identity may also preserve us from a society where cost-effectiveness is the only relevant consideration, from the sort of society prepared to stand impassively by in the face of medical crises because it is disposed to let present victims die for the sake of future possibilities. At least such a medicine will force the rest of us to ask whether a society which can ignore a cry for help even as it "maximizes protection" is the sort of society we want to be or to become.

Medicine must be true to itself — for its own sake and for ours. The financial crisis may be an opportunity for medicine to reassert its identity, not as a Promethean character denying the limits of our resources and of our mortality, not as a way of overcoming tragedy, but as a way to signal care for one another in the midst of tragedy.

Such a medicine will nurture and sustain certain virtues. One virtue is sensitivity to economic factors. The physician and the nurse, with integrity to their loyalty to the patient, can make contributions to the careful use of resources. They can have — and should have — a "cost conscience." They can cultivate diagnostic and therapeutic "elegance," not accepting the technologic that "if we can, we must," avoiding the shotgun workups and roulette therapies. These produce excessive costs and are indefensible both economically and clinically. A physician and a nurse with a "cost-conscience" will not give in to the patient's every whim as little more than hired hands on the marketplace model. That is poor — and costly — medicine. These are not tragic choices. These are choices coherent with the definition of medicine as a profession committed to the care of the patient. But these are not final solutions to the problem of scarce resources either; they will not finally eliminate the necessity of tragic choices.

We cannot eliminate tragedy when scarcity and sanctity meet, but we must not deny it either. A second virtue is truthfulness; doctors and nurses and hospital administrators should not deny the truth about our world, about the limits imposed by our mortality or the finitude of our resources, either to their patients or to themselves.

Joined to truthfulness is humility, the acknowledgment that we are not gods, but the creatures of God, finite and mortal creatures, human beings loved and cherished by God, so that in what is most basic, we are all equal.

Truthfulness and humility can sustain another virtue — care. Without them, without acknowledging limits, without an appropriate sense of the tragic, the capacity and responsibility to care (and to care intensively) may not be sustainable. And intensive care in response to crisis, it will be recalled, is what inspired and prompted medicine in the first place.

Let me add, finally, piety to this catalogue of virtues. There is nothing alien about piety to medicine. After all, the oath was sworn by Apollo, Asclepius, Panaceia, Hygeia, and all the gods and goddesses. The story of medicine has its beginnings among the gods and it will end with the story of a new heaven and a new earth when death and disease and pain will be no more. While we wait and watch for that day, piety can nurture and sustain truthfulness about our finitude, gratitude for the opportunities within our limitations, respect and care for the sanctity of each human life, and a sense of God's forgiveness in the midst of moral ambiguity.

Such a medicine will allocate the resources provided and limited by public policy in a way determined by its character, its identity, its virtue. That way, I suggest, will not rely on the marketplace to make the allocation decision and will not deny sanctity by using the criteria of social worth or potential social benefit. It will rely instead first on medical criteria and medical judgment. Techniques and procedures will be used only on persons who may and probably will benefit from them. But medical criteria may only define the candidates for medical procedures or techniques. The final allocation decision should be based on *random* selection. When scarcity makes allocation necessary, sanctity requires random selection and forbids godlike judgments that one life is worth more than another. Random selection alone will nurture medicine's capacity to care even when it may not cure. Random selection alone will sustain a relationship of truthfulness and trust between physician and patient. Random selection alone will encourage us to find less costly ways of responding to those threats to human life which menace those about whom we care intensively but may not cure.

When goods collide and evils gather, we may not deny scarcity, we may not deny sanctity; the best we can do is to act with integrity. The financial crisis is an identity crisis, and the allocation decisions it forces are decisions about the character and virtues of medicine. May medicine be true to the integrity of its character, to care when it cannot or may not cure.

126 The Ethical Legitimacy of Excluding the Elderly When Medical Resources Are Limited

John F. Kilner

As Fred Horn thought ahead to the Heart Transplant Patient Selection Committee meeting scheduled later that morning, he was reminded of some of the patient selection decisions he had been involved in during the early days of kidney dialysis. Once medical factors like tissue and blood typing had been accounted for, he mused, the two types of decisions were rather similar. In fact, he had heard talk that patients might again be excluded from dialysis on the basis of old age, even as the present committee sometimes barred older patients from heart transplants.

Fred's mind wandered to a particularly disturbing decision he had been a part of, when the age of a potential dialysis patient was very much in question. He could remember the committee chairperson, Paul Sims, picking up the first of five applications from patients who were hoping to be given the opportunity to take the place of a patient who had just elected to discontinue dialysis. . . .

"Roger Algers," Mr. Sims announced. "He's a fifty-three-year-old lawyer with three grown children. His wife is still alive, and he's still married to

From *The Annual of the Society of Christian Ethics* (Washington, D.C.: Georgetown University Press, 1988), pp. 179-204. Used by permission.

her. He's a member of the Rotary Club and the Elks, and a former scout-master."

"From the practical point of view," said Dr. Craine, "he would be a good candidate. He's intelligent and educated and understands what's involved in dialysis."

"I think he's definitely the sort of person we want to help," said Mrs. Langfore. "He's a real asset to the community."

"Wait a minute," said Mr. Sims. "I don't think fifty-three is old — I'd better not, because I'm fifty-two myself. Still, his children are grown, he's led a good life. I'm not sure I wouldn't give the edge to some younger fellow." "I agree," nodded Mr. Brewster. "His contributions to the community are history. Let's save someone who can remain active for a long time. Besides, his age might hamper the effectiveness of his treatment. . . ."

Fred recalled how hard the selection decision had been on that occasion. He knew that with fifty-four-year-old Bill Dever among those to be considered later that morning for a heart transplant, the present decision would not likely be any easier.[1]

This disagreement over the merits of selecting the "aging" Mr. Algers is indicative of current disputes over the place of an age criterion in patient selection — whether involving heart transplants, dialysis, or other such resources. The contributions for which Mr. Algers is appreciated in the community are largely in the past. Others are now taking over many of his responsibilities. Also, he has had the opportunity to live longer than most, and there are doubts concerning how well he will do on dialysis. Such factors establish the appropriateness of an age criterion in the eyes of many, but others are uncomfortable at the prospect of writing off any age group where life itself is at stake.

The elderly are usually in view when an age criterion is proposed, though occasionally the issue of infancy or youth is raised where the benefit of treatment is dubious. For the purpose of focus, the present analysis will concentrate upon the merits of excluding the elderly (rather than children) from certain treatments under particular circumstances. My conclusion will be that an age criterion *per se* is unjustified, though age may play a carefully defined role in medical assessments relevant to patient selection. I am concerned here with the access of specific persons or groups to particular existing resources; I am not going to address the problem of priorities in research funding (though that also is a crucial issue).

In light of the growing prominence of an age criterion in patient selection,[2] it is important to scrutinize the ethical legitimacy of arguments being offered both for and against the criterion. Accordingly, I will first explore the primary justifications for an age criterion, then examine its faults. In order to make the nature and significance of its faults clear, I will (1) discuss the major weaknesses of the justifications, (2) offer two broader critiques of the dubious assumptions upon which enthusiasm for the age criterion rests, and (3) consider the criterion in light of the Christian Scriptures in order to suggest its unacceptability from a Christian perspective. Finally, I will propose a way forward in the midst of the present controversy.

For the sake of convenience, justifications will be characterized and legitimacy will be assessed in terms of productivity-oriented or person-oriented styles of reasoning. A productivity-oriented argument is one that is concerned with promoting the achievement of some good such as efficiency or happiness. In contrast, a person-oriented argument is one that is concerned with respecting people for their own sake, irrespective of the goods they produce. Admittedly, there is a resemblance here to the classical contrasts of teleological against deontological, or utilitarian against egalitarian/libertarian, styles of reasoning. The problem with employing such categories, however, is that many egalitarians and libertarians approve of pursuing utility to some degree, and many utilitarians approve, to some degree, of basic values like equality and liberty. Not only are productivity-oriented and person-oriented categories more readily applicable to particular arguments, but they are also better suited to the cross-cultural comparisons to be introduced later in this essay. Even so, any categories are helpful only in a general way and will not be strained beyond their proper limits.

Justifications

Many arguments can be made in behalf of an age criterion. Some of them essentially equate this criterion with some form of medical criterion.[3] According to this approach, where the elderly will not benefit medically from treatment, they should be excluded. (Medical benefit typically involves a significant likelihood that a patient's life will be significantly lengthened or qualitatively improved as a direct result of treatment for a disease or illness.) While this approach is widely accepted, it really supports a medical criterion rather than an age criterion *per se*. The relation of age to medical considerations will be discussed further at the end of this essay.

Age criteria can also be justified in their own right. To many they seem obvious — often apparently for productivity reasons.[4] Explicitly productivity-oriented justifications are of several types. One type involves the contention that an age criterion will help to insure the best possible return on the investment of resources.[5] The young are more likely to contribute more to society — and for a longer time — than the elderly. Another type of justification focuses upon the convenience of an age criterion. Whereas many medical judgments are uncertain and somewhat subjective, a patient's age is an objective and precise basis for selection.[6] Moreover, an age criterion can be applied with rather little resistance from the elderly, who as individuals (even if not collectively) tend to be relatively unassertive. Finally, the financial savings that can be achieved if the elderly are excluded are also noteworthy. For example, if only those over fifty-five years of age were excluded from treatment for renal disease in the U.S., 45 percent of the costs of the renal disease program would be saved.[7] In other areas such as intensive care, the elderly use such a disproportionate amount of resources that there is a great financial gain where they are excluded. After all — though it is a tragically stark fact to acknowledge — death is the ultimate economy in health care expenditures.[8]

From a more person-oriented perspective, an age criterion may also have great appeal. Part of its appeal, interestingly, stems from what it is not. In the face of some lifesaving medical care today which is prone to dehumanize people by trying desperately to forestall death at all costs, an age criterion recognizes that it is appropriate to accept death when old age arrives.[9] The criterion also avoids much of the criticism directed against racism and sexism, for everyone (if death does not intervene first) is subject to old age. The evil of racism and sexism lies largely in the fact that only certain people are penalized by deprivations attached to race or sex.[10]

An age criterion may actually be seen as promoting equality. One form of this argument contends that the most important equality at issue here is the equal opportunity to live to the same age as others.[11] Some notion of a *prima facie* right to a minimum number of life-years may be involved.[12] An alternative version holds that there is a natural life span (perhaps seventy, perhaps eighty years) — a span which functions normatively rather than merely representing a statistical average at the present moment in history. Once people have reached this age, medicine should generally no longer be concerned with saving (extending) their lives.[13] This argument has a less person-oriented form as well, in which each year of life, rather than each person *per se*, is equally valued. From this perspective, the concern is to maximize the number of life-years saved by employing an age criterion.[14]

Another egalitarian proposal is that people should be treated equally not so much in the present moment as over a lifetime. Health care should be provided in the way that enables all people to live as long as possible.[15] To achieve this end, the resources available must be distributed throughout each person's lifetime in a way that will protect against early death. Expensive lifesaving resources, then, might be made available only to the young, with personal care services enhanced for the elderly (and preventive as well as other basic care perhaps provided to all).[16] Alternatively, all resources might be channeled to the young to increase their prospects, with the elderly encouraged to commit assisted suicide.[17] Unlike a more utilitarian concern to maximize the total number of life-years saved — often helping some at the expense of others — this type of justification adopts the perspective of the typical individual and seeks the most prudent distribution of limited resources throughout that person's lifetime.[18]

Weaknesses of the Justifications

The foregoing justifications of an age-criterion are far from universally accepted.[19] In fact, in circumstances where this criterion is most commonly employed — such as the provision of dialysis in Great Britain — physicians appear reluctant to admit its use. Confronted with a patient who is over the unofficial maximum age, British physicians will often tell the patient that nothing of medical benefit can be done, even when something can be done.[20] Some justify this practice with the half-truth that everyone over fifty-five is "a bit crumbly,"[21] but others admit to some deception.[22] If physicians do not succeed in deterring older patients and these patients apply to a clinic for dialysis, they will often be treated.[23] So, given limited resources, some means of curtailing the number seeking treatment is needed. Sensing the unacceptability of excluding patients on non-medical grounds, physicians disguise their use of an age criterion. British physicians are hardly unique in this respect — they are merely the most publicized case. The problem is more general to contemporary medicine.[24]

One reason many physicians, British and otherwise, regard an age criterion as morally unacceptable is that they find its justifications unconvincing. Their concerns are largely person-oriented. Consider first the productivity-oriented justifications. Excluding the elderly will indeed insure a better return on the investment of health care resources. But it may in the process unacceptably demean people — as if the only concern is to get the most productivity out of a group of machines.[25] Age is admittedly an objective index, but so are many other characteristics of persons. Objectivity says nothing necessarily about appropriateness as a selection criterion. An age criterion is also convenient in that the elderly may well be the weakest and easiest to exclude from treatment; but some find this a reason for special care, not less care.[26] The argument that disproportionate cost-savings may result from employing an age criterion also may be acknowledged; however, disproportionate spending on an age group is not necessarily a reason for cutbacks if legitimate needs vary by age groups. The appropriateness of spending educational dollars disproportionately on children is a possible parallel.[27]

The more person-oriented justifications may also be disputed. For instance, the need to accept death when it cannot be avoided can be seen as a good reason to adopt instead a medical-benefit criterion. The truth that we must all eventually die may be no more pertinent to the situation of an elderly patient than to the situation of a middle-aged patient, for an elderly person may have decades left to live if treated. On the other hand, the difference between selection by age and selection by race or sex may be simply acknowledged without saying anything one way or another about the justification of an age criterion. Moreover, when we denounce racism and sexism on moral grounds, we do so not only because of the selectivity of criteria that have subjected only certain populations to unusual and disproportionate burdens, but also because racist and sexist criteria disadvantage people for illegitimate reasons. Accordingly, ageism may need to be guarded against as fastidiously as racism and sexism, particularly when the victims are already in the vulnerable condition of sickness.[28]

The three remaining justifications focus upon equal opportunity, life span, and prudence respectively. They require somewhat more detailed attention.

Equal Opportunity

This justification involves giving people an equal opportunity to live to a certain age, thereby maximizing the life-years saved. The most controversial issue here is the way life-years rather than lives (persons) are valued. In the eyes of many, persons are more than sums of life-years which have been accumulated like property.[29] Persons are entities of equal value who must be treated as such.[30] Murderers, some note, are not generally punished less for killing victims who are sixty-five than for killing victims who are twenty-five.[31] While it is indeed better to preserve someone's life for a longer rather than a shorter time, this is arguably a different matter from preserving one person's life for a long time at the price of denying any chance of continuing existence to another.[32]

An age criterion seeking a maximum savings in life-years would also have the curious effect of saving fewer lives in certain cases. Where long-term and reusable resources like dialysis and intensive care are in view, this would mean that an age criterion would save fewer people for a longer time. In other words, the benefits of scarce resources (some minimum benefit — e.g., a set number of months — being assumed for each patient) would be confirmed to a few young rather than distributed to many of various ages.

Two problems unrelated to maximizing life-years also appear when we invoke selection by age in an attempt to equalize the opportunity people have to live a long life. Compare, first of all, two women, one of whom is a year older but has been in a coma for more than a year. Could it be plausibly argued that the best grounds for a decision to save the younger woman in preference to the older comatose woman is that the younger woman has had less opportunity to experience life? It would appear, rather, that the younger is the one who has experienced more. But if this is admitted, then a problematically large number of imprecise qualitative considerations need to be included in any assessment of who has had the least opportunity to experience life. One supporter of this approach admits that such assessments would be "an overwhelmingly complicated task," calling it "procedurally and administratively a nightmare."[33] It may be that other factors, such as one's socio-economic or spiritual condition, have much more to do with one's lifetime experience of well-being than does age. Age provides too rough a measure of lifetime well-being (or present physical health for that matter) to be used where something as important as life is at stake.[34]

The other problem related to equalizing opportunity for long life concerns the past access of patients to resources. Perhaps a younger person has already received a great deal of medical care, while an older person has received very little. It may not be accurate to say that the younger person should be saved because she or he has not been given as great an opportunity to live as the older person. It would appear that the opposite is the case.[35]

Life Span

One variation of the equal-opportunity justification limits lifesaving care to those who have not yet reached the end of their natural life span; this version is no more attractive than the others. The very notion of a normative life span is questionable. The "natural" human life span has lengthened through the years as life-extending care for the elderly has improved. An age criterion of the sort envisioned here would significantly hinder medicine from extending even good-quality years at the end of life.

Such an age criterion would also demean those living beyond the natural life span. One supporter candidly admits this problem, given the world as it presently is.[36] But this problem is not an accident of circumstance; it is intrinsic to the justification. The justification's supporters assume that life-extending care beyond the natural life span is not warranted because everything of significance to the individual has by that time been "accomplished" and "achieved."[37] An implicit productivity orientation is revealed here. What matters is what one succeeds in doing. But the significance of life is arguably as much a matter of "being" as of "doing" — it consists as much of relating to others as of completing tasks. Also, life goals are repeatedly altered to reflect different values at different ages.[38] To suggest that people at a later stage of life usually have no goals left to be realized is to assume wrongly that the (often productivity-oriented) life goals of earlier years are the last word.

While this productivity bias is not generally perceived by supporters, the quality-of-life orientation of this justification is readily acknowledged. In fact, this justification may in the end really support a quality-of-life criterion rather than an age criterion. One supporter admits that an age criterion to exclude elderly patients would not be warranted unless their quality of life was low.[39] Whether a quality-of-life or age criterion is in view, applying the criterion in practice is quite problematic. It is no easier to assess another person's quality of life accurately than it is to determine whether people have attained their life goals — in both cases we have to rely on patients' own statements. There is little reason to assume that all elderly patients will value continued life less than younger persons do.[40] Moreover, neither the old nor the young are likely to be particularly forthright in their assessment of their lives when their very lives are at stake. An alternative, of course, is to withhold resources only from those of any age who voluntarily forgo treatment.

Prudence

This last justification of an age criterion also raises a debatable issue. Is it truly prudent to distribute health care resources throughout life so that only certain resources are available at each stage of life? Two clarifications are called for here. First, a policy decision to make more personal care services available to the elderly does not in any way necessitate invoking an age criterion for acute care. All that is needed is to place greater priority on personal care services when macro-allocation decisions are being made. Second, utilization of an age criterion in the form of rationing medical resources according to patient age does not involve comparing individuals in order to favor the younger; it involves excluding entire groups from consideration for a scarce resource. Is such exclusion warranted on prudential grounds?

The potential strength of the proposal lies in envisioning the resource problem as a problem of distributing resources throughout an individual's lifetime. Ideally the proposal looks good, but even proponents admit that it would be wrong to introduce it in one health care setting and not in another.[41] They also admit that it may be politically unacceptable in any setting.[42] Politically the issue is perceived in terms of which groups will gain greatest access to the most resources. Moreover, were the proposal applied throughout an entire nation such as the United States, injustices in the system could cause the application of an age criterion to make things worse.[43] These concerns are so compelling that one theoretical supporter of age-rationing frankly concludes: "This is in no way a recommendation for the introduction of such practices in our present world."[44]

Apart from such pragmatic concerns, though, age-rationing is harmful in other ways as well. While it might not be as thoroughly discriminatory as racism or sexism, it is subtly discriminatory. It assumes that all persons move through all age categories, whereas many people are born with congenital, genetic, or environmentally-created conditions which ensure that they will not live as long as most.[45] Age-rationing more particularly appears to discriminate against those whose health has been robust throughout youth and middle-age. It puts those elderly persons who have never required health care, but find themselves now being denied needed lifesaving treatment, at odds with younger persons who may or may not have used other medical resources in addition to the scarce lifesaving treatment now also available to them. The proposal would also impose constraints on liberty and welfare during the elderly stage of life that would probably be experienced as unbearably harsh, even if they were in fact objectively prudent.[46]

At the same time a serious injustice would seem to be done in the first generation of its adoption. The transitional generation of elderly would be denied lifesaving resources without having previously received the special benefits accorded younger generations in order to justify denial of these resources in old age. Moreover, in their youth they would have paid for lifesaving resources for the elderly, only to find that when they became old the youth would not provide such resources for them.[47] It would hardly be prudent for them to support such a system. Some members of this generation of elderly would be forced to give up their lives for the good of all generations — a classic utilitarian form of injustice. To compensate them fairly during the transitional period would seem to require shifting resources from elsewhere, thereby creating new injustices. This is not merely a theoretical problem. When Social Security legislation was first passed, the idea of giving the then-current generation of elderly less income support than future generations was soundly rejected — even though the contemporary elderly had not paid into the system from which they would be receiving.[48] This problem is not a strictly transitory one. A similar structural inequity would occur every time a new lifesaving technology is introduced. The current elderly would be given no access to it — though the justification of this exclusion probably requires that they previously have had priority access to it.[49]

The approach becomes still less attractive if it is understood to entail active (even if voluntary) euthanasia for the elderly. The specter of doctors, not to mention society in general, encouraging people to die so that health-care resources can be saved is a potentially ominous one.[50] For euthanasia decisions to be truly voluntary, proponents admit, some of the savings generated when many older persons choose to be killed would have to be made available to provide decent health care for the elderly who choose not to be killed.[51] But in that case the approach becomes self-defeating, since fewer and fewer patients would opt to die if they still had decent health care available. In fact, it is far from obvious that most people would opt for death over illness, even if supportive services were limited.[52]

Overarching Critiques

Implicit in the foregoing responses to possible justifications for an age criterion — and going beyond them — are two basic critiques. One has to do with values and the other concerns the matter of rights.

Values

An age criterion in most of its forms, first of all, reflects certain non-medical values.[53] Among these, the value of youth is prominent. The United States is an example of a country in which such a high view is placed upon youth that it affects the practice of medicine generally.[54] Research indicates that the older patients are, the less likely they are to be treated — even resuscitated — under the same medical circumstances.[55] So it is not surprising to learn that some people originally supported funding dialysis for all because it looked as if primarily young adults would be the beneficiaries.[56] No more surprising is the enthusiasm over allocating health-care resources generally on the basis of maximizing the quality-adjusted life-years to be saved — an approach necessarily biased toward funding treatments that are mainly beneficial to the young.[57]

Youthfulness is attractive for various reasons, but especially for the productivity which normally accompanies it. Economic productivity is highly prized in many countries — so much so that those like the elderly who are less economically productive and thus less independent are looked down upon.[58] This devaluing translates directly into reduced medical care from the medical profession.[59] Viewed against this background, the age criterion for patient selection presents itself as a social-worth criterion.[60] The relative devaluing of old age can be quite subtle. For instance, the objective fact that elderly years are generally more subject to health-related limitations than younger years can be used to support the idea that it is better to save the lives of the younger rather than the old — as if there was no more to life than healthiness.[61]

The limited value placed on the elderly and their correspondingly limited access to scarce lifesaving medical resources are largely the product of various cultural and religious values.[62] This point becomes clearer when the view of the elderly common in a country like the United States is contrasted with that traditionally characteristic of, for example, the Akamba people of Kenya. (Western influences are now altering the Akamba view somewhat.) According to the Akamba, persons are much more than economic beings. A poor person in old age deserves as much respect as a rich or otherwise socially important person. In fact, old age calls forth a unique veneration.[63]

The high level of respect accorded to older people in Akamba society is intimately bound up with that culture's view of the relationship of the individual and the community. Whereas the utilitarian view common in the U.S. conceives of the social good atomistically in terms of individual (mainly job-related) contributions summed over the breadth of society, the Akamba view presupposes a social network of interpersonal relations within which one becomes more and more essential the older one becomes. The more personally interwoven a person becomes with others, the greater the damage done to the social fabric when that person is torn away by death. This extended-kinship social system commands a sort of spiritual loyalty and is ceremonially celebrated in various practices and rituals.[64]

A different set of cultural values surrounding old age leads many Akamba to age-related resource allocation decisions that are very different from those supported by many in the U.S. In my own study of Akamba medical personnel, I asked them whether an older or a younger man should be preferred when there are resources enough to save one only.[65] Faced with such a dilemma, many Akamba argue that the older man should be saved because he, not the young man, "has more responsibilities" and "is a father to many people."[66] European countries such as Sweden could also be cited as examples of places where greater respect for the elderly leads to age criteria (when they even exist) which are much less restrictive than in the U.S.[67]

Opponents of an age criterion employ these facts to argue that alternative attitudes toward the elderly are possible and that, for a variety of reasons, society should resist the temptation to discard its elderly. The first reason is that if economic productivity is important, then the elderly are more deserving of reward than anyone else; their contribution stretches over a lifetime.[68] Second, their crowning lifetime achievements may still be before them.[69] Third, the elderly are important to society for reasons other than their economic productivity. They often have wisdom to share,[70] patient love to bestow,[71] and various (though perhaps unspectacular) services to provide.[72] Even claims about their diminished mental abilities have been challenged by recent studies.[73] Should they be penalized simply because their society overlooks, perhaps inadvertently, the true value of their contribution? But the very attempt to justify the continued existence of the elderly in terms of their social contributions may itself be misplaced. People have different *worths* in a social sense, but many see their human work as persons to be intrinsic to their personhood.[74] Moreover, by systematically cultivating in people a sense of obligation to die when they are first thought to be terminally ill,[75] we would deny the intrinsic value of persons, substituting unstable instrumental value in its place.

Rights

The notion of intrinsic value points us toward another fundamental problem with an age criterion: it is a direct violation of basic human rights. A person's life arguably should be preserved simply because it is a human life. According to this argument, the age attached to that life is irrelevant,[76] otherwise, one's right to life would diminish with every day that one lives. Rooted in personhood *per se,* basic human rights do not vary with age. A year of life at any stage of life can be equally precious.[77] One response to this criticism is to argue that the basic right needing protection is the right to humane termination procedures rather than the right to continue living.[78] Unfortunately, such a response seems more sensitive to conserving society's resources than to how persons are treated.

Since an age criterion is often applied by excluding all patients above a certain age,[79] it also can be seen as violating basic rights in its discriminating between patients when there is no just basis for doing so. According to statistics, elderly patients do not fare well with certain treatments. Yet, a particular elderly person may be in better physical condition to undergo treatment than a younger person.[80] Certain elderly patients also have a strength of mind and heart that makes them better candidates for treatment than some who are half their age.[81] Finding a magic cut-off age beyond which people do not warrant lifesaving treatment simply because of their age is necessarily problematic.[82] Any such cut-off is arbitrary and unfair.[83]

The terminology of rights, however, may be misleading where the resources necessary to honor these rights fully do not exist or have not been made available. Under such circumstances the related language of equal respect (especially in the context of equal needs) may be more precise. In these terms, an age criterion can be said to be disrespectful of the elderly as persons. In being excluded as a class from treatment, individual differences that would make some much better candidates for treatment than others are not recognized.[84] In the process of showing such disrespect to an entire group of people, society itself can become brutalized. Even under schemes where the focus of concern is not age *per se* but some related problem, such as distributing limited resources prudently throughout people's lifetimes, an important symbol may be at stake. Where the elderly are left to die with no access to lifesaving treatments that are available to others, people actually practice abandoning the elderly and in that sense exclude them from communal care. Although philosophical justifications might be offered, in such situations society's sense of responsibility for all of its members is irreparably damaged.[85]

These criticisms may lose some of their force where the resources in view are not at least potentially lifesaving. But where life is at stake, the same fundamental human need and thus rightful claim on available resources arguably comes into play.[86] In fact, should the elderly have some particular difficulty making use of needed resources, then need itself can be seen to dictate that special efforts be made to overcome these difficulties.[87] Most people do not regard special need — if it can be compensated for — as the basis for less care. So, for instance, where the elderly have found it difficult to withstand the immunosuppressive regimen employed with kidney transplants, a frequent response has been to try different immunosuppressive regimens on them until workable treatments have been found, rather than simply excluding them from consideration.[88]

Insights from the Christian Scriptures

Many arguments, then, can be marshalled both for and against the use of an age criterion in selecting recipients of vital but limited health-care resources. Where medical condition rather than age *per se* is really in view, there is not much controversy. (I will comment on that case later.) Where age *per se* is at issue, though, the weaknesses of the criterion are quite compelling. Since many of the justifications of the criterion are productivity-oriented, this conclusion should come as no surprise from a Christian perspective. As I have suggested elsewhere, a Christian ethical outlook rooted in the Christian Scriptures must give due place to producing human well-being, but this consideration is strictly limited by other more person-oriented concerns.[89] To be sure, some justifications of an age criterion are genuinely person-oriented. These too, however, are flawed in their own right, as well as brought into question by the overarching critiques just examined.

Such refutations and critiques are not irrelevant from a Christian perspective. They expose the internal problems of the justifications themselves. At the same time they bring those justifications into question on the basis of fundamental and widely shared ethical concerns. Yet, one may still wonder whether these concerns, commended by reason, are indeed in harmony with an explicitly Christian understanding of the world. The present brief reflections, focused upon the Christian Scriptures, can only be suggestive. The insights presented here are not unique to Christian ethics; many are, in fact, widely espoused. Moreover, they are by no means the only ethical considerations conceivably relevant from an explicitly Christian perspective. Far more than scriptural materials would have to be addressed in order to develop fully a Christian perspective. In fact, greater attention to the diverse nuances in the various scriptural writings would be necessary merely to convey a complete scriptural account. Yet because the scriptural themes identified here disclose deep and important truths about aging and about the nature of life itself, they are likely to be prominent among Christianity's contributions to the debate at hand — at least to the extent that Christianity reflects such basic perspectives recurring in its Scriptures as those noted here.

The Elderly

To begin with, who are the elderly? Two characteristics stand out at various points in the biblical writings. First, they are generally wise. "Is not wisdom found among the aged?" Job reminds. "Does not long life bring understanding?" (Job 12:12; cf. 15:10; 32:7). The elders (normally elderly) are therefore in the best positions to give good counsel (Deut. 32:7; 1 Kings 12:6ff.), and a family that has lost all of its elderly has been severely punished (1 Sam. 2:31). Wisdom is generally presented as a function of the life experience that only the elderly have; however, because it is also a product of righteousness and God's Spirit, it is possible occasionally for the young to have it (Job 32:8-9; Eccl. 4:13) and the old to lack it (Prov. 16:31; Job 12:20).

A second characteristic of many of the elderly — at least at some point — is weakness. Old age is acknowledged in the Scriptures as a time of suffering and vulnerability (Eccl. 12:2-5; 2 Sam. 19:35). Knowing that insensitive people take advantage of the weakness of the elderly, the psalmist prays, "Do not cast me away when I am old; do not forsake me when my strength is gone" (Ps. 71:9; cf. v. 18).

Both the wisdom and the weakness of the elderly call for appropriate Christian responses. An appropriate response to wisdom is respect. Evil people are sometimes characterized by their lack of respect for the elderly (Deut. 28:50; 2 Chron. 36:17; Isa. 47:6). It is an evil day when "the young will rise up against the old" (Isa. 3:5) — when elders are shown no respect (Lam. 5:12). Instead, "rise in the presence of the aged," says the Lord. "Show respect for the elderly and revere your

God" (Lev. 19:32). Such texts recognize that the monetary (economic) value of the young is greater than that of the old (Lev. 27:1-7), but that the way people are to be valued and treated has to do with more than economic worth. The elderly are to be respected for their wisdom — but also simply for who they are as elderly persons (Prov. 20:29). To be sure, this special value placed on the elderly is likely the same sort of culturally relative value found among the Akamba. As such, it calls into question intuitive (Western) preferences for the young rather than simply serving as a transcultural normative guideline.

An appropriate response to the relative weakness of the elderly, on the other hand, is protection. God is frequently portrayed in biblical writings as the protector of the weak (Exod. 22:22-27; Ps. 10:14, 35:10, 140:12; Acts 20:35; 1 Cor. 8:9-12; 2 Cor. 12:9-10), and God's people are challenged to be the same (Prov. 31:8-9; 1 Thess. 5:14). So it is not at all surprising to find God affirming: "Even to your old age and gray hairs I am he, I am he who will sustain you" (Isa. 46:4). God's identification with the plight of the helpless, therefore, has understandably been heralded as a theological cornerstone for treatment of today's elderly.[90]

From this perspective the elderly are as worthy of lifesaving care as anyone else. In fact, whether a particular culture values the wisdom of the elderly or not is ultimately beside the point. All persons are God's creation in God's own image (Gen. 1:27) and are the objects of God's sacrificial love in Christ (John 3:16). It is this basic equal worth of all that demands that all be respected and that the weak accordingly receive special protection.

If anything, the tendency of the elderly to be physically weak and separated from the power that accompanies culturally-recognized economic productivity makes them especially worthy of Christian concern. Their equal claim upon society's lifesaving resources needs to be protected. As noted earlier, even if theoretical justifications for excluding the elderly were not flawed in their own right, they would engage people in the practice of abandoning the elderly and in that sense excluding them from communal care. This would serve as a destructive precedent,[91] and would be a high social price to pay for a chance to promote some particular value (opportunity, prudence, etc.). If individual elderly persons volunteer to let younger persons have priority over them in the distribution of limited lifesaving resources, such volunteering may be an admirable expression of sacrificial love. To require such sacrifice, however, is to demean the elderly as a group and to take from them the opportunity to give.

Life

Just as the biblical materials cast light on who the elderly are, they also illumine the nature of life itself in a way relevant to the assessment of age criteria in health care. Two characteristics of life stand out in opposition to non-religious views of life. The first is that *life* is *spiritual*. Linked to God, life includes but transcends the material sphere. The spirituality of life contrasts with common views of life at several important points.

First, people tend to live by what they see — by sight rather than by faith. As a result, the elderly appear to be relatively unproductive and insignificant. However, if what matters is not economic achievement but, for example, righteous character and relationship with God, then the elderly can be as fruitful as anyone (Ps. 92:14; cf. 2 Cor. 4:16).

Second, people tend to categorize people in ways calculated to elevate themselves and put down others. A spiritual perspective looks beyond such worldly classifications as Jew vs. Greek or barbarian vs. Scythian and views all peoples as loved and sought by God (John 4:11; Matt. 28:19) and potentially one in Christ (1 Cor. 12:13; Gal. 3:28; Col. 3:11). From this perspective, efforts to classify certain people by age groups in order to exclude them from access to health care should at least be suspect. Moreover, those of us steeped in the youth-oriented values of North America need to be challenged by alternative values in other cultures. We cannot assume that our culture is gospel. It is possible for North Americans to move significantly in a person-oriented direction, I would submit, without swinging completely over to an indifference toward productivity, which may be destructive of persons in its extreme.

A third point at which a spiritual perspective on life contrasts with other common outlooks has to do with the sinfulness of the world. For some, the world is essentially good or must be presumed to be so if their idealistic proposals are to work.

According to the spiritual perspective of the Christian Scriptures, however, people, as well as the policies and institutions they establish, are less than God intends them to be because people are fundamentally self-oriented rather than God-and-other oriented (Ps. 14:2-3; Jer. 17:9; Rom. 3:10-12, 23). While it is possible to turn from self-centeredness to God and others, experience and the Scriptures alike testify that the majority of people will never do so (Matt. 7:13-14; Luke 13:23-24). That being the case, social strategies are needed that take this reality into account and seek to promote the best possible policies in light of it. Good intentions and commitment to laudable concerns such as equal opportunity, a natural life span, or prudence are not enough. Proposals advocating age criteria that would be immoral if implemented "in our present world" may be misleading and even dangerous if they require the imminent arrival of a world much different from the world we actually have.

The second special characteristic of life often acknowledged in the Christian Scriptures is that *life is eternal.* Again, this characteristic of life contrasts with common views of life at several important points.

First, people tend to view temporal life as all there is, such that maximizing one's length of life becomes a matter of ultimate importance. Where an "afterlife" is acknowledged it is often viewed as something subsequent to "this life" and thoroughly different from it in nature. The perspective of some biblical writers adds a further insight. While some writers do focus upon the future dimension of eternal life, others add the conviction that eternal life does not begin later but now. A person who believes in God "has eternal life" already and "has crossed over from death to life" (John 5:24; cf. 1 John 3:14). In this perspective, physical death is not nearly so significant a transition as it is commonly considered to be. As sleep is merely a transition from one day to the next, so death may be simply referred to as "being asleep" (1 Cor. 15:6, 18, 20, 51). To be able to sleep and so go to be with Christ is actually "better by far" than living long (Phil. 1:23). In other words, if the good of a person is at issue, access to a long life pales in significance compared with access to an eternal life. (The lives of those who do not choose life with God also apparently continue eternally — albeit separated from God in accordance with their choice [Matt. 8:11-12; 25:46; Luke 14:15-24; 16:26, 31]).

There is a second way in which an eternal perspective on life minimizes the significance of attempts to lengthen life. In the face of eternity, a lifetime is but a few hours (Ps. 90:4, cf. 2 Pet. 3:8) — a momentary breath (Ps. 39:5; cf. James 4:14) — a fleeting shadow (Job 14:1-2; Ps. 144:4; Eccl. 6;12). To extend life by years, in a sense, is ultimately just to extend it by a few seconds. The two aspects of an eternal perspective noted so far are not direct arguments against the use of age criteria in health care. However, they do tend to neutralize the strong tendency to idolize length of life, and they provide a better frame of reference for considering the other numerous arguments against age criteria.

The final implication of an eternal perspective is closely related to the second but is somewhat more directive. Given its brevity in the face of eternity, temporal life may end at any moment. When one least expects it, the end may be at hand (Luke 12:16-20; I Thess. 5:1-4). Accordingly, ethical living in the present is crucial (Rom. 13:8-12). The point here is not that planning for the future is unnecessary but that immediate needs that can in fact be met must be attended to with special seriousness. Health care has traditionally reflected this perspective by directing the major portion of available resources (preventively and therapeutically) to present needs that can demonstrably be met, while at the same time devoting significant resources to research for the future.

In this light it may well be appropriate to emphasize diseases of the young when allocating research funds, for a variety of future-oriented ends are appropriately pursued in research. However, excluding the elderly from receiving specified health care resources in order to improve the life prospects of the young is a different matter. It morally compromises our capacity to meet definite medical needs, and it does so by making decisions about who receives care subordinate to the pursuit of other goods. In the biblical writings, a full life span may be understood as a good given by God, as is food, water, etc. (e.g. Exod. 23:25-26). Using patient selection to pursue any such goods is fundamentally a utilitarian (or misplaced egalitarian) endeavor that dilutes health care's commitment to respond to medical need.

A Way Forward

There are strong and varied reasons, then, to reject an age criterion which is essentially non-medical in nature. However, many of those who favor an age criterion do so for medical reasons. They are concerned in particular that critical resources should not be wasted if the elderly cannot benefit from them. Opponents of an age criterion share this concern.

The challenge is to find a more adequate way to respond to this concern. Perhaps the best way is to be careful about how language is used and to identify as "medical" all matters and criteria that are in fact medical. As noted earlier, age *per se* is not a medically relevant factor in that medical problems which make one elderly person a bad candidate may not affect another. Even a short life expectancy for any given elderly person cannot be taken for granted.[92] For this reason age is probably best not referred to as a medical criterion or supported as a criterion on those grounds.[93] The medical liabilities commonly associated with old age are themselves the potential reasons for exclusion — not age itself. Many elderly, for example, are so physically weakened that they make poor candidates for organ transplantation or intensive care; but others bear up fairly well in these circumstances.[94] In fact, studies show that many elderly do well even with dialysis, from which they are so often excluded.[95]

Accordingly, age is best not identified as a separate patient selection criterion at all. Rather, its most widely acceptable role is probably as one of many "symptoms" to be looked for by the physician making the medical assessment required by a medical-benefit criterion. Age constitutes a symptom in this sense whenever elderly persons do not tend (statistically) to receive significant medical benefit from the treatment in question. Just as any observed symptom can be an indicator of a possible medical problem, so can age. It may serve as a tool the physician uses in applying a medical criterion, not as a criterion in its own right. From this perspective it is inappropriate to single out age during a discussion of selection criteria because age is only one among many symptoms considered in the medical assessment. It is more a rule of thumb for this assessment than for patient selection in general.[96]

Even in such a restricted role, age considerations must be carefully handled to insure that they are not accorded more influence than is warranted medically. It is easy enough to underestimate the ability of some elderly to endure treatment when life is at stake; and technological developments repeatedly make treatments of all more endurable.[97] In the end, it may well be that the only way to know with confidence how well the elderly will bear up under a given treatment is to treat them in large numbers, as was done during the early days of dialysis in Italy.[98] Where possible in particular cases, a therapeutic trial can be employed to facilitate more individualized assessment.

The issues raised by the conversation depicted at the beginning of this essay can now be better appreciated. Some of the arguments in support of an age criterion appeal to considerations of social value, over which there is little agreement ("his contributions to the community are history. . . ."). Others appeal to a more egalitarian perspective (equality of opportunity) that is itself controversial even among egalitarians. The best hope for an ethically sound, broadly supportable inclusion of age-related considerations, as we have seen, lies in the medical arena.[99]

But the common form in which the medical justifications arise in this case is misleading. It is not the man's age that might hamper his treatments, as implied here; rather, it is the kind of physical limitations to which a man of fifty-three is prone. The difference is important. Were age *per se* a selection criterion, then a younger candidate could rightfully be preferred on the spot. If age is only a symptom, though, then the man's age should only serve as a reminder that a careful medical assessment is needed. If exclusion turns out to be medically warranted, then it should be justified solely upon medical grounds, without appeal to age considerations.

Notes

1. Adapted from Ronald Munson, *Intervention and Reflection*, 2nd ed. (Belmont, Calif.: Wadsworth, 1983), 476. The author and *The Annual* are grateful to Wadsworth Publishing Company for granting us permission to print this adaptation.

2. John F. Kilner, "Selecting Patients When Resources Are Limited: A Study of U.S. Medical Directors of Kidney Dialysis and Kidney Transplant Facilities," *American Journal of Public Health* 78 (February 1988): 144-47; Pacific Presbyterian Medical Center, "Who Lives, Who Dies, Who Decides? — National Poll Results" (San Francisco: Pac. Presb. Med. Ctr., January 20, 1987), 1-2; *National Kidney Dialysis and Kidney Transplantation Study* (Seattle: Battelle Human Affairs Research Centers, 1986), ch. 2, p. 17; Roger W. Evans et al., "National Policies for the Treatment of End-Stage Renal Disease" (Seattle: Battelle Human Affairs Research Centers, 1984), 6, 12; S. Challah et al., "Negative Selection of Patients for Dialysis and Transplantation in the United Kingdom," *British Medical Journal* 288 (April 14, 1984): 1120; Roger W. Evans, "Health Care Technology and the Inevitability of Resource Allocation and Rationing Decisions" (2 parts), *Journal of the American Medical Association* 249 (April 15 and 22/29, 1983): 2209.

3. Timothy M. Smeeding, "Artificial Organs, Transplants and Long-Term Care for the Elderly: What's Covered? Who Pays?," in *Should Medical Care Be Rationed by Age?*, ed. Timothy M. Smeeding (Totowa, N.J.: Rowman & Littlefield, 1987), 143; William A. Knaus et al., "The Use of Intensive Care: New Research Initiatives and Their Implications for National Health Policy," *Millbank Memorial Fund Quarterly/Health and Society* 61 (Fall 1983): 574; Gerald R. Winslow, *Triage and Justice* (Berkeley: University of California Press, 1982), 67; Marc D. Basson, "Choosing Among Candidates for Scarce Medical Resources," *The Journal of Medicine and Philosophy* 4 (September 1979): 324-25; Harry Moody, "Is It Right to Allocate Health Care Resources on Grounds of Age?" *Bioethics and Human Rights*, ed. Elsie L. Bandman and Bertram Bandman (Boston: Little, Brown and Co., 1978), 199-200.

4. Nicholas Rescher, "The Allocation of Exotic Medical Lifesaving Therapy," *Ethics* 79 (1969): 178-79; Robert Young, "Some Criteria for Making Decisions Concerning the Distribution of Scarce Medical Resources," *Theory and Decision* 6 (November 1975): 447; John Lachs, "Questions of Life and Death," *Wall Street Journal*, March 31, 1976, p. 8; David S. David, "The Agony and the Ecstacy of the Nephrologist," *Journal of the American Medical Association* 222 (1972): 584.

5. C. R. Stiller, "Ethics of Transplantation," *Transplantation Proceedings* 17, no. 6, suppl. 3 (December 1985): 135; Rescher, 182; Young, 448.

6. David H. Taube et al., "Successful Treatment of Middle Aged and Elderly Patients with End-Stage Renal Disease," *British Medical Journal* 286 (June 25, 1983): 2020; Albert R. Jonsen et al., *Clinical Ethics* (New York: Macmillan, 1982), 31; Paul Freund, "Introduction" *Daedalus* 98 (Spring 1969): xiii.

7. Michael Waldholz, "Cost of Using Kidney Device Sparks Debate," *Wall Street Journal*, February 5, 1981, p. 32.

8. Harry Schwartz, cited in Glenn Richards, "Technology Costs and Rationing Issues," *Hospitals* 58 (June 1, 1984): 81.

9. Daniel Callahan, *Setting Limits: Medical Goals in an Aging Society* (New York: Simon and Schuster, 1987), 65ff; E. Lovell Becker, "Finite Resources and Medical Triage," *American Journal of Medicine* 66 (April 1979): 550.

10. Norman Daniels, *Just Health Care* (London: Cambridge University Press, 1985), 96-7; David Thomasma, cited in Jeff Lyon, "Organ Transplants: Conundra Without End," *Second Opinion* 2 (March 1986): 59.

11. Robert M. Veatch, "Justice and Valuing Lives," in *Life Span*, ed. Robert M. Veatch (San Francisco: Harper & Row, 1979), 218; Veatch, "Ethical Foundations for Valuing Lives: Implications for Life-Extending Technologies," in *A Technology Assessment of Life-Extending Technologies*, Supplementary Report, vol. 6 (Glastonbury, Conn.: The Futures Group, 1977), 232; The Hastings Center Research Group, "Values and Life-Extending Technologies," in *Life Span*, 54-6, 82; Phil Bundy, "Media-Abetted Liver Transplants Raise Questions of 'Equity and Decency,'" *Journal of the American Medical Association* 249 (April 15, 1983): 1982.

12. Paul T. Menzel, *Medical Costs, Moral Choices* (New Haven, Conn.: Yale University Press, 1983), 191.

13. Callahan, 137ff.

14. Jonathan Glover, *Causing Death and Saving Lives* (New York: Penguin Books, 1977), 220; Menzel, 191.

15. Norman Daniels, "Am I My Parents' Keeper?," in *Securing Access to Health Care*, vol. 2, ed. President's Commission for the Study of Ethical Problems in Medicine and Biomedical and Behavioral Research (Washington, D.C.: Government Printing Office, March 1983); Daniels, "Is Age-Rationing Just?" (Paper delivered at the Pacific Section of the American Philosophical Association, San Francisco, March 1986), 16-18; Daniels, *Am I My Parents' Keeper? An Essay on Justice Between the Young and Old* (New York: Oxford University Press, 1988), ch. 5; Robert M. Veatch, "From Fae to Schroeder: The Ethics of Allocating High Technology," *Spectrum* 16 (April 1985): 17-18; Veatch, "Distributive Justice and the

Allocation of Technological Resources to the Elderly," Contract report prepared for the Office of Technology Assessment, U.S. Congress, Washington, D.C. (December 1985), 77.

16. National Heart Transplantation Study (Seattle: Battelle Human Affairs Research Centers, 1984), ch. 38, p. 26; Daniels, *Am I My Parents' Keeper? An Essay,* 8-9; cf. Callahan, 148ff.

17. Margaret P. Battin, "Age Rationing and the Just Distribution of Health Care: Is There a Duty to Die?," *Ethics* 97 (January 1987): 324ff.

18. Daniels, "Is Age-Rationing Just?," 19-20; Daniels, *Just Health Care,* 96-97.

19. National Heart, ch. 44, p. 30; James F. Childress, "Who Shall Live When Not All Can Live?," *Soundings* 53 (Winter 1970): 343.

20. Arthur L. Caplan, "Obtaining and Allocating Organs for Transplantation," in *Human Organ Transplantation,* ed. Dale H. Corvan et al. (Ann Arbor, Mich.: Health Administration Press, 1987), 13-14; James F. Childress, "Ensuring Care, Respect, and Fairness for the Elderly," *Hastings Center Report* 14 (October 1984): 29; William B. Schwartz and Henry J. Aaron, "Rationing Hospital Care: Lessons from Britain," *New England Journal of Medicine* 310 (January 5, 1984): 54; Henry J. Aaron and William B. Schwartz, *The Painful Prescription: Rationing Hospital Care* (Washington, D.C.: Brookings Institution, 1984), 101.

21. Aaron and Schwartz, *Painful Prescription,* 35.

22. Anthony Wing, in Annabel Ferriman, "1000 Kidney Patients Die 'Because Treatment Unavailable,'" *London Times,* March 20, 1980, p. 4.

23. J. D. Swales, "Medical Ethics: Some Reservations," *Journal of Medical Ethics* 8 (September 1982): 117-18; Schwartz and Aaron, "Rationing Hospital Care," 54.

24. Caplan, "Obtaining and Allocating," 6-7.

25. Guido Calabresi and Philip Bobbitt, *Tragic Choices* (New York: W. W. Norton & Co., 1978), 185.

26. Mark Siegler, "Should Age Be a Criterion in Health Care?," *Hastings Center Report* 14 (October 1984): 27.

27. James Stacey, "Name of 'New Game': Allocation of Resources," *American Medical News,* January 7, 1983, p. 7.

28. Office of Technology Assessment, U.S. Congress, *Life-Sustaining Technologies and the Elderly,* OTA-BA-306 (Washington, D.C.: U.S. Government Printing Office, 1987), 159; Hastings Center, *Guidelines on the Termination of Life-Sustaining Treatment and the Care of the Dying* (Briarcliff Manor, N.Y.: Hastings Center, 1987), 135.

29. Nora K. Bell, *Ethical Considerations in the Allocation of Scarce Medical Resources* (Ph.D. dissertation, University of North Carolina at Chapel Hill, 1978), 69.

30. Helmut Thielicke, "The Doctor as Judge of Who Shall Live and Who Shall Die," in *Who Shall Live?,* ed. Kenneth Vaux (Philadelphia: Fortress Press, 1970), 172; Office of Technology Assessment, 158-59.

31. Bell, *Ethical Considerations in the Allocation,* 71.

32. "Scarce Medical Resources," *Columbia Law Review* 69 (April 1969): 665.

33. Veatch, "Distributive Justice," 43; Veatch, *The Foundations of Justice* (New York: Oxford University Press, 1986), 146.

34. Leslie P. Francis, "Poverty, Age Discrimination, and Health Care," in *Poverty, Justice and the Law,* ed. George R. Lucas (Lanham, Md.: University Press of America, 1986), 121.

35. Daniels, "Is Age-Rationing Just?," 17; Francis, 127.

36. Callahan, 197-98.

37. Ibid., 66, 172.

38. Daniels, *Am I My Parents' Keeper? An Essay,* 59ff.

39. Callahan, 184-85.

40. Francis, 121.

41. Daniels, *Just Health Care,* 111; Daniels, *Am I My Parents' Keeper? An Essay,* 96; Battin, 340.

42. Daniels, *Am I My Parents' Keeper? An Essay,* 97; cf. Daniel Wikler, "Comments on Battin's 'Age Rationing,'" in *Should Medical Care Be Rationed by Age?,* ed. Timothy M. Smeeding (Totowa, N.J.: Rowman & Littlefield, 1987), 98.

43. Daniels, "Am I My Parents' Keeper?," 289-91; Daniels, *Just Health Care,* 113; Daniels, *Am I My Parents' Keeper? An Essay,* 96; Battin, 340.

44. Battin, 340.

45. Francis, 124.

46. Daniels (*Just Health Care,* 99) admits the possibility of this problem. Cf. Office of Technology Assessment, 159; Veatch, "Distributive Justice," 21, 48.

47. Veatch, "Distributive Justice," 56.

48. Daniels, *Am I My Parents' Keeper? An Essay,* 129.

49. Childress, "Ensuring Care," 29; contra generalization in Daniels, *Am I My Parents' Keeper? An Essay,* 129.

50. Callahan, 194.

51. Battin, 337.

52. Wikler, 96-97.

53. Working Group on Mechanical Circulatory Support of the National Heart, Lung and Blood Institute, *Artificial Heart and Assist Devices: Directions, Needs,*

Costs, Societal and Ethical Issues (Bethesda, Md.: National Institutes of Health, 1985), 26; Swales, 117-18; Phillip G. Clark, "The Social Allocation of Health Care Resources: Ethical Dilemmas in Age-Group Competition," *The Gerontologist* 25 (April 1985): 121; Jay Katz and Alexander M. Capron, *Catastrophic Disease: Who Decides What?* (New York: Russell Sage Foundation, 1975), 192. In the early Seattle hemodialysis days, age was considered at the second stage by the social committee rather than at the first stage by the medical committee; see Shana Alexander, "They Decide Who Lives, Who Dies," *Life* 53 (November 9, 1962): 106.

54. Louis Lasagna, "Physicians' Behavior Toward the Dying Patient," in *The Dying Patient,* ed. Orville B. Brim, Jr. et al. (New York: Russell Sage Foundation, 1970), 83; Clark, 122.

55. A. A. Scitovsky and A. M. Capron, "Medical Care at the End of Life: The Interaction of Economics and Ethics," *Annual Review of Public Health* 7 (1986): 72-73; William D. Spector and Vincent Mor, "Utilization and Charges for Terminal Cancer Patients in Rhode Island," *Inquiry* 21 (Winter 1984): 332-34; James Lubitz and Ronald Prihoda, "The Use and Costs of Medicare Services in the Last Two Years of Life," *Health Care Financing Review* 5 (Spring 1984): 117-31; David Hilfiker, "Allowing the Debilitated to Die: Facing Our Ethical Choices," *New England Journal of Medicine* 308 (March 24, 1983): 717; Diana Crane, *The Sanctity of Social Life: Physicians' Treatment of Critically Ill Patients* (New Brunswick, N.J.: Transaction Books, 1977), 58-61; Crane, "Decisions to Treat Critically Ill Patients: A Comparison of Social Versus Medical Considerations," in *Law and Ethics in Health Care,* ed. John B. McKinlay (Cambridge, Mass.: MIT Press, 1982), 392.

56. J. Wesley Robb, "The Allocation of Limited Medical Resources: An Ethical Perspective," *Pharos* 44 (Spring 1981): 29; John Sadler, cited in Gina B. Kolata, "Dialysis after Nearly a Decade," *Science* 208 (May 2, 1980): 473.

57. Jerry Avorn, "Benefit and Cost Analysis in Geriatric Care: Turning Age Discrimination into Health Policy," *New England Journal of Medicine* 310 (May 17, 1984); Daniels, "Is Age-Rationing Just?," 19-20; Roger Evans, cited in Dee J. Canale et al., "Panel Discussion," *Life and Death Issues,* ed. James Hammer III and Barbara Jacobs (Memphis: University of Tennessee, 1986), 49-50.

58. J. Gordon Harris, *God and the Elderly* (Philadelphia: Fortress, 1987), 110; Clark, 122; Nancy Foner, "Old and Frail and Everywhere Unequal," *Hastings Center Report* 15 (April 1985), 27-31; David J. Maitland, *Aging: A Time for New Learning* (Atlanta: John Knox, 1987), 2ff.

59. Terrie T. Wetle, "Ethical Aspects of Decision Making for and with the Elderly," in *Legal and Ethical Aspects of Health Care for the Elderly,* ed. Marshall B. Kapp et al. (Ann Arbor, Mich.: Health Administration Press, 1985), 263; Crane, *The Sanctity,* 60; cf. Christine K. Cassel, "Health Care for the Elderly: Meeting the Challenges," in *Legal and Ethical Aspects of Health Care,* 9.

60. John G. Francis and Leslie P. Francis, "Rationing of Health Care in Britain: An Ethical Critique of Public Policy-making," in *Should Medical Care Be Rationed By Age?,* ed. Timothy M. Smeeding (Totowa, N.J.: Rowman & Littlefield, 1987), 129; Lu Ann Aday and Romand M. Andersen, "Equity and Access to Medical Care: A Conceptual and Empirical Overview," *Medical Care* 19 (December 1981 Suppl.): 9; National Heart, ch. 36, p. 33; "Human Rights and Scientific and Technological Developments," United Nations 30th Session, Item 70 of the Provisional Agenda (July 28, 1975), 32; "Patient Selection for Artificial and Transplanted Organs," *Harvard Law Review* 82 (April 1969): 1330; "Scarce Medical Resources," 658-9.

61. Daniels, *Am I My Parents' Keeper? An Essay,* 145-46.

62. Ira Greifer, "Triage: From Departments to Patients," *Mount Sinai Journal of Medicine* 51 (January-February 1984): 111.

63. Kivuto Ndeti, *Elements of Akamba Life* (Nairobi: East Africa Publishing House, 1972), 104.

64. W. T. W. Morgan, "Kikuyu and Kamba: The Tribal Background," in *Nairobi: City and Region,* ed. W. T. W. Morgan (Nairobi: Oxford University Press, 1967), 65; Robert B. Edgerton, "An Ecological View of Witchcraft in 4 East African Societies," paper prepared for the Neuropsychiatric Institute, University of California, Los Angeles (1965): 4-5; Exposition Press, 1973), 74; Kivuto Ndeti, "The Role of Akamba Kithitu in Questions of Human Justice," *Proceedings of the Fifth Annual Conference* (University of East Africa, Social Science Council, Nairobi, 1969), 1186; John Middleton and Greet Kershaw, *The Central Tribes of the North-Eastern Bantu* (*The Kikuyu . . . and the Kamba*), rev. ed. (London: International African Institute, 1965), 72.

65. John F. Kilner, "Who Shall Be Saved? An African Answer," *Hastings Center Report* 14 (June 1984): 18-22.

66. Ibid. The expressions here are taken from the author's interviews with Kiua Mulela (Muvuti Location) and Esther Nthenya (Mbiuni Location).

67. Howard Brody, *Ethical Decisions in Medicine*, 2nd ed. (Boston: Little, Brown & Co., 1981), 225; Jerome B. Hallan and Benjamin S. H. Harris, "Estimation of a Potential Hemodialysis Population," *Medical Care* 8 (May-June 1970): 212; Al Katz, "Process Design for Selection of Hemodialysis and Organ Transplant Recipients," *Buffalo Law Review* 22 (1973): 418; Ramon Velez et al. "Treatment of End-Stage Renal Disease," *New England Journal of Medicine* 304 (February 5, 1981): 356.

68. Gerald Perkoff et al., "Decisions Regarding the Provision or Withholding of Therapy," *American Journal of Medicine* 61 (1976): 918.

69. John L. Horn, "Comments on Gillund's 'Memory Processes in the Aged,'" in *Should Medical Care Be Rationed by Age?*, ed. Timothy M. Smeeding (Totowa, N.J.: Rowman & Littlefield, 1987), 62-67; G. M. Berlyne, "Over 50 and Uraemic = Death," *Nephron* 31 (1982): 189.

70. Office of Technology Assessment, 1957; Maitland, ch. 3; Harris, 110; Veatch, "Distributive Justice," 40; Cassel, 8; Susan Porter, "Ethics and the Elderly — Care at What Cost?" *The Ohio State Medical Journal* 81 (June 1985): 406.

71. William F. May, "The Virtues and Vices of the Elderly," in *What Does It Mean to Grow Old?*, ed. Thomas R. Cole and Sally A. Gadow (Durham: Duke University, 1986), 51-61; Joseph A. Califano, Jr., *America's Health Care Revolution: Who Lives? Who Dies? Who Pays?* (New York: Random House, 1986), 175.

72. Renee C. Fox and Judith P. Swazey, *The Courage to Fail*, 2nd ed. (Chicago: University of Chicago Press, 1978), 238.

73. Gary Gillund, "Memory Processes in the Aged," in *Should Medical Care Be Rationed by Age?* ed. Timothy M. Smeeding (Totowa, N.J.: Rowman & Littlefield, 1987); Horn, 61-68.

74. Paul Ramsey, *Ethics at the Edges of Life* (New Haven: Yale University Press, 1978), xii-xiii; Ramsey, *The Patient as Person* (New Haven: Yale University Press, 1970), 258-59; Tom L. Beauchamp and James F. Childress, *Principles of Biomedical Ethics* (Oxford: Oxford University Press, 1979), 196; Office of Technology Assessment, 154-55; Callahan, 116.

75. E.g., by Battin, 335.

76. H. J. J. Leenen, "Selection of Patients," *Journal of Medical Ethics* 8 (March 1982): 34; Margaret A. Somerville, "Ethics and the Nephrologist," *Lancet* 1 (May 16, 1981): 1110; Eugene D. Robin, "Rapid Scientific Advances Bring New Ethical Questions," *Journal of the American Medical Association* 189 (August 24, 1964): 624.

77. Berlyne, 189; David M. Roxe, "Is Patient Rationing in Our Future? Hidden Issues," *Dialysis and Transplantation* 12 (December 1983): 832.

78. Battin, 336.

79. Calabresi and Bobbitt, 184-5; "Scarce Medical Resources," 620-92.

80. Norman G. Levinsky, "The Doctor's Master," *New England Journal of Medicine* 311 (December 13, 1984): 1574; Hastings Center, *Guidelines*, 136; Arthur L. Caplan, "Equity in the Selection of Recipients for Cardiac Transplants," *Circulation* 75 (January 1987): 16; Leenen, "Selection of Patients," 34; H. J. J. Leenen, "The Selection of Patients in the Event of a Scarcity of Medical Facilities — An Unavoidable Dilemma," *International Journal of Medicine and Law* 12 (Fall 1979): 169; Nora K. Bell, "Triage in Medical Practices: An Unacceptable Model?" *Social Science and Medicine* 15F (December 1981): 155.

81. Catherine Lyons, *Organ Transplants: The Moral Issues* (Philadelphia: Westminster Press, 1970), 96.

82. Norman Levinsky, cited in Timothy Johnson et al., "Medical Miracles: Can We Afford the Bill?" ABC News Nightline (August 29, 1985).

83. J. S. Murray et al., "A Community Hemodialysis Center for the Treatment of Chronic Uremia," *Transactions of the American Society for Artificial Internal Organs* 8 (1962): 316; Charles P. Hayes and J. Caulie Gunnells, Jr., "Selection of Recipients and Donors for Renal Transplantation," *Archives of Internal Medicine* 123 (May 1969): 522; Ramsey, *The Patient*, 244; Beauchamp and Childress, 193-94; Young, 445; Ramsey, *The Patient*, 252.

84. Massachusetts Task Force on Organ Transplantation, *Report* (Boston: Boston University Schools of Public Health and Medicine, October 1984), 78; George J. Annas, "The Prostitute, the Playboy, and the Poet: Rationing Schemes for Organ Transplantation," *American Journal of Public Health* 75 (February 1985): 188; Horn, 63-66; Veatch, "Distributive Justice," 50-51; Childress, "Ensuring Care," 28; Robert H. Binstock, "The Aged as Scapegoat," *The Gerontologist* 23 (April 1983): 136-43; Carol D. Austin and Martin B. Loeb, "Why Age is Relevant in Social Policy and Practice," in *Age or Need?*, ed. Bernice I. Neugarten (Beverly Hills: Sage, 1982), 264-65.

85. Calabresi and Bobbitt, 39; Childress, "Ensuring Care," 29. (Cf. Maitland on the importance of symbols in shaping the way the elderly are treated in society.)

86. H. E. De Wardener, "Some Ethical and Economic Problems Associated with Intermittent Haemodialysis," in *Ethics in Medical Progress: With Special Reference to*

Transplantation, ed. G. F. W. Wolstenholme (Boston: Little, Brown and Co., 1966), 108.

87. Katz, 415.

88. D. E. R. Sutherland et al., "The High-Risk Recipient in Transplantation," *Transplantation Proceedings* 14 (March 1982): 24-25.

89. John F. Kilner, "A Pauline Approach to Ethical Decision Making," *Interpretation* 43 (October, 1989).

90. Harris, 108.

91. James F. Childress, "Artificial and Transplanted Organs," in *Biolaw,* vol. 1, ed. James F. Childress et al. (Frederick, Md.: University Publications of America, 1986), 318; "Task Force on Transplantation," *Organ Transplantation: Issues and Recommendations* (Rockville, Md.: U.S. Dept. of Health and Human Services, 1986), 90.

92. Perkoff et al., 917; George J. Annas, "Allocation of Artificial Hearts in the Year 2002: Minerva v. National Health Agency," *American Journal of Law and Medicine* 3 (Spring 1977): 72-73.

93. Leenen, "Selection of Patients," 34; Leenen, "The Selection of Patients in the Event," 169; National Heart, ch. 9, pp. 2-3; James F. Childress, *Priorities in Medical Ethics* (Philadelphia: Westminster Press, 1981), 92.

94. Roger W. Evans and Junichi Yagi, "Social and Medical Considerations Affecting Selection of Transplant Recipients: The Case of Heart Transplantation," in *Human Organ Transplantation,* ed. Dale H. Cowan et al. (Ann Arbor, Mich.: Health Administration Press, 1987), 29; National Heart, ch. 36, p. 34; Callahan, 126; Albert G. Mulley, "The Allocation of Resources for Medical Intensive Care," in *Securing Access to Health Care,* vol. 3, ed. President's Commission for the Study of Ethical Problems in Medicine and Biomedical and Behavioral Research (Washington, D.C.: U.S. Government Printing Office, March 1983), 304; G. E. Thibault et al., "Physicians' Ability to Predict Outcome of Medical Intensive Care," *Clinical Research* 28 (1980): 301A.

95. European Dialysis Transplantation Association, *Annual Report* (London: Pitman Medical, 1981); Alexander C. Chester et al., "Hemodialysis in the 8th and 9th Decades of Life," *Archives of Internal Medicine* 139 (1979): 1001-5; Tom A. Hutchinson et al., "Predicting Survival in Adults with End-Stage Renal Disease: An Age Equivalence Index," *Annals of Internal Medicine* 139 (April 1982): 417-23; John M. Weller et al., "Analysis of Survival of End-Stage Renal Disease Patients," *Kidney International* 21 (January 1982): 78-83; Taube, 2018-20. Cf. Swales, 117-18; Martin S. Knapp, "Renal Failure — Dilemmas and Developments," *British Medical Journal* 284 (March 20, 1982): 847; Arthur L. Caplan, "The Selection of Patients for Dialytic Therapy — Should Treatment Be Left to Chance?" *Dialysis and Transplantation* 13 (March 1984): 158; Rodney Deitch, "UK's Poor Record in Treatment of Renal Failure," *Lancet* 2 (July 7, 1984): 53; Richard M. Freeman, cited in Waldholz, 23.

96. Cf. Task Force, 90; James F. Childress, "The Scarcity of Human Organs for Transplantation: Charity, Justice, and Public Policy" (Paper presented at a colloquium at The Wilson Center, July 9, 1985), 22.

97. E. Bergsten et al., "A Study of Patients on Hemodialysis," *Scandinavian Journal of Social Medicine* 11 (suppl. 1977): 8; Victor Parsons, "The Ethical Challenges of Dialysis and Transplantation," *Practitioner* 220 (June 1978): 873; Hayes and Gunnells, 521-30.

98. Calabresi and Bobbitt, 230.

99. Even supporters of a non-medical age criterion such as Callahan (p. 139) admit that a consensus seems to be emerging against it.

127 A Pathology of Medical Ethics: Economic Medical Rationing in a Morally Incoherent Society

L. Gregory Jones

In Kurt Vonnegut's *God Bless You, Mr. Rosewater,* one of the main characters is a writer. And in one of his science fiction novels, he looked into the future to an "America in which almost all of the work was done by machines, and the only people who could get work had three or more Ph.D.'s. There was a serious overpopulation problem, too. All serious diseases had been conquered. So death was voluntary, and the government, to encourage volunteers for death, set up a purple-roofed Ethical Suicide Parlor at every major intersection, right next door to an orange-roofed Howard Johnson's. There were pretty hostesses in the parlor, and Barca-Loungers, and Muzak, and a choice of 14 painless ways to die. The suicide parlors were busy places, because so many people felt silly and pointless, and because it was supposed to be an unselfish, patriotic thing to do, to die. The suicides also got free last meals next door. And so on . . . One of the characters asked a death stewardess if he would go to heaven, and she told him that of course he would. He asked if he would see God, and she said, 'Certainly, honey.' And he said, 'I sure hope so. I want to ask Him something I was never able to find out down here.' 'What's that?' she said, strapping him in. 'What in hell are people for?'"[1]

Such a story undoubtedly appears to be an odd way to begin a essay on "The Effects of Economic Medical Rationing on Ethical Problems in Medicine." After all, shouldn't such a topic focus on questions of DRGs and Medicare/Medicaid and malpractice litigation and catastrophic care coverage and non-profit versus profit hospitals and the like? I do not mean to deny the importance or relevance of dealing with such questions, and my essay will touch on some of them at least tangentially. But the issues of economics and medicine, particularly as they focus on contemporary moves toward containment and rationing, are bound up in a rather bewildering maze of statistics, studies, arguments and counter-arguments, such that it is often difficult to know where to begin.

It is not possible in one essay to begin to sort out all of the empirical data or even to evaluate policy recommendations. But even if it were possible, I'm not sure how useful it would be. For I think that the real problems and issues lie deeper than questions of empirical data and public policy. Indeed I think the contemporary debate about economic medical rationing reveals a deeper and more fundamental set of questions than we often assume.

That is to say, I think that one of the reasons economic medical rationing seems to present such intractable problems in our society is that we have no real way of addressing the question "What in hell are people for?" For example, Michael Ignatieff contends that "We have created a new need, the need to live an examined life; we pursue its satisfaction in the full babble of conflicting opinions about what life is for, and we pursue it in a collectively held silence about the meaning of death."[2]

Three Sets of Issues

In what follows, I want to identify rather briefly three sets of issues which indicate why our society's failure to deal with "what people are for" has made not only the practice of medicine, but also medical ethics, problematic. At the end, I want to suggest how we — at least those of us who presume to be followers of Jesus Christ — might

From *The Linacre Quarterly* 57, no. 2 (March 1990): 59-67. Used by permission.

begin to envision an alternative way of thinking and acting. I do not have any grand solutions, or even the outline of one, but I hope that identifying the problems can help us get a clearer grasp of the issues.

The first set of issues surrounds the difficult time our society has in dealing with issues at the beginning and at the end of life. We don't seem to have a great deal of difficulty thinking about issues "between the 20-year lines" of life; most of our bioethical attention is centered on questions of birth (e.g., abortion, genetic engineering, in vitro fertilization) and death (e.g., euthanasia, definitions of brain death, withdrawal of food and water). What makes those issues so seemingly unresolvable is that, as a culture, we are unsure "what people are for." In the absence of attention to that question, it is difficult to know how and/or what we should think and do about the beginnings and endings of life.

The trouble is that, with the advances in technology which we have seen in this century — advances that have (at least for the most part) resulted in improvements in health and the lessening of suffering — it has become increasingly possible to keep people alive. We have often presumed that one of the primary goals of medicine ought to be to prolong life. But if we do not know *why* we are doing so, and/or if we do not have means of understanding *when* we perhaps ought not to do so, then we run the risk of watching the costs of technology spiral out of control. That is true in general, and it is even more true given the increasing number of elderly in our society.

Indeed that is the concern of Daniel Callahan, director of The Hastings Center and author of the widely-discussed *Setting Limits*.[3] Callahan rightly insists that "medical need" is not a fixed concept but a "function of technological possibility and regnant social expectations."[4] In a death-defying and death-denying culture such as ours, that is a recipe for disaster. In response, Callahan's argument is two-pronged. On the one hand, he wants to develop a social vision of the aged in which they have a recognized and valued status such that we are willing to accept increased moral and financial obligations for their welfare. On the other hand, he wants us to develop a sense of a "natural span of life" as a means of rationing our medical resources. Beyond a certain point, for Callahan around 75-80 years, we ought to say that a person has lived a full life. Hence that person ought not to have a claim on technological interventions designed simply to prolong life.

Points Worth Noting

This is not the place to go into analysis of Callahan's proposal in detail, but three points are worth noting about the structure of his argument. First, his diagnosis is important. The elderly are placing increasing demands on medical resources, and we are caught in the double-bind of claiming that everything that can be done ought to be done while simultaneously insisting that we don't want to be the ones who pay for it.

Second, his analysis of the need for far-reaching changes is significant. He recognizes that we have an "almost complete inability to find a meaningful place in public discourse for suffering and decline in life,"[5] much less death. Moreover, he recognizes that in order for us to begin to overcome the problems faced by advancing technologies, economic restraints, and large numbers of elderly people, we need to alter some of our society's current presumptions (and lack thereof) about health, medicine, and the nature and purpose of human life.

But, third, Callahan's prognosis of how we should go about doing so is unpersuasive. I do not believe that his notion of a "natural life span" is coherent in and of itself. He develops the notion of a "biographical" rather than a "biological" definition of life. I agree that we need to attend at least as much to people's biographies as we do their biologies. But what he fails adequately to recognize is that people's "biographies" vary greatly as to the point at which life is fulfilled. Even more importantly, he fails to recognize that many people in our society — particularly the poor and the marginalized — are forced to live in ways that make any kind of biographical "unity" or "fulfillment" virtually impossible.

Even if Callahan's proposal for a "natural span of life" were developed in a coherent fashion, however, I still think it would be highly unlikely to win assent in our culture. Callahan underestimates the degree to which we as a culture are committed to technologically developed crisis interventions designed to stave off death. Part of what makes questions of allocating medical resources so terrifyingly difficult — indeed, virtually incorrigible to social and moral reasoning — is that we are always willing to debunk technology in the abstract while simultaneously trying to ensure that the best technology will be available to us when we need it.

Callahan is to be commended for a courageous foray into the minefield of economics, technology, and medicine. Callahan, unlike so many who write about these issues, is aware of the complexities of the problems and the need for some dramatic rethinking of our approaches to health, medicine, suffering, and death — in short, for more attention to the question of "what people are for." But I think that ultimately his own constructive proposal is predicated on the kinds of presumptions that undermine any such thinking.

A second set of issues surrounds the ways in which our failure to attend to the question of "what people are for" are affecting doctor-patient relations. Indeed this failure is part of the problem that is undermining such relationships and ultimately fueling the economic problems in medicine. At the heart of the classical understanding of medicine as a "profession" is the conviction that the physician is to be of service to the community by being present to, and caring for, his or her patients. This is based on the presumption that, though suffering isolates people from communities and often from themselves, we ought not to abandon those who are suffering.

Presence to Suffering

That commitment to be present to those who are suffering has undergone many shifts and changes over time. Over the past two centuries, as care has been increasingly moved from the homes of nuclear and extended family members to hospitals, and as there have been dramatic advances in scientific medicine, there has been a correlative shift in the presumptions about caring and curing. Increasingly the medical profession has been looked on not simply to care for people (and cure when they can), but rather as people charged with fighting illnesses and curing people. The story of these transformations in expectations is complex, and we do not as yet adequately understand how the story should be told.

Even so, one result of that story is that there has been a dislocation in the understanding of the relationship between physicians and patients. It has long been presumed that physicians and patients are bound to one another through such virtues as fidelity and trust. Increasingly, however, as the organization of medicine has become increasingly scientific, bureaucratic, and structured according to the canons of managerial and economic efficiency, the bonds between physicians and patients have been weakened and even sundered. It is not uncommon now, particularly in an era of medical rationing, to hear that physicians are simply purveyors of "goods and services" and that patients are consumers who enter into contract with such purveyors as they see fit.

What has happened, at least in part, is that economic considerations and even economic language have become more and more central to the health care system[6] As Dennis McCann suggests, what has happened at the level of social policy is that "the health care preference of the American people quickly sorted themselves out in two directions: on the one hand, we expected the government to pick up the bill for lavish expansion of health care services to all sectors of society, especially our own; on the other hand, we were appalled at the rapid inflation of health care costs and began to wonder whether we were getting our money's worth. Continually whipsawed between these two conflicting sentiments, health care administrators in both private and public institutions have been forced to experiment with a variety of 'cost-containment' measures."[7] Consequently, in the midst of such cost-consciousness and contractual relations, the *manager* has become the most important ideal not only for health care administrators, but, increasingly, for physicians as well. Unfortunately, ideals of managerial efficiency tend to preclude moral questions as irrelevant; hence, moral questions rarely (if ever) arise in discussions of economic rationing in medicine.

The celebrated exchange of letters between Uwe Reinhardt, professor of Economics and Public Affairs at Princeton, and Arnold Relman, editor of *The New England Journal of Medicine,* centers on the question of whether the institution of medicine in general, and physicians in particular, can adequately be described in economic categories.[8] Part of their disagreement turns on the descriptive question of whether physicians tend to act as "purveyors of goods and services." Reinhardt certainly has a point that the institution of medicine has brought some of the problems of perception upon itself. Its concern for economic self-interest and power and status, described quite powerfully by Paul Starr in his *The Social Transformation of American Medicine*,[9] has sometimes led people to suggest that physicians are, in fact, little more than highly successful purveyors of goods and services.

An Important Point

But Reinhardt misses an important normative point about casting physicians in managerial and corporate terms. Though Relman does not adequately characterize the point, his emphasis on the importance of medicine as a profession is a reminder that the relationship between physicians and patients must be understood differently from other producer-consumer relations, because medicine is fundamentally a *tragic profession*.[10] The very nature of medicine is such that, no matter how virtuous and technically skilled is a physician, no matter how sophisticated is the technology we use, medical practice sometimes results in failure. Handicapped babies are born. People die.

These are tragic situations (not to be confused with malpractice), and they require the presence of communal bonds sufficient to sustain us through the tragedies. When those communal bonds are absent (e.g., when people do not have shared understandings about the meaning and purpose of human life), then the relation between physicians and patients becomes a contractual agreement which does not leave room for tragedy. Consequently, as Stephen Fowl suggests, "When the patient does not trust the medical profession to act in her or his own best interest . . . the patient will respond to tragic situations with litigation."[11]

That can be seen perhaps most graphically with respect to OB-GYNs. In a society where we are not sure what it means to have children or why we are doing so, we place intolerable burdens on physicians. Couples now presume that they have entered into a contract with a physician, and the implied presumption of that contract is that the physician will deliver a "Gerber baby" — perfect in every way. When, as often happens, the baby is not a "Gerber baby," the couple presumes it must be the physician's fault and thus they typically sue for malpractice. The deleterious effects of such situations on the practice of medicine have been amply documented.

What is surprising, however, is that we have failed to recognize the ways in which economic presumptions about human life and human relationships undermine our ability to cope with the tragedies that are inherent in human life and, more particularly, in the practice of medicine. We have put physicians in a peculiar double-bind: we expect more and more from physicians in terms of cures and life-enhancing and life-extending technologies, but we also complain that the costs are too high and that physicians ought to quit trying to play God by keeping people alive at any cost. Is it any wonder that our conceptions of medicine seem to be rather chaotic?

A third set of issues surrounds our various forms of cost-containment. In good managerial fashion, we are trying to make medical care more efficient. But while there are certainly benefits to cost-containment (if by that we mean genuine institutional and systematic reforms designed to improve health), what we are doing is better described as "expenditure control." By that I mean that we are really focused more on reducing our expenditures than in reforming structures, and that is being done all too frequently in haphazard fashion. As Rashi Fein has noted, we are cutting costs by "defining people out of the health system and by shifting costs among the various payers. But shifting costs is hardly equitable, and cutting back on Medicare, Medicaid, and private insurance is a form of rationing. The fact that access is allocated by an impersonal market and invisible hand may make it more acceptable. It hardly makes it more virtuous."[12]

What we have not developed and, in the absence of attention to those larger questions about the meaning and purpose of human life, what I think we will not develop, is a way of talking in our society about how to deal with the fact that we can provide only "finite care in a world of infinite needs."[13] Were we to do that, we would need to attend far more carefully, for example, to what is known as "preventive medicine" as well as to the primary health care needs of the poor. That is unlikely to happen in our society at large, however. For if there is anything that seems to be clear, it is that we have agreed that we do not want to pay for equal access to health care — in any of the possible ways which could be understood.

Organizations Which are Significant

And yet, it is significant that there are organizations such as the Catholic Physicians' Guild. Presumably the fact that there are physicians who are Catholic or, more generally understood, that there are physicians who are Christians, is significant to their identity as physicians. I think it is so and ought to be so. The fact that organizations such as the CPG exist, may provide a context in which we can begin to look at these issues in a somewhat different light.

Christians have — or at least ought to have — a witness about each of the sets of issues I have identified. We are a people who believe that we have glimpsed in the life, death, and resurrection of Jesus of Nazareth an understanding of "what people are for." That is to say, Christians believe that the stories of our lives — however incoherent and/or fragmented they may be — are bounded by a narrative more determinative than anything we can create. That narrative is the story of God's creation, redemption, and promised consummation of the Kingdom. That gives us a lens through which we can understand both the great importance of medicine and also its limited task.

Christians should know that medicine cannot be expected to save us from death, for only God can do that. We should know that death is not the worst thing that can happen to a person, that far more important than whether we live or die is that we be faithful to God. Given that presumption, we ought to be willing to forego extraordinary means of extending life in the knowledge that death does not have the final word about our lives.

Moreover, Christians should know that there are tragedies which happen, and that we can cope with those tragedies if we are willing to be people who know how to embody forgiveness and reconciliation. That requires that we be people of virtue, people capable of the kinds of communal bonds which animate physician-patient relations at their best. That requires not only that physicians be virtuous people (which is often understood to be important), but also that patients be virtuous (to which we pay considerably less attention). Without the formation of such communal bonds, we are likely to be caught in cycles of vengeance and self-deception as we seek to protect ourselves from becoming vulnerable to other people's intrusions.

Christians should also know that such bonds entail that we learn to see things from the perspective of those who suffer. We cannot rest easily with any systems of medical care which fail to attend to the primary health care needs of the poor and those who are ill. We are, or at least ought to be, people who would rather accept our own death than use up precious resources if preventing our death would mean that others will go without care.

I do not pretend that the theological perspectives I have been suggesting will resolve any of the problems I have identified or that physicians face in their practices. But I do want to suggest that *if* we are going to make any progress at all in dealing with ethical problems in medicine and the effects of economic rationing on those problems, it will be done by recovering the distinctive witness of Jesus Christ. How we go about doing that in relation to contemporary issues in medicine is a complex matter, and would require another (and different) essay.

Even so, I think that recovering such a witness would entail, so it seems to me, that the hospitals founded by various churches (and, in different ways, synagogues) ought to reclaim their identities as institutions designed to be of service to God. It would entail that physicians who are Christians reclaim the significance of that identity for their vocation. And perhaps most determinatively, it would also entail that all of us who are Christians, health-care workers and laity alike, be willing to revise and reform our understandings of life and death and our expectations of the medical care system such that we might be able to provide a witness to a world which knows not God.

Notes

1. Vonnegut, Kurt, *God Bless You, Mr. Rosewater* (New York: Dell, 1971), p. 29.

2. Ignatieff, Michael, *The Needs of Strangers* (New York: Penguin Books, 1984) pp. 78-79.

3. Callahan, Daniel, *Setting Limits* (New York: Simon and Schuster, 1987).

4. Ibid., p. 134.

5. Ibid., p. 32.

6. Cf. Eli Ginzberg, *American Medicine: The Power Shift* (Totowa, N.J.: Rowman and Littlefield, 1985).

7. McCann, Dennis, "'Am I Still My Brother's Keeper?' Theological Reflections on the Crisis in Health Care Management," *Second Opinion* 8 (1988): 91.

8. The exchange can be found in Bradford H. Gray, ed., *For-Profit Enterprise in Health Care* (Washington, D.C.: National Academy Press, 1986), pp. 209-23.

9. Starr, Paul, *The Social Transformation of American Medicine* (New York: Basic Books, 1982).

10. For a powerful description of medicine as a tragic profession, cf. Stanley Hauerwas, *Truthfulness and Tragedy* (Notre Dame: University of Notre Dame Press, 1977), pp. 184-203.

11. Fowl, Stephen, "The Problematic Practice of Medicine in a Fragmented Society," manuscript p. 9. My thinking on tragedy and community in relation to medicine is indebted to Fowl's paper.

12. Fein, Rashi, *Medical Care, Medical Costs* (Cambridge, Mass.: Harvard University Press, 1986), p. 215, cited in Callahan, op. cit., 213.

13. I owe this phrase to Stanley Hauerwas.

128 Sick of Being Poor

Teresa Maldonado

I woke up early one morning with strong pains in my stomach. As I lay in bed, the pain would come and go. When it came, I doubled over and broke out in a sweat. My husband was out of town, and I was at home with my five children. After about an hour, I realized I had to do something.

I thought about what I could do. I thought of walking to one of the medical clinics just around the corner from my house, but we were broke. I thought of going to a hospital emergency room, but we didn't have health insurance. If I couldn't pay a doctor, I certainly couldn't pay a hospital emergency room bill either. My only remaining choice was to go to the Board of Health clinic.

I panicked. Although I was a registered patient there and had taken my children there many times, I had gone there only once or twice for myself. I was afraid because I knew I needed help, yet I knew that getting into the clinic might not be easy.

If I called and made my condition sound too serious, they would say, "Honey, don't come in. You're too sick. Go straight to the hospital." If I didn't communicate how sick I was, they would say, "Sure you can come in. How about a week from Friday?"

The pain was too intense to ignore, so I took a deep gulp and called. A gentlemen in the Adult Medicine department answered. I explained my

From David Caes, *Caring for the Least of These: Serving Christ Among the Poor* (Scottdale, Penn.: Herald Press, 1992), pp. 17-24. Reprinted by permission of the Christian Community Health Fellowship, 803 N. 64th Street, P.O. Box 12548, Philadelphia, Penn. 19151-0548.

situation and asked for permission to come in. His response was, "You've called the wrong place. You belong in Family Planning."

Family Planning! The effort I was making to hide my pain kept me from blowing up. "I know the difference between my stomach and my uterus," I said. He got flustered and put me on hold.

Within a few minutes a nurse was on the line. I had to start all over. When I was through, she said the same thing: "You belong in Family Planning."

"I am a registered patient with Adult Medicine. I do not belong in Family Planning," I repeated. "I'm not going to have any more babies. Please let me come in."

The nurse put me on hold again. When she came back, she was clearly annoyed with me. I could not come in until 1:00 p.m., she said. And if I did come in, she wouldn't guarantee I would see the doctor, even if I waited until closing time that evening.

After hanging up, I decided my pain wasn't bad enough to be worth enduring such treatment all day. I was powerless. I never did go in. The pain eventually subsided.

To be poor is to be powerless, to be boxed in, to have no choices. The professionals who live and work in my community are there by choice. They have the option of walking away into the regular job market and earning more somewhere else. The very fact that professionals are providing services implies a position of power. Such people are not poor, no matter how frugally they choose to live.

Those of us who receive those services are powerless, perhaps because we lack education, good communication skills, or marketable job skills. We cannot walk away from our neighborhood into the land of success and prosperity.

The health care system illustrates the lack of options for the poor. I am forced to seek health care for myself and my children in a system that is dehumanizing, impersonal, belittling, and blaming.

Health Care Which Dehumanizes

A typical visit to the Board of Health Clinic includes at least six, and sometimes as many as ten, lines to wait in. When one of my children gets sick and I call to ask permission to bring my child in, I brace myself for a three-to-five-hour ordeal.

When I arrive, I go to the nurse's desk and wait my turn. When I see the nurse, I assure her that I called and let her know that I have arrived. She puts a check next to my name and sends me to the records counter.

I then wait my turn to get my records. When I receive my child's medical records, I shuffle back to the nurse's station and wait my turn again. She pulls out a computer sheet that will be filled out by every person who sees my child and attaches it to the records.

I go back to the first desk to see the person who will prepare my bill. I go to the other side of the clinic and wait my turn to pay the fee. Next I go to a waiting room to get my child's weight and temperature checked.

After that I gather everything together and wait in the waiting room for the doctor. If the doctor feels a lab test is necessary, I go to the lab. I have to wait longer there than in all the other lines combined. When I am through at the lab, I go back to the doctor and wait for her to see me again.

If the doctor feels a prescription and follow-up visit are needed, I must go to the other side of the center to wait for my prescription, then back to the records counter for the clerk to give me another appointment.

Through all this I am juggling my infant and two toddlers as I shuffle from line to line. If it is winter, I'm also toting four sets of hats, coats, scarves, and gloves. As if there weren't enough waiting in line already, during my first visits I got in wrong lines several times.

By the time I leave the clinic, I feel exhausted, disgusted, and worthless. At every station I have had to endure intolerance, indifference, and impatience from those "helping" me. Through body language, tone of voice, or lack of eye contact, I get the message loud and clear that I am a nobody. It seems every time I go in at least one person is angry with me for daring to ask for service. When a child is sick, my only choices are to endure this treatment or decide that I can't handle it that day and stay home with my sick child.

When you have to go through this dehumanizing process time after time, it eventually becomes a part of you. You begin to believe you really *are* nobody.

When I shared my experiences with a friend, she pointed out that Dr. Martin Luther King, Jr., had said, "They no longer have to tell us to go to the rear of the bus; we will fight to get there." In other words, when you are treated like that again and again, it becomes a part of your being, and you begin to do only what is expected of you.

Health Care Which Is Impersonal

When I go to the corner store, the grocer knows me, my children, and my husband. She knows my neighbors and their families. If I haven't been to each of the businesses in my neighborhood at least a dozen times, I have passed them on my way to the others. If I don't know the owners by name, I at least know them by sight. I know them and they know me.

During the warm weather we live outside our houses as much as we do inside. I have a neighbor who always sits outside his house. He is our neighborhood patriarch — a solid, consistent fixture. I see him whenever I get my mail. I see him when I go outside to call my children. I see him when I open my door to see what the weather is like. He knows everybody — who they are, where they live, who lives with them, and what is going on in their lives.

Impersonal service is foreign to my community, where I know I belong. But this security withers when I have to go to the Women, Infants, and Children program (WIC), the Public Aid office, or the Board of Health Clinic. Once inside these offices, I am anonymous. I become a number, and that anonymity hurts.

When I am in touch with that pain, all I want to do is run out and go home. Whatever I am there to get doesn't seem worth it. I avoid those places if at all possible. After two years on WIC, I got to the point where I couldn't stand the dehumanizing treatment any more; I gave up my benefits.

Health Care Which Belittles

When I go to the clinic, any of ten doctors could be on duty. The doctor doesn't know me and may not see me again for a year. To the doctor, I am just another face.

Because I don't have money, I am treated as though I cannot think for myself, or make appropriate choices for my family. It would seem that relating to a child's mother would be a key part of diagnosing the child's illness. After all, I know my child better than she does. But when I say, "I think my child has this," the doctor doesn't listen and treats me as if I don't count.

I don't go to the clinic unless my child is very sick, so that at least they will believe me when I say my child is ill. I have a daughter who just turned five years old. Before her third birthday, she had pneumonia twelve times. She never had a cold or flu; whenever she got sick she got pneumonia, and that would eventually be verified at the clinic.

After her second or third bout with pneumonia, I began to recognize the symptoms. I would call for permission to go into the clinic and plan on being there for three to five hours. I thought going in before the pneumonia got bad was the responsible thing to do.

Each time all I would hear was, "Yes, your daughter has a fever. Yes, she is coughing. But no, she does not have pneumonia."

In my mind I'd say, *Yes, but give her a day or two.* I'd get Sudafed and Tylenol and be sent home. Two days later, my daughter would be sicker. I would have to hold my limp, little girl in my arms while I tried to work the system. That is powerlessness.

One year we actually had health insurance. When our daughter started to have trouble breathing one evening, my husband and I were pleased to realize we didn't have to wait until the next day to go to the clinic — we could take her to the hospital emergency room for a shot of adrenaline. After the doctor finally examined her two hours later, he said she had asthma and gave her a shot. He also said she had a touch of pneumonia; he wanted to hospitalize her.

That confused me. Hospitalize her for a touch of pneumonia? I said that I knew how to take care of her at home. My husband said there was no way we would leave her in the hospital because all they would do was give her an antibiotic and some Tylenol. We said no.

The doctor left. When he came back five

minutes later, he dropped a bomb. "We think your daughter has cystic fibrosis." What could we do? We gave in and let them hospitalize her.

My husband and I took turns staying with her days and evenings. By the fifth day, we still had not seen the doctor. He somehow managed to examine my daughter in the ten minutes it took one of us to get a sandwich. She was never tested for cystic fibrosis.

When we called the doctor, he said, "I don't have confidence in this hospital's ability to test for cystic fibrosis. When I release her, I'll give you an order, and you can take her to Children's Memorial Hospital."

My daughter was in the hospital for ten days. During that time she got Tylenol regularly and an antibiotic every eight hours. A respiratory therapist came and pounded on her back once a day. I could have done that! When we got the bill, the insurance company refused to pay $3,000 because it was a preexisting condition. This kind of experience is belittling.

Health Care Which Blames the Victim

When our children get sick, we parents naturally feel responsible. But when we take our children in for care, it is devastating to be told it is all our fault.

When my son was six months old, he got a high fever. When I took him in, I found out he had an ear and throat infection. That infection and fever seemed to last until after his first birthday. As I think back on that time, my only memories are of being in the bathroom with my son in the tub (trying to bring his fever down), or at the doctor's office getting him a prescription for an antibiotic. Toward the end of those six months, the doctor looked me squarely in the face. He said if I could not get my child well and keep him well, he was going to have my son taken away from me.

Now I know children get sick in the suburbs. Why else would there be so many pediatricians and hospitals out there? Do the pediatricians in the suburbs blame the child's mother every time a child is sick? Do pediatricians in the suburbs threaten to take a child away from its mother because the child is sick? Why am I always to blame when my child is sick? I am told that decisions I make, the food I prepare, the way I dress my children, and where we live is all my fault. That is why my child is sick.

When I was asked to share my experiences, I was afraid. What if people agreed with the doctor at the clinic? But as I was working on this, I showed it to some of my neighbors and relatives. As they read about my experiences, their mouths fell open. They were amazed that I had been able to name something deep inside of them — something that was tearing them up. "That's me," they said. "Go ahead and say it."

So I decided to risk it. And what I have to say is that most of the time the health care system's treatment of the poor in this county is dehumanizing, impersonal, belittling, and blaming. But it doesn't have to be. Empowered by God's Spirit, people can learn to serve the poor with compassion and without paternalism.